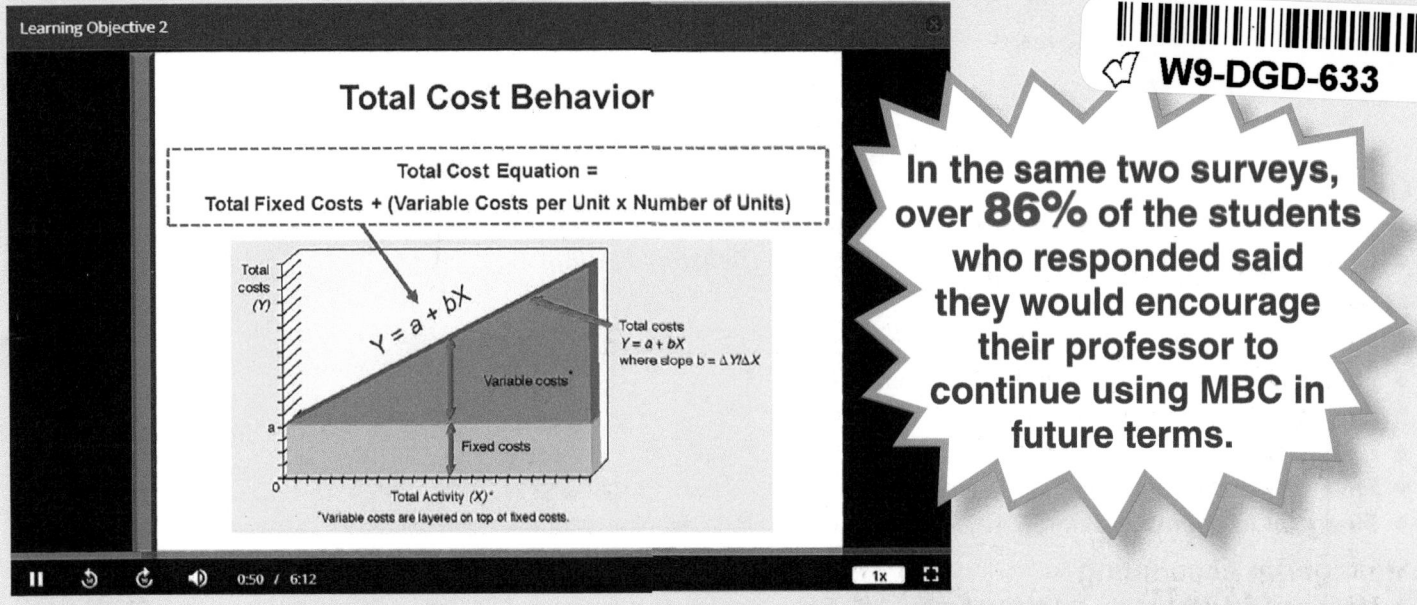

Make Instruction Needs-Based

◆ Identify where your students are struggling and customize your instruction to address their needs.

◆ Gauge how your entire class or individual students are performing by viewing the easy-to-use gradebook.

◆ Ensure your students are getting the additional reinforcement and direction they need between class meetings.

Provide Instruction and Practice 24/7

◆ Assign homework from your Cambridge Business Publishers' textbook and have myBusinessCourse grade it for you automatically.

◆ With our eLectures, your students can revisit accounting topics as often as they like or until they master the topic.

◆ Guided Examples show students how to solve select problems.

◆ Make homework due before class to ensure students enter your classroom prepared.

◆ For an additional fee, upgrade MBC to include the eBook and you have all the tools needed for an online course.

LMS Integration

myBusinessCourse integrates with many learning management systems, including **Canvas**, **Blackboard**, **Moodle**, **D2L**, **Schoology**, and **Sakai**. Your gradebooks sync automatically.

Getting Started is as EASY as 1, 2, 3 . . . 4!

1. Sign Up
Instructors register with myBusinessCourse.com

2. Setup Your Course
Add your class details and additional materials.

3. Invite Your Students
Students register using your unique course code.

4. Manage Your Course
Study, test, and grade assignments. It's simple!

Want to learn more about myBusinessCourse?
Contact your sales representative or visit www.mybusinesscourse.com.

Cambridge
BUSINESS PUBLISHERS
Series in Accounting

Computerized Accounting
◆ **QuickBooks Online: *2019 Update*,** by Williams & Johnson
◆ **Computerized Accounting with QuickBooks® 2019 *(Desktop version)*,** by Williams

Financial Accounting
◆ **Financial Accounting for Undergraduates, 4e** by Wallace, Nelson, and Christensen
◆ **Financial Accounting for Decision Makers, 2e** by DeFond
◆ **Financial Accounting, 6e** by Hanlon, Magee, Pfeiffer, and Dyckman
◆ **Financial Accounting for MBAs, 7e** by Easton, Wild, Halsey, and McAnally
◆ **Financial Accounting for Executives & MBAs, 4e** by Simko, Ferris, and Wallace
◆ **Financial Accounting Using IFRS, 2e** by Wong, Dyckman, Hanlon, Magee, and Pfeiffer

Managerial Accounting
◆ **Managerial Accounting for Undergraduates, 2e** by Christensen, Hobson, Wallace, and Matthews
◆ **Managerial Accounting, 8e** by Hartgraves & Morse

Combined Financial & Managerial Accounting
◆ **Financial & Managerial Accounting for Undergraduates, 2e** by Wallace, Nelson, Christensen, Hobson, and Matthews
◆ **Financial & Managerial Accounting for Decision Makers, 3e** by Dyckman, Hanlon, Magee, Pfeiffer, Hartgraves, and Morse
◆ **Financial & Managerial Accounting for MBAs, 5e** by Easton, Halsey, McAnally, Hartgraves, and Morse

Intermediate Accounting
◆ **Intermediate Accounting, 2e** by Hanlon, Hodder, Nelson, Roulstone, and Dragoo
◆ **Guide to Intermediate Accounting Research, 2e** by Collins

Cost Accounting
◆ **Cost Accounting: Foundations and Evolutions, 10e** by Kinney & Raiborn **(COMING 2020)**

Auditing
◆ **Alpine Cupcakes: An Audit Case with Data Analytics, 2e** by Dee, Durtschi, and Mindak

Financial Statement Analysis & Valuation
◆ **Financial Statement Analysis & Valuation, 5e** by Easton, McAnally, Sommers, and Zhang
◆ **Corporate Valuation, 2e** by Holthausen & Zmijewski
◆ **Valuation Using Financial Statements, 1e** by Sommers & Easton

Advanced Accounting
◆ **Advanced Accounting, 4e** by Hamlen
◆ **Advanced Accounting, 4e** by Hopkins & Halsey

Taxation
◆ **Scholes & Wolfson's Taxes and Business Strategy, 6e** by Erickson, Hanlon, Maydew, and Shevlin

Governmental and Not-For-Profit Accounting
◆ **Accounting for Governmental and Nonprofit Organizations, 1e** by Patton, Patton, and Ives
◆ **Governmental and Not-for-Profit Accounting: An Active Learning Workbook, 2e** by Convery

FASB Codification and eIFRS
◆ **Skills for Accounting Research: Text & Cases, 4e** by Collins

Casebooks
◆ **Cases in Financial Reporting, 8e** by Drake, Engel, Hirst, and McAnally
◆ **Cases in Managerial and Cost Accounting, 1e** by Allen, Brownlee, Haskins, and Lynch

my BusinessCourse

FREE WITH NEW COPIES OF THIS TEXTBOOK*

Scratch here for access code

kbcmjEheamSh82xp

Scratch here for access code

Start using my BusinessCourse Today: www.mybusinesscourse.com

my BusinessCourse is a web-based learning and assessment program intended to complement your textbook and faculty instruction.

Student Benefits

- **eLectures**: These videos review the key concepts of each Learning Objective in each chapter.
- **Guided examples**: These videos provide step-by-step solutions for select problems in each chapter.
- **Auto-graded assignments**: Provide students with immediate feedback on select assignments. **(with Instructor-Led course ONLY)**.
- **Quiz and Exam preparation**: myBusinessCourse provides students with additional practice and exam preparation materials to help students achieve better grades and content mastery.

You can access my BusinessCourse 24/7 from any web-enabled device, including iPads, smartphones, laptops, and tablets.

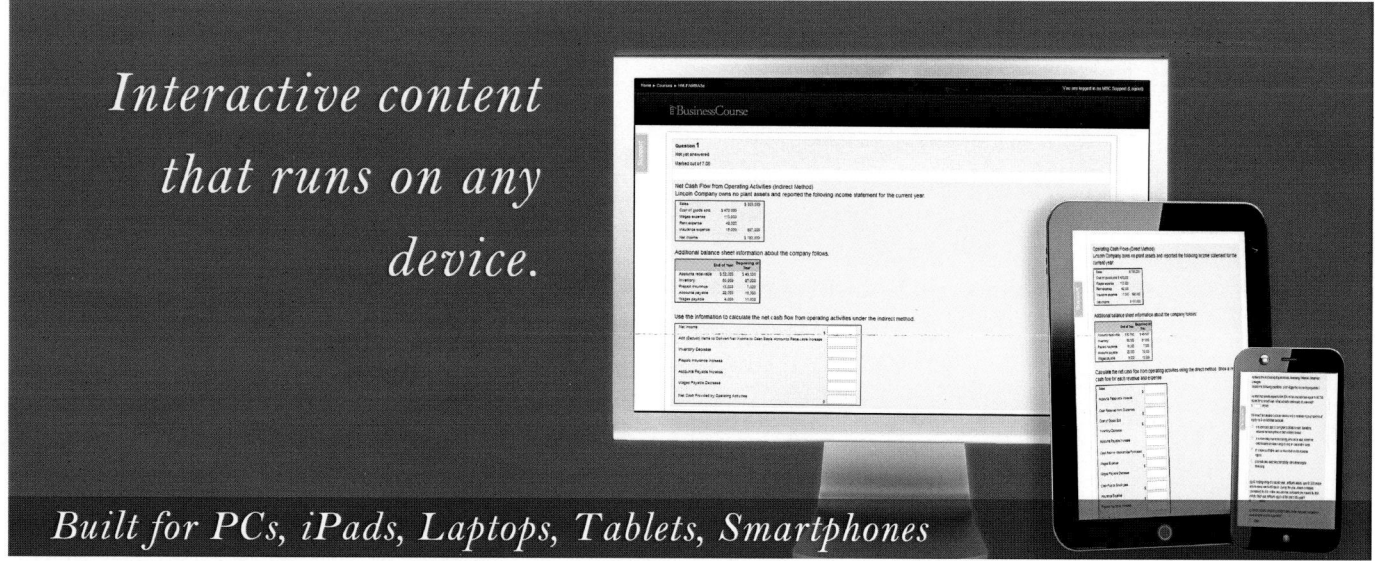

Interactive content that runs on any device.

Built for PCs, iPads, Laptops, Tablets, Smartphones

Financial & Managerial Accounting
for Undergraduates

Second Edition

James S. Wallace
The Peter F. Drucker and Masatoshi Ito
Graduate School of Management
Claremont Graduate University

Karen K. Nelson
M. J. Neeley School of Business
Texas Christian University

Theodore E. Christensen
Terry College of Business
University of Georgia

L. Scott Hobson
The Marriott School of Management
Brigham Young University

Jason W. Matthews
Terry College of Business
University of Georgia

Photo Credits

Ch 1 Opener: Arne Beruldsen/Shutterstock.com
Ch 1 p 5: Shutterstock.com.com for all 3 photos
Ch 1 p 6: Shutterstock.com for all photos
Ch 1 p 7: Shutterstock.com for all photos
Ch 1 p 8: Shutterstock.com for all photos
Ch 1 p 11: Shutterstock.com for all photos
Ch 1 p 8: REDPIXEL.PL/Shutterstock.com
Ch 2 opener: Intuit
Ch 2 p 8 and Ch 3 p 126: Creative Caliph/
   Shutterstock.com
Ch 3 Opener: Eric Broder Van Dyke/Shutterstock.com
Ch 4 Opener: iStock.com/AdrianHancu
Ch 4 p 198: Shutterstock.com
Ch 5 Opener: iStock.com/jetcityimage
Ch 6 Opener: iStock.com/Jorge Villalba
Ch 6 p 275 all photos: iStock
Ch 6 p 290: Shutterstock.com
Ch 7 Opener: iStock.com/fluxfoto

Ch 8 Opener: iStock.com/f11photo
Ch 8 p 381 Balance Sheet: iStock.com
Ch 8 p 381 and p 382 income statement: Shutterstock.com
Ch 8 p 386: Shutterstock.com
Ch 9 Opener: iStock.com/coffeekai
Ch 9 p 421 both photos: Shutterstock.com
Ch 9 p 423 construction vehicle: Joseph M. Arseneau/
   Shutterstock.com
Ch 9 p 423 tax button: Shutterstock.com
Ch 9 p 441: Shutterstock.com
Ch 10 Opener: iStock.com/rvolkan
Ch 10 p 446: Shutterstock.com
Ch 10 p 471: Shutterstock.com
Ch 11 Opener: pinglabel/iStock
Ch 11 p 554: Shutterstock.com
Ch 12 Opener: felixmizioznikov/iStock
Ch 12 p 588: Shutterstock.com
Ch 13 Opener: Procter & Gamble

Permissions Statement:

Materials from the Certified Management Accountant Examinations, Copyright © 2015, 2016, 2017, and 2018 by the Institute of Certified Management Accountants, are reprinted and/or adapted with permission.

All Fezzari photos courtesy of Fezzari Bicycles.

AICPA material and logo used with permission from the American Institute of Certified Public Accountants.

FINANCIAL & MANAGERIAL ACCOUNTING FOR UNDERGRADUATES, Second Edition, by James Wallace, Karen Nelson, Theodore Christensen, Scott Hobson, and Jason Matthews

ISBN 978-1-61853-310-4

Bookstores & Faculty: To order this book, contact the company via email customerservice@cambridgepub.com or call 800-619-6473.

Students & Retail Customers: To order this book, please visit the book's Website and order directly online.

Printed in the United States of America.
10 9 8 7 6 5 4 3 2 1

About the Authors

JAMES S. WALLACE is an Associate Professor at The Peter F. Drucker and Masatoshi Ito Graduate School of Management at The Claremont Graduate University. He received his B.A. from the University of California, Santa Barbara, his M.B.A. from the University of California, Davis, and his Ph.D. from the University of Washington. Professor Wallace also holds a CPA certification from the state of California. He previously served on the faculty of the University of California, Irvine and has served as a visiting professor at the University of California, San Diego. Professor Wallace's work has appeared in leading academic journals including the *Journal of Accounting and Economics*, the *Journal of Corporate Finance*, and *Information Systems Research*, along with leading applied journals such as the *Journal of Applied Corporate Finance*, the *Journal of Accountancy*, *Issues in Accounting Education*, and *Accounting Horizons*. Prior to his career in academics, Professor Wallace worked in public accounting and in industry with a Fortune 500 company. He has done consulting work with numerous companies in multiple industries.

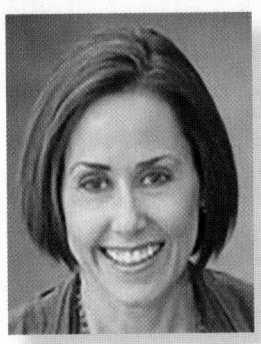

KAREN K. NELSON is the M. J. Neeley Professor of Accounting in the M. J. Neeley School of Business at Texas Christian University. She earned her Ph.D. from the University of Michigan and a bachelor's degree (summa cum laude) from the University of Colorado. Prior to joining TCU, Karen was on the faculty at Stanford University and Rice University, and a Visiting Professor at the University of Michigan. A Certified Public Accountant in Colorado, she is a member of the Standing Advisory Group of the Public Company Accounting Oversight Board.

Her research focuses on financial reporting and disclosure issues, including the role of regulators, auditors, and private securities litigation in monitoring financial reporting quality. She has held research seminars at over 50 leading business schools in the U.S. and abroad. Her research has been published in a variety of leading academic journals and has been featured in the financial press. Karen has taught financial accounting and reporting for undergraduate, MBA, and Ph.D. students, and is the recipient of numerous awards for teaching excellence.

THEODORE E. CHRISTENSEN is director and Terry Distinguished Chair of Business in the J. M. Tull School of Accounting at the University of Georgia. Prior to coming to UGA, he was on the faculty at Brigham Young University and at Case Western Reserve University. He was a visiting professor at the University of Michigan, the University of Utah, and Santa Clara University. He received a B.S. degree in accounting at San Jose State University, a M.Acc. degree in tax at Brigham Young University, and a Ph.D. in accounting from the University of Georgia. Professor Christensen has authored and coauthored articles published in many journals including *The Accounting Review*, *Journal of Accounting and Economics*, *Journal of Accounting Research*, *Review of Accounting Studies*, *Contemporary Accounting Research*, and *Accounting Organizations and Society*. He is also the author of an advanced financial accounting textbook. Professor Christensen has taught financial accounting at all levels, financial statement analysis, business valuation, both introductory and intermediate managerial accounting, and corporate taxation. He is the recipient of numerous awards for both teaching and research. He has been active in serving on various committees of the American Accounting Association and is a CPA.

L. SCOTT HOBSON is a Teaching Professor of Accounting at Brigham Young University (BYU), where he joined the faculty in 2003. He received his B.S. in accounting and Master of Accountancy degrees from BYU. Prior to his career in academics, Professor Hobson was the founder and owner of Hilton Farnkopf & Hobson (now HFH Consultants), a management consulting firm headquartered in Walnut Creek, California, for 14 years. He also worked in public accounting at Price Waterhouse for 5.5 years in both audit and consulting. While at Price Waterhouse, he taught for 2 years as an adjunct faculty at San Jose State University. He has taught accounting at all levels, from principles to M.B.A. courses, including managerial accounting, financial accounting, governmental and not-for-profit accounting, and management consulting. Professor Hobson is a CMA and is licensed as a CPA in California. Professor Hobson has published a case titled "Managing the CPA Firm at Dodge Company" in *Issues in Accounting Education*.

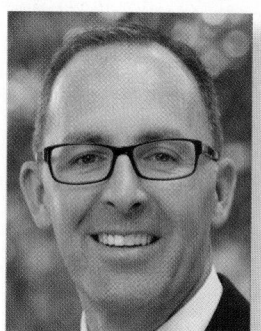

JASON W. MATTHEWS is a Senior Lecturer of Accounting and Director of Undergraduate Programs in the J. M. Tull School of Accounting at the University of Georgia (UGA). He received his B.S. from Missouri State University, his M.Acc. from North Carolina State University, and a Ph.D. from the University of Georgia. Prior to his career in academics, Professor Matthews was the interim Chief Financial Officer at Roark Capital Group, Director and Chief Financial Officer at United Coal Company, and Director and Chief Financial Officer of Oculan Corporation. Professor Matthews has taught across all levels at UGA including undergraduate financial accounting, managerial accounting, cost accounting and auditing; and graduate financial accounting and accounting information systems. He is the recipient of numerous teaching awards, including most recently the 2018 Terry College of Business Instructional Excellence award and the 2018 Pearcy B. Yeargin Outstanding Undergraduate Teacher of the Year award. He has been active in serving on committees in the Teaching Learning and Curriculum section of the American Accounting Association and is a CMA.

Preface

"THE MOST COMPELLING VALUE PROPOSITION OFFERED IN THE FINANCIAL AND MANAGERIAL ACCOUNTING MARKET!"

That has been our goal since this product's inception, and we have made that value proposition even more compelling with the Second Edition of *Financial & Managerial Accounting for Undergraduates*. We created this product to satisfy the needs of students taking an introductory course in financial and managerial accounting by providing a **high-quality**, **contemporary**, and **engaging** textbook and online learning system at an **affordable** price. With a net price of **$130** for the hardbound, full-color textbook with **free access** to myBusinessCourse for two terms, we challenge faculty to find a better overall value for their students.

Read on to learn why *Financial & Managerial Accounting for Undergraduates* has become a best-seller, and why you should use it in your introductory financial and managerial accounting classes.

PEDAGOGY THAT ENCOURAGES STUDENT SUCCESS

Accounting can be challenging—especially for students lacking business experience or previous exposure to business courses. To help students succeed in the course, we use a number of pedagogical devices throughout the textbook, and we provide a wealth of resources through our online learning and homework system, **myBusinessCourse** (MBC).

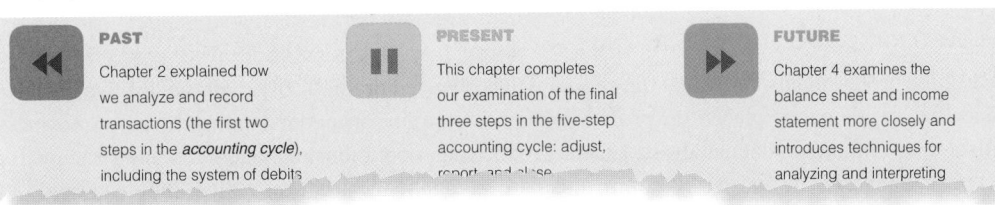

◀◀ PAST	**⏸ PRESENT**	**▶▶ FUTURE**
Chapter 2 explained how we analyze and record transactions (the first two steps in the *accounting cycle*), including the system of debits	This chapter completes our examination of the final three steps in the five-step accounting cycle: adjust, report, and close.	Chapter 4 examines the balance sheet and income statement more closely and introduces techniques for analyzing and interpreting

The Past/Present/Future feature puts each chapter in context.

Road Map

LO	Learning Objective	Page	eLecture	Guided Example	Assignments
LO1	Describe the nature of liabilities and discuss various current liabilities.	464	E10-1	YT10.1	SS1, SS2, SS4, E1A, E2A, E3A, E4A, E5A, E6A, E7A, E1B, E2B, E3B, E4B, E5B, E6B, E7B, P1A, P2A, P3A, P4A, P5A, P6A, P1B, P2B, P3B, P4B, P5B, P6B
LO2	Illustrate the accounting for long-term liabilities.	470	E10-2	YT10.2	SS8, SE2, SE8, SE9, SE10, E8A, E9A, E10A, E11A, E14A, E15A, E16A, E17A, E18A, E19A, E21A, E8B, E9B, E10B, E11B, E14B, E15B, E16B, E17B, E18B, E19B, E21B, P7A, P7B
LO3	Define contingent liabilities and explain the rules for their accounting and disclosure in the financial statements.	480	E10-3	YT10.3	SS3, SS5, SE1, SE3, E1A, E7A, E7B E12A, E12B, P6A, P6B

Road Maps outline each chapter and provide a quick reference table that summarizes the print and digital resources for that chapter.

The following inventory information is gathered from the accounting records of Tucker Enterprises:

Beginning inventory	4,000 units at $5 each
Purchases	6,000 units at $7 each
Sales	9,000 units at $10 each

Calculate (a) ending inventory, (b) cost of goods sold, and (c) the gross profit using each of the following methods (i) FIFO, (ii) LIFO, and (iii) weighted-average cost.

YOUR TURN! 6.2

The solution is on page 320.

Your Turns provide hands-on practice after each major concept to ensure mastery of a topic before proceeding to the next concept.

v

We use color and other visual cues pedagogically to help students learn and retain important concepts.

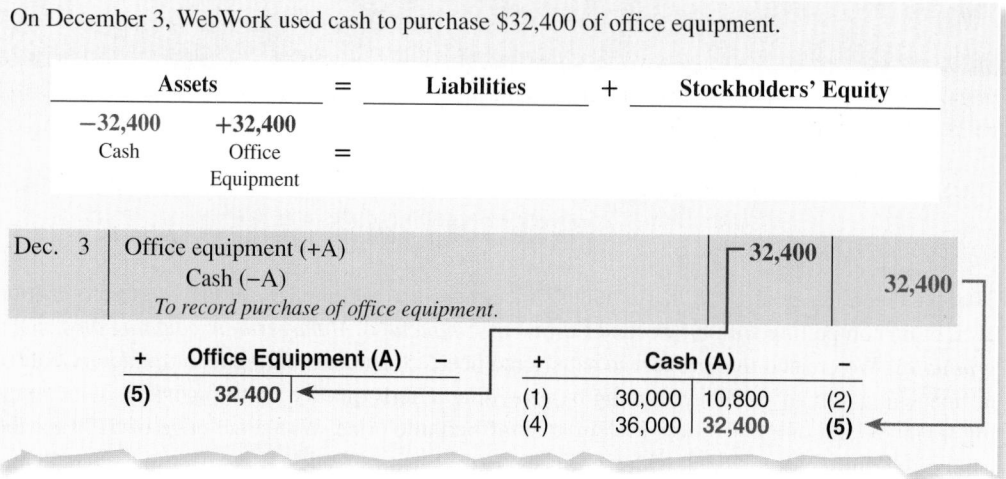

On December 3, WebWork used cash to purchase $32,400 of office equipment.

Assets		=	Liabilities	+	Stockholders' Equity
−32,400	+32,400				
Cash	Office Equipment	=			

Dec.	3	Office equipment (+A)		32,400	
		Cash (−A)			32,400
		To record purchase of office equipment.			

+	Office Equipment (A)	−		+	Cash (A)	−	
(5)	32,400			(1)	30,000	10,800	(2)
				(4)	36,000	32,400	(5)

Margin notes provide hints and identify commonly used alternative terms.

Hint: In contrast to the percentage of net sales method, the accounts receivable aging method takes into account the beginning balance of the Allowance for Doubtful Accounts.

A.K.A. The Allowance for Doubtful Accounts is also often referred to as the Allowance for Uncollectible Accounts.

RELEVANCE

Business professionals know that the economy has changed dramatically over the last two decades and that the demands placed on professionals now require an understanding of broad business disciplines, including data analysis, finance, marketing, operations management, and strategy. By exposing students to real-world companies and the challenges that they face, they can begin to understand the need to integrate accounting information with other business information in making good decisions.

The following features are used throughout the textbook to help students understand how accounting principles are used in real businesses today.

Real Company Examples

Environmental Business Consultants

Students are more likely to engage in the learning process and retain the concepts taught if the examples used are real companies with which they are familiar. In each financial accounting chapter, we incorporate a wide range of examples using real companies that students are familiar with, such as **Amazon, Microsoft,** and **Google.** In addition, the **Extending Your Knowledge** section in the financial accounting assignments require students to use the financial statements of **Columbia Sportswear Company, Under Armour Corporation, General Mills,** and **LVMH Moet Hennessey-Louis Vuitton S.A.**

Throughout the managerial accounting chapters, we incorporate a wide range of examples using real companies such as **Apple, Microsoft, Boeing,** and the **California State Bar.** In addition, two companies are used consistently throughout the managerial accounting chapters. Environmental Business Consultants, LLC, is a fictitious consulting company that gives students an opportunity to apply what they have learned within the service industry; and Fezzari is a custom bike manufacturer. These two continuous examples allow students to apply new skills to familiar organizations as they move through the managerial accounting concepts in the text.

Service Industry in Focus

The service sector is the fastest growing segment of the U.S. economy. The **Service Industry in Focus** inserts help students understand how managerial accounting is applied to improve the competitiveness of service companies.

| **SERVICE AND MERCHANDISING** | Environmental Business Consultants, LLC (EBC) worked on and completed two projects during June 2019: a review of appropriate rates for solid waste and recycling collection within Klamath County, and a competitive procurement of landfill disposal services for the City of Redding. The following information relates to these two projects: |

	Rate Review Project—Klamath	Procurement Project—Redding
WIP Inventory balance at June 1, 2019	$46,320	$85,318
Hours worked during June	100	74
Payroll cost per hour:		
Partner	$ 60	$ 60
Manager	$ 38	$ 38
Staff.	$ 24	$ 24
Overhead rate per labor hour	$ 25	$ 25

During June, the partner charged 10 hours to the rate review project and 20 hours to the procurement project; the manager charged 30 hours to the rate review project and 24

Accounting in Practice

These boxed inserts help students bridge the gap between the classroom and what students encounter in the real world. **Accounting in Practice** illustrations document situations a student will likely encounter and present choices that companies face in making decisions.

ACCOUNTING IN PRACTICE	**Factory Supplies versus Indirect Materials**
	Factory supplies are different from indirect materials. Factory supplies are used in the factory but are not part of the product itself. Lubricant used on the machine that stamps the sheet metal used in a laptop computer would be a factory supply. Indirect materials are part of the product but are difficult to trace to each individual product. Solder used to attach computer chips to a motherboard would be an indirect material. Both factory supplies and indirect materials can become part of manufacturing overhead.

CMA® Examination Questions

The Certified Management Accountant (CMA®) is a professional certification administered by the Institute of Management Accountants (IMA®). The purpose of the CMA certificate is to prepare accountants to be strategic thinkers and to analyze data in order to make better business decisions. We include past CMA questions at the end of each managerial chapter. These questions will help students experience how concepts are applied in realistic business situations and give them an advantage if they choose to pursue a career in management accounting and become a CMA. CMA questions are identified by a CMA icon in the margin.

Additional Features

Throughout the text these additional features emphasize the relevance of the current business environment on accounting concepts:

- **Corporate Social Responsibility** boxes help students understand how corporate social responsibility is being embraced by forward-thinking companies as part of their long-term business models.

- **Principle Alerts** discuss upcoming or new accounting pronouncements and changes in accounting principles.

- **Forensic Accounting** boxes highlight how financial accounting knowledge can help aid in the prevention of errors and fraud.

- **Thinking Globally** boxes emphasize the similarities and differences in business practices between companies in the U.S. and companies in other countries.

- **Ethics** is discussed where appropriate and select assignments raise ethical issues relevant to the material.

- **Service Industry Margin Callouts** identify sections of the text that apply managerial accounting concepts to the service industry

CURRENT DEVELOPMENTS AND ENGAGING EXAMPLES

Data Analytics and Blockchain Technology

The basics of accounting haven't changed much in hundreds of years, but the world in which we live has changed dramatically. Technology is rapidly altering how accounting is performed and what can be done with the data once they are collected. In this edition, we introduce students to Data Analytics and Blockchain Technology in **Chapter 1** and demonstrate data analysis concepts in Excel for the managerial chapters.

Data Analytics and Blockchain Technology

Accounting skills are not stagnant; rather they are constantly evolving. What was once done by hand is now done with the aid of specialized software. Programs like **Quick-Books** from **Intuit** have automated the basic accounting job of transaction recording, and programs like **Microsoft Excel** have greatly aided in the analysis of accounting data. While some industry observers had predicted these technological advances would replace the need for accountants, these applications have simply changed the way accountants perform their jobs. Newer technologies such as data analytics and blockchain are further

Where appropriate, we include boxed features highlighting new technologies.

Blockchain and the Future of Accounting

When most people hear the word *blockchain*, they likely think of Bitcoin. What makes blockchain so important for cybercurrencies like Bitcoin also makes it likely to revolutionize the future of accounting. Blockchain technology, which is also known as distributed ledger technology, allows multiple parties to a transaction to securely share a database. Blockchain has the potential to create a completely traceable audit trail, and could potentially automate the entire financial audit. While the future possibilities appear endless, current applications in addition to auditing include cybersecurity and financial planning and analysis.

For an expanded introduction to Data Analytics and Blockchain Technology, we added a new **Appendix F** that provides more detail and assignments that require the use of Excel and Tableau.

The authors demonstrate data analysis concepts in Excel, including:

- Guided example videos that demonstrate how to solve problems in Excel.
- Excel templates that are provided for select assignments and identified by an Excel icon.
- An expanded discussion of regression analysis using Excel to develop cost formulas is included in Chapter 19.
- Accompanying Excel tutorial videos covering Excel basics and the time value of money.

New Accounting Standards

In addition to the changes brought about by technology, several new accounting standards have gone into effect since the last edition of this book, including standards on revenue recognition, inventory measurement methods (lower-of-cost-or-net realizable value), leases, and investments. The Second Edition has been updated to incorporate the new standards. However, we recognize that the goal of the introductory course is to expose students to the general principles and processes of accounting without overwhelming them with the details that are more appropriately covered in intermediate accounting courses. Consequently, we utilize examples and applications that avoid the technical detail students will learn in future courses.

Revenue Recognition

Applying the revenue recognition principle can be quite straightforward for simple situations such as the sale of a dozen donuts at a Krispy Kreme store. More complex situations, however, can lead to more difficulty in applying the five-step revenue recognition process. For example, when Xerox Corp. sells a photocopy machine along with a three-year maintenance agreement as part of a packaged deal, the five-step process would be applied as follows:

Step 1: Identify the contract with the customer. The revenue recognition standard treats every revenue transaction as a contract between the seller to provide goods or services and the buyer to provide payment to the seller. Contracts may be informal and implicit such as the contract to purchase a dozen donuts from Krispy Kreme, or formal and explicit such as a written contract to purchase a photocopier with a maintenance agreement from Xerox.

TECHNOLOGY THAT IMPROVES LEARNING AND COMPLEMENTS FACULTY INSTRUCTION

myBusinessCourse is an online learning and assessment program intended to complement your textbook and faculty instruction. Access to **myBusinessCourse** is FREE ONLY with the purchase of a new textbook, but can be purchased separately.

MBC is ideal for faculty seeking opportunities to augment their course with an online component. MBC is also a turnkey solution for online courses. The following are some of the features of MBC.

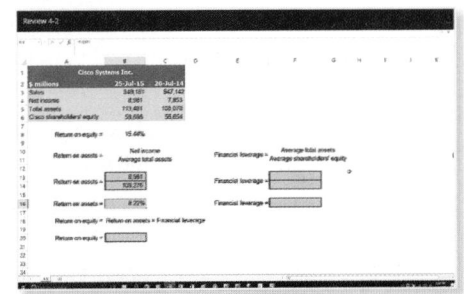

Increase Student Readiness

In two recent surveys of students who used MBC, **95%** responded that MBC helped them learn accounting.*

- **eLectures** cover each chapter's learning objectives and concepts. Consistent with the text and created by the authors, these videos are ideal for remediation and online instruction.
- **Guided Examples** are narrated video demonstrations created by the authors that show students how to solve select problems from the textbook.
- Immediate feedback with **auto-graded homework**.
- **Test Bank** questions that can be incorporated into your assignments.
- Instructor **gradebook** with immediate grade results.

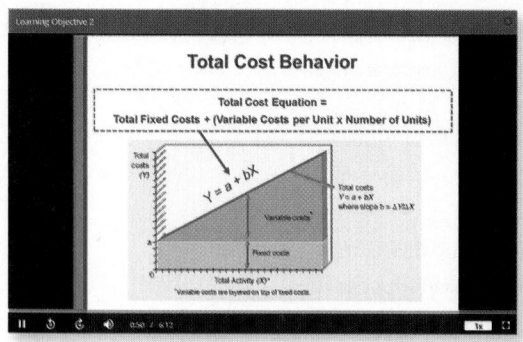

Make Instruction Needs-Based

- Identify where your students are struggling and customize your instruction to address their needs.
- Gauge how your entire class or individual students are performing by viewing the easy-to-use gradebook.
- Ensure your students are getting the additional reinforcement and direction they need between class meetings.

Provide Instruction and Practice 24/7

- Assign homework from your Cambridge Business Publishers' textbook and have MBC grade it for you automatically.

In the same two surveys, over **86%** of the students who responded said they would encourage their professor to continue using MBC in future terms.*

- With our eLectures, your students can revisit accounting topics as often as they like or until they master the topic.
- Guided Examples show students how to solve select problems.
- Make homework due before class to ensure students enter your classroom prepared.
- For an additional fee, upgrade MBC to include the eBook and you have all the tools needed for an online course.

Integrate with LMS

*my*BusinessCourse integrates with many learning management systems, including **Canvas**, **Blackboard**, **Moodle**, **D2L**, **Schoology**, and **Sakai**. Your gradebooks sync automatically.

NEW TO THIS EDITION

- **Road Map:** Each chapter opens with a quick reference grid that identifies each learning objective for the chapter, the related pages, eLecture and Guided Example videos, and end of chapter assignments. This allows students and faculty to quickly identify the chapter content and to efficiently navigate to the desired resource.
- Added discussions of **Data Analytics** and **Blockchain Technology** where appropriate, and added **Appendix F**, which provides a more in-depth exploration of Data Analytics and Blockchain Technology.
- Excel templates are provided for select assignments throughout the text and are identified by an EXCEL icon.
- A series of **tutorial videos covering Excel basics and the time value of money** accompany the text.

* These statistics are based on the results of two surveys in which 2,330 students participated.

- New **pedagogical use of color** in Chapter 3 to help students differentiate between the 4 types of end-of-period adjustments (accruals and deferrals).
- In the financial accounting chapters, we added **visual cues** to journal entries and T-accounts to help students understand the type of account being affected by transactions (A, L, SE, R, E, D) and the impact the transaction has on the account (+/−).
- Updated **revenue recognition** coverage for the standard change.
- Chapter 6: Updated the inventory coverage to reflect the new standard on **lower-of-cost-or-net realizable** value.
- Chapter 9: Added coverage on **natural resources** and depletion.
- Chapter 10: Updated the appendix on **leases** to reflect the new standard.
- **Data Analysis:** Cost-Volume-Profit Relationships (Chapter 19) includes an expanded discussion of regression analysis using Excel to develop cost formulas.
- Updated Appendix D on **Investments** to reflect the new standard.
- Updated **real financial data** throughout the text and assignments.
- Expanded the number of **Guided Example videos** and assignments included in MBC.
- **More Your Turn! Boxes** giving students even more opportunities to practice.
- **Additional Assignments** were added to ensure adequate reinforcement of each learning objective.
- **Additional Test Bank Questions** were added to ensure adequate assessment of each topic.

SUPPLEMENT PACKAGE

For Instructors

myBusinessCourse: A web-based learning and assessment program intended to complement your textbook and classroom instruction.

Solutions Manual: Created by the authors, the *Solutions Manual* contains complete solutions to all the assignment material in the text.

PowerPoint: The PowerPoint slides outline key elements of each chapter.

Test Bank: The Test Bank includes multiple-choice items, matching questions, short essay questions, and problems.

Excel Templates: We provide Excel spreadsheets for select assignments. These spreadsheets will save time in data entry and allow students to dedicate additional time to learning the material. The assignments accompanied by Excel spreadsheets are identified by the Excel icon.

Website: All instructor materials are accessible via the book's Website (password protected) along with other useful links and marketing information: www.cambridgepub.com

For Students

myBusinessCourse: A web-based learning and assessment program intended to complement your textbook and faculty instruction. This easy-to-use program grades homework automatically and provides you with additional help when your instructor is not available. Assignments with the in the margin are available in myBusinessCourse. Access is free with new copies of this textbook (look for page containing the access code towards the front of the book). If you buy a used copy of the book, you can purchase access at www.mybusinesscourse.com.

Excel Templates: We provide Excel spreadsheets for select assignments. These spreadsheets will save time in data entry and allow students to dedicate additional time to learning the material. The assignments accompanied by Excel spreadsheets are identified by the Excel icon.

Website: Updates and other useful links are available to students free of charge on the book's Website.

ACKNOWLEDGEMENTS

This book benefited greatly from the valuable feedback of focus group attendees, reviewers, students, and colleagues. We are extremely grateful to them for their help in making this project a success.

Markus Ahrens
James Aitken
Dave Alldredge
Bam Alling
David Ambrosini
Matthew Anderson
Adam Baker
Felicia Baldwin
James Bannister
Richard Barnhart
Gerhard Barone
Robyn Barrett
Sara Barritt
Melody Barta
Nancy Batch
Vernon Bell
James Benjamin
Debbie Benson
Christine Betts
Swati Bhandarkar
Jim Borden
Lydia Botsford
Amy Bourne
Robert Bowen
Scott Boylan
Rada Brooks
Marilyn Brooks-Lewis
Stephen Brown
Amy Browning
Helen Brubeck
Patricia Burnett
Ian Burt
Sandra Byrd
Jeffrey Byrne
Jennifer Cainas
Michael Calegari
Mike Campbell
John Capka
Tommy Carnes
Jackie Casey
Melissa Chadd
Christy Chauvin
Betty Chavis
Alan Cherry
Catherine Chiang
Gerald Childs
Jay Chittal
Alice Chu
Lawrence Chui
Howard Clampman
Leslie Cohen
Scott Collins
Margaret Combs
Erin Cornelsen
Nancy Coster
John Coulter
Rachel Cox
Timothy Creel
Cheryl Crespi

Jim Crumbacher
Richard Culp
Dori Danko
Emmanuel Danso
Lois Darga
Judy Daulton
Annette Davis
Patricia Davis
Susan Davis
Regina Derzon
Rosemond Desir
Glenn Dickerson
Vicky Dominguez
Pamela Donahue
Doris Donovan
Tom Downen
Chan Du
Peggy Eaton
Jeanne Eibes
Lisa Eiler
Jerrilyn Eisenhauer
Ahmed El-Zayaty
James Emig
Li Li Eng
Cole Engel
Michael Fagan
Connie Fajardo
Alan Falcon
Lucile Faurel
Kevin Feeney
Bud Fennema
Cathy Finger
Julie Finnegan
Linda Flaming
Charlene Foley-Deno
Gary Ford
David Forester
Jackie Franklin
Mitchell Franklin
Carolyn Galantine
Rena E. Galloway
Dennis George
Julie Gilbert
Lisa Gillespie
Brian Gilligan
Julie Gittelman
Alan Glazer
Hubert Glover
Julie Goodin
Marina Grau
Lisa Gray
Yvette Green
Timothy Griffin
Thomas Guarino
Wendy Gunn
Bruce Gunning
Joo Ha
Deborah Habel
James Halstead

Lorna Hardin
David Harr
Bob Hartman
Rosemary Hayward
Haihong He
Joshua Herbold
Merrily Hoffman
Cynthia Hollenbach
Steven Hornik
Jana Hosmer
Marsha Huber
Carol Hughes
Kathy Hurley
Kim Hurt
Helen Hurwitz
Laura Ilcisin
Stephen Jablonsky
Sharon Jackson
Shirin Jahanian
Paul Jaijairam
Marianne James
Ching-Lih Jan
Mark Jasonowicz
Bill Jefferson
Catherine Jeppson
Gene Johnson
Randy Johnston
Jane Jollineau
Thomas Kam
Kathryn Kapka
Jocelyn Kauffunger
Tom Kelley
Janis Kendziorski
Sara Kern
Suzanne Kiess
Christine Kloezeman
Aaron Knape
Becky Knickel
Dennis Knutson
John Koeplin
Paul Koulakov
Elida Kraja
Mary-Jo Kranacher
Lynn Krausse
Harold Krul
Christopher Kwak
Steven LaFave
Benjamin Lansford
Cathy Larson
Doug Larson
Greg Lauer
Gary Laycock
Ron Lazer
Joan Lee
Charles LeFlar
Zawadi Lemayian
Jennifer LeSure
Elliott Levy
Christine Li

Siyi Li
Zining Li
Lihong Liang
Emily Lindsay
Sara Linton
John Long
Suzanne Lozano
Debbie Luna
Heather Lynch
Nancy Lynch
Susan Lynn
David Manifold
Jeff Mankin
William J. Mann
Joe Manzo
Ariel Markelevich
Thomas Marsh
Dawn Massey
Michele Matherly
Clarice McCoy
Molly McFadden-May
Sarah McGaha
Terra McGhee
Florence McGovern
Michele McGowan
Allison McLeod
Jeff McMillan
Kate McNeil
Michelle McNeil-Brown
Casey McNellis
Cathryn Meegan
Lindsay Meermans
Sara Melendy
Michael Meyer
Linda Miller
Jill Mitchell
April Mohr
Michelle Moshier
Sheila Muller
Johnna Murray
Patricia Naranjo
Lisa Nash
Anne Mary
     Nash-Haruna
Tammie Neeley
Pam Neely
Joshua Neil
Bruce Neumann
Monica Newman
Joseph Nicassio
Micki Nickla
Tracie Nobles
Hossein Noorian
Lisa Novak
Sarah Nutter
Barbara Nyden
Joanne Orabone
Roshelle Overton
Ken O'Brien

Kalpana Pai
Abbie Gail Parham
Laurel Parrilli
Jeff Paterson
Keith Patterson
Paige Paulsen
Sy Pearlman
Mary Pearson
Ron Pearson
Aaron Pennington
Kimberly Perkins
Julie Petherbridge
Kathy Petroni
Marietta Peytcheva
Robert Picard
Gary Pieroni
April Poe
Ronald Premuroso
Jean Price
M. Jeff Quinlan
Allan Rabinowitz
Arwyna Randall-Gay
Ann Randolph
Kathy Rankin
Melinda Ratliff
Paul Recupero
Aaron Reeves
Vernon Richardson
Cecile Roberti
Shani Robinson
Andrea Roerdink
Gregg Romans
Lydia Rosencrants
Mark Ross
John Rossi
Eric Rothenburg
Maria Roxas
Ron Sabado
Alfredo Salas
John Sanders
Roby Sawyers
Albert Schepanski
Arnold Schneider
Robert Schweikle
Steve Sefcik
Jamie Seitz
Perry Sellers
Randy Serrett
Cathy Sevigny
Tracy Sewell
Ray Shaffer
Vikram Sharma
Carol Shaver
Dennis Shea
Regina Shea
John Shon
Gregory Sinclair
Ken Sinclair
Bhaskar Singh

Eric Slayter
Gene Smith
Gerald Smith
Nancy Snow
Robin Soffer
Liang Song
Marilyn Stansbury
George Starbuck
Ronald Stone
Carolyn Strauch
Rick Street
Scott Stroher
Rob Stussie
John Suckow
John Susenburger
Stephanie Swaim
Aida Sy
Mary Sykes
Ted Takamura
Robert Tallo
Diane Tanner
Linda Tarrago
Jay Thibodeaux
Randall Thomas
Robin Thomas
Dalton Tong
Sheri Trumpfheller
Anthony Tuan
Michael Tydlaska
Joan Van Hise
Marcia Viet
George Violette
Marcia Vorholt
Robert Walsh
Doris Warmflash
Brian Watkins
Randi Watts
Debra Webb
Andrea Weickgenannt
Patricia Wellmeyer
Donna Whitten
Monica Widdig
Idalene Williams
Paula Wilson
Michele Wiltsie
Wanda Wong
Douglas Woods
Maef Woods
Daryl Woolley
Susan Wright
Rong Yang
Kathryn Yarbrough
Robert Yu
Amy Yurko
Judith Zander
Jian Zhou

We thank Ken Ferris for his contribution to the First Edition, and we hope he enjoys a long and active retirement. In addition, we are extremely grateful to George Werthman, Lorraine Gleeson, Jill Sternard, Marnee Fieldman, Jocelyn Mousel, Katie Jones-Aiello, Beth Gilgen Nodus, Debbie McQuade, Terry McQuade, and the entire team at Cambridge Business Publishers for their encouragement, enthusiasm, and guidance. Feedback is always welcome. Please feel free to contact us with your suggestions or questions.

Jim Wallace   Karen Nelson   Ted Christensen   Scott Hobson   Jason Matthews

February 2019

Brief Contents

Contents

CHAPTER **15**

Managerial Accounting Concepts and Cost Flows **708**

CHAPTER **16**

Cost Accounting Systems: Job Order Costing **754**

CHAPTER **17**

Cost Accounting Systems: Process Costing **802**

CHAPTER **18**

Activity-Based Costing **856**

CHAPTER **19**

Cost-Volume-Profit Relationships **900**

CHAPTER **20**

Variable Costing: A Tool for Decision Making **954**

CHAPTER **21**

Relevant Costs and Short-Term Decision Making   **978**

CHAPTER **22**

Planning and Budgeting   **1020**

CHAPTER **23**

Standard Costing and Variance Analysis   **1066**

CHAPTER **24**

Flexible Budgets, Segment Reporting, and Performance Analysis   **1104**

CHAPTER **25**

Capital Budgeting   **1158**

APPENDIX **A**

Columbia Sportswear Company   **A-1**

Chapter 1

Financial Accounting and Business Decisions

A **Focus Company** *introduces each chapter and illustrates the relevance of accounting in everyday business.*

PRESENT

This chapter explains business formation, the uses and users of accounting information, the types of activities companies pursue, and financial statements that report on business.

FUTURE

The next chapters more fully explain financial statements, including how they are prepared, constructed, analyzed, and interpreted.

Past/Present/Future *provides an overview of where the chapter fits within the context of the whole book.*

It is often said that accounting is the language of business. Like all companies, **Columbia Sportswear Company** (Columbia.com), a maker of clothing for dedicated lovers of the greater outdoors, relies upon accounting for its success. It uses financial reports to judge its performance and that of its managers. It uses accounting controls to monitor its inventory. It uses accounting data to assess the amount and timing of dividend payments to shareholders.

This first chapter introduces many basic relations and principles underlying financial statements. It also identifies many key users of accounting information and discusses how that information is useful in businesses globally.

Road Map

Road Maps *summarize each chapter's resources and categorize them by learning objective.*

eLectures *are videos available in MBC that provide 3-5 minute reviews of each learning objective.*

Assignments *reinforce learning and can be completed by hand or within MBC.*

LO	Learning Objective	Page	eLecture	Guided Example	Assignments
LO1	Explain the three forms of business organizations.	4	E1-1	YT1.1	SE1, E1A, E1B, P1A, P1B
LO2	Describe business activities.	5	E1-2	YT1.2	SE5, SE10, E6A, E6B
LO3	Indicate who uses accounting information.	6	E1-3	YT1.3 YT1.4	SE3, SE8, E3A, E14A, E3B, P8A, P8B
LO4	Explain the accounting process and generally accepted accounting principles.	10	E1-4	YT1.5	SE2, SE4, SE9, SE15, SE19, E2A, E5A, E15A, E2B, E5B, E15B
LO5	Describe the accounting equation and each financial statement.	12	E1-5	YT1.6	SE6, SE11, SE12, SE13, SE14, E4A, E7A, E9A, E10A, E11A, E12A, E19A, E4B, E7B, E8B, E9B, E10B, E11B, E12B, 19B, P2A, P3A, P4A, P5A, P6A, P7A, P9A, P10A, P2B, P3B, P4B, P5B, P6B, P7B, P9B, P10B
LO6	Explain additional disclosures that accompany financial statements.	19	E1-6	YT1.7	SE7, E13A, E13B, P9A, P9B
LO7	Describe careers in accounting.	20	E1-7		
LO8	Appendix 1A: Discuss FASB's conceptual framework.	23	E1-8		SE16, SE17, SE18, SE20, SE21, E16A, E17A, E18A, E19A, E20A, E16B, E17B, E18B, E19B, E20B, P11A, P11B

Learning Objectives *identify the key learning goals of the chapter.*

Guided Examples *are videos that demonstrate how to solve various types of problems and are available in MBC.*

Chapter Organization charts visually depict the key topics and their sequence within the chapter.

FINANCIAL ACCOUNTING AND BUSINESS DECISIONS

Forms of Business Organizations	Business Activities	Accounting Information and Its Use	Information Dissemination	Other Annual Report Components	FASB Conceptual Framework (Appendix 1A)
• Sole proprietorship • Partnership • Corporation	• Financing • Investing • Operating	• External users • Internal users • Ethics and accounting	• Accounting process • Generally Accepted Accounting Principles • International Financial Reporting Standards • Financial statements	• Notes to financial statements • Independent auditor's report • Management's Discussion and Analysis	• Objectives • Elements • Characteristics • Recognition and Measurement

*eLecture icons denote the availability of an instructional video in **myBusinessCourse** (MBC). See the Preface for more information on MBC.*

BUSINESS ORGANIZATION

LO1 **Explain** the three forms of business organizations.

Learning Objectives are repeated at the start of the section covering that topic.

The first decision every business faces is deciding what form of organization it will take. The three principal forms of business organization are the sole proprietorship, the partnership, and the corporation. Although each of these organizational forms is treated as an accounting entity, only the corporation is viewed under the law as a legal entity separate and distinct from its owners. A corporation has an unlimited life, which means that it will continue to exist indefinitely unless it is formally dissolved. The life of a sole proprietorship or partnership is limited by the participation of the existing owners. If an owner dies or withdraws, the business typically ends as well.

A **sole proprietorship** is a business owned by one person; it is the most common of the three forms of business organization. The primary advantage of the sole proprietorship is its ease of formation. As the only owner, the sole proprietor makes all of the decisions affecting the business. This organizational form also enjoys certain income tax advantages relative to a corporation in that the income of that business is not taxed; instead, its income is included as part of the owner's income that is reported to the taxation authorities.

Key Terms are highlighted in bold, red font.

A **partnership** is a voluntary association of two or more persons for the purpose of conducting a business. Partnerships and sole proprietorships differ principally with respect to the number of owners. Partnerships can be as small as two people or as large as the biggest accounting or legal firms, which have hundreds or even thousands of partners. Partnerships are also easy to establish. Because a partnership involves multiple owners, the partners should establish the rights and obligations of each partner to avoid any misunderstandings that might lead to disputes and lawsuits. An advantage of the partnership form over the sole proprietorship is the broader skill set that multiple partners can bring to a business. Partnerships also enjoy the same income tax advantage as sole proprietorships.

A **corporation** is a legal entity created under the laws of a state or the federal government. A corporation can have as few as one owner but most have many owners. The owners of a corporation receive shares of stock as evidence of their ownership interest in the business, and consequently, they are referred to as **stockholders** (or *shareholders*). Since corporations are a separate legal entity, they must pay income taxes on their profits. This leads to a situation of double taxation because the income of the corporation is taxed and stockholders also pay taxes on dividends they receive from the corporation. The corporation is the dominant organizational form in terms of the volume of business activity conducted in the United States and worldwide.

While most businesses start off as either a sole proprietorship or as a partnership, some outgrow these organizational forms and convert to the corporate form. For example, **Columbia Sportswear Company** was incorporated in 1961 after beginning as a sole proprietorship in 1938. Two primary reasons for converting a sole proprietorship or a partnership to the corporate form of business are the relative ease of raising capital to grow the business and the protection afforded to stockholders against personal liability. A third advantage of the corporate form is the relative ease of selling ownership shares. For example, stock exchanges, such as the **New York Stock Exchange (NYSE)**, exist to enable stockholders to readily buy and sell their ownership shares. No such exchanges exist for sole proprietors or partners, and thus, selling an ownership interest in a sole proprietorship or a partnership is a more difficult, time-consuming event.

Proprietorship	Partnership	Corporation
• One owner control	• Shared owner control	• All types of owner control
• Business not taxed, but owner taxed	• Business not taxed, but owners taxed	• Business taxed and owners taxed
• Not legal entity	• Not legal entity	• Separate legal entity
• Limited life	• Limited life	• Unlimited life

© Shutterstock.com

Identify three characteristics for each of the principal forms of business organizations.

1. sole proprietorship
2. partnership
3. corporation

Your Turn! boxes reinforce the material just presented with self-study questions. To aid learning, solutions are provided at the end of the chapter.

YOUR TURN! 1.1

The solution is on page 53.

ACTIVITIES OF A BUSINESS

eLectures
MBC

Every business, regardless of its organizational form, its industry, or its size, is involved in three types of business activities—financing, investing, and operating.

LO2   **Describe** business activities.

Financing Activities

Before a company can begin operations, it must acquire money to support its operations. Employees need to be hired, buildings constructed, raw materials purchased, and machinery put in place. Companies can obtain the necessary funds to undertake these activities in several ways. These **financing activities** are generally categorized as either debt financing or equity financing.

    Debt financing involves borrowing money from sources such as a bank by signing a note payable or directly from investors by issuing bonds payable. The individuals or financial institutions that lend money to companies are called their **creditors**. Debt financing involves an obligation to repay a creditor both the amount initially borrowed, called the **principal**, and an interest fee for the use of the funds.

    Equity financing involves selling shares of stock to investors. In contrast to creditors who lend money to a business and expect to receive that money back with interest, investors that purchase shares of stock are buying an ownership interest in the company. Investors hope that their stock will increase in value so that they can earn a profit when they sell their shares. The owners of a company's stock may also receive dividend payments when the company decides to distribute some of its profits.

Investing Activities

Before a company can begin operations, it must purchase the long-term resources necessary to conduct its business, such as land, buildings and equipment. **Investing activities** involve the acquisition and disposition of factories, office furniture, computer and data systems, delivery vehicles, and other items that will be used to carry out the company's business plans. These items are referred to as assets.

Companies can obtain the money needed to make these investments from either the financing activities discussed previously or from any excess cash accumulated from operating the business profitably.

Operating Activities

The day-to-day activities of producing and selling a product or providing a service are referred to as **operating activities**. Operating activities are critical for a business because if a company is unable to generate income from its operations it is very likely that the business will fail. If creditors and stockholders do not believe that a company will be able to generate a profit, they are unlikely to provide the financing needed to start, or maintain, its operations.

Exhibit 1-1 provides a summary of the three types of business activities. Arrows are pointing both toward, and away from, operating activities. This is because financing and investing activities are necessary to carry out a company's operating activities; however, if a company's operating activities generate excess cash, then the excess cash can be used to either finance additional investments, repay the company's creditors, or pay dividends to shareholders.

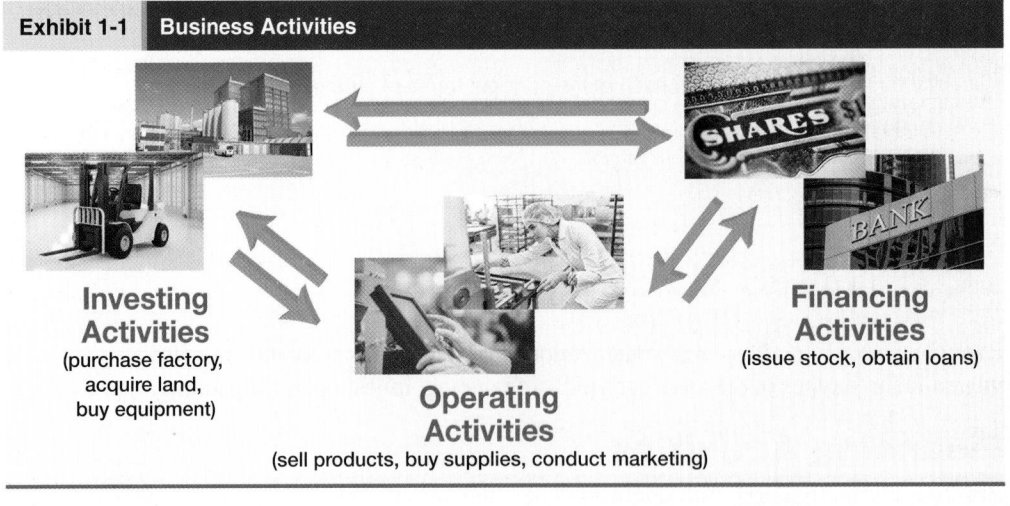

Exhibit 1-1 | **Business Activities**

Investing Activities
(purchase factory, acquire land, buy equipment)

Operating Activities
(sell products, buy supplies, conduct marketing)

Financing Activities
(issue stock, obtain loans)

© Shutterstock.com

YOUR TURN! 1.2

The solution is on page 53.

Classify each of the following activities as a financing, investing, or operating activity.

1. Receiving a loan from a bank.
2. Selling merchandise online.
3. Purchasing a delivery truck.
4. Purchasing merchandise for resale to customers.
5. Issuing shares of stock in exchange for cash.
6. Paying employee salaries.

ACCOUNTING INFORMATION AND ITS USE

LO3 Indicate who uses accounting information.

In today's society, many individuals and agencies are involved in the economic life of a business. The information needs of these parties are fulfilled, in part, by accounting information. The users of accounting information are classified by their relation to a business as either *external users* or *internal users*.

External Users of Accounting

An important function of the accounting process is to accumulate and report accounting information that details a business's results of operations, cash flows, and financial position. By U.S. law, publicly owned businesses must publish financial statements annually and quarterly. The subset of accounting that produces these publicly available financial statements is referred to as **financial accounting**.

Financial accounting information serves a variety of users. Potential investors and investment professionals need financial data to compare prospective investments to determine which, if any, they should invest in, and at what price. Creditors must consider the financial strength of a business before lending it funds, and stockholders must evaluate whether to remain invested in a business, buy more shares, or sell their existing shares of stock.

The financial statements issued by a company are the main source of financial information for these external users. Because financial statements are often used to evaluate the management team running the business, their objectivity is sometimes called into question because the reports are prepared by the management team itself. To establish the validity of financial statements, most businesses have their financial data audited by an independent public accountant. Publicly owned businesses are required to have their financial statements audited. The independent public accountant, or independent auditor, examines the financial statements and recommends any changes or improvements that are warranted. The independent auditor then expresses a professional opinion as to whether the financial statements are fairly presented "in conformity with generally accepted accounting principles." External users have greater confidence in financial statements that have been audited by an independent, certified public accountant.

ACCOUNTING IN PRACTICE

The Big Four

Independent auditors are licensed by the state in which they do their auditing work and are identified as **certified public accountants (CPAs)**. To qualify as a CPA, an individual must pass a rigorous examination that is administered nationally and must meet the educational and work experience requirements set by each state to ensure high standards of accounting and auditing performance. The four largest U.S. public accounting firms, referred to as the *Big Four*, have offices located throughout the world and employ thousands of auditors. These firms are **Deloitte & Touche**, **Ernst & Young**, **KPMG, LLP**, and **PricewaterhouseCoopers**.

Accounting In Practice boxes describe how accounting is used in real companies.

There are many other external users of a company's accounting information. For example, a business's customers may want information to help them determine if a company like **Whirlpool** will be able to honor its product warranties. Labor unions require information to determine the level of pay raises that they can demand from companies like **United Parcel Service**. **Exhibit 1-2** illustrates the kind of accounting information that is required by a company's external users.

Real Companies and Institutions are highlighted in bold, blue font.

Exhibit 1-2	Accounting Information Needs of External Users	
User Group		**Accounting Information Used to Answer Questions such as:**
Potential investors and current stockholders		How does the profitability of **Target** compare to that of **WalMart**? How does **Bank of America Corporation** compare with **Wells Fargo & Company** in terms of firm size?
Creditors and lenders		Will **Delta Airlines** be able to repay its creditors in a timely fashion? Is it safe to provide a bank loan to the **Federal Express Corporation**?
Taxation authorities and regulators	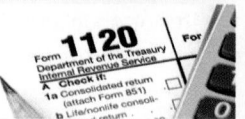	Is **Tesla Motors, Inc.** reporting the proper amount of taxable income? Is **Duke Energy**'s rate hike justified by its operating costs?

Internal Users of Accounting

A major function of accounting is to provide the internal management of a company with the data needed for decision making and the efficient management of the business. While managers have an interest in the information reported to external users, managers also require various other types of information, such as the cost of its products, estimates of the income to be earned from a sales campaign, cost comparisons of alternative courses of action, and long-range budgets. Because of the strategic nature of much of this information, it is usually only available to a company's top-level management. The process of generating and analyzing such data is referred to as **managerial accounting**. **Exhibit 1-3** illustrates the various types of accounting information that are required by a company's internal users.

Exhibit 1-3	Accounting Information Needs of Internal Users
User Group	**Accounting Information Used to Answer Questions such as:**
Marketing Department	What is the optimal price to sell the **Samsung** Galaxy phone to maximize the company's sales revenue? Was the promotional campaign by **Netflix** successful in promoting the company's *Stranger Things* series?
Management Team 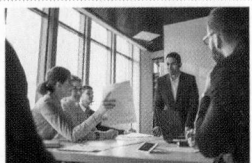	How much is the Olive Garden restaurant chain contributing to the overall profitability of its parent company, the **Darden Restaurant Group**? What is the projected profitability of the **General Motors'** Chevrolet brand for the coming year?
Finance Department	Is there sufficient cash available for **Hewlett Packard** to buy back a large amount of its outstanding common stock? Will **General Electric** have sufficient cash flow to pay its short-term expenses?

© Shutterstock.com

YOUR TURN! 1.3

The solution is on page 53.

1. Are financial statements the primary output of managerial or financial accounting? Explain.
2. Identify at least two internal users and explain why they need accounting information.
3. Identify at least two external users and explain why they need accounting information.

Ethics and Accounting

Ethics deals with the values, rules, and justifications that govern one's way of life. Although fundamental ethical concepts such as right and wrong, good and evil, justice and morality are abstract, many issues in our daily lives have ethical dimensions. The way that we respond to these issues defines our ethical profile. In both our personal and professional lives, our goal is to act ethically and responsibly.

Ethical behavior has not always been the rule in business. Business history reveals unethical activities such as price gouging of customers, using inside information for personal gain, paying bribes to government officials for favors, ignoring health and safety regulations, selling arms and military equipment to aggressor governments, polluting the environment, and issuing misleading financial information. Well-known accounting scandals at such companies as **Enron**, **WorldCom**, and **Lehman Brothers** have again brought ethics to the forefront.

Increasingly, business managers recognize the importance and value of ethical behavior by their employees. It is now commonplace for businesses to develop a written code of ethics to help guide the behavior of employees. Similarly, professional organizations of accountants have written ethics codes. The **American Institute of Certified Public Accountants (AICPA)**, for example, has a professional code of ethics to guide the conduct of its member CPAs. Similarly, the **Institute of Management Accountants (IMA)** has written standards of ethical conduct for accountants employed in the private sector.

Unethical behavior that results in misleading financial statements has the potential to erode public confidence and trust in accounting information. In response to this decline in public confidence, the U.S. Congress passed the **Sarbanes-Oxley Act** in 2002 with the goal of restoring investor trust by reducing the likelihood of future accounting scandals. Among the many changes required by this legislation is that a company's top management must certify in writing the accuracy of its reported financial statement information, and these executives risk criminal prosecution for fraudulent certification. In addition, companies must now report on the internal controls put into place to help deter errors in the financial reporting process and to detect them should they occur.

A.K.A. The Sarbanes-Oxley Act of 2002 is often referred to as SarBox or SOX.

Accountant as Detective—CSI in Real Life

FORENSIC ACCOUNTING

Law enforcement personnel are not the only people who perform criminal investigations. A branch of accounting known as **forensic accounting** is vitally important in many types of criminal investigations, from financial statement fraud, to money laundering, to massive investment frauds such as the one perpetrated by Bernard Madoff (who is currently serving a 150-year prison sentence). Unlike law enforcement personnel, forensic accountants are involved both before and after the commission of a crime.

Forensic Accounting boxes highlight how financial accounting knowledge can help aid in the prevention of errors and fraud.

Accountants face several unique ethical dilemmas, such as:

1. The output produced by accountants has financial implications for individuals, as well as businesses. These situations generate considerable pressure on the accountant to "improve" the reported results. The amount of income taxes to be paid by an individual or business, the amount of a bonus to be received by an employee, the price to be paid by a customer, and the amount of money to be distributed to a business's owners are examples of situations in which the financial implications can lead to efforts to influence the outcome. *Ethical behavior mandates that accountants ignore these pressures.*

2. Accountants have access to confidential, sensitive information. Tax returns, salary data, details of financial arrangements, planned acquisitions, and proposed price changes are examples of this type of information. *Ethical behavior mandates that accountants respect the confidentiality of information.*

3. A criticism of U.S. business practices is that they are too "bottom-line" (that is, short-term profit) oriented. This orientation can lead to unethical actions by management to increase reported short-term profits. Because accountants measure and report a firm's profit, they must be particularly concerned about these ethical breakdowns. *Both accountants and management must recognize the importance of a long-run perspective.* Studies indicate that, over the long term, successful companies and ethical practices go hand in hand.

YOUR TURN! 1.4

As an accountant for the Madoff Corporation, you are responsible for measuring and reporting the company's net income. It appears that actual results are going to be less than was expected by Wall Street analysts. Your supervisor has asked that you report some of next period's sales revenue early so that the current period's net income will be in line with analyst expectations. You know that reporting revenue like this represents a violation of generally accepted accounting principles. Your supervisor states that you will not really be doing anything wrong because the sales revenues are real—the company will just be reporting the revenue earlier than accounting guidelines allow. What should you do?

The solution is on page 54.

THE ACCOUNTING PROCESS

LO4   **Explain** the accounting process and generally accepted accounting principles.

Accounting is *the process of measuring economic activity of an entity in monetary terms and communicating results to users.* The accounting process consists of two principal activities—measurement and communication.

The measurement process must (1) identify the relevant economic activities of a business, (2) quantify these economic activities, and (3) record the resulting measures in a systematic manner. Measurement is done in monetary terms. In the United States, measurements are stated in U.S. dollars. In other countries, measurements are expressed in the local currency.

Because the purpose of accounting is to provide useful financial information, the communication process is extremely important. Accordingly, the accounting process (1) prepares financial reports to meet the needs of the user and (2) helps interpret the financial results for that user. To provide reports that serve users effectively, managers must be aware of how these users are likely to apply the reports. The needs of the various users differ; as such, there are different types of accounting reports. Managers employ various techniques to help users interpret the content of reports. These techniques include the way the report is formatted, the use of charts and graphs to highlight trends, and the calculation of ratios to emphasize important financial relations.

Thinking Globally *boxes emphasize the similarities and differences in business practices between companies in the U.S. and companies in other countries.*

THINKING GLOBALLY

Companies measure their operating performance using the currency of their principal place of business. The **Johnson & Johnson Company**, a well-known maker of baby shampoo and Band-Aids, is headquartered in New Jersey, and reports its financial results using the U.S. dollar. On the other hand, **Moet Hennessy Louis Vuitton**, the luxury goods manufacturer, is headquartered in Paris, France, and reports its financial results using the euro. Some companies prepare "convenience translations" of their financial statements in the currency and language of other countries so that potential foreign investors can more readily understand the company's financial performance and condition.

Generally Accepted Accounting Principles

It is important that financial statements be prepared under a set of rules that is understood by the users of those reports. Imagine if every business were free to determine exactly how it measured and communicated its financial health and operating performance. How would a user of this information be able to compare one company's results to another if each played by a different set of rules? Financial statement users who rely on accounting data expect that all companies will follow the same standards and procedures when preparing their statements. In the United States these standards and procedures are called **generally accepted accounting principles (GAAP)**.

Generally accepted accounting principles are guides to action that can (and do) change over time. Sometimes specific accounting principles must be altered or new principles formulated to fit a changing set of economic circumstances or changes in business practices.

A.K.A. Generally accepted accounting principles are often referred to as GAAP (pronounced like the clothing store "Gap").

Financial Accounting Oversight

The **Financial Accounting Standards Board (FASB)**, the American Institute of Certified Public Accountants (AICPA), and the **U.S. Securities and Exchange Commission (SEC)** are instrumental in the development of generally accepted accounting principles in the United States. As a federal agency, the SEC's primary focus is to regulate the interstate sale of stocks and bonds. The SEC requires companies under its jurisdiction to submit audited annual financial statements to the agency which it then makes available to the general public. The SEC has the power to set the accounting principles used by these companies, but the agency has largely delegated that principle-setting responsibility to the FASB.

The FASB is a nongovernmental entity whose pronouncements establish U.S. GAAP.[1] The FASB consists of a seven-member board and follows a process that allows for input from interested parties as it considers a new or changed accounting principle (see the appendix to this chapter for additional information on the conceptual framework the FASB has developed to formulate accounting standards). A new or changed principle requires the support of at least a majority of the board members. More recently, the **Public Company Accounting Oversight Board (PCAOB)** was established. The PCAOB approves auditing standards, known as **generally accepted auditing standards (GAAS)**, and monitors the quality of financial statements and audits. **Exhibit 1-4** illustrates the structure of financial accounting oversight in the United States.

Exhibit 1-4	Financial Accounting Oversight

Infographics *illustrate difficult concepts and procedures.*

© Shutterstock.com

The FASB completed the Accounting Standards Codification in 2009 concerning how GAAP is organized and communicated. This codification represents the authoritative U.S. GAAP for non-governmental entities and is easily researched through an online database maintained by the FASB. A major justification for the codification project was to ease the convergence of U.S. GAAP and international standards.

International Financial Reporting Standards

The past few decades have witnessed a steady acceptance of international financial reporting standards. This acceptance coincides with the increasing globalization of business. Although several organizations are working to increase international harmonization in accounting, the organization that has taken the lead in formulating international accounting principles is the **International Accounting Standards Board (IASB)**. The accounting standards formulated by the IASB are referred to as the **International Financial Reporting Standards (IFRS)**. Approximately 120 nations or reporting jurisdictions either require or permit the use of IFRS. This includes the European Union, Australia, New Zealand, Israel, and Canada.

A.K.A. International financial reporting standards are often referred to as IFRS (pronounced "eye furs").

U.S. companies are not currently allowed to report their financial statements using IFRS. However, the FASB and IASB coordinate their standard-setting activities in an effort to reduce or eliminate as many differences as possible.

---

[1] Paralleling the FASB structure, the **Governmental Accounting Standards Board (GASB)** was organized in 1984 to formulate generally accepted accounting principles for state and local governments.

YOUR TURN! 1.5

The solution is on page 54.

Match the items from column 1 with the correct item in column 2.

1. Accounting	*a.* Guides to action for financial reporting
2. Generally Accepted Accounting Principles (GAAP)	*b.* Responsible for formulating international accounting standards
3. Public Company Accounting Oversight Board (PCAOB)	*c.* The process of measuring economic activity of an entity in monetary terms and communicating the results to users
4. International Accounting Standards Board (IASB)	*d.* The organization empowered to approve auditing standards

FINANCIAL STATEMENTS

LO5 **Describe** the accounting equation and each financial statement.

There are four basic financial statements: the balance sheet, the income statement, the statement of stockholders' equity, and the statement of cash flows. Each financial statement begins with a heading. The heading provides the name of the company, the name of the financial statement, and the date or time period of the statement.

Balance Sheet

A.K.A. The balance sheet is also referred to as the statement of financial position.
A.K.A. The accounting equation is also called the balance sheet equation.

The **balance sheet** is a listing of a firm's assets, liabilities, and stockholders' equity as of a given date, usually the end of an accounting period. The balance sheet depicts a framework called the **accounting equation**. The accounting equation states that the sum of a business's economic resources must equal the sum of any claims on those resources. That is, a business obtains resources that it utilizes in its operations from outside sources, principally creditors and stockholders, who maintain claims on those resources. Consequently, the accounting equation can be written as:

Resources of a company = Claims on resources

Assets refer to a company's resources, liabilities refer to creditor claims on those resources, and stockholders' equity refers to owner claims on those resources. Using these terms, the accounting equation can be reformulated as:

Assets = Liabilities + Stockholders' equity

This equation states that the firm's assets equals the sum of its liabilities plus its stockholders' equity—see **Exhibit 1-5**. Throughout the accounting process, the accounting equation must always remain in balance.

Hints help explain difficult concepts.

Hint: Only resources that can be expressed in monetary terms are included among the assets reported on the balance sheet. There exist some assets that cannot be expressed in monetary terms, such as the value of a company's workforce, and, therefore, are not reported on a balance sheet.

Exhibit 1-5	**Accounting Equation for a Business**				
Economic Terms	Resources	=	Creditor claims on resources	+	Stockholder (owner) claims on resources
Business Terms	Assets	=	Liabilities	+	Stockholders' equity

Assets are the economic resources of a business that can be expressed in monetary terms. Assets take many forms. Cash is an asset, as are claims to receive cash payments from customers for goods or services provided, called accounts receivable. Other types of assets include inventory, supplies, land, buildings, and equipment. The key characteristic of any asset is that it represents a probable future economic benefit to a business.

Liabilities are the obligations or debts that a business must pay in cash or in goods and services at some future time as a consequence of past transactions or events. For example, a business can borrow money and sign a promissory note agreeing to repay the borrowed amount in six months. The business reports this obligation as a liability called notes payable. Similarly, if a business owes money to various suppliers for goods or services already provided, it is called accounts payable, or if it owes wages to its employees for work already performed, it is called wages payable. The business reports these obligations as liabilities on its balance sheet.

Stockholders' equity refers to the ownership (stockholder) claims on the assets of the business. Stockholders' equity represents a *residual claim* on a business's assets; that is, it is a claim on the assets of a business that remain after all liabilities to creditors have been satisfied. For this reason, stockholders' equity is sometimes referred to as a business's **net assets**, where net assets equal the difference between total assets and total liabilities. In equation format,

$$\text{Assets} - \text{Liabilities} = \text{Stockholders' equity}$$

and,

$$\text{Net assets} = \text{Stockholders' equity}$$

Columbia's balance sheet is shown in **Exhibit 1-6** and reports the company's assets, liabilities, and stockholders' equity. (All Columbia Sportswear amounts are in thousands of dollars.) Columbia's assets totaled $2,212,902 at year-end 2017, with the largest asset being cash of $673,166 followed by inventories of $457,927. Total assets ($2,212,902) are equal to the sum of liabilities ($560,643) and stockholders' equity ($1,652,259). This equality must always exist as required by the accounting equation.

Exhibit 1-6	Columbia Sportswear Balance Sheet

COLUMBIA SPORTSWEAR COMPANY
Balance Sheet
December 31, 2017
(In thousands)

Real financial data for focus companies illustrate key concepts of each chapter.

Assets

Cash	$ 673,166
Investments	94,983
Accounts receivable	364,862
Inventories	457,927
Prepaid expenses and other current assets	58,559
Property, plant, and equipment, net	281,394
Other assets	282,011
Total assets	$2,212,902

Hint: Final totals in the financial statements are double underlined. Follow this format whenever asked to prepare a financial statement.

Liabilities and Stockholders' Equity

Liabilities

Accounts payable	$ 252,301
Income taxes payable	77,211
Other liabilities	231,131
Total liabilities	560,643

Stockholders' Equity

Common stock	45,829
Retained earnings	1,606,430
Total stockholders' equity	1,652,259
Total liabilities and stockholders' equity	$2,212,902

Columbia's balance sheet indicates that the company principally depends on stockholders' equity to finance its operations since liabilities totaled only $560,643 at 2017 year-end, or approximately 25 percent of total assets.

TAKEAWAY 1.1	Concept	Method	Assessment
Takeaways summarize the key concepts before proceeding to the next topic.	What mix of financing does a company use?	The balance sheet provides information regarding the various forms of financing, both debt financing and equity financing. Compare the amount of liabilities appearing on the balance sheet to the amount of equity appearing on the balance sheet.	A higher ratio of liabilities to equity implies a higher use of creditor financing, and vice versa. Creditor financing is viewed by users as more risky.

Income Statement

A.K.A. The income statement is also called the statement of operations, the statement of income, and the earnings statement.

A.K.A. Sales revenue is also referred to as revenue, sales, net sales, or net revenue.

A.K.A. Net income is also referred to as net earnings or net profit.

The **income statement** reports the results of operations for a business for a given time period, usually a quarter or a year. The income statement lists the revenues and expenses of the business. **Sales revenue** are increases to a company's resources that result when goods or services are provided to customers. The amount of sales revenue earned is measured by the value of the assets received in exchange for the goods or services delivered.

Expenses are decreases in a company's resources from generating revenue. Expenses are generally measured by the value of the assets used up or exchanged as a result of a business's operating activities. Common examples of expenses include the cost of the items sold, referred to as cost of goods sold, selling expense, marketing expense, administrative expense, interest expense, and income tax. When total revenue exceeds total expenses, the resulting amount is called **net income**; when total expenses exceed sales revenue, the resulting amount is called a **net loss**.

Columbia's income statement is presented in **Exhibit 1-7**. The statement begins with the business's name, statement title, and time period covered. For Columbia, total revenue in 2017 is reported to be $2,477,329 (remember amounts are rounded to the nearest $1,000). Next, Columbia subtracts a series of expenses totaling $2,372,206, yielding net income of $105,123.

Exhibit 1-7   Columbia Sportswear Income Statement

COLUMBIA SPORTSWEAR COMPANY
Income Statement
For Year Ended December 31, 2017
(In thousands)

Revenue	
Sales	$2,466,105
Other revenue	11,224
Total revenue	2,477,329
Expenses	
Cost of goods sold	1,306,143
Selling, general, and administrative expense	910,894
Income tax expense	154,419
Other expenses	750
Total expenses	2,372,206
Net income	$ 105,123

Concept →	Method →	Assessment	TAKEAWAY 1.2
Is a company profitable?	The income statement reports a company's performance for a given period of time. Compare reported sales revenue to reported expenses.	Sales revenue in excess of expenses yields net income, implying a profitable company. If expenses exceed revenue, the company has a net loss.	

Statement of Stockholders' Equity

The **statement of stockholders' equity** reports the events causing an increase or decrease in stockholders' equity during a given time period. The statement of stockholders' equity consists of two parts—contributed capital and earned capital. **Contributed capital** is a measure of the capital contributed by the stockholders of a company when they purchase ownership shares in the company. Ownership shares are called *common shares* or *common stock*. **Earned capital** is a measure of the capital that is earned by the company, reinvested in the business, and not distributed to its stockholders—that is, its *retained earnings*.

Retained earnings are increased when operations produce net income and decreased when operations produce a net loss. Retained earnings also decrease when a company pays a dividend to its stockholders.

A company's retained earnings for a period is determined as follows (sometimes called *statement of retained earnings*):

Retained earnings, beginning of period	$1,527,710
Add: Net income (loss)	105,123
Less: Dividends and other	(26,403)
Retained earnings, end of period	$1,606,430

Note: According to a 2011 survey of 500 companies, nearly 98% (489 out of 500) of the companies surveyed issue a Statement of Stockholders' Equity, while only 1% issue a separate Statement of Retained Earnings. Source: Accounting Trends & Techniques, 2011.

Columbia's statement of stockholders' equity appears in **Exhibit 1-8**. We focus here on Columbia's retained earnings from its statement of stockholders' equity to emphasize two important concepts: (1) the relation between the income statement and the balance sheet and (2) the components of retained earnings. Columbia's statement of stockholders' equity in **Exhibit 1-8** begins with its ending retained earnings from 2016 of $1,527,710. The beginning balance of retained earnings is then increased by its net income of $105,123 from 2017. (Can you find this amount on Columbia's income statement in **Exhibit 1-7**?) Next, earnings that were distributed as a dividend to Columbia's stockholders in 2017 ($26,403) are subtracted to yield an ending retained earnings balance of $1,606,430 as of December 31, 2017. (Can you find this amount on Columbia's balance sheet in **Exhibit 1-6**?)

Exhibit 1-8	Columbia Sportswear Statement of Stockholders' Equity

COLUMBIA SPORTSWEAR COMPANY
Statement of Stockholders' Equity
For Year Ended December 31, 2017

(In thousands)	Common Stock	Retained Earnings	Total
Balance, December 31, 2016	$53,801	$1,527,710	$1,581,511
Add: Common stock issued	27,570		27,570
Net income		105,123	105,123
Less: Common stock repurchased	(35,542)		(35,542)
Dividends and other		(26,403)	(26,403)
Balance, December 31, 2017	$45,829	$1,606,430	$1,652,259

TAKEAWAY 1.3	Concept →	Method →	Assessment
	What portion of a company's current period net income is distributed to its stockholders, and what portion is retained?	The statement of stockholders' equity reports both a company's net income and the amount of dividends distributed to stockholders. Compare the company's dividends to its net income.	A higher ratio of dividends to net income implies that a company is distributing more of its net income to its stockholders, whereas a lower ratio implies it is retaining more of its income for purposes such as growing its business.

CORPORATE SOCIAL RESPONSIBILITY

Corporate Social Responsibility *boxes showcase how forward-thinking companies are embracing CSR as part of their long-term business models.*

Reporting on Triple Bottom Line

Companies worldwide are focused on more than just the bottom line. Research shows that financial responsibility goes hand in hand with social responsibility. This is labeled a "virtuous cycle" because financial success provides the means to act in a socially responsible manner, and acting socially responsible increases a company's financial performance. Financial statements are not well suited for measuring social performance. To aid in the pursuit of socially responsible behavior, accountants have developed a **triple bottom line** framework in which the single bottom line of financial performance on the income statement is supplemented with a social bottom line and an environmental bottom line. The triple bottom line standard for urban and community accounting has been ratified by the United Nations and has become widely used in public sector accounting.

Statement of Cash Flows

The **statement of cash flows** reports a business's cash inflows and cash outflows during a given period of time. The cash flows are grouped into the three business activities of operating, investing, and financing. Cash flow from operating activities includes the cash received from the sale of goods and services and the cash spent on operating expenses. Cash flow from investing activities includes cash payments and receipts from the business buying and selling certain assets that it uses in its operations. Cash flow from financing activities includes the issuance and repurchase of the business's own shares and the amounts borrowed and repaid to creditors.

Columbia's statement of cash flows is in **Exhibit 1-9**. This statement shows that Columbia's cash balance increased during 2017 by $121,777 from $551,389 on December 31, 2016, to $673,166 on December 31, 2017. Columbia's operating activities provided $341,128 in cash while Columbia's investing activities used $147,784 and Columbia's financing activities used $71,567. Adding the changes in cash for the three types of activities produces the increase of $121,777. The statement of cash flows always concludes with this reconciliation of the cash balance from the beginning of the year to the end of the year. (Can you find the ending cash balance on Columbia's balance sheet in **Exhibit 1-6**?)

Exhibit 1-9	Columbia Sportswear Statement of Cash Flows

COLUMBIA SPORTSWEAR COMPANY Statement of Cash Flows For Year Ended December 31, 2017 (In thousands)	
Cash flows from operating activities.	$341,128
Cash flows from investing activities	(147,784)
Cash flows from financing activities	(71,567)
Net increase (decrease) in cash.	121,777
Cash at beginning of year.	551,389
Cash at end of year	$673,166

Concept ➤	Method ➤	Assessment	TAKEAWAY 1.4
What are the major sources and uses of a company's cash?	The statement of cash flows reports a company's sources and uses of cash separated into three activities: operating, investing, and financing. Identify a company's sources and uses of cash as reported in the statement of cash flows.	Sources of cash are reported as positive numbers and uses of cash as negative numbers. Larger positive numbers represent major cash sources and larger negative numbers represent major cash uses.	

Relations Among the Financial Statements

The income statement, the statement of stockholders' equity, the balance sheet, and the statement of cash flows are linked to one another. That is, the financial statements *articulate*. To illustrate the linkages, refer to the financial statements of Columbia Sportswear in **Exhibit 1-10**. Observe that Ⓐ, the company's net income (or net loss) for a period is an input to the statement of stockholders' equity, and that Ⓑ, the ending common stock, retained earnings, and total equity are inputs to the balance sheet. The statement of cash flows Ⓒ explains the change in the cash balance on the balance sheet for a period.

Exhibit 1-10	Financial Statements for Columbia Sportswear Company

Columbia Sportswear Company
Income Statement
For Year Ended December 31, 2017

Revenue	
Sales	$2,466,105
Other revenue	11,224
Total revenue	2,477,329
Expenses	
Cost of sales	1,306,143
Selling, general, and administrative	910,894
Income tax expense	154,419
Other expenses	750
Total expenses	2,372,206
Net income	$ 105,123

Columbia Sportswear Company
Statement of Stockholders' Equity
For Year Ended December 31, 2017

	Common Stock	Retained Earnings	Total
Balance, December 31, 2016	$53,801	$1,527,710	$1,581,511
Add: Common stock issued	27,570		27,570
Net income		105,123	105,123
Less: Common stock repurchased	(35,542)		(35,542)
Dividends and other		(26,403)	(26,403)
Balance, December 31, 2017	$45,829	$1,606,430	$1,652,259

Columbia Sportswear Company
Balance Sheet
December 31, 2017

Assets		Liabilities	
Cash	$ 673,166	Accounts payable	$ 252,301
Investments	94,983	Income taxes payable	77,211
Accounts receivable	364,862	Other liabilities	231,131
Inventories	457,927	Total liabilities	560,643
Prepaid expenses and other current assets	58,559	**Stockholders' Equity**	
Property, plant, and equipment, net	281,394	Common stock	45,829
Other assets	282,011	Retained earnings	1,606,430
		Total stockholders' equity	1,652,259
Total assets	$2,212,902	Total liabilities and stockholders' equity	$2,212,902

Columbia Sportswear Company
Statement of Cash Flows
For Year Ended December 31, 2017

Cash flows from operating activities	$341,128
Cash flows from investing activities	(147,784)
Cash flows from financing activities	(71,567)
Net increase in cash	121,777
Cash at beginning of year	551,389
Cash at end of year	$673,166

When financial statements are prepared, the sequence suggested by these relations is customarily followed; that is, (1) the income statement is prepared first, followed by (2) the statement of stockholders' equity, then (3) the balance sheet, and finally (4) the statement of cash flows.

Three of these financial statements present information covering a specific period of time: the income statement, the statement of stockholders' equity, and the statement of cash flows. For this reason, these financial statements are referred to as **period-of-time statements**. In contrast, the balance sheet reports information as of a specific date. The balance sheet, therefore, is referred to as a **point-in-time statement**. (Illustrated in **Exhibit 1-11**.)

Exhibit 1-11   Financial Statement Links Across Time

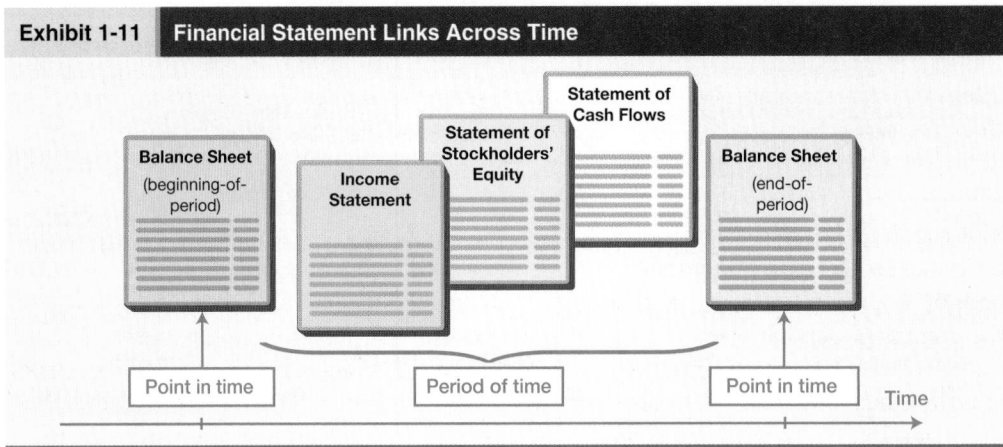

YOUR TURN! 1.6

The solution is on pages 54–55.

Guided Example icons denote the availability of a demonstration video in **myBusinessCourse** (MBC). See the Preface for more on MBC.

Kanzu Corporation started business on January 1. The following information was compiled by Kanzu as of December 31.

Sales revenue	$20,000	Accounts payable	$ 4,000
Expenses	12,000	Notes payable	33,000
Dividends	3,000	Common stock	20,000
Cash	1,500	Retained earnings	?
Accounts receivable	2,500	Cash flow from operating activities	6,500
Inventory	3,000	Cash flow from investing activities	(55,000)
Equipment	15,000	Cash flow from financing activities	50,000
Building	40,000		

Prepare the company's year-end financial statements: an income statement, a statement of stockholders' equity, a balance sheet, and a statement of cash flows.

OTHER ANNUAL REPORT COMPONENTS

Columbia Sportswear Company, like all publicly traded companies in the United States, must file an **annual report** called a **Form 10-K** with the U.S. Securities and Exchange Commission (SEC). Some companies also send a less detailed version of their annual report to their stockholders. The four financial statements explained in this chapter are essential components of this report. Additional components of the annual report are the notes to the financial statements, the auditor's report, and the Management's Discussion and Analysis.

Notes to Financial Statements

A skilled financial statement user wants to know more than just the numbers reported in the financial statements. That user also wants to know assumptions and estimates that were used in preparing the statements, the measurement procedures that were followed, and the details behind certain summary numbers. The notes to the financial statements, which are quantitative as well as qualitative, provide a great deal more information than just the numbers alone. For example, notes usually contain a description regarding how the company determined the value of its inventory, a detailed chart to explain the property, plant, and equipment account, and a description of any pending lawsuits. No analysis of the annual report is complete without a careful reading of the notes to the financial statements. The following is a short excerpt from Columbia's notes:

LO6   **Explain** additional disclosures that accompany financial statements.

> **Accounts receivable**   Accounts receivable have been reduced by an allowance for doubtful accounts. The Company makes ongoing estimates of the collectability of accounts receivable and maintains an allowance for estimated losses resulting from the inability of the Company's customers to make required payments.

The notes are considered a key part of the financial statements and, with the four basic financial statements, are audited by the company's independent auditor.

Excerpts from recent financial statements and notes are used to illustrate and reinforce concepts.

Independent Auditor's Report

The report of the independent auditor, commonly referred to as the auditor's report, describes the activities undertaken by a company's independent auditor and provides that auditor's opinion regarding whether the financial statements fairly present the results of the company's operations and financial health. A short excerpt from the auditor's report included with Columbia Sportswear's annual report follows. Deloitte & Touche, which is Columbia's independent auditor, reports that the financial statements of Columbia are, in its opinion, fairly presented. The independent auditor has intentionally avoided using language such as the statements are "correctly presented" or are "exactly correct." As we will see in subsequent chapters, the financial statements are prepared only after the management team makes a number of assumptions, estimates, and accounting policy decisions. As a consequence, it is inappropriate to describe the statements as being right or wrong since the reported numbers are dependent on the accounting policies selected and the assumptions and estimates made by management.

> **Report of Independent Registered Public Accounting Firm**
> In our opinion, such financial statements present fairly, in all material respects, the financial position of the Company as of December 31, 2017 and 2016, and the results of its operations and its cash flows for each of the three years in the period ended December 31, 2017, in conformity with accounting principles generally accepted in the United States of America.
> *DELOITTE & TOUCHE LLP*

Management's Discussion and Analysis

In addition to the financial statements and notes, the SEC requires companies to provide other information, such as a description of its business, the properties it owns, and the risks it faces. Unlike the financial statements and notes, however, this information is not audited by the company's independent auditor. An important component of this other information is the Management's Discussion and Analysis, or MD&A, which contains management's interpretation of the company's recent performance and financial condition. This interpretation helps financial statement users gain context to help frame their own analysis and interpretation of the numbers that appear in the financial statements.

The MD&A is also where a company's management provides its view regarding what the future holds for its business. Discussions of future opportunities and risks are called "forward-looking" and are helpful to any financial statement user interested in learning about such things as potential new markets for the company's products or potential new competitors. Obviously these forward-looking statements are subjective in nature, and the financial statement user must do his or her own independent analysis.

The following is a short excerpt from Columbia's MD&A.

Business Outlook

The global business climate continues to present us with a great deal of uncertainty, making it difficult to predict future results. Consistent with the historical seasonality of the business, we anticipate 2018 profitability to be heavily concentrated in the second half of the year. Factors that could significantly affect our full year 2018 financial results include:

- Performance and profitability of our global direct-to-consumer operations;
- Unseasonable weather conditions or other unforeseen factors affecting consumer demand and the resulting effect on cancellations of advance wholesale orders, sales returns, wholesale customer accommodations, replenishment orders and reorders, direct-to-consumer sales, changes in mix and volume of full price sales in relation to promotional and closeout product sales, and suppressed wholesale and end-consumer demand in subsequent seasons;
- Industry trends affecting consumer traffic and spending in brick and mortar retail channels, which are creating uncertainty regarding the long-term financial health of several of our U.S. wholesale customers;
- The effects of changes in foreign currency exchange rates on sales, gross margin, operating income, and net income;
- Difficult economic and competitive environments in certain key markets within our Latin America and Asia Pacific ("LAAP") region, in particular, Korea;
- Continued sales growth and profitability contributed by our Europe, Middle East and Africa ("EMEA") region;
- Performance of our Mountain Hardwear business as we work to re-invigorate that brand in the marketplace;
- The financial impact of activities associated with and resulting from Project CONNECT;
- Further refinement of our 2017 TCJA provisional income tax estimates; and
- The financial impact of executing our Consumer-First platform.

These factors and others may have a material effect on our financial condition, results of operations or cash flows, particularly with respect to quarterly comparisons.

YOUR TURN! 1.7

The solution is on page 55.

Match each of the items in the left column with the appropriate annual report component where we would find that item, from the right column.

1. An opinion regarding the fair presentation of financial statements.
2. Information regarding the procedures followed to value a company's assets.
3. A discussion of new markets that a company plans to enter.

   a. Management Discussion and Analysis
   b. Notes to the Financial Statements
   c. Auditor's report

CAREERS IN ACCOUNTING

Describe careers in accounting.

Job prospects after graduation are one of the primary considerations students have when selecting a major. The good news for accounting majors is that the present is very good and the future looks even brighter. According to the

Bureau of Labor Statistics, accounting jobs are expected to grow by 13 percent annually through 2022, assuring accounting majors will be in demand for the foreseeable future.

Accounting opportunities are present in multiple areas. **Exhibit 1-12** lists some typical job titles in (1) private accounting; (2) public accounting; and (3) government. Accountants working in the private sector work for a particular company, whereas accountants working in public accounting spend most of their time working for clients of their employer.

Accounting professionals are not just in high demand, they are also held in high regard by the public. Accounting professionals often earn various certificates in order to further distinguish themselves. The most sought after certification is the Certified Public Accountant (CPA) certificate. This certification requires both education and professional experience, passing an examination, and the highest ethical standards. Three other important certifications are the Certified Management Accountant (CMA), the Certified Internal Auditor (CIA), and the Certified Fraud Examiner (CFE) certificates.

Exhibit 1-12	Careers in Accounting		
	Private Accounting	**Public Accounting**	**Government Accounting**
Typical Positions	Internal audit Tax Financial reporting Analyst Budgeting Cost accounting	Auditor Tax Consulting Strategy	Auditor Tax Budgeting Criminal investigation

One of the reasons that accounting graduates find great opportunities upon graduation is because their accounting courses provide specific skills that can be applied immediately on the job. It is therefore quite apparent that when one compares the advantages and disadvantages of an accounting career, the positive job outlook and the high salaries are often listed. Accountants also have a great deal of mobility and upward advancement potential.

According to the U.S. Bureau of Labor Statistics, the 2017 median pay for the 1.4 million accounting jobs in their database was $69,350. **Exhibit 1-13** compares the 2018 salaries of starting accountants, accountants with a couple years of experience, and more senior accountants in both public accounting and in large corporations.

Exhibit 1-13	Accounting Salaries	
Area of Employment	**Position and Experience**	**Midpoint of Salary Range**
Private Accounting	Bookkeeper	$ 37,500
	Financial Analyst < 1 year	$ 50,000
	Financial Analyst 1–3 years	$ 65,000
	Financial Analyst Manager	$100,000
	Corporate Controller	$170,000
	Chief Financial Officer	$192,000
Public Accounting	Junior Accountant < 1 year	$ 46,000
	Senior Accountant	$ 70,000
	Senior Manager	$132,000

Source: Robert Half 2018 Salary Guide

Data Analytics and Blockchain Technology

Accounting skills are not stagnant; rather they are constantly evolving. What was once done by hand is now done with the aid of specialized software. Programs like **Quick-Books** from **Intuit** have automated the basic accounting job of transaction recording, and programs like **Microsoft Excel** have greatly aided in the analysis of accounting data. While some industry observers had predicted these technological advances would replace the need for accountants, these applications have simply changed the way accountants perform their jobs. Newer technologies such as data analytics and blockchain are further changing the way accountants do their jobs. However, knowledge of these technologies and the related skills needed to use them are often lacking among current accountants. That was the key finding in a recently released joint report, *Building a Team to Capitalize on the Promise of Big Data*, by the human resource consulting firm Robert Half and the Institute of Management Accountants (IMA).

Data analytics (DA) can broadly be defined as the process of examining sets of data with the goal of discovering useful information from patterns found in the data. Accountants employing data analytics can glean important insights from a company's financial data and identify areas where improvements can be made.

Blockchain was made famous as the underpinning technology used for digital currencies, such as **Bitcoin** and **Ethereum**. **Blockchain** is a distributed digital ledger that provides a secure means, for those that have permission, to view recorded transactions. This technology has wide-ranging implications for business and is expected to greatly affect the way accountants perform audits.

Understanding what data analytics and blockchain technology are and how they are used is the first step towards developing marketable skills in each area, so we have included examples of each at various points in the book. In addition, **Appendix F** at the end of this book provides a more detailed discussion of both topics.

COMPREHENSIVE PROBLEM

You have been approached by Janet Jones about helping her assemble a set of December 31 financial statements for her new business. Janet began the operations of her bakery shop on January 1, 2019. Janet decided that she did not want to risk any personal liability resulting from operating the business; consequently, she organized the bakery, called Sweet Pleasures, as a corporation.

Required

Use the format of **Exhibits 1-6** through **1-9** to prepare an income statement, statement of stockholders' equity, balance sheet, and statement of cash flows for Sweet Pleasures as of December 31, 2019. Use the account titles and balances provided below. Be sure to use proper underlining and double underlining.

Sales of goods	$200,000	Dividends	$ 10,000
Cash	99,000	Bank loan payable	20,000
Rent expense	16,000	Accounts receivable	40,000
Interest payable	1,600	Cash received from operating activities	160,000
Cash received from issuance of common stock	50,000	Cash payments for operating activities	94,000
Insurance expense	20,000	Salary expense	40,000
Purchase of equipment	27,000	Cash received from borrowing from bank	20,000
Equipment	27,000	Interest expense	1,600
Common stock	50,000	Administrative expense	18,000
Cash dividends paid	10,000		

Solution

SWEET PLEASURES CORPORATION
Income Statement
For Year Ended December 31, 2019

Revenue		
Sales of goods		$200,000
Expenses		
Rent expense	$16,000	
Insurance expense	20,000	
Salary expense	40,000	
Administrative expense	18,000	
Interest expense	1,600	
Total expenses		95,600
Net income		$104,400

SWEET PLEASURES CORPORATION
Statement of Stockholders' Equity
For Year Ended December 31, 2019

	Common Stock	Retained Earnings	Total
Balance, January 1	$ 0	$ 0	$ 0
Add: Common stock issued	50,000		50,000
Net income		104,400	104,400
Less: Dividends		(10,000)	(10,000)
Balance, December 31	$50,000	$ 94,400	$144,400

SWEET PLEASURES CORPORATION
Balance Sheet
December 31, 2019

Assets		Liabilities	
Cash	$ 99,000	Bank loan payable	$ 20,000
Accounts receivable	40,000	Interest payable	1,600
Equipment	27,000	Total liabilities	21,600
		Stockholders' Equity	
		Common stock	50,000
		Retained earnings	94,400
		Total stockholders' equity	144,400
Total assets	$166,000	Total liabilities and stockholders' equity	$166,000

SWEET PLEASURES CORPORATION
Statement of Cash Flows
For Year Ended December 31, 2019

Cash flow from operating activities		
Cash received from operating activities	$160,000	
Cash payments for operating activities	(94,000)	
Cash provided by operating activities		$66,000
Cash flow from investing activities		
Purchase of equipment	(27,000)	
Cash used by investing activities		(27,000)
Cash flow from financing activities		
Borrowing from bank	20,000	
Issuance of common stock	50,000	
Cash dividends paid	(10,000)	
Cash provided by financing activities		60,000
Net increase of cash		99,000
Cash at January 1		0
Cash at December 31		$99,000

APPENDIX 1A: FASB's Conceptual Framework

The FASB has developed a conceptual framework, in coordination with the International Accounting Standards Board. The **conceptual framework** is a cohesive set of interrelated objectives and fundamentals for external financial reporting whose purpose is to guide the formulation of specific U.S. accounting principles. This framework, outlined in **Exhibit 1A-1**, consists of (1) financial reporting objectives, (2) financial statement elements,

LO8 Appendix 1A: **Discuss** FASB's conceptual framework.

(3) qualitative characteristics of accounting information, and (4) recognition and measurement criteria for financial statements. A recurrent theme in the conceptual framework is the importance of providing information that is useful to financial statement users.

| Exhibit 1A-1 | Summary of Conceptual Framework |

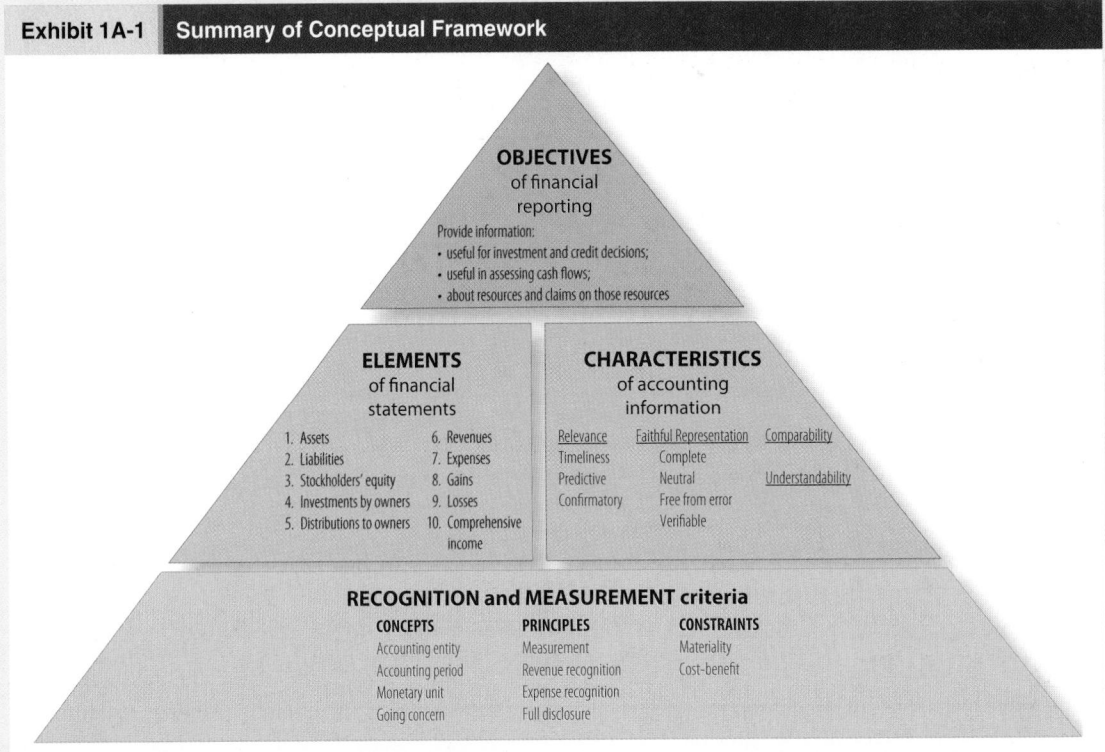

Financial Reporting Objectives

The **financial reporting objectives** focus on information useful to investors and creditors. Accordingly, financial statements have the principal objective of providing information that is (1) useful in making investment, credit, and similar decisions and (2) helpful in assessing the ability of enterprises to generate future cash flows. Financial statements should also (3) contain information about a company's economic resources, the claims on those resources, and the effects of events that change those resources and claims. This helps to identify a company's financial strengths and weaknesses, predict future performance, and evaluate earlier expectations.

Financial Statement Elements

The **financial statement elements** are the components of financial statements. These elements include assets, liabilities, stockholders' equity, investments by owners, distributions to owners, revenues, expenses, gains, losses, and comprehensive income.

Qualitative Characteristics

The **qualitative characteristics of accounting information** are depicted in **Exhibit 1A-2**. These qualities are intended to contribute to decision usefulness. The two primary qualities are **relevance** and **faithful representation**. To be relevant, accounting information must make a difference in a user's decisions. Relevant information must be timely and contribute to the predictive and evaluative decisions made by investors and creditors. Faithful representation has the characteristics of being complete, neutral, free from error, and verifiable.

Additional enhancing qualitative characteristics of accounting information are comparability and understandability. In order to enable users to most effectively compare financial results across companies, U.S. GAAP requires that companies disclose in the notes to financial statements the accounting policy choices they elected to use in the preparation of their financial statements. **Comparability** aids users to understand similarities and differences among items. Related to comparability is **consistency**, although they are not the same. Comparability relates to making comparisons among more than one item, whereas consistency relates to a single item and means the same accounting methods are used from one accounting period to the next. U.S. GAAP requires that when a firm changes a method of reporting its financial results that the financial impact of the method change be revealed in its notes to financial statements. **Understandability** is enhanced if information is classified, characterized, and presented clearly and concisely.

Exhibit 1A-2   **Qualitative Characteristics of Accounting Information**

Recognition and Measurement Criteria

The **recognition and measurement criteria** specify the conditions that must be satisfied before a particular asset, liability, revenue, or expense can be recorded in the financial records. An item under consideration must meet the definition of an element and be measurable, and information about the item must achieve the primary qualitative characteristics of accounting information. The recognition and measurement criteria consist of four concepts, four principles, and two constraints.

Concepts

A fundamental concept in accounting is the entity. An **accounting entity** is an economic unit with identifiable boundaries for which we accumulate and report financial information. Before we can analyze and report activities, we must identify the particular entity. Each sole proprietorship, partnership, and corporation is an entity, and separate accounting records must be maintained for each unit. In accumulating financial information, we maintain a record of the activities of the accounting entity separately from the economic and personal activities of its owners. The operations of most businesses are virtually continuous. Yet, the economic life of a company can be divided into specific periods of time, known as the **accounting period**, which is typically one year for purposes of preparing financial statements. Although the division of the total life of a business into segments based on annual periods is artificial, the concept of the accounting period is useful for financial reporting. The **monetary unit concept** specifies that a monetary unit (for example, the dollar in the United States and the euro in the European Union) is to be used to measure and record an entity's economic activity. Only items that can be expressed in these monetary units are included in the financial statements. When all assets, liabilities, and stockholders' equity are stated in monetary terms, they can be added or subtracted to prepare financial statements. Also, relations among financial statement components can be calculated and presented to help interpret the statements. In the absence of evidence to the contrary, a business is assumed to have an indefinite life. The **going concern concept** presumes that an enterprise will continue to operate indefinitely and will not be sold or otherwise liquidated.

Principles

Four principles frame financial accounting information: measurement, revenue recognition, expense recognition, and full disclosure. U.S. GAAP is a mixed measurement system. It is primarily founded on the **cost principle**, meaning assets and liabilities are initially recorded at the amount paid or obligated to pay. Historical acquisition cost is considered the proper initial measurement because, for example, at the time an asset is acquired, it represents the fair value of the asset as agreed upon by both the buyer and seller. However, the fair value principle is sometimes applied after acquisition, which is a "market-based" measurement system for assets and liabilities. In 2014, the FASB and IASB issued a joint **revenue recognition** standard with the intention of improving financial reporting by providing consistent principles for recognizing revenue regardless of the company's industry or geography. The rule replaces a patchwork of previous standards and is based on a five-step process that broadly considers when a performance obligation has been satisfied. This generally occurs when goods or services are transferred from the seller to the buyer. The amount of revenue recognized is the amount that reflects the consideration to which the seller expects to be entitled in exchange for those goods or services. The **expense recognition principle** states that net income is determined by linking any expenses incurred with the related earned sales revenues. Thus, expenses are recorded in the period that they help to generate the revenues.

Together, the revenue recognition principle and the expense recognition principle define the **accrual basis of accounting**. It is important to observe that recording revenues and expenses do not depend upon the receipt or payment of cash. The accrual basis of accounting is widely used. Under the **cash basis of accounting**, revenues are recorded when cash is received from operating activities and expenses are recorded when cash payments are made for operating activities. Net income, therefore, becomes the difference between operating cash receipts and operating cash payments. The cash basis is not considered generally accepted.

All information necessary for a user's understanding of financial statements should be disclosed in a company's annual report. The purpose of accounting is to provide useful information to those parties interested in a firm's financial health. Sometimes, facts or conditions exist that, although not specifically part of the data in the accounting system, have considerable influence on a full understanding and interpretation of financial statements. To properly inform financial statement users, the **full disclosure principle** requires that a business disclose all significant financial facts and circumstances.

Constraints

Two factors constrain the qualitative characteristics of accounting information: materiality and cost-benefit. Applying accounting procedures requires effort and costs money. When amounts involved are too small to affect the financial picture, the application of theoretically correct accounting procedures is hardly worth its cost. The concept of **materiality** permits a firm to expense the cost of such assets as small tools, office equipment, and furniture when acquired because their cost is "immaterial" in amount. The **cost-benefit constraint** requires that the benefit derived from the information outweighs the cost of providing it.

Summaries *review key bullet points for each Learning Objective and summarize each section's Takeaway.*

SUMMARY OF LEARNING OBJECTIVES

LO1   **Explain the three forms of business organizations. (p. 4)**

- There are three primary organizational forms that a business can take: proprietorship, partnership, and corporation.

- A sole proprietorship consists of a single owner. It is the most common form of business and the easiest to establish.

- A partnership is similar to a sole proprietorship except that there is more than one owner. Partnerships are also relatively easy to establish. An advantage of the partnership form over the sole proprietorship is the broader set of skills and resources that multiple partners can bring to an enterprise.

- A corporation is the most complex of the three organizational forms. The advantages of the corporate form of business include the ease of transferring ownership interests and the ease of raising funds. Another advantage is the limited liability protection it offers its owners. A disadvantage of the corporate form is the possibility of double taxation of the company's net income.

LO2   **Describe business activities. (p. 5)**

- Companies engage in three types of business activities: operating, investing, and financing.

- Operating activities consist of selling products or providing services to generate sales revenue and using economic resources to manufacture goods or provide services.

- Investing activities consist of those activities needed to provide the infrastructure to run a company's operations. Also included in this activity category are investments of excess cash.
- Financing activities consist of both debt financing and equity financing. Debt financing involves the procurement of a bank loan, whereas equity financing involves the sale of shares of stock to investors.

Indicate who uses accounting information. (p. 6)   LO3

- Accounting information is important to both internal and external users.
- Financial accounting produces publicly available financial statements for external users including investors, creditors, taxation authorities, regulatory agencies, labor unions, and customers.
- The process of generating and analyzing data for internal management use is referred to as managerial accounting.
- Business leaders recognize the importance of ethical behavior.

Explain the accounting process and generally accepted accounting principles. (p. 10)   LO4

- Accounting is the process of measuring the economic activities of an enterprise in monetary terms and communicating the results to interested parties.
- The basic purpose of accounting is to provide financial information that is useful in making economic decisions.
- The Financial Accounting Standards Board (FASB) is a private sector organization that has responsibility for formulating generally accepted accounting principles in the United States.
- Generally accepted accounting principles (GAAP) are the standards and procedures that guide the preparation of financial statements.
- The International Accounting Standards Board (IASB) has taken the lead role in formulating International Accounting Reporting Standards (IFRS).

Describe the accounting equation and each financial statement. (p. 12)   LO5

- The accounting equation, Assets = Liabilities + Stockholders' Equity, is the fundamental framework within which accounting analysis takes place.
  - Assets are the economic resources of a business that can be expressed in monetary terms.
  - Liabilities are the obligations that a business must pay in money or services in the future as a consequence of past transactions or events.
  - Stockholders' equity is the residual interest of the owners in the assets of a business.
- The *income statement* presents a company's sales revenues and expenses for a period of time.
- The *statement of stockholders' equity* reports the financial events causing a change in stockholders' equity during a period of time, and includes retained earnings and common stock.
- The *balance sheet* presents a company's assets, liabilities, and stockholders' equity as of a given date.
- The *statement of cash flows* reports a company's cash inflows and outflows during a period of time.

Explain additional disclosures that accompany financial statements. (p. 19)   LO6

In addition to the basic financial statements, the annual report includes notes to the financial statements, an independent auditor's report, and Management's Discussion and Analysis.

- The notes to the financial statements provide both a quantitative and a qualitative description of a company's financial statements and explain the numbers reported in those financial statements.
- The independent auditor's report provides a degree of assurance that a company's financial statements are presented fairly and can be relied upon for decision-making purposes.
- The Management's Discussion and Analysis (MD&A) provides management with an opportunity to both analyze past performance and discuss future opportunities and concerns involving a company.

Describe careers in accounting. (p. 20)   LO7

- Accounting graduates are in high demand and can anticipate bright employment prospects.
- Accountants can find jobs in public accounting, private corporations, or the government.

Appendix 1A: Discuss FASB's conceptual framework. (p. 23)   LO8

- The conceptual framework provides a guide to the formulation of U.S. generally accepted accounting principles.
- The framework consists of interrelated objectives, elements, characteristics, and recognition and measurement criteria.
- The financial reporting objectives focus on information useful to investors and creditors.

- The financial statement elements are the components of financial statements.
- The qualitative characteristics of accounting information are intended to contribute to decision usefulness.
- The recognition and measurement criteria specify the conditions that must be satisfied before a particular asset, liability, revenue, or expense can be recorded in the financial records.

SUMMARY	Concept ⟶	Method ⟶	Assessment
TAKEAWAY 1.1	What mix of financing does a company use?	The balance sheet provides information regarding the various forms of financing, both debt financing and equity financing. Compare the amount of liabilities appearing on the balance sheet to the amount of equity appearing on the balance sheet.	A higher ratio of liabilities to equity implies a higher use of creditor financing, and vice versa. Creditor financing is viewed by users as more risky.
TAKEAWAY 1.2	Is a company profitable?	The income statement reports a company's performance for a given period of time. Compare reported sales revenue to reported expenses.	Sales revenue in excess of expenses yields net income, implying a profitable company. If expenses exceed revenue, the company has a net loss.
TAKEAWAY 1.3	What portion of a company's current period net income is distributed to its stockholders, and what portion is retained?	The statement of stockholders' equity reports both a company's net income and the amount of dividends distributed to stockholders. Compare the company's dividends to its net income.	A higher ratio of dividends to net income implies that a company is distributing more of its net income to its stockholders, whereas a lower ratio implies that it is retaining more of its income for purposes such as growing its business.
TAKEAWAY 1.4	What are the major sources and uses of a company's cash?	The statement of cash flows reports a company's sources and uses of cash separated into three activities: operating, investing, and financing. Identify a company's sources and uses of cash as reported in the statement of cash flows.	Sources of cash are reported as positive numbers and uses of cash as negative numbers. Larger positive numbers represent major cash sources and larger negative numbers represent major cash uses.

Key Terms *are listed for each chapter with references to page numbers within the chapter.*

KEY TERMS ←

Accounting (p. 10)

Accounting entity (p. 25)

Accounting equation (p. 12)

Accounting period (p. 25)

Accrual basis of
accounting (p. 26)

American Institute of Certified
Public Accountants
(AICPA) (p. 9)

Annual report (p. 18)

Assets (p. 12)

Auditor's report (p. 19)

Balance sheet (p. 12)

Blockchain (p. 22)

Cash basis of accounting (p. 26)

Certified public accountants
(CPAs) (p. 7)

Comparability (p. 24)

Conceptual framework (p. 23)

Consistency (p. 24)

Contributed capital (p. 15)

Corporation (p. 4)

Cost-benefit constraint (p. 26)

Cost principle (p. 26)

Creditors (p. 5)

Data analytics (p. 22)

Debt financing (p. 5)

Earned capital (p. 15)

Equity financing (p. 5)

Ethics (p. 8)

Expense recognition (matching) principle (p. 26)

Expenses (p. 14)

Faithful representation (p. 24)

Financial accounting (p. 7)

Financial Accounting Standards Board (FASB) (p. 10)

Financial reporting objectives (p. 24)

Financial statement elements (p. 24)

Financing activities (p. 5)

Forensic accounting (p. 9)

Form 10-K (p. 18)

Full disclosure principle (p. 26)

Generally accepted accounting principles (GAAP) (p. 10)

Generally accepted auditing standards (GAAS) (p. 11)

Going concern concept (p. 25)

Governmental Accounting Standards Board (GASB) (p. 11)

Income statement (p. 14)

Institute of Management Accountants (IMA) (p. 9)

International Accounting Standards Board (IASB) (p. 11)

International Financial Reporting Standards (IFRS) (p. 11)

Investing activities (p. 6)

Liabilities (p. 13)

Management's Discussion and Analysis (p. 19)

Managerial accounting (p. 8)

Materiality (p. 26)

Monetary unit concept (p. 25)

Net assets (p. 13)

Net income (p. 14)

Net loss (p. 14)

New York Stock Exchange (NYSE) (p. 5)

Notes to the financial statements (p. 19)

Operating activities (p. 6)

Partnership (p. 4)

Period-of-time statements (p. 18)

Point-in-time statement (p. 18)

Principal (p. 5)

Public Company Accounting Oversight Board (PCAOB) (p. 11)

Qualitative characteristics of accounting information (p. 24)

Recognition and measurement criteria (p. 25)

Relevance (p. 24)

Retained earnings (p. 15)

Revenue recognition principle (p. 26)

Sales revenue (p. 14)

Sarbanes-Oxley Act (p. 9)

Sole proprietorship (p. 4)

Statement of cash flows (p. 16)

Statement of stockholders' equity (p. 15)

Stockholders (p. 4)

Stockholders' equity (p. 13)

Triple bottom line (p. 16)

Understandability (p. 25)

U.S. Securities and Exchange Commission (SEC) (p. 10)

Homework *icons indicate which assignments are available in* **myBusinessCourse** *(MBC). This feature is only available when the instructor incorporates MBC in the course.*

Self-Study Questions *in multiple-choice format with answers provided at the end of each chapter.*

Assignments with the ⟨MBC⟩ **logo in the margin are available in** BusinessCourse.
See the Preface of the book for details.

SELF-STUDY QUESTIONS

(Answers to Self-Study Questions are at the end of this chapter.)

1. **Which form of business organization is characterized by limited liability?**   **LO1**
   a. Sole proprietorship
   b. Partnership
   c. Corporation
   d. Both sole proprietorship and partnership

2. **Which of the following processes best defines accounting?**   **LO4**
   a. Measuring economic activities
   b. Communicating results to interested parties
   c. Preventing fraud
   d. Both a and b.

3. **Generally accepted accounting principles are:**   **LO4**
   a. A set of guidelines to aid in the financial reporting process
   b. A set of laws to prevent financial fraud
   c. A set of standards for ethical conduct
   d. A set of voluntary "best business practices"

4. **To which area of accounting are generally accepted accounting principles primarily relevant?**   **LO3**
   a. Managerial accounting
   b. Financial accounting
   c. Tax accounting
   d. Financial reporting to all regulatory agencies

LO2 5. **Which of the following is not one of the three types of business activities?**
   - *a.* Investing
   - *b.* Financing
   - *c.* Marketing
   - *d.* Operating

LO5 6. **If assets total $140,000 and liabilities total $50,000, how much are net assets?**
   - *a.* $40,000
   - *b.* $90,000
   - *c.* $140,000
   - *d.* $50,000

LO5 7. **What are increases in resources that a firm earns by providing goods or services to its customers?**
   - *a.* Assets
   - *b.* Revenues
   - *c.* Expenses
   - *d.* Liabilities

LO6 8. **Which of the following items is not required to be included as part of a company's annual report?**
   - *a.* Notes to the financial statements
   - *b.* Management discussion and analysis
   - *c.* Detailed history of the company
   - *d.* Auditor's report

LO3 9. **Which of the following situations presents ethical challenges to accountants?**
   - *a.* Pressure by superiors to produce a "good" number
   - *b.* Avoiding the disclosure of confidential information
   - *c.* An emphasis on short-term results
   - *d.* All the above present ethical challenges to accountants

LO1 10. **Match the following organizational attributes in the left column with the organizational form in the right column that the attribute is most often associated with.**

1. Tax advantages	*a.* Sole proprietorship
2. Unlimited liability	*b.* Partnership
3. Shared control	*c.* Corporation
4. Most complex to set up	
5. Easiest to raise a large amount of funds	
6. Single owner	

LO5 11. **The financial statements of People Company contain the following. How much is net income?**

Accounts payable	$12,000
Revenues	27,000
Accounts receivable	10,000
Expenses	8,000
Cash	7,000

   - *a.* $6,000
   - *b.* $11,000
   - *c.* $19,000
   - *d.* $17,000

LO5 12. **If Bing Company reports its year-end total liabilities to be $40,000, and its year-end stockholders' equity to be $60,000, how much are Bing Company's year-end total assets?**
   - *a.* $15,000
   - *b.* $185,000
   - *c.* $100,000
   - *d.* Cannot be determined from the given information

LO5 13. **Puff Company began the year with a retained earnings balance of $50,000, reported net income for the year of $45,000, and reported ending retained earnings of $60,000. How much dividends did Puff Company report for the year?**
   - *a.* $135,000
   - *b.* $35,000
   - *c.* $15,000
   - *d.* $30,000

QUESTIONS

1. Define *accounting*. What is the basic purpose of accounting?

2. What is the distinction between *financial* accounting and *managerial* accounting?

3. Who are some of the outside groups that may be interested in a company's financial data and what are their particular interests?

4. What are *generally accepted accounting principles* and what organization has primary responsibility for their formulation in the United States?

5. What are the main advantages and disadvantages of the corporate form of business?

6. What role does financial accounting play in the allocation of society's financial resources?

7. What is the accounting equation? Define *assets, liabilities,* and *stockholders' equity.*

8. What are the three principal business activities and how do they differ?

9. What is meant by corporate social responsibility?

10. What is the difference between generally accepted accounting principles (GAAP) and international financial reporting standards (IFRS)?

11. What are *revenues* and *expenses*?

12. What is the purpose of an income statement? The statement of stockholders' equity? The balance sheet? The statement of cash flows?

13. What is a *period-of-time statement*? Give three examples.

14. What is a *point-in-time statement*? Give one example.

15. On December 31, the Hill Company had $800,000 in total assets and owed $230,000 to creditors. If the corporation's common stock amounted to $400,000, what amount of retained earnings should appear on its December 31 balance sheet?

16. What are three aspects of the accounting environment that may create ethical pressure on an accountant?

17. What type of information might you find in the Management's Discussion and Analysis (MD&A) section of the annual report?

18. What is the purpose of having the financial statements audited by an independent auditor?

19. Determine whether the following statements are true or false and explain why:
    - *a.* The accounting process is only interested in communicating economic activity.
    - *b.* There are few potential users of financial accounting information.
    - *c.* Financial accounting is primarily used to communicate to outside users.
    - *d.* Auditors ensure the validity of a company's financial statements.

20. Why did the FASB develop a conceptual framework?

21. What are two primary qualities of accounting information that contribute to decision usefulness?

22. How would you describe, in one sentence, each of the following accounting principles, concepts and constraints?

Accounting entity	Consistency
Accounting period	Revenue recognition
Monetary unit	Expense recognition (matching)
Cost-benefit	Materiality
Going concern	Full disclosure

23. Which of the following is a primary qualitative characteristic of accounting information?
    - *a.* Relevance
    - *b.* Faithful representation
    - *c.* Comparability
    - *d.* All of the above are important characteristics.

SHORT EXERCISES

LO1   **SE1-1.**   **Forms of Business Organization** Match the following forms of business organization with the set of attributes that best describes that form of business: sole proprietorship, partnership, or corporation.

LOs link assignments to the Learning Objectives of each chapter.

    a.   Shared control, unlimited liability, tax advantages, increased skills and resources
    b.   Best for raising large amounts of funds, double taxation, limited liability, easiest to transfer ownership interests
    c.   Sole ownership, easiest to establish, tax advantages, unlimited liability

LO4   **SE1-2.**   **Accounting Processes** Identify the following processes as either measuring or communicating.

    a.   Prepare financial statements for the entity
    b.   Identify relevant economic activities of the entity
    c.   Record relevant economic activities of the entity
    d.   Interpret financial results of the entity
    e.   Quantify relevant economic activities of the entity

LO3   **SE1-3.**   **Types of Statements** Match the following type of report with the most likely statement user: management, taxation authority, regulatory agency, or investor.

    a.   Financial statements
    b.   Tax return
    c.   Annual budget
    d.   Special report on a bank's financial health

LO4   **SE1-4.**   **Accounting Organizations** Match the following organizations with the set of accounting guidelines: Financial Accounting Standards Board (FASB), International Accounting Standards Board (IASB).

    a.   Generally accepted accounting principles (GAAP)
    b.   International financial reporting standards (IFRS)

LO2   **SE1-5.**   **Business Activities** Match the following activities with the type of activity: Operating, Investing, Financing.

    a.   Day-to-day business activities
    b.   Purchase of land for a new warehouse
    c.   Sale of merchandise inventory
    d.   Obtain a new bank loan
    e.   Payment of dividends
    f.   Invest excess cash
    g.   Purchase office supplies
    h.   Sell old equipment that is no longer needed

LO5   **SE1-6.**   **Financial Statement Items** Identify the financial statement (or statements) in which each of the following items would appear: income statement (IS), statement of stockholders' equity (SSE), balance sheet (BS), or statement of cash flows (SCF).

    a.   Assets
    b.   Revenues
    c.   Cash flow from investing activities
    d.   Stockholders' equity
    e.   Expenses
    f.   Net change in cash
    g.   Net income
    h.   Liabilities

LO6   **SE1-7.**   **Annual Report Components** Which of the following would not be part of the notes to the financial statements in a company's annual report?

    a.   Qualitative information about potential lawsuits
    b.   Additional information about the reported total of notes payable
    c.   Details about potential new products to be introduced during the next year
    d.   Details of estimates used to compute the expected amount of warranty expense

SE1-8. **Sarbanes-Oxley Act** The Sarbanes-Oxley Act of 2002 was enacted to help restore confidence in financial reporting. Which of the following was **not** part of the legislation?   **LO3**

  a. Severe penalties for fraudulent reporting
  b. A requirement for certification of the financial statements by top management
  c. A new statement of social responsibility
  d. A report on internal controls to help prevent and detect errors in the reporting process

SE1-9. **Financial Accounting and Generally Accepted Accounting Principles** Answer the following multiple-choice questions: **LO4**

  1. What is not a primary function of financial accounting in society?
     a. Provide comedy material for late-night talk shows.
     b. Aid in the proper allocation of financial resources in a free enterprise economic system.
     c. Aid users to make better investing decisions.
  2. IFRS refers to:
     a. A random set of letters.
     b. A set of standards and procedures that form guidelines for international financial accounting.
     c. A set of standards and procedures that form guidelines for international managerial accounting.
  3. GAAP:
     a. Is the distance between two objects.
     b. Is a set of guidelines for preparing managerial reports in the United States.
     c. Is a set of guidelines for preparing financial reports in the United States.

SE1-10. **Cash Flow Activity Classification** Classify each activity as financing, investing, or operating: **LO2**

  1. Repay a loan from a bank.
  2. Sell merchandise from a storefront operation.
  3. Dispose of an old delivery truck.
  4. Pay rent on a company warehouse.
  5. Repurchase shares of stock from stockholders.
  6. Pay utilities.

SE1-11. **Using the Basic Accounting Equation** Use the basic accounting equation to answer the following: **LO5**

  a. Hawkins Company has total assets of $150,000 and total liabilities of $110,000. How much is the company's total stockholders' equity?
  b. Paul Company has total liabilities of $170,000 and total stockholders' equity of $105,000. How much total assets does the company have?
  c. If Black Company's total assets increased by $35,000 during the year, and its total liabilities decreased during the same year by $20,000, what was the change in the company's total stockholders' equity?

SE1-12. **Using the Basic Accounting Equation** Floyd Company had beginning-of-the-year total assets of $320,000 and total liabilities of $180,000.   **LO5**

  a. If during the year total assets increased by $15,000 and total liabilities increased by $40,000, what is the end-of-year total stockholders' equity?
  b. If during the year total assets increased by $60,000 and total liabilities decreased by $5,000, what is the end-of-year total stockholders' equity?
  c. If during the year total liabilities increased by $40,000 and total stockholders' equity increased by $35,000, what are the end-of-year total assets?

SE1-13. **Financial Statements** Indicate which statement (or statements) you would examine to locate the following items: balance sheet (BS), income statement (IS), statement of stockholders' equity (SSE), or statement of cash flows (SCF).   **LO5**

  a. Expenses for the period
  b. Cash at year-end
  c. Cash used to purchase new equipment
  d. Dividends for the period

LO5   **SE1-14. Financial Statements** Indicate which statement (or statements) you would examine to locate the following items: balance sheet (BS), income statement (IS), statement of stockholders' equity (SSE), or statement of cash flows (SCF).

   a.   Revenues for the period

   b.   Cash at year-end

   c.   Cash used to pay back borrowings

   d.   Dividends for the period

LO4   **SE1-15. International Accounting Principles** The worldwide acceptance of a global set of international accounting principles will provide certain benefits.

   a.   Which group has taken the lead in developing a set of international accounting principles?

   b.   Identify and briefly discuss a benefit that would result from the adoption of a global set of international accounting principles.

LO8   **SE1-16. Principles of Accounting** Which of the following accounting principles applies to the statement of (Appendix 1A) cash flows?

   a.   Materiality

   b.   Conservatism

   c.   Accrual basis of accounting

   d.   Cash basis of accounting

LO8   **SE1-17. Generally Accepted Accounting Principles** Select the best answer to each of the following (Appendix 1A) questions:

   1.   Accounting rules are developed to provide:

     a.   Simplicity

     b.   Useful information

     c.   Complexity

     d.   Ability to change over time

   2.   The conceptual framework consists of each of the following except:

     a.   Financial reporting objectives

     b.   Financial statement elements

     c.   Ratio analysis guidelines for analysts

     d.   Recognition criteria for financial statement items

   3.   Which of the following is a financial statement element?

     a.   Income statement

     b.   Liabilities

     c.   Balance sheet

     d.   Statement of cash flows

LO8   **SE1-18. Basic Accounting Principles** Match the following list of accounting concepts, principles, and as-(Appendix 1A) sumptions with the definitions below:

Accounting period concept	Consistency	Cost principle
Going concern concept	Materiality constraint	Full disclosure principle
	Comparability	

   1.   Ability to compare the financial performance of different companies.

   2.   Assumption that a company will continue to operate beyond the current period.

   3.   Only items large enough to make a difference to a user must be disclosed in the financial statements.

   4.   Prepare financial statements at set time intervals.

   5.   Record assets on the balance sheet at an amount equal to what was paid for them.

   6.   A company prepares its financial statements using the same methods used in prior periods.

   7.   All items of importance to the users of financial statements should be disclosed in the annual report.

SE1-19. FASB Codification A major reason for the codification project completed by the FASB in 2009 was to: **LO4**

    a. ease the convergence between financial and managerial accounting

    b. ease the convergence between U.S. GAAP and IFRS

    c. ease the convergence between financial and tax accounting

    d. ease the convergence between U.S. GAAP and GASB

SE1-20. Basic Accounting Principles Which of the following is not considered a qualitative characteristic of accounting information?   **LO8 (Appendix 1A)**

    a. faithful representation

    b. comparability

    c. assets must equal liabilities and stockholders' equity

    d. relevance

SE1-21. Basic Accounting Principles Identify whether the following statements are true or false.   **LO8 (Appendix 1A)**

    1. Together the revenue recognition principle and the expense recognition (matching) principle define the accrual basis of accounting.

    2. The cash basis of accounting is only used in the preparation of the statement of cash flows.

    3. The accrual basis of accounting is used in the preparation of the income statement and the balance sheet.

EXERCISES—SET A

E1-1A. Forms of Business Organization Match the following organizational attributes in the left column with the organizational form in the right column. More than one organizational form may be associated with a given attribute.   **LO1**

1. Unlimited liability	*a.* Sole proprietorship
2. Full control	*b.* Partnership
3. Business income combined with owner(s) income for income tax purposes	*c.* Corporation
4. Relatively more difficult to establish	
5. Easier to raise funds	

E1-2A. Accounting Process Establish the correct sequence of steps in the accounting measurement process.   **LO4**

    a. Record in a systematic fashion

    b. Identify relevant economic activity

    c. Quantify economic activity

E1-3A. Types of Accounting Identify the type of accounting associated with each type of report: Managerial, Financial, Tax, or some combination as needed.   **LO3**

    a. Budget for internal use by management

    b. Tax return for state income taxes

    c. Audited financial statements

    d. Special reports for regulators of a public utility

E1-4A. Corporate Social Responsibility Which of the following is not part of the triple bottom line reporting framework?   **LO5**

    a. Economic bottom line

    b. Social bottom line

    c. Competitive bottom line

    d. Environmental bottom line

E1-5A. Generally Accepted Accounting Principles Identify whether the following statements are true or false: **LO4**

    a. U.S. GAAP is universally accepted in all countries in the world.

    b. U.S. GAAP is established by the IASB.

    c. Once established, U.S. GAAP is rarely, if ever, modified.

    d. The international counterpart to the FASB is the IASB.

LO2 **E1-6A.** **Business Activities** Identify each of the following activities as operating (O), investing (I), or financing (F):

a. Payment of employee salaries
b. Repayment of a loan
c. Issuance of common stock
d. Purchase of equipment to manufacture a company's products
e. Sale of merchandise inventory
f. Investment of excess cash in the shares of another company

LO5 **E1-7A.** **The Accounting Equation** Determine the missing amount in each of the following cases:

Assets	Liabilities	Stockholders' Equity
$190,000	$62,000	?
?	$53,000	$31,000
$115,000	?	$61,000

LO5 **E1-8A.** **Determining Net Income** The beginning and ending balances of retained earnings for the year were $50,000 and $65,000, respectively. If dividend payments during the year were $0, determine the net income or net loss for the year.

a. $19,000 net loss
b. $19,000 net income
c. $15,000 net income
d. $11,000 net income

LO5 **E1-9A.** **Determining Retained Earnings and Net Income** The following information appears in the records of Becker Corporation at year-end:

Accounts receivable	$ 32,000	Retained earnings	$?
Accounts payable	12,000	Supplies	8,000
Cash	7,000	Equipment, net	145,000
Common stock	115,000		

a. Calculate the balance in retained earnings at year-end.
b. If the amount of the retained earnings at the beginning of the year was $38,000, and $13,000 in dividends is paid during the year, calculate net income for the year.

LO5 **E1-10A.** **Determining Stockholders' Equity and Assets** Determine the following:

a. The stockholders' equity of a corporation that has assets of $600,000 and liabilities of $306,000.
b. The assets of a corporation that has liabilities of $250,000, common stock of $125,000, and retained earnings of $85,000.

LO5 **E1-11A.** **Financial Statements** Fred Flores operates a golf driving range. For each of the following financial items related to his business, indicate the financial statement (or statements) in which the item would be reported: balance sheet (BS), income statement (IS), statement of stockholders' equity (SSE) or statement of cash flows (SCF).

a. Accounts receivable
b. Cash received from the sale of land
c. Net income
d. Cash invested in the business by Flores
e. Notes payable
f. Supplies expense
g. Land
h. Supplies

E1-12A. Omitted Financial Statement Data For the following four unrelated situations, A through D, calculate the unknown amounts appearing in each column: **LO5**

	A	B	C	D
Beginning				
Assets	$45,000	$32,000	$53,000	?
Liabilities	32,000	15,000	49,000	19,000
Ending				
Assets	50,000	30,000	41,000	52,000
Liabilities	22,000	?	20,000	24,000
During Year				
Sales revenue	?	30,000	31,000	27,000
Expenses	12,000	22,000	12,000	19,000
Dividends	2,000	3,000	?	8,000

E1-13A. Other Components of the Annual Report Identify where the following items will appear in a company's annual report: Management's Discussion and Analysis (MD&A), notes to the financial statements, or the auditor's report, or indicate that the item is not disclosed.   **LO6**

   a.   A comment that the financial statements appear to be fairly presented
   b.   A discussion about new competition likely to occur next year
   c.   A quantitative summary of notes payable appearing on the balance sheet
   d.   The "secret" ingredients in the company's special sauce

E1-14A. Ethics In each of the following cases, (a) identify the aspect of the accounting environment primarily responsible for the ethical pressure on the accountant as pressure to achieve a favorable outcome, to disclose confidential information, or to report good short-term results, and (b) indicate the appropriate behavioral response for the accountant.   **LO3**

   1.   James Jehring, a tax accountant, is preparing an income tax return for a client. The client asks Jehring to take a sizable deduction on the tax return for business-related travel even though the client states that he has no documentation to support the deduction. "I don't think the IRS will audit my return," declares the client.

   2.   Willa English, an accountant for Dome Construction Company, has just finished putting the numbers together for a construction project on which the firm is going to submit a bid next month. At a social gathering that evening, a friend casually asks English what Dome's bid is going to be. Ms. English knows that the friend's brother works for a competitor of Dome.

   3.   The manager of Cross Department Store is ending his first year with the firm. December's business was slower than expected, and the firm's annual results are trailing last year's results. The manager instructs Kyle Tarpley, the store accountant, to include sales revenues from the first week of January in the December data. "This way, we'll show an increase over last year," declares the manager.

Ethics assignments are denoted by this icon.

E1-15A. International Accounting Principles Identify whether the following statements are true or false.   **LO4**

   1.   One argument for IFRS is that there is less globalization in the world.
   2.   IFRS is accepted as GAAP in every country of the world.
   3.   The United States is working to converge its standards with IFRS.

E1-16A. The Conceptual Accounting Framework The Financial Accounting Standards Board worked many years to develop a conceptual framework for U.S. GAAP.   **LO8 (Appendix 1A)**

   a.   What is the purpose of a conceptual framework?
   b.   Identify the financial reporting objectives that are specified in the conceptual framework.

E1-17A. Recognition and Measurement Criteria Indicate the accounting concepts, principles, or constraints that underlie each of the following independent situations: accounting entity concept, going concern concept, cost-benefit constraint, expense recognition (matching principle), materiality constraint, revenue recognition principle, full disclosure principle, cost principle.   **LO8 (Appendix 1A)**

   a.   Dr. Lynn is a practicing pediatrician. Over the years, she has accumulated a personal investment portfolio of securities, virtually all of which have been purchased from her earnings as a pediatrician. The investment portfolio is not reflected in the accounting records of her medical practice.

b. A company purchases a desk tape dispenser for use by the office secretary. The tape dispenser cost $25 and has an estimated useful life of 15 years. The purchase is immediately expensed on the company's income statement.

c. A company sells a product that has a two-year warranty covering parts and labor. In the same period that revenues from product sales are recorded, an estimate of future warranty costs is recorded on the company's income statement.

d. A company is sued for $1.5 million by a customer claiming that a defective product caused an accident. The company believes that the lawsuit is without merit. Although the case will not be tried for a year, the company adds a note describing the lawsuit to its current financial statements.

LO8
(Appendix 1A)

E1-18A. Revenue Recognition Principle For each of the following situations, determine whether the criteria for revenue recognition have been met by December 31, 2018.

a. A manufacturing company received $60,000 cash on December 31, 2018, as an advance payment on a special order for a piece of equipment. The equipment will be manufactured by March 31, 2019.

b. A television dealer acquired six new high-definition television sets for $7,800 cash on December 31, 2018, and advertised their availability, at $2,000 each, in that evening's newspaper.

c. A snow removal service signed a contract on November 15, 2018, with a shopping mall to clear its parking lot of all snowfalls over 1 inch during the months of December 2018 through March 2019. The cost is $900 per month and payment is due in two $1,800 installments: January 2, 2019, and February 1, 2019. By December 31, 2018, no snowfall over 1 inch had occurred.

LO5, 8
(Appendix 1A)

E1-19A. Accrual Basis of Accounting versus Cash Basis of Accounting On December 31, Greg Jones completed his first year as a financial planner. The following data are available from his accounting records:

Fees billed to clients for services rendered	$131,000	Rent expense for year just ended	$12,000
Cash received from clients	119,000	Utility expenses incurred	4,500
Supplies purchased for cash	7,100	Utility bills paid	3,300
Supplies used during the year	6,100	Salary earned by assistant	39,400
Cash paid for rent (rent is paid through Mar. of next year)	15,000	Salary paid to assistant	35,100

a. Compute Greg's net income for the year just ended using the accrual basis of accounting.

b. Compute Greg's net income for the year just ended using the cash basis of accounting.

c. Which net income amount is computed in accordance with generally accepted accounting principles?

LO8
(Appendix 1A)

E1-20A. Recognition and Measurement Criteria The following are unrelated accounting practices:

1. Pine Company purchased a new $30 snow shovel that is expected to last six years. The shovel is used to clear the firm's front steps during the winter months. The shovel's cost is recorded on the company's balance sheet as an asset.

2. Penny Corporation has been named as the defendant in a $50 million pollution lawsuit. Because the lawsuit will take several years to resolve and the outcome is uncertain, Penny's management decides not to mention the lawsuit in the current year financial statements.

Required

For each of the given practices, indicate which accounting concepts, principles, or constraints apply and whether they have been applied appropriately. For each inappropriate accounting practice, indicate the proper accounting procedure.

EXERCISES—SET B

LO1

E1-1B. Forms of Business Organization Match the following organizational attributes in the left column with the organizational form in the right column. More than one organizational form may be associated with a given attribute.

1.	Limited liability	*a.* Sole proprietorship
2.	Shared control	*b.* Partnership
3.	Double taxation	*c.* Corporation
4.	Easiest to form	
5.	Easier to transfer ownership	

E1-2B. **The Accounting Process** Establish the correct sequence of steps in the accounting measurement process.   **LO4**

a.   Quantify economic activity

b.   Identify relevant economic activity

c.   Record in a systematic fashion

E1-3B. **Types of Accounting** Identify the type of accounting associated with each type of report: Managerial, Financial, Tax, or some combination as needed.   **LO3**

a.   Cost report for a new product

b.   Tax return for federal income taxes

c.   Unaudited financial statements requested for a bank loan

d.   Special report for banking regulators

E1-4B. **Corporate Social Responsibility** Which of the following is not part of the triple bottom line reporting framework?   **LO5**

a.   Social bottom line

b.   Environmental bottom line

c.   Economic bottom line

d.   Efficiency bottom line

E1-5B. **Generally Accepted Accounting Principles** Identify whether the following statements are true or false.   **LO4**

a.   GAAP can differ from one country to another.

b.   U.S. GAAP is established by the FASB.

c.   U.S. GAAP is a guide to action that may change over time.

d.   At this time there is no international counterpart to the FASB.

E1-6B. **Business Activities** Identify each of the following activities as operating (O), investing (I), or financing (F).   **LO2**

a.   Payment of rent on the company headquarters

b.   Repurchase of the company's common stock

c.   Obtain a long-term bank loan

d.   Sale of an empty warehouse

e.   Delivery of consulting service

f.   Sale of short-term investments

E1-7B. **The Accounting Equation** Determine the missing amount in each of the following cases: **LO5**

Assets	Liabilities	Stockholders' Equity
$350,000	?	$225,000
$155,000	$95,000	?
?	$40,000	$ 59,000

E1-8B. **Determining Net Income** The beginning and ending balances of retained earnings for the year were $63,000 and $82,000, respectively. If dividend payments during the year were $8,000, determine the net income or net loss for the year.   **LO5**

a. $14,000 net loss

b. $27,000 net income

c. $35,000 net income

d. $14,000 net income

LO5 **E1-9B. Determining Retained Earnings and Net Income** The following information appears in the records of Poco Corporation at year-end:

Accounts receivable	$ 42,000	Retained earnings	$?
Accounts payable	21,000	Supplies	30,000
Cash	18,000	Equipment, net	105,000
Common stock	139,000		

a. Calculate the amount of retained earnings at year-end.
b. If the amount of the retained earnings at the beginning of the year was $25,000, and $10,000 in dividends is paid during the year, calculate net income for the year.

LO5 **E1-10B. Determining Stockholders' Equity and Assets** Determine the following:

a. The stockholders' equity of a corporation that has assets of $850,000 and liabilities of $190,000.
b. The assets of a corporation that has liabilities of $195,000, common stock of $90,000, and retained earnings of $80,000.

LO5 **E1-11B. Financial Statements** Julie Jason operates a bakery. For each of the following financial statement items related to her business, indicate the financial statement (or statements) in which the item would be reported: balance sheet (BS), income statement (IS), statement of stockholders' equity (SSE) or statement of cash flows (SCF).

a. Accounts payable
b. Cash received from the sale of equipment
c. Net loss
d. Cash invested in the business by Jason
e. Notes receivable
f. Rent expense
g. Building
h. Inventory

LO5 **E1-12B. Omitted Financial Statement Data** For the following four unrelated situations, A through D, calculate the unknown amounts appearing in each column:

	A	B	C	D
Beginning				
Assets	$38,000	$22,000	$38,000	?
Liabilities	22,000	15,000	29,000	19,000
Ending				
Assets	40,000	36,000	44,000	65,000
Liabilities	22,000	?	27,000	24,000
During Year				
Sales revenue	?	26,000	31,000	27,000
Expense	12,000	22,000	12,000	19,000
Dividends	2,000	5,500	?	4,000

LO6 **E1-13B. Other Components of the Annual Report** Identify where the following items will appear in a company's annual report: Management's Discussion and Analysis (MD&A), notes to the financial statements, or the auditor's report, or indicate that the item is not disclosed.

a. A comment that the statements are presented in conformity with generally accepted accounting principles
b. A discussion about new products to be introduced next year
c. A quantitative summary of property, plant, and equipment appearing on the balance sheet
d. The salaries of every employee

LO3 **E1-14B. Ethics** In each of the following cases, (a) identify the aspect of the accounting environment primarily responsible for the ethical pressure on the accountant as pressure to achieve a favorable outcome, to disclose confidential information, or to report good short-term results, and (b) indicate the appropriate behavioral response for the accountant.

1. Jenny Jones, a tax accountant, is preparing an income tax return for a client. The client asks Jones to omit some income she received for consulting services because the amount was paid in cash. "I don't think the IRS will audit my return," declares the client. "And even if they do, what are the chances they would catch this?"

2. Fred French, an accountant for Top Electronics Company, has just finished estimating the cost for a new iPod device that the company plans to introduce. Cost estimates help the company to determine the price it can charge for new products. At a social gathering that evening, a friend casually asks Fred what Top's cost for the iPod device came out to be. Fred knows that the friend's brother works for a competitor of Top Electronics.

3. The manager of Jazz Department Store is ending his first year with the firm. December's business was slower than expected, and the firm's annual results are below Wall Street's expectations. The manager instructs Chris Green, store accountant, to record some of December's expenses in the following year. "This way, we'll meet Wall Street's expectations," declares the manager.

E1-15B. International Accounting Principles Although there are obstacles to the worldwide acceptance of a global set of international accounting principles, the potential benefits appear significant.

LO4

Identify and briefly discuss three potential benefits to the worldwide acceptance of a global set of international accounting principles.

E1-16B. The Conceptual Framework The Financial Accounting Standards Board worked many years to develop a conceptual framework for U.S. GAAP.

LO8
(Appendix 1A)

a. Identify the financial statement elements that are specified in the conceptual framework.

b. Before a financial statement element may be recorded in the accounts, certain recognition criteria must be met. What are those recognition criteria?

E1-17B. Recognition and Measurement Criteria Indicate the accounting concepts, principles, or constraints that underlie each of the following independent situations: accounting entity concept, going concern concept, cost-benefit constraint, expense recognition (matching principle), materiality constraint, revenue recognition principle, full disclosure principle, cost principle.

LO8
(Appendix 1A)

a. General Motors reports in its annual report to stockholders that revenues from automotive sales "are recorded by the company when products are shipped to dealers."

b. The annual financial report of Fiat Chrysler Corporation and subsidiaries includes the financial data of its significant subsidiaries, including Chrysler Financial Corporation (which provides financing for dealers and customers), Chrysler Technologies Corporation (which manufactures high-technology electronic products), and Pentastar Transportation Group, Inc. (which includes Thrifty Rent-A-Car System, Inc., and Dollar Rent A Car Systems, Inc.).

c. A company purchased a parcel of land several years ago for $70,000. The land's estimated current market value is $80,000. The Land account balance is not increased but remains at $70,000.

d. A company has a calendar-year fiscal year-end. On January 8, 2019, a tornado destroyed its largest warehouse, causing a $2,000,000 loss. This information is reported in a footnote to the 2018 financial statements.

E1-18B. Revenue Recognition Principle For each of the following situations, determine whether the criteria for revenue recognition have been met by December 31, 2018.

LO8
(Appendix 1A)

a. A manufacturing company received $85,000 cash on December 31, 2018, as an advance payment on a special order for a piece of equipment. The equipment will be manufactured by March 31, 2019.

b. An appliance dealer acquired ten new washer/dryer sets for $6,800 cash on December 31, 2018, and advertised their availability, at $1,000 for each set, in that evening's newspaper.

c. A yard maintenance service signed a contract on October 15, 2018, with an apartment complex to maintain its grounds during the months of November 2018 through June 2019. The cost is $750 per month and payment is due in two $3,000 installments: December 15, 2018 and March 15, 2019.

E1-19B. Accrual Basis of Accounting versus Cash Basis of Accounting On December 31, John Bush completed his first year as a financial planner. The following data are available from his accounting records:

LO5, 8
(Appendix 1A)

Fees billed to clients for services rendered	$137,000	Rent expense for year just ended	$12,000
Cash received from clients	115,000	Utility expense incurred	3,100
Supplies purchased for cash	9,000	Utility bills paid	3,200
Supplies used during the year	6,800	Salary earned by assistant	39,000
Cash paid for rent (rent is paid through Feb. of next year)	14,000	Salary paid to assistant	35,000

   a. Compute John's net income for the year just ended using the accrual basis of accounting.

   b. Compute John's net income for the year just ended using the cash basis of accounting.

   c. Which net income amount is computed in accordance with generally accepted accounting principles?

LO8
(Appendix 1A)

E1-20B. Recognition and Measurement Criteria The following are unrelated accounting practices:

1. A recession has caused a slowing of business activity and lower profits for Penn Company. Consequently, the firm delays making its payments for December's rent and utilities until January and does not record either of these expenses in December.

2. Joan Jeffrey, a consultant operating as a sole proprietorship, used her business car for a personal, month-long vacation. A full year's gas and oil expenditures on the car are charged to the firm's gas and oil expense account.

Required

For each of the given practices, indicate which accounting concepts, principles, or constraints apply and whether they have been applied appropriately. For each inappropriate accounting practice, indicate the proper accounting procedure.

PROBLEMS—SET A

LO1

P1-1A. Forms of Business Organization Presented below are four independent situations:

   a. Kent Jones, a senior in college looking for summer employment, decided to start a dog-walking business. Each morning and evening he picks up a group of dogs and walks them around the city park.

   b. Brothers Jack and Jim Stevens each owned a separate electronics repair shop. They decided to combine their talents and resources in order to expand the amount of business they could undertake.

   c. Three chemists at a large engineering company decided to start their own business based on an experimental chemical process they had developed outside the company. The process had the potential to be very successful; however, it was quite dangerous and could result in large legal problems.

   d. Jason King ran a small, but successful holistic healing spa. The spa has gained a strong reputation beyond the community where it is located. Jason decided to open a chain of similar spas across the state to capitalize on his reputation. This will require a substantial investment in supplies and employee training. In addition, since Jason will not be able to closely supervise each location, he is worried about potential liability.

Required

Explain the form of organization that would be best in each situation—sole proprietorship, partnership, or corporation. Explain what factors you considered important in each situation.

LO5

P1-2A. Financial Statements While each of the financial statements is likely to aid in any business decision, it is often the case that a particular financial statement may be best suited to help in a particular decision. Consider each decision below independently:

   a. You are trying to determine whether a particular firm is a good investment. You understand that share price increases are impacted heavily by a company's earnings potential.

   b. You are employed in the lending department of a large bank. You are trying to determine if you should lend to a potential customer. If you do make the loan you are especially concerned that the company will have sufficient collateral in the event that it is unable to repay the loan.

   c. You wish to invest in a firm that provides you with a steady source of income. You especially want a firm that pays out a large part of its net income as dividends.

d. You are trying to determine if a particular firm will have sufficient cash flow in order to keep expanding without relying too heavily on external sources of financing.

Required

Determine which of the financial statements contains the most useful information to help in your decision. Explain what information you used from each statement to help you make your decision.

P1-3A. **Balance Sheet** The following balance sheet data are for Brintany Coastal Catering Service, a corporation, at May 31, 2019:   **LO5**

Accounts receivable	$27,300	Accounts payable	10,200
Notes payable	29,000	Cash	16,300
Equipment, net	61,000	Common stock	41,500
Supplies	15,400	Retained earnings	?

Required

Prepare a balance sheet for Brintany as of May 31, 2019.

P1-4A. **Statement of Stockholders' Equity and Balance Sheet** The following is balance sheet information for Tuttle Janitorial Service, Inc., at the end of 2019 and 2018:   **LO5**

	December 31, 2019	December 31, 2018
Accounts payable	$ 6,000	$ 9,000
Cash	25,000	22,000
Accounts receivable	39,000	31,000
Land	56,000	46,000
Building, net	250,000	260,000
Equipment, net	44,000	46,000
Mortgage payable	93,000	88,000
Supplies	18,000	16,000
Common stock	225,000	225,000
Dividends	12,000	0
Retained earnings	?	?

Required

a. Prepare a balance sheet as of December 31 of each year.

b. Prepare a statement of stockholders' equity for 2019. (*Hint:* The increase in retained earnings is equal to the net income less the dividend.)

P1-5A. **Statement of Stockholders' Equity and Balance Sheet** The following is balance sheet information for Flush Janitorial Service, Inc., at the end of 2019 and 2018:   **LO5**

	December 31, 2019	December 31, 2018
Accounts payable	$ 17,000	$ 18,000
Cash	50,000	44,000
Accounts receivable	78,000	62,000
Land	92,000	92,000
Building, net	500,000	520,000
Equipment, net	75,000	77,000
Mortgage payable	175,000	205,000
Supplies	27,000	22,000
Common stock	420,000	420,000
Dividends	20,000	0
Retained earnings	?	?

Required

a. Prepare a balance sheet as of December 31 of each year.

b. Prepare a statement of stockholders' equity for 2019. (*Hint:* The increase in retained earnings is equal to the net income less the dividend.)

LO5   **P1-6A.**   **Income Statement and Balance Sheet** On March 1, 2019, Janet Dodge began Dodge Delivery Service, which provides delivery of bulk mailings to the post office, neighborhood delivery of weekly newspapers, data delivery to computer service centers, and various other delivery services using leased vans. On February 28, Dodge invested $20,000 of her own funds in the firm and borrowed $8,000 from her father on a six-month, non-interest-bearing note payable. The following information is available at March 31:

Excel icons *denote assignments with Excel templates available.*

Accounts receivable	$10,700	Delivery fees earned	$23,300
Rent expense	2,500	Cash	12,700
Advertising expense	1,100	Supplies inventory	14,800
Supplies expense	2,500	Notes payable	8,000
Accounts payable	1,400	Insurance expense	900
Salaries expense	6,200	Common stock	20,000
Miscellaneous expense	1,300	Retained earnings	?

Required

a.   Prepare an income statement for the month of March.
b.   Prepare a balance sheet as of March 31, 2019.

LO5   **P1-7A.**   **Statement of Cash Flows** Shown below is selected information from the financial records of Merris Corporation as of December 31:

Inventory	$165,000	Cash purchase of equipment	$ 29,000
Cash collected from customers	350,000	Buildings, net	810,000
Equipment, net	355,000	Sales revenue	910,000
Retained earnings	480,000	Cash paid for operating activities	225,000
Cash dividends paid	38,000	Principal payments on existing note payable	41,000
Salary expense	215,000	Common stock	529,000

Required

a.   Determine which of the above items will appear on the statement of cash flows and then prepare the statement for Merris Corporation for the year ended December 31, 2019.
b.   Comment on the adequacy of Merris's operations to provide cash for its investing and financing activities.

LO3   **P1-8A.**   **Ethics** In each of the following cases, (a) identify the aspect of the accounting environment primarily responsible for the ethical pressure on the accountant as pressure to achieve a favorable outcome, to disclose confidential information, or to report good short-term results, and (b) indicate the appropriate behavioral response that the accountant should take.

1. Patricia Kelly, an accountant for Wooden Company, is reviewing the costs charged to a government contract that Wooden worked on this year. Wooden is manufacturing special parts for the government and is allowed to charge the government for its actual manufacturing costs plus a fixed fee. Kelly notes that $75,000 worth of art objects purchased for the president's office is buried among the miscellaneous costs charged to the contract. Upon inquiry, the firm's vice president replies, "This sort of thing is done all the time."

2. Barry Marklin, accountant for Smith & Wesson partnership, is working on the 2016 year-end financial data. The partnership agreement calls for Smith and Wesson to share the firm's 2016 net income equally. In 2017, the partners will share the net income 60 percent to Smith and 40 percent to Wesson. Wesson plans to cut back his involvement in the firm. Smith wants Marklin to delay recording sales revenue from work done at the end of 2016 until January 2017. "We haven't received the cash yet from those services," declares Smith.

3. The St. Louis Wheelers, a professional football franchise, just signed its first-round draft pick to a multiyear contract that is reported in the newspapers as a four-year, $20 million contract. Johanna Factor, the Wheelers' accountant, receives a call from an agent of another team's first-round pick. "Just calling to confirm the contract terms reported in the papers," states the agent. "My client should receive a similar contract, and I'm sure you don't want him to get shortchanged."

P1-9A.   **Financial Statements and Other Components** Match each of the items in the left column with the appropriate annual report component from the right column:

LO5, 6

1. The company's total liabilities	a. Income Statement
2. The sources of cash during the period	b. Balance Sheet
3. An opinion about whether the financial statements are fairly stated	c. Statement of Cash Flows
4. The amount of dividends that are distributed to the company's stockholders	d. Statement of Stockholders' Equity
5. A discussion of potential new products to be introduced the next year	e. Notes to the Financial Statements
	f. Management's Discussion and Analysis (MD&A)
6. Information regarding accounting methods used	g. Auditor's report
7. The company's total revenue for the period	

P1-10A. **Income Statement, Statement of Stockholders' Equity, and Balance Sheet** Petty Corporation started business on January 1, 2019. The following information was compiled by Petty's accountant on December 31, 2019:

LO5

Sales revenue.	$32,000	Equipment, net.	$25,000
Expenses	20,000	Building, net	59,000
Dividends	8,000	Accounts payable	7,000
Cash	3,250	Notes payable.	50,500
Accounts receivable	2,750	Common stock	33,000
Inventory.	4,500	Retained earnings	?

Required

a.   You have been asked to assist the accountant for the Petty Corporation in preparing year-end financial statements. Use the above information to prepare an income statement, statement of stockholders' equity, and a balance sheet as of December 31, 2019.

b.   Comment on the decision to pay an $8,000 dividend.

P1-11A. **Recognition and Measurement Criteria** The following are unrelated accounting situations and the accounting treatment that was followed in each firm's records:

LO8
(Appendix 1A)

1.   John Company mounts an $800,000 year-long advertising campaign on a national cable television network. The firm's annual accounting period is the calendar year. The television network required full payment in December at the beginning of the campaign. Accounting treatment is
   Increase Advertising Expense, $800,000
   Decrease Cash, $800,000

2.   Because of a local bankruptcy, machinery worth $225,000 was acquired at a "bargain" purchase price of $170,000. Accounting treatment is
   Increase Machinery, $170,000
   Decrease Cash, $170,000

3.   Tony Voes, a consultant operating a sole proprietorship, withdrew $30,000 from the business and purchased stocks as an investment gift to his wife. Accounting treatment is
   Increase Investments, $30,000
   Decrease Cash, $30,000

4.   Channy Company received a firm offer of $96,000 for a parcel of land it owns that cost $50,000 two years ago. The offer was refused, but the indicated gain was recorded in the accounts. Accounting treatment is
   Increase Land, $46,000
   Increase Revenue from Change in Land Value, $46,000

Required

In each of the given situations, indicate which accounting concepts, principles or constraints apply and whether they have been applied appropriately. If you decide the accounting treatment is not generally accepted, discuss the effect of the departure on the balance sheet.

PROBLEMS—SET B

LO1 P1-1B. Forms of Business Organization

Presented below are four independent situations:

a. Larry Jordon, a photography major in college, decided to start a photography business specializing in weddings and similar occasions. Larry is still able to go to school full-time as all of his jobs are on weekends or holidays.

b. Joe Friday and Jay Holmes each owned a separate detective agency. They decided to combine their talents and resources in order to expand the amount of business they could undertake.

c. Three business school professors at a large university decided to start their own consulting business based on their combined talents. They feel that the insurance they can obtain will satisfy any possible legal issues they may face. They plan to use one professor's home office to meet clients, so start-up costs should be minimal.

d. Verna Zilver runs a small, but successful beauty salon. The salon has gained a strong reputation beyond the community where it is located. Verna has decided to open a chain of similar salons across the state to capitalize on her reputation. This will require a substantial investment in facilities and supplies. In addition, since Verna will not be able to closely supervise each location, she is worried about potential liability.

Required

Explain the form of organization that would be best in each situation—sole proprietorship, partnership, or corporation. Explain what factors you considered important in each situation.

LO5 P1-2B. Financial Statements While each of the financial statements is likely to aid in any business decision, it is often the case that a particular financial statement may be best suited to help in a particular decision. Consider each decision below independently:

a. You are trying to determine whether a particular firm is a good investment. You want to invest in a firm that has strong revenue growth.

b. You are employed as a financial analyst for a large investment firm. You are trying to assess the riskiness of a particular investment opportunity. You understand that the more debt a firm has relative to its stockholders' equity, the riskier the firm is.

c. You are trying to determine how much of a firm's net income it distributes to its stockholders.

d. You are trying to determine how a particular firm was able to finance its large expansion during the year.

Required

Determine which of the financial statements contains the most useful information to help in your decision. Explain what information you used from each statement to help you make your decision.

LO5 P1-3B. Balance Sheet The following balance sheet data are for Better Plumbing Contractors, Inc., a corporation, at May 31, 2019:

Accounts payable	$ 9,900	Common stock	$101,000
Cash	15,700	Retained earnings	?
Equipment, net	100,000	Notes payable	31,000
Supplies	28,500	Accounts receivable	9,200
Land	31,000		

Required

Prepare a balance sheet for Better as of May 31, 2019.

LO5 P1-4B. Statement of Stockholders' Equity and Balance Sheet The following is balance sheet information for Bryant Packaging Service at the end of 2019 and 2018:

	December 31, 2019	December 31, 2018
Accounts payable	$ 2,800	$ 2,600
Cash	11,000	12,000
Accounts receivable	23,800	19,500
Equipment, net	33,000	31,000
Notes payable	21,000	21,000
Supplies	5,700	5,200
Common stock	6,000	6,000
Dividends	13,000	0
Retained earnings	?	?

Required

a. Prepare a balance sheet as of December 31 of each year.

b. Prepare a statement of stockholders' equity for 2019. (*Hint:* The increase in retained earnings is equal to the net income less the dividend.)

P1-5B. Statement of Stockholders' Equity and Balance Sheet The following is balance sheet information for Philip Packaging Service at the end of 2019 and 2018:

LO5

	December 31, 2019	December 31, 2018
Accounts payable	$ 16,000	$ 14,000
Cash	53,000	49,000
Accounts receivable	80,000	64,000
Equipment, net	76,000	78,000
Notes payable	175,000	175,000
Supplies	29,000	31,000
Common stock	30,000	30,000
Dividends	15,000	0
Retained earnings	?	?

Required

a. Prepare a balance sheet as of December 31 of each year.

b. Prepare a statement of stockholders' equity for 2019. (*Hint:* The increase in retained earnings is equal to the net income less the dividend.)

P1-6B. Income Statement and Balance Sheet The first year records of R. Levitt, Interior Decorator, show the following information for the year-end December 31, 2019:

LO5

Notes payable	$ 6,000	Supplies	$ 6,500
Decorating fees earned	57,600	Cash	6,200
Insurance expense	1,600	Accounts receivable	8,600
Supplies expense	8,100	Advertising expense	700
Miscellaneous expense	1,200	Salaries expense	36,000
Common stock	7,000	Rent expense	4,500
Retained earnings	?	Accounts payable	2,800

Required

a. Prepare an income statement for the year.

b. Prepare a balance sheet as of December 31, 2019.

P1-7B. Statement of Cash Flows Shown below is selected information from the financial records of Willy Corporation as of December 31, 2019:

LO5

Inventory	$155,000	Cash purchase of equipment	$129,000
Cash collected from customers	670,000	Buildings, net	860,000
Equipment, net	255,000	Sales revenue	940,000
Retained earnings	580,000	Cash paid for operating activities	425,000
Cash dividends paid	90,000	Principal payments on existing note payable	128,000
Salary expense	226,000	Common stock	329,000

Required

a.   Determine which of the above items will appear on the statement of cash flows and then prepare the statement for Willy Corporation for the year ended December 31, 2019.

b.   Comment on the adequacy of Willy's operations to provide cash for its investing and financing activities.

LO3   **P1-8B.**   **Ethics**   In each of the following cases, (a) identify the aspect of the accounting environment primarily responsible for the ethical pressure on the accountant as pressure to achieve a favorable outcome, to disclose confidential information, or to report good short-term results, and (b) indicate the appropriate behavioral response that the accountant should take:

1.   Jim Miller, an accountant for the Geary Company, is reviewing costs charged to a big government contract to supply logistical support. The contract specifies that Geary is entitled to its cost plus 10 percent extra for profit. Jim notices that gardening services at the home of the company president, Stuart Geary, are included under miscellaneous expenses. The company's vice president, Slick Herve, tells you not to worry about this since the government expects a little bit of fancy accounting to be included in all of its contracts.

2.   Juan Salles, an accountant for the law partnership Dewy and Suem, is working on the year-end financial statements. Currently the two partners, Dewy and Suem, each receive one-half of the firm's net income. Next year the allocation will change to a two-thirds, one-third split since Suem will be taking considerable time off to do pro bono work, something Dewy never does. Dewy suggested to Salles that he delay booking a large partial settlement the partnership received in December until January of next year when they will receive the final cash payment. Dewy commented that it would be "cleaner" to keep it all together.

3.   Pete Jackson is the accountant for a large professional services firm. Part of his responsibility is to complete payroll tax reports based on the salaries paid to all the employees. Pete received a call from a friend at a search firm that specializes in personnel such as those employed at Pete's place of employment. Pete's friend casually asked how much certain employees were making, explaining he wanted to be able to calibrate market wages for work he was doing.

LO5, 6   **P1-9B.**   **Financial Statements and Other Components**   Match each of the items in the left column with the appropriate annual report component from the right column:

1. The company's total assets	a. Income Statement
2. An opinion regarding whether the financial statements followed GAAP	b. Statement of Stockholders' Equity
	c. Balance Sheet
3. Information regarding the estimates used in the financial statements	d. Statement of Cash Flows
	e. Management's Discussion and Analysis (MD&A)
4. The use of cash during the period	
5. The company's total expenses for the period	f. Notes to the Financial Statements
6. A discussion of potential risks that a company may encounter in the future	g. Auditor's report
7. The amount of a company's earnings that are distributed to the company's stockholders	

LO5   **P1-10B.**   **Income Statement, Statement of Stockholders' Equity, and Balance Sheet**   Pick Corporation started business on January 1, 2019. The following information was compiled by Pick's accountant on December 31, 2019:

Sales revenue.	$52,000	Equipment, net.	$31,000
Expenses	41,000	Building, net	49,000
Dividends	4,000	Accounts payable.	8,000
Cash.	5,250	Notes payable.	49,500
Accounts receivable	6,750	Common stock	33,000
Inventory.	5,500	Retained earnings	?

Required

a.   You have been asked to assist the accountant for the Pick Corporation in preparing year-end financial statements. Use the above information to prepare an income statement, statement of stockholders' equity, and a balance sheet as of December 31, 2019.

b.   Comment on the decision to pay a $4,000 dividend.

P1-11B. Recognition and Measurement Criteria The following are unrelated accounting situations and the accounting treatment that was followed in each firm's records:

LO8
(Appendix 1A)

1. The Buchanan Company mounts a $900,000 year-long advertising campaign on a new national cable television network. The firm's annual accounting period is the calendar year. The television network required full payment in December at the beginning of the campaign. Accounting treatment is

    Increase Advertising Expense, $900,000
    Decrease Cash, $900,000

2. Because of a local bankruptcy, machinery worth $320,000 was acquired at a "bargain" purchase price of $150,000. Accounting treatment is

    Increase Machinery, $150,000
    Decrease Cash, $150,000

3. J.R. Brown, a consultant operating a sole proprietorship, withdrew $50,000 from the business and purchased stocks as an investment gift to his wife. Accounting treatment is

    Increase Investments, $50,000
    Decrease Cash, $50,000

4. Puite Company received a firm offer of $106,000 for a parcel of land it owns that cost $56,000 two years ago. The offer was refused, but the indicated gain was recorded in the accounts. Accounting treatment is

    Increase Land, $50,000
    Increase Revenue from Change in Land Value, $50,000

Required

In each of the given situations, indicate which accounting concepts, principles or constraints apply and whether they have been applied appropriately. If you decide the accounting treatment is not generally accepted, discuss the effect of the departure on the balance sheet.

SERIAL PROBLEM: KATE'S CARDS

SP1. Kate Collins has always been good at putting together rhymes for any occasion. Kate is a recent college graduate with a double major in business and art. Kate has always had a bit of an entrepreneurial streak and has decided to open her own business designing and selling greeting cards.

Kate decided that she would rent a small studio where she would design the cards on a new Apple iMac that she is planning to purchase. Kate also decided to offer classes in greeting card design to other aspiring greeting card producers. After much thought, Kate decided to name her business "Kate's Cards."

Required

a. What form of business—sole proprietorship, partnership, or corporation—should Kate choose? Discuss why the organizational form that you selected is most appropriate for Kate.
b. What accounting information will Kate need to run her business?
c. What balance sheet accounts—assets, liabilities, and stockholders' equity—and income statement accounts—revenues and expenses—will Kate likely need to use?
d. Should Kate use her personal bank account or open a separate business bank account?

Kate's Cards is a continuous problem that requires students to apply the concepts from the current chapter. There is a Kate's Cards assignment in each chapter.

EXTENDING YOUR KNOWLEDGE

REPORTING AND ANALYSIS

EYK1-1. Financial Reporting Problem: Columbia Sportswear Company Financial statements for the **Columbia Sportswear Company** are reported in **Appendix A** at the end of the textbook.

COLUMBIA
SPORTSWEAR
COMPANY

Required

Refer to Columbia Sportswear's financial statements to answer the following questions:

a. How much did Columbia's total assets increase or decrease from December 31, 2016, to December 31, 2017?

Extending Your Knowledge assignments require use of real world financial statements and critical thinking skills.

  b. How much did Columbia's cash and cash equivalents increase or decrease from December 31, 2016, to December 31, 2017, and how much cash did Columbia report on its December 31, 2017, balance sheet?

  c. How much accounts receivable and accounts payable did Columbia report on December 31, 2017?

  d. Did Columbia experience sales growth in 2017?

  e. Was Columbia profitable in 2017? How does the company's 2017 net income compare to 2016?

COLUMBIA
SPORTSWEAR
COMPANY

UNDER ARMOUR

Financial Statements
*for Columbia
Sportswear and Under
Armour are located at
the end of the book
in Appendix A and
Appendix B.*

EYK1-2. **Comparative Analysis Problem: Columbia Sportswear Company vs. Under Armour, Inc.** Simplified financial statements for the Columbia Sportswear Company are reported in **Exhibit 1-10** and Under Armour's financial statements are presented in **Appendix B** at the end of this book.

Required

  1. Based on the information in these financial statements, compare the following for each company as of December 31, 2017:

  a. Total assets

  b. Sales

  c. Net income

  d. Cash flow from operations

  2. From this information, what can you conclude about the relative size and operating performance of each company?

EYK1-3. **Business Decision Problem** Paul Seger, a friend of yours, is negotiating the purchase of an exterminating company called Complete Pest Control. Seger has been employed by a national pest control service and knows the technical side of the business. However, he knows little about accounting, so he asks for your assistance. The owner of Complete Pest Control, Greg Krum, provided Seger with income statements for the past three years, which showed an average net income of $75,000 per year. The latest balance sheet shows total assets of $360,000 and liabilities of $60,000. Seger brings the following matters to your attention:

  1. Krum is asking $375,000 for the firm. He told Seger that because the firm has been earning a 20 percent return on stockholders' equity, the price should be higher than the net assets reported on the balance sheet. (Note: The return on stockholders' equity is calculated as net income divided by total stockholders' equity.)

  2. Seger noticed that there was no salary expense reported for Krum on the income statements, even though he worked half-time in the business. Krum explained that, because he had other income, he withdrew only $15,000 each year from the firm for personal use. If he purchases the firm, Seger will hire a full-time manager to run the firm at an annual salary of $30,000.

  3. Krum's tax returns for the past three years report a lower net income for the firm than the amounts shown in the financial statements. Seger is skeptical about the accounting principles used in preparing the company's financial statements.

Required

  a. If Seger accepts Krum's average annual income figure of $75,000, what would Seger's return on stockholders' equity be, assuming that the net income remained at the same level and that the firm was purchased for $375,000?

  b. Should Krum's withdrawals of $15,000 per year affect the net income reported in the financial statements? What will Seger's percentage return be if he takes into consideration the $30,000 salary he plans to pay a full-time manager?

  c. Could there be legitimate reasons for the difference between net income as shown in the financial statements and net income as reported on the tax returns, as mentioned in point 3? How might Seger obtain additional assurances about the propriety of the company's financial statements?

EYK1-4. **Financial Analysis Problem** Todd Jansen is deciding among several job offers. One job offer he is considering is in the marketing department at Columbia Sportswear. Before he makes his decision, he decides to review the financial reports of the company.

Required

Use the Columbia Sportswear annual report located in Appendix A at the end of this book to answer the following questions:

   a. Were the financial statements of Columbia audited? If so, what firm performed the audit?

   b. What was the amount of Columbia's 2017 net income? How does this compare with 2016 net income?

   c. How much cash was provided or used for investing activities? What were the major sources and uses of cash from investing activities?

   d. How much were accrued liabilities in 2017? What makes up this balance?

   e. What are some of the more significant estimates used in the preparation of the company's financial statements?

   f. To what amount are the financial statements rounded?

CRITICAL THINKING

EYK1-5. **Accounting Research Problem** Go to this book's Website and locate the annual report of **General Mills, Inc.** for the year ending May 28, 2017 (fiscal year 2017).

GENERAL MILLS, INC.

Required

   a. Refer to the company's balance sheet.

      1. What form of business organization does General Mills use? What evidence supports your answer?

      2. What is the date of the most recent balance sheet?

      3. For the most recent balance sheet, what is the largest asset reported? The largest liability?

   b. Refer to the company's income statement.

      1. What time period is covered by the fiscal year 2017 statement of earnings?

      2. What total amount of sales revenue did General Mills generate in the most recent period? What is the change in sales revenues from last year to the current report year?

      3. What is the net income (i.e., net earnings, including earnings attributable to noncontrolling interests) for the most recent period?

   c. Refer to the company's statement of cash flows.

      1. For the most recent period, what is the amount and trend of the cash flow from operating activities?

      2. For the most recent period, what is the amount and trend of the cash flow from investing activities?

      3. For the most recent period, what is the amount and trend of the cash flow from financing activities?

EYK1-6. **Accounting Communication Activity** Bruce Smith is an intern for the Start Company. He knows the company's balance sheet is supposed to balance, but he is not having much luck getting it to balance. Bruce knows that you are taking a course in accounting so he asks for your help. Bruce provides you with the following balance sheet that is currently out of balance:

START COMPANY			
Balance Sheet			
December 31, 2019			
Assets		**Liabilities**	
Cash......................	15,000	Inventory...........................	20,000
Accounts receivable...........	30,000	Notes payable......................	34,000
Equipment, net...............	28,000	**Stockholders' Equity**	
Accounts payable.............	(22,000)	Dividends	(11,000)
		Common stock	10,000
		Retained earnings, beginning of year......	10,000
Total	51,000	Total	67,000

In addition, Bruce provides you with a correct income statement that reports a net income for 2019 of $28,000.

Required

   a. Prepare a corrected balance sheet for the Start Company.

   b. Write a memo to Bruce explaining what he did wrong.

   c. In the memo explain the purpose of the balance sheet.

Writing *assignments are denoted by this icon.*

EYK1-7. **Accounting Ethics Case** Jack Hardy, CPA, has a brother, Ted, in the retail clothing business. Ted ran the business as a sole proprietor for 10 years. During this 10-year period, Jack helped Ted with various accounting matters. For example, Jack designed the accounting system for the company, prepared Ted's personal income tax returns (which included financial data about the clothing business), and recommended various cost control procedures. Ted paid Jack for all of these services. A year ago, Ted expanded the business and incorporated. Ted is president of the corporation and also chairs the corporation's board of directors. The board of directors has overall responsibility for corporate affairs. When the corporation was formed, Ted asked Jack to serve on its board of directors. Jack accepted. In addition, Jack now prepares the corporation's income tax returns and continues to advise his brother on accounting matters.

Recently, the corporation applied for a large bank loan. The bank wants audited financial statements for the corporation before it will decide on the loan request. Ted asked Jack to perform the audit. Jack replied that he cannot do the audit because the code of ethics for CPAs requires that he be independent when providing audit services.

Required

Why is it important that a CPA be independent when providing audit services? Which of Jack's activities or relationships impair his independence?

EYK1-8. **Ethics** As the accountant for Minkow Corporation, you are responsible for reporting the company's profit. It appears that the company's actual results are much better than was expected by Wall Street analysts. Your supervisor has requested that you report some of next period's expenses now so that this period's profits will be in line with analyst expectations. He states that you are not really doing anything wrong since the reported results will be more conservative. In addition, this will make it easier to make next year's numbers. What should you do?

**COLUMBIA
SPORTSWEAR
COMPANY**

EYK1-9. **Corporate Social Responsibility Problem** Go to the **Columbia Sportswear Company** Website and find the section on their commitment to corporate and environmental responsibility. These sections can be found near the bottom of their home page under the section "About Us."

Required

Answer the following questions.

a. How does Columbia describe the company's efforts at corporate responsibility?
b. How is the Higg Index used by Columbia's environmental responsibility efforts?
c. What featured initiative has Columbia embarked upon?
d. Why do you think that Columbia makes these efforts to be a good corporate citizen? Why do you think they devote so much space on their Website to promote these efforts?

EYK1-10. **Forensic Accounting Problem** Go to the Association of Certified Fraud Examiners Website and find their description of a forensic accountant. This can be found under the Career tab, Career Paths, then click on Accounting followed by Forensic Accountant (www.acfe.com/career-path-forensic-accountant.aspx).

Forensic Accounting
assignments are denoted by this icon.

Required

Answer the following questions.

a. What do forensic accountants do?
b. What knowledge, skills, and abilities should a forensic accountant possess?
c. How might the knowledge learned from this course help you to become a forensic accountant?

**LVMH MOET
HENNESSEY-
LOUIS VUITTON
S.A.**

EYK1-11. **Analyzing IFRS Financial Statements** The 2017 financial statements of **LVMH Moet Hennessey-Louis Vuitton S.A.** are presented in **Appendix C** at the end of this book. LVMH is a Paris-based holding company and one of the world's largest and best-known luxury goods companies. As a member of the European Union, French companies are required to prepare their consolidated (group) financial statements using International Financial Reporting Standards (IFRS). After reviewing LVMH's consolidated financial statements, consider the following questions:

a. What is LVMH's second largest asset account on its 2017 balance sheet? What percentage of total assets does this asset represent?
b. Is LVMH principally debt financed or equity financed in 2017? What percentage of LVMH's assets is financed with debt?

     c.   Is LVMH profitable in 2017? What percentage of the company's sales revenue in 2017 is represented by its "profit for the year," or its net income?

     d.   How much is LVMH's cash flow from operating activities in 2017? How does LVMH's profit for the year (net income) compare with its cash flow from operating activities?

EYK1-12.   **Working with the Takeaways**   You have just learned that you inherited a large sum of money. You know that it is important to invest this money wisely, and you have decided to invest in the shares of several different companies. One of those companies is the Columbia Sportswear Company.

     Required

     Answer the following questions regarding your potential investment in Columbia Sportswear shares:

     a.   Should you request financial statements from the company, and if so, which ones?

     b.   Is it important that the financial statements be audited by an independent auditor? Explain.

     c.   What does each of the four financial statements tell you about Columbia's financial health or operating performance?

ANSWERS TO SELF-STUDY QUESTIONS:

1. c, (p. 4)   2. d, (p. 10)   3. a, (p. 10)   4. b, (pp. 10–11)   5. c, (pp. 5–6)   6. b, (p. 13)   7. b, (p. 14)

8. c, (pp. 19–21)   9. d, (pp. 8–9)   10. (pp. 4–5)

     1.   Sole proprietorship and partnership

     2.   Sole proprietorship and partnership

     3.   Partnership

     4.   Corporation

     5.   Corporation

     6.   Sole proprietorship

11. c, (p. 14)   12. c, (pp. 12–13)   13. b, (pp. 15–16)

YOUR TURN! SOLUTIONS

Solution 1.1

Sole proprietorship: Easiest to set up, owner controlled, and tax advantages.

Partnership: Relatively easy to establish, larger skill set, and tax advantages.

Corporations: Easiest to raise capital, easiest to transfer ownership, and protection against personal liability.

Solution 1.2

1. Financing	4. Operating
2. Operating	5. Financing
3. Investing	6. Operating

Solution 1.3

1. The financial statements are the primary output of financial accounting. External users require information on a business's performance and financial position. This is the type of information provided by the financial statements. Managerial accounting involves the process of generating and analyzing financial data to use for internal decision making and management of the business.

2. Internal users include management, the marketing department, and the finance department, among others. Each of these groups require data to help them run their departments and make good business decisions.

3. External users include, among others, investors, lenders, and regulators. These external groups require accounting information to help them make decisions regarding a company's performance and financial position.

Solution 1.4

Your supervisor is asking you to participate in the preparation of fraudulent financial statements. This is not only unethical it is also illegal and could subject you to criminal prosecution. By reporting the sales revenue early, the financial statements will mislead users into thinking the company is doing better than it actually is. This in turn may lead them to make erroneous investment decisions. You should not follow your supervisor's request. Instead you should explain to your supervisor why reporting sales revenue prior to when it is earned is unethical. If your supervisor continues to pressure you, you should report your supervisor's request to a higher level of management in the company.

Solution 1.5

1. c
2. a
3. d
4. b

Solution 1.6

KANZU CORPORATION Income Statement For Year Ended December 31, 2019	
Sales revenue.	$20,000
Expenses	12,000
Net income	$ 8,000

KANZU CORPORATION
Statement of Stockholders' Equity
For Year Ended December 31, 2019

	Common Stock	Retained Earnings	Total
Balance, January 1.	$ 0	$ 0	$ 0
Add: Common stock issued	20,000		20,000
Net income		8,000	8,000
Less: Dividends		(3,000)	(3,000)
Balance, December 31.	$20,000	$5,000	$25,000

KANZU CORPORATION
Balance Sheet
December 31, 2019

Assets		Liabilities		
Cash.	$ 1,500	Accounts payable.	$ 4,000	
Accounts receivable	2,500	Notes payable.	33,000	
Inventory.	3,000	Total liabilities		$37,000
Building.	40,000	**Stockholders' Equity**		
Equipment	15,000	Common stock	20,000	
Total assets	$62,000	Retained earnings	5,000	
		Total stockholders' equity.		25,000
		Total liabilities and stockholders' equity		$62,000

KANZU CORPORATION Statement of Cash Flows For Year Ended December 31, 2019	
Cash flow from operating activities.	$ 6,500
Cash flow from investing activities	(55,000)
Cash flow from financing activities	50,000
Net increase in cash.	1,500
Cash at January 1, 2019	0
Cash at December 31, 2019.	$ 1,500

Solution 1.7

1. c
2. b
3. a

Chapter 2

Processing Accounting Information

PAST

Chapter 1 described the environment of financial accounting. It also introduced the financial statements and how they are related.

PRESENT

This chapter explains the accounting system, including transaction analysis, the system of debits and credits, and the journalizing of transactions.

FUTURE

Chapter 3 describes accounting adjustments, the construction of financial statements, and the period-end closing process.

While not everyone is familiar with the company **Intuit Inc.**, nearly everyone that works in the business world is familiar with some of its products. Intuit is a software company based in Mountain View, California, that develops the popular financial and tax preparation software QuickBooks, Mint, and TurboTax.

This chapter describes the details of the accounting system of debits and credits that is applied throughout the world and is the foundation for all accounting software. This chapter also explains the process of journalizing and posting transactions so that financial statements can be prepared for both internal and external users of accounting.

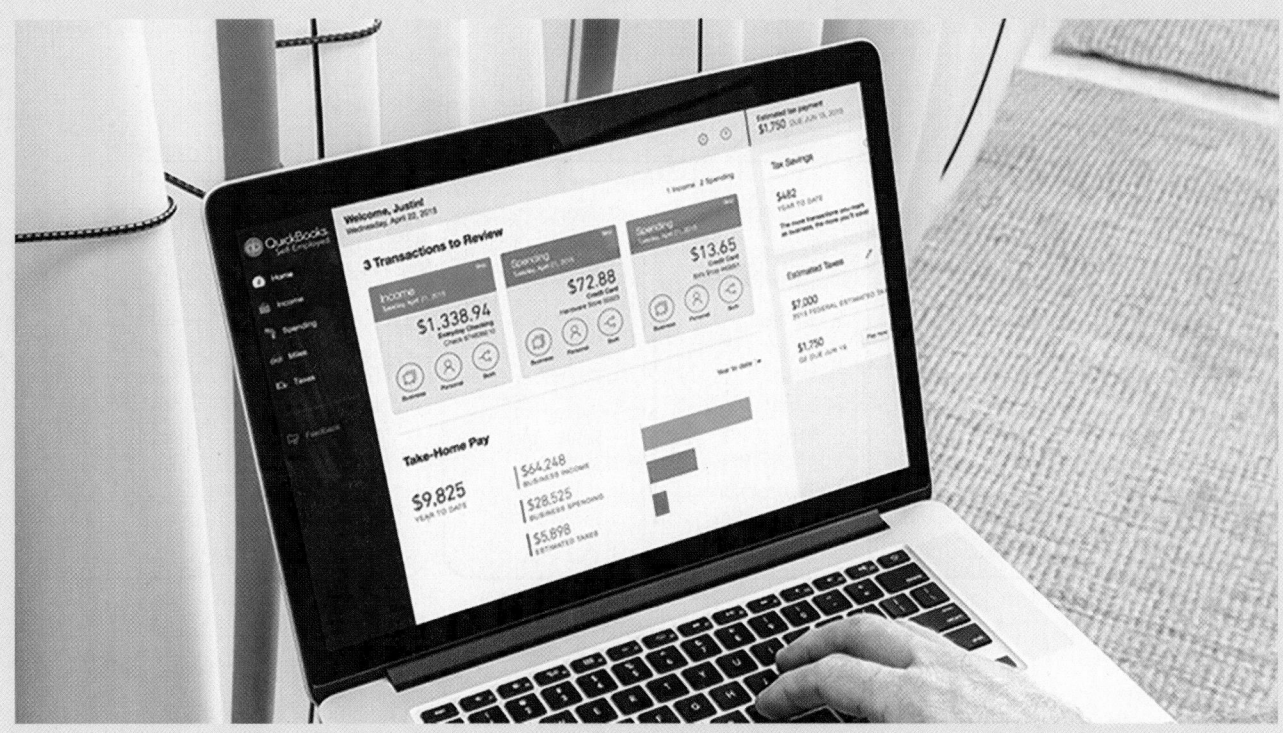

Road Map

LO	Learning Objective	Page	eLecture	Guided Example	Assignments
LO1	Identify the five major steps in the accounting cycle.	58	E2-1	YT2.1	SS15, SS17, SE10
LO2	Analyze and record transactions using the accounting equation.	59	E2-2	YT2.2	SS1, SS2, SS3, SS16, SE6, E1A, E2A, E3A, E4A, E11A, E15A, E1B, E2B, E3B, E4B, E11B, E15B, P1A, P2A, P3A, P4A, P5A, P6A, P7A, P8A, P9A, P10A, P11A, P1B, P2B, P3B, P4B, P5B, P6B, P7B, P8B, P9B, P10B, P11B
LO3	Explain the nature, format, and purpose of an account.	66	E2-3		SS4, SE11, E14A, E14B
LO4	Describe the system of debits and credits and its use in recording transactions.	66	E2-4	YT2.3, YT2.4	SS5, SS6, SS7, SS8, SS9, SS10, SE1, SE2, SE3, SE4, SE5, E5A, E8A, E9A, E10A, E11A, E5B, E8B, E9B, E10B, E11B, P12A, P13A, P14A, P15A, P16A, P12B, P13B, P14B, P15B, P16B
LO5	Explain the process of journalizing and posting transactions.	69	E2-5	YT2.5	SS11, SS13, SS14, SE7, E4A, E6A, E7A, E8A, E9A, E10A, E12A, E13A, E16A, E4B, E6B, E7B, E8B, E9B, E10B, E12B, E13B, E16B, P12A, P13A, P14A, P15A, P16A, P17A, P12B, P13B, P14B, P15B, P16B, P17B
LO6	Describe the trial balance.	77	E2-6	YT2.6	SS12, SE8, SE9, E12A, E13A, E12B, E13B, P12A, P13A, P14A, P15A, P16A, P17A, P12B, P13B, P14B, P15B, P16B, P17B

ACCOUNTING CYCLE

LO1 **Identify** the five major steps in the accounting cycle.

Businesses engage in economic activities. The role of accounting is to analyze these activities for their impact on a company's accounting equation, and then enter the results of that analysis in the company's accounting system. When a company's management team needs financial data for decision-making purposes and for reports to external parties, the company's financial statements are prepared and communicated. At the end of the accounting period, the "books are closed," a process that prepares the accounting records for the next accounting period. These accounting activities constitute the major steps in the **accounting cycle**—a sequence of activities undertaken by accountants to accumulate and report the financial information of a business. Stated succinctly, these steps are analyze, record, adjust, report, and close. **Exhibit 2-1** shows the sequence of the major steps in the accounting cycle.

Exhibit 2-1	Five Major Steps in the Accounting Cycle

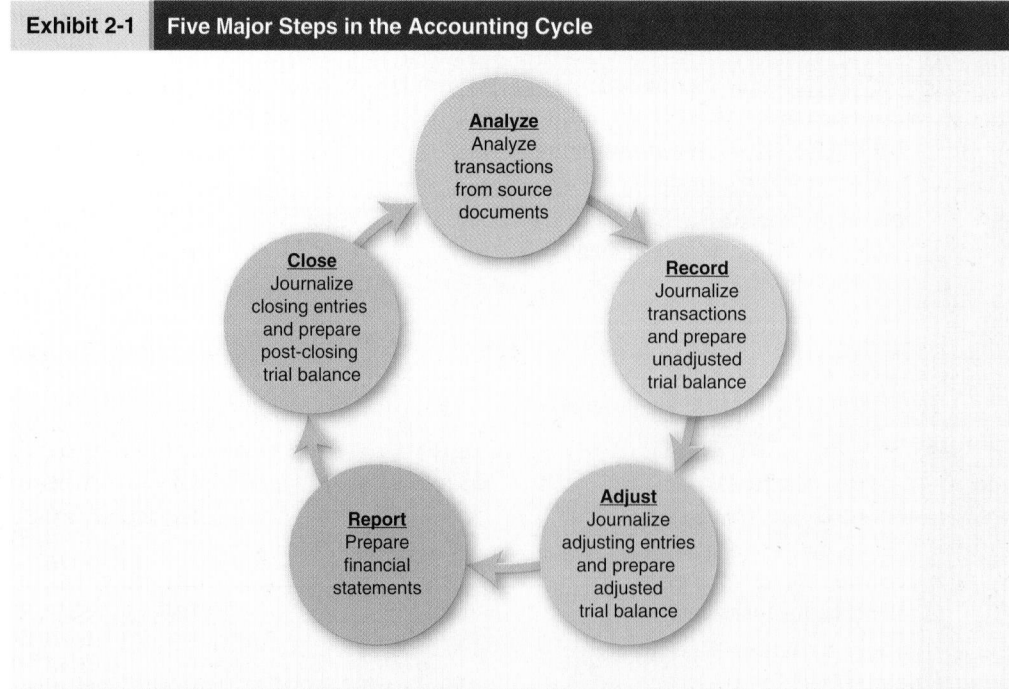

The five steps in the accounting cycle do not occur with equal frequency. A business analyzes and records financial transactions daily during the accounting period. It adjusts and reports accumulated financial data whenever management needs financial information, usually at weekly, monthly, or quarterly intervals, but at least annually. Closing the books occurs just once, at the end of the accounting period. This chapter focuses on the first two steps of the accounting cycle—analyze and record. In Chapter 3, we examine the final three steps of the cycle.

This chapter explains the accounting cycle using WebWork, a Website development and consulting business launched on December 1, 2019.

ACCOUNTING IN PRACTICE

Accounting Periods

The annual accounting period is known as a **fiscal year**. Businesses with fiscal year-ends on December 31 are said to be on a **calendar year**. About 60 percent of U.S. businesses are on a calendar year. Many companies prefer to have their accounting year coincide with their "natural" year—that is, at a point in time when business activity is at a low point. For example, many retailers conclude their fiscal year when inventory quantities are low and easier to count, as year-end accounting procedures are more efficiently accomplished when there is less inventory. The "natural" year does not necessarily coincide with the calendar year. For example, **Gap**, a retailer, ends its fiscal year on the Friday nearest January 31. The company's busiest period is November through January, when its customers are holiday shopping. Similarly, the **Boston Celtics**, a professional basketball team, concludes its fiscal year on June 30, following completion of the NBA finals.

YOUR TURN! 2.1

The solution is on page 116.

Place the following five major steps in the accounting cycle in the proper order:

a) Report   c) Close   e) Adjust

b) Record   d) Analyze

ANALYZING TRANSACTIONS

Many companies utilize a computer-based accounting system to record their financial transactions. You may have some personal experience using accounting software programs like QuickBooks by **Intuit**. While these computer-based accounting systems are not as sophisticated as the systems used by major corporations, they work in much the same way. Similarly, manual systems might lack the sophistication of large accounting systems utilized by companies like **Ford Motor Company**, but the basic process remains the same.

LO2 Analyze and record transactions using the accounting equation.

As we saw in Chapter 1, the accounting equation is written as:

$$\text{Assets (A)} = \text{Liabilities (L)} + \text{Stockholders' equity (SE)}$$

The accounting equation provides a convenient way to analyze and summarize a company's financial transactions and data. The first step in the accounting cycle—analyze—is to determine what information (if any) must be recorded in a company's accounting records. Only items that can be expressed in monetary terms are recorded in financial statements. (The monetary unit concept was discussed in Appendix 1A.) For example, the payment of salary to Jeff Bezos, the CEO of **Amazon**, is recorded because it can be expressed in monetary terms.

An **accounting transaction** is an economic event that must be recorded in the company's accounting records. In general, an event that affects any of the elements of the accounting equation—assets, liabilities, or stockholders' equity—must be recorded in a company's accounting records. Some activities—for example, ordering supplies, bidding on a contract, or negotiating the purchase of an asset—may represent a business activity, but an accounting transaction does not occur until such activities result in a change in an asset, liability, or stockholders' equity account.

An accounting transaction affects at least two elements of the accounting equation, so that the equation always remains in balance. This is where the term **double-entry accounting** comes from. For example, if an asset account such as Cash is increased, one of the following financial events must also occur to keep the accounting equation in balance:

   a. Another asset, such as Accounts Receivable, must decrease; or

   b. A liability, such as Notes Payable, must increase; or

   c. Stockholders' equity, such as Common Stock, must increase.

Accounting Equation Expanded

Stockholders' equity has two primary components—the amount invested by stockholders (common stock) and the cumulative net income of the business that has not been distributed to stockholders as a dividend (retained earnings). Common stock is increased when the company issues shares of stock. Retained earnings is increased by revenues and decreased by expenses (revenues and expenses are the elements of a company's net income or net loss). Retained earnings is also decreased by a company's payment of dividends. Incorporating these components into stockholders' equity, the *expanded accounting equation* is illustrated in **Exhibit 2-2**.

Exhibit 2-2 The Accounting Equation Expanded

Transactions and the Accounting Equation: An Illustration

We now consider the transactions of WebWork, Inc., a developer of web-based applications, to illustrate how various economic activities and events lead to financial statements.

Steve Gates first established WebWork on December 2, 2019. The company's transactions for December, the first month of operations, are analyzed on the following pages. The accounting equation for WebWork is shown after each transaction so that the financial effects of each transaction can be examined. The accounting equation remains in balance following each transaction. This is not a coincidence; it is the result of the fundamental structure of the accounting system.

The following pages illustrate eleven transactions that occurred at WebWork during December 2019. Avoid the temptation to skip any of these transactions because each transaction is included to illustrate a particular concept or approach to recording an economic event utilizing the accounting equation.

Transaction 1. Issued Stock

On December 2, 2019, Steve Gates invested $30,000 cash in exchange for all of the company's common stock. This transaction increased the company's assets, Cash, by $30,000 and increased its stockholders' equity, Common Stock, by $30,000, as illustrated below using the accounting equation. (For each transaction that impacts stockholders' equity, we add a brief description—in this case "Issued stock.")

	Assets	=	Liabilities	+	Stockholders' Equity	
	Cash	=			Common Stock	
(1)	+30,000	=			+30,000	Issued stock
	$30,000				$30,000	

It is important to verify the equality of the accounting equation following each transaction. After the above transaction is recorded, both sides of the equation total $30,000.

Transaction 2. Paid Rent in Advance

On December 2, WebWork prepaid its office rent for the next six months, December 2019 through May 2020. WebWork's rent is $1,800 per month; meaning it paid a total of $10,800 cash (6 × $1,800). This transaction decreased Cash by $10,800 and increased Prepaid Rent by $10,800.

	Assets			=	Liabilities	+	Stockholders' Equity
	Cash	+	Prepaid Rent	=			Common Stock
Balance	30,000						30,000
(2)	−10,800		+10,800				
	19,200	+	10,800				30,000
		$30,000		=			$30,000

The expenditure for prepaid rent is recorded as an asset because the advance payment is a future economic benefit to the company. This outlay of cash has value to the business beyond the current accounting period, but any rent that is used up in the current accounting period will be recorded as an expense for the month of December.

Transaction 3. Purchased Office Supplies on Account

On December 2, WebWork purchased office supplies on account totaling $2,850. Businesses often extend credit to their customers. Credit allows businesses to pay for goods or services at a later date. When credit is used to purchase goods or services, the purchase is said to be made *on account*. This transaction increased Office Supplies by $2,850 and increased Accounts Payable by the same amount.

	Assets					=	Liabilities	+	Stockholders' Equity
	Cash	+	Office Supplies	+	Prepaid Rent	=	Accounts Payable	+	Common Stock
Balance	19,200				10,800				30,000
(3)			+2,850				+2,850		
	19,200	+	2,850		+10,800	=	2,850	+	30,000
			$32,850			=		$32,850	

Office supplies are recorded as an asset because they are expected to be used by the business in future periods beyond the current accounting period. Any supplies that are used up in the current accounting period will be recorded as an expense for the month of December. Following the purchase of office supplies, WebWork's assets total $32,850, which is equal to the sum of total liabilities of $2,850 plus stockholders' equity of $30,000.

Transaction 4. Signed Bank Note in Exchange for Cash

On December 2, WebWork obtained a two-year bank loan in the amount of $36,000, after signing a note payable. Annual interest charges on the note amount to 10 percent and are due each November 30. As a consequence of this loan, the company's Cash account increased by $36,000 and the Notes Payable account, a liability, increased by $36,000.

	Assets			=	Liabilities		+	Stockholders' Equity
	Cash +	Office Supplies +	Prepaid Rent	=	Accounts Payable +	Notes Payable +		Common Stock
Balance	19,200	2,850	10,800		2,850			30,000
(4)	+36,000					+36,000		
	55,200 +	2,850 +	10,800	=	2,850 +	36,000 +		30,000
		$68,850				$68,850		

Transaction 5. Purchased Equipment With Cash

On December 3, WebWork used cash to purchase office equipment costing $32,400. This transaction decreased Cash by $32,400 and increased Office Equipment by the same amount. The accounting equation remains in balance because an equal amount, $32,400, is added to one asset (Equipment) and subtracted from another asset (Cash).

	Assets				=	Liabilities		+	Stockholders' Equity
	Cash +	Office Supplies +	Prepaid Rent +	Equipment	=	Accounts Payable +	Notes Payable +		Common Stock
Balance	55,200	2,850	10,800			2,850	36,000		30,000
(5)	−32,400			+32,400					
	22,800 +	2,850 +	10,800 +	32,400	=	2,850 +	36,000 +		30,000
		$68,850					$68,850		

Transaction 6. Received Customer Prepayment

A.K.A. Unearned revenue is also called **deferred revenue**.

On December 5, WebWork received a prepayment in the amount of $3,000 for services to be performed over the next few months. Because WebWork has not yet performed the services, it does not record the $3,000 payment as revenue. This practice follows the revenue recognition principle discussed in Appendix 1A. Instead, a liability account, **Unearned Revenue**, is increased by $3,000, and the Cash account is increased by $3,000. Unearned revenue is a liability because the company accepted payment for goods or services that have not yet been provided. Once WebWork performs the services, the unearned revenue liability will be reduced and revenue will be recognized.

	Assets				=	Liabilities			+	Stockholders' Equity
	Cash +	Office Supp. +	Prepd. Rent +	Equip-ment	=	Accts. Pay. +	Unearned Revenue +	Notes Pay. +		Common Stock
Bal.	22,800	2,850	10,800	32,400		2,850		36,000		30,000
(6)	+3,000						+3,000			
	25,800 +	2,850 +	10,800 +	32,400	=	2,850 +	3,000 +	36,000 +		30,000
			$71,850					$71,850		

Non-Accounting Transaction. Hired an Employee

On December 6, WebWork hired an employee to provide administrative help in the office. The employee will be paid $1,620 every two weeks and begins work Monday, December 9. At the time the employee is hired there is no immediate financial effect on the assets, liabilities, or stockholders' equity of the company. There is only an employment agreement between the employee and the company. The employee has not yet performed any work, nor has the employee received any wages.

Transaction 7. Provided Services to Customers for Cash

On December 10, WebWork performed services for several customers and was paid $13,510 cash. This transaction increased Cash by $13,510 and increased Fee Revenue by the same amount.

	Assets				=	Liabilities			+	Stockholders' Equity	
	Cash +	Office Supp. +	Prepd. Rent +	Equip- ment =		Accts. Pay. +	Unearned Revenue +	Notes Pay. +	Comm. Stock +	Retained Earnings	
										Rev. −Exp.−Div.	
Bal.	25,800	2,850	10,800	32,400		2,850	3,000	36,000	30,000		
(7)	+13,510									+13,510	Fee revenue
	39,310+ 2,850 + 10,800+ 32,400 = 2,850 + 3,000 + 36,000+ 30,000 + 13,510										
	$85,360					$85,360					

This transaction is recorded as earned revenue because WebWork has performed the services for which it was paid.

Transaction 8. Provided Services for Cash and on Account

On December 18, WebWork performed $4,740 of services and received $1,000 in cash with the remaining $3,740 to be paid to WebWork by customers within 90 days. As previously noted in transaction 3 above, businesses often extend credit to customers, allowing them to pay for goods or services at a later date. Under accrual accounting, revenue must be recorded when goods or services are transferred from the seller to the buyer, regardless of when payment is received. Consequently, this transaction increased Cash by $1,000, and Accounts Receivable by $3,740, and it increased Fee Revenue by the total amount of $4,740. The accounting equation remains in balance because both sides of the equation are increased by $4,740.

A.K.A. Delivering goods or services in advance of payment is referred to as providing goods or services "on account" or "on credit."

	Assets					=	Liabilities			+	Stockholders' Equity	
	Cash +	Accts. Rec. +	Office Supp. +	Prepd. Rent +	Equip- ment =		Accts. Pay. +	Unearned Revenue +	Notes Pay. +	Comm. Stock +	Retained Earnings	
											Rev. −Exp.−Div.	
Bal.	39,310		2,850	10,800	32,400		2,850	3,000	36,000	30,000	13,510	
(8)	+1,000	+3,740									+4,740	Fee revenue
	40,310+ 3,740+ 2,850+10,800+ 32,400 = 2,850 + 3,000 + 36,000+ 30,000 + 18,250											
	$90,100						$90,100					

Transaction 9. Paid Employee Wages

On December 20, WebWork paid the employee after she completed her first two weeks on the job. This transaction decreased Cash by $1,620, and increased Wage Expense by $1,620. By definition, an increase in expenses decreases stockholders' equity.

	Assets				=	Liabilities			+	Stockholders' Equity		
Cash +	Accts. Rec. +	Office Supp. +	Prepd. Rent +	Equip-ment	=	Accts. Pay. +	Unearned Revenue +	Notes Pay. +	Comm. Stock +	Retained Earnings Rev.	− Exp.	−Div.
Bal. 40,310	3,740	2,850	10,800	32,400		2,850	3,000	36,000	30,000	18,250		
(9) −1,620											−1,620	Wage expense
38,690 + 3,740 +	2,850 +	10,800 +	32,400 =			2,850 +	3,000 +	36,000 +	30,000 +	18,250 −	1,620	

$88,480 $88,480

Transaction 10. Received Payment on Account from Customer

On December 27, WebWork received a payment of $2,400 cash from a customer that had previously received services performed on account (see Transaction 8). This transaction increased Cash by $2,400, and decreased Accounts Receivable by $2,400.

	Assets				=	Liabilities			+	Stockholders' Equity		
Cash +	Accts. Rec. +	Office Supp. +	Prepd. Rent +	Equip-ment	=	Accts. Pay. +	Unearned Revenue +	Notes Pay. +	Comm. Stock +	Retained Earnings Rev.	− Exp.	− Div.
Bal. 38,690	3,740	2,850	10,800	32,400		2,850	3,000	36,000	30,000	18,250	1,620	
(10) +2,400	−2,400											
41,090 +	1,340 +	2,850 +	10,800 +	32,400 =		2,850 +	3,000 +	36,000 +	30,000 +	18,250 −	1,620	

$88,480 $88,480

After recording this transaction, the balance in Accounts Receivable is $1,340. This represents the amount still owed to WebWork for services that were previously performed on account but remain unpaid.

Transaction 11. Paid Cash Dividend

On December 30, WebWork paid a cash dividend. Dividends are not a business expense, and are not included in the calculation of net income. Rather, dividends are a distribution of the company's accumulated net income to its stockholders. Payment of the dividend decreased Cash by $500 and increased Dividends by $500. By definition, an increase in dividends causes a decrease in stockholders' equity.

	Assets				=	Liabilities			+	Stockholders' Equity		
Cash +	Accts. Rec. +	Office Supp. +	Prepd. Rent +	Equip-ment	=	Accts. Pay. +	Unearned Revenue +	Notes Pay. +	Comm. Stock +	Retained Earnings Rev.	− Exp.	− Div.
Bal. 41,090	1,340	2,850	10,800	32,400		2,850	3,000	36,000	30,000	18,250	1,620	
(11) −500												−500 Dividends
40,590 +	1,340 +	2,850 +	10,800 +	32,400 =		2,850 +	3,000 +	36,000 +	30,000 +	18,250 −	1,620 −	500

$87,980 $87,980

Transaction Summary

Exhibit 2-3 provides a summary of the eleven accounting transactions for WebWork, for the month of December. The exhibit illustrates the financial effect of each transaction using the accounting equation. It is important that the accounting equation remains in balance at all times, and that the equality between total assets and the sum of total liabilities and stockholders' equity is maintained following each transaction.

Exhibit 2-3	Summary of December Transactions and Their Effect on the Expanded Accounting Equation

	Assets					=	Liabilities			+	Stockholders' Equity			
	Cash	Accts. Rec.	Office Supp.	Prepd. Rent	Equip- ment		Accts. Pay.	Unearned Revenue	Notes Pay.		Comm. Stock	Retained Earnings		
												Rev.	Exp.	Div.
(1)	+30,000										+30,000			
(2)	−10,800			+10,800										
(3)			+2,850				+2,850							
(4)	+36,000								+36,000					
(5)	−32,400				+32,400									
(6)	+3,000							+3,000						
(7)	+13,510											+13,510		
(8)	+1,000	+3,740										+4,740		
(9)	−1,620												−1,620	
(10)	+2,400	−2,400												
(11)	−500													−500
	40,590 +	1,340+	2,850+	10,800+	32,400 =		2,850+	3,000 +	36,000 +		30,000 +	18,250 −	1,620 −	500
			$87,980									$87,980		

Concept	⟶	Method	⟶	Assessment	TAKEAWAY 2.1
When should an event be recorded in a company's accounting records?		Review the event details. Does the event affect the company's assets, liabilities, or stockholders' equity?		If the event affects any of the elements of the accounting equation, it must be recorded in a company's accounting records.	

Ford Aerobics Studio, Inc., operates as a corporation. The firm rents studio space (including a sound system) and specializes in offering aerobics classes to individuals and groups. On January 1, the assets, liabilities, and stockholders' equity of the business were as follows: Cash, $5,000; Accounts Receivable, $5,200; Accounts Payable, $1,000; Notes Payable, $2,500; Common Stock, $5,500; and Retained Earnings, $1,200. The January business activities for the studio were as follows:

YOUR TURN! 2.2

The solution is on page 116.

1. Paid $600 cash on accounts payable.
2. Paid January rent of $3,600 cash.
3. Billed clients for January classes in the amount of $11,500.
4. Received a $500 invoice from a supplier for T-shirts given free to January's class members as an advertising promotion.
5. Collected $10,000 cash on account from clients for prior aerobics classes.
6. Paid employee wages of $2,400 cash.
7. Received a $680 invoice for January's utilities.
8. Paid $20 cash to the bank as January interest on an outstanding note payable.
9. Paid $900 cash in dividends to stockholders.
10. Paid $4,000 cash on January 31 to purchase a sound system to replace the rented system.

Required

a. Set up an expanded accounting equation in columnar form with the following individual assets, liabilities, and stockholders' equity accounts: Cash, Accounts Receivable, Equipment, Accounts Payable, Notes Payable, Common Stock, and Retained Earnings. Enter the January 1 balances below each account. (The beginning balance in the Equipment account is $0.)

b. Record the financial impact (increase or decrease) of each transaction (1) through (10) on the beginning account balances. Then total the columns to demonstrate that total assets equal the sum of total liabilities plus stockholders' equity as of January 31.

THE "ACCOUNT" SYSTEM

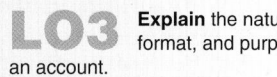

Explain the nature, format, and purpose of an account.

The basic component of an accounting system is the **account**, which is an individual record of the increases and decreases in a specific asset, liability, or stockholders' equity item. An account is created for each individual asset, liability, and stockholders' equity item on a company's financial statements. Some common account titles are Cash, Accounts Receivable, Notes Payable, Fee Revenue, and Rent Expense.

Chart of Accounts

Businesses maintain a chart of accounts to facilitate the analysis of a company's business activities. A **chart of accounts** is a list of the titles of all accounts in a business's accounting system. Account titles are grouped by, and in the order of, the six major components of the expanded accounting equation: assets, liabilities, stockholders' equity, revenues, expenses, and dividends. **Exhibit 2-4** shows the chart of accounts for WebWork and indicates the account numbers that will be used throughout this illustration. (Each company maintains its own unique set of accounts and its own numbering system.)

Exhibit 2-4	Chart of Accounts for WebWork

Assets	**Equity**
110 Cash	310 Common Stock
120 Accounts Receivable	320 Retained Earnings
130 Office Supplies	330 Dividends
150 Prepaid Rent	
170 Office Equipment	**Revenues**
175 Accumulated Depreciation— Office Equipment	410 Fee Revenue
	Expenses
Liabilities	510 Supplies Expense
210 Accounts Payable	520 Wage Expense
220 Interest Payable	530 Rent Expense
230 Wages Payable	540 Depreciation Expense— Office Equipment
250 Unearned Revenue	550 Interest Expense
260 Notes Payable	
	Dividends
	610 Dividends

System of Debits and Credits

LO4 **Describe** the system of debits and credits and its use in recording transactions.

One basic characteristic of all accounts is that data entries separately record the increases and decreases to an account. The method of recording data entries in the accounts is a matter of convention; that is, a simple set of rules is followed, which involves debits and credits.

A **T-account** is a simplified form of an account which is used to capture these effects. T-accounts are so named because they resemble the letter "T" as shown below:

Account Title (e.g., Cash)

Debit	Credit
Always the left side	Always the right side

The terms **debit** and **credit** refer to the left side and the right side, respectively, of an account. Regardless of what amount is recorded in an account, any entry made on the left side is a debit to the account while any entry recorded on the right side is a credit to the account. The words *debit* and *credit* are abbreviated *dr.* (from the Latin *debere*) and *cr.* (from the Latin *credere*), respectively.

The system of debits and credits identifies which side of the account, debit or credit, is used to increase the account and which side of the account is used to decrease the account. **Exhibit 2-5** summarizes these rules for each of the six primary categories of accounts: assets, liabilities, stockholders' equity, revenues, expenses, and dividends.

Observe the following relations in **Exhibit 2-5**:

1. Debit always refers to the left side of an account; credit always refers to the right side.

2. The pattern of increases and decreases in accounts derives from the accounting equation. Assets are on the left side of the accounting equation and increase with debit (or left side) entries. Assets decrease with credit entries.

3. Liabilities and stockholders' equity are on the right side of the accounting equation and increase with credit (or right side) entries. Liabilities and stockholders' equity decrease with debit entries.

4. The **normal balance** of an account is the side on which increases to the account are recorded. This is because increases in an account are usually greater than, or equal to, decreases in an account. Asset accounts normally have debit balances while liability and stockholders' equity accounts normally have credit balances.

5. Revenue, expense, and dividends are temporary subdivisions of retained earnings. The pattern of increases and decreases in these accounts derives from their relation to retained earnings. Revenues increase earnings, and just like the retained earnings account, revenue accounts increase with credit entries and decrease with debit entries. On the other hand, expenses decrease earnings, and so have the opposite pattern as retained earnings; expense accounts increase with debit entries and decrease with credit entries.

6. Dividends are distributions of retained earnings to shareholders, and like expense accounts have the opposite pattern as retained earnings; dividends increase with debit entries and decrease with credit entries.

Exhibit 2-5	System of Increases and Decreases, Debits and Credits, and Normal Balances

YOUR TURN! 2.3

The solution is on page 116.

For each of the following accounts, identify whether the account's normal balance is a debit or a credit.

a. Cash
b. Common stock
c. Wage expense
d. Notes payable
e. Dividends
f. Sales revenue
g. Inventory

As an example of the system of debits and credits, the Cash T-account with the December transactions for WebWork is presented in **Exhibit 2-6**.

Exhibit 2-6	Cash T-account

+		Cash (A)		–
(1)	30,000	10,800	(2)	
(4)	36,000	32,400	(5)	
(6)	3,000	1,620	(9)	
(7)	13,510	500	(11)	
(8)	1,000			
(10)	2,400			
	85,910	45,320		
Bal.	40,590			

To compute the T-account balance, sum the numbers in each column and subtract the smaller total from the larger total. In this example, subtract 45,320 from 85,910 to compute the 40,590 balance.

Note that amounts are not indicated with either a plus (+) or minus (-) sign in a T-account because, as shown in **Exhibit 2-5**, the type of the account and whether the data entry is a debit or credit to that account tell us if the amount is an increase or decrease. Because Cash is an asset, increases are always shown on the left as debits and decreases on the right as credits.

A T-account consists of: (1) the account title (such as Cash), (2) amounts reflecting increases and decreases, and (3) cross-references to other accounting records. It is customary to reference (or link) the data entries in a T-account with a number or a letter to identify the related accounting transaction that originated the data. This permits a systematic review of the data entries in the event of a recording error. It also enables a company, and its independent auditor, to review the company's set of accounts and match the account information with the related accounting transactions. The numerical references in the Cash T-account above are the ones used to identify the December transactions for WebWork from **Exhibit 2-3**.

YOUR TURN! 2.4

The solution is on page 116.

Using the information in **Exhibit 2-3**, construct the T-account for Accounts Receivable in proper form.

CORPORATE SOCIAL RESPONSIBILITY

What to Record?

An important element of the conceptual framework discussed in Appendix 1A in Chapter 1 is the monetary unit concept, which states that only those items that can be expressed in monetary terms are reported in financial statements. This causes many items of interest to be excluded from financial statements. Reporting of a company's social responsibility activities, for example, would be compromised if it were constrained to the activities that can be expressed in monetary terms. Reporting guidelines established by the Global Reporting Initiative, the organization that pioneered the world's most widely used sustainability reporting framework, allow for a wider range of activities to be measured and reported. For example, **Bayer Group**, a global healthcare company, reports such items as greenhouse emissions, net water usage, and employee safety records in its annual sustainable development report.

RECORDING TRANSACTIONS

Earlier in this chapter we analyzed the transactions of WebWork using the accounting equation. This approach enabled us to see how accounting transactions affect a company's financial position and operations. This approach is not feasible, however, for even a modest-sized business because of the large number of transactions and accounts involved. Consequently, we now explain the process of analyzing and recording accounting information in an actual accounting system.

LO5 Explain the process of journalizing and posting transactions.

An initial step in the analysis and recording process is to identify evidence of a business transaction. This usually comes in the form of a source document. **Source documents** are printed forms or computer records that are generated when a firm engages in a business transaction. At a minimum, a source document usually specifies the dollar amount involved, the date of the transaction, and possibly the party dealing with the firm. Some examples of source documents include (1) a supplier's invoice showing evidence of a purchase of supplies on account, (2) a bank check indicating the payment of an obligation, (3) a deposit slip showing the amount of cash deposited in a bank, and (4) a cash receipt indicating the amount of cash received from a customer for services rendered. An example of an invoice follows. Regardless of its form, the source document serves as the basis for the analysis of the underlying business event.

WebWork, Inc.   INVOICE

137 Technology Lane
Irvine, CA 92614
Phone (949) 727-3555

INVOICE # [100]
DATE: DECEMBER 18, 2019

TO:
Pick Enterprises
1055 Kinrose Ave.
Los Angeles, CA 90024
(310) 208-5570

FOR:
Web design

DESCRIPTION	HOURS	RATE	AMOUNT
Design work for Website, including motion graphics	16	$150	$2,400
		TOTAL	$2,400

Make all checks payable to WebWork, Inc.
Total due in 15 days. Overdue accounts subject to a service charge of 1% per month.

Thank you for your business!

Once the source document has been analyzed to determine the accounts affected and the amounts involved, we then record the transaction. All accounting transactions are initially recorded in a journal. A **journal**, or *book of original entry,* is a tabular record in which a business's activities are reflected in terms of debits and credits and recorded in chronological order. A journal organizes information by date, and thus, serves as a chronological diary of a company's business activities. The word *journalize* means to record a transaction in a journal. An entry in a journal is called a **journal entry**.

A.K.A. A company's journals are also referred to as its "books."

A.K.A. Another term often used to describe the recording of a transaction is to "book" the transaction.

General Journal

The **general journal** is a record with enough flexibility that any type of business transaction can be recorded in it. Like all journals in an accounting system, the general journal is a book of original entry in which accounting data are entered into a company's accounting system. **Exhibit 2-7** shows the first transaction as it is recorded in WebWork's general journal. The procedure for recording entries in the general journal follows:

❶ Indicate the year, month, and date of entry. (Usually the year and month are rewritten only at the top of each page of the journal or at the point in the journal where the year and month change.)

❷ Enter the titles of accounts affected (from the chart of accounts) in the Description column. Accounts to receive debits are entered close to the left margin and are recorded first. Accounts to receive credits are recorded next and indented slightly to the right.

❸ Enter dollar amounts in the left (Debit) and right (Credit) columns.

❹ Record an explanation of the transaction below the account titles; it should be brief, disclosing information necessary to understand the event recorded.

Exhibit 2-7	General Journal with First Entry of WebWork		
	GENERAL JOURNAL		
Date	Description	Debit	Credit
2019 ❶ Dec. 2	Cash ❷	30,000 ❸	
	Common stock		30,000
	Issued stock in exchange for cash. ❹		

A journal entry that involves more than two accounts is called a **compound journal entry**. (As shown on page 73, the journal entry for Transaction 8 is an example of a compound journal entry involving three accounts.) Any number of accounts can appear in a compound entry; but, regardless of how many accounts are used, the sum of the debit amounts always equals the sum of the credit amounts. Accordingly, each transaction entered in the general journal is recorded with equal dollar amounts of debits and credits. The account titles cited in the Description column should correspond to those from the chart of accounts. (To delineate between journal entries made in the general journal, we leave a blank line between each transaction entry.)

Posting Journal Entries to the General Ledger

After an accounting transaction is journalized in the general journal, the debits and credits in each journal entry are immediately transferred to another component of the accounting system called the general ledger. A **general ledger** is a listing of each account of a company and the amounts making up each account. While the general journal organizes transactions in chronological order, the general ledger organizes transactions by account. This makes it easier to determine the balance of each account, which in turn facilitates the preparation of the company's financial statements. Although businesses can use various ledgers to accumulate detailed accounting information, all firms have a general ledger.

The process of transferring the debit and credit information from the general journal to the general ledger is called **posting**. It is important to be able to trace each data entry appearing in a general ledger account to the general journal location from which it was posted; consequently, both the general journal and general ledger accounts have a **posting reference** code. The posting reference of the general journal indicates the account to which the related debit or credit has been posted. The posting references in the general journal and ledger accounts are entered when the journal entries are posted to the ledger accounts (automatically when computerized, or by hand for a manual system). We will use the transaction number as the posting reference in the examples that follow.

Illustration of the Recording Process

We now apply the recording process to the transactions of WebWork, that were summarized in **Exhibit 2-3**. For each transaction, we (1) **analyze** the transaction using the accounting equation, (2) **journalize** the transaction, and (3) **post** journal entries to the general ledger (for simplicity, we use the T-account structure for each ledger account).

Transaction 1   Issued Stock

On December 2, Steve Gates invested $30,000 in exchange for common stock of WebWork.

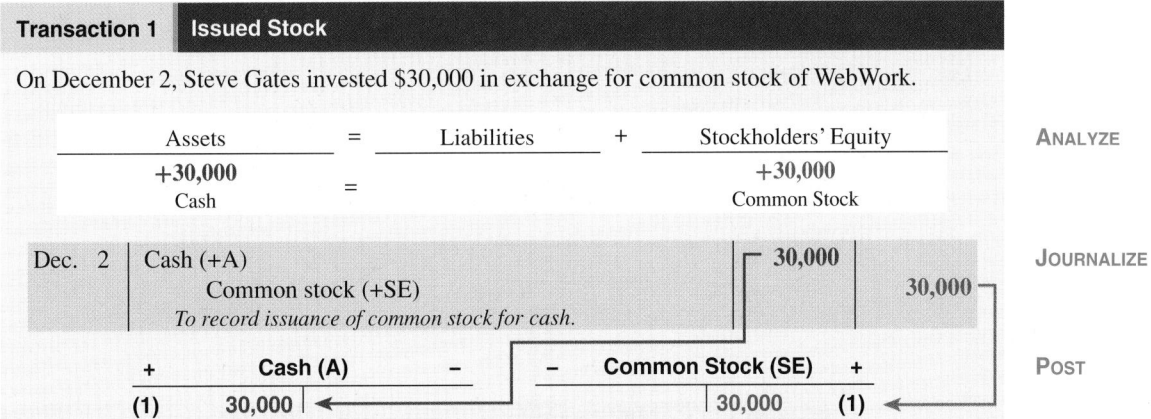

Transaction 2   Paid Rent in Advance

On December 2, WebWork prepaid rent for the office covering the next six months, December 2019 through May 2020. Monthly rent is $1,800; the total amount prepaid was $10,800 cash.

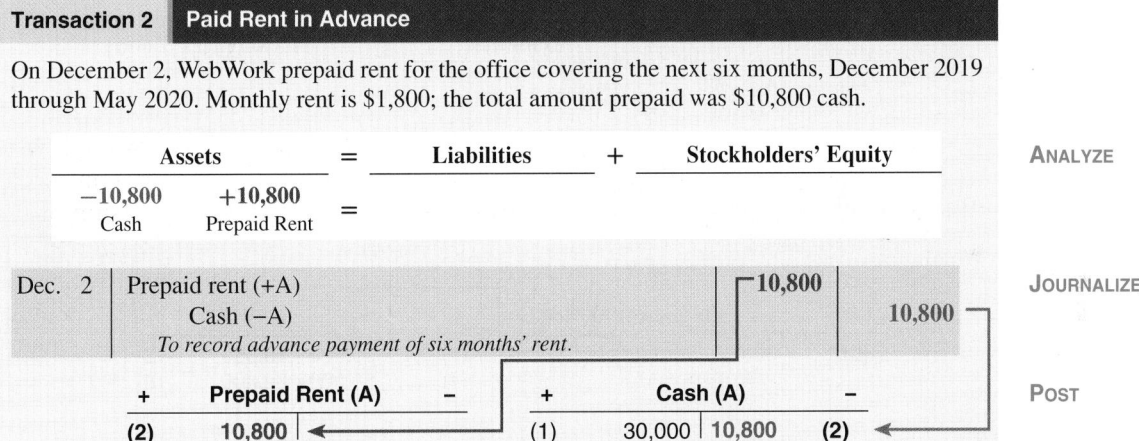

Transaction 3   Purchased Office Supplies on Account

On December 2, WebWork purchased $2,850 of office supplies on account.

Transaction 4	Signed Bank Note in Exchange for Cash

On December 2, WebWork obtained a two-year bank loan for $36,000, signing a note payable. Annual interest of 10 percent is due each November 30.

ANALYZE

Assets	=	Liabilities	+	Stockholders' Equity
+36,000		+36,000		
Cash	=	Notes Payable		

JOURNALIZE

Dec. 2	Cash (+A)		36,000	
	Notes payable (+L)			36,000
	To record borrowing of funds.			

POST

+	Cash (A)	–		–	Notes Payable (L)	+
(1)	30,000	10,800 (2)			36,000	(4)
(4)	36,000					

Transaction 5	Purchased Equipment with Cash

On December 3, WebWork used cash to purchase $32,400 of office equipment.

ANALYZE

Assets		=	Liabilities	+	Stockholders' Equity
−32,400	+32,400				
Cash	Office	=			
	Equipment				

JOURNALIZE

Dec. 3	Office equipment (+A)		32,400	
	Cash (−A)			32,400
	To record purchase of office equipment.			

POST

+	Office Equipment (A)	–		+	Cash (A)	–
(5)	32,400			(1)	30,000	10,800 (2)
				(4)	36,000	32,400 (5)

Transaction 6	Received Customer Prepayment

On December 5, WebWork received $3,000 cash for services to be performed in the future.

ANALYZE

Assets	=	Liabilities	+	Stockholders' Equity
+3,000		+3,000		
Cash	=	Unearned Revenue		

JOURNALIZE

Dec. 5	Cash (+A)		3,000	
	Unearned revenue (+L)			3,000
	To record advance payment from a customer.			

POST

+	Cash (A)	–		–	Unearned Revenue (L)	+
(1)	30,000	10,800 (2)			3,000	(6)
(4)	36,000	32,400 (5)				
(6)	3,000					

Transaction 7   **Provided Services to Customers for Cash**

On December 10, WebWork performed services for several customers and was paid $13,510 cash.

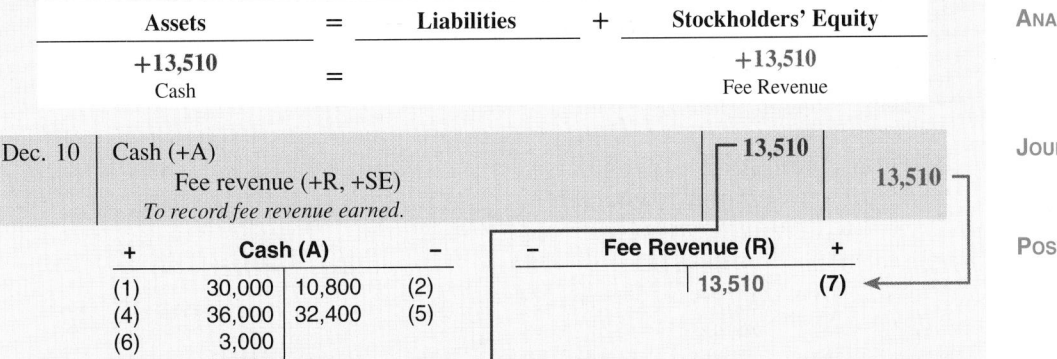

Transaction 8   **Provided Services for Cash and on Account**

On December 18, WebWork performed $4,740 of services for which it received $1,000 cash with the remaining $3,740 to be paid in the future.

Transaction 9   **Paid Employee Wages**

On December 20, WebWork paid its employee $1,620 cash upon completion of her first two weeks on the job.

ANALYZE

JOURNALIZE

POST

ANALYZE

JOURNALIZE

POST

Summary Illustration of Journalizing and Posting Transactions

Exhibit 2-8 presents the general journal for WebWork for the month of December 2019. Also, **Exhibit 2-9** presents the general ledger for WebWork as of December 31, 2019. All journal entries appearing in **Exhibit 2-8** have been posted to the general ledger accounts in **Exhibit 2-9**. The accounts in WebWork's general ledger are grouped by category as follows: (1) assets, (2) liabilities, (3) stockholders' equity, (4) dividends, (5) revenues, and (6) expenses. Each general ledger account in **Exhibit 2-9** has been totaled with the ending balance appearing in green. Note that total assets ($87,980) is equal to the sum of total liabilities ($41,850) and stockholders' equity ($46,130).

Exhibit 2-8	General Journal for WebWork		
	General Journal		
Date	**Account Titles and Explanation**	**Debit**	**Credit**
2019			
(1) Dec. 2	Cash (+A)	30,000	
	Common stock (+SE)		30,000
	To record issuance of common stock for cash.		
(2) 2	Prepaid rent (+A)	10,800	
	Cash (–A)		10,800
	To record advance payment of six months' rent.		
(3) 2	Office supplies (+A)	2,850	
	Accounts payable (+L)		2,850
	To record purchase of office supplies.		
(4) 2	Cash (+A)	36,000	
	Notes payable (+L)		36,000
	To record borrowing of funds.		
(5) 3	Office equipment (+A)	32,400	
	Cash (–A)		32,400
	To record purchase of office equipment.		
(6) 5	Cash (+A)	3,000	
	Unearned revenue (+L)		3,000
	To record advance payment from a customer.		
(7) 10	Cash (+A)	13,510	
	Fee revenue (+R, +SE)		13,510
	To record fee revenue earned.		
(8) 18	Cash (+A)	1,000	
	Accounts receivable (+A)	3,740	
	Fee revenue (+R, +SE)		4,740
	To record fee revenue earned.		
(9) 20	Wage expense (+E, –SE)	1,620	
	Cash (–A)		1,620
	To record payment of employee wages.		
(10) 27	Cash (+A)	2,400	
	Accounts receivable (–A)		2,400
	To record receipt of payment on account.		
(11) 30	Dividends (+D, –SE)	500	
	Cashe (–A)		500
	To record payment of cash dividends.		

Exhibit 2-9 | **General Ledger for WebWork**

General Ledger

Assets	=	Liabilities	+	Stockholders' Equity

Assets

+ Cash (A) −

(1)	30,000	10,800	(2)
(4)	36,000	32,400	(5)
(6)	3,000	1,620	(9)
(7)	13,510	500	(11)
(8)	1,000		
(10)	2,400		
Bal.	**40,590**		

+ Accounts Receivable (A) −

(8)	3,740	2,400	(10)
Bal.	**1,340**		

+ Office Supplies (A) −

(3)	2,850		
Bal.	**2,850**		

+ Prepaid Rent (A) −

(2)	10,800		
Bal.	**10,800**		

+ Office Equipment (A) −

(5)	32,400		
Bal.	**32,400**		

Liabilities

− Accounts Payable (L) +

	2,850	(3)
	2,850	**Bal.**

− Unearned Revenue (L) +

	3,000	(6)
	3,000	**Bal.**

− Notes Payable (L) +

	36,000	(4)
	36,000	**Bal.**

Stockholders' Equity

− Common Stock (SE) +

	30,000	(1)
	30,000	**Bal.**

+ Dividends (D) −

(11)	500	
Bal.	**500**	

− Fee Revenue (R) +

	13,510	(7)
	4,740	(8)
	18,250	**Bal.**

+ Wage Expense (E) −

(9)	1,620	
Bal.	**1,620**	

Assets = $87,980	=	Liabilities = $41,850	+	Stockholders' Equity = $46,130

YOUR TURN! 2.5

The solution is on pages 116–117.

For each of the transactions below, complete the following requirements.
1. Record the effect of each transaction using the accounting equation.
2. Prepare journal entries for each transaction.
3. Post the journal entries for each transaction to the appropriate T-accounts.

Transactions:

a. The company received $1,300 cash from clients for services rendered.
b. The company paid $2,400 cash for wages to employees.
c. The company collected $600 cash from clients on account.
d. The company paid a $400 cash dividend.
e. The company purchased $700 of office supplies on account.
f. The company billed clients $900 for services rendered, which were unpaid.
g. The company paid $500 cash to suppliers on account.

ACCOUNTING IN EVERYDAY LIFE | **Careers at Intuit**

A company like Intuit obviously needs employees with a strong knowledge of accounting. However, understanding accounting and how accounting is used is important for many career paths. For example, sales and marketing uses accounting to track and forecast sales activity, human resources uses accounting in employee performance evaluation, and corporate strategy uses accounting to research investment opportunities and communicate with corporate stakeholders. Clearly, knowledge of accounting will help you go far whatever your chosen career.

TRIAL BALANCE

LO6 **Describe** the trial balance.

A **trial balance** is a listing of all accounts from the general ledger with their respective debit or credit balance. A trial balance is prepared at the end of an accounting period after all transactions have been recorded. **Exhibit 2-10** shows the trial balance for WebWork, Inc. The heading provides the name of the company and the date the trial balance was prepared, December 31, 2019. The sequence of the accounts and the dollar amounts are taken directly from the general ledger T-accounts in **Exhibit 2-9** (which follow the order of the account numbering system in WebWork's chart of accounts). The debit and credit columns from the trial balance are in balance; that is, the $90,100 sum of the debit account balances equals the $90,100 sum of the credit account balances.

The two principal reasons for preparing a trial balance are:

1. To serve as a check on whether the sum of the debit balances and the sum of the credit balances from the general ledger accounts are equal. If the totals are not equal, it would indicate the presence of some type of recording error.

2. To show all general ledger account balances in one location, which facilitates the preparation of financial statements. The trial balance, however, is *not* a financial statement.

A trial balance must be dated. In **Exhibit 2-10**, the trial balance of WebWork, Inc., was prepared as of December 31, 2019.

While it is required that a trial balance be in balance—that is, that the total of the debit column equal the total of the credit column—this equality does not guarantee that the accounting data is error-free. Potential data errors could still exist as a consequence of (1) transactions not being journalized, (2) journal entries not being posted, (3) journal entries being posted in the wrong amount, and (4) journal entries being posted to the wrong accounts.

Exhibit 2-10	Unadjusted Trial Balance for WebWork	
WEBWORK, INC. **Unadjusted Trial Balance** **December 31, 2019**	**Debit**	**Credit**
Cash..	$40,590	
Accounts receivable........................	1,340	
Office supplies	2,850	
Prepaid rent	10,800	
Office equipment	32,400	
Accounts payable...........................		$ 2,850
Unearned revenue		3,000
Notes payable...............................		36,000
Common stock		30,000
Dividends	500	
Fee revenue..................................		18,250
Wage expense	1,620	
Totals	$90,100	$90,100

It is required that the sum of all debits equal the sum of all credits in the trial balance.

TAKEAWAY 2.2	Concept	➝	Method	➝	Assessment
	Is the trial balance in balance?		Ending balances for all of the general ledger accounts entered on the trial balance. Total the debit column and the credit column on the trial balance.		Verify the equality of the sum of the debit account balances and the sum of the credit account balances.

YOUR TURN! 2.6

The solution is on page 117.

Each of the following accounts from the Devin Company has a normal balance. The account balances are as of December 31, the end of Devin's first year of operations:

Cash............................	1,500	Common stock	7,500
Accounts receivable	4,500	Sales revenue.................	12,000
Inventory........................	3,750	Salary expense.................	4,500
Property, plant, and equipment........	11,250	Administrative expenses.........	750
Accounts payable..................	2,250	Dividends	1,500
Notes payable....................	6,000		

Prepare a trial balance for the Devin Company as of December 31.

ACCOUNTING IN PRACTICE

Big Data and AI

While accountants are often known as paper pushers, the future of accounting is likely much different. According to an article in Forbes, the digital world for accountants will look much different. We already see accounting software such as QuickBooks replacing paper ledgers and services such as **PayPal** replacing paper checks. But what does the future hold with Big Data and Artificial Intelligence (AI) becoming more and more mainstream?

The audits of tomorrow will benefit from the speed and rigorous checking provided by computers programed with AI. Computers with AI will also aid in regulatory compliance by ensuring transactions comply. Machine readable receipts will make quick order of reconciliations. And computers and AI, already becoming very good at fraud detections, will excel at risk management in the future.

Does this spell the demise of the accounting profession? Quite the contrary. Accountants willing to accept this future will learn to work with, rather than compete with these technologies. Just as the spreadsheet proved to make accountants more efficient at their jobs, so will Big Data and AI.

Marr, Bernard (Oct. 7, 2016) Big Data, AI And The Uncertain Future For Accountants. Retrieved from https://www.forbes .com/sites/bernardmarr/2016/10/07/big-data-ai-and-the-uncertain-future-for-accountants/2/#5294388e43f2

FORENSIC ACCOUNTING

Fraudulent Reporting

 Verifying that the sum of the debit account balances from the general ledger is equal to the sum of the credit account balances is not sufficient to guarantee accuracy of financial records. The infamous accounting scandal at **WorldCom** provides a case in point. To inflate its net income, WorldCom improperly "capitalized expenses"—that is, they inappropriately debited property, plant, and equipment, an asset account, when they should have debited an expense account. While the sum of the debit account balances on WorldCom's books did equal the sum of the credit account balances, assets were overstated and expenses were understated by almost $7 billion. WorldCom's CEO Bernard Ebbers, the mastermind of this fraudulent accounting scheme, was convicted of conspiracy to commit fraud, securities fraud, and making false filings with the SEC. Mr. Ebbers was sentenced to 25 years in prison.

COMPREHENSIVE PROBLEM

Juan Rios acted upon his entrepreneurial spirit and started a graphic design business called Juan's Designs. Based on an excellent business plan, Juan was able to raise sufficient capital to begin operations in October 2019. During the month of October, the following events occurred related to the business.

1. Stockholders invested $40,000 cash in the business in exchange for common stock.
2. Paid $2,500 cash for rent on an office suite for the month of October.
3. Purchased two desktop computers, software, and a printer for $10,000 cash.
4. Purchased miscellaneous supplies for $500 that will be used during the month, all on account.
5. Purchased an advertisement in a local newspaper for $300 cash, announcing the opening of his new business.
6. Performed $5,500 of design work on account.
7. Received $3,500 cash from customers for design work previously completed.
8. Paid $350 cash toward the company's accounts payable balance.
9. Paid $2,500 cash for wages of Juan Rios.

Required

a. Use the following accounts to create a general ledger using T-accounts.

Cash	Common Stock	Wage Expense
Accounts Receivable	Service Revenue	Advertising Expense
Equipment	Supplies Expense	Rent Expense
Accounts Payable		

Prepare journal entries and post the above accounting transactions to their general ledger T-accounts.

b. Prepare an unadjusted trial balance as of October 31, 2019.

Solution

Date	Description	Post Ref.	Debit	Credit
October	Cash (+A)	1	40,000	
	Common stock (+SE)	1		40,000
	Owner purchased shares for cash.			
	Rent expense (+E, −SE)	2	2,500	
	Cash (−A)	2		2,500
	Paid rent for office suite.			
	Equipment (+A)	3	10,000	
	Cash (−A)	3		10,000
	Purchased office equipment.			
	Supplies expense (+E, −SE)	4	500	
	Accounts payable (+L)	4		500
	Purchased supplies on account to be used in current month.			
	Advertising expense (+E, −SE)	5	300	
	Cash (−A)	5		300
	Purchased advertising.			
	Accounts receivable (+A)	6	5,500	
	Service revenue (+R, +SE)	6		5,500
	Performed design work on account.			
	Cash (+A)	7	3,500	
	Accounts receivable (−A)	7		3,500
	Received cash from previously billed work.			
	Accounts payable (−L)	8	350	
	Cash (−A)	8		350
	Paid cash towards accounts payable.			
	Wage expense (+E, −SE)	9	2,500	
	Cash (−A)	9		2,500
	Paid wages.			

+	Cash (A)	–		+	Accounts Receivable (A)	–
(1)	40,000	2,500	(2)	(6)	5,500	3,500	(7)
(7)	3,500	10,000	(3)	Bal.	2,000	
		300	(5)			
		350	(8)			
		2,500	(9)			
Bal.	27,850					

–	Accounts Payable (L)	+
(8)	350	500	(4)
		150	Bal.

+	Equipment (A)	–
(3)	10,000	

–	Service Revenue (R)	+
		5,500	(6)

–	Common Stock (SE)	+
		40,000	(1)

+	Wage Expense (E)	–
(9)	2,500	

+	Supplies Expense (E)	–
(4)	500	

+	Rent Expense (E)	–
(2)	2,500	

+	Advertising Expense (E)	–
(5)	300	

JUAN'S DESIGNS Unadjusted Trial Balance October 31, 2019		
	Debit	Credit
Cash	$27,850	
Accounts receivable	2,000	
Equipment	10,000	
Accounts payable		$ 150
Common stock		40,000
Service revenue		5,500
Supplies expense	500	
Wage expense	2,500	
Advertising expense	300	
Rent expense	2,500	
Totals	$45,650	$45,650

SUMMARY OF LEARNING OBJECTIVES

LO1 Identify the five major steps in the accounting cycle. (p. 58)

■ Five major steps in the accounting cycle are:
1. Analyze.
2. Record.
3. Adjust.
4. Report.
5. Close.

LO2 Analyze and record transactions using the accounting equation. (p. 59)

■ The accounting equation provides a convenient way to summarize the recording of financial information.

■ The initial step in the accounting process—analyze—is to determine which transactions (if any) need to be recorded.

■ An *accounting transaction* is an economic event that requires accounting recognition. An event that affects any of the elements of the basic accounting equation (assets, liabilities, or stockholders' equity) must be recorded.

Explain the nature, format, and purpose of an account. (p. 66)   **LO3**

- An account is an individual record of the increases and decreases in specific assets, liabilities, stockholders' equity, dividends, revenues, or expenses.
- Information provided by the account includes its title, amounts reflecting increases and decreases, cross-references to other accounting records, and dates and descriptive notations.

Describe the system of debits and credits and its use in recording transactions. (p. 66)   **LO4**

- The left side of an account is always the debit side; the right side of an account is always the credit side.
- Increases in assets, dividends, and expenses are debit entries; increases in liabilities, stockholders' equity, and revenues are credit entries. Decreases are the opposite.
- The normal balance of any account appears on the account side used for recording account increases.
- For each accounting transaction, the sum of the debit amounts must always equal the sum of the credit amounts.
- All accounting transactions are analyzed using one or more of the basic account categories: (1) assets, (2) liabilities, (3) stockholders' equity, (4) dividends, (5) revenues, and (6) expenses.

Explain the process of journalizing and posting transactions. (p. 69)   **LO5**

- Source documents provide the basis for analyzing business transactions.
- Accounting entries are initially recorded in a journal in chronological order; the journal is a book of original entry and acts like a diary of a business's activities.
- A general ledger is a grouping of all of the accounts that are used to prepare the basic financial statements.
- Posting is the transfer of information from a journal to the general ledger accounts.
- Posting references are used to cross-reference the information in journals and the general ledger accounts.

Describe the trial balance. (p. 77)   **LO6**

- A trial balance is a list of the accounts in the general ledger with their respective debit or credit balance.
- A trial balance is prepared after all transactions have been recorded for an accounting period.
- A trial balance serves as a mechanical check to evaluate the equality of the sum of the debit account balances and the sum of the credit account balances.
- A trial balance facilitates the preparation of the financial statements by showing all account balances in one concise record.

Concept	⟶	Method	⟶	Assessment	SUMMARY
When should an event be recorded in a company's accounting records?		Review the event details. Does the event affect the company's assets, liabilities, or stockholders' equity?		If the event affects any of the elements of the accounting equation, it must be recorded in a company's accounting records.	TAKEAWAY 2.1
Is the trial balance in balance?		Ending balances for all of the general ledger accounts entered on the trial balance. Total the debit column and the credit column on the trial balance.		Verify the equality of the sum of the debit account balances and the sum of the credit account balances.	TAKEAWAY 2.2

KEY TERMS

Account (p. 66)

Accounting cycle (p. 58)

Accounting transaction (p. 59)

Calendar year (p. 59)

Chart of accounts (p. 66)

Compound journal entry (p. 70)

Credit (p. 66)

Debit (p. 66)

Deferred revenue (p. 62)

Double-entry accounting (p. 60)

Fiscal year (p. 59)

General journal (p. 69)

General ledger (p. 70)

Journal (p. 69)

Journal entry (p. 69)

Normal balance (p. 67)

Posting (p. 70)

Posting reference (p. 70)

Source documents (p. 69)

T-account (p. 66)

Trial balance (p. 77)

Unearned revenue (p. 62)

Assignments with the ⊙ logo in the margin are available in BusinessCourse.
See the Preface of the book for details.

SELF-STUDY QUESTIONS

(Answers to Self-Study Questions are at the end of this chapter.)

LO2 1. **Which of the following transactions does not affect the balance sheet totals?**
   a.   Purchased $500 supplies on account
   b.   Paid off a $3,000 note payable
   c.   Received $4,000 cash from a bank after signing a note payable
   d.   Ordered a new machine that will be paid for upon its delivery in two months

LO2 2. **Tobias Company purchased inventory on account. This transaction will affect:**
   a.   Only the balance sheet
   b.   Only the income statement
   c.   The income statement and the statement of retained earnings
   d.   The income statement, balance sheet, and statement of retained earnings

LO2 3. **If assets increase by $50 and liabilities decrease by $30, stockholders' equity must:**
   a.   Remain unchanged
   b.   Increase by $80
   c.   Decrease by $70
   d.   Decrease by $130

LO3 4. **A T-account consists of how many parts?**
   a.   One
   b.   Two
   c.   Three
   d.   Four

LO4 5. **Which of the following is true?**
   a.   The debit is on the right side of an asset account
   b.   The debit is on the left side of an asset account
   c.   The credit is on the left side of a liability account
   d.   The debit is on the right side of an expense account

LO4 6. **Which of the following accounts has a normal debit balance?**
   a.   Accounts Payable
   b.   Notes Payable
   c.   Common Stock
   d.   Advertising Expense

LO4 7. **Which of the following accounts is increased by a credit?**
   a.   Accounts Receivable
   b.   Sales Revenue
   c.   Dividends
   d.   Advertising Expense

LO4 8. **Which of the following is true?**
   a.   A debit will increase a liability account
   b.   A credit will increase an asset account
   c.   A credit will increase a revenue account
   d.   A debit will decrease an expense account

LO4 9. **In applying the rules of debits and credits, which of the following statements is correct?**
   a.   The word *debit* means to increase and the word *credit* means to decrease
   b.   Asset, expense, and common stock accounts are debited for increases
   c.   Liability, revenue, and common stock accounts are debited for increases
   d.   Asset, expense, and dividends are debited for increases

LO4 10. **Which of these accounts has a normal debit balance?**
   a.   Assets, expenses, dividends
   b.   Assets, revenues, common stock
   c.   Liabilities, revenues, common stock
   d.   Assets, liabilities, dividends

11. **The general ledger includes accounts for all but which of the following?**   **LO5**
    a. Assets
    b. Expenses
    c. Dividends
    d. All of the above are in the general ledger

12. **Which of the following will cause a trial balance to be out of balance?**   **LO6**
    a. Mistakenly debiting an asset account instead of an expense account
    b. Posting $123 as $213 to both a debit and a credit account
    c. Posting the same transaction twice by mistake
    d. Posting only the debit part of a transaction

13. **A journal entry that contains more than just two accounts is called:**   **LO5**
    a. A posted journal entry
    b. An adjusting journal entry
    c. An erroneous journal entry
    d. A compound journal entry

14. **Posting refers to the process of transferring information from:**   **LO5**
    a. A journal to the general ledger accounts
    b. General ledger accounts to a journal
    c. Source documents to a journal
    d. A journal to source documents

15. **Which of the following is not one of the five steps in the accounting cycle?**   **LO1**
    a. Analyze
    b. Adjust
    c. Eliminate
    d. Report

16. **The purchase of $500 of supplies on account will:**   **LO2**
    a. Increase both assets and stockholders' equity by $500
    b. Increase assets and decrease liabilities by $500
    c. Increase assets and decrease stockholders' equity by $500
    d. Increase both assets and liabilities by $500

17. **Matching steps in the accounting cycle to their definitions.**   **LO1**

1. Analyze	a. Prepare financial statements
2. Record	b. Analyze transactions from source documents
3. Adjust	c. Journalize closing entries and prepare post-closing trial balance
4. Report	d. Journalize adjusting entries and prepare adjusted trial balance
5. Close	e. Journalize transactions and prepare unadjusted trial balance

QUESTIONS

1. List the five major steps in the accounting cycle in their proper order.

2. Define the term *fiscal year*.

3. Provide three examples of source documents that underlie business transactions.

4. Provide an example of a transaction that would:
    a. Increase one asset account but not change the amount of total assets.
    b. Decrease an asset account and a liability account.
    c. Decrease an asset account and increase an expense account.
    d. Increase an asset account and a liability account.

5. Explain the financial effect (increase, decrease, or no effect) of each of the following transactions on stockholders' equity:

   a. Purchased supplies for cash.
   b. Paid an account payable.
   c. Paid salaries.
   d. Purchased equipment for cash.
   e. Invested cash in business.
   f. Rendered services to customers, on account.
   g. Rendered services to customers, for cash.

6. The retained earnings on a balance sheet are $80,000. Without seeing the rest of the balance sheet, can you conclude that stockholders should be able to receive a dividend in the amount of $80,000 cash from the business? Justify your answer.

7. On December 31, the Milers Company had $800,000 in total assets and owed $300,000 to creditors. If the corporation's common stock amounted to $250,000, what amount of retained earnings should appear on the company's December 31 balance sheet?

8. Some accounting students believe that debits are good and credits are bad. Explain why this is not an accurate way to think about debits and credits.

9. What is an account?

10. What information is recorded in an account?

11. What does the term *debit* mean? What does the term *credit* mean?

12. What type of account—asset, liability, stockholders' equity, dividend, revenue, or expense—is each of the following accounts? Indicate whether a debit entry or a credit entry increases the balance of the account.

Professional Fees Earned	Common Stock
Accounts Receivable	Advertising Expense
Accounts Payable	Supplies
Cash	Dividends

13. How is the normal side of an account determined?

14. What is the normal balance (debit or credit) of each of the accounts in Discussion Question 12?

15. Describe the nature and purpose of a general journal.

16. What is the justification for the use of posting references?

17. Describe a compound journal entry.

18. What is a chart of accounts?

19. Explain the terms *general ledger* and *trial balance*. What are the primary reasons for preparing a trial balance?

20. Explain how it is possible for a trial balance to be in balance but still be in error.

21. What is a T-account and how is it used?

22. Is it possible for an accounting transaction to only affect the left side of the accounting equation and still leave the equation in balance? If so, provide an example.

23. Would a company record a transaction in its general ledger when an order is placed for the purchase of a machine that will be paid for at the time of its delivery in three months? Explain your answer.

SHORT EXERCISES

LO4   **SE2-1.   Normal Balances** Indicate for each of the following accounts whether the normal balance is a debit or a credit:

   a. Accounts Receivable   *e.* Inventory
   b. Accounts Payable   *f.* Interest Income
   c. Dividends   *g.* Retained Earnings
   d. Wage Expense

SE2-2. Debit and Credit Effects Indicate the account that will be debited for each of the following transactions: **LO4**

 a.   Issued common stock for cash
 b.   Borrowed money from a bank
 c.   Provided services on account
 d.   Purchased inventory on account
 e.   Collected cash from customers that owed a balance due

SE2-3. Debit and Credit Effects Indicate the account that will be credited for each of the following transactions: **LO4**

 a.   Issued common stock for cash
 b.   Borrowed money from a bank
 c.   Provided services on account
 d.   Purchased inventory on account
 e.   Collected cash from customers that owed a balance due

SE2-4. Determine a Transaction The Pearce Company recorded a transaction by debiting Accounts Receivable and crediting Sales Revenue. What event was being recorded?   **LO4**

SE2-5. Determine the Cash Balance The beginning-of-the-period cash balance for the Taylor Company was a $12,000 debit. Cash sales for the month were $8,000 and sales on account were $8,000. The company paid $2,500 cash for current-period purchases and also paid $3,000 cash for amounts due from last month. What is the ending debit or credit balance in the Cash account?   **LO4**

SE2-6. Recording Transactions with the Accounting Equation During the year, the Flight Company experienced the following accounting transactions: **LO2**

 1.   Issued common stock in the amount of $150,000
 2.   Paid a $30,000 cash dividend
 3.   Borrowed $25,000 from a bank
 4.   Made a principal payment of $3,500 on an outstanding bank loan
 5.   Made an interest payment of $1,200 on an outstanding bank loan

Using the accounting equation, record each of the transactions in columnar format using the following template:

Assets	=	Liabilities	+	Stockholders' Equity		
Cash	=	Notes Payable	+	Common Stock	+	Retained Earnings

SE2-7. Posting Transactions to T-accounts Using the data from short exercise SE2-6, prepare journal entries and post your transaction analysis to the appropriate T-accounts.   **LO5**

SE2-8. Prepare a Trial Balance The following balances were taken from the general ledger of Doogie Corporation as of December 31. All balances are normal. Prepare a trial balance.   **LO6**

Cash............................	$ 6,000	Accounts receivable................	$10,800
Accounts payable.................	6,000	Common stock....................	51,000
Equipment	45,000	Dividends	2,400
Utilities expense..................	2,000	Administrative expense	8,000
Sales revenue....................	17,200		

SE2-9. Prepare a Corrected Trial Balance The following trial balance for Hill Company has errors that cause it to be out of balance. Prepare a corrected version of the trial balance for Hill Company.   **LO6**

HILL COMPANY Unadjusted Trial Balance December 31, 2019		
	Debit	**Credit**
Cash.	$ 20,000	
Inventory.		$ 85,000
Accounts receivable	42,000	
Accounts payable.		12,000
Common stock		52,000
Retained earnings		58,000
Sales revenue.	100,000	
Utilities expense	60,000	
Selling expenses	15,000	
Totals	$237,000	$207,000

LO1   **SE2-10. The Accounting Cycle** The following is the correct order of the five steps in the accounting cycle:

   a.   Analyze; adjust; record; report; close
   b.   Analyze; record; adjust; report; close
   c.   Analyze; record; adjust; close; report
   d.   Analyze; report; adjust; record; close

LO3   **SE2-11. The Account** Which of the following is not part of the T-account?

   a.   Title
   b.   Amount
   c.   Cross-reference
   d.   Analysis

EXERCISES—SET A

LO2   **E2-1A. Accounting Equation** Determine the missing amount in each of the following cases:

	Assets	**Liabilities**	**Stockholders' Equity**
a.	$420,000	$175,000	?
b.	?	$ 31,000	$42,000
c.	$121,000	?	$90,000

LO2   **E2-2A. Transaction Analysis** Following the example shown in (a) below, indicate the accounting effects of the listed transactions on the assets, liabilities, and stockholders' equity of Martin & Company, a corporation:

   a.   Purchased, for cash, a desktop computer for use in the office.
          ANSWER: Increase assets (Office Equipment)
                      Decrease assets (Cash)
   b.   Rendered services and billed the client.
   c.   Paid rent for the month.
   d.   Rendered services to a client for cash.
   e.   Received amount due from a client in Transaction (b).
   f.   Purchased an office desk on account.
   g.   Paid employees' salaries for the month.
   h.   Paid for desk purchased in Transaction (f).
   i.   The company paid a dividend.

E2-3A. **Analysis of Accounts** Calculate the unknown amount in each of the following five independent situations. The answer to situation *(a)* is given as an example.

LO2

	Account	Beginning Balance	Ending Balance	Other Information
a.	Cash	$ 7,000	$ 5,250	Total cash disbursed, $5,400.
b.	Accounts receivable	11,000	9,300	Services on account, $16,500.
c.	Notes payable.	17,500	23,000	Borrowed funds by issuing a note, $30,000.
d.	Accounts payable	2,500	1,720	Payments on account, $3,900.
e.	Stockholders' equity	29,000	46,000	Capital contribution, $7,000.

Unknown Amounts Required	
a. Total cash received.	$3,650
b. Total cash collected from credit customers.	_____
c. Notes payable repaid during the period	_____
d. Goods and services received from suppliers on account	_____
e. Net income, assuming that no dividends were paid	_____

E2-4A. **Transaction Analysis** The accounts below are from the general ledger of The Bast Company. For each letter given in the T-accounts, describe the type of business transaction(s) or event(s) that would most likely be reflected by entries on that side of the account. For example, the answer to (a) is amounts for services performed for clients on account.

LO2, 5

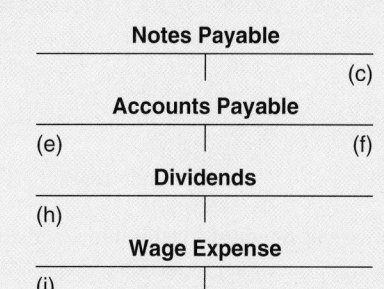

E2-5A. **Transaction Analysis** Match each of the following transactions of Lesch & Company with the appropriate letters, indicating the debits and credits to be made. The key for the letters follows the list of transactions. The correct answer for Transaction (1) is given as an illustration:

LO4

                                                                    Answer

1. Purchased supplies on account.   *a, d*
2. Paid interest on note payable.   _____
3. Paid cash dividend to stockholders.   _____
4. Returned some defective supplies and received a reduction in the amount owed.   _____
5. Made payment to settle note payable.   _____
6. Received an invoice for utilities used.   _____
7. Received payment in advance from client for work to be done next month.   _____
8. Received additional capital contribution from stockholders.   _____

Financial Effect of Transaction

a. Debit an asset	*g.* Debit dividends
b. Credit an asset	*h.* Credit dividends
c. Debit a liability	*i.* Debit a revenue
d. Credit a liability	*j.* Credit a revenue
e. Debit common stock	*k.* Debit an expense
f. Credit common stock	*l.* Credit an expense

LO5 **E2-6A.** **Transaction Entries** Unique Designs, a firm providing art services for advertisers, began business on June 1. The following accounts in its general ledger are needed to record the transactions for June: Cash; Accounts Receivable; Supplies; Office Equipment; Accounts Payable; Common Stock; Dividends; Service Fees Earned; Rent Expense; Utilities Expense; and Salaries Expense.

a. Using the accounting equation, record each of the transactions in columnar format.

b. Use journal entries to record the following transactions for June in the general journal.

June 1 Emily Holmes invested $8,000 cash to begin the business; she received common stock for her investment.

2 Paid rent for June, $375.

3 Purchased office equipment on account, $2,800.

6 Purchased art materials and other supplies costing $2,500; paid $900 down with the remainder due within 30 days.

11 Billed clients for services, $4,750.

17 Collected $2,600 from clients on account.

19 Paid $2,000 on account to office equipment company (see June 3 transaction).

25 Emily Holmes received a $750 dividend.

30 Paid utility bill for June, $525.

30 Paid salaries for June, $2,750.

LO5 **E2-7A.** **Source Documents** For each transaction in E2-6A, indicate the related source document or documents that provide evidence supporting the transaction.

LO4, 5 **E2-8A.** **Nature of Accounts, Debit and Credit Rules** For each of the accounts listed below, indicate whether the account is increased by a debit or a credit:

Accounts Payable	Dividends
Advertising Expense	Equipment
Cash	Land
Common Stock	Service Fees Earned

LO4, 5 **E2-9A.** **Nature of Accounts, Debit and Credit Rules** In columns, enter *debit* or *credit* to describe the journal entry necessary to increase and decrease the account shown on the left, and which side of the account represents its normal balance.

	Increase	Decrease	Normal Balance
Asset.	_____	_____	_____
Liability	_____	_____	_____
Common stock	_____	_____	_____
Dividends	_____	_____	_____
Revenue.	_____	_____	_____
Expense	_____	_____	_____

LO4, 5 **E2-10A.** **Nature of Accounts, Debit and Credit Rules** For each of the accounts listed below, indicate whether the account is increased by a debit or a credit:

Accounts Receivable	Notes Payable
Advertising Revenue	Retained Earnings
Building	Supplies
Common Stock	Utilities Expense

LO2, 4 **E2-11A.** **Transaction Analysis** Match each of the following transactions of L. Boyd & Company with the appropriate letters, indicating the debits and credits to be made. The key for the letters follows the list of transactions. The correct answer for Transaction 1 is given as an illustration:

		Answer
1.	Stockholders contributed cash to the business.	*a,f*
2.	Purchased equipment on account.	____
3.	Received and immediately paid advertising bill.	____
4.	Purchased supplies for cash.	____
5.	Borrowed money from a bank, giving a note payable.	____
6.	Billed customers for services rendered.	____
7.	Made a partial payment on account for equipment.	____
8.	Paid employee's salary.	____
9.	Collected amounts due from customers billed in Transaction 6.	____

Financial Effect of Transaction

a.	Debit an asset	*f.*	Credit common stock
b.	Credit an asset	*g.*	Debit a revenue
c.	Debit a liability	*h.*	Credit a revenue
d.	Credit a liability	*i.*	Debit an expense
e.	Debit common stock	*j.*	Credit an expense

E2-12A. Transaction Analysis and Trial Balance Make T-accounts for the following accounts that appear in the general ledger of Dave Jennings, an attorney: Cash; Accounts Receivable; Office Equipment; Legal Database Subscription; Accounts Payable; Common Stock; Dividends; Legal Fees Earned; Salaries Expense; Rent Expense; and Utilities Expense. Using the accounting equation, record each of the transactions in columnar format. Prepare journal entries and record the following October transactions in the T-accounts and key all entries with the number identifying the transaction. Determine the balance in each account and prepare a trial balance sheet as of October 31. **LO5, 6**

1 Jennings started his law practice by contributing $21,500 cash to the business on October 1, receiving shares of common stock in the company.
2 Purchased office equipment on account, $11,400.
3 Paid office rent for October, $1,100.
4 Paid $9,750 to access online legal database for two years.
5 Billed clients for services rendered, $14,000.
6 Made $6,000 payment on account for the equipment purchased on October 2.
7 Paid legal assistant's salary, $2,800.
8 Collected $7,500 from clients previously billed for services.
9 Received invoice for October utilities, $190; it will be paid in November.
10 Paid stockholders $1,500 as a cash dividend.

E2-13A. Transaction Analysis and Trial Balance Make T-accounts for the following accounts that appear in the general ledger of Miller Cat Hospital, owned by R. Miller, a veterinarian: Cash; Accounts Receivable; Supplies; Office Equipment; Accounts Payable; Common Stock; Dividends; Professional Fees Earned; Salaries Expense; and Rent Expense. Using the accounting equation, record each of the transactions in columnar format. Prepare journal entries and record the following December transactions in the T-accounts and key all entries with the number identifying the transaction. Finally, determine the balance in each account and prepare a trial balance as of December 31. **LO5, 6**

1 Miller opened a checking account on December 1 at United Bank in the name of Miller Cat Hospital and deposited $25,000 cash. Miller received common stock for his investment.
2 Paid rent for December, $1,500.
3 Purchased office equipment on account, $2,900.
4 Purchased supplies for cash, $1,900.
5 Billed clients for services rendered, $7,300.
6 Paid secretary's salary, $1,950.
7 Paid $1,500 on account for the equipment purchased on December 3.
8 Collected $5,800 from clients previously billed for services.
9 Paid stockholders $3,000 as a cash dividend.

LO3 **E2-14A. The Account** The following transactions occurred during December, the first month of operations for Farly Company. Prepare journal entries and create a T-account for accounts payable that includes the following five transactions.

1. Purchased $900 of inventory on account.
2. Purchased $200 of inventory on account.
3. Paid suppliers $550.
4. Purchased $500 of inventory on account.
5. Paid suppliers $300.

LO2 **E2-15A. Recording Transactions with the Accounting Equation** During the year, the Riley Company experienced the following accounting transactions:

1. Purchased equipment with cash in the amount of $165,000.
2. Purchased supplies on account in the amount of $15,000.
3. Collected $19,500 cash from customers.
4. Paid a cash dividend of $11,000.

Using the accounting equation, record each of the transactions in columnar format using the following template:

Assets				=	Liabilities	+	Stockholders' Equity
Cash +	Accounts Receivable	+ Supplies +	Equipment =		Accounts Payable	+	Retained Earnings

LO5 **E2-16A. Posting Transactions to T-accounts** Using the data from short exercise E2-15A, prepare journal entries and post your transaction analysis to the appropriate T-accounts.

EXERCISES—SET B

LO2 **E2-1B. Accounting Equation** Determine the missing amount in each of the following cases:

	Assets	Liabilities	Stockholders' Equity
a.	$425,000	$115,000	?
b.	?	$ 79,000	$19,000
c.	$152,000	?	$93,000

LO2 **E2-2B. Transaction Analysis** Following the example shown in (a) below, indicate the effects of the listed transactions on the assets, liabilities, and stockholders' equity of John Dallmus, certified public accountant, a corporation:

a. Purchased, for cash, a desktop computer for use in the office.
ANSWER: Increase assets (Office Equipment)
　　　　　　　Decrease assets (Cash)
b. Rendered accounting services and billed client.
c. Paid utilities for month.
d. Rendered tax services to client for cash.
e. Received amount due from client in Transaction (b).
f. Purchased a copying machine on account.
g. Paid employees' salaries for month.
h. Paid for copying machine purchased in Transaction (f).
i. The company paid a dividend.

LO2 **E2-3B. Analysis of Accounts** Compute the unknown amount required in each of the following five independent situations. The answer to situation (a) is given as an illustration:

	Account	Beginning Balance	Ending Balance	Other Information
a.	Cash	$ 8,100	$ 5,250	Total cash disbursed, $6,100.
b.	Accounts receivable	8,500	7,500	Services on account, $17,000.
c.	Notes payable.	17,000	14,000	Borrowed funds by issuing a note, $33,000.
d.	Accounts payable	5,280	1,750	Payments on account, $5,500.
e.	Stockholders' equity	29,500	41,000	Capital contribution, $6,100.

	Unknown Amounts Required	
a.	Total cash received.	$3,250
b.	Total cash collected from credit customers.	_____
c.	Notes payable repaid during the period	_____
d.	Goods and services received from suppliers on account	_____
e.	Net income, assuming that no dividends were paid	_____

E2-4B. Transaction Analysis The accounts below are from the general ledger of Andrew Miller & Company, an architectural firm. For each letter given in the T-accounts, describe the type of business transaction(s) or event(s) that would most likely be reflected by entries on that side of the account. For example, the answer to (a) is amounts for services performed for clients on account.

LO2, 5

E2-5B. Transaction Analysis Match each of the following transactions of Ardon Peralta & Company, a landscape design firm, with the appropriate letters, indicating the debits and credits to be made. The key for the letters follows the list of transactions. The correct answer for Transaction 1 is given as an illustration:

LO4

		Answer
1.	Purchased supplies on account.	*a, d*
2.	Paid interest on a bank loan.	_____
3.	The business paid the stockholders a dividend.	_____
4.	Returned some defective supplies and received a reduction in the amount owed.	_____
5.	Made payment to repay bank loan.	_____
6.	Received an invoice for supplies used.	_____
7.	Received payment in advance from client for work to be done next month.	_____
8.	Paid employee's salary.	_____
9.	Peralta contributed additional capital to the business.	_____

Financial Effect of Transaction

a.	Debit an asset		g.	Debit dividends
b.	Credit an asset		h.	Credit dividends
c.	Debit a liability		i.	Debit a revenue
d.	Credit a liability		j.	Credit a revenue
e.	Debit common stock		k.	Debit an expense
f.	Credit common stock		l.	Credit an expense

LO5 **E2-6B.** **Transaction Entries** Final Clean, a firm providing house-cleaning services, began business on April 1. The following accounts in its general ledger are needed to record the transactions for April: Cash; Accounts Receivable; Supplies; Prepaid Van Lease; Equipment; Accounts Payable; Notes Payable; Common Stock; Retained Earnings; Dividends; Cleaning Fees Earned; Wage Expense; Advertising Expense; and Fuel Expense.

a. Using the accounting equation, record each of the transactions in columnar format.
b. Use journal entries to record the following transactions for April in the general journal.

April 1 Randy Smith invested $14,000 cash to begin the business; he received common stock for his investment.
2 Paid six months' lease on a van, $2,850.
3 Borrowed $10,000 from a bank and signed a note payable agreeing to repay the $10,000 in one year plus 10 percent interest.
3 Purchased $5,500 of cleaning equipment; paid $2,000 down with the remainder due within 30 days.
4 Purchased cleaning supplies for $4,300 cash.
7 Paid $350 for newspaper advertisements to run during April.
21 Billed customers for services, $3,500.
23 Paid $1,500 on account to cleaning equipment firm (see April 3 transaction).
28 Collected $2,300 from customers on account.
29 Randy Smith received a $1,000 cash dividend.
30 Paid wages for April, $1,750.
30 Paid service station for gasoline used during April, $350.

LO5 **E2-7B.** **Source Documents** For each transaction in E2-6B indicate the related source document or documents that provide evidence supporting the transaction.

LO4, 5 **E2-8B.** **Nature of Accounts, Debit and Credit Rules** For each of the accounts listed below, indicate whether the account is increased by a debit or a credit:

Accounts Receivable	Common Stock
Supplies Expense	Dividends
Cash	Building
Equipment	Professional Fees Earned

LO4, 5 **E2-9B.** **Nature of Accounts, Debit and Credit Rules** In the three columns, enter *debit* or *credit* to describe the journal entry necessary to increase and decrease the account shown to the left, and indicate which side of the account represents its normal balance.

	Increase	Decrease	Normal Balance
Cash............................	_____	_____	
Accounts payable...................	_____	_____	_____
Common stock.....................	_____	_____	_____
Retained earnings	_____	_____	_____
Fee revenue......................	_____	_____	_____
Wage expense....................	_____	_____	_____

LO4, 5 **E2-10B.** **Nature of Accounts, Debit and Credit Rules** For each of the accounts listed below, indicate whether the account is increased by a debit or a credit:

Accounts Receivable	Notes Payable
Sales Revenue	Retained Earnings
Equipment	Inventory
Common Stock	Rent Expense

LO2, 4 **E2-11B.** **Transaction Analysis** Match each of the following transactions of R. Couche & Company, a printing company, with the appropriate letters, indicating the debits and credits to be made. The key for letters follows the list of transactions. The correct answer for Transaction (1) is given as an illustration:

		Answer
1.	Stockholders contributed cash to the business.	*a, f*
2.	Purchased inventory on account.	____
3.	Received and immediately paid a utility bill.	____
4.	Purchased supplies for cash.	____
5.	Borrowed money from a bank, giving a note payable.	____
6.	Billed customers for services rendered.	____
7.	Made a partial payment on account.	____
8.	Paid employee's salary.	____
9.	Collected amounts due from customers billed in Transaction 6.	____

Financial Effect of Transaction

a.	Debit an asset	*f.*	Credit common stock
b.	Credit an asset	*g.*	Debit a revenue
c.	Debit a liability	*h.*	Credit a revenue
d.	Credit a liability	*i.*	Debit an expense
e.	Debit common stock	*j.*	Credit an expense

E2-12B. Transaction Analysis and the Trial Balance Make T-accounts for the following accounts that appear in the general ledger of Matt Langley, an attorney: Cash; Accounts Receivable; Office Equipment; Legal Database Subscription; Accounts Payable; Common Stock; Dividends; Legal Fees Earned; Salaries Expense; Rent Expense; and Utilities Expense. Using the accounting equation, record each of the transactions in columnar format. Prepare journal entries and record the following October transactions in the T-accounts and key all entries with the number identifying the transaction. Determine the balance in each account and prepare a trial balance as of October 31.   **LO5, 6**

1. Langley started his law practice by contributing $18,000 cash to the business on October 1; he received common stock for his investment.
2. Purchased office equipment on account, $14,000.
3. Paid office rent for October, $700.
4. Paid $12,500 to access online legal database for two years.
5. Billed clients for services rendered, $11,300.
6. Made $6,000 payment on account for the equipment purchased on October 2.
7. Paid legal assistant's salary, $3,100.
8. Collected $9,400 from clients previously billed for services.
9. Received invoice for October utilities, $250; it will be paid in November.
10. The firm paid stockholders $1,500 cash as a dividend.

E2-13B. Transaction Analysis and Trial Balance Make T-accounts for the following accounts that appear in the general ledger of The Canine Hospital, owned by Kali Wells, a veterinarian: Cash; Accounts Receivable; Supplies; Office Equipment; Accounts Payable; Common Stock; Dividends; Professional Fees Earned; Salaries Expense; and Rent Expense. Using the accounting equation, record each of the transactions in columnar format. Prepare journal entries and record the following December transactions in the T-accounts and key all entries with the number identifying the transaction. Finally, determine the balance in each account and prepare a trial balance as of December 31.   **LO5, 6**

1. Wells opened a checking account on December 1 at Biltmore Bank in the name of The Canine Hospital and deposited $31,000 cash; Wells received common stock for her investment.
2. Paid rent for December, $2,750.
3. Purchased office equipment on account, $2,900.
4. Purchased supplies for cash, $1,800.
5. Billed clients for services rendered, $8,300.
6. Paid secretary's salary, $1,950.
7. Paid $1,500 on account for the equipment purchased on December 3.
8. Collected $4,900 from clients previously billed for services.
9. The firm paid stockholders $1,500 cash as a dividend.

E2-14B. The Account The following transactions occurred during January, the first month of operations for Red Corporation. Prepare journal entries and create a T-account for inventory that includes the   **LO3**

following five transactions. (*Hint:* When inventory is sold, it should be expensed to a Cost of Goods Sold expense account.)

1. Purchased $1,100 of inventory on account.
2. Purchased $1,800 of inventory on account.
3. Sold inventory with an original cost of $450.
4. Purchased $1,100 of inventory on account.
5. Sold inventory with an original cost of $1,750.

LO2   **E2-15B. Recording Transactions with the Accounting Equation** During the year, the Fletcher Company experienced the following accounting transactions:

1. Purchased equipment with cash in the amount of $130,000.
2. Purchased supplies on account in the amount of $16,500.
3. Collected $37,000 cash from customers.
4. Paid a cash dividend of $17,000.

Using the accounting equation, record each of the transactions in columnar format using the following template:

Assets				=	Liabilities	+	Stockholders' Equity
Cash +	Accounts Receivable	+ Supplies +	Equipment =		Accounts Payable	+	Retained Earnings

LO5   **E2-16B. Posting Transactions to T-accounts** Using the data from E2-15B, (a) prepare journal entries and (b) post your transactions to the appropriate T-accounts.

PROBLEMS—SET A

LO2   **P2-1A. Transaction Analysis** The accounting equation of L. Lee & Company as of the beginning of the accounting period is given below, followed by seven transactions whose effects on the accounting equation are shown. Describe each transaction that occurred. Of the transactions affecting Retained Earnings, transaction (e) had no effect on net income for the period.

	Cash	+	Accounts Receivable	+ Supplies	=	Accounts Payable	+	Notes Payable	+	Common Stock	+	Retained Earnings
Balance	$4,100	+	$9,000	+ $700	=	$800	+	$2,500	+	$2,000	+	$8,500
(a)	+8,000		−8,000									
(b)	−400			+400								
(c)			+7,000									+7,000
(d)	−750					−750						
(e)	−4,900											−4,900
(f)	−300			+300								
(g)	+2,200							+2,200				

LO2   **P2-2A. Transaction Analysis** An analysis of the transactions of Pruitt Detective Agency for the month of May appears below. Line 1 summarizes the company's accounting equation data as of May 1; lines 2–10 represent the transactions for May:

	Cash	+	Accounts Receivable	+	Supplies	+	Equipment	=	Accounts Payable	+	Notes Payable	+	Common Stock	+	Retained Earnings
(1)	$2,400	+	$7,600	+	$1,500	+	$8,000	=	$300	+	$6,000	+	$10,000	+	$3,200
(2)	+2,000										+2,000				
(3)	+6,100		−6,100												
(4)					+980				+980						
(5)			+5,200												+5,200
(6)	−300								−300						
(7)	+1,500														+1,500
(8)	−800														−800
(9)	−900						+900								
(10)	−2,500										−2,500				

Required

a. Show that assets equal liabilities plus stockholders' equity as of May 1.

b. Describe the apparent transaction indicated by each line. (For example, line 2: Borrowed $2,000, giving a note payable.) If any line could reasonably represent more than one type of transaction, describe each type. Transaction (8) does not affect net income.

c. Show that assets equal liabilities plus stockholders' equity as of May 31.

P2-3A. Transaction Analysis Grand Appraisal Service provides commercial and industrial appraisals and feasibility studies. On January 1, the assets and liabilities of the business were the following: Cash, $11,700; Accounts Receivable, $15,800; Accounts Payable, $600; and Notes Payable, $3,500. Common Stock had a balance of $18,400. Assume that Retained Earnings as of January 1 were $5,000. The following transactions occurred during the month of January:

LO2

1 Paid rent for January, $950.
2 Received $8,800 payment on customers' accounts.
3 Paid $750 on accounts payable.
4 Received $2,500 for services performed for cash customers.
5 Borrowed $5,000 from a bank and signed a note payable for that amount.
6 Billed the city $6,200 for a feasibility study performed; billed various other credit customers, $1,900.
7 Paid the salary of an assistant, $3,500.
8 Received invoice for January utilities, $410.
9 Paid $6,000 cash for employee salaries.
10 Purchased a van (on January 31) for business use, $7,200.
11 Paid $150 to bank as January interest on the outstanding notes payable.

Required

a. Set up an accounting equation in columnar form with the following individual assets, liabilities, and stockholders' equity accounts: Cash, Accounts Receivable, Van, Accounts Payable, Notes Payable, Common Stock, and Retained Earnings. Enter the January 1 balances below each item. (*Note:* The beginning Van account balance is $0.)

b. Show the impact (increase or decrease) of transactions 1–11 on the beginning balances, and total the columns to show that assets equal liabilities plus stockholders' equity as of January 31.

P2-4A. Transaction Analysis On June 1, a group of bush pilots in Thunder Bay, Ontario, Canada, formed the Thunder Fly-In Service, Inc., by selling $80,000 of common stock for cash. The group then leased several amphibious aircraft and docking facilities, equipping them to transport campers and hunters to outpost camps owned by various resorts. The following transactions occurred during June:

LO2

1 Sold common stock for cash, $80,000.
2 Paid June rent for aircraft, dockage, and dockside office, $4,250.
3 Received invoice for the cost of a reception the firm gave to entertain resort owners, $1,600.
4 Paid for June advertising in various sports magazines, $800.
5 Paid insurance premium for June, $1,800.
6 Rendered fly-in services for various groups for cash, $26,500.

7   Billed the Canadian Ministry of Natural Resources for transporting mapping personnel, $1,900, and billed various firms for fly-in services, $14,000.

8   Paid $1,500 on accounts payable.

9   Received $13,200 on account from clients.

10   Paid June wages, $21,000.

11   Received invoice for the cost of fuel used during June, $3,500.

12   Paid a cash dividend, $4,000.

Required

a.   Set up an accounting equation in columnar form with the following column headings: Cash, Accounts Receivable, Accounts Payable, Common Stock, and Retained Earnings.

b.   Show how the June transactions affect the items in the accounting equation, and total all columns to show that assets equal liabilities plus stockholders' equity as of June 30. (*Note:* Revenues, expenses, and dividends affect Retained Earnings.)

LO2   **P2-5A.   Accounting Equation**   Determine the following:

a.   The stockholders' equity of a company that has assets of $625,000 and liabilities of $310,000.

b.   The retained earnings of a company that has assets of $725,000, liabilities of $325,000, and common stock of $225,000.

c.   The assets of a corporation that has liabilities of $375,000, common stock of $425,000, and retained earnings of $185,000.

LO2   **P2-6A.   Transaction Analysis**   Following the example shown in (a) below, indicate the effects of the listed transactions on the assets, liabilities, and stockholders' equity of Martin Andrews & Company.

a.   Rendered legal services to clients for cash.
ANSWER: Increase assets (Cash)
                      Increase stockholders' equity (increase Revenue)

b.   Purchased office supplies on account.

c.   Andrews invested cash into the firm and received stock for his investment.

d.   Paid amount due on account for office supplies purchased in (b).

e.   Borrowed cash from a bank and signed a six-month note payable.

f.   Rendered services and billed clients.

g.   Purchased, for cash, a desk lamp for the office.

h.   Paid interest on a note payable to the bank.

i.   Received invoice for the current month's utilities.

LO2   **P2-7A.   Transaction Analysis**   On October 1, Alice Rodstein started a consulting firm. The asset, liability, and stockholders' equity account balances **after** each of her first six transactions are shown below. Describe each of these six transactions:

			Amounts after Transaction					
	Cash	+ Accounts Receivable +	Supplies +	Equipment =	Notes Payable +	Common Stock +	Retained Earnings
(a)	$7,000 +	$ 0 +	$ 0 +	$ 0 =	$ 0 +	$7,000 +	$ 0
(b)	5,000 +	0 +	2,000 +	0 =	0 +	7,000 +	0
(c)	8,500 +	0 +	2,000 +	0 =	3,500 +	7,000 +	0
(d)	3,000 +	0 +	2,000 +	5,500 =	3,500 +	7,000 +	0
(e)	3,000 +	1,000 +	2,000 +	5,500 =	3,500 +	7,000 +	1,000
(f)	3,400 +	600 +	2,000 +	5,500 =	3,500 +	7,000 +	1,000

LO2   **P2-8A.   Determination of Omitted Financial Statement Data**   For the four unrelated situations, A-D, calculate the unknown amounts indicated by the letters appearing in each column:

	A	B	C	D
Beginning				
Assets..................................	$28,000	$12,000	$28,000	$ (d)
Liabilities..............................	18,600	6,000	19,000	6,500
Ending				
Assets..................................	31,000	26,000	36,000	40,000
Liabilities..............................	17,300	(b)	15,000	19,000
During the Year				
Common stock	2,000	4,500	(c)	2,500
Sales revenues.........................	(a)	28,000	18,000	24,000
Dividends	5,000	1,750	2,000	6,500
Expenses	9,000	21,000	11,000	17,000

P2-9A. Transaction Analysis Appearing below is an analysis of the June transactions for Island Consulting   **LO2**
Services. Line 1 summarizes the company's accounting equation data as of June 1; lines 2-10 are the
transactions for the month of June:

	Cash	+	Accounts Receivable	+	Supplies	+	Equipment	=	Accounts Payable	+	Notes Payable	+	Common Stock	+	Retained Earnings
(1)	$3,500	+	$6,000	+	$820	+	$9,000	=	$600	+	$3,000	+	$10,920	+	$4,800
(2)			+670						+670						
(3)							3,750				3,750				
(4)	+4,200		−4,200												
(5)			+7,800												+7,800
(6)	−600								−600						
(7)	−200				+200										
(8)	−5,500														−5,500
(9)	+2,000										+2,000				
(10)							+750						+750		

Required

a. Show that assets equal liabilities plus stockholders' equity as of June 1.

b. Describe the transaction indicated by each line. For example, line 2: Purchased supplies on account, $670. If any line could reasonably represent more than one type of transaction, describe
each type.

c. Show that assets equal liabilities plus stockholders' equity as of June 30.

P2-10A. Transaction Analysis Grace Stewart began the Stewart Answering Service in December. The firm   **LO2**
provides services for professional people and is currently operating with leased equipment. On January 1, the assets and liabilities of the business were: Cash, $6,400; Accounts Receivable, $6,900; Accounts Payable, $1,600; and Notes Payable, $1,500. Assume that Retained Earnings as of January 1
were zero. The balance of Common Stock was $10,200. The following transactions occurred during
the month of January:

1   Paid rent on office and equipment for January, $1,800.
2   Collected $6,000 on account from clients.
3   Borrowed $3,000 from a bank and signed a note payable for that amount.
4   Billed clients for work performed on account, $12,500.
5   Paid $1,400 on accounts payable.
6   Received invoice for January advertising, $800.
7   Paid January salaries, $3,200.
8   Paid January utilities, $430.
9   Paid stockholders a dividend of $3,600 cash.
10 Purchased a printer (on January 31) for business use, $1,400.
11 Paid $30 to the bank as January interest on the outstanding notes payable.

Required

a.   Set up an accounting equation in columnar form with the following individual assets, liabilities, and stockholders' equity accounts: Cash, Accounts Receivable, Equipment, Accounts Payable, Notes Payable, Common Stock, and Retained Earnings. Enter the January 1 balances below each item. (*Note:* The beginning Equipment account balance is $0.)

b.   Show the impact (increase or decrease) of the January transactions on the beginning balances, and total all columns to show that assets equal liabilities plus stockholders' equity as of January 31.

LO2   **P2-11A.** **Transaction Analysis** On December 1, Fred Allen started Job Services Inc., providing career and vocational counseling services. The following transactions took place during the month of December:

1   Allen invested $7,000 in the business, receiving common shares.
2   Paid rent for December on furnished office space, $1,750.
3   Received invoice for December advertising, $660.
4   Borrowed $16,000 from a bank and signed a note payable for that amount.
5   Received $1,200 for counseling services rendered for cash.
6   Billed certain governmental agencies and other clients for counseling services, $7,150.
7   Paid secretary's salary, $2,200.
8   Paid December utilities, $910.
9   Paid stockholders a dividend of $900 cash.
10 Purchased land for cash to use as a site for a new facility, $13,000.
11 Paid $950 to the bank as December interest on a note payable.

Required

a.   Set up an accounting equation in columnar form with the following column headings: Cash, Accounts Receivable, Land, Accounts Payable, Notes Payable, Common Stock, and Retained Earnings.

b.   Show how the December transactions affect the items in the accounting equation, and total all columns to show that assets equal liabilities plus stockholders' equity as of December 31.

LO4, 5, 6   **P2-12A.** **Transaction Analysis and the Effect of Errors on the Trial Balance** The following T-accounts contain numbered entries for the May transactions of Carol Miller, a market analyst, who opened her business on May 1:

	Cash					Common Stock		
(1)	13,000	4,800	(2)				13,000	(1)
(9)	3,150	810	(4)					
		1,950	(6)					
		600	(8)					

	Accounts Receivable					Dividends		
(5)	6,400	3,150	(9)		(8)	600		

	Office Supplies					Professional Fees Earned		
(3)	3,100						6,400	(5)

	Office Equipment					Rent Expense		
(2)	4,800				(4)	810		

	Accounts Payable					Utilities Expense		
(6)	1,950	3,100	(3)		(7)	355		
		355	(7)					

Required

a.   Give a description of each of the nine numbered transactions entered in the above T-accounts. Example: (1) Carol Miller invested $13,000 of her personal funds in her business.

b.   The following trial balance, prepared from Miller's data as of May 31, contains several errors. Itemize the errors and indicate the correct totals for the trial balance.

CAROL MILLER & COMPANY Unadjusted Trial Balance May 31		
	Debit	Credit
Cash	$ 9,790	
Accounts receivable	4,250	
Office supplies	3,100	
Office equipment	4,800	
Accounts payable		$ 1,505
Common stock		13,000
Dividends		600
Professional fees earned		6,400
Rent expense	810	
Totals	$22,750	$21,505

P2-13A. Transaction Analysis and Trial Balance Pam Black owns Artsy Graphics, a firm providing designs for advertisers and market analysts. On July 1, the business's general ledger showed the following normal account balances:

LO4, 5, 6

Cash	$ 6,800	Accounts payable	$ 2,100
Accounts receivable	10,700	Notes payable	4,200
		Common stock	2,000
		Retained earnings	9,200
Total Assets	$17,500	Total Liabilities and Stockholders' Equity	$17,500

The following transactions occurred during the month of July:

1 Paid July rent, $510.
2 Collected $7,100 on account from customers.
3 Paid $1,800 installment due on the $3,300 noninterest-bearing note payable.
4 Billed customers for design services rendered on account, $18,100.
5 Rendered design services and collected from cash customers, $1,200.
6 Paid $1,400 to creditors on account.
7 Collected $12,750 on account from customers.
8 Paid a delivery service for delivery of graphics to commercial firms, $650.
9 Paid July salaries, $5,300.
10 Received invoice for July advertising expense, to be paid in August, $600.
11 Paid utilities for July, $250.
12 Paid stockholders a dividend of $2,000 cash.
13 Received invoice for supplies used in July, to be paid in August, $2,260.
14 Purchased computer for $7,000 cash to be used in the business starting next month.

Required

a. Set up accounts for the general ledger accounts with July 1 balances and enter the beginning balances. Also provide the following accounts: Equipment; Service Fees Earned; Rent Expense; Salaries Expense; Delivery Expense; Advertising Expense; Utilities Expense; Supplies Expense; and Dividends. Prepare journal entries and record the listed transactions in the appropriate T-accounts.
b. Prepare a trial balance as of July 31.

P2-14A. Transaction Analysis and Trial Balance Fly-In Service, Inc., operates leased amphibious aircraft and docking facilities, equipping the firm to transport campers and hunters from Vancouver, Canada, to outpost camps owned by various resorts. On August 1, the firm's trial balance was as follows:

LO4, 5, 6

FLY-IN SERVICE, INC. Unadjusted Trial Balance August 1		
	Debit	Credit
Cash	$48,600	
Accounts receivable	24,000	
Accounts payable		$ 2,500
Notes payable		3,000
Common stock		50,000
Retained earnings		17,100
Totals	$72,600	$72,600

During the month of August, the following transactions occurred:

1   Paid August rental cost for aircraft, dockage, and dockside office, $5,000.
2   Paid insurance premium for August, $1,200.
3   Paid for August advertising in various sports magazines, $1,000.
4   Rendered fly-in services for various groups for cash, $15,500.
5   Billed the Canadian Ministry of Natural Resources for services in transporting mapping personnel, $4,400.
6   Received $17,400 on account from clients.
7   Paid $2,100 on accounts payable.
8   Billed various clients for services, $16,400.
9   Paid interest on a note payable for August, $25.
10 Paid August wages, $12,800.
11 Received invoice for the cost of fuel used during August, $3,800.
12 Paid a cash dividend, $5,000.

Required

a.   Set up accounts for each item in the August 1 trial balance and enter the beginning balances. Also provide accounts for the following items: Service Fees Earned, Wage Expense, Advertising Expense, Rent Expense, Fuel Expense, Insurance Expense, and Interest Expense. Prepare journal entries and record the transactions for August in the appropriate T-accounts, using the references given.

b.   Prepare a trial balance as of August 31.

LO4, 5, 6

P2-15A. **Transaction Analysis and Trial Balance** Mary Baker opened a tax practice on June 1. The following accounts will be needed to record her transactions for June: Cash; Accounts Receivable; Office Supplies; Tax Library; Office Furniture and Fixtures; Accounts Payable; Notes Payable; Common Stock; Dividends; Professional Fees Earned; Rent Expense; Salaries Expense; Advertising Expense; Utilities Expense; and Interest Expense. The following transactions occurred during the month of June:

1   Baker opened a business checking account at a local bank, investing $13,500 in her practice in exchange for common stock.
2   Purchased office furniture and fixtures for $9,800, paid $2,800 cash, and gave a note payable for the balance.
3   Purchased books and software for a tax library on account, $4,500.
4   Purchased office supplies for cash, $950.
5   Paid rent for June, $750.
6   Returned $300 of books with defective bindings. The return reduced the amount owed to the supplier.
7   Billed clients for professional services rendered, $9,200.
8   Paid $1,700 on account for the library items purchased on June 3.
9   Collected $5,900 on account from clients billed on June 7.
10 Paid June salaries, $4,900.
11 Received invoice for June advertising, to be paid in July, $300.
12 Paid stockholders $800 cash as a dividend.
13 Paid utilities for June, $160.
14 Paid interest for June on note payable, $310.

Required

a. Prepare journal entries and record the above transactions in T-accounts, and key entries with the number of the transactions.

b. Prepare a trial balance as of June 30.

P2-16A. Transaction Analysis and the Effect of Errors on the Trial Balance   **LO4, 5, 6**

The following T-accounts contain numbered entries for the May transactions of Gomez Corporation, an architectural firm, which opened its offices on May 1:

Cash					Accounts Payable			
(1)	25,000	1,400	(4)	(5)	400	1,530	(3)
(10)	5,200	5,950	(7)	(8)	750	290	(9)
		750	(8)				

Accounts Receivable					Common Stock		
(6)	8,750	5,200	(10)			25,000	(1)

Supplies					Professional Fees Earned		
(3)	1,530	400	(5)			8,750	(6)

Office Equipment			Rent Expense	
(2)	5,000		(4)	1,400

Notes Payable				Utilities Expense	
		5,000	(2)	(9)	290

Salaries Expense	
(7)	5,950

Required

a. Give a description of each of the 10 numbered transactions entered in the above accounts. Example: (1) Gomez Corporation issued common stock for cash, $25,000.

b. The following trial balance, prepared for Gomez Corporation as of May 31, contains several errors. Itemize the errors, and indicate the correct totals for the trial balance.

GOMEZ CORPORATION		
Unadjusted Trial Balance		
May 31		
	Debit	Credit
Cash	$21,200	
Accounts receivable	3,550	
Supplies	1,130	
Office equipment		$ 5,000
Accounts payable		670
Notes payable		50,000
Common stock		2,500
Professional fees earned		8,570
Rent expense	1,400	
Utilities expense	290	
Salaries expense	5,950	
Totals	$33,520	$66,740

P2-17A. Transaction Analysis and Trial Balance James Green, electrical contractor, began business on   **LO5, 6**
May 1. The following transactions occurred during the month of May:

1 Green invested $15,500 of his personal funds in the business in exchange for common stock.

2 Purchased equipment on account, $4,200.

3 Returned $1,500 of equipment that was not satisfactory. The return reduced the amount owed to the supplier.

4 Purchased supplies on account, $860.

5 Purchased a truck for $9,500. Green paid $6,000 cash and gave a note payable for the balance.

6 Paid rent for May, $875.

7   Paid fuel cost for truck, $90.
8   Billed customers for services rendered, $13,700.
9   Paid $2,500 on account for equipment purchased on May 2.
10 Paid utilities for May, $210.
11 Received invoice for May advertising, to be paid in June, $350.
12 Paid employees' wages, $3,350.
13 Collected $8,600 on accounts receivable.
14 Paid stockholders $2,000 cash as a dividend.
15 Paid interest for May on an outstanding note payable, $30.

Required

a. Prepare journal entries and record the above transactions in T-accounts, and key entries with the numbers of the transactions. The following accounts will be needed to record the transactions for May: Cash; Accounts Receivable; Supplies; Equipment; Truck; Accounts Payable; Notes Payable; Common Stock; Dividends; Service Revenue; Rent Expense; Wages Expense; Utilities Expense; Truck Expense; Advertising Expense; and Interest Expense.
b. Prepare a trial balance as of May 31.

PROBLEMS—SET B

LO2   P2-1B.   Transaction Analysis The accounting equation of Matthew Thomas, attorney, at the beginning of an accounting period is given below, followed by seven transactions whose effects on the accounting equation are shown. Describe each transaction that occurred. Of the transactions affecting retained earnings, transaction (e) had no effect on net income for the period.

	Cash	+	Accounts Receivable	+	Supplies	=	Accounts Payable	+	Notes Payable	+	Common Stock	+	Retained Earnings
Balance	$4,100	+	$9,000	+	$900	=	$1,000	+	$2,500	+	$7,500	+	$3,000
(a)	+7,500		−7,500										
(b)					+400		+400						
(c)			+8,000										+8,000
(d)	−800						−800						
(e)	−4,900												−4,900
(f)	−300				+300								
(g)	+3,200								+3,200				

LO2   P2-2B.   Transaction Analysis An analysis of the transactions of Pickett Shipping Services for the month of May appears below. Line 1 summarizes Pickett's accounting equation data as of May 1; lines 2–10 represent the transactions for the month of May:

	Cash	+	Accounts Receivable	+	Supplies	+	Equipment	=	Accounts Payable	+	Notes Payable	+	Common Stock	+	Retained Earnings
(1)	$3,500	+	$6,700	+	$2,100	+	$9,000	=	$ 700	+	$6,000	+	$4,400	+	$10,200
(2)	+3,500										+3,500				
(3)	+5,200		−5,200												
(4)					+1,500				+1,500						
(5)			+4,600												+4,600
(6)	−300								−300						
(7)	+1,900														+1,900
(8)	−800														−800
(9)	−750						+750								
(10)	−2,500										−2,500				

Required

a. Show that assets equal liabilities plus stockholders' equity as of May 1.

b. Describe the apparent transaction indicated by each line. (For example, line 2: Borrowed $3,500, giving a note payable.) If any line could reasonably represent more than one type of transaction, describe each type. Transaction (8) does not affect net income.

c. Show that assets equal liabilities plus stockholders' equity as of May 31.

P2-3B. Transaction Analysis Wesson Appraisal Service provides commercial and industrial appraisals and feasibility studies. On January 1, the assets and liabilities of the business were the following: Cash, $8,700; Accounts Receivable, $18,800; Accounts Payable, $5,200; and Notes Payable, $6,500. Assume that Retained Earnings as of January 1 were $1,000. The balance of Common Stock was $14,800. The following transactions occurred during the month of January:

1 Paid rent for January, $1,500.
2 Received $9,800 on customers' accounts.
3 Paid $900 on accounts payable.
4 Received $900 for services performed for cash customers.
5 Borrowed $8,000 from a bank and signed a note payable for that amount.
6 Billed the city $7,800 for a feasibility study performed; billed various other credit customers, $3,500.
7 Paid salary of assistant, $4,500.
8 Received invoice for January utilities, $610.
9 Paid $6,000 cash for employees salaries.
10 Purchased a van (on January 31) for business use, $9,800 cash.
11 Paid $400 to the bank as January interest on an outstanding note payable.

Required

a. Set up an accounting equation in columnar form with the following individual assets, liabilities, and stockholders' equity accounts: Cash, Accounts Receivable, Van, Accounts Payable, Notes Payable, Common Stock, and Retained Earnings. Enter January 1 balances below each item. (*Note:* The beginning Van amount is $0.)

b. Show the impact (increase or decrease) of transactions 1–11 on the beginning balances, and total the columns to show that assets equal liabilities plus stockholders' equity as of January 31.

P2-4B. Transaction Analysis On June 1, a group of bush pilots in British Columbia, Canada, formed the Adventure Airlines, Inc., by selling $51,000 of common stock for cash. The group then leased several aircraft and docking facilities, equipping them to transport campers and hunters to outpost camps owned by various resorts. The following transactions occurred during June:

1 Sold common stock for cash, $51,000.
2 Paid June rent for aircraft, dockage, and dockside office, $5,500.
3 Received invoice for the cost of a reception the firm gave to entertain resort owners, $3,100.
4 Paid for June advertising in various sports magazines, $1,900.
5 Paid insurance premium for June, $2,750.
6 Rendered services for various groups for cash, $25,000.
7 Billed the Canadian Ministry of Natural Resources for transporting mapping personnel, $4,900, and billed various firms for services, $16,750.
8 Paid $1,200 on accounts payable.
9 Received $14,200 on account from clients.
10 Paid June wages, $16,000.
11 Received an invoice for the cost of fuel used during June, $3,500.
12 Paid a cash dividend, $6,000.

Required

a. Set up an accounting equation in columnar form with the following column headings: Cash, Accounts Receivable, Accounts Payable, Common Stock, and Retained Earnings.

b. Show how the June transactions affect the items in the accounting equation, and total all columns to show that assets equal liabilities plus stockholders' equity as of June 30.

LO2 **P2-5B.** **Accounting Equation** Determine the following:
 a. The stockholders' equity of a company that has assets of $480,000 and liabilities of $360,000.
 b. The retained earnings of a company that has assets of $625,000, liabilities of $225,000, and common stock of $165,000.
 c. The assets of a corporation that has liabilities of $500,000, common stock of $350,000, and retained earnings of $255,000.

LO2 **P2-6B.** **Transaction Analysis** Following the example shown in (a) below, indicate the effects of the listed transactions on the assets, liabilities, and stockholders' equity of McKay & Company:
 a. Rendered services to clients for cash.
   ANSWER: Increase assets (Cash)
       Increase stockholders' equity (increase Revenue)
 b. Invested cash in the firm in exchange for common stock.
 c. Purchased a document scanner on account.
 d. Borrowed cash from a bank and signed a nine-month note.
 e. Paid amount due on account for scanner purchased in (c).
 f. Rendered services and billed clients.
 g. Paid stockholders a cash dividend.
 h. Paid interest on note payable to bank.
 i. Received payment from clients billed in (f).

LO2 **P2-7B.** **Transaction Analysis** On October 1, Deloitte & Coopers Price started a consulting firm. The asset, liability, and stockholders' equity account balances **after** each of the firm's first six transactions are shown below. Describe each of these six transactions.

	Cash	+	Accounts Receivable	+	Supplies	+	Equipment	=	Notes Payable	+	Common Stock	+	Retained Earnings
(a)	$7,000	+	$ 0	+	$ 0	+	$ 0	=	$ 0	+	$7,000	+	$ 0
(b)	4,500	+	0	+	2,500	+	0	=	0	+	7,000	+	0
(c)	7,500	+	0	+	2,500	+	0	=	3,000	+	7,000	+	0
(d)	1,400	+	0	+	2,500	+	6,100	=	3,000	+	7,000	+	0
(e)	1,400	+	1,750	+	2,500	+	6,100	=	3,000	+	7,000	+	1,750
(f)	2,950	+	200	+	2,500	+	6,100	=	3,000	+	7,000	+	1,750

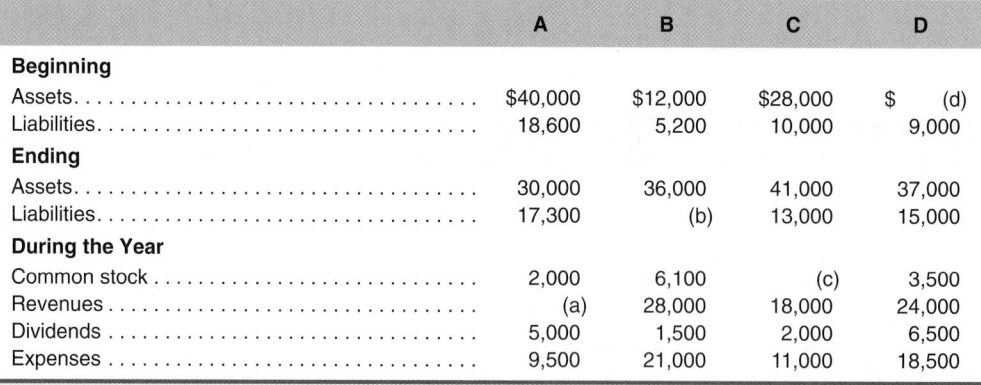

LO2 **P2-8B.** **Determination of Omitted Financial Statement Data** For the four unrelated situations, A–D, below, calculate the unknown amounts indicated by the letters appearing in each column:

	A	B	C	D
Beginning				
Assets.....................................	$40,000	$12,000	$28,000	$ (d)
Liabilities..................................	18,600	5,200	10,000	9,000
Ending				
Assets.....................................	30,000	36,000	41,000	37,000
Liabilities..................................	17,300	(b)	13,000	15,000
During the Year				
Common stock............................	2,000	6,100	(c)	3,500
Revenues..................................	(a)	28,000	18,000	24,000
Dividends..................................	5,000	1,500	2,000	6,500
Expenses..................................	9,500	21,000	11,000	18,500

LO2 **P2-9B.** **Transaction Analysis** Appearing below is an analysis of the June transactions for Fisk Communications Company. Line 1 summarizes the company's accounting equation data as of June 1; lines 2-10 are the transactions for June:

	Cash	+	Accounts Receivable	+	Supplies	+	Equipment	=	Accounts Payable	+	Notes Payable	+	Common Stock	+	Retained Earnings
(1)	$3,500	+	$5,200	+	$1,100	+	$12,000	=	$600	+	$3,000	+	$11,200	+	$7,000
(2)					+670				+670						
(3)							+6,000				+6,000				
(4)	+6,000		−6,000												
(5)			+7,800												+7,800
(6)	−600								−600						
(7)	−200				+200										
(8)	−4,600														−4,600
(9)	+3,000										+3,000				
(10)	−500						+500								

Required

a. Show that assets equal liabilities plus stockholders' equity as of June 1.

b. Describe the apparent transaction indicated by each line. For example, line 2: Purchased supplies on account, $670. If any line could reasonably represent more than one type of transaction, describe each type.

c. Show that assets equal liabilities plus stockholders' equity as of June 30.

P2-10B. Transaction Analysis Torrey Peoples began the Peoples Word Processing Service in December. The firm provides word-processing services for businesses and is currently operating with leased equipment. On January 1, the assets and liabilities of the business were: Cash, $6,400; Accounts Receivable, $7,500; Accounts Payable, $900; and Notes Payable, $3,500. Assume that Retained Earnings as of January 1, were zero. Common Stock balance was $9,500. The following transactions occurred during the month of January:

1 Paid rent on office and equipment for January, $1,100.
2 Collected $8,200 on account from clients.
3 Borrowed $5,000 from a bank and signed a note payable for that amount.
4 Billed clients for work performed on account, $9,150.
5 Paid $600 on accounts payable.
6 Received invoice for January advertising, $750.
7 Paid January salaries, $3,750.
8 Paid January utilities, $230.
9 Paid stockholders a dividend in the amount of $3,100.
10 Purchased a printer (on January 31) for business use, $1,750.
11 Paid $150 to bank as January interest on the outstanding notes payable.

Required

a. Set up an accounting equation in columnar form with the following individual assets, liabilities, and stockholders' equity accounts: Cash, Accounts Receivable, Equipment, Accounts Payable, Notes Payable, Common Stock, Retained Earnings. Enter the January 1 balances below each item. (*Note:* The beginning Equipment amount is $0.)

b. Show the impact (increase or decrease) of the January transactions on the beginning balances, and total all columns to show that assets equal liabilities plus stockholders' equity as of January 31.

P2-11B. Transaction Analysis On December 1, Molly Frick started Advancement Career Services, which provided career and vocational counseling services to individuals. The following transactions took place during the month of December:

1 Frick invested $10,000 in the business in exchange for common stock.
2 Paid rent for December on furnished office space, $1,250.
3 Received invoice for December advertising, $600.
4 Borrowed $27,000 from a bank and signed a note payable for that amount.
5 Received $4,200 for counseling services rendered for cash.
6 Billed certain governmental agencies and other clients for counseling services, $9,800.

7 Paid secretary's salary, $2,700.

8 Paid December utilities, $370.

9 Paid stockholders a dividend in the amount of $900.

10 Purchased land for cash to use as a site for the company's future offices, $28,000.

11 Paid $100 to the bank as December interest on the outstanding note payable.

Required

a. Set up an accounting equation in columnar form with the following column headings: Cash, Accounts Receivable, Land, Accounts Payable, Notes Payable, Common Stock, and Retained Earnings.

b. Show how the December transactions affect the items in the accounting equation, and total all columns to show that assets equal liabilities plus stockholders' equity as of December 31.

LO4, 5, 6 **P2-12B. Transaction Analysis and the Effect of Errors on the Trial Balance** The following T-accounts contain numbered entries for the May transactions of Valerie Vance who opened a consulting services business on May 1:

Cash					Common Stock		
(1)	20,000	4,800	(2)			20,000	(1)
(9)	3,700	810	(4)				
		1,950	(6)				
		600	(8)				

Accounts Receivable					Dividends		
(5)	6,700	3,700	(9)		(8)	600	

Office Supplies				Professional Fees Earned		
(3)	4,000				6,700	(5)

Office Equipment				Rent Expense		
(2)	4,800			(4)	810	

Accounts Payable					Utilities Expense		
(6)	1,950	4,000	(3)		(7)	510	
		510	(7)				

Required

a. Give a description of each of the nine numbered transactions entered in the above accounts. Example: (1) Valerie Vance invested $20,000 of her personal funds in the business in exchange for common stock.

b. The following trial balance, prepared for Rankine's firm as of May 31, contains several errors. Itemize the errors and indicate the correct totals for the trial balance.

VANCE CONSULTING SERVICES Unadjusted Trial Balance May 31	Debit	Credit
Cash	$15,450	
Accounts receivable	4,000	
Office supplies	4,000	
Office equipment	4,800	
Accounts payable		$ 2,560
Common stock		20,000
Dividends		600
Professional fees earned		6,700
Rent expense	810	
Totals	$29,060	$29,860

P2-13B. **Transaction Analysis and Trial Balance** Ashley Conners owns La Jolla Art Company, a firm providing designs for advertisers, market analysts, and others. On July 1, the business's general ledger
showed the following normal account balances:

LO4, 5, 6

Cash......................	$14,500	Accounts payable.......................		$ 2,100
Accounts receivable...........	9,800	Notes payable........................		7,000
		Common stock		11,200
		Retained earnings		4,000
Total assets	$24,300	Total Liabilities and Stockholders' Equity.....		$24,300

The following transactions occurred during the month of July:

1   Paid July rent, $670.
2   Collected $8,100 on account from customers.
3   Paid $3,500 installment due on the $7,000 noninterest-bearing note payable to a relative.
4   Billed customers for design services rendered on account, $21,000.
5   Rendered design services and collected from cash customers, $1,400.
6   Paid $1,900 to creditors on account.
7   Collected $16,500 on account from customers.
8   Paid a delivery service for delivery of graphics to commercial firms, $400.
9   Paid July salaries, $4,600.
10   Received invoice for July advertising expense, to be paid in August, $620.
11   Paid utilities for July, $350.
12   The business paid a $2,000 cash dividend.
13   Received invoice for supplies used in July, to be paid in August, $1,575.
14   Purchased a computer for $4,300 cash to be used in the business starting next month.

Required
a.   Set up accounts for the general ledger accounts with July 1 balances and enter the beginning
balances. Also provide the following accounts: Equipment; Dividends; Service Fees Earned;
Rent Expense; Salaries Expense; Delivery Expense; Advertising Expense; Utilities Expense; and
Supplies Expense. Prepare journal entries and record the listed transactions in the appropriate
T-accounts.
b.   Prepare a trial balance as of July 31.

P2-14B. **Transaction Analysis and Trial Balance** Great Outdoors Airlines, Inc., operates leased amphibious aircraft and docking facilities, equipping the firm to transport campers and hunters from British
Columbia, Canada, to outpost camps owned by various resorts. On August 1, the firm's trial balance
was as follows:

LO4, 5, 6

GREAT OUTDOORS AIRLINES, INC. Unadjusted Trial Balance August 1		
	Debit	Credit
Cash..	$ 88,600	
Accounts receivable.......................................	23,200	
Accounts payable...		$ 1,700
Notes payable..		6,000
Common stock		83,000
Retained earnings		21,100
Totals	$111,800	$111,800

During August the following transactions occurred:

1   Paid August rental cost for aircraft, dockage, and dockside office, $8,100.
2   Paid the insurance premium for August, $2,800.
3   Paid for August advertising in various sports magazines, $1,500.
4   Rendered services for various groups for cash, $15,900.

5   Billed the Canadian Ministry of Natural Resources for services in transporting mapping personnel, $5,100.

6   Received $21,000 on account from clients.

7   Paid $1,700 on accounts payable.

8   Billed various clients for services, $19,400.

9   Paid interest on an outstanding note payable for August, $95.

10   Paid August wages, $14,800.

11   Received invoice for the cost of fuel used during August, $5,600.

12   Paid a cash dividend, $2,500.

Required

a.   Set up accounts for each item in the August 1 trial balance and enter the beginning balances. Also provide similar accounts for the following items: Service Fees Earned, Dividends, Wages Expense, Advertising Expense, Rent Expense, Fuel Expense, Insurance Expense, and Interest Expense. Create journal entries and record the transactions for August in the appropriate T-accounts, using the references given.

b.   Prepare a trial balance as of August 31.

LO4, 5, 6   **P2-15B.** **Transaction Analysis and Trial Balance** Bill Williams opened a tax practice, (Bill Williams, Tax Accounting, Inc.), on June 1. The following accounts will be needed to record the business's transactions for June: Cash; Accounts Receivable; Office Supplies; Tax Library; Office Furniture and Fixtures; Accounts Payable; Notes Payable; Common Stock; Dividends; Professional Fees Earned; Rent Expense; Salaries Expense; Advertising Expense; Utilities Expense; and Interest Expense. The following transactions occurred in June:

1   Williams opened a business checking account at a local bank, investing $22,000 in his practice in exchange for common stock.

2   Purchased office furniture and fixtures for $9,800, paid $4,800 cash, and gave a note payable for the balance.

3   Purchased books and software for a tax library on account, $6,700.

4   Purchased office supplies for cash, $390.

5   Paid rent for June, $850.

6   Returned $300 of books with defective bindings. The return reduced the amount owed to the supplier.

7   Billed clients for professional services rendered, $18,600.

8   Paid $1,700 on account for the library items purchased on June 3.

9   Collected $17,250 on account from clients billed on June 7.

10   Paid June salaries, $4,900.

11   Received an invoice for June advertising, to be paid in July, $400.

12   The business paid stockholders a cash dividend of $800.

13   Paid utilities for June, $210.

14   Paid interest for June on an outstanding note payable, $160.

Required

a.   Prepare journal entries and record the above transactions in T-accounts, and key entries with the numbers of the transactions.

b.   Prepare a trial balance from the general ledger as of June 30.

LO4, 5, 6   **P2-16B.** **Transaction Analysis and the Effect of Errors on the Trial Balance**

The following T-accounts contain numbered entries for the May transactions of the Upland Corporation, an architectural firm, which opened its offices on May 1:

	Cash					Accounts Payable		
(1)	50,000	1,610	(4)		(5)	440	1,280	(3)
(10)	5,200	5,950	(7)		(8)	1,000	290	(9)
		1,000	(8)					

	Accounts Receivable					Common Stock		
(6)	8,750	5,200	(10)				50,000	(1)

	Supplies					Professional Fees Earned		
(3)	1,280	440	(5)				8,750	(6)

Office Equipment			Rent Expense	
(2)	5,000		(4)	1,610

Notes Payable			Utilities Expense	
	5,000	(2)	(9)	290

Salaries Expense	
(7)	5,950

Required

a. Give a description of each of the 10 numbered transactions entered in the above accounts. Example: (1) Upland Corporation issued common stock for cash, $50,000.

b. The following trial balance, prepared for Upland Corporation as of May 31, contains several errors. Itemize the errors, and indicate the correct totals for the trial balance.

UPLAND CORPORATION Unadjusted Trial Balance May 31		
	Debit	**Credit**
Cash	$46,460	
Accounts receivable	3,550	
Supplies	840	
Office equipment		$ 5,000
Accounts payable		130
Notes payable		50,000
Common stock		50,000
Professional fees earned		8,570
Rent expense	1,610	
Utilities expense	290	
Salaries expense	5,950	
Totals	$58,700	$113,700

P2-17B. Transaction Analysis and Trial Balance Huff & Company, Electrical Contractors began operations on May 1. The following transactions occurred during the month of May: **LO5, 6**

1 Stockholders invested $65,000 in the business in exchange for common stock.
2 Purchased equipment on account, $4,200.
3 Returned $200 of equipment that was not satisfactory. The return reduced the amount owed to the supplier.
4 Purchased supplies on account, $940.
5 Purchased a truck for $12,500. The company paid $5,500 cash and gave a note payable for the balance.
6 Paid rent for May, $875.
7 Paid fuel cost for truck, $60.
8 Billed customers for services rendered, $15,700.
9 Paid $4,400 on account for equipment purchased on May 2.
10 Paid utilities for May, $210.
11 Received invoice for May advertising, to be paid in June, $280.
12 Paid employees' wages, $5,350.
13 Collected $8,600 on accounts receivable.
14 The company paid stockholders a dividend of $2,500 cash.
15 Paid interest for May on an outstanding note payable, $75.

Required

a. Create journal entries and record the above transactions in T-accounts, and key entries with the numbers of the transactions. The following accounts will be needed to record the transactions for May: Cash; Accounts Receivable; Supplies; Equipment; Truck; Accounts Payable; Notes Payable; Common Stock; Dividends; Service Revenue; Rent Expense; Wages Expense; Utilities Expense; Truck Expense; Advertising Expense; and Interest Expense.

b. Prepare a trial balance as of May 31.

SERIAL PROBLEM: KATE'S CARDS

(Note: This is a continuation of the Serial Problem: Kate's Cards from Chapter 1.)

SP2. In September 2019, Kate incorporated Kate's Cards after investigating different organizational forms, and began the process of getting her business up and running. The following events occurred during the month of September 2019:

1. Kate deposited $10,000 that she had saved into a newly opened business checking account. She received common stock in exchange.
2. Kate designed a brochure that she will use to promote her greeting cards at local stationery stores.
3. Kate paid Fred Simmons $50 to critique her brochure before undertaking her final design and printing.
4. Kate purchased a new iMac computer tablet, specialized graphic arts software, and commercial printer for the company, paying $4,800 in cash. She decided to record all of these items under the same equipment account.
5. Kate purchased supplies such as paper and ink for $350 at the local stationery store. She opened a business account with the store and was granted 30 days credit on all purchases, including the one she just made.
6. Kate designed her first 5 cards and prepared to show them to potential customers.
7. The owner of the stationery store where Kate opened her account was impressed with Kate's work and ordered 1,000 of each of the five card designs at a cost of $1 per card, or $5,000 total. Kate tells the customer that she will have them printed and delivered within the week.
8. Kate purchased additional supplies, on account, in the amount of $1,500.
9. Kate delivered the 5,000 cards. Because the owner knows that Kate is just starting out, he paid her immediately in cash. He informed her that if the cards sell well that he will be ordering more, but would expect a 30-day credit period like the one he grants to his own business customers.
10. The cost to Kate for the order was $1,750 of the supplies she had purchased. (*Hint:* This cost should be recorded as a debit to an expense called Cost of Goods Sold.)
11. Kate paid her balance due for the supplies in full.
12. Kate purchased a one-year insurance policy for $1,200, paying the entire amount in cash. (*Hint:* Two accounts will need to be debited here, one for the current month expense and one for the prepaid amount.)
13. Kate determined that all of her equipment will have a useful life of 4 years (48 months) at which time it will not have any resale or scrap value. (*Hint:* Kate will expense 1/48th of the cost of the equipment each month to Depreciation Expense. The credit will be to Accumulated Depreciation.)
14. Kate paid herself a salary of $1,000 for the month.
15. Kate paid rent expense for the month in the amount of $1,200.

Required

a. Prepare a general ledger with the following accounts: Cash; Accounts Receivable; Supplies Inventory; Prepaid Insurance; Equipment; Accumulated Depreciation; Accounts Payable; Common Stock; Retained Earnings; Sales Revenue; Cost of Goods Sold; Consulting Expense; Insurance Expense; Depreciation Expense; Wages Expense; Rent Expense. Prepare journal entries for the above transactions using these accounts.

b. Post the accounting transactions for the month of September 2019 to the general ledger T-accounts.

c. Prepare a trial balance for Kate's Cards as of September 30, 2019.

EXTENDING YOUR KNOWLEDGE

REPORTING AND ANALYSIS

COLUMBIA
SPORTSWEAR
COMPANY

EYK2-1. **Financial Reporting Problem: Columbia Sportswear Company** The financial statements for the **Columbia Sportswear Company** can be found in Appendix A at the end of this book. The following selected accounts, in thousands, are from those statements:

Common stock	$1,585,009
Accounts payable	252,301
Accounts receivable	364,862
Inventories	457,927
Prepaid expenses and other current assets	58,559
Property, plant, and equipment	281,394
Net sales	2,466,105

Required

a. For each of these accounts, indicate whether a debit or a credit is required to increase its balance.

b. What other account is likely involved when:
   1. Accounts receivable is increased?
   2. Accounts payable is decreased?
   3. Net sales are increased?

EYK2-2. Comparative Analysis Problem: Columbia Sportswear Company vs. Under Armour, Inc.

COLUMBIA SPORTSWEAR COMPANY

UNDER ARMOUR, INC.

The financial statements for the **Columbia Sportswear Company** can be found in Appendix A and **Under Armour, Inc.**'s financial statements can be found in Appendix B at the end of this book.

Required

a. Each of the following accounts is listed in the company's financial statements:

Columbia Sportswear		Under Armour, Inc.	
1	Accounts receivable	1	Inventories
2	Property, plant, and equipment	2	Income tax expense
3	Accounts payable	3	Long term debt
4	Common stock	4	Retained earnings
5	Interest income	5	Cost of goods sold

Determine the normal balance (debit or credit) for each of the accounts listed above.

b. Identify the probable other account involved when:
   1. Cost of goods sold is increased.
   2. Interest income is increased.
   3. Accounts receivable is decreased.
   4. Income taxes payable is increased.

EYK2-3. Business Decision Problem

Mary Hernandez operates the Wildlife Image Gallery, selling original art and signed prints received on consignment (rather than purchased) from recognized wildlife artists throughout the country. The firm receives a 30 percent commission on all art sold and remits 70 percent of the sales price to the artist. All art is sold on a cash basis.

Mary began the business on March 1, 2019. She received a $20,000 loan from a relative to help her get started. Mary signed a note agreeing to repay the loan in one year. No interest is being charged on the loan, but the relative does expect to receive a set of financial statements each month. On April 1, 2019, Sarah asks for your help in preparing the financial statements for the first month.

Mary has carefully kept the firm's checking account up to date and provides you with the following complete listing of the cash receipts and disbursements for March 2019:

Cash Receipts

Original investment by Mary Hernandez in exchange for common stock	$ 6,500
Loan from relative	20,000
Sales of art	95,000
Total cash receipts	$121,500

Cash Disbursements

Payments to artists for sales made	$ 56,500
Payment of March rent for gallery space	900
Payment of March staff wages	4,900
Payment of airfare for personal vacation of Mary Hernandez (vacation will be taken in April)	500
Total cash disbursements	62,800
Cash balance, March 31, 2019	$ 58,700

Mary also gives you the following documents she has received:

1. A $350 invoice for March utilities; payment is due by April 15, 2019.
2. A $1,700 invoice from Careful Express for the shipping of the artwork sold during March; payment is due by April 10, 2019.
3. The one-year lease she signed for the gallery space; as an incentive to sign the lease, the landlord reduced the first month's rent by 25 percent; the monthly rent starting in April is $1,200.

In your discussions with Mary, she tells you that she has been so busy that she is behind in sending artists their share of the sales proceeds. She plans to catch up within the next week.

Required

From the above information, prepare the following financial statements for Wildlife Image Gallery: (a) income statement for the month of March 2019; (b) statement of stockholders' equity for the month of March 2019; and (c) balance sheet as of March 31, 2019. To obtain the data needed, you may wish to use T-accounts to construct the company's accounts.

EYK2-4. **Financial Analysis Problem** Tim Johnson runs a local photography studio, Action Images, Inc. Action Images is organized as a corporation. Tim's primary sources of revenue are from the events he is contracted to photograph, mostly sporting events, and from photography lessons given at a local community college. Most of Tim's photographic event customers pay him soon after they receive an invoice from Tim, approximately one week after the event, although in some cases Tim receives payment on the day of the event. The community college pays Tim at the end of each month that he teaches a class. Tim maintains the following accounts to account for these revenue transactions: Cash, Accounts Receivable, Photographic Revenue, Teaching Revenue.

Tim leases the studio where he does most of his work. He owns all his equipment, which consists of cameras, lenses, lighting, a computer, printer, furniture, and miscellaneous office equipment. These assets are accounted for in the following accounts: Photographic Equipment, Office Equipment, and Furniture.

Tim does most of the work himself, but he does employ part-time help on days of his photo events, and he also employs a part-time bookkeeper. Most months Tim has expenses for the studio rent, utilities, advertising, supplies, and insurance. The following accounts are used to account for these expenses: Rent Expense, Utilities Expense, Salaries Expense, Advertising Expense, Supplies Expense, and Insurance Expense.

Tim pays himself a monthly salary. In addition, if his business does well, he will receive a dividend from Action Images. The following stockholders' equity accounts are maintained by Tim: Common Stock and Retained Earnings.

During the month of November, Tim hired a new bookkeeper while his regular bookkeeper was away on vacation. The new bookkeeper was inexperienced, and Tim is concerned that things may not have been recorded correctly. He has asked you to review the following transactions. For each transaction, Tim provides you with the account, the amount either debited or credited, and an explanation for the transaction. In each case, the explanation is correct.

	Account	Debit	Credit
1	Cash	5,000	
	Photographic revenue		5,000
	Issued common stock in exchange for cash.		
2	Cash	2,000	
	Teaching revenue		2,000
	Received $2,000 from the community college for course taught.		
3	Cash	4,500	
	Accounts receivable		5,400
	Received $4,500 from customers for work done last month.		
4	Supplies expense	1,600	
	Cash		1,600
	Purchase of a new camera for $1,600.		
5	Rent expense	3,000	
	Cash		3,000
	To pay the month's rent on the studio.		
6	Supplies expense	150	
	Accounts receivable		150
	Purchased printing supplies on account.		
7	Salaries expense	3,000	
	Cash		3,000
	Paid the salaries for the month.		

Required

a. For each entry, state if it is correct. If the entry is in error, make the necessary correction.

b. Will any of the errors cause the trial balance to be out of balance?

c. What effect did the errors have on Tim's net income for November?

CRITICAL THINKING

EYK2-5. Accounting Research Problem Go to this book's Website and locate the annual report of General Mills, Inc. for the year ending May 28, 2017 (fiscal year 2017).

GENERAL MILLS, INC.

Required

1. For each of the income statement accounts, indicate the normal balance.
2. For each of the balance sheet accounts, indicate the normal balance.

EYK2-6. Accounting Communication Activity Jason Timmons is struggling with some accounting concepts and has come to you for help. In particular he does not understand what is meant by a debit and a credit. He was especially confused when he learned that sometimes debits result in account increases and sometimes debits result in account decreases.

Required

Write a short memorandum to Jason that explains what is meant by debits and credits as it applies to accounts used by a company.

EYK2-7. Accounting Ethics Case Devon Myers and his supervisor are sent on an out-of-town assignment by their employer. At the supervisor's suggestion, they stay at the Spartan Inn, across the street from the Luxury Inn. After three days of work, they settle their lodging bills and leave. On the return trip, the supervisor gives Devon what appears to be a copy of a receipt from the Luxury Inn for three nights of lodging. Actually, the supervisor indicates that he prepared the Luxury Inn receipt on his office computer and plans to complete his expense reimbursement request using the higher lodging costs from the Luxury Inn.

Required

What are the ethical considerations that Devon faces when he prepares his expense reimbursement request?

EYK2-8.   **Corporate Social Responsibility Problem** The Global Reporting Initiative (GRI) is a network-based organization that has pioneered the development of the world's most widely used sustainability reporting framework. The GRI Website is located at http://www.globalreporting.org/. Sustainability reporting differs from financial reporting in several areas. One difference that is readily apparent is that sustainability reports contain performance metrics that are measured in units other than dollars. For example, greenhouse emissions may be measured in metric tons and employee in-kind volunteering may be measured in hours.

Required

Go to the GRI Website and near the bottom, left of the page, under Useful Pages, select Disclosure Database. Use the Search feature in the middle of the page to select a report of one of the listed firms. What are some of the areas that the company reports on, and what measures do they use?

EYK2-9.   **Forensic Accounting Problem** Accrual accounting is based on the idea that revenue should be recognized when earned and that any resources consumed in the revenue-generating process (expenses) should be matched with those revenues in the same period. Another basic principle on which GAAP is based is that of the accounting period. This principle sets the time period for which the revenues and expenses are to be measured and matched. For many firms, this date is December 31. Revenues earned after December 31 are to be reported in the following period, and expenses in the following period are then matched to those revenues. One way that companies have been found to misrepresent their reported performance is to violate these principles by "holding the books open" beyond December 31. In other words, the firm will improperly record revenue earned after year-end as if it were earned in the current year, and at the same time, fail to properly match the expenses associated with those revenues. How might a forensic accountant who has been hired to investigate improper financial reporting catch this type of activity?

EYK2-10.   **IFRS Financial Statements** Thomson Reuters is a global information company created by the 2008 merger of the Thomson Corporation, a Canadian company, with the Reuters Company, a United Kingdom-based company. The company operates in over 100 countries and has over 50,000 employees. The company provides financial, legal, scientific, and tax information services to the public on a fee basis. The shares of Thomson Reuters are listed on the New York Stock Exchange and the Toronto Stock Exchange. The company prepares its financial statements using IFRS but also reconciles this information to various non-IFRS measures. You can view the company's financial statements and the Canadian GAAP-IFRS reconciliation at www.thomsonreuters.com.

Required

1. What are the advantages of having a single, global set of accounting standards like IFRS?
2. A competitor of Thomson Reuters is U.S.-based Bloomberg L.P, a closely held financial software, news, and data company founded by Michael Bloomberg, former mayor of New York City. Bloomberg prepares its financial statements using U.S. GAAP. What constraints would you face in trying to compare the financial results of Thomson Reuters to Bloomberg?

EYK2-11.   **Working with the Takeaways**

Part A

Each of the following accounts from the Canam Company has a normal balance as of December 31, 2019, the end of Canam's first year of operations.

Cash	$ 100	Common stock	$1,500
Accounts receivable	300	Dividends	100
Inventory	250	Sales revenue	800
Property, plant, and equipment	1,750	Selling expenses	300
Accounts payable	150	Administrative expenses	50
Notes payable	400		

Required

Prepare a trial balance for Canam Company as of December 31, 2019.

Part B

Landers Distributors was formed to serve as a distributor of fine furnishings imported from overseas manufacturers. Assume the following trial balance was prepared as of December 31, 2019, at the end of Landers' first year of operations:

LANDERS DISTRIBUTORS Unadjusted Trial Balance December 31, 2019	Debit	Credit
Cash.	$ 23,000	
Accounts receivable	4,500	
Buildings.	75,500	
Equipment	20,500	
Inventory.	38,000	
Accounts payable.		$ 5,500
Notes payable.		47,750
Common stock		45,000
Dividends	6,000	
Sales revenue.		280,250
Wage expense	100,000	
Selling expenses	31,000	
Rent expense	23,000	
Administrative expenses.	15,750	
Tax expense	23,000	
Totals	$360,250	$378,500

It is apparent that there is an error somewhere in the company's accounts since the sum of the debit account balances ($360,250) does not equal the sum of the credit account balances ($378,500). After further research, we learn the following:

1. A cash purchase of $20,000 in inventory, occurring near year-end, was not recorded.
2. By mistake, $10,000 that should have been recorded as Accounts Payable was recorded as Notes Payable.
3. A credit of $16,000 was accidentally recorded in the Wage Expense account rather than in Sales Revenue.
4. A sale on account of $18,750 was correctly recorded as Sales Revenue, but the other side of the entry was mistakenly never recorded.

Required

a. Which of the four errors, if any, is the reason that the trial balance is not in balance?
b. Which of the errors, if any, must be corrected?
c. Prepare a corrected trial balance.

ANSWERS TO SELF-STUDY QUESTIONS:

1. d, (pp. 59–65) 2. a, (pp. 59–65) 3. b, (pp. 59–65) 4. c, (p. 68) 5. b, (p. 67) 6. d, (p. 67)
7. b, (p. 67) 8. c, (p. 67) 9. d, (p. 67) 10. a, (p. 67) 11. d, (p. 70) 12. d, (p. 77) 13. d, (p. 70)
14. a, (p. 70) 15. c, (p. 58) 16. d, (pp. 59–60) 17. 1. (b), 2. (e), 3. (d), 4. (a), 5. (c), (p. 58)

YOUR TURN! SOLUTIONS

Solution 2.1

d, b, e, a, c

Solution 2.2

		Cash	+	Accounts Receivable	+	Equipment	=	Accounts Payable	+	Notes Payable	+	Common Stock	+	Retained Earnings
a.		$ 5,000	+	$ 5,200	+	$ 0	=	$1,000	+	$2,500	+	$5,500	+	$1,200
b.	(1)	−600						−600						
	(2)	−3,600												−3,600
	(3)			+11,500										+11,500
	(4)							+500						−500
	(5)	+10,000		−10,000										
	(6)	−2,400												−2,400
	(7)							+680						−680
	(8)	−20												−20
	(9)	−900												−900
	(10)	−4,000				+4,000								
		$ 3,480	+	$ 6,700	+	$4,000	=	$1,580	+	$2,500	+	$5,500	+	$4,600

$14,180 $14,180

Solution 2.3

a. Debit

b. Credit

c. Debit

d. Credit

e. Debit

f. Credit

g. Debit

Solution 2.4

+	Accounts Receivable (A)	−
(8)	3,740	2,400 (10)
Bal.	1,340	

Solution 2.5

1.

		Cash	+	Accounts Receivable	+	Office Supplies	=	Accounts Payable	+	Revenues	−	Expenses	−	Dividends	
		Assets						**Liabilities**		**Equity** — Retained Earnings					
a.		$ 1,300								$1,300					Service revenue
b.		−2,400										−2,400			Wages expense
c.		600		−600											
d.		−400												−400	Dividends
e.						700		700							
f.				900						900					Service revenue
g.		−500						−500							

2. a. | Cash (+A) | 1,300 |
| Service revenue (+R, +SE) | | 1,300 |
| *Revenue payment for services rendered.* | | |

b. | Wages expense (+E, −SE) | 2,400 |
| Cash (−A) | | 2,400 |
| *Paid employee wages.* | | |

c. | Cash (+A) | 600 |
| Accounts receivable (−A) | | 600 |
| *Received payment from clients.* | | |

d. | Dividends (+D, −SE) | 400 |
| Cash (−A) | | 400 |
| *Paid cash dividend.* | | |

e. | Office supplies (+A) | 700 |
| Accounts payable (+L) | | 700 |
| *Purchased office supplies on account.* | | |

f. | Accounts receivable (+A) | 900 |
| Service revenue (+R, +SE) | | 900 |
| *Billed clients for services rendered.* | | |

g. | Accounts payable (−L) | 500 |
| Cash (−A) | | 500 |
| *Paid suppliers.* | | |

3.

+	Cash (A)	−
(a)	1,300	2,400	(b)
(c)	600	400	(d)
		500	(g)

+	Accounts Receivable (A)	−
(f)	900	600	(c)

+	Office Supplies (A)	−
(e)	700	

−	Accounts Payable (L)	+
(g)	500	700	(e)

−	Service Revenue (R)	+
		1,300	(a)
		900	(f)

+	Wages Expense (E)	−
(b)	2,400	

+	Dividends (D)	−
(d)	400	

Solution 2.6

Devin Company Unadjusted Trial Balance December 31	Debit	Credit
Cash	$ 1,500	
Accounts receivable	4,500	
Inventory	3,750	
Property, plant, and equipment	11,250	
Accounts payable		$ 2,250
Notes payable		6,000
Common stock		7,500
Dividends	1,500	
Sales revenue		12,000
Salary expense	4,500	
Administrative expenses	750	
Totals	$27,750	$27,750

Chapter 3

Accrual Basis of Accounting

PAST

Chapter 2 explained how we analyze and record transactions (the first two steps in the *accounting cycle*), including the system of debits and credits.

PRESENT

This chapter completes our examination of the final three steps in the five-step accounting cycle: adjust, report, and close.

FUTURE

Chapter 4 examines the balance sheet and income statement more closely and introduces techniques for analyzing and interpreting financial statements.

Krispy Kreme is similar to other companies when it comes to the end-of-year accounting process. As it closes its books for the year, its employees must get the accounting information organized to prepare the financial statements for its annual report. That process normally requires several accounting adjustments to properly determine how well a company performed and its financial condition.

Accounting adjustments involve many estimates, assumptions, and judgments. They are important to investors and others that rely on financial statements for valuing a company's stock. Not long ago, Krispy Kreme was a high-flying company with a stock price of nearly $50 per share. Today, its stock is selling for less than half of that price.

What precipitated such a dramatic drop in its stock price? One reason suggested by Wall Street pundits is Krispy Kreme's accounting methods. It appears that some adjustments that Krispy Kreme made propped up its earnings much like the yeast in its donuts. When investors began to question the "quality" of Krispy Kreme's earnings, a sharp sell-off of its stock followed as worried stockholders moved their money to alternative investments.

Why are accounting adjustments so important? This chapter focuses on the importance of those adjustments for financial statements. It also shows how companies account for adjustments and how financial statements are prepared from the final adjusted numbers.

Road Map

ACCRUAL BASIS OF ACCOUNTING				
Accrual Accounting	**Accounting Adjustments**	**Adjusted Trial Balance and Financial Statements**	**Closing Process**	**Assessing the Accounting Numbers**
• Revenue recognition • Expense recognition	• Allocating prepaid assets to expense • Allocating deferred revenue to revenue • Accruing expenses • Accruing revenue	• Adjusted trial balance • Preparing financial statements from adjusted trial balance	• Closing the accounts and closing entries • Post-closing trial balance • Accounting cycle • Closing to the Income Summary account (Appendix 3A) • Using a worksheet (Appendix 3B)	• Quality of earnings concept • Conservative versus aggressive accounting

ACCRUAL BASIS OF ACCOUNTING

LO1 **Explain** the accrual basis of accounting and contrast it with the cash basis with reference to revenue and expense recognition.

Most individuals, and some small businesses, measure their financial performance by looking at their cash flow. For example, an individual is likely to evaluate her financial well-being in terms of her available cash. If she ends the period with a higher cash balance than she started with, she is likely to conclude that she generated a profit.

The cash basis of accounting is not considered generally accepted for most businesses. Generally accepted accounting principles require that companies use the accrual basis of accounting. The accrual basis of accounting requires a business to measure and report its operating performance regardless of whether all revenues have been collected in cash and all expenses have been paid with cash.

Revenue Recognition Principle

Under the cash basis of accounting, the receipt and payment of cash are the determining factors for when sales revenue is recognized and when expenses are deducted. Under the accrual basis of accounting, sales revenue is recognized as the amount the seller expects to be paid for the transfer of promised goods or services to customers. The selling company needs to apply the following five steps to determine the proper revenue to recognize:

1. Identify the contract with a customer.

2. Identify the performance obligations (or promises) in the contract.

3. Determine the transaction price.

4. Allocate the transaction price to the performance obligations in the contract.

5. Recognize revenue at the point the performance obligations have been satisfied.

For most businesses, this means that sales revenue is recognized at the time that goods and services are delivered to the customer. Revenue may be recognized before, after, or at the same time that cash is received.

Revenue Earned *When* Cash Is Received

For most sales, **Krispy Kreme** will receive cash at the same time that the customer receives donuts. Under these circumstances, accrual accounting recognizes sales revenue at the same time that the company receives payment for its product. As a consequence, Krispy Kreme will debit Cash and credit Sales Revenue.

April 30	Cash (+A)	100	
	Sales revenue (+R, +SE)		100
	To record revenue at time of cash receipt.		

$$A = L + SE$$
$$+100 \qquad + 100 \text{ Rev.}$$

Revenue Earned *Before* Cash Is Received

Safeway purchases large quantities of Krispy Kreme donuts for resale in its grocery stores. Assume that Safeway agrees to pay for the donuts thirty days after delivery. Even though Krispy Kreme has not received payment for the delivered donuts, the company has earned the right to receive the cash, and consequently, Krispy Kreme must recognize the sales revenue prior to cash collection. In this case, it will debit Accounts Receivable and credit Sales Revenue at the time of the sale. The subsequent collection of cash on the account does not result in sales revenue being recognized.

April 30	Accounts receivable (+A)	100	
	Sales revenue (+R, +SE)		100
	To recognize revenue earned.		

$$A = L + SE$$
$$+100 \qquad + 100 \text{ Rev.}$$

May 30	Cash (+A)	100	
	Accounts receivable (−A)		100
	To recognize cash received.		

$$A = L + SE$$
$$+100$$
$$-100$$

Revenue Earned *After* Cash Is Received

Assume that **Albertsons** prepays for its donut purchases by giving Krispy Kreme a cash payment prior to receiving any donuts. Even though Krispy Kreme has received cash, it has not delivered the donuts, and thus, will defer the recognition of sales revenue until it does. Krispy Kreme will record a liability account, Unearned Revenue, for the cash received. When the donuts are delivered to Albertsons, it will recognize the revenue.

April 30	Cash (+A)	100	
	Unearned revenue (+L)		100
	To recognize the receipt of cash prior to revenue being earned.		

$$A = L + SE$$
$$+100 \quad +100$$

May 30	Unearned revenue (−L)	100	
	Sales revenue (+R, +SE)		100
	To recognize earned revenue.		

$$A = L + SE$$
$$-100 + 100 \text{ Rev.}$$

As these examples demonstrate, the timing of revenue recognition is determined by the revenue recognition principle, and not the timing of the cash collection.

Concept ⟶	Method ⟶	Assessment	TAKEAWAY 3.1
When should sales revenue be recognized?	Apply the five steps of the revenue recognition process.	Early recognition of revenue overstates current period revenue; recognizing revenue too late understates current period revenue.	

Revenue Recognition	PRINCIPLE ALERT

Applying the revenue recognition principle can be quite straightforward for simple situations such as the sale of a dozen donuts at a Krispy Kreme store. More complex situations, however, can lead to more difficulty in applying the five-step revenue recognition process. For example, when Xerox Corp. sells a photocopy machine along with a three-year maintenance agreement as part of a packaged deal, the five-step process would be applied as follows:

    Step 1: Identify the contract with the customer. The revenue recognition standard treats every revenue transaction as a contract between the seller to provide goods or services and the buyer to provide payment to the seller. Contracts may be informal and implicit such as the contract to purchase a dozen donuts from Krispy Kreme, or formal and explicit such as a written contract to purchase a photocopier with a maintenance agreement from Xerox.

continued

continued from previous page

Step 2: Identify the separate performance obligations in the contract. Every contract requires the seller to perform at least one performance obligation, while some contracts may require multiple obligations. The purchase of a dozen donuts simply requires Krispy Kreme to deliver to the buyer the donuts in exchange for payment from the buyer. In contrast, the contract with Xerox contains two performance obligations: (1) the delivery of a photocopier and (2) the maintenance of the photocopier over a three-year period.

Step 3: Determine the transaction price. The transaction price is the amount the seller expects to receive for satisfying the performance obligations in the contract. The transaction price is easy to compute for the dozen donuts from Krispy Kreme. It is simply the price Krispy Kreme charges for the donuts. Determining the transaction price in the Xerox contract is more complex because it must be allocated between the two performance obligations in the contract as discussed in the following step.

Step 4: Allocate the transaction price to the separate performance obligations in the contract. Step 4 is quite easy in the case of single performance obligation contracts such as the donut sale. Krispy Kreme simply allocates the entire transaction price to the sale of the donuts. A more complex allocation is necessary for the Xerox contract with two performance obligations. A widely used method in a contract like this is for Xerox to base the allocation on the price that would be charged for each performance obligation if they were sold separately.

For example, assume the contract with Xerox is for $15,000. Further assume that if sold separately the two performance obligations in the contract would be priced as follows:

Photocopier	$12,000
Maintenance agreement	4,000
Total	$16,000

The $15,000 transaction price would be allocated $11,250 to the sale of the photocopier and $3,750 to the sale of the maintenance agreement as follows:

$$\text{Photocopier} = \text{Transaction price} \times \frac{\text{Separate price of Photocopier}}{\text{Total separate prices of photocopier and maintenance agreement}}$$

$$\text{Photocopier} = \$15,000 \times \frac{\$12,000}{\$16,000} = \$11,250$$

$$\text{Maintenance agreement} = \text{Transaction price} \times \frac{\text{Separate price of maintenance agreement}}{\text{Total separate prices of photocopier and maintenance agreement}}$$

$$\text{Maintenance agreement} = \$15,000 \times \frac{\$4,000}{\$16,000} = \$3,750$$

Step 5: Recognize revenue at the point the performance obligations have been satisfied. The seller should recognize revenue separately as each performance obligation is satisfied. In the simple Krispy Kreme example, revenue would be recognized by Krispy Kreme at the time the donuts are delivered to the buyer. In the more complex example, Xerox will recognize revenue for the sale of the photocopier at the time the buyer takes possession of the machine, and the revenue for the maintenance agreement over the three-year period of the agreement.

Continuing the example from above, the $11,250 revenue from the sale of the photocopier would be recognized by Xerox when the photocopier is delivered to the customer since the performance obligation is fulfilled at that point in time. The $3,750 revenue from the maintenance agreement would be recognized in the amount of $1,250 per year for each of the three years of the agreement.

Expense Recognition (Matching) Principle

Accounting requires that the expenses incurred to generate revenues be recognized (matched) in the same period. In other words, business expenses are recognized (matched) with sales revenues so that they are reported on the same income statement. Like the recognition of revenue, the recognition of expenses can occur prior to, simultaneously with, or subsequent to the receipt of cash. It is the recognition of revenue, and not the payment of cash, that determines when expenses are recognized under the accrual basis of accounting.

Referring again to Krispy Kreme, assume the company pays $50 cash to acquire baking supplies for its donuts. A cash purchase is not considered to be a business expense until Krispy Kreme sells the donuts it produces. The cash purchase of materials prior to sale would be accounted for as a reduction of cash and an increase in supplies, both assets.

May 15	Baking supplies (+A)	50	
	Cash (−A)		50
	To record cash payment for supplies.		

A = L + SE
+50
−50

In this case, the cash payment precedes the recognition of revenue and the matching of expense. But what happens if the materials are purchased on account and used in donuts sold before Krispy Kreme pays for the baking materials? In this case, the accrual basis of accounting dictates the recognition of expense prior to the cash payment for the materials so that the expense is properly matched with the revenue recognized in the same accounting period.

May 15	Baking supplies (+A)	50	
	Accounts payable (+L)		50
	To record purchase of supplies on account.		

A = L + SE
+50 +50

In each of the above cases the expense for the cost of goods sold is recognized when the donuts are sold with the following journal entry:

May 15	Cost of goods sold (+E, −SE)	50	
	Baking supplies (−A)		50
	To record cost of product sold.		

A = L + SE
−50   −50
         Exp.

The key point is that under accrual accounting the recognition of expense is matched to the recognition of revenue in the same period. This may occur after the cash expenditure, before the cash expenditure, or at the same time as the cash expenditure. In addition, it should be stressed that the purpose of accrual accounting is to adjust cash flows such that revenues and expenses are recognized in the period the revenue is earned and the corresponding resources to earn the revenue are used up. Such matching would not necessarily occur under the cash basis of accounting. Ultimately both cash-basis accounting and accrual-basis accounting will yield the same results; however, the results will likely differ period by period.

Concept	Method	Assessment	TAKEAWAY 3.2
When should expenses be recognized?	Recognize expenses with the related revenue in the same accounting period.	Early recognition of expenses overstates current period expenses; recognizing expenses too late understates current period expenses.	

YOUR TURN! 3.1

The solution is on page 182.

Prepare journal entries for Sawyer Enterprises for each of the following accrual accounting adjustments on June 30.
1. Sawyer Enterprises sells $600 of merchandise to Apollo Inc. with terms of cash due in 30 days.
2. Apollo Inc. prepays Sawyer Enterprises $700 for merchandise that will be delivered in 30 days.
3. Sawyer Enterprises purchases and receives inventory of $400 from its supplier Adamo Co. The terms are cash due in 45 days.

ADJUSTING ACCOUNTS

LO2 **Describe** the adjusting process.

In Chapter 2, we analyzed a series of accounting transactions for WebWork, Inc., that occurred during the month of December. We prepared journal entries for those transactions and recorded them in the general journal. We then posted the company's journal entry data to the general ledger, which we set up in T-account form. Many of the general ledger account balances from Chapter 2, however, require an end-of-period adjustment to bring them to the correct balance for the preparation of WebWork's financial statements. For example, WebWork prepaid six months of rent for its office space on December 1. By December 31, one month's rent has expired. The prepaid rent account must be adjusted so that the account balance reflects the remaining amount of rent that is still prepaid and rent expense is recognized for the month of December. When it is time to prepare a company's financial statements, the company must review account balances and make any necessary end-of-period adjustments to bring those (unadjusted) accounts to their proper balance.

Unadjusted Trial Balance

The end-of-period adjustment process begins with the preparation of a trial balance of all general ledger accounts. Because this trial balance reports the account balances before any adjustments have been made, it is referred to as the **unadjusted trial balance**. An unadjusted trial balance is prepared to ensure that the general ledger is in balance before the end-of-period adjusting process begins. Accumulating all general ledger account balances in one location makes it easier to review the accounts and determine which account balances must be adjusted. The unadjusted trial balance of WebWork, Inc., as of December 31 is in **Exhibit 3-1**.

Exhibit 3-1	**Unadjusted Trial Balance for WebWork, Inc.**

WEBWORK, INC. Unadjusted Trial Balance December 31, 2019	Debit	Credit
Cash	$40,590	
Accounts receivable	1,340	
Office supplies	2,850	
Prepaid rent	10,800	
Office equipment	32,400	
Accounts payable		$ 2,850
Unearned revenue		3,000
Notes payable		36,000
Common stock		30,000
Dividends	500	
Fee revenue		18,250
Wage expense	1,620	
Totals	$90,100	$90,100

Types of Adjustments

There are four types of accounting adjustments made at the end of an accounting period:

Prepaid Expenses	Unearned Revenues	Accrued Expenses	Accrued Revenues
Allocating previously recorded assets to expenses to reflect the proper expenses incurred during the period.	Allocating previously recorded unearned revenue to revenue to reflect revenue earned during the period.	Recording operating expenses that have not yet been paid or recorded to reflect expenses incurred during the period.	Recording revenues that have not yet been received or recorded to reflect revenue earned during the period.

Journal entries to record accounting adjustments are known as **adjusting entries**. Each adjusting entry affects one or more balance sheet accounts (an asset or liability account) and one or more income statement accounts (a revenue or expense account).

Adjustments in the first two categories—prepaid expenses and unearned revenues—are referred to as **deferrals**. The distinguishing characteristic of a deferral is that the adjustment deals with an amount that has previously been recorded, or deferred, in a balance sheet account. The adjusting entry, in effect, decreases the balance sheet account and increases an income statement account. Adjustments in the last two categories—accrued expenses and accrued revenues—are referred to as **accruals**. The unique characteristic of an accrual is that the adjustment deals with an amount that has not previously been recorded in an account. Consequently, the adjusting entry increases both a balance sheet account and an income statement account.

Match the transaction from the first column with the type of accounting adjustment from the second column.

1. Record depreciation for the month on buildings.
2. Record rental income for the month on equipment rented on a long-term rental agreement. Payment will be received next month.
3. Record rental income at month-end on amounts that had been prepaid at the beginning of the month.
4. Record utility expense at the end of the month for amounts that had previously been paid in advance and recorded as an asset.

a. Prepaid expenses
b. Unearned revenue
c. Accrued expenses
d. Accrued revenues

YOUR TURN! 3.2

The solution is on page 183.

DEFERRAL ADJUSTING ENTRIES

Allocating Previously Recorded Assets to Expenses

LO3

Illustrate deferral adjustments.

Prepaid Expenses

Many expenditures benefit multiple accounting periods. These expenditures must be allocated over the periods benefited. Common examples include purchases of buildings, equipment, and supplies; prepayments of rent and advertising; and prepayments of insurance premiums. Outlays for these expenditures are normally debited to an asset account at the time of payment. Then, at the end of each accounting period, the estimated portion of the expenditure that has expired, or that has been used up, during the period is transferred from the asset account to an expense account to achieve a proper recognition of revenue and expenses.

These adjustments are commonly identified by inspecting the unadjusted trial balance for costs that benefit multiple accounting periods. For example, by looking at the

December 31 trial balance of WebWork (**Exhibit 3-1**), we observe that adjustments are required to allocate costs of the purchased office supplies, the prepaid rent, and the office equipment to the current period (December) and subsequent accounting periods that benefit from these expenditures. The next three sections illustrate those adjustments.

Office Supplies

WebWork purchased office supplies on account and recorded the expenditure in an asset account, Office Supplies, as follows:

A = L + SE
+2,850 + 2,850

Dec. 1	Office supplies (+A)	2,850	
	Accounts payable (+L)		2,850
	To record the purchase of office supplies.		

During December, office supplies were used as services were provided. The cost of office supplies used is an expense for December that reduces the amount of supplies available. It is unnecessary to record an expense as each individual supply item, such as a copier cartridge or LCD cleaner, is used. Instead, at the end of December, the company physically counts the supplies still available and then subtracts that amount from the total amount purchased to determine the amount used. For example, assume that a physical count of the office supplies reveals that $1,530 worth of WebWork's office supplies are available at the end of the month. This implies that $1,320 ($2,850 − $1,530) worth of supplies were used during December. An adjusting entry is needed to transfer this amount to an expense account, Supplies Expense, as follows:

A = L + SE
−1,320 −1,320
Exp.

Dec. 31	Supplies expense (+E, −SE)	1,320	
	Office supplies (−A)		1,320
	To record expense of office supplies used in December.		

Office Supplies			
Unadjusted	2,850		
		1,320	(a)
Adjusted	1,530		

Supplies Expense		
Unadjusted	0	
(a)	1,320	
Adjusted	1,320	

When this adjusting entry is posted, it properly shows the $1,320 December expense for office supplies and reduces the asset account, Office Supplies, to $1,530, the amount of the asset remaining as of December 31.

Prepaid Rent

On December 1, WebWork paid six months' rent in advance and debited the $10,800 payment to Prepaid Rent, an asset account. As each day passes and the rented space is occupied, rent expense is being incurred, and the balance of the prepaid rent is decreasing. It is unnecessary to record rent expense on a daily basis because financial statements are not prepared daily; however, at the end of the accounting period, an adjusting entry is necessary to recognize the correct amount of rent expense for the period and to decrease the Prepaid Rent account. Specifically, on December 31, one month of WebWork's prepaid rent has been used up; consequently, WebWork will transfer $1,800 ($10,800/6 months) from the Prepaid Rent account to the Rent Expense account, as follows:

A = L + SE
−1,800 −1,800
Exp.

Dec. 31	Rent expense (+E, −SE)	1,800	
	Prepaid rent (−A)		1,800
	To record rent expense for December.		

Prepaid Rent			
Unadjusted	10,800		
		1,800	(b)
Adjusted	9,000		

Rent Expense		
Unadjusted	0	
(b)	1,800	
Adjusted	1,800	

The posting of this adjusting entry shows the correct rent expense ($1,800) for December in the Rent Expense account and reduces the Prepaid Rent account balance to the correct balance ($9,000) that remains prepaid as of December 31. (Examples of other prepaid expenses for which similar adjustments are made include prepaid insurance and prepaid advertising.)

Depreciation

The process of allocating the cost of buildings, equipment, and vehicles to the periods benefiting from their use is called **depreciation**. Because these long-lived assets help generate revenue for a company over many years, each accounting period in which the assets are used must reflect a portion of their cost as an expense. The allocation of the cost of revenue-generating assets over the many periods that they help produce revenues is an application of the expense recognition principle. This periodic expense is known as *depreciation expense*.

There is no exact way to measure the amount of these assets used each period, which means that the periodic depreciation expense is an estimate. The procedure used in this chapter estimates the annual amount of depreciation expense by dividing the acquisition cost of the asset by its estimated useful life in years. This method is called **straight-line depreciation**. (We will explore other depreciation methods in a later chapter.)

When recording depreciation expense, the asset account is not reduced directly. Instead, the reduction is recorded in a contra account called **Accumulated Depreciation**. **Contra accounts** are so named because they are used to record reductions in, or offsets against, a controlling account. In this case, the Accumulated Depreciation contra account offsets the controlling account, Office Equipment, which has a normal debit balance. Accumulated depreciation therefore has a normal credit balance and appears in the balance sheet as a deduction against Office Equipment. Use of the contra account Accumulated Depreciation allows the original cost of the related asset to be reported in the company's balance sheet, followed by the accumulated amount of depreciation taken to date. Users of financial statements want to see both of these amounts so that they can estimate how much of an asset has been used and how much remains to benefit the business in future periods.

Hint: A contra account is increased and decreased in the opposite way of its controlling account. Also, the normal balance of a contra account is opposite to the normal balance of its controlling account.

To illustrate, assume that the office equipment purchased by WebWork for $32,400 is expected to last six years. Straight-line depreciation is $5,400 per year ($32,400/6 years), or $450 per month ($5,400/12 months). At the end of December, WebWork would make the following adjusting entry:

Dec. 31	Depreciation expense (+E, −SE)	450	
	Accumulated depreciation—Office equipment (+XA, −A)		450
	To record December depreciation expense.		

When the preceding adjusting entry is posted, it shows the estimated cost of using the asset during December, and shows the estimated expense ($450) in the company's December income statement. On the balance sheet, the accumulated depreciation is subtracted from the related asset account (Office Equipment). The resulting balance (acquisition cost less accumulated depreciation) is called the asset's **book value** and represents the unexpired asset cost to be applied as an expense against future periods. For example, the December 31, 2019, balance sheet shows WebWork's office equipment with a book value of $31,950, presented as follows:

$$A = L + SE$$
$$-450 \qquad -450 \; Exp$$

Accumulated Depreciation— Office Equipment	
	0 Unadjusted
	450 (c)
	450 Adjusted

Depreciation Expense	
Unadjusted 0	
(c) 450	
Adjusted 450	

 A.K.A. Book value is also called **carrying value.**

Office equipment	$32,400
Less: Accumulated depreciation.	450
Office equipment, net	$31,950

Allocating Previously Recorded Unearned Revenue to Revenue

Unearned Revenues

Sometimes a business receives fees for services or products before the services or products are rendered. Such transactions are initially recorded by debiting the Cash account and crediting a liability account called **Unearned Revenue**. The Unearned Revenue account is also called **Deferred Revenue** and represents an obligation to perform a service, or provide a product, in the future. Once the service or product is provided, the revenue is recognized. The required adjusting entry is a debit to the Unearned Revenue account, which reduces the liability account, and a credit to the Revenue account for the amount of revenue earned in the current period.

Deferred Service Revenue

On December 5, WebWork signed a four-month contract to perform work for $750 per month, with the entire contract price of $3,000 received in advance. The journal entry made on December 5 was:

Dec. 5	Cash (+A)	3,000	
	Unearned revenue (+L)		3,000
	Received $3,000 advance payment on a four-month contract.		

On December 31, the following adjusting entry transfers $750 ($3,000/4 months), the revenue earned in December, to Fee Revenue and it reduces the liability Unearned Revenue by the same amount:

Dec. 31	Unearned revenue (−L)	750	
	Fee revenue (+R, +SE)		750
	To record portion of fee advance earned in December.		

After the journal entry is posted to the general ledger accounts, the liability account shows a balance of $2,250, the amount of future services still owed by WebWork and the Fee Revenue account reflects the $750 earned in December.

Other examples of revenues received in advance include rental prepayments by real estate management companies, insurance premiums received in advance by insurance companies, subscription revenues received in advance by magazine and newspaper publishers, and membership fees received in advance by health and fitness clubs. In each case, a liability account is established when the prepayment is initially received. Later, an adjusting entry is made to reflect the revenues earned from the services provided or products delivered during the current accounting period.

YOUR TURN! 3.3

The solution is on page 183.

Prepare journal entries for each of the following end-of-year accounting adjustments.

1. Record depreciation expense adjustment of $700 on the company's buildings.
2. Record $1,500 for rent expense that was previously recorded as part of a $2,000 advance rent payment to the company's landlord.

ACCRUAL ADJUSTING ENTRIES

LO4   Illustrate accrual adjustments.

Recording Previously Unrecorded Expenses

Accrued Expenses

A company often incurs expenses before paying for them. Employee wages, utilities, and income taxes are all examples of expenses that are typically incurred by a business before payment is made. Usually the cash payments are made at regular time intervals, such as weekly, monthly, quarterly, or annually. If the accounting period ends on a date that does not coincide with a scheduled cash payment date, an adjusting entry must be recorded to reflect the expense incurred during the period. Such expenses are referred to as **accrued expenses**. WebWork has two such adjustments to make on December 31, one for its employee wages and the other for interest on its bank loan.

Accrued Wages

WebWork's employee is paid every two weeks at the rate of $810 per week. The employee was paid $1,620 on Friday, December 20. At the close of business on Friday, December 27, the employee has worked one week during December for which wages are not paid until January. Because the employee's wages are $810 per week, an additional wage expense of $810 must be reflected in WebWork's income statement for December. The adjusting entry at the end of December to accrue one week of wage expense follows:

Dec. 31	Wage revenue (+R, +SE)	810	
	Wages payable (+L)		810
	To record accrued wages for the final week of December.		

A = L + SE
  + 810   −810
            Exp

Wages Payable
	0	Unadjusted
	810	(e)
	810	Adjusted

Wage Expense
Unadjusted	1,620	
(e)	810	
Adjusted	2,430	

This adjustment enables WebWork's December income statement to show the cost of all wages *incurred* during the month rather than just the wages *paid*. Also, WebWork's balance sheet will correctly show a liability for unpaid wages at the end of December.

When the employee is paid on the next regular payday in January, WebWork must ensure that the one week of accrued wages for December is not again charged to expense. When the employee is paid $1,620 on Friday, January 3, the following entry is made:

Jan. 3	Wages payable (−L)	810	
	Wage expense (+E, −SE)	810	
	Cash (−A)		1,620
	To record two weeks wages paid.		

A = L + SE
−1,620 −810   −810
             Exp.

This entry eliminates the liability recorded in Wages Payable at the end of December and debits January Wage Expense for only those wages earned by the employee in January.

Accrued Interest

On December 1, 2019, WebWork obtained a bank loan in the amount of $36,000 and signed a two-year note payable. The annual interest rate on the note is 10 percent, with interest payable each November 30. The amount of interest expense must be reflected in net income for the period. Interest expense (or interest revenue) is computed based on three factors: (1) the principal amount of the money borrowed (or loaned); (2) the rate of interest expressed as an annual rate; and (3) the amount of time in the calculation. The first year's interest of $3,600 ($36,000 × 10 percent) is due on November 30, 2020. Because interest accumulates as time passes, an adjusting entry is needed on December 31, 2019, to reflect the interest expense for December. December's interest is $300 ($3,600/12 months), and the computation and adjusting entry at December 31 follow:

Principal Amount of Note	×	Annual Interest Rate	×	Time as a fraction of a year	=	Interest
$36,000	×	10%	×	1/12	=	$300

Dec. 31	Interest expense (+E, −SE)	300	
	Interest payable (+L)		300
	To record accrued interest expense for December.		

A = L + SE
  +300   −300
            Exp

Interest Payable
	0	Unadjusted
	300	(f)
	300	Adjusted

Interest Expense
Unadjusted	0	
(f)	300	
Adjusted	300	

When this adjusting entry is posted to the general ledger, the correct interest expense for December is shown as well as a liability for one month's interest that has accrued as of December 31.

When the first year's interest of $3,600 is paid on November 30, 2020, WebWork must remember that $300 of that amount relates to 2019. On November 30, 2020, the following entry records the interest payment:

Nov. 30	Interest payable (−L)	300	
	Interest expense (+E, −SE)	3,300	
	Cash (−A)		3,600
	To record payment of annual interest.		

A = L + SE
−3,600 −300   −3,300
             Exp.

This entry eliminates the interest payable that was accrued on December 31, 2019, and debits the Interest Expense account for $3,300 ($300 times 11 months), the correct interest expense for the first 11 months of 2020.

Accrued Revenues

Recording Previously Unrecorded Revenues

Revenues from selling a product or providing a service must be recognized in the period in which the goods are sold or the services are performed. A company, however, may provide services during a period that are neither paid for by customers nor billed at the end of the period. The value of these services represents revenue that must be included in the current period income statement. To accomplish this, end-of-period adjusting entries are made to reflect any revenues for the period that have been earned but have not yet been paid or billed. Such accumulated revenue is often called **accrued revenue**.

Accrued Fees

WebWork entered into a contract with a local company on December 2 that requires a December 31 adjusting entry to accrue revenue. Under the one-year contract, WebWork agreed to maintain that company's Website in exchange for a monthly fee of $150, payable at the end of every three months. By December 31, WebWork has earned one month of fee revenue, and the following adjusting entry is made:

$$
\begin{array}{ll}
A & = L + \quad SE \\
+150 & \qquad +150 \ Rev.
\end{array}
$$

Accounts Receivable

Unadjusted	1,340	
(g)	150	
Adjusted	1,490	

Fee Revenue

		18,250	Unadjusted
		750	(d)
		150	(g)
		19,150	Adjusted

Dec. 31	Accounts receivable (+A)	150	
	Fee revenue (+R, +SE)		150
	To record accrued fee revenue earned in December.		

When WebWork receives the first $450 payment on February 29, 2020, the company must remember that $150 was previously earned and recorded in 2019. The following entry records the payment received on that date:

$$
\begin{array}{ll}
A & = L + \quad SE \\
+450 & \qquad +300 \ Rev. \\
-150 &
\end{array}
$$

Feb. 29	Cash (+A)	450	
	Accounts receivable (−A)		150
	Fee revenue (+R, +SE)		300
	To record receipt of quarterly payment.		

This entry eliminates the accounts receivable established on December 31, 2019, and records $300 of fee revenue earned for the first two months of 2020.

Accrued Interest

Another example of accrued revenue involves a company that has loaned money to another entity on which interest has been earned but that has not yet been collected at the end of the accounting period. Assume WebWork loaned $2,000 to James Corporation on November 1, 2019, with annual interest at the rate of 6 percent. The loan balance, along with interest, is to be repaid one year later. On December 31, 2019, WebWork would make the following adjusting entry:

$$
\begin{array}{ll}
A & = L + \quad SE \\
+20 & \qquad +20
\end{array}
$$

Dec. 31	Interest receivable (+A)	20	
	Interest income (+R, +SE)		20
	To record interest earned on note.		

The $20 interest is computed as follows:

Principal Amount of Note	×	Annual Interest Rate	×	Time as a fraction of a year	=	Interest
$2,000	×	6%	×	2/12	=	$20

Since WebWork did not actually have a loan to James Corporation, the adjustment calculated above will not be posted to the general ledger.

Summary of Accounting Adjustments

Exhibit 3-2 summarizes the adjusting entries for WebWork as recorded in its general journal. These adjustments would be posted to the company's general ledger.

Exhibit 3-2	Adjusting Entries for WebWork, Inc.

GENERAL JOURNAL

Date	Description	Debit	Credit	
2019				
Dec. 31	Supplies expense (+E, −SE)	1,320		**(a)**
	Office supplies (−A)		1,320	
	To record expense of office supplies used in December.			
Dec. 31	Rent expense (+E, −SE)	1,800		**(b)**
	Prepaid rent (−A)		1,800	
	To record rent expense for December.			
Dec. 31	Depreciation expense (+E, −SE)	450		**(c)**
	Accumulated depreciation—Office equipment (+XA, −A)		450	
	To record December depreciation.			
Dec. 31	Unearned revenue (−L)	750		**(d)**
	Fee revenue (+R, +SE)		750	
	To record portion of advance earned in December.			
Dec. 31	Wage expense (+E, −SE)	810		**(e)**
	Wages payable (+L)		810	
	To record accrued wages for the final week of December.			
Dec. 31	Interest expense (+E, −SE)	300		**(f)**
	Interest payable (+L)		300	
	To record accrued interest expense for December.			
Dec. 31	Accounts receivable (+A)	150		**(g)**
	Fee revenue (+R, +SE)		150	
	To record accrued fee revenue earned in December.			

Exhibit 3-3 lists the four types of accounting adjustments and also shows (1) examples of how each type of adjustment arises, (2) the generic adjusting entry for each type of adjustment, and (3) what accounts are overstated or understated *prior to* any adjustment. As we explained, each adjustment affects at least one balance sheet (asset or liability), which we show in blue in Exhibit 3-3, account and at least one income statement account (expense or revenue), which we show in red.

Exhibit 3-3	Four Types of Accounting Adjustments

Accounting Adjustment	Examples	Adjusting Entry	Financial Effects If *Not* Adjusted	
			Balance Sheet	Income Statement
Deferrals				

Prepaid expenses	Expiration of prepaid rent, insurance, and advertising; depreciation of buildings and equipment	Dr. Expense
		  Cr. Asset
		    (or contra asset)
			Asset overstated
			Equity overstated
				Expense understated

Unearned revenues	Recognition of prepayments on customer orders, gift cards, and subscriptions	Dr. Liability Cr. Revenue	Liability overstated Equity understated	Revenue understated
Accruals				
Accrued expenses	Incurred but not yet paid amounts for wages, interest, and tax expenses	Dr. Expense Cr. Liability	Liabilty understated Equity overstated	Expense understated
Accrued revenues	Earned but not yet received amounts for service, sales, and interest revenues	Dr. Asset Cr. Revenue	Asset understated Equity understated	Revenue understated

> Deals with amounts that have previously been recorded in a balance sheet account.

> Deals with amounts that have not been previously recorded in an account.

TAKEAWAY 3.3	Concept	Method	Assessment
	When should an adjusting entry be made?	Individual account balances and transaction details such as contracts and agreements. Knowledge of the proper account balance is needed. Adjustments involve (1) allocating assets to expense, (2) allocating unearned revenue to revenue, (3) accruing expenses, or (4) accruing revenues.	Record an adjusting entry so that accounts are correctly reported; otherwise income and assets (and/or liabilities) are incorrectly reported.

YOUR TURN! 3.4

The solution is on page 183.

Prepare journal entries for each of the following end-of-year accounting adjustments.

1. Record $400 of revenue earned that was previously recorded as unearned revenue due to an advance payment from a customer.
2. Record $500 of accrued interest expense that applies to the company's bank loan. The $500 is part of the company's annual cash interest payment that is due next period.

ADJUSTED TRIAL BALANCE AND FINANCIAL STATEMENTS

After the end-of-period adjustments are recorded in the general journal and posted to the general ledger, the company prepares an adjusted trial balance. The company then uses the adjusted trial balance to prepare financial statements.

LO5 Explain the adjusted trial balance and use it to prepare financial statements.

Preparing the Adjusted Trial Balance

The **adjusted trial balance** lists all the general ledger account balances after the end-of-period adjustments have been posted. **Exhibit 3-4** presents WebWork's adjusted trial balance as of December 31 in the two right-hand columns of the exhibit. This exhibit begins with the unadjusted trial balance, shown in the two left-hand columns, and lists the seven adjustments in the middle columns. For example, the first adjusting entry adjusted office supplies for the $1,320 of supplies used in December. This adjustment is highlighted in **Exhibit 3-4**. Office Supplies has a $2,850 debit balance in the unadjusted trial balance column. The adjustment of a $1,320 credit appears in the credit column of the adjustments. This leads to a $1,530 debit balance in the adjusted trial balance.

The adjusting entry also affects supplies expense, as shown in the exhibit. Supplies expense has a zero balance in the unadjusted trial balance. The adjustment appears as a $1,320 debit in the adjustments column, leading to a $1,320 debit balance in the adjusted trial balance for supplies expense. Using this presentation, managers can readily see the adjustments made and their impact on the financial accounting numbers. (Another common format for the adjusted trial balance is to only show the two right-hand columns as shown in **Exhibit 3-5**—either format is acceptable.)

ACCOUNTING IN EVERYDAY LIFE	**Getting a Loan**
	Because of the size of many corporations like **McDonald's Corp.** and **Amazon.com Inc.**, it is easy to believe that corporations are the primary form of businesses in the United States. In reality, sole proprietorships, with a single owner, comprise about 70 percent of U.S. businesses according to the Small Business Administration (SBA). A common form of financing for these businesses is a 7(a) loan guaranteed by the SBA. While the procedures learned in this chapter needed to produce financial statements may seem like something only an accountant would need to know, this skill set is very useful for anybody applying for a loan. Listed near the top of the 7(a) loan application checklist is the preparation of personal and business financial statements.

Exhibit 3-4	Adjusted Trial Balance for WebWork, Inc.

WEBWORK, INC.
Adjusted Trial Balance
December 31, 2019

	Unadjusted Trial Balance		Adjustments		Adjusted Trial Balance	
	Debit	Credit	Debit	Credit	Debit	Credit
Cash.	$40,590				$40,590	
Accounts receivable	1,340		(g) $ 150		1,490	
Office supplies	2,850			(a) $1,320	1,530	
Prepaid rent	10,800			(b) 1,800	9,000	
Office equipment	32,400				32,400	
Accumulated depreciation—						
Office equipment.				(c) 450		$ 450
Accounts payable		$ 2,850				2,850
Interest payable				(f) 300		300
Wages payable.				(e) 810		810
Unearned revenue		3,000	(d) 750			2,250
Notes payable.		36,000				36,000
Common stock		30,000				30,000
Dividends	500				500	
Fee revenue		18,250		(d) 750		19,150
				(g) 150		
Supplies expense			(a) 1,320		1,320	
Wage expense	1,620		(e) 810		2,430	
Rent expense			(b) 1,800		1,800	
Depreciation expense.			(c) 450		450	
Interest expense.			(f) 300		300	
Totals	$90,100	$90,100	$5,580	$5,580	$91,810	$91,810

Preparing Financial Statements

The adjusted trial balance is used to prepare the income statement, the statement of stockholders' equity, and the balance sheet. (It is also helpful in preparing the statement of cash flows although other information is also necessary to complete this financial statement.) We illustrate the preparation of financial statements for WebWork in **Exhibit 3-5**. Recall from Chapter 1 that financial statements are prepared in the following sequence: (1) the income statement, (2) the statement of stockholders' equity, (3) the balance sheet, and (4) the statement of cash flows.

STEP 1: Income Statement

The income statement presents a company's revenues and expenses and shows whether the company operated at a profit or a loss. WebWork's adjusted trial balance contains one revenue account and five expense accounts. The revenue and expense accounts are reported in WebWork's income statement located in the lower right side of **Exhibit 3-5**. The income statement shows its net income for December is $12,850.

STEP 2: Statement of Stockholders' Equity

The statement of stockholders' equity reports the transactions and events causing a company's stockholders' equity to increase or decrease during an accounting period. The middle right side of **Exhibit 3-5** presents WebWork's statement of stockholders' equity for December. The stockholders' equity accounts in the general ledger provide some of the information for this statement, including the common stock and retained earnings balances at the beginning of the period, new common stock issuances, and dividends during the period. Since December was the first month of operations for WebWork, the beginning

Exhibit 3-5	Financial Statements Prepared from the Adjusted Trial Balance

retained earnings balance is zero. The net income (or net loss) amount is obtained from the company's income statement.

STEP 3: Balance Sheet

The balance sheet reports a company's assets, liabilities, and stockholders' equity. The assets and liabilities for WebWork as of December 31, 2019, shown in the upper right side of **Exhibit 3-5**, come from the adjusted trial balance. The $12,350 amount reported as retained earnings is taken from the statement of stockholders' equity as of December 31.

STEP 4: Statement of Cash Flows

The statement of cash flows reports information regarding a company's cash inflows and outflows. The statement of cash flows classifies cash flows into three activity categories: operating, investing, and financing. The procedures for preparing a statement of cash flows are discussed in Chapter 12.

PRINCIPLE ALERT

Accounting Period Concept

The income statement, the statement of stockholders' equity, and the statement of cash flows are financial statements covering periods of time. These statements illustrate the *accounting period concept* that useful financial statements can be prepared for arbitrary time periods within a company's total life span. Since a company does not complete all of its transactions by the end of an accounting period, accounting principles must provide a process to account for a company's continuing transactions. The end-of-period adjusting procedures provided by the accrual basis of accounting are that process. A major purpose of adjusting entries is to ensure that correct amounts of revenue and expense are reported for each accounting period.

Cassi Company prepared the following adjusted trial balance to assist in the preparation of its December 31, 2019, financial statements.

YOUR TURN! 3.5

The solution is on pages 183–184.

CASSI COMPANY Adjusted Trial Balance December 31, 2019	Debit	Credit
Cash	$ 4,000	
Accounts receivable	15,000	
Inventory.	18,000	
Prepaid rent	5,000	
Equipment	50,000	
Accumulated depreciation		$ 10,000
Accounts payable.		8,000
Salaries payable.		9,000
Dividends payable		2,000
Unearned revenue		5,000
Long-term debt.		35,000
Common stock		15,000
Retained earnings		5,000
Sales revenue.		52,000
Cost of goods sold	30,000	
Salaries expense	5,000	
Rent expense	6,000	
Depreciation expense.	6,000	
Dividends	2,000	
Totals	$141,000	$141,000

Required

Prepare an income statement, a statement of stockholders' equity, and a balance sheet for Cassi Company using its December 31, 2019, adjusted trial balance. There were no changes in stockholders' equity during the year other than for net income and dividends.

The following section illustrates closing temporary accounts directly to Retained Earnings. Appendix 3A presents an alternative process that closes temporary accounts using the Income Summary account. Your instructor can choose to cover either one or both processes. If the process using Retained Earnings is skipped, then read Appendix 3A and return to the section (four pages ahead) titled, "Quality of Accounting Numbers."

CLOSING PROCESS

LO6   **Describe** the closing process and **summarize** the accounting cycle.

All accounts can be identified as either permanent accounts or temporary accounts. **Permanent accounts** are the accounts presented on the balance sheet. They consist of the asset, liability, and stockholders' equity accounts. The distinguishing feature of a permanent account is that any balance in the account at the end of an accounting period is carried forward to the following accounting period. **Temporary accounts** are used to gather information for a particular accounting period. Revenue, expense, and dividend accounts are temporary subdivisions of stockholders' equity. At the end of the accounting period, temporary account balances are transferred to Retained Earnings, which is a permanent stockholders' equity account. The process of transferring the balances in temporary accounts to Retained Earnings is referred to as the **closing process** or **closing procedures**.

A.K.A. The closing process is also known as **closing the books**.

A temporary account is *closed* when an entry is made that changes its account balance to zero—that is, the entry is equal in amount to the account's ending balance but is opposite to the balance as a debit or credit. An account that is closed is said to be closed *to* the account that receives the offsetting debit or credit. Thus, a closing entry simply transfers the balance of one account to another account. Because closing entries bring temporary account balances to zero, the temporary accounts are then ready to start accumulating data for the next accounting period. In essence, closing the temporary accounts prevents information from the current accounting period from being carried forward to a subsequent period, which enables financial statement users to make meaningful comparisons of revenues and expenses from one period to the next. The following summarizes the classification of permanent and temporary accounts.

Permanent Accounts	Temporary Accounts
Assets	Revenues
Liabilities	Expenses
Common Stock	Dividends
Retained Earnings	

YOUR TURN! 3.6

The solution is on page 184.

For each of the following accounts, identify whether the account is either a permanent account or a temporary account:

a. Cash   e. Dividends
b. Common Stock   f. Sales Revenue
c. Wage Expense   g. Inventory
d. Notes Payable   h. Prepaid Expense

Journalizing and Posting the Closing Entries

The Retained Earnings account is used to close the temporary revenue, expense, and Dividends accounts. The closing entries occur only at the end of an accounting period and consist of three steps, which are graphically shown below.

1. **Close the revenue accounts.** Debit each revenue account for an amount equal to its current credit balance, and credit the Retained Earnings account for the total amount of earned revenue.

2. **Close the expense accounts.** Credit each expense account for an amount equal to its current debit balance, and debit the Retained Earnings account for the total amount of expenses.

3. **Close the Dividends account.** Debit the Retained Earnings account and credit the Dividends account for an amount equal to the balance in the Dividends account.

Closing Process for WebWork

Exhibit 3-6 illustrates the closing entries for WebWork as recorded in the company's general journal. The financial information in these entries is posted to the appropriate general ledger accounts, which is represented using T-accounts.

Exhibit 3-6	Closing Revenue, Expense, and Dividends Accounts—WebWork, Inc.		
	GENERAL JOURNAL		
Date	**Description**	**Debit**	**Credit**
2019			
① Dec. 31	Fee revenue (−R)	19,150	
	Retained earnings (+SE)		19,150
	To close the revenue account.		
② Dec. 31	Retained earnings (−SE)	6,300	
	Supplies expense (−E)		1,320
	Wage expense (−E)		2,430
	Rent expense (−E)		1,800
	Depreciation expense (−E)		450
	Interest expense (−E)		300
	To close the expense accounts.		
③ Dec. 31	Retained earnings (−SE)	500	
	Dividends (−D)		500
	To close the dividends account.		

The financial effect of posting these entries on the general ledger is diagrammed below.

Preparing the Post-Closing Trial Balance

After closing entries are recorded in the general journal and posted to the general ledger, all of the temporary accounts have zero balances. At this point a **post-closing trial balance** is prepared. The post-closing trial balance provides evidence that an equality of debits and credits has been maintained in the general ledger throughout the adjusting and closing processes, and that the general ledger is in balance to start the next accounting period. Because the temporary accounts have been closed, only the balance sheet (or permanent) accounts appear in the post-closing trial balance. **Exhibit 3-7** presents the post-closing trial balance for WebWork.

Exhibit 3-7	Post-Closing Trial Balance for WebWork, Inc.

WEBWORK, INC.
Post-Closing Trial Balance
December 31, 2019

	Debit	Credit
Cash	$40,590	
Accounts receivable	1,490	
Office supplies	1,530	
Prepaid rent	9,000	
Office equipment	32,400	
Accumulated depreciation—Office equipment		$ 450
Accounts payable		2,850
Interest payable		300
Wages payable		810
Unearned revenue		2,250
Notes payable		36,000
Common stock		30,000
Retained earnings		12,350
Totals	$85,010	$85,010

Summary of the Accounting Cycle

The sequence of accounting procedures known as the *accounting cycle* occurs each fiscal period and represents a systematic process for accumulating and reporting the financial data of a business. **Exhibit 3-8** summarizes the five major steps in the accounting cycle as described in this and the preceding chapter.

Exhibit 3-8	The Accounting Cycle: A Summary

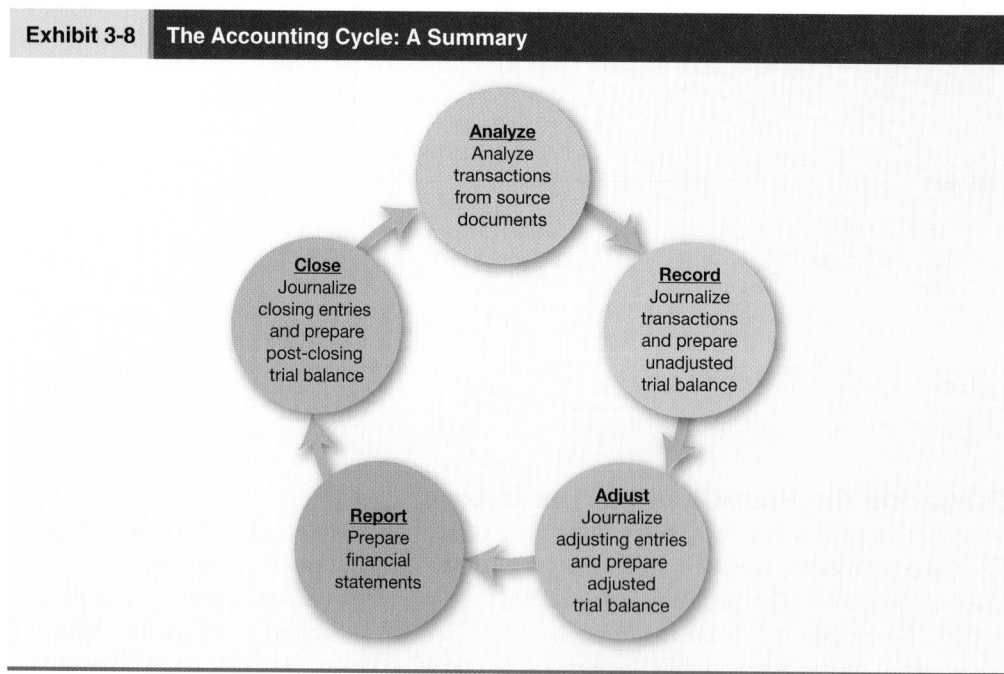

YOUR TURN! 3.7

The solution is on page 184.

Prior to closing its books, the Morgan Company has the following balances in its temporary accounts as of December 31.

	Debit	**Credit**
Sales revenue.		$79,000
Cost of goods sold	$41,000	
Wage expense	22,000	
Rent expense	3,000	
Depreciation expense.	2,000	
Interest expense.	4,000	
Dividends	5,000	

Required
Prepare closing entries as of December 31 for the Morgan Company.

For readers skipping the closing process using Retained Earnings, please resume reading here.

QUALITY OF ACCOUNTING NUMBERS

Earnings quality is a phrase used to characterize the degree to which a company's financial statements reflect its true financial condition and performance. The better the statements represent the company's actual financial condition and performance, the higher a company's earnings quality is assumed to be.

While many end-of-period adjustments discussed in this chapter are based on direct calculations, such as the time remaining for a prepaid insurance policy or the interest rate on an outstanding loan, many other adjustments that we discuss in later chapters involve judgments on the part of the company's management. Examples of judgments leading to adjusting entries are the amount of future warranty work associated with a company's product, the amount of a company's accounts receivable that will not be collected, and the estimated depreciable lives of a company's plant and equipment. Each of these items involves estimates of future events that cannot be known with certainty. Consequently, each of these estimates can have a material affect on a company's reported financial results in any given period, and can result in either higher or lower earnings quality for the company depending on how accurately management estimates these amounts.

Wall Street analysts often evaluate a company's quality of earnings by the degree to which these estimates are considered conservative or aggressive. Conservative estimates are those that are more pessimistic, leading to lower reported net income and net asset values, while aggressive estimates are those that result in higher reported net income and net asset values. The more conservative a company's estimates are judged to be, the higher a company's earnings quality is often assumed to be, although being overly conservative can also be viewed as a sign of low earnings quality. Investors may punish a company that is judged to have a low quality of earnings, as we saw in this chapter's opening feature story regarding **Krispy Kreme**, because they worry that a company using aggressive accounting estimates can surprise them with poor future performance that will cause the company's stock price to fall.

COMPREHENSIVE PROBLEM

Balke Laboratory began operations on July 1, 2017, and provides diagnostic services for physicians and medical clinics. The company's fiscal year ends on June 30, and the accounts are adjusted annually on this date. Balke's unadjusted trial balance as of June 30, 2019, is as follows:

BALKE LABORATORY Unadjusted Trial Balance June 30, 2019		
	Debit	**Credit**
Cash.	$ 1,000	
Accounts receivable	9,200	
Prepaid insurance.	6,000	
Supplies	31,300	
Laboratory equipment.	270,000	
Accumulated depreciation—Laboratory equipment		$ 30,000
Accounts payable		3,100
Diagnostic fees received in advance		4,000
Common stock		90,000
Retained earnings		50,000
Diagnostic fees revenue.		220,400
Wage expense	58,000	
Rent expense	22,000	
Totals	$397,500	$397,500

The following information is also available:

1. The Prepaid Insurance account balance represents a premium paid on January 1, 2019, for two years of fire and casualty insurance coverage. Before 2019, Balke Laboratory had no insurance protection.
2. The supplies were physically counted at June 30, 2019. The count totaled $6,300.
3. All laboratory equipment was purchased on July 1, 2017. It is expected to last nine years.
4. Balke Laboratory received a $4,000 cash payment on April 1, 2019, from Boll Clinic for diagnostic services to be provided uniformly over the four months beginning April 1, 2019. Balke credited the payment to Diagnostic Fees Received in Advance. The services for April, May, and June have been provided to Boll Clinic.
5. Unpaid wages at June 30, 2019, were $600.
6. Balke Laboratory rents facilities for $2,000 per month. Because of cash flow problems, Balke was unable to pay the rent for June 2019. The landlord gave Balke permission to delay the payment until July.

Required
a. Make the necessary adjusting entries as of June 30, 2019.
b. Prepare the adjusted trial balance as of June 30, 2019.
c. Prepare the Income Statement, Balance Sheet, and Statement of Stockholders' Equity for Balke Laboratory at June 30, 2019.
d. Make the necessary closing entries as of June 30, 2019.
e. Prepare the post-closing trial balance as of June 30, 2019.

Solution

a.

		Posting Ref.		
June 30	Insurance expense (+E, −SE)	1	1,500	
	Prepaid insurance (−A)	1		1,500
	To record 6 months' insurance expense.			
	($6,000/4 = $1,500).			
30	Supplies expense (+E, −SE)	2	25,000	
	Supplies (−A)	2		25,000
	To record supplies expense for the year.			
	($31,300 − $6,300 = $25,000).			
30	Depreciation expense—Laboratory equipment (+E, −SE)	3	30,000	
	Accumulated depreciation—Laboratory equipment (+XA, −A)	3		30,000
	To record depreciation for the year.			
	($270,000/9 years = $30,000).			
30	Diagnostic fees received in advance (−L)	4	3,000	
	Diagnostic fees revenue (+R, +SE)	4		3,000
	To record portion of advance payment that has been earned.			
	($4,000 × 3/4 = $3,000).			
30	Wage expense (+E, −SE)	5	600	
	Wages payable (+L)	5		600
	To record unpaid wages at June 30.			
30	Rent expense (+E, −SE)	6	2,000	
	Rent payable (+L)	6		2,000
	To record rent expense for June.			

b.

Balke Laboratory
Adjusted Trial Balance
June 30, 2019

	Unadjusted Trial Balance		Adjustments		Adjusted Trial Balance	
	Debit	Credit	Debit	Credit	Debit	Credit
Cash.	$ 1,000				$ 1,000	
Accounts receivable.	9,200				9,200	
Prepaid insurance.	6,000			[1] $ 1,500	4,500	
Supplies	31,300			[2] 25,000	6,300	
Laboratory equipment.	270,000				270,000	
Accumulated depreciation—						
Laboratory equipment.		$ 30,000		[3] 30,000		$ 60,000
Accounts payable.		3,100				3,100
Wages payable.				[5] 600		600
Rent payable				[6] 2,000		2,000
Diagnostic fees received in						
advance		4,000	[4] $ 3,000			1,000
Common stock		90,000				90,000
Retained earnings		50,000				50,000
Diagnostic fees revenue.		220,400		[4] 3,000		223,400
Wage expense	58,000		[5] 600		58,600	
Rent expense.	22,000		[6] 2,000		24,000	
Insurance expense.			[1] 1,500		1,500	
Supplies expense.			[2] 25,000		25,000	
Depreciation expense—			[3] 30,000		30,000	
Laboratory equipment.						
Totals	$397,500	$397,500	$62,100	$62,100	$430,100	$430,100

c.

Balke Laboratory
Income Statement
For the year ended June 30, 2019

Revenues		
Diagnostic fees revenue...		$223,400
Expenses		
Wage expense	58,600	
Rent expense	24,000	
Insurance expense	1,500	
Supplies expense	25,000	
Depreciation expense...	30,000	
Total expenses		139,100
Net income		$ 84,300

Balke Laboratory
Statement of Stockholders' Equity
For the year ended June 30, 2019

	Common Stock	Retained Earnings	Total
Balance, June 30, 2018	$90,000	$ 50,000	$140,000
Net income		84,300	84,300
Balance, June 30, 2019	$90,000	$134,300	$224,300

Balke Laboratory
Balance Sheet
June 30, 2019

Assets		Liabilities	
Cash..........................	$ 1,000	Accounts payable	$ 3,100
Accounts receivable	9,200	Wages payable........................	600
Prepaid insurance..................	4,500	Rent payable	2,000
Supplies	6,300	Diagnostic fees received in advance	1,000
Total current assets	21,000	Total liabilities	6,700
		Stockholders' equity	
Laboratory equipment..............	270,000	Common stock	90,000
Less: Accumulated depreciation.......	(60,000)	Retained earnings	134,300
Laboratory equipment, net	210,000	Total stockholders' equity	224,300
Total assets	$231,000	Total liabilities and stockholders' equity	$231,000

d.	June 30	Diagnostic fees revenue (−R)	223,400	
		Retained earnings (+SE)		223,400
		To close the revenue account.		
		Retained earnings (−SE)	139,100	
		Wage expense (−E)		58,600
		Rent expense (−E)		24,000
		Insurance expense (−E)		1,500
		Supplies expense (−E)		25,000
		Depreciation expense—Laboratory equipment (−E)		30,000
		To close the expense accounts.		

e.

Balke Laboratory **Post-Closing Trial Balance** **June 30, 2019**		
	Debit	**Credit**
Cash.	$ 1,000	
Accounts receivable	9,200	
Prepaid insurance.	4,500	
Supplies	6,300	
Laboratory equipment.	270,000	
Accumulated depreciation—Laboratory equipment		$ 60,000
Accounts payable		3,100
Wages payable.		600
Rent payable		2,000
Diagnostic fees received in advance		1,000
Common stock		90,000
Retained earnings		134,300
Totals	$291,000	$291,000

APPENDIX 3A: Closing Process—Using Income Summary Account

All accounts can be identified as either permanent accounts or temporary accounts. **Permanent accounts** are the accounts presented on the balance sheet. They consist of the asset, liability, and stockholders' equity accounts. The distinguishing feature of a permanent account is that any balance in the account at the end of an accounting period is carried forward to the following accounting period. **Temporary accounts** are used to gather information for a particular accounting period. Revenue, expense, and dividend accounts are temporary subdivisions of stockholders' equity. At the end of the accounting period, temporary account balances are transferred to retained earnings, which is a permanent stockholders' equity account. The process of transferring the balances in temporary accounts to retained earnings is referred to as the **closing process** or **closing procedures**.

LO7 Appendix 3A: **Describe** the process of closing to the Income Summary account and **summarize** the accounting cycle.

A temporary account is *closed* when an entry is made that changes its account balance to zero—that is, the entry is equal in amount to the account's ending balance but is opposite to the balance as a debit or credit. An account that is closed is said to be closed *to* the account that receives the offsetting debit or credit. Thus, a closing entry simply transfers the balance of one account to another account. Because closing entries bring temporary account balances to zero, the temporary accounts are then ready to start accumulating data for the next accounting period. In essence, closing the temporary accounts prevents information from the current accounting period from being carried forward to a subsequent period, which enables financial statement users to make meaningful comparisons of revenue and expenses from one period to the next. The following summarizes the classification of permanent and temporary accounts.

A.K.A. The closing process is also known as **closing the books**.

Permanent Accounts	Temporary Accounts
Assets	Revenues
Liabilities	Expenses
Common Stock	Dividends
Retained Earnings	Income Summary

YOUR TURN! 3A.1

The solution is on page 184.

For each of the following accounts, identify whether the account is either a permanent account or a temporary account:

a. Cash
b. Common Stock
c. Wage Expense
d. Notes Payable

e. Dividends
f. Sales Revenue
g. Inventory
h. Prepaid Expense

Journalizing and Posting the Closing Entries

A summary account is traditionally used to close the temporary revenue and expense accounts. We use an account titled Income Summary (alternative titles for this account include Revenue and Expense Summary, Income and Expense Summary, and Profit and Loss Summary). The closing entries occur only at the end of an accounting period and consist of four steps, which are graphically shown as follows.

1. **Close the revenue accounts.** Debit each revenue account for an amount equal to its current credit balance, and credit the Income Summary account for the total amount of earned revenue.
2. **Close the expense accounts.** Credit each expense account for an amount equal to its current debit balance, and debit the Income Summary account for the total amount of expenses.

After steps 1 and 2, the balance of the Income Summary account equals the current period net income (if a credit balance) or net loss (if a debit balance).

3. **Close the Income Summary account.** In the case of net income, debit the Income Summary account and credit the Retained Earnings account for an amount equal to net income. In the case of a net loss, debit the Retained Earnings account and credit the Income Summary account for an amount equal to the net loss.
4. **Close the Dividends account.** Debit the Retained Earnings account and credit the Dividends account for an amount equal to the balance in the Dividends account.

Closing Process for WebWork

Exhibit 3A-1 illustrates the closing entries for the revenue and expense accounts for WebWork as recorded in the company's general journal. The financial information in these entries is posted to the appropriate general ledger accounts, which is represented using T-accounts.

Exhibit 3A-1   Closing Revenue and Expense Accounts—WebWork, Inc.

GENERAL JOURNAL

Date	Description	Debit	Credit
2019			
Dec. 31	Fee revenue (−R)	19,150	
1	Income summary (+SE)		19,150
	To close the revenue account.		
Dec. 31	Income summary (−SE)	6,300	
	Supplies expense (−E)		1,320
	Wage expense (−E)		2,430
2	Rent expense (−E)		1,800
	Depreciation expense (−E)		450
	Interest expense (−E)		300
	To close the expense accounts.		

After steps 1 and 2, the Income Summary account has a credit balance equal to WebWork's net income of $12,850. Steps 3 and 4 close the Income Summary account and the Dividends account to the Retained Earnings account. These two entries are recorded in WebWork's general journal in **Exhibit 3A-2**. The financial effect of posting these entries on the general ledger is diagrammed below.

Exhibit 3A-2	Closing the Income Summary and Dividends Accounts—WebWork, Inc.

GENERAL JOURNAL

	Date	Description	Debit	Credit
	2019			
3	Dec. 31	Income summary (−SE)	12,850	
		Retained earnings (+SE)		12,850
		To close the Income Summary account.		
4	Dec. 31	Retained earnings (−SE)	500	
		Dividends (−D)		500
		To close the Dividends account.		

Preparing the Post-Closing Trial Balance

After closing entries are recorded in the general journal and posted to the general ledger, all of the temporary accounts have zero balances. At this point a **post-closing trial balance** is prepared. The post-closing trial balance provides evidence that an equality of debits and credits has been maintained in the general ledger throughout the adjusting and closing processes, and that the general ledger is in balance to start the next accounting period. Because the temporary accounts have been closed, only the balance sheet (or permanent) accounts appear in the post-closing trial balance. **Exhibit 3A-3** presents the post-closing trial balance for WebWork.

Exhibit 3A-3	Post-Closing Trial Balance for WebWork, Inc.

WebWork, Inc.
Post-Closing Trial Balance
December 31, 2019

	Debit	Credit
Cash.	$40,590	
Accounts receivable	1,490	
Office supplies	1,530	
Prepaid rent	9,000	
Office equipment	32,400	
Accumulated depreciation—Office equipment		$ 450
Accounts payable		2,850
Interest payable		300
Wages payable		810
Unearned revenue		2,250
Notes payable		36,000
Common stock		30,000
Retained earnings		12,350
Totals	$85,010	$85,010

Summary of the Accounting Cycle

The sequence of accounting procedures known as the *accounting cycle* occurs each fiscal period and represents a systematic process for accumulating and reporting the financial data of a business. **Exhibit 3A-4** summarizes the five major steps in the accounting cycle as described in this and the preceding chapter.

Exhibit 3A-4	The Accounting Cycle: A Summary

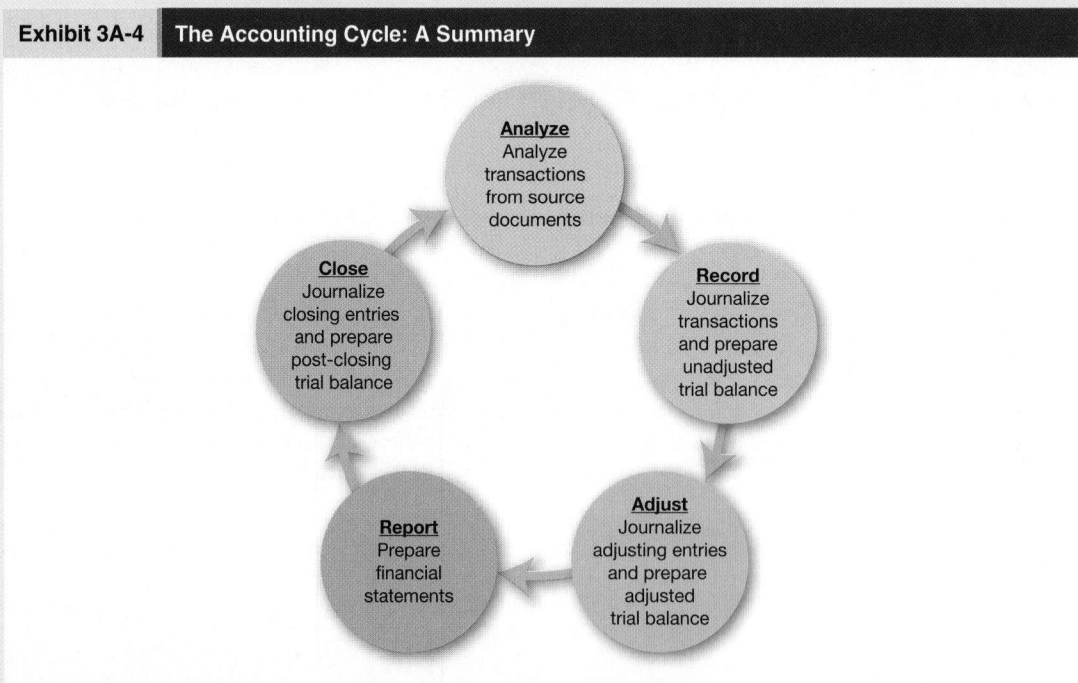

Prior to closing its books, the Morgan Company has the following balances in its temporary accounts as of December 31.

YOUR TURN! 3A.2

The solution is on page 185.

	Debit	Credit
Sales revenue.		$79,000
Cost of goods sold	$41,000	
Wage expense	22,000	
Rent expense	3,000	
Depreciation expense.	2,000	
Interest expense.	4,000	
Dividends	5,000	

Required

Prepare closing entries as of December 31 for the Morgan Company.

APPENDIX 3B: Using a Worksheet

A worksheet can be used to facilitate the adjusting and closing processes, and ultimately, the preparation of a company's financial statements. A **worksheet** is an informal document that helps accumulate the accounting information needed to prepare the financial statements. A worksheet is a tool; it is not part of a company's formal accounting records. In this section, we explain how a worksheet can be used to help compile information for a set of financial statements. Computer programs such as Microsoft Excel can simplify the preparation of a worksheet.

LO8   Appendix 3B: Explain how to use a worksheet in the adjusting and closing process.

Preparing a Worksheet

A worksheet is prepared at that stage in the accounting cycle when it is time to adjust the accounts and prepare the financial statements. The basic structure of a worksheet is illustrated in **Exhibit 3B-1**, which includes an explanation of the format used. The worksheet is prepared in the order indicated by the numbered boxes in the exhibit.

Exhibit 3B-1

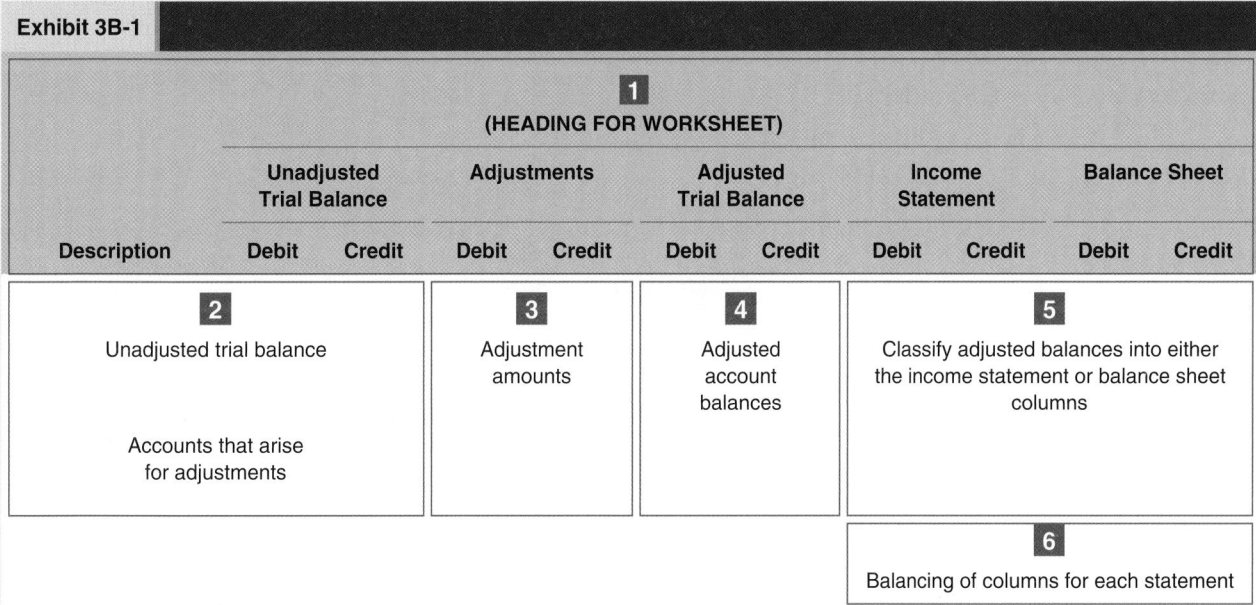

1 **Heading**   The worksheet *heading* includes (1) the name of the entity, (2) the term *Worksheet* to indicate the type of analysis being performed, and (3) a date describing the period covered. The worksheet includes both income statement data (for the period described) and balance sheet data (for the end of the period described). **Exhibit 3B-2** illustrates the heading for WebWork's worksheet. The worksheet has a description column and 10 amount (monetary) columns. A set of Debit and Credit columns is provided for each of the five headings: Unadjusted Trial Balance, Adjustments, Adjusted Trial Balance, Income Statement, and Balance Sheet.

2 **Unadjusted Trial Balance**   The unadjusted trial balance is the starting point for the accounting analysis on the worksheet. It is entered in the worksheet's description column and the first pair of monetary columns. Once the trial balance is entered in the worksheet and double-ruled, it reflects the general ledger at the time the worksheet is prepared. **Exhibit 3B-2** shows the worksheet placement of WebWork's unadjusted trial balance as of December 31, 2019.

3 **Adjustments**   *When a worksheet is used, all adjustments are first entered on the worksheet.* This procedure permits the adjustments to be reviewed for completeness and accuracy. To adjust accounts already appearing in the unadjusted trial balance, we simply enter the amounts in the appropriate side (debit or credit) of the adjustments columns on the lines containing the accounts. When accounts not appearing in the unadjusted trial balance require adjustment, their titles are listed as needed in the Description column below the accounts already listed. Adjustments entered on the worksheet are not yet journalized; journalizing the adjustments occurs later. The adjustments recorded on WebWork's worksheet in **Exhibit 3B-2** are identical to those illustrated in the chapter (see **Exhibit 3-2**). After recording all the adjusting entries on the worksheet, we total the adjustments columns to verify that the sum of the debit entries equals the sum of the credit entries.

Exhibit 3B-2

WEBWORK, INC.
Worksheet
For Month Ended December 31, 2019

	Unadjusted Trial Balance Debit	Unadjusted Trial Balance Credit	Adjustments Debit	Adjustments Credit	Adjusted Trial Balance Debit	Adjusted Trial Balance Credit	Income Statement Debit	Income Statement Credit	Balance Sheet Debit	Balance Sheet Credit
Cash................	$40,590				$40,590				$40,590	
Accounts receivable....	1,340		(g) $ 150		1,490				1,490	
Office supplies........	2,850			(a) $1,320	1,530				1,530	
Prepaid rent..........	10,800			(b) 1,800	9,000				9,000	
Office equipment......	32,400				32,400				32,400	
Accumulated depreciation— Office equipment.....				(c) 450		$ 450				$ 450
Accounts payable......		$ 2,850				2,850				2,850
Interest payable.......				(f) 300		300				300
Wages payable........				(e) 810		810				810
Unearned revenue.....		3,000	(d) 750			2,250				2,250
Notes payable........		36,000				36,000				36,000
Common stock........		30,000				30,000				30,000
Dividends............	500				500				500	
Fee revenue..........		18,250		(d) 750 (g) 150		19,150		$19,150		
Supplies expense......			(a) 1,320		1,320		1,320			
Wage expense........	1,620		(e) 810		2,430		$ 2,430			
Rent expense.........			(b) 1,800		1,800		1,800			
Depreciation expense...			(c) 450		450		450			
Interest expense.......			(f) 300		300		300			
Totals	$90,100	$90,100	$5,580	$5,580	$91,810	$91,810	6,300	19,150	85,510	72,660
Net income...........							12,850			12,850
Totals							$19,150	$19,150	$85,510	$85,510

4 **Adjusted Trial Balance**   Once the adjustments have been entered on the worksheet, there is sufficient information available to complete an adjusted trial balance. The adjusted figures are determined by combining horizontally, line by line, the amounts in the first four money columns—that is, the unadjusted trial balance and the adjustments. We review the calculations for two lines of **Exhibit 3B-2** to illustrate this process. The first line shows the Cash account with a debit amount of $40,590 in the unadjusted trial balance. Because Cash is not affected by any of the adjustments, the $40,590 appears in the debit column of the adjusted trial balance. On the third line, the Office Supplies account begins with a debit of $2,850 in the unadjusted trial balance and then shows a credit of $1,320 in the adjustments column. The $1,320 credit is subtracted from the $2,850 debit, and the remaining $1,530 is shown as a debit in the adjusted trial balance.

After calculating the adjusted trial balance amounts for all accounts on the worksheet, we total the two columns of the adjusted trial balance to verify that they are equal and that our worksheet is in balance.

5 **Extension of the Adjusted Trial Balance**   The amounts in the adjusted trial balance columns are extended into the two remaining pairs of columns as follows:

Expenses	→	Debit column of income statement
Revenues	→	Credit column of income statement
Assets and cash dividends	→	Debit column of balance sheet
Liabilities, Common Stock, Retained Earnings, and contra assets	→	Credit column of balance sheet

Expense and revenue account balances are extended to the income statement columns because these accounts will be used to prepare the income statement. Similarly, asset, contra asset, liability, and stockholders' equity accounts are balance sheet accounts, so their balances are extended to the balance sheet columns. In addition, the Dividends debit balance is extended to the balance sheet debit column, and the credit balances in the Common Stock and Retained Earnings accounts are extended to the balance sheet credit column. **Exhibit 3B-2** shows the extension of WebWork's adjusted trial balance to the worksheet's income statement and balance sheet columns. Once the proper extensions are made, the worksheet is complete except for balancing the two pairs of statement columns containing the adjusted balances.

6 **Balancing the Worksheet**   The first step in balancing is to add each of the income statement and balance sheet columns and record their respective totals on the same line as the totals of the adjusted trial balance columns. The difference between the total debits and total credits in the income statement columns is the difference between total revenues and total expenses—that is, the net income or net loss for the period. The net income or net loss must be the amount by which the debit and credit columns for the balance sheet differ. This is true because the Retained Earnings account balance, as extended, does not yet reflect the net income or net loss for the current period.

When revenues exceed expenses, we balance the two pairs of statement columns by adding the net income figure to both the debit column of the income statement and the credit column of the balance sheet. **Exhibit 3B-2** illustrates this balancing situation with WebWork's net income for December of $12,850. If expenses exceed revenues, we add the amount of net loss to the credit column of the income statement and to the debit column of the balance sheet. After we have added the net income (or loss) to the proper columns, we total and double-rule the four columns. The worksheet is now complete.

A completed worksheet aids in the last three steps of the accounting cycle—adjust, report, and close.

Adjust: The adjusting entries to be journalized and posted can be taken from the information in the adjustments columns. Because adjustments have first been entered on the worksheet, they can be reviewed for their financial effects before being journalized. Thus, the likelihood of incorrect adjustments appearing in the formal accounting records is reduced.

Report: The income statement can be prepared from the data in the income statement columns. Two pieces of information for the statement of stockholders' equity are available in the worksheet—the net income (or net loss) and dividends. The assets and liabilities needed for the balance sheet are available in the balance sheet columns (the ending Retained Earnings balance for the balance sheet is obtained from the statement of stockholders' equity).

Close: The closing entries to be journalized and posted can be prepared from data in the worksheet because it displays all of the temporary account balances. The revenue and expense account balances are shown in the income statement columns and the cash dividends account balance is shown in the balance sheet debit column.

SUMMARY OF LEARNING OBJECTIVES

LO1   Explain the accrual basis of accounting and contrast it with the cash basis with reference to revenue and expense recognition. (p. 120)

- Revenue is recognized on an accrual basis by the transfer of promised goods or services to customers in an amount that reflects the consideration to which the seller expects to be paid in exchange for those goods or services. This may be prior to the receipt of cash, at the same time as the receipt of cash, or following the receipt of cash.

- Expenses are matched against revenues in the same accounting period that the associated revenue is recognized. This may be prior to cash payment, at the same time as cash payment, or following cash payment.

- Revenue recognition and the corresponding matching of expenses may differ in timing on an accrual basis versus on a cash basis.

LO2   Describe the adjusting process. (p. 124)

- Adjusting entries are made to achieve the appropriate recognition of revenues and matching of expenses with revenues, and consist of four general types of adjustments:

  1. Allocating previously recorded assets to operating expenses to reflect the total expenses incurred during the period.

  2. Allocating previously recorded unearned revenue to revenue to reflect revenues earned during the period.

  3. Recording operating expenses to reflect expenses incurred during the period that have not yet been paid or recorded.

  4. Recording revenues to reflect revenue earned during the period that has not yet been received or recorded.

LO3   Illustrate deferral adjustments. (p. 125)

- Deferral adjustments deal with amounts that have previously been recorded on the balance sheet and require adjustment to their correct amounts.

- The adjustment decreases the balance sheet amount and increases an income statement amount.

- Deferral adjustments include adjustments to prepaid expenses and adjustments to unearned revenues.

LO4   Illustrate accrual adjustments. (p. 128)

- Accrual adjustments deal with amounts that have not been previously recorded in an account.

- The adjustment increases both a balance sheet account and an income statement account.

- Accrual adjustments include adjustments to accrue expenses and adjustments to accrue revenues.

LO5   Explain the adjusted trial balance and use it to prepare financial statements. (p. 132)

- An income statement, statement of stockholders' equity, balance sheet, and statement of cash flows may be prepared from an adjusted trial balance and other information.

- The stockholders' equity accounts may need to be reviewed to obtain information regarding the beginning balances and additional capital contributions during the period for the statement of stockholders' equity.

LO6   Describe the closing process and summarize the accounting cycle. (p. 136)

- *Closing the books* means closing the revenue, expense, and dividend accounts by transferring the balances to the Retained Earnings account.

LO7   Appendix 3A: Describe the process of closing to the Income Summary account and summarize the accounting cycle. (p. 143)

- *Closing the books* means closing the revenue, expense, and other temporary accounts. Revenue and expense account balances are transferred to the Income Summary account. The balances of the Income Summary account and the Dividends account are then transferred to the Retained Earnings account.

LO8   Appendix 3B: Explain how to use a worksheet in the adjusting and closing process. (p. 147)

A worksheet is an informal document that helps in compiling the information needed for the preparation of the financial statements. A worksheet is a tool of the accountant; it is not part of a company's formal accounting records. The worksheet consists of a heading, along with the following columns:

 a. Unadjusted trial balance   *d.* Income statement

 b. Adjustments   *e.* Balance sheet

 c. Adjusted trial balance

A completed worksheet aids in the last three steps of the accounting cycle: adjust, report, and close.

Concept	→	Method	→	Assessment	SUMMARY
When should sales revenue be recognized?		Apply the five steps of the revenue recognition process.		Early recognition of revenue overstates current period revenue; recognizing revenue too late understates current period revenue.	**TAKEAWAY 3.1**
When should expenses be recognized?		Recognized expenses with the related revenue in the same accounting period.		Early recognition of expenses overstates current period expenses; recognizing expenses too late understates current period expenses.	**TAKEAWAY 3.2**
When should an adjusting entry be made?		Individual account balances and transaction details such as contracts and agreements. Knowledge of the proper account balance is needed. Adjustments involve (1) allocating assets to expense, (2) allocating unearned revenue to revenue, (3) accruing expenses, or (4) accruing revenues.		Record an adjusting entry so that accounts are correctly reported; otherwise income and assets (and/or liabilities) are incorrectly reported.	**TAKEAWAY 3.3**

KEY TERMS

Accruals (p. 125)

Accrued expenses (p. 128)

Accrued revenue (p. 130)

Accumulated depreciation (p. 127)

Adjusted trial balance (p. 132)

Adjusting entries (p. 125)

Book value (p. 127)

Carrying value (p. 127)

Closing procedures (p. 136, 143)

Closing process (p. 136, 143)

Closing the books (p. 136, 143)

Contra accounts (p. 127)

Deferrals (p. 125)

Deferred revenue (p. 127)

Depreciation (p. 126)

Earnings quality (p. 139)

Permanent accounts (p. 136, 143)

Post-closing trial balance (p. 137, 145)

Straight-line depreciation (p. 127)

Temporary accounts (p. 136, 143)

Unadjusted trial balance (p. 124)

Unearned revenue (p. 127)

Worksheet (p. 147)

Assignments with the ⓜ logo in the margin are available in 𝒎𝒚 BusinessCourse.
See the Preface of the book for details.

SELF-STUDY QUESTIONS

(Answers to the Self-Study Questions are available at the end of the chapter.)

1. **Which of the following is an example of an adjusting entry?**
   a.   Recording the purchase of supplies on account
   b.   Recording depreciation expense on a truck
   c.   Recording the billing of customers for services rendered
   d.   Recording the payment of wages to employees

   LO3

2. **An adjusting entry to record utilities used during a month for which no bill has yet been received is an example of**
   a.   Allocating assets to expense to reflect the actual operating expenses incurred during the accounting period
   b.   Allocating revenues received in advance to revenue to reflect actual revenues earned during the accounting period

   LO4

c.   Accruing expenses to reflect expenses incurred during the accounting period that are not yet paid or recorded

d.   Accruing revenues to reflect revenues earned during the accounting period that are not yet received or recorded

LO6 3. **Which of the following is not an example of a closing entry?**
a.   Close each revenue account to the Retained Earnings account
b.   Close each expense account to the Retained Earnings account
c.   Close the Dividends account to the Retained Earnings account
d.   Close Unearned Revenue to Retained Earnings

LO1 4. **Which of the following transactions does not affect total assets, total liabilities, or total stockholders' equity on the balance sheet?**
a.   Purchasing $500 supplies on account
b.   Paying a $3,000 note payable
c.   Collecting $4,000 from customers on account
d.   Payment of an $800 dividend

LO5 5. **The beginning and ending balances of retained earnings for the year were $30,000 and $41,000, respectively. If yearly dividends totaled $3,000, what was the net income or net loss for the year?**
a. $8,000 net loss
b. $14,000 net income
c. $2,000 net income
d. $8,000 net income

LO2 6. **The ending balance of the Accounts Receivable account was $7,800. Services billed to customers for the period were $21,500, and collections on account from customers were $23,600. What was the beginning balance of Accounts Receivable?**
a. $33,500   c. $9,900
b. $14,100   d. $33,100

LO1 7. **Kelly Corporation received an advanced payment of $30,000 in 2018 from Rufus Company for consulting services. Kelly performed half of the consulting in 2018 and the remainder in 2019. Kelly reports using the accrual basis of accounting. How much revenue from this consulting project will Kelly report in 2018?**
a. $20,000   c. $0
b. $10,000   d. $15,000

QUESTIONS

1. Why is the adjusting step of the accounting cycle necessary?
2. What four different types of adjustments are frequently necessary at the close of an accounting period? Provide an example of each type.
3. On January 1, Prepaid Insurance was debited with the cost of a two-year premium in the amount of $3,744. What adjusting entry should be made on January 31 before the January financial statements are prepared?
4. What is a contra account? What contra account is used in reporting the book value of a depreciable asset?
5. At the beginning of January, the first month of the accounting year, the Supplies account had a debit balance of $825. During January, purchases of $260 of supplies were debited to the account. Although only $530 of supplies was on hand at the end of January, the necessary adjusting entry was omitted. How will the omission affect (a) the income statement for January and (b) the balance sheet prepared as of January 31?
6. The publisher of *International View*, a monthly magazine, received two-year subscriptions totaling $12,240 on January 1. (a) What entry should be made to record the receipt of the $12,240? (b) What entry should be made at the end of January before financial statements are prepared for the month?
7. Globe Travel Agency pays an employee $600 in wages each Friday for a five-day work week ending on that day. The last Friday of January falls on January 27. What adjusting entry should be made on January 31, the fiscal year-end?
8. The Bayou Company earns interest amounting to $425 per month on its investments. The company receives the interest every six months, on December 31 and June 30. Monthly financial statements are prepared. What adjusting entry should be made on January 31?
9. Define *permanent account*. Provide an example.
10. Define *temporary account*. Provide an example.

11. Which group of accounts is closed at the end of the accounting year? Why?

12. What is the purpose of a post-closing trial balance? Which of the following accounts should not appear in the post-closing trial balance: Cash, Unearned Revenue, Dividends, Depreciation Expense, Utilities Payable, Supplies Expense, Retained Earnings?

SHORT EXERCISES

SE3-1. Steps in the Accounting Cycle Listed below, out of order, are the steps in an accounting cycle.   **LO6**

1. Prepare the unadjusted trial balance.
2. Post journal entries to general ledger accounts.
3. Analyze transactions from source documents.
4. Journalize and post adjusting entries.
5. Prepare the financial statements.
6. Record transactions in a journal.
7. Prepare the post-closing trial balance.
8. Prepare the adjusted trial balance.
9. Journalize and post closing entries.

(a) Place the numbers from the above list in the order in which the steps in the accounting cycle are performed, and (b) identify the steps in the accounting cycle that occur daily.

SE3-2. Accrual Accounting Evan Corporation provided consulting services for Kensington Company   **LO1** in 2018. Evan incurred costs of $60,000 associated with the consulting and billed Kensington $130,000. Evan paid $40,000 of its costs in 2018 and the remaining $20,000 in 2019. Evan received $45,000 of its billing in 2018. Kensington paid the remaining $85,000 in 2019. Evan reports on the accrual basis of accounting. How much is Evan's 2018 and 2019 profit related to the Kensington consulting?

SE3-3. Adjusting Accounts MacKenzie Enterprises includes the following accounts in its general ledger.   **LO2** Explain why each of these accounts may need to be adjusted.

    a. Rent Payable
    b. Unearned Revenue
    c. Prepaid Subscriptions
    d. Depreciation Expense

SE3-4. Adjusting Entry for Depreciation Cowley Company just completed its first year of operations.   **LO3** The December 31 equipment account has a balance of $20,000. There is no balance in the Accumulated Depreciation—Equipment account or in the Depreciation Expense account. The accountant estimates the yearly equipment depreciation to be $5,000. Prepare the required adjusting entry to record the yearly depreciation for equipment.

SE3-5. Adjusting Entry for Prepaid Insurance Cooper Inc. recorded the purchase of a three-year insur-   **LO3** ance policy on July 1 in the amount of $4,800 by debiting Prepaid Insurance and crediting Cash. Prepare the necessary December 31 year-end adjusting entry.

SE3-6. Accrual Adjusting Entries Prepare adjusting journal entries for Sparky Electronics for the fol-   **LO3, 4** lowing items:

    a. Salaries for employees in the amount of $2,750 have not been paid.
    b. Interest expense of $1,400 for an outstanding note.
    c. Work performed but not yet billed for $3,800.

SE3-7. Analyze an Adjusted Trial Balance The trial balance of Fisher Supplies contains the following   **LO3, 4** balance sheet accounts that require adjustment. Identify the likely income statement account that   will be used to adjust these accounts.

    a. Prepaid Insurance
    b. Accumulated Depreciation
    c. Supplies
    d. Unearned Revenue
    e. Interest Payable

LO5 **SE3-8.** **Prepare an Income Statement from an Adjusted Trial Balance** The Decade Company's adjusted trial balance contains the following balances as of December 31: Retained Earnings $8,500; Dividends $2,000; Sales $22,000; Cost of Goods Sold $8,000; Selling and Administrative Expenses $3,000; Interest Expense $1,500. Prepare an income statement for the year.

LO6 **SE3-9.** **Prepare Closing Entries to Retained Earnings** Use the data from SE3-8 to prepare the closing entries for The Decade Company. Close the temporary accounts straight to retained earnings. The balance of $8,500 in the retained earnings account is from the beginning of the year. What is the ending retained earnings balance after posting the closing entries?

LO5 **SE3-10.** **Identify Financial Statements from Adjusted Trial Balance Accounts** Trownel Corp reports the following accounts in its adjusted trial balance. Identify which financial statement each account would appear on:

a. Cash
b. Sales
c. Accounts Payable
d. Unearned Revenue
e. Retained Earnings
f. Interest Income

LO7
(Appendix 3A) **SE3-11.** **Prepare Closing Entries Using the Income Summary Account** Use the data from SE3-8 to prepare the closing entries for The Decade Company. Close the temporary accounts to income summary. The balance of $8,500 in the retained earnings account is from the beginning of the year. What is the ending retained earnings balance after posting the closing entries?

LO8
(Appendix 3B) **SE3-12.** **The Accounting Worksheet** The adjusted trial balance section of Menlo Company's worksheet shows a $1,500 debit balance in utility expense. At the end of the accounting period the accounting manager accrues an additional $300 of utility expense for the last week of the period. This will result in the following amounts appearing on Menlo's worksheet for utilities expense:

a. $300 debit adjustment; $1,800 debit adjusted trial balance; $1,800 debit balance sheet
b. $300 debit adjustment; $1,800 debit adjusted trial balance; $1,800 debit income statement
c. $300 credit adjustment; $1,200 debit adjusted trial balance; $1,800 debit income statement
d. $300 credit adjustment; $1,800 debit adjusted trial balance; $1,800 debit income statement

EXERCISES—SET A

LO4 **E3-1A.** **Transaction Entries and Adjusting Entries** Deluxe Building Services offers janitorial services on both a contract basis and an hourly basis. On January 1, Deluxe collected $42,000 in advance on a six-month contract for work to be performed evenly during the next six months.

a. Provide the general journal entry on January 1 to record the receipt of $42,000 for contract work.
b. Provide the adjusting entry to be made on January 31, for the contract work done during January.
c. At January 31, a total of 40 hours of hourly rate janitor work was unbilled. The billing rate is $25 per hour. Provide the adjusting entry needed on January 31. (*Note:* The firm uses the account Fees Receivable to reflect amounts due but not yet billed.)

LO3, 4 **E3-2A.** **Adjusting Entries** Selected accounts of Ideal Properties Inc., a real estate management firm, are shown below as of January 31, before any adjusting entries have been made:

	Debit	Credit
Prepaid insurance	$7,200	
Supplies	2,100	
Office equipment	7,680	
Unearned rent revenue		$ 5,400
Salaries expense	3,250	
Rent revenue		16,000

Monthly financial statements are prepared. Using the following information, record in a general journal the adjusting entries necessary on January 31:

a. Prepaid Insurance represents a three-year premium paid on January 1.
b. Supplies of $975 were on hand January 31.
c. Office equipment is expected to last eight years. Depreciation is recorded monthly.

    d.   On January 1, the firm collected six months' rent in advance from a tenant renting space for $925 per month.

    e.   Accrued salaries not recorded as of January 31 are $625.

E3-3A. **Adjusting Entries** For each of the following unrelated situations, prepare the necessary adjusting entry in general journal form: **LO3, 4**

    a.   Unrecorded depreciation on equipment is $800.

    b.   The Supplies account has a balance of $3,100. Supplies on hand at the end of the period totaled $1,200.

    c.   On the date for preparing financial statements, an estimated utilities expense of $425 has been incurred, but no utility bill has been received.

    d.   On the first day of the current month, rent for four months was paid and recorded as a $2,800 debit to Prepaid Rent and a $2,800 credit to Cash. Monthly statements are now being prepared.

    e.   Nine months ago, Solid Insurance Company sold a one-year policy to a customer and recorded the receipt of the premium by debiting Cash for $800 and crediting Unearned Premium Revenue for $800. No adjusting entries have been prepared during the nine-month period. Annual financial statements are now being prepared.

    f.   At the end of the accounting period, employee wages of $1,050 have been incurred but not paid.

    g.   At the end of the accounting period, $411 of interest has been earned but not yet received on notes receivable that are held.

E3-4A. **Statement of Stockholders' Equity** On January 1, the credit balance of the Retained Earnings account was $51,000. The company's Common Stock account had an opening balance of $65,000, and $8,000 in new capital contributions were made during the year. On December 31, at year-end, the Dividends account had a debit balance of $12,000 before closing. The income statement shows net income of $30,500. Prepare a statement of stockholders' equity for Stede & Company, architectural design firm.   **LO5**

E3-5A. **Closing Entries** The adjusted trial balance prepared as of December 31, for Phyllis Howell & Company, Consultant, contains the following revenue and expense accounts: **LO6**

	Debit	Credit
Service fees earned		$91,000
Rent expense	$20,800	
Salaries expense	52,000	
Supplies expense	6,000	
Depreciation expense	11,300	
Retained earnings		72,000
Dividends	10,000	

Prepare journal entries to close the accounts directly to Retained Earnings. After these entries are posted, what is the balance in the Retained Earnings account?

E3-6A. **Revenue Recognition** Identify the proper point to recognize revenue for each of the following transactions.   **LO1**

    a.   Honey Industries sells a machine in January with terms of no payment due until six months later.

    b.   Platt Company collects an advance deposit of $700 in July toward the purchase of a $3,000 piece of equipment that is delivered to the customer the following September.

    c.   Naomi Corporation receives payment in October at the time of delivery of a rebuilt engine for a tractor.

E3-7A. **Expense Matching** Identify the proper point to recognize expense for each of the following transactions.   **LO1**

    a.   Kat Inc. purchases on credit six custom sofas for $800 each in June. Two of the sofas are sold for $1,200 each in June. One of the sofas is sold for $1,200 in July and the remaining three sofas are sold for $1,500 each in August. All sales are for cash. Kat pays its supplier in July.

    b.   Kira Co. purchases $500 of supplies in January. Half the supplies are used in January with the remaining half used in February.

    c.   Joseph Co. purchases $2,000 of inventory for cash in September. The entire inventory is sold in November.

LO6 **E3-8A. Closing Entries** In the midst of closing procedures, Echo Corporation's accountant became ill and was hospitalized. You have volunteered to complete the closing of the books. You find that all the revenue and expense accounts have zero balances. The Dividends account has a debit balance of $17,000. The Retained Earnings account has a beginning credit balance of $120,000. Expenses totaled $308,500, and revenues totaled $347,400. Prepare journal entries to complete the closing procedures as of year-end directly to Retained Earnings. After these entries are posted, what is the balance in the Retained Earnings account?

LO3, 4 **E3-9A. Analysis of Adjusted Data** Selected T-account balances for Coyle Company are shown below as of January 31; adjusting entries have already been posted. The firm uses a calendar-year accounting period and makes monthly adjustments.

Supplies	Supplies Expense
Jan. 31 . . . . . Bal. 800	Jan. 31 . . . . . Bal. 960

Prepaid Insurance	Insurance Expense
Jan. 31 . . . . . Bal. 492	Jan. 31 . . . . . . Bal. 82

Wages Payable	Wages Expense
Bal. 650 . . . . . Jan. 31	Jan. 31 . . . .Bal. 3,300

Truck	Accumulated Depreciation—Truck
Jan. 31 . . . .Bal. 8,700	Bal. 2,610 . . . . Jan. 31

a. If the amount in Supplies Expense represents the January 31 adjustment for the supplies used in January, and $825 worth of supplies were purchased during January, what was the January 1 balance of Supplies?

b. The amount in the Insurance Expense account represents the adjustment made at January 31 for January insurance expense. If the original insurance premium was for one year, what was the amount of the premium and on what date did the insurance policy start?

c. If we assume that no balance existed in Wages Payable or Wages Expense on January 1, how much cash was paid as wages during January?

d. If the truck has a useful life of five years, what is the monthly amount of depreciation expense and how many months has Coyle owned the truck?

LO3, 4 **E3-10A. Analysis of the Impact of Adjustments on Financial Statements** At the end of the first month of operations, the Stephan Company's accountant prepared financial statements that showed the following amounts:

Assets.	$60,000
Liabilities.	20,000
Stockholders' equity	40,000
Net income	9,000

In preparing the statements, the accountant overlooked the following items:

a. Depreciation for the month, $925.
b. Service revenue earned but unbilled at month-end, $1,500.
c. Employee wages earned but unpaid at month-end, $410.

Determine the correct amounts of assets, liabilities, and stockholders' equity at month-end and net income for the month.

E3-11A. Closing Entries The adjusted trial balance of the Petal Corporation, prepared as of December 31, contains the following accounts:

LO6

	Debit	Credit
Service fees earned		$87,500
Interest income		2,600
Salaries expense	$41,800	
Advertising expense	6,300	
Depreciation expense	8,700	
Income tax expense	11,000	
Common stock		75,000
Retained earnings		60,000
Cash dividends	15,000	

Prepare journal entries to close the accounts directly to Retained Earnings. After these entries are posted, what is the ending balance in the Retained Earnings account?

E3-12A. Closing Entries Use the information provided in E3-5A to prepare journal entries to close the accounts using the Income Summary account. After these entries are posted, what is the balance in the Retained Earnings account?

LO7
(Appendix 3A)

E3-13A. Closing Entries In the midst of closing procedures, Park Corporation's accountant became ill and was hospitalized. You have volunteered to complete the closing of the books, and you find that all revenue and expense accounts have zero balances and that the Income Summary account has a single debit entry for $320,000 and a single credit entry for $352,000. The Dividends account has a debit balance of $17,500, and the Retained Earnings account has a credit balance of $120,000. Prepare journal entries to complete the closing procedures as of year-end.

LO7
(Appendix 3A)

E3-14A. Worksheet Identify each of the 10 amount columns of the worksheet and indicate to which column the adjusted balance of the following accounts would be extended:

LO8
(Appendix 3B)

a.	Accounts Receivable	*f.*	Rent Receivable
b.	Accumulated Depreciation	*g.*	Prepaid Insurance
c.	Dividends	*h.*	Service Fees Earned
d.	Wages Payable	*i.*	Common Stock
e.	Depreciation Expense	*j.*	Retained Earnings

E3-15A. Closing Entries Use the information provided in E3-11A to prepare journal entries to close the accounts using the Income Summary account. After these entries are posted, what is the balance in the Retained Earnings account?

LO7
(Appendix 3A)

E3-16A. Worksheet The adjusted trial balance columns of a worksheet for Bond Corporation are shown below. The worksheet is prepared for the year ended December 31.

LO8
(Appendix 3B)

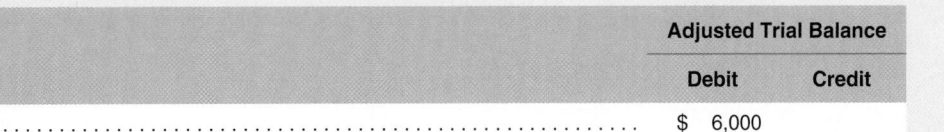

	Adjusted Trial Balance	
	Debit	Credit
Cash	$ 6,000	
Accounts receivable	6,500	
Equipment	83,000	
Accumulated depreciation		$ 14,000
Notes payable		12,500
Common stock		48,000
Retained earnings		20,600
Cash dividends	8,000	
Service fees earned		71,900
Rent expense	18,000	
Salaries expense	38,500	
Depreciation expense	7,000	
Totals	$167,000	$167,000

Complete the worksheet by (a) entering the adjusted trial balance, (b) putting in the worksheet income statement and balance sheet columns, (c) extending the adjusted trial balance to the income statement and balance sheet columns, and (d) balancing the worksheet.

EXERCISES—SET B

LO4 **E3-1B. Transaction Entry and Adjusting Entries** Burne Building Services offers janitorial services on both a contract basis and an hourly basis. On January 1, Burne collected $90,000 in advance on a six-month contract for work to be performed evenly during the next six months.

    a. Provide the general journal entry on January 1 to record the receipt of $90,000 for contract work.

    b. Provide the adjusting entry to be made on January 31, for the contract work done during January.

    c. At January 31, a total of 35 hours of hourly rate janitor work was unbilled. The billing rate is $31 per hour. Provide the adjusting entry needed on January 31. (*Note:* The firm uses the account Fees Receivable to reflect amounts due but not yet billed.)

LO3, 4 **E3-2B. Adjusting Entries** Judy Rock began Rock Refinishing Service on July 1. Selected accounts are shown below as of July 31, before any adjusting entries have been made:

	Debit	Credit
Prepaid rent	$6,000	
Prepaid advertising.	930	
Supplies	3,000	
Unearned refinishing fees.		$ 800
Refinishing fees revenue		2,500

Using the following information, record in a general journal the necessary adjusting entries on July 31:

    a. On July 1, the firm paid one year's rent of $6,000.

    b. On July 1, $930 was paid to a local newspaper for an advertisement to run daily for the months of July, August, and September.

    c. Supplies on hand at July 31 total $1,100.

    d. At July 31, refinishing services of $975 have been performed but not yet billed to customers. The firm uses the account Fees Receivable to reflect amounts due but not yet billed.

    e. One customer paid $1,100 in advance for a refinishing project. At July 31, the project is one-half complete.

LO3, 4 **E3-3B. Adjusting Entries** For each of the following unrelated situations, prepare the necessary adjusting entry in general journal form:

    a. Unrecorded depreciation on equipment is $1,850.

    b. The Supplies account has a balance of $5,000. Supplies on hand at the end of the period total $2,500.

    c. On the date for preparing financial statements, an estimated utilities expense of $550 has been incurred, but no utility bill has been received.

    d. On the first day of the current month, rent for four months was paid and recorded as a $2,800 debit to Prepaid Rent and a $2,800 credit to Cash. Monthly statements are now being prepared.

    e. Nine months ago, Macke Insurance Company sold a one-year policy to a customer and recorded the receipt of the premium by debiting Cash for $624 and crediting Unearned Premium Revenue for $624. No adjusting entries have been prepared during the nine-month period. Annual financial statements are now being prepared.

    f. At the end of the accounting period, employee wages of $700 have been incurred but not paid.

    g. At the end of the accounting period, $800 of interest has been earned but not yet received on notes receivable that are held.

LO5 **E3-4B. Statement of Stockholders' Equity** On January 1, the credit balance of the Retained Earnings account was $60,000. The company's common stock account had an opening balance of $85,000 and new contributions during the year totaled $9,000. On December 31, at year-end, the Dividends account had a debit balance of $6,500. The income statement shows net income of $40,000. Prepare a statement of stockholders' equity for Kim & Company, architectural design firm.

E3-5B.   Closing Entries   The adjusted trial balance prepared December 31, for Cheryl Lester & Company, shipping agent, contains the following accounts: **LO6**

	Debit	Credit
Commissions earned		$94,900
Wages expense	$36,000	
Insurance expense	3,000	
Utilities expense	9,500	
Depreciation expense	9,800	
Dividends	12,000	
Common stock		90,000
Retained earnings		22,100

Prepare journal entries to close the accounts directly to Retained Earnings. After these entries are posted, what is the ending balance in the Retained Earnings account?

E3-6B.   Revenue Recognition   Identify the proper point to recognize revenue for each of the following transactions.   **LO1**

    a.   Creed Industries sells a machine in January with terms of 50 percent due on delivery in January and the remaining balance due three months later.

    b.   Pia Company collects an advance deposit of $950 in May toward the purchase of a $4,000 piece of equipment that is delivered to the customer the following month.

    c.   Juan Corporation receives payment in March at the time of delivery of a rebuilt engine for a forklift.

E3-7B.   Expense Matching   Identify the proper point to recognize expenses for each of the following transactions.   **LO1**

    a.   Julio Inc. purchases for cash five custom dining tables for $1,200 each in March. Three tables are later sold for $1,750 each in April, and the remaining two tables are sold for $1,500 each in May.

    b.   Craig Company purchases $400 of office supplies that are both paid for and used in August.

    c.   Kerra Company purchases $500 of inventory on account in July. The inventory is sold for $650 in August. Kerra pays its suppliers the $500 due in September.

E3-8B.   Closing Entries   In the midst of closing procedures, La Verne Corporation's accountant became ill and was hospitalized. You have volunteered to complete the closing of the books. You find that all the revenue and expense accounts have zero balances. The Dividends account has a debit balance of $35,000. The Retained Earnings account has a beginning credit balance of $191,000. Expenses totaled $328,800, and revenues totaled $347,400. Prepare journal entries to complete the closing procedures as of year-end directly to Retained Earnings. After these entries are posted, what is the balance in the Retained Earnings account?   **LO6**

E3-9B.   Analysis of Adjusted Data   Selected T-account balances for the Rome Company are shown below as of January 31; adjusting entries have already been posted. The firm uses a calendar-year accounting period and makes monthly adjustments.   **LO3, 4**

Supplies		Supplies Expense	
Jan. 31 . . Bal. 1,050		Jan. 31 . . Bal. 2,540	

Prepaid Insurance		Insurance Expense	
Jan. 31 . . . Bal. 910		Jan. 31 . . . Bal. 182	

Wages Payable		Wages Expense	
	Bal. 650 . . . Jan. 31	Jan. 31 . . Bal. 2,700	

Truck		Accumulated Depreciation—Truck	
Jan. 31 . . Bal. 8,700			Bal. 2,610 . . Jan. 31

    a.   If the amount in Supplies Expense represents the January 31 adjustment for the supplies used in January, and $700 worth of supplies were purchased during January, what was the January 1 balance of Supplies?

b. The amount in the Insurance Expense account represents the adjustment made at January 31 for January insurance expense. If the original insurance premium was for one year, what was the amount of the premium and on what date did the insurance policy start?

c. If we assume that no balance existed in Wages Payable or Wages Expense on January 1, how much cash was paid as wages during January?

d. If the truck has a useful life of five years, what is the monthly amount of depreciation expense and how many months has Rome owned the truck?

LO3, 4

E3-10B. Analysis of the Impact of Adjustments on Financial Statements At the end of the first month of operations, the Lamar Company's accountant prepared financial statements that showed the following amounts:

Assets.	$90,000
Liabilities.	30,000
Stockholders' equity	50,000
Net income	11,000

In preparing the statements, the accountant overlooked the following items:

a. Depreciation for the month, $4,500.

b. Service revenue earned but unbilled at month-end, $1,850.

c. Employee wages earned but unpaid at month-end, $450.

Determine the correct amounts of assets, liabilities, and stockholders' equity at month-end and net income for the month.

LO6

E3-11B. Closing Entries The adjusted trial balance of the Murray Corporation, prepared December 31, contains the following accounts:

	Debit	Credit
Service fees earned		$102,500
Interest income.		7,000
Salaries expense	$49,800	
Advertising expense.	4,300	
Depreciation expense.	9,500	
Income tax expense	1,100	
Common stock		80,000
Retained earnings		57,700
Cash dividends.	17,000	

Prepare journal entries to close the accounts directly to Retained Earnings. After these entries are posted, what is the ending balance in the Retained Earnings account?

LO7
(Appendix 3A)

E3-12B. Closing Entries Use the information provided in E3-5B to prepare journal entries to close the accounts using the Income Summary account. After these entries are posted, what is the balance in the Retained Earnings account?

LO7
(Appendix 3A)

E3-13B. Closing Entries In the midst of closing procedures, La Verne Corporation's accountant became ill. You have volunteered to complete the closing of the books, and you find that all revenue and expense accounts have zero balances and that the Income Summary account has a single debit entry for $318,800 and a single credit entry for $370,000. The Cash Dividends account has a debit balance of $14,000, and the Retained Earnings account has a credit balance of $117,000. Prepare journal entries to complete the closing procedures as of year-end.

LO8
(Appendix 3B)

E3-14B. Worksheet Identify each of the 10 amount columns of the worksheet and indicate to which column the adjusted balance of the following accounts would be extended:

a. Accounts Receivable

b. Accumulated Depreciation

c. Dividends

d. Salaries Payable

e. Wages Expense

f. Interest Receivable

g. Prepaid Rent

h. Service Fees Earned

i. Common Stock

j. Retained Earnings

E3-15B. Closing Entries Use the information provided in E3-11B to prepare journal entries to close the accounts using the Income Summary account. After these entries are posted, what is the balance in the Retained Earnings account?

LO7
(Appendix 3A)

E3-16B. Worksheet The adjusted trial balance columns of a worksheet for Levitt Corporation are shown below. The worksheet is prepared for the year ended December 31.

LO8
(Appendix 3B)

	Adjusted Trial Balance	
	Debit	Credit
Cash	$ 16,000	
Accounts receivable	18,500	
Equipment	76,000	
Accumulated depreciation		$ 24,000
Notes payable		16,000
Common stock		43,000
Retained earnings		20,600
Cash dividends	8,000	
Service fees earned		79,000
Rent expense	18,000	
Salaries expense	37,100	
Depreciation expense	9,000	
Totals	$182,600	$182,600

Complete the worksheet by (a) entering the adjusted trial balance, (b) putting in the worksheet income statement and balance sheet columns, (c) extending the adjusted trial balance to the income statement and balance sheet columns, and (d) balancing the worksheet.

PROBLEMS—SET A

P3-1A. Transaction Entries, Posting, Trial Balance, and Adjusting Entries Mark Gold opened Gold Roofing Service on April 1. Transactions for April are as follows:

LO3, 4

1 Gold contributed $15,000 of his personal funds in exchange for common stock to begin the business.
2 Purchased a used truck for $6,100 cash.
3 Purchased ladders and other equipment for a total of $3,100, paid $1,000 cash, with the balance due in 30 days.
4 Paid two-year premium on liability insurance, $6,000.
5 Purchased supplies on account, $1,200.
6 Received an advance payment of $1,800 from a customer for roof repair work to be done during April and May.
7 Billed customers for roofing services, $9,000.
8 Collected $6,500 on account from customers.
9 Paid bill for truck fuel used in April, $75.
10 Paid April newspaper advertising, $100.
11 Paid assistants' wages, $4,500.
12 Billed customers for roofing services, $5,000.

Required
a. Set up a general ledger with the following accounts: Cash; Accounts Receivable; Supplies; Prepaid Insurance; Trucks; Accumulated Depreciation—Trucks; Equipment; Accumulated Depreciation—Equipment; Accounts Payable; Unearned Roofing Fees; Common Stock; Roofing Fees Earned; Fuel Expense; Advertising Expense; Wages Expense; Insurance Expense; Supplies Expense; Depreciation Expense—Trucks; and Depreciation Expense—Equipment.
b. Record these transactions in the general journal and post to the ledger accounts.
c. Prepare an unadjusted trial balance as of April 30.

d.   Prepare the journal entries to adjust the books for insurance expense, supplies expense, depreciation expense on the truck, depreciation expense on the equipment, and roofing fees earned. Supplies on hand on April 30 amounted to $950. Depreciation for April was $155 on the truck and $35 on the equipment. One-fourth of the roofing fee received in advance was earned by April 30. Post the adjusting entries.

LO3, 4   **P3-2A.**   **Transaction Entries, Posting, Trial Balance, and Adjusting Entries**   The Healthy Catering Service had the following transactions in July, its first month of operations:

1   Kelly Foster contributed $18,000 of personal funds to the business in exchange for common stock.
2   Purchased the following items for cash from a catering firm that was going out of business (make a compound entry): delivery van, $3,780; equipment, $3,240; and supplies, $1,700.
3   Paid premium on a one-year liability insurance policy, $2,160.
4   Entered into a contract with a local service club to cater weekly luncheon meetings for one year at a fee of $1,000 per month. Received eight months' fees in advance.
5   Paid rent for July, August, and September, $2,340.
6   Paid employees' two weeks' wages (five-day week), $2,400.
7   Billed customers for services rendered, $5,000.
8   Purchased supplies on account, $3,000.
9   Paid employees' two weeks' wages, $1,800.
10   Paid July bill for gas, oil, and repairs on delivery van, $850.
11   Collected $3,700 from customers on account.
12   Billed customers for services rendered, $5,400.
13   Foster received a $2,000 dividend.

Required

a.   Set up a general ledger that includes the following accounts: Cash; Accounts Receivable; Supplies; Prepaid Rent; Prepaid Insurance; Delivery Van; Accumulated Depreciation—Delivery Van; Equipment; Accumulated Depreciation—Equipment; Accounts Payable; Wages Payable; Unearned Catering Fees; Common Stock; Dividends; Catering Fees Revenue; Wages Expense; Rent Expense; Supplies Expense; Insurance Expense; Delivery Van Expense; Depreciation Expense—Delivery Van; and Depreciation Expense—Equipment.

b.   Record July transactions in the general journal and post to the ledger accounts.

c.   Prepare an unadjusted trial balance as of July 31.

d.   Record adjusting journal entries in the general journal and post to the ledger accounts. The following information is available on July 31:

  Supplies on hand, $1,600
  Accrued wages, $550
  Estimated life of delivery van, three years (Assume van was purchased July 1)
  Estimated life of equipment, six years (Assume equipment was purchased July 1)

Also, make any necessary adjusting entries for insurance, rent, and catering fees indicated by the July transactions. Assume original transactions occurred July 1.

LO3, 4   **P3-3A.**   **Trial Balance and Adjusting Entries**   Image, Inc., a commercial photography studio, has just completed its first full year of operations on December 31. The general ledger account balances before year-end adjustments follow. No adjusting entries have been made to the accounts at any time during the year. Assume that all balances are normal.

Cash	$ 2,150	Accounts payable	$ 2,710
Accounts receivable	3,600	Unearned photography fees	2,600
Prepaid rent	12,600	Common stock	24,000
Prepaid insurance	2,970	Photography fees earned	34,480
Supplies	5,250	Wages expense	11,000
Equipment	22,800	Utilities expense	3,420

An analysis of the firm's records discloses the following items:

1.   Photography services of $1,250 have been rendered, but customers have not yet been billed. The firm uses the account Fees Receivable to reflect amounts due but not yet billed.
2.   The equipment, purchased January 1, has an estimated life of 10 years.

Assets		Liabilities	
Cash	$ 4,800	Accounts payable	$12,000
Accounts receivable	14,700		
Land	67,000	**Stockholders' Equity**	
		Common stock	27,000
		Retained earnings	47,500
		Total Liabilities and	
Total Assets	$86,500	Stockholders' Equity	$86,500

a. At the end of the year, Azuza had the following assets and liabilities: Cash, $7,800; Accounts Receivable, $17,400; Land, $67,000; and Accounts Payable, $5,500; and Common Stock, $27,000. Prepare a year-end balance sheet for Azuza's Parking Lots.

b. Assume that stockholders did not invest any money in the business during the year but received $8,000 as a dividend; what was Azuza's net income or net loss the year?

LO5 P3-11A. Determination of Retained Earnings and Net Income The following information appears in the records of Stern Corporation at the end of the year:

Accounts receivable	$ 25,000	Retained earnings	$?
Accounts payable	13,000	Supplies	9,000
Cash	8,000	Equipment	138,000
Common stock	115,000		

a. Calculate the amount of retained earnings at the end of the year.

b. Using your answer from part a, if the amount of the retained earnings at the beginning of the year was $30,000, and $15,000 in dividends was paid during the year, what was the company's net income for the year?

4, 5, 6 P3-12A. Transaction Analysis, Trial Balance, and Financial Statements Angela Mica operates the Mica Dance Studio. On June 1, the business's general ledger contained the following information:

Cash	$ 5,930	Accounts payable	$ 480
Accounts receivable	8,400	Notes payable	3,980
		Common stock	7,870
		Retained earnings	2,000
	$14,330		$14,330

The following transactions occurred during the month of June:

1 Paid June rent for practice studio, $875.
2 Paid June piano rental, $240 (Rent Expense).
3 Collected $5,320 from students on account.
4 Borrowed $1,500 and signed a promissory note payable due in six months.
5 Billed students for June instructional fees, $7,500.
6 Paid interest for June on notes payable, $30.
7 Paid $375 for advertising ballet performances.
8 Paid costume rental, $550 (Rent Expense).
9 Collected $2,100 admission fees from ballet performances given during the month.
10 Paid $480 owed on account.
11 Received invoice for June utilities, to be paid in July, $510.
12 Paid stockholders $900 cash as a dividend.
13 Purchased piano for $5,500 cash, to be used in business starting in July.

Required

a. Set up accounts for the general ledger with June 1 balances and enter the beginning balances. Also provide the following accounts: Piano; Dividends; Instructional Fees Earned; Performance Revenue; Rent Expense; Utilities Expense; Advertising Expense; and Interest Expense. Record the listed transactions in the accounts.

b. Prepare a trial balance as of June 30.

c. Prepare an income statement for the month of June.

3. Utilities expense for December is estimated to be $750, but the bill will not arrive until January of next year.
4. The balance in Prepaid Rent represents the amount paid on January 1, for a two-year lease on the studio.
5. In November, customers paid $2,600 in advance for pictures to be taken for the holiday season. When received, these fees were credited to Unearned Photography Fees. By December 31, all fees are earned.
6. A three-year insurance premium paid on January 1 was debited to Prepaid Insurance.
7. Supplies on hand at December 31 are $1,750.
8. At December 31, wages expense of $650 has been incurred but not paid.

Required

a. Prove that the sum of the debits equals the sum of the credits for Image's unadjusted account balances by preparing an unadjusted trial balance as of December 31.

b. Record adjusting entries in the general journal.

P3-4A. Adjusting Entries Foote Carpet Cleaners ended its first month of operations on June 30. Monthly **LO3, 4** financial statements will be prepared. The unadjusted account balances are as follows:

FOOTE CARPET CLEANERS Unadjusted Trial Balance June 30, 2018		
	Debit	Credit
Cash	$ 1,180	
Accounts receivable	450	
Prepaid rent	3,100	
Supplies	2,520	
Equipment	4,440	
Accounts payable		$ 760
Common stock		2,500
Retained earnings		5,200
Dividends	400	
Service fees earned		4,650
Wages expense	1,020	
	$13,110	$13,110

The following information is also available:

1. The balance in Prepaid Rent was the amount paid on June 1 for the first two months' rent.
2. Supplies on hand at June 30 were $1,250.
3. The equipment, purchased June 1, has an estimated life of five years.
4. Unpaid wages at June 30 were $450.
5. Utility services used during June were estimated at $650. A bill is expected early in July.
6. Fees earned for services performed but not yet billed on June 30 were $500. The firm uses the account Fees Receivable to reflect amounts due but not yet billed.

Required

Prepare the adjusting entries needed at June 30 for the general journal.

P3-5A. Adjusting Entries The following information relates to December 31 adjustments for Best Print, a **LO3, 4** printing company. The firm's fiscal year ends on December 31.

1. Weekly salaries for a five-day week total $3,000, payable on Fridays. December 31 of the current year is a Tuesday.
2. Best Print has $25,000 of notes payable outstanding at December 31. Interest of $275 has accrued on these notes by December 31, but will not be paid until the notes mature next year.
3. During December, Best Print provided $1,000 of printing services to clients who will be billed on January 2. The firm uses the account Fees Receivable to reflect amounts due but not yet billed.

4. Starting December 1, all maintenance work on Best Print's equipment is handled by Prompt Repair Company under an agreement whereby Best Print pays a fixed monthly charge of $125. Best Print paid six months' service charge in advance on December 1, debiting Prepaid Maintenance for $750.

5. The firm paid $900 on December 15 for a series of radio commercials to run during December and January. One-third of the commercials have aired by December 31. The $900 payment was debited to Prepaid Advertising.

6. Starting December 16, Best Print rented 400 square feet of storage space from a neighboring business. The monthly rent of $0.90 per square foot is due in advance on the first of each month. Nothing was paid in December, however, because the neighbor agreed to add the rent for one-half of December to the January 1 payment.

7. Best Print invested $7,500 in securities on December 1 and earned interest of $62 on these securities by December 31. No interest will be received until January.

8. The annual depreciation on the firm's equipment is $2,600. No depreciation has been recorded during the year.

Required
Prepare the required December 31 adjusting entries in the general journal.

LO3, 4   P3-6A.   Adjusting Entries   The following selected accounts appear in the Bullard Company's unadjusted trial balance as of December 31, the end of the fiscal year (all accounts have normal balances):

Prepaid advertising	$ 1,400	Unearned service fees	$ 5,400
Wages expense	43,800	Service fees earned	87,000
Prepaid insurance	3,420	Rental income	4,900

Required
Prepare the necessary adjusting entries in the general journal as of December 31, assuming the following:

1. Prepaid advertising at December 31 is $950.
2. Unpaid wages earned by employees in December are $1,800.
3. Prepaid insurance at December 31 is $2,750.
4. Unearned service fees at December 31 are $2,800.
5. Rent revenue of $1,250 owed by a tenant is not recorded at December 31.

LO3, 4   P3-7A.   Adjusting Entries   The following selected accounts appear in the Birch Company's unadjusted trial balance as of December 31, the end of the fiscal year (all accounts have normal balances):

Prepaid maintenance	$2,700	Commission fees earned	$86,000
Supplies	9,400	Rent expense	10,800
Unearned commission fees	9,000		

Required
Prepare the necessary adjusting entries in the general journal as of December 31, assuming the following:

1. On September 1, the company entered into a prepaid equipment maintenance contract. Birch Company paid $2,700 to cover maintenance service for six months, beginning September 1. The $2,700 payment was debited to Prepaid Maintenance.
2. Supplies on hand at December 31 are $2,900.
3. Unearned commission fees at December 31 are $4,000.
4. Commission fees earned but not yet billed at December 31 are $3,500. (*Note:* Debit Fees Receivable.)
5. Birch Company's lease calls for rent of $900 per month payable on the first of each month, plus an annual amount equal to 2 percent of annual commissions earned. This additional rent is payable on January 10 of the following year. (*Note:* Be sure to use the adjusted amount of commissions earned in computing the additional rent.)

LO5, 6   P3-8A.   Financial Statements and Closing Entries   The adjusted trial balance shown below is for Sharpe Consulting Service as of December 31. Byran Sharpe made no capital contributions during the year.

Adjusted Trial Bala...

	Debit	Cre...
Cash	$ 2,900	
Accounts receivable	3,270	
Supplies	5,060	
Prepaid insurance	1,500	
Equipment	6,400	
Accumulated depreciation—Equipment		$ 1
Accounts payable		7
Long-term notes payable		2
Common stock		5
Retained earnings		
Dividends	2,900	
Service fees earned		62
Rent expense	15,500	
Salaries expense	33,400	
Supplies expense	4,200	
Insurance expense	3,250	
Depreciation expense—Equipment	720	
Interest expense	630	
Totals	$79,730	$79

Required
a. Prepare an income statement and a statement of stockholders' equity for the year, and a b... sheet as of December 31.
b. Prepare closing entries directly to Retained Earnings in general journal form.

P3-9A.   Closing Entries   The adjusted trial balance shown below is for Batton, Inc., at December 31:

Adjusted Trial Bala...

	Debit	Cre...
Cash	$ 4,000	
Accounts receivable	8,000	
Prepaid insurance	3,600	
Equipment	75,000	
Accumulated depreciation		$ 12
Accounts payable		30
Common stock		14
Retained earnings		7,000
Cash dividends	7,000	
Service fees earned		10
Miscellaneous income		2
Salaries expense	42,800	
Rent expense	12,900	
Insurance expense	1,800	
Depreciation expense	8,000	
Income tax expense	8,300	
Income tax payable		8
Totals	$171,400	$171

Required
a. Prepare closing entries directly to Retained Earnings in general journal form.
b. After the closing entries are posted, what is the ending balance in the Retained Earnings ac...
c. Prepare a post-closing trial balance.

P-10A.   Balance Sheet and Net Income   At the beginning of the year, Azuza's Parking Lots had the f... ing balance sheet:

   d. Prepare a statement of stockholders' equity for the month of June.

   e. Prepare a balance sheet as of June 30.

   f. Prepare closing entries.

   g. Prepare a post-closing trial balance.

P3-13A. Transaction Analysis, Trial Balance, and Financial Statements On December 1, a group of individuals formed a corporation to establish the *Local,* a neighborhood weekly newspaper featuring want ads of individuals and advertising of local firms. The free paper will be mailed to about 8,000 local residents; revenue will be generated from advertising and want ads. The December transactions are summarized as follows:

LO3, 4, 5

  1 Sold common stock of Beeper, Inc., for cash, $40,000.

  2 Paid December rent on furnished office, $1,200.

  3 Purchased for $750, on account, T-shirts displaying company logo. The T-shirts were distributed at a grand opening.

  4 Paid to creditor on account, $750.

  5 Collected "Help wanted" ad revenue in cash, $5,000.

  6 Paid post office for cost of bulk mailing, $910.

  7 Billed various firms for advertising in the first two issues of the newspaper, $5,600.

  8 Paid Acme Courier Service for transporting newspapers to post office, $50.

  9 Paid for printing newspaper, $2,900.

10 Collected "Help wanted" ad revenue in cash, $2,570.

11 Received invoice for December utilities, to be paid in January, $890.

12 Paid for printing newspaper, $2,900.

13 Paid December salaries, $4,100.

14 Billed various firms for advertising in two issues of the newspaper, $8,850.

15 Paid post office for cost of bulk mailing, $775.

16 Paid Acme Courier Service for transporting newspapers to post office, $350.

17 Collected $5,100 on accounts receivable.

18 Purchased a printer for office in exchange for a six-month note payable, $1,400.

Required

   a. Set up accounts for the following items: Cash, Accounts Receivable, Office Equipment, Accounts Payable, Notes Payable, Common Stock, Advertising Revenue, Want Ad Revenue, Printing Expense, Advertising Expense, Utilities Expense, Salaries Expense, Rent Expense, and Delivery Expense. Prepare journal entries in a general journal and record the foregoing transactions in the accounts.

   b. Prepare a trial balance as of December 31.

   c. Prepare an income statement for the month of December.

   d. Prepare a balance sheet as of December 31. (*Note:* In this problem, the net income for December becomes the amount of retained earnings at December 31.)

P3-14A. Balance Sheets for a Corporation The following balance sheet data are given for Norman Catering Service, a corporation, as of May 31:

LO5

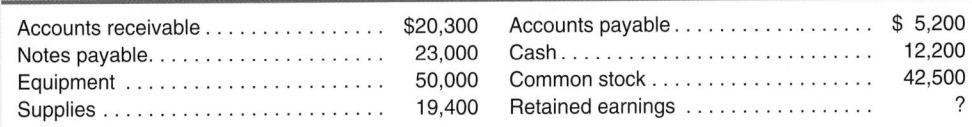

Accounts receivable	$20,300	Accounts payable	$ 5,200
Notes payable	23,000	Cash	12,200
Equipment	50,000	Common stock	42,500
Supplies	19,400	Retained earnings	?

Assume that on June 1, the following transactions occurred:

June 1   Purchased additional equipment costing $18,000, giving $3,000 cash and a $15,000 note payable.

       1   Paid a cash dividend of $8,000.

Required

   a. Prepare a balance sheet as of May 31.

   b. Prepare a balance sheet as of June 2.

P3-15A. Determination of Net Income and Retained Earnings The following selected income statement and balance sheet information is available for Floyd Appraisers at the end of the current month:

LO5

Supplies	$ 6,500	Accounts payable	$ 4,000
Accounts receivable	17,800	Salaries expense	17,000
Utilities expense	700	Appraisal fees earned	31,000
Supplies expense	1,400	Common stock	10,000
Rent expense	3,000	Retained earnings (beginning)	5,000
Cash	3,600		

a. Calculate the net income or net loss for the month.
b. If Mr. Floyd made no additional investment in the business during the month but received $6,000 as a dividend, what is the balance in Retained Earnings at the end of the month?

LO5 **P3-16A. Trial Balance and Financial Statements** The following account balances were taken (out of order) from the general ledger of Howe & Company as of January 31. Howe trains dogs for competitive championship field trials. The firm's accounting year began on January 1. All accounts have normal balances.

Land	$22,810	Office rent expense	$ 800
Maintenance expense	950	Supplies expense	760
Supplies	1,200	Utilities expense	200
Advertising expense	380	Fees earned	18,400
Common stock	20,000	Accounts receivable	8,200
Retained earnings	9,000		
Cash	7,300	Salaries expense	4,480
Accounts payable	880	Dividends	1,200

Required
a. Prepare a trial balance from the given data.
b. Prepare an income statement for the month of January.
c. Prepare a statement of stockholders' equity for the month of January.
d. Prepare a balance sheet as of January 31.

LO5 **P3-17A. Trial Balance and Financial Statements** The following account balances, in alphabetical order, are from the general ledger of Milo's Waterproofing Service at January 31. The firm began business on January 1. All accounts have normal balances.

Accounts payable	$ 3,500	Notes payable	$ 5,000
Accounts receivable	19,000	Rent expense	1,500
Advertising expense	1,420	Salaries expense	8,000
Cash	12,600	Service fees earned	25,760
Common stock	29,740	Supplies	8,860
Dividends	2,000	Supplies expense	10,250
Interest expense	50	Utilities expense	320

Required
a. Prepare a trial balance from the given data.
b. Prepare an income statement for the month of January.
c. Prepare a statement of stockholders' equity for the month of January.
d. Prepare a balance sheet as of January 31.

LO5, 7 **P3-18A. Financial Statements and Closing Entries** Use the information provided in P3-8A.
(Appendix 3A)

Required
a. Prepare an income statement, a statement of stockholders' equity, and a balance sheet as of December 31.
b. Prepare closing entries using the Income Summary account.

LO7 **P3-19A. Closing Entries** Use the information provided in P3-9A.
(Appendix 3A)

Required
a. Prepare closing entries in general journal form using the Income Summary account.
b. After the closing entries are posted, what is the ending balance in the Retained Earnings account?
c. Prepare a post-closing trial balance.

P3-20A. Worksheet The following unadjusted trial balance was prepared as of March 31:

LO8
(Appendix 3B)

FOCUS TRAVEL AGENCY Unadjusted Trial Balance March 31		
	Debit	**Credit**
Cash	$ 2,400	
Commissions receivable	8,000	
Supplies	2,200	
Prepaid insurance	1,800	
Equipment	16,000	
Accumulated depreciation		$ 7,600
Accounts payable		550
Unearned commissions		700
Common stock		4,000
Retained earnings		9,300
Dividends	900	
Commissions earned		18,990
Salaries expense	6,500	
Rent expense	1,870	
Advertising expense	850	
Utilities expense	620	
Totals	$41,140	$41,140

Focus Travel Agency's fiscal year ends on March 31. The following additional information is available:

1. Depreciation for the year is $1,500.
2. Supplies on hand at March 31 amount to $820.
3. By March 31, the entire $700 of the unearned commissions was earned.
4. Insurance expense for the year is $1,200.
5. Accrued salaries payable total $1,100 at March 31.

Required

Enter the trial balance on a worksheet and complete the worksheet using the adjustment data given above.

PROBLEMS—SET B

P3-1B. Transaction Entries, Posting, Trial Balance, Adjusting Entries Zhou Karate School began business on June 1. Transactions for June were as follows:

LO3, 4

1 Po Zhou contributed $10,000 of his personal funds in exchange for common stock to begin the business.
2 Purchased equipment for $4,750, paying $950 cash, with the balance due in 30 days.
3 Paid six months' rent, $6,450.
4 Paid one-year premium on liability insurance, $876.
5 Paid June newspaper advertising, $715.
6 Billed participants for karate lessons to date, $2,200.
7 Received $885 from a local company to conduct a special three-session class on self-defense for its employees. The three sessions will be held on June 29, July 6, and July 13, at $295 per session.
8 Collected $3,000 on account from participants
9 Paid $275 to repair damage to wall caused by an errant kick.
10 Billed participants for karate lessons to date, $2,000.
11 Paid assistant's wages, $950.

Required

a. Set up a general ledger with the following accounts: Cash; Accounts Receivable; Prepaid Rent; Prepaid Insurance; Equipment; Accumulated Depreciation—Equipment; Accounts Payable;

Utilities Payable; Unearned Karate Fees; Common Stock; Karate Fees Earned; Advertising Expense; Repairs Expense; Wages Expense; Rent Expense; Insurance Expense; Depreciation Expense—Equipment; and Utilities Expense.

b. Record these transactions in general journal form and post to the ledger accounts.

c. Prepare an unadjusted trial balance as of June 30.

d. Prepare the adjusting entries for rent expense, insurance expense, depreciation expense, utilities expense, and karate fees earned. Depreciation expense for June is $175, and estimated utilities expense for June is $320. Post the adjusting entries.

LO3, 4   **P3-2B.**   **Transaction Entries, Posting, Trial Balance, and Adjusting Entries** Market-Tech, a market research firm, had the following transactions in June, its first month of operations.

1 J. Witson invested $28,000 of personal funds in the firm in exchange for common stock.
2 The firm purchased the following from an office supply company: office equipment, $11,040; office supplies, $2,840. Terms called for a cash payment of $3,500, with the remainder due in 60 days. (Make a compound entry.)
3 Paid June rent, $1,275.
4 Contracted for five months' advertising in a local newspaper at $325 per month and paid for the advertising in advance.
5 Signed a six-month contract with an electronics firm to provide research consulting services at a rate of $3,200 per month. Received two months' fees in advance. Work on the contract started immediately.
6 Billed various customers for services rendered, $8,000.
7 Paid two weeks' salaries (five-day week) to employees, $3,600.
8 Paid J. Witson's travel expenses to business conference, $1,440.
9 Paid $520 cash for postage to mail questionnaire.
10 Paid two weeks' salaries to employees, $3,600.
11 Billed various customers for services rendered, $7,200.
12 Collected $7,900 from customers on account.
13 J. Witson received a $2,500 cash dividend.

Required

a. Set up a general ledger that includes the following accounts: Cash; Accounts Receivable; Office Supplies; Prepaid Advertising; Office Equipment; Accumulated Depreciation—Office Equipment; Accounts Payable; Salaries Payable; Unearned Service Fees; Common Stock; Dividends; Service Fees Earned; Salaries Expense; Advertising Expense; Supplies Expense; Rent Expense; Travel Expense; Depreciation Expense—Office Equipment; and Postage Expense.

b. Record June transactions in general journal form and post to the ledger accounts.

c. Prepare an unadjusted trial balance as of June 30.

d. Record adjusting journal entries in general journal form, and post to the ledger accounts. The following information is available on June 30:

Office supplies on hand, $1,830.
Accrued salaries, $875.
Estimated life of office equipment, eight years. (Assume equipment was purchased June 1)

Also, make any necessary adjusting entries for advertising and for service fees indicated by the June transactions. Assume original transactions occurred June 1.

LO3, 4   **P3-3B.**   **Trial Balance and Adjusting Entries** Sendall, a mailing service, has just completed its first full year of operations on December 31, 2018. The firm's general ledger account balances before year-end adjustments are given below. No adjusting entries have been made to the accounts at any time during the year. Assume that all balances are normal.

Cash	$ 2,600	Accounts payable	$ 2,700
Accounts receivable	5,120	Common stock	7,530
Prepaid advertising	1,680	Mailing fees earned	86,000
Supplies	6,570	Wages expense	38,800
Equipment	42,240	Rent expense	4,700
Notes payable	8,500	Utilities expense	3,020

An analysis of the firm's records reveals the following:

1. The balance in Prepaid Advertising represents the amount paid for newspaper advertising for one year. The agreement, which calls for the same amount of space each month, covers the period from February 1, 2018, to January 31, 2019. Sendall did not advertise during its first month of operations.

2. The equipment, purchased January 1, has an estimated life of eight years.

3. Utilities expense does not include expense for December, estimated at $525. The bill will not arrive until January 2019.

4. At year-end, employees have earned $1,750 in wages that will not be paid until January.

5. Supplies on hand at year-end amounted to $1,720.

6. At year-end, unpaid interest of $500 has accrued on the notes payable.

7. The firm's lease calls for rent of $525 per month payable on the first of each month, plus an amount equal to 1 percent of annual mailing fees earned. The rental percentage is payable within 15 days after the end of the year.

Required

a. Demonstrate that the sum of the debits equals the sum of the credits for the unadjusted account balances shown above by preparing an unadjusted trial balance as of December 31, 2018.

b. Record adjusting entries in general journal form.

P3-4B. Adjusting Entries The Spoke Place, Inc., began operations on March 1 to provide automotive wheel alignment and balancing services. On March 31, the unadjusted balances of the firm's accounts are as follows: **LO3, 4**

THE SPOKE PLACE, INC. Unadjusted Trial Balance March 31		
	Debit	**Credit**
Cash...	$ 1,900	
Accounts receivable......................................	5,820	
Prepaid rent...	4,770	
Supplies..	4,100	
Equipment...	36,180	
Accounts payable...		$ 4,510
Unearned service revenue...............................		1,500
Common stock..		38,800
Service revenue...		12,360
Wages expense...	4,400	
Totals...	$57,170	$57,170

The following information is also available.

1. The balance in Prepaid Rent was the amount paid on March 1 to cover the first six months' rent.

2. Supplies on hand on March 31 amounted to $2,100.

3. The equipment has an estimated life of nine years.

4. Unpaid wages at March 31 were $660.

5. Utility services used during March were estimated at $650. A bill is expected early in April.

6. The balance in Unearned Service Revenue was the amount received on March 1 from a new car dealer to cover alignment and balancing services on all new cars sold by the dealer in March and April. The Spoke Place agreed to provide the services at a fixed fee of $750 each month.

Required

Prepare the adjusting entries needed at March 31 in general journal form.

P3-5B. Adjusting Entries The following information relates to the December 31 adjustments for Liquid Barrier, a firm providing waterproofing services for commercial and residential customers. The firm's fiscal year ends December 31; no adjusting entries have been made during the year. **LO3, 4**

1. The firm paid a $4,500 premium for a three-year insurance policy, coverage to begin October 1. The premium payment was debited to Prepaid Insurance.

2. Weekly wages for a five-day work week total $1,250, payable on Fridays. December 31 is a Thursday.

3. Liquid Barrier received $3,000 in November for services to be performed during December through February of the following year. When received, this amount was credited to Unearned Service Fees. By December 31, one-third of this amount was earned.

4. Liquid Barrier receives a 6 percent commission from the manufacturer on sales of a waterproofing agent to Liquid Barrier's customers. By December 31, Liquid Barrier had sales of $10,000 (during November and December) for which no commissions had been received or recorded.

5. During December, fuel oil costs of $650 were incurred to heat the firm's buildings. Because the monthly bill from the oil company has not yet arrived, no entry has been made for this amount (fuel oil costs are charged to Utilities Expense).

6. The Supplies account has a balance of $17,500 on December 31. A count of supplies on December 31 indicates that $3,500 worth of supplies are still on hand.

7. On December 1, Liquid Barrier borrowed $10,000 from the bank, giving a note payable. Interest is not payable until the note is due near the end of the following January. However, the interest for December is $115.

8. Liquid Barrier rents parking spaces in its lot to firms in the office building next door. On December 1, Liquid Barrier received $7,500 as advance payments to cover parking privileges in the lot for December through March of the following year. When received, the $7,500 was credited to Unearned Parking Fees.

Required

Prepare the necessary December 31 adjusting entries in general journal form.

LO3, 4 **P3-6B.** **Adjusting Entries** The following selected accounts appear in the Gloria Company's unadjusted trial balance as of December 31, the end of the fiscal year (all accounts have normal balances):

Prepaid advertising..............	$ 3,600	Unearned service fees.............	$ 4,800
Wages expense..................	45,800	Service fees earned...............	88,000
Prepaid insurance................	6,420	Rental income....................	4,900

Required

Make the necessary adjusting entries in general journal form as of December 31 assuming the following:

a. Prepaid advertising at December 31 is $900.
b. Unpaid wages earned by employees in December are $1,900.
c. Prepaid insurance at December 31 is $2,380.
d. Unearned service fees at December 31 are $2,500.
e. Rent revenue of $4,200 owed by a tenant is not recorded at December 31.

LO3, 4 **P3-7B.** **Adjusting Entries** The following selected accounts appear in the Hawkes Company's unadjusted trial balance as of December 31, the end of the fiscal year (all accounts have normal balances):

Prepaid maintenance..............	$ 6,000	Commission fees earned...........	$97,000
Supplies........................	10,800	Rent expense....................	11,200
Unearned commission fees.........	10,700		

Required

Make the necessary adjusting entries in general journal form at December 31, assuming the following:

1. On September 1, the company entered into a prepaid equipment maintenance contract. The Hawkes Company paid $6,000 to cover maintenance service for six months, beginning September 1. The $6,000 payment was debited to Prepaid Maintenance.

2. Supplies on hand at December 31 are $3,500.

3. Unearned commission fees at December 31 are $5,500.

4. Commission fees earned but not yet billed at December 31 are $4,100. (*Note:* Debit Fees Receivable.)

5. The Hawkes Company's lease calls for rent of $900 per month payable on the first of each month, plus an annual amount equal to 4 percent of annual commissions earned. This additional rent is payable on January 10 of the following year. (*Note:* Be sure to use the adjusted amount of commissions earned in calculating the additional rent.)

P3-8B.   **Financial Statements and Closing Entries**   Outside, Inc., publishes magazines for skiers and hikers.   **LO5, 6**
The firm has the following adjusted trial balance at December 31:

OUTSIDE, INC. Adjusted Trial Balance December 31		
	Debit	**Credit**
Cash	$ 5,400	
Accounts receivable	19,000	
Supplies	4,200	
Prepaid insurance.	930	
Office equipment	70,000	
Accumulated depreciation		$ 13,000
Accounts payable.		17,000
Unearned subscription revenue		10,000
Salaries payable.		3,500
Common stock		21,000
Retained earnings		17,620
Subscription revenue		188,300
Advertising revenue		55,400
Salaries expense	120,230	
Printing and mailing expense	85,600	
Rent expense	5,400	
Supplies expense.	6,100	
Insurance expense.	1,860	
Depreciation expense.	5,500	
Income tax expense	1,600	
Totals	$325,820	$325,820

Required

a.   Prepare an income statement for the year and a balance sheet as of December 31.

b.   Prepare closing entries directly to Retained Earnings in general journal form.

LO6 **P3-9B.** **Closing Entries** The adjusted trial balance for Barry Moving Service as of December 31 is as follows:

	Adjusted Trial Balance	
	Debit	Credit
Cash.	$ 5,400	
Accounts receivable	5,250	
Supplies	5,300	
Prepaid advertising.	3,000	
Trucks.	30,300	
Accumulated depreciation—Trucks		$ 10,000
Equipment	7,600	
Accumulated depreciation—Equipment		2,100
Accounts payable.		1,200
Unearned service fees		6,700
Common stock		11,000
Retained earnings		16,750
Dividends	7,700	
Service fees earned		81,000
Wages expense	31,200	
Rent expense	10,200	
Insurance expense.	4,900	
Supplies expense.	5,100	
Advertising expense.	8,000	
Depreciation expense—Trucks.	4,000	
Depreciation expense—Equipment	800	
Totals	$128,750	$128,750

Required

a. Prepare the closing entries at December 31 directly to Retained Earnings in general journal form.

b. After the closing entries are posted, calculate the ending balance in the Retained Earnings account.

c. Prepare a post-closing trial balance.

LO5 **P3-10B.** **Balance Sheet and Net Income Determination** At the beginning of the year, Acme Parking Services had the following balance sheet:

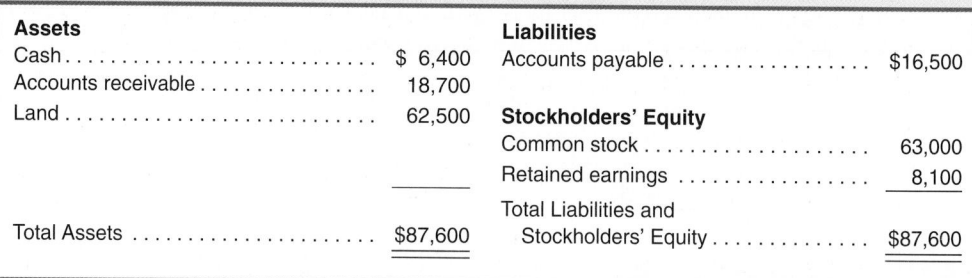

Assets		**Liabilities**	
Cash.	$ 6,400	Accounts payable.	$16,500
Accounts receivable	18,700		
Land	62,500	**Stockholders' Equity**	
		Common stock	63,000
		Retained earnings	8,100
		Total Liabilities and	
Total Assets	$87,600	Stockholders' Equity	$87,600

a. At the end of the year, Acme Parking Services had the following assets and liabilities: Cash, $9,200; Accounts Receivable, $18,400; Land, $62,500; and Accounts Payable, $11,750. Prepare a year-end balance sheet for Luxury Parking Services assuming that no additional stock was issued.

b. Assuming that stockholders did not invest any money in the business during the year but received a $12,000 dividend, what was the company's net income or net loss for the year?

P3-11B. Determination of Retained Earnings and Net Income The following information appears in the records of the Aukland Corporation at year-end: **LO5**

Accounts receivable	$ 40,000	Retained earnings	$?
Accounts payable	8,000	Supplies	9,000
Cash	7,000	Equipment	140,000
Common stock	130,000		

   a. Calculate the amount of retained earnings at the end of the year.
   b. Using your answer to part *a*, if the amount of the retained earnings at the beginning of the year was $30,000, and $6,000 in dividends was paid during the year, what was the net income for the year?

P3-12B. Transaction Analysis, Trial Balance, and Financial Statements Kate Smith operates the Smith Dance Studio. On June 1, the studio's general ledger contained the following information: **LO3, 4, 5, 6**

Cash	$10,930	Accounts payable	$ 480
Accounts receivable	18,200	Notes payable	3,000
		Common stock	11,870
		Retained earnings	13,780
	$29,130		$29,130

The following transactions occurred during the month of June:

   1 Paid June rent for practice studio, $3,000.
   2 Paid June piano rental, $800 (Rent Expense).
   3 Collected $14,320 from students on account.
   4 Borrowed $6,500 and signed a promissory note payable due in six months.
   5 Billed students for June instructional fees, $9,600.
   6 Paid interest for June on the outstanding notes payable, $110.
   7 Paid $550 for advertising ballet performances.
   8 Paid costume rental, $800 (Rent Expense).
   9 Collected $6,300 admission fees from ballet performances given during June.
   10 Paid $780 owed on account.
   11 Received invoice for June utilities, to be paid in July, $480.
   12 The studio paid stockholders a cash dividend of $900.
   13 Purchased piano for $6,000 cash, to be used in business starting in July.

   Required
   a. Set up accounts for the general ledger with June 1 balances and enter the beginning balances. Also provide the following accounts: Piano; Dividends; Instructional Fees Earned; Performance Revenue; Rent Expense; Utilities Expense; Advertising Expense; and Interest Expense. Record the listed transactions in the accounts.
   b. Prepare a trial balance as of June 30.
   c. Prepare an income statement for the month of June.
   d. Prepare a statement of stockholders' equity for the month of June.
   e. Prepare a balance sheet as of June 30.
   f. Prepare closing entries.
   g. Prepare a post-closing trial balance.

P3-13B. Transaction Analysis, Trial Balance, and Financial Statements On December 1, a group of individuals formed a corporation to establish the *Humbolt News,* a neighborhood newspaper featuring "Help wanted" ads by individuals and advertising by local firms. The free paper will be mailed to about 20,000 local residents; revenue will be generated from advertising and the want ads. The December transactions are summarized below: **LO3, 4**

1 Sold common stock for cash, $65,000.
2 Paid December rent on furnished office, $5,000.
3 Purchased for $550, on account, T-shirts displaying company logo. The T-shirts were distributed at a grand opening.
4 Paid to creditor on account, $475.
5 Collected want ad revenue in cash, $2,800.
6 Paid post office for cost of bulk mailing, $810.
7 Billed various firms for advertising in the first two issues of the newspaper, $6,300.
8 Paid Tucson Courier Service for transporting newspapers to the post office, $70.
9 Paid for printing newspaper, $3,900.
10 Collected want ad revenue in cash, $4,570.
11 Received invoice for December utilities, to be paid in January, $510.
12 Paid for printing newspaper, $4,400.
13 Paid December salaries, $6,100.
14 Billed various firms for advertising in two issues of the newspaper, $8,950.
15 Paid post office for cost of bulk mailing, $630.
16 Paid Tucson Courier Service for transporting newspapers to the post office, $90.
17 Collected $5,100 on accounts receivable.
18 Purchased a printer for the office in exchange for a six-month note payable, $3,100.

Required

a. Set up accounts for the following: Cash, Accounts Receivable, Office Equipment, Accounts Payable, Notes Payable, Common Stock, Advertising Revenue, Want Ad Revenue, Printing Expense, Advertising Expense, Utilities Expense, Salaries Expense, Rent Expense, and Delivery Expense. Prepare journal entries in a general journal and record the foregoing transactions in the accounts.
b. Prepare a trial balance as of December 31.
c. Prepare an income statement for the month of December.
d. Prepare a balance sheet as of December 31. (*Note:* In this problem, the net income for December becomes the amount of retained earnings at December 31.)

LO5 **P3-14B. Balance Sheets** The following balance sheet data are given for Harvard Catering Service, a corporation, at May 31:

Accounts receivable	$30,300	Accounts payable	$ 5,200
Notes payable	20,000	Cash	12,200
Equipment	60,000	Common stock	62,500
Supplies	16,400	Retained earnings	?

Assume that on June 1, the following transactions occurred:

June 1 Purchased additional equipment costing $26,000, giving $2,000 cash and a $24,000 note payable.
      2 Paid a cash dividend of $7,000.

Required

a. Prepare a balance sheet as of May 31.
b. Prepare a balance sheet as of June 2.

LO5 **P3-15B. Determination of Net Income and Stockholders' Equity** The following selected income statement and balance sheet information is available for Xin Land Appraisers at the end of the current month:

Supplies	$ 7,400	Accounts payable	$ 4,500
Accounts receivable	24,600	Salaries expense	15,000
Utilities expense	700	Appraisal fees earned	31,000
Supplies expense	1,300	Common stock	15,000
Rent expense	2,900	Retained earnings (beginning)	5,000
Cash	3,600		

a. Calculate the net income or net loss for the month.
b. If stockholders made no additional investment during the month but received $6,000 as a dividend, what is the amount of retained earnings at the end of the month?

P3-16B. Trial Balance and Financial Statements The following account balances were prepared (out of order) from the general ledger of The Cat Whisperer, Inc. as of January 31. The company trains cats having behavioral problems. The firm's business began on January 1. All accounts have normal balances.

LO5

Facilities	$32,000	Office rent expense	$ 800
Maintenance expense	460	Supplies expense	1,760
Supplies	1,640	Utilities expense	200
Advertising expense	550	Fees earned	20,470
Common stock	37,600	Accounts receivable	8,200
Cash	7,300	Salaries expense	4,480
Accounts payable	1,420	Dividends	2,100

Required
a.   Prepare a trial balance from the given data.
b.   Prepare an income statement for the month of January.
c.   Prepare a statement of stockholders' equity for the month of January.
d.   Prepare a balance sheet as of January 31.

P3-17B. Trial Balance and Financial Statements The following account balances, in alphabetical order, are from the general ledger of The Nina Service Company at January 31. The firm's business began on January 1. All accounts have normal balances.

LO5

Accounts payable	$ 9,200	Notes payable	$12,000
Accounts receivable	39,000	Rent expense	2,900
Advertising expense	840	Salaries expense	16,000
Cash	20,800	Service fees earned	53,020
Common stock	56,180	Supplies	17,920
Dividends	11,000	Supplies expense	20,500
Interest expense	800	Utilities expense	640

Required
a.   Prepare a trial balance from the given data.
b.   Prepare an income statement for the month of January.
c.   Prepare a statement of stockholders' equity for the month of January.
d.   Prepare a balance sheet as of January 31.

P3-18B. Financial Statements and Closing Entries Use the information provided in P3-8B.

LO5, 7
(Appendix 3A)

Required
a.   Prepare an income statement, a statement of stockholders' equity, and a balance sheet as of December 31.
b.   Prepare closing entries in general journal form using the Income Summary account.

P3-19B. Closing Entries Use the information provided in P3-9B.

LO7
(Appendix 3A)

Required
a.   Prepare closing entries at December 31 in general journal form using the Income Summary account.
b.   After the closing entries are posted, calculate the ending balance in the Retained Earnings account.
c.   Prepare a post-closing trial balance.

LO8
(Appendix 3B)

P3-20B.   Worksheet The July 31 unadjusted trial balance of Lake Outfitters, a firm renting various types of equipment to canoeists and campers, follows.

LAKE OUTFITTERS Unadjusted Trial Balance July 31		
	Debit	**Credit**
Cash	$ 3,750	
Supplies	8,600	
Prepaid insurance.	3,200	
Equipment	91,000	
Accumulated depreciation		$ 16,500
Accounts payable.		3,500
Unearned rental fees		8,850
Common stock		33,000
Retained earnings		3,000
Dividends	1,200	
Rental fees earned.		78,150
Wages expense	28,800	
Rent expense	3,300	
Advertising expense.	2,300	
Travel expense	850	
	$143,000	$143,000

Lake Outfitters' fiscal year ends on July 31. The following additional information is available:

1. Supplies on hand at July 31 amount to $2,300.
2. Insurance expense for the year is $1,600.
3. Depreciation for the year is $8,750.
4. The unearned rental fees consist of deposits received from customers in advance when reservations are made. During the year, $4,850 of the unearned rental fees were earned. The remaining deposits apply to rentals for August and September.
5. At July 31, revenue from rental services earned during July but not yet billed or received amounts to $3,500. (*Note:* Debit Fees Receivable.)
6. Accrued wages payable for equipment handlers and guides amounts to $700 at July 31.

Required
Enter the trial balance in a worksheet and complete the worksheet using the adjustment data given above.

SERIAL PROBLEM: KATE'S CARDS

(*Note: This is a continuation of the Serial Problem: Kate's Cards from Chapters 1 and 2.*)

SP3.   Getting ready for the upcoming holiday season is traditionally a busy time for greeting card companies, and it was no exception for Kate. The following transactions occurred during the month of October:

1. Hired an assistant at an hourly rate of $10 per hour to help with some of the computer layouts and administrative chores.
2. Supplements her business by teaching a class to aspiring card designers. She charges and receives a total of $450.
3. Delivers greeting cards to several new customers. She bills them a total of $3,500.
4. Pays a utility bill in the amount of $250 that she determines is the business portion of her utility bill.

5. Receives an advance deposit of $500 for a new set of cards she is designing for a new customer.

6. Pays her assistant $200 for the work done this month.

7. Determines that the assistant has worked 10 additional hours this month that have not yet been paid.

8. Ordered and receives additional supplies in the amount of $1,000. These were paid for during the month.

9. Counts her remaining inventory of supplies at the end of the month and determines the balance to be $300. Don't forget to consider the supplies inventory balance at September 30, from Chapter 2. (*Hint:* This expense will be a debit to Cost of Goods Sold.)

10. Records the adjusting entries for depreciation and insurance expense for the month.

11. Pays herself a salary of $1,000.

12. Paid monthly rent of $1,200 in cash.

13. Receives her next utility bill during December and determines $85 applies to October's operations.

14. Deciding she needs a little more cash, Kate pays herself a $100 dividend.

Required
Using the information that you gathered and the general ledger accounts that you prepared through Chapter 2, plus the new information above, complete the following:

a. Journalize the above transactions and adjusting entries.

b. Post the October transactions and adjusting entries. (Use the general ledger accounts prepared in Chapter 2 and add any new accounts that you may need.)

c. Prepare a trial balance as of October 31, 2018.

d. Prepare an income statement and a statement of stockholders' equity for the two-month period ending October 31, 2018, and a balance sheet as of October 31, 2018.

e. Prepare the closing entries as of October 31, 2018.

f. Prepare a post-closing trial balance.

EXTENDING YOUR KNOWLEDGE

REPORTING AND ANALYSIS

EYK3-1. **Financial Reporting Problem: Columbia Sportswear Company** The financial statements for the **Columbia Sportswear Company** can be found in Appendix A at the end of this book.

COLUMBIA
SPORTSWEAR
COMPANY

Required
Answer the following questions using Columbia's Consolidated Financial Statements and the Notes to the consolidated financial statements:

a. Identify an item that likely requires adjusting entries for prepayments.

b. Identify an item that likely requires an adjusting accrual.

c. Examine the statement of cash flows and identify the amount of depreciation and amortization expense for 2017. Where on the balance sheet was this accrual likely also shown?

d. Identify the items that will require closing entries. What account will they be ultimately closed to?

EYK3-2. **Comparative Analysis Problem: Columbia Sportswear Company vs. Under Armour, Inc.** The financial statements for the **Columbia Sportswear Company** can be found in Appendix A, and **Under Armour, Inc.'s** financial statements can be found in Appendix B at the end of this book.

COLUMBIA
SPORTSWEAR
COMPANY

UNDER ARMOUR,
INC.

Required
a. Examine the balance sheet of Columbia Sportswear and identify three items that indicate that the company uses the accrual method of accounting. In each case, identify the likely income statement account that is affected by these accruals.

b. Examine the balance sheet of Under Armour, Inc. and identify three items that indicate the company uses the accrual method of accounting. In each case, identify the likely income statement account that is affected by these accruals.

EYK3-3.   **Business Decision Problem** Gilbert Consulting Services, a firm started three years ago by Bruce Gilbert, offers consulting services for material handling and plant layout. The balance sheet prepared by the firm's accountant at the close of 2018 is shown here.

GILBERT CONSULTING SERVICES Balance Sheet As of December 31, 2018					
Assets			**Liabilities**		
Cash........................		$ 3,400	Notes payable.............		$30,000
Accounts receivable.............		22,875	Accounts payable..........		4,200
Supplies		13,200	Unearned consulting fees....		11,300
Prepaid insurance...............		4,500	Wages payable............		400
Equipment	$68,500		Total Liabilities		45,900
Less: Accumulated depreciation....	(23,975)	44,525	**Stockholders' Equity**		
			Common stock		20,000
			Retained earnings		22,600
			Total Stockholders' Equity ...		42,600
			Total Liabilities and		
Total Assets		$88,500	Stockholders' Equity		$88,500

Earlier in the year, Gilbert obtained a bank loan of $30,000 for the firm. One of the provisions of the loan is that the year-end debt-to-equity ratio (ratio of total liabilities to total stockholders' equity) shall not exceed 1.0. Based on the above balance sheet, the ratio at the end of 2018 is 1.08 ($45,900/$42,600).

Gilbert is concerned about being in violation of the loan agreement and asks your assistance in reviewing the situation. Gilbert believes that his rather inexperienced accountant may have overlooked some items at year-end.

In discussions with Gilbert and the accountant, you learn the following:

1. On January 1, 2018, the firm paid a $4,500 insurance premium for two years of coverage. The amount in Prepaid Insurance has not been adjusted.

2. Depreciation on the equipment should be 10 percent of cost per year. The accountant inadvertently recorded 15 percent for 2018.

3. Interest on the bank loan has been paid through the end of 2018.

4. The firm concluded a major consulting engagement in December, doing a plant layout analysis for a new factory. The $6,000 fee has not been billed or recorded in the accounts.

5. On December 1, 2018, the firm received an $11,300 advance payment from Croy Corporation for consulting services to be rendered over a two-month period. This payment was credited to the Unearned Consulting Fees account. One-half of this fee was earned by December 31, 2018.

6. Supplies costing $4,800 were on hand on December 31. The accountant filed the record of the count but made no entry in the accounts.

Required

a. What is the correct debt-to-equity ratio at December 31, 2018? Is the firm in violation of the loan agreement? Prepare a schedule to support your computation of the correct total liabilities and total stockholders' equity as of December 31, 2018.

b. Why might the loan agreement have contained the debt-to-equity provision?

EYK3-4.   **Financial Analysis Problem** Purpose: To learn more about the Financial Accounting Standards Board (FASB)

Address: http://www.fasb.org

Required

Use the information on the FASB site to answer the following questions:

a. When was the FASB established?

b. What is the mission of the FASB?

c. Who has oversight responsibility for the FASB?

d. What are some of the current projects of the FASB?

CRITICAL THINKING

EYK3-5. **Accounting Research Problem** Refer to the annual report of General Mills, Inc. for the year ending May 28, 2017 (fiscal year 2017), available on this book's Website. Review the consolidated balance sheets.

GENERAL MILLS, INC.

Required
a. Identify two assets listed in the consolidated balance sheets that indicate that General Mills uses the accrual basis of accounting. Which income statement accounts of General Mills are affected by adjustments to these assets accounts?
b. Identify two liabilities listed in the consolidated balance sheets that indicate that General Mills uses the accrual basis of accounting. Which income statement accounts of General Mills are affected by these adjustments?

EYK3-6. **Accounting Communications Activity** Many people do not understand the concept of accrual accounting and how it differs from accounting on a cash basis. In particular, they are confused as to why a company's results in any one accounting period can differ so much between the two methods of accounting. Because the cash basis is understood to a far larger degree, many people argue that the cash basis should be the primary basis of accounting.

Required
Write a short memorandum that explains the difference between accrual accounting and the cash basis of accounting. In your memo give a simple example of how the accrual basis can give a clearer picture of a company's performance in a given period.

EYK3-7. **Accounting Ethics Case** It is the end of an accounting year for Juliet Kravetz, controller of a medium-sized, publicly held corporation specializing in toxic waste cleanup. Within the corporation, only Kravetz and the president know that the firm has been negotiating for several months to land a very large contract for waste cleanup in Western Europe. The president has hired another firm with excellent contacts in Western Europe to help with the negotiations. The outside firm charges an hourly fee plus expenses, but has agreed not to submit a bill until the negotiations are in their final stages (expected to occur in another three to four months). Even if the contract falls through, the outside firm is entitled to receive payment for its services. Based upon her discussion with a member of the outside firm, Kravetz knows that its charge for services provided to date will be $150,000. This is a material amount for the company.

Kravetz knows that the president wants the negotiations to remain as secret as possible so that competitors will not learn of the European contract that the company is pursuing. Indeed, the president recently stated to her, "This is not the time to reveal our actions in Western Europe to other staff members, our auditors, or readers of our financial statements; securing this contract is crucial to our future growth." No entry has been made in the accounting records for the cost of the contract negotiations. Kravetz now faces an uncomfortable situation. The company's outside auditor has just asked her if she knows of any year-end adjustments that have not yet been recorded.

Required
What are the ethical considerations that Kravetz faces in answering the auditor's question? How should she respond to the question?

EYK3-8. **Corporate Social Responsibility Problem** Unlike financial reporting that requires all reported amounts to be expressed in monetary terms, Corporate Social Responsibility (CSR) reporting is often more qualitative than quantitative. This has caused some individuals to discount the CSR reports as too subjective.

Required
a. Can you identify any subjective areas within a financial statement prepared under GAAP?
b. Discuss the reasons both financial reporting, and to a larger extent CSR reporting, allow subjective estimates to be part of the report.

EYK3-9. **Forensic Accounting Problem** Most employees that choose to commit fraud against their employers feel justified in doing so. For example, a demotion with a corresponding pay cut can provide motivation to produce what is called "wages in kind," where the employee creates his or her own wages.

Required

What actions might an organization take to prevent "wages in kind"?

EYK3-10. **Analyzing IFRS Financial Statements** The 2017 financial statements of LVMH Moet Hennessey-Louis Vuitton S.A. are presented in Appendix C at the end of this book. LVMH is a Paris-based holding company and one of the world's largest and best-known luxury goods companies. As a member of the European Union, French companies are required to prepare their consolidated (group) financial statements using International Financial Reporting Standards (IFRS). After reviewing LVMH's consolidated financial statements, consider the following questions.

Required

a. Identify two assets listed in the group balance sheets that indicate that LVMH uses the accrual basis of accounting. Which income statement accounts of LVMH are affected by adjustments to these assets accounts?

b. Identify two liabilities listed in the group balance sheets that indicate that LVMH uses the accrual basis of accounting. Which income statement accounts of LVMH are affected by these adjustments?

EYK3-11. **Working with the Takeaways** The Vail Company has the following items that require adjustments as of December 31.

a. Service revenue of $600 had been received prior to work being performed. This amount was properly recorded as unearned revenue. At year-end, $500 of the services have now been performed.

b. Interest expense of $975 has not been recorded.

c. Services in the amount of $350 have been performed but not yet billed.

d. A physical count determined that supplies still available were $250. The Supplies asset account shows a balance of $800.

Required

Provide the adjusting entry needed to correct the balance in each of the affected accounts.

ANSWERS TO SELF-STUDY QUESTIONS:

1. b, (pp. 126–127) 2. c, (pp. 128–129) 3. d, (pp. 136–137) 4. c, (p. 121) 5. b, (pp. 133–134)
6. c, (pp. 124–125) 7. d, (pp. 120–121)

YOUR TURN! SOLUTIONS

Solution 3.1

1. June 30	Accounts receivable (+A)	600	
	Sales revenue (+R, +SE)		600
	To recognize revenue earned.		
2. June 30	Cash (+A)	700	
	Unearned revenue (+L)		700
	To recognize cash prior to revenue being earned.		
3. June 30	Inventory (+A)	400	
	Accounts payable (+L)		400
	To record the purchase of inventory on account.		

Solution 3.2

1. c, 2. d, 3. b, 4. a

Solution 3.3

1. Dec. 31	Depreciation expense (+E, −SE)	700	
	Accumulated depreciation—Buildings (+XA, −A)		700
	To record depreciation on buildings.		
2. Dec. 31	Rent expense (+E, −SE)	1,500	
	Prepaid rent (−A)		1,500
	To record rent expense.		

Solution 3.4

1. Dec. 31	Unearned revenue (−L)	400	
	Revenue (+R, +SE)		400
	To recognize revenue earned on a previously recorded advance payment from a customer.		
2. Dec. 31	Interest expense (+E, −SE)	500	
	Interest payable (+L)		500
	To accrue interest expense.		

Solution 3.5

THE CASSI COMPANY Income Statement For the Year Ended December 31, 2019		
Sales revenues		$52,000
Expenses		
Cost of goods sold	$30,000	
Salaries expense	5,000	
Rent expense	6,000	
Depreciation expense	6,000	
Total expenses		47,000
Net income		$ 5,000

THE CASSI COMPANY Statement of Stockholders' Equity For the Year Ended December 31, 2019			
	Common Stock	Retained Earnings	Total
Balance, December 1, 2019	$15,000	$5,000	$20,000
Add: Net income for December		5,000	5,000
Less: Dividends in December		(2,000)	(2,000)
Balance, December 31, 2019	$15,000	$8,000	$23,000

THE CASSI COMPANY
Balance Sheet
As of December 31, 2019

Assets			Liabilities		
Current assets			Current liabilities		
Cash.....................	$ 4,000		Accounts payable.......	$ 8,000	
Accounts receivable.........	15,000		Salaries payable........	9,000	
Inventory..................	18,000		Dividends payable	2,000	
Prepaid rent	5,000		Unearned service.......	5,000	
Total current assets........		$42,000	Total current liabilities ..		$24,000
			Long-term debt.........		35,000
Equipment	50,000		Total liabilities..........		59,000
Less: Accumulated					
depreciation	(10,000)	40,000	**Stockholders' Equity**		
			Common stock.........	15,000	
			Retained earnings	8,000	
			Total stockholders'		
			equity		23,000
Total Assets		$82,000	Total Liabilities and		
			Stockholders' Equity...		$82,000

Solution 3.6

a. Permanent

b. Permanent

c. Temporary

d. Permanent

e. Temporary

f. Temporary

g. Permanent

h. Permanent

Solution 3.7

Dec. 31	Sales revenue (−R)	79,000	
	Retained earnings (+SE)		79,000
	To close the revenue account.		
Dec. 31	Retained earnings (−SE)	72,000	
	Cost of goods sold (−E)		41,000
	Wage expense (−E)		22,000
	Rent expense (−E)		3,000
	Depreciation expense (−E)		2,000
	Interest expense (−E)		4,000
	To close the expense accounts.		
Dec. 31	Retained earnings (−SE)	5,000	
	Dividends (−D)		5,000
	To close the dividends account.		

Solution 3A.1

a. Permanent

b. Permanent

c. Temporary

d. Permanent

e. Temporary

f. Temporary

g. Permanent

h. Permanent

Solution 3A.2

Dec. 31	Sales revenue (−R)	79,000	
	Income summary (+SE)		79,000
	To close the revenue account.		
Dec. 31	Income summary (−SE)	72,000	
	Cost of goods sold (−E)		41,000
	Wage expense (−E)		22,000
	Rent expense (−E)		3,000
	Depreciation expense (−E)		2,000
	Interest expense (−E)		4,000
	To close the expense accounts.		
Dec. 31	Income summary (−SE)	7,000	
	Retained earnings (+SE)		7,000
	To close the Income Summary account.		
Dec. 31	Retained earnings (−SE)	5,000	
	Dividends (−D)		5,000
	To close the Dividends account.		

Chapter 4

Understanding Financial Statements

PAST

Chapters 1 through 3 explained the five-step accounting cycle: analyze, record, adjust, report, and close.

PRESENT

This chapter introduces classified financial statements and some key ratios computed from those statements.

FUTURE

Later chapters expand on ratios used in analyzing financial statements, starting in Chapter 5, which focuses on analyzing and recording merchandising transactions.

After a visit to one of **Apple**'s many retail stores, you will likely find it hard to believe that the company ever faced financial difficulties. The company has a cult-like following for its products including its Macintosh computer, the iPod, the iPhone, the iPad, and the Watch. Business has not always been so good for the company. In fact, Apple suffered crippling financial losses and record low stock prices in the mid-1990s. Steve Jobs, who left the company in 1985 to start another business, was brought back to Apple in 1997 as chief executive officer (CEO). Over the next few years, Jobs was able to return the company to profitability.

Being a profitable company has allowed Apple to benefit from what some refer to as a virtuous cycle in which the company is able to both do good financially and do good socially. The company's solid financial resources provide the ability to do good, whereas doing good helps the company do well financially.

But what if we decide to consider investing in a company like Apple? How should we go about determining whether Apple is a good investment? We first want to do some research to determine if the company is profitable and financially sound. In this, and future chapters, we will begin to accumulate the financial skills needed to evaluate the financial health and operating performance of companies such as Apple.

Road Map

LO	Learning Objective	Page	eLecture	Guided Example	Assignments
LO1	Describe a classified balance sheet.	188	E4-1	YT4.1	SS1, SS2, SS3, SS4, SS5, SE1, E1A, E4A, E1B, E4B, P1A, P2A, P4A, P1B, P2B, P4B
LO2	Describe a single-step and multi-step income statement.	193	E4-2	YT4.2	SS13, SE10, E2A, E2B, P3A, P6A, P10A, P3B, P6B, P10B
LO3	Discuss use of a balance sheet and ratios to assess liquidity and solvency.	197	E4-3	YT4.3	SS6, SS7, SS11, SE3, SE4, SE7, E3A, E5A, E6A, E3B, E5B, E6B, P5A, P8A, P9A, P5B, P8B, P9B
LO4	Discuss use of the income statement and ratios to assess profitability.	199	E4-4	YT4.4	SS8, SS9, SE2, SE9, E3A, E5A, E8A, E3B, E5B, E8B, P5A, P6A, P8A, P9A, P5B, P6B, P8B, P9B
LO5	Explain the components of the statement of stockholders' equity.	201	E4-5	YT4.5	SS10, SS12, E7A, E10A, E7B, E10B, P7A, P7B
LO6	Explain use of the statement of cash flows to help assess solvency.	202	E4-6	YT4.6	SE5, SE6, SE8, SE11, E3A, E5A, E9A, E3B, E5B, E9B, P4A, P4B

BALANCE SHEET CLASSIFICATION AND ANALYSIS

eLectures
MBC

LO1 **Describe** a classified balance sheet.

A **classified balance sheet** presents the assets and liabilities of a business in separate subgroups. Such classification aids our financial analysis and business decision making. **Exhibit 4-1** presents a list of the typical components of a classified balance sheet. A company need not use all of the components, and each company will use only those components necessary to report its financial position. **Exhibit 4-1** shows that a company's assets are commonly classified into two subgroups: current assets and long-term assets. Similarly, liabilities are classified into two subgroups: current liabilities and long-term liabilities. Classified balance sheets are presented by most businesses.

| Exhibit 4-1 | Typical Components of a Classified Balance Sheet |

Current Assets

Current assets consist of cash and other assets that will be converted into cash or used within the normal operating cycle of a business or one year, whichever is longer. The **normal operating cycle** of a business is the average period of time between the payment of cash to deliver a service or to buy goods for resale and the subsequent collection of cash from customers who purchase those services or products. For most businesses, the normal operating cycle is less than one year. For example, the normal operating cycle for a grocery store chain like **Safeway** might be as short as a week or two, on average, and even only a day or two for perishable products like bread and fresh sliced vegetables.

Current assets are listed on a classified balance sheet in the order of their expected liquidity. **Liquidity** is the ability of an asset to be readily converted into cash. **Exhibit 4-1** lists five examples of current assets in the order of their expected liquidity: cash, short-term marketable securities, accounts receivable, inventory, and other current assets. Short-term marketable securities represent short-term investments in the securities of other firms that can be quickly sold for cash. Accounts receivable and inventory are converted into cash as part of the normal operations of a business; that is, inventory is sold for cash or on credit (accounts receivable) that is subsequently collected as cash from customers. Other current assets, such as supplies, are consumed during the normal operating cycle rather than converted into cash, and thus, represent the least liquid of the current assets. The following excerpt shows the current asset section of **Apple**'s balance sheet.

APPLE INC. Balance Sheet (Partial) September 30, 2017 (in millions)	
Cash	$ 20,289
Short-term investments	53,892
Accounts receivable	35,673
Inventory	4,855
Other current assets	13,936
Total current assets	$128,645

Assets that will be converted into cash or used within the normal operating cycle of a business or one year, whichever is longer.

Long-Term Assets

Long-term assets are assets that the company does not expect to convert into cash within the next year or use during the course of the normal operating cycle, whichever is longer. As shown in **Exhibit 4-1**, long-term assets include property, plant, and equipment, intangible assets, and other long-term assets.

Property, Plant, and Equipment

Property, plant, and equipment consists of the land, buildings, equipment, vehicles, furniture, and fixtures that a company uses in its day-to-day operations. Investments into property, plant, and equipment, or PP&E, are often referred to as *capital expenditures* or capital investments. The following excerpt shows the PP&E section of **Apple**'s balance sheet.

APPLE INC. Balance Sheet (Partial) September 30, 2017 (in millions)		
Property, plant, and equipment		
Land and buildings	$13,587	
Equipment	54,210	
Leasehold improvements	7,279	$75,076
Less: accumulated depreciation and amortization		41,293
Total property, plant, and equipment		$33,783

Intangible Assets

Intangible assets consist of brand names, copyrights, patents, and trademarks that a company acquires. These assets are referred to as "intangible" because, unlike buildings and equipment, they lack a physical presence. But, like buildings and equipment, intangible assets enable a company to generate revenue from its customers who recognize the quality associated with products bearing a brand name or trademark. The following excerpt shows the intangible asset section of **Apple**'s balance sheet.

APPLE INC. Balance Sheet (Partial) September 30, 2017 (in millions)	
Intangible assets	
Goodwill	$5,717
Acquired technology	2,298
	$8,015

Other Long-Term Assets

Other long-term assets consist of resources that a company consolidates into a single miscellaneous category for purposes of presentation on the balance sheet. We discuss and illustrate the various types of assets that comprise this category of assets in later chapters. The following excerpt shows the other long-term assets section of **Apple**'s balance sheet.

APPLE INC. Balance Sheet (Partial) September 30, 2017 (in millions)	
Other long-term assets	
Long-term marketable securities.	$194,714
Other assets	10,162
	$204,876

Current Liabilities

Current liabilities consist of liabilities that must be settled within the normal operating cycle or one year, whichever is longer. **Exhibit 4-1** lists four types of current liabilities: accounts payable, accrued expenses payable, short-term notes payable, and other current liabilities. Accounts payable reflects the amounts owed for inventory that was purchased from suppliers on credit. Accrued expenses payable include wages, utilities, interest, income tax, and property taxes that are legally owed by a company but which have not yet been paid. Short-term notes payable represent amounts owed that are specified in a formal contract called a note. Other current liabilities consist of current obligations that the company aggregates into a single miscellaneous category. One example is the advance payments received from customers (deferred revenue), such as for goods under a layaway plan that will be recognized as revenue within the normal operating cycle or one year, whichever is longer. The following excerpt shows the current liabilities section of **Apple**'s balance sheet.

APPLE INC. Balance Sheet (Partial) September 30, 2017 (in millions)	
Current liabilities	
Accounts payable	$ 49,049
Accrued expenses	25,744
Deferred revenue	7,548
Short-term loans	18,473
Total current liabilities	$100,814

Liabilities that must be settled within the normal operating cycle or one year, whichever is longer.

Long-Term Liabilities

Long-term liabilities consist of debt obligations not due to be settled within the normal operating cycle or one year. Long-term notes payable and bonds payable are two examples of long-term liabilities. Other long-term liabilities include unfunded employee retirement plans that will be funded by the company in the future, or deferred revenue that will be recognized as revenue over longer periods. The following excerpt shows the long-term liabilities section of **Apple**'s balance sheet.

A.K.A. Long-term liabilities are also referred to as **noncurrent liabilities**.

APPLE INC. Balance Sheet (Partial) September 30, 2017 (in millions)	
Long-term liabilities	
Deferred revenue	$ 2,836
Long-term debt	97,207
Other long-term liabilities	40,415
Total long-term liabilities	$140,458

Stockholders' Equity

Stockholders' equity is the residual ownership interest in the assets of a business after its liabilities have been settled. The stockholders' equity of a corporation is divided into two main categories: amounts invested by stockholders (common stock) and the cumulative net income of a business that has not yet been distributed to its stockholders as a dividend (retained earnings). The following excerpt shows the stockholders' equity section of **Apple**'s balance sheet.

A.K.A. Stockholders' equity is also referred to as **shareholders' equity**.

APPLE INC. Balance Sheet (Partial) September 30, 2017 (in millions)	
Stockholders' equity	
Common stock	$ 35,867
Retained earnings	98,330
Other equity	(150)
Total stockholders' equity	$134,047

Presentation Format

There are two generally accepted formats for presenting a classified balance sheet—the account form and the report form. In the **account form**, assets are displayed on the left side and liabilities and stockholders' equity are displayed on the right side. In the **report form**, assets are displayed at the top, followed by liabilities, and finally by stockholders' equity. Apple's 2017 and 2016 balance sheets in report form are presented in **Exhibit 4-2**. The report form is the more widely used format.

Hint: According to Accounting Trends and Techniques, a recent survey of 600 large U.S. companies shows that 88% use the report form for their balance sheet while 12% use the account form.

Exhibit 4-2	Report Form of a Classified Balance Sheet

APPLE INC.
Balance Sheet
September 30, 2017, and September 24, 2016 (in millions)

(in millions)	2017	2016
Assets		
Current assets		
Cash	$ 20,289	$ 20,484
Short-term investments	53,892	46,671
Accounts receivable	35,673	29,299
Inventory	4,855	2,132
Other current assets	13,936	8,283
Total current assets	128,645	106,869
Long-term assets		
Property, plant and equipment	33,783	27,010
Intangible assets	8,015	8,620
Other noncurrent assets	204,876	179,187
Total long-term assets	246,674	214,817
Total assets	$375,319	$321,686
Liabilities		
Current liabilities		
Accounts payable	$ 49,049	$ 37,294
Other current liabilities	51,765	41,712
Total current liabilities	100,814	79,006
Long-term liabilities	140,458	114,431
Total liabilities	241,272	193,437
Stockholders' Equity		
Common stock	35,867	31,251
Retained earnings	98,330	96,364
Other equity	(150)	634
Total stockholders' equity	134,047	128,249
Total liabilities and stockholders' equity	$375,319	$321,686

IFRS ALERT

Go to Appendix C at the end of this book and review the classified balance sheet of LVMH Moet Hennessy, Louis Vuitton. LVMH is a Paris-based holding company and one of the world's largest and best-known luxury goods companies. As a member of the European Union, French companies are required to prepare their consolidated (group) financial statements using International Financial Reporting Standards (IFRS). After reviewing LVMH's balance sheet, prepare a list of differences between LVMH's IFRS balance sheet and Apple's U.S. GAAP balance sheet in **Exhibit 4-2**. Differences include: (1) LVMH presents noncurrent assets before its current assets—that is, it lists the company's assets in reverse order of liquidity; (2) LVMH presents shareholders' equity before liabilities; (3) LVMH presents noncurrent liabilities before current liabilities; and (4) LVMH uses slightly different labeling for some of its balance sheet accounts—for instance common stock is referred to as "share capital."

The President of Musicland Company requests that you prepare a classified balance sheet in report form for the company. The following financial data are available from the company's accounting records as of December 31, 2019.

Other current liabilities	$ 2,000	Other current assets	$ 1,500
Long-term notes payable	20,000	Inventory	12,200
Stockholders' equity	17,500	Property, plant, & equipment, net	25,000
Accounts payable	2,500	Accounts receivable	3,000
Cash	300		

YOUR TURN! 4.1

The solution is on page 227.

INCOME STATEMENT CLASSIFICATION AND ANALYSIS

A **single-step income statement** is the simplest form of an income statement. The name originates from the way the statement is constructed. The sum of the expenses is subtracted from the sum of the revenues in a single step to arrive at net income. An example of a single-step income statement for **Apple** for the years ended September 30, 2017, and September 24, 2016, is in **Exhibit 4-3**.

LO2

Describe a single-step and multi-step income statement.

Exhibit 4-3	Single-Step Income Statement for Apple Inc.

APPLE INC.
Income Statement
For Years Ended September 30, 2017, and September 24, 2016

(in millions)	2017	2016
Revenues		
Net sales	$229,234	$215,639
Other income	2,745	1,348
Total revenues	231,979	216,987
Expenses		
Cost of goods sold	141,048	131,376
Research and development expenses	11,581	10,045
Selling, general and administrative	15,261	14,194
Income tax expenses	15,738	15,685
Total expenses	183,628	171,300
Net income	$ 48,351	$ 45,687

Specifically, Apple's 2017 revenues are totaled, yielding $231,979 million. Next, Apple's 2017 expenses of $183,628 million are totaled and subtracted from total revenues to yield Apple's 2017 net income of $48,351 million.

A **multi-step income statement** presents revenues and expenses in distinct categories to facilitate financial analysis and management decision making. A multi-step income statement provides financial statement users with more information, and thus, enables them to make better and more informed decisions about a business. A multi-step income statement is divided into two main sections; the operating section and the non-operating section. The operating section contains revenues and expenses related to the principal business activities of the company. The non-operating section contains revenues and expenses that are incidental to the company's principal business activities, such as gains or losses on the sale of equipment and interest revenue or expense.

The format of a multi-step income statement will differ somewhat depending on whether the company is a service firm or a merchandising firm. The difference in format between

A.K.A A multi-step income statement is also known as a **classified income statement**.

service firms and merchandising firms results because service firms do not sell a physical product and therefore do not have cost of goods sold. Examples of service companies include accounting firms, health care providers, and architects. In contrast, merchandising companies sell goods to customers. We discuss merchandisers in more detail in Chapter 5.

For a service company, its total operating expenses are subtracted from its service revenues to determine its income from operations. Operating expenses are those expenses that relate to the primary operating activities of a business. Operating expenses are commonly classified as selling, general and administrative expenses. Revenue and expense items that do not relate to the primary operating activities of the company appear in a separate category called *Other Income and Expense*. The net amount of other income and expense is either added to or subtracted from income from operations to determine pretax income.

A.K.A. Gross profit is often referred to as **gross margin**.

For a merchandising company, the cost of goods sold is subtracted from the firm's net sales to determine its gross profit on sales. **Gross profit**, or gross profit on sales, is defined as the difference between net sales and cost of goods sold and reveals the amount of sales revenue remaining after subtracting the cost of products sold. **Net sales** are total sales less an estimate of **sales returns and allowances** and **sales discounts**. Sales returns and allowances represent the expected amount given to the customer for the return of merchandise or in lieu of a return. Sales discounts represent an expected amount allowed to the buyer for early payment. These items will be discussed further in Chapter 5. Gross profit also reveals how much sales revenue remains to cover a business's operating expenses. The remainder of the structure of a merchandising company's multi-step income statement (following gross profit) is the same as the structure of the service company's multi-step income statement.

A.K.A. Income before income tax is also known as **pretax income**.

Exhibit 4-4 presents a multi-step income statement for **Apple**. Apple's multi-step income statement provides more detail to the financial statement user with four measures of company performance: gross profit on sales, income from operations, income before income taxes, and net income. Gross profit on sales indicates how well the company performed in terms of purchasing goods, warehousing those goods, and pricing the goods for sale. Income from operations reports Apple's performance after considering the cost of running its stores, paying its employees, advertising to its customers, and administering the business. The income before income taxes reports the company's performance after considering various nonoperating items like interest expense and interest income but before subtracting the expected cost of

Exhibit 4-4	Multi-Step Income Statement for a Merchandising Company		
APPLE INC. **Income Statement** **For Years Ended September 30, 2017, and September 24, 2016**			
(in millions)		**2017**	**2016**
Net sales.		$229,234	$215,639
Less cost of goods sold		141,048	131,376
Gross profit on sales		88,186	84,263
Operating expenses			
Research and development expenses		11,581	10,045
Selling, general and administrative.		15,261	14,194
Total operating expenses		26,842	24,239
Income from operations.		61,344	60,024
Other income and expenses.		2,745	1,348
Income before income taxes		64,089	61,372
Income tax expense		15,738	15,685
Net income		$ 48,351	$ 45,687

A multi-step income statement for a service firm will not have cost of goods sold nor will it have a subtotal for gross profit on sales income taxes. Income tax is then subtracted from income before income taxes to compute net income. Income tax is computed as a percentage of income before income taxes.

Net sales for Apple consists primarily of sales of hardware, software, digital content, and support contracts. Apple records reductions from these amounts for estimated future product returns. Cost of goods sold represents the cost to Apple for the items sold. Cost of goods sold is typically the largest expense for a retail company such as Apple. Cost of goods sold is subtracted directly from net sales to highlight the gross profit on sales. The gross profit on sales is an important financial indicator for investment professionals who follow retail companies like Apple. Analysts compare the gross profit on sales between retailers as a way to assess the effectiveness of the retailer's pricing and purchasing policies.

The operating expenses section includes expenses that relate to the primary operating activities of a business. Operating expenses consist primarily of selling expenses and administrative expenses. Examples of Apple's selling, general and administrative expenses include salaries expense, delivery expense, advertising expense, depreciation expense, rent expense, and supplies expense.

The other income and expense section of the income statement is sometimes labeled nonoperating activities. Examples of revenues and expenses that do not relate to the primary operating activities of a merchandising firm include:

Other Revenues and Gains	Other Expenses and Losses
• Interest revenue	• Interest expense
• Gains on asset sales	• Losses on asset sales
• Dividend income	

These items are reported in the other income and expense section that follows the financial information regarding a business's primary operating activities.

Net income measures Apple's bottom-line performance—that is after all costs of running the business are subtracted. Net income is the same whether the company uses a single-step or multi-step income statement format.

Exhibit 4-5 presents the components of a multi-step income statement for Webwork (a service company) and for Apple (a merchandising company). We see the absence of the cost of goods sold section, including the gross profit subtotal, in the service company's income statement. Otherwise, the income statements follow the same format.

Exhibit 4-5	Classified Income Statements for Service and Merchandising Companies		
WEBWORK, INC. **Income Statement** **For Year Ended December 31, 2019**		**APPLE INC.** **Income Statement** **For Year Ended September 30, 2017**	
Revenues	$19,150	Net sales.	$229,234
		Less cost of goods sold	141,048
		Gross profit on sales	88,186
Operating expenses		Operating expenses	
Wage, rent and supplies expenses. . . .	5,550	Research and development expenses	11,581
Depreciation and interest expenses . . .	750	Selling, general and administrative	15,261
Total operating expenses	6,300	Total operating expenses	26,842
Income from operations	12,850	Income from operations	61,344
Other income and expenses.	—	Other income and expenses.	2,745
Income before income taxes	12,850	Income before income taxes	64,089
Income tax expense	2,570	Income tax expense	15,738
Net income	$10,280	Net income	$ 48,351

IFRS ALERT

Appendix C at the end of this book presents the multi-step income statement for LVMH Moet Hennessy, Louis Vuitton. LVMH is a Paris-based holding company and one of the world's largest and best-known luxury goods companies. As a member of the European Union, French companies are required to prepare their consolidated (group) financial statements using International Financial Reporting Standards (IFRS). Make a list of the similarities and any differences between LVMH's multi-step income statement and Apple's multi-step income statement in **Exhibit 4-4**. Like Apple, LVMH reports several measures of company performance: gross margin, profit from recurring operations, operating profit, net financial income (expense). Differences include (1) LVMH including more subsections; (2) LVMH uses the word "profit" instead of "income"; (3) LVMH separates out minority interest (less than 100 percent owned subsidiaries that are consolidated with the parent LVMH); (4) LVMH refers to its interest expense as "cost of financial debt." Other than these labeling differences, LVMH's multi-step income statement under IFRS is strikingly similar to Apple's U.S. GAAP multi-step income statement.

YOUR TURN! 4.2

The solution is on page 227.

Musicland provides the following information and requests that we prepare a multi-step income statement for the year ended December 31. Musicland pays income tax at the rate of 30 percent of income.

Selling, general and administrative expenses. . .	$25,000	Cost of goods sold.	$ 45,000
Research & development expense.	10,000	Net sales	100,000
Interest expense	5,000		

WORKING WITH FINANCIAL STATEMENTS

So far we have introduced the basic financial statements. We now demonstrate how financial statements are used to address questions about a company's operating performance and financial health.

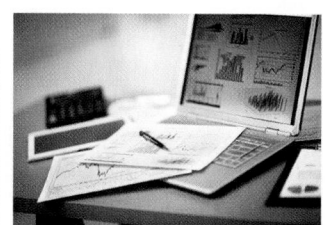

Analysis Based on Ratios

If Apple's net income in 2017 totaled $48,351 million, would we conclude that the company had a good year or a bad year? While $48,351 million is a large number, some frame of reference is needed before we can conclude that this amount represents a good, bad, or mediocre level of operating performance. For example, $48,351 million is a phenomenal performance if the company had only $1 million in assets to operate with during the year. But it is not as exceptional if the company had $100,000 million in assets to operate with during the year.

Investment professionals use a variety of methods to get a better understanding of how to interpret a net income number like $48,351 million. One such method involves ratio analysis. **Ratio analysis** expresses the relation of one relevant accounting number to another relevant accounting number through the process of division. The result of the division is expressed as a percentage, a rate, or as a proportion.

To illustrate how a ratio can provide additional meaning to Apple's net income of $48,351 million, we can divide Apple's net income by its total assets of $375,319 million, which is known as its **return on assets (ROA)**.

$$\text{Return on Assets (ROA)} = \frac{\text{Net income}}{\text{Total Assets}}$$

The result tells us that Apple earned a rate of return of 12.9 percent on each dollar of assets invested in the business in 2017.

Although a single number like Apple's net income is difficult to interpret in isolation, a single ratio is also difficult to interpret without some point of reference or benchmark. Business professionals often use one of two techniques to further their understanding of ratios. **Trend analysis** compares a company's results, or the results of a ratio, over time. This technique helps the financial statement user identify any readily observable trends in a company's performance. **Benchmarking analysis** compares a company's performance, or a ratio, to that of its competitors, or to an industry average. Under benchmarking analysis, we are trying to compare, or benchmark, a company's performance against similar companies, or against an industry standard. Trend analysis and benchmarking analysis are powerful tools to place a company's results into a meaningful context.

Working with the Balance Sheet

The balance sheet helps users evaluate the financial health of a company. The balance sheet also provides information on how the company finances the acquisition of its assets, with debt or with equity.

LO3 **Discuss** use of a balance sheet and ratios to assess liquidity and solvency.

Terms such as liquidity and solvency refer to the financial well-being of a company. For a company to remain in business, it must be able to pay its bills when they come due. Before a bank such as **Bank of America** will commit to extend a loan to a company like Apple, it needs to assess the likelihood that it will be repaid the amount borrowed and be paid the interest due on the amount borrowed, both in a timely manner. This assessment involves evaluating Apple's *liquidity*, the ability to pay obligations that come due in the current year, and *solvency*, the ability to pay obligations over the long term.

Liquidity

Liquidity refers to a company's ability to pay its short-term financial obligations. It depends on several factors, including the level of cash a company has and how quickly it can generate cash from operations or its assets.

Current Ratio   One widely used measure of a company's liquidity is the **current ratio**. The current ratio is defined as current assets divided by current liabilities. Current assets provide a measure of the cash available and expected to be generated in the current period. Current liabilities provide a measure of the cash that will be needed in the current period to pay existing or expected obligations.

$$\text{Current ratio} = \frac{\text{Current assets}}{\text{Current liabilities}}$$

A current ratio greater than one implies that a company has more cash and current assets than needed to pay off its current obligations, and a ratio less than one implies the opposite. While this interpretation is overly simplistic, it does provide an easily understood assessment of a company's liquidity. In general, the greater the current ratio, the more liquid a company is, and the less concern a lender has in extending a loan to the company.

One of Apple's competitors is **Hewlett-Packard Inc.**, an online retailer of personal computers. The current ratios for both Apple and for Hewlett-Packard are shown in **Exhibit 4-6**. Both companies report current ratios greater than one in 2017 and over one for Apple and just under one for Hewlett-Packard in 2016. Based on this ratio, we would conclude that Apple is more liquid than Hewlett-Packard in both years and that each company appears to be sufficiently liquid to satisfy currently due obligations.

Exhibit 4-6	Current Ratio		
Current Ratio		**2017**	**2016**
Apple		$\dfrac{\$128{,}645}{\$100{,}814} = 1.28{:}1$	$\dfrac{\$106{,}869}{\$79{,}006} = 1.35{:}1$
Hewlett-Packard.		$\dfrac{\$22{,}318}{\$22{,}412} = 1.00{:}1$	$\dfrac{\$18{,}468}{\$18{,}808} = 0.98{:}1$

TAKEAWAY 4.1	Concept	➡ Method	➡ Assessment
	Can a company meet its short-term obligations?	Current assets and current liabilities from the balance sheet. $\text{Current ratio} = \dfrac{\text{Current assets}}{\text{Current liabilities}}$	A larger current ratio implies greater liquidity and a greater ability to pay short-term obligations.

Solvency

Lenders often provide loans that have repayment terms that extend over several years. In such cases the lender is interested in evaluating a company's solvency. **Solvency** refers to a company's ability to pay its long-term financial obligations. It depends on several factors, including the level of assets a company has. Solvency, therefore, is a measure of a company's ability to survive over the long term. (Both liquidity and solvency are important indicators of financial health, but a company must first be liquid. If a company is unable to pay its bills in the short term, it is irrelevant whether it is solvent in the long term.)

Debt-to-Total-Assets Ratio   In general, the more debt a company uses to finance its assets and day-to-day operations, the riskier it is. This follows because the amount borrowed and the interest on that amount must be paid on a regular schedule. If a company is unable to meet the cash outflows required to satisfy its debt repayment schedule or meet its regular interest payments, a lender can legally demand immediate repayment of a loan, potentially forcing a company into bankruptcy if it is unable to repay that amount. The **debt-to-total-assets ratio**, calculated as total liabilities divided by total assets, provides a measure of this risk and is one ratio used to assess a company's solvency.

$$\textbf{Debt-to-total-assets ratio} = \frac{\textbf{Total liabilities}}{\textbf{Total assets}}$$

The greater the debt-to-total-assets ratio, the greater is a company's risk of not being able to pay its interest payments or principal repayments on a timely basis, and the lower is the company's solvency. Like the current ratio, the debt-to-total-assets ratio should not be used in isolation. There are many factors that must be considered when judging a company's solvency.

Exhibit 4-7 shows the debt-to-total-assets ratios for Apple and Hewlett-Packard. This exhibit reveals that in both 2017 and 2016, Hewlett-Packard used considerably more debt to finance its assets than did Apple (110.4 percent versus 64.3 percent in 2017). Consequently, Hewlett-Packard would be considered a riskier, less solvent company. A lender such as **Citibank** would likely be more concerned about the solvency of Hewlett-Packard than the solvency of Apple.

Exhibit 4-7	Debt-to-Total-Assets Ratio		
(in millions)		**2017**	**2016**
Apple		$\dfrac{\$241,272}{\$375,319} = 64.3\%$	$\dfrac{\$193,437}{\$321,686} = 60.1\%$
Hewlett-Packard...........................		$\dfrac{\$36,321}{\$32,913} = 110.4\%$	$\dfrac{\$32,876}{\$28,987} = 113.4\%$

Concept →	Method →	Assessment	TAKEAWAY 4.2
Can a company meet its long-term obligations?	Total assets and total liabilities from the balance sheet. $\text{Debt-to-total-assets ratio} = \dfrac{\text{Total liabilities}}{\text{Total assets}}$	A larger ratio implies reduced solvency and a reduced ability to repay outstanding obligations over the long term.	

The following information is available from the financial statements of the Philips Company

	2019	2018
Net sales..	$120,000	$110,000
Net income......................................	20,000	15,000
Cash provided by operating activities....................	25,000	22,000
Expenditures on property, plant, and equipment	7,000	6,000
Current assets	75,000	65,000
Current liabilities..................................	50,000	45,000
Total assets	220,000	190,000
Total liabilities...................................	$150,000	$145,000

Compute the current ratio and the debt-to-total-assets ratio and comment on any trends observed between 2018 and 2019.

YOUR TURN! 4.3

The solution is on pages 227-228.

Working with the Income Statement

Apple generates income by selling computers, iPads, iPods, iPhones, peripherals, and downloads from its iTunes store. The company's income statement provides a report detailing how much net income Apple was able to generate from these activities. A review of a company's income and its components is called profitability analysis. Apple's net income of $48,351 million for the year ended September 30, 2017, indicates that Apple was able to sell these products at a price that exceeded the cost of manufacturing. Apple's income statement, presented in **Exhibit 4-4**, also shows that the company's profitability increased from 2016 to 2017.

LO4 Discuss use of the income statement and ratios to assess profitability.

Apple's net income increased by $2,664 million, from $45,687 million in 2016 to $48,351 million in 2017. During a similar period, Hewlett-Packard's net income increased by $30 million, from $2,496 million to $2,526 million. This suggests that Apple outperformed one of its leading competitors during this period. How was that possible? Perhaps Apple's success reflects its superior product line or possibly its greater product focus. Alternatively, it might reflect the superior operating acumen of Apple's management team.

Measures for Profitability Analysis

There are many ways to measure a company's success. One such measure is profitability. Profitability indicates whether or not a company is able to bring its products or services to the market efficiently, and whether it produces products or services that are valued by the market. The more profitable a company is, the better are its long-term prospects. Consistently unprofitable companies are on a path to failure.

Return on Sales Ratio (Profit Margin)   It is somewhat unfair, and potentially misleading, to compare two companies of differing size on the basis of net income. A larger company is expected to generate a larger net income. But a large net income does not necessarily indicate that a company is performing more efficiently than a company with a smaller net income. One measure that facilitates a comparison of the profitability between companies of different size is the return on assets ratio, which we already explained. Another useful measure is the **return on sales (ROS) ratio (profit margin)**, calculated as net income divided by net sales.

$$\text{Return on sales ratio} = \frac{\text{Net income}}{\text{Net sales}}$$

Exhibit 4-8 shows the calculation of return on sales for both Apple and Hewlett-Packard. Apple is larger than Hewlett-Packard based on sales generated in 2017 ($229,234 million for Apple versus $52,056 million for Hewlett-Packard). Apple also generates much more net income than Hewlett-Packard ($48,351 million for Apple versus $2,526 million for Hewlett-Packard in 2017). Together, this translates into a much higher return on sales for Apple (21.1 percent for Apple versus 4.9 percent for Hewlett-Packard in 2017). An ROS of 21.1 percent indicates Apple has 21.1 cents left over for each dollar of sales revenue after subtracting all of its expenses. This is over four times as much as Hewlett-Packard, which generates just 4.9 cents for each dollar of sales revenue. This result suggests that Apple is a more profitable company than Hewlett-Packard, possibly because it is able to command a premium price for its products and/or because it runs a more efficient operation than does Hewlett-Packard.

Exhibit 4-8	Return on Sales		
(in millions)		**2017**	**2016**
Apple		$\frac{\$48,351}{\$229,234} = 21.1\%$	$\frac{\$45,687}{\$215,639} = 21.2\%$
Hewlett-Packard		$\frac{\$2,526}{\$52,056} = 4.9\%$	$\frac{\$2,496}{\$48,238} = 5.2\%$

TAKEAWAY 4.3	Concept	→ Method	→ Assessment
	How much net income does a company generate from each dollar of sales revenue?	Net sales and net income from the income statement. $$\text{Return on sales ratio} = \frac{\text{Net income}}{\text{Net sales}}$$	A larger ratio indicates that a company is more profitable on each sales dollar because it commands a premium price for its products and/or is more operationally efficient.

YOUR TURN! 4.4

The solution is on
page 228.

The following information is available from the financial statements of the Philips Company.

	2019	2018
Net sales.	$120,000	$110,000
Net income	20,000	15,000
Cash provided by operating activities.	25,000	22,000
Expenditures on property, plant, and equipment	7,000	6,000
Current assets	75,000	65,000
Current liabilities.	50,000	45,000
Total assets	220,000	190,000
Total liabilities.	150,000	145,000

Compute the return on sales ratio and comment on any trends observed between 2018 and 2019.

Working with the Statement of Stockholders' Equity

Chapter 1 introduced the statement of stockholder's equity, which summarizes the changes in a company's stockholders' equity during the period. The statement of stockholders' equity consists of two parts—contributed capital and earned capital. **Contributed capital** is a measure of the capital contributed by the stockholders of a company when they purchase ownership shares in the company. Ownership shares are called common shares or common stock. **Earned capital** is a measure of the capital that is earned by the company, reinvested in the business, and not distributed to its stockholders—that is, its retained earnings. Retained earnings at the end of a fiscal period is calculated as retained earnings at the start of the period, plus net income for the period, less any dividends paid during the period.

LO5   **Explain** the components of the statement of stockholders' equity.

Retained earnings, beginning of period
+ Net income
− Dividends

Retained earnings, end of period

   Exhibit 4-9 presents the statement of stockholders' equity for Apple. The column labeled Common Stock represents the change in Apple's contributed capital during the period covered by the statement. The change to common stock resulted from the issuance of additional shares to Apple's existing stockholders, to new stockholders, or possibly to Apple's employees.

   The column labeled Retained Earnings in **Exhibit 4-9** represents Apple's earned capital. The primary adjustments in this column are Apple's net income and the dividends Apple distributes to its shareholders.

Investing with a Social Conscience

CORPORATE SOCIAL RESPONSIBILITY

Not all investors are singularly focused on the financial performance of businesses they invest in. For a segment of the investing community, Corporate Social Responsibility goes hand in hand with financial performance in choosing an investment. **Socially Responsible Investing (SRI)**, also known as sustainable investing, considers a firm's environmental stewardship, consumer protection, human rights, and diversity, along with its financial performance. Investments in SRI funds are near $3 trillion and have grown in recent years at a pace almost six times greater than the growth of professionally managed investments.

Exhibit 4-9	Statement of Stockholders' Equity

APPLE INC.
Statement of Stockholders' Equity

(in millions)	Common Stock	Retained Earnings	Other Equity	Total Equity
Balance at September 26, 2015........	$27,416	$92,284	$(345)	$119,355
Issuance of common stock............	3,835			3,835
Net income........................		45,687		45,687
Dividends.........................		(12,188)		(12,188)
Other adjustments		(29,419)	979	(28,440)
Balance at September 24, 2016........	31,251	96,364	634	128,249
Issuance of common stock............	4,616			4,616
Net income........................		48,351		48,351
Dividends.........................		(12,803)		(12,803)
Other adjustments		(33,582)	(784)	(34,366)
Balance at September 30, 2017........	$35,867	$98,330	$(150)	$134,047

YOUR TURN! 4.5

The solution is on page 228.

The following information is available for the Owner Company:

Beginning of the year common stock	$120,000
Beginning of the year retained earnings	85,000
Additional common stock issued during the year	7,500
Net income.......................................	16,000
Dividends..	4,000

Prepare a statement of stockholders' equity for the Owner Company. How much of the total equity is considered contributed capital and how much is considered earned capital?

Working with the Statement of Cash Flows

LO6 **Explain** use of the statement of cash flows to help assess solvency.

A common refrain heard from business people is that "cash is king!" While net income is eventually converted into cash, it is the cash available that a company uses to run its business and pay its bills. The statement of cash flows provides information on a company's sources and uses of cash.

The statement of cash flows aids us in understanding the change in cash reported by a company over a period of time. It explains the change in the cash reported between two balance sheet dates, segmented into three activity categories: (1) cash flow from operating activities, (2) cash flow from investing activities, and (3) cash flow from financing activities. The separation into these three activities increases the statement's usefulness. For example, knowing that cash increased is not as useful as knowing that cash increased because of increased operating cash flow or because of a bank loan.

Exhibit 4-10 shows a simplified version of Apple's statement of cash flows. Apple reported a decrease of $195 million in cash in 2017, decreasing from $20,484 million in 2016 to $20,289 million in 2017. These cash balances are on Apple's balance sheet in **Exhibit 4-2**. Most of Apple's cash flow in 2017 was generated from operating activities ($63,598 million). Apple used much of its cash flow in its investing activities, with a net of $33,147 million used for purchase of investments and $12,451 used to purchase additional property, plant, and equipment. Apple also used a significant amount of cash in its financing activities. The largest of these financing activities was the repurchase of $32,900 million of its common stock.

Exhibit 4-10	Statement of Cash Flows

APPLE INC.
Statement of Cash Flows
For Years Ended September 30, 2017, and September 24, 2016

(in millions)	2017	2016
Cash flow provided by operating activities		
Cash receipts less cash disbursements from operating activities. . . .	$ 63,598	$ 65,824
Net cash provided by operations.	63,598	65,824
Cash flow provided by investing activities		
Net purchases of investments.	(33,147)	(30,634)
Net payments for property, plant, and equipment.	(12,451)	(12,734)
Other cash payments	(848)	(2,609)
Net cash used by investing.	$(46,446)	$(45,977)
Cash flow provided by financing activities		
Net cash from issuance of common stock	$ (692)	$ (668)
Net cash from issuance of debt	25,162	22,454
Payment of dividends	(12,769)	(12,150)
Repurchase of common stock	(32,900)	(29,722)
Other receipts	3,852	(397)
Net cash used by financing	(17,347)	(20,483)
Net increase (decrease) in cash.	(195)	(636)
Cash at beginning of year.	20,484	21,120
Cash at year-end	$ 20,289	$ 20,484

Free Cash Flow

The level of cash flow provided by operating activities is valuable information on a company's ability to generate cash from its day-to-day operations. One measure of cash flow health is **free cash flow**. Free cash flow is often calculated by subtracting a company's capital expenditures for PP&E from its cash flow provided by operating activities. A company's free cash flow is an indicator of its ability to expand operations, repay lenders, or pay stockholders a dividend after replacing the value of any property, plant and equipment used in operations. In general, the larger a company's free cash flow, the healthier a company is in terms of operating cash flow.

Hint: When calculating a firm's free cash flow, "capital expenditures" amount is the cash spent for purchases of PP&E less the cash proceeds received from sale of PP&E. Both amounts are reported on a statement of cash flows.

Free cash flow = Cash flow from operations – Capital expenditures

We calculate Apple's free cash flow in 2017 and 2016 with information reported in Apple's statement of cash flows in **Exhibit 4-10**.

(in millions)	2017	2016
Cash flow provided by operating activities	$63,598	$65,824
Less: Expenditures on property, plant, and equipment	(12,451)	(12,734)
Free cash flow	$51,147	$53,090

Apple's free cash flow of $51,147 in 2017 and $53,090 in 2016 indicates that it generates a healthy free cash flow. It also suggests that Apple should have no trouble financing future purchases of property, plant, and equipment, repaying its lenders, or paying dividends to its stockholders, using its operating cash flow.

TAKEAWAY 4.4	Concept →	Method →	Assessment
	How much free cash flow does a company generate?	Cash provided by operating activities less cash expended on purchases of property, plant, and equipment. Cash provided by operations — Capital expenditures = Free cash flow	Larger free cash flow indicates a greater ability to expand operations, repay debt, or pay dividends without external financing.

YOUR TURN! 4.6

The solution is on page 228.

The following information is available from the financial statements of the Philips Company.

	2019	2018
Net sales.	$120,000	$110,000
Net income.	20,000	15,000
Cash provided by operating activities.	25,000	22,000
Expenditures on property, plant, and equipment	7,000	6,000
Current assets	75,000	65,000
Current liabilities.	50,000	45,000
Total assets	220,000	190,000
Total liabilities.	150,000	145,000

Compute the free cash flow and comment on any trends observed between 2018 and 2019.

FORENSIC ACCOUNTING

Accountant as Detective—Cash Fraud Schemes

Frauds involving cash are the most common frauds, and are more common than corruption or fraudulent financial statements. The more common cash schemes include (1) skimming, where an employee accepts cash from a customer but does not record a sales transaction, (2) cash larceny, where an employee steals cash from the daily receipts before they are deposited in a bank, (3) check tampering, where an employee steals blank company checks and makes them out to him/herself or an accomplice, and (4) cash register disbursement, where an employee fraudulently voids a sale on his or her cash register and steals the cash.

COMPREHENSIVE PROBLEM

Following are items reported on the financial statements of **Microsoft Corporation** as of June 30, 2017. (Some of the reported accounts have been combined for simplicity.) Amounts given are in millions of dollars.

MICROSOFT
CORPORATION

Cash flow provided by operating activities	$ 39,507
Cash at June 30, 2016	6,510
Cash at June 30, 2017	7,663
Net revenue	89,950
Cash flow from investing activities	(46,781)
Inventory	2,181
Accounts receivable	19,792
Cost of goods sold	34,261
Cash flow from financing activities	8,427
Other current assets	130,215
Property, plant, and equipment	23,734
Operating expenses	33,363
Other income	823
Intangible assets	45,228
Other long-term assets	12,273
Income tax expense	1,945
Accounts payable	7,390
Other current liabilities	57,137
Long-term liabilities	104,165
Common stock	69,315
Retained earnings	2,648
Other stockholders' equity	431

a. Prepare a multi-step income statement, a classified balance sheet, and a statement of cash flows using the accounts listed above.

b. Compute the following ratios:
 Current ratio
 Debt-to-total-assets ratio
 Return on sales ratio

Solution

a.

MICROSOFT CORPORATION Income Statement For Year Ended June 30, 2017 (in millions)	
Net revenue	$89,950
Less cost of goods sold	34,261
Gross profit on sales	55,689
Operating expenses	33,363
Income from operations	22,326
Other income	823
Income before income taxes	23,149
Income tax expense	1,945
Net income	$21,204

MICROSOFT CORPORATION
Balance Sheet
June 30, 2017 (in millions)

Assets

Current assets

Cash	$ 7,663	
Accounts receivable	19,792	
Inventory	2,181	
Other current assets	130,215	
Total current assets		$159,851
Property, plant, and equipment		23,734
Intangible assets		45,228
Other long-term assets		12,273
Total assets		$241,086

Liabilities and Stockholders' Equity

Current liabilities

Accounts payable	$ 7,390	
Other current liabilities	57,137	
Total current liabilities		$ 64,527
Long-term liabilities		104,165
Total liabilities		168,692
Stockholders' equity		
Common stock	69,315	
Retained earnings	2,648	
Other stockholders' equity	431	
Total stockholders' equity		72,394
Total liabilities and stockholders' equity		$241,086

MICROSOFT CORPORATION
Statement of Cash Flows
For Year Ended June 30, 2017 (in millions)

Cash flow provided by operating activities	$39,507
Cash flow used by investing activities	(46,781)
Cash flow used by financing activities	8,427
Net increase in cash	1,153
Cash at June 30, 2016	6,510
Cash at June 30, 2017	$ 7,663

b.

Current ratio	$\dfrac{\$159,851}{\$64,527} = 2.48:1$
Debt-to-total-assets ratio	$\dfrac{\$168,692}{\$241,086} = 70.0\%$
Return on sales ratio	$\dfrac{\$21,204}{\$89,950} = 23.6\%$

SUMMARY OF LEARNING OBJECTIVES

Describe a classified balance sheet. (p. 188) **LO1**

- A classified balance sheet contains two subgroups of assets (current assets and long-term assets) and two subgroups of liabilities (current liabilities and long-term liabilities).
- A classified balance sheet can be presented in account form or report form.

Describe a single-step and multi-step income statement. (p. 193) **LO2**

- A multi-step income statement classifies items into subgroups in order to facilitate analysis and decision making.
- A multi-step income statement for a merchandising firm often includes one section for sales revenue; two sections for expenses: cost of goods sold and operating expenses; and a section for other income and expenses.
- A multi-step income statement for a service firm is similar, but does not have a section for cost of goods sold.

Discuss use of a balance sheet and ratios to assess liquidity and solvency. (p. 197) **LO3**

- Ratio analysis involves expressing the relation of one relevant accounting number with another relevant accounting number through the process of division. This process helps to provide a context to interpret a particular number.
- Two techniques that are often used in ratio analysis are (1) trend analysis where ratios are examined over time and (2) benchmarking analysis where a company's ratios are compared to those of another company or to an average of an industry as a whole.
- Liquidity refers to a company's ability to pay those obligations that are expected to come due in the next year.
- The current ratio, or current assets divided by current liabilities, provides a measure of a company's liquidity.
- Solvency refers to a company's ability to repay its debts over the long term.
- The debt-to-total-assets ratio, calculated as total debt divided by total assets, provides one measure of a company's solvency.

Discuss use of the income statement and ratios to assess profitability. (p. 199) **LO4**

- Return on sales, or net income divided by net sales, provides a measure of a company's profitability by indicating how much net income a company earns on each dollar of sales revenue.

Explain the components of the statement of stockholders' equity. (p. 201) **LO5**

- Stockholders' equity comprises two parts: (1) contributed capital and (2) earned capital.
- Contributed capital is the capital contributed to a firm by stockholders when they purchase ownership shares in the company.
- Earned capital represents the net income that has been earned by a company and not distributed to stockholders as a dividend.

Explain use of the statement of cash flows to help assess solvency. (p. 202) **LO6**

- The statement of cash flows provides information regarding a company's sources and uses of cash.
- Free cash flow, calculated as cash provided from operating activities less cash expended on property, plant, and equipment, provides information regarding management's ability to expand operations, repay debt, or make distributions to stockholders, using a firm's operating cash flow.

SUMMARY	Concept	Method ➜	Assessment
TAKEAWAY 4.1	Can a company meet its short-term obligations?	Current assets and current liabilities from the balance sheet. $$\text{Current ratio} = \frac{\text{Current assets}}{\text{Current liabilities}}$$	A larger current ratio implies greater liquidity and a greater ability to pay short-term obligations.
TAKEAWAY 4.2	Can a company meet its long-term obligations?	Total assets and total liabilities from the balance sheet. $$\text{Debt-to-total-assets ratio} = \frac{\text{Total liabilities}}{\text{Total assets}}$$	A larger ratio implies reduced solvency and a reduced ability to repay outstanding obligations over the long term.
TAKEAWAY 4.3	How much net income does a company generate from each dollar of sales revenue?	Net sales and net income from the income statement. $$\text{Return on sales ratio} = \frac{\text{Net income}}{\text{Net sales}}$$	A larger ratio indicates that a company is more profitable on each sales dollar because it commands a premium price for its products and/or is more operationally efficient.
TAKEAWAY 4.4	How much free cash flow does a company generate?	Cash provided by operating activities less cash expended on purchases of property, plant, and equipment. Cash provided by operations − Capital expenditures ───────────────── Free cash flow	Larger free cash flow indicates a greater ability to expand operations, repay debt, or pay dividends without external financing.

KEY TERMS

Account form (p. 191)

Benchmarking analysis (p. 197)

Classified balance sheet (p. 188)

Classified income statement (p. 193)

Contributed capital (p. 201)

Current assets (p. 188)

Current liabilities (p. 190)

Current ratio (p. 197)

Debt-to-total-assets ratio (p. 198)

Earned capital (p. 201)

Free cash flow (p. 203)

Gross margin (p. 194)

Gross profit (p. 194)

Intangible assets (p. 189)

Liquidity (p. 189, 197)

Long-term liabilities (p. 191)

Multi-step income statement (p. 193)

Net sales (p. 194)

Noncurrent liabilities (p. 191)

Normal operating cycle (p. 188)

Pretax income (p. 194)

Property, plant, and equipment (p. 189)

Ratio analysis (p. 196)

Report form (p. 191)

Return on assets (ROA) (p. 196)

Return on sales (ROS) ratio (profit margin) (p. 200)

Sales discounts (p. 194)

Sales returns and allowances (p. 194)

Shareholders' equity (p. 191)

Single-step income statement (p. 193)

Socially Responsible Investing (SRI) (p. 201)

Solvency (p. 198)

Stockholders' equity (p. 191)

Trend analysis (p. 197)

Assignments with the (MBC) logo in the margin are available in BusinessCourse.
See the Preface of the book for details.

SELF-STUDY QUESTIONS

(Answers to Self-Study Questions are at the end of this chapter.)

1. **Which of the following items will not be reported on a classified balance sheet?**   LO1
   a. Current assets
   b. Net income
   c. Total liabilities
   d. Common stock

2. **Which of the following would not be considered a current asset?**   LO1
   a. Inventory
   b. Accounts receivable
   c. Property, plant, and equipment
   d. Cash

3. **For the balance sheet to be in balance, the following must exist:**   LO1
   a. Total assets must be greater than total liabilities.
   b. Total assets must be less than total liabilities.
   c. Total assets must equal total liabilities plus stockholders' equity.
   d. Total liabilities must equal total stockholders' equity.

4. **Which of the following would be considered an intangible asset?**   LO1
   a. Cash
   b. Land
   c. Accounts payable
   d. Patents

5. **Which of the following would most likely be classified as a long-term liability?**   LO1
   a. Accounts payable
   b. Notes payable
   c. Accounts receivable
   d. Common stock

6. **Ratio analysis always involves which type of arithmetic operation?**   LO3
   a. Addition
   b. Subtraction
   c. Multiplication
   d. Division

7. **Which of the following is not a true statement?**   LO3
   a. Benchmarking analysis involves comparing a company to its industry's averages.
   b. Benchmarking analysis involves comparing a company to its competitors.
   c. Trend analysis involves comparing a company's ratios over time.
   d. Benchmarking analysis involves comparing a company's ratios over time.

8. **A company reported net income of $200 on net sales of $2,000. The company's return on sales is:**   LO4
   a. $1,800.
   b. 10 percent.
   c. 0.1 percent.
   d. None of the above.

9. **The return on sales ratio does *not* provide insight on which of the following?**   LO4
   a. A company's net income per dollar of sales
   b. A measure of a company's financial performance
   c. A measure of a company's cash flow flexibility
   d. A measure of a company's operating efficiency

10. **Which of the following is not shown on the statement of stockholders' equity?**   LO5
    a. Contributed capital
    b. Retained earnings
    c. Common stock
    d. Total liabilities

LO3   **11.** **The following data appear in the financial statements of a company. Calculate its current ratio.**

Current assets	$10,000
Current liabilities.	$5,000

   a.   2:1
   b.   1:2
   c. $5,000
   d.   ($5,000)

LO5   **12.** **The following data pertains to Smith Consulting, Inc. for 2018. Compute its ending retained earnings.**

Beginning-of-year retained earnings	$120,000
Net income	37,500
Dividends paid	5,000

   a. $157,500
   b. $152,500
   c. $162,500
   d. $115,000

LO2   **13.** **A merchandising company's multi-step income statement differs from that of a service company in what way?**
   a.   There is no difference.
   b.   A service company does not include a line for cost of goods sold.
   c.   A service company has a line for selling expenses whereas a merchandising company does not.
   d.   A merchandising company will have a line for income from operations whereas a service company will not.

QUESTIONS

1. List three subgroups of assets that may be found in the asset section of a classified balance sheet.
2. Define *current asset* and *normal operating cycle*.
3. Which of the following are current assets: land, cash, prepaid expense, building, accounts receivable, inventory, equipment?
4. What is meant by Corporate Social Responsibility?
5. Define the following ratios: current ratio, debt-to-total-assets ratio, and return on sales ratio.
6. What is meant by socially responsible investing?
7. Which of the following measures are best computed using a classified balance sheet?
   a.   Liquidity
   b.   Solvency
   c.   Free cash flow
   d.   Both a. and b.
8. Which of the following is a correct statement?
   a.   The current ratio is a measure of firm solvency.
   b.   The current ratio is a measure of firm liquidity.
   c.   The debt-to-total-assets ratio is a measure of firm liquidity.
   d.   None of the above is correct.
9. Free cash flow is measured using information from which financial statement?
   a.   Balance sheet
   b.   Income statement
   c.   Statement of cash flows
   d.   Statement of retained earnings
10. Socially Responsible Investing
   a.   Means making as much money on your investments as you can as your only goal.
   b.   Means investing in companies that adhere to environmental and social policies in their operations.
   c.   Is too small of a concept to matter much.

SHORT EXERCISES

SE4-1. **Preparing a Classified Balance Sheet** Desi Company, a merchandising firm, reports the following data as of January 31, 2019: **LO1**

Stockholders' equity	$ 5,700
Property, plant, and equipment	10,000
Inventory	3,500
Accounts receivable	1,200
Other current liabilities	600
Accounts payable	800
Long-term notes payable	8,000
Cash	400

Prepare a classified balance sheet for Desi Company as of January 31, 2019.

SE4-2. **Evaluating Firm Profitability** The following financial information is taken from the annual reports of the Billy Company and the Ball Company: **LO4**

	Billy	Ball
Net income	$10,000	$100,000
Net sales	40,000	500,000

Calculate the return on sales ratio for each company and determine which firm is more profitable.

SE4-3. **Evaluating Firm Liquidity** The following financial information is taken from the balance sheets of the Peter Company and the Paul Company: **LO3**

	Peter	Paul
Current assets	$200,000	$50,000
Current liabilities	40,000	20,000

Calculate the current ratio for each company and determine which firm has the higher level of liquidity.

SE4-4. **Evaluating Firm Solvency** The following financial information is taken from the balance sheets of the Benny Company and the Walter Company: **LO3**

	Benny	Walter
Total debt	$400,000	$ 900,000
Total assets	500,000	1,000,000

Calculate the debt-to-total-assets ratio and determine which firm has the higher level of solvency.

SE4-5. **Calculating Free Cash Flow** The following financial information is taken from the annual reports of the Ira Company and the Paul Company: **LO6**

	Ira	Paul
Cash flow from operating activities	$300,000	$650,000
Cash investment in property & equipment	75,000	240,000

Calculate the free cash flow for each company and determine which firm has better cash flow health.

LO6 **SE4-6.** **Statement of Cash Flows** Which of the following would not appear on a company's statement of cash flows?

a. Cash flow from operating activities
b. Net change in cash
c. Total assets
d. Cash flow for investing activities

LO3 **SE4-7.** **Debt-to-Total-Assets Ratio** Red Company's balance sheet reports the following totals: Assets = $80,000; Liabilities = $50,000; Stockholders' Equity = $30,000. Determine the company's debt-to-total-assets ratio.

a. 37.5%
b. 62.5%
c. $15,000
d. 166.7%

LO6 **SE4-8.** **Free Cash Flow** Debra Linens reports the following items on its statement of cash flows:

Cash flow provided by operating activities = $100,000
Cash flow used by investing activities = $50,000
Cash flow used by financing activities = $25,000
Capital expenditures = $40,000

Determine Debra's free cash flow:

a. $40,000
b. $5,000
c. 40%
d. $60,000

LO4 **SE4-9.** **Return on Sales** The following data are from the financial statements of Pluto Wines, Inc. Compute Pluto's return on sales ratio for 2019.

Total revenues for 2019: $3,500,000
Total expenses for 2019: $2,800,000

a. 125%
b. 80%
c. 25%
d. 20%

LO2 **SE4-10.** **The Multi-step Income Statement** Robert Company, a merchandising firm, reports the following data for the month ended January 31:

Operating expenses	$ 7,000
Cost of goods sold	4,000
Net sales	15,000
Income tax expense	900
Other income	500

Prepare a multi-step income statement for Robert Company for the month of January.

LO6 **SE4-11.** **Statement of Cash Flows** Identify whether the following statements are true or false.

a. The statement of cash flows provides information about whether a firm is "rich" or not.
b. The statement of cash flows provides information about a firm's financial health.
c. The statement of cash flows provides information about a firm's liquidity.
d. The statement of cash flows provides information about a firm's solvency.

EXERCISES—SET A

E4-1A. Preparing a Classified Balance Sheet From the following accounts, listed in alphabetical order, prepare a classified balance sheet for Oakland Wholesalers as of December 31. All accounts have normal balances.

LO1

Accounts payable	$ 50,000	Inventory	$117,000
Accounts receivable	40,000	Land	39,000
Building	67,000	Mortgage payable (long term)	79,000
Cash	28,000	Office supplies	1,000
Common stock	120,000	Retained earnings	?
		Salaries payable	7,000

E4-2A. Multi-step Income Statement From the following accounts, listed in alphabetical order, prepare a multi-step income statement for Carl Distributors for the year ended December 31. All accounts have normal balances.

LO2

Selling, general and administrative expense	$225,000	Sales revenue	$580,000
Cost of goods sold	335,000	Income tax expense	10,000
Interest expense	5,000		

E4-3A. Evaluating the Liquidity and Solvency of a Company Identify whether the following statements are true or false.

LO3, 4, 6

a. The current ratio is a measure of a firm's liquidity.
b. Free cash flow is a measure of a firm's solvency.
c. The return on sales ratio is a measure of a firm's liquidity.
d. The debt-to-total-assets ratio is a measure of a firm's liquidity.

E4-4A. Classified Balance Sheet The George Company collected the following information for the preparation of its December 31 classified balance sheet:

LO1

Accounts receivable	$22,000	Property, plant, and equipment	$200,000
Cash	17,000	Inventory	57,000
Other current assets	25,000	Other long-term assets	40,000
Accounts payable	25,000	Common stock	92,000
Long-term liabilities	60,000	Retained earnings	?
Other current liabilities	19,000		

Prepare a classified balance sheet for the George Company.

E4-5A. Profitability, Liquidity, and Solvency Ratios Alex Corporation gathered the following information from its financial statements:

LO3, 4, 6

Net sales	$175,000
Net income	35,000
Cash provided by operating activities	40,000
Expenditures on property, plant, and equipment	15,000
Current assets	47,250
Current liabilities	27,000
Total assets	135,000
Total liabilities	94,500

Using the above data, calculate the following: (1) return on sales ratio, (2) current ratio, (3) debt-to-total-assets ratio, and (4) free cash flow.

LO3 **E4-6A.** **Return on Assets** The following information was taken from **Apple Inc.**'s 2017 financial statements. Numbers are in millions.

APPLE INC.
AAPL

	2017	2016
Net income	$ 48,351	$ 45,687
Total assets	375,319	321,686

Required

a. What was Apple's return on assets for 2017 and 2016?
b. Based on your answer from part *a*, how did the company's performance change from 2016 to 2017?

LO5 **E4-7A.** **Statement of Stockholders' Equity** You have been asked to assist with the preparation of a statement of stockholders' equity for Minimus Company for the year ended December 31, 2019. You determine the following balances:

Common stock at December 31, 2018	$10,000
Retained earnings at December 31, 2018	7,500
Net income during 2019	6,000
Dividends during 2019	900
Issuance of common stock during 2019	600

Required

Prepare a statement of stockholders' equity for Minimus Company for 2019.

LO4 **E4-8A.** **Return on Sales** Peyton Co.'s sales rose 12 percent over prior year sales of $100,000; however, net income increased by only 5 percent over the prior year's net income. If Peyton's prior year return on sales ratio was 8 percent, what is the current year return on sales ratio?

LO6 **E4-9A.** **Free Cash Flow** Katty Co. reports the following financial data for the current year:

Cash flow from operating activities	$23,200
Cash flow from investing activities	(10,555)
Cash flow from financing activities	5,000
Cash disbursed for capital expenditures	(4,325)

Compute Katty's free cash flow.

LO5 **E4-10A.** **Statement of Stockholders' Equity** Jay Co. reported the following financial data for its most current year:

Beginning-of-year common stock	$105,000
Beginning-of-year retained earning	175,400
Net income	33,400
Dividends paid	10,500
Issuance of common stock	24,000

Compute Jay's end-of-year total stockholders' equity.

EXERCISES—SET B

LO1 **E4-1B.** **Preparing a Classified Balance Sheet** From the following accounts, listed in alphabetical order, prepare a classified balance sheet for Halford Wholesalers as of December 31. All accounts have normal balances.

Accounts payable....................	$ 55,000	Inventory.....................	$142,000
Accounts receivable.................	61,000	Land.........................	58,000
Building and equipment..............	87,000	Mortgage payable (long-term).....	82,000
Cash........................	40,000	Office supplies.................	2,000
Common stock....................	125,000	Retained earnings..............	?
		Salaries payable...............	8,000

E4-2B. Multi-step Income Statement From the following accounts, listed in alphabetical order, prepare a multi-step income statement for Moto Wholesale for the year ended December 31. All accounts have normal balances.

LO2

Sellling, general, and administrative expenses ...	$260,000	Sales revenue..........	$580,000
Cost of goods sold........................	275,000	Income tax expense......	6,000
Interest expense.........................	10,000		

E4-3B. Evaluating the Liquidity and Solvency of a Company Identify whether the following statements are true or false.

LO3, 4, 6

a. The current ratio is a measure of a firm's solvency.
b. Free cash flow is a measure of a firm's liquidity.
c. The return on sales ratio is a measure of a firm's solvency.
d. The debt-to-total-assets ratio is a measure of a firm's solvency.

E4-4B. Classified Balance Sheet The Oxford Company collected the following information for the preparation of its December 31 classified balance sheet:

LO1

Accounts receivable...............	$26,000	Property, plant, and equipment.......	$200,000
Cash...........................	20,000	Inventory........................	75,000
Other current assets...............	32,000	Other long-term assets.............	40,000
Accounts payable..................	30,000	Common stock...................	115,000
Long-term liabilities................	60,000	Retained earnings................	?
Other current liabilities.............	18,000		

Prepare a classified balance sheet for Oxford Company.

E4-5B. Profitability, Liquidity, and Solvency Ratios O'Reilly Corporation gathered the following information from its financial statements:

LO3, 4, 6

Net sales................................	$300,000	Current assets..........	$ 75,000
Net income............................	90,000	Current liabilities........	25,000
Cash provided by operating activities...........	100,000	Total assets............	140,000
Expenditures on property, plant, and equipment ...	19,000	Total liabilities...........	112,000

Using the above data, calculate the following: (1) return on sales ratio, (2) current ratio, (3) debt-to-total-assets ratio, and (4) free cash flow.

E4-6B. Return on Assets Sue Company reports the following information in its financial statements. Numbers are in thousands.

LO3

	2019	2018
Net sales....	$42,075	$44,100
Net income....	12,780	15,732
Total assets	63,900	87,400

There were 5,000 outstanding shares at December 31, 2019.

Required

a. What was Sue's return on assets ratio for 2019 and 2018?

b. Based on your answer from part *a*, how did the company's performance change from 2018 to 2019?

LO5   E4-7B. Statement of Stockholders' Equity You have been asked to assist with the preparation of a statement of stockholders' equity for Pal Company for the year ended December 31, 2019. You determine the following balances:

Common stock at December 31, 2018	$47,000
Retained earnings at December 31, 2018	19,500
Net income during 2019	23,400
Dividends during 2019	7,800
Issuance of common stock during 2019	5,000

Required
Prepare a statement of stockholders' equity for Pal Company for 2019.

LO4   E4-8B. Return on Sales Trevor Co.'s sales rose 10 percent over prior year sales of $300,000; however net income increased by 6 percent over the prior year's net income. If Trevor's prior year return on sales ratio was 25 percent, what is the current year return on sales ratio?

LO6   E4-9B. Free Cash Flow Madison Co. reports the following financial data for the current year:

Cash flow from operating activities	$41,500
Cash flow from investing activities	30,100
Cash flow from financing activities	21,175
Cash disbursed for capital expenditures	(12,500)

Compute Madison's free cash flow.

LO5   E4-10B. Statement of Stockholders' Equity Wally Co. reported the following financial data for its most current year:

Beginning-of-year common stock	$140,000
Beginning-of-year retained earnings	325,500
Net income	10,500
Dividends paid	10,000
Issuance of common stock	15,000

Compute Wally's end-of-year total stockholders' equity.

PROBLEMS—SET A

LO1   P4-1A. Preparing a Classified Balance Sheet The following financial data for Kravis Distributors was collected as of December 31. All accounts have normal balances.

Accounts payable	$ 80,000	Accounts receivable	$120,200
Delivery equipment	90,000	Accumulated depreciation	55,000
Inventory	114,000	Cash	15,200
Retained earnings	?	Common stock	130,000
Supplies	6,400	Prepaid insurance	4,000

Required
Prepare a classified balance sheet as of December 31 for Kravis Distributors.

P4-2A. **Preparing a Classified Balance Sheet** The following financial data for the Revel Corporation was collected as of December 31. All accounts have normal balances.

LO1

Furniture and equipment	$107,000	Accumulated depreciation—furniture and equipment	$ 48,800
Cash	61,000	Accounts receivable	95,200
Common stock	190,000	Accounts payable	19,200
Prepaid insurance	300	Inventory	93,000
Retained earnings	?		

Required
Prepare a classified balance sheet as of December 31.

P4-3A. **Multi-step Income Statements** The adjusted trial balance of Molly Distributors on December 31 is shown below.

LO2

MOLLY DISTRIBUTORS Adjusted Trial Balance December 31	Debit	Credit
Cash	$ 30,200	
Accounts receivable	110,200	
Inventory	94,000	
Prepaid insurance	2,400	
Supplies	6,400	
Delivery equipment	85,000	
Accumulated depreciation		$ 35,000
Accounts payable		100,000
Common stock		105,000
Retained earnings		22,800
Sales revenue		791,000
Cost of goods sold	513,400	
Salaries expense	123,000	
Rent expense	40,000	
Supplies expense	6,400	
Utilities expense	4,000	
Depreciation expense	16,000	
Insurance expense	6,800	
Income tax expense	16,000	
	$1,053,800	$1,053,800

Required
Prepare a multi-step income statement for the year ended December 31. Combine all the operating expenses into one line on the income statement for selling, general and administrative expenses.

P4-4A. **Preparing the Financial Statements** Listed below are items reported on the financial statements of the Irvine Company as of June 30, 2019:

LO1, 6

Cash flow provided by operating activities	$39,000	Other long-term assets	$17,500
Cash at June 30, 2018	8,000	Cash flow from financing activities	1,300
Cash at June 30, 2019	38,000	Current liabilities	24,000
Inventory	5,500	Long-term liabilities	16,250
Accounts receivable	15,200	Intangible assets	9,500
Cash flow from investing activities	(10,300)	Common stock	60,000
Other current assets	1,500	Retained earnings	?
Property, plant and equipment	60,000		

Required

Prepare a classified balance sheet as of June 30, 2019, and statement of cash flows for 2019.

LO3, 4 **P4-5A.** **Assessing a Firm's Profitability, Liquidity and Solvency** Presented below is financial data for the Outback Company as of year-end 2018 and 2019:

	2018	2019
Current assets	$ 68,750	$ 70,000
Total assets	100,000	130,000
Current liabilities	27,500	40,000
Total liabilities	80,000	91,000
Net sales	140,000	190,000
Net income	22,400	26,600

Required

Calculate Outback's current ratio, debt-to-total-assets ratio, and return on sales ratio. Comment on the trend in the company's profitability, liquidity, and solvency from 2018 to 2019.

LO2, 4 **P4-6A.** **Profitability and the Income Statement** Presented below is income statement data for Short & Company as of year-end 2019:

Income tax expense	$ 5,400	Net revenue	$62,950
Cost of goods sold	14,300	Operating expenses	27,000
Other expenses	500		

Required

Prepare a multi-step income statement for 2019 and calculate the company's return on sales ratio. If Short's return on sales was 16 percent in 2018, is the company's profitability improving or declining?

LO5 **P4-7A.** **Preparing the Statement of Stockholders' Equity** Presented below is financial data for Jason & Co. as of year-end 2019:

Cash	$ 8,500	Accumulated depreciation	$(14,000)
Retained earnings, Jan. 1, 2019	17,000	Net income	35,000
Intangible assets	25,000	Stockholders' equity, Jan. 1, 2019	67,000
Common stock	50,000	Retained earnings, Dec. 31, 2019	38,000
Accounts payable	4,000	Stockholders' equity, Dec. 31, 2019	88,000
Dividends paid	14,000	Building	72,500

Required

Prepare a statement of stockholders' equity for Jason & Co. as of December 31, 2019.

LO3, 4 **P4-8A.** **Interpreting Liquidity, Solvency, and Profitability Ratios** Presented below are financial data for two retail companies:

	Company A	Company B
Return on sales ratio	15.5%	13.9%
Current ratio	0.4	2.0
Debt-to-total-assets	65%	35%

Required

Consider the financial ratio data for the two companies. Which company represents the better investment opportunity in your view and why?

P4-9A.   Ratio Analysis The following balances were reported in the financial statements for Nadir Company.   **LO3, 4**

	2019	2018
Net sales.	$1,000,000	$750,000
Net income	120,000	75,000
Current assets	220,000	270,000
Current liabilities.	80,000	90,000
Total liabilities	250,000	240,000
Total assets	800,000	600,000

Required
1. Compute the following ratios for 2019 and 2018 for Nadir Company.
   a. Return on sales ratio
   b. Current ratio
   c. Debt-to-total-assets ratio
2. Comment on changes to Nadir Company's profitability, liquidity, and solvency.

P4-10A.   Multi-step Income Statement and Adjusting Entries The New England Trading Company, whose   **LO2**
accounting year ends on December 31, had the following normal balances in its general ledger at December 31:

Cash.	$17,000	Sales revenue.	$620,000
Accounts receivable	56,600	Cost of goods sold	394,000
Inventory.	74,000	Utilities expense	4,800
Prepaid insurance.	3,000	Sales salaries expense.	77,000
Office supplies	4,200	Delivery expense	10,800
Furniture and fixtures	21,000	Advertising expense	5,600
Accumulated depreciation—		Rent expense	9,400
furniture and fixtures.	7,000	Office salaries expense	56,000
Delivery equipment.	86,000	Income tax expense	9,000
Accumulated depreciation—			
delivery equipment	12,000		
Accounts payable.	37,000		
Long-term notes payable	28,000		
Common stock	70,000		
Retained earnings	56,400		

During the year, the accounting department prepared monthly statements but no adjusting entries were
made in the journals and ledgers. Data for the year-end procedures are as follows:

1. Prepaid insurance, December 31, was $1,800.
2. Depreciation expense on furniture and fixtures for the year was $2,200.
3. Depreciation expense on delivery equipment for the year was $11,000.
4. Salaries payable, December 31 ($1,900 sales and $1,200 office), was $3,100.
5. Unused office supplies on December 31 were $1,400.

Required
a. Record the necessary adjusting entries at December 31.
b. Prepare a multi-step income statement for the year. Combine all the operating expenses into one
line on the income statement for selling, general and administrative expenses.

PROBLEMS—SET B

LO1 **P4-1B.** **Preparing a Classified Balance Sheet** The following financial data for Brandon & Company was collected as of December 31. All accounts have normal balances.

Accounts receivable..............	$223,000	Accumulated depreciation..........	$110,000
Inventory........................	268,000	Cash...........................	40,000
Common stock...................	200,000	Accounts payable................	155,000
Prepaid insurance................	7,000	Supplies	12,800
Retained earnings	?	Delivery equipment...............	160,000

Required

Prepare a classified balance sheet as of December 31 for Brandon & Company.

LO1 **P4-2B.** **Preparing a Classified Balance Sheet** The following financial data for the St. Joseph Corporation was collected as of December 31. All accounts have normal balances.

Accounts receivable...............	$203,400	Furniture and equipment	$196,000
Accounts payable.................	36,800	Cash.........................	92,800
Prepaid insurance.................	900	Accumulated Depreciation—	
Common stock...................	410,000	furniture and equipment	77,600
Retained earnings	?	Inventory.....................	175,000

Required

Prepare a classified balance sheet as of December 31.

LO2 **P4-3B.** **Multi-step Income Statement** The adjusted trial balance of Patton Corporation on December 31 is shown below.

PATTON CORPORATION Adjusted Trial Balance December 31		
	Debit	**Credit**
Cash...	$ 50,400	
Accounts receivable.................................	95,200	
Inventory...	87,000	
Prepaid insurance...................................	1,300	
Furniture and fixtures	32,000	
Accumulated depreciation—furniture and fixtures		$ 6,800
Delivery equipment..................................	66,000	
Accumulated depreciation—delivery equipment		34,000
Accounts payable...................................		17,400
Common stock.....................................		208,000
Retained earnings		50,000
Sales revenue......................................		381,000
Cost of goods sold	214,800	
Salaries expense	97,000	
Rent expense......................................	20,800	
Utilities expense....................................	6,800	
Insurance expense..................................	1,500	
Depreciation expense—furniture and fixtures	3,200	
Depreciation expense—delivery equipment...........................	18,000	
Income tax expense.................................	3,200	
	$697,200	$697,200

Required

Prepare a multi-step income statement for the year ended December 31. Combine all the operating expenses into one line on the income statement for selling, general and administrative expenses.

P4-4B. Preparing the Financial Statements Listed below are items reported on the financial statements of the La Playa Company as of June 30, 2019:

Cash flow provided by operating activities	$ 50,000	Other long-term assets	$ 35,000
Cash at June 30, 2018	21,000	Cash flow from financing activities	2,600
Cash at June 30, 2019	43,000	Current liabilities	46,000
Inventory	12,000	Long-term liabilities	36,500
Accounts receivable	24,400	Intangible assets	19,000
Cash flow from investing activities	(30,600)	Common stock	102,000
Other current assets	3,000	Retained earnings	?
Property, plant and equipment	85,000		

Required

Prepare a classified balance sheet as of June 30, 2019, and statement of cash flows for 2019.

P4-5B. Assessing a Firm's Profitability, Liquidity and Solvency Presented below is financial data for the Lite Company as of year-end 2018 and 2019:

	2018	2019
Current assets	$ 90,000	$112,000
Total assets	250,000	350,000
Current liabilities	60,000	140,000
Total liabilities	160,000	227,500
Net sales	265,000	375,000
Net income	35,775	50,250

Required

Calculate Lite's current ratio, debt-to-total-assets ratio, and return on sales ratio. Comment on the trend in the company's profitability, liquidity, and solvency from 2018 to 2019.

P4-6B. Profitability and the Income Statement Presented below are income statement data for Poole & Company for 2019:

Income tax expense	$16,000	Sales revenue	$150,000
Cost of goods sold	30,000	Operating expenses	57,000
Other expenses	2,000		

Required

Prepare a multi-step income statement for 2019 and calculate the company's return on sales ratio. If Poole's return on sales was 26 percent in 2018, is the company's profitability improving or declining?

P4-7B. Preparing a Statement of Stockholders' Equity Presented below is financial data for Thomas & Co. as of December 31:

LO5

Cash	$ 25,000	Inventory	$ 14,000
Retained earnings, Jan. 1, 2019	31,000	Net income	60,000
Building	150,000	Stockholders' equity, Jan. 1, 2019	151,000
Common stock	120,000	Retained earnings, Dec. 31, 2019	?
Accrued expenses payable	8,000	Stockholders' equity, Dec. 31, 2019	181,000
Dividends paid	30,000		

Required

Prepare a statement of stockholders' equity as of December 31, 2019.

LO3, 4   **P4-8B.**   **Interpreting Profitability, Liquidity, and Solvency Ratios** Presented below is financial data for two furniture manufacturing companies:

	Company B	Company D
Return on sales ratio	9.0%	10.9%
Current ratio	2.1	1.0
Debt-to-total-assets ratio	41%	72%

Required

Consider the financial data of the two companies. Which company represents the better investment opportunity in your opinion and why?

LO3, 4   **P4-9B.**   **Ratio Analysis** The following balances were reported in the financial statements for Rudy Company.

	2019	2018
Net sales	$1,700,000	$1,750,000
Net income	170,000	204,750
Current assets	408,000	525,000
Current liabilities	170,000	210,000
Total liabilities	496,000	661,500
Total assets	1,550,000	2,450,000

Required

1. Compute the following ratios for 2019 and 2018 for Rudy Company.
   a. Return on sales ratio
   b. Current ratio
   c. Debt-to-total-assets ratio
2. Comment on changes to Rudy Company's profitability, liquidity, and solvency.

LO2   **P4-10B.**   **Multi-step Income Statement and Adjusting Entries** Washington Distributors, whose accounting year ends on December 31, had the following normal balances in its ledger accounts at December 31:

Cash	$45,750	Common stock	$ 125,000
Accounts receivable	92,000	Retained earnings	?
Inventory	84,400	Sales revenue	1,170,000
Prepaid insurance	7,200	Cost of goods sold	822,200
Office supplies	4,800	Utilities expense	5,600
Furniture and fixtures	28,000	Sales salaries expense	108,000
Accumulated depreciation—		Delivery expense	37,000
furniture and fixtures	10,800	Advertising expense	28,200
Delivery equipment	70,000	Rent expense	30,000
Accumulated depreciation—		Office salaries expense	72,000
delivery equipment	24,400		
Accounts payable	69,400		
Long-term notes payable	30,000		
Income tax expense	11,000		

During the year, the accounting department prepared monthly statements, but no adjusting entries were made in the journals and ledgers. Data for the year-end procedures are as follows:

1. Prepaid insurance, December 31, was $2,800.
2. Depreciation expense on furniture and fixtures for the year was $3,000.
3. Depreciation expense on delivery equipment for the year was $10,000.
4. Salaries payable, December 31 ($2,300 sales and $800 office), was $3,100.
5. Office supplies on hand, December 31, were $1,900.

Required

   a. Record the necessary adjusting entries in general journal form at December 31.

   b. Prepare a multi-step income statement for the year. Combine all the operating expenses into one line on the income statement for selling, general and administrative expenses.

SERIAL PROBLEM: KATE'S CARDS

(Note: This is a continuation of the Serial Problem: Kate's Cards from Chapter 3.)

SP4. In order to learn more about the industry and to meet people who could give her advice, Kate attended several industry trade shows. At the most recent trade show, Kate was introduced to Fred Abbott, operations manager of "Sentiments," a national card distributor. After much discussion, Fred asked Kate to consider being one of Sentiments' card suppliers. He provided Kate with a copy of the company's recent financial statements. Fred indicated that he expects that Kate will need to supply Sentiments with approximately 50 card designs per month. Kate is to send Sentiments a monthly invoice, and she will be paid approximately 30 days from the date the invoice is received in Sentiments' corporate office. Naturally, Kate was thrilled with this offer, since this will certainly give her business a big boost.

Required

Kate has several questions. Answer the following questions for Kate.

   a. What type of information does each of Sentiments' financial statements provide to Kate?

   b. What financial statements would Kate need to evaluate whether Sentiments will have enough cash to meet its current liabilities? Explain what to look for.

   c. What financial statement would Kate need to evaluate whether Sentiments will be able to survive over a long period of time? Explain what to look for.

   d. What financial statement would Kate need to evaluate Sentiments' profitability? Explain what to look for.

   e. Where can Kate find out whether Sentiments has outstanding debt? How can Kate determine whether Sentiments will be able to meet its interest and principal payments on any debts that it has?

   f. How could Kate determine whether Sentiments pays a dividend?

   g. In deciding whether to go ahead with this opportunity, are there other areas of concern that Kate should be aware of?

EXTENDING YOUR KNOWLEDGE

REPORTING AND ANALYSIS

EYK4-1. **Financial Reporting Problem: Columbia Sportswear Company** The financial statements for **Columbia Sportswear** can be found in Appendix A at the end of this textbook.

COLUMBIA SPORTSWEAR COMPANY

Required

Answer the following questions using the Consolidated Balance Sheet and the Notes to the consolidated financial statements:

   a. What were the combined totals of Columbia's liabilities and stockholders' equity for 2017 and 2016?

   b. How do these amounts compare with Columbia's total assets for each year?

   c. What was the largest, in dollar value, of Columbia's assets each year? What does this asset represent?

   d. What is the balance of accrued liabilities made up of?

EYK4-2. **Comparative Analysis Problem: Columbia Sportswear Company vs. Under Armour, Inc.** The financial statements for **Columbia Sportswear** can be found in Appendix A and **Under Armour**'s financial statements can be found in Appendix B at the end of this textbook.

COLUMBIA SPORTSWEAR COMPANY

UNDER ARMOUR, INC.

Required

a. Calculate for each company the following ratios for 2017:
  1. Current ratio
  2. Debt-to-total-assets ratio
  3. Return on sales ratio
b. Comment on the companies' relative profitability, liquidity, and solvency.

EYK4-3. **Business Decision Problem** Memoryman, a maker of computer memory devices, reports the following information in its financial statements. Assume that you are a loan officer at a major bank and have been assigned the task of evaluating whether to extend a loan for a plant expansion to the company.

(in millions)	2019	2018	2017
Current assets	$ 4,356	$4,033	$2,915
Total assets	10,175	8,777	6,002
Current liabilities	1,093	960	871
Total liabilities	3,114	2,997	2,093
Retained earnings	1,797	813	(487)
Net sales	5,662	4,827	3,567
Cost of goods sold	3,223	2,565	2,282
Net income	987	1,300	415
Cash flow from operating activities	1,054	1,452	488
Cash flow from investing activities	(667)	(2,715)	(375)
Cash flow from financing activities	(48)	991	25
Expenditures for property, plant, and equipment	(193)	(108)	(60)

Required

a. Calculate the company's current ratio, debt-to-total-assets ratio, return on sales ratio, and free cash flow for each year.
b. Comment on Memoryman's liquidity, solvency, and profitability.
c. Based on what you have learned about Memoryman, would you recommend offering the company a loan?

EYK4-4. **Financial Analysis Problem** As part of your internship at Howe Inc. you have been assigned the job of developing a few important ratios from the company's financial statements. This information is intended to be used by the company to help Howe obtain a large bank loan. In particular, the data will need to convince the bank that Howe is a good loan risk based on its liquidity, solvency, and profitability. Below are the data you pulled together:

	2019	2018
Current ratio	2.4:1	1.5:1
Debt-to-total-assets ratio	57 percent	66 percent
Return on sales ratio	9.3 percent	9.2 percent
Free cash flow	Up 18 percent	Up 19 percent
Net income	Up 16 percent	Down 12 percent

Required

Prepare brief comments that discuss how each of these items can be used to support the argument that Howe is showing improving financial health.

CRITICAL THINKING

GENERAL MILLS, INC.

EYK4-5. **Accounting Research Problem** Go to this book's Website and locate the annual report of General Mills, Inc. for the year ending May 28, 2017 (fiscal year 2017).

Required

1. Calculate the company's return on sales for 2015, 2016, and 2017. What is the trend?
2. Calculate the company's current ratio for 2016 and 2017. What is the trend?

3. Calculate the company's debt-to-total-assets ratio for 2016 and 2017. What is the trend?
4. Calculate the company's free cash flow for 2015, 2016, and 2017. What is the trend? (*Hint:* Proceeds from disposal of land, buildings, and equipment offset capital expenditures.)

EYK4-6. **Accounting Communication Activity** V. J. Simmons is the President of Forward Engineering Associates. He is a very good engineer, but his accounting knowledge is quite limited.

Required
V. J. has heard that ratio analysis can help him determine the financial condition of his company. In particular, he would like you to explain to him in a memo how to calculate and interpret the following three ratios: (1) return on sales ratio, (2) current ratio, and (3) debt-to-total-assets ratio. Prepare a memo for V. J.

EYK4-7. **Accounting Ethics Case** In the post-Enron environment, and with the enactment of the Sarbanes-Oxley legislation, many firms are proactively portraying themselves as being "ethical." Ethical behavior is, for example, part of the Corporate Social Responsibility movement. This behavior includes many dimensions, from the ethical treatment of employees and the environment, to ethical financial reporting. Academic research has found a positive correlation between a firm's reputation and its financial performance. Do you feel that strong ethics makes good business sense? Why do you think that there is a positive correlation between ethical behavior and successful corporate financial performance?

EYK4-8. **Corporate Social Responsibility Problem** Many investors consider past performance, fees, and investment objectives as the sole criteria for selecting a mutual fund for investment purposes. A growing number of investors are also asking about the actions and philosophies of the companies that form a fund's underlying investment portfolio. Socially responsible mutual funds have been developed to fill this need. These funds are designed for investors who want to align their investments with their religious, political, or social convictions.

Because there is no universally accepted definition as to what makes a company responsible or an investment a socially responsible investment, socially responsible funds are quite diverse. Not surprisingly different funds may take opposite positions on certain controversial issues such as family planning, gay rights, or animal testing.

For the most part, socially responsible funds select their underlying investment firms through either a negative filter or a positive filter. A negative filter is used to screen out firms that are not considered acceptable to the positions advocated by the fund. Examples of firms that may be screened out include firms that are involved in gambling, alcohol, tobacco, or weapons. A positive filter is used to include firms that are seen to be leaders in areas advocated by the fund, such as environmental, diversity, or human rights records.

Required
a. Go to the Websites of three socially responsible mutual funds
   1. Calvert Signature Funds: https://www.calvert.com/calvert-responsible-indexes.php
   2. Domini Social Equity Fund: http://www.domini.com/investing-for-impact/impact-investment-standards
   3. Green Century Balanced Fund: http://www.greencentury.com/funds/Green-Century-Balanced-Fund
b. Compare the screening criteria used by each fund. How do they differ and how are they alike?

EYK4-9. **Forensic Accounting Problem** Debra Day, a business major at a local college, was recently hired for the summer at Sweet Delights, a popular ice cream parlor near the campus. Debra spent most of her time tending the cash register where she noticed that most of the customers paid in cash and never seemed to care about getting a receipt. Debra soon figured out that she could ring up a much lesser amount on the register, charge the customer the full amount, then toss the receipt. For example, on a $7 order she would charge and collect the full $7 from the customer, but only ring up $5. She would then deposit $5 in the register so that it would agree with the register tape and pocket the $2.

Required

a. What type of fraud is Debra committing?

b. The store manager recently hired you as a forensic accountant to critique the controls at Sweet Delights. He has noticed that while the store seems as busy as ever, and the cash in the register agrees with the tapes, the store is not as profitable as it previously was. What control would you recommend to help prevent the type of fraud being committed by Debra?

LOGITECH INTERNATIONAL

EYK4-10. **Working with the Takeaways** Throughout this chapter we have considered the financial statements of Apple Inc. and have undertaken select financial analysis using the Takeaways. Utilize these same tools to analyze the financial data of **Logitech International**, a manufacturer of computer peripherals. The following information was reported by Logitech in the company's financial statements as of year-end March 31, 2017 and 2016:

March 31 (in thousands)	2017	2016
Current assets	$1,027,845	$ 926,247
Total assets	1,498,677	1,324,147
Current liabilities	507,078	414,930
Total liabilities	642,566	564,199
Net sales	2,221,427	2,018,100
Net income	205,876	119,317
Cash provided by operating activities	278,728	183,111
Expenditures on property, plant, and equipment	31,804	56,615

Required

1. Calculate the return on sales ratio for each year and comment on Logitech's profitability.
2. Calculate the current ratio for each year and comment on Logitech's liquidity.
3. Calculate the debt-to-total-assets ratio for each year and comment on Logitech's solvency.
4. Calculate the free cash flow for each year and comment on what this means for Logitech.
5. Apple's fiscal year-end occurs near the end of September, whereas Logitech uses a March year-end. How might this affect a comparison of the financial results of the two companies?

LVMH MOET HENNESSEY-LOUIS VUITTON S.A.

EYK4-11. **Evaluating Firm Liquidity, Solvency, Profitability and Free Cash Flow: IFRS Financial Statements** The 2017 financial statements of **LVMH Moet Hennessey-Louis Vuitton S.A.** are presented in Appendix C at the end of this book. LVMH is a Paris-based holding company and one of the world's largest and best-known luxury goods companies. As a member of the European Union, French companies are required to prepare their consolidated (group) financial statements using International Financial Reporting Standards (IFRS). Using this financial data, calculate the company's (a) return on sales ratio using net profit, group share, (b) current ratio, (c) debt-to-total-assets ratio, and (d) free cash flow for 2016 and 2017. Comment on the trend in LVMH's liquidity, solvency, profitability, and free cash flow from 2016 to 2017.

ANSWERS TO SELF-STUDY QUESTIONS:

1. b, (pp. 188–191) 2. c, (pp. 188–189) 3. c, (p. 188) 4. d, (pp. 189–190) 5. b, (p. 191) 6. d, (p. 196)
7. d, (p. 197) 8. b, (p. 200) 9. c, (p. 200) 10. d, (p. 201) 11. a, (p. 197) 12. b, (p. 201)
13. b, (pp. 193–194)

YOUR TURN! SOLUTIONS

Solution 4.1

MUSICLAND COMPANY Balance Sheet December 31, 2019	
Assets	
Current assets	
Cash	$ 300
Accounts receivable	3,000
Inventory	12,200
Other current assets	1,500
Total current assets	17,000
Property, plant, & equipment, net	25,000
Total assets	$42,000
Liabilities and Stockholders' Equity	
Current liabilities	
Accounts payable	$ 2,500
Other current liabilities	2,000
Total current liabilities	4,500
Long-term notes payable	20,000
Total liabilities	24,500
Stockholders' equity	17,500
Total liabilities and stockholders' equity	$42,000

Solution 4.2

MUSICLAND COMPANY Income Statement For Year Ended December 31, 2019	
Net sales	$100,000
Less cost of goods sold	45,000
Gross profit on sales	55,000
Operating expenses	
Selling, general and administrative	25,000
Research and development expenses	10,000
Total operating expenses	35,000
Income from operations	20,000
Other income and expense	
Interest expense	5,000
Income before income taxes	15,000
Income tax expense	4,500
Net income	$ 10,500

Solution 4.3

	2019	2018
Current ratio	$\dfrac{75,000}{50,000} = 1.50{:}1$	$\dfrac{65,000}{45,000} = 1.44{:}1$
Debt-to-total-assets ratio	$\dfrac{150,000}{220,000} = 68.2\%$	$\dfrac{145,000}{190,000} = 76.3\%$

The Philips Company has improved its performance on both measures. Both its liquidity as reflected by the current ratio and its solvency as reflected by the debt-to-total-assets ratio are trending in a positive direction (the current ratio is increasing and the debt-to-total assets ratio is decreasing).

Solution 4.4

	2019	2018
Return on sales	$\dfrac{20{,}000}{120{,}000} = 16.7\%$	$\dfrac{15{,}000}{110{,}000} = 13.6\%$

The Philips Company has improved its performance from 2018 to 2019. The company is earning a higher amount of net income on every dollar of sales revenue as indicated by its return on sales ratio.

Solution 4.5

Owner Company Statement of Stockholders' Equity			
	Common Stock	Retained Earnings	Total Equity
Balance at beginning of the year	$120,000	$85,000	$205,000
Issuance of common stock...................	7,500		7,500
Net income................................		16,000	16,000
Dividends		(4,000)	(4,000)
Balance at the end of the year	$127,500	$97,000	$224,500

Contributed capital amounted to $127,500 and earned capital amounted to $97,000.

Solution 4.6

2019	2018
25,000 − 7,000 = 18,000	22,000 − 6,000 = 16,000

The Philips Company has improved its performance from 2018 to 2019. The company has more cash for a possible plant expansion as seen in its increasing free cash flow.

Chapter 5

Accounting for Merchandising Operations

PAST

Chapters 1 through 4 explained the five-step accounting cycle: analyze, record, adjust, report, and close.

PRESENT

This chapter focuses on analyzing and recording merchandising transactions.

FUTURE

Chapter 6 describes the accounting for inventory, including cost assumptions, the lower of cost or market approach, and inventory analysis.

Target Corporation is one of the largest merchandising companies in the world with over 1,800 stores and with sales of aproximately $70 billion. Target sells products, often referred to as *inventory*. However, Target does not manufacture or make its inventory. Instead, it buys this inventory from manufacturers such as **Sony** and **Panasonic**, and then resells that inventory to consumers. Some refer to companies such as Target as "middlemen."

This chapter describes the most common inventory accounting system used by merchandising companies such as that used by Target. This system *perpetually* tracks all purchases and sales of inventory. Such tracking is important for managers to effectively manage this key asset and to regularly compute measures that report on management's ability to generate profit from inventory.

Road Map

LO	Learning Objective	Page	eLecture	Guided Example	Assignments
LO1	Explain the operations of a merchandising company and contrast that with the operations of a service company.	232	E5-1	YT5.1	SS9, SE1
LO2	Describe the accounting for purchases of merchandise.	235	E5-2	YT5.2	SS1, SS2, SS3, SS5, SS6, SE2, SE3, SE4, SE5, E3A, E4A, E5A, E3B, E4B, E5B, P1A, P2A, P3A, P4A, P1B, P2B, P3B, P4B
LO3	Describe the accounting for sales of merchandise.	239	E5-3	YT5.3	SE6, E1A, E2A, E4A, E1B, E2B, E4B, P1A, P2A, P3A, P4A, P1B, P2B, P3B, P4B
LO4	Define the gross profit percentage and the return on sales ratio, and explain their use in profitability analysis.	242	E5-4	YT5.4	SS4, SS7, SS8, SE7, SE8, E6A, E6B, P5A, P5B
LO5	Appendix 5A: Describe and illustrate a periodic inventory system.	246	E5-5	YT5A.1, 5A.2, 5A.3	SS10, SS11, SE9, SE10, SE11, E7A, E8A, E9A, E7B, E8B, E9B, P6A, P7A, P6B, P7B
LO6	Appendix 5B: Describe and illustrate the revenue recognition standard for sales returns and allowances and sales discounts.	249	E5-6	YT5B.1	SE12, SE13, E10A, E11A, E10B, E11B

ACCOUNTING FOR MERCHANDISING OPERATIONS

Merchandising	Accounting for Purchases of Merchandise	Accounting for Sales of Merchandise	Profitability Analysis	Periodic Inventory System (Appendix 5A)	New Revenue Recognition Standard (Appendix 5B)
• Operating cycle • Cost flows • Inventory systems—perpetual and periodic	• Transportation costs • Purchase returns and allowances • Purchase discounts • Credit period	• Sales returns and allowances • Sales discounts • Net sales	• Gross profit percentage • Return on sales ratio	• Purchases of merchandise • Sales of merchandise • Comparing periodic and perpetual systems • Cost of good sold using a periodic system	• Sales discounts • Sales returns and allowances

THE NATURE OF MERCHANDISING

LO1 **Explain** the operations of a merchandising company and **contrast** that with the operations of a service company.

Manufacturers are companies that make goods for sale. **Merchandisers** buy the finished products, warehouse or display them for varying periods of time, and then resell the products to consumers. Merchandising firms do not manufacture products nor do they consume the products that they purchase. Merchandising firms often provide additional services to their customers, but their primary business is the resale of goods produced by other companies. **Exhibit 5-1** illustrates the typical relationship among these types of companies and the final consumer.

Exhibit 5-1 | **Distribution of Products to Individual Consumers**

Manufacturer	Merchandiser	Consumer
Produce goods	Purchase finished goods and resell	Consume product

© Shutterstock.com

Manufacturers convert raw materials and component parts into a finished product through the application of skilled labor and machine operations. **Ford Motor Company**, for example, converts raw materials such as sheets of steel and components such as tires into automobiles and trucks. Similarly, **Del Monte** converts raw materials such as fresh peaches and components such as metal cans into canned peaches.

Wholesalers and retailers are types of merchandising firms. **Wholesalers** buy finished products from manufacturing firms in large quantities. Manufacturers typically only sell their products to wholesalers in what is referred to as a business-to-business or "B2B" transaction. The wholesaler then sells and ships the product to various retailers in smaller quantities to satisfy the local demand for the product. Some wholesalers handle the products of only one manufacturer, while others handle the products of many manufacturers. Retailers typically buy products from wholesalers and resell the finished products to individual consumers in what is referred to as a business-to-consumer transaction (a "B2C" transaction). Retailers often have multiple store locations, including the Internet, where they display the products they are offering for sale, enabling customers to view and buy the products. Radio, television, newspaper, and online advertisements inform potential customers of product availability and price. Retailers may range in size from small, with only one store location, to large, with thousands of store locations along with an online Website, such as Target.com.

Operating Cycle of a Merchandising Firm

Exhibit 5-2 presents the operating cycle of a merchandising firm. There are three primary transactions involved in a merchandising firm's operating cycle: ❶ purchase merchandise and place in inventory; ❷ sell merchandise inventory to customers; and ❸ receive cash from customers. These transactions involve three current asset accounts—cash, accounts receivable, and inventory—and one current liability account—accounts payable. The merchandising firm purchases products with cash or on credit. Purchasing on credit creates an accounts payable. The purchased merchandise becomes part of the merchandiser's inventory until sold. An accounts receivable is created when the merchandise is sold to a customer on credit with cash received later when the customer pays the amount owed on account. In cases where the customer pays immediately with cash for the purchased merchandise, no accounts receivable is created. The merchandising firm uses the cash received from customers to pay the balances owed on accounts payable and to purchase more merchandise to resell, beginning a new operating cycle.

Exhibit 5-2	Comparison of Operating Cycle for a Merchandising Firm and a Service Firm

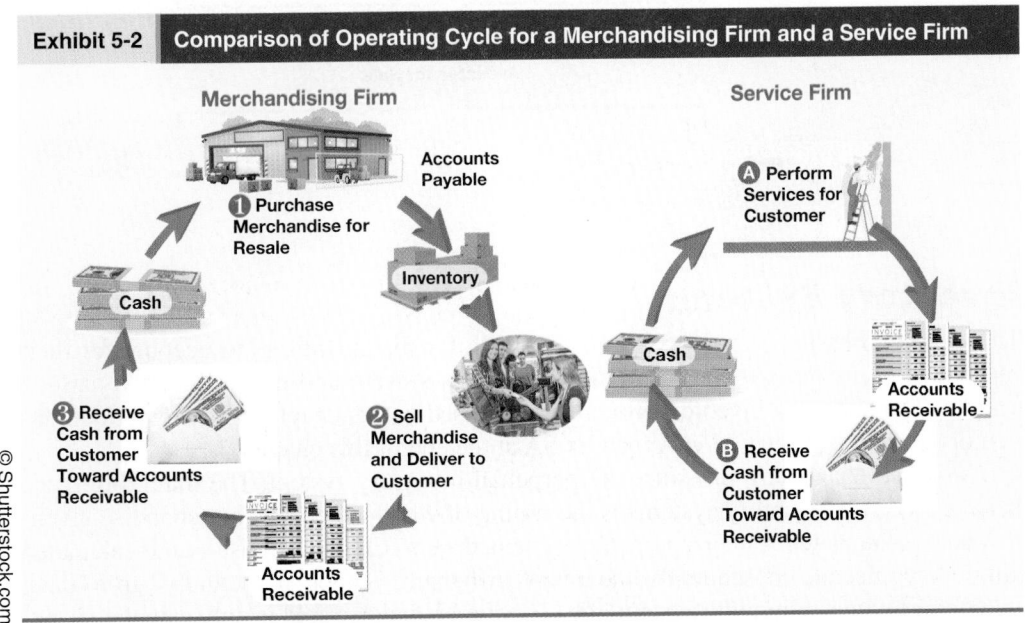

In contrast, there are only two primary transactions involved in the operating cycle of a service firm: ❹ perform service, and ❺ receive cash from the customer. Service firms have no inventory to warehouse or display, and consequently, the length of their operating cycle is typically much shorter than that of a merchandising firm.

The three primary transactions for a merchandising firm repeat frequently, creating the cycle depicted in Exhibit 5-2. The timing of the cash collection depends upon the credit terms associated with the sale. When a wholesaler sells to a retailer, a B2B transaction, the sale is usually concluded on a credit basis. That is, the retailer is allowed some period of time following the sale, frequently 30 days or more, to pay the wholesaler for the purchased goods. Some retailers call a credit sale a **sale on account** (also referred to as **sale on credit**). "On account" means on a credit basis.

When retailers such as **Nordstrom** sell to individual consumers, the consumer can (1) pay cash at the time of the sale; (2) use a credit card such as **Discover**, **MasterCard**, or **Visa**; or (3) use an "open account" with the retailer. An **open account** is a charge account provided by a retailer for its customers. Many retailers such as Nordstrom have their own private label credit card to facilitate open account sales. If a customer pays cash, the retailer receives cash immediately. If the customer uses a major credit card issued by a financial institution like **Citibank**, the retailer transmits the credit card information to the card-issuing financial institution and collects the cash either on the same day or within a few days following the credit-sale transaction. If the customer uses an open account, the retailer may not collect the cash from the customer for 30 to 60 days or longer, depending upon the length of the credit terms allowed by the retailer.

Cost Flows

The costs of inventory for merchandisers flow through its accounting system as shown in the diagram below. Specifically, a company adds its *costs of goods purchased* to any *beginning inventory* balance it might have. These two components make up the company's *cost of goods available for sale*. The portion of the goods available for sale that the company sells during the period is recorded in *cost of goods sold*. The portion that is not sold is the *ending inventory* balance that is carried forward into the next period.

The mathematical representation of this cost flow relation is:

Beginning inventory
+ Cost of goods purchased
= Cost of goods available for sale
− Ending inventory
= Cost of goods sold

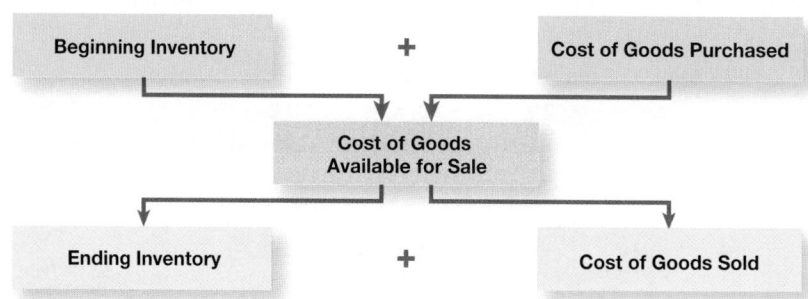

Inventory Systems

There are two basic inventory systems available for merchandisers to account for their **merchandise inventory**: the **perpetual inventory system** and the **periodic inventory system**. The perpetual inventory system is discussed in this chapter, and the periodic inventory system is discussed in Appendix 5A at the end of this chapter.

Most merchandising firms use the perpetual inventory system. The main difference between the two inventory systems is the timing of when the cost of merchandise inventory sold is calculated. Under a perpetual system, the cost of merchandise sold is calculated after every sale, and consequently, the inventory balance is kept "perpetually" up-to-date. In contrast, under a periodic system, the cost of merchandise sold is only calculated "periodically" when a physical count of the inventory is done. A physical inventory count is time consuming and usually occurs only at the end of a fiscal period. As a consequence, the actual inventory balance remains unknown until the end of a fiscal period.

A major advantage of the perpetual system is the increased control it provides over the inventory. Since the inventory is being continuously updated, management is able to determine whether current inventory levels are adequate to satisfy pending or expected sales. In addition, having a record of exactly how much inventory is available allows management to compare these amounts to a physical count of the inventory. Management can then investigate any difference between the amounts to identify the presence of theft or spoilage (in the case of perishable goods).

YOUR TURN! 5.1

The solution is on page 267.

Jenny Company begins the year with $110,000 of inventory and purchased an additional $245,000 of inventory during the year. At year end, a physical count of inventory revealed that Jenny Company still had $90,000 of inventory.

   a. How much was Jenny's cost of goods available for sale for the year?

   b. How much was Jenny's cost of goods sold for the year?

ACCOUNTING FOR PURCHASES OF MERCHANDISE

The first step of the merchandiser's operating cycle is the purchase of merchandise inventory. When a company using the perpetual inventory system purchases merchandise, it debits the Inventory account for the acquisition cost of the merchandise purchased to reflect an increase in the amount of inventory and credits the Accounts Payable account to reflect an increase in the amount owed to the supplier. For example, the Barton Wholesale Electronics' purchase invoice for inventory shown in **Exhibit 5-3** requires Barton to record the company's purchase of merchandise from Malibu Manufacturing on November 10 with the following journal entry:

LO2   **Describe** the accounting for purchases of merchandise.

Nov. 10	Inventory (+A)	21,000	
	Accounts payable (+L)		21,000
	To record the purchase of 100 disk drives from Malibu Manufacturing with credit terms of 2/10, n/30.		

A   =   L   +   SE
+21,000   +21,000

Transportation Costs

Transportation Costs Incurred by Buyer

Transportation costs are sometimes incurred by a merchandising company when it acquires goods, and this cost is included as part of the acquisition cost of the inventory. When the buyer is responsible for shipping costs, it is referred to as **FOB shipping point**. An example of an invoice that specifies the shipping and payment terms is shown in **Exhibit 5-3**. (Shipping terms are explained further in Chapter 6.) Assume Barton (buyer) pays $126 to a freight company on November 11, for transportation costs on the 100 disk drives purchased from Malibu Manufacturing (seller). Barton makes the following journal entry to record the payment of $126:

Nov. 11	Inventory (+A)	126	
	Cash (−A)		126
	To record the payment of $126 of transportation costs for the purchase of 100 disk drives.		

A   =   L   +   SE
+126

−126

Cost Principle   **PRINCIPLE ALERT**

The inclusion of transportation costs in the acquisition cost of inventory is consistent with the *cost principle*. The cost principle states that an asset is initially recorded at the amount paid to acquire the asset. There can be multiple expenditures associated with an asset acquisition, and all expenditures that are reasonable and necessary to acquire an asset are added to the asset's initial recorded cost.

Exhibit 5-3	Invoice for Inventory Purchase

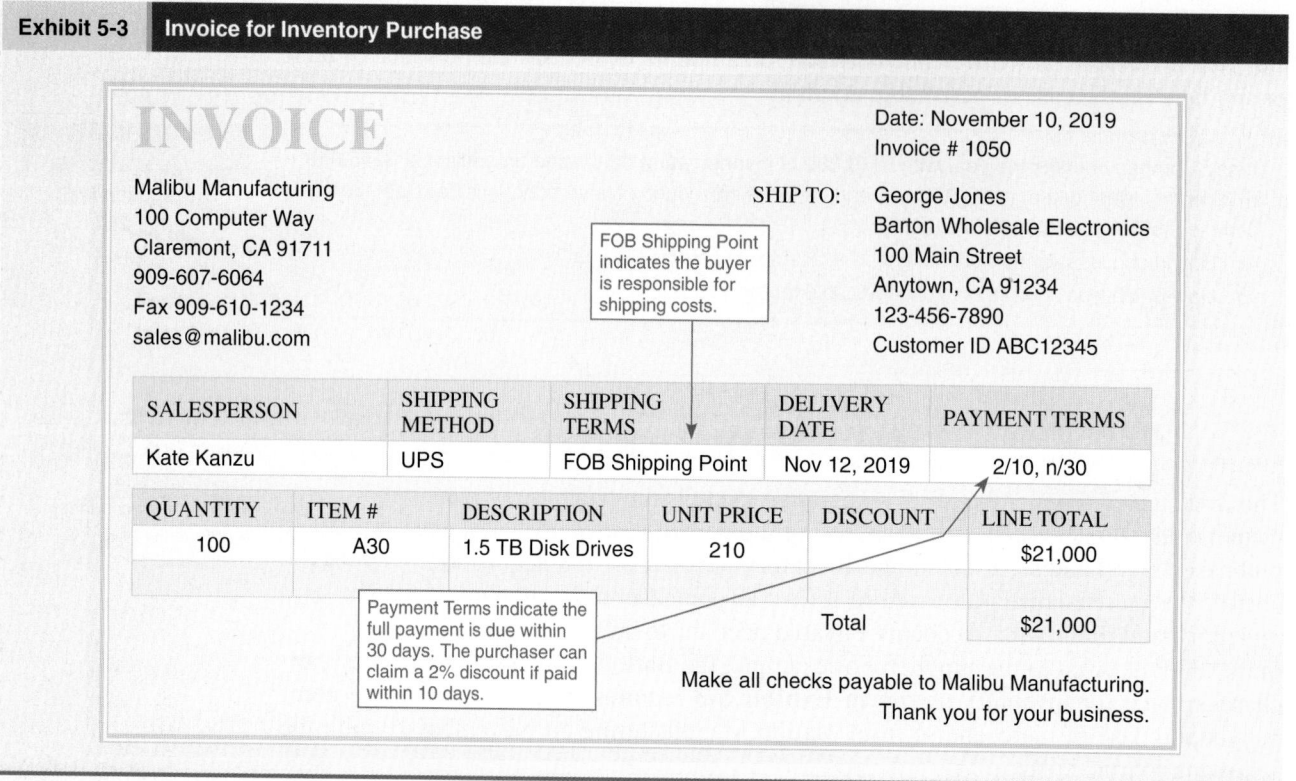

Transportation Costs Incurred by Seller

When the seller is responsible for shipping costs, it is referred to as **FOB destination**. Instead of the shipping terms stated in the invoice above, assume that the seller, Malibu Manufacturing, is responsible for and paid the $126 transportation costs. In this case the transportation cost would be considered an operating expense of the seller, and Malibu Manufacturing would debit an expense account titled Freight-out Expense as follows:

A	=	L	+	SE			
−126				−126 Exp			

	Nov. 11	Freight-out expense (+E, −SE))		126	
		Cash (−A)			126
		To record payment for the transportation cost for goods sold.			

Malibu paid the freight charges on the Barton purchase of disk drives, and it will attempt to pass on this cost to the buyer in the form of a higher sales price for the items purchased.

Purchase Returns and Allowances

Occasionally, a purchaser is dissatisfied with some or all of the merchandise purchased because, for example, the merchandise was manufactured poorly, the wrong merchandise was shipped, or the merchandise was damaged during shipping. When such circumstances are encountered, the purchaser and the seller can remedy the problem by agreeing to treat the value of the unwanted items either as a purchase return or as a purchase allowance.

With a **purchase return**, the purchaser ships the unsatisfactory merchandise back to the seller and receives a credit against the amount due equal to the **invoice price** of the returned merchandise. With a **purchase allowance**, the purchaser retains the merchandise, and the seller reduces the amount that the purchaser owes the seller for the shipment, in effect reducing the sales price.

As an example of a purchase return, assume that on November 15, Barton returns 10 of the 100 disk drives purchased on November 10. Barton has not yet paid Malibu

Manufacturing for the goods purchased. Accordingly, Barton makes the following journal entry on November 15 to record the purchase return:

Nov. 15	Accounts payable (−L)	2,100	
	Inventory (−A)		2,100
	To record a purchase return of 10 disk drives at an invoice price of		
	$210 each to Malibu Manufacturing.		

A   =   L   + SE
−2,100   −2,100

This entry reduces the Inventory account balance and reduces the amount owed. When the purchaser and seller reach agreement on how to handle a purchase return, they also must agree on which party pays the freight charges on the returned merchandise. (Usually the seller pays freight charges when goods are returned, in an attempt to maintain a positive customer relationship and to increase the likelihood of future repeat business.)

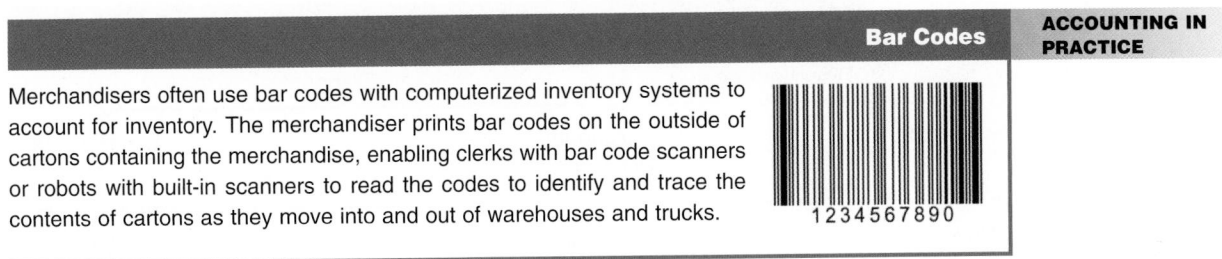

ACCOUNTING IN PRACTICE

Bar Codes

Merchandisers often use bar codes with computerized inventory systems to account for inventory. The merchandiser prints bar codes on the outside of cartons containing the merchandise, enabling clerks with bar code scanners or robots with built-in scanners to read the codes to identify and trace the contents of cartons as they move into and out of warehouses and trucks.

Purchase Discounts

Credit Period

When merchandise is sold on credit, the **credit period** is the maximum amount of time, often stated in days, that a purchaser can take to pay a seller for the purchased items. A typical credit period for a wholesale distributor is 30 days. The credit period is frequently described as the *net credit period*, or net terms. Merchandisers use the notation "**n/**" followed by the number of days in the credit period to designate the time period that a customer can take before paying cash for purchased goods. For example, **n/30** indicates a credit period of 30 days, and n/45 indicates a credit period of 45 days.

To encourage the early payment of unpaid bills, many firms offer their customers a cash discount if payment is made within a designated discount period. A **cash discount**, or **sales discount**, is the amount that the seller deducts from the invoice price if payment is made within the allowed discount period. Some refer to the cash discount offered to credit customers as a "quick-pay incentive." Sellers usually state cash discounts as a percent of the invoice price. The **discount period** is the maximum amount of time, stated in days, that a purchaser has to pay the seller if the purchaser wants to claim the cash discount. The discount period is always shorter than the credit period. Most merchandisers use the format "cash discount percent/discount period" to designate the cash discount and the discount period. For example, 1/10 indicates a cash discount of 1 percent of the invoice price and a discount period of ten days following the invoice date. Finally, merchandisers usually combine the notation for the cash discount and the discount period with the notation for the credit period. For example, 1/10, n/30 represents a cash discount of 1 percent if paid within ten days of the sale with a total credit period of 30 days following the date of the sale.

To illustrate, let's return to the Barton example in which Malibu Manufacturing and Barton agree on terms of 2/10, n/30, for the sale on November 10. Barton deducts 2 percent of the $21,000 invoice price ($420) if it pays Malibu by November 20. In that case, Barton pays $20,580 cash [computed as $21,000 × (1 − 0.02)]. If Barton pays Malibu after November 20 but no later than December 10, the amount that Barton must pay is $21,000. After December 10, the $21,000 amount would become overdue and often incurs additional interest cost depending on the invoice terms. **Exhibit 5-4** illustrates this example.

Discounts are normally attractive to merchandisers. For instance, if Barton did not take the discount offered by Malibu, this is like Barton paying an interest rate of 2 percent on the $21,000 for 20 days (30-day credit period less 10-day discount period). This is similar to paying an annual interest rate of 36.5 percent, computed as 2 percent × 365/20. Barton can borrow money at lower rates.

Exhibit 5-4	**Purchase Discounts**

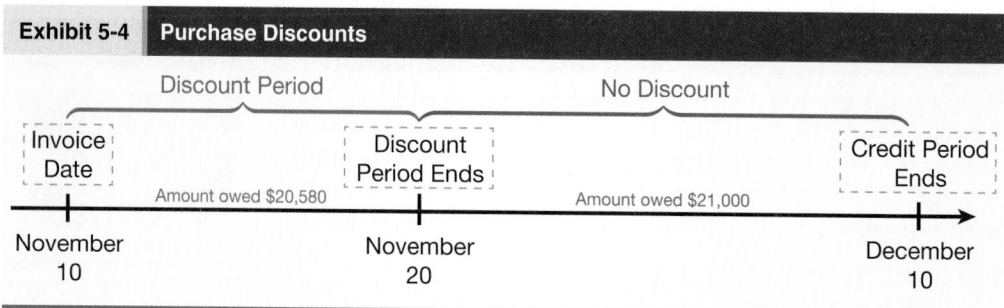

Accounting for Discounts

Let's extend the prior example where Barton owes $18,900 to Malibu Manufacturing; recall that Barton made a $21,000 purchase, then had a $2,100 purchase return, yielding an amount owed of $18,900. See T-account in the margin.

Accounts Payable

		21,000	Nov. 10
Nov. 15	2,100		
		18,900	**Balance**

Pay Within Discount Period Assume that Barton makes a cash payment to Malibu on November 20, the last day of the discount period. (November 11, the first day following the date of sale, is the first day of the discount period, and November 20 is the tenth or last day of the discount period.) Barton records the cash payment, less the cash discount, with the following journal entry:

A	=	L	+ SE
−378		−18,900	
−18,522			

Nov. 20	Accounts payable (−L)	18,900	
	Inventory (−A)		378
	Cash (−A)		18,522
	To record the purchase discount and payment to Malibu Manufacturing within the discount period.		

This entry reduces to zero the amount that Barton owes Malibu Manufacturing. It also records the purchase discount of 2 percent ($18,900 × 2 percent = $378) as a reduction of the cost in the Inventory account. The entry reveals that $18,522 in cash was paid by Barton to Malibu Manufacturing ($18,900 − $378 = $18,522). Two aspects of this transaction should be noted. First, the cash discount applies only to the cost of the merchandise and not to the transportation cost. Second, the invoice price of the returned merchandise is subtracted from the total invoice price before the cash discount is calculated.

The net total cost reflected in Barton's Inventory account for the disk drives follows:

		+	Inventory (A)		−	
Purchase (+100 units)	**Nov 10**	21,000				
Freight-in	**Nov 11**	126				
				2,100	**Nov 15**	**Purchase return (−10 units)**
				378	**Nov 20**	**Purchase discount**
	Balance	18,648				

A total cost of $18,648 is assigned to the 90 disk drives in Barton's inventory (100 purchased less 10 returned). This results in an average cost per disk drive of $207.20 ($18,648/90).

Pay After Discount Period If Barton made a cash payment to Malibu sometime between November 21 and December 10, after the discount period expired, Barton is not eligible to receive the 2 percent purchase discount. Consequently, Barton would record a full cash payment on November 25 with the following journal entry:

Nov. 25	Accounts payable (−L)	18,900	
	Cash (−A)		18,900
	To record full payment to Malibu Manufacturing following expiration of the discount period.		

A = L + SE
−18,900 −18,900

When Barton makes the payment to Malibu outside of the allowed discount period, the net total cost in Barton's Inventory account for the 90 disk drives is:

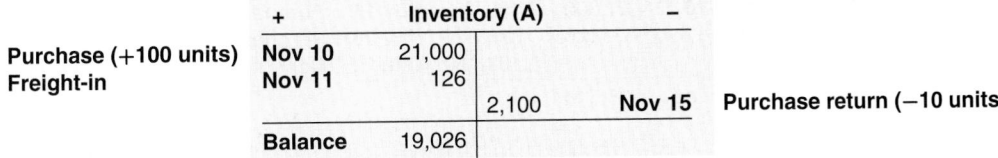

+	Inventory (A)	−	
Purchase (+100 units)	Nov 10	21,000	
Freight-in	Nov 11	126	
		2,100	Nov 15 Purchase return (−10 units)
	Balance	19,026	

A total cost of $19,026 is assigned to the 90 disk drives in Barton's inventory, resulting in an average cost per disk drive of $211.40 ($19,026/90). The cost per disk drive is higher in this situation because Barton did not make the payment for the inventory in a timely fashion to make it eligible for the cash discount.

On June 1, Musicland Inc. purchases 125 CDs at $4.08 each on account from its distributor for a total of $510. The credit terms of the purchase were 2/10, n/30. Also on June 1, Musicland paid freight charges of $22.18 cash for delivery of the CDs. On June 4, Musicland returned 15 defective CDs for an account credit of $61.20. On June 8, Musicland paid for the remaining 110 CDs. Record these transactions in journal entry form for Musicland.

YOUR TURN! 5.2
The solution is on pages 267–268.

ACCOUNTING FOR SALES OF MERCHANDISE

LO3 **Describe** the accounting for sales of merchandise.

The second step of the merchandiser's operating cycle is the sale of inventory to customers. Merchandising firms credit Sales Revenue when they sell products, regardless of whether the sales transaction is for cash or on credit. The Sales Revenue account has a normal credit balance.

Let's return to our example and assume that Barton sells 15 disk drives purchased from Malibu Manufacturing (the assumed cost per unit = $18,648/90 disk drives = $207.20 per disk drive) to The Computer Outlet Store at a sales price of $280 per unit. Barton makes the credit sale on December 12, with terms of 1/10, n/15, and The Computer Outlet Store pays shipping costs. Barton makes the following *two* journal entries to record the sale:

Dec. 12	Accounts receivable (+A)	4,200	
	Sales revenue (+R, +SE)		4,200
	To record sale of 15 disk drives at a sales price of $280 each to The Computer Outlet Store with credit terms of 1/10, n/15.		

A = L + SE
+4,200 +4,200 Rev

Dec. 12	Cost of goods sold (+E, −SE)	3,108	
	Inventory (−A)		3,108
	To record sale of 15 disk drives with a unit cost of $207.20 to The Computer Outlet Store.		

A = L + SE
−3,108 −3,108 Exp

Revenue Side The first journal entry records $4,200 of sales revenue ($280 × 15 disk drives) from the sale to Computer Outlet. The debit to Accounts Receivable increases the amount due from customers, and the credit to Sales Revenue increases the total revenue from sales of merchandise during the accounting period.

Cost Side The second journal entry transfers the $3,108 cost of merchandise sold ($207.20 × 15 disk drives) from the Inventory account, an asset account, to the Cost of Goods Sold account, an expense account. The debit to Cost of Goods Sold increases the total cost of merchandise sold during the accounting period, and the credit to Inventory removes the cost of the merchandise sold from the Inventory account. Cost of goods sold is the total cost of merchandise sold to customers during the accounting period.

After recording this sale, the net cost in Barton's Inventory account related to the disk drives is $15,540, as follows:

	+	Inventory (A)		–	
Purchase (+100 units)	Nov 10	21,000	2,100	Nov 15	Purchase return (−10 units)
Freight-in	Nov 11	126	378	Nov 20	Purchase discount
			3,108	Dec 12	Cost of goods sold (−15 units)
	Balance	15,540			

The $15,540 cost relates to the 75 disk drives (100 purchased − 10 returned − 15 sold) remaining in inventory. The average cost per disk drive remains $207.20 ($15,540/75 disk drives).

PRINCIPLE ALERT	**Revenue and Expense Recognition**

The entry to record sales revenue when 15 disk drives are sold to The Computer Outlet Store illustrates the *revenue recognition principle*. Under the revenue recognition principle, a merchandising firm will record revenue when goods are sold. Normally, this is the earliest point in time that the company has satisfied its performance obligation by delivering the goods to the customer. The entry to record the cost of goods sold illustrates the *expense recognition (matching) principle*. Under the expense recognition principle, expenses should be recorded in the same accounting period as the revenues they help generate.

Sales Returns and Allowances

When customers have returns and allowances, there are sellers that must record those same returns and allowances. With a sales return, the customer ships the merchandise back to the seller and the customer receives a reduction in the amount due to the seller. For example, textbook publishers often allow college bookstores to return any unsold textbooks to publishers at the conclusion of a term. With a sales allowance, the customer retains the merchandise, and the seller reduces the amount the customer owes, in effect reducing the sales price.

Accounting for **sales returns** requires two journal entries. The first entry offsets the sales revenue generated from the transaction and reduces the amount owed by the customer. The second entry transfers the cost of merchandise from Cost of Goods Sold back to the Inventory account. In the case of a **sales allowance**, the goods are not returned to the seller. As a result, only the first of these two entries is required.

Extending the previous example, assume that on December 15, The Computer Outlet Store returned five of the disk drives that it had purchased on December 12. Computer Outlet returned the units because it ordered five units too many; there is nothing wrong with the disk drives. Barton records the sales return by making the following two journal entries:

Dec. 15	Sales returns and allowances (+XR, −SE)	1,400	
	Accounts receivable (−A)		1,400
	To record the return of 5 disk drives by The Computer Outlet Store,		
	with a sales price of $280 each.		

A	=	L	+	SE
				−1,400
−1,400				Contra-Rev

Dec. 15	Inventory (+A)	1,036	
	Cost of goods sold (−E, +SE)		1,036
	To record the return of 5 disk drives with a unit cost of $207.20 from		
	The Computer Outlet Store.		

A	=	L	+	SE
				+1,036
+1,036				Exp

The first entry offsets the revenue generated from the sale by debiting Sales Returns and Allowances and it reduces the amount the customer owes by crediting Accounts Receivable. The Sales Returns and Allowances account is a *contra-revenue account* and is subtracted from gross sales revenue on the income statement.

The second journal entry transfers the cost of the merchandise from Cost of Goods Sold back to the Inventory account by debiting Inventory (increasing it) and by crediting Cost of Goods Sold (decreasing it). After recording the transfer from Cost of Goods Sold to Inventory, the net total cost in Barton's Inventory account related to the disk drives is:

Hint: Contra accounts, such as the contra-revenue account, are useful because they provide more information than if the related account were used by itself. For example, by using both the revenue and the contra-revenue accounts, it is possible to track how much of the original sales have had associated returns or allowances.

+		Inventory (A)		−	
Purchase (+100 units)	Nov 10	21,000	2,100	Nov 15	Purchase return (−10 units)
Freight-in	Nov 11	126	378	Nov 20	Purchase discount
Sales return (+5 units)	Dec 15	1,036	3,108	Dec 12	Cost of goods sold (−15 units)
	Balance	16,576			

The $16,576 total cost relates to 80 units (100 purchased − 10 purchase return − 15 sold + 5 sales return); and the average cost of the inventory remains $207.20 ($16,576/80).

Monitoring Sales Returns and Allowances

ACCOUNTING IN PRACTICE

Companies accumulate sales revenue in one account and sales returns and allowances in another account so that they can separately monitor both types of activities. A high ratio of sales returns and allowances to sales revenue is undesirable, often indicating a problem in the quality of the merchandise or its packaging. A company can compare the ratio for the current year to prior-year ratios, or to a target ratio set for the current year, to determine how well the company is managing its product and packaging quality.

Sales Discounts

When making a cash payment for purchased goods, a customer is entitled to take a cash discount only if the payment is made during the allowed discount period. If a cash discount is taken, the seller records it in a separate account called Sales Discounts.

Pay Within Discount Period

Returning to the previous example, assume that The Computer Outlet Store agrees to terms of 1/10, n/15, and it then pays the amount due Barton after deducting the 1 percent cash discount on December 22, the last day of the cash discount period. (December 13 is the first day of the discount period, and December 22 is the tenth or last day of the discount period.) Barton makes the following journal entry to record the cash received from Computer Outlet:

Dec. 22	Cash (+A)	2,772	
	Sales discounts (+XR, −SE)	28	
	Accounts receivable (−A)		2,800
	To record the sales discount and cash payment from The Computer		
	Outlet Store within the allowed discount period.		

A	=	L	+	SE
+2,772				−28
−2,800				Contra-Rev

This entry reduces the amount the customer, Computer Outlet, owes the seller, Barton, to zero. The total undiscounted amount due from The Computer Outlet Store was $2,800 ($4,200 sale − $1,400 sales return). With terms of 1/10, n/15, the sales discount is $28 ($2,800 × 1 percent) and the cash collected is $2,772 ($2,800 − $28).

Companies accumulate sales discounts in a separate account. This enables management to monitor the dollar amount of sales discounts being taken by customers. Sales Discounts is a *contra-revenue account* like Sales Returns and Allowances. Both accounts are contra to, or subtracted from, gross Sales Revenue on the income statement.

There are two important aspects of the sales discount calculation. First, the cash discount applies only to the sales price of the merchandise sold and not to any transportation cost. Second, the sales price of any merchandise returned must be subtracted from the total amount before calculating the cash discount.

Pay After Discount Period

If The Computer Outlet Store makes a cash payment after December 22 (after the discount period has expired), the cash discount does not apply. For example, if cash is received in full payment from Computer Outlet on December 27, Barton would record the following journal entry:

A = L + SE
+2,800

−2,800

Dec. 27	Cash (+A)	2,800	
	Accounts receivable (−A)		2,800
	To record cash received from The Computer Outlet Store outside the allowed discount period.		

Net Sales

Gross sales revenue
− Sales returns and allowances
− Sales discounts
= Net sales

Net sales is the gross sales revenue generated through merchandise sales less any sales returns and allowances and any sales (cash) discounts. A company calculates its net sales for the period by subtracting the balances of the Sales Returns and Allowances account (normal debit balance) and the Sales Discounts account (normal debit balance) from the balance of the Sales Revenue account (normal credit balance).

YOUR TURN! 5.3

The solution is on page 268.

On June 15, a customer buys 75 CDs on account from Musicland for $10 each, for a total of $750. The **list price** of the CDs is $12 each, but Musicland gave the customer a $2 per CD discount because of the large order. On June 20, the customer returned, unopened, five of the CDs and was given a purchase credit of $50. The customer paid its full balance of $700 on June 25. Record these transactions in journal entry form for Musicland. The unit cost of the CDs in inventory is $4.20 each.*

*$4.20 is calculated from the prior Your Turn! as follows:
  Inventory cost = $510.00 + $22.18 − $61.20 − $8.98 = $462.00
  Inventory quantity = 125 − 15 = 110
  Cost per unit = $462.00/110 = $4.20

PROFITABILITY ANALYSIS

LO4 **Define** the gross profit percentage and the return on sales ratio, and **explain** their use in profitability analysis.

Gross Profit Percentage

Managers, investment professionals, and stockholders closely monitor a company's gross profit on sales. They know that if gross profit on sales declines from one year to the next, net income for the current and following year is also likely to decline. A declining gross profit can indicate problems in a company's purchasing activities or problems selling its goods at an acceptable price. **Gross profit (gross margin)**, or **gross profit on sales**, is defined as the difference between Net Sales and Cost

A.K.A. Gross profit is often referred to as gross margin.

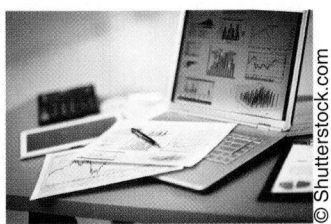

of Goods Sold and reveals the amount of sales revenue remaining after subtracting the cost of products sold. (Recall that net sales equals gross sales revenue less any sales returns and allowances and sales discounts.)

Financial statement users who monitor a company's gross profit are also interested in its **gross profit percentage**—that is, the rate at which a company earns gross profit on its sales revenue. The gross profit percentage is computed as follows:

$$\text{Gross profit percentage} = \frac{\text{Gross profit on sales}}{\text{Net sales}}$$

Using the data in **Exhibit 5-5**, the 2017 gross profit percentage for **Target** is 28.9 percent.

Financial analysis of the gross profit percentage frequently involves comparing the company against its performance in prior years and against the performance of competitor companies. Gross profit percentages for a two-year period are presented in **Exhibit 5-5** for both **Target Corporation** and one of its chief competitors, **Walmart Corporation**.

Exhibit 5-5	Gross Profit Percentage for Target Corporation and Walmart Corporation	
(in millions)	**2017**	**2016**
Target	$\dfrac{\$20,754}{\$71,879} = 28.9$ percent	$\dfrac{\$20,350}{\$69,495} = 29.3$ percent
Walmart	$\dfrac{\$126,947}{\$500,343} = 24.4$ percent	$\dfrac{\$124,617}{\$485,873} = 25.6$ percent

Target's gross profit percentage decreased 0.4 percent, from 29.3 percent in 2016 to 28.9 percent in 2017; however, in both years Target has a higher gross profit percentage than Walmart. Walmart's gross profit percentage is only 25.6 percent in 2016 and 25.4 percent in 2017. One explanation for the large difference between the gross profit percentages of the two companies is their different business strategies. Target attempts to sell higher-quality products at a reasonable price, whereas Walmart focuses more on low prices and less on product quality.

Concept ⟶	Method ⟶	Assessment	TAKEAWAY 5.1
Is a company able to maintain prices on its goods consistent with changes in the cost of its inventory?	Gross profit and net sales $\text{Gross profit percentage} = \dfrac{\text{Gross profit on sales}}{\text{Net sales}}$	A higher ratio suggests the company has market power to command higher retail prices. A lower ratio suggests competitive pressures on price setting.	

Return on Sales Ratio (Profit Margin)

First introduced in Chapter 4, the **return on sales ratio (profit margin)** reveals the net income earned on each dollar of net sales and is computed by dividing net income by net sales:

A.K.A. Return on sales is often referred to as profit margin.

$$\textbf{Return on sales ratio} = \frac{\textbf{Net income}}{\textbf{Net sales}}$$

Return on sales ratios for **Target Corporation** and **Walmart Corporation** are presented in **Exhibit 5-6**. Target's return on sales ratio for 2017 is 4.1 percent.

Exhibit 5-6	Return on Sales Ratios for Target Corporation and Walmart Corporation	
(in millions)	**2017**	**2016**
Target	$\dfrac{\$2,934}{\$71,879} = 4.1\,\text{percent}$	$\dfrac{\$2,737}{\$69,495} = 3.9\,\text{percent}$
Walmart . . .	$\dfrac{\$10,523}{\$500,343} = 2.1\,\text{percent}$	$\dfrac{\$14,293}{\$485,873} = 2.9\,\text{percent}$

Walmart's return on sales ratio for 2017 indicates that it earned 2.1 cents for each dollar of sales. The return on sales ratio allows us to compare a company's ability to earn profits on its sales regardless of company size. Walmart generates nearly seven times the sales revenue as does Target ($71,879 million for Target versus $500,343 for Walmart), yet Walmart has a return on sales ratio that is smaller than Target's. A company has a number of ways to improve its return on sales ratio, for example, by raising its retail prices or by purchase discounts from buying in larger quantities. It could also reduce operating expenses by reducing salaries, administrative costs, or selling and marketing costs, or discontinuing poorly performing segments of the business. Analysts like to compare return on sales ratios for a company over time to detect any trends. They also like to compare the ratio with those of competitors.

TAKEAWAY 5.2	Concept ⟶	Method ⟶	Assessment
	Is a company able to maintain prices on its goods consistent with changes in its total expenses?	Net income and net sales $\text{Return on sales ratio} = \dfrac{\text{Net income}}{\text{Net sales}}$	A higher ratio suggests the company is providing a higher net income on each dollar of net sales.

YOUR TURN! 5.4

The solution is on page 268.

The President of Musicland has asked for help to evaluate the company's performance during the current year. In particular, we are requested to calculate Musicland's gross profit and its return on sales ratio and then explain what these measures indicate. The following information is from Musicland's financial statements:

Net sales.	$100,000
Cost of goods sold	45,000
Net income	10,500

CORPORATE SOCIAL RESPONSIBILITY

Governance and Conflicts of Interest

An important component of good corporate responsibility is strong corporate governance. **Target** publishes a Business Conduct Guide for its employees as part of its governance program. Included in this handbook are guidelines concerning conflicts of interest. The list below provides examples of potential conflicts of interest:

- Owning a substantial amount of stock in any competing business or in any organization that does business with us.
- Serving as a director, manager, consultant, employee or independent contractor for any organization that does business with us, or is a competitor—except with our company's specific prior knowledge and consent.
- Accepting or receiving gifts of any value or favors, compensation, loans, excessive entertainment or similar activities from any individual or organization that does business or wants to do business with us, or is a competitor.
- Representing the company in any transaction in which you or a related person has a substantial interest.

continued

continued from previous page

- Disclosing or using for your benefit confidential or non-public information about Target or other organizations with which we do business.
- Taking personal advantage of a business opportunity that is within the scope of Target's business—such as by purchasing property that Target is interested in acquiring.

COMPREHENSIVE PROBLEM

Williams Distributing Company is a merchandising company. Williams uses the perpetual inventory system. Record each of the following transactions related to the company's purchasing and selling of merchandise:

March   1   Purchased merchandise on account for $6,000; terms were 2/10, n/30.
       3   Paid $200 cash for freight on the March 1 purchase.
       6   Returned merchandise costing $300 (part of the $6,000 purchase).
      10   Paid for merchandise purchased on March 1.
      12   Sold merchandise on account costing $8,000 for $10,000; terms were 2/10, n/30.
      15   Accepted returned and undamaged merchandise from a customer costing $400 that had been sold on account for $500 (part of the $10,000 sale).
      20   Received payment from customer for merchandise sold on March 12.

Solution

March	1	Inventory (+A)	6,000	
		Accounts payable (+L)		6,000
		Purchased merchandise with 2/10, n/30 terms.		
	3	Inventory (+A)	200	
		Cash (−A)		200
		Paid freight on March 1 purchase.		
	6	Accounts payable (−L)	300	
		Inventory (−A)		300
		Returned merchandise from March 1 purchase.		
	10	Accounts payable (−L)	5,700	
		Inventory (−A)		114
		Cash (−A)		5,586
		Paid for merchandise purchased on March 1 within the discount period [($6,000 − $300) × 2% = $114].		
	12	Accounts receivable (+A)	10,000	
		Sales revenue (+R, +SE)		10,000
		To record revenue from sale of merchandise.		
	12	Cost of goods sold (+E, −SE)	8,000	
		Inventory (−A)		8,000
		To record cost of merchandise sold and to reduce inventory.		
	15	Sales returns and allowances (+XR, −SE)	500	
		Accounts receivable (−A)		500
		To record revenue lost from return by customer.		
	15	Inventory (+A)	400	
		Cost of goods sold (−E, +SE)		400
		To record cost of goods returned by customer.		
	20	Cash (+A)	9,310	
		Sales discounts (+XR, −SE)	190	
		Accounts receivable (−A)		9,500
		To record receipt of cash from customer within the discount period [($10,000 − $500) × 2% = $190].		

APPENDIX 5A: Periodic Inventory System

LO5 Appendix 5A: **Describe** and **illustrate** a periodic inventory system.

An alternative to the perpetual inventory system illustrated in the chapter is the periodic inventory system. The **periodic inventory system** does not update the Inventory account or the Cost of Goods Sold account as merchandise transactions occur during the year. Instead, the Inventory account and the Cost of Goods Sold account are updated only at the end of the accounting period when a physical count of the inventory on hand is undertaken. The periodic inventory system is unacceptable for most companies because up-to-date inventory amounts are not available during the year for managerial decision making. The following section illustrates the journal entries that Barton Wholesale Electronics would make if it used the periodic inventory system. We utilize the same data used in the chapter to illustrate the perpetual inventory system to facilitate an easy comparison of the two systems.

Accounting for Purchases of Merchandise

When a company uses the periodic inventory system, it records the purchase of merchandise by debiting the cost of the merchandise to the Purchases account, rather than the Inventory account, and crediting the cost to Accounts Payable. (The Purchases account has a normal debit balance.) On November 10, Barton records the purchase of 100 disk drives with a list price of $210 each and terms of 2/10, n/30 by making the following journal entry:

A = L + SE		
+21,000 −21,000		

Nov. 10	Purchases (−SE)	21,000	
	Accounts payable (+L)		21,000
	To record the purchase of 100 disk drives from Malibu		
	with 2/10, n/30 terms.		

Transportation Costs

When a purchaser using the periodic inventory system bears the cost of transporting the merchandise from the seller, the purchaser records the transportation cost in the Freight In account, rather than in the Inventory account. (The Freight In account has a normal debit balance.) Barton makes the following journal entry on November 12 to record payment of $126 of transportation costs on the purchase of 100 disk drives:

A = L + SE		
−126	−126 Exp	

Nov. 12	Freight in (+E, −SE)	126	
	Cash (−A)		126
	To record the payment of $126 of transportation costs on the		
	purchase of 100 disk drives.		

Purchase Returns and Allowances

If a purchaser is dissatisfied with merchandise that was purchased and a purchase return or allowance is granted, the purchaser records the purchase return or allowance using the Purchase Returns and Allowances account, rather than the Inventory account. (Purchase Returns and Allowances is a contra-purchases account with a normal credit balance.) On November 15, Barton records the return of 10 disk drives to Malibu Manufacturing by making the following journal entry:

A = L + SE		
−2,100 +2,100		

Nov. 15	Accounts payable (−L)	2,100	
	Purchase returns and allowances (+SE)		2,100
	To record the return of 10 disk drives at a list price of $210.		

Purchase Discounts

If a purchaser makes a cash payment to the seller before the end of the allowed discount period, the purchaser deducts a cash discount. Otherwise, the purchaser pays the full invoice price. When a purchaser takes a cash discount, the purchaser credits the Purchase Discounts account, rather than the Inventory account. (Purchase Discounts is a contra-purchases account with a normal credit balance.) Barton makes the following journal entry on November 20 to record its cash payment to Malibu Manufacturing after deducting the cash discount:

A = L + SE		
−18,522 −18,900 +378		

Nov. 20	Accounts payable (−L)	18,900	
	Purchase discounts (+SE)		378
	Cash (−A)		18,522
	To record the payment to Malibu Manufacturing within the allowed		
	discount period.		

If Barton makes payment between November 21 and December 10, after the discount period has expired, the cash discount does not apply. In this case, Barton records a cash payment on November 25 with the following journal entry:

| Nov. 25 | Accounts payable (–L) | 18,900 | | |
| | Cash (–A) | | 18,900 | |

To record the payment to Malibu Manufacturing outside the allowed discount period.

$$A = L + SE$$
$$-18,900 \quad -18,900$$

YOUR TURN! 5A.1

The solution is on pages 268-269.

Assume that Musicland uses the *periodic system*. On June 1, Musicland purchased 125 CDs at $4.08 each on account from its distributor for $510. The terms of the purchase were 2/10, n/30. Also on June 1, Musicland paid in cash a freight charge of $22.18 for delivery of the CDs. On June 4, Musicland returned 15 defective CDs for a credit of $61.20. On June 8, Musicland paid for the remaining 110 CDs. Record the transactions in journal entry form for Musicland.

Accounting for Sales of Merchandise

Under the periodic inventory system, a seller makes only one journal entry to record a sale of merchandise. The entry records an account receivable (or Cash) from the customer and the sales revenue from the sale by debiting Accounts Receivable and crediting Sales Revenue. Barton records the December 12 sale of 15 disk drives to The Computer Outlet Store at a sales price of $280 each with terms of 1/10, n/15 by making the following entry:

| Dec. 12 | Accounts receivable (+A) | 4,200 | | |
| | Sales revenue (+R, +SE) | | 4,200 | |

To record the sale of 15 disk drives at a sales price of $280 each to The Computer Outlet Store with credit terms of 1/10, n/15.

$$A = L + SE$$
$$+4,200 \qquad +4,200$$
$$Rev$$

The same journal entry is made under the perpetual inventory system. Under the periodic inventory system, however, there is no concurrent entry to transfer the cost of merchandise sold from the Inventory account to the Cost of Goods Sold account.

Sales Returns and Allowances

Under the periodic inventory system, only one journal entry is used to record a sales return or allowance. The entry records the reduction of the revenue from the sale and the reduction of the account receivable from the customer by debiting Sales Returns and Allowances and crediting Accounts Receivable. Barton records the December 15 return by The Computer Outlet Store of five disk drives by making the following journal entry:

| Dec. 15 | Sales returns and allowances (+XR, –SE) | 1,400 | | |
| | Accounts receivable (–A) | | 1,400 | |

To record the return of 5 disk drives by The Computer Outlet Store; sales price was $280 each.

$$A = L + SE$$
$$-1,400 \qquad -1,400$$
$$Rev$$

This entry is the same as the first journal entry under the perpetual inventory system; however, Barton does not make the second journal entry that was made under the perpetual inventory system. Under the periodic inventory system, there is no immediate reinstatement of the returned merchandise to the Inventory account or corresponding reduction in the Cost of Goods Sold account.

Sales Discounts

The journal entry to record the receipt of a cash payment from a customer is exactly the same under either the perpetual inventory system or the periodic inventory system. If the payment is made within the allowed discount period, the entry includes a debit to Sales Discounts, a contra-sales account. Barton records the cash received from The Computer Outlet Store on December 22 (within the discount period) as follows:

Dec. 22	Cash (+A)	2,772		
	Sales discounts (+XR, –SE)	28		
	Accounts receivable (–A)		2,800	

To record the cash payment from The Computer Outlet Store within the discount period.

$$A = L + SE$$
$$+2,772 \qquad -28$$
$$-2,800 \qquad Rev$$

If The Computer Outlet Store makes its cash payment any time between December 13 and December 27 (after the discount period), the cash discount does not apply. Barton records the cash received from Computer Outlet on December 27 with the following journal entry:

A = L + SE
+2,800

–2,800

Dec. 27	Cash (+A)	2,800	
	Accounts receivable (–A)		2,800
	To record the cash payment from The Computer Outlet Store outside the discount period.		

YOUR TURN! 5A.2

The solution is on page 269.

Assume Musicland uses the *periodic system*. On June 15, a customer buys on account 75 CDs from Musicland for $10 each, for a total of $750. The list price of the CDs is $12 each, but Musicland provided the customer with a $2 per CD discount because of the large order. On June 20, the customer returned, unopened, five of the CDs and was given a credit of $50. The customer paid its full balance of $700 on June 25. Record these transactions on Musicland's books. The unit cost of the CDs in inventory is $4.20 each.*

*$4.20 is computed from Your Turn 5A.1 as follows:
  Inventory cost = $510.00 + $22.18 – $61.20 – $8.98 = $462.00
  Inventory quantity = 125 – 15 = 110
  Cost per unit = $462.00/110 = $4.20

Comparison of Entries Under the Perpetual and Periodic Systems

Exhibit 5A-1 summarizes all key journal entries under both the perpetual and periodic inventory systems for purchases and sales of merchandise.

Exhibit 5A-1	Comparison of Journal Entries under the Perpetual and Periodic Systems					
Date	**Transaction**	**Perpetual Inventory System**			**Periodic Inventory System**	

Nov 10	Purchase of merchandise on credit	Inventory
		  Accounts payable
			21,000	21,000	Purchases
					  Accounts payable
						21,000
						
							21,000

Nov 11	Freight cost	Inventory
		  Cash
			126	126	Freight In
					  Cash
						126	126

Nov 15	Purchase returns	Accounts payable
		  Inventory
			2,100	2,100	Accounts payable
					  Purchase returns and allowances
						2,100	2,100

Nov 20	Purchase discount and payment	Accounts payable
		  Inventory
		  Cash
			18,900	378
				18,522
					Accounts payable
					  Purchase discounts
					  Cash
						18,900	378
							18,522

Dec 12	Sale of merchandise on credit	Accounts receivable
		  Sales revenue
			4,200	4,200	Accounts receivable
					  Sales revenue
						4,200	4,200

		Cost of goods sold Inventory	3,108	3,108	No entry		

Dec 15	Return of sales merchandise	Sales returns and allowances
		  Accounts receivable
			1,400	1,400	Sales returns and allowances
					  Accounts receivable
						1,400	1,400

		Inventory Cost of goods sold	1,036	1,036	No entry		

Dec 22	Sales discount and payment	Cash
		Sales discounts
		  Accounts receivable
			2,772
			28
				2,800	Cash
					Sales discounts
					  Accounts receivable
						2,772
						28
							2,800

Cost of Goods Sold Using a Periodic System

If a firm uses a periodic system rather than a perpetual system, it does not record cost of goods sold at the time sales revenue is recorded. Instead, cost of goods sold is calculated periodically at the end of the accounting period when the inventory is physically counted. Cost of goods sold is then backed into by subtracting the ending inventory from the cost of goods available for sale, which represents the total inventory that was available to be sold. The calculation of cost of goods sold using the periodic method is shown in **Exhibit 5A-2**.

Exhibit 5A-2	Cost of Goods Sold Computation Using the Periodic Method

	Beginning inventory
+	Cost of goods purchased during the period
=	Cost of goods available for sale
−	Ending inventory
=	Cost of goods sold

One additional difference between the periodic method and the perpetual method is how a company keeps track of items that affect the Inventory account. Under the perpetual system, items such as transportation charges, purchase returns, and purchase discounts are recorded directly to the Inventory account. Under the periodic system, separate accounts are used for each of these items, which are then added to beginning inventory to arrive at the cost of goods available for sale. An illustration of this is shown in **Exhibit 5A-3**, assuming that there was no beginning inventory.

Exhibit 5A-3	Cost of Goods Sold Illustration Using the Periodic Method

BARTON WHOLESALE ELECTRONICS
Cost of Goods Sold
For Year Ended December 31, 2019

Inventory, January 1..			$ 0
Purchases...		$21,000	
Less: Purchase returns and allowances	$2,100		
Purchase discounts	378	2,478	
Net purchases		18,522	
Add: Freight-in		126	
Cost of goods purchased			18,648
Cost of goods available for sale			18,648
Less: Inventory, December 31			16,576
Cost of goods sold			$ 2,072

Assume that Musicland uses a periodic inventory system. Prepare a schedule of cost of goods sold as of December 31, 2018, using the following information:

Inventory, January 1, 2018...................................	$10,000
Purchases..	50,000
Purchase returns and allowances	2,000
Freight-in	200
Purchase discounts	1,000
Inventory, December 31, 2018	12,200

YOUR TURN! 5A.3

The solution is on page 269.

APPENDIX 5B: The Revenue Recognition Standard

The core principle behind the revenue recognition standard is that a company should recognize revenue when it transfers goods or services to a customer, and the amount of revenue that the company recognizes should reflect the consideration that the entity expects to receive in exchange for those goods or services.

    Consequently, end-of-period adjusting entries are used to reduce the gross amounts to the net amounts that the company expects to receive after sales discounts are taken and returns and allowances are made. A company must use its judgment to estimate the amount of sales discounts that will be taken and sales returns and allowances that will be made in future periods for sales that occur in the current period. It is reasonable to assume that nearly all customers will take the sales discounts because of the financial benefits of doing so. It is also likely that companies will use past experience to estimate sales returns and allowances.

LO6 Appendix 5B: **Describe** and **illustrate** the new revenue recognition standard for sales returns and allowances and sales discounts.

eLectures
MBC

The following example illustrates the accounting for sales of merchandise for Barton Wholesale Electronics using the approach required in the revenue recognition standard. Barton's fiscal year-end is December 31.

Assume that during the year Barton sells merchandise on account totaling $500,000. Further assume the cost to Barton of this merchandise was $400,000. The following two journal entries summarize Barton's credit sales during the year, along with the associated cost of goods sold.

Various dates	Accounts receivable (+A)	500,000	
	Sales revenue (+R, +SE)		500,000
	To record sale of merchandise on account.		
Various dates	Cost of goods sold (+E, −SE)	400,000	
	Inventory (−A)		400,000
	To record cost of goods sold.		

The revenue recognition standard requires Barton to estimate the amount of both sales discounts and sales returns and allowances. Below we illustrate three adjusting journal entries made at year-end to comply with the revenue recognition standard. The first adjusting journal entry applies to estimated sales discounts, and the other two adjusting journal entries apply to estimated sales returns and allowances.

Adjusting Journal Entry for Sales Discounts

Barton offers credit terms of 1/10, n/15 to encourage early payment. At year-end, Barton recognizes that there are $9,000 of sales on account still eligible for the 1 percent discount. Barton believes that all companies will pay within the discount period to receive the 1 percent discount. Barton makes the following adjusting journal entry at the year-end to provide for these estimated sales discounts:

Dec. 31	Sales discounts (+XR, −SE)	90	
	Allowance for sales discounts (+XA, −A)		90
	To record the estimated sales discount taken of 1 percent on credit		
	sales still eligible for discount at year-end ($9,000 × 0.01).		

This adjusting journal entry debits Sales discounts for the amount of discounts Barton estimates will be taken. The Sales discounts account is a contra account to Sales revenue. The credit in this entry is to the Allowance for sales discounts, which is a contra account to Accounts receivable.

Adjusting Journal Entry for Sales Returns and Allowances

Barton allows a 60-day return privilege for the merchandise it sells. At year-end, Barton estimates there remain $100,000 of sales (with a cost to Barton of $80,000) that are still within the 60-day return period and that, from past experience, 10 percent of this merchandise will be returned. Barton makes the following adjusting journal entries at year-end to provide for these estimated returns.

Dec. 31	Sales returns and allowances (+XR, −SE)	10,000	
	Sales refunds payable (+L)		10,000
	To record the estimated return of 10 percent of the merchandise sold		
	that is still eligible for return at year-end ($100,000 × 0.10).		
Dec. 31	Estimated inventory return (+A)	8,000	
	Cost of goods sold (−E, +SE)		8,000
	To record the estimated return of 10 percent of the merchandise sold		
	that is still eligible for return at year-end ($80,000 × 0.10).		

The first adjusting journal entry debits Sales returns and allowances for the amount of merchandise that Barton estimates will be returned within the return period. Sales returns and allowance represents a contra account to Sales revenue. The credit in this entry is to Sales refunds payable, a liability account representing the refund that will be due upon the return of the merchandise.

The second adjusting journal entry debits Estimated inventory return for the amount of inventory Barton estimates will be returned. Estimated inventory return is an asset account.

In subsequent periods, management will assess these three important accounts: Allowance for Sales Discounts, Sales Refunds Payable, and Estimated Inventory Return. Management would adjust upward or downward as necessary during the year-end adjustment process to report balances for these accounts that reflect economic circumstances. All other entries during the period for returns, allowances, and discounts are identical to those described in the chapter.

YOUR TURN! 5B.1

The solution is on page 269.

WikiTech's fiscal year-end is December 31. Assume that during the year, WikiTech sells merchandise on account totaling $1,000,000. Further assume the cost to WikiTech of this merchandise was $300,000. WikiTech offers credit terms of 2/10, n/30 to encourage early payment. At year-end, WikiTech recognizes that there are $150,000 of sales on account still eligible for the 2 percent discount. WikiTech believes that all companies will pay within the discount period to receive the 2 percent discount. In addition, WikiTech allows a 90-day return privilege for the merchandise it sells. At year-end, WikiTech estimates there remain $200,000 of sales (with a cost to WikiTech of $60,000) that are still within the 90-day return period and that, from past experience, 7.5 percent of this merchandise is expected to be returned. Prepare the period-end adjusting journal entries needed for WikiTech to comply with the revenue recognition standard.

SUMMARY OF LEARNING OBJECTIVES

Explain the operations of a merchandise company and contrast that with the operations of a service company. (p. 232)　　**LO1**

- Merchandise inventory is a stock of products that a company buys from another company and makes available for sale to its customers.
- Merchandising firms sell merchandise. There are two types of merchandising firms: wholesale distributors and retailers.
- Manufacturing companies convert raw materials and components into finished products through the application of skilled labor and machine operations; wholesale distributors buy finished product from manufacturing firms in large quantities and sell smaller quantities to retailers; retailers sell the products to individual consumers.
- The operating cycle of a merchandising firm consists of three types of transactions: purchase merchandise for resale and warehouse the inventory, remove goods from inventory and ship to the customer at sale, and receive cash from the customer.
- The primary revenue source for a service firm is from providing services to customers, rather than manufacturing or selling a physical product.

Describe the accounting for purchases of merchandise. (p. 235)　　**LO2**

- The perpetual inventory system records the cost of merchandise in the Inventory account at the time of purchase and updates the Inventory account for subsequent transactions as they occur.
- When the perpetual inventory system is used, the Inventory account is affected by merchandise transactions as follows:
  - Debited for the invoice price of purchases.
  - Debited for transportation costs.
  - Credited for the cost of purchase returns and allowances.
  - Credited for cash discounts taken.
  - Credited for the cost of the merchandise sold.
  - Debited for the cost of any sales returns.

Describe the accounting for sales of merchandise. (p. 239)　　**LO3**

- When a perpetual inventory system is used, the following procedure is followed to account for the sale of merchandise:
  - Credit Sales Revenue at the time of the sale, and debit Cash or Accounts Receivable.
  - Debit Cost of Goods Sold and credit Inventory at the time of sale to match expenses with revenue and to update the inventory balance.

Define the gross profit percentage and the return on sales ratio, and explain their use in profitability analysis. (p. 242)　　**LO4**

- The gross profit percentage is the rate at which a company earns gross profit on net sales.
- The gross profit percentage is calculated as net sales less the cost of goods sold, all divided by net sales.
- The return on sales ratio reveals how much of each dollar of net sales is earned by the company after subtracting all expenses.
- The return on sales ratio is calculated by dividing net income by net sales.

LO5 **Appendix 5A: Describe and illustrate a periodic inventory system. (p. 246)**

- The periodic inventory system updates both the Inventory account and the Cost of Goods Sold account at the end of the accounting period when a physical count of the inventory is taken.
- Under the periodic inventory system separate accounts are used to record merchandise purchases, transportation costs, purchase returns and allowances, and purchase discounts, rather than recording these items to the Inventory account.
- The periodic inventory system does not update the Inventory account or the Cost of Goods Sold account as merchandise transactions occur during the year. Instead, the Inventory account and the Cost of Goods Sold account are updated only at the end of the accounting period when a physical count of the inventory is taken. Other accounts are used to record purchases, transportation costs, purchase returns and allowances, and purchase discounts.
- Cost of goods sold is calculated by subtracting the remaining inventory on hand from the cost of goods available for sale, which represents the aggregate inventory that was available to be sold.
- The basic formula for calculating the cost of goods sold under the periodic system is to calculate goods available for sale consisting of beginning inventory plus net purchases during the period, less purchase returns and allowances and less purchase discounts, and then subtract ending inventory from this amount.

LO6 **Appendix 5B: Describe and illustrate the revenue recognition standard for sales returns and allowances and sales discounts. (p. 249)**

- The core principle underlying the revenue recognition standard is that a company should recognize revenue in the amount of consideration it expects to receive in exchange for the transfer of goods or services to a customer.

SUMMARY	Concept	→ Method →	Assessment
TAKEAWAY 5.1	Is a company able to maintain prices on its goods consistent with changes in the cost of its inventory?	Gross profit and net sales $\text{Gross profit percentage} = \dfrac{\text{Gross profit on sales}}{\text{Net sales}}$	A higher ratio suggests the company has market power to command higher retail prices. A lower ratio suggests competitive pressures on price setting.
TAKEAWAY 5.2	Is a company able to maintain prices on its goods consistent with changes in its total expenses?	Net income and net sales $\text{Return on sales ratio} = \dfrac{\text{Net income}}{\text{Net sales}}$	A higher ratio suggests the company is providing a higher net income on each dollar of net sales.

KEY TERMS

Cash discount (p. 237)
Cost of goods available for sale (p. 248)
Cost of goods sold (p. 240)
Credit period (p. 237)
Discount period (p. 237)
FOB destination (p. 236)
FOB shipping point (p. 235)
Gross profit (gross margin) (p. 242)
Gross profit on sales (p. 242)
Gross profit percentage (p. 243)

Invoice price (p. 236)
List price (p. 242)
Manufacturers (p. 232)
Merchandise inventory (p. 234)
Merchandisers (p. 232)
Net sales (p. 242)
Open account (p. 234)
Operating cycle (p. 233)
Periodic inventory system (p. 234)
Perpetual inventory system (p. 234)

Purchase allowance (p. 236)
Purchase return (p. 236)
Retailers (p. 233)
Return on sales ratio (profit margin) (p. 243)
Sale on account (p. 234)
Sale on credit (p. 234)
Sales allowance (p. 240)
Sales discount (p. 237)
Sales returns (p. 240)
Wholesalers (p. 232)

Assignments with the ⊙ logo in the margin are available in BusinessCourse.
See the Preface of the book for details.

SELF-STUDY QUESTIONS

(Answers to Self-Study Questions are at the end of this chapter.)

1. On March 1, Kate Company purchased merchandise with an invoice price of $2,700 and 2/10, n/30 terms. On March 3, Kate pays $98 transportation cost on the purchased goods. On March 10, Kate pays for the merchandise. What is Kate's total cost of the purchased merchandise?   **LO2**

   a. $2,700   c. $2,746
   b. $2,744   d. $2,800

2. Angle Company started business on January 1. During the year, the company purchased merchandise with an invoice price of $500,000. Angle also paid $20,000 freight on the merchandise. During the year, Angle also returned $80,000 of the merchandise to its suppliers. All purchases were paid for in a timely manner, and a $10,000 cash discount was taken. $418,000 of the merchandise was sold for $627,000. What is the December 31 balance in the Inventory account?   **LO2**

   a. $82,000   c. $12,000
   b. $32,000   d. $2,000

3. Samuel Company uses the perpetual inventory system. Samuel purchased merchandise with an invoice price of $800, terms 2/10, n/30. If Samuel returns merchandise with an invoice price of $200 to the supplier, what should the journal entry to record the return include?   **LO2**

   a. Debit to Inventory of $200
   b. Debit to Inventory of $196
   c. Credit to Inventory of $200
   d. Credit to Inventory of $100

4. Jackson Company reports net sales of $500, cost of sales of $300, and net income of $50. What is the gross profit percentage and return on sales ratio for Jackson?   **LO4**

   a. Gross profit percentage is 10 percent and return on sales ratio is 40 percent.
   b. Gross profit percentage is 60 percent and return on sales ratio is 10 percent.
   c. Gross profit percentage is 40 percent and return on sales ratio is 10 percent.
   d. Gross profit percentage is 40 percent and return on sales ratio is 25 percent.

5. Jefferson & Sons purchased $5,000 of merchandise from the Claremont Company with terms of 3/10, n/30. How much discount is Jefferson & Sons entitled to take if it pays within the allowed discount period of 10 days?   **LO2**

   a. $50   c. $150
   b. $100   d. $300

6. Adams Inc. purchased merchandise with a list price of $6,000 from the Sprague Company. Sprague offers its customers credit terms of 2/10, n/30. What amount should Adams pay if the cash discount is taken?   **LO2**

   a. $5,940   c. $6,120
   b. $6,060   d. $5,880

7. The Eureka Company is a merchandiser and reports the following data at year-end: **LO4**

Net sales.	$100,000
Cost of goods sold	60,000
Net income	15,000

   What is the company's gross profit percentage?

   a. 40 percent   c. 15 percent
   b. 60 percent   d. None of the above

8. Using the data in Question 7, what is The Eureka Company's return on sales ratio?   **LO4**

   a. 40 percent   c. 15 percent
   b. 60 percent   d. None of the above

LO1 9. **Which of the following statements regarding cost flows is true?**
a. Cost of goods available for sale is equal to beginning inventory minus cost of goods purchased.
b. Cost of goods available for sale is equal to beginning inventory plus cost of goods purchased.
c. CGAS = beginning inventory minus ending inventory.
d. CGAS = cost of goods sold minus cost of goods purchased.

LO5
(Appendix 5A)
10. **Daniel Co. uses the periodic inventory system. When goods are purchased, Daniel will:**
a. debit freight costs to Inventory.
b. debit purchase returns and allowance for returned items.
c. debit the Purchases account for purchases on account.
d. debit the Inventory account for purchases on account.

LO5
(Appendix 5A)
11. **Bleu Company began the period with $20,000 in inventory. The company also purchased an additional $20,000 of inventory and returned $2,000 for a full credit. A physical count of the inventory at year-end revealed an inventory on hand of $16,000. What was Bleu's cost of goods sold for the period?**
a. $16,000
c. $48,000
b. $22,000
d. $50,000

QUESTIONS

1. Describe the differences between (a) a manufacturer, (b) a wholesale distributor, and (c) a retailer.
2. Describe the three primary transactions in the operating cycle of a merchandising firm.
3. What is the difference between a credit period and a discount period? What is a cash discount?
4. Spink Company purchased merchandise with a list price of $4,000 from the Thompson Company. Thompson offers a 2 percent cash discount if payment is received within 10 days. What is the payment amount if the cash discount is taken?
5. Carole Company purchased $6,000 of merchandise and paid $300 in transportation costs to deliver the merchandise. Carole then returned $1,000 of the merchandise before paying the supplier within the discount period. Carole was entitled to a 2 percent cash discount. How much did Carole pay the supplier?
6. What is the primary difference between a merchandise return and a merchandise allowance?
7. Define the *return on sales ratio*. What does this ratio measure?
8. Define *gross profit on sales*.
9. Define *gross profit percentage*. How is this percentage used by analysts and investors?
10. When merchandisers and manufacturers prepare income statements for their annual reports to shareholders, they usually begin the statement with net sales. For internal reporting purposes, however, the income statements will show gross sales and the related contra-revenue accounts of sales returns and allowances and sales discounts. What might explain this difference in the financial information disclosed to external parties and management? Do you consider the more limited disclosure in the annual reports to be inconsistent with the full disclosure principle? Briefly explain your point of view.

SHORT EXERCISES

LO1 **SE5-1.** **Merchandising versus Service Firm** For each of the following accounts, indicate whether it would be found in the records of a merchandising firm, a service firm, or both.
a. Cost of goods sold.
b. Service revenue.
c. Purchase returns and allowances.
d. Inventory.
e. Accounts receivable.
f. Accounts payable.
g. Sales revenue.
h. Freight-out.

SE5-2. Accounting for Purchase Transactions Donna Company began operations on June 1. The following transactions took place in June: LO2

a. Purchases of merchandise on account were $750,000.
b. The cost of freight to receive the inventory was $20,000. This was paid in cash.
c. Donna returned $10,000 of the merchandise due to an ordering error. Donna received a full credit for the return.
d. Donna paid the remaining balance for the merchandise.

Calculate the dollar amount that Donna will have in inventory at the end of the month. Assume Donna uses the perpetual inventory system and there were no sales.

SE5-3. Accounting for Purchase Transactions Use the data from SE5-2 and prepare the journal entries to record the June transactions. LO2

SE5-4. Accounting for Purchase Discounts Kurt Company purchased $5,000 of merchandise from Marilyn Company with terms of 2/10 n/40. What percent discount will Kurt Company get if it pays within the allowed discount period? If Kurt Company fails to pay within the discount period, how many days does Kurt Company have from the date of purchase before the payment is considered to be late? LO2

SE5-5. Accounting for Purchase Discounts Using the information in SE5-4, what amount will Kurt Company pay to Marilyn Company if Kurt Company takes advantage of the purchase discount? LO2

SE5-6. Accounting for Sales Transactions Madison Company uses the perpetual inventory system. Record the journal entries for the following transactions: LO3

a. On July 16, Madison sold $500 of merchandise with terms of 3/10, n/30. The cost of the merchandise was $200.
b. On July 19, the customer returned $100 of the merchandise from (a). The cost of the merchandise was $40.
c. On July 22, the customer paid the entire balance due to Madison.

SE5-7. Gross Profit Percentage Using the data below, compute Ian's gross profit percentage for the month of January. LO4

Net sales.	$12,000
Cost of goods sold	3,000
Operating expenses	7,000
Other income	500
Income tax expense	1,000

SE5-8. Return on Sales Ratio Using the data in SE5-7, compute Ian's return on sales ratio for the month of January. LO4

SE5-9. Cost of Goods Sold and the Periodic System Kuyu Company uses the periodic inventory system. Kuyu started the period with $12,000 in inventory. The company purchased an additional $25,000 of merchandise, and returned $1,500 for a full credit. A physical count of inventory at the end of the period revealed that there was an ending inventory balance of $6,000. What was Kuyu's cost of goods sold during the period? LO5 (Appendix 5A)

SE5-10. Cost of Goods Sold and the Periodic System Layla Company uses the periodic inventory system. Layla started the period with $22,000 in inventory. The company purchased an additional $25,000 of merchandise and returned $3,000 for a full credit. If Layla's cost of goods sold during the period was $31,000, what must have been the total of the physical inventory count? LO5 (Appendix 5A)

SE5-11. Journalize Periodic Inventory Entries Prepare the journal entries to record the following transactions for the Kristen Company using a periodic inventory system. LO5 (Appendix 5A)

a. On June 2, Kristen purchased $250,000 of merchandise from the Ferway Company with terms, 3/15, n/30.
b. On June 5, Kristen returned $50,000 of the merchandise purchased on June 2.
c. On June 13, Kristen paid the balance due to Ferway.

SE5-12. Revenue Recognition Standard—Adjusting Journal Entry–Sales Discounts Douglas Corporation reports it sold merchandise on account for a total of $800,000 for the current year. The cost to Douglas for the merchandise was $300,000. To encourage early payment, Douglas offers its customers credit LO6 (Appendix 5B)

terms of 1/10, n/30. At year-end, there is $150,000 of sales on account still eligible for the 1 percent discount. Douglas believes that all customers will pay within the discount period to receive the discount. Prepare the adjusting journal entry needed for Douglas Corporation to comply with the revenue recognition standard. Assume Douglas' fiscal year-end is December 31.

LO6
(Appendix 5B)

SE5-13. **Revenue Recognition Standard—Adjusting Journal Entries–Sales Returns and Allowances** During the year, Raul Company sells merchandise on account totaling $2,000,000 (the cost to Raul for this merchandise was $800,000). Raul allows a 60-day return privilege for the merchandise it sells. At year-end, Raul estimates there remain $400,000 of sales (with a cost to Raul of $160,000) that are still within the 60-day return period. Based on past experience, Raul expects 5 percent of this merchandise to be returned. Prepare the period-end adjusting journal entries needed for Raul Company to comply with the revenue recognition standard. Raul's fiscal year-end is December 31.

EXERCISES—SET A

LO3

E5-1A. **Cash Discount Calculations** On June 1, Meadow Company sold merchandise with a list price of $40,000. For each of the sales terms below, determine the proper amount of cash received:

	Credit Terms	Date Paid
1.	2/10, n/30	June 8
2.	1/10, n/30	June 15
3.	1/15, n/30	June 14
4.	n/30	June 28

LO3

E5-2A. **Journal Entries for Sale, Return, and Remittance—Perpetual System** On September 13, Tomas Company sold merchandise with an invoice price of $1,200 ($600 cost), with terms of 2/10, n/30, to Dalton Company. On September 17, $250 of the merchandise ($80 cost) was returned because it was the wrong model. On September 23, Tomas Company received a check for the amount due from Dalton Company.

Required
Prepare the journal entries made by Tomas Company for these transactions. Tomas uses the perpetual inventory system.

LO2

E5-3A. **Journal Entries for Purchase, Return, and Remittance—Perpetual System** On April 13, the Albert Company purchased $26,000 of merchandise from the Krausman Company, with terms of 1/10, n/30. On April 15, Albert paid $400 to Ace Trucking Company for freight on the shipment. On April 18, Albert Company returned $900 of merchandise for credit. Final payment was made to Krausman on April 22. Albert Company records purchases using the perpetual inventory system.

Required
Prepare the journal entries that Albert Company should make on April 13, 15, 18, and 22.

LO2, 3

E5-4A. **Journal Entries for Merchandise Transactions on Seller's and Buyer's Books—Perpetual System**
The following are selected transactions for Kim, Inc., during the month of June:

June 21 Sold and shipped on account to Lowery Company, $4,000 ($2,000 cost) of merchandise, with terms of 2/10, n/30.
　　28 Lowery Company returned defective merchandise billed at $400 on June 21 ($200 cost).
　　30 Received from Lowery Company a check for full settlement of the June 21 transaction.

Required
Prepare the necessary journal entries for (a) Kim, Inc., and (b) Lowery Company. Both companies use the perpetual inventory system.

LO2

E5-5A. **Recording Purchases—Perpetual System** On July 1, Hernandez, Inc. purchased merchandise for $2,500, with terms of 1/10, n/30. On July 5, the firm returned $1,000 of the merchandise to the seller. Payment of the account occurred on July 8. Hernandez uses the perpetual inventory system.

Required

a. Prepare the journal entries for July 1, July 5, and July 8.

b. Assuming that the account was paid on July 14, prepare the journal entry for payment on that date.

E5-6A. Profitability Analysis Erin Enterprises reports the following information on its year-end income statement: **LO4**

Net sales.	$200,000	Operating expenses	$40,000
Cost of goods sold	110,000	Other income	25,000

Required

Calculate Erin's gross profit percentage and return on sales ratio.

E5-7A. Journal Entries for Sale, Return, and Remittance—Periodic System On June 8, James Company sold merchandise listing for $1,850 to Dalton Company, terms 3/10, n/30. On June 12, $550 worth of the merchandise was returned because it was the wrong color. On June 18, James Company received a check for the amount due. **LO5 (Appendix 5A)**

Required

Record the journal entries made by James Company for these transactions. James uses the periodic inventory system.

E5-8A. Journal Entries for Purchase, Return, and Remittance—Periodic System On March 10, Horne Company purchased $21,000 worth of merchandise from James Company, terms 1/10, n/30. On March 12, Horne paid $300 freight on the shipment. On March 15, Horne returned $300 of merchandise for credit. Final payment was made to James on March 19. Horne Company uses the periodic inventory system. **LO5 (Appendix 5A)**

Required

Prepare the journal entries that Horne should make on March 10, March 12, March 15, and March 19.

E5-9A. Journal Entries for Merchandise Transactions on Seller's and Buyer's Records—Periodic System The following are selected transactions for Jefferson, Inc., during the month of April: **LO5 (Appendix 5A)**

April 20 Sold and shipped on account to Lind Stores merchandise for $3,000, with terms of 1/10, n/30.

27 Lind Stores returned defective merchandise billed at $300 on April 20.

29 Received from Lind Stores a check for full settlement of the April 20 transaction.

Required

Prepare the necessary journal entries for (a) Jefferson, Inc., and (b) Lind Stores. Both companies use the periodic inventory system.

E5-10A. Revenue Recognition Standard—Adjusting Journal Entries TheOne sold $5,000,000 of merchandise on account during the current year. The cost for this merchandise to TheOne was $1,400,000. To encourage early payment from its customers, TheOne offers credit terms of 2/10, n/30. At year-end, TheOne recognizes that there are $500,000 of sales on account still eligible for the 2 percent discount. TheOne believes that all customers will pay within the discount period to receive this discount. In addition, TheOne allows a 60-day return privilege for the merchandise it sells. At year-end, TheOne estimates there remain $600,000 of sales (with a cost to TheOne of $168,000) that are still within the 60-day return period and that, based on past experience, 4 percent of this merchandise is expected to be returned. Prepare the period-end adjusting journal entries needed for TheOne to comply with the new revenue recognition standard. Assume TheOne's fiscal year-end is December 31. **LO6 (Appendix 5B)**

E5-11A. Revenue Recognition Standard—Adjusting Journal Entries During the year, Price Company sells merchandise on account totaling $10,000,000 with a cost of merchandise to Price of $5,000,000. Price offers its customers credit terms of 1/15, n/30. Price recognizes that there are $900,000 of sales on account still eligible for the 1 percent discount at year-end and believes that all customers will pay within the discount period. Additionally, Price allows a 90-day return privilege for the merchandise it sells. At year-end, Price estimates sales of $2,500,000 (with a cost to Price of $1,250,000) remain that are still within the 90-day return period. From past experience, 8 percent of this merchandise is expected to be returned. Prepare the period-end adjusting journal entries needed for Price Company to comply with the revenue recognition standard. Price's fiscal year-end is December 31. **LO6 (Appendix 5B)**

EXERCISES—SET B

LO3 **E5-1B.** **Cash Discount Calculations** On April 1, the Gerald Company sold merchandise with a list price of $75,000. For each of the sales terms below, determine the proper amount of cash received:

	Credit Terms	Date Paid
1.	1/15, n/30 . . .	April 14
2.	n/30.	April 28
3.	2/10, n/30 . . .	April 8
4.	1/10, n/30 . . .	April 15

LO3 **E5-2B.** **Journal Entries for Sale, Return, and Remittance—Perpetual System** On October 14, the Henry Company sold merchandise with an invoice price of $1,300 ($750 cost), with terms of 1/10, n/30, to the Baxter Company. On October 18, $300 of merchandise ($175 cost) was returned because it was the wrong size. On October 24, the Henry Company received a check for the amount due from the Baxter Company.

Required
Prepare the journal entries for the Henry Company using the perpetual inventory system.

LO2 **E5-3B.** **Journal Entries for Purchase, Return, and Remittance—Perpetual System** On May 15, Walter Company purchased $30,000 of merchandise from the Terrell Company, with terms of 1/10, n/30. On May 17, Walter paid $400 to Swift Trucking Company for freight on the shipment. On May 20, Walter Company returned $1,200 of merchandise for credit. Final payment was made to Terrell on May 24. Walter Company records purchases using the perpetual inventory system.

Required
Prepare the journal entries that Walter Company should make on May 15, 17, 20, and 24.

LO2, 3 **E5-4B.** **Journal Entries for Merchandise Transactions on Seller's and Buyer's Books—Perpetual System** The following are selected transactions of Candy, Inc., during the month of June:

June 18 Sold and shipped on account to Dante Company $5,000 ($3,000 cost) of merchandise, with terms of 2/10, n/30.
      25 Dante Company returned merchandise billed at $700 on June 18 ($300 cost).
      27 Received from Dante Company a check for full settlement of the June 18 transaction.

Required
Prepare the necessary journal entries for (a) Candy, Inc., and (b) Dante Company. Both companies use the perpetual inventory system.

LO2 **E5-5B.** **Recording Purchases—Perpetual System** On September 12, Burt, Inc., purchased merchandise for $4,800, with terms of 2/10, n/30. On September 16, the firm returned $500 of the merchandise to the seller. Payment of the account occurred on September 19. Burt uses the perpetual inventory system.

Required
a. Prepare the journal entries for September 12, September 16, and September 19.
b. Assuming that the account was paid on September 25, prepare the journal entry for payment on that date.

LO4 **E5-6B.** **Profitability Analysis** Shannon Enterprises reports the following information on its year-end income statement:

Net sales.	$200,000	Operating expenses	$20,000
Cost of goods sold	130,000	Other income	10,000

Required
Calculate Shannon's gross profit percentage and return on sales ratio.

LO5
(Appendix 5A) **E5-7B.** **Journal Entries for Sale, Return, and Remittance—Periodic System** On March 10, the Stone Company sold merchandise listing for $3,000 to the Dillard Company with terms of 1/10, n/30. On March 14, $200 of merchandise was returned because it was the wrong size. On March 20, Stone Company received a check for the amount due.

Required

Prepare the journal entries made by Stone Company for these transactions. Stone uses the periodic inventory system.

E5-8B. **Journal Entries for Purchase, Return, and Remittance—Periodic System** On August 15, the Ford Company purchased $17,500 of merchandise from Jason Company with terms of 2/10, n/30. On August 17, Ford paid $350 freight on the shipment. On August 20, Ford returned $500 worth of the merchandise for credit. Final payment was made to Jason on August 24. Ford Company records purchases using the periodic inventory system.

LO5
(Appendix 5A)

Required

Prepare the journal entries that Ford should make on August 15, August 17, August 20, and August 24.

E5-9B. **Journal Entries for Merchandise Transactions on Seller's and Buyer's Books—Periodic System** The following are selected transactions of Fedor, Inc., during the month of January:

LO5
(Appendix 5A)

Jan.   20   Sold and shipped on account to Lawrence Stores merchandise listing for $4,500 with terms of 2/10, n/30.
      27   Lawrence Stores was granted a $500 allowance on goods shipped January 20.
      29   Received from Lawrence Stores a check for full settlement of the January 20 transaction.

Required

Prepare journal entries for (a) Fedor, Inc., and (b) Lawrence Stores. Both companies use the periodic inventory system.

E5-10B. **Revenue Recognition Standard—Adjusting Journal Entries** Prime sold $2,000,000 of merchandise on account during the current year. The cost for this merchandise to Prime was $800,000. To encourage early payment from its customers, Prime offers credit terms of 2/10, n/30. At year-end, Prime recognizes that there are $350,000 of sales on account still eligible for the 2 percent discount. Prime believes that all customers will pay within the discount period to receive this discount. In addition, Prime allows a 60-day return privilege for the merchandise it sells. At year-end, Prime estimates there remain $450,000 of sales (with a cost to Prime of $180,000) that are still within the 60-day return period and that, based on past experience, 7 percent of this merchandise is expected to be returned. Prepare the period-end adjusting journal entries needed for Prime to comply with the revenue recognition standard. Assume Prime's fiscal year-end is December 31.

LO6
(Appendix 5B)

E5-11B. **Revenue Recognition Standard—Adjusting Journal Entries** During the year, Carrie Corporation sells merchandise on account totaling $4,000,000 with a cost of merchandise to Carrie of $2,000,000. Carrie offers its customers credit terms of 1/15, n/30. Carrie recognizes that there are $410,000 of sales on account still eligible for the 1 percent discount at year-end and believes that all companies will pay within the discount period. Additionally, Carrie allows a 90-day return privilege for the merchandise it sells. At year-end, Carrie estimates sales of $1,200,000 (with a cost to Carrie of $600,000) remain that are still within the 90-day return period. From past experience, 6 percent of this merchandise is expected to be returned. Prepare the period-end adjusting journal entries needed for Carrie Corporation to comply with the revenue recognition standard. Carrie Corporation's fiscal year-end is December 31.

LO6
(Appendix 5B)

PROBLEMS—SET A

P5-1A. **Journal Entries for Merchandise Transactions on Seller's and Buyer's Books—Perpetual System** The following transactions occurred between the Decker Company and Mann Stores, Inc., during March:

LO2, 3

Mar.   8   Decker sold $14,000 worth of merchandise ($9,600 cost) to Mann Stores with terms of 2/10, n/30.
     10   Mann Stores paid freight charges on the shipment from Decker Company, $500.
     12   Mann Stores returned $2,000 of the merchandise ($1,600 cost) shipped on March 8.
     17   Decker received full payment for the net amount due from the March 8 sale.
     20   Mann Stores returned goods that had been billed originally at $800 ($600 cost). Decker issued a check for $784.

Required

Prepare the necessary journal entries for (a) the books of Decker Company and (b) the books of Mann Stores, Inc. Assume that both companies use the perpetual inventory system.

LO2, 3 **P5-2A.** **Journal Entries for Merchandise Transactions—Perpetual System** Rockford Corporation, which began business on August 1, sells on terms of 2/10, n/30. Credit terms for its purchases vary with the supplier. Selected transactions for August are given below. Unless noted, all transactions are on account and involve merchandise held for resale. The perpetual inventory system is used.

Aug. 1 Purchased merchandise from Norris, Inc., $4,000, terms 2/10, n/30.
     5 Paid freight on shipment from Norris, Inc., $220.
     7 Sold merchandise to Denton Corporation, $5,500 ($4,100 cost).
     7 Paid $300 freight on August 7 shipment and billed Denton for the charges.
     9 Returned $800 worth of the merchandise purchased August 1 from Norris, Inc., because it was defective. Norris approved the return.
     9 Received $750 of returned merchandise ($500 cost) from Denton Corporation. Rockford approved the return.
    10 Paid Norris, Inc., the amount due.
    14 Purchased from Chambers, Inc., goods with a price of $9,000. Terms 1/10, n/30.
    15 Paid freight on shipment from Chambers, Inc., $320.
    17 Received the amount due from Denton Corporation.
    18 Sold merchandise to Weber, Inc., $9,600 ($6,600 cost).
    20 Paid $350 freight on August 18 shipment and billed Weber for the charges.
    24 Paid Chambers, Inc., the amount due.
    28 Received the amount due from Weber, Inc.

Required

Prepare journal entries for these transactions for Rockford Corporation.

LO2, 3 **P5-3A.** **Effects of Transactions on the Inventory Account—Perpetual System** Watt Wholesale Company purchases merchandise from a variety of manufacturers and sells the merchandise to a variety of retailers. All sales are subject to a cash discount (2/10, n/30). Watt uses a perpetual inventory system. The May 1 balance in Watt's Inventory account was a $70,000 debit. The following transactions occurred during May:

May 2 Purchased $5,500 of merchandise from Ajax Manufacturing; terms are 1/10, n/30.
     4 Paid $200 freight on the May 2 purchase.
    12 Paid Ajax for the May 2 purchase.
    14 Purchased $4,000 of merchandise from Baker Manufacturing; terms are 2/10, n/45.
    16 Received a $300 allowance on the May 14 purchase since some of the merchandise was the wrong color. All of the merchandise is salable at regular prices.
    18 Purchased $2,500 of merchandise from Charles Industries; terms are 2/10, n/30.
    19 Sold merchandise with a list price of $2,000 ($1,200 cost) to Daytime Industries.
    22 Daytime Industries returned 40 percent of the merchandise from the May 19 sale.
    26 Paid Baker Manufacturing for the May 14 purchase.
    29 Paid Charles Industries for the May 18 purchase.

Required

Prepare a schedule that shows the impact of these transactions on Watt's Inventory account. Use the following headings:

Date	Transaction	Debit Amount	Credit Amount	Account Balance

LO2, 3 **P5-4A.** **Journal Entries for Merchandise Transactions—Perpetual System** Cushing Distributing Company uses the perpetual inventory system. Cushing had the following transactions related to merchandise during the month of June:

June 1 Purchased on account merchandise for resale for $10,000; terms were 2/10, n/30.
     3 Paid $550 cash for freight on the June 1 purchase.
     7 Returned merchandise costing $600 (part of the $10,000 purchase).
    10 Paid for merchandise purchased on June 1.
    13 Sold merchandise on account costing $8,000 for $10,000; terms were 2/10, n/30.

June 16 Customer returned merchandise costing $750 that had been sold on account for $1,000 (part of the $10,000 sale).

22 Received payment from customer for merchandise sold on June 13.

Required

Prepare journal entries for each of the transactions for the Cushing Distributing Company.

P5-5A. Profitability Analysis Kolby Enterprises reports the following information on its income statement: **LO4**

Net sales..................	$250,000	Administrative expenses........	$10,000
Cost of goods sold	150,000	Other income	15,000
Selling expenses	50,000	Other expense	10,000

Required

Calculate Kolby's gross profit percentage and return on sales ratio. Explain what each ratio tells us about Kolby's performance. Kolby is planning to add a new product and expects net sales to be $45,000 and cost of goods to be $38,000. No other income or expenses are expected to change. How will this affect Kolby's gross profit percentage and return on sales ratio? What do you advise regarding the new product offering?

P5-6A. Journal Entries for Merchandise Transactions on Seller's and Buyer's Books—Periodic System   **LO5**
The following transactions occurred between Southwick Company and Mann Stores, Inc., during March: **(Appendix 5A)**

Mar. 8 Southwick sold $7,100 worth of merchandise to Mann Stores, terms 2/10, n/30.

10 Mann Stores paid freight charges on the shipment from Southwick Company, $200.

12 Mann Stores returned $700 of the merchandise shipped on March 8.

17 Southwick received full payment for the net amount due from the March 8 sale.

20 Mann Stores returned goods that had been billed originally at $400. Southwick issued a check for $392.

Required

Prepare the necessary journal entries for (a) the books of Southwick Company and (b) the books of Mann Stores, Inc. Assume that both companies use the periodic inventory system.

P5-7A. Journal Entries for Merchandise Transactions—Periodic System The Malvado Corporation sells goods on terms of 2/10, n/30. Credit terms for its purchases vary with the supplier. Selected transactions for August are given below. Unless noted, all transactions are on account and involve merchandise held for resale. The periodic inventory system is used.   **LO5**
(Appendix 5A)

Aug. 1 Purchased merchandise from Norris, Inc., $2,500; terms 2/10, n/30.

5 Paid freight on shipment from Norris, Inc., $120.

7 Sold merchandise to Denton Corporation, $3,100.

7 Paid freight on shipment to Denton Corporation, $150, and billed Denton for the charges.

9 Returned $400 worth of the merchandise purchased August 1 from Norris, Inc., because it was defective. Norris approved the return.

9 Received $500 of returned merchandise from Denton Corporation.

10 Paid Norris, Inc., the amount due.

14 Purchased from Chambers, Inc., goods with a price of $4,500. Terms 1/10, n/30.

15 Paid freight on shipment from Chambers, Inc., $160.

17 Received the amount due from Denton Corporation.

18 Sold merchandise to Weber, Inc., $4,800.

20 Paid freight on August 18 shipment to Weber, Inc., $160 and billed Weber.

24 Paid Chambers, Inc., the amount due.

28 Received the amount due from Weber, Inc.

Required

Prepare the necessary journal entries for the Malvado Corporation.

PROBLEMS—SET B

LO2, 3 **P5-1B.** **Journal Entries for Merchandise Transactions on Seller's and Buyer's Books—Perpetual System**
Ryan Distributing Company had the following transactions with Arlington, Inc., during the month of November:

Nov. 10 Ryan sold and shipped $8,000 worth of merchandise ($4,500 cost) to Arlington, terms 1/10, n/30.
12 Arlington, Inc., paid freight charges on the shipment from Ryan Company, $450.
14 Ryan received $600 of merchandise returned by Arlington ($340 cost) from the November 10 sale.
19 Ryan received payment in full for the net amount due on the November 10 sale.
24 Arlington returned goods that had originally been billed at $400 ($280 cost). Ryan issued a check for $396.

Required
Prepare the necessary journal entries (a) on the books of Ryan Distributing Company and (b) on the books of Arlington, Inc. Assume that both companies use the perpetual inventory system.

LO2, 3 **P5-2B.** **Journal Entries for Merchandise Transactions—Perpetual System** Webb Company was established on July 1. Its sales terms are 3/10, n/30. Credit terms for its purchases vary with the supplier. Selected transactions for the first month of operations are given below. Unless noted, all transactions are on account and involve merchandise held for resale. Webb Company uses the perpetual inventory system.

July 1 Purchased goods from Dawson, Inc., $2,500; terms 1/10, n/30.
2 Purchased goods from Penn Company, $5,500; terms 2/10, n/30.
3 Paid freight on shipment from Dawson, $300.
5 Sold merchandise to Ward, Inc., $1,400 ($1,100 cost).
5 Paid freight on shipment to Ward, Inc., $90. (*Hint:* debit Delivery Expense)
8 Returned $700 worth of the goods purchased July 1 from Dawson, Inc., because some goods were damaged. Dawson approved the return.
9 Received returned goods from Ward, Inc., worth $200 ($150 cost).
10 Paid Dawson, Inc., the amount due.
10 Purchased goods from Dorn Company with a list price of $3,000. Terms 2/10, n/30.
11 Paid freight on shipment from Dorn Company, $150.
15 Received the amount due from Ward, Inc.
15 Sold merchandise to Colby Corporation, $3,200 ($2,400 cost).
16 Mailed a check to Penn Company for the amount due on its July 2 invoice.
18 Received an allowance of $250 from Dorn Company for defective merchandise purchased on July 10.
19 Paid Dorn Company the amount due.
25 Received the amount due from Colby Corporation.

Required
Prepare the necessary journal entries for the Webb Company.

LO2, 3 **P5-3B.** **Effects of Transactions on the Inventory Account—Perpetual System** Rand Wholesale Company purchases merchandise from a variety of manufacturers and sells the merchandise to a variety of retailers. All sales are subject to a cash discount (2/10, n/30). Rand has a perpetual inventory system. The February 1 balance in Rand's Inventory account was a $50,000 debit. The following transactions occurred during February:

Feb. 2 Purchased $8,600 of merchandise from Sweet Manufacturing; terms are 1/10, n/30.
5 Paid $270 freight on the February 2 purchase.
11 Paid Sweet for the February 2 purchase.
13 Purchased $5,000 of merchandise from Tayler Manufacturing; terms are 2/10, n/45.
16 Received a $300 allowance on the February 13 purchase since some of the merchandise was the wrong size. All of the merchandise is salable at regular prices.
17 Purchased $5,200 of merchandise from Zorn Industries; terms are 2/10, n/30.
20 Sold merchandise with a list price of $3,000 ($1,200 cost) to Valley Mart.
22 Valley Mart returned 30 percent of the merchandise from the February 20 sale.
23 Paid Tayler Manufacturing for the February 13 purchase.
28 Paid Zorn Industries for the February 17 purchase.

Required

Prepare a schedule that shows the impact of these transactions on Rand's Inventory account. Use the following headings:

Date	Transaction	Debit Amount	Credit Amount	Account Balance

P5-4B. Journal Entries for Merchandise Transactions Jane Distributing Company uses the perpetual inventory system. Jane had the following transactions related to merchandise during the month of August:

LO2, 3

Aug. 10 Purchased on account merchandise for resale for $9,000; terms were 2/10, n/30.
     12 Paid $450 cash for freight on the August 10 purchase.
     16 Returned merchandise costing $800 (part of the $9,000 purchase).
     19 Paid for merchandise purchased on August 10.
     22 Sold merchandise on account costing $8,500 for $11,000; terms were 2/10, n/30.
     25 Customer returned merchandise costing $750 that had been sold on account for $900 (part of the $11,000 sale).
     31 Received payment from customer for merchandise sold on August 22.

Required

Record each of the transactions related to purchasing and selling merchandise for the Jane Distributing Company.

P5-5B. Profitability Analysis Emily Enterprises reports the following information on its income statement:

LO4

Net sales.	$400,000	Administrative expenses.	$20,000
Cost of goods sold	170,000	Other income	15,000
Selling expenses	50,000	Other expense	10,000

Required

Compute Emily's gross profit percentage and return on sales ratio. Explain what each ratio tells us about Emily's performance. Emily is planning to add a new product and expects net sales to be $40,000 and cost of goods to be $28,000. No other income or expenses are expected to change. How will this affect Emily's gross profit percentage and return on sales ratio? What do you advise regarding the new product offering?

P5-6B. Journal Entries for Merchandise Transactions on Seller's and Buyer's Books—Periodic System Fame Distributing Company had the following transactions with Arlington, Inc., during November:

LO5
(Appendix 5A)

Nov. 10 Fame sold and shipped $8,000 worth of merchandise to Arlington, terms 2/10, n/30.
     12 Arlington, Inc., paid freight charges on the shipment from Fame Company, $450.
     14 Fame received $850 of merchandise returned by Arlington from the November 10 sale.
     19 Fame received payment in full for the net amount due on the November 10 sale.
     24 Arlington returned goods that had originally been billed at $700. Fame issued a check for $686.

Required

Prepare the necessary journal entries (a) on the books of Fame Distributing Company and (b) on the books of Arlington, Inc. Assume that both companies use the periodic inventory system.

P5-7B. Journal Entries for Merchandise Transactions—Periodic System Drake Company was established on July 1. Its sales terms are 2/10, n/30. Credit terms for its purchases vary with the supplier. Selected transactions for the first month of operations are given below. Unless noted, all transactions are on account and involve merchandise held for resale. All purchases are recorded using the periodic inventory system.

LO5
(Appendix 5A)

July 1 Purchased goods from Dawson, Inc., $3,500; terms 1/10, n/30.
     2 Purchased goods from Penn Company, $5,100; terms 2/10, n/30.
     3 Paid freight on shipment from Dawson, $200.
     5 Sold merchandise to Ward, Inc., $1,700.
     5 Paid freight on shipment to Ward, Inc., $80. (*Hint:* debit Delivery Expense)

July   8 Returned $300 worth of the goods purchased July 1 from Dawson, Inc., because some goods were damaged. Dawson approved the return.

9 Received returned merchandise from Ward, Inc., $200.

10 Paid Dawson, Inc., the amount due.

10 Purchased goods from Dorn Company with a price of $2,200. Terms 2/10, n/30.

11 Paid freight on shipment from Dorn Company, $130.

15 Received the amount due from Ward, Inc.

15 Sold merchandise to Colby Corporation, $4,200.

16 Mailed a check to Penn Company for the amount due on its July 2 invoice.

18 Received an allowance of $100 from Dorn Company for defective merchandise purchased on July 10.

19 Paid Dorn Company the amount due.

25 Received the amount due from Colby Corporation.

Required

Prepare the necessary journal entries for Drake Company.

SERIAL PROBLEM: KATE'S CARDS

(Note: This is a continuation of the Serial Problem: Kate's Cards from Chapters 1 through 4.)

SP5.   Kate was a little worried about some of the practices of Fred Abbott, the CEO of Sentiments, and decided that an association with Sentiments could damage the reputation of her own company. Kate is very concerned that her business be viewed as socially responsible and any damage to her reputation at this early stage could prove very difficult to overcome. She therefore decided to concentrate her efforts on producing a quality product that consumers would be proud to purchase and send to their loved ones.

As expected, November saw a boom in Kate's greeting card business. She invested in additional computer graphics equipment, which she partially funded with a bank loan of $15,000 and an additional investment of her own funds into the business. The loan carries an interest rate of six percent with interest payments required semiannually. The entire principal balance is due in one balloon payment in two years. Kate uses a perpetual inventory system. As of December 2, 2018, Kate's Cards had the following account balances:

Cash.	$11,900	Accumulated depreciation	$ 1,600
Accounts receivable	16,800	Accounts payable	13,800
Inventory.	16,000	Other current liabilities	900
Other current assets	3,600	Long-term note payable	15,000
Computer equipment	38,900	Common stock	25,000
		Retained earnings	30,900

The company had the following transactions during December 2018:

Dec   1 Paid $1,200 rent for the month.

7 Paid $1,800 to employees. Of this amount, $900 was for an amount owed from November. Wages due to employees at the end of each month are recorded as Other Current Liabilities.

9 Received $5,400 from customers as payment on account.

12 Sold, for cash, $11,000 of greeting cards. This merchandise had cost $6,000 to produce.

14 Purchased additional inventory totaling $7,000 on account with terms of 2/10, n/45.

15 Paid cash for supplies (listed as Other Current Assets) in the amount of $600.

19 Sold, on account with terms of 2/10, n/30, greeting cards totaling $6,000. The merchandise had cost $4,000 to produce.

21 Paid additional wages of $1,400.

25 Paid the total owed for the merchandise that was purchased on December 14.

28 Received payment in full from the customer that purchased the merchandise on December 19.

31 Depreciation for the month totaled $900.

31 A physical count of inventory and supplies revealed that $13,000 and $2,000, respectively, were on hand at year-end. Assume that Other Current Assets consists only of the cost of supplies.

Required
a. Prepare journal entries for the December transactions.
b. Prepare a classified income statement for the month of December 2018.
c. Calculate Kate's gross profit percentage and return on sales ratio for December 2018.

EXTENDING YOUR KNOWLEDGE

REPORTING AND ANALYSIS

EYK5-1. **Financial Reporting Problem: The Columbia Sportswear Company** The financial statements for the Columbia Sportswear Company are in Appendix A at the end of this book.

COLUMBIA
SPORTSWEAR
COMPANY

Required
Using the company's Consolidated Statement of Operations (which is another name for Income Statement), answer the following questions.
a. What was the change in net sales and in net income from 2016 to 2017?
b. What was the gross profit percentage in each of the three years, 2015 through 2017? Comment on the trend in this ratio.
c. What was the return on sales ratio in each of the three years, 2015 through 2017? Comment on the trend in this ratio.

EYK5-2. **Comparative Analysis Problem: The Columbia Sportswear Company vs. Under Armour, Inc.** The financial statements for the Columbia Sportswear Company and Under Armour, Inc. are in Appendix A and B, respectively, at the end of this book.

COLUMBIA
SPORTSWEAR
COMPANY

UNDER ARMOUR,
INC.

Required
a. Based on the information you find in these financial statements, determine the following values for each company:
  1. Gross profit for 2017
  2. Gross profit percentage for 2017
  3. Net income for 2017
  4. Return on sales ratio for 2017
b. Based on this information, what can you say about the relative performance of these two companies?

EYK5-3. **Business Decision Problem** Northern Corporation started a retail clothing business on July 1, 2018. During 2018, Northern Corporation had the following summary transactions related to merchandise inventory:

	Purchases	Sales
July.	$240,000	$ 360,000
August	384,000	696,000
September	312,000	576,000
October.	360,000	660,000
November.	900,000	1,020,000
December.	264,000	1,344,000

On average, Northern's cost of goods sold is 50 percent of sales. Assume that there were no sales returns and allowances or purchases returns and allowances during this six-month time period.

Required
a. Calculate the ending merchandise inventory for each of the six months.
b. Northern's purchases peaked during November; its sales peaked during December. Did Northern plan its purchases wisely? Should Northern expect a similar pattern in future years?

EYK5-4. **Financial Analysis Problem** Johnson & Johnson is a worldwide manufacturer of health care products, including Band-Aid bandages and Mylanta antacid. It reported the following results for three recent years:

JOHNSON &
JOHNSON

(in millions)	2017	2016	2015
Net sales.	$76,450	$71,890	$70,074
Cost of goods sold	25,354	21,685	21,536

Assume that similar-sized companies in the same basic industries have experienced an average gross profit percentage of 65 percent each year.

Required

a. Calculate the gross profit percentage for Johnson & Johnson for the three years.

b. Compare the three-year trend in gross profit percentage for Johnson & Johnson to the assumed industry average. Analyze the trend and evaluate the performance of Johnson & Johnson compared to the assumed industry average.

CRITICAL THINKING

GENERAL MILLS, INC.

EYK5-5. **Accounting Research Problem** Refer to the fiscal year 2017 annual report of **General Mills, Inc.**, available on this book's Website.

Required

a. How much sales revenue did General Mills report in 2016 and 2017?

b. What was the company's gross profit percentage in 2016 and 2017?

c. How much net income did the company earn in 2016 and 2017?

d. What was the company's return on sales for 2016 and 2017? What can we conclude about the company's performance over the two-year period?

EYK5-6. **Accounting Communication Activity** Geary Company produces custom machinery that has few competitors. As such, Geary is able to charge a large markup that is reflected in its large gross profit percentage. Recently the marketing director proposed offering a new set of products that are more generic in nature, and therefore will not allow large markups. The accounting department has, however, determined the products will add to Geary's overall net income. The following table provides estimates of Geary's profitability both with and without the new product:

	Without New Product	With New Product
Net sales.	$250,000	$350,000
Cost of goods sold	125,000	210,000
Net income	25,000	31,500

Required

The President of Geary, Jack Brown, has asked you to write a memo answering the following questions.

a. How will the new product line affect the company's profitability as measured by its gross profit percentage and the return on sales ratio?

b. How is it possible for net income to improve, while at the same time these profitability ratios may deteriorate?

c. Should the company expand by offering this new product line?

EYK5-7. **Accounting Ethics Case** During the last week of 2017, George Green, controller of We 'R' Appliances, received a memorandum from the firm's president, Jane Anderson. The memorandum stated that Anderson had negotiated a very large sale with a new customer and directed Green to see that the order was processed and the goods shipped before the end of the year. Anderson noted that she had to depart from the usual credit terms of n/30 and allow terms of n/60 to clinch the sale. Although the credit terms were unusual for the company, Green was particularly pleased with the news because business had been somewhat slow. The goods were shipped on December 29 and the sale was incorporated into the 2017 financial data.

It is now mid-February 2018, and two events have occurred recently that, together, cause concern for Green. First, he was inadvertently copied on a letter from the firm's bank to Anderson. The letter stated that the bank had reconsidered its decision to deny a loan to the company and is now granting the loan based on the new, and favorable, sales data supplied by the president. The bank was "particularly impressed with the sales improvement shown in December." Although Green had been involved in the initial loan application that was denied, he had been unaware that the president had reapplied for the loan.

The second event was that all of the goods shipped on December 29, 2017, to the new customer had just been returned.

Required
What are the ethical considerations George Green faces as a result of the recent events?

EYK5-8. **Corporate Social Responsibility Problem** Target is one of a large growing number of companies that publish an annual corporate social responsibility report. Go to the Target Website and navigate to the section on corporate responsibility to download Target's latest corporate responsibility report. Discuss some of the ways that Target documents its good citizenship.

EYK5-9. **Analyzing IFRS Financial Statements** The 2017 financial statements of LVMH Moet Hennessey-Louis Vuitton S.A. are presented in Appendix C at the end of this book. LVMH is a Paris-based holding company and one of the world's largest and best-known luxury goods companies. As members of the European Union, French companies are required to prepare their consolidated (group) financial statements using International Financial Reporting Standards (IFRS). Using the company's financial statements, calculate the company's (a) gross profit percentage and (b) return on sales ratio for 2016 and 2017. Comment on the trend in the company's profitability over the two-year period.

EYK5-10. **Working with the Takeaways** Costco Wholesale Corporation is the largest membership warehouse club chain in the world based on sales volume. It is the fifth largest general retailer in the United States. Costco is also one of the fastest growing retailers, having grown to over 600 locations since its start in 1983. A look at Costco's income statement reveals the following data:

COSTCO WHOLESALE CORPORATION		
(in millions)	2017	2016
Net sales.	$126,172	$116,073
Cost of goods sold	111,882	102,901
Net income	2,679	2,350

Required
Evaluate Costco's performance in terms of gross profit percentage and return on sales ratio. How does Costco compare to Target and Walmart? (See **Exhibits 5-5** and **5-6** on pages 243 and 244.)

ANSWERS TO SELF-STUDY QUESTIONS:

1. b, (pp. 235–239)   2. c, (pp. 235–239)   3. c, (pp. 236–237)   4. c, (pp. 242–244)   5. c, (pp. 237–239)
6. d, (pp. 237–239)   7. a, (pp. 242–243)   8. c, (p. 243–244)   9. b, (p. 234)   10. c, (p. 246)
11. b, (pp. 248–249)

YOUR TURN! SOLUTIONS

Solution 5.1
a. Cost of goods available for sale = $110,000 + $245,000 = $355,000.
b. Cost of goods sold = $355,000 − $90,000 = $265,000.

Solution 5.2

June 1	Inventory (+A)	510.00	
	Accounts payable (+L)		510.00
	To record merchandise purchased on account (125 CDs @ $4.08 each)		

June 1	Inventory (+A)	22.18	
	Cash (−A)		22.18
	To record payment of freight charges on merchandise purchased.		

June 4	Accounts payable (−L)	61.20	
	Inventory (−A)		61.20
	To record the return of defective merchandise		
	(15 units @ $4.08 per unit).		

June 8	Accounts payable (−L)	448.80	
	Cash (−A)		439.82
	Inventory (−A)		8.98
	To record full payment within discount period. Cash discount		
	earned = $8.98.		

Solution 5.3

June 15	Accounts receivable (+A)	750.00	
	Sales revenue (+R, +SE)		750.00
	To record the sale of 75 CDs on account.		

June 15	Cost of goods sold (+E, −SE)	315.00	
	Inventory (−A)		315.00
	To record cost of goods sold for 75 CDs.		

June 20	Sales returns and allowances (+XR, −SE)	50.00	
	Accounts receivable (−A)		50.00
	To record the return of 5 CDs for credit.		

June 20	Inventory (+A)	21.00	
	Cost of goods sold (−E, +SE)		21.00
	To record the return of 5 CDs for credit.		

June 25	Cash (+A)	700.00	
	Accounts receivable (−A)		700.00
	To record cash payment from customer.		

Solution 5.4

Gross profit percentage = ($100,000 − $45,000)/$100,000 = 55 percent
Return on sales ratio = $10,500/$100,000 = 10.5 percent

A gross profit percentage of 55 percent indicates that Musicland was able to earn 55 cents for each dollar of net sales after considering just its cost of goods sold. In other words, Musicland still has 55 cents available from each dollar of net sales to cover its remaining expenses and to earn a net profit.

A return on sales ratio of 10.5 percent indicates that Musicland was able to earn 10.5 cents in net income from each dollar of net sales after subtracting all of the business's expenses.

Solution 5A.1

June 1	Purchases (−SE)	510.00	
	Accounts payable (+L)		510.00
	To record merchandise purchased on account (125 @ $4.08 each) with		
	2/10, n/30 terms.		

June 1	Freight in (+E, −SE)	22.18	
	Cash (−A)		22.18
	To record payment of freight charge on merchandise purchase.		

June 4	Accounts payable (−L)	61.20	
	Purchase returns and allowances (+SE)		61.20
	To record the return of defective merchandise (15 units).		

continued

June 8	Accounts payable (−L)	448.80	
	Cash (−A)		439.82
	Purchase discounts (+SE)		8.98
	To record payment for merchandise purchased.		

Solution 5A.2

June 15	Accounts receivable (+A)	750.00	
	Sales revenue (+R, +SE)		750.00
	To record the sale of 75 CDs on account.		

June 20	Sales returns and allowances (+XR, −SE)	50.00	
	Accounts receivable (−A)		50.00
	To record the return of 5 CDs for credit.		

June 25	Cash (+A)	700.00	
	Accounts receivable (−A)		700.00
	To record cash payment from customer.		

Solution 5A.3

MUSICLAND COMPANY
Cost of Goods Sold
For Year Ended December 31, 2018

Cost of goods sold			
Inventory, January 1			$10,000
Purchases.		$50,000	
Less: Purchase returns and allowances.	$2,000		
Purchase discounts	1,000	3,000	
Net purchases.		47,000	
Add: Freight-in		200	
Cost of goods purchased			47,200
Cost of goods available for sale			57,200
Less: Inventory, December 31			12,200
Cost of goods sold.			$45,000

Solution 5B.1

Adjusting Journal Entry for Sales Discount

Dec. 31	Sales discounts (+XR, −SE)	3,000	
	Allowance for sales discounts (+XA, −A)		3,000
	To record the estimated sales discount taken of 2 percent on credit		
	sales still eligible for discount at year-end ($150,000 × 0.02).		

Adjusting Journal Entry for Sales Returns

Dec. 31	Sales returns and allowances (+XR, −SE)	15,000	
	Sales refunds payable (+L)		15,000
	To record the estimated return of 7.5 percent of the merchandise sold		
	that is still eligible for return at year-end ($200,000 × 0.075).		

Dec. 31	Estimated inventory return (+A)	4,500	
	Cost of goods sold (−E, +SE)		4,500
	To record the estimated return of 7.5 percent of the merchandise sold		
	that is still eligible for return at year-end ($60,000 × 0.075).		

Chapter 6

Accounting for Inventory

PAST

Chapter 5 focused on accounting for merchandising transactions.

PRESENT

This chapter explains the accounting for inventory and the cost flow assumptions we make to simplify computations.

FUTURE

Chapter 7 focuses on fraud risks faced by businesses and internal controls used to combat fraud and errors.

The period following the financial crisis of 2008 will likely be remembered as some of the most difficult years ever in the retail industry. Retail company bankruptcies during this time period include **Linens 'n Things**, **Mervyn's**, **Sharper Image**, **Steve and Barry's**, and **Wickes Furniture**. However, the bankruptcy of **Circuit City** was perhaps the biggest surprise. Circuit City had over 500 stores throughout the United States that were full of the latest flat screen TVs and electronics. What could explain the failure of Circuit City when the company's biggest rival, **Best Buy**, reported nearly $5 million in profits during the same time period? One key explanation, according to **Time** magazine, was ineffective inventory management.

Circuit City was unable to sell its existing inventory quickly enough, thereby failing to generate the necessary cash flow to enable the company to pay off its huge debt load and creating a backlog that prevented the company from ordering the newer models that consumers preferred. Best Buy, on the other hand, spent considerable time and effort revamping its supply chain and inventory management system to avoid such a fate. The Vice President of Logistics and Transportation with Best Buy observed that "Without better inventory management, Best Buy would have been a thing of the past."

With inventory comprising over one-third of Best Buy's assets, it is readily apparent why effective inventory management is so crucial to its financial health (and that of Circuit City). But how is Best Buy's inventory valued and recorded on its balance sheet? What measures exist for management and financial statement users to evaluate how effectively those inventories are being managed? We discuss answers to both of these important questions and others in this chapter.

Source: "Why Circuit City Busted, While Best Buy Boomed," by Anita Hamilton, Time.com, November 11, 2008; Best Buy 10-K report; Circuit City 10-K report.

Road Map

LO	Learning Objective	Page	eLecture	Guided Example	Assignments
LO1	Explain inventory concepts and modern inventory practices.	272	E6-1	YT6.1	SS1, SS4, SE3, E1A, E3A, E1B, E3B, P1A, P6A, P9A, P1B, P6B, P9B
LO2	Describe inventory costing using specific identification, FIFO, LIFO, and weighted-average cost.	276	E6-2	YT6.2	SS2, SE2, SE8, SE9, SE11, E2A, E4A, E7A, E8A, E2B, E4B, E7B, E8B, P2A, P4A, P8A, P2B, P4B, P8B
LO3	Analyze the financial effects of different inventory costing methods on company profit.	281	E6-3	YT6.3	SS3, SS6, SS7, SS8, SS9, SE10, E5A, E5B, P4A, P4B
LO4	Apply the lower-of-cost-or-net realizable value method.	286	E6-4	YT6.4	SS5, SS10, SE1, SE4, SE5, E6A, E9A, E10A, E12A, E6B, E9B, E10B, E12B, P3A, P7A, P3B, P7B
LO5	Define inventory turnover and days' sales in inventory and explain the use of these ratios.	288	E6-5	YT6.5	SS11, SE6, SE7, E9A, E11A, E9B, E11B, P5A, P5B
LO6	Appendix 6A: Describe inventory costing under a perpetual inventory system using specific identification, FIFO, LIFO, and weighted-average cost.	291	E6-6	YT6A.1	SS13, SE12, SE13, E14A, E15A, E16A, E14B, E15B, E16B, P10A, P11A, P13A, P10B, P11B, P13B
LO7	Appendix 6B: Define the LIFO reserve and explain how it is used to compare the performance of companies using LIFO and FIFO inventory costing methods.	296	E6-7	YT6B.1	SS12, SE14, E13A, E13B, P12A, P12B, EYK11

ACCOUNTING FOR INVENTORY

Inventory Concepts	Inventoriable Items	Inventory Costing Methods (Under Periodic Inventory System)	Inventory Analysis
• Inventory categories • Inventory management methods and objectives	• Goods in transit • Consignment goods • Physical inventory count • Inventory shrinkage and overage	• Specific identification • First-In, first-out (FIFO) • Last-In, first-out (LIFO) • Weighted-average cost • Gross profit effects • Income tax effects • Inventory errors • Lower-of-cost-or-net realizable value • Perpetual Inventory System (Appendix 6A)	• Inventory turnover • Days' sales in inventory • LIFO inventory reserve (Appendix 6B)

INVENTORY CATEGORIES AND CONCEPTS

LO1 **Explain** inventory concepts and modern inventory practices.

This section explains the basic categories of inventory and introduces basic concepts of inventory management.

Categories of Inventory

We define *merchandise inventory* as the inventory of goods that a merchandising company buys from a manufacturing company and makes available for sale to its customers. All necessary costs incurred to acquire the merchandise inventory and deliver it to the buyer's place of business are included in the buyer's cost of inventory. This includes the purchase price of the merchandise, plus any transportation or freight-in costs, less any purchase returns and allowances and any purchase discounts. Wholesale distributors and retailing firms are two major types of merchandising firms.

Unlike merchandising firms, manufacturing firms do not purchase merchandise that is ready for sale. Instead, they purchase various raw materials and components and convert them into salable merchandise. At any point in time, manufacturing firms have units of merchandise at various stages of completion. Consequently, a manufacturing firm usually maintains three separate categories of inventory: raw materials inventory, work-in-process inventory, and finished goods inventory.

Raw materials inventory includes raw materials and components that have been purchased for use in the production of a product but that have not yet been placed into the production process. Sheets of steel are an example of raw material, and computer chips are an example of a component. A *component* is an item in the raw materials inventory account that was a finished product for the manufacturer that produced it. For example, **Intel Corporation** manufactures computer chips that other manufacturers incorporate into their final products. **Dell Inc.**, a computer manufacturer, is an example of a company that incorporates the finished goods of Intel into the computers that it manufactures.

Work-in-process inventory consists of units of product that have been placed into production but that are not fully assembled. All of the costs related to raw materials and components, human labor in the factory, factory utilities, and other factory-related costs are included in the work-in-process inventory. Items in this inventory category are not ready for sale since they are not yet a finished product.

Finished goods inventory includes all units that have been fully manufactured and are ready to be sold to customers. The cost of each item in the finished goods inventory is accumulated in the work-in-process inventory account and is then transferred to the finished goods inventory when the inventory is ready for sale.

© iStock.com

| Raw Materials | Work-in-Process | Finished Goods |

Concepts of Inventory Management

Merchandising and manufacturing companies often find it desirable to maintain a large and varied inventory of merchandise to satisfy the diverse needs and preferences of their customers. Not having enough inventory to meet customer demand can result in missed sales opportunities, called **stock-out costs**. At the same time, carrying more inventory than is needed to meet demand also leads to additional costs. Companies will use inventory management techniques to control these costs.

Just-in-Case Inventory

Manufacturing companies have traditionally maintained inventories as a buffer against unforeseen shipping delays and unforeseen demand by customers. This extra quantity is known as **just-in-case inventory**. Just-in-case inventories create **inventory carrying costs**, which include insurance, building usage costs, and the cost of the capital invested in the inventory.

Just-in-Time Manufacturing

Just-in-time (JIT) manufacturing seeks to eliminate or minimize inventory quantities and their related costs. The key to just-in-time manufacturing involves careful raw material purchase planning and careful management of the manufacturing and sales processes to avoid stock-out costs.

Quick Response Systems   **ACCOUNTING IN PRACTICE**

Many retailers have installed point-of-sale checkout systems to assist in inventory management. These systems either read Universal Product Code bar codes or specially-formed characters using either a plate scanner built into the checkout counter or a handheld scanner (or "wand") to identify the product being sold. Retailers also use a quick response system to optimize their inventory. A **quick response system** is designed to ensure that the retailer quickly reorders items that are being sold and quickly eliminates from inventory any items that are not selling. Special software on a business's computer identifies fast-selling and slow-selling items. The retailer reviews the list and orders more of the highly desirable items that are selling quickly. A retailer typically uses one (or both) of the following approaches to eliminate slow-moving items: (1) return the item to the supplier (if possible) and (2) reduce the unit selling price to (hopefully) induce a quick sale. Quick response systems tend to reduce both the size of inventory that a company must maintain and increase the dollar amount of its sales revenue.

INVENTORY OWNERSHIP AND PHYSICAL COUNT

To determine the quantity of inventory, it is necessary to take a physical count of the inventory, usually at the end of a fiscal period. This involves not only physically counting the inventory, but also determining ownership of the inventory.

Ownership of Inventory

Goods in Transit

Goods in transit can present some uncertainty when trying to determine the end-of-period inventory quantities. It is important to include all inventory items that are owned by a company and exclude any items that are no longer owned, regardless of whether a company has the merchandise in its physical possession or not. When merchandise is shipped by a common carrier—a railroad, trucking company, or an airline—the carrier prepares a *freight bill* in accordance with the instructions of the party making the transportation arrangements. The accountant could look at the freight bill or the invoice, such as the one illustrated in **Exhibit 5-3** (p. 238), to determine which party bears the shipping costs and which party has ownership of the merchandise that is being shipped, referred to as **goods in transit**.

These documents usually show shipping terms of **F.O.B. shipping point** or **F.O.B. destination**. *F.O.B.* is an abbreviation for "free on board." When the freight terms are F.O.B. shipping point, the buyer assumes ownership of the merchandise at the time the common carrier accepts the items from the seller. When the terms are F.O.B. destination, the seller maintains ownership of the merchandise until the buyer takes possession at delivery. In sum, ownership of goods in transit is directly linked to the freight terms when goods are shipped from a seller to a buyer, as illustrated in **Exhibit 6-1**.

Exhibit 6-1 | Ownership of Goods In Transit

F.O.B. Shipping Point

F.O.B. Destination

- Ownership transferred when goods are shipped
- Buyer pays shipping costs

- Ownership transferred when goods are delivered
- Seller pays shipping costs

© Shutterstock.com

ACCOUNTING IN PRACTICE | **Goods in Transit**

As a practical matter most companies ignore inventory in transit for inventory purchases because it has no profit effect. In a perpetual inventory system, the accounts affected are accounts payable and inventory. In a periodic inventory system, purchases and ending inventory are both increased so there is no change in cost of goods sold.

Consignment Goods

Another uncertainty when assessing inventory ownership involves consignment goods. **Consignment goods** are items held for sale by parties other than the owner. An example of a consignment good is used cars held for sale at a used car lot specializing in selling cars for private parties. The car lot does not assume ownership of the cars, but simply attempts to sell the cars, collecting a commission on any completed sales. Since consignment goods do not involve a transfer of title, they are included in the determination of the end-of-period inventory quantity by the owner until sold.

Physical Count of Inventory

A company takes a **physical count of inventory** to verify the balance of inventory. It is possible that changes in the quantity of particular items could have taken place without a transaction being recognized. For example, quantities of various items may have been stolen, damaged, or destroyed. Also, the seller might have shipped an incorrect quantity to a customer even though the seller reflected the correct quantity in a journal entry. The physical count of inventory is often taken at year-end and consists of the following steps:

1. Count the number of individual items of merchandise inventory available at the end of the period.

2. Determine the unit cost of each individual item and multiply the unit cost times the quantity to obtain the total cost for each individual inventory item.

3. Add the total cost of all the individual inventory items to obtain the total cost of the aggregate inventory available.

In a perpetual inventory system, if the physical count of inventory results in a total that does not agree with the balance in the Inventory account, the company makes a year-end adjusting entry. If the physical inventory total is less than the Inventory account balance, the company makes an adjusting entry debiting Cost of Goods Sold and crediting Inventory for the difference between the physical inventory total and the balance in the Inventory account. This entry decreases the balance in the Inventory account and adds the cost of the inventory shortage to Cost of Goods Sold. The cost associated with an inventory shortage is known as **inventory shrinkage**.

Employee Theft of Inventory

FORENSIC ACCOUNTING

Inventory shrinkage arises from employee and/or customer theft, physical damage or deterioration, and obsolescence. Shrinkage is typically discovered following a physical count of inventory. Shrinkage for U.S. retailers is estimated at over $40 billion, and the largest part, nearly $20 billion, is employee theft. Preventing inventory theft is difficult. However, there are several ways that companies can help prevent it, such as:

- Give different passwords to each cashier. Using separate passwords and log-ins reveals which employee was manning the cash register at the times when theft occurs.
- Verify any transaction that is voided or canceled. This is a common way for inventory to be removed from a store.
- Review inventory reports daily to be sure sales match current inventory quantities.
- Install an alarm system on a store's back door that is activated each time the door is opened without authorization.
- Inspect the garbage nightly. Use clear, plastic bags so that the contents are easily inspected to ensure that no inventory is hidden inside.
- Install security cameras in the store and in the back storage to allow the store manager to keep an eye on items on the store racks as well as in stock.

If the physical inventory total is greater than the Inventory account balance, the company makes an adjusting entry debiting Inventory and crediting Cost of Goods Sold for the difference between the physical inventory and the Inventory account balance. This entry increases the balance in the Inventory account and subtracts the cost of this **inventory overage** from Cost of Goods Sold.

To illustrate shrinkage (the usual situation), assume that the December 31 balance of the Inventory account (including all items) is $120,600. Also assume that a physical count of the inventory produced a total cost at December 31 of $120,000. The following period-end adjusting entry is required at December 31 to adjust the balance in the Inventory account from $120,600 to $120,000:

A	=	L	+	SE		Dec. 31	Cost of Goods Sold (+E, −SE)		600	
−600				−600 Exp			Inventory (−A)			600

To adjust the inventory account balance to the total cost determined by a physical inventory count in a perpetual inventory system.

YOUR TURN! 6.1

The solution is on page 320.

The Counter Company just completed the year-end physical count of its inventory. The total value of inventory was determined to be $300,000. The following additional information came to light following the conclusion of the physical count:

1. The company included $20,000 of inventory that was shipped F.O.B. destination.
2. The company included $15,000 of inventory that was shipped F.O.B. shipping point.
3. The company did not include $25,000 of inventory that was being sold on consignment by Johnson Sales, a consignment dealer. The inventory is located at Johnson Sales, but it was still owned by The Counter Company at the time of its physical count of inventory.

Discuss how this additional information affects the $300,000 value that The Counter Company initially determined to be the value of its ending inventory.

INVENTORY COSTING METHODS

LO2 **Describe** inventory costing using specific identification, FIFO, LIFO, and weighted-average cost.

In general, the value of a company's inventory is entered into the accounting records at its acquisition cost. Inventory costing is simple when the acquisition cost remains constant. For example, assume that the Fletcher Motor Company purchased electric motors four times during the year, as shown in **Exhibit 6-2**.

Exhibit 6-2	Illustration of Cost Flows When Prices Do Not Change
February 10 purchase	100 motors at $180 each
April 25 purchase	150 motors at $180 each
July 16 purchase	150 motors at $180 each
October 8 purchase	200 motors at $180 each
December 31 ending inventory.	40 motors at $_?_ each

The December 31 ending inventory of 40 electric motors includes some from the July 16 purchase and some from the October 8 purchase. In this case, it is easy to determine the cost to be assigned to the 40 motors (40 × $180 = $7,200) because all of the inventory purchases were made at the exact same purchase price of $180. In real business situations, however, the purchase price of an item of inventory often changes. The trend is usually toward increasing prices, although in some cases purchase prices may actually decline. When purchase prices change during the year, a company must either keep track of the acquisition cost of each specific unit or make an assumption about which units have been sold and which units remain in inventory. Most companies choose the latter option and make an assumption about which units have been sold and which are still available because the cost of keeping track of exactly which units are sold can be prohibitively expensive.

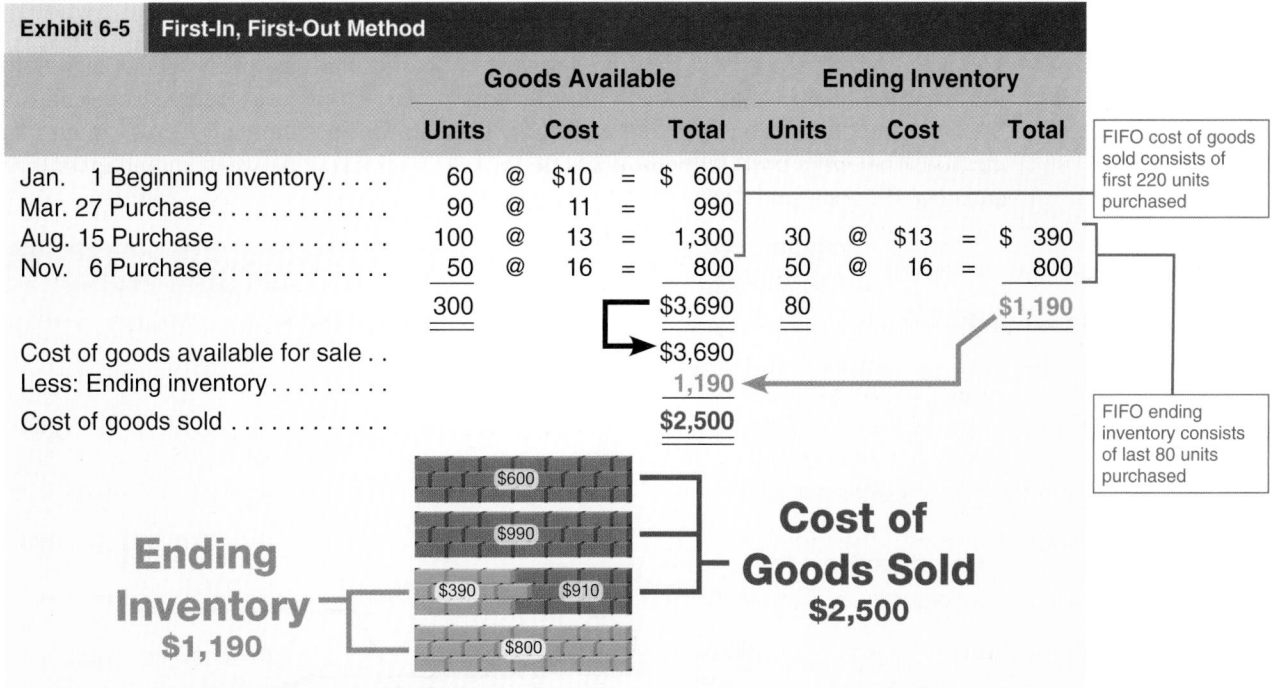

Exhibit 6-5   First-In, First-Out Method

	Goods Available			Ending Inventory			
	Units	Cost	Total	Units	Cost	Total	
Jan. 1 Beginning inventory.....	60 @	$10 =	$ 600				FIFO cost of goods sold consists of first 220 units purchased
Mar. 27 Purchase.............	90 @	11 =	990				
Aug. 15 Purchase.............	100 @	13 =	1,300	30 @	$13 =	$ 390	
Nov. 6 Purchase.............	50 @	16 =	800	50 @	16 =	800	
	300		$3,690	80		$1,190	
Cost of goods available for sale ..			$3,690				
Less: Ending inventory.........			1,190				FIFO ending inventory consists of last 80 units purchased
Cost of goods sold			$2,500				

Ending Inventory $1,190

$600
$990
$390 $910
$800

Cost of Goods Sold $2,500

Last-In, First-Out (LIFO) Method

The **last-in, first-out (LIFO) method** assumes that the most recent purchases are sold first. **Exhibit 6-6** illustrates the calculation of LIFO cost of goods sold. LIFO assumes that the 220 units last (most recently) purchased are sold first, and that the 80 oldest units available for sale remain in inventory at the end of the period.

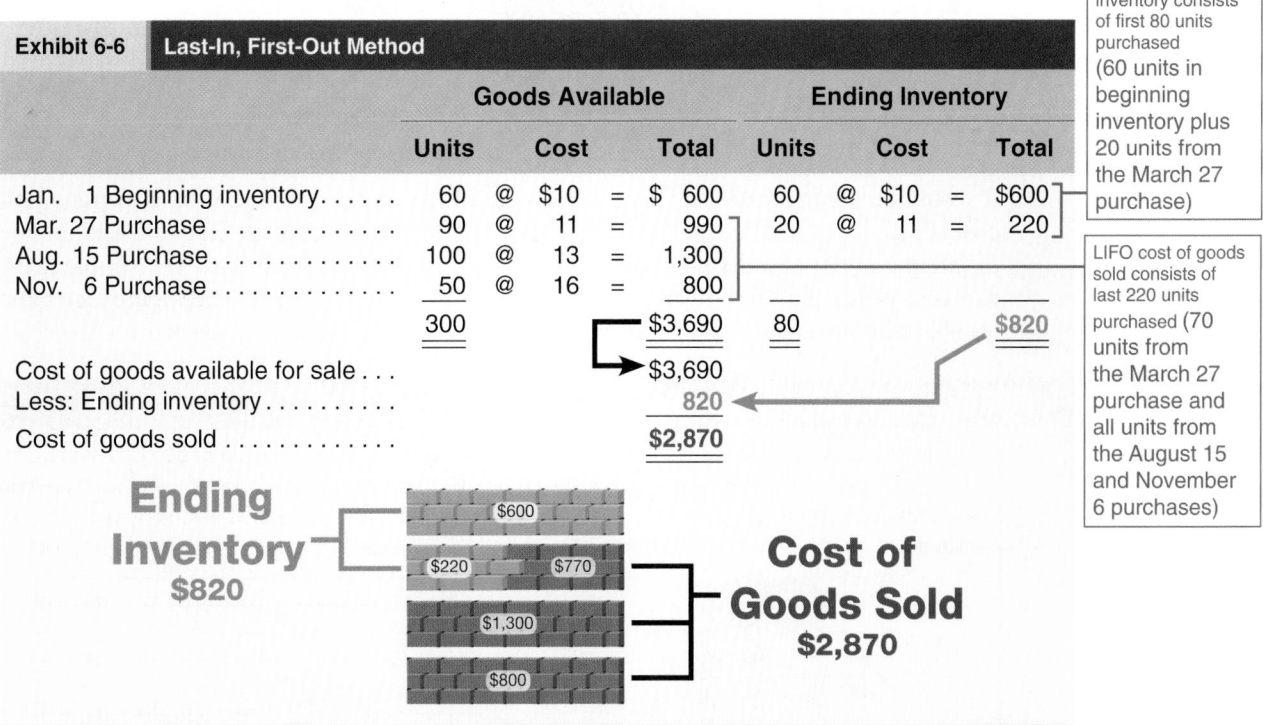

Exhibit 6-6   Last-In, First-Out Method

	Goods Available			Ending Inventory			
	Units	Cost	Total	Units	Cost	Total	
Jan. 1 Beginning inventory......	60 @	$10 =	$ 600	60 @	$10 =	$600	LIFO ending inventory consists of first 80 units purchased (60 units in beginning inventory plus 20 units from the March 27 purchase)
Mar. 27 Purchase..............	90 @	11 =	990	20 @	11 =	220	
Aug. 15 Purchase..............	100 @	13 =	1,300				
Nov. 6 Purchase..............	50 @	16 =	800				
	300		$3,690	80		$820	LIFO cost of goods sold consists of last 220 units purchased (70 units from the March 27 purchase and all units from the August 15 and November 6 purchases)
Cost of goods available for sale ...			$3,690				
Less: Ending inventory..........			820				
Cost of goods sold			$2,870				

Ending Inventory $820

$600
$220 $770
$1,300
$800

Cost of Goods Sold $2,870

Weighted-Average Cost Method

The **weighted-average cost method** spreads the total dollar cost of the goods available for sale equally among all units. In our illustration, the weighted-average cost per unit is $12.30, computed as $3,690/300. **Exhibit 6-7** diagrams the assignment of costs under this method. The entire cost of goods available for sale is allocated between ending inventory and cost of goods sold.

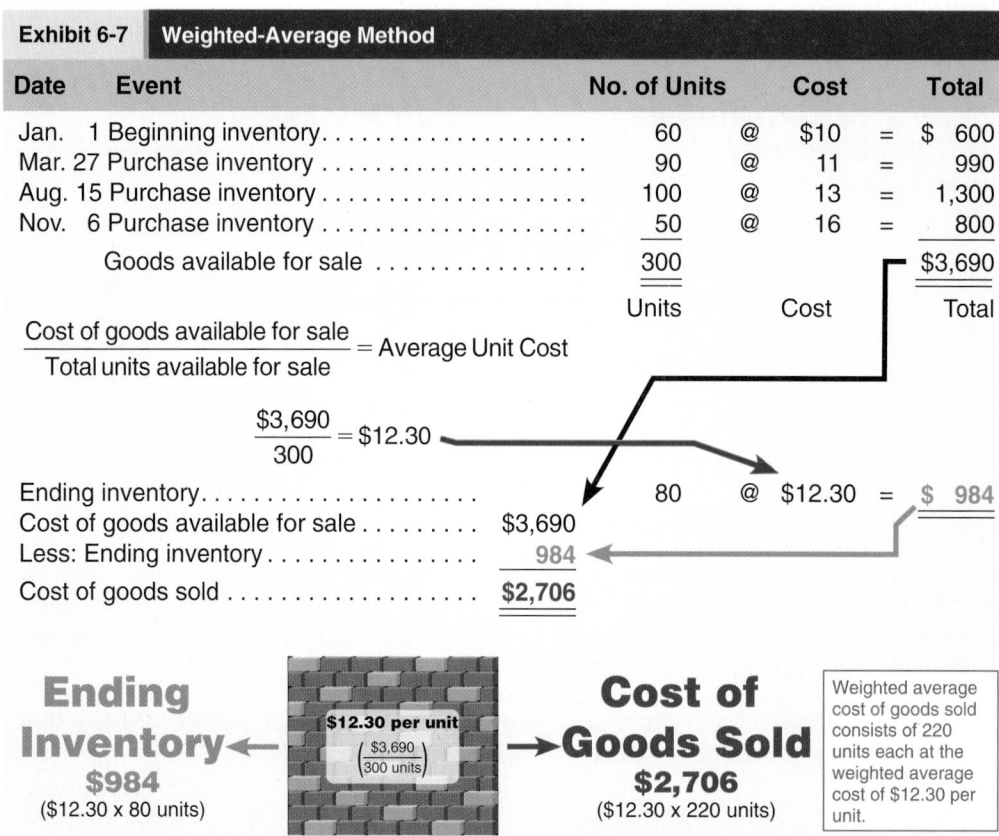

Exhibit 6-7	Weighted-Average Method			
Date Event		**No. of Units**	**Cost**	**Total**
Jan. 1 Beginning inventory.		60	@ $10 =	$ 600
Mar. 27 Purchase inventory		90	@ 11 =	990
Aug. 15 Purchase inventory		100	@ 13 =	1,300
Nov. 6 Purchase inventory		50	@ 16 =	800
Goods available for sale		300		$3,690
		Units	Cost	Total

$$\frac{\text{Cost of goods available for sale}}{\text{Total units available for sale}} = \text{Average Unit Cost}$$

$$\frac{\$3,690}{300} = \$12.30$$

Ending inventory.	80 @ $12.30 =	$ 984
Cost of goods available for sale	$3,690	
Less: Ending inventory.	984	
Cost of goods sold	**$2,706**	

Weighted average ending inventory consists of 80 units, each at the weighted average cost of $12.30 per unit.

Ending Inventory ← $12.30 per unit $\left(\frac{\$3,690}{300 \text{ units}}\right)$ → **Cost of Goods Sold**

$984
($12.30 x 80 units)

$2,706
($12.30 x 220 units)

Weighted average cost of goods sold consists of 220 units each at the weighted average cost of $12.30 per unit.

It would be incorrect to use a *simple* average of the unit costs. The simple average unit cost is $12.50, or [($10 + $11 + $13 + $16)/4]. This figure does not take into account the different number of units purchased and available at the various prices. The simple average cost yields the same result as the weighted-average cost only when the exact same number of units is purchased at each unit price.

ACCOUNTING IN PRACTICE

Inventory Costing Methods

The following chart identifies the inventory costing methods used by a sample of 600 U.S. firms. The most frequently used method is FIFO, followed by LIFO and then weighted-average cost. (The total exceeds 100% because some firms use more than one method to value their inventory, which is permitted under GAAP.) [Source: Accounting Trends and Techniques]

	FIFO	LIFO	Weighted-average	Other
70%				
60%				
50%				
40%				
30%				
20%				
10%				
0%				

YOUR TURN! 6.2

The solution is on page 320.

The following inventory information is gathered from the accounting records of Tucker Enterprises:

Beginning inventory	4,000 units at $5 each
Purchases	6,000 units at $7 each
Sales	9,000 units at $10 each

Calculate (a) ending inventory, (b) cost of goods sold, and (c) the gross profit using each of the following methods (i) FIFO, (ii) LIFO, and (iii) weighted-average cost.

Comparative Analysis of Inventory Costing Methods and Gross Profit

LO3 **Analyze** the financial effects of different inventory costing methods on company profit.

The purchase price data used in the Claremont Company illustration has an important characteristic: the purchase price of the inventory increased each time that a purchase was made, from $11 per unit to $13 per unit to $16 per unit. Increasing inventory prices are frequently encountered in the real world where price inflation is common and price deflation is uncommon. **Exhibit 6-8** summarizes the results of applying the four inventory costing methods to the Claremont Company data and reveals that the FIFO method produces the lowest cost of goods sold ($2,500), while the LIFO method produces the highest cost of goods sold ($2,870). The exhibit also reveals that FIFO produces the highest year-end value of ending inventory ($1,190), while LIFO produces the lowest year-end value of ending inventory ($820). Weighted-average cost produces ending inventory values and cost of goods sold values that fall in between the results obtained using FIFO and LIFO.

These results, however, are highly dependent on the purchase prices for the inventory. If the inventory's purchase price had been decreasing rather than increasing, the financial effects would have been just the opposite, with LIFO producing the lowest cost of goods sold and FIFO the highest. If the purchase prices had been perfectly stable, there would be no difference between the cost of goods sold or the ending inventory for any of the four methods.

Exhibit 6-8	Results of Different Inventory Costing Methods			
	Specific Identification	FIFO	LIFO	Weighted-Average
Cost of goods sold	$2,530	$2,500	$2,870	$2,706
Ending inventory	1,160	1,190	820	984

To illustrate the financial effects of the different inventory costing methods, assume that the 220 units sold by the Claremont Company were sold for $20 each, producing sales of $4,400 ($20 × 220). **Exhibit 6-9** shows the difference in gross profit under each of the four inventory costing methods. Remember that the difference in reported gross profit results from the assumptions made about cost flow, not from any difference in the physical flow of goods. In each case, 220 units were sold and 80 units remained. Each of the inventory costing methods is in accord with generally accepted accounting principles, yet the methods have different financial effects on gross profit and net income.

Exhibit 6-9	Gross Profit Using Alternative Inventory Costing Methods			
	Specific Identification	FIFO	LIFO	Weighted-Average
Sales (220 units @ $20)...................	$4,400	$4,400	$4,400	$4,400
Cost of goods sold	2,530	2,500	2,870	2,706
Gross profit............................	$1,870	$1,900	$1,530	$1,694
Increased gross profit compared with LIFO ..	$ 340	$ 370		$ 164

Income Statement and Balance Sheet Effects

As **Exhibit 6-9** reveals, LIFO results in the smallest gross profit ($1,530), with FIFO producing the highest ($1,900) gross profit. This result occurs because the purchase price of inventory was increasing throughout the year, from $11 per unit to $13 per unit to $16 per unit. When costs are rising, FIFO tends to overstate gross profit (and income) because older, lower unit costs are included in the cost of goods sold and matched with current sales prices. In other words, in the illustration, the units sold are charged to costs of goods sold under FIFO at unit costs of $10, $11, and $13. If the latest purchase price reflects the inventory's current acquisition cost, the units sold must be replaced by units costing $16 (or more if costs continue to rise).

It is frequently argued that LIFO provides a better matching of current costs with current revenues since the cost of the most recent purchases constitutes the LIFO cost of goods sold. While LIFO associates the current, higher unit costs with cost of goods sold, it assigns costs to ending inventory using the older, lower unit costs. As a consequence, the value of the LIFO ending inventory on the balance sheet is often undervalued in terms of the inventory's current value. When inventory quantities are maintained or increased, the LIFO method prevents older costs from appearing in the cost of goods sold. No doubt, some firms still carry LIFO inventories at unit costs that existed more than 10 years ago. Under FIFO, the ending inventory is measured at relatively recent costs.

Selecting Inventory Methods

Under generally accepted accounting principles, a company is permitted to select one or more of the four methods for purposes of assigning cost to its ending inventory and its cost of goods sold. Which method (or methods, since a company may elect to value some of its inventory using FIFO, some using LIFO, and some using weighted-average cost) is selected by a company depends upon a number of factors, including the type of product, the cost of the product, whether the product is perishable, whether the company desires to report a high or a low net income, and income tax considerations.

Specific Identification Method

Companies might choose to use specific identification for unique items with small volume and high unit cost, such as fine art or jewelry, that would justify the cost of tracking the specific unit cost of each inventory item. Specific identification is usually not cost-justified for inventories that have a low unit cost or involve high volumes of similar products.

FIFO Method

Many companies, especially those with perishable, time-dated, or style-affected merchandise, attempt to sell their oldest merchandise first. This is especially true for companies that sell food products, chemicals, and drugs. For these types of companies, the cost flow produced by the FIFO method most closely matches the physical goods flow. However, a company is not required to use the cost flow assumption that most closely matches its physical goods flow. When costs are rising, FIFO will result in the lowest cost of goods sold, and therefore, the highest net income. The desire to show a higher net income by some companies partly explains the popularity of the FIFO method.

LIFO Method

Although LIFO does not reflect the physical goods flow for most businesses, its popularity is likely linked to the potential income tax savings associated with its use. We illustrate the income tax advantages of the LIFO method in the next section. For some industries, however, LIFO does depict the physical goods flow. For example, in industries that extract natural resources, such as mining, the product is frequently dumped onto a storage pile from an overhead trestle, and sold inventory is taken from the top of the pile. One disadvantage of using LIFO when the quantity of beginning inventories has been maintained or increased is that a firm's ending inventory can be substantially undervalued since old purchase prices tend to be retained on a company's books under the LIFO method. This, in turn, will cause a firm's current assets and total assets to likewise be undervalued.

Weighted-Average Cost Method

Weighted-average cost is best suited for businesses that warehouse a large volume of undifferentiated goods in a common area. Liquid fuels, grains, and other commodities are examples. Weighted-average cost typically generates a cost of goods sold amount that is neither high nor low as compared to the other methods, as is revealed in **Exhibit 6-8**.

Summary

We can broadly summarize the choice among the cost flow assumptions as follows:

1. Specific identification identifies the actual cost of goods sold and ending inventory but can be costly to implement.

2. FIFO approximates the actual physical flow of goods for most firms.

3. LIFO is popular because of the income tax savings associated with its use.

4. Weighted-average cost is most often associated with businesses in which undifferentiated goods are commingled in a common area like a warehouse.

Consistency and Full Disclosure	**PRINCIPLE ALERT**

Inventory costing requires the application of *consistency* and *full disclosure*. Because of the possible variation in gross profit and ending inventory values that result from the use of different inventory costing methods, it is important that a firm use the same inventory costing method from one fiscal period to the next. This application of consistency enhances the comparability of a firm's cost of goods sold, gross profit, net income, inventory, current assets, and total assets over time. In addition, a firm should disclose which inventory costing method it is using, either in its financial statements or in the notes to the statements. This information is required by the full disclosure principle and is important to users who compare financial data across firms.

For readers skipping the periodic system, please resume reading here.

Income Tax Effects

During periods of rising purchase prices, LIFO results in a lower gross profit than any of the alternative inventory costing methods. A lower gross profit, and net income, means that lower amounts of income taxes need to be paid. Hence, the desire to reduce current income tax payments is a major reason for widespread use of LIFO.

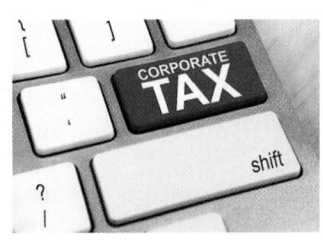

To illustrate LIFO's income tax advantage, assume that the Huntington Corporation has beginning inventory of 10 units costing $500 each, and that only two transactions occur. In the first transaction, it purchases 10 more units costing $630 each, for a total cash purchase price of $6,300. In the second transaction, it sells 10 units for $700 each, for a total cash sale of $7,000. Both transactions are for cash and, for simplicity, we assume that the company's operating expenses are zero and the applicable income tax rate is 20 percent. **Exhibit 6-10** presents the income statements and cash flows for Huntington under both FIFO and LIFO.

Exhibit 6-10	FIFO vs. LIFO Comparison: Phantom Profit Effect and Tax Benefit			
	FIFO		**LIFO**	
	Income Statement	Cash In (Out)	Income Statement	Cash In (Out)
Sales (10 @ $700)	$ 7,000	$7,000	$ 7,000	$7,000
Cost of goods sold				
Beginning inventory (10 @ $500)	5,000		5,000	
Purchases (10 @ $630)	6,300	(6,300)	6,300	(6,300)
Goods available (20 units)	11,300		11,300	
Ending inventory				
10 @ FIFO	6,300			
10 @ LIFO.			5,000	
Cost of goods sold	5,000		6,300	
Pretax income.	2,000		700	
Income tax (at 20%)	400	(400)	140	(140)
Net income	$ 1,600		$ 560	
Net cash proceeds		$ 300		$ 560

Under FIFO, Huntington reports $1,300 of net income, but cash from sales ($7,000) is only enough to replace the inventory sold ($6,300) and pay the income tax ($700) on the $2,000 in FIFO pretax net income. The net income of $1,300 is not realized in cash, and consequently, is unavailable to pay dividends or be reinvested in the business or replace the sold inventory. As a consequence, FIFO net income is sometimes referred to as *phantom profit.*

Under LIFO, Huntington reports net income of $455 as a consequence of its higher cost of goods sold ($6,300). With a lower net income, it incurs a smaller cash outflow ($245) for income taxes. The attractiveness of LIFO during periods of rising inventory purchase prices is evidenced by LIFO's more favorable net cash flow ($455) as compared with FIFO ($0). Use of LIFO during times of falling inventory purchase prices, however, has the opposite income tax effect.

Management is usually free to select different accounting treatments for financial reporting to shareholders and for income tax reporting to the Internal Revenue Service (IRS). For example, it is acceptable for a business to use different methods of computing depreciation when reporting under GAAP on the income statement and for reporting under income tax regulations on a company's income tax return. An exception to this flexibility occurs when a company chooses to use LIFO for income tax reporting to benefit from the lower income taxes that result when purchase prices are rising. A U.S. federal tax regulation known as the **LIFO conformity rule** requires any company that selects LIFO for income tax reporting to also use LIFO for financial reporting to shareholders. In other words, it is currently not possible to report lower taxable income to the IRS using LIFO while also reporting higher net income to shareholders using FIFO.

Errors in the Inventory Count

A physical count of inventory is necessary to determine the value of a company's ending inventory regardless of what inventory method is used. Unfortunately, errors in the inventory count, for example failing to count some items or counting some items twice, can occur. These errors affect not only the value of ending inventory reported on the balance sheet in the period of the error, but also cost of goods sold and gross profit. Further, the error is not limited to only the current period—cost of goods sold and gross profit in the following period are also affected. To illustrate, assume that the Arrow Company began operations in 2014. **Exhibit 6-11** summarizes Arrow's 2018 and 2019 transactions.

Exhibit 6-11	Inventory Transactions for Arrow Company	Inventory Units	Inventory Balance
2018	Beginning inventory	0	0
	Purchased 1,000 units of merchandise inventory for $3 per unit	1000	$3,000
	Sold 400 units of merchandise inventory	(400)	(1,200)*
	Ending inventory	600	$1,800
2019	Beginning inventory	600	$1,800
	Purchased 2,000 units of merchandise inventory for $3 per unit	2,000	6,000
	Sold 1,500 units of merchandise inventory	(1,500)	(4,500)*
	Ending inventory	1,100	$3,300

* Cost of goods sold.

Assume that Arrow Company made an error in its physical count of inventory at the end of 2018, mistakenly double-counting 40 units of inventory, and consequently, overstating ending inventory by $120 (40 units × $3). As illustrated in **Exhibit 6-12**, both the value of ending inventory and cost of goods sold in 2018 are affected. Further, because ending inventory in 2018 becomes beginning inventory in 2019, cost of goods sold in 2019 is also misstated. **Exhibit 6-12** illustrates these effects on both the 2018 and 2019 Arrow Company income statements.

Exhibit 6-12	Inventory Error Effects				
Cost of goods sold	=	**Beginning Inventory**	+ **Purchases**	− **Ending Inventory**	
2018: $1,080 (instead of $1,200)	=	$ 0	+ $3,000	− $1,920**	
2019: $4,620 (instead of $4,500)	=	$1,920	+ $6,000	− $3,300	

Key figures	No Error	With Error
2018		
Cost of goods sold	$1,200	$1,080 ↓
Gross profit (under)/over stated		$ 120
2019		
Cost of goods sold	$4,500	$4,620 ↑
Gross profit (under)/over stated		$ (120)

** ($1,800 + $120)

In sum, an error in the ending inventory account in the current year affects the value of ending inventory in the current year, as well as current year gross profit through cost of goods sold. The error also affects, in an opposite direction, gross profit in the following year (through its effect on cost of goods sold). To show this using the example in **Exhibit 6-12**, notice that the combined cost of goods sold for both years is $5,700, without the error ($1,200 + $4,500) or with the error ($1,080 + $4,620). Further, we see that ending inventory was overstated in 2018 by $120, which resulted in: 2018 ending inventory being overstated by $120, 2018 cost of goods sold being understated by $120, and 2018 gross profit being overstated by $120. The same $120 error is carried through to 2019 where it causes cost of goods sold to be overstated by $120 (because of the overstatement of beginning inventory), and gross profit to be understated by $120.

FORENSIC ACCOUNTING	**Fraudulent Reporting**

 Most errors in inventory result from honest mistakes; however, there are inventory counts that have been intentionally overstated. One such case involved a retail company called **Crazy Eddie**, which was a discount electronics store. Court records indicate that Eddie, the founder, hired his nephew, Sammy, who had earned a degree in accounting, to inflate sales by $15 to $20 million per year, and falsified inventories to justify the inflated figures. The U.S. Securities and Exchange Commission ultimately charged Eddie with securities fraud and he was sentenced to 8 years in prison and ordered to pay more than $150 million in fines.

YOUR TURN! 6.3

The solution is on page 321.

Assume Pointer Company began operations in 2018. The table below summarizes Pointer's 2018 and 2019 transactions. For simplicity assume that cost of goods sold is the only expense that occurs.

		Inventory Units	Inventory Balance	Sales
2018	Beginning inventory	0	0	
	Purchased 2,000 units of merchandise for $5 per unit	2,000	$10,000	
	Sold 1,500 units of merchandise for $10 per unit	(1,500)	(7,500)	$15,000
	Ending inventory	500	$ 2,500	
2019	Beginning inventory	500	$ 2,500	
	Purchased 3,000 units of merchandise for $5 per unit	3,000	$15,000	
	Sold 2,500 units of merchandise for $10 per unit	(2,500)	(12,500)	$25,000
	Ending inventory	1,000	$ 5,000	

Assume that Pointer made an error in its physical count of inventory at the end of 2018, mistakenly omitting 100 units of inventory, and consequently, understating ending inventory by $500 (100 units × $5). Determine Pointer's 2018 and 2019 ending inventory without the error. Also compute Pointer's sales, cost of goods sold, and net income for 2018 and 2019 both with and without the error.

LOWER-OF-COST-OR-NET REALIZABLE VALUE METHOD

MBC eLectures

LO4 **Apply** the lower-of-cost-or-net realizable value method.

In general, inventory is valued at its acquisition cost using one of the generally accepted inventory costing methods explained earlier in this chapter. However, it can be necessary to report inventory at a lower value if there is evidence that the inventory's utility to a business—that is, the inventory's revenue-generating ability—has fallen below its acquisition cost. Such *inventory write-downs* can occur when (1) merchandise must be sold at reduced prices because it is damaged or otherwise not in normal salable condition or when (2) the cost of replacing the ending inventory has declined below the inventory's recorded acquisition cost.

Net Realizable Value

Damaged, physically deteriorated, or obsolete merchandise should be measured and reported at its net realizable value on the balance sheet when this value is less than the inventory's acquisition cost. **Net realizable value (NRV)** is an item's estimated selling price less the expected cost of the eventual sale or disposal of the item. For example, assume that an inventory item cost $300 but can be sold for only $200 because it is damaged. If the related selling costs are estimated to be $20, the inventory should be written down to $180 ($200 estimated selling price less $20 estimated disposal cost) and a $120 inventory write-down loss ($300 − $180) should be reported on the income statement for the current period.

Lower-of-Cost-or-Net Realizable Value

The **lower-of-cost-or-net realizable value** method provides for the recognition of an inventory write-down loss when the inventory's net realizable value declines below its recorded acquisition cost. Under this method, a loss is reported in the period when the inventory's net realizable value declines, rather than during a subsequent period when the actual sale of the inventory takes place. This procedure assumes that decreases in the net realizable value of inventory will be accompanied by proportionate decreases in the selling price of the inventory. The lower-of-cost-or-net realizable value method values the ending inventory at its lower NRV. Consequently, income decreases by the amount that the ending inventory is written down.

To illustrate, assume that an inventory item that cost $80 has been selling at a retail price of $100, yielding a gross profit percentage of 20 percent. Assume also that by year-end, the item's net realizable value has declined to $60 (calculated as a sales price of $64 with an estimated cost of $4 to sell the item). In this case, the inventory is written down to its $60 net realizable value and the current period's net income is reduced by a $20 write-down loss ($80 − $60). If the inventory is sold in a subsequent period for $75 (assuming the normal gross profit percentage of 20 percent on sales), a gross profit of $15 will be reported ($75 − $60).

The lower-of-cost-or-net realizable value method can be applied to each individual item in inventory or to the total of all inventory. In **Exhibit 6-13**, if the lower-of-cost-or-net realizable value method is applied on an individual item basis, the value of ending inventory is $6,820. If the lower-of-cost-or-net realizable value method was instead applied to all inventory, the value of ending inventory is $7,120.

Exhibit 6-13	Application of the Lower-of-Cost-or-Net Realizable Value					
		Per Unit		**Total**		**Lower-of-Cost-or-Net Realizable Value**
Inventory Item	Quantity	Cost	NRV	Cost	NRV	Individual Item
Cameras						
Model V70...	40	$80	$75	$3,200	$3,000	$3,000
Model V85...	30	60	64	1,800	1,920	1,800
Subtotal...				$5,000	$4,920	—
Calculators						
Model C20...	90	13	15	$1,170	$1,350	1,170
Model C40...	50	20	17	1,000	850	850
Subtotal...				$2,170	$2,200	—
Total				$7,170	$7,120	$6,820

**PRINCIPLE
ALERT**

Conservatism

The lower-of-cost-or-net realizable value method for inventory is a good illustration of *conservatism*. When the net realizable value for an inventory item falls below its acquisition cost, there is increased uncertainty about the future profitability of the item. Conservatism is the reaction to significant uncertainties in the measurement of net assets and net income. In choosing between alternative financial measures, conservatism causes the least optimistic measure to be selected. When an item's net realizable value falls below its historical acquisition cost, the least optimistic measure is its lower NRV. The lower-of-cost-or-net realizable value method applies to all inventory methods except LIFO. For LIFO inventory, companies report inventory at the lower of cost or market, where market is typically the replacement cost of the inventory. The replacement cost is never greater than net realizable value.

IFRS ALERT

Under IFRS, LIFO is not generally accepted. Further, under U.S. GAAP, inventory may not be revalued upward, even if it has been revalued downward. IFRS permits reversal of inventory write-downs, with the reversal limited to the amount of the original write-down.

YOUR TURN! 6.4

The solution is on page 321.

GuidedExamples

MBC

The Images Company sells three types of video equipment—DSLR cameras, Point and Shoot cameras, and Camcorders. The cost and net realizable value of its inventory of video equipment follow:

	Cost	NRV
DSLR	$110,000	$125,000
Point and Shoot	73,000	92,000
Camcorders	57,000	48,000

Compute the value of the Images Company's ending inventory under the lower-of-cost-or-net realizable value method applied on an item-by-item basis.

eLectures

MBC

INVENTORY ANALYSIS

Inventory Turnover and Days' Sales in Inventory

LO5 Define *inventory turnover* and *days' sales in inventory* and **explain** the use of these ratios.

The **inventory turnover ratio** indicates how many times a year, on average, a firm sells its inventory, and it is calculated as:

$$\text{Inventory turnover} = \frac{\text{Cost of goods sold}}{\text{Average inventory}}$$

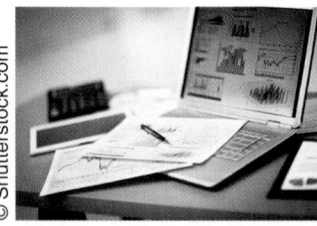

© Shutterstock.com

This ratio relates data from two financial statements: the income statement and the balance sheet. Cost of goods sold is taken from the income statement, while the average inventory is calculated from balance sheet data—that is, the beginning and ending inventories are summed and the total is divided by two.

In general, the faster a company can turn over its inventory, the more profitable the company will be. Further, the higher the inventory turnover ratio, the less time a firm has its funds tied up in its inventory and the less risk the firm faces from trying to sell out-of-date merchandise. What is considered to be a satisfactory inventory turnover varies from industry to industry. A grocery store chain like **Safeway**, for example, should have a much higher inventory turnover than a jewelry store like **Zales**.

To illustrate the inventory turnover ratio, **Best Buy** reported the following financial data:

($ millions)	2017	2016
Cost of goods sold	$32,275	$29,963
Beginning inventory	4,864	5,051
Ending inventory	5,209	4,864

Best Buy's inventory turnover in 2017 is 6.41, computed as $32,275/[($4,864 + $5,209)/2]. A similar calculation reveals that Best Buy's inventory turnover was 6.04 in 2016, indicating an improvement from 2016 to 2017.

The inventory turnover ratio can be influenced by a firm's choice of inventory costing method. Inventory amounts calculated using LIFO, for example, will typically be smaller than the same inventory calculated using FIFO. An investor comparing inventory turnover ratios between different firms will need to verify that the firms are using the same inventory costing method; otherwise, any ratio comparisons will be apples-to-oranges rather than apples-to-apples.

An extension of the inventory turnover ratio is the **days' sales in inventory**, calculated as:

$$\text{Days' sales in inventory} = \frac{365}{\text{Inventory turnover}}$$

This ratio indicates how many days it takes, on average, for a firm to sell its inventory. During 2017, for example, Best Buy's days' sales in inventory was 56.9 days, or 365/6.41; that is, Best Buy took over 56 days to sell its inventory. Similar calculations reveal it took an average of 60.4 days for Best Buy to sell its inventory in 2016. Do these ratio results indicate that Best Buy is doing a good job of managing its investment in inventory? Without comparable ratio data from a competitor like Target Corporation, it is difficult to conclude whether a days' sales in inventory ratio of 56.9 days indicates that Best Buy is doing a good or bad job of managing its inventory.

A.K.A. The days' sales in inventory ratio is also referred to as the days' inventory-on-hand ratio and the inventory-on-hand period.

Concept	Method	Assessment	TAKEAWAY 6.1
How long, on average, does it take to sell the inventory?	Cost of goods sold, beginning inventory, and ending inventory $$\text{Inventory turnover} = \frac{\text{Cost of goods sold}}{\text{Average inventory}}$$ $$\text{Days' sales in inventory} = \frac{365}{\text{Inventory turnover}}$$	A higher inventory turnover or a lower days' sales in inventory indicates that the company is able to sell its inventory more quickly.	

YOUR TURN! 6.5

The solution is on page 321.

Flip Company installed a new inventory management system at the beginning of 2019. Shown below are financial data from the company's accounting records:

	2018	2019
Sales revenue	$4,000,000	$4,400,000
Cost of goods sold	2,000,000	2,300,000
Beginning inventory	450,000	430,000
Ending inventory	430,000	320,000

Calculate the inventory turnover and days' sales in inventory for 2018 and 2019. Discuss your findings.

Best Buy and an Ethical Supply Chain

Many businesses strive to not only do well financially, but also to do good environmentally and socially. **Best Buy** serves as the ultimate seller of many products manufactured by other companies, such as TVs by **Sony**, cameras by **Nikon**, and computers by **Dell**. Best Buy also sells its exclusive brands. As the manufacturer of these products, Best Buy faces decisions on how and where these products are produced. Best Buy's Corporate Responsibility Report states, "While manufacturing expertise, lower labor costs and an efficient global supply chain make production in southeastern Asia a viable proposition, our operations there have not been without challenges." Best Buy meets these challenges through their ethical manufacturing program that includes supplier compliance standards that embody standards of the Fair Labor Association Workplace Code of Conduct and the core labor standards of the International Labor Organization. Best Buy also has a factory audit program to identify environmental and social problems at its suppliers.

COMPREHENSIVE PROBLEM

The Montclair Corporation had the following inventory transactions for its only product during 2018:

Purchases	
February 15.	2,000 units @ $27.00 each
April 20	3,000 units @ $28.40 each
October 25	1,200 units @ $31.25 each
Sales	
March 1.	1,200 units @ $50.00 each
June 12.	2,000 units @ $52.00 each
August 10	1,000 units @ $53.00 each
December 14	1,600 units @ $55.00 each

The Montclair Corporation had 1,000 units in its January 1, 2018, beginning inventory with a unit cost of $24 each. Montclair uses the periodic inventory system.

Required

a. Determine the cost assigned to Montclair's December 31, 2018, ending inventory and Montclair's cost of goods sold for 2018 under each of the following inventory costing methods:
1. Weighted-average cost
2. FIFO
3. LIFO

b. Determine Montclair's gross profit for 2018 under each of the following inventory costing methods:
1. Weighted-average cost
2. FIFO
3. LIFO

c. Determine Montclair's inventory turnover and days' sales in inventory for 2018 under each of the following inventory costing methods:
1. Weighted-average cost
2. FIFO
3. LIFO

Solution

a. Units available:

1,000	units @ $24.00 =	$ 24,000	
2,000	units @ $27.00 =	54,000	
3,000	units @ $28.40 =	85,200	
1,200	units @ $31.25 =	37,500	
7,200		$200,700	

1. **Weighted-average cost:**

   Weighted-average unit cost: $200,700/7,200 units = $ 27.875

   Ending inventory: 1,400 units × $27.875 = $ 39,025

   Cost of goods sold: $200,700 − $39,025 = $161,675

2. **FIFO:**

   Ending inventory: 1,200 units @ $31.25 = $ 37,500

                   200 units @ $28.40 =   5,680

                1,400 $ 43,180

   Cost of goods sold: $200,700 − $43,180 = $157,520

3. **LIFO:**

   Ending inventory: 1,000 units @ $24.00 = $ 24,000

                   400 units @ $27.00 =   10,800

                1,400 $ 34,800

   Cost of goods sold: $200,700 − $34,800 = $165,900

b. Sales revenue:

           1,200 units @ $50.00 = $ 60,000

           2,000 units @ $52.00 = 104,000

           1,000 units @ $53.00 =   53,000

           1,600 units @ $55.00 =   88,000

           5,800 $305,000

   1. Weighted-average gross profit = $305,000 − $161,675 = $143,325
   2. FIFO gross profit = $305,000 − $157,520 = $147,480
   3. LIFO gross profit = $305,000 − $165,900 = $139,100

c.

	Inventory Turnover	Days' Sales in Inventory
Weighted-average cost	5.13	71.15 days
FIFO	4.69	77.83 days
LIFO	5.64	64.72 days

APPENDIX 6A: Inventory Costing Methods and the Perpetual Inventory System

This appendix illustrates the accounting for inventories using the perpetual inventory system under the four costing methods of: (1) specific identification; (2) first-in, first-out; (3) last-in, first-out; and (4) weighted-average cost. All four methods are illustrated using the following data for Claremont Company.

Date	Event	No. of Units	Unit Cost		Total Cost
Jan. 1	Beginning inventory	60	@ $10	=	$ 600
Mar. 27	Purchase inventory.	90	@ 11	=	990
	Goods available for sale.	150			$1,590
May 2	Sell inventory	(130)			
Aug. 15	Purchase inventory.	100	@ 13	=	1,300
Nov. 6	Purchase inventory.	50	@ 16	=	800
	Goods available for sale.	170			$3,690
Dec. 10	Sell inventory	(90)			
Dec. 31	Ending inventory.	80			

LO6 **Describe** inventory costing under a perpetual inventory system using specific identification, FIFO, LIFO, and weighted-average cost.

Under all four inventory costing methods, the Inventory account is increased each time a purchase occurs for the amount of the purchase and is decreased each time a sale occurs by an amount equal to the cost of goods sold. The methods differ only in the computation of cost of goods sold, consisting of 220 units (130 + 90 = 220), and the year-end Inventory account balance, consisting of 80 units remaining.

Specific Identification Method

Under the specific identification method, the actual cost of the specific units sold is identified and used to compute the cost of goods sold. To illustrate, assume that (1) 50 of the 130 units sold on May 2 came from the beginning inventory of 60 units and the remaining 80 units sold (50 + 80 = 130) came from the purchase of 90 units on March 27, and that (2) 10 of the 90 units sold on December 10 came from the purchase of 90 units on March 27 and the remaining 80 units sold (10 + 80 = 90) came from the purchase of 100 units on August 15. **Exhibit 6A-1** illustrates the calculation of cost of goods sold and ending inventory using specific identification. The cost of goods sold is $2,530 (sum of the Sold Total column), and the ending inventory of 80 units is valued at $1,160 (final amount in the Inventory Balance Total column).

Exhibit 6A-1	Specific Identification Method (Perpetual Inventory System)								
	Purchased			**Sold**			**Inventory Balance**		
Date	**Units**	**Unit Cost**	**Total**	**Units**	**Unit Cost**	**Total**	**Units**	**Unit Cost**	**Total**
Jan. 1							60	$10	$ 600
Mar. 27	90	$11	$ 990				60	10	
							90	11	1,590
May 2				50	$10	$ 500	10	10	
				80	11	880	10	11	210
Aug. 15	100	13	1,300				10	10	
							10	11	1,510
							100	13	
Nov. 6	50	16	800				10	10	
							10	11	
							100	13	2,310
							50	16	
Dec. 10				10	11	110	10	10	
				80	13	1,040	20	13	1,160
							50	16	
Total						$2,530			

First-In, First-Out (FIFO) Method

Under the first-in, first-out (FIFO) method, each time that a sale is made the cost of the oldest goods are charged to cost of goods sold.

Results of the FIFO method are in **Exhibit 6A-2**. FIFO handles the May 2 sale of 130 units as follows: The oldest units are the units in the January 1 beginning inventory. These are the first 60 units assumed to be sold. The next oldest units are the units purchased on March 27 and 70 units are needed from this purchase (130 sold – 60 from January 1) to provide all of the units sold on May 2. After the May 2 sale, only 20 units remain, all from the March 27 purchase.

The December 10 sale of 90 units is handled in a similar manner. The oldest units at December 10 are the 20 units remaining from the March 27 purchase. These are the first units assumed to be sold. The next oldest units are the 100 units purchased on August 15 and 70 additional units are needed for the sale (90 sold − 20 from the March 27 purchase). Therefore, 70 of the 100 units purchased on August 15 are assumed to be included in the units sold on December 10. After the December 10 sale, 30 units remain from the August 15 purchase and 50 units remain from the November 6 purchase.

Cost of goods sold using the FIFO method is $2,500 (sum of the Sold Total column), and the ending inventory is $1,190 (final amount in the Inventory Balance Total column).

Exhibit 6A-2	First-In, First-Out Method (Perpetual Inventory System)								
	Purchased			**Sold**			**Inventory Balance**		
Date	**Units**	**Unit Cost**	**Total**	**Units**	**Unit Cost**	**Total**	**Units**	**Unit Cost**	**Total**
Jan. 1							60	$10	$ 600
Mar. 27	90	$11	$ 990				60 90	10 11	1,590
May 2				60 70	$10 11	$ 600 770	20	11	220
Aug. 15	100	13	1,300				20 100	11 13	1,520
Nov. 6	50	16	800				20 100 50	11 13 16	2,320
Dec. 10				20 70	11 13	220 910	**30** **50**	**13** **16**	**1,190**
Total						$2,500			

Last-In, First-Out (LIFO) Method

When the last-in, first-out (LIFO) method is used, the cost of the most recent inventory purchased is charged to cost of goods sold when a sale occurs.

Exhibit 6A-3 illustrates the results using LIFO. The LIFO method handles the May 2 sale of 130 units as follows: The most recently purchased units (newest units) are the units from the March 27 purchase. These are the first 90 units assumed to be sold. The next newest units are the units in the January 1 beginning inventory and 40 units from the January 1 units are needed (130 sold − 90 from the March 27 purchase) to provide all of the units sold on May 2. After the May 2 sale, only 20 units remain, all from the January 1 beginning inventory.

The December 10 sale of 90 units is handled in a similar manner. The newest units at December 10 are the 50 units purchased on November 6. These are the first units assumed to be sold. The next newest units are the 100 units purchased on August 15 and 40 additional units are needed for the sale (90 sold − 50 from the November 6 purchase). Therefore, 40 of the 100 units purchased on August 15 are assumed to be included in the units sold on December 10. After the sale, 20 units remain from the January 1 inventory and 60 units remain from the August 15 purchase.

Cost of goods sold using LIFO is $2,710 (sum of the Sold Total column), and the ending inventory is $980 (final amount in the Inventory Balance Total column).

Exhibit 6A-3	Last-In, First-Out Method (Perpetual Inventory System)								
	Purchased			**Sold**			**Inventory Balance**		
Date	**Units**	**Unit Cost**	**Total**	**Units**	**Unit Cost**	**Total**	**Units**	**Unit Cost**	**Total**
Jan. 1							60	$10	$ 600
Mar. 27	90	$11	$ 990				60 90	10 11	1,590
May 2				90 40	$11 10	$ 990 400	20	10	200
Aug. 15	100	13	1,300				20 100	10 13	1,500
Nov. 6	50	16	800				20 100 50	10 13 16	2,300
Dec. 10				50 40	16 13	800 520	**20** **60**	**10** **13**	**980**
Total						$2,710			

Weighted-Average Cost Method

When the weighted-average cost method is used, a new weighted-average unit cost is calculated for the goods (**equal to the total cost divided by total units**) each time that goods are purchased and added to inventory. The cost of goods sold for each sale is calculated by multiplying the weighted-average unit cost at the time of sale by the number of units sold. **Exhibit 6A-4** illustrates the calculation of cost of goods sold and ending inventory under the weighted-average cost method. The weighted-average unit cost is calculated three times in **Exhibit 6A-4**. On March 27, 90 units were purchased at a unit cost of $11, and the updated weighted-average unit cost on this date is:

$$[\$600 + \$990]/[60 \text{ Units} + 90 \text{ Units}] = \$10.60$$

On August 15, 100 units were purchased at a unit cost of $13. The updated weighted-average unit cost on this date is:

$$[\$212 + \$1,300]/[20 \text{ Units} + 100 \text{ Units}] = \$12.60$$

On November 6, 50 units were purchased at a unit cost of $16. The updated weighted-average unit cost on this date is:

$$[\$1,512 + \$800]/[120 \text{ Units} + 50 \text{ Units}] = \$13.60$$

The cost of goods sold is $2,602 (sum of the Sold Total column), and the ending inventory is $1,088 (final amount in the Inventory Balance Total column).

Exhibit 6A-4	Weighted-Average Cost Method (Perpetual Inventory System)								
	Purchased			**Sold**			**Inventory Balance**		
Date	**Units**	**Unit Cost**	**Total**	**Units**	**Unit Cost**	**Total**	**Units**	**Unit Cost**	**Total**
Jan. 1							60	$10.00	$ 600
Mar. 27	90	$11	$ 990				150	10.60	1,590
May 2				130	$10.60	$1,378	20	10.60	212
Aug. 15	100	13	1,300				120	12.60	1,512
Nov. 6	50	16	800				170	13.60	2,312
Dec. 10				90	13.60	1,224	80	13.60	1,088
Total						$2,602			

Comparative Analysis of Inventory Costing Methods

The purchase price data used in the Claremont Company illustration has an important characteristic: the purchase price of the inventory increased each time that a purchase was made, from $11 per unit to $13 per unit to $16 per unit. Increasing inventory prices are frequently encountered in the real world where price inflation is common and price deflation is uncommon. **Exhibit 6A-5** summarizes the results of applying the four inventory costing methods to the Claremont Company data and reveals that the FIFO method produces the lowest cost of goods sold ($2,500), while the LIFO method produces the highest cost of goods sold ($2,710). The exhibit also reveals that FIFO produces the highest year-end value of ending inventory ($1,190), while LIFO produces the lowest year-end value of ending inventory ($980). Weighted-average cost produces ending inventory values and cost of goods sold values that fall in between the results obtained using FIFO and LIFO.

These results, however, are highly dependent on the purchase prices for the inventory. If the inventory's purchase price had been decreasing rather than increasing, the financial effects would have been just the opposite, with LIFO producing the lowest cost of goods sold and FIFO the highest. If the purchase prices had been perfectly stable, there would be no difference between the cost of goods sold or the ending inventory for any of the four methods.

Exhibit 6A-5	Results of Different Inventory Costing Methods			
	Specific Identification	FIFO	LIFO	Weighted-Average
Cost of goods sold	$2,530	$2,500	$2,710	$2,602
Ending inventory.	1,160	1,190	980	1,088

To illustrate the financial effects of the different inventory costing methods, assume that the 220 units sold by the Claremont Company were sold for $20 each, producing sales of $4,400 ($20 × 220). **Exhibit 6A-6** shows the difference in gross profit under each of the four inventory costing methods. Remember that the difference in reported gross profit results from the assumptions made about cost flow, not from any difference in the physical flow of goods. In each case, 220 units were sold and 80 units remained. Each of the inventory costing methods is in accord with generally accepted accounting principles, yet the methods have different financial effects on gross profit and net income.

Exhibit 6A-6	Gross Profit Using Alternative Inventory Costing Methods			
	Specific Identification	FIFO	LIFO	Weighted-Average
Sales (220 units @ $20).	$4,400	$4,400	$4,400	$4,400
Cost of goods sold	2,530	2,500	2,710	2,602
Gross profit.	$1,870	$1,900	$1,690	$1,798
Increased gross profit compared with LIFO	$ 180	$ 210		$ 108

Income Statement and Balance Sheet Effects

As **Exhibit 6A-6** reveals, LIFO results in the smallest gross profit ($1,690) with FIFO producing the highest ($1,900) gross profit. This result occurs because the purchase price of inventory was increasing throughout the year, from $11 per unit to $13 per unit to $16 per unit. Most agree that when costs are rising, FIFO tends to overstate gross profit (and income) because older, lower unit costs are included in the cost of goods sold and matched with current sales prices. In other words, in the illustration, the units sold are charged to costs of goods sold under FIFO at unit costs of $10, $11, and $13. If the latest purchase price reflects the inventory's current acquisition cost, the units sold must be replaced by units costing $16 (or more if costs continue to rise).

It is frequently argued that LIFO provides a better matching of current costs with current revenues since the cost of the most recent purchases constitutes the LIFO cost of goods sold. While LIFO associates the current, higher unit costs with cost of goods sold, it assigns costs to ending inventory using the older, lower unit costs. As a consequence, the value of the LIFO ending inventory on the balance sheet is often undervalued in terms of the inventory's current value. When inventory quantities are maintained or increased, the LIFO method prevents older costs from appearing in the cost of goods sold. No doubt, some firms still carry LIFO inventories at unit costs that existed more than 10 years ago. Under FIFO, the ending inventory is measured at relatively recent costs.

Comparison of Inventory Costing Methods

Exhibit 6A-7 summarizes the results of applying the periodic and perpetual costing methods to the same Claremont data. The specific identification method and the FIFO method yield the exact same results for ending inventory and cost of goods sold regardless of whether the periodic or the perpetual method is being used. Only the LIFO and weighted-average methods produce different results under the periodic and perpetual systems.

Exhibit 6A-7	Summary Results of Different Inventory Costing Methods		
Costing Method		**Ending Inventory**	**Cost of Goods Sold**
Specific identification			
Periodic		$1,160	$2,530
Perpetual		1,160	2,530
FIFO			
Periodic		1,190	2,500
Perpetual		1,190	2,500
LIFO			
Periodic		820	2,870
Perpetual		980	2,710
Average			
Periodic		984	2,706
Perpetual		1,088	2,602

Choice of a periodic versus perpetual system does *not* affect specific identification or FIFO

Choice of a periodic versus perpetual system does affect LIFO and weighted-average results

YOUR TURN! 6A.1

The solution is on pages 321–322.

MBC
GuidedExamples

The following information applies to the Kensington Company.

Jan. 1 Beginning inventory 1,000 units at $5 each

Jan. 5 Purchased 600 units at $6 each

Jan. 15 Sold 200 units

Jan. 17 Purchased 300 units at $7 each

Jan. 25 Sold 400 units

Kensington Company utilizes a perpetual inventory system. Calculate the cost of goods sold and ending inventory using the following methods.

a. FIFO

b. LIFO

c. Weighted-average

APPENDIX 6B: LIFO Reserve

eLectures
MBC

L07 **Define** the LIFO reserve and **explain** how it is used to compare the performance of companies using LIFO and FIFO inventory costing methods.

As shown in this chapter, the LIFO inventory costing method can produce significantly different results relative to other inventory costing methods for both ending inventory and cost of goods sold, and therefore gross profit and net income. The difference is greatest when compared to results obtained using FIFO. When costs are rising, FIFO will result in higher reported ending inventory, lower cost of goods sold, and higher net income relative to LIFO.

To make comparisons between companies using LIFO and companies using FIFO, we need to use the **LIFO inventory reserve**, or simply *LIFO reserve*. Companies that use LIFO are required under generally accepted accounting principles to report the difference between ending inventory using LIFO and the inventory that would have been reported under FIFO. This difference is called the LIFO inventory reserve and is disclosed in notes to financial statements.

Referring again to **Exhibit 6-8**, FIFO ending inventory is valued at $1,190 and LIFO ending inventory at $820. The LIFO reserve is $370 ($1,190 − $820). Use of LIFO can have a material impact on many ratios, and one way to compensate for these effects is to use the LIFO reserve to restate the reported inventory and cost of goods sold to a FIFO basis. To illustrate, assume that Claremont Company, whose inventory costing method results are compared in **Exhibit 6-8**, has current assets of $2,100 and current liabilities of $1,400 under the LIFO method. **Exhibit 6B-1** calculates the current ratio (current assets divided by current liabilities) under both LIFO and FIFO. (The current ratio is discussed in Chapter 2.)

Exhibit 6B-1	Impact of the LIFO Inventory Reserve on the Current Ratio	
	LIFO	**FIFO**
Current ratio	$\dfrac{\$2,100}{\$1,400} = 1.50$	$\dfrac{(\$2,100 + \$370)}{\$1,400} = 1.76$

Hint: The LIFO reserve is also used to restate the LIFO cost of goods sold to that under FIFO. The LIFO cost of goods sold minus the change in the LIFO reserve from the beginning to the end of the period equals FIFO cost of goods sold.

As shown in **Exhibit 6B-1**, the current ratio is much higher under FIFO (1.76) than under LIFO (1.50). Differences occur between LIFO and FIFO companies for many ratios, with FIFO resulting in more favorable ratios in most cases since FIFO generally results in higher inventory values and higher net earnings. For some ratios, however, LIFO produces more favorable results. Two examples are the inventory turnover ratio and the days' sales in inventory ratio. Because LIFO results in lower inventory values, the inventory turnover (and consequently, the days' sales in inventory) under LIFO appears higher (lower) than it does under FIFO. (The LIFO reserve also affects cost of goods sold and therefore the numerator of the inventory turnover ratio; in most cases the adjustment to cost of goods sold is much smaller than the adjustment to average inventory, leading to a higher inventory turnover under LIFO than under FIFO.)

Concept ➞	Method ➞	Assessment	TAKEAWAY 6.2
What effect does the use of LIFO have on ending inventory relative to the use of FIFO?	Ending inventory and the LIFO inventory reserve The value of LIFO ending inventory + the LIFO inventory reserve = The value of FIFO ending inventory	If the LIFO reserve is material, it can have a significant impact on many ratios when compared to FIFO. The calculation of these ratios can be adjusted using the LIFO inventory reserve to provide a more comparable set of results.	

Adams Inc. reports ending inventory under the LIFO method at $165,000. Adams also discloses a LIFO reserve of $20,000. What would Adams have reported for ending inventory if it had used FIFO rather than LIFO?.

YOUR TURN! 6B.1

The solution is on page 322.

SUMMARY OF LEARNING OBJECTIVES

Explain inventory concepts and modern inventory practices. (p. 272)

LO1

- Merchandise inventory is a stock of goods that a merchandising company buys from a manufacturer and makes available for sale to its customers.
- A manufacturing firm maintains three different inventory categories: raw materials inventory, work-in-process inventory, and finished goods inventory.
- Traditionally, manufacturers have maintained just-in-case inventories of raw materials and components to provide for unplanned production or delayed raw material shipments, resulting in high levels of inventory carrying costs.
- Today, many manufacturers have adopted the just-in-time (JIT) manufacturing philosophy, which is designed to eliminate or minimize raw materials, work-in-process, and finished goods inventories. The key to JIT manufacturing is careful inventory order planning and sophisticated production management.
- Ownership of goods in transit depends on the shipping terms. The buyer assumes ownership of goods in transit shipped F.O.B. shipping point, whereas the seller maintains ownership of goods shipped F.O.B. destination until the buyer assumes possession at delivery.
- Consignment goods are goods held for sale by parties other than the owner. The owner maintains legal ownership of these inventory items while they are held for sale by the consignment seller.
- The year-end physical count of inventory is taken to verify the inventory balance. It consists of three steps:
  - Count the number of individual items of merchandise on hand at the end of the year.
  - Determine the unit cost of each individual item and multiply the unit cost times the quantity on hand to obtain the total cost for each individual item of merchandise.
  - Add together the total cost of all the individual items to obtain the total cost of the inventory on hand.

LO2 **Describe inventory costing under specific identification, FIFO, LIFO, and weighted-average cost. (p. 276)**

- To assign cost to units sold (cost of goods sold) and units available (inventory), a company must either keep track of the cost of each specific unit (specific identification method) or make an assumption about which units have been sold (weighted-average cost, FIFO, and LIFO methods).
- The weighted-average cost method assumes that a mix of the goods available is sold; the FIFO method assumes that the oldest goods are sold first; and the LIFO method assumes that the newest goods are sold first.

LO3 **Analyze the financial effects of different inventory costing methods on company profit. (p. 281)**

- Each of the alternative inventory costing methods produces a different cost of goods sold and gross profit unless purchase prices have been perfectly stable.
- When costs are rising, the LIFO method does the best job of matching current costs with revenues; LIFO also produces a lower gross profit and lower income taxes than either weighted-average cost or FIFO.

LO4 **Apply the lower-of-cost-or-net realizable value method. (p. 286)**

- Damaged, physically deteriorated, or obsolete merchandise should be valued and reported at its net realizable value—that is, its estimated selling price less the expected cost of disposal.
- The lower-of-cost-or-net realizable value method provides for inventory write-downs to be recorded in the period that the net realizable value of inventory declines below the inventory's acquisition cost.

LO5 **Define *inventory turnover* and *day's sales in inventory* and explain the use of these ratios. (p. 288)**

- Inventory turnover and days' sales in inventory indicate, respectively, how many times on average during the year a firm sells its inventory and how many days on average it takes a firm to sell its inventory.
- Inventory turnover and days' sales in inventory provide evidence regarding a firm's ability to sell its inventory and its ability to effectively manage its investment in inventory.

LO6 **Appendix 6A: Describe inventory costing under a perpetual inventory system using specific identification, FIFO, LIFO, and weighted-average cost. (p. 291)**

- To assign cost to units sold (cost of goods sold) and units available (inventory), a company must either keep track of the cost of each specific unit (specific identification method) or make an assumption about which units have been sold (weighted-average cost, FIFO, and LIFO methods).
- The weighted-average cost method assumes that a mix of the goods available is sold; the FIFO method assumes that the oldest goods are sold; and the LIFO method assumes that the newest goods are sold.
- The specific identification method and the FIFO method yield the exact same results for ending inventory and for cost of goods sold regardless of whether the periodic or the perpetual method is being used. Only LIFO and weighted-average methods produce different results.

LO7 **Appendix 6B: Define the LIFO reserve and explain how it is used to compare the performance of companies using LIFO and FIFO inventory costing methods. (p. 296)**

- The LIFO inventory reserve represents the difference between the value of LIFO ending inventory and what the value of ending inventory would have been under FIFO.
- The LIFO inventory reserve can cause a material effect on many ratios. These ratios should be adjusted for the LIFO inventory reserve when comparing a company using LIFO with a FIFO company.

SUMMARY	Concept ⟶	Method ⟶	Assessment
TAKEAWAY 6.1	How long, on average, does it take to sell the inventory?	Cost of goods sold, beginning inventory, and ending inventory $$\text{Inventory turnover} = \frac{\text{Cost of goods sold}}{\text{Average inventory}}$$ $$\text{Days' sales in inventory} = \frac{365}{\text{Inventory turnover}}$$	A higher inventory turnover or a lower days' sales in inventory indicates that the company is able to sell its inventory more quickly.
TAKEAWAY 6.2	What effect does the use of LIFO have on ending inventory relative to the use of FIFO?	Ending inventory and the LIFO inventory reserve The value of LIFO ending inventory + the LIFO inventory reserve = The value of FIFO ending inventory	If the LIFO reserve is material, it can have a significant impact on many ratios when compared to FIFO. The calculation of these ratios can be adjusted using the LIFO inventory reserve to provide a more comparable set of results.

KEY TERMS

Consignment goods (p. 274)

Cost flow (p. 277)

Days' sales in inventory (p. 289)

Finished goods inventory (p. 273)

First-in, first-out (FIFO) method (p. 278, 292)

F.O.B. destination (p. 274)

F.O.B. shipping point (p. 274)

Goods flow (p. 277)

Goods in transit (p. 274)

Inventory carrying costs (p. 273)

Inventory overage (p. 275)

Inventory shrinkage (p. 275)

Inventory turnover ratio (p. 288)

Just-in-case inventory (p. 273)

Just-in-time (JIT) manufacturing (p. 273)

Last-in, first-out (LIFO) method (p. 279, 293)

LIFO conformity rule (p. 284)

LIFO inventory reserve (p. 296)

Lower-of-cost-or-net realizable value (p. 287)

Net realizable value (NRV) (p. 287)

Physical count of inventory (p. 275)

Quick response system (p. 273)

Raw materials inventory (p. 272)

Specific identification method (p. 278, 292)

Stock-out costs (p. 273)

Weighted-average cost method (p. 280, 294)

Work-in-process inventory (p. 272)

Assignments with the ⓜⒷⒸ logo in the margin are available in ᵐʸBusinessCourse.
See the Preface of the book for details.

SELF-STUDY QUESTIONS

(Answers to Self-Study Questions are at the end of this chapter.)

1. **Which of the following concepts relates to the elimination or minimization of inventories by a manufacturing firm?**   **LO1**
   a. Quick response
   b. Just-in-time
   c. Just-in-case
   d. Specific identification

2. **Which inventory costing method assumes that the most recently purchased merchandise is sold first?**   **LO2**
   a. Specific identification
   b. Weighted-average cost
   c. FIFO
   d. LIFO

3. **Which inventory costing method results in the highest-valued ending inventory during a period of rising unit costs?**   **LO3**
   a. Specific identification
   b. Weighted-average cost
   c. FIFO
   d. LIFO

4. **Under which of the following freight terms does the seller retain ownership of the shipped goods?**   **LO1**
   a. F.O.B. shipping point
   b. F.O.B. destination

5. **When should ending inventory be written down below its acquisition cost on the balance sheet?**   **LO4**
   a. When units are damaged, physically deteriorated, or obsolete.
   b. When the inventory's net realizable value exceeds its acquisition cost.
   c. When the inventory's net realizable value is below its acquisition cost.
   d. Both a and c.

6. **Which inventory costing method results in the highest net income during a period of rising unit prices?**   **LO3**
   a. Specific identification
   b. Weighted-average cost
   c. FIFO
   d. LIFO

LO3

7. **Which inventory costing method is expensive to implement?**
   a. Specific identification
   b. Weighted-average cost
   c. FIFO
   d. LIFO

LO3

8. **Which inventory costing method is frequently used when undifferentiated units are stored in a common area?**
   a. Specific identification
   b. Weighted-average cost
   c. FIFO
   d. LIFO

LO3

9. **Which inventory costing method results in the lowest net income during a period of rising unit prices?**
   a. Specific identification
   b. Weighted-average cost
   c. FIFO
   d. LIFO

LO4

10. **Which inventory costing method does not require the use of the lower-of-cost-or-net realizable value method?**
    a. Specific identification
    b. Weighted-average cost
    c. FIFO
    d. All methods require the use of LCM.

LO5

11. **Mack Corp. reported annual cost of goods sold of $30,000 and average inventory on hand during the year of $3,750. What was Mack's inventory turnover?**
    a. 0.125 times
    b. 8.0 times
    c. $26,250
    d. 8.0%

LO7
(Appendix 6B)

12. **The Molly Company reports ending inventory under the LIFO method of $15,000. Had Molly used FIFO, the ending inventory would have been reported as $16,500. Molly's LIFO inventory reserve is:**
    a. $31,500
    b. $15,000
    c. $1,500
    d. 91%

LO6
(Appendix 6A)

13. **The periodic inventory system differs from the perpetual inventory system:**
    a. because the periodic system is not compatible with modern technology.
    b. because the perpetual system continually updates inventory, while the periodic inventory system only updates inventory at the end of the period.
    c. because the periodic system continually updates inventory, while the perpetual inventory system only updates inventory at the end of the period.
    d. because the periodic system is more complex and costly.

QUESTIONS

1. What are the three inventory accounts maintained by a manufacturing firm? Define each.
2. ShopMart Stores uses point-of-sale equipment at its checkout counters to read universal bar codes. It also uses a quick response system. What is a quick response system?
3. What are *just-in-case inventory* and *inventory carrying costs?*
4. What is the *just-in-time manufacturing philosophy?* Describe it.
5. What is meant by *goods flow* and *cost flow?*
6. Describe how each of the following inventory costing methods is used with the perpetual inventory system: (a) Specific identification; (b) Weighted-average cost; (c) First-in, first-out; and (d) Last-in, first-out.

7. Describe the type of inventory for which the goods flow would most naturally correspond to the cost flow for each of the inventory costing methods: (a) Specific identification, (b) Weighted-average cost, (c) FIFO, and (d) LIFO.

8. Why do relatively stable purchase prices reduce the significance of the choice of an inventory costing method?

9. What is the nature of FIFO *phantom profits* during periods of rising inventory purchase prices?

10. If costs have been rising, which inventory costing method—weighted-average cost; first-in, first-out; or last-in, first-out—yields (a) the lowest ending inventory value? (b) the lowest net income? (c) the largest ending inventory value? (d) the largest net income?

11. Even though it does not represent their goods flow, why might firms adopt last-in, first-out inventory costing during periods when inventory costs are rising?

12. Describe a situation in which merchandise must be valued on the balance sheet at an amount less than its acquisition cost.

13. Which of the following is not an inventory costing method?
    a. Specific identification
    b. Weighted-average cost
    c. Just-in-time manufacturing
    d. FIFO

14. What is the effect on reported net income of applying the lower-of-cost-or-net realizable value method to ending inventory?

15. How do the accounting principles of consistency and full disclosure apply to inventory costing?

16. Which party, the seller or the buyer, bears the freight cost when the terms are F.O.B. shipping point? When the terms are F.O.B. destination?

17. What is a LIFO inventory reserve and how can it be useful to an analyst?

18. Moyer Company has an inventory turnover of 4.51. What is Moyer's days' sales in inventory?

19. In an annual report, **Craftmade International, Inc.**, describes its inventory accounting policies as follows: CRAFTMADE INTERNATIONAL, INC.

> Inventories are stated at the lower-of-cost-or-net realizable value, with inventory cost determined using the first-in, first-out (FIFO) method. The cost of inventory includes freight-in and duties on imported goods.

Also in an annual report, **Kaiser Aluminum Corporation** made the following statement in discussing its inventories: KAISER ALUMINUM CORPORATION

> The Company recorded pretax charges of approximately $19.4 million because of a reduction in the carrying values of its inventories caused principally by prevailing lower prices for alumina, primary aluminum, and fabricated products.

What accounting principle did Craftmade International follow when it included the costs of freight-in and duties on imported goods in its Inventory account? Briefly describe how a firm determines which costs to include in its inventory account. What accounting principle did Kaiser Aluminum follow when it recorded the $19.4 million pretax charge? Briefly describe the rationale for this principle.

20. What are the three steps that make up the year-end physical count of inventory?

SHORT EXERCISES

SE6-1.   Departures from Acquisition Cost   At year-end, The Kitchen Shop has a refrigerator that has been   LO4
used as a demonstration model. The refrigerator cost $375 and sells for $550 when new. In its present condition, the refrigerator will be sold for $330. Related selling costs are an estimated $15. At what amount should the refrigerator be carried in inventory?

    a. $350   *c.* $325
    b. $335   *d.* $315

LO2   SE6-2.   Inventory Costing Methods Which inventory costing method requires that a company keep track of the cost of each specific unit of inventory?

    a.   Specific identification
    b.   Lower of cost or market method
    c.   LIFO
    d.   All of the above

LO1   SE6-3.   Identify Goods to Be Included in Inventory Lisa Company has the following items at year-end. Identify which items should be included in Lisa's year-end inventory count.

    1. Goods held on consignment by Sell For You Company.
    2. Goods held by Lisa on consignment that will be sold for another company.
    3. Goods in transit sent to a client F.O.B. shipping point.
    4. Goods in transit sent to a client F.O.B. destination.

LO4   SE6-4.   Lower-of-Cost-or-Net Realizable Value Method The Claremont Company's ending inventory is composed of 50 units that had cost $20 each and 100 units that had cost $15 each. If all 150 units have an NRV of $16 each, what value should be assigned to the company's ending inventory assuming that it applies lower-of-cost-or-net realizable value on a group-wise basis?

LO4   SE6-5.   Lower-of-Cost-or-Net Realizable Value Method The McQuenny Company's ending inventory is composed of 100 units that had an acquisition cost of $25 per unit and 50 units that had an acquisition cost of $30 per unit. If 150 units have an NRV of $27 per unit, what value should be assigned to the company's ending inventory assuming that it applies the lower-of-cost-or-net realizable value method on an individual item basis?

LO5   SE6-6.   Inventory Turnover and Days' Sales in Inventory Bass & Company reported the following information in its recent annual report:

	2018	2019
Cost of goods sold	$4,000,000	$4,600,000
Beginning inventory	880,000	860,000
Ending inventory.	860,000	760,000

Calculate the company's inventory turnover and days' sales in inventory for both years.

LO5   SE6-7.   Inventory Turnover and Days' Sales in Inventory Hamm & Company disclosed the following information in its recent annual report:

	2018	2019
Cost of goods sold	$16,000,000	$22,000,000
Beginning inventory	2,000,000	4,000,000
Ending inventory.	3,000,000	5,000,000

Calculate the company's inventory turnover and days' sales in inventory for both years.

LO2   SE6-8.   Inventory Costing Methods and the Periodic Method Lamb Company experienced the following events in January:

Date	Event	Units		Unit Cost	Total Cost
Jan. 10	Purchased inventory.	100	@	$14	$1,400
Jan. 20	Purchased inventory.	200	@	16	3,200
Jan. 30	Sold inventory.	150			

If the Lamb Company uses the FIFO inventory costing method, calculate the company's cost of goods sold and its ending inventory as of January 31 assuming the periodic method.

SE6-9. **Inventory Costing Methods and the Periodic Method** Deer Company experienced the following events in February:

Date	Event	Units		Unit Cost	Total Cost
Feb. 1	Purchased inventory........................	100	@	$18	$1,800
Feb. 4	Sold inventory...............................	50			
Feb. 9	Purchased inventory........................	100	@	$21	$2,100
Feb. 27	Sold inventory..............................	100			

If the Deer Company uses the LIFO inventory costing method, calculate the company's cost of goods sold and ending inventory as of February 28 assuming the periodic method.

SE6-10. **Errors in Inventory Count** Pow Corp. accidentally overstated its 2018 ending inventory by $750. Assume that ending 2019 inventory is accurately counted. The error in 2018 will have what effect on Pow Corp.?

a. 2018 net income is understated by $750.
b. 2018 net income is overstated by $750.
c. 2019 net income is understated by $750.
d. Both *b* and *c* are correct.

SE6-11. **Inventory Costing Methods and the Periodic Method** Kay & Company experienced the following events in March:

Date	Event	Units		Unit Cost	Total Cost
Mar. 1	Purchased inventory........................	100	@	$16	$1,600
Mar. 3	Sold inventory...............................	60			
Mar. 15	Purchased inventory........................	100	@	$18	$1,800
Mar. 20	Sold inventory..............................	40			

If Kay & Company uses the weighted-average cost method, calculate the company's cost of goods sold and ending inventory as of March 31 assuming the periodic method.

SE6-12. **Inventory Costing Methods and the Perpetual Method** Refer to the information in SE6-11 and assume the perpetual inventory system is used. Use the weighted-average inventory costing method to calculate the company's cost of goods sold and ending inventory as of March 31. Round your final answers to the nearest dollar.

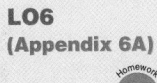

SE6-13. **Inventory Costing Methods and the Perpetual Method** Refer to the information in SE6-9 and assume the perpetual inventory system is used. Use the LIFO inventory costing method to calculate the company's cost of goods sold and ending inventory as of February 28.

SE6-14. **LIFO Inventory Reserve** Lamar Company reports ending inventory of $150,000 on a LIFO basis and also reports a LIFO inventory reserve of $32,000. If Lamar had used FIFO rather than LIFO, ending inventory would have been:

a. $123,000.
b. $150,000.
c. $177,000.
d. $182,000.

EXERCISES—SET A

E6-1A. **Just-in-Time Inventories** Mitch Manufacturing Company uses the perpetual inventory system and plans to use raw materials costing $1,200,000 in manufacturing its products. Mitch will operate its factory 300 days during the year. Currently, Mitch follows the just-in-case philosophy with its raw materials inventory, keeping raw materials costing $12,000 in its raw materials inventory. Mitch plans to switch to the just-in-time manufacturing philosophy by keeping only the raw materials needed for the next two days of production. Calculate the new raw materials inventory level after Mitch implements the just-in-time manufacturing philosophy in its factory.

LO2   **E6-2A.   Inventory Costing Methods—Periodic Method** The Luann Company uses the periodic inventory system. The following July data are for an item in Luann's inventory:

July   1   Beginning inventory, 30 units @ $9 per unit.
       10   Purchased 50 units @ $11 per unit.
       15   Sold 60 units.
       26   Purchased 25 units @ $13 per unit.

Calculate the cost of goods sold for July and ending inventory at July 31 using (a) first-in, first-out, (b) last-in, first-out, and (c) the weighted-average cost methods. Round the cost per unit to 3 decimal places and your final answers to the nearest dollar.

LO1   **E6-3A.   Year-End Physical Inventory** The December 31 inventory for the Jeremy Company included five products. The year-end physical count revealed the following:

Product	Quantity Available
A	26
B	50
C	71
D	75
E	55

The related unit costs were: A, $10; B, $6; C, $9; D, $8; and E, $11.

Required
Calculate the total cost of the December 31 physical inventory.

LO2   **E6-4A.   Inventory Costing Methods—Periodic Method** Arrow Company is a retailer that uses the periodic inventory system. On August 1, it had 80 units of product A at a total cost of $1,600. On August 5, Arrow purchased 100 units of A for $2,116. On August 8, it purchased 200 units of A for $4,416. On August 11, it sold 170 units of A for $4,800. Calculate the August cost of goods sold and the ending inventory at August 31 using (a) first-in, first-out, (b) last-in, first-out, and (c) the weighted-average cost methods. Round your final answers to the nearest dollar.

LO3   **E6-5A.   Errors in Inventory Counts** The following information was taken from the records of Tinker Enterprises:

	2019	2018
Beginning inventory	$ 60,000	$ 50,000
Cost of goods purchased	420,000	400,000
Cost of goods available for sale	480,000	450,000
Ending inventory	55,000	60,000
Cost of goods sold	$425,000	$390,000

The following two errors were made in the physical inventory counts:

1. 2018 ending inventory was understated by $8,000.
2. 2019 ending inventory was overstated by $4,000.

Compute the correct cost of goods sold for both 2018 and 2019.

LO4   **E6-6A.   Departures from Acquisition Cost** Determine the proper total inventory value for each of the following items in Viking Company's ending inventory:

a.   Viking has 500 video games in stock. The games cost $36 each, but their year-end net realizable value is $28.

b.   Viking has 400 rolls of camera film that are past the expiration date marked on the film's box. The films cost $1.65 each and are normally sold for $3.30. To clear out these old films, Viking will drop their selling price to $1.30. There are no related selling costs.

    c. Viking has seven cameras in stock that have been used as demonstration models. The cameras cost $180 and normally sell for $280. Because these cameras are in used condition, Viking has set the selling price at $160 each. Expected selling costs are $15 per camera.

E6-7A. **Inventory Costing Methods—Periodic Method** The following information is for the Bud Company; the company sells just one product: **LO2**

		Units	Unit Cost
Beginning inventory		200	$10
Purchases:	Feb. 11	500	14
	May 18	400	16
	October 23	100	22

At year-end, there was an ending inventory of 340 units. Assume the use of the periodic inventory method. Calculate the value of ending inventory and the cost of goods sold for the year using (a) first-in, first-out, (b) last-in, first-out, and (c) the weighted-average cost method.

E6-8A. **Inventory Costing Methods—Periodic Method** The following data are for the Vista Company, which sells just one product: **LO2**

		Units	Unit Cost
Beginning inventory, January 1		200	$10
Purchases:	February 11	500	14
	May 18	400	17
	October 23	100	18
Sales	March 1	400	
	July 1	380	

Calculate the value of ending inventory and cost of goods sold using the periodic method and (a) first-in, first-out, (b) last-in, first-out, and (c) weighted-average cost method. Round your final answers to the nearest dollar.

E6-9A. **Applying IFRS** LVMH is a Paris-based manufacturer of luxury goods that prepares its financial statements using IFRS. During the year, the management of the company undertook a review of the fair value of its inventory and found that the inventory had appreciated above its book value of 12 million euros. According to the company's management, the inventory was undervalued by 3 million euros. (*Hint:* Credit Asset, revaluation reserve. Prepare the journal entry to revalue the company's inventory. How would the revaluation immediately affect the company's (a) current ratio, (b) inventory turnover, and (c) days' sales in inventory?   **LO4, 5**

E6-10A. **Lower-of-Cost-or-Net Realizable Value Method** The following data are taken from the Browning Corporation's inventory accounts: **LO4**

Item Code	Quantity	Unit Cost	Net Realizable Value
ACE	100	$27	$25
BDF	300	29	31
GHJ	400	22	18
MBS	200	23	27

Calculate the value of the company's ending inventory using the lower-of-cost-or-net realizable value method applied to each item of inventory.

E6-11A. **Inventory Turnover and Days' Sales in Inventory** The Northern Company installed a new inventory management system at the beginning of 2018. Shown below are data from the company's accounting records as reported out by the new system: **LO5**

	2018	2019
Sales revenue.	$8,000,000	$11,000,000
Cost of goods sold	4,000,000	4,800,000
Beginning inventory	510,000	540,000
Ending inventory.	550,000	600,000

Calculate the company's (a) inventory turnover and (b) days' sales in inventory for 2018 and 2019. Comment on your results.

LO4

E6-12A. Lower-of-Cost-or-Net Realizable Value Method The following data refer to the Ian Company's ending inventory:

Item Code	Quantity	Unit Cost	Net Realizable Value
ABX	80	$50	$55
TYG	200	38	42
JIL.	175	28	24
GGH	90	44	38

Calculate the value of the company's ending inventory by using the lower-of-cost-or-net realizable value applied to each item of inventory.

LO7
(Appendix 6B)

E6-13A. The LIFO Inventory Reserve Southeast Steel Company uses the LIFO inventory costing method to value its ending inventory. The following data were obtained from the company's accounting records:

Current assets (under FIFO)	$9,000,000
Current liabilities.	6,000,000
Inventory under LIFO	2,200,000
Inventory under FIFO	2,800,000

Calculate the company's (a) LIFO inventory reserve and (b) the current ratio assuming (i) FIFO and (ii) LIFO.

LO6
(Appendix 6A)

E6-14A. Inventory Costing Methods—Perpetual Method Refer to the information in E6-2A and assume the perpetual inventory system is used. Calculate the cost of goods sold for the July 15 sale using (a) first-in, first-out, (b) last-in, first-out, and (c) the weighted-average cost methods. Round your final answers to the nearest dollar.

LO6
(Appendix 6A)

E6-15A. Inventory Costing Methods—Perpetual Method Refer to the information in E6-4A and assume the perpetual inventory system is used. Calculate the inventory cost of product A on August 11 (after the sale) using (a) first-in, first-out, (b) last-in, first-out, and (c) the weighted-average cost methods. Round your final answers to the nearest dollar.

LO6
(Appendix 6A)

E6-16A. Inventory Costing Methods—Perpetual Method Refer to the information in E6-8A and assume the perpetual inventory system is used. Calculate the value of ending inventory and cost of goods sold using the perpetual method and (a) first-in, first-out, (b) last-in, first-out, and (c) weighted-average cost method. Round the cost per unit to 3 decimal places and round your final answers to the nearest dollar.

EXERCISES—SET B

LO1

E6-1B. Just-in-Time Inventories Nevada Manufacturing Company uses the perpetual inventory system and plans to use raw material costing $2,100,000 in making its products. Nevada will operate its factory 300 days during the year. Currently, Nevada follows the just-in-case philosophy with its raw materials inventory, keeping raw materials costing $20,000 in its raw materials inventory. Nevada plans to switch to the just-in-time manufacturing philosophy by keeping only the raw materials needed for the next two days of production. Calculate the new raw materials inventory level after Nevada implements the just-in-time manufacturing philosophy.

E6-2B. **Inventory Costing Methods—Periodic Method** Mary Company uses the periodic inventory sys- LO2
tem. The following May data are for an item in Mary's inventory:

May   1 Beginning inventory, 150 units @ $30 per unit.
    12 Purchased 100 units @ $35 per unit.
    16 Sold 180 units.
    24 Purchased 170 units @ $40 per unit.

Calculate the cost of goods sold for May and ending inventory at May 31 using (a) first-in, first-out,
(b) last-in, first-out, and (c) the weighted-average cost method. Round the cost per unit to 3 decimal places
and your final answers to the nearest dollar.

E6-3B. **Year-End Physical Inventory** The December 31 inventory for the Simpson Company included five LO1
products. The year-end physical count revealed the following quantities on hand:

Product	Quantity Available
K	40
L	42
M	60
N	52
P	55

The related unit costs were: K, $7; L, $10; M, $9; N, $5; and P, $7.

Required
Calculate the total cost of the December 31 physical inventory.

E6-4B. **Inventory Costing Methods—Periodic Method** Spanner Company is a retailer that uses the pe- LO2
riodic inventory system. On March 1, it had 100 units of product M at a total cost of $1,590. On
March 6, Spanner purchased 200 units of M for $3,600. On March 10, it purchased 125 units of M for
$3,000. On March 15, it sold 200 units of M for $6,000. Calculate the March cost of goods sold and
the ending inventory at March 31 using (a) first-in, first-out, (b) last-in, first-out, and (c) the weighted-
average cost method. Round your final answers to the nearest dollar.

E6-5B. **Errors in Inventory Counts** The following information was taken from the records of Hawk LO3
Enterprises:

	2019	2018
Beginning inventory	$ 55,000	$ 75,000
Cost of goods purchased	540,000	500,000
Cost of goods available for sale	595,000	575,000
Ending inventory	85,000	55,000
Cost of goods sold	$510,000	$520,000

The following two errors were made in the physical inventory counts:

1. 2018 ending inventory was overstated by $28,000.
2. 2019 ending inventory was understated by $17,000.

Compute the correct cost of goods sold for both 2018 and 2019.

E6-6B. **Departures from Acquisition Cost** Determine the proper total inventory value for each of the fol- LO4
lowing items in Parker Company's ending inventory:

a. Parker has 70 model X3 cameras in stock. The cameras cost $160 each, but their year-end net
realizable value is only $140.
b. Parker has 600 rolls of film that are past the expiration date since film is now a slow moving
item. The film cost $2.00 each and normally sells for $4.00. Parker has put the expired film on
clearance and is selling it for $1.50 per roll. There are no related selling costs.
c. Parker has five computers in stock that have been used as demonstration models. These computers cost $400 and normally sell for $550. Because they are used, Parker is selling them for $350
each. Expected selling costs are $10 per computer. New models of the computer (on order Z) will
cost Parker $420 and will be priced to sell at $590.

LO2   **E6-7B.** **Inventory Costing Methods—Periodic Method** The Caitlin Company, which uses the periodic inventory system, has the following records:

		Units	Unit Cost
Beginning inventory		100	$49
Purchases:	Jan. 6	650	42
	July 15	550	38
	Dec. 28	200	36

Ending inventory was 400 units. Compute the ending inventory and the cost of goods sold for the year using (a) first-in, first out, (b) weighted-average cost, and (c) last-in, first-out.

LO2   **E6-8B.** **Inventory Costing Methods—Periodic Method** The following data are for the Lite Corporation, which sells just one product:

		Units	Unit Cost
Beginning inventory, January 1		200	$12
Purchases	February 11	500	13
	May 18	400	15
	October 23	100	17
Sales	March 1	350	
	July 1	440	

Calculate the value of ending inventory and cost of goods sold using the periodic method and (a) first-in, first-out, (b) last-in, first-out, and (c) weighted-average cost method. Round your final answers to the nearest dollar.

LO4, 5   **E6-9B.** **Applying IFRS** The French Petroleum Company is a Paris-based oil and gas company that prepares its financial statements using IFRS. During the year, the management of the company undertook a review of the fair value of its oil and gas inventory and found that the inventory had appreciated above its book value of 55 million euros. According to the company's management, the oil and gas inventory was undervalued by 8 million euros. Prepare the journal entry to revalue the company's inventory. (*Hint:* Credit Asset, revaluation reserve.) How would the revaluation immediately affect the company's (a) current ratio, (b) inventory turnover, and (c) days' sales in inventory?

LO4   **E6-10B.** **Lower-of-Cost-or-Net Realizable Value Method** The following data are taken from the Smith & Barney Corporation's inventory accounts:

Item Code	Quantity	Unit Cost	Net Realizable Value
ZKE	100	$22	$16
XYF	300	33	37
MNJ	400	23	18
UBS	220	33	39

Calculate the value of the company's ending inventory using the lower-of-cost-or-net realizable value method applied to each item of inventory.

LO5   **E6-11B.** **Inventory Turnover and Days' Sales in Inventory** The Western Company installed a new inventory management system at the beginning of 2018. Shown below are data from the company's accounting records as reported by the new system:

	2018	2019
Sales revenue	$11,000,000	$14,000,000
Cost of goods sold	5,000,000	6,000,000
Beginning inventory	620,000	630,000
Ending inventory	630,000	750,000

Calculate the company's (a) inventory turnover and (b) days' sales in inventory for 2018 and 2019. Comment on your results.

E6-12B. Lower-of-Cost-or-Net Realizable Value Method The following data refer to the Fanning Company's ending inventory:

LO4

Item Code	Quantity	Unit Cost	Net Realizable Value
LXC.	60	$40	$48
KWT	260	38	34
MOR	400	25	20
NES	100	26	32

Calculate the value of the company's ending inventory by using the lower-of-cost-or-net realizable value method applied to each item of inventory.

E6-13B. The LIFO Inventory Reserve Eastern Steel Company uses the LIFO inventory costing method to value its ending inventory. The following data were obtained from the company's accounting records:

LO7
(Appendix 6B)

Current assets (under FIFO)	$9,500,000
Current liabilities	7,500,000
Inventory under LIFO	4,000,000
Inventory under FIFO	5,700,000

Calculate the company's (a) LIFO inventory reserve and (b) current ratio assuming (i) FIFO and (ii) LIFO.

E6-14B. Inventory Costing Methods—Perpetual Method Refer to the information in E6-2B and assume the perpetual inventory system is used. Calculate the cost of goods sold for the May 16 sale using (a) first-in, first-out, (b) last-in, first-out, and (c) the weighted-average cost method. Round your final answers to the nearest dollar.

LO6
(Appendix 6A)

E6-15B. Inventory Costing Methods—Perpetual Method Refer to the information in E6-4B and assume the perpetual inventory system is used. Calculate the ending inventory cost of product M on March 15 (after the sale) using (a) first-in, first-out, (b) last-in, first-out, and (c) the weighted-average cost method. Round your final answers to the nearest dollar.

LO6
(Appendix 6A)

E6-16B. Inventory Costing Methods—Perpetual Method Refer to the information in E6-8B and assume the perpetual inventory system is used. Calculate the value of ending inventory and cost of goods sold using the perpetual method and (a) first-in, first-out, (b) last-in, first-out, and (c) weighted-average cost method. Round the cost per unit to 3 decimal places and your final answers to the nearest dollar.

LO6
(Appendix 6A)

PROBLEMS—SET A

P6-1A. Just-in-Time Inventory The Mason Manufacturing Company uses the perpetual inventory system with its raw material inventory. Mason plans to include raw material costing $2,700,000 in the products that it manufactures. John Mason, president of the company, wants to adopt the just-in-time manufacturing philosophy for the raw materials inventory. He wants to have only the raw material needed for the next day's production at the end of each day. The factory operates 300 days each year. Historically, the raw materials inventory balance at the end of the day has averaged $40,000 cost. Mason has an annual inventory carrying cost equal to 20 percent of total inventory cost.

LO1

Required

a. What is the anticipated inventory carrying cost (in dollars) if Mason does not adopt the just-in-time manufacturing philosophy?

b. Calculate the average level (in dollars) for the raw materials inventory if Mason adopts the just-in-time manufacturing philosophy.

c. Calculate the reductions in the raw materials inventory level and the raw materials inventory annual carrying cost if Mason adopts the just-in-time manufacturing philosophy.

d. What other factors or situations should Mason consider before deciding to have only one day's supply of raw material? (*Hint:* Consider factors and situations related to environment, supplier problems, labor problems, etc.)

LO2 **P6-2A.** **Inventory Costing Methods—Periodic Method** Tally Stores uses the periodic inventory system for its merchandise inventory. The April 1 inventory for one of the items in the merchandise inventory consisted of 120 units with a unit cost of $330. Transactions for this item during April were as follows:

April   9 Purchased 40 units @ $345 per unit.
        14 Sold 80 units @ $550 per unit.
        23 Purchased 20 units @ $360 per unit.
        29 Sold 40 units @ $550 per unit.

Required
a. Calculate the cost of goods sold and the ending inventory cost for the month of April using the weighted-average cost method. Round the cost per unit to 3 decimal places and your final answers to the nearest dollar.
b. Calculate the cost of goods sold and the ending inventory cost for the month of April using the first-in, first-out method.
c. Calculate the cost of goods sold and the ending inventory cost for the month of April using the last-in, first-out method.

LO4 **P6-3A.** **Lower-of-Cost-or-Net Realizable Value Method** The following data are taken from the Daley Corporation's inventory accounts:

Item Code	Quantity	Unit Cost	Net Realizable Value
Product 1			
ZKE.....................................	100	$22	$18
ZKF.....................................	300	31	36
Product 2			
MNJ....................................	400	22	19
MNS	250	31	37

Calculate the value of the company's ending inventory using the lower-of-cost-or-net realizable value method applied to each item of inventory.

LO2, 3 **P6-4A.** **Inventory Costing Methods—Periodic Method** Chou Sales Corporation uses the periodic inventory system. On January 1, 2018, Chou had 1,000 units of product A with a unit cost of $20 per unit. A summary of purchases and sales during 2018 follows:

	Unit Cost	Units Purchased	Units Sold
Feb. 2			400
Apr. 6	$22	1,800	
July 10			1,600
Aug. 9	25	800	
Oct. 23			800
Dec. 30	28	1,400	

Required
a. Assume that Chou uses the first-in, first-out method. Compute the cost of goods sold for 2018 and the ending inventory balance at December 31, 2018, for product A.
b. Assume that Chou uses the last-in, first-out method. Compute the cost of goods sold for 2018 and the ending inventory balance at December 31, 2018, for product A.
c. Assume that Chou uses the weighted-average cost method. Compute the cost of goods sold for 2018 and the ending inventory balance at December 31, 2018, for product A.
d. Assuming that Chou's products are perishable items, which of the three inventory costing methods would you choose to:
  1. Reflect the likely goods flow through the business?
  2. Minimize income taxes for the period?
  3. Report the largest amount of net income for the period?
Explain your answers.

P6-5A. **Inventory Turnover and Days' Sales in Inventory** The Southern Corporation installed a new inventory management system at the beginning of 2018. Shown below are data from the company's accounting records as reported by the new system:

	2018	2019
Sales revenue.	$19,000,000	$20,000,000
Cost of goods sold	8,600,000	9,200,000
Beginning inventory	2,500,000	2,530,000
Ending inventory.	2,530,000	2,600,000

Calculate the company's (a) inventory turnover (round to three decimal places) and (b) days' sales in inventory for 2018 and 2019. Comment on your results.

P6-6A. **Goods in Transit** The Yankee Wholesale Company sells merchandise to a variety of retailers. Yankee uses different freight terms with its various customers and suppliers. All sales are made on account.

Required

For each of the following transactions, indicate which company has ownership of the goods in transit:

a. Yankee sold merchandise to X-Mart Stores, with shipping terms of F.O.B. shipping point.

b. Yankee purchased merchandise from Zendo Manufacturing Company, with shipping terms of F.O.B. destination.

c. Yankee sold merchandise to Mary's Boutique, with shipping terms of F.O.B. destination.

d. Sunshine Manufacturing Company sold merchandise to Yankee, with shipping terms of F.O.B. shipping point.

e. Yankee purchased merchandise from Warfield Manufacturing Company, with freight terms of F.O.B. shipping point.

f. Stevenson Stores purchased merchandise from Yankee, with shipping terms of F.O.B. shipping point.

P6-7A. **Lower-of-Cost-or-Net Realizable Value Method** The Vandy Company had the following inventory at year-end:

		Unit Price	
	Quantity	Cost	Net Realizable Value
Fans			
Model X1.	300	$18	$19
Model X2.	250	23	24
Model X3.	450	29	25
Heaters			
Model B7.	500	24	30
Model B8.	290	35	32
Model B9.	100	41	37

Required

a. Determine the value of ending inventory after applying the lower-of-cost-or-net realizable value method to each item of inventory.

b. Would the net income be lower under the cost method or the lower-of-cost-or-net realizable value method?

LO2   **P6-8A.**   **Inventory Costing Methods—Periodic Method** The following data are for the Porter Corporation, which sells just one product:

		Units	Unit Cost
Beginning inventory, January 1		1,200	$ 8
Purchases	February 11	1,500	9
	May 18	1,400	12
	October 23	1,100	14
Sales	March 1	1,400	
	July 1	1,400	
	October 29	1,200	

Calculate the value of ending inventory and cost of goods sold at year-end using the periodic method and (a) first-in, first-out, (b) last-in, first-out, and (c) weighted-average cost method. Round the cost per unit to 3 decimal places and round your final answers to the nearest dollar. If the net realizable value of the inventory at year-end is $15, how will the cost of goods sold under each method be affected?

LO1   **P6-9A.**   **Physical Inventory Calculation** Comanche Stores conducted a physical inventory at December 31. The items counted during the physical inventory are listed below. Comanche's accountant provided the unit costs.

Item Description	December 31 Count	Unit Cost
Colorado wool sweaters	48	$32
Magnum wool sweaters	27	34
Johnson jackets	50	30
Magnum caps	45	12
Evans caps	30	10
Colorado shirts	72	20
Johnson shirts	68	25
Magnum boots	45	60

Required

Prepare a schedule to determine the total cost of each item in the inventory and the total cost of the complete inventory at December 31.

LO6   **P6-10A.**   **Inventory Costing Methods—Perpetual Method** Refer to the information in P6-2A and assume the
(Appendix 6A)   perpetual inventory system is used.

Required

a.   Calculate the cost of goods sold and the ending inventory cost for the month of April using the weighted-average cost method.

b.   Calculate the cost of goods sold and the ending inventory cost for the month of April using the first-in, first-out method.

c.   Calculate the cost of goods sold and the ending inventory cost for the month of April using the last-in, first-out method.

LO6   **P6-11A.**   **Inventory Costing Methods—Perpetual Method** Refer to the information in P6-4A and assume the
(Appendix 6A)   perpetual inventory system is used.

Required

a.   Assume that Chou uses the first-in, first-out method. Compute the cost of goods sold for 2018 and the ending inventory balance at December 31, 2018, for product A.

b.   Assume that Chou uses the last-in, first-out method. Compute the cost of goods sold for 2018 and the ending inventory balance at December 31, 2018, for product A.

c.   Assume that Chou uses the weighted-average cost method. Compute the cost of goods sold for 2018 and the ending inventory balance at December 31, 2018, for product A.

    d. Assuming that Chou's products are perishable items, which of the three inventory costing methods would you choose to:
1. Reflect the likely goods flow through the business?
2. Minimize income taxes for the period?
3. Report the largest amount of net income for the period?

Explain your answers.

P6-12A. The LIFO Inventory Reserve   Alaska Manufacturing Company uses the LIFO inventory costing method to value its ending inventory. The following data were obtained from the company's accounting records:

Current assets (under FIFO)	$20,000,000
Current liabilities	15,000,000
Inventory under LIFO	7,000,000
Inventory under FIFO	7,700,000

Calculate the company's (a) LIFO inventory reserve and (b) current ratio assuming (i) FIFO and (ii) LIFO. If the company's LIFO gross profit was $10,000,000 and the change in the LIFO inventory reserve was $1,400,000, calculate the company's gross profit under FIFO.

LO7
(Appendix 6B)

P6-13A. Inventory Costing Methods—Perpetual Method   Using the data in P6-8A, assume that Porter Corporation uses the perpetual inventory system. Calculate the value of ending inventory and cost of goods sold at year-end using the perpetual method and (a) first-in, first-out, (b) last-in, first-out, and (c) weighted-average cost method. Round the cost per unit to 3 decimal places and round your final answers to the nearest dollar. If the net realizable value of the inventory at year-end is $15, how will the cost of goods sold under each method be affected?

LO6
(Appendix 6A)

PROBLEMS—SET B

P6-1B. Just-in-Time Inventory   The Track Manufacturing Company uses the perpetual inventory system for its raw materials inventory. Track plans to include raw material costing $2,500,000 in the products that it manufactures. Henry Track, president of the company, wants to adopt the just-in-time manufacturing philosophy for the raw materials inventory. He wants to have only the raw material needed for the next day's production at the end of each day. The factory operates 250 days each year. Historically, the raw materials inventory balance at the end of the day has averaged $55,000 cost. Track has an annual inventory carrying cost equal to 22 percent of total inventory cost.

LO1

Required
  a. What is the anticipated annual inventory carrying cost (in dollars) if Track does not adopt the just-in-time manufacturing philosophy?

  b. Calculate the average level (in dollars) for the raw materials inventory if Track adopts the just-in-time manufacturing philosophy.

  c. Calculate the reduction in the raw materials inventory level and the raw materials inventory annual carrying cost if Track adopts the just-in-time manufacturing philosophy.

  d. What other factors or situations should Track consider before deciding to have only one day's supply of material? (*Hint:* Consider factors and situations related to environment, supplier problems, labor problems, etc.)

P6-2B. Inventory Costing Methods—Periodic Method   The Kali Company uses the periodic inventory system for its merchandise inventory. The June 1 inventory for one of the items in the merchandise inventory consisted of 60 units with a unit cost of $45. Transactions for this item during June were as follows:

LO2

June   5   Purchased 40 units @ $50 per unit.
        13   Sold 50 units @ $95 per unit.
        25   Purchased 40 units @ $53 per unit.
        29   Sold 20 units @ $110 per unit.

Required
  a. Compute the cost of goods sold and the ending inventory cost for the month of June using the weighted-average cost method. Round the cost per unit to 3 decimal places and round your final answers to the nearest dollar.

b. Compute the cost of goods sold and the ending inventory cost for the month of June using the first-in, first-out method.

c. Compute the cost of goods sold and the ending inventory cost for the month of June using the last-in, first-out method.

LO4   **P6-3B.   Lower-of-Cost-or-Net Realizable Value Method** The following data are taken from the Hilton Corporation's inventory accounts:

Item Code	Quantity	Unit Cost	Net Realizable Value
Product 1			
XKE.	100	$32	$28
XKF.	400	43	44
Product 2			
ZNJ.	400	32	29
ZNS.	300	43	48

Calculate the value of the company's ending inventory using the lower-of-cost-or-net realizable value method applied to each item of inventory.

LO2, 3   **P6-4B.   Inventory Costing Methods—Periodic Method** The Glenn Sales Corporation uses the periodic inventory system. On January 1, 2018, Glenn had 2,600 units of product B with a unit cost of $40 per unit. A summary of purchases and sales during 2018 follows:

	Unit Cost	Units Purchased	Units Sold
Jan. 3 .			1,600
Mar. 8 .	$44	3,000	
June 13.			2,000
Sept. 19 .	46	800	
Nov. 23 .	50	1,200	
Dec. 28.			1,800

Required

a. Assume that Glenn uses the first-in, first-out method. Compute the cost of goods sold for 2018 and the ending inventory balance at December 31, 2018, for product B.

b. Assume that Glenn uses the last-in, first-out method. Compute the cost of goods sold for 2018 and the ending inventory balance at December 31, 2018, for product B.

c. Assume that Glenn uses the weighted-average cost method. Compute the cost of goods sold for 2018 and the ending inventory balance at December 31, 2018, for product B.

d. Assuming that Glenn sells items that quickly become obsolete, which of these three inventory costing methods would you choose to:
1. Reflect the likely goods flow through the business?
2. Minimize income tax for the period?
3. Report the largest amount of net income for the period?
Explain your answers.

LO5   **P6-5B.   Inventory Turnover and Days' Sales in Inventory** The Southwestern States Corporation installed a new inventory management system at the beginning of 2018. Shown below are data from the Southwestern States' accounting records as reported by the new system:

	2018	2019
Sales revenue.	$49,000,000	$42,000,000
Cost of goods sold	30,000,000	29,500,000
Beginning inventory	16,250,000	16,500,000
Ending inventory.	17,000,000	20,500,000

Calculate the company's (a) inventory turnover (round to three decimal places) and (b) days' sales in inventory for 2018 and 2019. Comment on your results.

P6-6B. **Goods in Transit** Field Distributors sells merchandise to a variety of retailers. Field uses different freight terms with its various customers and suppliers. All sales are made on account.

Required

For each of the following transactions, indicate which company has ownership of the goods in transit:

a. Field sold merchandise to Clay Boutique, with shipping terms of F.O.B. destination.

b. Field purchased merchandise from Campbell Manufacturing Company, with freight terms of F.O.B. shipping point.

c. Field sold merchandise to Save-A-Lot Stores, with shipping terms of F.O.B. shipping point.

d. Field purchased merchandise from Central Manufacturing Company, with shipping terms of F.O.B. destination.

e. Levinson Stores purchased merchandise from Field, with shipping terms of F.O.B. shipping point.

f. Connor Manufacturing Company sold merchandise to Field, with shipping terms of F.O.B. shipping point.

P6-7B. **Lower-of-Cost-or-Net Realizable Value Method** The Crow Company had the following inventory at year-end:

	Quantity	Unit Price Cost	Unit Price Net Realizable Value
Desks			
Model 9001	70	$190	$215
Model 9002	45	310	268
Model 9003	20	345	360
Cabinets			
Model 7001	120	60	68
Model 7002	80	95	85
Model 7003	60	135	126

Required

a. Determine the value of the ending inventory after applying the lower-of-cost-or-net realizable value method to each item of inventory.

b. Would the net income be lower under the cost method or the lower-of-cost-or-net realizable value method?

P6-8B. **Inventory Costing Methods—Periodic Method** The following data are for the Cracker Corporation, which sells just one product:

		Units	Unit Cost
Beginning inventory, January 1		1,200	$18
Purchases	February 11	1,500	19
	May 18	1,400	20
	October 23	1,100	23
Sales	March 1	1,400	
	July 1	1,400	
	October 29	1,000	

Calculate the value of ending inventory and cost of goods sold for the year using the periodic method and (a) first-in, first-out, (b) last-in, first-out, and (c) weighted-average cost method. Round the cost per unit to 3 decimal places and round your final answers to the nearest dollar. If the replacement cost of the inventory at year-end is $25, how will the cost of goods sold under each method be affected?

P6-9B. **Physical Inventory Calculation** Household City conducted a physical inventory at December 31. The items counted during the physical inventory are listed below. Household City's accountant provided the unit costs.

Item Description	December 31 Count	Unit Cost
Taylor sofas	10	$250
Georgia sofas	8	300
Taylor chairs	22	175
Taylor recliners	16	200
Georgia recliners	4	220
Carolina lamps	16	30
Chicago lamps	20	28
Georgia tables	10	155

Required
Prepare a schedule to determine the total cost of each item in the inventory and the total cost of the complete inventory at December 31.

LO6
(Appendix 6A)

P6-10B. Inventory Costing Methods—Perpetual Method Refer to the information in P6-2B and assume the perpetual inventory system is used.

Required
a. Compute the cost of goods sold and the ending inventory cost for the month of June using the weighted-average cost method.
b. Compute the cost of goods sold and the ending inventory cost for the month of June using the first-in, first-out method.
c. Compute the cost of goods sold and the ending inventory cost for the month of June using the last-in, first-out method.

LO6
(Appendix 6A)

P6-11B. Inventory Costing Methods—Perpetual Method Refer to the information in P6-4B and assume the perpetual inventory system is used.

Required
a. Assume that Glenn uses the first-in, first-out method. Compute the cost of goods sold for 2018 and the ending inventory balance at December 31, 2018, for product B.
b. Assume that Glenn uses the last-in, first-out method. Compute the cost of goods sold for 2018 and the ending inventory balance at December 31, 2018, for product B.
c. Assume that Glenn uses the weighted-average cost method. Compute the cost of goods sold for 2018 and the ending inventory balance at December 31, 2018, for product B.
d. Assuming that Glenn sells items that quickly become obsolete, which of these three inventory costing methods would you choose to:
    1. Reflect the likely goods flow through the business?
    2. Minimize income tax for the period?
    3. Report the largest amount of net income for the period?
    Explain your answers.

LO7
(Appendix 6B)

P6-12B. The LIFO Inventory Reserve The Midwestern Manufacturing Company uses the LIFO inventory costing method to value its ending inventory. The following data were obtained from the company's accounting records:

Current assets (under FIFO)	$50,000,000
Current liabilities	38,000,000
Inventory under LIFO	16,000,000
Inventory under FIFO	18,700,000

Calculate the company's (a) LIFO inventory reserve and (b) current ratio assuming (i) FIFO and (ii) LIFO. If the company's LIFO gross profit was $18,000,000 and the change in the LIFO inventory reserve was $3,000,000, calculate the company's gross profit under FIFO.

LO6
(Appendix 6A)

P6-13B. Inventory Costing Methods—Perpetual Method Using the data in P6-8B, assume that Cracker Corporation uses the perpetual inventory system. Calculate the value of ending inventory and cost of goods sold for the year using the perpetual method and (a) first-in, first-out, (b) last-in, first-out, and

(c) weighted-average cost method. Round the cost per unit to 3 decimal places and round your final answers to the nearest dollar. If the net realizable value of the inventory at year-end is $25, how will the cost of goods sold under each method be affected?

SERIAL PROBLEM: KATE'S CARDS

(Note: This is a continuation of the Serial Problem: Kate's Cards from Chapters 1 through 5.)

SP6.   As expected, the holiday season was very busy for Kate and her greeting card company. In fact, most of her supplies were fully depleted by year-end, necessitating a restocking of inventory. Assume that Kate uses the periodic method of accounting for inventory and that her January beginning inventory was $0. The following transactions occurred for Kate's Cards during January of the New Year:

Purchases	Units		Unit Cost	Total Cost
Jan. 10	400	@	$3.00 per unit	$1,200
Jan. 17	500	@	$3.50 per unit	1,750
Jan. 23	300	@	$4.00 per unit	1,200
Total	1,200			$4,150

Sales	Units			
Jan. 15	360			
Jan. 21	420			
Jan. 27	380			
Total	1,160			

Required

a.   Calculate the company's cost of goods sold and value of ending inventory for the month of January using (1) FIFO, (2) LIFO, and (3) the weighted-average cost method. Round the cost per unit to 3 decimal places and round your final answers to the nearest dollar.

b.   If the net realizable value of Kate's inventory is $4.00 per unit on January 31, what value should be reported for her ending inventory on the January 31 balance sheet under each of the three inventory costing methods?

EXTENDING YOUR KNOWLEDGE

REPORTING AND ANALYSIS

EYK6-1.   **Financial Reporting Problem: The Columbia Sportswear Company** The financial statements for the **Columbia Sportswear Company** can be found in Appendix A at the end of this textbook.

COLUMBIA
SPORTSWEAR
COMPANY

Required

Answer the following questions using Columbia's Consolidated Financial Statements:

a.   How much inventory does Columbia carry on its balance sheet? What percentage of Columbia's total assets does inventory represent in 2017 and 2016?

b.   Compute the inventory turnover and days' sales in inventory for 2017 and 2016. Calculate inventory turnover using end of year inventory.

c.   Is Columbia's inventory management improving?

EYK6-2.   **Comparative Analysis Problem: Columbia Sportswear Company vs Under Armour, Inc.** The financial statements for **Columbia Sportswear Company** can be found in Appendix A at the end of this textbook, and the financial statements of **Under Armour, Inc.** can be found in Appendix B.

COLUMBIA
SPORTSWEAR
COMPANY

UNDER ARMOUR,
INC.

Required

a.   Compare the dollar value of inventory carried on the balance sheet by each company in 2017 and 2016. Which company carries the greatest dollar amount of inventory? Compare the ratio of inventory divided by total assets for each company for 2017 and 2016. Which company carries the largest relative investment in inventory?

b. Calculate the inventory turnover and days' sales in inventory for 2017 and 2016 for each company. Inventory at December 31, 2015, for Columbia and Under Armour, Inc. was $473.6 million and $783.0 million, respectively.

c. Which company appears to be doing the better job of managing its investment in inventory?

EYK6-3. Business Decision Problem Margaret Company is a wholesaler that uses the perpetual inventory system. On January 1, 2018, Margaret had 3,000 units of its product at a cost of $5 per unit. Transactions related to inventory during 2018 were as follows:

Purchases				Sales			
Feb. 5	9,000 units	@	$6	March 8	8,000 units	@	$ 9
May 19	20,000 units	@	7	June 21	19,000 units	@	10
Dec. 15	3,000 units	@	9	Dec. 28	4,000 units	@	12

Margaret is trying to decide whether to use the first-in, first-out (FIFO) inventory costing method or the last-in, first-out (LIFO) inventory costing method.

Required

a. Assume that Margaret decides to use the FIFO inventory costing method.
   1. What would gross profit be for 2018?
   2. How would Margaret's gross profit and ending inventory for 2018 change if the December 15, 2018, purchase had been made on January 3, 2019, instead?
   3. How would Margaret's gross profit and ending inventory for 2018 change if the December 15, 2018, purchase had been for 6,000 units instead of 3,000 units?

b. Assume that Margaret decides to use the LIFO inventory costing method.
   1. What would gross profit be for 2018?
   2. How would Margaret's gross profit and ending inventory for 2018 change if the December 15, 2018, purchase had been made on January 3, 2019, instead?
   3. How would Margaret's gross profit and ending inventory for 2018 change if the December 15, 2018, purchase had been for 6,000 units instead of 3,000 units?

c. Which inventory costing method should Margaret choose and why?

EYK6-4. Financial Analysis Problem Purpose: To use annual financial report filings to learn about how a company accounts for its inventory.

Select any publicly traded company not discussed in this chapter and go to its Website. Find the section on investor information and download its latest annual report (you may download its 10K report rather than the annual report).

Required

Using this report, answer the following questions.

a. What is the name of the company you chose and what is the primary industry that it operates in?

b. Does the company list inventory on its balance sheet? If so, where on the balance sheet does it appear?

c. Does the company have a separate note in the notes to the financial statements that provides a more detailed breakdown of the amount of inventory listed? If so, what is that breakdown?

d. What inventory method does the company use?

e. Calculate the inventory turnover ratio and days' sales in inventory for the most current year shown.

CRITICAL THINKING

GENERAL MILLS, INC.

EYK6-5. Accounting Research Problem The fiscal year 2017 annual report of General Mills, Inc. is available on this book's Website.

Required

a. What percentage of total assets is represented by General Mills' investment in inventory in 2017 and 2016?

    b. Compute the inventory turnover and days' sales in inventory for General Mills for 2017 and 2016. Calculate inventory turnover using end of year inventory.

    c. Is the company doing a better job of managing its investment in inventory in 2017?

    d. What inventory costing method does General Mills use?

    e. What is the value of the company's LIFO reserve at year-end 2017? General Mills labels its LIFO reserve as the "Excess of FIFO over LIFO cost" in Note 17. (Appendix 6B)

EYK6-6. **Accounting Communications Activity** **Pactiv Corporation** is a leader in the consumer and foodservice packaging market. In December 2009 the company announced a change in the accounting for inventories. www.businesswire.com/news/home/20091221005622/en/ Pactiv-Announces-Inventory-Accounting-Change-LIFO-FIFO

PACTIV CORPORATION

Required

Sarah Jenkins, CEO of a competing firm, read this announcement, but was confused about what exactly Pactiv was doing. She asked that you write a memo explaining the following items.

    a. What about its accounting for inventory was Pactiv changing?

    b. Why does Pactiv believe the new method is preferable?

    c. What benefit does Pactiv believe will be realized from the change?

EYK6-7. **Accounting Ethics Case** Reed Kohler is in his final year of employment as controller for Quality Sales Corporation; he hopes to retire next year. As a member of top management, Kohler participates in an attractive company bonus plan. The overall size of the bonus is a function of the firm's net income before bonus and income taxes—the larger net income, the larger the bonus.

    Due to a slowdown in the economy, Quality Sales Corporation has encountered difficulties in managing its cash flow. To improve its cash flow by reducing cash payments for income taxes, the firm's auditors have recommended that the company change its inventory costing method from FIFO to LIFO. This change would cause a significant increase in the cost of goods sold for the year. Kohler believes the firm should not switch to LIFO this year because its inventory quantities are too large. He believes that the firm should work to reduce its inventory quantities and then switch to LIFO (the switch could be made in a year or two). After expressing this opinion to the firm's treasurer, Kohler is stunned when the treasurer replies: "Reed, I can't believe that after all these years with the firm, you put your personal interests ahead of the firm's interests."

    Explain why Kohler may be viewed as holding a position that favors his personal interests. What can Kohler do to increase his credibility when the possible change to LIFO is discussed at a meeting of the firm's top management next week?

EYK6-8. **Corporate Social Responsibility Problem** The Corporate Social Responsibility highlight in this chapter discussed how **Best Buy** is working to make sure its supply chain complies with the company's high ethical standards. One of the ways this is done is for Best Buy's Global Sourcing team to work with their Social and Environmental Responsibility team.

BEST BUY

    Go to the Best Buy Website and its page on Corporate Responsibility & Sustainability (https://corporate.bestbuy.com/sustainability/) and locate Best Buy's Fiscal Year 2017 Sustainability Report. Open the report and scroll down to the section entitled: "Responsible Sourcing." The Supply Chain Sustainability (SCS) Program seeks to control risk, enhance the partnership with suppliers (by building their capacity for responsible business practices), and to create value for all stakeholders. The supplier code of conduct and the audit methodology are intended to create business value by improving working and environmental conditions in the supply chain. Explain the six parts of the code of conduct and the factory audit program utilized in the SCS program.

EYK6-9. **Forensic Accounting Problem** The chapter highlights an inventory fraud case at **Crazy Eddie**. Unfortunately there have been many other serious inventory frauds where the auditors were fooled by illegal acts. A few of these cases include (1) **Comptronix Corporation**, (2) **Leslie Fay Company**, (3) **Laribee Manufacturing Company**, and (4) **Phar-Mor** drug stores.

CRAZY EDDIE
COMPTRONIX CORPORATION
LESLIE FAY COMPANY
LARIBEE MANUFACTURING COMPANY
PHAR-MOR

    Do a computer search of one of these cases and explain how inventory was used to commit the fraud. List some ways the auditors can lessen the chance such frauds could go undetected.

EYK6-10. **Inventory Turnover and Days' Sales in Inventory: IFRS Financial Statements** The 2017 financial statements of LVMH Moet Hennessey-Louis Vuitton S.A. are presented in Appendix C at the end of this book. LVMH is a Paris-based holding company and one of the world's largest and best-known luxury goods companies. As a member of the European Union, French companies are

LO5
IFRS

required to prepare their consolidated (group) financial statements using International Financial Reporting Standards (IFRS). LVMH's IFRS financial statements are presented in Appendix C at the end of this textbook. Using these financial statements, calculate the company's (a) inventory turnover and (b) days' sales in inventory for 2016 and 2017. Comment on the company's trend in inventory management effectiveness.

LO7
(Appendix 6B)

EYK6-11. **Working with the Takeaways** Unger Company uses the LIFO inventory costing method to value inventory. The following financial data were obtained from its accounting records for the current year:

Current assets (including inventory)..	$4,000
Current liabilities...	2,000
Inventory under LIFO...	575
Inventory under FIFO...	775

Compute (a) the current ratio assuming (i) LIFO and (ii) FIFO and (b) the LIFO inventory reserve.

ANSWERS TO SELF-STUDY QUESTIONS:

1. b, (p. 275)   2. d, (p. 281)   3. c, (pp. 280–281)   4. b, (p. 276)   5. d, (p. 289)   6. c, (pp. 283–284)
7. a, (p. 285)   8. b, (p. 285)   9. d, (pp. 283–284)   10. d, (pp. 288–290)   11. b, (pp. 290–291)
12. c, (pp. 298–299) 13. b, (pp. 297–298)

YOUR TURN! SOLUTIONS

Solution 6.1

The $15,000 of goods shipped F.O.B. shipping point should be deducted from the inventory valuation, and the $25,000 of consignment goods should be included in the inventory valuation. The corrected ending inventory total should be $310,000 ($300,000 − $15,000 + $25,000).

Solution 6.2

a. Ending inventory using:

   i. FIFO: 1,000 × $7 = $7,000
   ii. LIFO: 1,000 × $5 = $5,000
   iii. Weighted-average cost: 1,000 × [(4,000 × $5) + (6,000 × $7)]/10,000 = 1,000 × $6.20 = $6,200

b. Cost of goods sold using:

   i. FIFO: (4,000 × $5) + (5,000 × $7) = $55,000
   ii. LIFO: (6,000 × $7) + (3,000 × $5) = $57,000
   iii. Weighted-average cost: 9,000 × [(4,000 × $5) + (6,000 × $7)]/10,000 = 9,000 × $6.20 = $55,800

c. Gross profit using:

   i. FIFO: $90,000 − $55,000 = $35,000
   ii. LIFO: $90,000 − $57,000 = $33,000
   iii. Weighted-average cost: $90,000 − $55,800 = $34,200

Solution 6.3

	Cost of Goods Sold	Beginning Inventory		Purchases		Ending Inventory
2018	$7,000 (instead of $7,500)	$ —	+	$10,000	−	$3,000
2019	$13,000 (instead of $12,500)	$ 3,000	+	$15,000	−	$5,000

		With Error	Without Error
2018			
	Sales.	$15,000	$15,000
	Cost of goods sold	7,500	7,000
	Net income	$ 7,500	$ 8,000
2019			
	Sales.	$25,000	$25,000
	Cost of goods sold	12,500	13,000
	Net income	$12,500	$12,000

Solution 6.4

The lowest value for each inventory item is: DSLR $110,000, Point and Shoot $73,000, and Camcorders $48,000. The total of the inventory is therefore valued under LCM at $231,000 ($110,000 + $73,000 + $48,000).

Solution 6.5

	2018	2019
Inventory turnover.	$\dfrac{\$2,000,000}{(\$450,000 + \$430,000)/2} = 4.55$	$\dfrac{\$2,300,000}{(\$430,000 + \$320,000)/2} = 6.13$
Days' sales in inventory	365/4.55 = 80.22 days	365/6.13 = 59.54 days

The company increased its sales by $400,000 from 2018 to 2019, and at the same time, decreased its average inventory by $65,000 ($440,000 − $375,000) as a consequence of improved inventory management. This resulted in a significantly improved inventory turnover (6.13 versus 4.55) and 20.68 (80.22 − 59.54) less days' sales in inventory. It appears that the new inventory management system is a financial success.

Solution 6A.1

FIFO

		Purchased			Sold			Inventory Balance		
Date	Units	Unit Cost	Total	Units	Unit Cost	Total	Units	Unit Cost	Total
Jan. 1							1,000	$5.00	$5,000
Jan. 5	600	$6.00	$3,600				1,000	5.00	8,600
							600	6.00	
Jan. 15 . . .				200	$5.00	$1,000	800	5.00	7,600
							600	6.00	
Jan. 17 . . .	300	7.00	2,100				800	5.00	9,700
							600	6.00	
							300	7.00	
Jan. 25 . . .				400	5.00	2,000	400	5.00	7,700
							600	6.00	
						$3,000	300	7.00	

LIFO

Date	Units	Purchased Unit Cost	Total	Units	Sold Unit Cost	Total	Units	Inventory Balance Unit Cost	Total
Jan. 1							1,000	$5.00	$5,000
Jan. 5	600	$6.00	$3,600				1,000 / 600	5.00 / 6.00	8,600
Jan. 15 ...				200	$6.00	$1,200	1,000 / 400	5.00 / 6.00	7,400
Jan. 17 ...	300	7.00	2,100				1,000 / 400 / 300	5.00 / 6.00 / 7.00	9,500
Jan. 25 ...				300 / 100	7.00 / 6.00	2,700	1,000 / 300	5.00 / 6.00	6,800
						$3,900			

Weighted Average

Date	Units	Purchased Unit Cost	Total	Units	Sold Unit Cost	Total	Units	Inventory Balance Unit Cost	Total
Jan. 1							1,000	$5.000	$5,000
Jan. 5	600	$6.00	$3,600				1,600	5.375	8,600
Jan. 15 ...				200	$5.375	$1,075	1,400	5.375	7,525
Jan. 17 ...	300	7.00	2,100				1,700	5.662	9,625
Jan. 25 ...				400	5.662	2,265	1,300	5.662	7,360
						$3,340			

Solution 6B.1
$165,000 + $20,000 = $185,000

Chapter 7
Internal Control and Cash

PAST

Chapter 6 explained the accounting for inventory. We described and applied the costing methods of specific identification, FIFO, LIFO, and weighted-average.

PRESENT

In this chapter, we focus our attention on another current asset, cash. In addition, we study how internal control can be used to prevent errors and fraud associated with assets such as cash and inventory.

FUTURE

Chapter 8 explains the accounting for accounts and notes receivable. We will explain the reporting of uncollectible accounts and how managers monitor such accounts.

If you were given the list of checks shown in the table to the right and were asked if you noticed anything unusual, what would you say? The list represents the checks that a manager at the Arizona State Treasurer wrote to embezzle funds for his own use. All the vendors to whom these checks were written were fictitious.[1]

If you were a forensic accountant trained in such techniques as Benford's Law (see Forensic Accounting box on page 330 of this chapter), you would have had no trouble noticing that the amounts on these checks were made to look random, but were anything but random. In fact, the pattern of the check amounts is almost the direct opposite of what Benford's Law would predict.

Benford's Law is one of many techniques forensic accountants use to catch fraud. It is estimated that the typical organization loses 5 percent of its revenue to fraud each year. According to the Association of Certified Fraud Examiners, this percentage loss translates to nearly $4 trillion worldwide. Although detecting fraud is important, it is far better to keep fraud from occurring in the first place. Developing a knowledge of the elements of fraud and understanding how internal controls can prevent fraud are critical to all organizations.

In this chapter, we study internal controls. Perhaps this discussion will inspire some of you to embark on a career in forensic accounting. Who knows, you may even inspire a new television series, "CSI Accounting!"

Date of Check	Amount
October 9	$ 1,927.48
	27,902.31
October 14	86,241.90
	72,117.46
	81,321.75
	97,473.96
October 19	93,249.11
	89,658.17
	87,776.89
	92,105.83
	79,949.16
	87,602.93
	96,879.27
	91,806.47
	84,991.67
	90,831.83
	93,766.67
	88,338.72
	94,639.49
	83,709.28
	96,412.21
	88,432.86
	71,552.16
TOTAL	**$1,878,687.58**

[1] Mark J. Nigrini, I've Got Your Number, *Journal of Accountancy*, April 30, 1999.

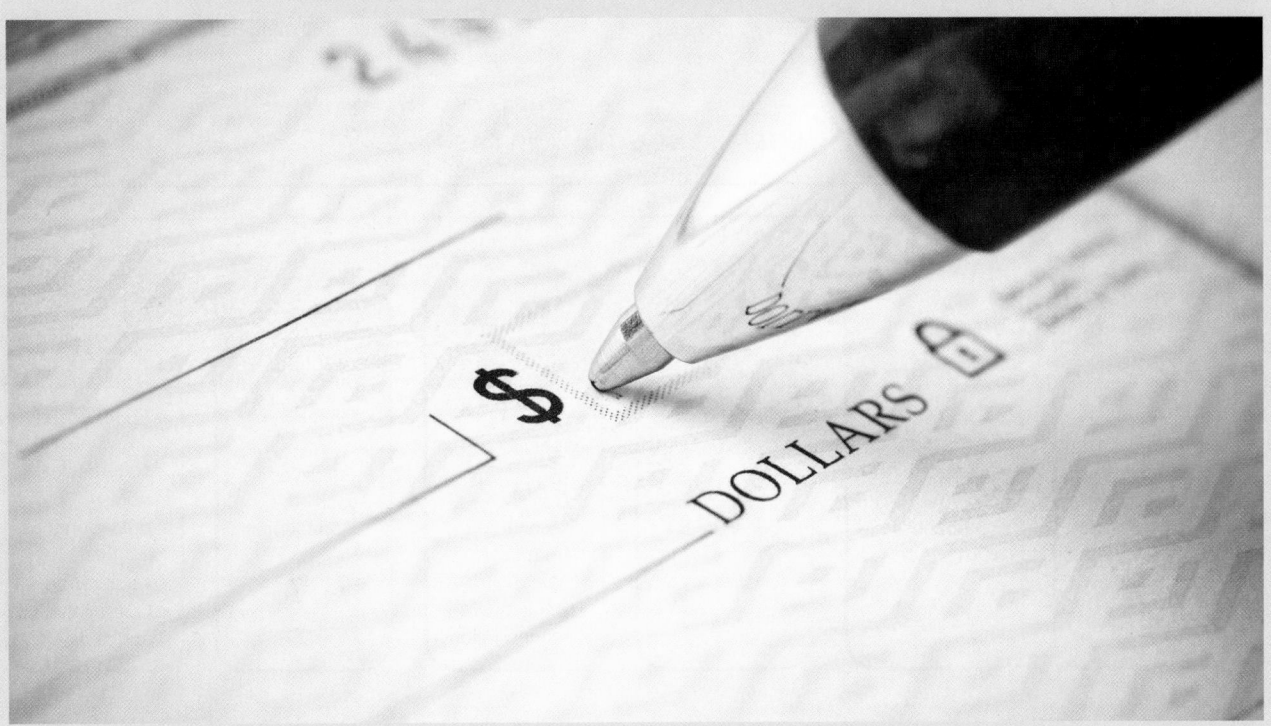

Road Map

LO	Learning Objective	Page	eLecture	Guided Example	Assignments
LO1	Define the three elements of fraud.	326	E7-1	YT7.1	SS1, SE1
LO2	Discuss how the COSO framework helps prevent fraud, identify potential internal control failures, and discuss SOX regulations.	327	E7-2	YT7.2	SS2, SS3, SS4 SE2, SE3, SE4, SE5, E1A, E5A, E1B, E5B, P1A, P2A, P7A, P8A, P1B, P2B,P7B, P8B
LO3	Define cash and discuss the accounting for cash.	333	E7-3	YT7.3	SS6, SE6, SE7, E7A, E7B, P6A, P6B
LO4	Describe the internal controls for cash.	335	E7-4	YT7.4	SS7, SS10, SE8, SE9, E2A, E2B, P1A, P2A, P3A, P8A, P1B, P2B, P3B, P8B
LO5	Illustrate the bank reconciliation process.	341	E7-5	YT7.5	SS8, SS9, E3A, E4A, E3B, E4B, P4A, P5A, P9A, P4B, P5B, P9B
LO6	Describe the four primary activities of effective cash management.	346	E7-6	YT7.6, YT7.7	SE10, E6A, E6B, P10A
LO7	Appendix 7A: Describe financial statement audits and operational audits.	349	E7-7	YT7A.1	SS5, SE4, E8A, E9A, E8B, E9B

FRAUD

Infamous stories of fraud involving **Enron Corporation** and **Madoff Investment Securities LLC** illustrate the potential cost that fraud can have on so many people. Unfortunately, it is nearly impossible to completely prevent fraud; however, we do know much about why fraud is committed and what can be done to lower the risk of it occurring. Research has shown that any individual, under the right circumstances, can commit fraud. This does not mean, however, that everyone will commit fraud. What it does mean is that it is very difficult to determine prior to the commission of a fraud exactly which employee will be the one to commit fraud.

Fraud refers to any act by the management or employees of a business involving an intentional deception for personal gain. Fraud may include, among other acts, embezzlement of a business's cash, theft of assets, filing false insurance claims, filing false health claims, and financial statement fraud. Fraud is a punishable crime and is also a violation of civil law.

Fraud Triangle

Research has shown that three elements are almost always present when a fraud occurs. These elements are often referred to as the **fraud triangle** and include (1) a perceived pressure, (2) some way to rationalize the fraudulent act, and (3) a perceived opportunity. Reducing or suppressing any of the three elements of the fraud triangle reduces the likelihood of fraud occurring in a business.

Unfortunately, the fraud triangle is not well understood. Because of this, nearly all fraud prevention efforts by businesses are devoted to the third element—reducing the opportunity to commit fraud. Too often, little effort is expended on the other elements of fraud even though it has been shown that efforts in any one area can reduce the effort needed in the other two areas.

Pressure

Pressure can be divided into several categories, but research has shown that nearly all frauds are committed by individuals who feel perceived pressure from some sort of financial need. Financial pressure could come from living beyond one's means and being unable to pay one's bills, experiencing large medical bills, or the financial pressure from vices like gambling, drugs, or alcohol. The latter pressure is sometimes referred to as vice pressure.

Financial statement fraud, such as the overstatement of revenues or the understatement of expenses, usually occurs because of pressure on management to "make the numbers," either to satisfy Wall Street analyst expectations or to attain a company-sponsored monetary bonus.

Although it is not possible to completely eliminate this element of fraud, numerous methods have proven successful at lowering the risk of financial statement fraud. An obvious action is to perform careful personnel screening before hiring any employee to reduce the likelihood of employing individuals with known histories of fraud.

Rationalization

Very few individuals want to commit fraud since they recognize that it is wrong. In order to overcome this tremendous feeling of guilt, most employees need to come up with some form of rationalization so that they can live with the knowledge of what they did. Common rationalizations include such attitudes as (1) I am underpaid and the company owes it to me; (2) Everyone else is doing it; or (3) I am only borrowing the money and I will pay it back later.

The best way to reduce this element of fraud is to create an environment in which it is difficult to rationalize unethical behavior. A company that promotes a culture of honesty and integrity, within which unethical behavior is considered unacceptable, is much less likely to encounter fraudulent behavior by management or its employees. The key to building organization-wide attitudes regarding ethical behavior starts with the "tone at the top"—that is, the behaviors and attitudes displayed by a company's CEO or president.

Opportunity

The third element of the fraud triangle is perceived opportunity. An individual will only attempt to commit a fraud if he or she perceives that there is an opportunity to succeed. Of course this element is related to the other two elements. For example, if an employee is under tremendous pressure either at work or outside the workplace, he may attempt to commit a fraud even if he perceives only a small chance of success, while an individual under much less pressure will likely only attempt the fraud if it is perceived to be easy to commit.

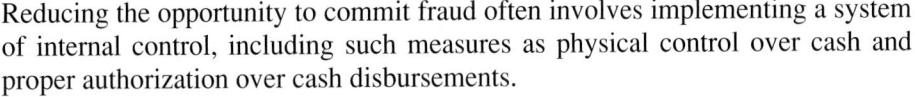

Identify the element of the fraud triangle associated with each of the following statements:
1. "I take full responsibility for what happened. But saying that, I know in my mind that I did nothing criminal."
2. "We were constantly told we would end up working for McDonald's. If we did not make the sales quotas, we had to stay for what felt like after-school detention, or report to a call session on Saturdays."
3. "The attitude was sort of, 'If you're doing something wrong, we don't want to know.'"

YOUR TURN! 7.1

The solution is on page 371.

eLectures
MBC

INTERNAL CONTROL

Reducing the opportunity to commit fraud often involves implementing a system of internal control, including such measures as physical control over cash and proper authorization over cash disbursements.

LO2 **Discuss** how the COSO framework helps prevent fraud, **identify** potential internal control failures, and **discuss** SOX regulations.

COSO Framework

In 1992, the Committee on Sponsoring Organizations of the Treadway Commission (COSO) released a framework to help companies structure and evaluate their internal controls. Twenty years later, in 2013, COSO updated their framework to reflect changes in business environments brought about by developments such as technological advancements and increasing globalization.

The COSO framework identifies five internal control components: (1) the control environment, (2) risk assessment, (3) control activities, (4) information and communication, and (5) monitoring activities.

1. Control Environment

The **control environment** sets the tone of the organization. An environment of ethical values and integrity is crucial to keeping employees from feeling that it is acceptable to commit fraud. The control environment provides the foundation for all other components of internal control. Included in the control environment are management's philosophy and management style; the organizational structure and assignment of authority and responsibility; the process for attracting and developing competent employees; and the rewards to drive accountability for performance.

CORPORATE SOCIAL RESPONSIBILITY	**Governance and Conflicts of Interest**

Much of what was done at **Enron** was perfectly legal. Enron's management became very skilled at staying within the letter of the law, even if it meant violating the spirit of the law. For example, Enron used specialized accounting rules that allowed them to mask the true level of its debt so that financial statement users would be unable to obtain a transparent view of the company's financial position. Top executives at Enron created a culture of deceit within the company that provided employees with an easy rationalization for their own misdeeds. Corporate Social Responsibility, by way of contrast, espouses the notion that not only is it important to make money, but it is important to do so in a responsible way. Cutting corners and playing fast and loose with the rules may work in the short term, but it is not sustainable in the long run as the Enron saga reveals. Creating a culture of ethical behavior within a business is perhaps the most important internal control that exists to not only prevent fraud, but to provide a foundation for a sustainable enterprise.

2. Risk Assessment

Every organization faces a variety of different risks from both internal and external sources. Risk is defined as the possibility that an event will occur that has a negative impact on the organization's objectives. **Risk assessment** involves identifying and analyzing relevant risks to an organization's objectives. Because items external to the organization such as the economic conditions, industry competitors, and regulations, along with internal items such as operating conditions are constantly changing, risk assessment must be an ongoing dynamic and iterative process.

3. Control Activities

The accounting system represents a cornerstone of the control environment that is necessary to reduce the opportunity for, and success of, fraudulent behavior. A critical aspect of the accounting system is a strong system of internal controls. **Internal controls** are the measures undertaken by a business to ensure the reliability of its accounting data, protect its assets from theft or unauthorized use, ensure that employees are following the company's policies and procedures, and evaluate the performance of employees, departments, divisions, and the company as a whole. Management is responsible for designing, installing, and monitoring internal controls throughout the business with the intent of attaining "reasonable assurance," rather than "absolute assurance," that the controls will meet their objectives.

Control activities are the specific policies and procedures designed to reduce risk. A control activity can be either a prevention control or a detection control. A **prevention control** is intended to deter a problem or fraud before it can arise. A **detection control**, on the other hand, is designed to discover any problems or fraud shortly after it arises. Prevention controls are generally more desirable and preferred than detection controls, reflecting the old saying that "an ounce of prevention is worth a pound of detection."

A company should incorporate the following elements when it designs its prevention and detection controls:

- Establish clear lines of authority and responsibility.
- Implement segregation of duties.
- Hire competent personnel.
- Use control numbers on all business documents.
- Develop plans and budgets.
- Maintain adequate accounting records.
- Provide physical and electronic controls.

We consider each of these elements in the following paragraphs and provide examples of their use.

Establish Clear Lines of Authority and Responsibility

The organizational structure of a company defines the lines of authority and responsibility within the company. It informs employees about who is in charge of which functions and to whom each person reports.

The existence of an identified supervisor is a prevention control. Employees know that the supervisor is evaluating their performance; consequently, they are more likely to perform according to a company's established policies and rules. Supervision is also a detection control. A supervisor is likely to discover errors or irregularities when he or she reviews the work performance of employees.

Implement Segregation of Duties

Segregation of duties requires that when allocating various duties within the accounting system, management should make sure that no employee is assigned too many different responsibilities. As a general rule, no individual employee should be able to perpetrate and conceal irregularities in the transaction processing system. To accomplish this, management must separate three functions: the authorization function, the recording function, and the custody function.

When an employee prepares a purchase order to buy merchandise, that employee is effectively "authorizing" the transaction. When the merchandise is received, a second employee should prepare the receiving report when he or she gains "custody" of the merchandise. And, neither of these two employees should be allowed to "record" the purchase order, the receipt of the merchandise, or the payment of cash for the goods in the accounting records. Separating the work functions in this manner will reduce the likelihood of fraud occurring because committing a fraud when work duties are separated requires collusion among multiple employees. Proper segregation of duties is a prevention control.

Hire Competent Personnel

Because people are the most important element of an accounting system, it is vital that a company hire competent personnel. Management must screen each job applicant to determine that he or she has sufficient education, training, and experience to qualify for the job. After hiring an employee, the company should provide specific formal training so that the employee is able to complete all of the tasks that the job requires. The training should refer to written policy statements, procedure manuals, and job descriptions so that the employee can become familiar with all aspects and expectations of his or her job. Hiring and training employees is a prevention control.

Some companies routinely rotate personnel among various jobs. For example, a company might switch jobs between an employee working exclusively with the accounts receivable and an employee working exclusively with accounts payable. This rotation may disclose errors or irregularities resulting from over-familiarity with a job or just carelessness. Requiring employees to take vacations of at least one week in duration may also disclose errors or irregularities when another employee performs the vacationing employee's duties. These personnel policies act as a detection control.

ACCOUNTING IN PRACTICE	**Job Rotation and Mandatory Vacations as Internal Controls**

Job rotation and mandatory vacations are some of the best internal controls for uncovering fraud. For many frauds, it is necessary for the perpetrator to actively cover up his or her misdeeds through the falsification of accounting records. Requiring job rotation and vacations allows another employee to perform these job responsibilities, often leading to the discovery of fraud. And you thought your employer was only giving you that vacation to be nice!

Source: Association of Certified Fraud Examiners 2008 Report.

Use Control Numbers on All Business Documents

All business documents such as purchase orders, sales invoices, credit memos, and checks should have **control numbers** preprinted on them. Each control number should be unique for that type of document. For example, the bank checks that you use to pay your personal expenses have control numbers on them, usually in the upper right-hand corner of the check, referred to as a *check number*. These numbers act as a detection control enabling you to track each check written, and to ensure that no one has written an improper check against your account.

Develop Plans and Budgets

Top management should initiate the planning and budgeting process to establish forward thinking about the business and to provide a basis for evaluating department and employee

FORENSIC ACCOUNTING	**Benford's Law and Data Analytics Aids Accounting Sleuths**

How often should the number 9 appear as the first digit of an amount reported on a financial statement? If you say one out of ten times you, like most people, would be wrong. It turns out the number 9 should appear less than 5 percent of the time, whereas the number 1 will appear as the first digit of a reported amount over 30 percent of the time! This numerical phenomenon, known as Benford's Law, was discovered by Frank Benford while working as a physicist at the GE Research Laboratories.

An intuitive explanation of Benford's Law appeared in the *Journal of Accountancy* in the article "I've Got Your Number" written by Mark Nigrini. Nigrini offered an explanation that considered "the total assets of a mutual fund that is growing at 10 percent per year. When the total assets are $100 million, the first digit of total assets is 1. The first digit will continue to be 1 until total assets reach $200 million. This will require a 100 percent increase (from 100 to 200), which, at a growth rate of 10 percent per year, will take about 7.3 years (with compounding). At $500 million the first digit will be 5. Growing at 10 percent per year, the total assets will rise from $500 million to $600 million in about 1.9 years, significantly less time than assets took to grow from $100 million to $200 million. At $900 million, the first digit will be 9 until total assets reach $1 billion, or about 1.1 years at 10 percent. Once total assets are $1 billion the first digit will again be 1, until total assets again grow by another 100 percent. The persistence of a 1 as a first digit will occur with any phenomenon that has a constant (or even an erratic) growth rate."

The expected frequency of the first digits in a dataset of numbers is as follows:

1	2	3	4	5	6	7	8	9
30.1%	17.6%	12.5%	9.7%	7.9%	6.7%	5.8%	5.1%	4.6%

An excellent example of accountants at KPMG leveraging data analytics occurred when Benford's Law was used in the audit of a call center. The call center allowed hundreds of operators to issue refunds up to $50 without manager approval. What the audit found was that there were way too many refunds that began with a 4. The accountants soon found that several operators were issuing refunds just under the $50 limit to friends, family members, and even more boldly, to themselves. The total fraud, uncovered with the aid of data analytics and Benford's Law, amounted to hundreds of thousands of dollars of fraudulent refunds.

performance. Every company should prepare an annual operating plan and budget. These items provide guidance for all levels of management regarding how to respond to various situations. The budget also provides a basis for comparing actual operating results to planned results when management evaluates operating unit performance. An example of evaluating performance involves comparing the actual advertising expense to the budgeted advertising expense. When variances between actual and budgeted amounts are observed, those variances should be investigated by management. This type of control activity is both a prevention control and a detection control.

Maintain Adequate Accounting Records

In previous chapters, we discussed a number of detection controls that help ensure that a business has adequate accounting records. These controls include using the double-entry approach to record transactions (debits must equal credits), preparing trial balances (total debits must equal total credits), and taking a physical count of the inventory on hand (physical inventory total should equal perpetual inventory total).

Many control activities related to maintaining accurate accounting records involve comparisons of various amounts. For instance, each business should periodically make a physical inspection of its plant assets to compare the data in the plant assets' ledger account to the plant assets actually in use. This inspection identifies any missing assets and any assets not recorded in the asset account. Similarly, a business should periodically confirm the amounts owed to suppliers (Accounts Payable) and the amounts due from customers (Accounts Receivable) by contacting the suppliers and customers to verify any amounts owed or to be received. This internal control process is known as accounts receivable confirmation and accounts payable confirmation.

Provide Physical and Electronic Controls

Physical and electronic controls are prevention controls that take many forms. Locked doors are an important physical control. Locked doors help prevent the theft of assets and protect the integrity of the accounting system. Many companies install safes and vaults to store cash prior to depositing it in a bank and to hold important business documents such as mortgages and securities. Any installed safes and vaults should be of sufficient quality that they can withstand fire and such natural disasters as flooding and tornados. Fencing off company property and assigning security guards at the gates are other commonly used physical controls.

Electronic controls are also widely used by businesses. Merchandising firms use electronic cash registers to ensure that each salesperson records each transaction as it occurs and that the salesperson stores cash in a locked drawer. Retailers, convenience stores, and banks use observation cameras to monitor their operations. Retailers also attach special plastic tags to merchandise, which activate electronic sensors and set off alarms if an individual attempts to leave a store without having the plastic tag removed by a salesperson.

4. Information and Communication

The fourth control component of the COSO framework involves communication. It is important that individuals receive a clear message from senior management that control responsibilities must be taken seriously. To do this, management must obtain or generate relevant and quality information from both internal and external sources. This information must then be communicated in a continual and iterative process of providing, sharing, and then obtaining new information.

5. Monitoring Activities

It is necessary for the internal control system to be monitored in order to assess the quality of the system's performance over time. Monitoring activities involve ongoing evaluations, special evaluations, or some combination of each. Ongoing evaluations are built into the business processes at various levels of the organization and provide timely information.

Special evaluations are conducted periodically and vary in scope and frequency based on risk assessments, results from ongoing evaluations, and other management considerations.

Internal Audits

Internal audits are one type of monitoring activity. In a small company, internal auditing is a function typically assigned to an employee who has other duties as well. In a large company, internal auditing is an activity assigned to an independent department that reports to top management or the board of directors of the corporation. **Internal auditing** is a company function that provides independent appraisals of the company's financial statements, its internal control, and its operations.

The evaluation of a company's internal control involves two phases. First, the internal auditor determines whether sufficient internal controls are in place. Second, the internal auditor determines whether the internal controls in place are actually functioning as planned. After completing the appraisal, the internal auditor makes recommendations to management regarding additional controls that are needed or improvements that are required for existing controls.

ACCOUNTING IN PRACTICE

Blockchain and the Future of Accounting

When most people hear the word *blockchain*, they likely think of Bitcoin. What makes blockchain so important for cybercurrencies like Bitcoin also makes it likely to revolutionize the future of accounting. Blockchain technology, which is also known as distributed ledger technology, allows multiple parties to a transaction to securely share a database. Blockchain has the potential to create a completely traceable audit trail, and could potentially automate the entire financial audit. While the future possibilities appear endless, current applications in addition to auditing include cybersecurity and financial planning and analysis.

Control Failures

Occasionally, internal controls fail. For example, an employee may forget to lock an exterior door and a thief will steal some merchandise. Or, an employee with custody responsibilities steals cash received from customers. A company cannot completely prevent these types of incidents from occurring. Consequently, many businesses purchase insurance to compensate the company if any of these types of incidents do occur. Casualty insurance provides financial compensation to a business for losses from fire, natural disasters, and theft. A **fidelity bond** is an insurance policy that provides financial compensation for theft by employees specifically covered by the insurance.

Another reason that internal controls fail is **employee collusion**. When two or more employees work together to circumvent or avoid prescribed internal controls, this act is known as *employee collusion*. For example, an employee with custody of an asset (like cash) can work with an employee with recording responsibilities to steal the asset and cover up the theft in the accounting records. Employee collusion is difficult to prevent or detect. Hiring high-quality employees and paying them market wages is the best approach to avoid collusion. Close employee supervision is also important.

THINKING GLOBALLY

While it might appear that financial fraud occurs only in the United States, that is far from the truth. For example, in 2008, India's leading software services firm, **Satyam Computer Services**, was found to have defrauded stockholders for more than a decade by overstating the company's revenues and its cash by over $1 billion. The company's independent auditors, **PricewaterhouseCoopers**, were arrested shortly thereafter on charges of being an accomplice to the financial fraud.

As with employee collusion, senior management can often circumvent internal controls. Additionally, in small companies where proper segregation of duties is not possible, the owner must serve as the mitigating control. This requires the owner to be present most of the time and also provides opportunity for the owner to circumvent internal controls.

The Sarbanes-Oxley Act

For public companies, strong internal controls like those described above are no longer simply a matter of good business practice; they are required by law. Following the **Enron** and **WorldCom** accounting scandals, the U.S. Congress passed landmark legislation called the Sarbanes-Oxley Act (SOX). This act mandates that all publicly traded U.S. corporations maintain an adequate system of internal controls. Further, top management must ensure the reliability of these controls and outside independent auditors must attest to the adequacy of the controls. Failing to do so can result in prison sentences of up to 20 years and/or monetary fines of up to $5 million.

Concept ➝	Method ➝	Assessment	TAKEAWAY 7.1
Are the internal controls adequate?	The COSO framework identifies five internal control components: (1) the control environment, (2) risk assessment, (3) control activities, (4) information and communication, and (5) monitoring activities.	Monitoring activities include appraisals of the company's internal control system. If weaknesses are reported, be cautious in relying on the reported financial statements.	

YOUR TURN! 7.2

The solution is on page 371.

Identify which internal control concept is being violated and explain how this may cause an opportunity for fraud to occur within a business:

1. The supervisor for the purchasing department has not taken a vacation in three years.
2. Inventory is left in a receiving area at the back of the store by an open door.
3. The purchasing supervisor has the authority to order a purchase and also to receive the merchandise, record its receipt, and authorize the accounting department to issue a check.

ACCOUNTING FOR CASH

eLectures
MBC

Cash includes coins, currency (paper money), checks, money orders, traveler's checks, and funds on deposit at a financial institution in a company's checking and savings accounts. An item is considered to be an element of cash if (1) it is accepted by a bank or other financial institution (brokerage firm or credit union) for deposit, and (2) it is free from restrictions that would prevent its use for paying debts.

LO3 **Define** cash and **discuss** the accounting for cash.

Many near-cash items such as certificates of deposit, postdated checks, not-sufficient-funds checks, and IOUs are not considered to be cash. **Certificates of deposit** (CDs) are securities issued by a bank when cash is invested for a short period of time, typically three months to one year. CDs pay a fixed rate of interest on any deposited funds. A **postdated check** is a check from another person or company with a date that is later than the current date. A postdated check does not become equivalent to cash until the actual calendar date on the check. A **not-sufficient-funds check** (**NSF** check) is a check from an individual or company that had an insufficient cash balance in the bank when the holder of the check presented it to the bank for payment. IOU is a slang term for a note receivable—that is, a written document that states that one party promises to pay another party a certain amount of cash on a certain date. CDs are accounted for as investments, whereas postdated checks, NSF checks, and IOUs are accounted for as Other Receivables.

Reporting Cash

A company may have only one Cash account in the general ledger or it may have multiple cash accounts, such as Cash in Bank, Cash on Hand, and Petty Cash. Cash in Bank includes any cash held in a company's checking and savings accounts, while Cash on Hand includes cash items not yet deposited in the bank. Petty Cash is an example of cash on hand that is used for small disbursements and is maintained at the company's business location.

When a company has several bank accounts, it may maintain a separate general ledger account for each account or use a single Cash in Bank account. Although a company may prepare for internal use only a balance sheet that shows each individual bank account separately, the balance sheet that the company prepares for external users typically shows the combined balances of all bank accounts and other cash accounts under a single heading of Cash. Management is likely to want to see the detail involving the multiple cash accounts that the company maintains so that it can monitor and control the various accounts and on hand amounts. Most external users, however, are only interested in the total amount of cash and its relationship to other items on the balance sheet.

ACCOUNTING IN PRACTICE	**Balance Sheet Title for Cash**

Cash is cash, or is it? Companies often include many other items, such as certificates of deposit, that are very similar to cash in their Cash account. Companies also vary in the title they use for their Cash account on their balance sheet. In fact, Cash is not the most common term used. Cash and Cash Equivalents is by far the most commonly used label. The following table identifies the label used by a sample of 600 large U.S. firms for their Cash account on the balance sheet:

Source: Accounting Trends and Techniques

Cash is a current asset and is shown first in the balance sheet listing of assets. Some of a company's cash may be **restricted cash**, meaning that the cash is restricted for a special purpose. For example, a company may have a restriction on its cash to cover a litigation settlement. Restricted cash should be reported separately on the balance sheet as either a current or noncurrent asset depending on the length of the restriction. Sometimes a company's total cash includes one or more compensating balances. A **compensating balance** is a minimum cash balance that a bank requires a firm to maintain in its bank account as part of a borrowing arrangement. Compensating balances related to short-term borrowings are current assets, which, if significant, are reported separately from the cash amount among the current assets. Compensating balances related to long-term borrowings are reported as long-term assets.

Cash and Cash Equivalents

A company may combine certain short-term, highly liquid investments with cash and present a single amount called **cash and cash equivalents** on the balance sheet. Cash equivalents are highly liquid, short-term investments of 90 days maturity or less in such risk-free securities as U.S. Treasury bills and money market funds. A company presents this combined amount on the balance sheet so that it reconciles with the change in cash and cash equivalents appearing on the company's statement of cash flows. The statement of cash flows explains the changes in a firm's total cash and cash equivalents during an accounting period.

Concept	→	Method	→	Assessment	TAKEAWAY 7.2
Are there any restrictions on a company's use of its cash and cash equivalents?		Balance sheet and the notes to the financial statements. Are there any restrictions to cash or compensating cash balances reported?		Any assessments of liquidity should consider any existing cash restrictions.	

All of the following are typically included in the cash and cash equivalents account except:
a. Cash
b. Marketable securities
c. Money market funds
d. 30-day U.S. Treasury bills

YOUR TURN! 7.3

The solution is on page 371.

INTERNAL CONTROL OF CASH RECEIPTS TRANSACTIONS

Most companies develop elaborate internal controls to protect their cash because it is their most liquid asset, and in all likelihood, an important operating asset. Cash is highly desirable, easily taken and concealed, and quickly converted into other assets. In addition, a high percentage of a company's transactions involve cash. Cash is received from customers following a sale and cash is paid to suppliers and employees for goods and services. A company receives cash from customers, for example, as payment on account and as payment for cash sales. The following sections describe cash handling procedures and the related internal controls for these two types of cash receipts.

LO4 Describe the internal controls for cash.

Cash Received on Account

A company receives cash through the mail from customers who are making payments on their accounts receivable balance. Four departments play major roles in processing cash receipts that arrive via the mail: the mailroom, the treasurer's department, the controller's department, and the internal audit department. **Exhibit 7-1** and the following paragraphs describe the role that each department plays in processing mailed cash receipts.

Mailroom

A company often sets up a separate post office box and requests that its customers mail any cash payments on account to that post office box. All other mail and company correspondence are directed to another company address or a different post office box. This approach automatically sorts a company's mail into two groups: (1) cash receipts from customers and (2) all other mail.

Mailroom employees open the envelopes containing cash receipts from customers. Each envelope should contain two items: a check and a remittance advice. A **remittance advice** is a form that accompanies a check to inform the company receiving the check about the purpose of the check. The remittance advice includes the customer's name, the amount paid, and such reference numbers as the invoice number and the customer account number.

Mailroom employees ensure that the dollar amount on each check and the related remittance advice are the same and then place the two documents in separate piles. An employee then endorses each check "For Deposit Only" so that no one can cash the check. The mailroom employees also prepare a remittance list. A **remittance list** is a list of all of the checks received on a given day. For each check, the remittance list includes the customer name and/or account number, the check number, and the amount received.

A separate mailroom employee compares the remittance list total to a list totaling the checks and another list totaling the remittance advices to ensure that the check amounts are listed correctly and that they agree with the remittance advices. The mailroom then sends the checks to the treasurer's department and the remittance list and the remittance advices to the controller's department.

Exhibit 7-1	Processing Cash Received on Account Through the Mail

Mailroom

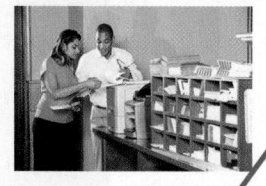

1. Opens mail from separate post office box.
2. Compares checks to remittance advices.
3. Endorses checks.
4. Prepares remittance list and compares it to total of checks.
5. Sends checks to treasurer.
6. Sends remittance list and remittance advices to controller.

Treasurer (Custody)

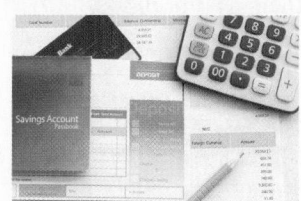

1. Prepares deposit slip.
2. Sends deposit slips and checks to bank.
3. Sends copy of deposit slip to controller.
4. Files a copy of the deposit slip.

Controller (Recording)

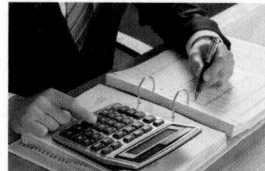

1. Compares deposit slip from treasurer to remittance list total.
2. Uses the total on the remittance list to prepare the journal entry to record the cash receipt.
3. Uses the remittance advices to post to the accounts receivable subsidiary ledger.
4. Files the remittance list, remittance advices, and deposit slip copy.

Internal Audit

1. Receives monthly bank statement directly from the bank through the mail.
2. Prepares bank reconciliation.
3. Prepares adjusting entries.

Treasurer

The treasurer's department is a *custodial* department. It maintains custody of the received customer checks. It has no responsibilities for any recording or posting activities. The duties of this department include preparing a bank deposit slip (original plus two copies) for each batch of checks received and sending the original deposit slip and the customer checks to the bank. One copy of the deposit slip is forwarded to the controller's department, and the treasurer's department files the second copy for future reference.

Controller

The controller's department is a *recording* department. It records the cash receipts in a journal and posts the cash receipts to the company's general ledger and the Accounts

Receivable account. The controller's department never has access to, or custody of, the received customer checks.

Before recording and posting the cash receipts, the controller's department compares the total on the deposit slip copy from the treasurer's department to the remittance list obtained from the mailroom to ensure that the treasurer's department deposited all of the checks sent from the mailroom. The controller's department then prepares a journal entry (debit Cash and credit Accounts Receivable) to record the cash receipts. The dollar amount of the debit and credit is the total from the deposit slip.

The controller's department uses the individual remittance advices to post the cash payments to the Accounts Receivable account of each individual customer. After processing, the remittance list, the remittance advices, and the deposit slip copy are filed in the controller's department for future reference.

Internal Audit

Internal audit is an independent department; it has no recurring custody, recording, or authorization duties related to accounting transactions. Once each month, the internal audit department performs its independent review and **reconciliation** duties related to the cash received. The internal auditor receives the monthly bank statement directly from the bank through the mail. This ensures that no one can alter the information returned with the bank statement. The internal audit department uses the bank statement to prepare the monthly bank reconciliation and create any needed journal entries. These internally prepared bank reconciliations can be part of a good internal control environment and serve as schedules that the independent auditors can more easily verify and test as a part of their audit process. The preparation of the bank reconciliation and related journal entries are discussed later in this chapter.

Cash Received from Retail Cash Sales

A retailer receives cash from customers when the retailer sells merchandise. The retailer must design internal controls to protect any cash received. Five groups play major roles in collecting, protecting, processing, and recording cash received from retail customers: the retail sales area, the retail sales supervisor, the treasurer's department, the controller's department, and the internal audit department. **Exhibit 7-2** and the following paragraphs describe the role that each group plays.

Retail Sales Area

Sales associates use cash registers to record cash sales and to control and protect the cash collected from customers. Each sales associate uses a unique **password** or key to identify him- or herself to the cash register. Each associate should have a separate cash drawer for collecting cash from customers and making change. Each sales associate begins each business day with a fixed amount of change in his or her cash drawer. The sales associates enter details of each sale into the cash register and place any cash received from customers into the assigned cash drawer. The cash register prints a paper tape listing the description and price of the items sold and the total amount due. The cash register also records this information either in the memory of the cash register or in a computer memory that the cash register accesses.

Retail Sales Supervisor

The retail sales supervisor oversees the retail sales operations of a business. Throughout the day, the supervisor approves any unusual transactions such as merchandise returns. At the end of the day, the supervisor counts the contents of each cash drawer. He or she compares the amount of cash in each drawer in excess of the beginning amount to the sales total accumulated by the cash register for each sales associate. The supervisor then prepares a written report (three copies) to document the total sales and the total cash received.

The supervisor delivers the cash in excess of the initial change amount and a copy of the written report to the treasurer's department. The cash register tape and another copy of the written report are taken to the controller's department. The supervisor files the third copy of the written report for future use if needed.

Exhibit 7-2	Processing Cash Received from Retail Cash Sales

Retail Sales Area

1. Begin each day with a fixed amount of change in drawer of each cash register.
2. Sales associate enters details of each sale into a cash register and places cash received from the customer into the cash register drawer assigned to that sales associate.

Retail Sales Supervisor

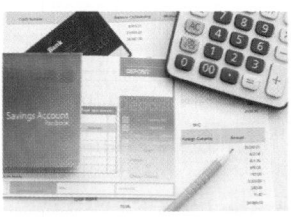

1. Observes the sales operation during the day.
2. Approves any unusual transactions during the day.
3. At the end of the day, counts the contents of each drawer with the sales associate responsible for the drawer.
4. Compares the amount in the drawer in excess of the beginning amount to the sales total accumulated by the cash register for that sales associate.
5. Prepares written report of sales and cash received.
6. Sends cash and a copy of the written report to the treasurer.
7. Sends cash register tape and a copy of the report to the controller.

Treasurer (Custody)

1. Prepares deposit slip.
2. Sends deposit slip and cash to bank.
3. Sends copy of deposit slip to controller.
4. Files a copy of the deposit slip.

Controller (Recording)

1. Compares deposit slip from treasurer to written report and cash register tape.
2. Uses the written report to prepare the journal entry to record cash sales.
3. Files written report and deposit slip.

Internal Auditor

1. Receives monthly bank statement directly from the bank through the mail.
2. Prepares bank reconciliation.
3. Prepares adjusting entries.

© Shutterstock.com

Treasurer

The treasurer's department takes custody of any cash from the retail sales supervisor after signing a receipt that the supervisor retains as proof of the cash delivery. Employees of the treasurer's department count the cash and prepare a deposit slip (original plus two copies). The employees then send the original deposit slip and cash to the bank for deposit. One copy of the deposit slip is sent to the controller's department, and the treasurer's department files the final copy for future reference.

Controller

The controller's department is responsible for recording cash sales. The controller's department never has access to or custody of the cash. Before recording and posting the cash receipts, the controller's department compares the total on the deposit slip copy from the treasurer's department to the written report from the retail sales supervisor to ensure that the treasurer's department deposited all of the cash received. The controller's department then prepares a journal entry to record the cash sales. This entry also reflects any shortage or overage of cash, should this occur. The written report and the deposit receipt are filed for future reference.

Internal Audit

The duties of the internal audit department with respect to cash received from retail sales are identical to its duties with respect to cash received on account. Note again that the bank sends the monthly bank statement directly to a company's internal auditor. If a company does not have an internal auditor, the bank sends the monthly bank statement to an appropriate person designated by the company, usually someone who does not have custody or recording responsibilities for cash. The internal audit department prepares a bank reconciliation statement and makes any needed journal entries.

Checks

When a company opens a checking account at a bank, the bank requires each company employee who will sign checks to sign a signature card. Occasionally, a bank employee compares the signatures on the checks presented for payment by various parties to the authorized signatures on the signature cards. This comparison provides an internal control for the bank that it is not cashing a check written by an unauthorized employee. The bank is responsible for any amounts erroneously paid out of a company's checking account.

A **check** is a written order signed by a checking account owner (also known as the *maker*) directing the bank (called the *payer*) to pay a specified amount of money to the person or company named on the check (called the *payee*). A check is a negotiable instrument; it can be transferred to another person or company by writing "pay to the order of" and the name of the other person or company on the back of the check and then signing the back of the check.

Exhibit 7-3 presents a sample check. As noted previously, proper internal control requires that business documents such as checks be prenumbered in numerical sequence. The printed check number appears in two locations in **Exhibit 7-3**: in standard type in the

| **Magnetic Characters on Checks** | **ACCOUNTING IN PRACTICE** |

The routing number on a check tells the various banks handling the check how to route it through the U.S. Federal Reserve System to properly transfer the cash between bank accounts. The routing number has two formats: the fraction format (item 3 in **Exhibit 7-3**) and the MICR format (item 4 in **Exhibit 7-3**). Both formats are printed on each check. In the fraction format in **Exhibit 7-3**, the number 79 represents the state in which the bank is located, the number 123 represents the number of the bank where the checking account is located, and the number 759 represents the Federal Reserve District and bank through which the check must clear. In the MICR format, the number 0759 identifies the Federal Reserve District and bank, the number 0123 identifies the specific bank, and the number 8 is the check digit.

upper right corner ❶ and in MICR (magnetic ink character recognition) form on the bottom of the check ❷. Also printed twice on the check are alternative formats of the routing number for the check, a fraction format ❸ and an MICR format ❹. (See Accounting in Practice, "Magnetic Characters on Checks," above.) The check printer also places the customer's account number on the check in MICR form ❺. When the check is processed by the banking system, the MICR check amount ❻ is added at the bottom right of the check. Banks use special equipment that reads MICR codes directly into computer files.

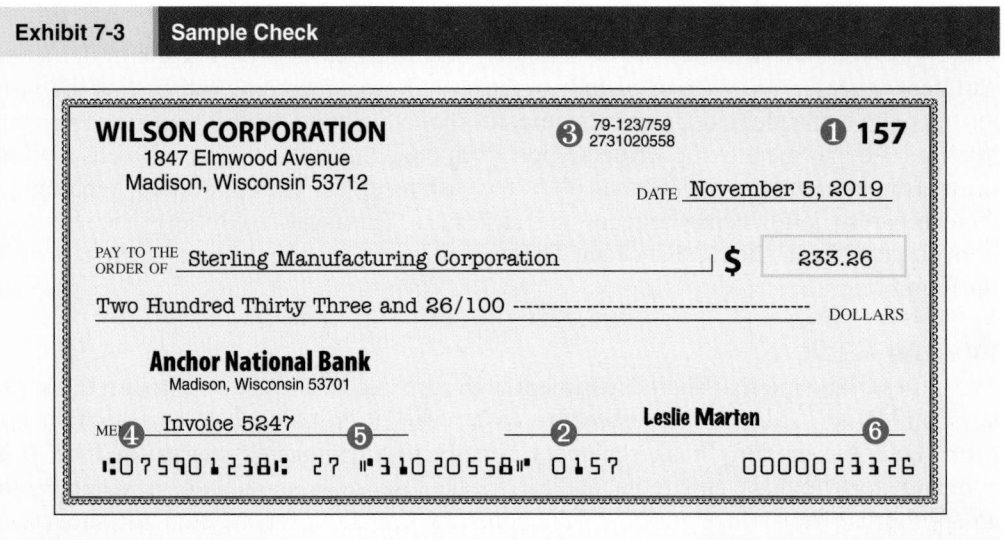

Exhibit 7-3 | Sample Check

Using Electronic Funds Transfer

Many companies receive payments from customers or make payments to suppliers using electronic funds transfer rather than writing and mailing checks. **Electronic funds transfer**, commonly known as EFT, involves sending an electronic message from one computer to another to cause a transfer of money from one financial institution to another, or directly to a company. Actually, two electronic messages are sent. To illustrate, assume that a company wants to use EFT to transfer money to a second company to pay an invoice. The paying company has its computer send a message to its bank's computer to request the funds transfer. This is known as *retail EFT*. Then, the paying company's bank uses EFT to transfer funds to the receiving company's bank. This is known as *wholesale EFT* or *bank-to-bank EFT*. Wholesale EFT usually involves a central bank (such as a Federal Reserve Bank) that acts as an automated clearinghouse by increasing the balance of one bank and decreasing the balance of the other bank.

The Petty Cash Fund

Most businesses find it inconvenient and expensive to write checks for small expenditures. Instead, these businesses establish a petty cash fund. A **petty cash fund** is a small amount of cash, for example $300, that is placed in a secure location on a business's premises to be used to pay for small expenditures such as postage, delivery service charges, and minor purchases of supplies. The size of the petty cash fund depends on how often it is used and the amount of the disbursements. Firms often select an amount that will last for three or four weeks.

Although the use of a petty cash fund violates the rule that all cash payments should be made by check or EFT, control can be maintained by handling the fund on an imprest basis with documented procedures. An imprest fund contains a fixed amount of cash. A business establishes a petty cash fund by writing a check against the firm's checking account and cashing the check at the bank. All replenishments of the petty cash fund are also made by check. As a result, all expenditures are ultimately controlled by check, providing a paper trail of all cash transfers to the petty cash fund.

Match the internal control function from the left-hand column with the area of responsibility in the right-hand column:
1. Prepares deposit receipt.
2. Approves unusual transactions.
3. Prepares remittance list.
4. Prepares bank reconciliation.
5. Compares deposit receipt to remittance list.

a. Retail sales supervisor
b. Mailroom
c. Treasurer's department
d. Controller's department
e. Internal audit department

The Bank Statement

At the end of each month, a company's bank prepares a bank statement for each checking account that the company maintains and then sends the statement to the internal audit department of the company that owns the checking account. **Exhibit 7-4** is the bank statement from Anchor National Bank for the Wilson Corporation's checking account as of November 30, 2019.

In the body of the bank statement, the bank lists Wilson's deposits and other credits on the left, Wilson's checks (in numerical order) and other debits in the center, and Wilson's daily account balance on the right. The daily account balance is the balance in the account as of the end of each day listed. The bank presents a summary calculation of Wilson's ending account balance near the bottom of the statement.

The bank defines a series of code letters at the bottom of the statement. These code letters identify debits and credits not related to paying checks or making deposits. These code letters are not standard from bank to bank. In **Exhibit 7-4**, EC identifies corrections of errors made by the bank; DM (debit memo) identifies automatic loan payments and bank charges for items such as collecting notes; CM (credit memo) identifies amounts collected by the bank for the depositor; SC (service charge) identifies fees charged by the bank for the checking account; OD (overdraft) indicates a negative balance in the account; RT (returned item) identifies items such as posted checks and NSF checks for which the bank could not collect cash; and IN (interest earned) identifies interest added to the account.

The Bank Reconciliation

The internal audit department prepares a bank reconciliation as of the end of each month. A **bank reconciliation** is a schedule that (1) accounts for all differences between the ending cash balance on the bank statement and the ending cash balance in the Cash account in the company's general ledger and (2) determines the reconciled cash balance as of the end of the month. The internal audit department employee preparing the bank reconciliation needs access to the bank statement, the general ledger, cash receipts records, and cash disbursements records to prepare the reconciliation.

LO5 **Illustrate** the bank reconciliation process.

Debits or Credits?　　　**ACCOUNTING IN PRACTICE**

Debit and credit terminology may seem backward on a bank statement. Debits decrease a bank account balance and credits increase a bank account balance. To understand this, realize that bank statements are prepared from the perspective of the bank, not the customer of the bank. In other words, when a company deposits cash in its checking account, the bank debits Cash and credits a liability account called a Customer Deposit. The bank statement sent to a company each month is a statement of its Customer Deposit account held by the bank. As with any liability, debits decrease its balance and credits increase its balance.

Exhibit 7-4	Bank Statement of Wilson Corporation

ANCHOR NATIONAL BANK
123 Center Street
Madison, Wisconsin 53701

Wilson Corporation
1847 Elmwood Avenue
Madison, Wisconsin 53712

Account Number   27-31020558
Statement Date   November 30, 2019

Deposits and Credits		Checks and Debits			Daily Balance	
Date	Amount	Number	Date	Amount	Date	Amount
Nov. 01	420.00	149	Nov. 02	125.00	Nov. 01	6,060.30
Nov. 02	630.00	154	Nov. 03	56.25	Nov. 02	6,565.30
Nov. 07	560.80	155	Nov. 10	135.00	Nov. 03	6,509.05
Nov. 10	480.25	156	Nov. 08	315.10	Nov. 07	6,801.19
Nov. 14	525.00	157	Nov. 07	233.26	Nov. 08	6,486.09
Nov. 17	270.25	158	Nov. 11	27.14	Nov. 10	6,831.34
Nov. 21	640.20	159	Nov. 18	275.00	Nov. 11	6,804.20
Nov. 26	300.00CM	160	Nov. 15	315.37	Nov. 14	7,329.20
Nov. 26	475.00	161	Nov. 17	76.40	Nov. 15	7,013.83
Nov. 30	471.40	162	Nov. 21	325.60	Nov. 17	7,207.68
		163	Nov. 21	450.00	Nov. 18	6,932.68
		164	Nov. 23	239.00	Nov. 21	6,731.58
		165	Nov. 21	65.70	Nov. 23	6,492.58
		166	Nov. 28	482.43	Nov. 26	7,262.58
		169	Nov. 28	260.00	Nov. 28	6,520.15
		170	Nov. 30	122.50	Nov. 30	6,488.95
		171	Nov. 30	370.10		
			Nov. 07	35.40RT		
			Nov. 26	5.00DM		
			Nov. 30	10.00SC		

Beginning Balance	+	Deposits and Credits	−	Checks and Debits	=	Ending Balance
$5,640.30	+	$4,772.90	−	$3,924.25	=	$6,488.95

Item Codes: EC: Error Correction   DM: Debit Memo   CM: Credit Memo
SC: Service Charge   OD: Overdraft   RT: Returned Item
IN: Interest Earned

Bank Reconciliation Structure

Exhibit 7-5 outlines the structure of a company's bank reconciliation. The bank reconciliation is really two schedules prepared side by side. The schedule on the left includes bank items, and the schedule on the right includes items related to the company's general ledger.

The schedule on the left begins with the ending cash balance from the bank statement (the month-end balance according to the bank's records). The internal audit department employee preparing the reconciliation adds (1) deposits not yet recorded by the bank, called **deposits in transit**, and (2) any corrections not yet made by the bank that will increase the bank balance. The preparer then subtracts (1) checks not yet recorded by the bank, called **outstanding checks**, and (2) any corrections not yet made by the bank that will decrease the bank balance. The resulting total is the reconciled cash balance at the end of the month.

The schedule on the right begins with the ending balance in the Cash account in the company's general ledger. The internal audit department employee adds (1) items recorded as cash receipts by the bank but not yet recorded in the company's journals and (2) any

Exhibit 7-5	Structure of a Company's Bank Reconciliation

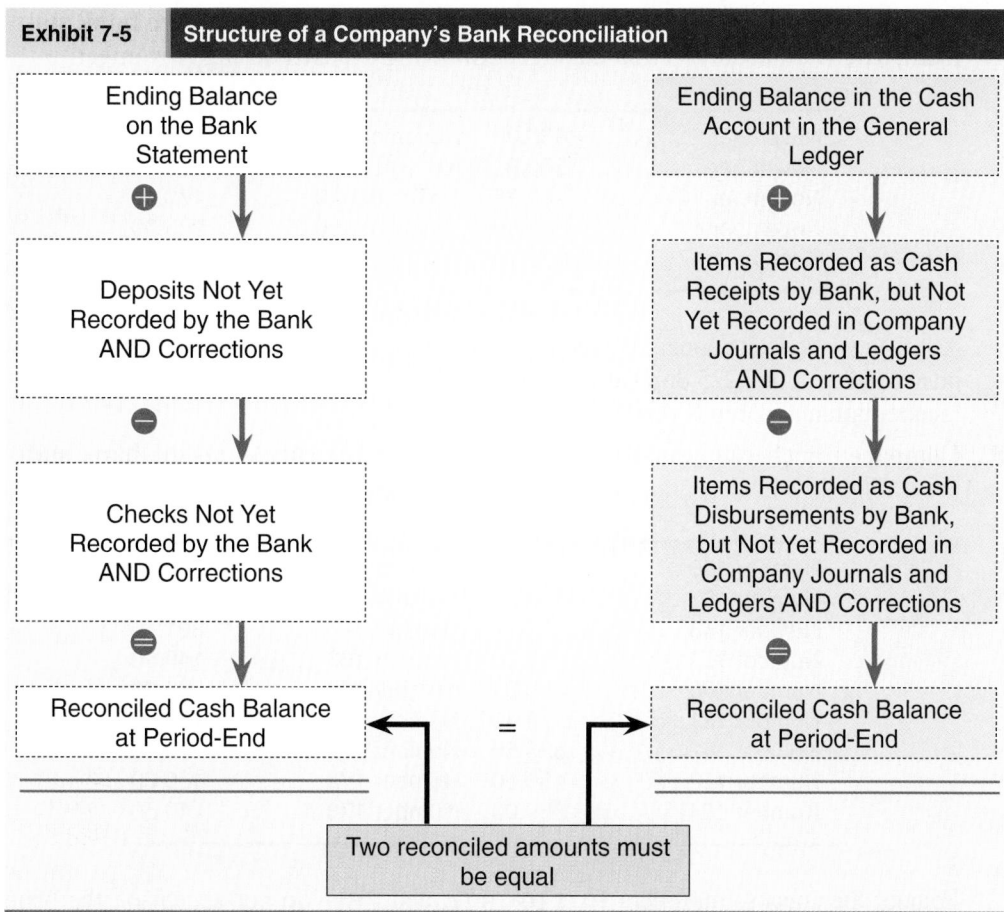

corrections not yet made by the company that will increase the general ledger cash balance. The preparer subtracts (1) items recorded as cash disbursements by the bank but not yet recorded in the company's journals and (2) any corrections not yet made by the company that will decrease the general ledger cash balance. The resulting total is the reconciled cash balance at the end of the month. The totals of the two schedules should be the same.

Bank Reconciliation Illustrated   Assume that the internal auditor of the Wilson Corporation is preparing the November 30, 2019, bank reconciliation. She uses the following procedures to reconcile the November 30 bank statement balance of $6,488.95 to the November 30 general ledger Cash account balance of $5,322.69:

1. **Trace outstanding items on the bank reconciliation for the previous month to the current bank statement.** Any items on the previous bank reconciliation that have still not been processed by the bank must appear on the current bank reconciliation. The October 31 reconciliation included the following:

Deposit in transit		$420.00
Outstanding checks:	Number 149	$125.00
	Number 154	56.25
	Number 155	135.00

The November 30 bank statement includes the $420 deposit and all three checks listed above. Therefore, none of these items will appear on the November 30 bank reconciliation.

2. **Compare the deposits made during the month to the deposits on the bank statement.** The Wilson Corporation made the following deposits during November:

November 2	$630.00	November 21	$640.20
November 7	560.80	November 26	475.00
November 10	480.25	November 29	471.40
November 14	525.00	November 30	225.00
November 17	270.25		

All of these deposits appear on the bank statement except for the November 30 deposit of $225. The $225 deposit will appear on the left side of the November 30 bank reconciliation as a deposit in transit.

3. **Compare the checks issued during the month to the checks on the bank statement.** The Wilson Corporation issued the following checks during November:

Number 156	$315.10	Number 165	$ 65.70
Number 157	233.26	Number 166	482.43
Number 158	27.14	Number 167	301.66
Number 159	275.00	Number 168	149.50
Number 160	315.37	Number 169	260.00
Number 161	76.40	Number 170	122.50
Number 162	325.60	Number 171	370.10
Number 163	450.00	Number 172	450.00
Number 164	239.00	Number 173	240.50

Four of the checks—numbers 167, 168, 172, and 173—do not appear on the bank statement. These four checks will appear on the left side of the November 30 bank reconciliation as outstanding checks.

4. **Scan the bank statement for charges and credits not yet reflected in the general ledger.** The Wilson Corporation's bank statement contains a charge of $35.40 for a returned item, a debit memo of $5.00, and a service charge of $10.00 in the checks and other debits column. The deposits and other credits column contains a credit memo for $300.00. Supplemental information sent by the bank with the bank statement reveals that the bank charged a $35.40 NSF check against Wilson's account, collected a $300.00 note for Wilson and charged a $5.00 collection fee, and that the service charge for the month of November was $10.00. These four items have not yet been recorded by Wilson Corporation. Therefore, they must be listed on the right side of the bank reconciliation.

5. **Check for errors.** The Wilson Corporation recorded check number 159 as $725.00. The correct amount of $275.00 appears on the bank statement. The check was written to pay for office supplies. The correction of the transposition in the amount of $450 must be listed on the right side of the bank reconciliation.

After the five preceding procedures have been completed, the November 30 bank reconciliation for the Wilson Corporation appears as shown in **Exhibit 7-6**. Note that both the left side and the right side of the reconciliation end with a reconciled cash balance and that the two amounts are the same. This reconciled cash balance of $5,572.29 is the amount that will appear on the November 30 balance sheet for the company.

Exhibit 7-6	November 30, 2019, Bank Reconciliation for Wilson Corporation

WILSON CORPORATION
Bank Reconciliation
November 30, 2019

Ending balance from bank statement....	$6,488.95	Balance from general ledger		$4,872.69
Add: Deposits in transit...............	225.00	Add: Check 159 for $275		
		recorded as $725		450.00
		Collection of note	$300.00	
	6,713.95	Less: Collection fee	5.00	295.00
				5,617.69
Less: Outstanding checks:				
No. 167 .... $301.66		Less: NSF check	35.40	
No. 168 .... 149.50		Service charge	10.00	45.40
No. 172 .... 450.00				
No. 173 .... 240.50	1,141.66			
Reconciled cash balance	$5,572.29	Reconciled cash balance		$5,572.29

Before the Wilson Corporation prepares its financial statements for November, Wilson must make journal entries to bring the balance in the Cash account into agreement with the reconciled cash balance on the bank reconciliation. These entries incorporate the items on the company's side of the bank reconciliation as follows:

Nov. 30	Cash (+A)	450.00		
	Office supplies expense (−E, +SE)		450.00	A = L + SE
	To correct recording error on check number 159.			+450.00
				+450.00 Exp

Nov. 30	Cash (+A)	295.00		
	Miscellaneous expense (+E, −SE)	5.00		A = L + SE
	Notes receivable(−A)		300.00	+295.00
	To record a note collected by the bank, less a collection fee.			−300.00 −5.00 Exp

Nov. 30	Accounts receivable (+A)	35.40		
	Cash (−A)		35.40	A = L + SE
	To reclassify an NSF check as an account receivable.			+35.40
				−35.40

Nov. 30	Miscellaneous expense (+E, −SE)	10.00		
	Cash (−A)		10.00	A = L + SE
	To record bank service charge for November.			−10.00 −10.00 Exp

Accounting Trick to Catch Transpositions	ACCOUNTING IN EVERYDAY LIFE

Transposing numbers is one of the most frequent causes of errors in bank reconciliations. Transposing numbers occurs when they are written in the wrong sequence. Recording 87 instead of 78 or 149 instead of 194 are examples of transposition errors. Anybody who has recorded lists of numbers has probably made these kinds of errors at some point. Fortunately there is an easy way to detect transposition errors. If, when doing a bank reconciliation, you find that the number you arrive at differs from the bank's number by a multiple of 9, chances are it is a transposition error. Assume you think you have $120 in your account, but the bank claims your balance is only $66. The difference between $120 and $66 is $54; a number evenly divisible by 9. There is a good chance that this difference is a result of a transposition error because all transpositions, no matter what numbers are transposed, will cause an error evenly divisible by 9. Recall our two examples above, 87 and 149 transposed as 78 and 194. The differences are 9 and 45, and both are evenly divisible by 9. Go ahead and try it with any number. Of course this trick can be used anytime you are recording numbers, not just with bank reconciliations.

Match the reconciling items from the left-hand column with the proper reconciling action from the right-hand column:

1. Deposits in transit
2. Outstanding checks
3. Bank service charge
4. Cash collected by bank on note

a. Add to bank statement balance
b. Subtract from bank statement balance
c. Add to cash general ledger account
d. Subtract from cash general ledger account

EFFECTIVE CASH MANAGEMENT

LO6 **Describe** the four primary activities of effective cash management.

Cash is typically one of a company's most important assets. Without cash, a company would be unable to pay its employees or its suppliers. In short, a company would be unable to continue operating. As a consequence, managers spend considerable time and effort managing and monitoring this key asset. Similarly, investors and lenders spend considerable time understanding where a company's cash came from and how the company spent it.

Monitoring Cash

The most effective tool for external parties to monitor a company's cash is the statement of cash flows.[2] As discussed in Chapter 1, the statement of cash flows identifies a company's cash inflows and cash outflows, segmenting them into the three business activities of operating, investing, and financing. **Exhibit 7-7** presents the statement of cash flows for WebWork Inc. for the month ended December 31, 2019.

Exhibit 7-7	Statement of Cash Flows for WebWork, Inc.

WEBWORK, INC.
Statement of Cash Flows
For Month Ended December 31, 2019

Cash flow from operating activities		
Cash received from clients	$19,910	
Cash paid to employees and suppliers	(1,620)	
Cash paid for rent	(10,800)	
Cash provided by operating activities		$ 7,490
Cash flow from investing activities		
Purchase of office equipment	(32,400)	
Cash used by investing activities		(32,400)
Cash flow from financing activities		
Stock issued	30,000	
Borrowing from bank	36,000	
Cash dividends	(500)	
Cash provided by financing activities		65,500
Net increase in cash		40,590
Cash at December 1, 2019		0
Cash at December 31, 2019		$40,590

The positive numbers on the statement of cash flows represent a company's cash inflows and the negative numbers represent a company's cash outflows. WebWork's

---

[2] The statement of cash flows provides an after-the-fact monitoring of cash sources and uses. Many companies use a cash budget in order to plan anticipated cash inflows and outflows so that they are able to manage the amount of cash on hand at an appropriate level. Cash budgets are covered in most managerial accounting textbooks.

primary cash inflows involved the sale of stock ($30,000) and its bank borrowings ($36,000). The company's primary uses of cash involved the purchase of office equipment ($32,400) and the payment of rent ($10,800). Not only does the statement of cash flows identify the sources and uses of cash, but it also identifies whether a company's cash balance increased or decreased for the period. **Exhibit 7-7** reveals that WebWork's cash account increased by $40,590 for the month of December.

While having some cash on hand is important to enable a company to pay its employees and its suppliers on a timely basis, having too much cash on hand may indicate that a company is not maximizing the return on its assets. Thus, it is important for managers to not only monitor a company's cash but also to manage it effectively to ensure that the company is earning an adequate return on this key asset.

Primary Activities of Effective Cash Management

Effective cash management generally involves four primary activities:

1. Manage accounts receivable. Since accounts receivable rarely include interest charges for late payment, the sooner that cash from sales can be collected, the sooner the cash can be used to pay suppliers, pay debt, or be invested in operations. Thus, managers should try to increase the rate at which accounts receivable are collected.

2. Manage inventory levels. Inventory should be maintained at levels that allow a company to satisfy customer needs while, at the same time, avoid having too much of the company's resources tied up in inventory for extended periods of time. Thus, managers should try to keep inventory levels as low as possible without losing any sales.

3. Manage accounts payable. Since accounts payable rarely include an interest charge for late payment, the longer a manager takes to pay off these accounts, the longer a company can use its cash to fund operations. Thus, managers should delay the payment of accounts payable. However, they should not be delayed beyond the point at which suppliers are no longer willing to do business with the company on reasonable terms. Where accounts payable have credit terms that provide a discount for prompt payment, managers must evaluate the trade-off involved by delaying the payment of accounts payable versus the reduced purchase price that results from timely payment.

4. Invest excess cash. Since cash on hand or in a bank account yields a very low rate of return, it is important to invest any excess cash. Thus, an important management activity is forecasting a company's cash needs by constructing a cash budget each period. Only a sufficient amount of cash necessary to cover a company's day-to-day needs should be kept on hand; any excess amounts should be invested in an effort to earn an adequate rate of return on this asset.

Match the activities from column 1 with the activities described in column 2.

1	2
a. Manage accounts receivable	1. Acquire additional production machinery using additional cash beyond what the company normally needs to fund day-to-day operations.
b. Manage inventory levels	2. Develop a forecast of demand for the company's products, taking into account factors such as seasonal fluctuations.
c. Manage accounts payable	3. Contact customers with a reminder the first day a payment is late rather than waiting until the next month.
d. Invest excess cash	4. Set up a schedule to pay invoices based on the credit terms offered by each vendor.

YOUR TURN! 7.6

The solution is on page 371.

COMPREHENSIVE PROBLEM

At December 31, 2019, the Cash account in the Tyler Company's general ledger had a debit balance of $18,434.27. The December 31, 2019, bank statement showed a balance of $19,726.40. In reconciling the two amounts, you discover the following:

1. Bank deposits made by Tyler on December 31 amounting to $2,145.40 do not appear on the bank statement.
2. A non-interest-bearing note receivable from the Smith Company for $2,000, left with the bank for collection, was collected by the bank at the end of December. The bank credited the proceeds, less a $5 collection charge, on the bank statement. Tyler Company has not recorded the collection.
3. Accompanying the bank statement is a debit memorandum indicating that John Miller's check for $450 was charged against Tyler's bank account on December 30 because of insufficient funds.
4. Check No. 586, written for advertising expense of $869.10, was recorded as $896.10 by Tyler Company.
5. A comparison of the paid checks returned by the bank with the recorded disbursements revealed that the following checks are still outstanding as of December 31:

No. 561.............	$306.63	No. 591.............	$190.00
No. 585.............	440.00	No. 592.............	282.50
No. 588.............	476.40	No. 593.............	243.00

6. The bank mistakenly charged Tyler Company's account for check printing costs of $30.50, which should have been charged to Taylor Company.
7. The bank charged Tyler Company's account $42.50 for the rental of a safe deposit box. No entry has been made in Tyler's records for this expense.

Required
a. Prepare a bank reconciliation as of December 31, 2019.
b. Prepare any necessary journal entries at December 31, 2019.

Solution
a.

TYLER COMPANY
Bank Reconciliation
December 31, 2019

Ending balance from bank statement.....		$19,726.40	Balance from general ledger		$18,434.27
Add: Deposits not credited by bank		2,145.40	Add: Collection of note	$2,000.00	
Error by bank (Check printing			Less: Collection charge	5.00	1,995.00
charge of Taylor Co.)		30.50	Error in recording check No. 586		27.00
		21,902.30			20,456.27
Less: Outstanding checks:			Less:		
No. 561........................	$306.63		NSF check	450.00	
No. 585........................	440.00		Charge for safe deposit box	42.50	492.50
No. 588........................	476.40				
No. 591........................	190.00				
No. 592........................	282.50				
No. 593........................	243.00	1,938.53			
Reconciled cash balance		$19,963.77	Reconciled cash balance		$19,963.77

b.	Dec. 31	Cash (+A)	1,995.00		A = L + SE
		Miscellaneous expense (+E, −SE)	5.00		+1,995.00 −5.00
		Notes receivable—Smith Company (−A)		2,000.00	−2,000.00
		To record collection of Smith Company's note by bank, less			
		collection charge.			
	31	Cash (+A)	27.00		A = L + SE
		Advertising expense (−E, +SE)		27.00	+27.00 +27.00
		To correct error in recording advertising expense.			
	31	Accounts receivable—John Miller (+A)	450.00		A = L + SE
		Cash (−A)		450.00	+450.00
		To reclassify NSF check as an account receivable.			−450.00
	31	Miscellaneous expense (+E, −SE)	42.50		A = L + SE
		Cash (−A)		42.50	−42.50 −42.50
		To record rental expense of safety deposit box.			

APPENDIX 7A: Auditing and Internal Control

One of the internal control concepts previously discussed is conducting internal company audits. Internal audits provide appraisals of a company's financial statements, its internal control, and its operations. Internal auditors, who are employees of the company that they audit, conduct internal audits under the direction of top management or a company's board of directors.

LO7   Appendix 7A
Describe financial statement audits and operational audits.

Parties outside the company, such as bankers and stockholders, prefer independent appraisals of a company's performance. These parties are usually unwilling to accept an audit report prepared by company-employed internal auditors because of possible bias and conflicts of interest. Consequently, creditors and stockholders usually require that an independent, professional auditing firm conduct an audit of the annual financial statements. Moreover, U.S. securities law requires that all corporations whose common stock is publicly traded have an independent firm of certified public accountants (CPAs) audit the company's annual financial statements.

Not Your Ordinary Audit	**FORENSIC ACCOUNTING**

The financial statement audit is performed to enable the independent auditor to express an opinion regarding whether the financial statements present fairly, in all material respects, the financial position and results of operations of a company. In so doing, the independent auditor is looking for material errors, whether the errors are a result of unintentional misstatement or fraud. To perform the audit, the auditor will perform statistical sampling of the reported transactions to make judgments regarding the fairness of the reported statements. The auditor is not specifically looking for fraud, and likely will not find it even if present, because the financial statement audit is not designed to uncover fraud. The forensic accountant, by way of contrast, is specifically looking for fraud. Forensic accountants concentrate their efforts where fraud is likely to occur or is suspected, rather than on the financial statements as a whole. The forensic accountant will also utilize additional investigative techniques and follow leads suggested by what appear to be immaterial items. The forensic accountant will often have additional skills not common to financial statement auditors, such as surveillance tactics and interviewing and interrogation skills.

Financial Statement Audits

A **financial statement audit** is an examination of a company's annual financial statements by a firm of independent certified public accountants. (The quarterly financial reports of U.S. publicly traded companies are "reviewed" by an independent audit firm but they are not subject to a full audit like the annual financial statements.) The independent audit firm conducts this examination so it can prepare a report that expresses an opinion regarding whether (or not) the financial statements fairly present the results of operations, cash flows, and financial position of a company.

Audit Procedures

The independent audit firm conducts the annual financial statement audit according to standards established by the **Public Company Accounting Oversight Board (PCAOB)**, a quasi-governmental agency established by the Sarbanes-Oxley Act. The PCAOB is responsible for establishing auditing standards, inspecting the auditing practices of independent audit firms, and disciplining those firms that fail to maintain acceptable audit standards and practices.

The annual financial statement audit includes many different stages of work. During the early stage of an audit, the independent auditor reviews and evaluates the internal controls imbedded in a company's accounting system and other systems. This review and evaluation help the auditor determine what additional investigative steps, if any, should be included in the audit. The auditor then collects and analyzes data that substantiate the amounts in the financial statements. The auditor obtains most of these data from accounting records (such as journals and ledgers), business documents (such as purchase orders, sales invoices, and payment approval forms), and outside sources (such as banks, insurance companies, and suppliers).

The Audit Report

The **audit report** that the independent auditor issues following the annual audit specifies the financial statements that were audited, summarizes the audit process, and states the auditor's opinion regarding the financial statement data. The opinion usually states that the financial statements "fairly present" the results of operations, cash flow, and financial position of the company. The independent auditor does not conduct the audit to determine whether the financial statements are absolutely correct. Instead, the audit is conducted to determine whether the financial statements are a fair representation of operating results, cash flow, and financial position.

The primary purpose of the annual financial statement audit is *not* the discovery of fraudulent acts by management or employees of the company. Many audit procedures use statistical samples of transactions and data rather than examining the complete population of transactions. The auditors use samples to minimize the time required to conduct the audit, and consequently, to minimize its cost. As a result, there is the possibility that some errors or irregularities will exist in the transactions and data that the auditor does not review or evaluate. However, the independent auditor carefully designs the sampling procedures to detect errors and irregularities that are material in relation to the financial statements.

Report of Independent Registered Public Accounting Firm
In our opinion, such consolidated financial statements present fairly, in all material respects, the financial position of the Company as of December 31, 2017 and 2016, and the results of its operations and its cash flows for each of the three years in the period ended December 31, 2017, in conformity with accounting principles generally accepted in the United States of America. Also, in our opinion, such a financial statement schedule, when considered in relation to the basic consolidated financial statements taken as a whole, presents fairly, in all material respects, the information set forth therein.

DELOITTE & TOUCHE LLP

Operational Audits

Both internal audit departments and independent audit firms perform operational audits. An **operational audit** is an evaluation of activities, systems, and internal controls within a company to determine their efficiency, effectiveness, and economy. Operational auditing goes beyond accounting records and financial statements to obtain a full understanding of the operations of a company. Companies dedicated to continuous quality improvement often use operational audits to identify specific areas where they need to improve the quality of their operations or products.

Auditors design operational audits to assess the quality and efficiency of operational performance, identify opportunities for improvement, and develop specific recommendations for improvement. The scope of an operational audit can be very narrow, such as a review and evaluation of the procedures for processing cash receipts, or quite broad, such as a review and evaluation of all of the internal controls in a computerized accounting system.

Match the description in the left-hand column with the type of audit in the right-hand column:

1. Conducted by company employees
2. Conducted by independent auditors
3. Conducted by both independent auditors and internal auditors
4. Primary purpose is to report on the fairness of a company's financial statements
5. Evaluation of the efficiency and effectiveness of company activities

a. Internal audit
b. Financial statement audit
c. Operational audit

YOUR TURN! 7A.1

The solution is on page 371.

SUMMARY OF LEARNING OBJECTIVES

Define the three elements of fraud. (p. 326)   **LO1**
- The fraud triangle consists of three parts: (1) pressure, (2) rationalization, and (3) opportunity.

Discuss how the COSO framework helps prevent fraud, identify potential internal control failures, and discuss SOX regulations. (p. 327)   **LO2**
- The COSO framework identifies five internal control components: (1) the control environment; (2) risk assessment; (3) control activities; (4) information and communication; and (5) monitoring activities.
- Internal controls are the measures undertaken by a company to ensure the reliability of its accounting data, protect its assets from theft or unauthorized use, ensure that employees follow the company's policies and procedures, and evaluate the performance of employees, departments, divisions, and the company as a whole.
- A prevention control is designed to deter problems before they arise. A detection control is designed to discover problems soon after they arise. Prevention controls are generally more desirable than detection controls.
- A company should incorporate the following concepts when it designs its internal control:
  - Establish clear lines of authority and responsibility.
  - Implement segregation of duties.
  - Hire competent personnel.
  - Use control numbers on all business documents.
  - Develop plans and budgets.
  - Maintain adequate accounting records.
  - Provide physical and electronic controls.
- The internal control system must be monitored in order to assess the quality of the system's performance over time. One type of monitoring activity is an internal audit.
- Occasionally, internal controls fail. To compensate, many businesses purchase a fidelity bond, an insurance policy that provides financial compensation for theft by employees specifically covered by the insurance.
- For public companies, strong internal controls are required by law. The Sarbanes-Oxley Act (SOX) mandates that all publicly traded U.S. corporations maintain an adequate system of internal controls, that top management ensures the reliability of these controls, and that outside independent auditors attest to the adequacy of the controls. Failing to do so can result in prison sentences of up to 20 years and/or monetary fines of up to $5 million.

Define cash and discuss the accounting for cash. (p. 333)   **LO3**
- Cash includes coins, currency (paper money), checks, money orders, traveler's checks, and funds on deposit at a financial institution in a company's checking accounts and savings accounts.
- A company can have one or more cash accounts in its general ledger. Cash is a current asset.
- A company may combine certain short-term, highly liquid investments with cash and present a single amount called *cash and cash equivalents*.
- Not all of the company's cash may be available for general use. Restricted cash represents cash that has been restricted for specific uses. A compensating balance is an amount that a company must maintain in a bank account as part of a loan agreement.

LO4 **Describe the internal controls for cash. (p. 335)**

- Companies develop elaborate internal controls to protect cash, their most liquid asset.
- Four departments play major roles in processing cash received on account: the mailroom (open mail, endorse checks, list checks), the treasurer's department (deposit checks), the controller's department (update general ledger accounts), and the internal audit department (reconcile bank statement).
- Five departments play major roles in processing cash received from retail sales: the retail sales area (enter sales in cash register and place cash in drawer), the retail sales supervisor (count cash and prepare reports), the treasurer's department (deposit cash), the controller's department (update general ledger), and the internal audit department (reconcile bank statement).
- Many companies receive payments from customers or make payments to suppliers using electronic funds transfer (EFT) rather than writing and mailing checks. EFT involves sending an electronic message from one computer to another to cause a transfer of money from one financial institution to another, or directly to a company.
- A petty cash fund is a small amount of cash placed in a secure location on a company's premises to be used to pay for small expenditures such as postage and delivery service.

LO5 **Illustrate the bank reconciliation process. (p. 341)**

- A bank reconciliation is a schedule that (1) accounts for all differences between the ending cash balance of the bank statement and the ending cash balance of the Cash account in a company's general ledger and (2) determines the reconciled cash balance as of the end of the month.
- The procedure used to prepare the bank reconciliation involves four steps:
  - Trace outstanding items on the bank reconciliation from the previous month to the current bank statement.
  - Compare the deposits made during the month to the deposits on the bank statement.
  - Compare the checks issued during the month to the checks on the bank statement.
  - Scan the bank statement for charges and credits not yet reflected in the general ledger.
  - Check for errors.

LO6 **Describe the four primary activities of effective cash management. (p. 346)**

- Effective cash management includes monitoring and managing accounts receivable, inventory, and accounts payable, and investing any excess cash.
- Cash should be monitored using the statement of cash flows.

LO7 **Appendix 7A: Describe financial statement audits and operational audits. (p. 349)**

- A financial statement audit is an examination of a company's financial statements by a firm of independent certified public accountants. The firm issues an audit report upon completion of the audit.
- An operational audit is an evaluation of activities, systems, and internal controls within a company to determine their efficiency, effectiveness, and economy.

SUMMARY	Concept ⟶	Method ⟶	Assessment ⟶
TAKEAWAY 7.1	Are the internal controls adequate?	The COSO framework identifies five internal control components: (1) the control environment, (2) risk assessment, (3) control activities, (4) information and communication, and (5) monitoring activities.	Monitoring activities include appraisals of the company's internal control system. If weaknesses are reported, be cautious in relying on the reported financial statements.
TAKEAWAY 7.2	Are there any restrictions on a company's use of its cash and cash equivalents?	Balance sheet and the notes to the financial statements. Are there any restrictions to cash or compensating cash balances reported?	Any assessments of liquidity should consider any existing cash restrictions.

KEY TERMS

Audit report (p. 350)
Bank reconciliation (p. 341)
Budget (p. 331)
Cash (p. 333)
Cash and cash
  equivalents (p. 334)
Certificates of deposit (p. 333)
Check (p. 339)
Compensating balance (p. 334)
Control activities (p. 328)
Control environment (p. 328)
Control numbers (p. 330)
Deposits in transit (p. 342)
Detection control (p. 328)

Electronic funds
  transfer (p. 340)
Employee collusion (p. 332)
Fidelity bond (p. 332)
Financial statement
  audit (p. 349)
Fraud (p. 326)
Fraud triangle (p. 326)
Internal auditing (p. 332)
Internal controls (p. 328)
Monitoring activities (p. 331)
Not-sufficient-funds
  check (p. 333)
Operational audit (p. 350)

Outstanding checks (p. 342)
Password (p. 337)
Petty cash fund (p. 340)
Postdated check (p. 333)
Prevention control (p. 328)
Public Company Accounting
  Oversight Board
  (PCAOB) (p. 350)
Reconciliation (p. 337)
Remittance advice (p. 335)
Remittance list (p. 336)
Restricted cash (p. 334)
Risk assessment (p. 328)
Segregation of duties (p. 329)

Assignments with the ⓜ logo in the margin are available in myBusinessCourse.
See the Preface of the book for details.

SELF-STUDY QUESTIONS

(Answers to the Self-Study Questions are at the end of the chapter.)

1. **Which of the following is not one of the three elements of the fraud triangle?** **LO1**
   a. Pressure
   b. Rationalization
   c. Embezzlement
   d. Opportunity

2. **Which of the following is not a common internal control concept?** **LO2**
   a. Establish clear lines of responsibility
   b. Provide physical and electronic controls
   c. Collusion among employees
   d. Separate work functions

3. **Which of the following are considered good internal control practice?** **LO2**
   a. Job rotation
   b. Required vacations
   c. Only promoting from within
   d. Both a and b

4. **Burton Company should utilize all except one of the following concepts related to placing control numbers on business documents. Which concept should Burton not use?** **LO2**
   a. Write the control number on the document when it is used.
   b. Place control numbers on all business documents.
   c. Use the documents in strict numerical sequence.
   d. Periodically account for all numbers used.

5. **An operational audit is:** **LO7**
   a. Just another word for a financial statement audit.
   b. Only performed by independent auditors.
   c. Used to assess the quality and efficiency of operational performance.
   d. Usually reported to the public along with the financial statements.

6. **Which of the following statements is correct regarding the reporting of cash?** **LO3**
   a. Restricted cash is always shown as a noncurrent asset.
   b. Cash is shown as the first asset on the balance sheet.
   c. Restricted cash is usually combined with unrestricted cash on the balance sheet.
   d. If a company maintains more than one bank account, each must be shown separately on the balance sheet.

7. The treasurer is responsible for each of the following except:
   a. Prepare the deposit slip.
   b. Send deposit slips and checks to the bank.
   c. Prepare the bank reconciliation.
   d. File a copy of the deposit receipt.

8. What is a bank reconciliation?
   a. A formal financial statement that lists all of a firm's bank account balances
   b. A merger of two banks that previously were competitors
   c. A statement sent monthly by a bank to a depositor that lists all deposits, checks paid, and other credits and charges to the depositor's account for the month
   d. A schedule that accounts for differences between a firm's cash balance as shown on its bank statement and the balance shown in its general ledger Cash account

9. In a bank reconciliation, outstanding checks are:
   a. Deducted from the bank balance.
   b. Added to the bank balance.
   c. Deducted from the general ledger balance.
   d. Added to the general ledger balance.

LO4

10. Which of the following statements about a petty cash fund is not true?
   a. The fund is managed on an imprest basis.
   b. The fund is used to pay for minor items such as postage and delivery charges.
   c. The fund should have a balance large enough to support one replenishment per year.
   d. All replenishments are made by check.

QUESTIONS

1. Describe the three elements of the fraud triangle and how they relate to each other.

2. Explain why supervision is an important internal control.

3. Define and contrast prevention controls and detection controls. Which are more desirable?

4. Yates Company is reviewing its internal procedures to try to improve the company's internal control. It specifically wants to separate work functions. What three types of work functions must be separated to improve internal control?

5. Janet Jones is considered one of the rising stars at Finch Company. Janet is very hard working and has not taken a vacation in three years. Explain why this is a violation of good internal control.

6. Why does the control environment provide the foundation for the entire internal control system?

7. In what way did the Sarbanes-Oxley Act impact the need for internal control?

8. How are a financial statement audit and an operational audit similar and different?

9. What types of items are included in cash? What are the two important characteristics of an item of cash?

10. Which of the following are considered to be cash: paper money, certificates of deposit, postdated checks, traveler's checks, funds in a checking account, and money orders?

11. What is a remittance advice? What types of data are included on a remittance advice?

12. What is electronic funds transfer (EFT)? What are retail EFT and wholesale EFT?

13. What is the purpose of a bank reconciliation?

14. In preparing a bank reconciliation, how should you determine (a) deposits not recorded in the bank statement and (b) outstanding checks?

15. Indicate whether the following bank reconciliation items should be (1) added to the bank statement balance, (2) deducted from the bank statement balance, (3) added to the ledger account balance, or (4) deducted from the ledger account balance:
   a. Bank service charge
   b. NSF check
   c. Deposit in transit
   d. Outstanding check
   e. Bank error charging company's account with another company's check
   f. Difference of $270 in amount of check written for $410 but recorded by the company as $140

16. Which of the items listed in Discussion Question 15 require a journal entry on the company's books?

17. What is an imprest petty cash fund? How is such a fund established and replenished?

18. Carter Manufacturing Company makes a variety of consumer products. For the year just ended (and the two prior years), sales of private-label product to Mega-Mart (1,200 stores nationwide) have made up 60 to 65 percent of total sales. On December 31 of the year just ended, Mega-Mart informed Carter that it would be buying all private-label products from another manufacturer under a five-year contract. Losing this business will result in a 50 to 55 percent reduction in total gross profit for Carter.
    a. What is the going concern concept and how does it apply to this situation?
    b. How should the full disclosure principle be applied when preparing the annual report for the year just ended?
    c. What is the independent auditor's responsibility in this situation?

SHORT EXERCISES

SE7-1. **The Fraud Triangle** Each of the following is part of the fraud triangle except: **LO1**
    a. pressure.
    b. opportunity.
    c. concealment.
    d. rationalization.

SE7-2. **Segregation of Duties** Having one person responsible for the related activities of ordering merchandise, receiving the merchandise, and paying for the merchandise: **LO2**
    a. provides increased security over the firm's assets.
    b. is an example of good internal control.
    c. is a good example of segregation of duties.
    d. increases the potential of fraud.

SE7-3. **Internal Control** Internal controls do each of the following except: **LO2**
    a. protect assets from theft.
    b. evaluate the performance of employees.
    c. guarantee the accuracy of the accounting records.
    d. increase the likelihood that any errors will be caught.

SE7-4. **Auditors** Which of the following is true?   **LO2, 7**
    a. Internal auditors are independent of the company they audit.
    b. Internal audits provide appraisals of a company's internal control.
    c. The company being audited cannot pay the external auditing firm since this would violate their independence.
    d. Outside parties prefer appraisals by internal auditors over those of external auditors since they know more about the company being audited.

SE7-5. **The COSO framework identifies five internal control components** Which of the following is not one of the five components: **LO2**
    a. segregation of duties
    b. risk assessment
    c. monitoring activities
    d. control activities

SE7-6. **Cash** Cash includes each of the following except: **LO3**
    a. a postdated check.
    b. currency.
    c. money orders.
    d. funds in a checking account.

SE7-7. **Restricted Cash** Restricted cash: **LO3**
    a. must be shown as a current asset.
    b. must be shown as a noncurrent asset.
    c. is shown as a liability.
    d. is reported separate from unrestricted cash.

SE7-8. **Electronic Funds Transfer** Electronic funds transfer (EFT) involves transferring cash from one location to another using: **LO4**

    a.   armored trucks.

    b.   computers.

    c.   bicycle messengers.

    d.   the mail service.

LO4   **SE7-9.** **Cash Internal Control** Good internal control over cash received on account involves the mailroom doing each of the following activities except:

    a.   Open the mail.

    b.   Prepare the deposit receipt.

    c.   Prepare the remittance list.

    d.   Send checks to the treasurer.

LO6   **SE7-10.** **Cash Management** Effective cash management involves all the following except:

    a.   Manage accounts receivable.

    b.   Manage inventory.

    c.   Invest excess cash.

    d.   Conduct internal audits.

EXERCISES—SET A

LO2   **E7-1A.** **Internal Control** Explain how each of the following procedures strengthens a company's internal control:

    a.   After preparing a check for a cash disbursement, the accountant for Timber Lumber Company cancels the supporting business documents (purchase order, receiving report, and invoice) by stamping them PAID.

    b.   The salespeople for Phinney Department Store give each customer a cash register receipt along with the proper change. A sign on each cash register states that no refunds or exchanges are allowed without the related cash register receipt.

    c.   The ticket-taker at the Sunrise Theater tears each admission ticket in half and gives one half back to the ticket purchaser. The seat number is printed on each half of the ticket.

    d.   John Verde's restaurant provides servers with prenumbered customers' checks. The servers are to void checks with mistakes on them and issue new ones rather than make corrections on them. Voided checks must be given to the manager every day.

LO4   **E7-2A.** **Internal Controls for Cash Received on Account** Oregon Company sells supplies to restaurants. Most sales are made on open account (credit sales). Oregon has requested your help in designing procedures for processing checks received from its customers. Briefly describe the procedures that should be used in each of the following departments:

    a.   Mailroom

    b.   Treasurer's department

    c.   Controller's department

LO5   **E7-3A.** **Bank Reconciliation** Use the following information to prepare a bank reconciliation for Fast Company at June 30:

    1.   Balance per Cash account, June 30, $7,015.40.

    2.   Balance per bank statement, June 30, $7,235.85.

    3.   Deposits not reflected on bank statement, $975.

    4.   Outstanding checks, June 30, $1,260.45.

    5.   Service charge on bank statement not recorded in books, $50.

    6.   Error by bank—Yertel Company check charged on Fast Company's bank statement, $375.

    7.   Check for advertising expense, $260, incorrectly recorded in books as $620.

LO5   **E7-4A.** **Bank Reconciliation Components** Identify the requested amount in each of the following situations:

    a.   Munster Company's May 31 bank reconciliation shows deposits in transit of $1,400. The general ledger Cash in Bank account shows total cash receipts during June of $55,600. The June bank statement shows total cash deposits of $54,300 (and no credit memos). What amount of deposits in transit should appear in the June 30 bank reconciliation?

    b.   Sanders Company's August 31 bank reconciliation shows outstanding checks of $1,850. The general ledger Cash in Bank account shows total cash disbursements (all by check) during September of \$49,800. The September bank statement shows \$49,200 of checks clearing the bank. What amount of outstanding checks should appear in the September 30 bank reconciliation?

    c. Burkle Corporation's March 31 bank reconciliation shows deposits in transit of \$700. The general ledger Cash in Bank account shows total cash receipts during April of \$41,000. The April bank statement shows total cash deposits of \$37,100 (including \$1,000 from the collection of a note; the note collection has not yet been recorded by Sanders). What amount of deposits in transit should appear in the April 30 bank reconciliation?

E7-5A. **Internal Control** Explain how each of the following actions strengthens a company's system of internal control: **LO2**

    a. Separate work functions.
    b. Hire competent personnel.
    c. Develop plans and budgets.
    d. Use control numbers on all business documents.

E7-6A. **Effective Cash Management** Explain how each of the following activities can improve a company's cash management: **LO6**

    a. Manage accounts receivable.
    b. Manage inventory.
    c. Manage accounts payable.
    d. Invest excess cash.

E7-7A. **Cash and Cash Equivalents** Identify each of the following items as either cash (C), cash equivalents (CE), or neither (N):   **LO3**

    a. Coin
    b. U.S. treasury bills
    c. Checks
    d. Six-month certificate of deposit
    e. Currency

E7-8A. **External versus Internal Audit** Explain why parties outside the company, such as bankers and stockholders, prefer an independent appraisal of the company's financial results rather than relying on the work of internal auditors.   **LO7**
   (Appendix 7A)

E7-9A. **Operational Audits** Explain the nature of an operational audit.   **LO7**
   (Appendix 7A)

EXERCISES—SET B

E7-1B. **Internal Control** Explain how each of the following procedures strengthens a company's internal control: **LO2**

    a. Susan Corporation's photocopy machines are activated by keying a code number. Each employee is assigned a different, confidential code number. Each copy machine keeps track of the number of copies run under each employee number.
    b. Pike Company's bank requires a signature card on file for each Pike Company employee who is authorized to sign checks.
    c. Speedy Stop Convenience Stores have programmed their cash registers to imprint a blue star on every 300th receipt printed. A sign by each cash register states that the customer will receive \$2 if his or her receipt has a blue star on it.
    d. Wurst Corporation has a policy that every employee must take two weeks of vacation each year.

E7-2B. **Internal Controls for Cash Received from Retail Sales** Dunn Company operates a retail department store. Most customers pay cash for their purchases. Edwards has asked you to help it design procedures for processing cash received from customers for cash sales. Briefly describe the procedures that should be used in each of the following departments: **LO4**

    a. Retail sales departments
    b. Retail sales supervisor
    c. Treasurer's department
    d. Controller's department

LO5   **E7-3B.   Bank Reconciliation** Use the following information to prepare a bank reconciliation for Dylan Company at April 30:

1. Balance per Cash account, April 30, $6,042.10.
2. Balance per bank statement, April 30, $6,428.28.
3. Deposits not reflected on bank statement, $575.
4. Outstanding checks, April 30, $1,340.18.
5. Service charge on bank statement not recorded in books, $19.
6. Error by bank—Dillard Company check charged on Dylan Company's bank statement, $450.
7. Check for advertising expense, $230, incorrectly recorded in books as $320.

LO5   **E7-4B.   Bank Reconciliation Components** Identify the requested amount in each of the following situations:

a. MaryAnn Company's August 31 bank reconciliation shows deposits in transit of $2,250. The general ledger Cash in Bank account shows total cash receipts during September of $86,050. The September bank statement shows total cash deposits of $87,000 (and no credit memos). What amount of deposits in transit should appear in the September 30 bank reconciliation?

b. Ginger Corporation's March 31 bank reconciliation shows deposits in transit of $1,400. The general ledger Cash in Bank account shows total cash receipts during April of $64,600. The April bank statement shows total cash deposits of $63,100 (including $700 from the collection of a note; the note collection has not yet been recorded by Ginger). What amount of deposits in transit should appear in the April 30 bank reconciliation?

c. Skipper Company's October 31 bank reconciliation shows outstanding checks of $2,400. The general ledger Cash in Bank account shows total cash disbursements (all by check) during November of $69,300. The November bank statement shows $67,200 of checks clearing the bank. What amount of outstanding checks should appear in the November 30 bank reconciliation?

LO2   **E7-5B.   Internal Control** Explain how each of the following items strengthens a company's system of internal control:

a. Conduct internal audits.
b. Establish clear lines of authority and responsibility.
c. Maintain adequate accounting records.
d. Provide physical and electronic controls.

LO6   **E7-6B.   Effective Cash Management** Presented below is the statement of cash flows for Professor & Sons for the month ended December 31. Identify (a) the major sources of cash, (b) the major uses of cash, and (c) the change in the cash balance during the month.

PROFESSOR & SONS Statement of Cash Flows For the Month Ended December 31	
Cash flows from operating activities	
Cash receipts from customers	$13,275
Cash payments for operating activities	(11,131)
Cash provided by operating activities	2,144
Cash flows from investing activities	
Net purchases of investments	(140)
Net capital expenditures	(30,000)
Cash used by investing activities	(30,140)
Cash flows for financing activities	
Repurchase of common stock	(7,300)
Cash dividends paid	(7,000)
Cash used in financing activities	(14,300)
Net decrease in cash	(42,296)
Cash at beginning of month	95,000
Cash at end of month	$52,704

E7-7B.   **Cash and Cash Equivalents**   Identify each of the following items as either cash (C), cash equivalents   **LO3**
(CE), or neither (N):

  a.   Money market funds
  b.   Euros
  c.   A postdated check
  d.   A savings account
  e.   Traveler's checks

E7-8B.   **External versus Internal Audit**   Compare the purpose of an external audit to that of an internal audit.   **LO7**
(Appendix 7A)

E7-9B.   **The External Audit and Fraud**   Explain why the external audit is not considered a fraud audit.   **LO7**
(Appendix 7A)

PROBLEMS—SET A

P7-1A.   **Internal Control**   Xiley Company encountered the following situations: **LO2, 4**

  a.   The person who opens the mail for Xiley, Bill Stevens, stole a check from a customer and cashed
it. To cover up the theft, he debited Sales Returns and Allowances and credited Accounts Receivable in the general ledger. He also posted the amount to the customer's account in the accounts
receivable subsidiary ledger.
  b.   The purchasing agent, Susan Martin, used a company purchase order to order building materials
from Lumber Mart. Later, she telephoned Lumber Mart and changed the delivery address to her
home address. She told Lumber Mart to charge the material to the company. At month-end, she
approved the invoice from Lumber Mart for payment.
  c.   Nash Supply Company sent two invoices for the same order: the first on June 10 and the second
on July 20. The accountant authorized payment of both invoices and both were paid.
  d.   On January 1, Jack Monty, a junior accountant for Xiley, was given the responsibility of recording all general journal entries. At the end of the year, the auditors discovered that Monty had
made 150 serious errors in recording transactions. The chief accountant was unaware that Monty
had been making mistakes.

Required
For each situation, describe any violations of good internal control procedures and identify the steps
that you would take to prevent each situation.

P7-2A.   **Internal Control**   Each of the following lettered paragraphs briefly describes an independent situa-   **LO2, 4**
tion involving some aspect of internal control.

Required
Answer the questions at the end of each paragraph or numbered section.

  a.   Robert Flynn is the office manager of Oakwood Company, a small wholesaling company. Flynn
opens all incoming mail, makes bank deposits, and maintains both the general ledger and the accounts receivable subsidiary ledger. An assistant records transactions in the credit sales journal
and the cash receipts journal. The assistant also prepares a monthly statement for each customer
and mails the statements to the customers. These statements list the beginning balance, credit
sales, cash receipts, adjustments, and ending balance for the month.

  1.   If Flynn stole Customer A's $200 check (payment in full) and made no effort to conceal his
embezzlement in the ledgers, how would the misappropriation be discovered?
  2.   What routine accounting procedure would disclose Flynn's $200 embezzlement in part (1),
even if Flynn destroyed Customer A's subsidiary ledger account?
  3.   What circumstances might disclose Flynn's theft if he posted a payment to Customer A's account in the accounts receivable subsidiary ledger and set up a $200 account for a fictitious
customer?
  4.   In part (3), why might Flynn be anxious to open the mail himself each morning?
  5.   In part (3), why might Flynn want to have the authority to write off accounts considered
uncollectible?

  b.   A bagel shop uses a cash register that produces a printed receipt for each sale. The register also
prints each transaction on a paper tape that is locked inside the cash register. Only the supervisor

has access to the cash-register tape. A prominently displayed sign promises a free bagel to any customer who is not given a cash-register receipt with his or her purchase. How is this procedure an internal control device for the bagel shop?

c. Jason Philber, a swindler, sent several businesses invoices requesting payment for office supplies that had never been ordered or delivered to the businesses. A 5 percent discount was offered for prompt payment. What internal control procedures should prevent this swindle from being successful?

d. The cashier for Downtown Cafeteria is located at the end of the food line. After customers have selected their food items, the cashier rings up the prices of the food and the customer pays the bill. The customer line frequently stalls while the person paying searches for the correct amount of cash. To speed things up, the cashier often collects money from the next customer or two who have the correct change without ringing up their food on the register. After the first customer finally pays, the cashier rings up the amounts for the customers who have already paid. What is the internal control weakness in this procedure? How might the internal control over the collection of cash from the cafeteria customers be strengthened?

LO4 **P7-3A.** **Internal Controls for Cash Received on Account** Blue Company sells plumbing supplies to plumbing contractors on account. The procedures that Blue uses to handle checks received from customers via the mail are described below:

a. Blue instructs its customers to send payment checks to its street address, 619 Main Street, Scottsdale, Arizona.

b. Blue does not provide a remittance advice to its customers for return with payment checks.

c. Checks are endorsed by the treasurer's office just prior to sending the checks to the bank for deposit.

d. The mailroom prepares a remittance list of all the checks received and files the only copy of the remittance list in a mailroom file cabinet.

e. The checks are sent to the controller's office. The controller's office uses the checks to post the accounts receivable subsidiary ledger and prepare the journal entry to record cash receipts. The checks are then sent to the treasurer's office.

f. The treasurer's office prepares the deposit slip (two copies) and sends one copy and the checks to the bank. The other copy of the deposit slip is filed in the treasurer's file cabinet.

g. The bank statement is sent to the controller, who prepares the bank reconciliation.

Required

Indicate how Blue Company could improve each of these procedures. (Refer to **Exhibit 7-1** in the chapter to help you generate ideas.)

LO5 **P7-4A.** **Bank Reconciliation** On July 31, Arthur Company's Cash in Bank account had a balance of $8,112.62. On that date, the bank statement indicated a balance of $10,170.62. A comparison of returned checks and bank advices revealed the following:

1. Deposits in transit July 31 amounted to $3,316.12.
2. Outstanding checks July 31 totaled $1,251.12.
3. The bank erroneously charged a $215 check of Solomon Company against the Arthur bank account.
4. A $15 bank service charge has not yet been recorded by Arthur Company.
5. Arthur neglected to record $4,000 borrowed from the bank on a 10 percent six-month note. The bank statement shows the $4,000 as a deposit.
6. Included with the returned checks is a memo indicating that J. Martin's check for $610 had been returned NSF. Martin, a customer, had sent the check to pay an account of $660 less a $50 discount.
7. Arthur Company recorded a $107 payment for repairs as $1,070.

Required

a. Prepare a bank reconciliation for Arthur Company at July 31.

b. Prepare the journal entry (or entries) necessary to bring the Cash in Bank account into agreement with the reconciled cash balance on the bank reconciliation.

LO5 **P7-5A.** **Bank Reconciliation** The bank reconciliation made by Thurman, Inc., on August 31 showed a deposit in transit of $1,170 and two outstanding checks, No. 597 for $650 and No. 603 for $710. The reconciled cash balance on August 31 was $14,110.

The following bank statement is available for September:

Bank Statement							
TO Thurman, Inc. St. Louis, MO						September 30 **STATE BANK**	
Date	**Deposits**	**No.**	**Date**	**Charges**	**Date**		**Balance**
					Aug.	31	$14,300
Sept. 1	$1,170	597	Sept. 1	$ 650	Sept.	1	14,820
2	1,120	607	5	1,850		2	15,940
5	850	608	5	1,100		5	13,840
9	744	609	9	552		8	13,200
15	585	610	8	640		9	13,392
17	1,540	611	15	817		15	13,160
25	1,028	612	17	488		17	14,212
30	680	614	25	920		25	14,320
		NSF	29	991		29	13,329
		SC	30	36		30	13,973

Item Codes:	EC: Error Correction	DM: Debit Memo	CM: Credit Memo
	SC: Service Charge	OD: Overdraft	RT: Returned Item
	IN: Interest Earned	NSF: Non-sufficient Funds	

A list of deposits made and checks written during September is shown below:

Deposits Made		**Checks Written**	
Sept. 1	$1,120	No. 607	$1,850
4	850	608	1,100
8	744	609	552
12	585	610	640
16	1,540	611	488
24	1,028	612	871
29	680	613	310
30	1,266	614	920
		615	386
	$7,813	616	420
			$7,537

The Cash in Bank account balance on September 30 was $14,386. In reviewing checks returned by the bank, the accountant discovered that check No. 612, written for $817 for advertising expense, was recorded in the cash disbursements journal as $871. The NSF check for $991, which Thurman deposited on September 24, was a payment on account from customer D. Walker.

Required
a. Prepare a bank reconciliation for Thurman, Inc., at September 30.
b. Prepare the necessary journal entries to bring the Cash in Bank account into agreement with the reconciled cash balance on the bank reconciliation.

P7-6A. Reporting Cash Tina Company has the following items at year-end. **LO3**

Currency and coin in safe.	$ 4,100
Funds in savings account (requires $2,500 compensating balance)	26,540
Funds in checking account.	6,750
Traveler's checks	625
Postdated check.	1,250
Not-sufficient-funds check	1,880
Money market fund.	35,100

Required
Identify the amount of the above items that should be reported as cash and cash equivalents on Tina Company's balance sheet.

LO2 **P7-7A.** **Internal Control** Bart Simons has worked for Dr. Homer Spring for many years. Bart has been a model employee. He has not taken a vacation in over four years, always stating that work was too important. One of Bart's primary jobs at the clinic is to open mail and list the checks received. He also collects cash from patients at the cashier's window as patients leave. There are times that things are so hectic that Bart does not bother to give the patient a receipt; however, he assures them that he will make sure their account is properly credited. When things slow down at the clinic, Bart often offers to help Lisa post payments to the patients' accounts receivable ledger. Lisa is always happy to receive help since she is also quite busy and because Bart is such a careful worker.

Required

Identify any internal control principles that may be violated in Dr. Spring's clinic.

LO2, 4 **P7-8A.** **Internal Control** Listed below are (a) four potential errors or problems that could occur in the processing of cash transactions and (b) internal control principles. Review each error or problem and identify an internal control principle that could reduce the chance of the error or problem occurring. You may also cite more than one principle if more than one applies, or write none if none of the principles will correct the error or problem.

1. An employee steals cash collected from a customer's accounts receivable and hides the theft by issuing a credit memorandum indicating the customer returned the merchandise.
2. An official with authority to sign checks is able to steal blank checks and issue them without detection.
3. Due to a labor shortage many employees are hired without sufficient skills with the thought they can "learn on the job."
4. A salesperson often rings up a sale for less than the actual amount and then pockets the additional cash collected from the customer.

Internal control principles:

a. Establish clear lines of authority and responsibility.
b. Segregation of duties.
c. Hire competent personnel.
d. Use control numbers on all business documents.
e. Develop plans and budgets.
f. Maintain adequate accounting records.
g. Provide physical and electronic controls.
h. Conduct internal audits.

LO5 **P7-9A.** **Bank Reconciliation** The Seattle First Company's bank statement for the month of September indicated a balance of $13,375. The company's cash account in the general ledger showed a balance of $10,030 on September 30. Other relevant information includes the following:

1. Deposits in transit on September 30 total $9,850.
2. The bank statement shows a debit memorandum for a $95 check printing charge.
3. Check number 238 payable to Simon Company was recorded in the accounting records for $496 and cleared the bank for this same amount. A review of the records indicated that the Simon account now has a $72 credit balance and the check to them should have been $568.
4. Outstanding checks as of September 30 totaled $11,600.
5. Check No. 276 was correctly written and paid by the bank for $574. The check was recorded in the accounting records as a debit to accounts payable and a credit to cash for $754.
6. The bank returned an NSF check in the amount of $1,110.
7. The bank included a credit memorandum for $2,620 representing a collection of a customer's note. The principal portion was $2,400 and the interest portion was $220. The interest had not been accrued.

Required

a. Prepare the September bank reconciliation for Seattle First Company.
b. Prepare any necessary adjusting entries.

P7-10A. **Effective Cash Management** Shorte LLP is a new law firm struggling to manage its cash flow. Like many new businesses, the firm has not yet developed a sufficient client base to cover its operating costs. Additionally, the firm faced a number of large initial, but nonrecurring, start-up costs at the beginning of the year. Ongoing monthly costs include office rent and salary for a paralegal staff member. Another problem that the firm faces is that several of its major clients have failed to pay their current, but overdue, bills. Mick Shorte, one of the two founding partners, has not taken any salary since the firm began operations over eight months ago, and has decided to maintain a part-time job bartending on weekends at a local resort to ensure that he has some cash to cover day-to-day expenses like travel.

LO6

Required
What suggestions would you make to Mick Shorte to improve his firm's cash management practices?

PROBLEMS—SET B

P7-1B. **Internal Control** Walt Company encountered the following situations:

LO2, 4

  a. Jenny Farrell, head of the receiving department, created a fictitious company named Speedy Forms and used it to send invoices to Walt Company for business documents that Walt never ordered or received. Farrell prepared receiving reports that stated that the business documents had been received. Walt's controller compared the receiving reports to the invoices and paid each one.

  b. Walt Company lost one day's cash receipts. An employee took the receipts to the bank after the bank's closing hours to deposit them in the night depository slot. A creative thief had placed a sign on the slot saying it was out of order and all deposits should be placed in a metal canister placed next to the building. Walt's employee placed the deposit in the canister and left. Employees from two other companies did the same thing. Later that night, the thief returned and stole the deposits from the canister. (This is an actual case.)

  c. Walt Company does not prenumber the sales invoices used for over-the-counter sales. A cashier pocketed cash receipts and destroyed all copies of the related sales invoices.

Required
For each situation, describe any violations of good internal control procedures and identify the steps that you would take to prevent each situation.

P7-2B. **Internal Control** The Mountain amusement ride has the following system of internal control over cash receipts. All persons pay the same price for a ride. A person taking the ride pays cash to the cashier and receives a prenumbered ticket. The tickets are issued in strict number sequence. The individual then walks to the ride site, hands the ticket to a ticket-taker (who controls the number of people getting on each ride), and passes through a turnstile. At the end of each day, the beginning ticket number is subtracted from the ending ticket number to determine the number of tickets sold. The cash is counted and compared with the number of tickets sold. The turnstile records how many people pass through it. At the end of each day, the beginning turnstile count is subtracted from the ending count to determine the number of riders that day. The number of riders is compared with the number of tickets sold.

LO2, 4

Required
Which internal control feature would reveal each of the following irregularities?

  a. The ticket-taker lets her friends on the ride without tickets.
  b. The cashier gives his friends tickets without receiving cash from them.
  c. The cashier gives too much change.
  d. The ticket-taker returns the tickets she has collected to the cashier. The cashier then resells these tickets and splits the proceeds with the ticket-taker.
  e. A person sneaks into the ride line without paying the cashier.

P7-3B. **Internal Controls for Cash Received from Retail Sales** Ocean Stores is a retailer of men's clothing. Most customers pay cash for their purchases. The procedures that Ocean uses for handling cash are described below:

LO4

  a. Each department begins the day with whatever amount of cash remains in the cash register from the prior day. This is not a predetermined amount.
  b. All sales associates share one cash drawer.

c.   Each sales associate can handle all transactions, including returns and unusual transactions, without approval from a supervisor.

d.   At the end of each day, one of the sales associates takes the cash drawer and the cash register totals to a private area where no one can observe what is being done, counts the cash in the drawer, and prepares a written report of sales and cash received. The cash, the register tape, and a copy of the report are sent to the controller's department.

e.   The controller prepares the deposit slip and sends the deposit to the bank. The controller then prepares the journal entry to record the cash sales.

f.   The controller does not keep any copies of the written report or the deposit slip.

g.   The bank statement is sent to the controller, who prepares the bank reconciliation.

Required

Indicate how Ocean could improve each of these procedures. (Refer to **Exhibit 7-2** in the chapter to help you generate ideas.)

LO5   P7-4B.   Bank Reconciliation On May 31, the Cash in Bank account of James Company, a sole proprietorship, had a balance of $5,950.30. On that date, the bank statement indicated a balance of $7,868.50. A comparison of returned checks and bank advices revealed the following:

1.   Deposits in transit May 31 totaled $2,603.05.
2.   Outstanding checks May 31 totaled $3,152.45.
3.   The bank added to the account $19.80 of interest income earned by James during May.
4.   The bank collected a $2,400 note receivable for James and charged a $30 collection fee. Both items appear on the bank statement.
5.   Bank service charges in addition to the collection fee, not yet recorded, were $65.
6.   Included with the returned checks is a memo indicating that L. Ryder's check for $686 had been returned NSF. Ryder, a customer, had sent the check to pay an account of $700 less a 2% discount.
7.   James Company incorrectly recorded the payment of an account payable as $360; the check was for $630.

Required

a.   Prepare a bank reconciliation for James Company at May 31.

b.   Prepare the journal entry (or entries) necessary to bring the Cash in Bank account into agreement with the reconciled cash balance on the bank reconciliation.

LO5   P7-5B.   Bank Reconciliation The bank reconciliation made by Adam Company, a sole proprietorship, on March 31 showed a deposit in transit of $1,300 and two outstanding checks, No. 797 for $550 and No. 804 for $690. The reconciled cash balance on March 31 was $12,020.

The following bank statement is available for April 30:

				Bank Statement			
TO	**Adam Company** **Fairbanks, AK**					**April 30** **FAIRBANKS NATIONAL BANK**	
Date	**Deposits**	**No.**	**Date**	**Charges**		**Date**	**Balance**
						Mar. 31	$11,960
Apr. 1	$1,300	804	Apr. 2	$ 690		Apr. 1	13,260
3	1,680	807	3	730		2	12,570
7	1,250	808	7	1,240		3	13,520
13	1,020	809	7	838		7	12,692
18	840	810	16	1,040		13	13,171
23	990	811	13	541		16	12,131
27	1,340	813	27	640		18	12,471
30	1,160	814	23	600		23	12,861
30	95IN	NSF	18	500		27	13,561
		SC	30	40		30	14,776
Item Codes:	EC: Error Correction		DM: Debit Memo			CM: Credit Memo	
	SC: Service Charge		OD: Overdraft			RT: Returned Item	
	IN: Interest Earned		NSF: Non-sufficient Funds				

A list of deposits made and checks written during April is shown below:

Deposits Made		Checks Written	
Apr. 2	$1,680	No. 807	$ 730
6	1,250	808	1,240
10	1,020	809	838
17	840	810	1,040
22	990	811	451
24	1,340	812	948
29	1,160	813	640
30	1,425	814	600
	$9,705	815	372
		816	875
			$7,734

The Cash in Bank account balance on April 30 was $13,991. In reviewing checks returned by the bank, the accountant discovered that check No. 811, written for $541 for delivery expense, was recorded in the cash disbursements journal as $451. The NSF check for $500 was that of customer R. Koppa, deposited in April. Interest for April added to the account by the bank was $95.

Required

a. Prepare a bank reconciliation for Adam Company at April 30.
b. Prepare the necessary journal entries to bring the Cash in Bank account into agreement with the reconciled cash balance on the bank reconciliation.

P7-6B. Reporting Cash Janzen Company has the following items at year-end: LO3

Currency and coin in safe...	$ 5,300
Funds in savings account (requires $2,500 compensating balance)	17,300
Funds in checking account...	1,750
Traveler's checks	1,900
Postdated check...	2,250
Not-sufficient-funds check	575
Money market fund...	12,600

Required

Identify the amount of the above items that should be reported as cash and cash equivalents on Janzen Company's balance sheet.

P7-7B. Internal Control Jerry Finch has worked for Jane Hardware for many years. Jerry has been a model LO2
employee. He has not taken a vacation in over three years, always stating that work was too important. One of Jerry's primary jobs at the store is to open mail and list the checks received. He also collects cash from customers at the store's outdoor nursery area. There are times that things are so hectic that Jerry does not bother to use the register, simply making change from cash he carries with him. When things slow down at the store Jerry often offers to help Cindy post payments to the customer's accounts receivable ledger. Cindy is always happy to receive help since she is also quite busy and because Jerry is such a careful worker.

Required

Identify any internal control principles that may be violated in the Jane Hardware store.

P7-8B. Internal Control Listed below are (a) four potential errors or problems that could occur in the pro- LO2, 4
cessing of cash transactions and (b) internal control principles. For each error or problem, identify an internal control principle that could reduce the chance of the error or problem occurring. You may also cite more than one principle if more than one applies, or write none if none of the principles will correct the error or problem.

1. Three cashiers use one cash register and the cash in the drawer is often short of the recorded balance.
2. The same employee is responsible for opening the mail, listing any checks received, preparing the deposit receipt, and recording to the accounts receivable journal. Several customers have complained that their balances are incorrect.
3. In an effort to save printing costs, generic receipts without numbers are used for customer sales.
4. Because things have been hectic, no budgets were prepared this year. One department seems to be doing less volume in revenue, but cost of goods sold appear to be high relative to sales.

Internal control principles:

   a. Establish clear lines of authority and responsibility.
   b. Segregation of duties.
   c. Hire competent personnel.
   d. Use control numbers on all business documents.
   e. Develop plans and budgets.
   f. Maintain adequate accounting records.
   g. Provide physical and electronic controls.
   h. Conduct internal audits.

LO5

P7-9B. **Bank Reconciliation** The Chicago Skate Company's bank statement for the month of June indicated a balance of $4,320. The company's cash account in the general ledger showed a balance of $2,464 on June 30. Other relevant information includes the following:

1. Deposits in transit on June 30 total $2,550.
2. The bank statement shows a debit memorandum for a $10 check printing charge.
3. Check No. 160 payable to Simon Company was recorded in the accounting records for $124 and cleared the bank for this same amount. A review of the records indicated that the Simon account now has a $28 credit balance and the check to them should have been $142.
4. Outstanding checks as of June 30 totaled $3,175.
5. Check No. 176 was correctly written and paid by the bank for $345. The check was recorded in the accounting records as a debit to accounts payable and a credit to cash for $354.
6. The bank returned an NSF check in the amount of $311.
7. The bank included a credit memorandum for $630 representing a collection of a customer's note. The principal portion was $610 and the interest portion was $20. The interest had not been accrued.

Required

   a. Prepare the June bank reconciliation for the Chicago Skate Company.
   b. Prepare any necessary adjusting entries.

SERIAL PROBLEM: KATE'S CARDS

(Note: This is a continuation of the Serial Problem: Kate's Cards from Chapters 1 through 6.)

SP7. On February 15, 2019, Kate Collins, owner of Kate's Cards, asks you to investigate the cash handling activities in her business. She believes that a new employee might be stealing funds. "I have no proof," she says, "but I'm fairly certain that the January 31, 2019, undeposited receipts amounted to more than $12,000, although the January 31 bank reconciliation prepared by the cashier (who works in the treasurer's department) shows only $7,238.40. Also, the January bank reconciliation doesn't show several checks that have been outstanding for a long time. The cashier told me that these checks needn't appear on the reconciliation because he had notified the bank to stop payment on them and he had made the necessary adjustment on the books. Does that sound reasonable to you?"

    At your request, Kate shows you the following (unaudited) January 31, 2019, bank reconciliation prepared by the cashier:

KATE'S CARDS Bank Reconciliation January 31, 2019					
Ending balance from bank statement...		$ 4,843.69	Balance from general ledger ...		$10,893.89
Add: Deposits in transit.		7,238.40			
		$12,082.09			
Less:			Less:		
Outstanding checks:			Bank service charge	$ 60.00	
No. 2351	$1,100.20		Unrecorded credit	1,200.00	(1,260.00)
No. 2353	578.32				
No. 2354	969.68	(2,448.20)			
Reconciled cash balance		$ 9,633.89	Reconciled cash balance		$ 9,633.89

You discover that the $1,200 unrecorded bank credit represents a note collected by the bank on Kate's behalf; it appears in the deposits column of the January bank statement. Your investigation also reveals that the December 31, 2018, bank reconciliation showed three checks that had been outstanding longer than 10 months: No. 1432 for $600, No. 1458 for $466.90, and No. 1512 for $253.10. You also discover that these items were never added back into the Cash account in Kate's books. In confirming that the checks shown on the cashier's January 31 bank reconciliation were outstanding on that date, you discover that check No. 2353 was actually a payment of $1,658.32 and had been recorded on the books for that amount.

To confirm the amount of undeposited receipts at January 31, you request a bank statement for February 1–12 (called a cutoff bank statement). This indeed shows a January 1 deposit of $7,238.40.

Required
a. Calculate the amount of funds stolen by the employee.
b. Describe how the employee concealed the theft.
c. What suggestions would you make to Kate about cash control procedures?

EXTENDING YOUR KNOWLEDGE

REPORTING AND ANALYSIS

EYK7-1. Financial Reporting Problem: Columbia Sportswear Company The financial statements for the **Columbia Sportswear Company** can be found in Appendix A at the end of this book.

COLUMBIA
SPORTSWEAR
COMPANY

Required
Use the financial statements and the accompanying notes to the financial statements to answer the following questions about Columbia Sportswear:
a. What title is used on Columbia's consolidated balance sheet for cash?
b. According to the information given in Note 2, what is the makeup of the cash and cash equivalents account?
c. According to information in Item 9A. Controls and Procedures, who is responsible for establishing and maintaining adequate internal control over financial reporting?
d. Deloitte and Touche, the independent auditor of Columbia Sportswear, issued a report on its audit of Columbia's internal control. What did Deloitte and Touche conclude?

EYK7-2. Comparative Analysis Problem: Columbia Sportswear Company vs. Under Armour, Inc. The financial statements for **Columbia Sportswear Company** can be found in Appendix A and **Under Armour, Inc.**'s financial statements can be found in Appendix B at the end of this book.

COLUMBIA
SPORTSWEAR
COMPANY

UNDER ARMOUR,
INC.

Required
Use the information in the companies' financial statements to answer the following questions:
a. What is the balance in cash and cash equivalents as of December 31, 2017?
b. What percentage of each company's total assets is made up of cash and cash equivalents as of December 31, 2017?
c. How much did cash and cash equivalents change during 2017 for each firm?
d. For each company, how did the change in cash for 2017 compare to its cash provided by operating activities?

EYK7-3. Business Decision Problem Quality Electronics Company is a distributor of microcomputers and related electronic equipment. The company has grown very rapidly. It is located in a large building near Chicago, Illinois. Jack Flanigan, the president of Quality, has hired you to perform an internal control review of the company. You conduct interviews of key employees, tour the operations, and observe various company functions. You discover the following:

1. Quality has not changed its ordering procedures since it was formed eight years ago. Anyone in the company can prepare a purchase order and send it to the vendor without getting any managerial approval. When the invoice arrives from the vendor, it is compared only to the purchase order before authorizing payment.

2. Quality does not have an organization chart. In fact, employees are encouraged to work on their own, without supervision. Flanigan believes that this approach increases creativity.

3. Business documents have been carefully designed by the controller. When the printer prints the documents, no control numbers are printed on them. Instead, employees using a form write the next sequential number on the form. The controller believes that this approach ensures that a proper sequencing of numbers will be maintained.

4. No budgets are prepared for the company.

5. All doors to the building remain unlocked from 7:00 a.m. to 11:00 p.m. Employees normally work from 7:30 a.m. to 5:00 p.m. A private security firm drives to the building to unlock it each morning and lock it each night. The security firm's employee leaves immediately after unlocking or locking. The company does not use time clocks or employee badges.

6. Flanigan believes that audits (either external or internal) are a waste of time. He has resisted the bank president's urging to hire a CPA firm to conduct an audit.

Required

Analyze the findings listed above. Then list all the internal control weaknesses that you can identify. For each weakness, describe one or more internal controls that Quality should install to overcome the weakness.

EYK7-4. **Financial Analysis Problem** The **Public Company Accounting Oversight Board (PCAOB)** was created as part of the Sarbanes-Oxley legislation to provide oversight to U.S. accounting firms. The PCAOB's address is http://www.pcaobus.org.

Required

Answer the following questions:

a. What is the mission of the PCAOB?
b. What is the title of the first auditing standard AS1001 issued by the PCAOB?
c. According to the rules section of the site, what is required for a PCAOB rule to take effect?

CRITICAL THINKING

EYK7-5. **Accounting Research Problem** Refer to the consolidated balance sheets in the fiscal year 2017 annual report of **General Mills, Inc.** available on this book's website.

Required

a. What was the amount of cash and cash equivalents as of May 28, 2017?
b. By what amount did cash and cash equivalents increase or decrease during the year?
c. What statement elsewhere in the annual report contains an explanation of the increase or decrease in the cash and cash equivalents amount? In that statement, what amount of cash was provided or used by (1) operating activities, (2) investment activities, and (3) financing activities?
d. What members of the company signed off as to the assessment of the company's internal control (see Reports of management and Independent Registered Public Accounting Firm)?
e. What firm conducted the audit of General Mills?
f. What opinion did the accounting firm express about General Mills' financial statements?
g. In addition to their audit of the financial statements, what else did the auditing firm audit?

EYK7-6. **Accounting Communication Activity** You were recently hired as the head of a company's ethics division. As one of your first acts, you decide to prepare a letter to the company's Chairman of the Board explaining the importance of ethics within the company. What are some of the items that should be included in your letter?

EYK7-7. **Accounting Ethics Case** Gina Pullen is the petty cash cashier for a large family-owned restaurant. She has been presented on numerous occasions with properly approved receipts for reimbursement from petty cash that she believes are personal expenses of one of the five owners of the restaurant. She reports to the controller of the company. The controller is also a family member and is the person who approves the receipts for payment out of petty cash.

Required

What are the accounting implications if Pullen is correct? What alternatives should she consider?

EYK7-8. **Corporate Social Responsibility Problem** Corporate Social Responsibility and fraud prevention are often related. One way that the two are connected is in the creation of a culture of honesty and the ethical treatment of employees. This is often the result of the tone from the top, where the company leaders not only talk about these concepts, but also practice them.

Required
Discuss how a culture of honesty and the ethical treatment of employees can reduce the risk of fraud.

EYK7-9.   **Forensic Accounting Problem**   Internal control follows the concept of reasonable assurance. Pete Simmons, the chief compliance officer of Salem Company, stated that he does not want simply reasonable assurance. He wants absolute assurance in all aspects that apply to the financial statements of the company. Specifically, Pete stated, "As long as I am working here, we will run a perfectly tight system that ensures absolutely no fraud in our financial statements." Betty Flint, the controller, disagreed with Pete and argued that anything more than reasonable assurance is both financially and practically impossible.

Required
Do you agree with Pete or Betty, and why?

EYK7-10.   **Forensic Accounting Problem**   Wayne James Nelson, a manager in the office of the Arizona State Treasurer, was found guilty of trying to defraud the state of nearly $2 million. Nelson's scheme involved issuing checks to bogus vendors. The amounts of the 23 checks issued are shown below:

The table lists the checks that a manager in the office of the Arizona State Treasurer wrote to divert funds for his own use. The vendors to whom the checks were issued were fictitious.

Date of Check	Amount
October 9, 1992	$ 1,927.48
	27,902.31
October 14, 1992	86,241.90
	72,117.46
	81,321.75
	97,473.96
October 19, 1992	93,249.11
	89,658.17
	87,776.89
	92,105.83
	79,949.16
	87,602.93
	96,879.27
	91,806.47
	84,991.67
	90,831.83
	93,766.67
	88,338.72
	94,639.49
	83,709.28
	96,412.21
	88,432.86
	71,552.16
TOTAL	**$1,878,687.58**

Required
Refer to the chart shown below that reports the occurrences of various digits in a number. Compare the first digit of the fraudulent checks to the table of Benford's Law. How do the two compare? Are there any other unusual patterns you detect in the check amounts?

Position of digit in number				
Digit	First	Second	Third	Fourth
0	.	.11968	.10178	.10018
1	.30103	.11389	.10138	.10014
2	.17609	.10882	.10097	.10010
3	.12494	.10433	.10057	.10006
4	.09691	.10031	.10018	.10002
5	.07918	.09668	.09979	.09998
6	.06695	.09337	.09940	.09994
7	.05799	.09035	.09902	.09990
8	.05115	.08757	.09864	.09986
9	.04576	.08500	.09827	.09982

Example: The number 147 has three digits, with 1 as the first digit, 4 as the second digit, and 7 as the third digit. The table shows that under Benford's Law the expected proportion of numbers with a first digit 1 is 30.103% and the expected proportion of numbers with a third digit 7 is 9.902%.

Source: "A Taxpayer Compliance Application of Benford's Law," by M. J. Nigrini. *The Journal of American Taxation Association* 18, 1996.

EYK7-11. Analyzing IFRS Financial Statements The 2017 financial statements of LVMH Moet Hennessey-Louis Vuitton S.A. are presented in Appendix C at the end of this book. LVMH is a Paris-based holding company and one of the world's largest and best-known luxury goods companies. As a member of the European Union, French companies are required to prepare their consolidated (group) financial statements using International Financial Reporting Standards (IFRS). After reviewing LVMH's consolidated financial statements, consider the following questions:

Required
a. What was the amount of cash and cash equivalents as of December 31, 2017?
b. By what amount did cash and cash equivalents increase or decrease during the year?
c. What statement elsewhere in the annual report contains an explanation of the increase or decrease in the cash and cash equivalents amount? In that statement, what amount of cash was provided or used by (1) operating activities, and (2) financing activities?

EYK7-12. Working with the Takeaways The following conditions of material weaknesses were reported in a prior year independent auditors' report on internal control of the U.S. Department of Transportation Highway Trust Fund (HTF):

1. Weaknesses with respect to journal entry preparation:
   a. Lack of indication of preparer
   b. Lack of supporting documentation
   c. Lack of proper review and approval
2. Weaknesses with respect to the consolidated financial statement preparation and analysis process:
   a. Inadequate analysis of abnormal balances
   b. Inadequate analysis of account relationships
   c. Inadequate controls over journal entry processing
   d. Lack of oversight related to allocation transfers

Required
a. What is the possible negative effect of these material weaknesses?
b. If you were the reporting auditor, what would you recommend be done?

ANSWERS TO SELF-STUDY QUESTIONS:

1. c, (pp. 326–327) 2. c, (pp. 328–329) 3. d, (p. 330) 4. a, (p. 330) 5. c, (p. 350) 6. b, (p. 334)
7. c, (pp. 336, 339) 8. d, (p. 341) 9. a, (p. 343) 10. c, (pp. 340–341)

YOUR TURN! SOLUTIONS

Solution 7.1

1. **Rationalization.** This quote is from CEO Kenneth Lay rationalizing his role in the accounting fraud at Enron.
2. **Pressure.** This quote is from an employee at Wells Fargo who was one of at least 5,000 employees pressured to open fake bank and credit card accounts.[3]
3. **Opportunity.** This quote is from Bernie Madoff describing how the "willful blindness" of regulators and investors provided the opportunity to keep his Ponzi scheme afloat.[4]

Solution 7.2

1. This is a personnel policy control violation. The supervisor may be committing a fraud and covering up his acts. If the supervisor were forced to take a vacation, the employee filling in might observe some suspicious activity and uncover the fraud.
2. This is a physical control violation. The unattended inventory could be stolen through the open door.
3. This is a segregation of duties violation. The supervisor is in a position to order an improper purchase, receive the goods for his own purposes, record the goods as received by the company, and then have the company pay for the purchase.

Solution 7.3

b. Marketable securities are often held for longer than 90 days and are reported separately from cash and cash equivalents.

Solution 7.4

1. (c) Treasurer's department
2. (a) Retail sales supervisor
3. (b) Mailroom
4. (e) Internal audit department
5. (d) Controller's department

Solution 7.5

1. (a) Add to bank statement balance
2. (b) Subtract from bank statement balance
3. (d) Subtract from cash general ledger account
4. (c) Add to cash general ledger account

Solution 7.6

a. 3   *b.* 2   *c.* 4   *d.* 1

Solution 7A.1

1. (a) Internal audit
2. (b) Financial statement audit
3. (c) Operational audit
4. (b) Financial statement audit
5. (c) Operational audit

---

[3] https://newrepublic.com/article/137571/wells-fargo-encouraged-employees-commit-fraud
[4] https://www.nytimes.com/2011/02/16/business/madoff-prison-interview.html

Chapter 8
Accounting for Receivables

PAST

In Chapter 7 we studied how companies can prevent errors and fraud with the use of internal controls.

PRESENT

In this chapter we turn our attention to the accounting for two important assets—accounts and notes receivable.

FUTURE

In Chapter 9 we will continue our study of a company's assets by looking at long-lived assets.

MGM Resorts International is among the largest gaming companies in the world. The company owns over 20 casino resorts, including Bellagio, MGM Grand Las Vegas, Mandalay Bay, Luxor, Excalibur, Monte Carlo, New York-New York, Circus Circus, and The Mirage, along with other properties such as golf courses and sports arenas. These establishments provide gaming, hotel accommodations, dining, and other entertainment for their clientele. Gaming, however, is the primary revenue-producing activity for these businesses.

Casino credit is an important marketing tool for gaming companies like MGM Resorts International. When used intelligently, it can result in significant increases in revenue since high-end casinos like Bellagio and The Mirage rely heavily on clientele that gamble on credit. Granting credit to gamblers also increases player loyalty because gamblers are inclined to play at casinos where they have a line of credit. Once credit is established, the gambler is allowed to write a marker and withdraw money to use to gamble. The credit, however, is only granted to clientele who utilize it. While there is no requirement that a gambler lose in order to maintain a line of credit, the credit is lost if it is not used. In other words, a casino grants credit to its clientele with the expectation that the more a gambler uses the line of credit, the more likely the casino is to win.

While credit lines clearly provide a boost to a casino's revenue, it is critical that the casino carefully manage these receivables. MGM Resorts International, for example, maintains strict controls over the issuance of markers and "aggressively pursues collection from those customers who fail to repay their markers on a timely basis." GAAP requires MGM Resorts International to recognize the likelihood that a casino may be unable to collect all of its outstanding markers on its financial statements. At year-end 2017, despite its collection efforts, MGM Resorts International reported nearly $93 million in casino doubtful accounts, representing 15% of casino accounts receivable.

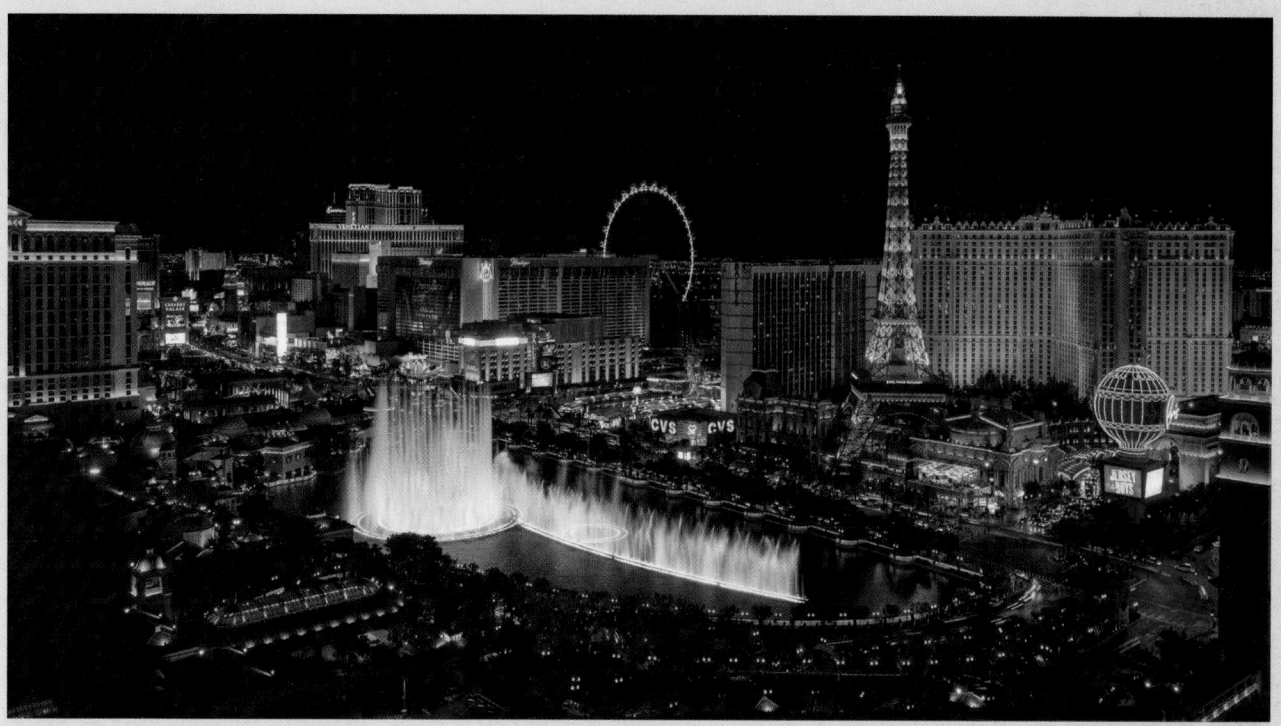

Road Map

LO	Learning Objective	Page	eLecture	Guided Example	Assignments
LO1	Define accounts receivable, explain losses from uncollectible accounts, and describe the allowance method of accounting for doubtful accounts.	374	E8-1	YT8.1	SS1, SS7, SS9, SE1, E2A, E3A, E9A, E2B, E3B, E9B, P2A, P7A, P2B, P7B
LO2	Describe and illustrate the percentage of net sales method and the accounts receivable aging method for estimating a business's bad debts expense.	379	E8-2	YT8.2 YT8.3	SS1, SS2, SS7, SS9, SE1, SE2, SE3, E1A, E2A, E8A, E9A, E1B, E2B, E8B, E9B, P1A, P2A, P3A, P5A, P6A, P7A, P8A, P10A, P1B, P2B, P3B, P5B, P6B, P7B, P8B, P10B
LO3	Discuss the accounting treatment of credit card sales.	384	E8-3	YT8.4	SS8, SE6, E4A, E11A, E4B, E11B, P4A, P9A, P4B, P9B
LO4	Illustrate a promissory note receivable, discuss the calculation of interest on notes receivable, and present journal entries to record notes receivable and interest.	384	E8-4	YT8.5	SS3, SS6, SS10, SE5, SE7, SE8, E5A, E6A, E12A, E13A, E5B, E6B, E12B, E13B, P5A, P10A, P5B, P10B
LO5	Define accounts receivable turnover and average collection period and explain their use in the analysis and management of accounts and notes receivable.	388	E8-5	YT8.6	SS4, SS5, SE4, SE9, E7A, E10A, E7B, E10B
LO6	Appendix 8A: Illustrate the direct write-off method and contrast it with the allowance method for accounting for doubtful accounts.	391	E8-6	YT8.7	SS9, SE10, E14A, E15A, E14B, E15B

ACCOUNTING FOR RECEIVABLES

Accounts Receivable	**Credit Card Sales**	**Notes Receivable**	**Analyzing and Managing Receivables**
• Recording accounts receivable • Allowance methods: percentage of net sales and aging of receivables • Direct write-off method (Appendix 8A)	• Recording receivables from credit card sales	• Promissory note • Interest on note • Maturity date • Recording entries • Disclosure of notes	• Accounts receivable turnover • Average collection period • Factoring and discounting

RECEIVABLES

Receivables are assets representing a company's right to receive cash or other assets at some point in the future. Receivables may be classified as either a current asset or a non-current asset, depending upon the date of the expected receipt of cash or other assets. The most common types of receivables are accounts receivable and notes receivable, which arise when a company sells its products or services to its customers on credit. Other types of receivables include loans to employees, loans to other companies, and any interest receivable on such outstanding loans.

ACCOUNTING IN PRACTICE	**Accounts Receivable**

Accounts receivable can amount to a large percentage of total assets for a company. Below are representative accounts receivable as a percentage of total assets appearing on recent balance sheets of four well-known companies in different industries.

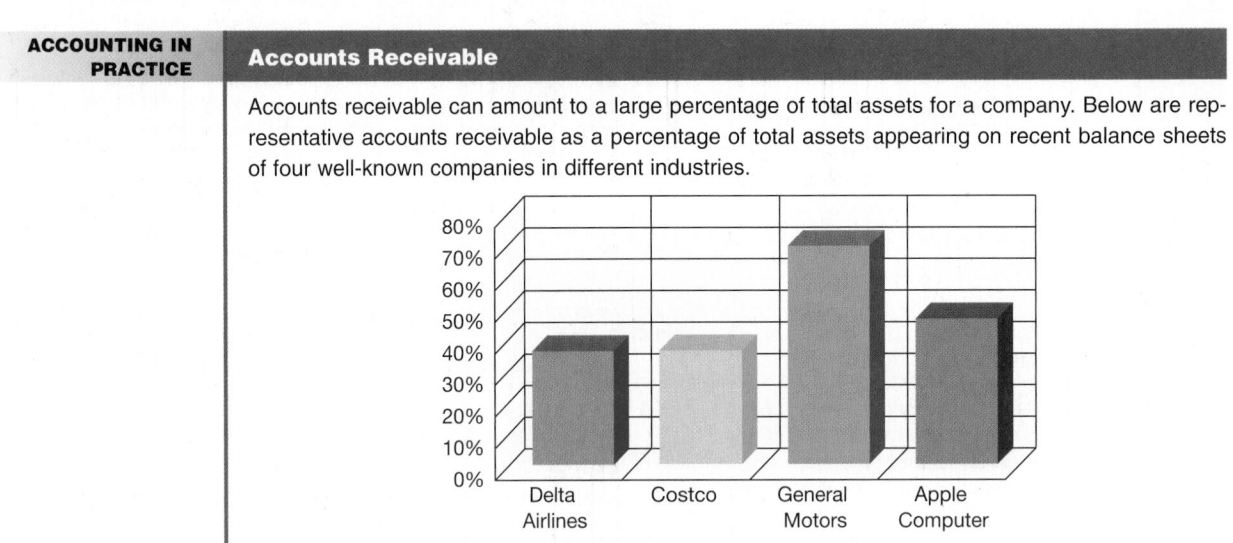

ACCOUNTS RECEIVABLE

LO1 **Define** accounts receivable, explain losses from uncollectible accounts, and **describe** the allowance method of accounting for doubtful accounts.

Many businesses sell goods and services to their customers on a credit basis, allowing customers to pay for their purchases over a period of time called the credit period. **Accounts receivable** is the asset, usually classified as current, that is created when a sale or service transaction is executed on a credit basis.

When a company executes a credit sale, it debits the Accounts Receivable account and credits the Sales Revenue account. When this transaction is posted to the general ledger, it increases both the Accounts Receivable and Sales Revenue balances. To illustrate, assume that on December 1, 2019, the Claremont Company sells $20,000 of merchandise on account. The company will make the following journal entry on its books for the credit sale transaction:

2019			
Dec. 1	Accounts receivable (+A)	20,000	
	Sales revenue (+R, +SE)		20,000
	To record credit sales to customers.		

A = L + SE
+20,000   +20,000
                 Rev

When the credit sale is collected on December 20, the following entry is made:

Dec. 20	Cash (+A)	20,000	
	Accounts receivable (−A)		20,000
	To record cash collection.		

A = L + SE
+20,000
−20,000

Accounts receivable includes only those amounts relating to credit sales of goods or services. Other amounts due, such as from advances to employees or loans to affiliated companies, should be included with the Other Receivables account on the balance sheet. Other Receivables may be either a current asset or a noncurrent asset.

A.K.A. Accounts receivable are also sometimes referred to as trade receivables.

Balance Sheet Title for Accounts Receivable

ACCOUNTING IN PRACTICE

Regardless of what it is called, accounts receivable are not cash until they are collected. So, what should we call these receivables? Uncollected cash may seem like an appropriate account title, but this title is not commonly used by businesses. Instead, companies use several other titles, as can be seen from a survey of 600 large U.S. companies:

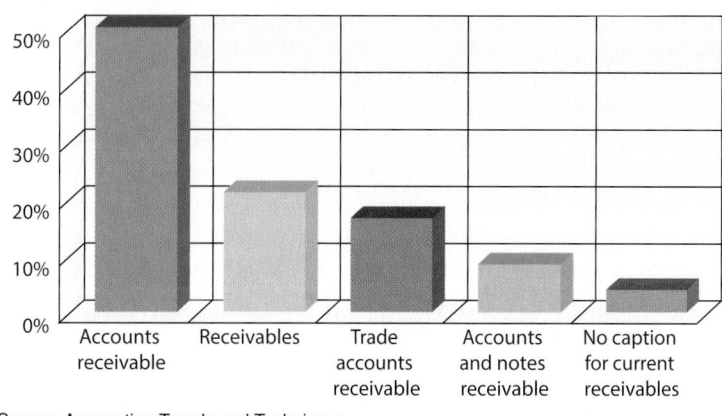

Source: Accounting Trends and Techniques

ACCOUNTING FOR BAD DEBTS

Businesses that extend credit to their customers anticipate some amount of credit losses—that is, losses from customers who fail to pay for their credit purchases. The magnitude of these losses is usually closely related to a firm's credit-granting policy. A **credit-granting policy** is a policy that a company follows to decide which customers should be allowed to buy goods and services on credit and how much credit those customers should be granted. Companies often base their credit-granting policy on a computerized credit score. (See Accounting in Practice: "Credit Scoring Systems" on the next page.) A company may deliberately relax its credit-granting policy to increase its sales, but should recognize that this will likely cause a corresponding increase in its credit losses.

Businesses must also establish a **credit-collection policy**; that is, a policy establishing the amount of time that its customers may take before they are required to pay their outstanding accounts receivable. In Chapter 5, we discussed the *credit period*, or the allowed time period that customers may take to pay for their credit purchases, and *sales discounts*, or the dollar amount that customers may deduct from the purchase price of goods if they pay within an allowed discount period. Together, any sales discount, the discount period, and the credit period constitute a company's credit-collection policy. Maintaining an effective credit-collection policy is important for those businesses that allow their customers to buy goods and services on credit, since companies can have millions of dollars of their cash tied up in uncollected accounts receivable.

Most large companies have credit departments that administer the company's credit-granting and credit-collection policies. Credit personnel conduct credit investigations, establish credit limits, and follow up on any unpaid accounts. They also decide, following written collection procedures, when an account receivable becomes uncollectible, and consequently, when it should be written off a company's balance sheet.

A.K.A. The Bad Debts Expense is also sometimes referred to as the Provision for Bad Debts.

Credit losses are considered to be an operating expense of a business, and consequently, they are debited to an account called **Bad Debts Expense**. Normally, the Bad Debts Expense account is classified as a selling expense on the income statement, although some companies include it as part of their administrative expenses.

ACCOUNTING IN PRACTICE	**Credit Scoring Systems**

Most companies use a computerized credit scoring system to decide whether to extend credit to their customers. The credit scoring system is based on a set of formulas with multiple variables. Data from a customer's credit application and from credit reporting agencies are used by the system to calculate a credit score. The system then compares the score to predetermined limits and recommends whether or not credit be extended.

If credit is extended, the scoring system often recommends an upper limit on the amount of credit to be extended. Scoring systems focus on a customer's ability to generate net income and cash flow, the customer's current level of debt and required repayment schedule, and current assets. Many of the financial statement ratios discussed throughout this text are incorporated into credit scoring systems.

Allowance Method

Credit losses are an unfortunate but predictable consequence of a business extending credit to its customers. At the time that a credit sale is made, the seller does not know whether the account receivable will be collected in full, in part, or not at all. Further, any loss from an uncollectible account may not be known for several months, or even a year or more, following the credit sale. To achieve a proper matching of sales revenues and expenses, however, a company's accountants must estimate the amount of the bad debts expense to report on the income statement. This estimate is recorded in an end-of-period adjusting entry. The process of estimating and recording the bad debts expense for a business is most often done using the **allowance method**.

PRINCIPLE ALERT	**Matching Concept**

The *matching concept* states that expenses should be linked with, or matched with, the revenues that they help to generate. A company sells its goods and services on credit because this business practice attracts more customers and, therefore, more sales revenue than if the company only permitted cash transactions. One of the costs associated with extending credit to customers is the bad debts expense. The matching concept requires that this expense be reported in the same accounting period as the related sales revenue. To accomplish the appropriate matching of sales revenue and expenses, accountants must estimate the bad debts expense because the specific accounts that will be uncollectible may not be known until a later accounting period.

Recording Estimated Bad Debts Expense Under the Allowance Method

The allowance method receives its name because the end-of-period adjusting entry credits a contra-asset account called the *Allowance for Doubtful Accounts*. The allowance method not only matches credit losses with the related credit sales in the same time period in which the sale occurs, but it also reports accounts receivable at their estimated realizable value in the end-of-period balance sheet. To illustrate, assume that the Claremont Corporation estimates its bad debts expense for 2019 to be $1,600 and makes the following adjusting entry in its general journal:

2019			
Dec. 31	Bad debts expense (+E, −SE)	1,600	
	Allowance for doubtful accounts (+XA, −A)		1,600
	To record the bad debts expense for the year.		

A	= L +	SE
−1,600		−1,600 Exp

Notice that the credit entry is made to the Allowance for Doubtful Accounts rather than directly against the Accounts Receivable account. The reason for this is because when a firm records its estimate of the amount of its uncollectible accounts, it does not know precisely which of its customer accounts included in the Accounts Receivable account will be uncollectible.

A.K.A. The Allowance for Doubtful Accounts is also often referred to as the Allowance for Uncollectible Accounts.

The Allowance for Doubtful Accounts is a contra-asset account with a normal credit balance. To report the amount of accounts receivable which the business expects to collect on the balance sheet, the Allowance for Doubtful Accounts is subtracted from the Accounts Receivable account. Assuming that the Claremont Corporation had $100,000 of accounts receivable (and a zero balance in the Allowance for Doubtful Accounts prior to the December 31, 2019, adjusting entry), the year-end balance sheet presentation would appear as follows:

Current Assets		
Cash		$ 52,000
Accounts receivable	$100,000	
Less: Allowance for doubtful accounts	1,600	
Accounts receivable, net.		98,400
Inventory.		125,000
Other current assets		31,000
Total Current Assets		$306,400

The Allowance for Doubtful Accounts of $1,600 is subtracted from the $100,000 of Accounts Receivable to obtain the net realizable value of $98,400. In other words, customers owe Claremont Corporation $100,000 but Claremont does not expect to collect $1,600 of this amount. Instead, Claremont only expects to collect $98,400, referred to as the net balance of Accounts Receivable.

Going Concern Concept

PRINCIPLE ALERT

Accounts receivable are reported on the balance sheet at the amount that a company expects to collect in the future from its credit customers. This presentation assumes that the company will be in existence long enough to collect its accounts receivable, and therefore, it is an example of the *going concern concept*. As a principle of accounting, the going concern concept assumes that a business entity will continue to operate indefinitely in the future.

Writing Off Specific Accounts Receivable under the Allowance Method   A company's credit department manager is usually the employee with the authority to determine when an account receivable is uncollectible, and hence, when a specific account receivable should be written off and removed from a company's balance sheet. This might occur, for example, if the customer has not made any payments on its account for a specified period of time, say four months, or if the customer has declared bankruptcy. Assume, for example, that the credit manager of the Claremont Corporation authorizes a $300 write-off of the Monroe Company's account receivable. When the accounting department is notified of the credit department manager's decision, it will make the following journal entry:

A = L + SE
+300
−300

2020			
Jan. 5	Allowance for doubtful accounts accounts (−XA, +A)	300	
	Accounts receivable—Monroe Company (−A)		300
	To write off the Monroe Company's account receivable.		

Notice that the journal entry to write off an account receivable does not affect a company's net income or total assets. Net income is reduced when the company records the year-end adjusting entry for bad debts expense. And because the Allowance for Doubtful Accounts is deducted from the Accounts Receivable account on the balance sheet, the *net* realizable value of accounts receivable is unchanged by the account write-off. After the Monroe Company's account receivable has been written off, the Accounts Receivable and the Allowance for Doubtful Accounts T-accounts of Claremont Corporation appear as follows:

+	Accounts Receivable (A)		–		– Allowance for Doubtful Accounts (XA) +			
Beg.	100,000	300	Jan. 5		Jan. 5	300	1,600	Beg.
Bal.	99,700						1,300	Bal.

As can be seen in the above T-accounts, the net realizable value of Claremont's accounts receivable as of January 1, 2020, is $98,400 ($100,000 less $1,600 allowance for doubtful accounts). Following the January 5, 2020, account write-off, the net realizable value of the Claremont Corporation's accounts receivable remains $98,400 ($99,700 less $1,300 allowance for doubtful accounts) since both the Accounts Receivable account and the Allowance for Doubtful Accounts are reduced by the same amount ($300). The following table summarizes the allowance method.

Action	Journal Entry	Balance Sheet Effect (Increase/Decrease)	Income Statement Effect (Increase/Decrease)
Recording Estimated Bad Debts Expense (In period when sale occurred)	**DEBIT** Bad debts expense **CREDIT** Allowance for doubtful accounts	▲ Allowance for doubtful accounts ▼ Accounts receivable, net	▲ Bad debts expense ▼ Net income
Writing-Off Bad Debt (When receivable is determined uncollectible)	**DEBIT** Allowance for doubtful accounts **CREDIT** Accounts receivable	▼ Accounts receivable ▼ Allowance for doubtful accounts No Change Accounts receivable, net	**No Change**

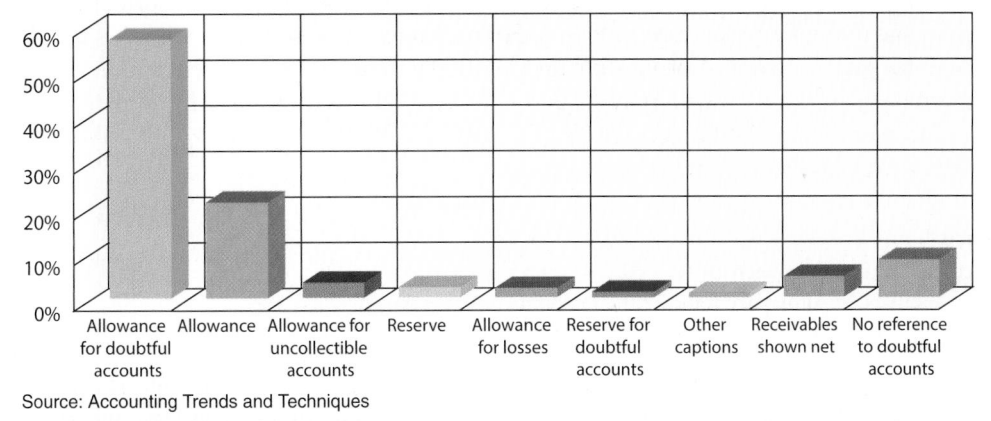

Balance Sheet Title for Uncollectible Accounts

No doubt about it, not all receivables will be collected! So how should a company title the amount that it likely will be unable to collect? Allowance for Doubtful Accounts is the most common account title, although several other titles are also used, as can be seen from a survey of 600 large U.S. companies:

Source: Accounting Trends and Techniques

Provide journal entries for the following transactions for the Turner Company:

May   2   Sold $40,000 of merchandise on account
May   17   Collected $35,000 of the May 2nd sale
May   31   Estimated $500 of the remaining accounts receivable may not be collected
June 15   Wrote off $200 of the existing accounts receivable

YOUR TURN! 8.1

The solution is on page 414.

ESTIMATING CREDIT LOSSES

When the allowance method is used, estimates of a company's expected credit losses are generally based on past business experience, with additional consideration given to forecasts of future sales activity, economic conditions, and any planned changes to a company's credit-granting policy. The most commonly used estimates of expected credit losses are related either to a company's credit sales for the period, or to the amount of accounts receivable outstanding at the end of a fiscal period. Companies may estimate credit losses using one or both methods, and a variety of different assumptions, before deciding on the best estimate that will be recorded in the financial statements.

LO2 **Describe** and **illustrate** the percentage of net sales method and the accounts receivable aging method for estimating a business's bad debts expense.

© Shutterstock.com

Percentage of Net Sales Method

Some companies estimate their expected credit losses as a percentage of their credit sales for a given period. Under this approach, the amount of the end-of-period adjusting entry for a business's expected bad debts expense is determined by multiplying the company's total credit sales for the period by a historical percentage that reflects past credit losses. For example, suppose that credit sales for 2019 for the Claremont Corporation are $80,000 and that past experience indicates that the company is likely to sustain a two percent loss on its credit sales. The adjusting entry for Claremont's expected credit losses of $1,600 for 2019 (2 percent × $80,000) would be recorded as follows in the general journal:

A = L + SE

−1,600   −1,600
                Exp

2019			
Dec. 31	Bad debts expense (+E, −SE)	1,600	
	Allowance for doubtful accounts (+XA, −A)		1,600
	To record the bad debts expense for the year.		

Because the periodic estimate for doubtful accounts under this procedure is related to credit sales, a firm should review its allowance account regularly to ensure that the account maintains a reasonable balance. If the allowance account balance is too large or too small, and does not reflect the amount the company thinks will prove uncollectible, the percentage used to estimate the periodic credit losses should be revised accordingly.

A company that uses the **percentage of net sales method** usually applies the estimated uncollectible percentage only to its credit sales, excluding cash sales, since only credit sales are subject to credit losses. Further, any sales discounts and sales returns and allowances should be deducted from total credit sales before applying the historical uncollectible percentage.

YOUR TURN! 8.2

The solution is on page 414.

MBC

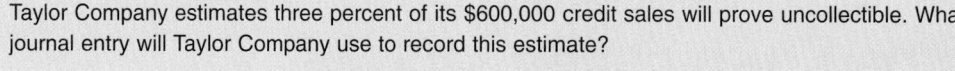

Taylor Company estimates three percent of its $600,000 credit sales will prove uncollectible. What journal entry will Taylor Company use to record this estimate?

Accounts Receivable Aging Method

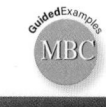

© iStock.com

A second approach to estimating a company's bad debts expense is to determine the appropriate balance for the Allowance for Doubtful Accounts account at year-end, and then calculate the appropriate estimate of the bad debts expense necessary to achieve this balance. The year-end balance in the Allowance for Doubtful Accounts represents a firm's estimate of the year-end accounts receivable that will prove uncollectible. By comparing this year-end estimate to the balance in the Allowance account just prior to making the adjustment for bad debts, it is possible to indirectly determine the appropriate current period estimate of the company's bad debts expense. This approach is called the **accounts receivable aging method**.

When using the accounts receivable aging method, a company determines the amount needed in the allowance account by analyzing the age structure of its outstanding accounts receivable balances using an aging schedule similar to the one in **Exhibit 8-1**. An **aging schedule** is simply an analysis that reveals how much time has elapsed since a credit sale originally occurred, and consequently, how long a customer's account receivable has remained unpaid. Assume, for example, that the firm whose aging schedule appears in **Exhibit 8-1** sells its goods on credit with a credit period of 30 days. The exhibit reveals that the Alton account is current, which means that the $320 billing was made within the last 30 days; however, the Bailey account is 0–30 days *past due,* which means that the account receivable is from 31 to 60 days old. The aging schedule also reveals that the Wall balance consists of a $50 billing made from 91 to 150 days ago and a $100 billing made from 151 days to seven months ago, and so on.

Exhibit 8-1	Aging Schedule of Customer Balances, December 31, 2019						

						Past Due		
Customer	Account Balance	Current	0–30 Days	31–60 Days	61–120 Days	121 Days to 6 Mos.	Over 6 Mos.
Alton, J.............	$ 320	$ 320					
Bailey, C.	400		$ 400				
many more accts ...	...	...	...	$ ...	$ ...	$ ...	$ ...
Wall, M............	150					50	100
Zorn, W..........	210			210			
	$50,000	$42,000	$4,000	$2,000	$1,000	$800	$200

Companies that analyze their uncollectible accounts experience using aged account balances develop probability-of-collection percentages to correspond with each age category. The probability of collection is subtracted from 100 percent to arrive at the probability of noncollection. At the end of each period, the probability-of-noncollection percentages are applied to the totals of each age category to determine the appropriate allowance account balance for a given category. For our example, these percentages are shown in the table below. As one might expect, the estimated probability of noncollection increases as the number of days past due increases. Applying the percentages to the totals in our aging schedule, we can calculate the required balance for the Allowance for Doubtful Accounts—that is, $1,560:

	Amount	Probability of Noncollection	Allowance Required
Current	$42,000	2%	$ 840
0–30 days past due	4,000	3%	120
31–60 days past due	2,000	5%	100
61–120 days past due	1,000	20%	200
121–180 days past due	800	25%	200
Over 180 days past due	200	50%	100
Total allowance required................			$1,560

Since the aging method is just an estimation process, estimation errors are likely to occur, causing the allowance account to sometimes be over- or underestimated. If, for example, the Allowance for Doubtful Accounts has an existing $400 credit balance (implying an overestimation error in the prior period), the year-end adjusting entry is:

2019			
Dec. 31	Bad debts expense (+E, −SE)	1,160	
	Allowance for doubtful accounts (+XA, −A)		1,160
	To record the bad debts expense for the period.		

A = L + SE
−1,160   −1,160 Exp

This entry brings the credit balance in the Allowance for Doubtful Accounts account to the required amount—$1,560, as shown below:

– Allowance for Doubtful Accounts (XA) +	
	400 · Beg.
	1,160 · Dec. 31
	1,560 · Bal.

Hint: In contrast to the percentage of net sales method, the accounts receivable aging method takes into account the beginning balance of the Allowance for Doubtful Accounts.

It is also possible to have a debit balance in the allowance account before the year-end adjustment, implying an underestimation error in the prior period. This would occur whenever the write-off of specific accounts receivable during the year exceeded the credit balance in the account as of the beginning of the year. Assume, for example, that the Allowance for Doubtful Accounts had a $350 debit balance prior to the recording of the December 31, 2019, adjusting entry, and that the aging schedule showed that the allowance account should have a $1,560 credit balance. The year-end adjusting entry would then be as follows:

A = L + SE	**2019**			
−1,910 −1,910 Exp	Dec. 31	Bad debts expense (+E, −SE)	1,910	
		Allowance for doubtful accounts (+XA, −A)		1,910
		To record the bad debts expense for the period.		

The following Allowance for Doubtful Accounts T-account shows that this entry creates the desired year-end credit balance in the allowance account of $1,560:

– Allowance for Doubtful Accounts (XA) +			
Beg.	350	1,910	Dec. 31
		1,560	Bal.

TAKEAWAY 8.1	Concept →	Method →	Assessment
	Are the accounts receivable being collected in a timely manner?	List of accounts receivable along with how long they have been outstanding. Prepare an aging schedule.	Accounts in the older categories require additional collection attention.

Recoveries of Accounts Written Off under the Allowance Method Occasionally, an account written off against the allowance for doubtful accounts as uncollectible will later prove to be wholly or partially collectible. In such situations, a firm must first reinstate the customer's account receivable for the amount recovered before recording the collection of cash. Then the cash payment can be recorded in the customer's account. The journal entry made for the original account write-off is reversed to the extent of the recovery amount and the receipt of cash is recorded in the usual manner. For example, assume that the Claremont Corporation is using the allowance method and wrote off the Monroe Company's $300 account on January 5, 2020, but subsequently received a $200 payment on April 20, 2020. The following journal entries illustrate the write-off and subsequent recovery procedure:

To write off the account

2020			
Jan. 5	Allowance for doubtful accounts (−XA, +A)	300	
	Accounts receivable—Monroe Company (−A)		300
	To write off the Monroe Company's account.		

$$A = L + SE$$
$$+300$$
$$-300$$

To reinstate the account

Apr. 20	Accounts receivable—Monroe Company (+A)	200	
	Allowance for doubtful accounts (−A)		200
	To reinstate the Monroe Company's account to the extent of the recovery.		

$$A = L + SE$$
$$+200$$
$$-200$$

To record receipt of cash

Apr. 20	Cash (+A)	200	
	Accounts receivable—Monroe Company (−A)		200
	To record collection of cash on account.		

$$A = L + SE$$
$$+200$$
$$-200$$

These last two journal entries are prepared the same way even if the recovery occurs more than a year following the period in which the account was originally written off.

Lapping

FORENSIC ACCOUNTING

One type of fraud that forensic accountants are trained to detect is "lapping." Lapping is not actually a fraud, but rather is a technique that a fraudster uses to cover up a fraud, typically involving the theft of funds. Under lapping, an employee who has access to incoming payments from the collection of accounts receivables will steal some of the cash received from credit customers. The employee then applies another customer's payment to the outstanding balance from the individual's account whose payment was stolen to cover up the theft. The process is repeated in an effort to cover up the original misappropriation. In other words, after the initial theft, the fraudster must continually "rob Peter to pay Paul." One audit procedure that may detect a lapping scheme involves the confirmation of accounts receivable. As part of the year-end independent audit, or as part of a regular internal audit, a company's accountant will send out confirmation letters to a sample of customers from the list of outstanding accounts receivable and pay particular attention to replies from customers disputing the timing of their payments or their outstanding balance.

Phisher, Inc., analyzed its accounts receivable at the end of 2018, and arrived at the aged balances listed below, along with the percentage that is estimated to be uncollectible:

YOUR TURN! 8.3

The solution is on page 414.

Age Group	Balance	Estimated Loss Percentage
0–30 days past due	$100,000	1
31–60 days past due	15,000	3
61–120 days past due	10,000	5
Over 120 days past due	20,000	10
	$145,000	

The company handles credit losses with the allowance method. The company has an existing credit balance in the Allowance account of $750.

a. Prepare the adjusting entry for estimated credit losses on December 31, 2018.

b. Prepare the journal entry to write off Phorest Company's account on May 12, 2019, in the amount of $480.

CREDIT CARD SALES

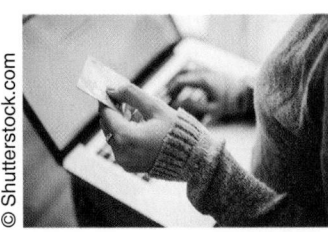

LO3   **Discuss** the accounting treatment of credit card sales.

Many businesses, especially retailers, allow their customers to use credit cards for their purchase transactions. Popular credit cards include VISA, MasterCard, Discover, and American Express. When a customer uses a credit card to make a purchase, the seller collects cash from the credit card company, and the customer pays cash to the credit card company when billed at a later date.

The issuer of a credit card, frequently a financial institution like **Chase Bank** or **Citibank**, will charge the seller a fee each time a card is used. The **credit card fee** usually ranges from one percent to five percent of the amount of the credit card purchase. Businesses are willing to incur this fee because credit cards provide considerable benefits to a seller. For example, the seller does not have to evaluate the creditworthiness of the customer using a credit card, and the business avoids any risk of noncollection of the account since this risk remains with the credit card issuer. Finally, the seller typically receives the cash from the credit card issuer faster than if the customer were granted trade credit by the seller.

To illustrate, the journal entry to record a $1,000 credit card sale on March 15, with a three percent credit card fee, is as follows:

A = L + SE			
+970	Mar. 15	Cash (+A)	970	
−30 Exp		Credit card fee expense (+E, −SE)	30	
+1,000 Rev		Sales revenue (+R, +SE)		1,000
		To record credit card sales and collection, less a three percent fee.		

YOUR TURN! 8.4

The solution is on page 415.

Nafooz Company pays a two percent credit card fee on all credit sales, and receives a cash deposit immediately following each credit card transaction. If credit sales for the company total $50,000, what journal entry should be recorded to recognize the receipt of cash and the credit card fee expense?

NOTES RECEIVABLE

LO4   **Illustrate** a promissory note receivable, **discuss** the calculation of interest on notes receivable, and **present** journal entries to record notes receivable and interest.

Promissory notes receivable are often used in sale transactions when the credit period is longer than the 30- to 60-day credit period that is typical for accounts receivable. Promissory notes are also used frequently in sales involving equipment and property because the dollar amount of these transactions can be quite large. Occasionally, a note will be substituted for an account receivable when an extension of the usual credit period is granted. Also, promissory notes are normally prepared when financial institutions make a loan to a business or an individual.

A **promissory note** is a written promise to pay a certain sum of money on demand or at a fixed (or determinable) future date. The note is signed by the **maker** and made payable to the order of either a specific **payee** or to the **bearer**. The interest rate specified on the note is typically an annual rate. **Exhibit 8-2** illustrates a promissory note.

A note from a debtor is called a **note receivable** by the noteholder. A note is usually regarded as a stronger claim against a debtor than an account receivable because the terms of payment are specified in writing.

Exhibit 8-2	A Promissory Note

PROMISSORY NOTE

$ __2,000.00__   __May 3__ 20 __19__

__60 days__ after the above date the undersigned promises to pay

to the order of __Susan Robinson__ , the

sum of __Two thousand no/100.............__ dollars, with __9__ %

interest. Payable at __First Bank of Los Angeles, CA__ .

__James Stone__

NAME OF BORROWER

Interest on Notes Receivable

Interest is a charge for the use of money over time. Interest incurred on a promissory note receivable is interest income to the noteholder or payee of the note and interest expense to the maker of the note. Businesses are required to distinguish between operating and non-operating items in their income statements; consequently, they place any interest expense or interest income on outstanding notes under the other income and expense heading in the income statement so that financial statement users will readily identify interest income or expense as being nonoperating in nature.

Interest on a short-term promissory note is paid at the maturity date of the note. The formula for determining the amount of interest expense to the maker and interest income to the noteholder is as follows:

$$\text{Interest} = \text{Principal} \times \text{Interest rate} \times \text{Interest time}$$

The principal is the face amount of a note and the interest rate is the annual rate of interest specified in the note agreement. Interest time is the fraction of a year that a note receivable is outstanding.

When a note is written for a certain number of months, interest time is expressed in twelfths of a year. For example, interest on a six-month note for $2,000 with a nine percent annual interest rate is calculated as:

$$\text{Interest} = \$2{,}000 \times 0.09 \times 6/12 = \$90$$

When a note's duration, or time to maturity, is given in days, interest time is expressed as a fraction of a year; the numerator is the number of days that the note receivable will be outstanding and the denominator is 360 days. (Some lenders use 360 days, while others use 365 days; we use 360 days in our examples, exercises, and problems.) For example, interest on a 60 day note for $2,000 with a nine percent annual interest rate is:

$$\text{Interest} = \$2{,}000 \times 0.09 \times 60/360 = \$30$$

Determining Maturity Date

When a note's duration is expressed in days, it is customary to count the exact number of days in each calendar month to determine the note's **maturity date**. For example, a 90 day note dated July 21 has an October 19 maturity date, which is determined as follows:

10	days in July (remainder of month—31 days minus 21 days)
31	days in August
30	days in September
19	days in October (number of days required to total 90)
90	

If the duration of a note is expressed in months, the maturity date is calculated simply by counting the number of months from the date of issue. For example, a two-month note dated January 31 would mature on March 31, a three-month note of the same date would mature on April 30 (the last day of the month), and a four-month note would mature on May 31.

Recording Notes Receivable and Interest

When a note is exchanged to settle an account receivable, a journal entry is made to reflect the note receivable and to reduce the balance of the related account receivable. For example, suppose that Jordon Company sold $12,000 of merchandise on account to Bowman Company. On October 1, after the regular credit period had elapsed, the Bowman Company gave the Jordon Company a 60 day, nine percent note receivable for $12,000. Jordon Company makes the following journal entry to record receiving the note:

A = L + SE
+12,000
−12,000

Oct. 1	Notes receivable—Bowman Company (+A)	12,000	
	Accounts receivable—Bowman Company (−A)		12,000
	Received 60 day, nine percent note in payment of account.		

If the Bowman Company pays its note receivable on the November 30 maturity date, the Jordon Company makes the following journal entry:

A = L + SE
+12,180 +180 Rev
−12,000

Nov. 30	Cash (+A)	12,180	
	Interest income (+R, +SE)		180
	Notes receivable—Bowman Company (−A)		12,000
	Collected Bowman Company note. ($12,000 × 0.09 × 60/360 = $180).		

Recording Dishonored Notes

In the prior example, interest for 60 days at nine percent is recorded on the maturity date of the note even if the maker of the note (Bowman Company) defaults on or dishonors the note. When a note is dishonored at maturity, the amount of the combined principal plus interest is converted to an account receivable. This procedure leaves only the current, unmatured notes in the noteholder's Notes Receivable account. If the Bowman Company, for example, failed to pay its note on November 30 as expected, the Jordon Company would make the following journal entry:

A = L + SE
+12,180 +180 Rev
−12,000

Nov. 30	Accounts receivable—Bowman Company (+A)	12,180	
	Interest income (+R, +SE)		180
	Notes receivable—Bowman Company (−A)		12,000
	To record the dishonoring of a note by Bowman Company.		

Adjusting Entry for Interest

When the term of a promissory note extends beyond the end of an accounting period, a year-end adjusting entry is necessary to reflect the interest earned. To illustrate, assume that Jordon Company has a note receivable outstanding at December 31, 2019. The note receivable from the Garcia Company is dated December 21, 2019, has a principal amount of $6,000, an interest rate of 12 percent, and a maturity date of February 19, 2020. The adjusting entry that Jordon Company makes at December 31, 2019, to record the earned, but uncollected, interest income is as follows:

Dec. 31	Interest receivable (+A)	20		A	= L +	SE
	Interest income (+R, +SE)		20	+20		+20 Rev
Ⓐ	*To accrue interest income on the note from Garcia Company*					
	($6,000 × 0.12 × 10/360 = $20).					

When the note is subsequently paid on February 19, 2020, Jordon Company makes the following journal entry:

Feb. 19	Cash (+A)	6,120		A	= L +	SE
	Interest income (+R, +SE)		100	+6,120		+100 Rev
	Interest receivable (−A)		20	−20		
Ⓑ	Notes receivable—Garcia Company (−A)		6,000	−6,000		
	Received payment of principal and interest from Garcia Company					
	($6,000 × 0.12 × 50/360 = $100).					

Revenue Recognition Principle   PRINCIPLE ALERT

The adjusting entry to accrue interest income on an outstanding promissory note receivable at year-end illustrates the *revenue recognition principle*. This principle states that revenue should be recognized when services are performed or goods are sold. The holder of a promissory note provides the maker of the note with a service—the use of money for a specified time period. This service is provided each day that a note is outstanding and interest is the payment for this service. Interest income is not recorded each day. Normally, interest income for a note's full term is recorded when it is collected at the note's maturity. If the accounting period ends before a note's maturity date, an adjusting entry is made to record the accrued interest income for the services provided in the current period.

Reporting Notes Receivable on the Balance Sheet

Short-Term Notes Receivable are a current asset on the balance sheet. Since these notes can normally be readily converted into cash, they are often placed below Accounts Receivable in the current asset section. As with accounts receivable, notes receivable are reported separately from other notes receivable from officers and employees and notes representing advances to affiliated companies. If the notes are not short term, they should be classified as noncurrent assets. Interest Receivable on a note receivable is also a current asset.

Sometimes companies with a large volume of notes receivable must provide for possible losses on the outstanding notes. Frequently, the Allowance for Doubtful Accounts also covers potential credit losses on notes as well. In such cases, the Allowance for Doubtful Accounts account is deducted from the aggregate total of Accounts Receivable and Notes Receivable on the balance sheet. Estimating the potential credit losses on outstanding notes receivable follows the same procedures as for accounts receivable.

Perhaps it may seem odd to equate good corporate citizenship with the gaming industry, but that does not mean that gaming companies should not do all that they can to be good citizens. MGM Resorts International's mission statement aims to portray the company as a responsible corporate citizen committed to sustainability:

> "MGM Resorts International is committed to be a global leader in sustainability and stewardship of the environment, bringing value to communities and shareholders alike. Our company operates smarter and more efficiently as we extend sustainable business practices to existing properties and new projects. The results we achieve include using resources more efficiently; reducing construction impact; minimizing waste; managing supply chains; and increasing awareness. This commitment helps our business grow responsibly."

YOUR TURN! 8.5

The solution is on page 415.

Ruby Company received a four month, five percent note receivable for $40,000 on October 1, 2019. How much interest income should be accrued on December 31, 2019?

ANALYZING AND MANAGING RECEIVABLES

LO5 **Define** accounts receivable turnover and average collection period and **explain** their use in the analysis and management of accounts and notes receivable.

Most companies transact the majority of their sales on credit, and doing so creates accounts receivable. Management and financial analysts closely monitor a company's accounts receivable using a variety of financial measures, including the accounts receivable turnover ratio and the average collection period. **Accounts receivable turnover** indicates how many times a year a firm collects its average accounts receivable, and thus, measures how fast accounts receivable are being converted into cash. Accounts receivable turnover is calculated as follows:

$$\text{Accounts receivable turnover} = \frac{\text{Net sales}}{\text{Average accounts receivable (net)}}$$

The numerator in this ratio is net sales. Ideally, the numerator should be net credit sales, but financial information available to financial statement users does not usually divide net sales into credit sales and cash sales. For many businesses like the **Johnson & Johnson Company**, the maker of Band-Aids and baby shampoo, over 99 percent of the company's sales are credit sales. Unless there is other information available on the amount of credit sales, it is common to assume that a company's net sales is a good proxy for its credit sales. Average accounts receivable (net of the allowance for doubtful accounts) is calculated by summing the beginning and ending accounts receivable (net) balances and dividing the sum by two.

To illustrate the calculation of this ratio, consider the financial results for the Claremont Corporation.

	2020	2019
Net sales.	$40,831	$33,548
Beginning accounts receivable (net)	1,848	1,948
Ending accounts receivable (net).	1,799	1,848

Claremont's accounts receivable turnover for 2020 is 22.39, or $40,831/[$1,848 + $1,799)/2], and for 2019 is 17.68, or $33,548/[($1,948 + $1,848)/2]. In general, the higher the accounts receivable turnover ratio, the faster a company is converting its receivables into cash. The increase in accounts receivable turnover from 2019 to 2020 is a positive sign regarding how well the Claremont Corporation is managing its accounts receivable.

An extension of the accounts receivable turnover ratio is the **average collection period**, calculated as follows:

$$\text{Average collection period} = \frac{365}{\text{Accounts receivable turnover}}$$

This ratio indicates how many days it takes on average to collect an account receivable. During 2020, Claremont's average collection period was 16.3 days, or 365/22.39. During 2019, Claremont's average collection period was 20.6 days, or 365/17.68. The ratio reveals that Claremont is taking four fewer days to collect its accounts receivable in 2020 than in 2019, another sign of improved accounts receivable management.

The average collection period may also be used to evaluate the effectiveness of a company's credit policies. One rule of thumb states that the average collection period should not exceed a business's allowed credit period by more than 15 days. Thus, if a firm grants credit terms of 30 days to its customers, its average collection period should not exceed 45 days.

YOUR TURN! 8.6

The solution is on page 415.

The Forrester Corporation disclosed the following financial information (in millions) in its recent annual report:

	2019
Net sales.	$30,000
Beginning accounts receivable (net)	2,800
Ending accounts receivable (net)	3,200

a. Calculate the accounts receivable turnover ratio for 2019.
b. Calculate the average collection period for 2019.

Factoring and Discounting

A company can accelerate the collection of cash on an account receivable or a note receivable by selling the receivable to a finance company or a financial institution. Selling an account receivable is called **factoring** and selling a note receivable is called **discounting**. Finance companies and financial institutions that buy receivables are called **factors**.

When receivables are sold, the factor pays the selling company the amount of the account receivable or note receivable less a fee, often ranging from two percent to five percent of the value of the sold receivable. The factor then collects the cash payments directly from the customer who originally purchased the goods or services on credit. This approach speeds the collection of cash to the selling company and releases it from the work of billing and collecting the account.

Accounts and notes receivable may be sold under two conditions—with recourse and without recourse. "With recourse" indicates that in the event that a factor is unable to collect a specific customer's account or note receivable, the factor has the right to request that the selling company return the amount of the uncollected receivable. "Without recourse" indicates that a factor is unable to request reimbursement from the selling company if the factor is unable to collect a specific account or note receivable. Selling receivables without recourse is more expensive than selling receivables with recourse because the factor is forced to assume additional collection risk.

TAKEAWAY 8.2	Concept	→ Method →	Assessment
	Are any of the existing accounts receivable in need of further attention?	Net sales and average accounts receivable $$\text{Accounts receivable turnover} = \frac{\text{Net sales}}{\text{Average accounts receivable (net)}}$$ $$\text{Average collection period} = \frac{365}{\text{Accounts receivable turnover}}$$	Compare the average collection period to the company credit policy. Longer collection periods suggest the need for management attention.

COMPREHENSIVE PROBLEM

At December 31, 2018, the following selected accounts appeared in Delta Company's unadjusted trial balance:

Accounts receivable	$81,000
Allowance for doubtful accounts.	1,200 (credit)
Notes receivable (Jason, Inc.)	12,000

Net credit sales for 2018 were $250,000. The $12,000 note receivable was a 90 day, eight percent note dated December 13, 2018. The following adjusting entries and transactions occurred at the end of 2018 and during 2019:

2018

Dec. 31   Recorded the adjusting entry for the bad debts expense, at $1\frac{1}{2}$ percent of net credit sales.
       31   Recorded the adjusting entry for interest on the $12,000 note receivable.

2019

Mar. 13   Received payment on the $12,000 note receivable from Jason, Inc., plus interest.
Apr.   5   Wrote off the account of Abilene Company, $2,850.
July   9   Wrote off the account of Acme Suppliers, $1,450.
Sept. 5   Received payment from Acme Suppliers, which is in bankruptcy proceedings, for $450 in final settlement of the account written off on July 9.
Dec.   6   Wrote off the account of Walton, Inc., $1,300.
       31   Changed from the percentage-of-net-sales method of providing for uncollectible accounts to an estimate based on the accounts receivable aging method. The account analysis indicated a desired credit balance of $4,500 in the Allowance for Doubtful Accounts.

Required
Prepare the journal entries for these adjustments and transactions.

Solution

2018			
Dec. 31	Bad debts expense (+E, −SE)	3,750	
	Allowance for doubtful accounts (+XA, −A)		3,750
	To provide for bad debts expense at $1\frac{1}{2}$ percent of net credit sales, $250,000.		
31	Interest receivable (+A)	48	
	Interest income (+R, +SE)		48
	To accrue interest on Jason, Inc., note receivable ($12,000 × 0.08 × 18/360 = $48).		

continued

2019			
Mar. 13	Cash (+A)	12,240	
	Interest income (+R, +SE)		192
	Interest receivable (−A)		48
	Notes receivable—Jason, Inc. (−A)		12,000
	To record receipt of payment of Jason, Inc., note receivable		
	($12,000 × 0.08 × 72/360 = $192).		
	(31 + 28 + 13 = 72 days)		
Apr. 5	Allowance for doubtful accounts (−XA, +A)	2,850	
	Accounts receivable—Abilene Company (−A)		2,850
	To write off the account of Abilene Company as uncollectible.		
July 9	Allowance for doubtful accounts (−XA, +A)	1,450	
	Accounts receivable—Acme Suppliers (−A)		1,450
	To write off the account of Acme Suppliers as uncollectible.		
Sept. 5	Accounts receivable—Acme Suppliers (+A)	450	
	Allowance for doubtful accounts (+XA, −A)		450
	To reinstate $450 of the account of Acme Suppliers that proved		
	collectible.		
5	Cash (+A)	450	
	Accounts receivable—Acme Suppliers (−A)		450
	To record payment of Acme Suppliers' account.		
Dec. 6	Allowance for doubtful accounts (−XA, +A)	1,300	
	Accounts receivable—Walton, Ince. (−A)		1,300
	To write off the account of Walton, Inc., as uncollectible.		
Dec. 31	Bad debts expense (+E, −SE)	4,700	
	Allowance for doubtful accounts (+XA, −A)		4,700
	To provide for bad debts expense		
	($4,500 desired balance + $200 existing debit balance = $4,700).		

Allowance for Doubtful Accounts	
Beginning balance	($1,200)
Bad Debts Expense, 12/31/2018	(3,750)
Write-offs ($2,850 + $1,450 + $1,300)	5,600
Recovery	(450)
Balance.	200
Bad Debts Expense, 12/31/2019	(4,700)
Ending Balance	($4,500)

APPENDIX 8A: Direct Write-Off Method

The direct write-off method of accounting for credit losses is an alternative to the allowance method. Under the **direct write-off method**, doubtful accounts are charged to the bad debts expense on the income statement in the period in which the accounts are determined to be uncollectible. Under this approach, there is no attempt to estimate the bad debts expense, nor is there any attempt to match this expense with sales revenues in the period in which the credit sales transaction originally occurred. As a consequence, U.S. GAAP does not permit the use of the direct write-off method unless the amount of the credit losses is immaterial. The reason for this is because the direct write-off method does not properly match credit losses with credit sales in the appropriate time period, violating the matching concept.

LO6 **Illustrate** the direct write-off method and **contrast** it with the allowance method for accounting for doubtful accounts.

For example, an account receivable may not be determined to be uncollectible, and therefore not written off, until several periods after the actual credit sales revenue is recorded. By way of contrast, the allowance method, through the use of an estimate of the bad debts expense, properly matches this expense with the associated sales revenue in the same period. The use of the direct write-off method also causes a consistent overstatement of accounts receivable on the balance sheet. Although not generally accepted for accounting purposes for most businesses, the direct write-off method is used by all companies for U.S. federal income tax purposes.

The journal entries made when the direct write-off method is used are illustrated below using data from the Claremont Corporation illustration appearing on pages 382–383:

To write off the account

		2020			
A	= L +	SE	Jan. 5	Bad debts expense (+E, −SE)	300	
−300		−300 Exp		Accounts receivable—Monroe Company (−A)		300
				To write off the Monroe Company's account.		

To reinstate the account

A	= L +	SE	Apr. 20	Accounts receivable—Monroe Company (+A)	200	
+200		+200 Exp		Bad debts expense (−E, +SE)		200
				To reinstate the Monroe Company's account to the extent of the recovery.		

To record receipt of cash

A	= L +	SE	Apr. 20	Cash (+A)	200	
+200				Accounts receivable—Monroe Company (−A)		200
−200				*To record collection of cash on account.*		

If an account receivable written off in a prior year is reinstated during the current year and the Bad Debts Expense account has no existing balance from other write-offs (and no more write-offs are expected), then the account credited in the reinstatement entry is the Doubtful Accounts Recovery, a revenue account.

**YOUR TURN!
8A.1**

The solution is on page 415.

Harley Company has determined an account receivable in the amount of $750 from Rhea Inc. will be uncollectible and has decided to write the account off. Harley Company uses the direct write-off method because write-offs are considered immaterial. Provide the journal entry to write off the Rhea account.

SUMMARY OF LEARNING OBJECTIVES

LO1 **Define accounts receivable, explain losses from uncollectible accounts, and describe the allowance method of accounting for doubtful accounts. (p. 374)**

- Accounts receivable is a current asset created when a sales transaction is executed on a credit basis.
- Accounts receivable does not include such receivables as loans to affiliate companies or advances to employees.
- The credit department of a company is responsible for conducting credit investigations of customers, establishing credit limits, and following up on overdue accounts.
- The allowance method is designed to record the bad debts expense in the same accounting period as the related credit sale.
- When the allowance method is used, specific accounts are written off by debiting the Allowance for Doubtful Accounts and crediting the Accounts Receivable account.

LO2 **Describe and illustrate the percentage of net sales method and the accounts receivable aging method for estimating a business's bad debts expense. (p. 379)**

- The percentage of net sales method is used to determine estimated credit losses directly. Estimated credit losses are determined by multiplying credit sales (net of any sales discounts and sales returns and allowances) times the estimated percentage of uncollectible credit sales.
- The accounts receivable aging method determines the estimated credit loss indirectly. The balance in the Accounts Receivable account is segmented into age categories. Then the balance of each category is multiplied by the estimated uncollectible percentage for that age category. The results are added to obtain the desired balance in the Allowance for Doubtful Accounts. The desired balance is then compared to the existing balance in the Allowance for Doubtful Accounts to determine the estimated credit losses and bad debts expense for the period.

- Occasionally, accounts written off against the Allowance for Doubtful Accounts later prove to be wholly or partially collectible. When this happens, the Accounts Receivable account is first reinstated to the extent of the recovery, and then the cash collection is recorded.

Discuss the accounting treatment of credit card sales. (p. 384)   LO3

- Credit card fee expense is recognized when the credit card sales transaction is recorded.
- Credit card fee expense reduces the amount of cash received by the company from the credit card issuer.

Illustrate a promissory note receivable, discuss the calculation of interest on notes receivable, and present journal entries to record notes receivable and interest. (p. 384)   LO4

- Interest on a short-term promissory note is determined using the following formula:

$$\text{Interest} = \text{Principal} \times \text{Interest rate} \times \text{Interest time}$$

- When a note is received in payment of an account receivable balance, the Notes Receivable account is debited and the Accounts Receivable account is credited.
- The noteholder recognizes interest income at the maturity date or in an end-of-period adjusting entry if the financial statements are prepared before the note matures.

Define *accounts receivable turnover* and *average collection period* and explain their use in the analysis and management of accounts and notes receivable. (p. 388)   LO5

- Accounts receivable turnover = Net sales/Average accounts receivable
- Average collection period = 365/Accounts receivable turnover
- *Accounts receivable turnover* indicates how many times a year, on average, that a firm collects its accounts receivable. *Average collection period* indicates how many days it takes, on average, to collect an account receivable.

Appendix 8A: Illustrate the direct write-off method and contrast it with the allowance method for accounting for doubtful accounts. (p. 391)   LO6

- Under the direct write-off method, uncollectible accounts are charged to the bad debts expense in the period in which they are determined to be uncollectible.
- For most companies, the direct write-off method is not a generally accepted method of accounting for credit losses; however, most companies use the direct write-off method for income tax purposes.
- U.S. GAAP does not permit the use of the direct write-off method unless the amount of the credit losses is immaterial.

Concept	Method	Assessment	SUMMARY
Are the accounts receivable being collected in a timely manner?	List of accounts receivable along with how long they have been outstanding. Prepare an aging schedule.	Accounts in the older categories require additional collection attention.	TAKEAWAY 8.1
Are any of the existing accounts receivable in need of further attention?	Net sales and average accounts receivable $\text{Accounts receivable turnover} = \dfrac{\text{Net sales}}{\text{Average accounts receivable (net)}}$ $\text{Average collection period} = \dfrac{365}{\text{Accounts receivable turnover}}$	Compare the average collection period to the company credit policy. Longer collection periods suggest the need for management attention.	TAKEAWAY 8.2

KEY TERMS

Accounts receivable (p. 374)

Accounts receivable aging method (p. 380)

Accounts receivable turnover (p. 388)

Aging schedule (p. 380)

Allowance for Doubtful Accounts (Allowance for Uncollectible Accounts) (p. 377)

Allowance method (p. 376)

Average collection period (p. 389)

Bad Debts Expense (Provision for Bad Debts) (p. 376)

Bearer (p. 384)

Credit card fee (p. 384)

Credit-collection policy (p. 375)

Credit-granting policy (p. 375)

Direct write-off method (p. 391)

Discounting (p. 389)

Factoring (p. 389)

Factors (p. 389)

Maker (p. 384)

Maturity date (p. 385)

Note receivable (p. 384)

Payee (p. 384)

Percentage of net sales method (p. 380)

Promissory note (p. 384)

Assignments with the (MBC) logo in the margin are available in myBusinessCourse.
See the Preface of the book for details.

SELF-STUDY QUESTIONS

(Answers to the Self-Study Questions are available at the end of this chapter.)

LO1, 2   **1.** A firm, using the allowance method of recording credit losses, wrote off a customer's account in the amount of $500. Later, the customer paid the account. The firm reinstated the account by means of a journal entry and then recorded the collection. What is the result of these procedures?
   a. Increases total assets by $500
   b. Decreases total assets by $500
   c. Decreases total assets by $1,000
   d. Has no effect on total assets

LO2   **2.** A firm has accounts receivable of $90,000 and a debit balance of $900 in the Allowance for Doubtful Accounts. Two-thirds of the accounts receivable are current and one-third is past due. The firm estimates that two percent of the current accounts and five percent of the past due accounts will prove to be uncollectible. The adjusting entry to provide for the bad debts expense under the aging method should be for what amount?
   a. $2,700   *c.* $1,800
   b. $3,600   *d.* $4,500

LO4   **3.** A firm receives a six-month note from a customer. The note has a face amount of $4,000 and an interest rate of nine percent. What is the total amount of interest to be received?
   a. $1,080
   b. $30
   c. $360
   d. $180

LO5   **4.** A business has net sales of $60,000, a beginning balance in Accounts Receivable of $5,000, and an ending balance in Accounts Receivable of $7,000. What is the company's accounts receivable turnover?
   a. 10.0
   b. 12.0
   c. 8.6
   d. 9.2

LO5   **5.** A business has an accounts receivable turnover of ten. What is the company's average collection period?
   a. 36.0
   b. 30.8
   c. 34.6
   d. 36.5

6. Lite Company received a 90 day, six percent note receivable for $10,000 on December 1. How much interest should be accrued on December 31?   **LO4**
   a. $150
   b. $90
   c. $50
   d. $25

7. Wesson Company uses the allowance method to record its expected credit losses. It estimates its losses at one percent of credit sales, which were $750,000 during the year. The Accounts Receivable balance was $220,000 and the Allowance for Doubtful Accounts had a credit balance of $1,000 at year-end. What amount is the debit to the Bad Debts Expense?   **LO1, 2**
   a. $7,500
   b. $8,500
   c. $6,500
   d. $3,200

8. Rufus & Company pays a three percent credit card fee on all credit sales, and receives a cash deposit immediately following each credit card transaction. If credit sales for the company total $15,000 on December 13, what journal entry should be recorded to recognize the receipt of cash and the credit card fee expense?   **LO3**
   a. Debit Cash $14,550; debit Credit Card Fee Expense $450.
   b. Debit Cash $15,000; credit Credit Card Fee Expense $450.
   c. Debit Cash $15,450; debit Credit Card Fee Expense $450.
   d. Debit Cash $15,450; credit Credit Card Fee Expense $450.

9. Which of the following statements is true?   **LO1, 2, 6**
   a. The direct write-off method is generally accepted.
   b. The percentage of net sales method estimates the bad debts expense indirectly.
   c. The accounts receivable aging method estimates the bad debts expense indirectly.
   d. None of the above is true.

10. On September 1, the Pavey Company accepted a $24,000, 60 day, nine percent, promissory note in exchange for overdue accounts receivable balance for the same amount from the Wagner Company. On November 30, the Wagner Company dishonored the note. What journal entry should be recorded on November 30?   **LO4**
    a. Debit Dishonored Note Receivable Expense; credit Notes Receivable.
    b. Debit Allowance for Doubtful Accounts; credit Notes Receivable.
    c. Debit Accounts Receivable; credit Interest Income; credit Notes Receivable.
    d. None of the above entries is correct.

QUESTIONS

1. In dealing with receivables, what do the terms *factoring* and *discounting* mean?
2. How does a credit scoring system work?
3. How do the allowance method and the direct write-off method of handling credit losses differ with respect to the timing of bad debts expense recognition?
4. When a firm provides for credit losses under the allowance method, why is the Allowance for Doubtful Accounts credited rather than Accounts Receivable?
5. What are the two most commonly used methods of estimating the bad debts expense when the allowance method is employed? Describe them.
6. Haley Company estimates its bad debts expense by aging its accounts receivable and applying percentages to various age groups of the accounts. Haley calculated a total of $2,100 in possible credit losses as of December 31. Accounts Receivable has a balance of $98,000, and the Allowance for Doubtful Accounts has a credit balance of $500 before adjustment at December 31. What is the December 31 adjusting entry to provide for credit losses? What is the net amount of accounts receivable that should be included in current assets?
7. On June 15, 2018, Vance, Inc. sold $750 worth of merchandise to Dell Company. On November 20, 2018, Vance, Inc., wrote off Dell's account. On March 10, 2019, Dell Company paid the account in full. What are the journal entries that Vance, Inc. should make for the write-off and the recovery assuming that Vance, Inc., uses (a) the allowance method of handling credit losses and (b) the direct write-off method?

8. Fiber Company sold a $675 refrigerator to a customer who charged the sale using a VISA credit card. Fiber Company deposits credit card sales slips daily; cash is deposited in Fiber Company's checking account at the same time. Fiber Company's bank charges a credit card fee of four percent of sales revenue. What journal entry should Fiber Company make to record the sale?

9. Volt Inc. received a 60 day, nine percent note for $15,000 on March 5 from a customer. What is the maturity date of the note?

10. Stafford Company received a 150 day, eight percent note for $15,000 on December 1. What adjusting entry is needed to accrue the interest due on December 31?

11. Define *accounts receivable turnover* and explain its use. How is the *average collection period* determined?

12. At a recent board of directors meeting of Ascot, Inc., one of the directors expressed concern over the Allowance for Doubtful Accounts appearing on the company's balance sheet. "I don't understand this account," he said. "Why don't we just show accounts receivable at the amount we would receive if we sold them to a financial institution and get rid of that allowance account?"

    Prepare a written response to the director. Include in your response (1) an explanation of why the company has an allowance account, (2) what the balance sheet presentation of accounts receivable is supposed to show, and (3) how the basic principles of accounting relate to the analysis and presentation of accounts receivable.

13. What generally accepted accounting principle is being implemented when a company estimates its potential credit losses from its outstanding accounts receivable?

14. Why is the direct write-off method of accounting for credit losses not generally accepted?

15. When a previously written-off account receivable is collected, it must first be reinstated by debiting the Accounts Receivable account and crediting the Allowance for Doubtful Accounts. Explain the credit portion of the reinstatement journal entry.

SHORT EXERCISES

LO1, 2 **SE8-1.** **Accounting for Doubtful Accounts** Randall Company estimates its bad debts expense by aging its accounts receivable and applying percentages to various age groups of the accounts. Randall calculated a total of $3,000 in possible credit losses as of December 31. Accounts Receivable has a balance of $128,000, and the Allowance for Doubtful Accounts has a credit balance of $500 before adjustment at December 31. What is the December 31 adjusting entry to provide for credit losses? What is the net amount of accounts receivable that should be included in current assets?

LO2 **SE8-2.** **Reinstating Written-Off Accounts** The Stonegate Company uses the allowance method of recording credit losses and wrote off a customer's account in the amount of $800. Later, the customer paid the account. The company reinstated the account by means of a journal entry and then recorded the collection. What is the result of these procedures?

    a. Increases total assets by $800

    b. Decreases total assets by $800

    c. Decreases total assets by $1,600

    d. Has no effect on total assets

LO2 **SE8-3.** **Estimating the Bad Debts Expense** Winter & Company has accounts receivable of $120,000 and a debit balance of $1,000 in the Allowance for Doubtful Accounts. Two-thirds of the accounts receivable are current and one-third is past due. The firm estimates that two percent of the current accounts and five percent of the past due accounts will prove to be uncollectible. The adjusting entry to provide for the bad debts expense under the aging method should be for what amount?

    a. $3,600   *c.* $2,600

    b. $4,600   *d.* $1,600

LO5 **SE8-4.** **Average Collection Period** Smyth & Sons has an accounts receivable turnover of 20. What is the company's average collection period?

    a. 18.25 days   *c.* 22.25 days

    b. 20.0 days   *d.* 24.25 days

SE8-5. **Recording Dishonored Promissory Notes Receivable** On October 1, the Humpback Company accepted a $50,000, 60 day, nine percent, promissory note in exchange for an overdue accounts receivable balance for the same amount from the Schwartz Company. On November 30, the Schwartz Company dishonored the note. What journal entry should be recorded on November 30?

LO4

 a. Debit Dishonored Note Receivable Expense; credit Notes Receivable.
 b. Debit Allowance for Doubtful Accounts; credit Notes Receivable.
 c. Debit Accounts Receivable; credit Interest Income; credit Notes Receivable.
 d. None of the above entries is correct.

SE8-6. **Accounting for Credit Card Sales** Carter & Company pays a three percent credit card fee on all credit sales, and receives a cash deposit immediately following each credit card transaction. If credit sales for the company total $30,000 on January 15, what journal entry should be recorded to recognize the receipt of cash and the credit card fee expense?

LO3

 a. Debit Cash $29,100; debit Credit Card Fee Expense $900.
 b. Debit Cash $29,100; credit Credit Card Fee Expense $900.
 c. Debit Cash $30,900; debit Credit Card Fee Expense $900.
 d. Debit Cash $30,900; credit Credit Card Fee Expense $900.

SE8-7. **Calculating Accrued Interest Income on Promissory Notes Receivable** Pickett Company received a 90 day, six percent note receivable for $20,000 on November 1. How much interest income should be accrued on December 31?

LO4

 a. $100
 b. $200
 c. $300
 d. $400

SE8-8. **Calculating Interest on Promissory Notes Receivable** Houston Company receives a six-month note from a customer. The note has a face amount of $8,000 and an interest rate of nine percent. What is the total amount of interest income to be received?

LO4

 a. $720
 b. $540
 c. $360
 d. $180

SE8-9. **Accounts Receivable Turnover** Taver Company has net sales of $120,000, a beginning balance in Accounts Receivable of $10,000, and an ending balance in Accounts Receivable of $14,000. What is the company's accounts receivable turnover?

LO5

 a. 10.0
 b. 12.0
 c. 8.6
 d. 9.2

SE8-10. **Direct Write-Off Method** The direct write-off method is not generally accepted because:

LO6
(Appendix 8A)

 a. The method overstates the bad debts expense.
 b. It is too complex.
 c. The method fails to match sales revenue with expenses in the appropriate time period.
 d. The method causes liabilities to be overstated.

EXERCISES—SET A

E8-1A. **Credit Losses Based on Credit Sales** Gregg Company uses the allowance method for recording its expected credit losses. It estimates credit losses at three percent of credit sales, which were $900,000 during the year. On December 31, the Accounts Receivable balance was $150,000, and the Allowance for Doubtful Accounts had a credit balance of $12,200 before adjustment.

LO2

 a. Prepare the adjusting entry to record the credit losses for the year.
 b. Show how Accounts Receivable and the Allowance for Doubtful Accounts would appear in the December 31 balance sheet.

LO1, 2   **E8-2A.**   **Credit Losses Based on Accounts Receivable** Hunter, Inc., analyzed its accounts receivable balances at December 31, and arrived at the aged balances listed below, along with the percentage that is estimated to be uncollectible:

Age Group	Balance	Probability of Noncollection
0–30 days past due	$ 90,000	1
31–60 days past due	20,000	2
61–120 days past due	11,000	5
121–180 days past due	6,000	10
Over 180 days past due	6,000	25
	$133,000	

The company handles credit losses using the allowance method. The credit balance of the Allowance for Doubtful Accounts is $820 on December 31, before any adjustments.

a. Prepare the adjusting entry for estimated credit losses on December 31.

b. Prepare the journal entry to write off the Rose Company's account on April 10 of the following year in the amount of $650.

LO1   **E8-3A.**   **Recognizing Accounts Receivable** On June 7, Pixer Co. sells $1,500 of merchandise to Jasmine Co. on account. Jasmine Co. pays for this merchandise on June 21.

a. Prepare the entry on Pixer's books to record the sale.

b. Prepare the entry on Pixer's books to record the receipt of payment.

LO3   **E8-4A.**   **Credit Card Sales** Jamie's Fabrics accepts cash, personal checks, and two credit cards when customers buy merchandise. With the Great American Bank Card, Jamie's Fabrics receives an immediate deposit in its checking account when credit card sales slips are deposited at the bank. The bank charges a three percent fee. With the United Merchants Card, Jamie's Fabrics mails the credit card sales slips to United Merchants' regional processing center each day. United Merchants accumulates these slips for two days and then mails a check to Jamie's Fabrics, after deducting a three percent fee. Prepare journal entries to record the following:

a. Sales for March 15 were as follows:

Cash and checks	$ 950
Great American Bank Card (Deposited at the end of the day)	1,200
United Merchants Card (Mailed at the end of the day)	700
	$2,850

b. Received a check for $1,900 from United Merchants on March 20.

LO4   **E8-5A.**   **Maturity Dates of Notes Receivable** Determine the maturity date and compute the interest for each of the following notes:

	Date of Note	Principal	Interest Rate (%)	Term
a.	August 5	$ 6,000	8	120 days
b.	May 10	16,800	7	30 days
c.	October 20	25,000	9	45 days
d.	July 6	4,500	11	60 days
e.	September 15	9,000	9	75 days

LO4   **E8-6A.**   **Computing Accrued Interest** Compute the interest accrued on each of the following notes receivable held by Southland, Inc., on December 31: (Round your answer to the nearest dollar.)

Maker	Date of Note	Principal	Interest Rate (%)	Term
Maple	11/21	$20,000	10	120 days
Wyman	12/13	14,000	9	90 days
Nahn.	12/24	21,000	6	60 days

E8-7A. **Accounts Receivable Turnover and Average Collection Period** The Outback Corporation disclosed the following financial information (in millions) in its recent annual report:

LO5

	2018	2019
Net sales.	$72,500	$83,750
Beginning accounts receivable (net)	3,896	4,100
Ending accounts receivable (net).	4,100	3,596

   a. Calculate the accounts receivable turnover ratio for both years.
   b. Calculate the average collection period for both years.
   c. Is the company's accounts receivable management improving or deteriorating?

E8-8A. **Credit Losses Based on Credit Sales** Fritters & Sons uses the allowance method of handling its credit losses. It estimates credit losses at three percent of credit sales, which were $1,900,000 during the year. On December 31, the Accounts Receivable balance was $300,000, and the Allowance for Doubtful Accounts had a credit balance of $23,200 before adjustment.

LO2

   a. Prepare the adjusting entry to record the credit losses for the year.
   b. Show how Accounts Receivable and the Allowance for Doubtful Accounts would appear in the December 31 balance sheet.

E8-9A. **Credit Losses Based on Accounts Receivable** Miller, Inc., analyzed its accounts receivable balances at December 31 and arrived at the aged balances listed below, along with the percentage that is estimated to be uncollectible:

LO1, 2

Age Group	Balance	Probability of Noncollection
0–30 days past due	$180,000	1
31–60 days past due	40,000	4
61–120 days past due	22,000	5
121–180 days past due	14,000	12
Over 180 days past due	8,000	25
	$264,000	

The company handles credit losses using the allowance method. The credit balance of the Allowance for Doubtful Accounts is $1,150 on December 31, before any adjustments.

   a. Prepare the adjusting entry for estimated credit losses on December 31.
   b. Prepare the journal entry to write off the Lyons Company's account on April 10 of the following year in the amount of $575.

E8-10A. **Accounts Receivable Turnover and Average Collection Period** Verne Corporation disclosed the following financial information (in millions) in its recent annual report:

LO5

	2018	2019
Net sales.	$167,096	$181,662
Beginning accounts receivable (net)	13,896	15,100
Ending accounts receivable (net).	15,100	13,598

   a. Calculate the accounts receivable turnover ratio for both years.
   b. Calculate the average collection period for both years.
   c. Is the company's accounts receivable management improving or deteriorating?

LO3 **E8-11A. Credit Card Sales** The Green Roof accepts cash, personal checks, and two credit cards when customers buy merchandise. With the Great American Bank Card, The Green Roof receives an immediate deposit in its checking account when credit card sales slips are deposited at the bank. The bank charges a two percent fee. With the United Merchants Card, The Green Roof mails the credit card sales slips to United Merchants' regional processing center each day. United Merchants accumulates these slips for three days and then mails a check to The Green Roof, after deducting a two percent fee. Prepare journal entries to record the following:

a. Sales for March 15 were as follows:

Cash and checks	$1,800
Great American Bank Card (Deposited at the end of the day)	2,500
United Merchants Card (Mailed at the end of the day)	1,400
	$5,700

b. Received a check for $4,050 from United Merchants on March 20.

LO4 **E8-12A. Maturity Dates of Notes Receivable** Determine the maturity date and compute the interest for each of the following notes:

	Date of Note	Principal	Interest Rate (%)	Term
a.	August 5	$12,000	9	120 days
b.	May 10	33,600	7	90 days
c.	October 20	48,000	12	45 days
d.	July 16	9,000	10	60 days
e.	September 15	19,000	7	75 days

LO4 **E8-13A. Computing Accrued Interest** Compute the interest accrued on each of the following notes receivable held by Kirkland, Inc., on December 31:

Maker	Date of Note	Principal	Interest Rate (%)	Term
Abel	11/21	$42,000	12	120 days
Baker	12/13	32,000	9	90 days
Charlie	12/19	25,000	6	60 days

LO6
(Appendix 8A)

E8-14A. Allowance Method versus Direct Write-Off Method On March 10, May, Inc., declared a $2,500 account receivable from Anders Company as uncollectible and wrote off the account. On November 18, May received an $800 payment on the account from Anders.

a. Assume that May uses the allowance method of handling credit losses. Prepare the journal entries to record the write-off and the subsequent recovery of Anders's account.

b. Assume that May uses the direct write-off method of handling credit losses. Prepare the journal entries to record the write-off and the subsequent recovery of Anders's account.

c. Assume that the payment from Anders arrives on the following February 5, rather than on November 18 of the current year. (1) Prepare the journal entries to record the write-off and subsequent recovery of Anders's account under the allowance method. (2) Prepare the journal entries to record the write-off and subsequent recovery of Anders's account under the direct write-off method.

LO6
(Appendix 8A)

E8-15A. Allowance Method versus Direct Write-Off Method On March 10, Chancey, Inc., declared a $700 account receivable from the Gates Company as uncollectible and wrote off the account. On November 18, Chancey received a $200 payment on the account from Gates.

a. Assume that Chancey uses the allowance method of handling credit losses. Prepare the journal entries to record the write-off and the subsequent recovery of Gates's account.

b. Assume that Chancey uses the direct write-off method of handling credit losses. Prepare the journal entries to record the write-off and the subsequent recovery of Gates's account.

c. Assume that the payment from Gates arrives on February 5 of the following year rather than on November 18 of the current year. (1) Prepare the journal entries to record the write-off and subsequent recovery of Gates's account under the allowance method. (2) Prepare the journal entries to record the write-off and subsequent recovery of Gates's account under the direct write-off method.

EXERCISES—SET B

E8-1B. **Credit Losses Based on Credit Sales** Lowland Company uses the allowance method of handling credit losses. It estimates losses at two percent of credit sales, which were $1,400,000 during the year. On December 31, the Accounts Receivable balance was $280,000, and the Allowance for Doubtful Accounts had a credit balance of $2,100 before adjustment.

LO2

    a. Prepare the adjusting entry to record credit losses for the year.

    b. Show how the Accounts Receivable account and the Allowance for Doubtful Accounts would appear on the December 31 balance sheet.

E8-2B. **Credit Losses Based on Accounts Receivable** Marvel, Inc. analyzed its accounts receivable balances at December 31 and arrived at the aged balances listed below, along with the percentage that is estimated to be uncollectible:

LO1, 2

Age Group	Balance	Probability of Noncollection
0–30 days past due	$100,000	1
31–60 days past due	20,000	2
61–120 days past due	20,000	6
121–180 days past due	9,000	11
Over 180 days past due	2,000	20
	$151,000	

The company handles credit losses with the allowance method. The credit balance of the Allowance for Doubtful Accounts is $840 on December 31, before any adjustments.

    a. Prepare the adjusting entry for estimated credit losses on December 31.

    b. Prepare the journal entry to write off Porter Company's account on the following May 12, in the amount of $680.

E8-3B. **Recognizing Accounts Receivable** On August 9, Gait Co. sells $980 of merchandise to Taylor Co. on account. Taylor Co. pays for this merchandise on September 1.

LO1

    a. Prepare the entry on Gait's books to record the sale.

    b. Prepare the entry on Gait's books to record the receipt of payment.

E8-4B. **Credit Card Sales** Historically, 60 percent of the customer bills at the Andrews' Supper Club have been paid with cash or check, and 40 percent have been paid using either the Great American Bank Card or the United Merchants Card. Andrews pays a four percent fee with both cards. Great American Bank deposits cash in Andrews' checking account when the credit card sales slips are deposited. United Merchants makes an electronic funds transfer three days after the sales slips are mailed. Prepare journal entries to record the following:

LO3

    a. Sales for September 10 were as follows:

Cash and checks	$1,340
Great American Bank Card (Deposited at the end of the day)	500
United Merchants Card (Mailed at the end of the day)	300
	$2,140

    b. On September 13, Andrews received an electronic funds transfer from United Merchants for the September 10 sales.

E8-5B. **Maturity Dates of Notes Receivable** Determine the maturity date and compute the interest for each of the following notes:

LO4

	Date of Note	Principal	Interest Rate (%)	Term
a.	July 10	$ 7,200	9	90 days
b.	April 25	12,000	5	120 days
c.	May 19	11,200	7	120 days
d.	June 10	5,400	11	45 days
e.	October 29	30,000	6	75 days

LO4   **E8-6B.   Computing Accrued Interest** Compute the interest accrued on each of the following notes receivable held by Gallow, Inc., on December 31: (Round your answer to the nearest dollar.)

Maker	Date of Note	Principal	Interest Rate (%)	Term
Barton.....................	12/14	$ 8,000	8	120 days
Lawson....................	12/13	26,000	9	90 days
Riley	12/19	12,000	11	60 days

LO5   **E8-7B.   Accounts Receivable Turnover and Average Collection Period** The Bud Miller Corporation disclosed the following financial information (in millions) in its recent annual report:

	2018	2019
Net sales..	$97,096	$111,662
Beginning accounts receivable (net)	6,450	6,355
Ending accounts receivable (net).....................................	6,355	6,598

a.   Calculate the accounts receivable turnover ratio for both years.
b.   Calculate the average collection period for both years.
c.   Is the company's accounts receivable management improving or deteriorating?

LO2   **E8-8B.   Credit Losses Based on Credit Sales** Ranch Company uses the allowance method of handling its credit losses. It estimates credit losses at 2.5 percent of credit sales, which were $2,700,000 during the year. On December 31, the Accounts Receivable balance was $475,000, and the Allowance for Doubtful Accounts had a credit balance of $30,600 before adjustment.

a.   Prepare the adjusting entry to record the credit losses for the year.
b.   Show how Accounts Receivable and the Allowance for Doubtful Accounts would appear in the December 31 balance sheet.

LO1, 2   **E8-9B.   Credit Losses Based on Accounts Receivable** Billy, Inc., analyzed its accounts receivable balances at December 31 and arrived at the aged balances listed below, along with the percentage that is estimated to be uncollectible:

Age Group	Balance	Probability of Noncollection
0–30 days past due	$320,000	1
31–60 days past due	60,000	3
61–120 days past due	33,000	6
121–180 days past due	18,000	10
Over 180 days past due.....................................	14,000	25
	$445,000	

The company handles credit losses using the allowance method. The credit balance of the Allowance for Doubtful Accounts is $1,560 on December 31, before any adjustments.

a.   Prepare the adjusting entry for estimated credit losses on December 31.
b.   Prepare the journal entry to write off the Matthews Company's account on the following April 10, in the amount of $460.

LO5   **E8-10B.   Accounts Receivable Turnover and Average Collection Period** The Yale Corporation disclosed the following financial information (in millions) in its recent annual report:

	2018	2019
Net sales..	$127,096	$112,550
Beginning accounts receivable (net)	8,896	8,120
Ending accounts receivable (net).....................................	8,120	6,598

a. Calculate the accounts receivable turnover ratio for both years.
b. Calculate the average collection period for both years.
c. Is the company's accounts receivable management improving or deteriorating?

E8-11B. Credit Card Sales The Kitchen Store accepts cash, personal checks, and two credit cards when customers buy merchandise. With the Great American Bank Card, The Kitchen Store receives an immediate deposit in its checking account when credit card sales slips are deposited at the bank. The bank charges a three percent fee. With the United Merchants Card, The Kitchen Store mails the credit card sales slips to United Merchants' regional processing center each day. United Merchants accumulates these slips for three days and then mails a check to The Kitchen Store, after deducting a two percent fee. Prepare journal entries to record the following: **LO3**

a. Sales for March 15 were as follows:

Cash and checks	$2,550
Great American Bank Card (Deposited at the end of the day)	3,300
United Merchants Card (Mailed at the end of the day)	2,100
	$7,950

b. Received a check for $9,250 from United Merchants on March 20.

E8-12B. Maturity Dates of Notes Receivable Determine the maturity date and compute the interest for each of the following notes: **LO4**

	Date of Note	Principal	Interest Rate (%)	Term
a.	August 5	$20,000	8	120 days
b.	May 10	50,400	7	90 days
c.	October 30	72,000	9	45 days
d.	July 6	13,750	11	60 days
e.	September 15	27,000	8	60 days

E8-13B. Computing Accrued Interest Compute the interest accrued on each of the following notes receivable held by Northland, Inc., on December 31: **LO4**

	Maker	Date of Note	Principal	Interest Rate (%)	Term
a.	Delta	11/21	$54,000	7	120 days
b.	Echo	12/13	42,000	9	90 days
c.	Foxtrot	12/17	63,000	8	60 days

E8-14B. Allowance Method versus Direct Write-Off Method On March 10, Barnes, Inc., declared a $3,700 account receivable from Lamas Company as uncollectible and wrote off the account. On November 18, Barnes received a $1,600 payment on the account from Lamas. **LO6** **(Appendix 8A)**

a. Assume that Barnes uses the allowance method of handling credit losses. Prepare the journal entries to record the write-off and the subsequent recovery of Lamas's account.
b. Assume that Barnes uses the direct write-off method of handling credit losses. Prepare the journal entries to record the write-off and the subsequent recovery of Lamas's account.
c. Assume that the payment from Lamas arrives on the following February 5, rather than on November 18 of the current year. (1) Prepare the journal entries to record the write-off and subsequent recovery of Lamas's account under the allowance method. (2) Prepare the journal entries to record the write-off and subsequent recovery of Lamas's account under the direct write-off method.

E8-15B. Allowance Method versus Direct Write-Off Method On April 12, Mitch Company declared a $2,000 account receivable from the Ward Company as uncollectible and wrote off the account. On December 5, Mitch received a $600 payment on the account from Ward. **LO6** **(Appendix 8A)**

a. Assume that Mitch uses the allowance method of handling credit losses. Prepare the journal entries to record the write-off and the subsequent recovery of Ward's account.
b. Assume that Mitch uses the direct write-off method of handling credit losses. Prepare the journal entries to record the write-off and the subsequent recovery of Ward's account.

c. Assume that the payment from Ward arrives on the following January 18, rather than on December 5 of the current year. (1) Prepare the journal entries to record the write-off and subsequent recovery of Ward's account under the allowance method. (2) Prepare the journal entries to record the write-off and subsequent recovery of Ward's account under the direct write-off method.

PROBLEMS—SET A

LO2 **P8-1A.** **Allowance Method** David Company, which has been in business for three years, makes all of its sales on account and does not offer cash discounts. The firm's credit sales, collections from customers, and write-offs of uncollectible accounts for the three-year period are summarized below:

Year	Sales	Collections	Accounts Written Off
2018	$300,000	$287,000	$2,200
2019	385,000	390,000	3,350
2020	430,000	407,000	3,650

Required

a. If David Company had used the allowance method of recognizing credit losses and had provided for such losses at the rate of 1.6 percent of credit sales, what amounts in accounts receivable and the allowance for doubtful accounts would appear on the firm's balance sheet at the end of 2020? What total amount of bad debts expense would have appeared on the firm's income statement during the three-year period?

b. Comment on the use of the 1.6 percent rate to provide for credit losses in part *a.*

LO1, 2 **P8-2A.** **Journal Entries for Credit Losses** At the beginning of the year, Portal Company had the following accounts on its books:

Accounts receivable	$140,000 (debit)
Allowance for doubtful accounts	8,000 (credit)

During the year, credit sales were $1,173,000 and collections on account were $1,175,000. The following transactions, among others, occurred during the year:

Feb.	17	Wrote off R. Lowell's account, $4,000.
May	28	Wrote off G. Boyd's account, $3,400.
Oct.	13	Received $600 from G. Boyd, who is in bankruptcy proceedings, in final settlement of the account written off on May 28. This amount is not included in the $1,175,000 collections.
Dec.	15	Wrote off K. Marshall's account, $1,600.
	31	In an adjusting entry, recorded the allowance for doubtful accounts at 0.9 percent of credit sales for the year.

Required

a. Prepare journal entries to record the credit sales, the collections on account, and the preceding transactions and adjustment.

b. Show how Accounts Receivable and the Allowance for Doubtful Accounts would appear on the December 31 balance sheet.

LO2 **P8-3A.** **Credit Losses Based on Accounts Receivable** At December 31, Mueller Company had a balance of $409,000 in its Accounts Receivable account and a credit balance of $4,200 in the Allowance for Doubtful Accounts account. The accounts receivable T-account consisted of $414,000 in debit balances and $5,000 in credit balances. The company aged its accounts as follows:

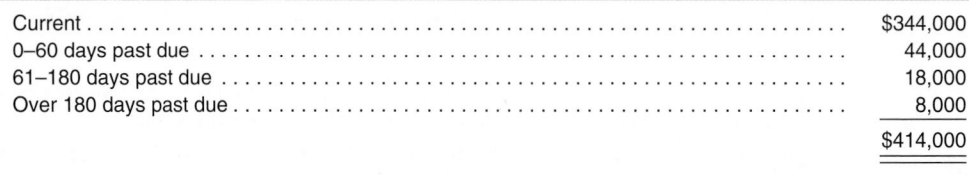

Current	$344,000
0–60 days past due	44,000
61–180 days past due	18,000
Over 180 days past due	8,000
	$414,000

In the past, the company has experienced credit losses as follows: one percent of current balances, five percent of balances 0–60 days past due, 18 percent of balances 61–180 days past due, and 30 percent of balances over six months past due. The company bases its allowance for doubtful accounts on an aging analysis of accounts receivable.

Required

a. Prepare the adjusting entry to record the allowance for doubtful accounts for the year.

b. Show how Accounts Receivable (including the credit balances) and the Allowance for Doubtful Accounts would appear on the December 31 balance sheet.

P8-4A. Credit Card Sales Katy's Gallery sells quality art work, with prices for individual pieces ranging from $300 to $25,000. Sales are infrequent, typically only three to five pieces per week. The following transactions occurred during the first week of June 2015. Perpetual inventory is used.

LO3

June   1   Sold a $900 framed print ($450 cost) to Kerwin Antiques on account, with 3/10, n/30 credit terms.

2   Sold three framed etchings totaling $2,400 ($1,500 cost) to Maria Alvado, who used the United Merchants Card to charge the cost of the etchings. Katy mailed the credit card sales slip to United Merchants the same day. United Merchants will send a check within seven days after deducting a one percent fee.

4   Sold a $1,900 oil painting ($1,000 cost) to Shaun Chandler, who paid with a personal check.

5   Sold a $2,100 watercolor ($1,500 cost) to Julie and John Malbie, who used their Great American Bank Card to charge the purchase of the painting. Katy deposited the credit card sales slip the same day and received immediate credit in the company's checking account. The bank charged a one percent fee.

6   Received payment from Kerwin Antiques for its June 1 purchase.

7   Received a check from United Merchants for the June 2 sale.

Required

Prepare journal entries to record the Katy Gallery transactions.

P8-5A. Journal Entries for Accounts and Notes Receivable Pomona Inc. began business on January 1. Certain transactions for the year follow:

LO2, 4

June   8   Received a $30,000, 60 day, six percent note on account from R. Elliot.

Aug.   7   Received payment from R. Elliot on her note (principal plus interest).

Sept.   1   Received an $18,000, 120 day, seven percent note from B. Shore Company on account.

Dec.   16   Received a $14,400, 45 day, eight percent note from C. Judd on account.

30   B. Shore Company failed to pay its note.

31   Wrote off B. Shore's account as uncollectible. Lancaster, Inc. uses the allowance method of providing for credit losses.

31   Recorded expected credit losses for the year by an adjusting entry. Accounts written off during this first year have created a debit balance in the Allowance for Doubtful Accounts of $24,500. An analysis of aged receivables indicates that the desired balance of the allowance account should be $21,300.

31   Made the appropriate adjusting entries for interest.

Required

Record the foregoing transactions and adjustments in general journal form.

P8-6A. Allowance Method The Irvine Company, which has been in business for three years, makes all of its sales on account and does not offer cash discounts. The firm's credit sales, collections from customers, and write-offs of uncollectible accounts for the three-year period are summarized below:

LO2

Year	Sales	Collections	Accounts Written Off
2018	$600,000	$574,000	$4,200
2019	770,000	740,000	6,900
2020	860,000	814,000	7,300

Required

a. If the Irvine Company had used the allowance method of recognizing credit losses and had provided for such losses at the rate of 1.3 percent of credit sales, what amounts in Accounts Receivable and the Allowance for Doubtful Accounts would appear on the firm's balance sheet at the end of 2020? What total amount of bad debts expense would have appeared on the firm's income statement during the three-year period?

b. Comment on the use of the 1.3 percent rate to provide for credit losses in part *a*.

LO1, 2   **P8-7A.**   **Journal Entries for Credit Losses**   At the beginning of the year, the Dallas Company had the following accounts on its books:

Accounts receivable	$264,000 (debit)
Allowance for doubtful accounts	16,500 (credit)

During the year, credit sales were $2,346,000 and collections on account were $2,350,000. The following transactions, among others, occurred during the year:

Feb.   17   Wrote off R. St. John's account, $7,500.

May   28   Wrote off G. Herberger's account, $4,800.

Oct.   13   Received $1,200 from G. Herberger, who is in bankruptcy proceedings, in final settlement of the account written off on May 28. This amount is not included in the $2,350,000 collections.

Dec.   15   Wrote off R. Clancy's account, $5,000.

       31   In an adjusting entry, recorded the allowance for doubtful accounts at 0.8 percent of credit sales for the year.

Required

a. Prepare journal entries to record the credit sales, the collections on account, and the preceding transactions and adjustment.

b. Show how Accounts Receivable and the Allowance for Doubtful Accounts would appear on the December 31 balance sheet.

LO2   **P8-8A.**   **Credit Losses Based on Accounts Receivable**   At December 31, the Azuza Company had a balance of $754,000 in its Accounts Receivable account and a credit balance of $9,000 in the Allowance for Doubtful Accounts account. The company aged its accounts as follows:

Current	$608,000
0–60 days past due	88,000
61–180 days past due	40,000
Over 180 days past due	18,000
	$754,000

In the past, the company has experienced credit losses as follows: one percent of current balances, five percent of balances 0–60 days past due, 20 percent of balances 61–180 days past due, and 40 percent of balances over six months past due. The company bases its allowance for doubtful accounts on an aging analysis of accounts receivable.

Required

a. Prepare the adjusting entry to record the allowance for doubtful accounts for the year.

b. Show how Accounts Receivable and the Allowance for Doubtful Accounts would appear on the December 31 balance sheet.

LO3   **P8-9A.**   **Credit Card Sales**   Le Kai Arts sells quality art work, with prices for individual pieces ranging from $1,000 to $50,000. Sales are infrequent, typically only six to ten pieces per week. The following transactions occurred during the first week of June. Perpetual inventory is used.

June   1   Sold an $1,800 framed print ($1,200 cost) to Likert Antiques on account, with 2/10, n/30 credit terms.

continued

June   2   Sold three framed etchings totaling $5,200 ($2,800 cost) to Annabelle Herrera, who used the United Merchants Card to charge the cost of the etchings. Le Kai mailed the credit card sales slip to United Merchants the same day. United Merchants will send a check within seven days after deducting a two percent fee.

4   Sold a $3,600 oil painting ($2,000 cost) to Ryan LaLander, who paid with a personal check.

5   Sold a $6,000 watercolor ($2,200 cost) to Julie and Bobby Herman, who used their Great American Bank Card to charge the purchase of the painting. Le Kai deposited the credit card sales slip the same day and received immediate credit in the company's checking account. The bank charged a one percent fee.

6   Received payment from Likert Antiques for its June 1 purchase.

7   Received a check from United Merchants for the June 2 sale.

Required
Prepare journal entries to record the Le Kai Gallery transactions.

P8-10A.   Journal Entries for Accounts and Notes Receivable Philly, Inc., began business on January 1. Certain transactions for the year follow: **LO2, 4**

June   8   Received a $15,000, 60 day, nine percent note on account from J. Albert.
Aug.   7   Received payment from J. Albert on his note (principal plus interest).
Sept.   1   Received a $40,000, 120 day, six percent note from R.T. Matthews Company on account.
Dec.   16   Received a $28,800, 45 day, ten percent note from D. LeRoy on account.
30   R.T. Matthews Company failed to pay its note.
31   Wrote off R.T. Matthews' account as uncollectible. Philly's, Inc., uses the allowance method of providing for credit losses.
31   Recorded expected credit losses for the year by an adjusting entry. Accounts written off during this first year have created a debit balance in the allowance for doubtful accounts of $45,200. An analysis of aged receivables indicates that the desired balance of the allowance account should be $42,000.
31   Made the appropriate adjusting entries for interest.

Required
Record the foregoing transactions and adjustments in general journal form.

PROBLEMS—SET B

P8-1B.   Allowance Method Brooke Company, which has been in business for three years, makes all of its sales on account and does not offer cash discounts. The firm's credit sales, collections from customers, and write-offs of uncollectible accounts for the three-year period are summarized as follows: **LO2**

Year	Sales	Collections	Accounts Written Off
2018	$751,000	$733,000	$5,300
2019	876,000	864,000	6,400
2020	980,000	938,000	6,500

Required
a.   If Brooke Company used an allowance method of recognizing credit losses and provided for such losses at the rate of one percent of credit sales, what amounts of accounts receivable and the allowance for doubtful accounts should appear on the firm's balance sheet at the end of 2020? What total amount of bad debts expense should appear on the firm's income statement during the three-year period?

b.   Comment on the use of the one percent rate to provide for credit losses in part *a*.

P8-2B.   Journal Entries for Credit Losses At January 1, the Blake Company had the following accounts on its books: **LO1, 2**

Accounts receivable	$130,000 (debit)
Allowance for doubtful accounts.	7,000 (credit)

During the year, credit sales were $850,000 and collections on account were $794,000. The following transactions, among others, occurred during the year:

Jan. 11 Wrote off J. Wolf's account, $3,000.
Apr. 29 Wrote off B. Avery's account, $2,000.
Nov. 15 Received $1,000 from B. Avery to pay a debt that had been written off April 29. This amount is not included in the $794,000 collections.
Dec. 5 Wrote off D. Wright's account, $2,250.
      31 In an adjusting entry, recorded the allowance for doubtful accounts at one percent of credit sales for the year.

Required
a. Prepare journal entries to record the credit sales, the collections on account, the transactions, and the adjustment.
b. Show how Accounts Receivable and the Allowance for Doubtful Accounts appear on the December 31 balance sheet.

LO2   **P8-3B.** **Credit Losses Based on Accounts Receivable** At December 31, Rhine Company had a balance of $307,000 in its Accounts Receivable account and a credit balance of $2,800 in the Allowance for Doubtful Accounts account. The accounts receivable T-account consisted of $310,600 in debit balances and $3,600 in credit balances. The company has aged its accounts as follows:

Current	$262,000
0–60 days past due	28,000
61–180 days past due	11,200
Over 180 days past due	9,400
	$310,600

In the past, the company has experienced credit losses as follows: two percent of current balances, six percent of balances 0–60 days past due, 15 percent of balances 61–180 days past due, and 30 percent of balances more than six months past due. The company bases its allowance for doubtful accounts on an aging analysis of accounts receivable.

Required
a. Prepare the adjusting journal entry to record the provision for credit losses for the year.
b. Show how Accounts Receivable (including the credit balances) and the Allowance for Doubtful Accounts appear on the December 31 balance sheet.

LO3   **P8-4B.** **Credit Card Sales** Captain Peter's Marina sells boats and other water recreational vehicles (approximately three vehicles are sold each week). The following transactions occurred during the third week of May:

May 15 Sold an $800 boat trailer ($500 cost) to Sam and Myrna Marston, who paid using a personal check.
16 Sold a $10,000 boat ($6,500 cost) to the Calumet Lake Patrol on account, with 2/10, n/30 terms.
18 Sold a $1,200 water scooter ($700 cost) to Kyle Bronson, who used the United Merchants Card to charge the cost of the water scooter. Captain Peter's mailed the credit card sales slip to United Merchants the same day. United Merchants will send a check within seven days, net of a two percent fee.
19 Sold a $6,000 fishing boat ($3,500 cost) to Michael Ferguson, who used the Great American Bank Card to pay for the boat. Captain Peter's deposited the credit card sales slip the same day and received an immediate credit in the company's checking account, net of a three percent fee.
20 Received payment from Calumet Lake Patrol for the boat purchased on May 16.
21 Received payment from United Merchants for the May 18 transaction.

Required
Prepare journal entries to record these transactions. Captain Peter's Marina uses the perpetual inventory system.

P8-5B. **Journal Entries for Accounts and Notes Receivable** Lance, Inc., began business on January 1.   **LO2, 4**
Several transactions for the year follow:

May	2	Received a $18,000, 60 day, ten percent note on account from the Holt Company.
July	1	Received payment from Holt for its note plus interest.
	1	Received a $30,000, 120 day, ten percent note from B. Rich Company on account.
Oct.	29	B. Rich failed to pay its note.
Dec.	9	Wrote off B. Rich's account as uncollectible. Lance, Inc., uses the allowance method of providing for credit losses.
	11	Received a $35,000, 90 day, nine percent note from W. Maling on account.
	31	Recorded expected credit losses for the year by an adjusting entry. The allowance for doubtful accounts has a debit balance of $28,300 as a result of accounts written off during this first year. An analysis of aged accounts receivables indicates that the desired balance of the allowance account is $5,800.
	31	Made the appropriate adjusting entries for interest.

Required

Record the foregoing transactions and adjustments in general journal form.

P8-6B. **Allowance Method** The Fallbrook Company, which has been in business for three years, makes all   **LO2**
of its sales on account and does not offer cash discounts. The firm's credit sales, collections from
customers, and write-offs of uncollectible accounts for the three-year period are summarized below:

Year	Sales	Collections	Accounts Written Off
2018	$1,602,000	$1,466,000	$10,600
2019	1,752,000	1,728,000	12,500
2020	2,050,000	1,876,000	14,000

Required

a.   If the Fallbrook Company used an allowance method of recognizing credit losses and provided for such losses at the rate of one percent of credit sales, what amounts of accounts receivable and the allowance for doubtful accounts should appear on the firm's balance sheet at the end of 2020? What total amount of bad debts expense should appear on the firm's income statement during the three-year period?

b.   Comment on the use of the one percent rate to provide for credit losses in part *a*.

P8-7B. **Journal Entries for Credit Losses** At January 1, the Sherry Company had the following accounts on   **LO1, 2**
its books:

Accounts receivable	$255,000 (debit)
Allowance for doubtful accounts	13,600 (credit)

During the year, credit sales were $1,750,000 and collections on account were $1,588,000. The following transactions, among others, occurred during the year:

Jan.	11	Wrote off J. Smith's account, $5,800.
Apr.	29	Wrote off B. Bird's account, $2,500.
Nov.	15	Received $1,500 from B. Bird to pay a debt that had been written off April 29. This amount is not included in the $1,588,000 collections.
Dec.	5	Wrote off D. Finger's account, $4,300.
	31	In an adjusting entry, recorded the allowance for doubtful accounts at three percent of credit sales for the year.

Required

a.   Prepare journal entries to record the credit sales, the collections on account, the transactions, and the adjustment.

b.   Show how Accounts Receivable and the Allowance for Doubtful Accounts appear on the December 31 balance sheet.

LO2 **P8-8B.** **Credit Losses Based on Accounts Receivable** At December 31, the Lange Company had a balance of $622,000 in its accounts receivable account and a credit balance of $7,500 in the allowance for doubtful accounts account. The company has aged its accounts as follows:

Current	$524,000
0–60 days past due	56,000
61–180 days past due	25,200
Over 180 days past due	16,800
	$622,000

In the past, the company has experienced credit losses as follows: two percent of current balances, six percent of balances 0–60 days past due, 20 percent of balances 61–180 days past due, and 30 percent of balances more than six months past due. The company bases its allowance for doubtful accounts on an aging analysis of accounts receivable.

Required

a. Prepare the adjusting journal entry to record the provision for credit losses for the year.

b. Show how Accounts Receivable and the Allowance for Doubtful Accounts appear on the December 31 balance sheet.

LO3 **P8-9B.** **Credit Card Sales** Lake Heart Marina sells boats and other water recreational vehicles (approximately three vehicles are sold each week). The following transactions occurred during the third week of May:

May 15 Sold a $1,500 boat trailer ($760 cost) to Ed and Jane Peeler, who paid using a personal check.

16 Sold a $20,000 boat ($13,000 cost) to the Lake Heart Lake Patrol on account, with 2/10, n/30 terms.

18 Sold a $2,800 water scooter ($1,500 cost) to Bryan Wagner, who used the United Merchants Card to charge the cost of the water scooter. Lake Heart Marina mailed the credit card sales slip to United Merchants the same day. United Merchants will send a check within seven days, net of a three percent fee.

19 Sold a $9,000 fishing boat ($5,000 cost) to Michael Moffett, who used the Great American Bank Card to pay for the boat. Lake Heart Marina deposited the credit card sales slip the same day and received an immediate credit in the company's checking account, net of a two percent fee.

20 Received payment from the Lake Heart Lake Patrol for the boat purchased on May 16.

21 Received payment from United Merchants for the May 18 transaction.

Required

Prepare journal entries to record these transactions. The Lake Heart Marina uses a perpetual inventory system.

LO2, 4 **P8-10B.** **Journal Entries for Accounts and Notes Receivable** Austin, Inc., began business on January 1. Several transactions for the year follow:

May 2 Received a $30,000, 60 day, ten percent note on account from the Haskins Company.

July 1 Received payment from Haskins for its note plus interest.

1 Received a $61,000, 120 day, nine percent note from R. Longo Company on account.

Oct. 29 R. Longo failed to pay its note.

Dec. 9 Wrote off R. Longo's account as uncollectible. Austin, Inc., uses the allowance method of providing for credit losses.

11 Received a $42,000, 90 day, 12 percent note from R. Canal on account.

31 Recorded expected credit losses for the year by an adjusting entry. Accounts written off during this first year have created a debit balance in the Allowance for Doubtful Accounts of $61,000. An analysis of aged accounts receivables indicates that the desired balance of the allowance account should be $13,200.

31 Made the appropriate adjusting entries for interest.

Required

Record the foregoing transactions and adjustments in general journal form.

SERIAL PROBLEM: KATE'S CARDS

(Note: This is a continuation of the Serial Problem: Kate's Cards from Chapters 1 through 7.)

SP8.   Kate has put a lot of time and effort into streamlining the process to design and produce a greeting card. She has documented the entire process in a QuickTime video she produced on her iMac. The video takes the viewer through the step-by-step process of selecting hardware and software, and shows how to design and produce the card. Kate has met many people who would like to get into the production of greeting cards, but are overwhelmed by the process. Kate has decided to sell the entire package (hardware, software, and video tutorial) to aspiring card producers. The cost of the entire package to Kate is $4,500 and she plans to mark it up by $500 and sell it for $5,000.

John Stevens, an individual Kate met recently at a greeting card conference, would like to buy the package from Kate. Unfortunately, John does not have this much cash and would like for Kate to extend credit.

Kate believes that many of her customers will not be able to pay cash and, therefore, she will need to find some way to provide financing. One option she is exploring is to accept credit cards. She learned that the credit card provider charges a 2.5 percent fee and provides immediate cash upon receiving the sales receipts.

Kate would like you to answer the following questions:

1. What are the advantages and disadvantages of offering credit?
2. What precautions should she take before offering credit to people like John?
3. If Kate grants credit to John, the terms will be 2/10, n/30. Assuming the payment is made during the 10-day discount period, what would be the journal entry to record the sale and then the subsequent payment?
4. If instead of paying early, John pays in 25 days, what would be the journal entry to record the payment?
5. Rather than providing the financing directly, assume that Kate decides to allow the use of credit cards. Further, assume that during the month there is $15,000 worth of credit card sales. Provide the journal entry to record the sales, along with the associated credit card fee. The cost of the goods sold total $13,500.

EXTENDING YOUR KNOWLEDGE

REPORTING AND ANALYSIS

EYK8-1.   **Financial Reporting Problem: Columbia Sportswear Company** The annual report of the Columbia Sportswear Company is presented in Appendix A at the end of this book.

    a.   What was the gross amount of Accounts Receivables and the Allowance for Doubtful Accounts at the end of 2016 and 2017?

    b.   What percent of net accounts receivables was the allowance for doubtful accounts at the end of 2016 and 2017?

EYK8-2.   **Comparative Analysis Problem: Columbia Sportswear Company vs. Under Armour, Inc.** The annual report of the Columbia Sportswear Company is presented in Appendix A at the end of this book and the complete annual report of Under Armour, Inc. is on this book's Website.

Required

    a.   Calculate the accounts receivable turnover and the average collection period for Columbia Sportswear and Under Armour, Inc. for 2017 and 2016. (To calculate the accounts receivable turnover, use the ending net accounts receivable balance as the denominator rather than average net accounts receivable.)

    b.   Compare the average collection periods for the two companies and comment on possible reasons for the difference in the average collection periods for the two companies.

EYK8-3.   **Business Decision Problem** Sally Smith owned a dance studio in San Francisco, California. Students could buy access to the dance classes by paying a monthly fee. Unfortunately, many of Sally's students were struggling actors and actresses who lacked the ability to pay their bills in a timely manner. Although the students were expected to pay for classes in advance, Sally had begun offering credit to many of her students in order to grow her business. This, however, created a serious liquidity problem for Sally.

Age Classification	Trade Receivables Outstanding Balance	Historical Estimate of Noncollection
0–30 days	$44,000	4%
31–60 days	31,000	8%
61–90 days	22,000	12%
91–120 days	13,000	14%
121–150 days	9,000	20%
> 150 days	5,000	50%

Sally's accountant, Matt Thomas, had tried to help her get a handle on the problem, but to little avail. One trick he had successfully used in the past to make Sally realize the seriousness of the problem was to overestimate the extent of Sally's debts; consequently, there currently existed a balance in the Allowance for Uncollectible Accounts totaling $2,700.

Required

1. The first step to help get Sally's business back on track is to write off all receivables having a very low probability of collection (i.e., those accounts over 150 days). Which accounts are affected and by what amount?
2. Prepare an aging of Sally's remaining accounts receivable. What should be the balance in the Allowance for Uncollectible Accounts?
3. Sally is in need of an immediate cash infusion and Matt has advised her to sell some of her receivables. A local bank has offered her two alternatives:
   a. Factor $40,000 of "current" receivables (i.e., 0–30 days old) on a nonrecourse basis at a flat fee of 11 percent of the receivables sold.
   b. Factor $40,000 of "current" receivables on a recourse basis at a flat fee of six percent of the receivables sold.
   Which option should Sally choose? Why?

ABBOTT
LABORATORIES
PFIZER INC.

EYK8-4. **Financial Analysis Problem** **Abbott Laboratories** is a diversified health care company devoted to the discovery, development, manufacture, and marketing of innovative products that improve diagnostic, therapeutic, and nutritional practices. Abbott markets products in more than 130 countries and employs 50,000 people. **Pfizer Inc.** is a research-based, global health care company. Its mission is to discover and develop innovative, value-added products that improve the quality of life of people around the world. Pfizer manufactures products in 31 countries and markets these products worldwide. These two companies reported the following information in their financial reports:

(in millions)	2017
Abbott Laboratories	
Net sales.	$27,390
Beginning accounts receivable (net).	3,248
Ending accounts receivable (net)	5,249
Pfizer Inc.	
Net sales.	$52,546
Beginning accounts receivable (net).	8,225
Ending accounts receivable (net)	8,221

Required

a. Calculate the accounts receivable turnover and the average collection period for Abbott Laboratories and Pfizer Inc. for 2017.
b. Compare the average collection periods for the two companies and comment on possible reasons for the difference in average collection periods for the two companies.

CRITICAL THINKING

GENERAL MILLS,
INC.

EYK8-5. **Accounting Research Problem** Access the fiscal year 2017 annual report of **General Mills, Inc.**, available on this book's Website.

Required

a. What was the amount of total Accounts Receivables and the Allowance for Doubtful Accounts at the end of fiscal-year 2017 and 2016? (Note: This information can be found in Note 17.)

    b.   What percent of total accounts receivables was the allowance for doubtful accounts at the end of 2017 and 2016?

    c.   Calculate the accounts receivable turnover and the average collection period for General Mills for 2017 and 2016. (For purposes of calculating the accounts receivable turnover, use the ending total accounts receivable balance [net] as the denominator rather than the average total accounts receivable [net].)

    d.   Comment on whether General Mills' management of accounts receivable improved (or not) over the two-year period.

EYK8-6.   **Accounting Communications Activity** You have been hired as the accounting manager of Taylor, Inc., a provider of custom furniture. The company recently switched its method of paying its salespeople from a straight salary to a commission basis in order to encourage them to increase sales. The salespeople receive ten percent of the sales price at the time of the sale. You have noticed that the company's accounts receivable balance is growing because the salespeople are granting more credit to their customers.

Required

Draft a memorandum explaining why it is important to closely monitor the company's accounts receivable balance and why a large balance could lead to cash flow problems.

EYK8-7.   **Accounting Ethics Case** Tractor Motors' best salesperson is Marie Glazer. Glazer's largest sales have been to Farmers Cooperative, a customer she brought to the company. Another salesperson, Bryan Blanchard, has been told in confidence by his cousin (an employee of Farmers Cooperative) that Farmers Cooperative is experiencing financial difficulties and may not be able to pay Tractor Motors what is owed.

    Both Glazer and Blanchard are being considered for promotion to a new sales manager position.

Required

What are the ethical considerations that face Bryan Blanchard? What alternatives does he have?

EYK8-8.   **Corporate Social Responsibility Problem** **MGM Resorts International** is committed to responsible gaming and strictly adheres to the Code of Conduct established by the American Gaming Association. The company's efforts include employee training, public awareness, and support for research initiatives through the National Center for Responsible Gaming.

MGM RESORTS
INTERNATIONAL

    Since MGM Resorts International makes money when people gamble, and the more people gamble, the more money the company makes, why would MGM Resorts International work to curtail gambling by some of the people it could make a lot of money from? Does this form of good citizenship run counter to the company's responsibilities to its stockholders?

EYK8-9.   **Forensic Accounting Problem** The chapter highlight on forensic accounting discussed the technique of covering up receivables theft by lapping (see Forensic Accounting: Lapping on page 383), where one account is credited with the receipt from another account. The highlight stated that lapping may be detected by an auditor through the confirmation of accounts receivables. While detection is important, it is far better to prevent lapping from occurring in the first place. Can you think of any controls that can be put in place to help prevent lapping?

EYK8-10. **Analyzing IFRS Financial Statements** The 2017 financial statements of **LVMH Moet Hennessey-Louis Vuitton S.A.** are presented in Appendix C at the end of this book. LVMH is a Paris-based holding company and one of the world's largest and best-known luxury goods companies. As a member of the European Union, French companies are required to prepare their consolidated (group) financial statements using International Financial Reporting Standards (IFRS). At year-end 2017 (2016), LVMH's allowance account was 343 (294) million euros. After reviewing LVMH's consolidated financial statements, consider the following questions. (Additional information can be found in LVMH's complete annual report provided on this book's Website.)

LVMH MOET
HENNESSEY-
LOUIS VUITTON
S.A.

IFRS

Required

    a.   What was the gross amount of Trade and Other Receivables at fiscal year-end 2016 and 2017?

    b.   What percent of total trade and other receivables were the provision for impairment and the provision for product returns combined as of the end of 2016 and 2017?

    c.   Calculate the accounts receivable turnover and the average collection period for the company for 2016 and 2017.

    d.   Comment on whether LVMH's management of its trade receivables improved (or not) over the two-year period.

EYK8-11. **Working with the Takeaways** Below are selected data from a recent **MGM Resorts International** financial statement. Amounts are in thousands.

Net sales:	$9,455,123
Beginning of year accounts receivable:	480,559
End of year accounts receivable:	542,924

Required
Calculate the MGM Resorts International (a) accounts receivable turnover, and (b) average collection period.

ANSWERS TO SELF-STUDY QUESTIONS:

1. d, (pp. 382–383) 2. b, (pp. 380–382) 3. d, (pp. 386–387) 4. a, (pp. 388–389) 5. d, (p. 389)
6. c, (pp. 386–387) 7. a, (p. 380) 8. a, (p. 384) 9. c, (p. 380–382) 10. c, (p. 386)

YOUR TURN! SOLUTIONS

Solution 8.1

May 2	Accounts receivable (+A)	40,000	
	Sales revenue (+R, +SE)		40,000
	To record credit sales.		
May 17	Cash (+A)	35,000	
	Accounts receivable (−A)		35,000
	To record cash collections.		
May 31	Bad debts expense (+E, −SE)	500	
	Allowance for doubtful accounts (+XA, −A)		500
	To record bad debts expense.		
June 15	Allowance for doubtful accounts (−XA, +A)	200	
	Accounts receivable (−A)		200
	To write off accounts receivable.		

Solution 8.2

Bad debts expense (+E, −SE)	18,000	
Allowance for doubtful accounts (+XA, −A)		18,000
To record the bad debts expense for the period.		

Solution 8.3

a.	Bad debts expense (+E, −SE)	3,200	
	Allowance for doubtful accounts (+XA, −A)		3,200
	To record the bad debts expense for the period.		

$$\text{Bad debt expense} = \frac{(\$100{,}000 \times 1\%) + (\$15{,}000 \times 3\%) +}{(\$10{,}000 \times 5\%) + (\$20{,}000 \times 10\%) - \$750}$$
$$= \$3{,}200$$

b.	Allowance for doubtful accounts (−XA, +A)	480	
	Accounts receivable—Phorest Company (−A)		480
	To write off the Phorest Company uncollectible account.		

Solution 8.4

Cash (+A)	49,000	
Credit card fee expense (+E, −SE)	1,000	
Sales revenue (+R, +SE)		50,000

To record credit sales and collection, less a two percent fee.

Solution 8.5

$40,000 × .05 × 3/12 = $500

Solution 8.6

a. Accounts receivable turnover = $30,000/[($2,800 + $3,200)/2] = 10
b. Average collection period = 365/10 = 36.5 days

Solution 8A.1

Bad debts expense (+E, −SE)	750	
Accounts receivable (−A)		750

To write off the Rhea Inc. uncollectible account.

Chapter 9

Accounting for Long-Lived and Intangible Assets

PAST

In Chapter 8 we studied how to account for accounts and notes receivable.

PRESENT

This chapter focuses on another important set of assets—long-lived and intangible assets.

FUTURE

Chapter 10 begins our study of the accounting for liabilities.

Facebook is perhaps the best known of all the social media and social networking services. Facebook has more than 2 billion monthly active users, a far cry from its humble origins when membership was initially limited to Harvard students. Since 2006, anyone can join as long as they are at least 13 years of age.

Along with expanding its user base, Facebook has also increased its asset base to accommodate all those users. As of December 31, 2017 Facebook had nearly $36 billion of plant and intangible assets; about 43 percent of its total assets. In this chapter we will study how companies like Facebook account for their plant and intangible assets along with some measures that can be used to analyze how well a company utilizes these assets.

Road Map

LO	Learning Objective	Page	eLecture	Guided Example	Assignments
LO1	Discuss the nature of plant assets and identify the accounting guidelines relating to their initial measurement.	419	E9-1	YT9.1	SS1, SE1, E1A, E2A, E1B, E2B, P1A, P2A, P4A, P6A, P8A, P1B, P2B, P4B, P6B, P8B
LO2	Discuss the nature of depreciation, illustrate three depreciation methods, and explain impairment losses.	422	E9-2	YT9.2	SS2, SE2, SE3, SE4, E3A, E4A, E5A, E3B, E4B, E5B, P2A, P3A, P4A, P6A, P8A, P9A, P2B, P3B, P4B, P6B, P8B, P9B
LO3	Discuss the distinction between revenue expenditures and capital expenditures.	431	E9-3	YT9.3	SS7, E6A, E6B, P4A, P8A, P9A, P4B, P8B, P9B
LO4	Explain and illustrate the accounting for disposals of plant assets.	433	E9-4	YT9.4	SS3, SS11, SE5, SE11, E7A, E7B, P5A, P5B
LO5	Discuss the nature of, and the accounting for, intangible assets and natural resources.	434	E9-5	YT9.5, YT9.6	SS4, SS5, SS6, SS12, SE6, SE7, SE13, E8A, E8B, P6A, P6B
LO6	Illustrate the balance sheet presentation of long-lived assets.	438	E9-6		SS8, SE12, E10A, E11A, E10B, E11B, P7A, P7B
LO7	Define the return on assets ratio and the asset turnover ratio and explain their use.	439	E9-7	YT9.7	SS9, SS10, SE8, SE9, SE10, E9A, E9B

```
┌─────────────────────────────────────────────────────────┐
│      ACCOUNTING FOR LONG-LIVED AND INTANGIBLE ASSETS      │
└─────────────────────────────────────────────────────────┘
```

Plant Assets	Intangible Assets and Natural Resources	Analyzing Long-Lived Assets
• Measuring acquisition cost • Recording plant assets • Computing depreciation • Revenue and capital expenditures • Disposing of plant assets	• Measuring intangible asset costs • Recording intangible assets • Computing amortization • Examples of intangibles • Accounting for natural resources • Balance sheet presentation	• Return on assets • Asset turnover

OVERVIEW OF LONG-LIVED ASSETS

A.K.A. Plant assets are often referred to as fixed assets.

A.K.A. Property, plant and equipment is often referred to simply as **PP&E**.

A.K.A. Natural resources are also known as wasting assets because they are consumed (exhausted) through extraction or removal from their natural setting.

Consider for a moment the asset structure of Facebook, Inc. Approximately 16 percent of the assets used to fulfill the company's mission of providing a platform for social media and networking are in the long-term asset category known as plant assets. **Plant assets** refer to a firm's *long-lived property, plant and equipment*. Facebook reports plant assets of over $13.7 billion. **Intangible assets** are those economic resources that benefit a company's operations but which lack the physical substance that characterizes plant assets. Examples of intangible assets include copyrights, franchises, and patents. Facebook's reported intangible assets are composed of such things as acquired technologies, patents, and trade names. Resources supplied by nature, such as timber stands, mineral deposits, and oil and gas deposits are **natural resources**. The benefits provided to a firm by these three types of long-lived assets extend over many accounting periods. In this chapter, we discuss the accounting for these long-lived assets.

The carrying value of long-lived assets is initially based on the asset's historical cost—that is, the cost incurred to acquire and place the asset into a revenue-producing state. The costs related to the use of long-lived assets must be matched with the revenues that they help to generate to ensure that a business's net income is correctly determined. The portion of an asset's cost that is consumed or used up in any given period is called *depreciation expense when referring to plant assets, amortization expense when referring to intangible assets,* and *depletion expense when referring to natural resources*. Depreciation, amortization, and depletion all refer to the process of allocating a portion of an asset's acquisition cost to expense on the income statement to reflect the consumption of the asset as it produces revenue for a business.

Exhibit 9-1 provides several examples of all three categories of long-lived assets. The exhibit also identifies the appropriate term for the periodic consumption of the asset and its write-off to expense. Note that the land on which a business is operated has an indefinite useful life, and therefore does not require any periodic write-off to expense.

Exhibit 9-1	Long-Lived Assets That Require Periodic Write-Off	
Asset Category	**Examples**	**Term for the Periodic Write-Off to Expense**
Plant Assets	*Buildings, equipment, tools, furniture, fixtures, vehicles*	Depreciation
Intangible Assets	*Patents, copyrights, leaseholds, franchises, trademarks, brand names*	Amortization
Natural Resources	*Timber, coal, oil and gas reserves, mineral deposits*	Depletion

MEASURING ACQUISITION COST OF PLANT ASSETS

Exhibit 9-2 is a graphic presentation of the accounting issues associated with plant assets during their useful life. The accounting issues include: ❶ Identifying the type, and amount, of expenditures that make up the acquisition cost of the asset. ❷ Determining the appropriate amount of an asset's cost to periodically charge against revenue to reflect the asset's consumption. This involves estimating the asset's useful life and its probable salvage value at disposal. ❸ Differentiating expenditures related to the maintenance of an asset from expenditures that increase an asset's productive capacity or extend its useful life. ❹ Determining any gain or loss to be recognized when a plant asset is disposed.

LO1   **Discuss** the nature of plant assets and **identify** the accounting guidelines relating to their initial measurement.

Exhibit 9-2	Issues Associated with the Accounting for Plant Assets

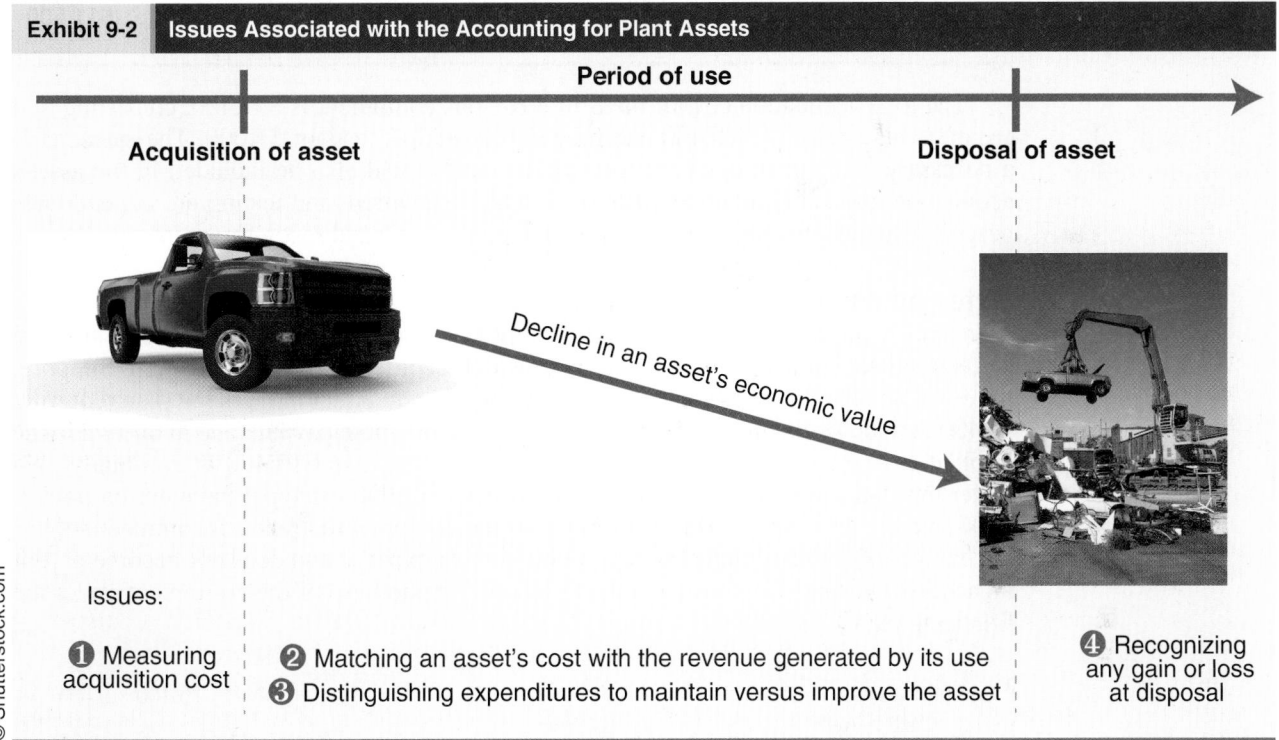

Acquisition Cost

Plant assets are initially recorded on the balance sheet at their acquisition cost. This measure is also called the asset's *historical cost* because it represents the amount expended when the asset was originally acquired. In general, the acquisition cost equals the cash and/or cash equivalent given up to acquire the asset *and* to prepare it for its intended use.

	Cost Principle	PRINCIPLE ALERT

The initial valuation of long-lived assets follows directly from the *cost principle* discussed in Chapter 1. To measure an asset's acquisition cost, accountants must not only identify the asset's cash-equivalent purchase price, but also identify whether any additional costs were incurred to get the asset to a company's place of business and in a condition for use by the business. Both costs are added to the asset's balance sheet value and are considered part of the asset's acquisition cost.

Cash Purchases

An asset's acquisition cost is often simply the amount of cash paid when the asset is acquired and readied for use by a business. Consider, for example, the following expenditures made by Smith & Sons to acquire a piece of equipment:

Purchase price components:		
Gross invoice price	$10,000	
Less: Cash discount (1/10, n/30)	(100)	
Sales tax	500	$10,400
Related expenditures:		
Freight charges	200	
Installation costs	500	
Testing of installed machine	300	1,000
Acquisition cost of equipment		**$11,400**

The total acquisition cost of the Smith & Sons equipment is $11,400, consisting of a cash purchase price of $10,400 and related preparation costs of $1,000. The sales tax is a necessary component of the purchase price and should also be included in the asset's acquisition cost. Similarly, the costs of freight, installation, and testing are expenditures necessary to get the asset to the desired business location and ready for its intended use.

Deferred Payment Purchases

If an asset's purchase price is not immediately paid in cash, the cash-equivalent purchase price at the date of acquisition is determined and recorded in the asset account. Suppose, for example, that Smith & Sons purchased its equipment under a financing plan requiring a $400 cash down payment and a nine percent, $10,000 note payable due in one year. The implied cash price remains $10,400 even though more than $10,400 is eventually paid under the financing plan ($400 down payment + $10,000 principal payment on note + $900 interest payment = $11,300). Because the equipment is ready for immediate use, the extra $900 paid as interest is charged to interest expense and does not become part of its acquisition cost. The journal entry to record the purchase of the equipment under the financing plan is as follows:

A = L + SE		
+10,400		
−400 +10,000		

Equipment (+A)	10,400	
Cash (−A)		400
Notes payable (+L)		10,000
To record purchase of equipment.		

As in the case of a cash purchase, the expenditures for freight, installation, and testing are debited to the Equipment account when incurred.

Package Purchases

Sometimes several long-lived assets are purchased as a package. For example, assume that Smith & Sons purchased a freight terminal that included land, a building, and some loading equipment for an aggregate price of $190,000. For accounting purposes, the total purchase price should be divided among the three assets because (1) they should be reported in different asset accounts on the balance sheet to properly reflect the company's asset structure, (2) only the building and equipment are subject to depreciation, and (3) the equipment is likely to have an estimated useful life different from that of the building.

The total package price is allocated among the acquired assets on the basis of their relative market or appraisal values. For example, if the estimated market value of the land, building, and equipment is $60,000, $120,000, and $20,000, respectively, the allocation of the $190,000 acquisition price would be as follows:

Asset	Estimated Market Value	Percent of Total	Allocation of Purchase Price	Estimated Useful Life
Land	$ 60,000	30	$ 57,000 (30% × $190,000)	Indefinite
Building.	120,000	60	114,000 (60% × $190,000)	30 years
Equipment	20,000	10	19,000 (10% × $190,000)	8 years
Totals	$200,000	100	$190,000	

Acquisition Costs Related to Land

The purchase of land often raises a number of accounting issues. Suppose, for example, that Smith & Sons retains a local real estate broker at a fee of $2,000 to locate an appropriate site for the company's new office building. Assume, also, that the property selected for purchase has an existing building on it which will need to be razed. The terms of the sale include a down payment of $40,000 to the seller, with the buyer paying off an existing mortgage of $10,000 and $300 of accrued interest. In addition, Smith & Sons agrees to pay accrued real estate taxes of $800 owed by the seller. Other related expenditures include legal fees of $400 and a title insurance premium of $500. A local salvage company will be hired to raze the old building, paying Smith & Sons $200 for reclaimed materials. Applying the cost principle, the acquisition cost of the land is calculated as follows:

© Shutterstock.com

Payment to the seller	$40,000
Commission to real estate agent	2,000
Payment of mortgage and accrued interest due at time of sale	10,300
Payment of property taxes owed by seller	800
Legal fees.	400
Title insurance premium	500
	$54,000
Less: Net recovery from material reclamation	200
Cost of land.	$53,800

Again, any expenditure for the property taxes, insurance, and legal fees should be capitalized, or added to, the acquisition cost of the land because they are necessary to complete the purchase transaction. Similarly, removing the old building also prepares the land for its intended use. The $200 net recovery from razing the existing structure, therefore, *reduces* the land's cost. A net payment to remove the old building would have *increased* the land's cost.

When a land site is acquired in an undeveloped area, a firm may pay a special assessment to the local government for such property improvements as streets, sidewalks, and sewers. These improvements are considered to be permanent improvements; and consequently, the special assessment is capitalized to (added to) the acquisition cost of the land.

A firm may also make property improvements that have limited lives. Classified as land improvements, they include such improvements as paved parking lots, driveways, private sidewalks, and fences. Expenditures for these assets are charged to a separate Land Improvement account on the balance sheet and depreciated over the estimated useful life of the improvements.

Leasehold Improvements

Expenditures made by a business to alter or improve leased property are called leasehold improvements. For example, a merchandising firm may make improvements, with the permission of the owner, to a leased building. The Home Depot, Inc., a home improvement retail chain, leases a significant portion of its more than 2,000 U.S. stores and reports nearly $1.6 billion of leasehold improvements on its balance sheet. The improvements, or alterations, become part of the leased property and revert to the owner of the property at the end of the lease. The cost of the leasehold improvements is capitalized to the Leasehold Improvements account on the balance sheet and is depreciated over the life of the lease or the life of the improvements, whichever is shorter.

YOUR TURN! 9.1

The solution is on page 460.

Kelly Company purchased manufacturing equipment for $20,000 cash. In addition to the $20,000 purchase price, Kelly paid sales tax of $1,600, freight costs of $400, installation costs of $600, testing costs of $100, and $300 for unrelated supplies from the same company. Explain the accounting treatment for each of the expenditures.

CORPORATE SOCIAL RESPONSIBILITY

It is unlikely that the first company that you think of when asked to name the top companies in an annual ranking of socially-responsible businesses was a manufacturer of diesel engines. Perhaps you may need to revise your thinking. **Cummins Inc.** is a perennial top 10 finisher among Business Ethics 100 Best Corporate Citizens, a prestigious annual ranking by *Business Ethics* magazine. In fact, Cummins placed number one in the ranking in 2005!

Cummins is one of the best manufacturing companies in the world when it comes to air-emissions reduction research. The company's research efforts have paid off with a 90 percent reduction in diesel-engine emissions. Cummins' ten-year goal is to achieve zero, or close to zero, engine emissions.

NATURE OF DEPRECIATION

LO2 **Discuss** the nature of depreciation, **illustrate** three depreciation methods, and **explain** impairment losses.

With the exception of land, the use of plant assets to generate revenue consumes the economic benefit provided by the assets. At some point—usually before they are totally worthless—these assets are disposed of, and often replaced. A diagram of a typical pattern of plant asset utilization is illustrated below:

In this example, a plant asset is acquired for $1,000, used for several accounting periods, and then sold for $100. The $900 decline in recorded value is called **depreciation** and is an expense of generating the revenues recognized during the periods that the asset was in use. Thus, if a company's net income is to be a meaningful representation of the business's operating performance, $900 of expense must be allocated to the periods of asset use and matched with sales revenue. Failure to do so would overstate the company's net income for these periods.

As part of this allocation process, it is first necessary to estimate the asset's useful life and its expected future salvage value. **Useful life** is the expected period of economic usefulness to the business—that is, the period from the date of acquisition to the expected date of disposal. **Salvage value** (or *residual value*) is the expected net recovery (sales proceeds less disposal costs) when the asset is sold or removed from service. When the salvage value is insignificant, it may be ignored in the depreciation process under the materiality concept.

A.K.A. The salvage value of a plant asset is also often referred to as its residual value or scrap value.

Allocation versus Valuation: Depreciation Accounting

Although the idea is theoretically appealing, accountants do not base an asset's periodic depreciation expense on changes in the asset's market value or on the measured wear of the asset, primarily because a reliable, objective, and practical source for such data rarely exists. Rather, the purpose of **depreciation accounting** is to allocate, in a *systematic* and *rational* manner, the difference between an asset's acquisition cost and its estimated salvage value over the *estimated* useful life of the asset. Consequently, depreciation accounting techniques are convenient expedients for estimating asset utilization and should not be considered precise. Although imperfect, depreciation estimates facilitate a better assessment of a business's net income than would result from expensing the asset at either its date of acquisition or its date of disposal.

Expense Recognition (Matching) Concept	PRINCIPLE ALERT

Depreciation accounting represents an application of the *expense recognition (matching) concept*. Depreciable plant assets are used in a business's operating activities to help generate revenues. Each period that benefits from the use of a plant asset is assigned part of the asset's cost as depreciation expense. In so doing, the depreciation expense is matched with the sales revenue that the asset helps to generate. The matching that occurs through this allocation process extends throughout the asset's useful life.

Several factors are related to the periodic allocation of depreciation, including wear from use, from natural deterioration, and from technical obsolescence. Each factor reduces the economic value of an asset. To some extent, maintenance (lubrication, adjustments, parts replacements, and cleaning) may partially arrest or offset wear and deterioration. Thus, when an asset's useful life and salvage value are estimated, a given level of maintenance is assumed.

Calculating Depreciation Expense

Estimating the periodic depreciation of a plant asset can be achieved in many ways. In this section, three widely used methods for calculating depreciation are illustrated.

1. Straight-line
2. Declining-balance
3. Units-of-production

For each method, we assume that equipment is purchased for $1,000. The equipment is assumed to have an estimated useful life of five years and has an estimated salvage value of $100.

Straight-Line Method

The **straight-line method** is the easiest depreciation method to understand and calculate, and it is the most widely used depreciation method by U.S. businesses. Under the straight-line method, an equal amount of depreciation expense is allocated to each period of an asset's useful life. Straight-line depreciation is calculated as follows:

$$\text{Annual depreciation} = \frac{(\text{Acquisition cost} - \text{Salvage value})}{\text{Estimated useful life (in months or years)}}$$

For the purchased equipment in our example, the annual straight-line depreciation expense is:

$$\frac{(\$1,000 - \$100)}{5 \text{ years}} = \$180 \text{ per year}$$

The journal entry to record the annual depreciation expense is:

Depreciation expense—Equipment (+E, −SE)	180	
Accumulated depreciation—Equipment (+XA, −A)		180
To record depreciation expense for the year.		

A	=	L	+	SE
−180				−180 Exp

A.K.A. The book value of an asset (acquisition cost less accumulated depreciation) is also referred to as the **net book value**.

Like other expense accounts, Depreciation Expense is deducted from sales revenue on the income statement and is closed at year-end to Retained Earnings. The offsetting credit entry is posted to a contra-asset account, Accumulated Depreciation, which is deducted from the Equipment account on the balance sheet to calculate the asset's book value. In this manner, as long as the asset is in service, the original acquisition cost of the asset is maintained in the asset account, and the cumulative balance of depreciation taken to date is carried in the contra-asset account. When an asset is disposed of, the asset's acquisition cost and accumulated depreciation are removed from the respective accounts.

The following table shows the depreciation schedule for the equipment's five-year life under the straight-line method:

			End-of-Period Balance	
Year of Useful Life	**Balance of Equipment Account**	**Annual Depreciation Expense**	**Accumulated Depreciation Account**	**Asset's Book Value**
1	$1,000	$180	$180	$820
2	1,000	180	360	640
3	1,000	180	540	460
4	1,000	180	720	280
5	1,000	180	900	100
Total		$900		

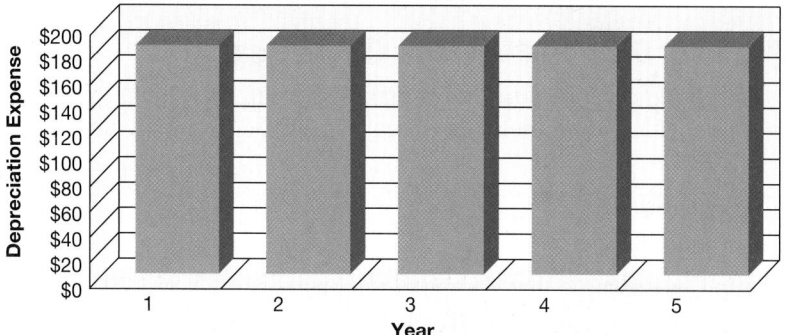

Notice that (1) the Equipment account always shows the original acquisition cost ($1,000) of the asset; (2) each period reflects $180 of depreciation expense; (3) the Accumulated Depreciation account balance is cumulative and shows the portion of the acquisition cost taken as depreciation to date; (4) the asset's book value is the original acquisition cost of the asset less the accumulated depreciation taken to date; and (5) the asset's book value at the end of the five-year period is equal to the asset's estimated salvage value. Thus, an asset's book value declines to its estimated salvage value as the asset is depreciated over its useful life.

For periods of less than one year, straight-line depreciation amounts are simply proportions of the annual depreciation charge. For example, if an asset is acquired on April 1, depreciation for the period ended December 31 would be $135, or 9/12 × $180. Assets acquired or disposed of during the first half of any month are usually treated as if the acquisition or disposal occurred on the first day of the month. When either event occurs during the last half of any month, it is assumed that the event occurred on the first day of the following month.

Note the role of the *going concern concept* in depreciation accounting. Absent evidence to the contrary, the going concern concept assumes that a business has an indefinite life. Depreciation accounting allocates an asset's acquisition cost to expense over the asset's useful life. Any depreciation method that allocates an asset's acquisition cost over many years—whether the useful life is five years or 25 years (or more)—implicitly assumes that a business will be in existence for at least that number of years.

Declining-Balance Method

The **declining-balance method** is an **accelerated depreciation method**. It calculates a company's depreciation expense as a constant percentage of an asset's book value as of the beginning of each period. The method takes its name from the fact that, over time, an asset's book value (acquisition cost − accumulated depreciation) declines as the asset is used up, yielding a decreasing depreciation expense. An asset's salvage value is *not* considered in the calculation of declining-balance depreciation, except that the depreciation of an asset stops when the asset's book value equals its estimated salvage value.

The declining-balance method is an "accelerated" method because the constant depreciation percentage it uses is a multiple of the straight-line depreciation rate (the straight-line depreciation rate = 100 percent/expected useful life in years). There are many versions of the declining-balance method because different multiples of the straight-line rate may be used. *Double-declining balance depreciation* uses a depreciation rate that is twice the straight-line rate; similarly, *150 percent-declining balance depreciation* uses a depreciation rate that is one and one-half times the straight-line rate.

For example, the straight-line depreciation rate for an asset with a five-year useful life is 20 percent per year (100 percent/5 years). Thus, to depreciate a five-year asset on an accelerated basis, the double-declining balance method uses a 40 percent depreciation rate (2 × 20 percent), while the 150 percent declining-balance method uses a 30 percent depreciation rate (1.5 × 20 percent).

Under the double-declining balance method, the annual depreciation expense is calculated as follows:

Annual depreciation = Book value at beginning of year × Double-declining balance rate

Referring to our example of the equipment purchased for $1,000, with a useful life of five years and an expected salvage value of $100, the periodic double-declining balance depreciation would be calculated as follows (amounts rounded to the nearest dollar):

Year of Useful Life	Acquisition Cost	Beginning Accumulated Depreciation	Beginning Book Value	Twice Straight-line Percentage		Annual Depreciation Expense
1	$1,000	$ 0	$1,000	× 40 percent	=	$400
2	1,000	400	600	× 40 percent	=	240
3	1,000	640	360	× 40 percent	=	144
4	1,000	784	216	× 40 percent	=	86
5	1,000	870	130	[exceeds limit]		30
Total						$900

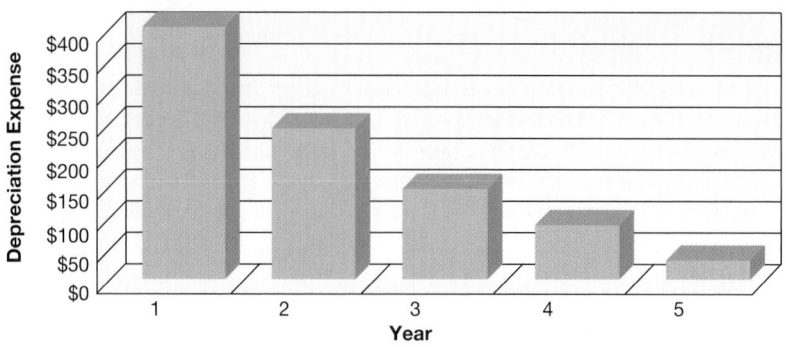

Hint: An asset's salvage value must be considered when calculating the depreciation expense for an asset using the straight-line method or the units-of-production method. Salvage value is not considered when calculating double-declining balance depreciation until the final year.

Notice in the fifth year that the depreciation expense is only $30, the amount needed to reduce the asset's book value to its estimated salvage value of $100. Assets are not depreciated below their estimated salvage value.

If an asset is purchased during a fiscal period, a pro-rata allocation of the first year's depreciation is calculated. If, for example, an asset is acquired on April 1, depreciation for the period ended December 31 would be $300, or [9/12 × (40 percent × $1,000)]. In subsequent periods, the usual procedure is followed; that is, the asset's book value at the beginning of the period is multiplied by the constant depreciation rate. For example, in the second year, depreciation on the asset would be $280, or [40 percent × ($1,000 − $300)].

Units-of-Production Method

The **units-of-production method** allocates depreciation in proportion to an asset's use in operations. Under this method, the depreciation per unit of production is first calculated by dividing the total depreciable cost of the asset (in our example, $1000 − $100 = $900) by the asset's total projected units-of-production capacity:

$$\text{Depreciation per unit} = \frac{(\text{Acquisition cost} - \text{Salvage value})}{\text{Total estimated units of production}}$$

The total estimated units of production may represent the total expected miles that an asset will be driven, the total tons expected to be hauled, the total hours expected to be used, or the total number of expected cuttings, drillings, or stampings of parts by a piece of equipment. To illustrate, assume that a drilling tool will drill an estimated 45,000 parts during its expected useful life. The tool is purchased for $1,000 and has an expected salvage value of $100. Consequently, the depreciation per unit of production is:

$$\frac{(\$1,000 - \$100)}{45,000 \text{ parts}} = \$0.02 \text{ per part}$$

To find the asset's annual depreciation expense, the depreciation per unit of production is multiplied by the number of units actually produced during a given year:

Annual depreciation = Depreciation per unit × Units of production for the period

Assuming that the number of parts drilled over the five years were 8,000, 14,000, 10,000, 4,000, and 9,000, respectively, in Year 1 through Year 5, the units-of-production depreciation expense is calculated as follows:

Year of Useful Life	Depreciation per Unit		Annual Units of Production		Annual Depreciation Expense
1	$0.02	×	8,000	=	$160
2	0.02	×	14,000	=	280
3	0.02	×	10,000	=	200
4	0.02	×	4,000	=	80
5	0.02	×	9,000	=	180
Total					$900

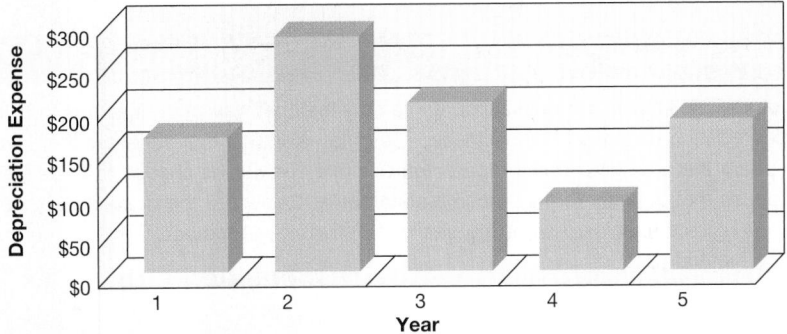

A Comparison of Alternative Depreciation Methods

The following charts compare the periodic depreciation expense and accumulated depreciation from our equipment illustration. The charts show the accelerated nature of the double-declining balance method relative to the straight-line method. Notice, for example, that the depreciation expense in Year 1 under the double-declining balance method is $400 but is only $180 under the straight-line method. In Year 2, the double-declining balance depreciation is $240 but again is only $180 for the straight-line method. It is not until Year 3 that the straight-line method produces a depreciation charge that exceeds the double-declining balance charge. Depreciation expense for the units-of-production method reflects the assumptions presented previously in the chapter. There is no general pattern for the annual depreciation expense under this method. The annual depreciation for the units-of-production method depends on the yearly productive activity of an asset, and this activity will vary from asset to asset. Finally, note that the total accumulated depreciation over the life of the asset is the same under all three methods, and is equal to the acquisition cost less salvage value, or $900.

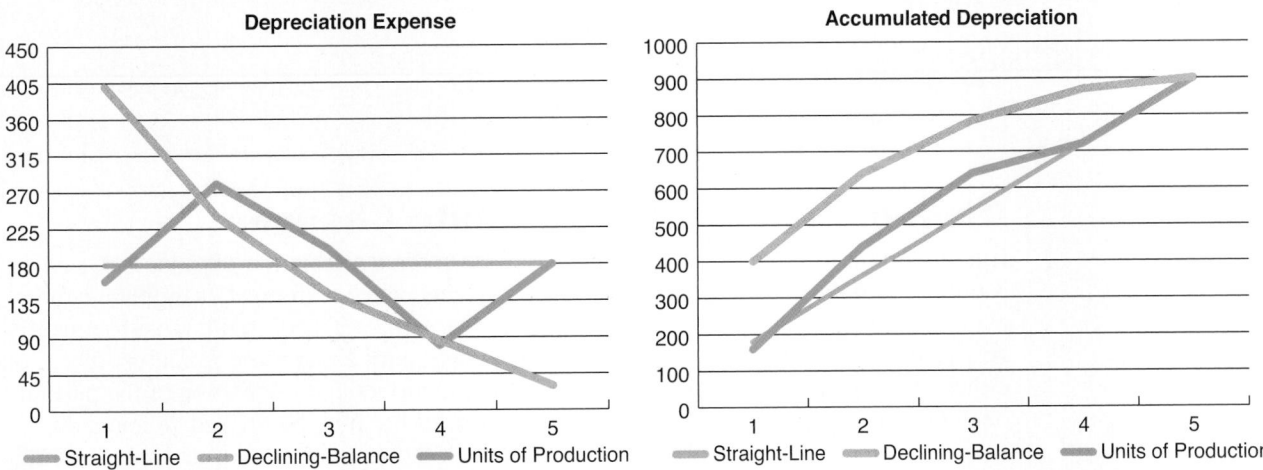

Annual Depreciation Expense			
Year	**Straight-Line**	**Declining-Balance**	**Units-of-Production**
1	$180	$400	$160
2	180	240	280
3	180	144	200
4	180	86	80
5	180	30	180
Total	$900	$900	$900

Depreciation Methods

So many assets, so little time. Some accountants may feel that way when it comes to calculating the periodic depreciation expense for a business. They may also feel that variety is the spice of life. At least it appears that way given the various methods that companies choose to calculate the depreciation expense that appears in their income statements. Below are the depreciation methods used by 600 large U.S. companies. As can be seen, the straight-line method is by far the most popular depreciation method used:

- Group/composite 1.8%
- Units-of-production 3.3%
- Accelerated method—not specified 4%
- Sum-of-the-years'-digits <1%
- Declining-balance 2.2%
- Straight-line 99%

*The totals exceed 100 percent because some firms use more than one method.
Source: Accounting Trends and Techniques

YOUR TURN! 9.2

The solution is on page 460.

The Salsbury Company purchased equipment costing $10,000 at the start of the year. The equipment has an estimated useful life of five years and a salvage value of $2,000. The CEO is unsure if the company should use the straight-line method or the double-declining balance method to depreciate the new equipment.

Required:
Prepare the journal entry for depreciation for the second year under each of the alternative depreciation accounting methods.

Depreciation Method Estimate Changes

It is important to remember that a business's periodic depreciation expense is based on estimates of both an asset's useful life and its salvage value. Circumstances change, however, and the estimates originally made when the asset was acquired may subsequently be found to be too high or too low. Once it is determined that the original estimates of either an asset's useful life or salvage value were incorrect, the calculation of the periodic depreciation expense for an asset's remaining useful life may be revised. When a depreciation estimate revision is found to be warranted, the revision is executed by allocating the undepreciated balance of the asset's book value over the revised remaining useful life and using the revised estimated salvage value. To illustrate this process, refer again to our example of equipment costing $1,000, with a five-year life, and an estimated salvage value of $100.

If, based on original estimates, straight-line depreciation of $180 has been recorded for each of the first three years of the asset's useful life, the accumulated depreciation to date would total $540, or 3 × $180. Now, suppose that just before recording the depreciation expense for the fourth year, circumstances indicate that the equipment's useful life will total six years instead of five, and that its salvage value at the end of the sixth year will be $40 instead of $100. The revised depreciation expense to be taken during the revised remaining useful life (Year Four through Year Six) of the equipment is calculated as follows:

Original acquisition cost	$1,000
Depreciation previously recorded (3 years @ $180)	(540)
Book value at start of fourth year	$ 460
Revised salvage value	(40)
Revised remaining depreciable cost	$ 420
Revised remaining useful life	3 years
Revised depreciation for fourth, fifth, and sixth years	$420/3 = $140 per year

Impairment Losses

Sometimes a change in the circumstances relating to a depreciable asset is so severe that the future cash flows from the asset's use and disposal are estimated to be *less* than its current book value. If an asset's remaining book value cannot be recovered through the future cash flows expected to be generated from the asset's use, the asset's value is said to be *impaired*. Under these circumstances, an impairment loss is recorded on the income statement, and the asset's book value on the balance sheet is reduced. The **impairment loss** is calculated as the difference between the asset's current book value and its current fair value.

To illustrate, assume that two years ago Facebook purchased computer servers costing $500,000, with an estimated useful life of six years and a salvage value of $20,000. The book value of the servers is currently $340,000 ($500,000 cost less $160,000 accumulated depreciation). Unanticipated technological advances in server technology used by competitors, however, now severely limits the use of Facebook's equipment. An analysis by the company's CFO indicates that Facebook now expects that the net future cash flows to be generated from the use and disposal of the equipment over the next four years is $300,000. The limited uses for the equipment cause its current fair value to be only $200,000.

Facebook's equipment is impaired because its book value is not recoverable through its expected future cash flows—the $300,000 of expected future cash flows is less than the equipment's $340,000 current book value. Thus, an impairment loss is computed by comparing the equipment's book value with its current fair value, as follows:

Equipment book value	$340,000
Equipment current fair value	(200,000)
Impairment loss	$140,000

The journal entry to record the impairment loss is as follows:

					A	= L +	SE
Impairment loss on equipment (+Loss, −SE)	140,000				−140,000		−140,000
Accumulated depreciation—Equipment (+XA, −A)		140,000					Loss
To record impairment loss on equipment.							

© Shutterstock.com

PRINCIPLE ALERT   **Conservatism Concept**

The accounting for impaired plant assets illustrates the *conservatism concept*. In selecting between alternative accounting measures, the conservatism concept states that the least optimistic measure should be used. When a plant asset is impaired, it is reported on the balance sheet at its current fair value, an amount lower than its book value before any impairment loss is recorded. Unimpaired plant assets remain on the balance sheet at their book value, however, even though current fair values may be higher. U.S. GAAP mandates that asset values be written down when impaired, but prohibits the write-up of assets when their value appreciates.

IFRS ALERT

While U.S. GAAP requires that long-lived assets be written down in value when they are judged to be impaired, they may not be written up in value if there is a subsequent recovery in their fair market value. Under International Financial Reporting Standards (IFRS), however, the accounting treatment of long-lived asset value recoveries is substantially different. Under IFRS, if an asset's value increases above its current book value, the asset's balance sheet value may be written up to the higher value by debiting the asset account for the amount of the increase. The balancing credit entry is to a stockholders' equity account called the asset revaluation reserve.

To illustrate, assume that Peabody International PLC, based in the United Kingdom, owns land in London that was originally purchased for 20 million British pounds. Current real estate appraisals, however, indicate that the fair market value of the land is now worth 50 million pounds. To recognize the increase in the land's fair market value, Peabody International would record the following journal entry:

Land (+A)	30 million pounds	
Asset revaluation reserve—Land (+SE)		30 million pounds
To record the revaluation of land.		

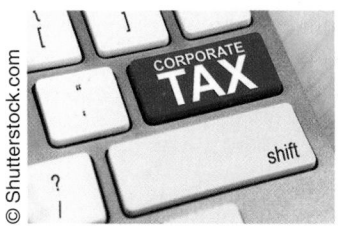

Depreciation for Income Tax Purposes

Depreciation expense may be deducted by a business on its federal income tax return as a normal business expense. As a consequence, some refer to the tax deductibility of depreciation as a "tax shield" since depreciation expense lowers a business's taxable income, and hence, lowers the actual income taxes that must be paid. The depreciation expense deducted on a business's income tax return, however, may differ substantially from the depreciation expense reported on a company's income statement because the calculation of tax depreciation follows income tax regulations referred to as the **modified accelerated cost recovery system (MACRS)**.

MACRS establishes several asset classes with prescribed useful lives ranging from three years to 31.5 years. Most machinery and equipment, for example, are in the seven-year asset class. When acquired, an asset is placed in the appropriate asset class (per MACRS guidelines) and depreciated over the prescribed useful life specified for that class.[1]

MACRS was introduced into U.S. tax law to encourage companies to invest in plant assets. Because the useful life specified under MACRS is usually shorter than an asset's accounting useful life, this method provides larger depreciation deductions during an asset's early years, much like the declining-balance method used for financial statement

---

[1] Depreciation in most asset classes must follow a half-year convention whereby one-half of the first year's depreciation expense is taken in the first year, regardless of when the asset was acquired, and one-half of the asset's last year's depreciation is taken in the year of disposal, regardless of when during the year the asset is disposed. The half-year convention means that assets in the three-year asset class are effectively depreciated over four different accounting periods, assets in the five-year property class are depreciated over six different accounting periods, and so on.

reporting. In a sense, the accelerated deductions under MACRS provide an interest-free loan to a business because they allow the firm to pay less income tax in the early years of an asset's life and more in the later years. During the intervening time period, the firm can use the postponed income tax payments to support the business's operations, without incurring any interest charges.

Change and modification characterize U.S. tax law. Tax depreciation guidelines will likely be modified again in the future. Keep in mind, however, that depreciation changes in the tax law do not affect the depreciation methods and estimates that a firm may use in preparing its financial statements using U.S. GAAP for its shareholders and lenders.

REVENUE VERSUS CAPITAL EXPENDITURES

Revenue Expenditures

LO3 **Discuss** the distinction between revenue expenditures and capital expenditures.

Revenue expenditures are expenditures relating to plant assets that are expensed when incurred. The following list identifies two common types of revenue expenditures:

1. Expenditures for ordinary maintenance and repairs of existing plant assets.
2. Expenditures to acquire low-cost items that benefit the firm for several periods.

Maintenance and Repairs

Some level of maintenance and repairs must be assumed when estimating the useful lives and salvage values of property, plant, and equipment. For example, a plant asset that is not maintained or repaired will have a shorter useful life than a similar asset that is properly maintained. Periodic upkeep—such as lubrication, cleaning, and replacement of minor parts—is necessary to maintain an asset's expected level and length of usefulness. These periodic upkeep costs—referred to as maintenance costs—are charged to expense as they are incurred.

Low-Cost Items

Most businesses purchase items that provide years of service at a relatively small cost, such as paperweights, staplers, and wastebaskets. Because of the small dollar amounts involved, establishing these items as assets on the balance sheet and depreciating them over their expected useful lives serves no useful purpose. The effect on the financial statements is insignificant and consequently, expensing these expenditures at the time of purchase is more efficient. The accounting for such low-cost items is thus completed in the period in which they are acquired.

Materiality Concept	PRINCIPLE ALERT

The practice of accounting for small dollar transactions in the most expedient fashion follows the *materiality concept*. Under this accounting concept, generally accepted accounting principles apply only to items of significance to the users of financial statements. Because the judgment of users will be unaffected by the accounting for immaterial dollar amounts, their immediate expensing does not diminish the usefulness of financial statements.

Capital Expenditures

Capital expenditures increase the book value of long-lived assets. To *capitalize* an amount means to increase an asset's book value by that amount. The following list identifies two typical capital expenditures related to property, plant, and equipment:

1. Initial acquisitions and additions.
2. Betterments.

Initial Acquisitions and Additions

At the beginning of this chapter, the accounting guidelines governing the initial measurement of long-lived assets were discussed. We noted that expenditures equal to an asset's implied cash purchase price, plus any costs necessary to prepare the asset for use, were debited to the asset account. These amounts are commonly referred to as capital expenditures.

These same accounting guidelines apply for additions to existing plant assets. Adding a new wing to a building or expanding the size of an asphalt parking lot are examples of additions. These capital expenditures should also be debited to an asset account. A separate account (and depreciation schedule) should be used for an addition when its estimated useful life differs from the remaining useful life of the existing plant asset.

Betterments

Betterments are expenditures that (1) extend the useful life of an asset, (2) improve the quality and/or quantity of the asset's output, or (3) reduce the asset's operating expenses. Examples include overhauling the engine or adding a power winch to a highway service truck, improving the precision of a machining device to reduce defects, or converting a building to solar power. Expenditures for betterments are generally debited to the appropriate asset account, and the subsequent periodic depreciation expense is increased to allocate the additional cost over the asset's remaining useful life.

<table>
<tr>
<td>

YOUR TURN! 9.3

The solution is on
page 460.

</td>
<td>

Hastings Company recorded the following expenditures during the year with regard to its delivery van:

1. Changed the engine oil
2. Repainted the van
3. Overhauled the engine that is expected to increase the useful life of the van
4. Repaired a dent in a fender
5. Converted the van to run on a biofuel with an estimated annual fuel cost savings of 30 percent.

Required:
Determine whether each of the above expenditures is a revenue expenditure or a capital expenditure.

</td>
</tr>
</table>

<table>
<tr>
<td>

**FORENSIC
ACCOUNTING**

</td>
<td>

WorldCom's Bad Accounting

</td>
</tr>
<tr>
<td></td>
<td>

 On the surface, the decision to capitalize or expense an expenditure related to a plant asset does not seem like the subject matter for one of the most infamous accounting scandals of all time. Unfortunately, to the many investors in **WorldCom** who saw the value of their investment disappear, this accounting decision had profound consequences.

Beginning in 2001, and continuing through mid-2002, WorldCom, under the direction of its CEO, CFO, Controller, and Director of General Accounting, used fraudulent accounting methods to portray a false picture of the company's financial health. The principal accounting gimmickry used by the company was to misclassify "line costs," a cost that should have been expensed each year, as a capital expenditure, thus adding to WorldCom's assets rather than adding to its expenses.

The fraud was discovered and brought to the attention of WorldCom's Board of Directors by a small team of internal auditors who had been conducting their investigation in secret, mostly at night. The Securities and Exchange Commission followed with its own investigation. The final conclusion—WorldCom's assets and pre-tax net income had been inflated by nearly $11 billion! Following a conviction for filing false financial reports with the SEC, WorldCom's CEO Bernard Ebbers was sentenced to 25 years in prison.

</td>
</tr>
</table>

DISPOSALS OF PLANT ASSETS

A business may dispose of its plant assets in a variety of ways. An asset may be sold, retired, or exchanged as partial payment for a new asset. The asset's usefulness to a firm may also be ended by an unfavorable or unanticipated event—the asset may be stolen or destroyed by a natural disaster.

LO4   **Explain** and **illustrate** the accounting for disposals of plant assets.

Depreciation must extend through an asset's total useful life to a business. Consequently, depreciation must be recorded up to the disposal date, regardless of the manner of the asset's disposal. Should the disposal date not coincide with the end of an accounting period, a journal entry must record depreciation for the partial period—that is, the period from the date that depreciation was last recorded to the asset's disposal date.

The following data is used to illustrate the disposal of plant assets:

Equipment's acquisition cost	$1,000
Estimated salvage value after five years	100
Annual straight-line depreciation	180

(Assume that depreciation to the date of disposal has been recorded.)

Sale of Plant Assets

Most sales of plant assets involve the following factors:

1. The sale transaction involves an exchange of a used plant asset for cash. Because the plant asset sold is no longer on hand, a journal entry must remove the asset account and the accumulated depreciation account from the books. These amounts together reflect the asset's book value.

2. Because plant assets are often sold for an amount higher or lower than their book value, a gain or loss will result. Sale proceeds in excess of book value create a gain, whereas book values in excess of sales proceeds create a loss.

Asset Sales for More Than Book Value

Assume that the equipment is sold for $230 midway through its fifth year of use. Depreciation was last recorded at the end of the fourth year. The journal entries to record the sale are:

Depreciation expense—Equipment (+E, −SE)	90	
Accumulated depreciation—Equipment (+XA, −A)		90
To record depreciation expense for six months ($180/2).		

A	=	L	+	SE
−90				−90 Exp

Cash (+A)	230	
Accumulated depreciation—Equipment (−XA, +A)	810	
Equipment (−A)		1,000
Gain on sale of plant assets (+Gain, +SE)		40
To record the sale of equipment for $230.		

A	=	L	+	SE
+230				+40 Gain
+810				
−1,000				

Note that recording depreciation to the date of sale adds $90 to the Accumulated Depreciation account, which totals $810, calculated as [(4 × $180) + $90]. To reflect the sale properly, it is necessary to remove the entire amount of accumulated depreciation ($810) from the books. The gain of $40 is calculated as the sale proceeds of $230 minus the asset's book value of $190 ($1,000 − $810).

Asset Sales for Less Than Book Value

Assume that the equipment is sold for $30 at the end of the fifth year. The journal entry to record this sale is:

				Cash (+A)	30	
A	= L +	SE		Loss on sale of plant assets (+Loss, −SE)	70	
+30		−70 Loss		Accumulated depreciation—Equipment (−XA, +A)	900	
+900				Equipment (−A)		1,000
−1,000				*To record the sale of equipment for $30.*		

The loss on the asset sale equals the book value of $100 minus the sales proceeds of $30. The cash received is recorded, and the balances from both the Equipment account and the Accumulated Depreciation account are removed from the books.

If the equipment is sold for an amount exactly equal to its book value, no gain or loss results. Should the equipment be abandoned, stolen, or destroyed (with no insurance coverage) before the end of its expected useful life, a loss equal to its book value is recorded.

Exchange of Plant Assets

A plant asset may be exchanged for another plant asset. The accounting for long-lived asset exchanges can be complex depending upon the relationship between the new asset and the asset being traded in. Consequently, the accounting for asset exchanges is covered in intermediate accounting textbooks.

YOUR TURN! 9.4

The solution is on page 460.

The Jones Company is self-insured, and consequently the company does not receive any insurance payments if it is involved in an accident. One of the Jones Company trucks was involved in a major accident and the company decided to sell the truck for scrap. At the time of the accident, the truck had a cost basis of $22,500 and accumulated depreciation of $15,000. The proceeds from the sale totaled $750.

Required:
Record the journal entry for the disposal of the truck.

ACCOUNTING IN EVERYDAY LIFE

Career Opportunities at Facebook

When one thinks of a career at Facebook, one probably first thinks of somebody with a computer engineering, data analytics, or marketing background. While Facebook certainly hires people with these skills, it is also constantly looking for people with accounting skills to support its mission. A recent search of career opportunities on Facebook's Website highlighted many accounting and finance positions. Among the requirements is a bachelor's degree and experience with accounting concepts.

INTANGIBLE ASSETS AND NATURAL RESOURCES

LO5 **Discuss** the nature of, and the accounting for, intangible assets and natural resources.

Intangible assets are the various resources that benefit a business's operations, but which lack physical characteristics or substance. Intangible assets include, for example, the exclusive rights or privileges obtained from a governmental unit or by legal contract, such as patents, copyrights, franchises, trademarks, and leaseholds. Another intangible asset is goodwill, which reflects the beneficial attributes acquired in the acquisition of another company that cannot be attributed to any other recorded asset.

By convention, only certain assets are included in the intangible asset category. Some resources that lack physical substance, such as prepaid insurance, accounts receivable, and investments, are not classified as intangible assets. Because intangible assets lack physical characteristics, the related accounting procedures are more subjective than for such tangible assets as property, plant, and equipment.

Measurement of Intangible Assets (Cost Determination)

A firm should record intangible assets acquired from outside entities at their acquisition cost. Similarly, some costs associated with intangible assets created internally by a firm are capitalized to the balance sheet. For example, the costs to secure a trademark or patent—such as attorney's fees and registration fees—are charged to an Intangibles Asset account, if they are material.

The accounting for other expenditures related to intangible assets varies depending upon the type of expenditure and the nature of the intangible asset. Notably, **research and development costs** are not capitalized to the balance sheet as an intangible asset because GAAP guidelines require that these expenditures be expensed when incurred. As a result of these accounting procedures, some companies may have important intangible assets that are carried at a nominal amount, or may even fail to appear at all on the firm's balance sheet. It is noteworthy that one U.S. industry is exempted from the conservative accounting treatment of research and development costs. Under U.S. GAAP, software development companies may capitalize some costs associated with the development of software.

IFRS ALERT

The accounting for some intangible assets under IFRS differs significantly from the accounting under U.S. GAAP. For instance, under U.S. GAAP, all research and development costs must be expensed when incurred; however, under IFRS, development costs may be capitalized if a commercially viable product results from the original research effort. A significant consequence of this alternative accounting treatment is that IFRS companies enjoy a more fairly presented balance sheet, since most intangible assets are fully disclosed. On the balance sheets of many U.S. GAAP companies, there are many unreported intangible assets.

Amortization of Intangibles

The **amortization** of an intangible asset carried on the balance sheet involves the periodic expensing of the asset's cost over the term of its expected useful life. Because salvage values are ordinarily not involved, the amortization of intangible assets typically entails (1) determining the asset's cost, (2) estimating the period over which it will benefit a company, and (3) allocating the cost in equal amounts to each accounting period involved. Straight-line amortization is typically used for intangible assets unless another method is shown to be more appropriate.

The amortization entry debits the Amortization Expense account and credits the Intangible Asset account. An Accumulated Amortization account could be used for the credit entry, but generally there is no particular benefit to financial statement users from accumulating amortization in a separate contra-asset account.

Not all intangible assets are amortized. Some intangible assets have a limited life because of legal or regulatory restrictions. Intangible assets classified as having a limited life are amortized over their expected useful life. Other intangible assets are considered to have an indefinite life because they are expected to generate cash flows for the company for the foreseeable future. Goodwill is an example of an intangible asset with an indefinite life. Intangible assets with an indefinite life are not amortized.

EXAMPLES OF INTANGIBLE ASSETS

Patents

A **patent** is an exclusive privilege granted to an inventor by the U.S. Patent Office for a period of 20 years from the date the patent application is filed. A patent gives the patent holder the right to exclude others from making, using, or selling the invention. Patent laws were originated to encourage inventors by protecting them from imitators who might usurp the invention for commercial gain. Just what qualifies as a patentable idea, however, has become quite complex in the modern realm of technical knowledge. Consequently, long periods of patent "searching," and frequently, successful defense of infringement suits may precede the validation of a patent. Even though patents have a legal life of 20 years from application date, changes in technology or consumer tastes may shorten their economic life. Because of their uncertain value, patents are accounted for conservatively by most businesses. For example, most businesses amortize patents over a shorter period than 20 years. When patents are purchased, the buyer enjoys patent protection for the patent's remaining legal life.

CORPORATE SOCIAL RESPONSIBILITY

Intangible assets include items such as patents that provide protection from competitors using the patented device or process for up to 20 years. It is not uncommon for firms to vigorously defend their patents through aggressive lawsuits. Tesla believes so strongly in what electric vehicles can do for the planet that it has chosen to freely share its patents. This allows Tesla's competitors, along with any engineers who wish to use these patents, to work with the technology with the aim, according to Tesla, of strengthening the development of sustainable technology.

Copyright

A copyright protects its owner against the unauthorized reproduction of a specific written work, recorded work, or artwork. A copyright lasts for the life of the author plus 70 years. The purchase price of valuable copyrights can be substantial, and proper measurement and amortization are necessary for valid business income determination.

Franchises

Franchises most often involve exclusive rights to operate or sell a specific brand of products in a given geographic area. Franchises may be for definite or indefinite periods. Although many franchises are agreements between two private firms, various governmental units award franchises for public utility operations within their legal jurisdictions. The right to operate a **Kentucky Fried Chicken (KFC)** restaurant or to sell **Midas Mufflers** in a specific area illustrates franchise agreements in the private sector.

ACCOUNTING IN PRACTICE

Types of Intangible Assets

Intangible assets are perhaps the most difficult asset category to fully comprehend. Intangible assets appearing on a company's balance sheet represent a varied collection of assets as can be seen from a sample of 600 large U.S. firms:

Type of Intangible Asset	Number	%
Goodwill	542	90%
Trademarks, brand names, copyrights	330	55%
Customer lists/relationships	320	53%
Technology	162	27%
Patents	161	27%
Licenses, franchises, memberships	114	19%
Non-compete covenants	112	18.7%
Contracts, agreements	104	17.3%
Other—described	65	10.8%

Source: Accounting Trends and Techniques.

Trademarks

Trademarks and trade names represent the exclusive and continuing right to use certain terms, names, or symbols, usually to identify a brand or family of products. An original trademark or trade name can be registered with the U.S. federal government for a nominal cost. A company may spend considerable time and money to determine an appropriate name or symbol for a product. Also, the purchase of well-known, and thus valuable, trademarks or trade names may involve substantial amounts of money. When the cost of a trademark or trade name is material, the amount is debited to an appropriate intangible asset account—Trademarks—and amortized over the period of expected benefit to a business.

Goodwill

Goodwill is an often misunderstood concept. In common usage, goodwill may represent the favorable reputation a firm has earned based on its prior operations, quality of service, or positive product characteristics. The term goodwill, however, has a much different meaning when used in accounting. Goodwill represents the amount paid by one company in the acquisition of another company above the amount that can be attributed to the identifiable net assets of the acquired company, including the other intangibles like those discussed above. The measurement of goodwill is complex because it can stem from many factors. Examples of such factors include exceptional customer relations, advantageous business location, operating efficiency, superior personnel, favorable financial sources, or perceived synergies between the acquiring company and the acquired company. Unlike most intangible assets, goodwill is not subject to periodic amortization because it is considered to have an indefinite life. Instead, goodwill is evaluated annually for any impairment in value. If a company's goodwill is found to be impaired, the Goodwill account is written down to its fair value and an Impairment Loss is recorded on the income statement.

Goodwill Can Be a Significant Asset	ACCOUNTING IN PRACTICE

Although accountants only record goodwill when another business entity is purchased (to the extent that the purchase price exceeds the fair value of the identifiable net assets acquired), the balance sheets of many major corporations contain significant amounts of goodwill. Recent balance sheets, for example, show the following amounts of goodwill: **Bank of America Corporation**, $68.9 billion; **General Electric Company**, $83.9 billion; **AT&T Inc.**, $105.4 billion; and **Procter & Gamble Company**, $49.7 billion. These amounts are evidence of the active acquisition efforts of these major corporations, and also of the large amounts that may be paid for goodwill in acquisition transactions.

Match the descriptive explanation below with the correct term:

Amortization	Patent	Copyright
Franchise	Trademark	

1. An exclusive right that protects an owner against the unauthorized reproduction of a specific written work.
2. The periodic write-off of an intangible asset to expense on the income statement.
3. An exclusive and continuing right to use a certain symbol to identify a brand or family of products.
4. An exclusive right to operate or sell a specific brand of products in a given geographic area.
5. An exclusive privilege granted to an inventor that gives the asset holder the right to exclude others from making, using, or selling the invention.

YOUR TURN! 9.5

The solution is on page 460.

NATURAL RESOURCES

Natural resources include assets such as standing timber, iron ore, coal, gold, silver, and other metal ores. Natural resource assets are recorded on the balance sheet at their acquisition cost plus exploration and development costs.[2] Similar to the units-of-production depreciation method for plant assets, GAAP requires natural resources to be *depleted* over the asset's expected useful life.

---

[2] The accounting for another type of natural resource—oil and gas reserves—is more complicated and depends on which of two available methods the company selects: the full cost method or the successful efforts method. These methods are described in advanced accounting textbooks.

Depletion represents the removal of the natural resource from the resource's natural setting and subsequent sale or placement into inventory for sale. Because it is not known with certainty the amount of natural resources in their natural state, the depletion recorded in an accounting period represents an estimate of the actual amount of natural resources extracted in the period.

To illustrate, assume that on January 1, Silverton Mining acquires for $1,000,000 a mineral deposit with an estimated 400,000 tons of ore. Silverton spends an additional $200,000 on exploration and development. Silverton expects zero salvage value once the ore is fully mined. The acquisition would be recorded with the following journal entry:

A   = L + SE
+1,200,000
−1,200,000

Jan. 1	Mineral deposits (+A)	1,200,000	
	Cash (−A)		1,200,000
	To record the purchase of mineral deposits and associated exploration and development costs.		

Assume Silverton mined a total of 60,000 tons of ore in the initial year. The depletion charge is computed as follows:

$$\text{Depletion rate} = \frac{\text{Cost of natural resource} - \text{Salvage}}{\text{Estimated total units of natural resource}} = \frac{\$1,200,000}{400,000} = \$3.00 \text{ per ton}$$

The current year depletion expense is $180,000 (60,000 tons × $3.00 per ton). The depletion expense would be recorded with the following journal entry.

A   = L + SE
−180,000   −180,000

Dec. 31	Depletion expense (+E, −SE)	180,000	
	Accumulated depletion (+XA, −A)		180,000
	To record the depletion of mineral deposits.		

In the above example it is assumed that Silverton sold all the $180,000 of ore that was mined during the year. If instead one-half of the mined ore was still unsold at year end, the proper journal entry to record depletion would be:

A   = L + SE
+90,000   −90,000
−180,000

Dec. 31	Inventory—mineral deposits (+A)	90,000	
	Depletion expense (+E, −SE)	90,000	
	Accumulated depletion (+XA, −A)		180,000
	To record the depletion of mineral deposits.		

YOUR TURN! 9.6

The solution is on page 461.

Hardwoods, Inc. purchased a tract of timber for a total cost of $500,000. The tract is estimated to contain 200,000 board feet of lumber once the timber is harvested. Hardwoods expects the land will be worth $100,000 once the timber is fully harvested. Hardwoods harvests 40,000 board feet of timber in the initial year and sells all but 5,000 board feet.

Record separate journal entries for the purchase of the tract of timber and for the recording of depletion.

BALANCE SHEET PRESENTATION

LO6 **Illustrate** the balance sheet presentation of long-lived assets.

Long-lived assets are presented on the balance sheet below the Current Assets category. (Recall that assets are listed on a classified balance sheet in descending order of liquidity.) Natural resources are usually shown on the balance sheet as either a part of plant assets or as a separate category among noncurrent assets with a title such as "oil reserves" or "timber stands." For example, **Boise Cascade** reports a separate line item titled "Timber deposits," while **ExxonMobil** includes natural resources with other property, plant, and equipment. In either case, natural resources are reported at their total cost less accumulated depletion. For example, **Exhibit 9-3** reveals how these assets appear on the balance sheet of **Weyerhaeuser Company**.

Exhibit 9-3	Weyerhaeuser Company

WEYERHAEUSER COMPANY
Balance Sheet (asset section only)
Dollar amounts in millions

	December 31	
	2017	**2016**
Current assets:		
Cash and cash equivalents.	$ 824	$ 676
Accounts receivable	410	474
Inventories	383	358
Prepaid expenses and other current assets	98	114
Total current assets	1,715	1,622
Property and equipment, less depreciation	1,618	1,562
Construction in progress.	225	213
Timber and timberlands at cost, less depletion	12,954	14,299
Minerals and mineral rights, less depletion	308	319
Goodwill	40	40
Other assets.	1,199	1,188
Total assets.	**$18,059**	**$19,243**

RETURN ON ASSETS AND ASSET TURNOVER

The ability of a firm to use its assets effectively and efficiently is a sign of a healthy, well-managed company. The rate of return generated on a company's assets, referred to as the *return on assets ratio,* is a widely used indicator that focuses on this dimension of a firm's financial performance. In practice, there is some variation in the calculation of this ratio, but one commonly used definition of **return on assets** is:

LO7 **Define** the return on assets ratio and the asset turnover ratio, and **explain** their use.

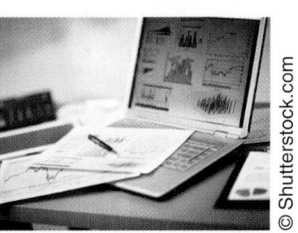

$$\text{Return on assets} = \frac{\text{Net income}}{\text{Average total assets}}$$

This ratio relates data from two financial statements—the income statement and the balance sheet. The numerator consists of the net income for the year from the income statement.[3] The denominator in the ratio is the average balance of total assets for the year (computed by adding the total assets at the beginning of the year to the total assets at the end of the year and dividing the sum by two) obtained from the balance sheet.

    To illustrate the calculation of the return on assets ratio, we use data from Ford Motor Company, a manufacturing firm with a large investment in long-lived assets. The company reported 2017 net income of $8,803 million, total assets at the beginning of the year of $237,951 million, and year-end total assets of $257,808 million. Ford's return on assets for the year is 3.6 percent; calculated as $8,803/[($237,951 + $257,808)/2]. To evaluate a firm's return on assets, it is useful to consider the trend in the ratio, the return for other firms in the same industry, the industry's average return on assets, and the company's economic environment.

---

[3] An alternative calculation of the return on assets ratio adds interest expense to net income in the ratio's numerator. This calculation keeps the method of financing a company's assets from influencing the calculation of the ratio.

TAKEAWAY 9.1	Concept ➞	Method ➞	Assessment
	How effective is a company in using its assets to produce net income?	Net income and average total assets $$\text{Return on assets ratio} = \frac{\text{Net income}}{\text{Average total assets}}$$	A higher ratio value implies a higher, more effective level of asset utilization.

The **asset turnover** ratio is another ratio that evaluates a company's effective use of its assets. This ratio measures how effectively a firm uses its assets to generate sales revenue. The asset turnover ratio is calculated as follows:

$$\textbf{Asset turnover} = \frac{\textbf{Net sales}}{\textbf{Average total assets}}$$

Referring again to the 2017 Ford data, the company reported net sales of $156,776 million. Consequently, Ford's asset turnover for the year is 0.63, or $156,776/[($237,951 + $257,808)/2], indicating that the company was able to generate $0.63 of sales revenue for every dollar invested in assets. A high asset turnover ratio indicates that a company is very effective in using its assets to generate sales revenue. For the preceding year, Ford's asset turnover was 0.66. Thus, Ford generated $0.66 in net sales in 2016 for each dollar invested in total assets. The slight decrease in Ford's asset turnover from 0.66 to 0.63 indicates that the firm used its assets less effectively in 2017 than in 2016 to generate sales revenue.

YOUR TURN! 9.7

The solution is on page 461.

Rollins Co. reported the following information in its 2018 financial statements:

Net sales.	$150,000
Net income	25,000
Beginning of year total assets	130,000
End of year total assets	120,000

Compute the return on assets and asset turnover for Rollins Co. in 2018.

TAKEAWAY 9.2	Concept ➞	Method ➞	Assessment
	How effective is a company in generating sales revenue using its assets?	Average total assets and net sales $$\text{Asset turnover ratio} = \frac{\text{Net sales}}{\text{Average total assets}}$$	A higher ratio value implies a higher level of sales revenue generated for each dollar invested in assets.

COMPREHENSIVE PROBLEM

Segman Company purchased a machine on January 2 for $24,300. The machine has an expected useful life of three years and an expected salvage value of $900. The company expects to use the machine for 1,400 hours in the first year, 2,000 hours in the second year, and 1,600 hours in the third year.

Required

 a. Calculate the depreciation expense for each year using each of the following depreciation methods: (1) straight-line, (2) units-of-production (assume that actual usage equals expected usage), (3) double-declining balance.

b. Assume that the machine was purchased June 1. Calculate the depreciation expense for each year using the following depreciation methods: (1) straight-line, (2) double-declining balance.

Solution

a. 1. Straight-line:
      Year 1: ($24,300 − $900)/3 = $7,800
      Year 2: ($24,300 − $900)/3 = $7,800
      Year 3: ($24,300 − $900)/3 = $7,800
   2. Units-of-production:
      Depreciation per hour = ($24,300 − $900)/5,000 hours = $4.68 per hour
      Year 1: 1,400 hours × $4.68 = $6,552
      Year 2: 2,000 hours × $4.68 = $9,360
      Year 3: 1,600 hours × $4.68 = $7,488
   3. Double-declining balance:
      Depreciation rate = (l00/3) × 2 = 66 2/3 percent
      Year 1: $24,300 × 66 2/3 percent = $16,200
      Year 2: ($24,300 − $16,200) × 66 2/3 percent = $5,400
      Year 3: ($24,300 − $21,600) × 66 2/3 percent = $1,800
b. 1. Straight-line: Refer to calculations in (a)1.
      Year 1: $7,800 × 7/12 = $4,550
      Year 2: $7,800 (full year's depreciation)
      Year 3: $7,800 (full year's depreciation)
      Year 4: $7,800 × 5/12 = $3,250
   2. Double-declining balance: Refer to calculations in (a)3.
      Year 1: $16,200 × 7/12 = $9,450
      Year 2: ($24,300 − $9,450) × 66 2/3 percent = $9,900
      Year 3: ($24,300 − $19,350) × 66 2/3 percent= $3,300
      Year 4: $750 [This amount reduces the machine's book value to its salvage value of $900 and is the maximum depreciation expense for the year. ($24,300 − $22,650) × 66 2/3 percent = $1,100 gives an amount in excess of the maximum $750 depreciation.]

SUMMARY OF LEARNING OBJECTIVES

Discuss the nature of long-lived assets and identify the accounting guidelines relating to their initial measurement. (p. 419)　　　　　LO1

- The accounting for long-lived assets involves the determination of an asset's acquisition cost, periodic depreciation expense, subsequent capital expenditures, and disposal.
- The initial cost of a plant asset is its implied cash price plus any expenditure necessary to prepare the asset for its intended use.

Discuss the nature of depreciation, illustrate three depreciation methods, and explain impairment losses. (p. 422)　　　　　LO2

- Depreciation is a cost allocation process; it allocates a plant asset's depreciable cost (acquisition cost less salvage value) in a systematic manner over the asset's estimated useful life.
- The most commonly used depreciation methods are straight-line, units-of-production, and declining-balance.
- Revisions of depreciation estimates are accomplished by recalculating depreciation charges for current and subsequent periods.
- When a plant asset is impaired, a loss is recognized equal to the difference between the asset's book value and its current fair value.

Discuss the distinction between revenue expenditures and capital expenditures. (p. 431)　　　　　LO3

- Revenue expenditures are expensed as incurred and include the cost of ordinary repairs and maintenance and the purchase of low-cost items.
- Capital expenditures, which increase a plant asset's book value, include initial acquisitions, additions, and betterments.

LO4 **Explain and illustrate the accounting for disposals of plant assets. (p. 433)**
- When a firm disposes of a plant asset, depreciation must be recorded on the asset up to the disposal date.
- Gains and losses on plant asset dispositions are determined by comparing an asset's book value to the proceeds received.

LO5 **Discuss the nature of, and the accounting for, intangible assets and natural resources. (p. 434)**
- Intangible assets acquired from other entities are initially valued at their acquisition cost. Some internally created intangible assets are also measured at their cost, but most expenditures related to internally developed intangible assets are expensed rather than capitalized.
- Research and development costs related to a firm's products and its production processes are expensed as incurred.
- Amortization is the periodic write-off to expense of an intangible asset's cost over the asset's useful life.
- Goodwill may be shown in the accounts only when it has been purchased as part of the acquisition of another business.
- Natural resources include assets such as standing timber, oil and gas reserves, and mineral ores.
- Depletion represents the removal of the natural resources from their natural setting.

LO6 **Illustrate the balance sheet presentation of long-lived assets. (p. 438)**
- Long-lived assets are shown on the balance sheet after long-term investments. Although technically an intangible asset, goodwill is reported separately on the balance sheet since it is not subject to amortization.

LO7 **Define the return on assets ratio and the asset turnover ratio, and explain their use. (p. 439)**
- The return on assets ratio is calculated by dividing net income by average total assets; it represents an overall measure of a firm's profitability and how efficiently a company is using its assets to generate net income.
- The asset turnover ratio is calculated by dividing net sales by average total assets; it provides an indication of the effective utilization of business assets to generate sales revenues.

SUMMARY	Concept ⟶	Method ⟶	Assessment
TAKEAWAY 9.1	How effective is a company in using its assets to produce net income?	Net income and average total assets $$\text{Return on assets ratio} = \frac{\text{Net income}}{\text{Average total assets}}$$	A higher ratio value implies a higher, more effective level of asset utilization.
TAKEAWAY 9.2	How effective is a company at generating sales using its assets?	Average total assets and net sales $$\text{Asset turnover ratio} = \frac{\text{Net sales}}{\text{Average total assets}}$$	A higher ratio value implies a higher level of sales revenue generated for each dollar invested in assets.

KEY TERMS

Accelerated depreciation method (p. 425)
Amortization (p. 435)
Asset turnover (p. 440)
Betterments (p. 432)
Capital expenditures (p. 431)
Copyright (p. 436)
Declining-balance method (p. 425)
Depletion (p. 438)
Depreciation (p. 422)
Depreciation accounting (p. 423)

Franchises (p. 436)
Goodwill (p. 437)
Impairment loss (p. 429)
Intangible assets (p. 418, 434)
Land improvements (p. 421)
Leasehold improvements (p. 421)
Modified accelerated cost recovery system (MACRS) (p. 430)
Natural resources (p. 418, 437)
Net book value (p. 424)
Patent (p. 435)

Plant assets (p. 418)
PP&E (p. 418)
Research and development costs (p. 435)
Return on assets (p. 439)
Revenue expenditures (p. 431)
Salvage value (p. 422)
Straight-line method (p. 423)
Trademarks (p. 436)
Trade names (p. 436)
Units-of-production method (p. 426)
Useful life (p. 422)

Assignments with the ⓂⒷⒸ logo in the margin are available in ᵐʸBusinessCourse.
See the Preface of the book for details.

SELF-STUDY QUESTIONS

(Answers for the Self-Study Questions are available at the end of this chapter.)

1. **The acquisition cost of a plant asset is equal to the asset's implied cash price and:**   **LO1**
   a. The interest paid on any debt incurred to finance the asset's purchase.
   b. The market value of any noncash assets given up to acquire the plant asset.
   c. The reasonable and necessary costs incurred to prepare the asset for its intended use.
   d. The asset's estimated salvage value.

2. **On January 1, Bush Company purchased a delivery truck for $10,000. The company estimates**   **LO2**
   the truck will be driven 80,000 miles over its eight-year useful life. The estimated salvage value
   is $2,000. The truck was driven 12,000 miles in its first year. Which method results in the largest
   depreciation expense for the first year?
   a. Units-of-production
   b. Straight-line
   c. Double-declining balance

3. **On the first day of the current year, Griffin Company sold equipment for less than its book value.**   **LO4**
   Which of the following is part of the journal entry to record the sale?
   a. A debit to Equipment
   b. A credit to Accumulated Depreciation—Equipment
   c. A credit to Gain on Sale of Plant Assets
   d. A debit to Loss on Sale of Plant Assets

4. **Accounting for the periodic amortization of intangible assets is similar to which depreciation**   **LO5**
   method?
   a. Straight-line
   b. Units-of-production
   c. Double-declining balance

5. **An exclusive right to operate or sell a specific brand of products in a given geographic area is called:**   **LO5**
   a. A franchise.   c. A patent.
   b. Goodwill.   d. A copyright.

6. **Which of the following statements is true?**   **LO5**
   a. Goodwill is subject to amortization.
   b. Research and development costs may be capitalized to the balance sheet.
   c. Intangible assets are amortized to expense on the income statement.
   d. Goodwill arises because of a company's positive corporate image among its customers.

7. **Which of the following statements is false?**   **LO3**
   a. Expenditures for ordinary repairs are a capital expenditure.
   b. Betterment expenditures are a capital expenditure.
   c. Expenditures to acquire low-cost assets are revenue expenditures.
   d. Material additions to a plant asset are capital expenditures.

8. **Which of the following statements is true?**   **LO6**
   a. Intangible assets are shown on the balance sheet net of the Accumulated Amortization account.
   b. Goodwill is shown on the balance sheet net of the Accumulated Amortization account.
   c. The Accumulated Depreciation account need not be used for plant assets.
   d. Plant assets are shown on the balance sheet net of the Accumulated Depreciation account.

9. **A company reports net income of $12,000, net sales of $30,000, and average total assets of $48,000.**   **LO7**
   What is the company's return on assets?
   a. 62.5 percent
   b. 25.0 percent
   c. 40.0 percent
   d. None of the above

LO7 10. **A company reports net income of $12,000, net sales of $30,000, and average total assets of $48,000. What is the company's asset turnover?**
  a. 0.625
  b. 0.250
  c. 0.400
  d. None of the above

LO4 11. **Davidson Company sold one of its worn-out delivery trucks on December 31, 2019. The truck was purchased on January 1, 2016, for $50,000 and was depreciated on a straight-line basis over a five-year life. There was no salvage value associated with the truck. If the truck was sold for $14,000, what was the amount of gain or loss recorded at the time of the sale?**
  a. $4,000 loss   *c.* $4,000 gain
  b. $14,000 gain   *d.* $6,000 loss

LO5 12. **Which of the following is not an example of a natural resource?**
  a. Oil reserves   *c.* Oil rig
  b. Standing timber   *d.* Mineral deposits

QUESTIONS

1. What are the three major types of long-term assets that require a periodic write-off? Present examples of each, and indicate for each type of asset the term that denotes the periodic write-off to expense.

2. In what way is land different from other plant assets?

3. In general, what amounts constitute the acquisition cost of plant assets?

4. Foss Company bought land with a vacant building for $400,000. Foss will use the building in its operations. Must Foss allocate the purchase price between the land and building? Why or why not? Would your answer be different if Foss intends to raze the building and build a new one? Why or why not?

5. Why is the recognition of depreciation expense necessary to match revenue and expense properly?

6. What is the pattern of plant asset utilization (or benefit) that corresponds to each of the following depreciation methods: (a) straight-line, (b) units-of-production, (c) double-declining balance?

7. How should a revision of depreciation charges due to a change in an asset's estimated useful life or salvage value be handled? Which periods—past, present, or future—are affected by the revision?

8. When is a plant asset considered to be impaired? How is an impairment loss calculated?

9. What is the benefit of accelerating depreciation for income tax purposes when the total depreciation taken is no more than if straight-line depreciation were used?

10. Identify two types of revenue expenditures. What is the proper accounting for revenue expenditures?

11. Identify two types of capital expenditures. What is the proper accounting for capital expenditures?

12. What factors determine the gain or loss on the sale of a plant asset?

13. Folger Company installed a conveyor system that cost $192,000. The system can be used only in the excavation of gravel at a particular site. Folger expects to excavate gravel at the site for 10 years. Over how many years should the conveyor be depreciated if its physical life is estimated at (a) 8 years and (b) 12 years?

14. What are five different types of intangible assets? Briefly explain the nature of each type.

15. How should a firm account for research and development costs?

16. Under what circumstances is goodwill recorded?

17. How is the *return on assets* ratio calculated? What does this ratio reveal about a business?

18. How is the *asset turnover ratio* calculated? What does this ratio reveal about a business?

SHORT EXERCISES

LO1 **SE9-1. Calculate Amount to Capitalize** The Bud Company paid $12,000 to acquire a 100 ton press. Freight charges to deliver the equipment amounted to $1,500 and were paid by Bud. Installation costs amounted to $570, and machine testing charges amounted to $400. Calculate the amount that should be capitalized to the Equipment account.

SE9-2. **Depreciation Expense Using the Straight-Line Method** The Peete Company purchased an office building for $4,500,000. The building had an estimated useful life of 25 years and an expected salvage value of $500,000. Calculate the depreciation expense for the second year using the straight-line method. **LO2**

SE9-3. **Depreciation Expense Using the Double-Declining Balance Method** The Peete Company purchased an office building for $4,500,000. The building had an estimated useful life of 25 years and an expected salvage value of $500,000. Calculate the depreciation expense for the second year using the double-declining balance method. **LO2**

SE9-4. **Depreciation Expense Using the Units-of-Production Method** The Sonya Company is a coal company based in West Virginia. The company recently purchased a new coal truck for $50,000. The truck had an expected useful life of 200,000 miles and an expected salvage value of $2,000. Calculate the depreciation expense using the units-of-production method assuming the truck travelled 40,000 miles on company business during the year. **LO2**

SE9-5. **Sale of a Building** The Mite Company sold a building for $350,000 that had a book value of $450,000. The building had originally cost the company $12,000,000 and had accumulated depreciation to date of $11,550,000. Prepare a journal entry to record the sale of the building. **LO4**

SE9-6. **Goodwill Impairment** Bruce Farms Equipment Company had goodwill valued at $80 million on its balance sheet at year-end. A review of the goodwill by the company's CFO indicated that the goodwill was impaired and was now only worth $45 million. Prepare a journal entry to record the goodwill impairment on the books of the company. **LO5**

SE9-7. **Amortization Expense** Smith & Daughters obtained a patent for a new optical scanning device. The fees incurred to file for the patent and to defend the patent in court against several companies which challenged the patent amounted to $90,000. Smith & Daughters concluded that the expected economic life of the patent was 12 years. Calculate the amortization expense that should be recorded in the second year, and record the journal entry for the amortization expense on the books of Smith & Daughters. **LO5**

SE9-8. **Return on Assets** The Queen Company reported net income of $80,000 and average total assets of $450,000. Calculate the company's return on assets. **LO7**

SE9-9. **Asset Turnover** The Kingwood Company reported sales revenue of $520,000 and average total assets of $500,000. Calculate the company's asset turnover. **LO7**

SE9-10. **Return on Assets and Asset Turnover** Last year, the Miller Company reported a return on assets of 15 percent and an asset turnover of 1.6. In the current year, the company reported a return on assets of 19 percent but an asset turnover of only 1.2. If sales revenue remained unchanged from last year to the current year, what would explain the two ratio results? **LO7**

SE9-11. **Sale of Equipment** Prepare the journal entry for the following transactions: (1) Geysler Company sold some old equipment that initially cost $30,000 and had $25,000 of accumulated depreciation and received cash in the amount of $2,000. (2) Assume the same facts except Geysler received $8,000. **LO4**

SE9-12. **Financial Statement Placement** Name the financial statement where each of the following will appear: (IS) Income Statement; (BS) Balance Sheet; (SCF) Statement of Cash Flows; (N) None. **LO6**

    a. Book value of equipment purchased five years ago
    b. Market value of equipment purchased five years ago
    c. Cash proceeds from the sale of land
    d. Gain on the sale of buildings
    e. Accumulated depreciation on equipment
    f. Impairment loss on land

SE9-13. **Depletion expense** Digger, Inc. paid $100,000 for the rights to mineral deposits containing an estimated 20,000 tons or ore. Digger paid an additional $20,000 for exploration and development and estimated there would be no salvage value once the ore was fulling extracted. Calculate depletion expense be if Digger extracted and sold 8,000 tons of ore? **LO5**

EXERCISES—SET A

LO1 **E9-1A. Acquisition Cost of Long-Lived Asset** The following data relate to a firm's purchase of a machine used in the manufacture of its product:

Invoice price	$34,000
Applicable sales tax	2,000
Cash discount taken for prompt payment	400
Freight paid	260
Cost of insurance coverage on machine while in transit	125
Installation costs	2,000
Testing and adjusting costs	475
Repair of damages to machine caused by the firm's employees	750
Prepaid maintenance contract for first year of machine's use	400

Determine the acquisition cost of the machine.

LO1 **E9-2A. Allocation of Package Purchase Price** Tamarack Company purchased a plant from one of its suppliers. The $1,000,000 purchase price included the land, a building, and factory machinery. Tamarack also paid $6,000 in legal fees to negotiate the purchase of the plant. An appraisal showed the following values for the items purchased:

Property	Assessed Value
Land	$126,000
Building	456,000
Machinery	318,000
Total	$900,000

Using the assessed value as a guide, allocate the total purchase price of the plant to the land, building, and machinery accounts in Tamarack Company's records.

LO2 **E9-3A. Depreciation Methods** A delivery truck costing $22,000 is expected to have a $2,000 salvage value at the end of its useful life of four years or 100,000 miles. Assume that the truck was purchased on January 2. Calculate the depreciation expense for the second year using each of the following depreciation methods: (a) straight-line, (b) double-declining balance, and (c) units-of-production. (Assume that the truck was driven 30,000 miles in the second year.)

LO2 **E9-4A. Revision of Depreciation** On January 2, 2015, Moser, Inc., purchased equipment for $100,000. The equipment was expected to have a $10,000 salvage value at the end of its estimated six-year useful life. Straight-line depreciation has been recorded. Before adjusting the accounts for 2019, Moser decided that the useful life of the equipment should be extended by three years and the salvage value decreased to $8,000.

a. Prepare a journal entry to record depreciation expense on the equipment for 2019.
b. What is the book value of the equipment at the end of 2019 (after recording the depreciation expense for 2019)?

LO2 **E9-5A. Impairment Loss** On July 1, 2015, Karen Company purchased equipment for $325,000; the estimated useful life was 10 years and the expected salvage value was $40,000. Straight-line depreciation is used. On July 1, 2019, economic factors cause the market value of the equipment to decrease to $90,000. On this date, Karen evaluates if the equipment is impaired and estimates future cash flows relating to the use and disposal of the equipment to be $195,000.

a. Is the equipment impaired at July 1, 2019? Explain.
b. If the equipment is impaired at July 1, 2019, calculate the amount of the impairment loss.
c. If the equipment is impaired at July 1, 2019, prepare the journal entry to record the impairment loss.

LO3 **E9-6A. Revenue and Capital Expenditures** Shriver Company built an addition to its chemical plant. Indicate whether each of the following expenditures related to the addition is a revenue expenditure or a capital expenditure:

   a.   Shriver's initial application for a building permit was denied by the city as not conforming to environmental standards. Shriver disagreed with the decision and spent $8,000 in attorney's fees to convince the city to reverse its position and issue the permit.

   b.   Due to unanticipated sandy soil conditions, and on the advice of construction engineers, Shriver spent $58,000 to extend the footings for the addition to a greater depth than originally planned.

   c.   Shriver spent $3,000 to send each of the addition's subcontractors a side of beef as a thank-you gift for completing the project on schedule.

   d.   Shriver invited the mayor to a ribbon-cutting ceremony to open the plant addition. It spent $40 to purchase the ribbon and scissors.

   e.   Shriver spent $4,100 to have the company logo sandblasted into the concrete above the entrance to the addition.

E9-7A.   **Sale of Plant Asset**   Lone Pine Company has a machine that originally cost $60,000. Depreciation has been recorded for four years using the straight-line method, with a $5,000 estimated salvage value at the end of an expected ten-year life. After recording depreciation at the end of four years, Lone Pine sells the machine. Prepare the journal entry to record the machine's sale for: **LO4**

   a. $39,000 cash.

   b. $38,000 cash.

   c. $28,000 cash.

E9-8A.   **Amortization Expense**   For each of the following unrelated situations, calculate the annual amortization expense and prepare a journal entry to record the expense: **LO5**

   a.   A patent with a 10-year remaining legal life was purchased for $350,000. The patent will be commercially exploitable for another eight years.

   b.   A patent was acquired on a device designed by a production worker. Although the cost of the patent to date consisted of $52,300 in legal fees for handling the patent application, the patent should be commercially valuable during its entire remaining legal life of 10 years and is currently worth $400,000.

   c.   A franchise granting exclusive distribution rights for a new solar water heater within a three-state area for five years was obtained at a cost of $70,000. Satisfactory sales performance over the five years permits renewal of the franchise for another three years (at an additional cost determined at renewal).

E9-9A.   **Return on Assets Ratio and Asset Turnover Ratio**   Northern Systems reported the following financial data (in millions) in its annual report: **LO7**

	2018	2019
Net income	$ 9,050	$ 7,500
Net sales.	52,350	37,200
Total assets	58,734	68,128

If the company's total assets are $55,676 in 2017, calculate the company's (a) return on assets and (b) asset turnover for 2018 and 2019.

E9-10A.   **Financial Statement Presentation**   Alexa Corp. reported the following amounts for the year just ended: **LO6**

Land	$150,000
Patents	25,000
Equipment	40,000
Buildings.	150,000
Goodwill	37,000
Accumulated amortization	13,000
Accumulated depreciation	90,000

Prepare a partial balance sheet for these amounts.

E9-11A.   **Natural Resources**   The Hollister Company acquires a silver mine at the cost of $1,300,000 on January 1. Along with the purchase price Hollister pays additional costs associated with development of   **LO6**

$50,000. Hollister expects the mine will have a salvage value of $100,000 once all the silver has been mined. Best estimates are that the mine contains 250,000 tons of ore.

Required

a. Prepare the entry to record the purchase of the silver mine.
b. Prepare the December 31 year-end adjusting entry to record depletion if 60,000 tons of ore are mined and all the ore is sold.
c. Prepare the December 31 year-end adjusting entry to record depletion if 60,000 tons of ore are mined but only 15,000 tons of the ore are sold.

EXERCISES—SET B

LO1 **E9-1B.** **Acquisition Cost of Long-Lived Asset** Derrick Construction purchased a used front-end loader for $32,000, terms 2/10, n/30, F.O.B. shipping point, freight collect. Derrick paid the freight charges of $330 and sent the seller a check for $31,360 one week after the machine was delivered. The loader required a new battery, which cost Fischer $180. Derrick also spent $240 to have the company name printed on the loader and $375 for one year's insurance coverage on it. Derrick hired a new employee to operate it at a wage of $20 per hour; the employee spent one morning (eight hours) practicing with the machine and went to work at a construction site that afternoon. Calculate the amount at which the front-end loader should be reported on the company's balance sheet.

LO1 **E9-2B.** **Allocation of Package Purchase Price** Joe Comey went into business by purchasing a car lubrication station, consisting of land, a building, and equipment. The seller's original asking price was $240,000. Comey hired an appraiser for $3,000 to appraise the assets. The appraised valuations were land, $43,000; building, $95,000; and equipment, $62,000. After receiving the appraisal, Comey offered $183,000 for the business. The seller refused this offer. Comey then offered $190,000 for the business, which the seller accepted. Using the appraisal values as a guide, allocate the total purchase price of the car lubrication station to the Land, Building, and Equipment accounts.

LO2 **E9-3B.** **Depreciation Methods** A machine costing $180,000 was purchased May 1. The machine should be obsolete after four years and, therefore, no longer useful to the company. The estimated salvage value is $15,000. Calculate the depreciation expense for each year of its expected useful life using each of the following depreciation methods: (a) straight-line, (b) double-declining balance.

LO2 **E9-4B.** **Revision of Depreciation** People's Clinic purchased a special machine for use in its laboratory on January 2, 2016. The machine cost $100,000 and was expected to last 10 years. Its salvage value was estimated to be $6,000. By early 2018, it was evident that the machine will be useful for a total of only seven years. The salvage value after seven years was estimated to be $7,500. People's Clinic uses straight-line depreciation. Compute the proper depreciation expense on the machine for 2018.

LO2 **E9-5B.** **Impairment Loss** On May 1, 2016, Smooth, Inc., purchased machinery for $360,000; the estimated useful life was eight years and the expected salvage value was $15,000. Straight-line depreciation is used. On May 1, 2018, economic factors cause the market value of the machinery to decrease to $190,000. On this date, Smooth evaluates whether the machinery is impaired.

a. Assume that on May 1, 2018, Smooth estimates future cash flows relating to the use and disposal of the machinery to be $270,000. Is the machinery impaired at May 1, 2018? Explain. If it is impaired, what is the amount of the impairment loss?
b. Assume that on May 1, 2018, Smooth estimates future cash flows relating to the use and disposal of the machinery to be $230,000. Is the machinery impaired at May 1, 2018? Explain. If it is impaired, what is the amount of the impairment loss?

LO3 **E9-6B.** **Revenue and Capital Expenditures** Indicate whether each of the following expenditures is a revenue expenditure or a capital expenditure for Linda Company:

a. Paid $300 to replace a truck windshield that was cracked by a stone thrown up by another vehicle while the truck was being used to make a delivery.
b. Paid $10 for a "No Smoking" sign for the conference room.
c. Paid $900 to add a hard disk to an employee's computer.
d. Paid $25 for a dust cover for a computer printer.

    e. Paid $280 to replace a cracked windshield on a used truck that was just purchased for company use. The company bought the truck knowing the windshield was cracked.

    f. Paid $750 for a building permit from the city for a storage shed the company is going to have built.

E9-7B. **Sale of Plant Asset** Shannon Company has equipment that originally cost $68,000. Depreciation has been recorded for six years using the straight-line method, with a $9,000 estimated salvage value at the end of an expected eight-year life. After recording depreciation at the end of six years, Shannon sells the equipment. Prepare the journal entry to record the equipment's sale for: **LO4**

    a. $30,000 cash.

    b. $23,750 cash.

    c. $21,000 cash.

E9-8B. **Amortization Expense** For each of the following unrelated situations, calculate the annual amortization expense and prepare a journal entry to record the expense: **LO5**

    a. A patent with a 15-year remaining legal life was purchased for $756,000. The patent will be commercially exploitable for another six years.

    b. A patent was acquired on a device designed by a production worker. Although the cost of the patent to date consisted of $88,200 in legal fees for handling the patent application, the patent should be commercially valuable during its entire remaining legal life of 15 years and is currently worth $720,000.

    c. A franchise granting exclusive distribution rights for a new wind turbine within a three-state area for four years was obtained at a cost of $72,000. Satisfactory sales performance over the four years permits renewal of the franchise for another four years (at an additional cost determined at renewal).

E9-9B. **Return on Assets Ratio and Asset Turnover Ratio** United Systems reported the following financial data (in millions) in its annual report: **LO7**

	2018	2019
Net income	$21,500	$16,134
Net sales	49,540	52,250
Total assets	68,734	78,128

If the company's total assets are $65,676 in 2017, calculate the company's (a) return on assets and (b) asset turnover for 2015 and 2016.

E9-10B. **Financial Statement Presentation** Olin Corp. reported the following amounts for the year just ended: **LO6**

Land	$ 90
Trademarks	16
Equipment	83
Buildings	110
Goodwill	32
Accumulated amortization	10
Accumulated depreciation	55

Prepare a partial balance sheet for these amounts.

E9-11B. **Natural Resources** The Stein Company acquires a copper mine at the cost of $$950,000 on January 1. Along with the purchase price Stein pays additional costs associated with development of $75,000. Stein expects the mine will have a salvage value of $125,000 once all the silver has been mined. Best estimates are that the mine contains 300,000 tons of ore.   **LO6**

Required

    a. Prepare the entry to record the purchase of the silver mine.

    b. Prepare the December 31 year-end adjusting entry to record depletion if 40,000 tons of ore are mined and all the ore is sold.

    c. Prepare the December 31 year-end adjusting entry to record depletion if 40,000 tons of ore are mined but only 10,000 tons of the ore are sold.

PROBLEMS—SET A

LO1 **P9-1A. Acquisition Cost of Long-Lived Assets** The following items represent expenditures (or receipts) related to the construction of a new home office for Norma Company.

Cost of land site, which included an old apartment building appraised at $75,000	$ 180,000
Legal fees, including fee for title search	2,100
Payment of apartment building mortgage and related interest due at time of sale	9,300
Payment for delinquent property taxes assumed by the purchaser	6,000
Cost of razing the apartment building.	19,000
Proceeds from sale of salvaged materials	(3,800)
Grading to establish proper drainage flow on land site	2,100
Architect's fees on new building	310,000
Proceeds from sales of excess dirt (from basement excavation) to owner of adjoining property (dirt was used to fill in a low area on property)	(2,000)
Payment to building contractor	5,000,000
Payment of medical bills of employee accidentally injured while inspecting building construction.	1,600
Special assessment for paving city sidewalks (paid to city)	20,000
Cost of paving driveway and parking lot.	30,000
Cost of installing lights in parking lot	9,500
Premium for insurance on building during construction	7,800
Cost of open house party to celebrate opening of new building.	10,000

Required

From the given data, calculate the proper balances for the Land, Building, and Land Improvements accounts of Norma Company.

LO1, 2 **P9-2A. Allocation of Package Purchase Price and Depreciation Methods** To expand its business, Renee Company paid $760,000 for most of the property, plant, and equipment of a small trucking company that was going out of business. Before agreeing to the price, Small hired a consultant for $10,000 to appraise the assets. The appraised values were as follows:

Land	$120,000
Building.	440,000
Trucks.	144,000
Equipment	96,000
Total	$800,000

Small issued two checks totaling $770,000 to acquire the assets and pay the consultant on July 1. Renee depreciated the assets using the straight-line method on the building and on the equipment, and the double-declining balance method on the trucks. Estimated useful lives and salvage values were as follows:

	Useful Life	Salvage Value
Building.	20 years	$42,000
Trucks.	4 years	15,000
Equipment	8 years	10,000

Required

a. Calculate the amounts allocated to the various types of plant assets acquired on July 1.

b. Prepare the July 1 journal entries to record the purchase of the assets and the payment to the consultant.

c. Prepare the December 31 journal entries to record depreciation expense for the year on the building, trucks, and equipment.

LO2 **P9-3A. Depreciation Methods** On January 2, 2018, Skyler, Inc. purchased a laser cutting machine to be used in the fabrication of a part for one of its key products. The machine cost $120,000, and its estimated useful life was four years or 920,000 cuttings, after which it could be sold for $5,000.

Required

a. Calculate each year's depreciation expense for the period 2018–2021 under each of the following depreciation methods:
   1. Straight-line.
   2. Double-declining balance.
   3. Units-of-production. Assume annual production in cuttings of 200,000; 350,000; 260,000; and 110,000.
b. Assume that the machine was purchased on July 1, 2018. Calculate each year's depreciation expense for the period 2018–2022 under each of the following depreciation methods:
   1. Straight-line.
   2. Double-declining balance.

P9-4A. **Accounting for Plant Assets** Ethan Corporation had the following transactions related to its delivery truck:

LO1, 2, 3

Year 1

Jan.	5	Purchased for $28,000 cash a new truck with an estimated useful life of four years and a salvage value of $4,000.
Feb.	20	Installed a new set of side-view mirrors at a cost of $80 cash.
June	9	Paid $325 for an engine tune-up, wheel balancing, and a periodic chassis lubrication.
Aug.	2	Paid a $410 repair bill for the uninsured portion of damages to the truck caused by Ethan's own driver.
Dec.	31	Recorded depreciation on the truck for the year.

Year 2

May	1	Installed a set of parts bins in the truck at a cost of $950 cash. This expenditure was not expected to increase the salvage value of the truck.
Dec.	31	Recorded depreciation on the truck for the year.

Year 3

Dec.	31	Recorded depreciation on the truck for the year.

Ethan's depreciation policies include (1) using straight-line depreciation, (2) recording depreciation to the nearest whole month, and (3) expensing all truck expenditures of $100 or less.

Required

Prepare journal entries to record these transactions and adjustments.

P9-5A. **Disposal of Plant Asset** Ben Company has a used executive charter plane that originally cost $1,000,000. Straight-line depreciation on the plane has been recorded for six years, with a $100,000 expected salvage value at the end of its estimated eight-year useful life. The last depreciation entry was made at the end of the sixth year. Eight months into the seventh year, Ben disposes of the plane.

LO4

Required

Prepare journal entries to record:

a. Depreciation expense to the date of disposal.
b. Sale of the plane for cash at its book value.
c. Sale of the plane for $300,000 cash.
d. Sale of the plane for $220,000 cash.
e. Destruction of the plane in a fire. Ben expects a $210,000 insurance settlement.

P9-6A. **Accounting for Intangible Assets and Leasehold Improvements** Jeffrey Company owns several retail outlets. During the year, it expanded operations and entered into the following transactions:

LO1, 2, 5

Jan.	2	Signed an eight-year lease for additional retail space for an annual rent of $32,000. Paid the first year's rent on this date. (*Hint:* Debit the first year's rent to Prepaid Rent.)
	3	Paid $23,600 to a contractor for installation of a new oak floor in the leased facility. The oak floor's life is an estimated 50 years with no salvage value.
Mar.	1	Paid $60,000 to obtain an exclusive area franchise for five years to distribute a new line of gourmet chocolates.

July 1 Paid $46,000 to LogoLab, Inc., for designing a trademark for a new line of gourmet chocolates that Jeffrey will distribute nationally. Jeffrey will use the trademark for as long as the firm remains in business. Jeffrey expects to be in business for at least another 50 years.

1 Paid $40,000 for advertisement in a national magazine (June issue) introducing the new line of gourmet chocolates and the trademark.

Required

a. Prepare journal entries to record these transactions.

b. Prepare the necessary adjusting entries on December 31 for these transactions. Jeffrey makes adjusting entries once a year. Jeffrey uses straight-line depreciation and amortization.

LO6 **P9-7A.** **Preparation of Balance Sheet** Ari Company's December 31 post-closing trial balance contains the following normal balances:

Cash.	$ 19,000
Accounts payable.	20,000
Building.	439,500
Long-term notes payable	785,000
Common stock	950,000
Retained earnings	75,000
Accumulated depreciation—Equipment.	180,000
Land	877,000
Accounts receivable	22,500
Accumulated depreciation—Building	135,000
Wages payable.	6,000
Patent (net of amortization)	120,000
Notes payable (short term).	131,000
Inventory.	206,000
Equipment	600,000
Allowance for doubtful accounts.	2,000

Required

Prepare a December 31 classified balance sheet for Ari Company.

LO1, 2, 3 **P9-8A.** **Journal Entries for Plant Assets** During the first few days of the year, Jules Company entered into the following transactions:

1. Purchased a parcel of land with a building on it for $900,000 cash. The building, which will be used in operations, has an estimated useful life of 20 years and a salvage value of $60,000. The assessed valuations for property tax purposes show the land at $80,000 and the building at $720,000.

2. Paid $31,200 for the construction of an asphalt parking lot for customers. The parking lot is expected to last 12 years and has no salvage value.

3. Paid $50,000 for the construction of a new entrance to the building.

4. Purchased store equipment, paying the invoice price (including seven percent sales tax) of $78,760 in cash. The estimated useful life of the equipment is eight years, and the salvage value is $6,000.

5. Paid $240 freight on the new equipment.

6. Paid $1,650 to repair damages to floor caused when the store equipment was accidentally dropped as it was moved into place.

7. Paid $75 for an umbrella holder to place inside front door (customers may place wet umbrellas in the holder). The holder is expected to last 20 years.

Required

a. Prepare journal entries to record these transactions.

b. Prepare the December 31 journal entries to record depreciation expense for the year. Double-declining balance depreciation is used for the equipment, and straight-line depreciation is used for the building and parking lot.

P9-9A. Revision of Depreciation and Capital Expenditure Eric Company uses straight-line depreciation for its equipment. On January 1, 2013, Eric purchased a new piece of equipment for $168,000
cash. The equipment's estimated useful life was eight years with $15,000 salvage value. In 2018,
the company decided its original useful life estimate should be increased by six years. Beginning in
2018, depreciation was based on a 14-year total useful life and no change was made in the salvage
value estimate. On January 3, 2019, Eric added a modification to the equipment that increased its
productivity at a cost of $21,100 cash. These modifications did not change the equipment's useful
life but did increase the estimated salvage value by $3,980.

LO2, 3

Required

a. Prepare journal entries to record (1) the purchase of the equipment, (2) 2013 depreciation expense, (3) 2018 depreciation expense, (4) the 2019 modification, and (5) 2019 depreciation
expense.

b. Calculate the book value of the equipment at the end of 2019 (that is, after recording the depreciation expense for 2019).

PROBLEMS—SET B

P9-1B. Acquisition Cost of Long-Lived Assets The following items represent expenditures (or receipts)
related to the construction of a new home office for Ryan Investment Company.

LO1

Cost of land site, which included an abandoned railroad spur	$ 185,000
Legal fees, including title search, relating to land purchase	4,300
Cost of surveying land to confirm boundaries	3,000
Cost of removing railroad tracks	7,000
Payment of delinquent property taxes assumed by the purchaser	6,000
Proceeds from sale of timber from walnut trees cut down to prepare site for construction	(20,000)
Proceeds from sale of salvaged railroad track	(4,700)
Grading to prepare land site for construction	4,000
Cost of basement excavation (contracted separately)	3,700
Architect's fees on new building	142,000
Payment to building contractor—original contract price	3,200,000
Cost of changes during construction to make building more energy efficient	91,000
Cost of replacing windows broken by vandals	3,400
Cost of paving driveway and parking lot	17,000
Out-of-court settlement for mud slide onto adjacent property	12,500
Special assessment for paving city sidewalks (paid to city)	22,000
Cost of brick and wrought iron fence installed across front of property	17,500

Required

From the given data, compute the proper balances for the Land, Building, and Land Improvements
accounts of Ryan Investment Company.

P9-2B. Allocation of Package Purchase Price and Depreciation Methods In an expansion move, James
Company paid $2,190,000 for most of the property, plant, and equipment of a small manufacturing
firm that was going out of business. Before agreeing to the price, James hired a consultant for $25,000
to appraise the assets. The appraised values were as follows:

LO1, 2

Land	$ 384,000
Building	912,000
Equipment	960,000
Trucks	144,000
Total	$2,400,000

James issued two checks totaling $2,215,000 to acquire the assets and pay the consultant on April 1.
James depreciated the assets using the straight-line method for the building and equipment, and the
double-declining balance method for the trucks. Estimated useful lives and salvage values were as
follows:

	Useful Life	Salvage Value
Building.	30 years	$86,000
Equipment	10 years	70,000
Trucks.	4 years	13,000

Required
a. Calculate the amounts allocated to the various types of plant assets acquired on April 1.
b. Prepare the April 1 journal entries to record the purchase of the assets and the payment of the consultant.
c. Prepare the December 31 journal entries to record the depreciation expense on the building, equipment, and trucks for the year.

LO2 **P9-3B. Depreciation Methods** On January 2, 2018, Javier Company purchased an electroplating machine to help manufacture a part for one of its key products. The machine cost $437,500 and was estimated to have a useful life of six years or 781,200 platings, after which it could be sold for $46,800.

Required
a. Calculate each year's depreciation expense for the period 2018–2023 under each of the following depreciation methods:
    1. Straight-line.
    2. Double-declining balance.
    3. Units-of-production. (Assume annual production in platings of 140,000; 180,000; 150,000; 125,000; 95,000; and 91,200.)
b. Assume that the machine was purchased on September 1, 2018. Calculate each year's depreciation expense for the period 2018–2024 under each of the following depreciation methods:
    1. Straight-line.
    2. Double-declining balance.

LO1, 2, 3 **P9-4B. Journal Entries for Plant Assets** Ediza Delivery Service had the following transactions related to its delivery truck:

Year 1
Mar. 1 Purchased for $32,500 cash a new delivery truck with an estimated useful life of five years and a $6,850 salvage value.
2 Paid $750 for painting the company name and logo on the truck.
Dec. 31 Recorded depreciation on the truck for the year.

Year 2
July 1 Installed air conditioning in the truck at a cost of $1,808 cash. Although the truck's estimated useful life was unaffected, its estimated salvage value was increased by $400.
Sept. 7 Paid $600 for truck tune-up and safety inspection.
Dec. 31 Recorded depreciation on the truck for the year.

Year 3
Sept. 3 Installed a set of front and rear bumper guards at a cost of $125 cash.
Dec. 31 Recorded depreciation on the truck for the year.

Year 4
Dec. 31 Recorded depreciation on the truck for the year.

Ediza's depreciation policies include (1) using straight-line depreciation, (2) recording depreciation to the nearest whole month, and (3) expensing all truck expenditures of $150 or less.

Required
Prepare journal entries to record these transactions and adjustments.

LO4 **P9-5B. Disposal of Plant Asset** Crystal Company has a used delivery truck that originally cost $24,200. Straight-line depreciation on the truck has been recorded for three years, with a $3,500 expected salvage value at the end of its estimated six-year useful life. The last depreciation entry was made at the end of the third year. Four months into the fourth year, Crystal disposes of the truck.

Required
Prepare journal entries to record:

    a.   Depreciation expense to the date of disposal.

    b.   Sale of the truck for cash at its book value.

    c.   Sale of the truck for $17,000 cash.

    d.   Sale of the truck for $10,000 cash.

    e.   Theft of the truck. Crystal carries no insurance for theft.

P9-6B.   **Accounting for Plant and Intangible Assets**   Selected transactions of Global Publishers, Inc., for   **LO1, 2, 5** 2019 are given below:

Jan.   2   Paid $170,000 to purchase copyrights to a series of romantic novels. The copyrights expire in 40 years, although sales of the novels are expected to stop after 10 years.

Mar.   1   Discovered a satellite dish antenna has been destroyed by lightning. The loss is covered by insurance and a claim is filed today. The antenna cost $18,360 when installed on July 1, 2018, and was being depreciated over 12 years with a $1,800 salvage value. Straight-line depreciation was last recorded on December 31, 2018. Global expects to receive an insurance settlement of $17,000.

April   1   Paid $140,000 to remodel space to create an employee exercise area on the lower level in a leased building. The building's remaining useful life is 40 years; the lease on the building expires in 12 years.

July   1   Paid $540,000 to acquire a patent on a new publishing process. The patent has a remaining legal life of 15 years. Global estimates the new process will be utilized for 6 years before it becomes obsolete.

Nov.   1   Paid $180,000 to obtain a four-year franchise to sell a new series of computerized do-it-yourself manuals.

Required

    a.   Prepare journal entries to record these transactions.

    b.   Prepare the December 31 journal entries to record depreciation and amortization expense for assets acquired during the year. Global uses straight-line depreciation and amortization.

P9-7B.   **Preparation of Balance Sheet**   Conner Corporation's December 31 post-closing trial balance contains the following normal account balances: **LO6**

Cash	$ 10,000
Accounts payable	13,000
Building	260,000
Long-term notes payable	940,000
Common stock	420,000
Retained earnings	342,000
Accumulated depreciation—Equipment	130,000
Land	1,129,000
Accounts receivable	21,000
Accumulated depreciation—Building	70,000
Interest payable	24,000
Patent (net of amortization)	60,000
Notes payable (short term)	80,000
Inventory	137,000
Equipment	266,000
Allowance for doubtful accounts	1,000
Accumulated depreciation - Leasehold improvements	22,000
Leasehold improvements	140,000
Trademark (net of amortization)	19,000

Required

Prepare a December 31 classified balance sheet for Conner Corporation.

P9-8B.   **Journal Entries for Plant Assets**   During the first few days of the year, Coastal Company entered   **LO1, 2, 3** into the following transactions:

    1.   Purchased a parcel of land with a building on it for $3,500,000 cash. The building, which will be used in operations, has an estimated useful life of 30 years and a salvage value of $200,000.

The assessed valuations for property tax purposes show the land at $280,000 and the building at $2,520,000.

2. Paid $180,000 for the construction of an asphalt parking lot for customers. The parking lot is expected to last 15 years and has no salvage value.

3. Paid $500,000 for the construction of a new entrance to the building.

4. Purchased store equipment, paying the invoice price (including seven percent sales tax) of $89,660 in cash. The estimated useful life of the equipment is five years, and the salvage value is $4,000.

5. Paid $640 freight on the new equipment.

6. Paid $1,200 to repair damages to floor caused when the store equipment was accidentally dropped as it was moved into place.

7. Paid $50 for an umbrella holder to place inside front door (customers may place wet umbrellas in the holder). The holder is expected to last 30 years.

Required

a. Prepare journal entries to record these transactions.

b. Prepare the December 31 journal entries to record depreciation expense for the year. Double declining balance depreciation is used for the equipment, and straight-line depreciation is used for the building and parking lot.

LO2, 3 **P9-9B.** **Revision of Depreciation and Capital Expenditure** Pinecrest Company uses straight-line depreciation in accounting for its machines. On January 2, 2013, Pinecrest purchased a new machine for $258,000 cash. The machine's estimated useful life was seven years with a $20,000 salvage value. In 2018, the company decided its original useful life estimate should be increased by three years. Beginning in 2018, depreciation was based on a 10-year total useful life, and no change was made in the salvage value estimate. On January 3, 2019, Pinecrest added an automatic cut-off switch and a self-sharpening blade mechanism to the machine at a cost of $9,200 cash. These improvements did not change the machine's useful life but did increase the estimated salvage value to $11,200.

Required

a. Prepare journal entries to record (1) the purchase of the machine, (2) 2013 depreciation expense, (3) 2018 depreciation expense, (4) the 2019 improvements, and (5) 2019 depreciation expense.

b. Calculate the book value of the machine at the end of 2019 (that is, after recording the depreciation expense for 2019).

SERIAL PROBLEM: KATE'S CARDS

(Note: This is a continuation of the Serial Problem: Kate's Cards from Chapters 1 through 8.)

SP9. Kate's business is growing faster than she had predicted. In order to keep up, she will need to purchase improved computer hardware. Kate has learned that the software that she uses runs much faster if her computer has a lot of memory. In addition, her files are very large and she is running out of free space on her existing hard drive. Finally, Kate has heard horror stories about hard disk drive crashes and the possibility that all of her work will be destroyed. In order to protect against this possibility, she has decided to invest in a large commercial grade backup system.

The cost of the memory and hard disk drive upgrade to Kate's computer will total $420. The cost of the backup system is $3,000. The memory and hard disk upgrade will increase the productivity of Kate's current computer; however, it will not extend its useful life. The backup system is expected to have a five-year useful life.

Kate would like to know the following items:

1. How should the expenditure for the memory and hard disk drive upgrade be recorded? Provide the journal entry.

2. Kate's current computer has 42 months remaining for depreciation purposes (under the straight-line method). The original cost of the computer was $4,800 and had a four-year useful life. The current monthly depreciation is $100. How will this current expenditure affect the monthly depreciation?

3. Kate would like to know how depreciation on the backup system under both the straight-line method and the double-declining method differ. She is assigning a $500 salvage value to the equipment. Construct a table showing yearly depreciation under both methods.

EXTENDING YOUR KNOWLEDGE

REPORTING AND ANALYSIS

EYK9-1. **Financial Reporting Problem: Columbia Sportswear Company** The financial statements for the Columbia Sportswear Company can be found in Appendix A at the end of this book.

Required
Answer the following questions.
  a. What was the total cost of Columbia's property, plant, and equipment at December 31, 2017?
  b. What was the total accumulated depreciation at December 31, 2017?
  c. What percentage of the total cost of property, plant, and equipment at December 31, 2017, was from building and improvements?
  d. How much depreciation and amortization expense was taken in 2017?
  e. What amount of property, plant, and equipment purchases (capital expenditures) occurred in 2017?

EYK9-2. **Comparative Analysis Problem: Columbia Sportswear Company vs. Under Armour, Inc.** The financial statements for the Columbia Sportswear Company can be found in Appendix A at the end of this book, and the financial statements of Under Armour, Inc. can be found in Appendix B (the complete annual report is available on this book's Website).

Required
  a. Calculate the following ratios for Columbia Sportswear and for Under Armour, Inc. for 2017:
    1. Return on assets
    2. Asset turnover
  b. Comment on your findings.

EYK9-3. **Business Decision Problem** Lyle Fleming, president of Fleming, Inc., wants you to resolve his dispute with Mia Gooden over the amount of a finder's fee due Gooden. Fleming hired Gooden to locate a new plant site to expand the business. By agreement, Gooden's fee was to be 15 percent of the "cost of the property (excluding the finder's fee), measured according to generally accepted accounting principles."

Gooden located Site 1 and Site 2 for Fleming to consider. Each site had a selling price of $150,000, and the geographic locations of both sites were equally acceptable to Fleming. Fleming employed an engineering firm to conduct the geological tests necessary to determine the relative quality of the two sites for construction. The tests, which cost $10,000 for each site, showed that Site 1 was superior to Site 2.

The owner of Site 1 initially gave Fleming 30 days—a reasonable period—to decide whether or not to buy the property. However, Fleming procrastinated in contracting the geological tests, and the results were not available by the end of the 30-day period. Fleming requested a two-week extension. The Site 1 owner granted Fleming the additional two weeks but charged him $6,000 for the extension (which Fleming paid). Fleming eventually bought Site 1.

Fleming sent Gooden a fee of $24,000, which was 15 percent of a cost computed as follows:

Sales price, Site 1	$150,000
Geological tests, Site 1	10,000
Total	$160,000

Gooden believes that she is entitled to $26,400, based on a cost computed as follows:

Sales price, Site 1	$150,000
Geological tests, Site 1	10,000
Geological tests, Site 2	10,000
Fee for time extension	6,000
Total	$176,000

COLUMBIA
SPORTSWEAR
COMPANY

COLUMBIA
SPORTSWEAR
COMPANY

UNDER ARMOUR,
INC.

Required

What fee is Gooden entitled to under the agreement? Explain.

EYK9-4.   Financial Analysis Problem Best Buy Co., Inc., is headquartered in Minneapolis, Minnesota. The company sells brand name consumer electronics, personal computers, home office products, major appliances, entertainment software, and photographic equipment. Selected financial data for Best Buy Co. follow (amounts in millions):

	2017	2016	2015
Total assets, beginning of year	$13,856	$13,519	$15,245
Total assets, end of year	$13,049	$13,856	$13,519
Revenues for the year	$42,151	$39,403	$39,529
Net income for the year	$ 1,000	$ 1,228	$ 897

Required

a.   Calculate the return on assets for 2015–2017.

b.   In 2017, Best Buy's revenues grew by 7 percent, but in 2016 they declined by 0.3%. How did this revenue growth correspond to Best Buy's ROA for 2017 and 2016?

CRITICAL THINKING

EYK9-5.   Accounting Research Problem The 2017 annual report of General Mills, Inc., for fiscal year 2017 is available on this book's Website. Review the consolidated statements of earnings, the consolidated balance sheets, and Notes 2 and 17.

Required

a.   What is General Mills' gross cost of land, buildings, and equipment at May 28, 2017?

b.   What depreciation method is used in the financial statements?

c.   How much depreciation and amortization were expensed in fiscal 2017?

d.   How much depreciation has accumulated by May 28, 2017?

e.   How much research and development cost was expensed in fiscal 2017?

f.   What is General Mills' return on assets for fiscal 2017?

EYK9-6.   Accounting Communication Activity Peggy Zimmer, a friend of yours taking her first accounting class, is confused as to why there is a separate accumulated depreciation account. She argues that it would be much simpler to just credit the asset that is being depreciated directly instead of crediting accumulated depreciation.

Required

Explain to your friend in an informal memo a possible advantage that keeping the cost and accumulated depreciation separate can have for an analyst.

EYK9-7.   Accounting Ethics Case Linda Tristan, assistant controller for Ag-Growth, Inc., a biotechnology firm, has concerns about the accounting analysis for the firm's purchase of a land site and building from Hylite Corporation. The price for this package purchase was $1,800,000 cash. A memorandum from the controller, Greg Fister, stated that the journal entry for this purchase should debit Land for $1,350,000, debit Building for $450,000, and credit Cash for $1,800,000. The building, a used laboratory facility, is to be depreciated over 10 years with a zero salvage value.

The source documents supporting the transaction include two appraisals of the property, one done for Ag-Growth and one done for Hylite Corporation. The appraisal for Ag-Growth valued the land at $1,000,000 and the building at $500,000. The appraisal for Hylite Corporation (done by a different appraiser) valued the land at $1,500,000 and the building at $750,000. Negotiations between the two firms finally settled on an overall price of $1,800,000 for the land and the building.

Tristan asked Fister how he arrived at the amounts to be recorded for the land and building since each appraisal valued the land at only twice the building's value. "Well," replied Fister, "I used the $1,500,000 land value from Hylite's appraiser and the $500,000 building value from our appraiser. That relationship shows the land to be worth three times the building's value. Using that relationship, I assigned 75 percent of our actual purchase price of $1,800,000 to the land and 25 percent of the purchase price to the building."

"But why do it that way?" asked Tristan.

"Because it will improve our profits, before income taxes, by $150,000 over the next decade," replied Fister.

"But it just doesn't seem right," commented Tristan.

Required

a.   How does the accounting analysis by Fister improve profits before income taxes by $150,000 over the next decade?

b.   Is the goal of improving profits a sufficient rationale to defend the accounting analysis by Fister?

c.   Do you agree with Fister's analysis? Briefly explain.

d.   What actions are available to Tristan to resolve her concerns with Fister's analysis?

EYK9-8.   Corporate Social Responsibility Problem Unlike Tesla Motors' emphasis on electric engines, Cummins, Inc. is best known for its design and manufacturing of diesel engines. Go to the **Cummins**' Website at http://cummins.com and navigate to the section on sustainability.

CUMMINS INC.

Required

1.   Articulate Cummins' approach to corporate responsibility.

2.   Cummins states that "corporate responsibility contributes directly to the long-term health, growth and profitability of our company." Explain how being a good corporate citizen may lead to increased growth and profitability.

EYK9-9.   Forensic Accounting Problem **Waste Management** is a leading provider of comprehensive trash and waste removal, recycling, and waste management services. In 2002, the Securities and Exchange Commission sued several members and former members of Waste Management's management team for fraud. Go to the S.E.C. press release at: http://www.sec.gov/news/headlines/wastemgmt6.htm to answer the following questions:

WASTE MANAGEMENT, INC.

1.   What does the complaint claim about Dean L. Buntrock, the company's founder, chairman of the board, and chief executive officer?

2.   What accounting methods does the complaint claim were used by Waste Management in order to perpetuate the fraud?

EYK9-10.   Analyzing IFRS Financial Statements The 2017 financial statements of **LVMH Moet Hennessey-Louis Vuitton S.A.** are presented in Appendix C at the end of this book. LVMH is a Paris-based holding company and one of the world's largest and best-known luxury goods companies. As a member of the European Union, French companies are required to prepare their consolidated (group) financial statements using International Financial Reporting Standards (IFRS). After reviewing LVMH's consolidated financial statements, consider the following questions. (Additional information can be found in LVMH's complete annual report provided on this book's Website.)

LVMH MOET HENNESSEY-LOUIS VUITTON S.A.

Required

a.   What is LVMH's net cost of property, plant, and equipment at December 31, 2017?

b.   What depreciation method is used in the company?

c.   What is LVMH's net cost of goodwill and other intangible assets at December 31, 2017?

d.   How does LVMH account for its research costs? Development costs?

e.   What is LVMH's return on assets for the year ended December 31, 2017?

EYK9-11.   Working with the Takeaways The following data (in millions) are taken from **Alphabet's (Google)** 2017 financial statements:

ALPHABET INC.

(in millions)	2017	2016
Net sales	$110,855	$ 90,272
Net income	12,662	19,478
Total assets	197,295	167,497

Calculate Alphabet's 2017 asset turnover and return on assets.

ANSWERS TO SELF-STUDY QUESTIONS:

1. c, (pp. 421–422)   2. c, (pp. 425–429)   3. d, (pp. 435–436)   4. a, (p. 437)   5. a, (p. 438)
6. c, (pp. 437–439)   7. a, (pp. 433–434)   8. d, (p. 441)   9. b, (pp. 441–442)   10. a, (p. 442)
11. c, (p. 435)   12. c, (p. 439)

YOUR TURN! SOLUTIONS

Solution 9.1

All of the costs, with the exception of the unrelated supplies, are considered to be part of the equipment's acquisition cost, and therefore should be capitalized to the equipment account. This includes the $20,000 purchase price, along with the $1,600 sales tax, $400 freight cost, $600 installation cost, and $100 testing cost, for a total acquisition cost of $22,700. The cost of the $300 of supplies should be accounted for as a supplies inventory (an asset) and allocated to expense on the income statement as it is used.

Solution 9.2

(a) Under the straight-line method, the annual depreciation expense is calculated as ($10,000 − $2,000)/5 years = $1,600 for each year. Thus, depreciation for the second year will require the following journal entry:

Depreciation expense (+E, −SE)	1,600	
Accumulated depreciation (+XA, −A)		1,600
To record depreciation expense.		

(b) The depreciation rate for a five-year asset under the double-declining balance method is 40 percent, or [(100 percent/5 years) × 2]. Depreciation expense is calculated as 40 percent times the book value of the asset as of the beginning of the year. Thus, the first year depreciation is $4,000 (40 percent × $10,000) and the second year depreciation is $2,400 [40 percent × ($10,000 − $4,000)]. Thus, the required journal entry is:

Depreciation expense (+E, −SE)	2,400	
Accumulated depreciation (+XA, −A)		2,400
To record depreciation expense.		

Solution 9.3

Items (1), (2), and (4) are revenue expenditures. Item (3) increases the van's useful life and item (5) reduces the van's operating costs, and thus these items are capital expenditures.

Solution 9.4

Cash (+A)	750	
Accumulated depreciation (−XA, +A)	15,000	
Loss on sale of truck (+E, −SE)	6,750	
Truck (−A)		22,500
To record the sale of truck.		

Solution 9.5

1. Copyright
2. Amortization
3. Trademark
4. Franchise
5. Patent

Solution 9.6

Standing timber (+A)	500,000	
Cash (−A)		500,000
To record the purchase of a tract of timber.		

Inventory—timber (+A)	10,000	
Depletion expense (+E, −SE)	70,000	
Accumulated depletion (+XA, −A)		80,000
To record the depletion of timber.		

$$\text{Depletion rate} = \frac{\$500,000 \ - \ \$100,000}{200,000} \quad = \$2.00 \text{ board foot}$$

Inventory $= 5,000 \times \$2.00$; Depletion expense $= 35,000 \times \$2.00$

Solution 9.7

Return on assets = \$25,000 / [(\$130,000 + \$120,000)/2] = 20 percent

Asset turnover = \$150,000 / [(\$130,000 + \$120,000)/2] = 1.20

Chapter 10
Accounting for Liabilities

PAST

Chapter 9 concluded our investigation of the accounting for assets.

PRESENT

In this chapter we turn our attention to the accounting for liabilities.

FUTURE

Chapter 11 examines the accounting for stockholders' equity.

Microsoft Corporation is one of the world's most well-recognized technology companies.

Until 2009, Microsoft remained largely debt free. The company's business model was so successful that it was unnecessary for the company to borrow money. The high profit margins on the company's products enabled Microsoft to finance its growth using internally generated operating cash flow. In 2009, however, the company issued its first bonds to the capital market. Wall Street analysts speculated that Microsoft really didn't need the cash but rather sold the bonds to take advantage of the extremely low interest rates available at that time and possibly to "bulk up" the company's cash position in anticipation of a major corporate acquisition.

In this chapter, we examine how companies, like Microsoft, value and disclose liabilities on their balance sheets. We consider current liabilities such as accounts payable and accrued expenses payable, noncurrent liabilities such as bonds payable and term loans payable, and contingent liabilities such as pending lawsuits and environmental cleanup obligations.

Road Map

LO	Learning Objective	Page	eLecture	Guided Example	Assignments
LO1	Describe the nature of liabilities and discuss various current liabilities.	464	E10-1	YT10.1	SS1, SS2, SS4, E1A, E2A, E3A, E4A, E5A, E6A, E7A, E1B, E2B, E3B, E4B, E5B, E6B, E7B, P1A, P2A, P3A, P4A, P5A, P6A, P1B, P2B, P3B, P4B, P5B, P6B
LO2	Illustrate the accounting for long-term liabilities.	470	E10-2	YT10.2	SS8, SE2, SE8, SE9, SE10, E8A, E9A, E10A, E11A, E14A, E15A, E16A, E17A, E18A, E19A, E21A, E8B, E9B, E10B, E11B, E14B, E15B, E16B, E17B, E18B, E19B, E21B, P7A, P7B
LO3	Define contingent liabilities and explain the rules for their accounting and disclosure in the financial statements.	480	E10-3	YT10.3	SS3, SS5, SE1, SE3, E1A, E7A, E7B E12A, E12B, P6A, P6B
LO4	Define the current ratio, quick ratio, and times-interest-earned ratio and explain their use.	484	E10-4	YT10.4	SS10, SS11, SE5, SE6, SE7, E13A, E13B, P8A, P8B
LO5	Appendix 10A: Explain bond pricing and illustrate the straight-line and effective interest methods of amortizing bond discounts/premiums.	487	E10-5	YT10A.1	SS6, SS7, E14A, E15A, E16A, E17A, E18A, E19A, E14B, E15B, E16B, E17B, E18B, E19B, P9A, P10A, P11A, P12A, P9B, P10B, P11B, P12B
LO6	Appendix 10B: Describe the accounting for leases.	496	E10-6	YT10B.1	SS9, SE4, E20A, E20B

ACCOUNTING FOR LIABILITIES

Current Liabilities	Long-Term Liabilities	Contingent Liabilities	Bond Pricing (Appendix 10A)	Leases (Appendix 10B)
• Accounts payable • Notes payable and interest • Current portion of long-term debt • Advance payments • Sales and excise taxes • Payroll-related liabilities • Income tax	• Notes payable • Bonds and bond pricing • Recording both discount and premium bonds • Retiring bonds • Accounting for notes and interest	• Defining contingent liabilities • Accounting for contingent liabilities • Examples of contingent liabilities • Current ratio and quick ratio • Times-interest-earned ratio	• Straight-line interest method • Effective interest method	• Financing with leases • Finance leases • Operating leases

CURRENT LIABILITIES

LO1 **Describe** the nature of liabilities and **discuss** *current liabilities.*

Liabilities are obligations resulting from past transactions or events that require a business to pay money, provide goods, or perform services in the future. **Current liabilities** are obligations that will require (1) the use of existing current assets or (2) the creation of other current liabilities. Most current liabilities are settled by using current assets, but sometimes a current liability is settled by the issuance of another current liability. A past due account payable, for example, may be settled by issuing a short-term note payable. Liabilities are classified as current using the same time frame used to classify current assets—the longer of one year or a firm's normal operating cycle. We discuss some typical current liabilities in this section.

Accounts Payable

In a balance sheet listing of current liabilities, amounts due to short-term creditors on accounts payable and notes payable are commonly shown first. Short-term creditors send invoices specifying the amount owed for goods or services that they have provided. As a result, the amount of any account or note payable is easily determined because it is based on the invoices received from a creditor.

At the end of an accounting period, accountants need to know whether any goods are in transit and what the shipping terms are for such goods. If the goods are shipped F.O.B. shipping point, ownership of the goods has transferred to the buyer and an account payable should be recorded at year-end (as well as an increase in inventory) even though the goods and an invoice have not yet arrived.

Notes Payable and Interest

Promissory notes are often issued in transactions when the credit period is longer than the 30 or 60 days typical for accounts payable. Although promissory notes are commonly used in credit sales transactions involving equipment and real property, a note may sometimes be exchanged for merchandise. A note payable may also be substituted for an account payable when an extension of the usual credit period is granted. And, a promissory note is prepared when a loan is obtained from a bank.

Interest is a charge for the use of money. Consequently, interest incurred on a promissory note is an expense to the maker of a note. Since businesses are required under GAAP to distinguish between operating and nonoperating expenses in their income statements, interest expense is reported under the Other Income and Expense category to highlight the fact that this expense is not considered to be an operating expense, and instead, is a financing expense of the business.

Interest on promissory notes can be structured in either of two ways: (1) as an amount paid in addition to the face amount of the note, called the *add-on interest method*, or (2) as an amount included in the face amount of the note, called the *discount method*. The add-on interest method is most commonly used, and consequently, we focus on that approach.

Add-On Interest Method

Interest on a short-term note payable using the *add-on interest method* is paid at the maturity date of the note. The formula for determining the amount of interest to be paid is as follows:

$$\textbf{Interest} = \textbf{Principal} \times \textbf{Interest rate} \times \textbf{Time}$$

The principal, or face amount, of a note is the amount borrowed. The interest rate is the annual rate of interest. Time is the fraction of a year that a note is outstanding.

When a note is written for a certain number of months, time is expressed in twelfths of a year. For example, interest on a three-month note for $4,000, with a nine percent annual interest rate is:

$$\textbf{Interest} = \textbf{\$4,000} \times \textbf{0.09} \times \textbf{3/12} = \textbf{\$90}$$

When a note's duration—that is, the length of the borrowing period—is given in days, time is expressed as a fraction of a year; the numerator is the number of days that the note will be outstanding and the denominator is 360 days. (Some lenders use 360 days, while others use 365 days; we will use 360 days in our examples.) For example, interest on a 60-day note for $3,000, with a nine percent annual interest rate is:

$$\textbf{Interest} = \textbf{\$3,000} \times \textbf{0.09} \times \textbf{60/360} = \textbf{\$45}$$

Determining the Maturity Date of a Note

When the duration of a note is expressed in months, the maturity date is determined by counting the number of months from the date of issue. For example, a two-month note dated January 31 matures on March 31, a three-month note of the same date matures on April 30 (the last day of the month), and a four-month note matures on May 31.

When a note's duration is expressed in days, the exact number of days in each calendar month is counted to determine the note's **maturity date**. For example, a 90-day note dated July 21 has an October 19 maturity date, determined as follows:

July (remainder of month, 31 days minus 21 days).......	10 days
August	31 days
September	30 days
October (number of days required to total 90)...........	19 days
	90

Recording Notes Payable and Interest Expense

When a note payable is exchanged to settle an account payable, a journal entry is made to reflect the note payable and to reduce the balance of the related account payable. For example, suppose that the Jordon Company sold $12,000 of merchandise on account to

Bowman Company. On October 1, after the regular credit period had expired, Bowman Company gave the Jordon Company a 60-day, nine percent note for $12,000. As a consequence, the Bowman Company makes the following journal entry on October 1:

A = L + SE
−12,000
+12,000

Oct. 1	Accounts payable—Jordon Company (−L)	12,000	
	Notes payable—Jordon Company (+L)		12,000
	Gave 60-day, 9 percent note in payment of account.		

If the Bowman Company pays the note on the November 30 maturity date, the company makes the following journal entry:

A = L + SE
−180
−12,180 −12,000 Exp

Nov. 30	Notes payable—Jordon Company (−L)	12,000	
	Interest expense (+E, −SE)	180	
	Cash (−A)		12,180
	Paid note to Jordon Company ($12,000 × 0.09 × 60/360 = $180).		

Interest Payable

At the end of the fiscal year, adjusting entries must be made to reflect any accrued, but unpaid, interest expense. For example, assume that the Bowman Company has one note payable outstanding at December 31, 2018, to Garcia Company. The note is dated December 21, 2018, has a principal amount of $6,000, an interest rate of 12 percent, and a maturity date of February 19, 2019. The adjusting entry that Bowman Company makes at December 31, 2018, is as follows:

A = L + SE
−20
+20 Exp

2018			
Dec. 31	Interest expense (+E, −SE)	20	
	Interest payable (+L)		20
	To accrue interest expense on the note to Garcia Company		
	($6,000 × 0.12 × 10/360 = $20).		

When the note payable to Garcia Company is subsequently paid on February 19, 2019, the Bowman Company makes the following entry:

A = L + SE
−6,120 −6,000 −100
−20 Exp

2019			
Feb. 19	Notes payable—Garcia Company (−L)	6,000	
	Interest payable (−L)	20	
	Interest expense (+E, −SE)	100	
	Cash (−A)		6,120
	Paid principal and interest to Garcia Company		
	($6,000 × 0.12 × 50/360 = $100).		

Current Portion of Long-Term Debt

The repayment of many long-term obligations involves a series of principal payment installments over several years. To report liabilities involving installments properly, any principal due within one year (or the operating cycle, if longer) is reported as a current liability on the balance sheet. Failure to reclassify the currently maturing portion of any long-term debt as a current liability can mislead readers regarding the total current obligations of a business.

Advance Payments—Unearned Revenue

Airline tickets, gift cards, cruise-line tickets, season football tickets, and cellular phone connection charges are examples of advance payments for services. A customer pays cash in advance for these services and the service provider agrees to provide future services. As an example, assume that **Southwest Airlines Co.** sells a ticket for $400 on March 20 for travel on May 25. Southwest makes the following entry when the ticket is sold:

Mar. 20	Cash (+A)	400		
	Unearned ticket revenue (+L)		400	
	To record the sale of an airline ticket.			

A = L + SE
+400 +400

When the passenger takes the scheduled flight, the airline makes the following entry:

May 25	Unearned ticket revenue (−L)	400		
	Ticket revenue (+R, +SE)		400	
	To record ticket revenue earned.			

A = L + SE
−400 +400
Rev

Sales and Excise Taxes Payable

Many products and services are subject to sales and excise taxes. The laws governing these taxes usually require the selling firm to collect the tax at the time of sale and to send the collections periodically to the appropriate tax collection agency. For example, assume that a particular product selling for $1,000 is subject to a six percent state sales tax and a ten percent federal excise tax. Each tax should be figured on the basic sale price only. The sale is recorded as follows:

	Accounts receivable (*or* Cash) (+A)	1,160		
	Sales revenue (+R, +SE)		1,000	
	Sales tax payable (+L)		60	
	Excise tax payable (+L)		100	
	To record sales and related taxes.			

A = L + SE
+1,160 +60 +1,000
+100 Rev

The selling firm will periodically complete a tax reporting form and send the period's tax collections to the appropriate collection agency. The tax liability accounts are then debited and the Cash account is credited.

Payroll-Related Liabilities

Salaries and wages represent a major outlay in the cost structure of many businesses. For service firms, the largest expense category is usually the compensation paid to employees and the related payroll taxes and fringe benefits paid by the employer. Three types of current liabilities arise from a company's payroll: (1) accrued salaries and wages payable (discussed in Chapter 4), (2) amounts withheld from employees' paychecks by the employer, and (3) payroll taxes and fringe benefits paid by the employer.

Amounts Withheld from Employee Paychecks

When a business hires an employee, the firm establishes the employee's rate of pay. At the end of each pay period, the employer uses the employee's salary to determine the employee's **gross pay**, the amount earned before any withholdings. The employer then subtracts any withheld amounts to determine the employee's **net pay**, the amount of the paycheck. **Exhibit 10-1** demonstrates these relations.

Amounts Withheld by Legal Mandate Some amounts withheld from an employee's gross pay are mandated by law. These amounts include federal income tax, state income tax, Social Security taxes, and Medicare taxes.

The amount of federal income tax withheld from an employee's paycheck is determined by referencing a table that uses the amount of the employee's gross pay, the employee's marital status, and the number of withholding allowances claimed by the employee. Most states require employers to use similar information in calculating state income tax withholding, although not all states have an income tax.

The Federal Insurance Contributions Act (FICA) dictates the percentages to be used in calculating the withholding amounts for Social Security and Medicare. The rates for employee withholding for 2018 were 6.2 percent of the first $128,400 of gross pay for Social Security and 1.45 percent of all gross pay for Medicare.

Amounts Withheld by Employee Request   Other amounts are withheld from an employee's gross pay by employee request. These amounts include premiums for life or health insurance, union dues, and payments into a self-funded retirement plan.

Recording Gross Pay and Net Pay

To illustrate the recording of employee gross and net pay, assume that the payroll for the week ended August 15 for Centerline Company totaled $6,000. Amounts withheld were $1,200 for federal income tax, $405 for state income tax, $372 for Social Security, and $87 for Medicare. In addition, Centerline withheld $100 for union dues and $320 for health insurance premiums. Centerline makes the following entry to record the payroll:

A = L + SE		
+1,200 −6,000		
Exp		
+405		
+459		
+100		
+320		
+3,516		

Aug. 15	Salaries and wage expense (+E, −SE)	6,000	
	Federal income tax withholding payable (+L)		1,200
	State income tax withholding payable (+L)		405
	FICA taxes payable (+L)		459
	Union dues payable (+L)		100
	Health insurance premiums payable (+L)		320
	Payroll payable (+L)		3,516
	To record the payroll for the week ended August 15.		

At the appropriate time, the employer will remit the amounts withheld from employees to the proper recipients. To the extent that any of the payable amounts are not paid at the end of an accounting period, they are reported as current liabilities.

Exhibit 10-1   **Determination of Net Pay**

FICA
$459

Federal Income Tax
$1,200

State Income Tax
$405

$6,000
Gross Pay

Health
Insurance Premiums
$320

Union Dues
$100

Net Pay = Gross Pay − Amounts Withheld

$3,516

Payroll Taxes Paid by the Employer

An employer pays three types of taxes on the gross payroll amount: FICA taxes (Social Security and Medicare), federal unemployment tax, and state unemployment tax.

Each employer is required to pay an amount equal to the FICA taxes withheld from the employees' gross pay (2018 rates were 6.2 percent of the first $128,400 of gross pay for Social Security and 1.45 percent of gross pay for Medicare). As a result, the total Social Security collected in 2018 for each employee was 12.4 percent of the first $128,400 of gross pay, and the total Medicare collected was 2.9 percent of all gross pay.

Federal and state unemployment taxes are levied only on employers as a percentage of the gross payroll, subject to various limits. The current federal unemployment tax rate is 6.0 percent of the first $7,000 of an employee's gross pay. However, an employer is entitled to a credit against this tax for unemployment taxes paid to the state. The maximum credit allowed is 5.4 percent of the first $7,000 of gross pay. Many states set their basic unemployment tax rate at this maximum credit. In these states, the effective federal unemployment tax rate is 0.6 percent (6.0 percent − 5.4 percent), and the effective state unemployment tax rate is 5.4 percent.

Recording Payroll Taxes Paid by the Employer   Assume that the payroll for the week ended August 15 for Centerline Company totaled $6,000. Amounts withheld included $372 for Social Security and $87 for Medicare. Federal unemployment tax payable for the week was $36 (0.6 percent) and state unemployment tax payable was $324 (5.4 percent). Centerline makes the following entry to record its payroll taxes:

Aug. 15	Payroll tax expense (+E, −SE)	819		
	FICA taxes payable (+L)		459	
	Federal unemployment tax payable (+L)		36	
	State unemployment tax payable (+L)		324	
	To record the payroll taxes for the week ended August 15.			

A = L + SE
　 +459 −819 Exp
　 +36
　 +324

If payroll taxes have not been remitted to the proper government agency by the end of the accounting period, they are classified as current liabilities in the balance sheet.

The solution is on page 520.

Archer Corporation had the following payroll data for April:

Office salaries.	$ 40,000
Sales salaries.	86,000
Federal income taxes withheld.	25,600
Health insurance premiums withheld	1,850
Union dues withheld.	950
Salaries (included above):	
Subject to both FICA taxes.	126,000
Subject to federal unemployment taxes	76,000
Subject to state unemployment taxes.	88,000

The combined FICA tax rate (for both employee withholding and employer) is 7.65 percent (6.2 percent plus 1.45 percent), the federal unemployment compensation tax rate is 0.6 percent, and the state unemployment compensation tax rate is 5.4 percent. The amounts subject to these taxes are given above.

Required
Prepare journal entries to record the following on April 30:
a. Accrual of the payroll.
b. Payment of the net payroll.
c. Accrual of the employer's payroll taxes.
d. Payment of all liabilities related to the payroll. (Assume that all liabilities are paid at the same time.)

Income Taxes Payable

The U.S. Federal Government, most states, and some municipalities levy income taxes against corporations, individuals, estates, and trusts. Sole proprietorships and partnerships are not taxable entities—their owners include any business income on the owner's personal income tax return.

The tax due is determined in accordance with tax law, rulings by taxing agencies, and court decisions. Because the administration of tax law is quite complex and many honest differences exist in their interpretation, the tax obligation reported on a tax return is only an estimate until the government reviews and accepts a firm's (or individual's) calculations.

Because corporations are separate taxable entities, they incur a legal obligation for income taxes whenever income is earned. Therefore, corporate financial statements routinely include income tax liabilities. For example, business income taxes of $8,000 are recorded as follows:

A = L + SE
+8,000 −8,000
Exp

Income tax expense (+E, −SE)	8,000	
Income tax payable (+L)		8,000
To record estimated income tax.		

Corporations usually pay their estimated income taxes quarterly, with an annual tax return and final payment due within a few months following the end of a calendar year. Thus, any liability for income taxes in the financial statements is classified as a current liability since payment is expected in the short term.

CORPORATE SOCIAL RESPONSIBILITY

Aligning Business and Citizenship

Being socially responsible does not mean trying to solve the world's problems single-handedly. To do things that one has no particular competence in is wasteful, and it makes far more sense and is far more responsible to do things to help others using one's strengths. Few would contest that one of **Microsoft Corporation**'s strengths is technology. Although technology has led to phenomenal advances in productivity and economic growth in developed countries, much of the world still has little access to this technology. Through partnerships, grants, investments, education, and advocacy, the Microsoft Affordable Access Initiative "helps to create technology solutions, business models, and policies that help close the digital divide, with projects in 17 countries over the last five years." Microsoft's 4Afrika Initiative "provides a set of programs to empower African youth, entrepreneurs, developers and business and civic leaders with skill development, access to technology, and support for local innovation."

eLectures
MBC

LONG-TERM LIABILITIES

LO2 **Illustrate** the accounting for long-term liabilities.

Most businesses will need to secure long-term funds to finance operations or the acquisition of various operating assets. When a business elects to finance with long-term debt, it may do so by borrowing money with long-term notes or issuing bonds. An obligation in the form of a written note due after the current period is referred to as a **term loan** or long-term note payable. The borrower typically signs a note payable and the debt is referred to as a term loan. Whereas long-term notes are usually arranged with a single lender, bonds are usually issued to the general public with a large number of buyers. A **bond** is a long-term debt instrument that promises to pay interest periodically as well as a principal amount at maturity, to the bond investor. In the United States, bond interest is usually paid semiannually. The principal amount is referred to as the bond's face value (because it is printed on the face of the bond certificate), par value, or maturity value.

Long-Term Notes (Term Loans)

Term loans are often repaid in equal periodic installments. The agreement may require installment payments to be made monthly, quarterly, or semiannually. Each payment contains an interest amount and a partial repayment of principal. Because the installment payments are equal, the amounts that are allocated to interest and principal repayments change over time. These component amounts change with each installment because the interest is computed on the unpaid principal, and the unpaid principal is reduced with each payment.

To illustrate, assume that on December 31, 2018, Reid, Inc., borrows $100,000 from a bank on a 12 percent, ten-year mortgage note payable. The note is to be repaid with equal quarterly installments of $4,326 (please see Appendix E for explanation on how to do this calculation). Thus, there will be 40 quarterly payments; and, the quarterly interest rate is three percent (12 percent/4 quarters). **Exhibit 10-2** presents the first eight quarterly payments (of the complete 40 quarterly payment schedule) and their division between interest expense and principal repayment. As the book value of the note declines over time (column D), the amount of interest expense also declines (column B). As a result, the amount of the fixed quarterly cash payment (column A) that is applied to repayment of the principal increases over time (column C). The entries to record the mortgage note payable and the first quarterly payment follow:

2018				
Dec. 31	Cash (+A)		100,000	
	Mortgage note payable (+L)			100,000
	To record mortgage loan.			

A = L + SE
100,000 100,000

2019				
Mar. 31	Interest expense (+E, −SE)		3,000	
	Mortgage note payable (−L)		1,326	
	Cash (−A)			4,326
	To record quarterly mortgage loan payment.			

A = L + SE
−4,326 −1,326 −3,000
Exp

Exhibit 10-2	**Partial Mortgage Note Payment Schedule**

$100,000 mortgage note payable with quarterly payments of $4,326 and quarterly interest rate of three percent

	A	B	C	D
Payment Date	**Cash Payment**	**Interest Expense (3% × D)***	**Principal Repaid (A − B)**	**Book Value of Note (Unpaid Principal)**
2018				
December 31 (issue date). . . .				$100,000
2019				
March 31.	$4,326	$3,000	$1,326	98,674
June 30	4,326	2,960	1,366	97,308
September 30	4,326	2,919	1,407	95,901
December 31	4,326	2,877	1,449	94,452
2020				
March 31.	4,326	2,834	1,492	92,960
June 30	4,326	2,789	1,537	91,423
September 30	4,326	2,743	1,583	89,840
December 31	4,326	2,695	1,631	88,209

* Three percent × Unpaid principal after previous payment (rounded to nearest dollar).

Types of Bonds

Companies issue different types of bonds to capitalize on certain lending situations, appeal to special investor groups, or provide special repayment patterns.

Secured bonds, for example, pledge specific property as security for meeting the terms of the bond agreement. The specific title of the bonds may indicate the type of property pledged—for example, real estate mortgage bonds (land or buildings), chattel mortgage bonds (machinery or equipment), and collateral trust bonds (negotiable securities).

Bonds that have no specific property pledged as security for their repayment are called **debenture bonds**. Buyers of debenture bonds rely on a borrower's general credit reputation. Because a lender's risk is usually greater than with secured bonds, the sale of unsecured bonds may require offering a higher rate of interest to attract bond buyers.

The maturity dates of **serial bonds** are staggered over a series of years. For example, a serial bond issue of $15 million may provide for $1 million of the bonds to mature each year for 15 years. An advantage of serial bonds is that bond investors can choose bonds with maturity dates that correspond with their desired length of investment.

Sinking fund bonds require that a borrower make payments each year to a trustee who is responsible for managing the funds needed to retire the bonds at maturity. The orderly retirement of bonds, or the accumulation of funds needed at maturity, as required by a sinking fund provision is generally viewed as making any bond safer (less risky) for the bondholders.

Convertible bonds grant the bondholder the right to convert the bonds into a company's common stock at some specific exchange (or conversion) ratio. This provision gives an investor the security of being a creditor during a certain stage of a firm's life, with the option of becoming a stockholder if the firm becomes sufficiently profitable. Because the conversion feature is attractive to potential investors, a company may issue convertible bonds at a lower interest rate than it would pay without the conversion feature.

Callable bonds allow the bond issuer to call in the bonds for redemption. Usually, an extra amount or premium must be paid to the holders of a called bond. A call provision offers borrowers additional financing flexibility that may be significant if funds become available at interest rates substantially lower than those currently being paid on the bonds. Borrowers can, in effect, also "call" any of their bonds by buying them in the open market.

ACCOUNTING IN PRACTICE

Bond Risk Ratings

The relative riskiness of different bonds may vary considerably. Bond investors who want to know the relative quality of a particular bond issue can consult a bond-rating service. Two major firms that rate the riskiness of bonds are **Standard & Poor's Corporation** (S&P) and **Moody's Investors Service** (Moody's). The rating categories used by these firms are similar. The schedule below shows the relationship between the ratings and the degree of risk using Standard & Poor's rating system:

Low Risk							High Risk
AAA	AA	A	BBB	BB	B	CCC	D

I- - - - - - - - - Investment Grade Bonds - - - - - - - - -I- - - - - - - - Junk Bonds - - - - - - - - -I

Investment grade bonds are highly-rated bonds with little risk that the issuing company will fail to pay interest as scheduled or fail to repay the principal at a bond's maturity. Junk bonds, on the other hand, are low-quality, high-yield bonds. In the S&P rating system, junk bonds are any bond rated BB and lower. Generally, bonds with poor credit ratings must offer higher interest rates than highly-rated bonds to attract potential buyers.

A.K.A. Junk bonds are often referred to as **high-yield bonds** because of the higher yield rates that typically accompany this type of debt investment.

A.K.A. A bond's face value is also referred to as its **maturity value**, stated value, or settlement value.

Bond Prices

Bonds are typically sold in units (denominations) of $1,000 face (maturity) value, and the market price is expressed as a percentage of face value. Thus, a $1,000 face value bond that is quoted at 98 will sell for $980. For example, in the bond certificate illustrated in **Exhibit 10-3**, General Electric issued a total of $5 billion of unsecured bonds in denominations of $1,000. The bonds were priced (issued) at 99.626. Generally, bond prices fluctuate in response to changes in market interest rates, which are determined by government monetary policies (managing the demand and supply of money) and economic expectations. Bond prices are also affected by the financial outlook for the issuing firm.

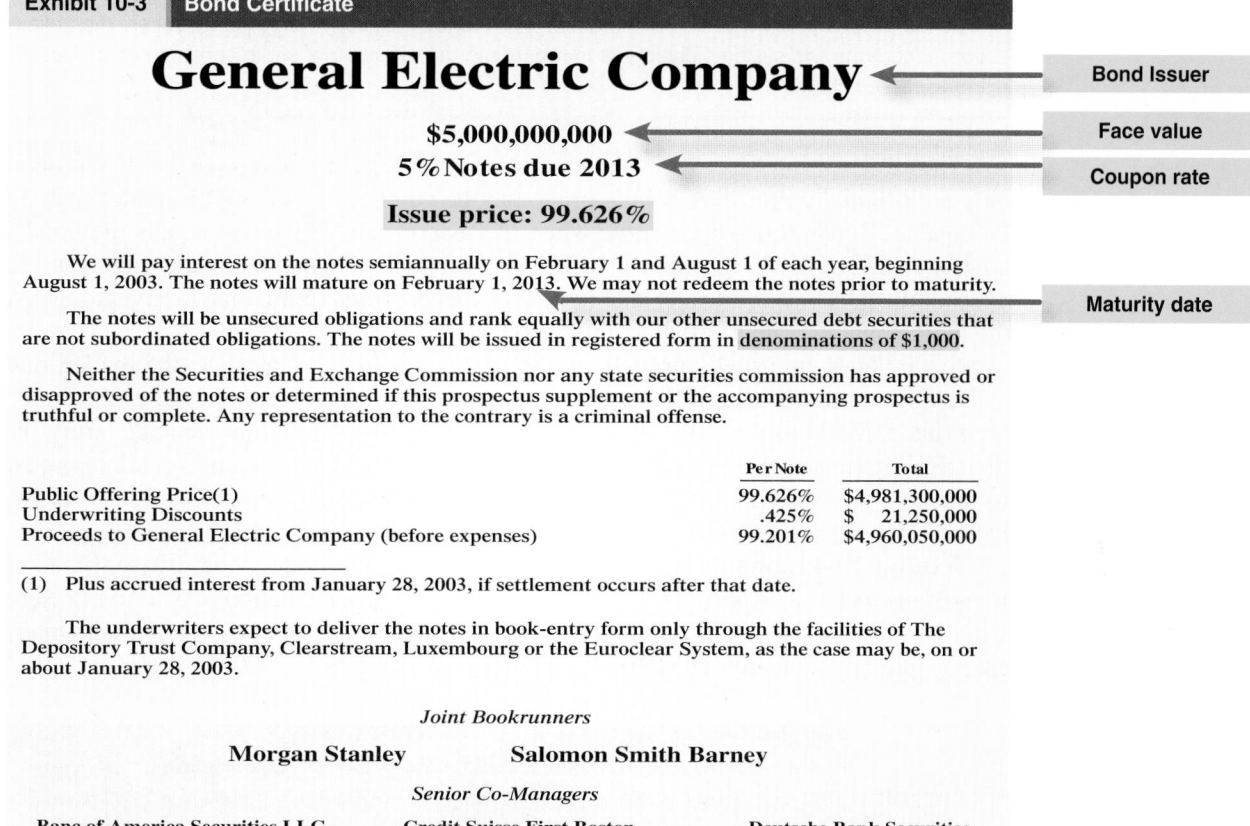

Exhibit 10-3   Bond Certificate

General Electric Company ← Bond Issuer

$5,000,000,000 ← Face value
5% Notes due 2013 ← Coupon rate
Issue price: 99.626%

We will pay interest on the notes semiannually on February 1 and August 1 of each year, beginning August 1, 2003. The notes will mature on February 1, 2013. We may not redeem the notes prior to maturity. ← Maturity date

The notes will be unsecured obligations and rank equally with our other unsecured debt securities that are not subordinated obligations. The notes will be issued in registered form in denominations of $1,000.

Neither the Securities and Exchange Commission nor any state securities commission has approved or disapproved of the notes or determined if this prospectus supplement or the accompanying prospectus is truthful or complete. Any representation to the contrary is a criminal offense.

	Per Note	Total
Public Offering Price(1)	99.626%	$4,981,300,000
Underwriting Discounts	.425%	$ 21,250,000
Proceeds to General Electric Company (before expenses)	99.201%	$4,960,050,000

(1)   Plus accrued interest from January 28, 2003, if settlement occurs after that date.

The underwriters expect to deliver the notes in book-entry form only through the facilities of The Depository Trust Company, Clearstream, Luxembourg or the Euroclear System, as the case may be, on or about January 28, 2003.

Joint Bookrunners

Morgan Stanley   Salomon Smith Barney

Senior Co-Managers

Banc of America Securities LLC	**Credit Suisse First Boston**	**Deutsche Bank Securities**
Goldman. Sachs & Co.	**JPMorgan**	**Merrill Lynch & Co.**
	UBS Warburg	

Co-Managers

Banc One Capital Markets, Inc.	**Barclays Capital**	**Blaylock & Partners, L.P.**
BNP PARIBAN	**Dresdner Kleinwort Wasserstein**	**Guzman & Company**
HSBC	**Loop Capital Markets**	**Ormes Capital Markets, Inc.**
Utendahl Capital Partners, L.P.	**The Williams Capital Group, L.P.**	

A bond specifies a pattern of future cash flows, usually a series of interest payments and a single payment at maturity equal to the bond's face value. The amount of the periodic interest payment is determined by the **coupon rate** stated on the bond certificate. The General Electric bonds have a coupon rate of five percent. Interest rates are usually quoted as annual rates, so the coupon rate will need to be converted to a per period interest rate when interest is paid more than once a year. For example, in the U.S., bond interest is usually paid semiannually, with the payments six months apart. The General Electric bonds pay interest semiannually on February 1 and August 1 of each year. Thus, the amount of interest paid semiannually is calculated by multiplying one-half the coupon rate of interest times the bond's face value.

A bond's market price is determined by discounting the bond's future cash flows (both its principal and interest payments) to the present using the current **market rate of interest** for the bond as the discount rate, a process known as *computing the bond's present value*. The market rate is the rate of return investors expect on their investment.

A.K.A. A bond's coupon rate of interest is also referred to as its nominal rate or stated rate of interest.

A.K.A. A bond's market rate of interest is also referred to as its real rate of interest or its effective yield rate.

U.S. GAAP and IFRS are substantially aligned when it comes to the reporting of liabilities. Under both accounting systems, for example, current liabilities, like Accounts Payable, are reported at their settlement or future value, or the amount of money required to satisfy the obligation when it becomes due. Similarly, both systems require that long-term liabilities, like Bonds Payable, be reported at their present value, or the amount of money necessary to currently satisfy the obligation. Where the two systems diverge is in regards to the reporting of some contingent liabilities (to be discussed shortly).

The **effective interest rate** is the market rate of interest used to price the bonds when they are originally issued. A bond's price may be equal to, less than, or greater than its face value. Bonds sell at *face value* when the market rate of interest equals the bond's coupon rate. Bonds sell at a *discount* (less than face value) when the market interest rate exceeds the bond's coupon rate; and, bonds sell at a *premium* (more than face value) when the market interest rate is less than the bond's coupon rate.

Since bonds are usually printed on one date and sold at a later date, the market rate and coupon rate will often differ due to a change in market interest rates after the bonds are printed. Market rates and coupon rates are frequently stated in percentage terms, although increasingly, these rates are stated as "basis points." One percentage point is equal to one hundred basis points. Thus, a bond with a coupon rate of three percent is said to have a coupon rate of 300 basis points.

Exhibit 10-4 shows the calculation of a bond's selling price using different market rates of interest. (See Appendix 10A for a discussion of the calculation of a bond's present value.) The bond is a $1,000, eight percent annual coupon rate, four-year bond with interest payable semiannually. The periodic interest payment is $40 ($1,000 × 0.08 × 1/2).

Exhibit 10-4	Calculation of Bond Selling Price at Different Market Rates		
Four-year $1,000 bond, eight percent annual coupon rate, interest payable semiannually. Eight semiannual interest payments of $40 ($1,000 × 0.08 × 1/2)			
	Yield Rate, Compounded Semiannually		
	10%	**8%**	**6%**
Present value of $1,000 at maturity			
$1,000 × 0.67684 present value factor* ..... =	$677		
$1,000 × 0.73069 present value factor ..... =		$ 731	
$1,000 × 0.78941 present value factor ..... =			$ 789
Present value of eight $40 interest payments (rounded to nearest dollar)			
$40 × 6.46321 present value factor* .... =	259		
$40 × 6.73274 present value factor .... =		269	
$40 × 7.01969 present value factor .... =			281
Bond selling price	$936	$1,000	$1,070
Bond priced at	**Discount**	**Face value**	**Premium**

*See Appendix 10A for a discussion of present value factors.

As shown in the exhibit, the bond will:

1. Sell at a *discount* ($936 bond price) when the market rate (ten percent) exceeds the coupon rate (eight percent).

2. Sell at *face value* ($1,000 bond price) when the market rate (eight percent) equals the coupon rate (eight percent).

3. Sell at a *premium* ($1,070 bond price) when the market rate (six percent) is less than the coupon rate (eight percent).

Recording Bonds

Bonds Issued at Face Value

To provide a simple illustration, we use a bond with a short period to maturity. Assume that on December 31, 2018, Reid, Inc., issues at face value $100,000 of eight percent bonds that mature in four years with interest paid on June 30 and December 31. The following entry records the bond, which is sold at its face value:

2018			
Dec. 31	Cash (+A)	100,000	
	Bonds payable (+L)		100,000
	To record the issuance of bonds.		

A = L + SE
+100,000 +100,000

Interest of $4,000 ($100,000 × 0.08 × 6/12) will be paid on each of the eight payment dates (four years, semiannual payments). For example, the entry on June 30, 2019, the first interest payment date, is:

2019			
June 30	Bond interest expense (+E, −SE)	4,000	
	Cash (−A)		4,000
	To record the payment of semiannual interest on bonds.		

A = L + SE
−4,000   −4,000
                    Exp

When the bonds mature, Reid, Inc., records their retirement as follows (this assumes the December 31 interest payment has already been recorded):

2019			
Dec. 31	Bonds payable (−L)	100,000	
	Cash (−A)		100,000
	To record the retirement of bonds.		

A = L + SE
−100,000 −100,000

Issuance Between Interest Dates

Not all bonds are sold on the exact day on which their interest payment period begins. Investors who buy bonds after the interest period begins are expected to "buy" any interest that has accrued on the bonds. Such bonds are said to be sold at a given price "plus accrued interest." The accrued interest is returned to the investor at the next interest payment date. This procedure simplifies the bond issuer's administrative work. Regardless of when bonds are issued, a full six months' interest is paid to all bondholders on each interest payment date.

To illustrate, assume that Reid, Inc. sold its $100,000, eight percent, four-year bonds at 100 plus accrued interest on February 28, 2019, instead of on December 31, 2018. The following journal entry is made:

A = L + SE
+101,333 +100,000
     +1,333

2019			
Feb. 28	Cash (+A)	101,333	
	Bonds payable (+L)		100,000
	Bond interest payable (+L)		1,333
	To record bond issuance at 100 plus two months' accrued interest.		

The interest accrued on the bonds on February 28 is $1,333 ($100,000 × 0.08 × 2/12, rounded). On the first interest payment date, June 30, 2019, Reid, Inc., makes the following entry:

A = L + SE
           −2,667
−4,000 −1,333 Exp

2019			
June 30	Bond interest payable (−L)	1,333	
	Bond interest expense (+E, −SE)	2,667	
	Cash (−A)		4,000
	To record the payment of semiannual interest on bonds payable.		

Bond interest expense recorded by Reid relates only to the four months since the bonds were issued.

Bonds Issued at a Discount

If the coupon rate of interest on the bonds issued is less than the current market rate, the bonds will be sold at a price less than their face value. In such cases, investors "discount" the price of the bonds to enable the buyer to earn the current market rate of interest. For example, assume that Reid, Inc.'s $100,000 issue of eight percent, four-year bonds is sold on December 31, 2018, for $93,537. This price permits investors to earn an effective interest rate of ten percent even though the bonds are only paying a cash coupon rate of eight percent. (For calculations, please see Appendix 10A.) The following entry records the issuance of the bonds at a discount:

A = L + SE
+93,537 −6,463
    +100,000

2018			
Dec. 31	Cash (+A)	93,537	
	Discount on bonds payable (+XL, −L)	**6,463**	
	Bonds payable (+L)		100,000
	To record the issuance of bonds.		

Discount on Bonds Payable is a contra account that reduces the value of Bonds Payable on the balance sheet. The $6,463 discount is not a loss or an expense to Reid, Inc. It represents an adjustment to interest expense that will be made over the life of the bonds. This can be illustrated by comparing the funds that Reid, Inc., receives with the funds it must pay to the bondholders. Regardless of their selling price, the bonds represent an agreement to pay $132,000 to the bondholders ($100,000 principal at maturity plus eight semiannual interest payments of $4,000 each).

Total funds paid to bondholders	$132,000
Total funds received from bond sale.	(93,537)
Difference equals total interest expense	38,463
Total semiannual interest payments ([$100,000 × 8% = $8,000] × 4 years) . .	(32,000)
Increase in interest expense beyond semiannual interest payments (*bond discount*).	$ **6,463**

The total interest expense for this four-year bond issue is $38,463, the difference between the total cash paid to the bondholders and the proceeds from the sale of the bonds. The semiannual interest payments to bondholders total $32,000, so an additional $6,463 must be recognized as interest expense over the life of the bonds. The $6,463 is the amount of the bond discount. To reflect the larger periodic interest expense, the bond discount is *amortized over the eight interest payment periods*. Amortization of a bond discount means that, periodically, an amount is transferred from the Discount on Bonds Payable account to the Bond Interest Expense account.

There are two methods of bond amortization: the straight-line method and the effective interest method. Under the **straight-line interest method**, equal amounts are transferred from bond discount to interest expense for each interest payment period. The **effective interest method**, on the other hand, reflects a constant rate of interest over the life of the bonds. Appendix 10A illustrates both methods, but the effective interest method is the more commonly used accounting method for bond amortization.

Zero-coupon bonds are a special type of discount bond. As the name implies, these bonds pay no periodic interest payments,which causes them to be issued at a substantial discount from their face value. The face value is paid to the bondholder at maturity. The total interest implicit in the bond contract is the difference between the bond's original issue price and its face value at maturity. For example, a five-year, $1,000 zero-coupon bond issued for $713 will pay the lender $1,000 at the end of the five years. The total interest associated with this bond is $287 ($1,000 − $713). Zero-coupon bonds are particularly helpful to a borrower when the project being financed with the bond proceeds provides no cash inflows until the bond maturity date.

Bonds Issued at a Premium

If the market rate of interest had been below the eight percent offered by Reid, Inc., investors would have been willing to pay a premium to buy the bonds. Suppose that the effective interest rate was six percent. Reid Inc.'s $100,000, eight percent, four-year bonds would sell for $107,020 (for calculations, please see Appendix 10A). The issuance of the bonds on December 31, 2018, is recorded as follows:

2018			
Dec. 31	Cash (+A)	107,020	
	Bonds payable (+L)		100,000
	Premium on bonds payable (+XL, +L)		**7,020**
	To record issuance of bonds.		

A	= L	+ SE
+107,020	+100,000	
	+7,020	

When bonds are issued at a premium, the book value of the bond liability is determined by adding the Premium on Bonds Payable account balance to the Bonds Payable account balance.

Premium on Bonds Payable is a contra account that increases the value of Bonds Payable on the balance sheet. Like a bond discount, a bond premium is considered an adjustment of interest expense over the life of the bonds. We saw that a bond discount represents the excess of total interest expense over the total semiannual interest payments. A similar analysis shows that a bond premium represents the amount by which the total semiannual interest payments exceed the total interest expense. The analysis begins by comparing the total funds that will be paid to the bondholders over the four years (again, it is $132,000) with the proceeds received when the bonds are issued:

Total funds paid to bondholders	$132,000
Total funds received from bond sale.	(107,020)
Difference equals total interest expense	24,980
Total semiannual interest payments ([$100,000 × 8% = $8,000] × 4 years) . . .	(32,000)
Decrease in interest expense below semiannual interest payments	
(***bond premium***).	$ 7,020

The total interest expense for this four-year bond issue is $24,980, an amount that is $7,020 less than the total semiannual interest payments to be made to bondholders. The

$7,020 is the amount of the bond premium. The bond premium is amortized to cause the periodic interest expense to be less than the semiannual interest payment.

Year-End Adjustments

When a periodic interest payment does not correspond with the fiscal year-end, an adjusting entry should be recorded reflecting the amount of interest expense incurred but not yet recorded. The adjusting entry includes a pro rata amortization of bond discount or bond premium for the portion of the year involved.

PRINCIPLE ALERT	**Matching Concept**
	The adjusting entry to record interest expense incurred but not yet recorded is an application of the *expense recognition (matching) concept.* This accounting concept states that all expenses incurred to generate sales revenue must be recorded, regardless of when the expense is paid in cash. Interest is a charge for the use of money, and this charge is incurred every day that a borrower has use of, and benefits from, borrowed funds.

Bonds Payable Disclosed on the Balance Sheet

Bonds payable that mature more than one year in the future are classified as long-term liabilities on the balance sheet. Bonds payable maturing within the next year, on the other hand, are classified as current liabilities. Discount on Bonds Payable and Premium on Bonds Payable are contra accounts that adjust the value of Bonds Payable on the balance sheet. Discount on Bonds Payable is a deduction from and Premium on Bonds Payable is an addition to the face value of the bonds reported in the balance sheet. Many companies do not separately disclose the Discount on Bonds Payable account or the Premium on Bonds Payable account on their balance sheet, but rather net these amounts against the Bonds Payable account.

At December 31, 2019, the Reid, Inc., bonds issued at a discount (see **Exhibit 10A-4**) appear on Reid's balance sheet as follows:

Bonds payable	$100,000
Less: Discount on bonds payable.	6,463
Bonds payable, net.	$ 93,537

On the same date, the Reid Inc. bonds issued at a premium (see **Exhibit 10A-5**) appear as follows:

Bonds payable	$100,000
Add: Premium on bonds payable	7,020
Bonds payable, net.	$107,020

Retirement of Bonds Before Maturity

Bonds are usually retired at their maturity dates with a journal entry debiting the Bonds Payable account and crediting the Cash account for the face value of the bonds. However, bonds can be retired before maturity—for example, to take advantage of more attractive financing terms. In accounting for the retirement of bonds before maturity, the following steps are used:

1. Remove the book value of the bonds being retired from the accounts (that is, remove the Bonds Payable amount and any related bond premium or discount).

2. Record the cash paid to retire the bonds.

3. Recognize any difference between the bonds' book value and the cash paid as a gain or loss on bond retirement.

To illustrate, assume that the Reid, Inc., bonds issued at a premium for $107,020 in our previous example were called for retirement at 105 at the end of 2021, after paying the semiannual interest on December 31, 2021. According to **Exhibit 10A-5**, the bonds' book value at the end of 2021 is $101,915. The following entry records the bond retirement:

2021			
Dec. 31	Bonds payable (−L)	100,000	
	Premium on bonds payable (−XL, −L)	1,915	
	Loss on bond retirement (+LOSS, −SE)	3,085	
	Cash (−A)		105,000
	To retire bonds at 105 and record loss on retirement.		

A   =   L   +   SE
−105,000 −100,000 −3,085
                      −1,915   Loss

Koby Company issued $300,000 of bonds for $325,000. (a) Prepare the journal entry to record the issuance of the bonds, and (b) illustrate how the bonds will be shown on the Koby Company's balance sheet at the issuance date.

YOUR TURN! 10.2

The solution is on page 520.

Advantages and Disadvantages of Long-Term Bonds and Notes

Issuing bonds and notes versus issuing common stock is an alternative way for a corporation to obtain needed long-term funds. The advantages of obtaining long-term funds by issuing bonds and notes instead of common stock include:

1. **No dilution of ownership interest.** Bondholders and noteholders are creditors, not shareholders, of a corporation. Issuing bonds and notes rather than common stock maintains the number of outstanding shares of stock at their current level.

2. **Tax deductibility of interest expense.** Interest expense is deductible as an expense on a corporation's income tax return. Dividend payments to shareholders are not tax deductible.

3. **Income to common shareholders can increase.** Leverage refers to the use of borrowed funds, particularly long-term debt, to finance a business's growth. When a firm is able to earn a return on its borrowed funds that exceeds the cost of borrowing the funds, then leverage is said to build shareholder value.

For example, assume that a firm can earn 15 percent on a $5,000,000 project financed by issuing bonds and notes that have a ten percent interest rate. If the firm pays income taxes at a 20 percent rate, its net income will increase $200,000 each year, as follows:

Earnings on funds borrowed: 15 percent × $5,000,000..................	$750,000
Interest cost on funds borrowed: 10 percent × $5,000,000	**(500,000)**
Increase in income before income tax expense.......................	$250,000
Income tax expense on increase: 20 percent × $250,000	**(50,000)**
Increase in net income...	$200,000

The $200,000 increase in net income accrues exclusively to the company's common stockholders.

Not all aspects of issuing bonds and notes, however, are necessarily desirable for the borrowing company. Among the disadvantages of issuing bonds and notes are the following:

1. **Interest expense is a contractual obligation.** In contrast with dividends on common stock, interest represents a fixed periodic expenditure that the firm is contractually obligated to pay.

2. **Funds borrowed have a specific repayment date.** Because bonds and notes normally have a defined maturity date, the borrower has a specific obligation to repay the borrowings at maturity.

3. **Borrowing agreement can restrict company actions.** The legal document setting forth the terms of a debt issue is called an *indenture*. Some of the provisions in an indenture may involve restrictions on dividend payments, restrictions on additional financing, and specification of minimum financial ratios that must be maintained. These provisions, called *debt covenants*, are intended to provide protection for debt-holders by limiting a company's flexibility to act.

ACCOUNTING IN PRACTICE	**Why Issue Bonds? Or Is Debt Really Bad?**

The opening vignette of this chapter mentions that Microsoft, a company with seemingly no need to borrow money, issued bonds to obtain additional cash. Microsoft is not alone in this behavior. Apple, on its 2017 balance sheet, reported nearly $300 billion in cash and marketable securities that could be readily converted to cash. Still, Apple has continued to issue debt, reporting slightly over $100 billion on its 2017 balance sheet. Nearly all of this debt was raised in the past few years. Why would companies like Microsoft and Apple take on more debt when they clearly have sufficient cash on hand? As finance theory teaches us, as long as a company can earn a higher rate of return on borrowed funds than the cost of those funds, the excess returns flow to the shareholders in the way of a higher return on equity. Of course this may be inconsistent with what a lot of people believe about debt.

CONTINGENT LIABILITIES

LO3   **Define** *contingent liabilities* and **explain** the rules for their accounting and disclosure in the financial statements.

Previously, we defined a liability as an obligation resulting from past transactions or events that require a firm to pay money, provide goods, or perform services in the future. Even though a past transaction or event has taken place, the existence of some liabilities still depends on the occurrence of a future event. These types of liability are called **contingent liabilities**. Whether or not a contingent liability is recorded in the accounts depends on the likelihood of the future event occurring and the measurability of the obligation.

If the future event will *probably occur* and the amount of the liability is known or can be *reasonably estimated,* an estimated liability should be recorded in the accounts. The estimated liability for product warranties is a good example of this situation. Many firms guarantee their products for a period of time following their sale. Customers are likely to make claims under a warranty for goods that they had purchased, and a reasonable estimate of the amount of the warranty obligation can usually be made.

Some contingent liabilities are not recorded in the accounts but must be disclosed in a note to the financial statements. Contingent liabilities disclosed in this manner are (1) those for which the likelihood of the future event occurring is probable but no reasonable estimate of the future obligation can be made or (2) those for which the likelihood of the future event occurring is only *reasonably possible* (but not probable), regardless of the ability to measure the future amount. When the future amount is not determinable, the note should state that the amount cannot be estimated.

**PRINCIPLE
ALERT**

Measuring Unit Concept and Full Disclosure Principle

The accounting guidelines for contingent liabilities illustrate the application of two principles of accounting: the *measuring unit concept* and the *full disclosure principle*. The measuring unit concept requires that information reported in the body of the financial statements be expressed in money terms. If a reasonable estimate of a contingent liability's dollar amount cannot be made, the measuring unit concept prevents the item from appearing in the balance sheet, even if its future occurrence is probable. However, the full disclosure principle requires that firms disclose all significant financial facts and circumstances to financial statement users. This principle leads to the reporting of likely but unmeasurable contingent liabilities in the notes to the financial statements.

If the likelihood of the future event occurring is *remote,* the contingent liability is neither recorded in the accounts nor disclosed in the notes to the financial statements, regardless of the ability to measure the future amount. One exception to this guideline, however, is when a company guarantees the credit of others (discussed in the following section). Even remote contingent liabilities associated with credit guarantees must be disclosed in the notes to the financial statements.

**ACCOUNTING IN
PRACTICE**

Estimated Liabilities Resulting from Lawsuits

Walmart Stores, Inc., is the world's largest retailer with over 11,000 stores around the globe. Each week, 200 million customers visit a Walmart store to take advantage of the company's low prices. But while Walmart may be cheered by consumers for its low prices, others are more critical of the company. Walmart, for example, has been criticized and sued by community groups, trade unions, and environmental groups for, among other things, its extensive foreign product sourcing, treatment of employees and product suppliers, environmental policies, and store impact on local communities. One such lawsuit alleges that female employees were discriminated against in pay. The following description of the lawsuit appeared in the company's 2016 annual report:

> ASDA Stores, Ltd., a wholly-owned subsidiary of the Company, is a defendant in over 10,000 "equal value" claims that are proceeding before an Employment Tribunal in Manchester in the United Kingdom on behalf of current and former ASDA store employees, who allege that the work performed by female employees in ASDA's retail stores is of equal value in terms of, among other things, the demands of their jobs to that of male employees working in ASDA's warehouse and distribution facilities, and that the disparity in pay between these different job positions is not objectively justified. Claimants are requesting differential back pay based on higher wage rates in the warehouse and distribution facilities and those higher wage rates on a prospective basis as part of these equal value proceedings.
>
> At present, the Company cannot predict the number of such claims that may be led, and cannot reasonably estimate any loss or range of loss that may arise from these proceedings.

Examples of Contingent Liabilities

Situations that may create contingent liabilities are discussed in the following sections. In each of these situations, accountants must assess the likelihood of the future event occurring and the measurability of the future amount because these factors determine the proper accounting treatment of the contingent liability.

Product Warranties

A proper matching of sales revenue and expenses requires that the estimated cost of honoring and servicing **product warranties** be recognized as an expense in the period of sale rather than in a later period when the warranty costs may actually be incurred and paid.

To illustrate, assume that a firm sells a product for $300 per unit, which includes a 30-day warranty against defects. Past experience indicates that three percent of the units will prove defective and that the average repair cost will be $40 per defective unit. Furthermore, during a particular month, product sales were $240,000, and 13 of the units sold during the month were defective and were repaired. Using this information, the accrued liability for product warranties at the end of the month can be calculated as follows:

Number of units sold ($240,000/$300)	800
Rate of projected defective units	× 0.03
Total units expected to fail	24
Less: Units that failed in the month of sale	13
Units expected to fail in the remainder of the warranty period	11
Average repair cost per unit	× $40
Estimated liability for product warranty at end of month	$440

This accrued liability is recorded at the end of the month of sale as follows:

A = L + SE
      +440 −440
             Exp

Product warranty expense (+E, −SE)	440	
Estimated liability for product warranty (+L)		440
To record estimated warranty expense.		

When a unit fails in a future period, the repair costs will be recorded by debiting the Estimated Liability for Product Warranty account and crediting Cash, Supplies, and so forth.

PRINCIPLE ALERT   **Matching Concept**

> The accounting for product warranties follows the *expense recognition (matching) concept*. This accounting concept states that expenses must be recorded in the same accounting period as the revenues they help generate. Product warranties make a company's products more attractive to buyers; consequently, product warranties help generate incremental sales revenues. Hence, one of the expenses that must be matched with sales revenues is the cost of honoring and servicing a product warranty. Because most warranty costs are incurred in periods following the period of sale, it is necessary to estimate these costs and record them in the same period when the sale of the product occurs to achieve a proper matching of revenues and expenses.

Lawsuits

In the course of its operations, a firm may be a defendant in one or more lawsuits involving potentially material financial settlements. Examples of litigation issues include product liability, patent infringement, unfair labor practices (see the Walmart Accounting in Practice on p. 483), and environmental matters. The resolution of a lawsuit may take many years. During the time a lawsuit is pending, the defendant has a contingent liability for any future financial settlement although it is impossible in most cases to arrive at a reasonable estimate of a company's possible losses. For this reason, lawsuit liabilities are most commonly disclosed in the notes to the financial statements and not on the face of the income statement or the balance sheet.

Environmental Cleanup Costs

Past actions by many companies in disposing of various types of industrial waste have caused subsequent environmental damage. Some estimates of the total cleanup costs for the United States run as high as $100 billion. Firms owning sites that require environmental remediation or that may require cleanup face a contingent liability for the remediation costs. Cleanup costs for a particular site may be very difficult to estimate. The party responsible for bearing the cost—the company or its insurance company—may also be at issue.

Credit Guarantees

To accommodate important but less financially secure suppliers or customers, a firm may create a **credit guarantee** by cosigning a note payable. Until the original debtor satisfies the obligation, the cosigning firm is contingently liable for the debt. Even when the likelihood of default by a debtor is considered remote, the contingent liability associated with credit guarantees must be disclosed in the notes to the financial statements.

IFRS ALERT

The accounting for some contingent liabilities under U.S. GAAP and IFRS differs significantly. For example, under U.S. GAAP, purchase commitments—that is, an agreement by one company to buy merchandise from another company at a future date—are not reported on the balance sheet but, if material in amount, are disclosed in the notes to the financial statements. Under IFRS, however, purchase commitments are reported on the balance sheet when a company has a clear and demonstrable commitment to a second company to buy its goods. In essence, IFRS adopts a broader definition of what constitutes an accounting liability than does U.S. GAAP. Under U.S. GAAP, while purchase commitments are acknowledged to be economic liabilities of a business, they do not constitute an accounting liability until an exchange of assets occurs between the two companies.

Summary of Accounting Treatment for Liabilities

Exhibit 10-5 summarizes the accounting for different types of liabilities according to their unique characteristics.

Exhibit 10-5	**Liabilities: Criteria and Financial Statement Treatment**					
Different Characteristics that Determine the Type of Liability and How it is Recorded	**Recorded in Accounts and Reported on Balance Sheet**		**Disclosed in Footnote to Financial Statements**		**No Disclosure Required**	
	Noncontingent	**Contingent**	**Contingent**	**Contingent**	**Contingent**	
Dependent on future event...	No	No	Yes	Yes	Yes	Yes
Likelihood of future event...............	Already Occurred	Already Occurred	**Probable**	**Probable**	**Reasonably possible**	**Remote**
Amount of future obligation..............	Known	Reasonably estimable	Known, or Reasonably estimable	Not reasonably estimable	Known, or Reasonably estimable, or Not reasonably estimable	Known, or Reasonably estimable, or Not reasonably estimable
Common examples.........	Notes payable, Accounts payable, Dividends payable	Income tax payable, Estimated liability for frequent use awards	Estimated liability for product warranty	Lawsuits, Environmental cleanup, Guarantee of others' credit	Lawsuits, Environmental cleanup, Guarantee of others' credit	Lawsuits, Environmental cleanup

YOUR TURN! 10.3

The solution is on
page 521.

For each of the following scenarios determine if the firm should (a) record as a liability; (b) disclose as a contingent liability; or (c) neither:

1. The Seco Co. has been sued by a group of individuals claiming the products they purchased from the company were defective and caused injuries. Seco's lawyers have determined that the product in question could not possibly have caused the types of damages claimed and further that the same group of individuals has unsuccessfully sued several other companies claiming their products caused the same injuries. The likelihood of losing this lawsuit is deemed remote.
2. The Everett Co. has guaranteed the loan of a subsidiary that is suffering minor financial distress. The chance that the loan will not be repaid is deemed remote.
3. Hiller Inc. has acquired a defunct mining company and assumed all its liabilities. Toxic waste from the defunct company was recently discovered to have leaked into some nearby wells. The evidence that the waste came from the mining company is very strong and the cost of cleanup is estimated to be $4 million.

TAKEAWAY 10.1	Concept	→ Method →	Assessment
	Does the company have any contingent liabilities?	Notes to the financial statements Read the notes to the financial statements to identify contingent liabilities	Consider the likely outcome and size of contingent liabilities. If significant, consider these items in the analysis of the firm's liabilities.

FORENSIC ACCOUNTING

Accounting Software

 One definition of forensic accounting is "the use of accounting records and documents to determine the legality of past activities." Possible uses of forensic accounting include financial statements, government investigations, contract disputes, or even culling through a shoebox of receipts in preparation for an IRS audit. As a business owner, would you rather defend yourself in an investigation with a shoebox full of documents or with a detailed set of accounting records? While some small business owners feel that entry-level accounting systems such as **Intuit**'s Quickbooks are fine for their needs, they may want to consider the benefits of a more robust accounting package, such as **Microsoft** Dynamics GP accounting system. In today's technology-driven society, a security breach is only a few keystrokes away. A hacker will have a much easier time penetrating the single layer of security in most entry-level packages than the eight levels of security in Microsoft Dynamics GP. In addition, the more robust accounting systems provide a richer data repository from which a forensic accountant can mine data in an effort to identify inconsistencies, a major weapon in the detection of fraud.

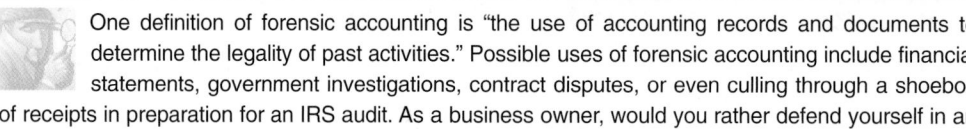

ANALYZING LIABILITIES

**eLectures
MBC**

LO4   Define the *current ratio, quick ratio,* and *times-interest-earned ratio* and **explain** their use.

Current Ratio and Quick Ratio

The **working capital** of a firm is the difference between the amount of its current assets and the amount of its current liabilities. In general, having a higher working capital position is preferred to having a lower working capital position. In analyzing the adequacy of a firm's working capital, the current ratio is a widely used financial metric. The **current ratio** is calculated as follows:

$$\text{Current ratio} = \frac{\text{Current assets}}{\text{Current liabilities}}$$

Historically, a current ratio of 2.00 has been considered an acceptable current ratio; however, this is a general guide only. Many businesses operate successfully with a

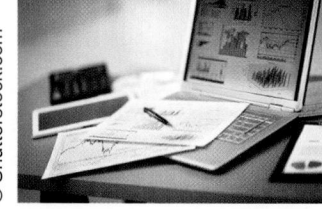

current ratio below 2.00, particularly service firms, because they do not need to maintain large amounts of inventory among their current assets. Similarly, many fast-food franchises operate successfully with a negative working capital position. These businesses produce large amounts of operating cash flow, have no accounts receivable, and extensively utilize the trade credit (accounts payable) provided by their suppliers.

The **quick ratio** is another ratio used to evaluate a company's working capital position. The quick ratio is calculated as follows:

$$\text{Quick ratio} = \frac{[\text{Cash and cash equivalents} + \text{Short-term investments} + \text{Accounts receivable}]}{\text{Current liabilities}}$$

Cash and cash equivalents, short-term investments, and accounts receivable are also known as quick assets. Quick assets are converted to cash more quickly than other current assets such as inventory or prepaid assets that are omitted from the numerator of the ratio. Consequently, the quick ratio is often preferred by investment professionals because it gives a more accurate picture of a company's ability to pay current liabilities.

The following are examples of the current and quick ratios for companies in different industries:

	Current Ratio	Quick Ratio
Verizon Communications (telecommunications)	0.91	0.77
Johnson & Johnson (health care products)	1.41	1.04
Duke Energy (utility)	0.66	0.25
Alphabet (technology)	5.14	4.99

As can be seen from the above data, the current and quick ratios vary dramatically between industries.

Forensic Accounting

FORENSIC ACCOUNTING

One of the key measures indicating the amount of liabilities, or leverage, used by a company is its net debt. Net debt is calculated as a firm's total liabilities minus its liquid (or quick) assets. The higher a firm's net debt, the higher the firm's leverage, or use of debt financing. Because of the widespread use of net debt as an indicator of a firm's use of leverage by investment professionals, some firms have attempted to manage the level of their reported net debt. To illustrate, consider the case of **Parmalat SpA**, an Italian dairy company. In late 2003, the company filed for bankruptcy after revealing that it had massively underreported its outstanding net debt. According to the company's forensic investigative auditor, **PricewaterhouseCoopers LLP**, Parmalat underreported its net debt position by overstating the amount of cash on hand and retaining worthless accounts receivable on the company's balance sheet.

Concept	Method	Assessment	TAKEAWAY 10.2
Can a firm pay its current liabilities?	Current assets, Quick assets, Current liabilities $\text{Current ratio} = \dfrac{\text{Current assets}}{\text{Current liabilities}}$ $\text{Quick ratio} = \dfrac{\text{Quick assets}}{\text{Current liabilities}}$	A higher current ratio and quick ratio indicate that a firm can readily pay its current liabilities.	

Times-Interest-Earned Ratio

A financial ratio of particular interest to current and potential long-term creditors is the times-interest-earned ratio. The **times-interest-earned ratio** is computed as follows:

$$\text{Times-interest-earned ratio} = \frac{\text{Income before interest expense and income taxes}}{\text{Interest expense}}$$

A.K.A. The times-interest-earned ratio is also referred to as the interest coverage ratio.

The principal on long-term debt, such as bonds payable, is not due until maturity, which may be many years into the future. Interest payments, however, are due every six months, and possibly monthly on term loans. Thus, creditors examine the times-interest-earned ratio to help assess the ability of a company to meet its periodic interest commitments. The ratio indicates the number of times that the fixed interest charges were earned during the year. Many investment professionals believe that the times-interest-earned ratio should be at least in the range of 3.0–4.0 for the extension of long-term credit to be considered a safe investment. The trend of the ratio in recent years and the nature of the industry (volatile or stable, for example) also influence the interpretation of this ratio.

Both the numerator and denominator in the times-interest-earned ratio are obtained from the income statement. The numerator uses income before interest expense and income taxes because that is the amount available to cover a business's current interest charges. The denominator is the business's total interest expense for the period. To illustrate, Reid, Inc., issued $100,000 of eight percent bonds at face value. The annual interest expense was $8,000. If this was Reid's only interest expense and Reid's income before interest expense and income taxes was $28,000, Reid's times-interest-earned ratio for the year would be 3.5, or $28,000/$8,000.

The times-interest-earned ratio may differ substantially among industries and firms, depending upon a company's decision to use leverage to finance its assets and operations. The following are examples of times-interest-earned ratios for several companies in different industries:

Kellogg Company (grocery products)	12.50
Kimberly-Clark Corporation (consumer goods)	10.41
Amazon.com Inc. (online retailing)	8.49
Cisco Systems, Inc. (computer communications equip.)	15.27

TAKEAWAY 10.3	Concept →	Method →	Assessment
	Can a firm pay its current periodic interest payments?	Income before income taxes and interest expense, Interest expense Times-interest-earned ratio $= \dfrac{\text{Income before income taxes and interest expense}}{\text{Interest expense}}$	A higher times-interest-earned ratio indicates that a firm will have less difficulty paying its current interest expense.

YOUR TURN! 10.4

The solution is on page 521.

Magee Company reports the following in its current year financial statements:

Current assets	$120,000
Current liabilities	80,000
Cash and cash equivalents	10,000
Short-term investments	25,000
Accounts receivable	30,000
Income before interest expense and income taxes	20,000
Interest expense	4,000

Compute the following ratios for Magee Company:
a. Current ratio
b. Quick ratio
c. Times-interest-earned ratio

COMPREHENSIVE PROBLEM

The following are selected transactions for Tyler, Inc., for 2017 and 2018. The firm closes its books on December 31.

2017
Dec. 31 Issued $500,000 of 12 percent, ten-year bonds for $562,360, yielding an effective rate of ten percent. Interest is payable June 30 and December 31.

2018
June 30 Paid semiannual interest and recorded semiannual premium amortization on bonds.
Dec. 31 Paid semiannual interest and recorded semiannual premium amortization on bonds.
   31 Called one-half of the bonds in for retirement at 104.

Required
Record the transactions using (a) straight-line amortization and (b) effective interest amortization. Round amounts to the nearest dollar. You should read Appendix 10A prior to attempting this comprehensive problem.

Solution:

		(a) Straight-line Amortization		(b) Effective Interest Amortization	
2017					
Dec. 31	Cash (+A)	562,360		562,360	
	Bonds payable (+L)		500,000		500,000
	Premium on bonds payable (+XL, +L)		62,360		62,360
	Issued $500,000 of 12 percent, ten-year bonds for $562,360.				
2018					
June 30	Bond interest expense (+E, −SE)	26,882		28,118	
	Premium on bonds payable (−XL, −L)	3,118		1,882	
	Cash (−A)		30,000		30,000
	To record semiannual interest payment and premium amortization.	*[$62,360 ÷ 20 = $3,118].*		*[$562,360 × 0.05 = $28,118].*	
Dec. 31	Bond interest expense (+E, −SE)	26,882		28,024	
	Premium on bonds payable (−XL, −L)	3,118		1,976	
	Cash (−A)		30,000		30,000
	To record semiannual interest payment and premium amortization.	*[$62,360 ÷ 20 = $3,118].*		*[($562,360 − $1,882) × 0.05 = $28,024, rounded].*	
31	Bonds payable (−L)	250,000		250,000	
	Premium on bonds payable (−XL, −L)	28,062		29,251	
	Cash (−A)		260,000		260,000
	Gain on bond retirement (+Gain, +SE)		18,062		19,251
	To record retirement of $250,000 of bonds; Retirement payment: $250,000 × 1.04 = $260,000.	*[$56,124 × 50% = $28,062].*		*[$58,502 × 50% = $29,251].*	

APPENDIX 10A: Bond Pricing

We explained that (1) a bond agreement specifies a pattern of future cash flows—usually a series of interest payments and a single payment at maturity equal to the face value—and that (2) bonds are often sold at premiums or discounts to adjust their stated or coupon interest rates to the prevailing market rate of interest when they are issued.

Because of the role played by interest, the selling price of a bond that is necessary to yield a specific rate can be determined as follows:

❶ Use Appendix E's Table III to calculate the present value of the future principal repayment at the bond's effective rate of interest.

L05 **Explain** bond pricing and **illustrate** the straight-line and effective interest methods of amortizing bond discounts/premiums.

② Use Appendix E's Table IV to calculate the present value of the future series of interest payments at the bond's effective rate of interest.

③ Add the two present value calculations obtained in steps one and two.

Exhibit 10A-1 illustrates the pricing of a $100,000 issue of eight percent, four-year bonds paying interest semiannually and sold on the date of issue to yield (1) eight percent, (2) ten percent, or (3) six percent. The price of the eight-percent bonds sold to yield eight percent equals the face (or par) value of the bonds. However, the bonds must sell for $93,537 to provide a yield of ten percent, whereas the bonds must sell for $107,020 to provide a yield of six percent.

Exhibit 10A-1	Calculating Bond Issue Price Using Present Value Tables

① $100,000 of eight percent, four-year bonds with interest payable semiannually sold to yield eight percent:

Future Cash Flows	Multiplier (Table III)	Multiplier (Table IV)	Present Values at 4% Semiannually
Principal repayment, $100,000 (a single amount received eight semiannual periods hence)	0.73069		$ 73,069
Interest payments, $4,000 at end of each of eight semiannual interest periods		6.73274	26,931
Total present value (or issue price) of bonds			$100,000

② $100,000 of eight percent, four-year bonds with interest payable semiannually sold to yield ten percent:

Future Cash Flows	Multiplier (Table III)	Multiplier (Table IV)	Present Values at 5% Semiannually
Principal repayment, $100,000 (a single amount received eight semiannual periods hence)	0.67684		$ 67,684
Interest payments, $4,000 at end of each of eight semiannual interest periods		6.46321	25,853
Total present value (or issue price) of bonds			$ 93,537

③ $100,000 of eight percent, four-year bonds with interest payable semiannually sold to yield six percent:

Future Cash Flows	Multiplier (Table III)	Multiplier (Table IV)	Present Values at 3% Semiannually
Principal repayment, $100,000 (a single amount received eight semiannual periods hence)	0.78941		$ 78,941
Interest payments, $4,000 at end of each of eight semiannual interest periods		7.01969	28,079
Total present value (or issue price) of bonds			$107,020

Straight-line Interest Method of Discount Amortization

When bonds are sold at either a discount or a premium, the amount of interest that the company pays to bondholders will differ from the amount of interest expense that is reported on the income statement. To see why this is the case, we will first consider the bond in **Exhibit 10A-1** that sells for $93,537; a discount of $6,463 from the face value of $100,000. This $6,463 discount represents an additional interest cost that the issuing company, Reid Inc., must pay because it borrowed $93,537 but will have to pay back $100,000 in addition to the semiannual $4,000 interest payments. To properly apply the matching principle, Reid, Inc. will recognize a portion of the $6,463 discount as additional interest expense each time it makes an interest payment, thus spreading the additional interest of $6,463 over the life of the bond.

Under the straight-line interest method an equal amount of the discount is amortized to expense at each payment date. **Exhibit 10A-2** presents an amortization table illustrating the straight-line method. The interest rates shown in columns A and B are one-half the annual rates. Column A lists the constant amount of interest paid each six months—that is, the coupon interest rate times the face value (4 percent × $100,000). The amounts in column B are obtained by dividing the $6,463 discount by the eight interest payments, or $808 per semiannual period. The total interest expense appearing in column C is the interest payment in column A *plus* the discount amortization in column B. The original $6,463 discount is reduced by $808 each period as shown in column D. The reported value of the bonds, shown in column E, changes each period. For discounted bonds, the reported value increases each period until it reaches the face value on the maturity date because the discount is being reduced each period until it becomes zero.

Exhibit 10A-2	Bonds Sold at a Discount: Straight-line Interest Method

$100,000 of 8% four-year bonds with interest payable semiannually
Issued on December 31, 2018, at $93,537 to yield 10%

Date	Interest Period	A Interest Paid (4% of face value)	B Additional Interest ($6,463 discount divided by 8 periods) (Rounded)	C Total Interest Expense (A + B)	D Balance of Unamortized Discount (D – B)	E Book Value of Bonds, End of Period ($100,000 – D)
Dec. 31, 2018 . . .	At issue				$6,463	$ 93,537
June 30, 2019 . . .	1	$4,000	$808	$4,808	5,655	94,345
Dec. 31, 2019 . . .	2	4,000	808	4,808	4,847	95,153
June 30, 2020 . . .	3	4,000	808	4,808	4,039	95,961
Dec. 31, 2020 . . .	4	4,000	808	4,808	3,231	96,769
June 30, 2021 . . .	5	4,000	808	4,808	2,423	97,577
Dec. 31, 2021 . . .	6	4,000	808	4,808	1,615	98,385
June 30, 2022 . . .	7	4,000	808	4,808	808	99,192
Dec. 31, 2022 . . .	8	4,000	808	4,808	0	100,000

The following journal entry records the interest expense and discount amortization each period:

2019				
June 30	Bond interest expense (+E, −SE)	4,808		
	Discount on bonds payable (−XL, +L)		808	
	Cash (−A)		4,000	
	To record semiannual interest payments and amortization.			

A = L + SE
−4,000 +808 −4,808

Amortizing the bond discount over the four-year life of the bonds leaves a zero balance in the Discount on Bonds Payable account on the maturity date of the bonds. The retirement of the bonds at maturity is then recorded by debiting Bonds Payable and crediting Cash for $100,000, the amount of their face value.

Straight-line Interest Method of Premium Amortization

When bonds are issued at a premium, the interest expense each period will be less than the amount of cash paid. We can see this by again considering the Reid, Inc. bond from **Exhibit 10A-1**, this time considering the bond issued for $107,020, a premium of $7,020 over the face value of $100,000. The $7,020 premium represents a reduction of interest cost to Reid, Inc., because Reid borrowed $107,020 but will have to pay back only $100,000 in addition to the semiannual $4,000 interest payments. As with the discount discussed above, to properly apply the matching principle, Reid, Inc. will recognize a portion of the $7,020 premium as a reduction of interest expense each time it makes an interest payment, thus spreading the $7,020 premium over the life of the bond.

Exhibit 10A-3 presents an amortization table illustrating the straight-line method. The interest rates shown in columns A and B are one-half the annual rates. Column A lists the constant amount of interest paid each six months—that is, the coupon interest rate times the face value (4 percent × $100,000). The amounts in column B are obtained by dividing the $7,020 premium by the eight interest payments, or $877.50 per semiannual period. The total interest expense appearing in column C is the interest payment in column A *minus* the premium amortization in column B. The original $7,020 premium is reduced by $877.50 each period as shown in column D. The reported value of the bonds, shown in column E, changes each period. For bonds issued at a premium, the value decreases each period until it reaches the face value on the maturity date because the premium is being reduced each period until it becomes zero.

Exhibit 10A-3	Bonds Sold at a Premium: Straight-line Interest Method

$100,000 of 8% four-year bonds with interest payable semiannually
Issued on December 31, 2018, at $107,020 to yield 6%

Date	Interest Period	A Interest Paid (4% of face value)	B Additional Interest ($7,020 premium divided by 8 periods)	C Total Interest Expense (A + B)	D Balance of Unamortized Premium (D − B)	E Book Value of Bonds, End of Period ($100,000 + D)
Dec. 31, 2018...	At issue				$7,020.00	$107,020.00
June 30, 2019...	1......	$4,000	$877.50	$3,122.50	6,124.50	106,142.50
Dec. 31, 2019...	2......	4,000	877.50	3,122.50	5,265.00	105,265.00
June 30, 2020...	3......	4,000	877.50	3,122.50	4,387.50	104,387.50
Dec. 31, 2020...	4......	4,000	877.50	3,122.50	3,510.00	103,510.00
June 30, 2021...	5......	4,000	877.50	3,122.50	2,632.50	102,632.50
Dec. 31, 2021...	6......	4,000	877.50	3,122.50	1,755.00	101,755.00
June 30, 2022...	7......	4,000	877.50	3,122.50	877.50	100,877.50
Dec. 31, 2022...	8......	4,000	877.50	3,122.50	0.00	100,000.00

The following journal entry records the interest expense and premium amortization each period:

A = L + SE				
−4,000.00 −877.50 −3,122.50	**2019** June 30	Bond interest expense (+E, −SE) Premium on bonds payable (−XL, −L) Cash (−A) *To record semiannual interest payments and amortization.*	3,122.50 877.50	 4,000

Amortizing the bond premium over the four-year life of the bonds leaves a zero balance in the Premium on Bonds Payable account on the maturity date of the bonds. The retirement of the bonds at maturity is then recorded by debiting Bonds Payable and crediting Cash for $100,000, the amount of their face value.

Effective Interest Method of Discount Amortization

A bond premium or discount can be amortized to interest expense using the straight-line method or the effective interest method. GAAP requires the effective interest method, except in cases where the differences between the two methods are not material. The **effective interest method** of amortization recognizes a constant percentage of the book value of a bond as interest expense for each interest payment period. For bonds issued at a discount, the book value of a bond is the balance in the Bonds Payable account less the balance in the Discount on Bonds Payable account. To obtain a period's interest expense under the effective interest method, we multiply the bond's book value at the beginning of each period by the effective interest rate. The **effective interest rate** is the market rate of interest used to price the bonds when they are originally issued. The difference between this amount and the amount of interest paid (coupon interest rate × face value of bonds) is the amount of discount amortized.

When using the effective interest method of amortization, accountants often prepare an amortization schedule similar to the one in **Exhibit 10A-4**. This schedule covers the four-year life of the Reid, Inc., bonds issued at a discount. The interest rates shown in columns A and B are one-half the annual rates. Column A lists the constant amounts of interest paid each six months—that is, the coupon interest rate times the face value (4 percent × $100,000). The amounts in Column B are obtained by multiplying the book value as of the beginning of each period (column E) by the 5 percent effective interest rate. For example, the $4,677 interest expense for the first period is 5 percent times $93,537; for the second period, it is 5 percent times $94,214, or $4,711, and so on. The reported value of the bonds changes each period. For discounted bonds, the value increases each period because the book value increases over the life of the bonds until it reaches the face value on the maturity date. The amount of discount amortization for each period, given in column C, is the difference between the corresponding amounts in columns A and B. Column D lists the amount of unamortized discount at the end of each period.

Exhibit 10A-4	Bonds Sold at a Discount: Effective Interest Method

$100,000 of 8%, four-year bonds with interest payable semiannually issued on December 31, 2018, at $93,537 to yield 10%

Date	Interest Period	A Interest Paid (4% of face value)	B Interest Expense (5% of bond book value)	C Periodic Amortization (B − A)	D Balance of Unamortized Discount (D − C)	E Book Value of Bonds, End of Period ($100,000 − D)
Dec. 31, 2018...	At issue				$6,463	$ 93,537
June 30, 2019 ..	1.......	$4,000	$4,677	$677	5,786	94,214
Dec. 31, 2019...	2.......	4,000	4,711	711	5,075	94,925
June 30, 2020 ..	3.......	4,000	4,746	746	4,329	95,671
Dec. 31, 2020...	4.......	4,000	4,784	784	3,546	96,454
June 30, 2021 ..	5.......	4,000	4,823	823	2,723	97,277
Dec. 31, 2021...	6.......	4,000	4,864	864	1,859	98,141
June 30, 2022 ..	7.......	4,000	4,907	907	952	99,048
Dec. 31, 2022...	8.......	4,000	4,952	952	0	100,000

The amounts recorded for each interest payment can be read directly from the amortization schedule. The following journal entries record the interest expense and discount amortization at the time of the first two interest payments:

2019 June 30	Bond interest expense (+E, −SE)	4,677	
	Discount on bonds payable (−XL, +L)		677
	Cash (−A)		4,000
	To record semiannual interest payment and amortization.		

A = L + SE
−4,000 +677 −4,677 Exp

Dec. 31	Bond interest expense (+E, −SE)	4,711	
	Discount on bonds payable (−XL, +L)		711
	Cash (−A)		4,000
	To record semiannual interest payment and amortization.		

A = L + SE
−4,000 +711 −4,711 Exp

Amortizing the bond discount over the four-year life of the bonds leaves a zero balance in the Discount on Bonds Payable account on the maturity date of the bonds. The retirement of the bonds at maturity is then recorded by debiting Bonds Payable and crediting Cash for $100,000, the amount of their face value.

Materiality Concept

PRINCIPLE ALERT

Under U.S. GAAP, the effective interest method is the preferred method of bond amortization. It is generally accepted because it uses the actual market rate of interest when the bonds were originally issued to determine the amount of the periodic amortization. The effective interest method, however, is somewhat more complex than the straight-line method. Accounting standards permit the straight-line method of amortization to be used when the results are not materially different from those achieved under the effective interest method. This exception represents an application of the *materiality concept*. As previously discussed, the materiality concept permits insignificant accounting transactions to be recorded most expediently. Here, the materiality concept permits a simpler (and, thus, more expedient) straight-line method to be used when it results in insignificant differences from the theoretically superior effective interest method.

Effective Interest Method of Premium Amortization

The **effective interest method** of amortizing a bond premium is handled the same way as a bond discount amortization. Each interest period, a constant percentage of the bonds' book value as of the beginning of the period is recognized as interest expense; the difference between the interest expense and the semiannual interest payment is the amount of the premium amortization.

Exhibit 10A-5 shows the amortization schedule for the four-year life of the Reid, Inc., bonds that were issued at a premium. The coupon rate of four percent in column A and the effective interest rate of three percent in column B are one-half the annual rates because the calculations are for six-month periods.

Exhibit 10A-5	**Bonds Sold at a Premium: Effective Interest Method**					
	$100,000 of 8%, four-year bonds with interest payable semiannually issued on December 31, 2018, at $107,020 to yield 6%					
		A	B	C	D	E
Date	**Interest Period**	**Interest Paid (4% of face value)**	**Interest Expense (3% of bond book value)**	**Periodic Amortization (A − B)**	**Balance of Unamortized Premium (D − C)**	**Book Value of Bonds, End of Period ($100,000 + D)**
Dec. 31, 2018. . .	At issue				$7,020	$ 7,020
June 30, 2019 . .	1	$4,000	$3,241	$789	6,231	6,231
Dec. 31, 2019. . .	2	4,000	3,187	813	5,418	5,418
June 30, 2020 . .	3	4,000	3,163	837	4,580	4,580
Dec. 31, 2020. . .	4	4,000	3,137	863	3,717	3,717
June 30, 2021 . .	5	4,000	3,112	888	2,829	2,829
Dec. 31, 2021. . .	6	4,000	3,085	915	1,914	1,914
June 30, 2022 . .	7	4,000	3,057	943	971	971
Dec. 31, 2022. . .	8	4,000	3,029	971	0	100,000

The journal entries for each interest payment are taken directly from the amortization schedule. The entries for the first two interest payments follow. Note that the periodic interest expense is less than the semiannual interest payment.

A = L + SE		**2019**			
−4,000 −789 −3,211 Exp		June 30	Bond interest expense (+E, −SE)	3,211	
			Premium on bonds payable (−XL, −L)	789	
			Cash (−A)		4,000
			To record semiannual interest payment and amortization.		

A = L + SE					
−4,000 −813 −3,187 Exp		Dec. 31	Bond interest expense (+E, −SE)	3,187	
			Premium on bonds payable (−XL, −L)	813	
			Cash (−A)		4,000
			To record semiannual interest payment and amortization.		

After amortizing the bond premium over the four-year life of the bonds, the balance in the Premium on Bonds Payable account is zero. When the bonds are retired at the end of four years, the journal entry to record the retirement debits Bonds Payable and credits Cash for the $100,000 face value of the bonds.

Exhibit 10A-6 shows the book value of the Reid, Inc. bonds from issuance to maturity. The bond issued at face value has a reported book value of $100,000 over its entire life. The book value of the bond sold at a premium is greater than the face value at issuance. As the premium is amortized over the life of the bond, the book value declines until it is equal to the face value. The book value of the bond sold at a discount behaves in the opposite fashion; it is less than the face value at issuance, and increases over time as the discount is amortized. At maturity, the book value of all three bonds is equal to the $100,000 face value.

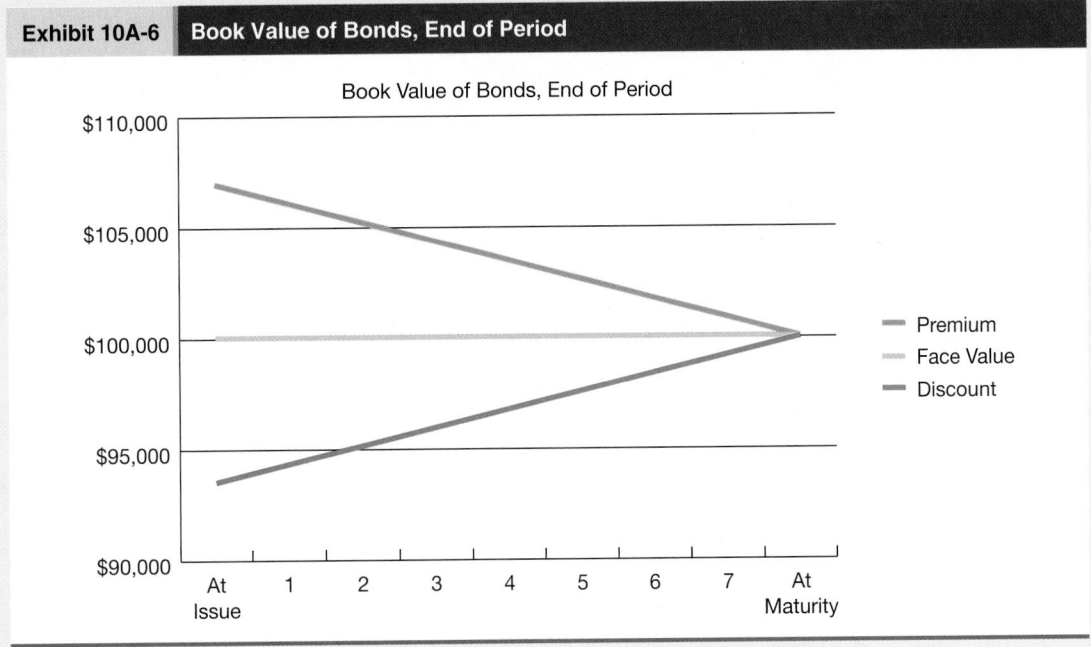

| Exhibit 10A-6 | Book Value of Bonds, End of Period |

Using a Financial Calculator

While present value tables can provide a handy method to solve some time value of money problems, they are not suitable for many real-world situations. For example, many real-world interest rates are not "even integers" like those appearing in Table I through Table IV of Appendix E, nor are many problems limited to the number of time periods appearing in the tables. While it is still possible to solve these problems with the provided formulas, a financial calculator provides a quicker solution. Financial calculators can be distinguished from other calculators by the presence of dedicated keys for present and future values, along with keys for the number of periods, interest rates, and annuity payments. There are many brands of financial calculators; however, all of them work in much the same way. We will illustrate the calculation of bond issuance prices from **Exhibit 10A-1** using a Hewlett-Packard 10BII financial calculator, as illustrated in **Exhibit 10A-7**. (It is usually necessary to do some preliminary setup on a financial calculator before performing time value of money calculations. For example, the HP 10BII calculator has a default setting of monthly compounding; this may need to be changed if the problem calls for a different number of compounding periods, such as annual. In addition, the calculator assumes interest payments occur at the end of each period; this will need to be changed if the problem requires beginning of period payments. See your calculator manual to determine how to make these setting changes.)

| Exhibit 10A-7 | Hewlett-Packard 10BII Financial Calculator |

To solve a time value of money problem using a financial calculator, input the known values and then press the key of the unknown value. **Exhibit 10A-8** illustrates the bond value calculations from **Exhibit 10A-1**. The interest payment (PMT = $4,000) and principal at maturity (FV = $100,000) are shown as negative numbers, indicating cash outflows. Solving for the present value (PV) of these cash flows yields the price of the bond which is equal to the amount of cash received at issuance. Financial calculators require cash outflows and inflows to be of opposite signs. If we were to enter PMT and FV as positive numbers, PV would be displayed as a negative number. Calculator solutions can be slightly different from the solutions using either the tables or the formulas due to rounding of the future value and present value multipliers.

Exhibit 10A-8	Calculating Bond Issue Prices Using a Financial Calculator

(1) $100,000 of eight percent, four-year bonds with interest payable semiannually sold to yield eight percent:

Enter		Display		
8	N	N	=	8
4	I/YR	I/YR	=	4
−4,000	PMT	PMT	=	−4,000
−100,000	FV	FV	=	−100,000
Press	PV	PV	=	100,000

(2) $100,000 of eight percent, four-year bonds with interest payable semiannually sold to yield ten percent:

Enter		Display		
8	N	N	=	8
5	I/YR	I/YR	=	5
−4,000	PMT	PMT	=	−4,000
−100,000	FV	FV	=	−100,000
Press	PV	PV	=	93,537

(3) $100,000 of eight percent, four-year bonds with interest payable semiannually sold to yield six percent:

Enter		Display		
8	N	N	=	8
3	I/YR	I/YR	=	3
−4,000	PMT	PMT	=	−4,000
−100,000	FV	FV	=	−100,000
Press	PV	PV	=	107,020

ACCOUNTING IN EVERYDAY LIFE	Getting a Car Loan

The expression "knowledge is power" certainly applies to the situation many of us face when shopping for a new car that we plan to finance. Sitting in the room with the car dealership's finance manager can be much more pleasant if one is armed with a financial calculator and the knowledge of how to calculate car payments. You no longer need to trust that the interest rate you are being quoted is the "real" interest rate you are being charged; you can simply do the calculation yourself and verify the number.

Using an Electronic Spreadsheet

In addition to present value tables and financial calculators, another way to solve time value of money problems is with an electronic spreadsheet such as Excel. Excel has several built-in functions that allow calculation of time value of money problems. Depending on the version of Excel, these functions are accessed differently. Within Excel, go to the Insert function *fx* in the Formulas ribbon. The required functions are located under the FINANCIAL option. Below are examples of how to use Excel to solve the same problems we previously solved using a financial calculator.

Example 1

Find the selling price (present value) of $100,000 of eight percent, four-year bonds with interest payable semiannually sold to yield eight percent. Use the PV function and enter the values as follows:

Example 2

Find the selling price (present value) of $100,000 of eight percent, four-year bonds with interest payable semi-annually sold to yield ten percent. Use the PV function and enter the values as follows:

Example 3

Find the selling price (present value) of $100,000 of eight percent, four-year bonds with interest payable semi-annually sold to yield six percent. Use the PV function and enter the values as follows:

YOUR TURN! 10A.1

The solution is on page 521.

Use an Excel spreadsheet to find the selling price (present value) of a three-year $100,000 face value bond with coupon semiannual payments at four percent that is issued when bonds of similar risk are yielding six percent.

APPENDIX 10B: Leases

A firm may rent property for a specified period of time under a contract called a **lease**. The company acquiring the right to use the property is the **lessee**, while the owner of the property is the **lessor**. The rights transferred to the lessee are called a **leasehold**. Examples of leased assets include land, buildings, factory machinery, and office equipment.

L06 Describe the accounting for leases.

The FASB updated its leasing standard effective for fiscal years beginning after December 15, 2019. The FASB believes the updated accounting standard for leases provides a more faithful representation of a lessee's rights and obligations arising from a lease. Before the update, companies were often able to structure a lease such that the leased asset and its corresponding liability failed to be reported on the balance sheet, a practice known as **off-balance sheet financing**.

Under the revised standard, a lessee's accounting treatment of a leased asset and lease liability depends on whether a lease is categorized as a **finance lease** or an **operating lease**. If any of the following five criteria are met, the lease is categorized as a finance lease. Otherwise the lease is categorized as an operating lease.

- Ownership of the leased asset is transferred to the lessee at the end of the lease.
- The lessee has the option to purchase the leased asset at a bargain price.
- The lease term is for a major part of the remaining economic life of the leased asset.
- The present value of the lease payments and any residual value guarantees is equal to, or more than, substantially all of the fair value of the leased asset.
- The leased asset has no alternative use to the lessor at the end of the term because of its specialized nature.

Under the revised standard, all leases will require the lessee to record the leased asset and its corresponding lease liability on the balance sheet at an amount equal to the present value of the future lease payments. For example, assume Microsoft leases a building for 10 years with annual lease payments of $129,505 when Microsoft's borrowing rate is five percent. The present value of these lease payments is $1,000,000.[1] Microsoft would therefore make the following journal entry to record the lease:

Right-of-Use Asset (Building) (+A)	1,000,000	
Lease liability (Building) (−A)		1,000,000

There are some differences in the income statement treatment between an operating and a finance lease. These differences are covered in an intermediate accounting textbook.

YOUR TURN! 10B.1

The solution is on page 521.

Huff Company leased a new forklift for four years. Huff Co. will return the forklift at the end of the four years. The estimated economic life of the forklift is five years. At the time of the lease, the fair value of the forklift is $45,000. The monthly lease payments are $1,000 and the lease has an implied interest rate of six percent, for a present value of $42,580.

Determine whether the lease will be categorized as a finance or operating lease and provide the journal entry to record the lease.

---

[1] Annual lease payment of $129,505 times present value of an ordinary annuity with a factor of 7.72173 (5% and 10 periods) equals 1,000,000 (rounded) (See Appendix E, Table IV)

Leases	ACCOUNTING IN PRACTICE

Although companies are not required to adopt the revised accounting standard for leases until essentially January 2020, Microsoft chose to adopt the standard early for their 2018 financial statements which have a fiscal year end of June 30, 2018. They disclose the following information about the accounting for leases:

We determine if an arrangement is a lease at inception. Operating leases are included in operating lease right-of-use ("ROU") assets, other current liabilities, and operating lease liabilities in our consolidated balance sheets. Finance leases are included in property and equipment, other current liabilities, and other long-term liabilities in our consolidated balance sheets.

ROU assets represent our right to use an underlying asset for the lease term and lease liabilities represent our obligation to make lease payments arising from the lease. Operating lease ROU assets and liabilities are recognized at commencement date based on the present value of lease payments over the lease term. As most of our leases do not provide an implicit rate, we use our incremental borrowing rate based on the information available at commencement date in determining the present value of lease payments. We use the implicit rate when readily determinable.

SUMMARY OF LEARNING OBJECTIVES

Describe the nature of liabilities and discuss various *current liabilities*. (p. 464)   LO1

- Liabilities are obligations resulting from past transactions or events that require a business to pay money, provide goods, or perform services in the future.
- Current liabilities are obligations that will require, within the coming year or the normal operating cycle, whichever is longer, (1) the use of existing current assets or (2) the creation of other current liabilities.

Illustrate the accounting for long-term liabilities. (p. 470)   LO2

- A bond is a long-term debt instrument used by many businesses to provide financing for operations or asset purchases.
- Discounts and premiums may be recorded when the bonds are issued.
- Bonds payable are shown in the long-term liabilities section of the balance sheet, with any unamortized premium added or unamortized discount deducted.
- The entry for the retirement of bonds removes both the bonds payable and any related bond premium or bond discount from the accounts at the date of retirement and recognizes any gain or loss on retirement.

Define *contingent liabilities* and explain the rules for their accounting and disclosure in the financial statements. (p. 480)   LO3

- Even though a past transaction or event has taken place, the existence of some liabilities, called contingent liabilities, depends on the occurrence of a future event. Whether or not a contingent liability is recorded in the accounts depends on the likelihood of the future event occurring and the measurability of the obligation:
  1. If the future event will probably occur and the amount of the liability is known or can be reasonably estimated, the contingent liability should be recorded in the accounts.
  2. If the likelihood of the future event occurring is probable, but no reasonable estimate of the future obligation is determinable, or the likelihood of the future event occurring is reasonably possible (but not probable), regardless of the ability to measure the future amount, the contingent liability should be disclosed in a note to the financial statements, but not recorded in the accounts.
  3. If the likelihood of the future event occurring is remote, the contingent liability is not recorded in the accounts or disclosed in a note to the financial statements. The only exception is a credit guarantee, which must be disclosed in a note to the financial statements.

LO4 **Define the *current ratio*, *quick ratio*, and *times-interest-earned ratio* and explain their use. (p. 484)**

- The current ratio is calculated as follows:

$$\text{Current ratio} = \frac{\text{Current assets}}{\text{Current liabilities}}$$

- The quick ratio is calculated as follows:

$$\text{Quick ratio} = \frac{[\text{Cash and cash equivalents} + \text{Short-term investments} + \text{Accounts receivable}]}{\text{Current liabilities}}$$

- Both the current and quick ratios measure a firm's ability to pay its current liabilities, as well as the strength of its working capital position.
- The times-interest-earned ratio measures the ability of a firm to meet its periodic interest commitments, and is calculated as:

$$\text{Times-interest-earned ratio} = \frac{\text{Income before income taxes and interest expense}}{\text{Interest expense}}$$

LO5 **Appendix 10A: Explain bond pricing and illustrate the straight-line and effective interest methods of amortizing bond discounts/premiums. (p. 487)**

- Because of the role played by interest, the selling price of the bond often differs from the face amount of the bond.
- We account for this difference by utilizing bond premium (when the market rate of interest is less than the coupon rate) and bond discount (when the market rate of interest is more than the coupon rate) accounts, which affect the book value of the liability.
- While the straight-line method may be simpler, the preferred method according to GAAP for amortizing bond premiums and discounts is the effective interest method.

LO6 **Appendix 10B: Describe the accounting for leases. (p. 496)**

- Leases are categorized as either finance leases or operating leases based on five criteria.
- Effective for fiscal years beginning after December 15, 2019, all leases require the lessee to record the leased asset (Right-of-Use Asset) and a corresponding lease liability on the balance sheet.

SUMMARY	Concept ⟶	Method ⟶	Assessment
TAKEAWAY 10.1	Does the company have any contingent liabilities?	Notes to the financial statements Read the notes to the financial statements to identify contingent liabilities	Consider the likely outcome and size of contingent liabilities. If significant, consider these items in the analysis of the firm's liabilities.
TAKEAWAY 10.2	Can a firm pay its current liabilities?	Current assets, Quick assets, Current liabilities $\text{Current ratio} = \dfrac{\text{Current assets}}{\text{Current liabilities}}$ $\text{Quick ratio} = \dfrac{\text{Quick assets}}{\text{Current liabilities}}$	A higher current ratio and quick ratio indicate that a firm can readily pay its current liabilities.
TAKEAWAY 10.3	Can a firm pay its current periodic interest payments?	Income before income taxes and interest expense, Interest expense Times-interest-earned ratio $= \dfrac{\text{Income before income taxes and interest expense}}{\text{Interest expense}}$	A higher times-interest-earned ratio indicates that a firm will have less difficulty paying its current interest expense.

KEY TERMS

Bond (p. 470)

Callable bonds (p. 472)

Contingent liabilities (p. 480)

Convertible bonds (p. 472)

Coupon rate (p. 473)

Credit guarantee (p. 483)

Current liabilities (p. 464)

Current ratio (p. 484)

Debenture bonds (p. 472)

Effective interest
  method (p. 477, 490, 492)

Effective interest rate (p. 474,
  490)

Finance lease (p. 496)

Gross pay (p. 467)

High-yield bonds (p. 472)

Lease (p. 496)

Leasehold (p. 496)

Lessee (p. 496)

Lessor (p. 496)

Leverage (p. 479)

Liabilities (p. 464)

Market rate of interest (Real
  rate of interest; effective
  yield rate) (p. 473)

Maturity date (p. 465)

Maturity value (p. 472)

Net pay (p. 467)

Off-balance sheet
  financing (p. 496)

Operating lease (p. 496)

Product warranties (p. 481)

Quick ratio (p. 485)

Secured bonds (p. 471)

Serial bonds (p. 472)

Sinking fund bonds (p. 472)

Straight-line interest
  method (p. 477, 488)

Term loan (p. 470)

Times-interest-earned
  ratio (p. 485)

Working capital (p. 484)

Zero-coupon bonds (p. 477)

Assignments with the ⓂⒷⒸ logo in the margin are available in ᵐʸBusinessCourse.
See the Preface of the book for details.

SELF-STUDY QUESTIONS

(Answers to the Self-Study Questions are available at the end of this chapter.)

1. **Goldsteen Corporation obtained a $5,000 loan from a bank on April 1. If the bank charges eight percent interest annually, how much interest will be accrued at December 31?**   **LO1**
   - *a.* $400
   - *b.* $300
   - *c.* $275
   - *d.* $250

2. **Wong, Inc., sold merchandise on account for $1,840, which is subject to a ten percent excise tax and a five percent sales tax. What would the entry to record this sale include?**   **LO1**
   - *a.* A debit of $1,600 to Accounts Receivable
   - *b.* A debit of $2,116 to Accounts Receivable
   - *c.* A credit of $1,600 to Sales
   - *d.* A debit of $1,840 to Sales

3. **Jansen Company sells a product for $400 per unit, which includes a 30-day warranty against product defects. Experience indicates that four percent of the units sold will prove defective, requiring an average repair cost of $50 per unit. During the first month of business, product sales were $320,000, and 20 of the units sold were found to be defective and repaired during the month. What is the accrued liability for product warranties at month-end?**   **LO3**
   - *a.* $1,000
   - *b.* $600
   - *c.* $1,600
   - *d.* $2,000

4. **Which of the following payroll-related taxes are not withheld from an employee's earnings?**   **LO1**
   - *a.* Medicare taxes
   - *b.* Income taxes
   - *c.* Federal unemployment taxes
   - *d.* Social Security taxes

5. **Which of the following is *not* considered to be a contingent liability?**   **LO3**
   - *a.* Environmental cleanup costs
   - *b.* Notes payable
   - *c.* Credit guarantees
   - *d.* Lawsuit

LO5
(Appendix 10A)

6. On May 1, 2019, a firm issued $400,000 of 12-year, nine percent bonds payable at 96 1/2 plus accrued interest. The bonds are dated January 1, and interest is payable on January 1 and July 1 of each year. The amount the firm receives on May 1 from the sale of the bonds (see Appendix 10A) is:
   a. $386,000.
   b. $422,000.
   c. $392,000.
   d. $398,000.

LO5
(Appendix 10A)

7. A firm issued $250,000 of ten-year, 12 percent bonds payable on January 1, for $281,180, yielding an effective rate of ten percent. Interest is payable on January 1 and July 1 each year. The firm records amortization on each interest date. Bond interest expense for the first six months using effective interest amortization (see Appendix 10A) is:
   a. $15,000.
   b. $16,871.
   c. $14,059.
   d. $14,331.

LO2

8. In financial statement presentations, the Discount on Bonds Payable account is:
   a. Added to Bond Interest Expense.
   b. Deducted from Bonds Payable.
   c. Added to Bonds Payable.
   d. Deducted from Bond Interest Expense.

LO6
(Appendix 10B)

9. An example of off-balance-sheet financing is a(n):
   a. Term loan.
   b. Operating lease.
   c. Zero-coupon bond.
   d. Capital lease.

LO4

10. Apolo Company reported year-end current assets of $75,000 and current liabilities of $25,000. The company's current ratio is:
   a. 1/3   c. 4
   b. 3   d. $50,000

LO4

11. Cristo Company reported net income of $50,000 after subtracting $10,000 for interest expense and $20,000 for taxes. Compute the company's times-interest-earned ratio:
   a. 2.5   c. 8
   b. 5   d. 3

QUESTIONS

1. For accounting purposes, how are liabilities defined?

2. At what amount are current liabilities presented on the balance sheet?

3. What does the term *current liabilities* mean?

4. What formula should Hardy Company use to calculate the total amount of interest on a note payable that uses add-on interest?

5. Gordon Company signed a note payable on November 20. Gordon has a December 31 year-end. It paid the note, including interest, on the maturity date, February 20. What accounts did Gordon debit and what account did it credit on February 20?

6. Jack Swanson gave a creditor a 90-day, eight percent note payable for $7,200 on December 16. What adjusting entry should Swanson make on December 31?

7. What are two examples of voluntary deductions from an employee's gross pay?

8. On whom is the FICA tax levied? What does the FICA tax finance?

9. What is the difference between accounting for product warranties on (a) failed units repaired in the month of sale and (b) failed units repaired in a subsequent month but that are still covered by warranty?

AMERICAN
PAGING, INC.

10. **American Paging, Inc.,** is the seventh largest paging company in the United States. In a recent balance sheet, it reported a current liability of $8,452,379 that was labeled Unearned Revenues and Deposits. A note to the financial statements explained:

Unearned revenues and deposits primarily represent monthly charges to customers for radio paging rental and dispatch billed in advance. Such revenues and deposits are recognized in the following month when service is provided or are applied against the customer's final bill or last month's rent.

What basic principle of accounting guides American Paging's handling of its unearned revenues and deposits?

11. What do the following terms mean? (a) term loan, (b) bonds payable, (c) trustee, (d) secured bonds, (e) serial bonds, (f) call provision, (g) convertible bonds, (h) face value, (i) coupon rate, (j) bond discount, (k) bond premium, and (l) amortization of bond premium or discount.

12. What are the advantages and disadvantages of issuing bonds rather than common stock?

13. A $3,000,000 issue of ten-year, nine percent bonds was sold at 98 plus accrued interest three months after the bonds were dated. What net amount of cash is received when the bonds are sold?

14. If the effective interest amortization method is used for bonds payable, how does the periodic interest expense change over the life of the bonds when they are issued (a) at a discount and (b) at a premium?

15. On April 30, one year before maturity, Eastern Company retired $200,000 of nine percent bonds payable at 101. The book value of the bonds on April 30 was $197,600. Bond interest was last paid on April 30. What is the gain or loss on the retirement of the bonds?

16. What are *contingent liabilities*? List three examples of contingent liabilities. When should contingent liabilities be recorded in the accounts?

17. What is the difference between an operating lease and a finance lease?

18. Define the terms *current ratio* and *quick ratio*. What does each ratio tell us?

19. Define the times-interest-earned ratio and explain how it is used.

SHORT EXERCISES

SE10-1.   Contingent Liabilities The CEO of Evans & Sons, Inc., negotiated with its principal supplier of raw materials to purchase 10,000 units for a total price of $100,000. The units are to be delivered in 90 days. The CEO is uncertain whether she should record the purchase commitment on the company's balance sheet as a liability or not. She asks for your advice. What would you advise her?   **LO3**

SE10-2.   Determining Bond Premium or Discount Evans & Sons, Inc., decides to sell $1,000,000 in bonds to finance the construction of a new warehouse. The bonds will carry an annual coupon rate of interest of three percent, to be paid semiannually, and will mature in five years. (a) If the market rate of interest at the time of issuance is five percent, will the bonds sell at their face value, a discount, or a premium? (b) If the market rate of interest at the time of issuance is three percent, will the bonds sell at their face value, a discount, or a premium? (c) If the market rate of interest at the time of issuance is two percent, will the bonds sell at their face value, a discount, or a premium?   **LO2**

SE10-3.   Contingent Liabilities Evans & Sons, Inc., received notification from a local attorney that the company was being sued for $5,000,000 for patent infringement. A review of the situation by the company's CEO led to the conclusion that Evans & Sons had indeed infringed upon the other company's patented product. Nonetheless, the CEO thought the amount of $5,000,000 was excessive and intended to litigate the issue. How should the lawsuit be reported in Evans & Sons' annual report?   **LO3**

SE10-4.   Operating and Capital Leases The CEO of Evans & Sons, Inc., was considering a lease for a new administrative headquarters building. The building was old, but was very well located near the company's principal customers. The leasing agent estimated that the building's remaining useful life was ten years, and at the end of its useful life, the building would probably be worth $100,000. The proposed lease term was eight years, and as an inducement to Smith & Sons' CEO to sign the lease, the leasing agent indicated a willingness to include a statement in the lease agreement that would allow Smith & Sons to buy the building at the end of the lease for only $75,000. As the CEO considered whether or not to sign the lease, she wondered whether the lease could be accounted for as a finance lease or an operating lease. What would you advise her?   **LO6**
(Appendix 10B)

The following information relates to SE10-5 through SE10-7:

EVANS & SONS, INC.
Income Statement
For Years Ended December 31, 2019 and 2018

(in millions)	2019	2018
Net sales.	$ 9,800	$ 9,300
Cost of goods sold	(5,500)	(5,200)
Gross profit.	4,300	4,100
Selling and administrative expenses	(2,800)	(2,700)
Income from operations	1,500	1,400
Interest expense.	(300)	(250)
Income before income taxes	1,200	1,150
Income tax expense	(220)	(200)
Net income	$ 980	$ 950

EVANS & SONS, INC.
Balance Sheet
December 31, 2019 and 2018

(in millions)	2019	2018
Assets		
Current assets		
Cash and cash equivalents	$ 100	$ 300
Accounts receivable	900	800
Inventory.	500	650
Other current assets.	400	250
Total current assets	1,900	2,000
Property, plant, & equipment (net)	2,600	2,500
Other assets.	5,700	5,900
Total Assets	$10,200	$10,400
Liabilities and Stockholders' Equity		
Current liabilities.	$ 3,000	$ 2,900
Long-term liabilities.	5,000	5,400
Total liabilities	8,000	8,300
Stockholders' equity – common	2,200	2,100
Total Liabilities and Stockholders' Equity	$10,200	$10,400

LO4 **SE10-5.** **Current Ratio** Calculate the current ratio for Evans & Sons, Inc., for 2018 and 2019, and comment on the company's working capital position. Did the company's ability to pay its current liabilities improve over the two years?

LO4 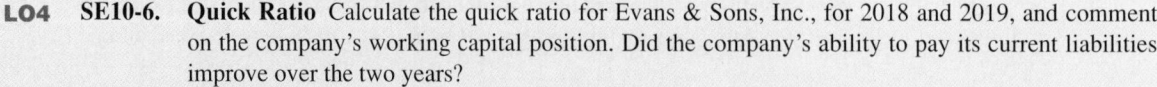 **SE10-6.** **Quick Ratio** Calculate the quick ratio for Evans & Sons, Inc., for 2018 and 2019, and comment on the company's working capital position. Did the company's ability to pay its current liabilities improve over the two years?

LO4 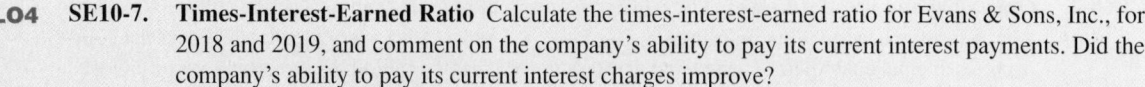 **SE10-7.** **Times-Interest-Earned Ratio** Calculate the times-interest-earned ratio for Evans & Sons, Inc., for 2018 and 2019, and comment on the company's ability to pay its current interest payments. Did the company's ability to pay its current interest charges improve?

LO2 **SE10-8.** **Premium and Discount of a Bond or Debenture** Evans & Sons, Inc. reported the following borrowings in a prior annual report:

	Borrowing ($ in millions)	Amount	Effective Interest Rate (%)
a.	4.00 percent, zero-coupon bond, due 2020	$202	4.00
b.	4.80 percent debentures, due 2033	500	5.00
c.	3.80 percent debentures, due 2017	500	3.95
d.	6.95 percent bonds, due 2025	293	6.85

For each borrowing, indicate whether the bond or debenture was originally sold at its face value, a discount, or a premium.

SE10-9. **Bond Interest Expense** Evans & Sons, Inc., sold $100,000 face value, six percent coupon rate, four-year bonds, for an aggregate issue price of $95,000. Calculate the total interest expense to be recorded by the company over the four-year life of the bonds.   **LO2**

SE10-10. **Bond Interest Expense** During 2019, Evans & Sons, Inc., issued $400 million of zero-coupon bonds, due in 2026. The proceeds from the bond issuance were $184.2 million. Calculate the total interest expense that the company will incur over the life of the bonds.   **LO2**

EXERCISES—SET A

E10-1A. **Liabilities on the Balance Sheet** For each of the following situations, indicate the amount shown as a liability on the balance sheet of Cooper, Inc., at December 31:   **LO1, 3**

    a. Cooper has accounts payable of $120,000 for merchandise included in the year-end inventory.

    b. Cooper agreed to purchase a $30,000 drill press in the following January.

    c. During November and December of the current year, Cooper sold products to a firm and guaranteed them against product failure for 90 days. Estimated costs of honoring this provision next year are $2,200.

    d. On December 15, Cooper declared a $60,000 cash dividend payable on January 15 of the following year to shareholders of record on December 31.

    e. Cooper provides a profit-sharing bonus for its executives equal to five percent of the reported before-tax income for the current year. The estimated before-tax income for the current year is $800,000.

E10-2A. **Maturity Dates of Notes Payable** Determine the maturity date and compute the interest for each of the following notes payable with add-on interest: **LO1**

	Date of Note	Principal	Interest Rate (%)	Term
a.	August 5	$20,000	9	120 days
b.	May 10	8,400	7	90 days
c.	October 5	12,000	6	45 days
d.	July 6	6,000	10	60 days
e.	September 15	12,000	8	75 days

E10-3A. **Accrued Interest Payable** Compute the interest accrued on each of the following notes payable owed by Northland, Inc., on December 31:   **LO1**

Lender	Date of Note	Principal	Interest Rate (%)	Term
Maple	11/21	$18,000	10	120 days
Wyman	12/13	5,000	8	90 days
Nahn	12/10	16,000	12	60 days

LO1 **E10-4A.** **Adjusting Entries for Interest** The following note transactions occurred during the year for Towne Company:

Nov. 25 Towne issued a 90-day, nine percent note payable for $8,000 to Hyatt Company for merchandise.
Dec. 7 Towne signed a 120-day, $30,000 note at the bank at ten percent.
22 Towne gave Barr, Inc., a $12,000, four percent, 60-day note in payment of account.

Prepare the general journal entries necessary to adjust the interest accounts at December 31.

LO1 **E10-5A.** **Excise and Sales Tax Calculations** Clifford Company has just billed a customer for $1,100, an amount that includes an eight percent excise tax and a two percent state sales tax.

a. What amount of revenue is recorded?
b. Prepare a general journal entry to record the transaction on the books of Clifford Company.

LO1 **E10-6A.** **Advance Payments for Goods** The Petaluma Daily Times Corporation (CDT) publishes a daily newspaper. A 52-week subscription sells for $260. Assume that CDT sells 100 subscriptions on January 1. None of the subscriptions are cancelled as of March 31.

a. Prepare a journal entry to record the receipt of the subscriptions on January 1.
b. Prepare a journal entry to record one week of earned revenue on March 25.

LO3 **E10-7A.** **Warranty Costs** Zealand Company sells a motor that carries a 3-month unconditional warranty against product failure. Based on a reliable statistical analysis, Milford knows that between the sale and the end of the product warranty period, four percent of the units sold will require repair at an average cost of $60 per unit. The following data reflect Milford's recent experience:

	October	November	December	Dec. 31 Total
Units sold	23,000	22,000	25,000	70,000
Known product failures from sales in:				
October...........................	120	180	160	460
November..........................		130	220	350
December..........................			210	210

Calculate, and prepare a journal entry to record, the estimated liability for product warranties at December 31. Assume that warranty costs of known failures have already been reflected in the records.

LO2 **E10-8A.** **Financial Statement Presentation of Bond Accounts** Indicate the proper financial statement classification for each of the following accounts:

Gain on Bond Retirement (material amount)
Discount on Long-term Bonds Payable
Mortgage Notes Payable
Long-term Bonds Payable
Bond Interest Expense
Bond Interest Payable
Premium on Long-term Bonds Payable

LO2 **E10-9A.** **Early Retirement of Bonds** Eaton Company issued $600,000 of eight percent, 20-year bonds at 106 on January 1, 2013. Interest is payable semiannually on July 1 and January 1. Through January 1, 2019, Eaton amortized $5,000 of the bond premium. On January 1, 2019, Eaton retired the bonds at 103 (after making the interest payment on that date). Prepare the journal entry to record the bond retirement on January 1, 2019.

LO2 **E10-10A.** **Installment Term Loan** On December 31, 2017, Eppel, Inc. borrowed $900,000 on an eight percent, 15-year mortgage note payable. The note is to be repaid in equal semiannual installments of $52,047 (payable on June 30 and December 31). Prepare journal entries to reflect (a) the issuance of the mortgage note payable, (b) the payment of the first installment on June 30, 2018, and (c) the payment of the second installment on December 31, 2018. Round amounts to the nearest dollar.

LO2 **E10-11A.** **Installment Term Loan** On December 31, 2016, Clarke, Inc. borrowed $900,000 on a seven percent, 10-year mortgage note payable. The note is to be repaid in equal annual installments of $128,140 (payable on December 31). Prepare journal entries to reflect (a) the issuance of the mortgage note payable, (b) the payment of the first installment on December 31, 2017, and (c) the payment of the second installment on December 31, 2018. Round amounts to the nearest dollar.

E10-12A. Contingent Liabilities Determine which of the following transactions represent contingent liabilities for Sawyer Rental and indicate the proper accounting treatment at the company's fiscal year-end, by placing the letter of the correct accounting treatment in the space provided.

LO3

a. Accrue a liability and disclose in the financial statement notes
b. Disclose in the financial statement footnotes only
c. No disclosure

1. Sawyer Rental cosigned a loan for $75,000 due in one year for Wyler Company. Wyler is a very profitable company and is very liquid, making it a remote chance Sawyer will have to pay the loan.	
2. One of Sawyer's rental tents collapsed at a wedding and injured the bride and groom. Sawyer's legal counsel believes it is probable that Sawyer will have to pay damages of $400,000.	
3. Sawyer Rental is being audited by the Internal Revenue Service. Its tax returns for the past two years are being examined. At the company's year-end, the audit is still in process. Sawyer's CPA believes that payment of significant taxes is possible.	

E10-13A. Ratio Analysis Presented below are summary financial data from Porter's annual report:

LO4

Amounts in millions	
Balance sheet	
Cash and cash equivalents	$ 1,850
Marketable securities	19,100
Accounts receivable (net)	9,367
Total current assets	39,088
Total assets	123,078
Current liabilities	38,450
Long-term debt	7,279
Shareholders' equity	68,278
Income Statement	
Interest expense	400
Net income before taxes	14,007

Calculate the following ratios:
a. Times-interest-earned ratio
b. Quick ratio
c. Current ratio

E10-14A. Issue Price of a Bond Matt Enterprises issued $200,000 of ten percent, five-year bonds with interest payable semiannually. Determine the issue price if the bonds are priced to yield (a) ten percent, (b) six percent, and (c) 12 percent.

LO2, 5
(Appendix 10A)

E10-15A. Issue Price of a Bond Abbott, Inc., plans to issue $500,000 of ten percent bonds that will pay interest semiannually and mature in five years. Assume that the effective interest rate is 12 percent per year compounded semiannually. Calculate the selling price of the bonds.

LO2, 5
(Appendix 10A)

E10-16A. Bonds Payable Journal Entries; Straight-Line Interest Amortization On December 31, 2017, Brown Company issued $750,000 of 20-year, eight percent bonds payable for $621,307, yielding an effective interest rate of ten percent. Interest is payable semiannually on June 30 and December 31. Prepare journal entries to reflect (a) the issuance of the bonds, (b) the semiannual interest payment and discount amortization (straight-line interest method) on June 30, 2018, and (c) the semiannual interest payment and discount amortization on December 31, 2018. Round amounts to the nearest dollar.

LO2, 5
(Appendix 10A)

E10-17A. Bonds Payable Journal Entries; Straight-Line Interest Amortization On December 31, 2017, Shade Company issued $250,000 of 20-year, eight percent bonds payable for $276,694, yielding an effective interest rate of seven percent. Interest is payable semiannually on June 30 and December 31. Prepare journal entries to reflect (a) the issuance of the bonds, (b) the semiannual interest payment and premium amortization (straight-line interest method) on June 30, 2018, and (c) the semiannual interest payment and premium amortization on December 31, 2018. Round amounts to the nearest dollar.

LO2, 5
(Appendix 10A)

LO2, 5
(Appendix 10A)

E10-18A. **Bonds Payable Journal Entries; Effective Interest Amortization** On December 31, 2017, Phillip Company issued $600,000 of ten-year, nine percent bonds payable for $496,771, yielding an effective interest rate of twelve percent. Interest is payable semiannually on June 30 and December 31. Prepare journal entries to reflect (a) the issuance of the bonds, (b) the semiannual interest payment and discount amortization (effective interest method) on June 30, 2018, and (c) the semiannual interest payment and discount amortization on December 31, 2018. Round amounts to the nearest dollar.

LO2, 5
(Appendix 10A)

E10-19A. **Bonds Payable Journal Entries; Effective Interest Amortization** On December 31, 2017, Karen Company issued $400,000 of 10-year, ten percent bonds payable for $454,361, yielding an effective interest rate of eight percent. Interest is payable semiannually on June 30 and December 31. Prepare journal entries to reflect (a) the issuance of the bonds, (b) the semiannual interest payment and premium amortization (effective interest method) on June 30, 2018, and (c) the semiannual interest payment and premium amortization on December 31, 2018. Round amounts to the nearest dollar.

LO6
(Appendix 10B)

E10-20A. **Leases** On January 1, Lorraine, Inc., entered into a lease contract. The lease contract was a ten-year lease for a computer with $15,000 annual lease payments due at the end of each year. Lorraine took possession of the computer on January 1. The present value of the lease payments under the lease contract is $108,703.

The lease contract is a finance lease. Prepare the journal entry for this lease on January 1.

LO2

E10-21A. **Coupon Rates, Yield Rates, and Bond Issuance Prices** The relation between a bond's coupon rate and yield rate is known to influence a bond's issuance price. Presented below are coupon rates and yield rates for a selection of corporate bonds. Identity whether each bond was sold at a discount, at its par value, or at a premium, and explain why.

Bond	Coupon Rate	Yield Rate
A.........................	7.5%	7.55%
B.........................	8.1	8.00
C.........................	6.0	6.00
D.........................	4.5	4.40
E.........................	9.0	9.15

EXERCISES—SET B

LO1

E10-1B. **Liabilities on the Balance Sheet** For each of the following situations, indicate the amount shown as a liability on the balance sheet of Anchor, Inc., at December 31:

a. Javier's general ledger shows a credit balance of $130,000 in Long-Term Notes Payable. Of this amount, a $30,000 installment becomes due on June 30 of the following year.

b. Javier estimates its unpaid income tax liability for the current year is $34,000; it plans to pay this amount in March of the following year.

c. On December 31, Javier received a $30,000 invoice for merchandise shipped on December 28. The merchandise has not yet been received. The merchandise was shipped F.O.B. shipping point.

d. During the year, Javier collected $10,500 of state sales tax. At year-end, it has not yet remitted $1,400 of these taxes to the state department of revenue.

e. On December 31, Javier's bank approved a $10,000, 90-day loan. Javier plans to sign the note and receive the money on January 2 of the following year.

LO1

E10-2B. **Maturity Dates of Notes Payable** Determine the maturity date and compute the interest for each of the following notes payable written in 2018:

	Date of Note	Principal	Interest Rate (%)	Term
a.	July 10	$ 8,400	9	90 days
b.	April 4	6,000	8	120 days
c.	May 19	5,600	7 ½	180 days
d.	June 10......................................	6,500	8	45 days
e.	October 29	10,000	3	60 days

E10-3B. **Accrued Interest Payable** Compute the interest accrued on each of the following notes payable **LO1**
owed by Galloway, Inc., on December 31:

Lender	Date of Note	Principal	Interest Rate (%)	Term
Barton.........................	12/4	$12,000	12	150 days
Lawson........................	12/13	14,000	10	90 days
Riley	12/19	15,000	11	90 days

E10-4B. **Adjusting Entries for Interest** The following note transactions occurred during the year for Zale **LO1**
Company:

Nov. 25 Zale issued a 120-day, 12 percent note payable for $9,000 to Porter Company for
merchandise.

Dec. 10 Zale's signed a 180-day, $7,200 note at the bank at ten percent.

23 Zale's gave Dale, Inc., a $9,000, six percent, 60-day note in payment of account.

Prepare the journal entries necessary to adjust the interest accounts at December 31.

E10-5B. **Excise and Sales Tax Calculations** Beck Company has just billed a customer for $1,400, an **LO1**
amount that includes an eight percent excise tax and a four percent state sales tax.

a. What amount of revenue is recorded?

b. Prepare a journal entry to record the transaction on the books of Beck Company.

E10-6B. **Advance Payment for Services** The Whitney Bluebirds football team sells a 15-game season ticket **LO1**
for $180. Assume that the team sells 2,000 season tickets on August 10. The tickets are all used for
admission.

a. Prepare a journal entry to record the sale of the season tickets on August 10.

b. Prepare a journal entry to record one game of earned revenue on September 12.

E10-7B. **Warranty Costs** Young Company sells an electric timer that carries a 3-month unconditional war- **LO3**
ranty against product failure. Based on a reliable statistical analysis, Young knows that between the
sale and the end of the product warranty period, four percent of the units sold will require repair at
an average cost of $50 per unit. The following data reflect Young's recent experience:

	October	November	December	Dec. 31 Total
Units sold	36,000	34,000	45,000	115,000
Known product failures from sales in:				
October........................	320	550	210	1,080
November......................		230	360	590
December......................			410	410

Calculate, and prepare a journal entry to record, the estimated liability for product warranties at December 31. Assume that warranty costs of known failures have already been reflected in the records.

E10-8B. **Bonds Payable on the Balance Sheet** The adjusted trial balance for the Mammoth Corporation at **LO2**
the end of 2018 contains the following accounts:

Bond interest payable...	$ 40,000
9% Bonds payable due 2020	600,000
10% Bonds payable due 2019	500,000
Discount on 9% bonds payable	19,000
Premium on 10% bonds payable	15,000
Zero coupon bonds payable due 2021......................................	170,500
8% Bonds payable due 2023	200,000

Prepare the long-term liabilities section of the balance sheet. Indicate the balance sheet classification
for any accounts listed above that do not belong in the long-term liabilities section.

E10-9B. **Early Retirement of Bonds** Navarro, Inc., issued $250,000 of eight percent, 20-year bonds at 98 **LO2**
on June 30, 2012. Interest is payable semiannually on December 31 and June 30. Through June 30,

2018, Navarro amortized $3,000 of the bond discount. On June 30, 2018, Navarro retired the bonds at 102 (after making the interest payment on that date). Prepare the journal entry to record the bond retirement on June 30, 2018.

LO2   **E10-10B. Installment Term Loan** On December 31, 2017, James, Inc., borrowed $500,000 on an eight percent, ten-year mortgage note payable. The note is to be repaid in equal quarterly installments of $18,278 (beginning March 31, 2018). Prepare journal entries to reflect (a) the issuance of the mortgage note payable, (b) the payment of the first installment on March 31, 2018, and (c) the payment of the second installment on June 30, 2018. Round amounts to the nearest dollar.

LO2   **E10-11B. Installment Term Loan** On December 31, 2017, James, Inc., borrowed $300,000 on a six percent, 20-year mortgage note payable. The note is to be repaid in equal semiannual installments of $12,979 (beginning July 1, 2018). Prepare journal entries to reflect (a) the issuance of the mortgage note payable, (b) the payment of the first installment on July 1, 2018, and (c) the payment of the second installment on December 31, 2018. Round amounts to the nearest dollar.

LO3   **E10-12B. Contingent Liabilities** Determine which of the following transactions represent contingent liabilities for June Leasing and indicate the proper accounting treatment at the company's fiscal year-end, by placing the letter of the correct accounting treatment in the space provided.

a.   Accrue a liability and disclose in the financial statement notes
b.   Disclose in the financial statement footnotes only
c.   No disclosure

1. June Leasing was sued by a customer who claimed the equipment they leased was not up to the standards described by June. June stands by its claims and can support all the item's specifications. June plans to vigorously defend itself and believes the chances of losing the lawsuit are remote.	
2. A government audit of June found that the company is in violation of several work safety regulations. June has been notified that it will be assessed a fine of $25,000. June has agreed to make the safety changes so that it will be in compliance with the regulations.	
3. June Leasing has been served a lawsuit by a customer that claims he was injured from one of the products leased from June. June plans to defend itself in court, but its lawyers believe there is a 50/50 chance that they will lose and be forced to pay $50,000.	

LO4   **E10-13B. Ratio Analysis** Presented below are summary financial data from the Smith Co. annual report:

Amounts in millions	
Balance sheet	
Cash and cash equivalents	$ 2,200
Marketable securities	16,200
Accounts receivable (net)	10,000
Total current assets	42,000
Total assets	155,000
Current liabilities	25,000
Long-term debt	52,500
Shareholders' equity	79,500
Income Statement	
Interest expense	6,400
Net income before taxes	37,800

Calculate the following ratios:

a.   Times-interest-earned ratio
b.   Quick ratio
c.   Current ratio

LO2, 5
(Appendix 10A)   **E10-14B. Issue Price of a Bond** May Enterprises issued $200,000 of six percent, five-year bonds with interest payable semiannually. Determine the issue price if the bonds are priced to yield (a) six percent, (b) ten percent, and (c) two percent.

E10-15B. Issue Price of a Bond Atlantic, Inc., plans to issue $700,000 of nine percent bonds that will pay interest semiannually and mature in ten years. Assume that the effective interest is eight percent per year compounded semiannually. Calculate the selling price of the bonds.

LO2, 5
(Appendix 10A)

E10-16B. Bonds Payable Journal Entries; Straight-Line Interest Amortization On December 31, 2017, Green Company issued $600,000 of 15-year, ten percent bonds payable for $517,411, yielding an effective interest rate of 12 percent. Interest is payable semiannually on June 30 and December 31. Prepare journal entries to reflect (a) the issuance of the bonds, (b) the semiannual interest payment and discount amortization (straight-line interest method) on June 30, 2018, and (c) the semiannual interest payment and discount amortization on December 31, 2018. Round amounts to the nearest dollar.

LO2, 5
(Appendix 10A)

E10-17B. Bonds Payable Journal Entries; Straight-Line Interest Amortization On December 31, 2017, Tan Company issued $400,000 of ten-year, 12 percent bonds payable for $449,849, yielding an effective interest rate of ten percent. Interest is payable semiannually on June 30 and December 31. Prepare journal entries to reflect (a) the issuance of the bonds, (b) the semiannual interest payment and premium amortization (straight-line interest method) on June 30, 2018, and (c) the semiannual interest payment and premium amortization on December 31, 2018. Round amounts to the nearest dollar.

LO2, 5
(Appendix 10A)

E10-18B. Bonds Payable Journal Entries; Effective Interest Amortization On December 31, 2017, Blair Company issued $600,000 of 20-year, 11 percent bonds payable for $554,861, yielding an effective interest rate of 12 percent. Interest is payable semiannually on June 30 and December 31. Prepare journal entries to reflect (a) the issuance of the bonds, (b) the semiannual interest payment and discount amortization (effective interest method) on June 30, 2018, and (c) the semiannual interest payment and discount amortization on December 31, 2018. Round amounts to the nearest dollar.

LO2, 5
(Appendix 10A)

E10-19B. Bonds Payable Journal Entries; Effective Interest Amortization On December 31, 2017, Kim Company issued $500,000 of five-year, 12 percent bonds payable for $538,609, yielding an effective interest rate of ten percent. Interest is payable semiannually on June 30 and December 31. Prepare journal entries to reflect (a) the issuance of the bonds, (b) the semiannual interest payment and premium amortization (effective interest method) on June 30, 2018, and (c) the semiannual interest payment and premium amortization on December 31, 2018. Round amounts to the nearest dollar.

LO2, 5
(Appendix 10A)

E10-20B. Leases On January 1, Cheryl, Inc., entered into a lease contract. The lease contract was an eight-year lease for a sound system with $28,000 annual lease payments due at the end of each year. Cheryl took possession of the sound system on January 1. The present value of the lease payments under the lease contract is $173,778.

The lease contract is a finance lease. Prepare the journal entry for this lease on January 1.

LO6
(Appendix 10B)

E10-21B. Coupon Rates, Yield Rates, and Bond Issuance Prices The relation between a bond's coupon rate and yield rate is known to influence a bond's issuance price. Presented below are coupon rates and yield rates for a selection of corporate bonds. Identity whether each bond was sold at a discount, at its par value, or at a premium, and explain why.

LO2

Bond	Coupon Rate	Yield Rate
A.	7.5%	7.45%
B.	8.1	8.40
C.	6.0	5.80
D.	4.4	4.40
E.	8.9	9.10

PROBLEMS—SET A

P10-1A. Journal Entries for Accounts and Notes Payable Lyon Company had the following transactions:

LO1

Apr.	8	Issued a 6,000, 60-day, six percent note payable in payment of an account with Bennett Company.
May	15	Borrowed $40,000 from Lincoln Bank, signing a 60-day note at nine percent.
June	7	Paid Bennett Company the principal and interest due on the April 8 note payable.
July	6	Purchased $14,000 of merchandise from Bolton Company; signed a 90-day note with ten percent interest.
July	14	Paid the May 15 note due Lincoln Bank.

Oct. 2 Borrowed $30,000 from Lincoln Bank, signing a 120-day note at nine percent.

4 Defaulted on the note payable to Bolton Company.

Required

a. Record these transactions in general journal form.

b. Record any adjusting entries for interest in general journal form. Lyon Company has a December 31 year-end.

LO1 P10-2A. Adjusting Entries for Interest At December 31, 2017, Eric Corporation had two notes payable outstanding (notes 1 and 2). At December 31, 2018, Eric also had two notes payable outstanding (notes 3 and 4). These notes are described below:

	Date of Note	Principal Amount	Interest Rate	Number of Days
December 31, 2017				
Note 1	11/16/2017	$30,000	8%	120
Note 2	12/4/2017	16,000	9	60
December 31, 2018				
Note 3	12/7/2018	9,000	10	60
Note 4	12/21/2018	18,000	12	30

Required

a. Prepare the adjusting entries for interest at December 31, 2017.

b. Assume that the adjusting entries were made at December 31, 2017. Prepare the 2018 journal entries to record payment of the notes that were outstanding at December 31, 2017.

c. Prepare the adjusting entries for interest at December 31, 2018.

LO1 P10-3A. Recording Payroll and Payroll Taxes Ruth Corporation had the following payroll for April:

Officers' salaries	$36,000
Sales salaries	67,000
Federal income taxes withheld	19,000
FICA taxes withheld	7,500
Health insurance premiums withheld	1,800
Union dues withheld	1,400
Salaries (included above) subject to federal unemployment taxes	55,000
Salaries (included above) subject to state unemployment taxes	58,000

Required

Prepare journal entries on April 30 to record:

a. Accrual of the monthly payroll.

b. Payment of the net payroll.

c. Accrual of employer's payroll taxes. (Assume that the FICA tax matches the amount withheld, the federal unemployment tax is 0.6 percent, and the state unemployment tax is 5.4 percent.)

d. Payment of all liabilities related to this payroll. (Assume that all are settled at the same time.)

LO1 P10-4A. Recording Payroll and Payroll Taxes The following data are taken from Stockton Wholesale Company's May payroll:

Administrative salaries	$50,000
Sales salaries	51,000
Custodial salaries	7,000
Total payroll	$108,000
Salaries subject to 1.45 percent Medicare tax	$108,000
Salaries subject to 6.2 percent Social Security tax	85,000
Salaries subject to federal unemployment taxes	14,000
Salaries subject to state unemployment taxes	21,000
Federal income taxes withheld from all salaries	17,800

Assume that the company is subject to a two percent state unemployment tax (due to a favorable experience rating) and a 0.6 percent federal unemployment tax.

Required
Record the following in general journal form on May 31:

a. Accrual of the monthly payroll.

b. Payment of the net payroll.

c. Accrual of the employer's payroll taxes. (Assume that the FICA tax matches the amount withheld).

d. Payment of these payroll-related liabilities. (Assume that all are settled at the same time.)

P10-5A.   **Excise and Sales Tax Calculations**   Fullerton Corporation initially records its sales at amounts that exclude any related excise and sales taxes. During June, Fullerton recorded total sales of $700,000. An analysis of June sales indicated the following:

LO1

1. Thirty percent of sales were subject to both a ten percent excise tax and a six percent sales tax.
2. Fifty percent of sales were subject only to the sales tax.
3. The balance of sales was for labor charges not subject to either excise or sales tax.

Required
a. Calculate the related liabilities for excise and sales taxes for June.

b. Prepare the necessary journal entry at June 30 to record the monthly payment of excise tax and sales tax to the government.

P10-6A.   **Noncontingent and Contingent Liabilities**   The following independent situations represent various types of liabilities:

LO1, 3

1. One of the employees of Martin Company was severely injured when hit by one of Martin's trucks in the parking lot. The 35-year-old employee will never be able to work again. Insurance coverage is minimal. The employee has sued Martin Company and a jury trial is scheduled.
2. A shareholder has filed a lawsuit against Sweitzer Corporation. Sweitzer's attorneys have reviewed the facts of the case. Their review revealed that similar lawsuits have never resulted in a cash award and it is highly unlikely that this lawsuit will either.
3. Armstrong Company signed a 60-day, ten percent note when it purchased merchandise from Fischer Company.
4. Richmond Company has been notified by the Department of Environment Protection (DEP) that a state where it has a plant is filing a lawsuit for groundwater pollution against Richmond and another company that has a plant adjacent to Richmond's plant. Test results have not identified the exact source of the pollution. Richmond's manufacturing process can produce by-products that pollute ground water.
5. Fredonia Company has cosigned a note payable to a bank for one of its customers. The customer received all of the proceeds of the note. Fredonia will have to repay the loan if the customer fails to do so. Fredonia Company believes that it is unlikely that it will have to pay the note.
6. Holt Company manufactured and sold products to Z-Mart, a retailer that sold the products to consumers. The manufacturer's warranty offers replacement of the product if it is found to be defective within 90 days of the sale to the consumer. Historically, 1.2 percent of the products are returned for replacement.

Required
Prepare a multicolumn analysis that presents the following information for each of these situations:

a. Number of the situation.

b. Type of liability: (1) noncontingent or (2) contingent.

c. Accounting treatment: (1) record in accounts, (2) disclose in a note to the financial statements, or (3) neither record nor disclose.

P10-7A.   **Bonds Payable Journal Entries; Issued at Par Plus Accrued Interest**   Ashton, Inc., which closes its books on December 31, is authorized to issue $800,000 of nine percent, 20-year bonds dated May 1, with interest payments on November 1 and May 1.

LO2

Required

Prepare journal entries to record the following events, assuming that the bonds were sold at 100 plus accrued interest on October 1:

a.   The bond issuance.
b.   Payment of the first semiannual period's interest on November 1.
c.   Accrual of bond interest expense at December 31.
d.   Payment of the semiannual interest on May 1 of the following year.
e.   Retirement of $400,000 of the bonds at 101 on May 1, Year 2 (immediately after the interest payment on that date).

LO4   **P10-8A.**   **Current Ratio, Quick Ratio, and Times-Interest-Earned Ratio**   The following data are from the current accounting records of Rome Company:

Cash...	$120
Accounts receivable (net of allowance of 40)..................................	200
Inventory..	150
Other current assets...	80
Accounts payable...	110
Other current liabilities..	170

The president of the company is concerned that the company is in violation of a debt covenant that requires the company to maintain a minimum current ratio of 2.0. He believes the best way to rectify this is to reverse a bad debt write-off in the amount of $10 that the company just recorded. He argues that the write-off was done too early, and that the collections department should be given more time to collect the outstanding receivables. The CFO argues that this will have no effect on the current ratio, so a better idea is to use $10 of cash to pay accounts payable early.

Required

a.   Which idea, the president's or the CFO's, is better for attaining a minimum 2.0 current ratio?
b.   Will either the quick ratio or the times-interest-earned ratios be affected by either of these ideas?

LO5   **P10-9A.**   **Effective Interest Amortization**   On December 31, Casper, Inc., issued $300,000 of eight percent,
(Appendix 10A)   ten-year bonds for $262,613, yielding an effective interest rate of ten percent. Semiannual interest
   is payable on June 30 and December 31 each year. The firm uses the effective interest method to amortize the discount.

Required

a.   Prepare an amortization schedule showing the necessary information for the first two interest periods. Round amounts to the nearest dollar.
b.   Prepare the journal entry for the bond issuance on December 31.
c.   Prepare the journal entry to record the bond interest payment and discount amortization at June 30 of the following year.
d.   Prepare the journal entry to record the bond interest payment and discount amortization at December 31 of the following year.

LO5   **P10-10A.**   **Effective Interest Amortization**   On January 1, Lowe, Inc., issued $500,000 of ten percent, 20-year
(Appendix 10A)   bonds for $598,964, yielding an effective interest rate of eight percent. Semiannual interest is pay-
   able on June 30 and December 31 each year. The firm uses the effective interest method to amortize the premium.

Required

a.   Prepare an amortization schedule showing the necessary information for the first two interest periods. Round amounts to the nearest dollar.
b.   Prepare the journal entry for the bond issuance on January 1.
c.   Prepare the journal entry to record the bond interest payment and premium amortization at June 30.
d.   Prepare the journal entry to record the bond interest payment and premium amortization at December 31.

P10-11A. Accounting for Bonds Sold at a Discount The Biltmore National Bank raised capital through the sale of $150 million face value of eight percent coupon rate, ten-year bonds. The bonds paid interest semiannually and were sold at a time when equivalent risk-rated bonds carried a yield rate of ten percent.

LO5
(Appendix 10A)

    a. Calculate the proceeds that The Biltmore National Bank received from the sale of the eight percent bonds.

    b. Calculate the interest expense on the bonds for the first year that the bonds are outstanding.

    c. Calculate the book value of the bonds at the end of the first year.

P10-12A. Accounting for Bonds Issues at a Premium The Longo Corporation issued $50 million maturity value of six percent coupon rate bonds, with interest paid semiannually. At the time of the bond issuance, equivalent risk-rated debt instruments carried a yield rate of four percent. The bonds matured in five years.

LO5
(Appendix 10A)

    a. Calculate the proceeds that the Longo Corporation would receive from the sale of the bonds.

    b. Calculate the interest expense on the bonds for the first year.

    c. Calculate the book value of the bonds at the end of the first year.

PROBLEMS—SET B

P10-1B. Journal Entries for Accounts Payable and Notes Payable Geary Company had the following transactions:

LO1

Apr.	15	Issued a $6,000, 60-day, eight percent note payable in payment of an account with Marion Company.
May	22	Borrowed $50,000 from Sinclair Bank, signing a 60-day note at nine percent.
June	14	Paid Marion Company the principal and interest due on the April 15 note payable.
July	13	Purchased $15,000 of merchandise from Sharp Company; signed a 90-day note with eight percent interest.
	21	Paid the May 22 note due Sinclair Bank.
Oct.	2	Borrowed $38,000 from Sinclair Bank, signing a 120-day note at 12 percent.
	11	Defaulted on the note payable to Sharp Company.

Required

    a. Record these transactions in general journal form.

    b. Record any adjusting entries for interest in general journal form. Geary Company has a December 31 year-end.

P10-2B. Adjusting Entries for Interest At December 31, 2017, Seattle Corporation had two notes payable outstanding (notes 1 and 2). At December 31, 2018, Seattle also had two notes payable outstanding (notes 3 and 4). These notes are described below.

LO1

	Date of Note	Principal Amount	Interest Rate	Number of Days
December 31, 2017				
Note 1.	11/25/2017	$35,000	8%	90
Note 2.	12/16/2017	16,800	10	60
December 31, 2018				
Note 3.	12/11/2018	15,400	9	120
Note 4.	12/7/2018	20,000	12	90

Required

    a. Prepare the adjusting entries for interest at December 31, 2017.

    b. Assume that the adjusting entries were made at December 31, 2017, and that no adjusting entries were made during 2018. Prepare the 2018 journal entries to record payment of the notes that were outstanding at December 31, 2017.

    c. Prepare the adjusting entries for interest at December 31, 2018.

LO1 **P10-3B.** **Recording Payroll and Payroll Taxes** England, Inc., had the following payroll for March:

Officers' salaries	$39,000
Sales salaries	60,000
Federal income taxes withheld	21,000
FICA taxes withheld	7,900
Health insurance premiums withheld	2,500
Salaries (included above) subject to federal unemployment taxes	55,000
Salaries (included above) subject to state unemployment taxes	65,000

Required

Prepare journal entries on March 31 to record:

a. Accrual of the monthly payroll.
b. Payment of the net payroll.
c. Accrual of employer's payroll taxes. (Assume that the FICA tax matches the amount withheld, the federal unemployment tax is 0.6 percent, and the state unemployment tax is 5.4 percent.)
d. Payment of all liabilities related to this payroll. (Assume that all are settled at the same time.)

LO1 **P10-4B.** **Recording Payroll and Payroll Taxes** The following data are taken from Madison Distribution Company's March payroll:

Administrative salaries	$34,000
Sales salaries	58,000
Custodial salaries	8,000
Total payroll	$100,000
Salaries subject to 1.45 percent Medicare tax	$100,000
Salaries subject to 6.2 percent Social Security tax	100,000
Salaries subject to federal unemployment taxes	66,000
Salaries subject to state unemployment taxes	76,000
Federal income taxes withheld from all salaries	18,600

Assume that the company is subject to a 5.2 percent state unemployment tax and an 0.6 percent federal unemployment tax.

Required

Record the following in general journal form on March 31:
a. Accrual of the monthly payroll.
b. Payment of the net payroll.
c. Accrual of the employer's payroll taxes. (Assume that the FICA tax matches the amount withheld).
d. Payment of these payroll-related liabilities. (Assume that all are settled at the same time.)

LO1 **P10-5B.** **Excise and Sales Tax Calculations** Adams Corporation initially records its sales at amounts that exclude any related excise and sales taxes. During May, Adams recorded total sales of $750,000. An analysis of May sales indicated the following:

1. Thirty percent of sales were subject to both a ten percent excise tax and a five percent sales tax.
2. Sixty-five percent of sales were subject only to the sales tax.
3. The balance of sales was for labor charges not subject to either excise or sales tax.

Required

a. Calculate the related liabilities for excise and sales taxes for May.
b. Prepare the necessary journal entry at May 31, to record the monthly payment of excise tax and sales tax to the government.

LO1, 3 **P10-6B.** **Noncontingent and Contingent Liabilities** The following independent situations represent various types of liabilities:

1. Marshall Company has a manufacturing plant located in a small, rural community. The only other major employer in the area is Baker Company, which is experiencing financial problems. Marshall agrees to guarantee a loan for Baker, so Baker will remain in the community. Baker will receive all the proceeds of the loan. However, Marshall will have to repay the loan if Baker fails to do so. Marshall believes that Baker will repay the loan.

2. The village of High Creek and the town of Middlebury have been jointly using a rural dump site for 25 years. The state Department of Natural Resources has notified the two municipalities that wells on the nearby farms are polluted and that the dump site will be closed while further testing is done. Cleanup could cost as much as $25 million.

3. Two people walking on the sidewalk in front of the building owned by First United Bank were injured when part of the building collapsed on them. They are 25 years old and both are totally disabled. The building had been in poor condition for a long time. Insurance coverage is minimal. Both are suing First United Bank, and a jury trial is scheduled.

4. Winters Company sells garden tractors through 120 dealers located throughout the United States. Winters provides a two-year warranty for all parts and labor on these tractors. Each year, the average warranty cost per tractor sold is approximately $40.

5. Cronnin Company signed a 90-day note when it bought a new delivery truck for $25,000.

6. The CPA firm of Boyd and Lampe is being sued by one of the owners of an audit client that went bankrupt three years after Boyd and Lampe conducted an audit. The CPA firm has no insurance for this type of lawsuit. The attorneys for the CPA firm have stated that similar cases have never been successful, and they expect the same result here.

Required

Prepare a multicolumn analysis that presents the following information for each of these situations:

a. Number of the situation.

b. Type of liability: (1) noncontingent or (2) contingent.

c. Accounting treatment: (1) record in accounts, (2) disclose in a note to the financial statements, or (3) neither record nor disclose.

P10-7B. Bonds Payable Journal Entries; Issued at Par Plus Accrued Interest Richard, Inc., which closes its books on December 31, is authorized to issue $600,000 of six percent, 20-year bonds dated March 1, with interest payments on September 1 and March 1.

LO2

Required

Prepare journal entries to record the following events, assuming that the bonds were sold at 100 plus accrued interest on July 1.

a. The bond issuance.

b. Payment of the semiannual interest on September 1.

c. Accrual of bond interest expense at December 31.

d. Payment of the semiannual interest on March 1 of the following year.

e. Retirement of $200,000 of the bonds at 104 on March 1, Year 3 (immediately after the interest payment on that date).

P10-8B. Current Ratio, Quick Ratio, and Times-Interest-Earned Ratio The following data are from the current accounting records of Crest Company:

LO4

Cash	$240
Accounts receivable (net of allowance of 80)	400
Inventory	300
Other current assets	160
Accounts payable	220
Other current liabilities	340

The president of the company is concerned that the company may be in violation of a debt covenant that requires the company to maintain a minimum current ratio of 2.0. He believes the best way to rectify the problem is to reverse a bad debt write-off in the amount of $20 that the company just recorded. He argues that the write-off was done too early and that the collections department should be given more time to collect the outstanding amounts. The CFO argues that this will have no effect on the current ratio, so a better idea is to use $20 of cash to pay accounts payable early.

Required

a. Which idea, the president's or the CFO's, is better for attaining a minimum 2.0 current ratio?

b. Will either the quick ratio or the times-interest-earned ratios be affected by either of these ideas?

LO5
(Appendix 10A)

P10-9B.   **Effective Interest Amortization**   On December 31, 2018, Edmand, Inc., issued $750,000 of 11 percent, five-year bonds for $722,400, yielding an effective interest rate of 12 percent. Semiannual interest is payable on June 30 and December 31 each year. The firm uses the effective interest method to amortize the discount.

Required

a.   Prepare an amortization schedule showing the necessary information for the first two interest periods. Round amounts to the nearest dollar.
b.   Prepare the journal entry for the bond issuance on December 31.
c.   Prepare the journal entry to record bond interest expense and discount amortization at June 30 of the following year.
d.   Prepare the journal entry to record bond interest expense and discount amortization at December 31 of the following year.

LO5
(Appendix 10A)

P10-10B.   **Effective Interest Amortization**   On January 1, 2018, Ranier, Inc., issued $300,000 of ten percent, 15-year bonds for $351,876, yielding an effective interest rate of eight percent. Semiannual interest is payable on June 30 and December 31 each year. The firm uses the effective interest method to amortize the premium.

Required

a.   Prepare an amortization schedule showing the necessary information for the first two interest periods. Round amounts to the nearest dollar.
b.   Prepare the journal entry for the bond issuance on January 1, 2018.
c.   Prepare the journal entry to record the bond interest payment and premium amortization at June 30.
d.   Prepare the journal entry to record the bond interest payment and premium amortization at December 31.

LO5
(Appendix 10A)

P10-11B.   **Accounting for Bonds Sold at a Discount**   The Peoples National Bank raised capital through the sale of $100 million face value of four percent coupon rate, ten-year bonds. The bonds paid interest semiannually and were sold at a time when equivalent risk-rated bonds carried a yield rate of six percent.

a.   Calculate the proceeds that The Peoples National Bank received from the sale of the six percent bonds.
b.   Calculate the interest expense on the bonds for the first year that the bonds are outstanding.
c.   Calculate the book value of the bonds at the end of the first year.

LO5
(Appendix 10A)

P10-12B.   **Accounting for Bonds Issues at a Premium**   The Miller Corporation issued $100 million maturity value of six percent coupon rate bonds, with interest paid semiannually. At the time of the bond issuance, equivalent risk-rated debt instruments carried a yield rate of four percent. The bonds matured in ten years.

a.   Calculate the proceeds that the Miller Corporation would receive from the sale of the bonds.
b.   Calculate the interest expense on the bonds for the first year.
c.   Calculate the book value of the bonds at the end of the first year.

SERIAL PROBLEM: KATE'S CARDS

(Note: This is a continuation of the Serial Problem: Kate's Cards from Chapters 1 through 9.)

SP10.   Recall that Kate previously obtained a $15,000 bank loan, signing a note payable, on November 30. The note required semiannual interest payments at the rate of six percent. The entire principal balance was due two years from the origination date of the note. Kate has been accruing interest on a monthly basis in the amount of $75. Kate would like to know how she should record the interest in May, the month she makes the first interest payment. She is unsure how much expense will need to be recorded in May.

    The upcoming interest payment is really not Kate's main concern right now. She was just notified by a lawyer that she is being sued for copyright infringement. Mega Cards Incorporated, one of the largest greeting card companies, believes that one of Kate's designs is too similar to one of Mega's designs for it to be coincidence, and has, therefore, decided to sue Kate's Cards. Mega has a prior reputation for suing small companies and settling out of court for lesser damages. Kate, however, knows that her design is original and that she had never previously seen the Mega design that is the subject of the lawsuit. She has determined to fight the lawsuit, regardless of the cost. She doesn't know, however, how this will affect her financial statements.

1. Record the May journal entry for Kate's first interest payment. How much interest expense is reported in May?
2. How should Kate report the copyright infringement lawsuit in her financial statements?

EXTENDING YOUR KNOWLEDGE

REPORTING AND ANALYSIS

EYK10-1. **Financial Reporting Problem: Columbia Sportswear Company** The financial statements for the **Columbia Sportswear Company** can be found in Appendix A at the end of this book.

COLUMBIA
SPORTSWEAR
COMPANY

Required
Answer the following questions:

a. How much were Columbia's current liabilities as of December 31, 2017?
b. What two items made up the largest percentage of Columbia's December 31, 2017, current liabilities?
c. What was the largest component of Columbia's December 31, 2017, accrued liabilities?
d. What was the largest component of Columbia's December 31, 2017, other long-term liabilities?

EYK10-2. **Comparative Analysis Problem: Columbia Sportswear Company vs Under Armour Inc.** The financial statements for the **Columbia Sportswear Company** can be found in Appendix A at the end of this book, and the financial statements of **Under Armour, Inc.** can be found in Appendix B (the complete annual report is available on this book's Website).

COLUMBIA
SPORTSWEAR
COMPANY

UNDER ARMOUR,
INC.

Required
Answer the following questions:

a. Compute the current ratio for Columbia Sportswear and Under Armour, Inc. as of December 31, 2017, and comment on what this ratio implies about each company's liquidity and working capital position.
b. Compute the debt-to-total assets ratio for Columbia Sportswear and Under Armour, Inc. as of December 31, 2017, and comment on what this ratio implies about each company's solvency.

EYK10-3. **Business Decision Problem** Kingston Corporation has total assets of $5,200,000 and has been earning an average of $800,000 before income taxes the past several years. The firm is planning to expand plant facilities to manufacture a new product and needs an additional $2,000,000 in funds, on which it expects to earn 18 percent before income tax. The income tax rate is expected to be 20 percent for the next several years. The firm has no long-term debt outstanding and presently has 75,000 shares of common stock outstanding. The firm is considering three alternatives:

1. Obtain the $2,000,000 by issuing 25,000 shares of common stock at $80 per share.
2. Obtain the $2,000,000 by issuing $1,000,000 of ten percent, 20-year bonds at face value and 12,500 shares of common stock at $80 per share.
3. Obtain the $2,000,000 by issuing $2,000,000 of ten percent, 20-year bonds at face value.

Required
As a shareholder of Kingston Corporation, which of the three alternatives would you prefer if your main concern is enhancing the firm's earnings per share? (Hint: Divide net income by the number of outstanding common shares to determine the company's earnings per share.)

EYK10-4. **Financial Analysis Problem** **Abbott Laboratories** is a diversified health care company devoted to the discovery, development, manufacture, and marketing of innovative products that improve diagnostic, therapeutic, and nutritional practices. The company's balance sheet for three recent years contains the following data:

ABBOTT
LABORATORIES

	2017	2016	2015
Cash and cash equivalents	$ 9,407,000	$18,620,000	$ 5,001,000
Short-term investments	203,000	155,000	1,124,000
Trade receivables (net of allowance)	5,249,000	3,248,000	3,418,000
Inventories	3,601,000	2,434,000	2,599,000
Other current assets	1,687,000	2,319,000	2,013,000
Total current assets	$20,147,000	$26,776,000	$14,155,000
Total current liabilities	$ 8,912,000	$ 6,660,000	$ 9,186,000

Required

a. Compute the current ratio for 2015–2017.
b. Compute the quick ratio for 2015–2017.
c. Comment on the three-year trend in these ratios.

CRITICAL THINKING

GENERAL MILLS,
INC.

EYK10-5. Financial Analysis on the Web: General Mills, Inc. The fiscal year 2017 annual report of General Mills, Inc. is available on this book's Website. Refer to the consolidated balance sheet, and Note 8.

Required

a. What was the total dollar amount of current liabilities as of May 28, 2017?
b. What percent of long-term debt was considered current as of May 28, 2017?
c. What were the current ratio and quick ratio as of May 28, 2017?
d. What is the total amount of long-term liabilities reported by General Mills as of May 28, 2017?
e. How much principal payments on the long-term debt is General Mills anticipating paying in fiscal year 2018?

EYK10-6. Accounting Communication Activity Cedric Salos is considering different ways to raise money for the expansion of his company's operations. Cedric is not sure about the advantages of issuing bonds versus issuing common stock. In addition, he is not sure which features he should consider including with the bonds if he selects that form of financing. He asks you to explain, in simple terms, the answers to his questions.

Required

Write a short memorandum to Cedric explaining the advantages of issuing bonds over issuing common stock and the features that should be considered for inclusion with the bonds.

EYK10-7. Accounting Ethics Case Sunrise Pools, Inc., is being sued by the Crescent Club for negligence when installing a new pool on Crescent Club's property. Crescent Club alleges that the employees of Sunrise Pools damaged the foundation of the clubhouse and part of the golf course while operating heavy machinery to install the pool.

The lawsuit is for $1.5 million. At the time of the alleged incident, Sunrise Pools carried only $600,000 of liability insurance.

While reviewing the draft of Sunrise Pools' annual report, its president deletes all references to this lawsuit. She is concerned that disclosure of this lawsuit in the annual report will be viewed by Crescent Club as admission of Sunrise's wrongdoing, even though she privately admits that Sunrise employees were careless and believes that Sunrise Pools will be found liable for an amount in excess of $1 million. The president sends the amended draft of the annual report to the vice president of finance with a note stating that the lawsuit will not be disclosed in the annual report and that the lawsuit will not be disclosed to the board of directors.

Required

Is the president's concern valid? What ethical problems will the vice president of finance face if he follows the president's instructions?

EYK10-8. **Corporate Social Responsibility Problem** The chapter highlight on **Microsoft**'s corporate social responsibility efforts (see page 472) discussed two of the company's efforts. Go to Microsoft's Website and navigate to the section "About Microsoft;" then select "What We Value," then navigate to the section on corporate social responsibility. Download the Corporate Citizenship Report. In addition to these efforts, what are some other ways that Microsoft demonstrates its commitment to being a good corporate citizen?

MICROSOFT

EYK10-9. **Forensic Accounting Problem** Billing schemes are frauds in which an employee causes the victim organization to issue fraudulent payments by submitting invoices for nonexistent goods or services, inflated invoices, or invoices for personal items. One type of billing scheme uses a shell company that is set up for the purpose of committing the fraud. The shell company is often nothing more than a fake corporate name and a post-office mailbox.

What are some of the ways that shell company invoices can be detected?

EYK10-10. **Working with the Takeaways** Below are selected data from **Microsoft**'s recent financial statements:

	2017	2016
Net income	$ 21,201	$ 16,798
Tax expense	1,945	2,953
Cash and cash equivalents	7,663	6,510
Short-term investments	125,318	106,730
Accounts receivable	19,792	18,277
Inventory.	2,181	2,251
Other current assets.	4,897	5,892
Current liabilities.	64,527	59,357

Required

Calculate the following ratios for 2017 and 2016 and comment on the trend:

a. Current ratio

b. Quick ratio

EYK10-11. **Analyzing IFRS Financial Statements** The 2017 financial statements of **LVMH Moet Hennessey-Louis Vuitton S.A.** are presented in Appendix C at the end of this book. LVMH is a Paris-based holding company and one of the world's largest and best-known luxury goods companies. As a member of the European Union, French companies are required to prepare their consolidated (group) financial statements using International Financial Reporting Standards (IFRS). Using LVMH's financial data for 2016 and 2017, calculate the company's (a) current ratio, (b) quick ratio, and (c) times-interest-earned ratio. Is LVMH's working capital position improving or declining over the two-year period? Can LVMH readily service its interest payments from its income before interest expense and income taxes? (*Hint:* LVMH's interest expense is labeled "cost of net financial debt" on its consolidated income statement.)

IFRS

LVMH MOET
HENNESSEY-
LOUIS VUITTON
S.A.

ANSWERS TO SELF-STUDY QUESTIONS:

1. b, (p. 466)   2. b, (p. 467)   3. b, (pp. 481–482)   4. c, (pp. 469–471)   5. b, (pp. 481–483)
6. d, (pp. 488–491)   7. c, (p. 492)   8. b, (p. 478)   9. b, (p. 496)   10. b, (p. 484)   11. c, (pp. 485–486)

YOUR TURN! SOLUTIONS

Solution 10.1

a.	Apr. 30	Office salaries expense (+E, −SE)	40,000	
		Sales salaries expense (+E, −SE)	86,000	
		Federal income tax withholding payable (+L)		25,600
		FICA tax payable (+L)		9,639
		Health insurance premiums payable (+L)		1,850
		Union dues payable (+L)		950
		Payroll payable (+L)		87,961
		To accrue payroll for April		
		(FICA taxes = 0.0765 × $126,000 = $9,639).		
b.	30	Payroll payable (−L)	87,961	
		Cash (−A)		87,961
		To pay April payroll.		
c.	30	Payroll tax expense (+E, −SE)	14,847	
		FICA tax payable (+L)		9,639
		Federal unemployment tax payable (+L)		456
		State unemployment tax payable (+L)		4,752
		To record employer's payroll taxes (FICA Tax = 0.0765 ×		
		$126,000 = $9,639; Federal Unemployment Tax = 0.006 ×		
		$76,000 = $456; State Unemployment Tax = 0.054 × $88,000		
		= $4,752).		
d.	30	Federal income tax withholding payable (−L)	25,600	
		FICA tax payable (−L)	19,278	
		Health insurance premiums payable (−L)	1,850	
		Union dues payable (−L)	950	
		Federal unemployment tax payable (−L)	456	
		State unemployment tax payable (−L)	4,752	
		Cash (−A)		52,886
		To record the payment of payroll-related liabilities.		

Solution 10.2

(a)	Cash (+A)		325,000	
	Bonds payable (+L)			300,000
	Premium on bonds payable (+XL, +L)			25,000
	To record the issuance of bonds payable			

(b)

Long-term liabilities	
Bonds payable	$300,000
Add: Premium on bonds payable	25,000
Bonds payable, net	$325,000

Solution 10.3

1. Because the likelihood of losing the lawsuit is deemed remote, it does not need to be recognized or disclosed by Seco Co.
2. Even though the contingency is deemed remote, credit guarantees must be disclosed in the notes to the financial statements.
3. The liability should be recorded on the balance sheet because the likelihood of payment is both high and can be estimated.

Solution 10.4

a. Current ratio = $120,000 / $80,000 = 1.50
b. Quick ratio = ($10,000 + $25,000 + $30,000) / $80,000 = 0.8125
c. Times-interest-earned ratio = $20,000 / $4,000 = 5.0

Solution 10A.1

The selling price will be $94,582.81

Solution 10B.1

The present value of the lease payments is $42,580, which is "substantially all" of the asset's fair value of $45,000. In addition, the four-year lease is for the "major part" of the asset's five-year economic life. Therefore the lease is a finance lease. The entry to record the lease is:

Right-of-Use Asset (Equipment)	42,580	
Lease liability (Equipment)		42,580

Chapter 11

Stockholders' Equity

PAST

Chapter 10 examined the accounting for liabilities.

PRESENT

In this chapter, we turn our attention to the accounting for stockholders' equity.

FUTURE

In Chapter 12, we shift our focus to the statement of cash flows.

The first **Starbucks** coffeehouse was opened in Seattle, Washington, in 1971 to sell high-quality coffee beans and equipment. Since that time, Starbucks has grown at an explosive rate. Starbucks is the largest coffeehouse company in the world with over 27,000 stores.

Where do firms get the necessary capital for expansion? While not every large firm is a corporation, many are, and one of the most important characteristics of the corporate form of organization is the ability to raise new capital by selling ownership shares in the company. Starbucks had its initial public offering of its common shares in 1992.

Without a doubt, the modern corporation dominates the national and international economic landscape. In the United States, corporations generate well over three-fourths of the combined sales revenue of all forms of business organization, even though less than one of every five businesses is organized as a corporation. The corporate form of organization is used in a variety of business settings—from large multinational corporations with more than a million stockholders operating in countries all over the world, to small, family-owned businesses operating only in their local community.

Why do fast-growing firms like Starbucks choose the corporate form of organization? There are several reasons, but certainly one of the primary reasons is the relative ease of attracting large amounts of capital as compared to other organizational forms of business.

Road Map

LO	Learning Objective	Page	eLecture	Guided Example	Assignments
LO1	Define the corporate form of organization and discuss its principal characteristics.	524	E11-1	YT11.1	SS1, SE1, E11A, E11B
LO2	Explain the difference between par value stock and no-par value stock.	527	E11-2	YT11.2	SE2
LO3	Identify and discuss the two types of capital stock and their respective stockholder rights.	528	E11-3	YT11.3	SS2, SS8, SE3, E8A, E8B
LO4	Describe the accounting for issuances of capital stock.	532	E11-4	YT11.4	SS3, SE4, E2A, E4A, E12A, E13A, E2B, E4B, E12B, E13B, P2A, P3A, P4A, P5A, P8A, P9A, P10A, P11A, P2B, P3B, P4B, P5B, P8B, P9B, P10B, P11B
LO5	Define and discuss the accounting for stock splits.	534	E11-5	YT11.5	SS6, SE5, E3A, E9A, E15A, E3B, E9B, E15B, P4A, P8A, P9A, P4B, P8B, P9B
LO6	Explain the accounting for treasury stock.	534	E11-6	YT11.6	SS4, SE6, E4A, E13A, E4B, E13B, P3A, P4A, P5A, P8A, P9A, P10A, P11A, P3B, P4B, P5B, P8B, P9B, P10B, P11B
LO7	Identify and distinguish between cash dividends and stock dividends.	536	E11-7	YT11.7	SS5, SS9, SE7, E1A, E5A, E6A, E14A, E15A, E1B, E5B, E6B, E14B, E15B, P1A, P6A, P7A, P10A, P1B, P6B, P7B, P10B
LO8	Illustrate the statement of retained earnings and the statement of stockholders' equity.	540	E11-8	YT11.8	SS10, SE11, E7A, E7B, P2A, P3A, P4A, P6A, P7A, P9A, P10A, P2B, P3B, P4B, P6B, P7B, P10B
LO9	Define the return on common stockholders' equity, dividend yield, and dividend payout ratio and explain their use.	542	E11-9	YT11.9	SS7, SE8, SE9, SE10, E10A, E10B

STOCKHOLDERS' EQUITY

Corporations	Capital Stock	Dividends	Financial Statement Presentation
• Formation • Advantages • Disadvantages	• Par value • Common stock • Preferred stock • Stock issuance • Stock splits • Treasury stock	• Cash dividends • Stock dividends	• Statement of retained earnings • Statement of stockholders' equity • Analyzing stockholders' equity

NATURE AND FORMATION OF A CORPORATION

LO1 Define the corporate form of organization and **discuss** its principal characteristics.

A **corporation** is a legal entity created with the approval of a governmental authority. The right to conduct business as a corporation is granted by the state in which a corporation is formed (or chartered). All states have laws specifying the requirements for creating a corporation.

To form a corporation, the incorporators (founders) must apply for a charter. The incorporators prepare and file the **articles of incorporation**, which define the basic structure of the corporation, including the purpose for which it is formed and the amount of capital stock to be authorized. If the incorporators meet the requirements of the law, the government issues a charter or certificate of incorporation. After a charter has been granted, the founders hold an organizational meeting to elect the first board of directors and adopt the corporation's bylaws.

Because assets are essential to starting any business, a corporation issues (or sells) *certificates of capital stock* to obtain the necessary funds to acquire its operating assets. As owners of a corporation, *stockholders* are entitled to a voice in the control and management of the company. Stockholders with voting stock may vote on specific issues at the annual meeting and participate in the election of the board of directors. The board of directors establishes the overall policies of a corporation and declares dividends. Normally, the board also hires a group of corporate officers, including a chief executive officer, a chief financial officer, one or more vice presidents, a controller, a treasurer, and a secretary, to execute the day-to-day operations of the company. The officers implement the policies of the board of directors and actively manage the affairs of the corporation. **Exhibit 11-1** depicts the responsibilities of these stakeholders in a corporation.

Advantages of the Corporate Form of Organization

A corporation has several advantages when compared with a sole proprietorship or partnership.

Separate Legal Entity

The corporation, as a separate legal entity, may acquire assets, incur debt, enter into contracts, sue, and be sued—all in its own name. The stockholders of a corporation are separate and distinct from the corporation. This characteristic contrasts with proprietorships and partnerships, which are accounting entities but not legal entities apart from their owners.

EXHIBIT 11-1 Responsibilities of Selected Corporate Stakeholders

Limited Liability

The liability of stockholders with respect to a company's business affairs is usually limited to the value of their investment in the corporation. By way of contrast, the owners of proprietorships and partnerships can be held financially responsible, separately and collectively, for any unsatisfied obligations of the business. To protect a corporation's creditors, state laws limit the distribution of contributed capital to stockholders. Distributions of retained earnings (undistributed profits) are not legal unless the board of directors formally votes to declare a dividend. Because of the legal constraints regarding the amount of stockholder capital available for distribution, corporations must maintain clear distinctions in the accounts to identify the various elements of stockholders' equity.

Transferability of Ownership

Shares in a corporation may be routinely transferred without affecting a company's operations. The corporation merely notes such transfers of ownership in the stockholder records. Although a corporation must have stockholder records to notify stockholders of meetings and to pay dividends, the price at which shares transfer between investors is not recognized in the corporation's accounts.

Continuity of Existence

Because routine transfers of ownership do not affect a corporation's affairs, the corporation is said to have continuity of existence. In a partnership, any change in ownership technically results in a discontinuation of the old partnership and the formation of a new one.

PRINCIPLE ALERT

Entity Concept and Going Concern Concept

Two characteristics of the corporate form of organization mesh well with the basic principles of accounting. The separate legal status conferred upon a corporation conforms, for example, with the *entity concept*. When the corporation is the unit of focus for accounting purposes, the entity concept requires that the economic activity of the corporation be accounted for separately from the activities of its owners. Legally, the corporate entity is also distinct from its owners. Consequently, the corporation's continuity of existence also aligns well with the *going concern concept*, which assumes that the accounting entity will continue indefinitely into the future.

Capital Raising Capability

The limited liability of stockholders and the ease with which shares of stock may be transferred from one investor to another are attractive features to potential stockholders. These characteristics enhance the ability of the corporation to raise large amounts of capital by issuing shares of stock. Since both large and small investors may acquire ownership interests in a corporation, there exists a wide spectrum of potential investors. Corporations with thousands of stockholders are not uncommon.

Separate Legal Entity

Limited Liability

Transferability of Ownership

Continuous Existence

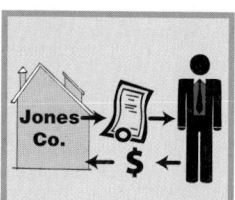
Capital Raising Capability

Disadvantages of the Corporate Form of Organization

There are some disadvantages to organizing as a corporation compared to a proprietorship or partnership.

Organization Costs

Creating a corporation is more costly than organizing a proprietorship or partnership. The expenditures incurred to organize a corporation are charged to Organization Costs and expensed on the income statement when incurred. These costs include attorney's fees, fees paid to the state, and the costs of promoting the enterprise.

Taxation

As separate legal entities, corporations are subject to federal income taxes on any earned income. Stockholders are likewise subject to income taxation on any income received from a corporation as dividends, leading to a situation of double taxation of a corporation's distributed earnings.

In addition, corporations are usually subject to state income taxes in the states in which they are incorporated or are doing business. They may also be subject to real estate, personal property, and franchise taxes.

THINKING GLOBALLY

The equity ownership structure of most U.S. and United Kingdom companies is characterized by small diffuse investors, each of whom owns only a small fraction of the firm. But the ownership structure of public companies in most of the rest of the world is strikingly different, and is more commonly characterized by the presence of a large investor who holds a controlling interest in the company's shares. These large owners usually consist of families and are typically directly involved in managing the company's operations. To illustrate, consider the following seven East Asian countries and the percentage of their public companies that are controlled by families. South Korea has the highest percentage of family-controlled public companies at 78 percent:

Country	Percentage of Family-Controlled Companies
Hong Kong	65%
Indonesia	75
Malaysia	71
Singapore	50
South Korea	78
Taiwan	55
Thailand	68

Regulation and Supervision

Corporations are subject to greater degrees of regulation and supervision than are proprietorships and partnerships. Each state maintains the right to regulate the corporations it charters. State laws also limit the powers a corporation may exercise, identify reports that must be filed by a corporation, and define the rights and liabilities of stockholders. If shares of stock are issued to the public, the corporation must comply with any securities laws governing the sale of corporate securities. Furthermore, corporations whose shares are listed and traded on organized security exchanges, such as the New York Stock Exchange, are subject to the various reporting and disclosure requirements of these exchanges.

Accounting for Stockholders' Equity in Alternative Organizational Forms

Differences exist between the accounting for the stockholders' equity of a corporation and for that of a sole proprietorship or partnership. In a sole proprietorship, only a single owner's capital account is needed to reflect increases from capital contributions and net income as well as decreases from owner withdrawals and net losses. A similar situation exists in most partnerships, which customarily maintain capital and drawing accounts for each partner.

A corporation, on the other hand, is subject to certain legal restrictions imposed by the government approving its creation. These restrictions focus on the distinction between contributed capital and retained earnings and make accounting for stockholders' equity somewhat more complex for corporations than for other types of business organizations.

The following attributes are associated with the corporate form of organization. Identify each one as either an advantage or a disadvantage of the corporate form over other forms of organization:

1. Taxation
2. Limited liability
3. Capital raising capability
4. Regulation
5. Cost to organize
6. Transferability of ownership

YOUR TURN! 11.1

The solution is on page 567.

PAR VALUE STOCK AND NO-PAR VALUE STOCK

A corporate charter may specify a face value, or **par value**, for each share of capital stock. In the early days of corporate stock issuances, par value represented the market value of the stock when it was issued. In more recent times, however, par values have typically been set at amounts well below a stock's fair market value on the date of issue. For example, the par value of Starbuck's common stock is $0.001 per share. As a consequence, a stock's par value has no economic significance today.

LO2 Explain the difference between par value stock and no-par value stock.

Par value, however, may have legal implications. In some states, par value may represent the minimum amount that must be contributed per share of stock. If stock is issued at a *discount* (that is, at less than its par value), the stockholder may have a liability for the amount of the discount should any creditor claims remain unsatisfied following a company's liquidation. Issuing stock at a discount rarely occurs, however, because boards of directors have generally established par values below fair market values at the time of issue.

Par value may also be used in some states to define a corporation's legal capital. *Legal capital* is the minimum amount of contributed capital that must remain in a corporation as a margin of protection for creditors. However, given the low par values typically assigned to common stock today, this protection has limited usefulness for creditors. Still, given the role that par value may play in defining legal capital, accountants carefully segregate and record the par value of stock transactions in an appropriate capital stock account.

Most states permit the issuance of capital stock without a par value, called **no-par value stock**. The company's board of directors, however, usually sets a **stated value** for the no-par stock. In such cases, the stated value will determine the corporation's legal capital. For accounting purposes, stated value amounts are treated similarly to par value amounts. In the absence of a stated value, the entire proceeds from the issuance of no-par value stock will likely establish a corporation's legal capital.

Starbucks

To some, corporate social responsibility (CSR) means doing things for non-stockholder stakeholders, even if it means a lower rate of return for stockholders. This sort of thinking pits CSR against stockholder gains, as if the two were competitors for the corporate dollar. Companies that truly understand CSR have come to see CSR in a more strategic light, where doing good can lead to doing well. Further, these companies realize that they would not have the resources to do good if they were not making money. Starbucks is known to be not only a highly profitable company with 2017 profits of nearly $3 billion U.S. dollars, but also a company on the leading edge of social responsibility. Starbucks believes businesses should have a positive impact on the communities they serve. The company has set goals in such areas as ethical sourcing, recycling, diversity, and philanthropy.

YOUR TURN! 11.2

The solution is on page 567.

Which of the following sentences is false?

a. In the early days of corporations, the par value represented the market value of the stock.

b. Par value represents the average value of the stock.

c. In recent times, par value is typically set well below a stock's market value.

d. Par value may be related to a corporation's legal capital.

TYPES OF CAPITAL STOCK

LO3 **Identify** and **discuss** the two types of capital stock and their respective stockholder rights.

The amounts and kinds of capital stock that a corporation may issue are specified in a company's charter of incorporation. Providing for the sale of several classes of capital stock permits a company to raise capital from different types of investors with diverse risk preferences. The charter also specifies a corporation's **authorized shares**—the maximum number of shares of each class of capital stock that may be issued. Shares that have been sold and issued to stockholders constitute the **issued shares** of a corporation. Some of these shares may be repurchased by the corporation. When shares are repurchased, they may be retired and cancelled or held for reissuance. Shares actually held by stockholders are called **outstanding shares**, whereas those reacquired by a corporation (and not cancelled) are called **treasury stock**. We will discuss treasury stock later in the chapter.

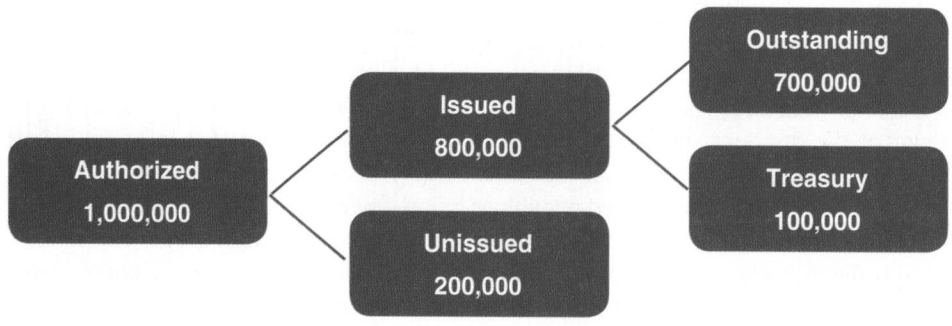

Common Stock

When only one class of stock is issued, it is called **common stock**. Common stockholders have the right to vote on corporate matters, to share in the corporation's net income, to participate in additional issuances of stock, and in the case of a corporate liquidation, to share in any asset distributions after any prior claims against the corporation by its creditors have been settled.

As the owners of a corporation, the common stockholders elect the board of directors and vote on all matters requiring the approval of the owners. Stockholders who do not attend the annual stockholders' meetings may vote by proxy.

A common stockholder has the right to a proportionate share of the corporation's earnings that are distributed as dividends. All earnings belong to the corporation, however, until the board of directors formally votes to declare a dividend.

Each stockholder of a corporation has a **preemptive right** to maintain his or her proportionate ownership interest in the corporation. If a company issues additional shares of stock, the current owners of that type of capital stock receive the first opportunity to acquire, on a pro rata basis, the new shares. In certain situations, management may request stockholders to waive their preemptive right. For example, a corporation may wish to issue additional shares of capital stock for use to acquire another company.

Preemptive Right Prevents Wealth Transfer	ACCOUNTING IN PRACTICE

A major reason for the preemptive right is to protect stockholders against a transfer of their wealth to new stockholders. To illustrate, assume that a firm has 10,000 shares of common stock outstanding with a market price of $20 per share. Thus, the firm's total market value is $200,000 (10,000 shares × $20). If the firm sells another 10,000 common shares at $10 per share (a price below its current market value), the additional $100,000 cash received would raise the firm's total market value to $300,000. With a new market value of $15 per share ($300,000/20,000 shares), the new share issuance causes the old stockholders to lose $5 per share and the new stockholders to gain $5 per share—that is, the sale of the new shares at a lower price caused a wealth transfer from the old stockholders to the new stockholders. The preemptive right protects the existing stockholders from such wealth transfers by enabling them to purchase any newly issued shares.

When a corporation liquidates, it converts its assets to a form suitable for distribution, usually cash, which it then distributes to all parties having claims on the corporate assets. Any assets remaining after all claims have been satisfied belong to the residual owners of the corporation—that is, the common stockholders. Common stockholders are entitled to the final distribution of the balance of any remaining assets in a corporate liquidation.

A company may occasionally issue *classified* common stock; that is, it may issue more than one class of common stock. For example, when two classes of common stock are issued, they are often identified as Class A and Class B. The two classes usually differ in either their respective dividend rights or their respective voting powers. Usually, classified common stock is issued when the founders of a corporation wish to acquire funds from the public while retaining voting control of the corporation. For example, Google originally issued two classes of common stock: Class A shares that were sold to the public and Class B shares that were retained by the Company's founders. The Class A shares have one vote per share while the Class B shares have 10 votes per share.

Preferred Stock

Preferred stock is a class of stock with characteristics that differentiate it from common stock. Preferred stock, for example, has one or more preferences over common stock, usually with reference to (1) the payment of dividends and (2) the distribution of assets when a corporation liquidates. To determine the features of a particular preferred stock issue, it is necessary to examine the preferred stock contract. The majority of preferred shares, however, have certain typical features, which are discussed below.

Dividend Preference

When the board of directors declares a distribution of the company's net income, preferred stockholders are entitled to an annual dividend before common stockholders may receive any dividend distribution. The amount is usually specified in the preferred stock contract as a percentage of the par value of the stock or in dollars per share if the stock lacks a par value. Thus, if the preferred stock has a $100 par value and a six percent dividend rate, the preferred stockholders receive $6 per share in dividends. However, the dividend is owed to the stockholders only if, and when, declared by the board of directors.

Preferred dividends are usually **cumulative**—that is, regular dividends to preferred stockholders omitted in the past must be paid in addition to the current year's dividend before any dividend distribution can be made to the common stockholders. If a preferred stock is **noncumulative**, omitted dividends do not carry forward.

To illustrate the difference between cumulative and noncumulative preferred stock, assume that a company ending its second year of operations has 1,000 shares of $100 par value, six percent preferred stock and 100,000 shares of $1 par value common stock outstanding. The company declared no dividends last year. This year a dividend of $27,000 is declared. The distribution of the $27,000 between the two stockholder classes depends on whether the preferred stock is cumulative or noncumulative. If the preferred stock is cumulative, preferred stockholders receive $12 per share before common stockholders receive anything, as illustrated below:

	Preferred	Common	Total
Total par value of outstanding shares.	$100,000	$100,000	$200,000
Preferred stock is cumulative			
Preferred dividends in arrears (6 percent)	$ 6,000		$ 6,000
Regular preferred dividend (6 percent).	6,000		6,000
Remainder to common.		$ 15,000	15,000
Total distribution.	$ 12,000	$ 15,000	$ 27,000
Preferred stock is noncumulative			
Regular preferred dividend (6 percent).	$ 6,000		$ 6,000
Remainder to common.		$ 21,000	21,000
Total distribution.	$ 6,000	$ 21,000	$ 27,000

Dividends in arrears (that is, dividends omitted in past years) on cumulative preferred stock are not an accounting liability and do not appear in the liability section of the balance sheet. They do not become an obligation of the corporation until the board of directors formally declares such dividends. Any dividends in arrears are disclosed to investors in the notes to the financial statements.

Asset Distribution Preference

Preferred stockholders normally have a preference over common stockholders with respect to the receipt of assets in the event of a corporate liquidation. When a corporation liquidates, any creditor claims are settled first. Preferred stockholders then have the right to receive assets equal to the par value of their shares, or a larger stated liquidation value per share, before any assets are distributed to common stockholders. The preferred stockholders' preference to assets in liquidation also includes any dividends in arrears.

Other Preferred Stock Features

Although preferred stockholders do not ordinarily have the right to vote in the election of the board of directors, this right can be accorded by contract. Some state laws require that all capital stock issued by a corporation be given voting rights. Further, preferred stock may contain features that cause the shares to resemble common stock. Preferred stock may, for example, be **convertible** into common stock at a specified conversion rate. When this feature is present, the market price of the preferred shares often moves in a fashion consistent with the related common shares. When the price of the common stock rises, the value of the conversion feature is enhanced, and consequently, the value of the preferred shares should also rise.

Preferred stock may be **participating**. A *participating preferred stock* shares any special dividend distributions with common stock beyond the regular preferred stock dividend rate. (Special dividends are discussed on p. 537.) After receiving its regular dividend preference, preferred stock normally does not participate in any special dividend distribution until the common stock is allowed a dividend amount corresponding to the regular preferred stock dividend rate At this point, the two classes of stock begin to share the special dividend distribution at the same rate. The preferred stock participation feature may be partial (which limits the participation to a certain amount) or full (which places no limit on the rate of participation).

Preferred stock may be **callable**, which means that a corporation can redeem the shares after a length of time and at a price specified in the stock contract. The call feature makes the preferred stock similar to a bond, since many bonds are callable or have a limited life. Most preferred stocks are callable, with the call or redemption price set slightly above the original preferred stock issuance price.

Using Forensic Accounting to Pick Stocks	**FORENSIC ACCOUNTING**

 A new investment product has been introduced for those who want to use the techniques of forensic accounting to help in their investing. The Forensic Accounting ETF is a fund that attempts to track the Del Vecchio Earnings Quality Index. This index looks at all 500 stocks in the S&P 500 and grades them from A through F based on the quality of their reported earnings. Earnings quality is defined based on judging the sustainability of the reported earnings. While the methodology that uses forensic accounting techniques is proprietary, some of the known factors are reserve concerns, cost of goods for inventory issues, and aggressive revenue recognition.

Preferred Shares and the Capital Market	**ACCOUNTING IN PRACTICE**

Although legally, and from an accounting standpoint, preferred shares are considered to be part of a company's stockholders' equity, the capital market takes a different point of view. Most investment professionals consider a company's preferred stock to be part of the company's debt structure. Thus, from a capital market perspective, the only true stockholders of a business are its common stockholders. This point of view is apparent in the calculation of such ratios as the return on common stockholders' equity, discussed shortly, which excludes a company's preferred stockholders' equity.

Match the description in the right column with the appropriate term in the left column:

1. Authorized	*a.*	The right to receive dividends omitted in prior years.
2. Outstanding	*b.*	The most basic class of stock ownership.
3. Common stock	*c.*	Stock with one or more preferences over common stock.
4. Preemptive right	*d.*	The maximum number of shares of each class of stock that may be issued.
5. Preferred stock		
6. Cumulative preference	*e.*	Shares actually held by stockholders.
	f.	The right to maintain a proportionate ownership interest in a corporation.

YOUR TURN! 11.3

The solution is on page 567.

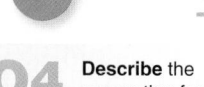

STOCK ISSUANCES FOR CASH

LO4 **Describe** the accounting for issuances of capital stock.

When issuing capital stock to investors, a corporation may use the services of an investment bank, a specialist in marketing securities to the capital market. The investment bank may *underwrite* a stock issue by agreeing to sell the shares on a firm commitment basis—that is, buying the shares from the corporation and then reselling them to investors. Under a firm commitment agreement, a corporation does not risk being unable to sell its stock. The underwriter bears this risk in return for the fees and profits generated by selling the shares to investors at a price higher than it paid to the corporation. An investment bank that is unwilling to underwrite a stock issue may handle the issuance of the shares on a *best efforts* basis. In this case, the investment bank agrees to sell as many shares as possible at a set price, but the corporation bears the risk of any unsold shares.

When capital stock is issued to investors, the appropriate capital stock account is credited for the par value of the stock issued, or if the stock is no-par value stock, with its stated value, if any. The asset received in exchange for the stock (usually cash) is debited, and any difference is credited to the Paid-in Capital in Excess of Par Value account.

To illustrate the journal entries to record various stock issuances in exchange for cash, assume that Smith & Sons issued two different types of capital stock during its first year of operations:

Issuing Stock at a Premium

1. Issued 1,000 shares of $100 par value, nine percent preferred stock at $107 cash per share:

A   = L +   SE
+107,000   +100,000
                 PS
                 +7,000
                 PS

Cash (+A)	107,000	
Preferred stock (+SE)		100,000
Paid-in capital in excess of par value—Preferred stock (+SE)		7,000

In this transaction, the preferred stock is issued at a price greater than its par value—that is, the shares were sold at a premium. The par value of the preferred stock issued is credited to the Preferred Stock account and the $7,000 premium is credited to the Paid-in Capital in Excess of Par Value account. If there is more than one class of par value stock, the account title may indicate the class of stock to which the premium relates, in this case Paid-in Capital in Excess of Par Value—Preferred Stock.

Issuing No-Par Stock

2. Issued 30,000 shares of no-par value common stock, stated value $5, at $8 cash per share:

A   = L +   SE
+240,000   +150,000
                 CS
                 +90,000
                 CS

Cash (+A)	240,000	
Common stock (+SE)		150,000
Paid-in capital in excess of stated value—Common stock (+SE)		90,000

When no-par value stock has a stated value, as in Entry 2, the stated value of the total shares issued is credited to the proper capital stock account, and any additional amount received is credited to the account Paid-in Capital in Excess of Stated Value. If there is no stated value for the no-par value stock, the entire proceeds are credited to the appropriate capital stock account. In the second journal entry, if the common stock had no stated value, the entire $240,000 amount would have been credited to the Common Stock account.

These two stock issuances are reflected in **Exhibit 11-2**, which presents the stockholders' equity section from Smith & Sons' year-end balance sheet. (Retained earnings are assumed to be $25,000.) The stockholders' equity section is divided into two major categories: ❶ Paid-in Capital and ❷ Retained Earnings. **Paid-in capital** is the amount of capital contributed to the corporation from various capital stock transactions such as the issuance of preferred stock and common stock. The capital contributed by stockholders through the issuance of stock is divided between the legal capital (the par value or stated value of the stock) and the amounts received in excess of the legal capital. Later in this chapter we discuss treasury stock transactions that may affect a corporation's paid-in capital. **Retained earnings** represent the cumulative net income and losses of the company that have not been distributed to stockholders as a dividend.

EXHIBIT 11-2	Stockholders' Equity Section of the Balance Sheet		
❶	Paid-in Capital		
	9% Preferred stock, $100 par value, 1,000 shares authorized, issued, and outstanding	$100,000	
	No-par common stock, stated value $5, 40,000 shares authorized; 30,000 shares issued and outstanding.	150,000	$250,000
	Additional paid-in capital.		
	In excess of par value—Preferred stock	7,000	
	In excess of stated value—Common stock	90,000	97,000
	Total Paid-in Capital.		347,000
❷	Retained earnings		25,000
	Total Stockholders' Equity		$372,000

Noncash Stock Issuances

Sometimes a corporation will exchange its common stock for services, operating assets, or for its own convertible debt or convertible preferred stock. For example, some start-up companies lacking cash will exchange their common stock for professional services provided by attorneys and accountants. When this occurs, a journal entry is made to debit the Professional Services Expense account and a credit is made to Common Stock—Par Value and to the Paid-in Capital in Excess of Par Value—Common Stock account for the fair value of the services received.

When common stock is exchanged for operating assets, a similar journal entry is made, although the debit in this case is to the Land or Equipment account. When common stock is exchanged for convertible bonds (discussed in Chapter 10), the value of the newly issued stock is assumed to be equal to the book value of the bonds. An exchange of convertible bonds for common stock is executed by debiting the Bonds Payable account and the Premium on Bonds Payable account (or crediting the Discount on Bonds Payable account) and crediting the Common Stock account and the Paid-in Capital in Excess of Par Value—Common Stock for any excess of the bonds' book value over the stock's par value.

When preferred stock is converted into a company's common stock, the newly issued common stock assumes the book value of the preferred stock. That is, the Preferred Stock—Par Value and the Paid-in Capital in Excess of Par Value—Preferred Stock are debited while the Common Stock—Par Value and Paid-in Capital in Excess of Par Value—Common Stock are credited.

Wyatt Industries began operations on June 1 by issuing 10,000 shares of $1 par value common stock for cash at $9 per share. How much Additional Paid-in Capital will be reported by Wyatt Industries?

YOUR TURN! 11.4

The solution is on page 568.

STOCK SPLITS

Occasionally, a corporation may issue additional shares of common stock to its stockholders through a **forward stock split**. The principal reason that companies execute a forward stock split is to reduce the market price of their shares. A forward stock split increases the number of shares outstanding and is accounted for by reducing the par value or stated value of the stock affected. A forward stock split does not change the balances of any of the stockholders' equity accounts; however, a memorandum entry is made in the general journal to show the altered par value or stated value of the stock and to note the increase in the number of shares issued and outstanding. For example, if Smith & Sons has 10,000 shares of $10 par value common stock outstanding and announces a 2-for-1 forward stock split, it would simply reduce the par value of its common stock to $5 per share and issue to its stockholders 10,000 new common shares. Thus, after the forward stock split, each stockholder would have twice the number of shares held prior to the split, and the value of the Common Stock account would remain unchanged at $100,000 (10,000 shares × 2 = 20,000 shares × $5 = $100,000). If you owned one share of Smith & Sons $10 par value stock before the 2-for-1 forward stock split, you would own two shares of Smith & Sons $5 par value stock after the stock split.

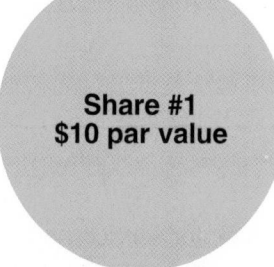

Before 2-for-1 forward stock split   **After 2-for-1 forward stock split**

Occasionally, a company may execute a **reverse stock split**, for example a 1-for-2 reverse stock split, which increases the par value of the stock and reduces the number of shares outstanding. Reverse stock splits are designed to increase a company's stock price. Most major stock exchanges have a minimum trading price that a company must meet or exceed in order to be traded on the exchange. When a company's stock price falls below the minimum trading price, the shares may be delisted, making it difficult for stockholders to find buyers for their shares. Meeting an exchange's minimum listing price is one of the principal reasons for reverse stock splits.

Aston Enterprises currently has 500,000 common shares outstanding with a par value of $3.00. Joe Smith owns 500 of those shares. If Aston were to execute a 3-for-1 split, what would be the resulting share information for both Aston and Smith?

TREASURY STOCK

When a corporation acquires its own outstanding shares and does not retire (cancel) them, the acquired shares are called **treasury stock**. Treasury stock may be purchased for a variety of reasons, including reissuing them to officers and employees in profit sharing programs or employee stock option plans. Whatever the purpose, treasury stock purchases reduce a company's stockholders' equity. Treasury shares do not carry voting privileges or preemptive rights, are not paid dividends, and do not receive assets in the event of a corporation's liquidation.

Corporations usually purchase their own shares by buying them through a brokerage firm on the open market or by making a tender offer to stockholders. Under a tender offer, the company offers to buy back its shares of stock at a specified price per share. Another way to acquire treasury stock is to negotiate a purchase of shares from a single large stockholder. In some cases, this latter technique may involve greenmail. *Greenmail* is a ploy in which an investor purchases a large number of a company's shares, threatens to take control of the company, and then sells the shares back to the company at a premium. Management pays the premium to entice the investor to "be quiet and go away." Although it is not illegal, payment of an unjustified greenmail premium is likely to upset other stockholders and may lead to legal action against a company.

Accounting for Treasury Stock

Accountants record treasury stock at its acquisition cost, debiting the Treasury Stock account and crediting the Cash account. The Treasury Stock account is a contra-stockholders' equity account, and its balance is deducted when deriving total stockholders' equity on the balance sheet. To illustrate the accounting for the purchase of treasury stock, assume that Smith & Sons had 20,000 shares of $10 par value common stock outstanding and then purchased 1,000 shares at $12 per share. The journal entry to record the purchase is:

Treasury stock (+XSE, −SE)	12,000	
Cash (−A)		12,000
To record purchase of 1,000 shares of treasury stock at $12 per share.		

$$A = L + SE$$
$$-12{,}000 \qquad\qquad -12{,}000$$
$$TS$$

If a balance sheet is prepared following this transaction, the stockholders' equity section would appear as follows (the values for Paid-in Capital in Excess of Par Value and Retained Earnings are assumed):

SMITH & SONS, INC. Stockholders' Equity	
Paid-in Capital	
Common stock, $10 par value, authorized and issued 20,000 shares;	
1,000 shares in treasury, 19,000 shares outstanding	$200,000
Paid-in capital in excess of par value	20,000
Total Paid-in Capital	220,000
Retained earnings	40,000
	260,000
Less: Treasury stock (1,000 shares) at cost	12,000
Total Stockholders' Equity.	$248,000

Note that the $200,000 par value of all *issued* stock is disclosed, although the 1,000 treasury shares are no longer outstanding. The total cost of the 1,000 shares, however, is later deducted as the last component in the presentation of total stockholders' equity.

If Smith & Sons subsequently resells 500 shares of its treasury stock at $14 per share, the following journal entry is made:

Cash (+A)	7,000	
Treasury stock (−XSE, +SE)		6,000
Paid-in capital—Treasury stock (+SE)		1,000

$$A = L + SE$$
$$+7{,}000 \qquad\qquad +6{,}000 \text{ TS}$$
$$+1{,}000 \text{ TS}$$

Note that the $1,000 "gain" on the resale of the treasury stock is accounted for as an increase in shareholders' equity and not as net income.

ACCOUNTING IN PRACTICE

Why Do Companies Buy Back Their Stock?

There are many potential reasons why firms buy back their own shares. The company may feel that its shares are currently undervalued by the market and repurchasing its own outstanding shares takes advantages of this possible mispricing. This not only allows the company to benefit if and when the share price ultimately rises, but perhaps more importantly it also sends a strong positive signal to the financial markets about the company's value. While it is one thing for the CEO to simply claim the company's stock is undervalued, it is a far more powerful signal to "put their money where their mouth is" by repurchasing the shares.

Some companies repurchase their own shares as a means to build shareholder value. Distributing this excess cash to the shareholders prevents management from using the cash in ways that destroy value, such as investing in a pet project with little chance of succeeding or wasting it on lavish management benefits such as a new corporate jet. Further, repurchasing stock benefits the shareholders because what the shareholder earns on shares sold back to the company is often taxed at lower capital gains rates than the ordinary income tax rate used to tax dividends.

Other possible reasons for share repurchases include the need to have a sufficient number of shares available to execute an acquisition through a share exchange, or to meet the demand for new shares when employees exercise their stock options. Alternatively, some companies repurchase as a takeover defense, for example, when the company's share price is below its intrinsic value per share and outsiders have been accumulating the shares.

Finally, share repurchases have the potential to improve the company's earnings per share calculation. Recall earnings per share is computed by dividing the company's earnings by the number of outstanding shares of common stock. Treasury stock is not counted as outstanding, and therefore reduces the denominator in the earnings per share calculation.

IFRS ALERT

Under IFRS and U.S. GAAP, treasury stock is reported on the balance sheet as a contra stockholders' equity account. That is, the repurchase cost of any treasury stock is subtracted from total stockholders' equity. In addition, both IFRS and U.S. GAAP preclude the recognition of any gain or loss by a company from stock transactions involving its own shares—that is, any "gain" or "loss" from trading in a company's own shares is recorded as part of Paid-in Capital in Excess of Par Value. By way of contrast, some countries permit treasury stock to be reported on the asset side of the balance sheet as an investment in marketable securities. Under IFRS and U.S. GAAP, treasury stock does not satisfy the definition of an asset, and therefore, cannot be reported on the balance sheet as marketable securities. It is also noteworthy that in some countries, treasury stock purchases are illegal because they are viewed as a form of stock price manipulation.

YOUR TURN! 11.6

The solution is on page 568.

GuidedExamples
MBC

The Fullerton Corporation purchased 5,000 shares of its outstanding $2 par value common stock for $75,000 cash on November 1. Management anticipates holding the stock in the treasury until it resells the stock. By how much would the Fullerton Corporation debit Treasury Stock for this purchase?

---

eLectures
MBC

CASH DIVIDENDS AND STOCK DIVIDENDS

LO7 **Identify** and **distinguish** between cash dividends and stock dividends.

Dividends are a distribution of assets or shares of stock from a corporation to its stockholders. A corporation can distribute dividends to stockholders only after its board of directors has formally voted to declare a distribution. Dividends are usually paid in cash but may also be paid as property or additional shares of stock in the firm.

Legally, declared dividends are an obligation of the firm, and an entry to record the dividend obligation is made on the *dividend declaration date*. Cash and property dividends payable are carried as liabilities, and stock dividends to be issued are shown in the stockholders' equity section of the balance sheet. At the date of declaration, a *record date* and *payment date* are also established. For example, assume that on April 25 (the declaration date), the board of directors of Smith & Sons declares a cash dividend payable on June 1 (the payment date) to those investors who own shares of stock on May 15 (the record date). Stockholders owning stock on the record date receive the dividend even if they dispose of their shares before the payment date. Therefore, shares sold between the record date and the payment date are sold *ex dividend*—that is, they are sold without the right to receive the dividend.

Most dividend declarations are accounted for by reducing retained earnings. Dividends are distributions of earnings and are not shown as expenses on the income statement. Also, dividends cannot be deducted as expenses for income tax purposes. Under certain conditions, however, state laws may permit distributions from additional paid-in capital. Stockholders should be informed of the source of such dividends, because, in a sense, any dividend paid from a company's paid-in capital is a nontaxable return of capital rather than a taxable distribution of earnings.

Declaration Date	Record Date	Payment Date
April 25	May 15	June 1
Balance sheet effects	No effect	**Balance sheet effects**
Increase dividends payable		Decrease cash
Decrease retained earnings		Decrease dividends payable

THINKING GLOBALLY

While U.S. corporations principally distribute cash and/or stock dividends, property dividend distributions are common among Japanese corporations. For example, **McDonald's Holding Company of Japan** annually distributes to its stockholders coupons for a free Big Mac as a property dividend. **DyDo Drinco, Inc.**, distributes to its stockholders samples of its beverage products as a property dividend. Companies that distribute their products or coupons for their products to stockholders as a property dividend believe that by making stockholders more familiar with the company's products, they will retain the investment commitment of their stockholders on a longer term basis than would otherwise be the case.

Cash Dividends

The majority of dividends distributed by corporations are paid in cash. Although companies may pay such dividends annually, many firms pay quarterly dividends. Dividends that are paid routinely are called regular dividends. The **Johnson & Johnson Company** and **PepsiCo, Inc.**, for example, pay regular quarterly dividends. Some companies occasionally pay a special dividend. Special dividends occur infrequently and represent the distribution of excess cash that has been accumulated by a business and for which the business has no immediate operational need.

When a company declares a **cash dividend**, the company must have both an appropriate amount of retained earnings and the necessary amount of cash on hand. Uninformed investors often believe that a large retained earnings balance automatically permits generous dividend distributions. A company, however, may successfully accumulate earnings and at the same time not be sufficiently liquid to pay large cash dividends. Many companies, especially new firms in growth industries, finance their expansion from assets generated through earnings and pay out small cash dividends or none at all.

Cash dividends are based on the number of shares outstanding. When a company's directors declare a cash dividend, an entry is made debiting the Cash Dividends account and crediting the Dividends Payable account. The Cash Dividends account is a temporary account that is closed to the Retained Earnings account at year-end.[1] To illustrate, assume that Smith & Sons has 1,000 shares of $100 par value, six percent preferred stock and 6,000 shares of $10 par value common stock outstanding. If the company declares the regular $6 dividend on the preferred stock and a $2 dividend on the common stock, the dividend payment totals $18,000. The following journal entry is made on the declaration date:

A = L + SE
+6,000 −18,000
+12,000   Div

Cash dividends (−SE)	18,000	
Dividends payable—Preferred stock (+L)		6,000
Dividends payable—Common stock (+L)		12,000
To record the declaration of $6 dividend on preferred stock and		
$2 dividend on common stock.		

Dividends Payable—Preferred Stock and Dividends Payable—Common Stock are reported as current liabilities on the balance sheet until paid. On the dividend payment date, the following journal entry is made:

A = L + SE
−18,000 −6,000
−12,000

Dividends payable—Preferred stock (−L)	6,000	
Dividends payable—Common stock (−L)	12,000	
Cash (−A)		18,000
To record the payment of dividends on preferred and common shares.		

Stock Dividends

Companies may also distribute shares of their own stock as dividends to stockholders in lieu of, or in addition to, cash dividends. A company may issue **stock dividends** when it does not wish to deplete its working capital by paying a cash dividend. Young and growing companies often issue stock dividends because cash is usually needed to acquire new facilities and to expand.

The accounting for a stock dividend results in a transfer of a portion of retained earnings to the paid-in capital accounts. Thus, the distribution of a stock dividend signals to investors management's desire to "plow back" earnings into the company. Although stock dividends may take a number of forms, usually common shares are distributed to common stockholders. We limit our discussion to this type of stock dividend distribution.

Small Stock Dividends

Small stock dividends are share distributions that involve less than 25 percent of the total number of shares previously outstanding. Small stock dividends are *recorded at the market value* of the shares issued, causing retained earnings to decrease and paid-in capital to increase by this amount. To illustrate the journal entries for a declaration of a small stock dividend, assume that the stockholders' equity of Smith & Sons is as follows prior to the declaration of a ten percent stock dividend:

Common stock, $5 par value, 20,000 shares issued and outstanding.	$100,000
Paid-in capital in excess of par value.	20,000
Total Paid-in Capital	120,000
Retained earnings	65,000
Total Stockholders' Equity.	$185,000

With 20,000 shares outstanding, the declaration of a ten percent stock dividend requires the issuance of an additional 2,000 shares (10 percent × 20,000 shares). If the

---

[1] Some companies, especially those paying regular dividends, debit the Retained Earnings account directly on the dividend declaration date.

current market price per share is $11, the total market value of the shares to be distributed is $22,000 (2,000 shares × $11), resulting in the following journal entry:

Stock dividends (−SE)	22,000	
Stock dividend distributable (+SE)		10,000
Paid-in capital in excess of par value (+SE)		12,000
To record declaration of 10 percent stock dividend on common shares.		

A = L + SE
−22,000
Div
+10,000
CS
+12,000
CS

The amount of the credit to the Stock Dividend Distributable account is the par value of the shares to be distributed (2,000 shares × $5). If a balance sheet is prepared between the declaration date and the distribution date of a stock dividend, the Stock Dividend Distributable account is shown in stockholders' equity immediately after the Common Stock account. When the shares are distributed, the following journal entry is made:

Stock dividend distributable (−SE)	10,000	
Common stock (+SE)		10,000
To record issuance of stock dividend on common shares.		

A = L + SE
−10,000
CS
+10,000
CS

The Stock Dividends account is a temporary account that is closed to the Retained Earnings account at year-end, as shown by the following journal entry:

Retained earnings (−SE)	22,000	
Stock dividends (+SE)		22,000
To close the Stock Dividends account.		

A = L + SE
−22,000
RE
+22,000
Div

A comparison of the stockholders' equity and outstanding shares, before and after the stock dividend, appears below. Note that retained earnings decreased by $22,000 and paid-in capital increased by $22,000, but total stockholders' equity remains unchanged:

	Before Stock Dividend	After Stock Dividend
Common stock, $5 par value	$100,000	$110,000
Paid-in capital in excess of par value	20,000	32,000
Total Paid-in Capital	120,000	142,000
Retained earnings	65,000	43,000
Total Stockholders' Equity.	$185,000	$185,000
Common shares issued and outstanding.	20,000	22,000

> Total stockholders' equity remains unchanged.

The relative ownership interest of a common stockholder is unaltered by the receipt of a common stock dividend. If a ten percent stock dividend is distributed, all stockholders increase their proportionate holdings by ten percent, and the total shares outstanding are increased in the same proportion. Small stock dividends rarely affect the market value of the underlying stock.

Large Stock Dividends

When the number of shares issued as a stock dividend is large enough to impact the stock's market value per share, stockholders may not perceive the same benefits as they do for a small stock dividend. This is because issuing a large number of shares is likely to reduce the market price of the shares, much the same way that a stock split, discussed earlier in the chapter, reduces the market price per share. To see this, note that a 100 percent large stock dividend is the same as a 2-for-1 forward stock split. Accordingly, the accounting for large stock dividends (those over 25 percent) differs from the accounting for small stock dividends. Large stock dividends are recorded *at the par value* of the shares issued. The journal entry to record the declaration of a large stock dividend debits the Stock Dividends account and credits the Stock Dividend Distributable account for the par or stated value of the shares issued. Once the stock is issued, the increase in paid-in capital is reflected in the Common Stock account.[2]

ACCOUNTING IN EVERYDAY LIFE

How Big Will That Bonus Be?

Investors and creditors are not the only people with a keen interest in a company's reported accounting results. Employees often have a big reason to care as well. The reason is that their own well-being could be directly tied to how much profit the company reports in a couple of ways. First, some companies believe in sharing some of the wealth with their employees through profit sharing plans. In addition, it is not uncommon to have the size of an employee's bonus based on some accounting measure, such as net income or return on assets. All the more reason to understand the accounting numbers.

YOUR TURN! 11.7

The solution is on page 568.

Fango Company's president would like to know the financial impact that a cash dividend and a stock dividend will have on the company's retained earnings account. The current balance in retained earnings is $500,000. The company has 10,000 shares of $1 par value common stock outstanding with a current market value of $20 per share. The potential cash dividend will be $3 per share and the potential stock dividend will be ten percent.

Required
Compute the Fango Company retained earnings balance after

a. A $3 per share cash dividend
b. A ten percent stock dividend

RETAINED EARNINGS AND THE STATEMENT OF STOCKHOLDER'S EQUITY

LO8 Illustrate the statement of retained earnings and the statement of stockholders' equity.

A **statement of retained earnings** presents an analysis of the Retained Earnings account for a given accounting period. An example of a statement of retained earnings is presented in **Exhibit 11-3**. The statement begins with the retained earnings balance as of the beginning of the period ❶, then reports the items that caused retained earnings to change during the period ❷, and ends with the end-of-period balance in retained earnings ❸.

EXHIBIT 11-3	Statement of Retained Earnings

GEYSER CORPORATION **Statement of Retained Earnings** **For Year Ended December 31, 2019**	
❶ Retained earnings, January 1, 2019..........................	$48,000
❷ Add: Net income.......................................	32,000
	80,000
Less: Cash dividends declared...............................	19,000
❸ Retained earnings, December 31, 2019.......................	$61,000

---

[2] A stock's par value or stated value per share is not changed by a stock dividend. However, a stock split reduces the par value or stated value in proportion to the increase in the number of shares issued. This difference leads to a difference in accounting treatment—only a memorandum entry is made for a stock split, whereas a large stock dividend requires a journal entry to transfer the legal capital of the shares to be issued from retained earnings to common stock.

Statement of Stockholders' Equity

Rather than reporting a statement of retained earnings, most corporations integrate the information regarding retained earnings into a more comprehensive statement called a **statement of stockholders' equity**. This statement shows an analysis of all of the stockholders' equity accounts for the period. **Exhibit 11-4** presents an example of a statement of stockholders' equity. The statement begins with the beginning balances of the various stockholders' equity accounts ❶, reports the items causing changes in these accounts ❷, and ends with the end-of-period balances ❸.

The statement of stockholders' equity in **Exhibit 11-4** reveals all of the events affecting the Geyser Corporation's stockholders' equity during 2019. These events are the earning of net income, the issuance of common stock, the issuance of treasury stock, the declaration of a cash dividend, and the acquisition of treasury stock. Note that the information in the retained earnings column (highlighted using a dotted red box) contains the same information as a statement of retained earnings.

EXHIBIT 11-4	Statement of Stockholders' Equity

GEYSER CORPORATION
Statement of Stockholders' Equity
For Year Ended December 31, 2019

		Common Stock	Paid-in Capital in Excess of Par Value	Paid-in Capital from Treasury Stock	Retained Earnings	Treasury Stock	Total
❶	Balance, January 1, 2019.	$200,000	$120,000	$18,000	$48,000	$(14,000)	$372,000
	Net income				32,000		32,000
	6,000 Common shares issued . . .	30,000	24,000				54,000
❷	500 Treasury shares issued			2,000		3,500	5,500
	Cash dividends declared				(19,000)		(19,000)
	200 Treasury shares acquired . . .					(2,000)	(2,000)
❸	Balance, December 31, 2019. . . .	$230,000	$144,000	$20,000	$61,000	$(12,500)	$442,500

IFRS ALERT

There are a number of significant terminology differences between U.S. GAAP and IFRS with respect to the reporting of stockholders' equity:

U.S. GAAP	IFRS
Common stock	Share capital
Paid-in capital in excess of par value	Share premium
Retained earnings	Retained profits
Accumulated other comprehensive income	Other reserve accounts

---

YOUR TURN! 11.8

The solution is on page 568.

Dior Company had beginning balances at January 1, 2019, of $100,000 Common Stock, $900,000 Paid-in Capital in Excess of Par Value, $50,000 Retained Earnings, and $10,000 Treasury Stock. Net income for the year was $30,000. Dior paid a cash dividend of $8,000. Dior also issued 1,000 new $1 par value common shares for $15 each.

Required
Prepare a statement of stockholders' equity for the Dior Company for 2019.

ANALYZING STOCKHOLDERS' EQUITY

LO9 **Define** the *return on common stockholders' equity, dividend yield*, and *dividend payout ratio* and **explain** their use.

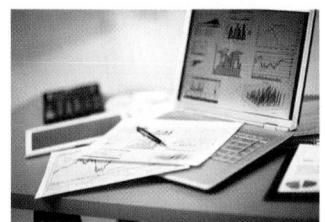

© Shutterstock.com

Return on Common Stockholders' Equity

A financial ratio of particular interest to common stockholders is the return on common stockholders' equity. This ratio measures the overall profitability of the common stockholders' investment in a company. The **return on common stockholders' equity** is calculated as follows:

$$\text{Return on common stockholders' equity} = \frac{(\text{Net income} - \text{Preferred stock dividends})}{\text{Average common stockholders' equity}}$$

By subtracting the preferred stock dividends from net income, the numerator represents the net income available exclusively to the common stockholders. The denominator averages the common stockholders' equity for the year (sum the beginning and ending common stockholders' equity and then divide by 2). If a company has preferred stock outstanding, the common stockholders' equity is calculated by subtracting the preferred stockholders' equity (the sum of the preferred stock par value and the preferred stock paid-in capital in excess of par value) from total stockholders' equity.

To illustrate the calculation of the return on common stockholders' equity, financial data from **Johnson Controls, Inc.**, is used. Johnson Controls manufactures automotive heating systems, environmental control systems, automotive batteries, and plastic packaging. The company's 2017 financial data are as follows (in millions of dollars):

Net income	$ 1,611
Preferred stock dividends.	0
Preferred stockholders' equity, beginning of year.	0
Preferred stockholders' equity, end of year	0
Common stockholders' equity, beginning of year.	20,447
Common stockholders' equity, end of year.	24,118

Johnson Controls' return on common stockholders' equity for the year is 7.2 percent, calculated as ($1,611 − $0)/[($20,477 + $24,118)/2].

TAKEAWAY 11.1	Concept ⟶	Method ⟶	Assessment
	How profitable is the stockholders' investment in a company?	Statement of stockholders' equity and the income statement. Calculate the return on common stockholders' equity.	The higher the return on common stockholders' equity, the higher the overall return on the stockholders' investment in a business.

Dividend Yield and Dividend Payout Ratio

Investors differ in their expectations regarding their investments—some investors are primarily interested in appreciation in the market value of their shares, while other investors focus on receiving current income in the form of dividends. Dividend yield and dividend payout ratio are ratios that are helpful to this latter group of investors.

Dividend Yield

Dividend yield measures the current rate of return in cash dividends from an investment in a company's shares. The ratio may be calculated for either common or preferred shares by dividing the latest annual dividend per share by the current market price of the stock:

$$\text{Dividend yield} = \frac{\text{Annual dividend per share}}{\text{Market price per share}}$$

To illustrate, **Worthington Industries**, a manufacturer of steel and plastic products, declared cash dividends per common share of $0.80. At its fiscal year-end, Worthington's common stock had a market price of $41.97 per share. Consequently, at year-end, the company's dividend yield was 1.9 percent, or $0.80/$41.97.

Dividend yields are included in the stock tables published in *The Wall Street Journal* and *Barrons,* as well as online resources such as Yahoo! Finance, so it is easy for investors to compare current dividend yields for different stocks. The following are 5-year average dividend yields for several well-known companies:

The Coca-Cola Company.	3.0 percent
AT&T.	5.1 percent
IBM Corporation.	2.9 percent
J.C. Penney Company.	0 percent
Chevron Corp.	3.9 percent
Wal-Mart Stores, Inc.	2.6 percent

Concept	Method	Assessment	TAKEAWAY 11.2
What is a company's current rate of return to stockholders in the form of dividends?	Statement of stockholders' equity and a company's current market price per share. Calculate the company's dividend yield by dividing the annual dividend per share by the company's market price per share.	The higher a company's dividend yield, the greater the rate of return to stockholders in the form of dividends.	

Dividend Payout Ratio

The **dividend payout ratio** measures the percentage of net income available to common stockholders that is paid out as dividends. The ratio is calculated as follows:

$$\text{Dividend payout ratio} = \frac{\text{Annual dividend per share}}{\text{Earnings per share}}$$

Dividend payout ratios vary considerably among corporations. Companies that are considered "growth" companies often have low payout ratios because they use the net income to help finance their growth. In contrast, "mature" companies that lack significant growth opportunities often distribute a high percentage of their net income as dividends. A good example of a mature company is the local utility company whose growth is limited by the net increase of new homes and businesses in the community and the approved rate increases by the local public utility commission.

Some corporations try to maintain a reasonably stable dividend payout ratio, so their payout ratios do not vary much from one year to the next. Other corporations try to keep their dividend per share either constant or increasing each year at a constant rate. If net income fluctuates quite a bit from year to year, these latter corporations will show dividend payout ratios that are quite variable over time. However, no company likes to cut its dividend per share because of the negative signal it sends to stockholders.

The following are the recent dividend payout ratios for some well-known corporations:

Best Buy Co. Inc. (retail).	33 percent
Microsoft Corporation (technology).	129 percent
Procter & Gamble Co. (consumer goods)	73 percent

YOUR TURN! 11.9

The solution is on page 568.

Century Co. reports the following information for the current year:

Net income	$150,000
Preferred stock dividends.	15,000
Beginning of year common stockholders' equity	650,000
End of year common stockholders' equity	700,000
Annual common dividend per share.	0.75
Market price of common shares.	33.00
Earnings per common share	3.00

Calculate Century's (a) return on common stockholders' equity; (b) dividend yield; and (c) dividend payout ratio.

TAKEAWAY 11.3	Concept	Method	Assessment
	What percentage of a company's net income is paid out to stockholders as a dividend?	Statement of stockholders' equity and the income statement. Calculate the dividend payout ratio by dividing the annual dividend per share by a company's earnings per share.	The higher the dividend payout ratio, the higher the percentage of net income paid to stockholders as a dividend.

COMPREHENSIVE PROBLEM

Following is the stockholders' equity section of Bayside Corporation's December 31 balance sheet:

Paid-in Capital		
7 Percent preferred stock, $50 par value, 5,000 shares authorized, issued, and outstanding	$ 250,000	
Common stock, $6 par value, 700,000 shares authorized; 200,000 issued, of which 10,000 shares are in the treasury	1,200,000	$1,450,000
Additional Paid-in Capital		
In excess of par value—Preferred stock	80,000	
In excess of par value—Common stock	1,000,000	
From treasury stock.	22,000	1,102,000
Total Paid-in Capital.		2,552,000
Retained earnings.		2,223,000
		4,775,000
Less: Treasury stock (10,000 common shares) at cost		140,000
Total Stockholders' Equity		$4,635,000

Required

a. What is Bayside's legal capital at December 31?

b. What is the number of common shares outstanding at December 31?

c. What is the average amount per share received from the original issuance of common stock?

d. Assuming that the preferred stock is cumulative with no dividends in arrears, what total dollar amount of preferred dividends needs to be declared at December 31, before the common stockholders may receive a dividend?

e. Has Bayside ever sold treasury stock for more than the treasury stock cost when it was acquired? Briefly explain.

f. Assume that Bayside splits its common stock 3-for-1 on the following January 1. What is the total amount of paid-in capital immediately after the split?

Solution

a. $1,450,000 (the par value of the issued preferred stock and common stock).

b. 190,000 shares (200,000 issued common shares less 10,000 shares in the treasury).

c. $11 [($1,200,000 par value of issued shares + $1,000,000 paid-in capital in excess of par value)/200,000 issued shares].

d. $17,500 (7 percent × $250,000).

e. Yes, the stockholders' equity section shows additional paid-in capital of $22,000 from treasury stock. This type of paid-in capital represents the excess of proceeds from the sale of treasury stock over that treasury stock's cost.

f. $2,552,000 (splitting the common stock does not change any of the account balances composing paid-in capital; the common stock's par value will decrease to $2 per share, and the common shares issued will increase to 600,000).

SUMMARY OF LEARNING OBJECTIVES

Define the corporate form of organization and discuss its principal characteristics. (p. 524)   LO1

- A corporation is a separate legal entity chartered by the state in which it is formed.
- The liability of corporate stockholders for the debts of a business is limited to the value of their ownership interest in a corporation, whereas claims against partners and sole proprietors may extend to their personal resources.
- Unlike sole proprietorships and partnerships, corporations must report paid-in capital separately from the accumulated balance of retained earnings. Distributions to stockholders are limited by the amount of retained earnings and other capital as specified by state law.

Explain the difference between par value stock and no-par value stock. (p. 527)   LO2

- Par value is the face value printed on a stock certificate. It has no economic significance but may have legal significance.
- No-par value stock has no face value printed on the stock certificate, although generally the board of directors sets a stated value for a corporation's capital stock.

Identify and discuss the two types of capital stock and their respective stockholder rights. (p. 528)   LO3

- Common stock represents a corporation's basic ownership class of stock; common shares carry the right to vote and may or may not pay a dividend.
- Preferred stock may differ from common stock in several ways. Typically, preferred stock has, at a minimum, some type of dividend preference and a prior claim to assets in the event of a corporate liquidation, relative to common stock.

Describe the accounting for issuances of capital stock. (p. 532)   LO4

- When capital stock is issued, the appropriate capital stock account is credited with the par value or stated value of the shares issued. The asset exchanged for the stock (usually cash) is debited for its fair value. Any difference is placed in the Paid-in Capital in Excess of Par Value account.

Define and discuss the accounting for stock splits. (p. 534)   LO5

- Stock splits change the par or stated value of capital stock and affect the number of shares outstanding. Only a memorandum notation records stock splits in the general journal. Forward stock splits increase the number of shares outstanding and lower its par or stated value, while reverse stock splits do the opposite.

Explain the accounting for treasury stock. (p. 534)   LO6

- Treasury stock represents reacquired shares of a firm's capital stock. It is commonly recorded at its acquisition cost and is deducted from total stockholders' equity on the balance sheet.

Identify and distinguish between cash dividends and stock dividends. (p. 536)   LO7

- Cash dividends reduce retained earnings and are a current liability when declared.
- Stock dividends are accounted for by a transfer of retained earnings to the appropriate capital stock and paid-in capital accounts at the fair market value of the shares distributed for small stock dividends and at par value for large stock dividends.

LO8 **Illustrate the statement of retained earnings and the statement of stockholders' equity. (p. 540)**

- A statement of retained earnings presents the financial effect of events causing retained earnings to change during an accounting period.

- A statement of stockholders' equity presents the financial effect of events causing each component of stockholders' equity (including retained earnings) to change during an accounting period.

LO9 **Define the *return on common stockholders' equity, dividend yield,* and *dividend payout ratio* and explain their use. (p. 542)**

- The return on common stockholders' equity is computed as (net income − preferred stock dividends)/ average common stockholders' equity. It indicates the profitability of the common stockholders' investment in a company.

- Dividend yield is computed by dividing a stock's annual dividend per share by its current market price per share. For investors, this ratio identifies the annual rate of return in dividends from an investment in a company's shares.

- The dividend payout ratio is computed by dividing the annual dividend per share by a company's earnings per share.

SUMMARY	Concept	Method	Assessment
TAKEAWAY 11.1	How profitable is the stockholders' investment in a company?	Statement of stockholders' equity and the income statement. Calculate the return on common stockholders' equity.	The higher the return on common stockholders' equity, the higher the overall return on the stockholders' investment in a business.
TAKEAWAY 11.2	What is a company's current rate of return to stockholders in the form of dividends?	Statement of stockholders' equity and a company's current market price per share. Calculate the company's dividend yield by dividing the annual dividend per share by the company's market price per share.	The higher a company's dividend yield, the greater the rate of return to stockholders in the form of dividends.
TAKEAWAY 11.3	What percentage of a company's net income is paid out to stockholders as a dividend?	Statement of stockholders' equity and the income statement. Calculate the dividend payout ratio by dividing the annual dividend per share by a company's earnings per share.	The higher the dividend payout ratio, the higher the percentage of net income paid to stockholders as a dividend.

KEY TERMS

Articles of
   incorporation (p. 524)
Authorized shares (p. 528)
Callable (p. 531)
Cash dividend (p. 537)
Common stock (p. 529)
Convertible (p. 531)
Corporation (p. 524)
Cumulative (p. 530)
Dividend payout ratio (p. 543)
Dividends (p. 536)
Dividends in arrears (p. 530)

Dividend yield (p. 542)
Forward stock split (p. 534)
Issued shares (p. 528)
Noncumulative (p. 530)
No-par value stock (p. 528)
Outstanding shares (p. 528)
Paid-in capital (p. 533)
Participating (p. 531)
Par value (p. 527)
Preemptive right (p. 529)
Preferred stock (p. 529)
Retained earnings (p. 533)

Return on common
   stockholders' equity (p. 542)
Reverse stock split (p. 534)
Stated value (p. 528)
Statement of retained
   earnings (p. 540)
Statement of stockholders'
   equity (p. 541)
Stock dividends (p. 538)
Treasury stock (p. 528, 534)

Assignments with the (MBC) logo in the margin are available in BusinessCourse.
See the Preface of the book for details.

SELF-STUDY QUESTIONS

(Answers to the Self-Study Questions are available at the end of this chapter.)

1. **What is the usual liability of stockholders for corporation actions?** LO1
   a. Unlimited
   b. Limited to the par value or stated value of the shares of stock they hold
   c. Limited to the amount of their investment in the corporation
   d. Limited to the amount of a corporation's retained earnings

2. **Which type of stock may have dividends in arrears?** LO3
   a. Cumulative preferred stock
   b. Common stock
   c. Noncumulative preferred stock
   d. Treasury stock

3. **Wyler Company issued 20,000 shares of $10 par value common stock in exchange for a building** LO4
   with a current fair value of $1,000,000. In recording this transaction, what amount should be
   credited to the Paid-in Capital in Excess of Par Value account?
   a. $1,000,000   c. $800,000
   b. $200,000   d. $980,000

4. **Which of the following accounts has a normal debit balance?** LO6
   a. Common Stock
   b. Paid-in Capital in Excess of Stated Value
   c. Preferred Stock
   d. Treasury Stock

5. **Which of the following events decreases a corporation's stockholders' equity?** LO7
   a. A payment of a previously declared cash dividend
   b. A declaration of a six percent stock dividend
   c. A 2-for-1 forward stock split
   d. A declaration of a $1 cash dividend per share on preferred stock

6. **When a company wants to reduce the market price per share of its stock, what action should it take?** LO5
   a. Issue a cash dividend
   b. Issue a stock dividend
   c. Do a reverse stock split
   d. Do a forward stock split

7. **What type of company is typically characterized by a high dividend payout ratio?** LO9
   a. Technology company
   b. High-growth company
   c. Mature, low-growth company
   d. All of the above

8. **Preferred stock that may be converted into common stock has which of the following characteristics?** LO3
   a. Call feature
   b. Cumulative feature
   c. Participation feature
   d. Convertible feature

9. **A dividend that is paid every quarter or every year is called?** LO7
   a. Regular dividend
   b. Special dividend
   c. Property dividend
   d. Stock dividend

10. **The statement of stockholders' equity includes each of the following except:** LO8
    a. Retained Earning
    b. Treasury Stock
    c. Paid-in Capital in Excess of Par Value
    d. Accounts Receivable

QUESTIONS

1. What is the meaning of each of the following terms: *corporation, articles of incorporation, corporate charter, board of directors, corporate officers,* and *organization costs*?

2. What is meant by the limited liability of a stockholder? Does this characteristic enhance or reduce a corporation's ability to raise capital?

3. Contrast the federal income taxation of a corporation with that of a sole proprietorship and a partnership. Which of the three types of organizations must file a federal income tax return?

4. Define *par value stock*. What is the significance of a stock's par value?

5. What is the preemptive right of a stockholder?

6. What are the basic differences between preferred stock and common stock? What are the typical features of preferred stock?

7. What features make preferred stock similar to debt? What features make it similar to common stock?

8. What is meant by dividends in arrears? If dividends are two years in arrears on $500,000 of six percent preferred stock and dividends are declared this year, what amount of total dividends must preferred stockholders receive before any distributions can be made to common stockholders?

9. Distinguish between authorized shares and issued shares. Why might the number of shares issued be more than the number of shares outstanding?

10. What are the different sources of paid-in capital?

11. Define a *forward stock split*. What is the major reason for a forward stock split?

12. Define *treasury stock*. Why might a corporation acquire treasury stock? How is treasury stock shown on the balance sheet?

13. If a corporation purchases 600 shares of its own common stock at $10 per share and resells the shares at $14 per share, where would the $2,400 [($14 − $10) × 600 shares] increase in capital appear in the financial statements? Why is no gain reported?

14. Assume that a corporation has preferred shares outstanding. How is the return on common stockholders' equity computed?

15. What is a stock dividend? How does a common stock dividend paid to common stockholders affect their respective ownership interests?

16. What is the difference between the accounting for a small stock dividend and the accounting for a large stock dividend?

17. What information is presented in a statement of retained earnings? What information is presented in a statement of stockholders' equity?

18. Where do the following accounts (and their balances) appear in the balance sheet?
    a. Dividends Payable—Common Stock
    b. Stock Dividend Distributable

19. How is a corporation's dividend yield calculated?

20. Bleaker Company declares and pays its annual dividend near the end of its fiscal year. For the current year, Bleaker's dividend payout ratio was 40 percent, its earnings per common share were $5.80, and it had 50,000 shares of common stock outstanding all year. What total amount of dividends did Bleaker declare and pay in the current year?

SHORT EXERCISES

LO1   **SE11-1.   Issuance of Common Stock** Evans & Sons, Inc., is authorized to issue one million shares of $1 par value common stock. In the company's initial public offering, 500,000 shares are sold to the investing public at a price of $5 per share. One month following Smith & Sons' initial public offering, 1,000 of its common shares were sold by one investor to another at a price of $15 per share. How should this transaction be recorded in the accounts of Evans & Sons? Why?

LO2   **SE11-2.   Issuance of No-Par Common Stock** Browne & Company issued 200,000 shares of $1 par value common stock at a price of $5 per share and issued 10,000 shares of no-par value common stock at a price of $10 per share. Prepare the journal entry to record the issuance of the no-par value common stock. How does this entry differ from the entry to record the $1 par value common stock?

SE11-3. **Allocating Liquidation Between Common Stockholders and Preferred Stockholders** The Azuza Company is liquidating. After paying off all of its creditors, the company has $1.5 million to distribute between its preferred stockholders and its common stockholders. The aggregate par value of the preferred stock is $900,000 and the aggregate par value of its common stock is $2 million. How much of the remaining $1.5 million in assets should be distributed to the preferred stockholders and how much should be distributed to the common stockholders? **LO3**

SE11-4. **Issuance of Common Stock** Evans & Sons, Inc., is authorized to issue one million shares of $1 par value common stock. The company actually sells 700,000 shares at $10 per share. Prepare the journal entry to record the issuance of the 700,000 shares. **LO4**

SE11-5. **Outstanding Shares** Willis & Company has 20 million shares of $1 par value common stock outstanding. The company believes that its current market price of $100 per share is too high and decides to execute a 4-for-1 forward stock split to lower the price. How many shares will be outstanding following the stock split, and what will be the new par value per share? **LO5**

SE11-6. **Treasury Stock Purchase** Browne & Company has no-par value common stock outstanding that is selling at $40 per share. The company's CEO believes that the stock price is undervalued and decides to buy back 10,000 shares. Prepare the journal entry to record the purchase of the treasury stock. **LO6**

SE11-7. **Dividends Paid and Dividends in Arrears** The Glendora Company has 200,000 shares of cumulative, five percent, $100 par value preferred stock outstanding. Last year the company failed to pay its regular dividend, but the board of directors would like to resume paying its regular dividend this year. Calculate the dividends in arrears and the total dividend that must be paid this year. **LO7**

The following information relates to SE11-8 through SE11-10:

Evans & Sons, Inc., disclosed the following information in a recent annual report:

	2018	2019
Net income	$ 35,000	$ 48,000
Preferred stock dividends.	3,000	3,000
Average common stockholders' equity.	1,000,000	1,500,000
Dividend per common share.	1.90	2.00
Earnings per share.	2.85	3.20
Market price per common share, year-end.	19.00	21.00

SE11-8. **Return on Common Stockholders' Equity** Calculate the return on common stockholders' equity for Evans & Sons for 2018 and 2019. Did the return improve from 2018 to 2019? **LO9**

SE11-9. **Dividend Yield** Calculate the dividend yield for Evans & Sons for 2018 and 2019. Did the dividend yield improve from 2018 to 2019? **LO9**

SE11-10. **Dividend Payout Ratio** Calculate the dividend payout for Evans & Sons for 2018 and 2019. Did the dividend payout increase from 2018 to 2019? **LO9**

SE11-11. **Change in Stockholders' Equity** Nikron Corporation issued 20,000 shares of $0.50 par value common stock during the year for $20 each. Nikron also repurchased treasury stock for $15,000. Net income for the year was $140,000. The company also paid cash dividends of $25,000. What was the total change in Nikron's stockholders' equity for the year? **LO8**

EXERCISES—SET A

E11-1A. **Dividend Distribution** Lake Company has the following shares outstanding: 20,000 shares of $50 par value, five percent cumulative preferred stock and 80,000 shares of $10 par value common stock. The company declared cash dividends amounting to $200,000. **LO7**

    a. If no dividends in arrears on the preferred stock exist, how much in total dividends, and in dividends per share, is paid to each class of stock?

    b. If one year of dividends in arrears exist on the preferred stock, how much in total dividends, and in dividends per share, is paid to each class of stock?

LO4 **E11-2A.** **Share Issuances for Cash** Minaret, Inc., issued 10,000 shares of $50 par value preferred stock at $68 per share and 12,000 shares of no-par value common stock at $15 per share. The common stock has no stated value. All issuances were for cash.

a. Prepare the journal entries to record the share issuances.

b. Prepare the journal entry for the issuance of the common stock assuming that it had a stated value of $4 per share.

c. Prepare the journal entry for the issuance of the common stock assuming that it had a par value of $2 per share.

LO5 **E11-3A.** **Forward Stock Split** On March 1 of the current year, Center Corporation has 500,000 shares of $10 par value common stock that are issued and outstanding. The general ledger shows the following account balances relating to the common stock:

Common stock	$5,000,000
Paid-in capital in excess of par value	3,500,000

On March 2, Center Corporation splits its stock 2-for-1 and reduces the par value to $5 per share.

a. How many shares of common stock are issued and outstanding immediately following the stock split?

b. What is the balance in the Common Stock account immediately following the stock split?

c. What is the balance in the Paid-in Capital in Excess of Par Value account immediately following the stock split?

d. Is a journal entry required to record the forward stock split? If yes, prepare the entry.

LO4, 6 **E11-4A.** **Treasury Stock** Inland Corporation issued 30,000 shares of $5 par value common stock at $15 per share and 8,000 shares of $50 par value, eight percent preferred stock at $85 per share. Later, the company purchased 3,000 shares of its own common stock at $20 per share.

a. Prepare the journal entries to record the share issuances and the purchase of the common shares.

b. Assume that Inland sold 2,000 shares of the treasury stock at $30 per share. Prepare the general journal entry to record the sale of this treasury stock.

c. Assume that Inland sold the remaining 1,000 shares of treasury stock at $18 per share. Prepare the journal entry to record the sale of this treasury stock.

LO7 **E11-5A.** **Cash Dividends** Bernard Corporation has the following shares outstanding: 8,000 shares of $50 par value, six percent preferred stock and 50,000 shares of $1 par value common stock. The company has $328,000 of retained earnings. At year-end, the company declares its regular $3 per share cash dividend on the preferred stock and a $2.20 per share cash dividend on the common stock. Three weeks later, the company pays the dividends.

a. Prepare the journal entry for the declaration of the cash dividends.

b. Prepare the journal entry for the payment of the cash dividends.

LO7 **E11-6A.** **Stock Dividends** White Corporation has 80,000 shares of $5 par value common stock outstanding. At year-end, the company declares a five percent stock dividend. The market price of the stock on the declaration date is $20 per share. Four weeks later, the company issues the shares of stock to stockholders.

a. Prepare the journal entry for the declaration of the stock dividend.

b. Prepare the journal entry for the issuance of the stock dividend.

c. Assume that the company declared a 30 percent stock dividend rather than a five percent stock dividend. Prepare the journal entries for (1) the declaration of the stock dividend and (2) the issuance of the stock dividend.

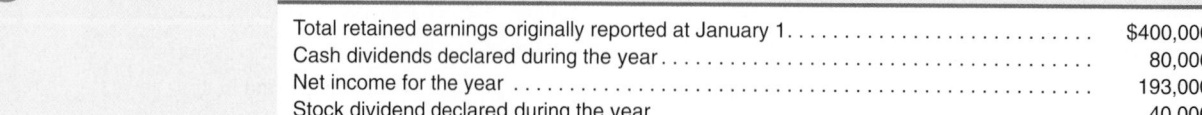

LO8 **E11-7A.** **Statement of Retained Earnings** Use the following data to prepare a statement of retained earnings for Barney Corporation.

Total retained earnings originally reported at January 1	$400,000
Cash dividends declared during the year	80,000
Net income for the year	193,000
Stock dividend declared during the year	40,000

E11-8A. Conversion of Preferred Stock into Common Stock Evans & Sons, Inc., has 20,000 shares of $100 par value, six percent preferred stock and 100,000 shares of $1.00 par value common stock outstanding. The preferred stock is convertible into the company's common stock at a conversion rate of 1-to-20; that is, each share of preferred stock is convertible into 20 shares of common stock. The preferred stock had been sold for its par value when issued. Prepare the journal entry to record the conversion of all of the company's preferred stock into common stock. **LO3**

E11-9A. Reverse Stock Split Upland Metals Company had 20,000,000 shares of $0.01 par value common stock outstanding which had been sold for an aggregate amount of $300,000,000. The company's shares are traded on the New York Stock Exchange, which has a minimum listing price of $1 per share. Recently, the company's common stock has been trading on the exchange below $1 per share, and the exchange has notified the company that its common stock would be delisted in 30 days if the stock price did not rebound above its minimum listing price. In response to this notification, Upland Metals authorized a 1-for-40 reverse stock split. Following the reverse stock split: **LO5**

a. How many common shares will be outstanding?
b. What will be the new par value per share?
c. How will the reverse stock split be recorded in the company's accounts?

E11-10A. Return on Common Stockholders' Equity, Dividend Yield, and Dividend Payout The following information relates to Ontario Components, Inc.: **LO9**

	2018	2019
Net income	$ 65,000	$ 100,000
Preferred stock dividends	5,000	5,000
Average common stockholders' equity	2,000,000	2,100,000
Dividend per common share	1.50	1.50
Earnings per share	2.90	3.00
Market price per common share, year-end	27.50	30.00

a. Calculate the company's return on common stockholders' equity for 2018 and 2019.
b. Calculate the company's dividend yield for 2018 and 2019.
c. Calculate the company's dividend payout for 2018 and 2019.

E11-11A. Characteristics of a Corporation Label each of the following characteristics of a corporation as either an (A) advantage or a (D) disadvantage: **LO1**

a. Limited liability
b. Taxation
c. Regulations
d. Transferability of ownership

E11-12A. Cash and Noncash Share Issuances Skelton Corporation was organized on June 1. The company's charter authorizes 500,000 shares of $5 par value common stock. On July 1, the attorney who helped organize the corporation accepted 600 shares of Skelton common stock in settlement for the services provided (the services were valued at $8,000). On July 15, Skelton issued 6,000 common shares for $65,000 cash. On September 15, Guild issued 2,000 common shares to acquire a vacant land site appraised at $28,000. Prepare the journal entries to record the stock issuances on July 1, July 15, and September 15. **LO4**

E11-13A. Stock Issuance and Treasury Stock Decade, Inc., recorded certain capital stock transactions shown in the following journal entries: (1) issued common stock for $25 cash per share, (2) purchased treasury shares at $40 per share, and (3) sold some of the treasury shares: **LO4, 6**

1.	Cash	500,000	
	Common stock		75,000
	Paid-in capital in excess of par value		425,000
2.	Treasury stock	100,000	
	Cash		100,000

3.	Cash	81,000	
	Treasury stock		75,000
	Paid-in capital from treasury stock		6,000

   a. How many shares were originally issued?
   b. What was the par value of the shares issued?
   c. How many shares of treasury stock were acquired?
   d. How many shares of treasury stock were sold?
   e. At what price per share was the treasury stock sold?

LO7 **E11-14A. Cash and Stock Dividends** Lester Corporation has 30,000 shares of $1 par value common stock outstanding. The company has $250,000 of retained earnings. At year-end, the company declares a cash dividend of $3.00 per share and a five percent stock dividend. The market price of the stock at the declaration date is $40 per share. Three weeks later, the company pays the dividends.

   a. Prepare the journal entry for the declaration of the cash dividend.
   b. Prepare the journal entry for the declaration of the stock dividend.
   c. Prepare the journal entry for the payment of the cash dividend.
   d. Prepare the journal entry for the payment of the stock dividend.

LO5, 7 **E11-15A. Large Stock Dividend and Forward Stock Split** High Corporation has 60,000 shares of $20 par value common stock outstanding and retained earnings of $800,000. The company declares a 100 percent stock dividend. The market price at the declaration date is $20 per share.

   a. Prepare the journal entries for (1) the declaration of the dividend and (2) the issuance of the dividend.
   b. Assume that the company splits its stock 2-for-1 and reduces the par value from $20 to $10 rather than declaring a 100 percent stock dividend. How does the accounting for the forward stock split differ from the accounting for the 100 percent stock dividend?

EXERCISES—SET B

LO7 **E11-1B. Dividend Distribution** Bowen Corporation has the following shares outstanding: 15,000 shares of $50 par value, six percent preferred stock and 50,000 shares of $5 par value common stock. During its first three years in business, the firm declared no dividends in the first year, $140,000 of dividends in the second year, and $60,000 of dividends in the third year.

   a. If the preferred stock is cumulative, determine the total amount of dividends paid to each class of stock in each of the three years.
   b. If the preferred stock is noncumulative, determine the total amount of dividends paid to each class of stock in each of the three years.

LO4 **E11-2B. Share Issuances for Cash** Chase, Inc., issued 10,000 shares of $20 par value preferred stock at $50 per share and 8,000 shares of no-par value common stock at $20 per share. The common stock has no stated value. All issuances were for cash.

   a. Prepare the journal entries to record the share issuances.
   b. Prepare the journal entry for the issuance of the common stock assuming that it had a stated value of $10 per share.
   c. Prepare the journal entry for the issuance of the common stock assuming that it had a par value of $2 per share.

LO5 **E11-3B. Forward Stock Split** On September 1, Cambridge Company has 500,000 shares of $15 par value common stock that are issued and outstanding. The general ledger shows the following account balances relating to the common stock:

Common stock	$7,500,000
Paid-in capital in excess of par value	$2,250,000

On September 2, Cambridge splits its stock 3-for-2 and reduces the par value to $10 per share.

   a. How many shares of common stock are issued and outstanding immediately following the stock split?

b. What is the balance in the Common Stock account immediately following the stock split?

c. What is the likely reason that Cambridge Company split its stock?

E11-4B. Treasury Stock Pomona Corporation issued 60,000 shares of $3 par value common stock at $21 per share and 9,000 shares of $30 par value, ten percent preferred stock at $85 per share. Later, the company purchased 2,000 shares of its own common stock at $23 per share. **LO4, 6**

a. Prepare the journal entries to record the share issuances and the purchase of the common shares.

b. Assume that Pomona sold 1,500 shares of the treasury stock at $30 per share. Prepare the general journal entry to record the sale of this treasury stock.

c. Assume that Pomona sold the remaining 500 shares of treasury stock at $20 per share. Prepare the journal entry to record the sale of this treasury stock.

E11-5B. Cash Dividends Sand Corporation has the following shares outstanding: 10,000 shares of $40 par value, ten percent preferred stock and 50,000 shares of $2 par value common stock. The company has $428,000 of retained earnings. At year-end, the company declares its regular $4 per share cash dividend on the preferred stock and a $3.20 per share cash dividend on the common stock. Two weeks later, the company pays the dividends. **LO7**

a. Prepare the journal entry for the declaration of the cash dividends.

b. Prepare the journal entry for the payment of the cash dividends.

E11-6B. Stock Dividends Mammoth Corporation has 100,000 shares of $10 par value common stock outstanding. At year-end, the company declares a five percent stock dividend. The market price of the stock on the declaration date is $30 per share. Three weeks later, the company issues the shares of stock to stockholders. **LO7**

a. Prepare the journal entry for the declaration of the stock dividend.

b. Prepare the journal entry for the issuance of the stock dividend.

c. Assume that the company declared a 50 percent stock dividend rather than a five percent stock dividend. Prepare the journal entries for (1) the declaration of the stock dividend and (2) the issuance of the stock dividend.

E11-7B. Statement of Retained Earnings Use the following data to prepare a statement of retained earnings for June Corporation. **LO8**

Total retained earnings originally reported as of January 1	$347,000
Stock dividends declared during the year	25,000
Cash dividends declared during the year	40,000
Net income for the year	70,000

E11-8B. Conversion of Preferred Stock into Common Stock Givens & Sons, Inc., has 20,000 shares of $50 par value, nine percent preferred stock and 100,000 shares of $0.50 par value common stock outstanding. The preferred stock is convertible into the company's common stock at a conversion rate of 1-to-40; that is, each share of preferred stock is convertible into 40 shares of common stock. The preferred stock had been sold for its par value when issued. Prepare the journal entry to record the conversion of all of the company's preferred stock into common stock. **LO3**

E11-9B. Reverse Stock Split The Crystal Company had 100,000,000 shares of $0.10 par value common stock outstanding which had been sold for an aggregate amount of $500,000,000. The company's shares are traded on the New York Stock Exchange, which has a minimum listing price of $1 per share. Recently, the company's common stock has been trading on the exchange below $1 per share, and the exchange has notified the company that its common stock would be delisted in 30 days if the stock price did not rebound above its minimum listing price. In response to this notification, Crystal authorized a 1-for-40 reverse stock split. Following the reverse stock split: **LO5**

a. How many common shares will be outstanding?

b. What will be the new par value per share?

c. How will the reverse stock split be recorded in the company's accounts?

E11-10B. Return on Common Stockholders' Equity, Dividend Yield, and Dividend Payout The following information relates to Menlo, Inc.: **LO9**

	2018	2019
Net income	$ 125,000	$ 200,000
Preferred stock dividends	15,000	18,000
Average common stockholders' equity	5,000,000	4,200,000
Dividend per common share	2.80	3.00
Earnings per share	5.80	6.00
Market price per common share, year-end	60.00	59.50

    a.   Calculate the company's return on common stockholders' equity for 2018 and 2019.
    b.   Calculate the company's dividend yield for 2018 and 2019.
    c.   Calculate the company's dividend payout for 2018 and 2019.

LO1   **E11-11B. Characteristics of a Corporation** Label each of the following characteristics of a corporation as either an (A) advantage or a (D) disadvantage:

    a.   Organizational costs
    b.   Continuity of existence
    c.   Capital raising capability
    d.   Separate legal entity

LO4   **E11-12B. Cash and Noncash Share Issuances** Channey Corporation was organized on July 1. The company's charter authorizes 100,000 shares of $2 par value common stock. On August 1, the attorney who helped organize the corporation accepted 950 shares of Channey common stock in settlement for the services provided (the services were valued at $9,800). On August 15, Channey issued 6,000 common shares for $75,000 cash. On October 15, Channey issued 3,000 common shares to acquire a vacant land site appraised at $50,000. Prepare the journal entries to record the stock issuances on August 1, August 15, and October 15.

LO4, 6   **E11-13B. Stock Issuance and Treasury Stock** Omaha, Inc., recorded certain capital stock transactions shown in the following journal entries: (1) issued common stock for $40 cash per share, (2) purchased treasury shares at $50 per share, and (3) sold some of the treasury shares:

1.	Cash	437,000	
	Common stock		43,700
	Paid-in capital in excess of par value		393,300
2.	Treasury stock	77,000	
	Cash		77,000
3.	Cash	63,360	
	Treasury stock		52,800
	Paid-in capital from treasury stock		10,560

    a.   How many shares were originally issued?
    b.   What was the par value of the shares issued?
    c.   How many shares of treasury stock were acquired?
    d.   How many shares of treasury stock were sold?
    e.   At what price per share was the treasury stock sold?

LO7   **E11-14B. Cash and Stock Dividends** Murphy Corporation has 50,000 shares of $10 par value common stock outstanding. The company has $450,000 of retained earnings. At year-end, the company declares a cash dividend of $2.10 per share and a five percent stock dividend. The market price of the stock at the declaration date is $35 per share. Four weeks later, the company pays the dividends.

    a.   Prepare the journal entry for the declaration of the cash dividend.
    b.   Prepare the journal entry for the declaration of the stock dividend.
    c.   Prepare the journal entry for the payment of the cash dividend.
    d.   Prepare the journal entry for the payment of the stock dividend.

LO5, 7   **E11-15B. Large Stock Dividend and Forward Stock Split** Kitch Corporation has 50,000 shares of $5 par value common stock outstanding and retained earnings of $820,000. The company declares a 100 percent stock dividend. The market price at the declaration date is $17 per share.

    a. Prepare the journal entries for (1) the declaration of the dividend and (2) the issuance of the dividend.

    b. Assume that the company splits its stock 5-for-1 and reduces the par value from $5 to $1 rather than declaring a 100 percent stock dividend. How does the accounting for the forward stock split differ from the accounting for the 100 percent stock dividend?

PROBLEMS—SET A

P11-1A. **Dividend Distribution** Ryan Corporation began business on March 1, 2016. At that time, it issued 20,000 shares of $60 par value, seven percent cumulative preferred stock and 100,000 shares of $5 par value common stock. Through the end of 2018, there had been no change in the number of preferred and common shares outstanding.

LO7

Required

    a. Assume that Ryan declared dividends of $0 in 2016, $195,000 in 2017, and $200,000 in 2018. Calculate the total dividends and the dividends per share paid to each class of stock in 2016, 2017, and 2018.

    b. Assume that Ryan declared dividends of $0 in 2016, $90,000 in 2017, and $190,000 in 2018. Calculate the total dividends and the dividends per share paid to each class of stock in 2016, 2017, and 2018.

P11-2A. **Stockholders' Equity: Transactions and Balance Sheet Presentation** Torey Corporation was organized on April 1, with an authorization of 25,000 shares of six percent, $50 par value preferred stock and 200,000 shares of $5 par value common stock. During April, the following transactions affecting stockholders' equity occurred:

LO4, 8

Apr. 1 Issued 80,000 shares of common stock at $40 cash per share.

       3 Issued 2,000 shares of common stock to attorneys and promoters in exchange for their services in organizing the corporation. The services were valued at $31,000.

       8 Issued 3,000 shares of common stock in exchange for equipment with a fair market value of $55,000.

     20 Issued 6,000 shares of preferred stock for cash at $80 per share.

Required

    a. Prepare journal entries to record the above transactions.

    b. Prepare the stockholders' equity section of the balance sheet at April 30. Assume that the net income for April is $60,000.

P11-3A. **Stockholders' Equity: Transactions and Balance Sheet Presentation** The stockholders' equity accounts of Willis Corporation at January 1 appear below:

LO4, 6, 8

8 Percent preferred stock, $10 par value, 50,000 shares authorized; 6,800 shares issued and outstanding . . .	$ 68,000
Common stock, $10 par value, 200,000 shares authorized; 50,000 shares issued and outstanding	500,000
Paid-in capital in excess of par value—Preferred stock	68,000
Paid-in capital in excess of par value—Common stock	200,000
Retained earnings	270,000

During the year, the following transactions occurred:

Jan. 10 Issued 35,000 shares of common stock for $18 cash per share.

     23 Purchased 10,000 shares of common stock as treasury stock at $19 per share.

Mar. 14 Sold one-half of the treasury shares acquired January 23 for $21 per share.

July 15 Issued 3,500 shares of preferred stock in exchange for equipment with a fair market value of $128,000.

Nov. 15 Sold 1,000 of the treasury shares acquired January 23 for $24 per share.

Dec. 31 Closed the net income of $59,000 to the Retained Earnings account.

Required

    a. Set up T-accounts for the stockholders' equity accounts as of the beginning of the year and enter the January 1 balances.

b.   Prepare journal entries to record the foregoing transactions and post to T-accounts (set up any additional T-accounts needed). Do not prepare the journal entry for the Dec. 31 transaction, but post the appropriate amount to the Retained Earnings T-account. Determine the ending balances for the stockholders' equity accounts.

c.   Prepare the December 31 stockholders' equity section of the balance sheet.

LO4, 5, 6, 8   **P11-4A.**   **Stockholders' Equity: Transactions and Balance Sheet Presentation** The stockholders' equity of Peak Corporation at January 1 follows:

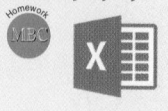

7 Percent preferred stock, $100 par value, 20,000 shares authorized;	
5,000 shares issued and outstanding......................................	$ 500,000
Common stock, $15 par value, 100,000 shares authorized;	
40,000 shares issued and outstanding.....................................	600,000
Paid-in capital in excess of par value—Preferred stock.........................	24,000
Paid-in capital in excess of par value—Common stock.........................	360,000
Retained earnings	325,000
Total Stockholders' Equity...	$1,809,000

The following transactions, among others, occurred during the year:

Jan.   12   Announced a 4-for-1 common stock split, reducing the par value of the common stock to $3.75 per share. The authorization was increased to 400,000 shares.

Mar.   31   Converted $40,000 face value of convertible bonds payable (the book value of the bonds was $43,000) to common stock. Each $1,000 bond converted to 125 shares of common stock.

June   1   Acquired equipment with a fair market value of $90,000 in exchange for 500 shares of preferred stock.

Sept.   1   Acquired 10,000 shares of common stock for cash at $10 per share.

Oct.   12   Sold 1,500 treasury shares at $12 per share.

Nov.   21   Issued 5,000 shares of common stock at $11 cash per share.

Dec.   28   Sold 1,200 treasury shares at $9 per share.

        31   Closed net income of $105,000 to the Retained Earnings account.

Required

a.   Set up T-accounts for the stockholders' equity accounts as of the beginning of the year and enter the January 1 balances.

b.   Prepare journal entries for the given transactions and post them to the T-accounts (set up any additional T-accounts needed). Do not prepare the journal entry for the Dec. 31 transaction, but post the appropriate amount to the Retained Earnings T-account. Determine the ending balances for the stockholders' equity accounts.

c.   Prepare the stockholders' equity section of the balance sheet at December 31.

LO4, 6   **P11-5A.**   **Stockholders' Equity: Information and Entries from Comparative Data** Comparative stockholders' equity sections from two successive years of balance sheets from Farrow, Inc., are as follows:

	Dec. 31, 2018	Dec. 31, 2017
Paid-in Capital		
8 Percent preferred stock, $40 par value, authorized 20,000 shares;		
issued and outstanding, 2017: 10,000 shares; 2018: 12,000 shares ...	$ 480,000	$ 400,000
Common stock, no-par value, $5 stated value, authorized 80,000		
shares; issued, 2017: 32,000 shares; 2018: 40,000 shares	200,000	160,000
Additional Paid-in Capital		
In excess of par value—Preferred stock........................	224,000	144,000
In excess of stated value—Common stock......................	232,000	160,000
From treasury stock......................................	21,000	
Retained earnings......................................	350,000	229,000
		$1,093,000
Less: Treasury stock (8,000 shares common) at cost	0	179,000
Total Stockholders' Equity...............................	$1,507,000	$ 914,000

No dividends were declared or paid during 2018.

Required

Prepare the journal entries for the transactions affecting stockholders' equity that occurred during 2018. Do not prepare the journal entry for closing net income to retained earnings. Assume that any share transactions were for cash.

P11-6A. **Retained Earnings: Transactions and Statement** The stockholders' equity accounts of Raymund Corporation as of January 1 appear below: **LO7, 8**

Common stock, $1 par value, 400,000 shares authorized; 160,000 shares issued and outstanding . . .	$160,000
Paid-in capital in excess of par value	920,000
Retained earnings	513,000

During the year, the following transactions occurred:

June   7 Declared a 20 percent stock dividend; market value of the common stock was $15 per share.
     28 Issued the stock dividend declared on June 7.

Dec.   5 Declared a cash dividend of $2.00 per share.
     26 Paid the cash dividend declared on December 5.

Required

a. Prepare journal entries to record the foregoing transactions.

b. Prepare a statement of retained earnings. The net income for the year is $435,000.

P11-7A. **Retained Earnings: Transactions and Statement** The stockholders' equity of Carly Corporation at January 1 follows: **LO7, 8**

6 Percent preferred stock, $10 par value, 40,000 shares authorized;	
25,000 shares issued and outstanding	$ 250,000
Common stock, $1 par value, 300,000 shares authorized; 80,000 shares	
issued and outstanding	80,000
Paid-in capital in excess of par value—Common stock	560,000
Retained earnings	830,000
Total Stockholders' Equity.	$1,720,000

The following transactions, among others, occurred during the year:

June   18 Declared a 70 percent stock dividend on all outstanding shares of common stock. The market value of the stock was $14 per share.

July   1 Issued the stock dividend declared on June 18.

Dec.   20 Declared the annual cash dividend on the preferred stock and a cash dividend of $1.80 per share on the common stock, payable on January 20 to stockholders of record on December 28.

Required

a. Prepare journal entries to record the foregoing transactions.

b. Prepare a statement of retained earnings. The net income for the year is $500,000.

P11-8A. **Stockholders' Equity Transactions, Journal Entries, and T-Accounts** The stockholders' equity of Black Corporation at January 1 follows: **LO4, 5, 6**

8 Percent preferred stock, $100 par value, 20,000 shares	
authorized; 5,000 shares issued and outstanding	$ 500,000
Common stock, $1 par value, 100,000 shares	
authorized; 40,000 shares issued and outstanding	40,000
Paid-in capital in excess of par value—Preferred stock	200,000
Paid-in capital in excess of par value—Common stock	800,000
Retained earnings	625,000
Total Stockholders' Equity.	$2,165,000

The following transactions, among others, occurred during the year:

Jan.	1	Announced a 4-for-1 common stock split, reducing the par value of the common stock to $0.25 per share.
Mar.	31	Converted $75,000 face value of convertible bonds payable (the book value of the bonds was $83,000) to common stock. Each $1,000 bond converted to 110 shares of common stock. (Record common stock entry in whole dollars. Round up.)
June	1	Acquired equipment with a fair market value of $90,000 in exchange for 300 shares of preferred stock.
Sept.	1	Acquired 15,000 shares of common stock for cash at $20 per share.
Nov.	21	Issued 5,000 shares of common stock at $22 cash per share.
Dec.	28	Sold 1,000 treasury shares at $23 per share.
	31	Closed net income of $145,000, to the Retained Earnings account.

Required

a. Set up T-accounts for the stockholders' equity accounts as of the beginning of the year and enter the January 1 balances.

b. Prepare journal entries for the given transactions and post them to the T-accounts (set up any additional T-accounts needed). Do not prepare the journal entry for the Dec. 31 transaction, but post the appropriate amount to the Retained Earnings T-account. Determine the ending balances for the stockholders' equity accounts.

LO4, 5, 6, 8   **P11-9A.**   **Stockholders' Equity Section of the Balance Sheet**   Using your analysis from P11-8A, prepare the stockholders' equity section of the Black Corporation's balance sheet.

LO4, 6, 7, 8   **P11-10A.**   **Stockholders' Equity: Transactions and Statement**   The stockholders' equity section of Day Corporation's balance sheet at January 1 follows:

Common stock, $5 par value, 300,000 shares authorized, 60,000 shares		
Issued, 6,000 shares in treasury...................................		$ 300,000
Additional paid-in capital...		
In excess of par value..	$480,000	
From treasury stock	30,000	510,000
Retained earnings		348,000
		1,158,000
Less: Treasury stock (6,000 shares) at cost........................		138,000
		$1,020,000

The following transactions affecting stockholders' equity occurred during the year:

Jan.	8	Issued 15,000 shares of previously unissued common stock for $42 cash per share.
Mar.	12	Sold all of the treasury shares for $56 cash per share.
June	30	Declared a five percent stock dividend on all outstanding shares of common stock. The market value of the stock was $50 per share.
July	10	Issued the stock dividend declared on June 30.
Oct.	7	Acquired 2,500 shares of common stock as treasury stock at $52 cash per share.
Dec.	18	Declared a cash dividend of $1.00 per outstanding common share, payable on January 9 to stockholders of record on December 31.

Required

a. Prepare journal entries to record the foregoing transactions.

b. Prepare a statement of stockholders' equity. Net income for the year is $351,000.

LO4, 6   **P11-11A.**   **Stockholders' Equity: Transaction Descriptions from Account Data**   The following T-accounts contain keyed entries representing five transactions involving the stockholders' equity of Riverside, Inc.:

	Cash		
(1)	90,000	15,600	(4)
(2)	120,000		
(5)	8,400		

	Paid-in Capital in Excess of Par Value—Common Stock	
		15,000	(3)

	Land	
(3)	105,000	

	Paid-in Capital from Treasury Stock	
		600	(5)

	Preferred Stock, $10 Par	
		30,000	(1)

	Paid-in Capital in Excess of Par Value—Preferred Stock	
		60,000	(1)

	Common Stock, $20 Par	
		120,000	(2)
		90,000	(3)

	Treasury Stock		
(4)	(600 shares of common)	7,800	(5)
	15,600		

Required

Using this information, give detailed descriptions, including number of shares and price per share when applicable, for each of the five transactions.

PROBLEMS—SET B

P11-1B. **Dividend Distribution** Chauncey Corporation began business on June 30, 2016. At that time, it issued 20,000 shares of $50 par value, six percent, cumulative preferred stock and 90,000 shares of $10 par value common stock. Through the end of 2018, there had been no change in the number of preferred and common shares outstanding.

LO7

Required

a. Assume that Chauncey declared dividends of $69,000 in 2016, $0 in 2017, and $354,000 in 2018. Calculate the total dividends and the dividends per share paid to each class of stock in 2016, 2017, and 2018.

b. Assume that Chauncey declared dividends of $0 in 2016, $120,000 in 2017, and $186,000 in 2018. Calculate the total dividends and the dividends per share paid to each class of stock in 2016, 2017, and 2018.

P11-2B. **Stockholders' Equity: Transactions and Balance Sheet Presentation** Baker Corporation was organized on July 1, with an authorization of 50,000 shares of $5 no-par value preferred stock ($5 is the annual dividend) and 100,000 shares of $10 par value common stock. During July, the following transactions affecting stockholders' equity occurred:

LO4, 8

July	1	Issued 62,000 shares of common stock at $21 cash per share.
	12	Issued 7,000 shares of common stock in exchange for equipment with a fair market value of $71,000.
	15	Issued 10,000 shares of preferred stock for cash at $40 per share.

Required

a. Prepare journal entries to record the foregoing transactions.

b. Prepare the stockholders' equity section of the balance sheet at July 31. The net income for July is $52,000.

P11-3B. **Stockholders' Equity: Transactions and Balance Sheet Presentation** The stockholders' equity accounts of Cooper Corporation at January 1 follow:

LO4, 6, 8

Common stock, $1 par value, 350,000 shares authorized; 150,000 shares issued and outstanding	$150,000
Paid-in capital in excess of par value	600,000
Retained earnings	366,000

During the year, the following transactions occurred:

Jan. 5 Issued 20,000 shares of common stock for $15 cash per share.

18 Purchased 4,000 shares of common stock as treasury stock at $14 cash per share.

Mar. 12 Sold one-fourth of the treasury shares acquired January 18 for $17 per share.

July 17 Sold 600 shares of the remaining treasury stock for $12 per share.

Oct. 1 Issued 5,000 shares of eight percent, $25 par value preferred stock for $35 cash per share. These are the first preferred shares issued out of 50,000 authorized shares.

Dec. 31 Closed the net income of $170,000 to the Retained Earnings account.

Required

a. Set up T-accounts for the stockholders' equity accounts as of the beginning of the year and enter the January 1 balances.

b. Prepare journal entries to record the foregoing transactions and post to T-accounts (set up any additional T-accounts needed). Do not prepare the journal entry for the Dec. 31 transaction, but post the appropriate amount to the Retained Earnings T-account. Determine the ending balances for the stockholders' equity accounts.

c. Prepare the December 31 stockholders' equity section of the balance sheet.

LO4, 5, 6, 8 **P11-4B.** **Stockholders' Equity: Transactions and Balance Sheet Presentation** The following is the stockholders' equity of Laker Corporation at January 1:

8 Percent preferred stock, $40 par value, 10,000 shares authorized; 7,000 shares issued and outstanding	$ 280,000
Common stock, $20 par value, 50,000 shares authorized; 25,000 shares issued and outstanding	500,000
Paid-in capital in excess of par value—Preferred stock	70,000
Paid-in capital in excess of par value—Common stock	385,000
Retained earnings	238,000
Total Stockholders' Equity	$1,473,000

The following transactions, among others, occurred during the year:

Jan. 15 Issued 2,000 shares of preferred stock for $65 cash per share.

20 Issued 4,000 shares of common stock at $40 cash per share.

31 Converted $20,000 face value of convertible bonds payable (the book value of the bonds is $18,500) to common stock. Each $1,000 bond converted to 25 shares of common stock.

May 18 Announced a 2-for-1 common stock split, reducing the par value of the common stock to $10 per share. The authorization was increased to 100,000 shares.

June 1 Acquired equipment with a fair market value of $50,000 in exchange for 2,000 shares of common stock.

Sept. 1 Purchased 3,500 shares of common stock as treasury stock at $19 cash per share.

Oct. 12 Sold 900 treasury shares at $21 per share.

Dec. 22 Issued 600 shares of preferred stock for $59 cash per share.

28 Sold 1,100 of the remaining treasury shares at $18 per share.

31 Closed net income of $150,000 to the Retained Earnings account.

Required

a. Set up T-accounts for the stockholders' equity accounts as of the beginning of the year and enter the January 1 balances.

b. Prepare journal entries for the given transactions and post them to the T-accounts (set up any additional T-accounts needed). Do not prepare the journal entry for the Dec. 31 transaction, but post the appropriate amount to the Retained Earnings T-account. Determine the ending balances for the stockholders' equity accounts.

c. Prepare the stockholders' equity section of the balance sheet at December 31.

LO4, 6 **P11-5B.** **Stockholders' Equity: Information and Entries from Comparative Data** Comparative stockholders' equity sections from two successive years of balance sheets from Kirkwood, Inc., are as follows:

	Dec. 31, 2018	Dec. 31, 2017
Paid-in Capital		
10 percent preferred stock, $20 par value, authorized 50,000 shares; issued and outstanding, 2017: 15,000 shares; 2018: 25,000 shares	$ 500,000	$ 400,000
Common stock, no-par value, $10 stated value, authorized 120,000 shares; issued, 2017: 48,000 shares; 2018: 65,000 shares	600,000	480,000
Additional Paid-in Capital		
In excess of par value—Preferred stock	225,000	160,000
In excess of stated value—Common stock	540,000	336,000
From treasury stock.	25,000	
Retained earnings	390,000	335,000
	2,275,000	1,711,000
Less: Treasury stock (10,000 shares common) at cost	0	136,000
Total stockholders' equity	$2,275,000	$1,575,000

No dividends were declared or paid during 2018.

Required

Prepare the journal entries for the transactions affecting stockholders' equity that occurred during 2018. Do not prepare the journal entry for closing net income to retained earnings. Assume that any share transactions were for cash.

P11-6B. **Retained Earnings: Transactions and Statement** The stockholders' equity of Ranger Corporation at January 1 appears below:

Common stock, $10 par value, 200,000 shares authorized; 80,000 shares issued and outstanding	$800,000
Paid-in capital in excess of par value	480,000
Retained earnings	305,000

During the year, the following transactions occurred:

May   12   Declared a 15 percent stock dividend; market value of the common stock was $22 per share.
June   6   Issued the stock dividend declared on May 12.
Dec.   5   Declared a cash dividend of $1.50 per share.
        30   Paid the cash dividend declared on December 5.

Required

a.   Prepare journal entries to record the foregoing transactions.
b.   Prepare a statement of retained earnings. Net income for the year is $275,000.

P11-7B. **Retained Earnings: Transactions and Statement** The stockholders' equity of Elsworth Corporation at January 1 is shown below:

5 Percent preferred stock, $100 par value, 10,000 shares authorized; 4,000 shares issued and outstanding	$ 400,000
Common stock, $5 par value, 200,000 shares authorized; 50,000 shares issued and outstanding	250,000
Paid-in capital in excess of par value—Preferred stock	40,000
Paid-in capital in excess of par value—Common stock	300,000
Retained earnings	656,000
Total Stockholders' Equity.	$1,646,000

The following transactions, among others, occurred during the year:

Apr.   1   Declared a 100 percent stock dividend on all outstanding shares of common stock. The market value of the stock was $16 per share.
        15   Issued the stock dividend declared on April 1.
Dec.   7   Declared a two percent stock dividend on all outstanding shares of common stock. The market value of the stock was $18 per share.

Dec.   17   Issued the stock dividend declared on December 7.

      20   Declared the annual cash dividend on the preferred stock and a cash dividend of $1.20 per common share, payable on January 15 to common stockholders of record on December 31.

Required

a.   Prepare journal entries to record the foregoing transactions.

b.   Prepare a statement of retained earnings. Net income for the year is $300,000.

LO4, 5, 6   **P11-8B.**   **Stockholders' Equity Transactions, Journal Entries, and T-Accounts** The stockholders' equity of Zhou Corporation at January 1 follows:

10 percent Preferred stock, $100 par value, 20,000 shares authorized; 4,000 shares issued and outstanding.	$ 400,000
Common stock, $4 par value, 100,000 shares authorized; 40,000 shares issued and outstanding.	160,000
Paid-in capital in excess of par value—Preferred stock.	400,000
Paid-in capital in excess of par value—Common stock	800,000
Retained earnings	850,000
Total Stockholders' Equity.	$2,610,000

The following transactions, among others, occurred during the year:

Jan.   1   Announced a 4-for-1 common stock split, reducing the par value of the common stock to $1.00 per share.

Mar. 31   Converted $100,000 face value of convertible bonds payable (the book value of the bonds was $103,000) to common stock. Each $1,000 bond converted to 110 shares of common stock.

June   1   Acquired equipment with a fair market value of $40,000 in exchange for 200 shares of preferred stock.

Sept. 1   Acquired 10,000 shares of common stock for cash at $21 per share.

Nov. 21   Issued 5,000 shares of common stock at $22 cash per share.

Dec. 28   Sold 500 treasury shares at $23 per share.

      31   Closed net income of $150,000 to the Retained Earnings account.

Required

a.   Set up T-accounts for the stockholders' equity accounts as of the beginning of the year and enter the January 1 balances.

b.   Prepare journal entries for the given transactions and post them to the T-accounts (set up any additional T-accounts needed). Do not prepare the journal entry for the Dec. 31 transaction, but post the appropriate amount to the Retained Earnings T-account. Determine the ending balances for the stockholders' equity accounts.

LO4, 5, 6, 8   **P11-9B.**   **The Stockholders' Equity Section of the Balance Sheet** Using your analysis from P11-8B, prepare the Stockholders' Equity section of the Zhou Corporation's balance sheet.

LO4, 6, 7, 8   **P11-10B.**   **Stockholders' Equity: Transactions and Statement** The stockholders' equity section of Light Corporation's balance sheet at January 1 follows:

Common stock, $10 par value, 200,000 shares authorized, 35,000 shares issued, 4,000 shares are in the treasury.		$350,000
Additional paid-in capital		
In excess of par value.	$315,000	
From treasury stock	18,000	333,000
Retained earnings		298,000
		981,000
Less: Treasury stock (4,000 shares) at cost.		84,000
Total Stockholders' Equity		$897,000

The following transactions affecting stockholders' equity occurred during the year:

Jan.   8   Issued 30,000 shares of previously unissued common stock for $23 cash per share.
Mar.   12   Sold all of the treasury shares for $29 cash per share.
June   30   Declared a six percent stock dividend on all outstanding shares of common stock. The market value of the stock was $35 per share.
July   10   Issued the stock dividend declared on June 30.
Oct.   7   Acquired 2,000 shares of common stock as treasury stock at $28 cash per share.
Dec.   18   Declared a cash dividend of $1.20 per outstanding common share, payable on January 9 to stockholders of record on December 31.

Required
a.   Prepare journal entries to record the foregoing transactions.
b.   Prepare a statement of stockholders' equity. Net income for the year is $200,000.

P11-11B. Stockholders' Equity: Transaction Descriptions from Account Data   The following T-accounts contain keyed entries representing five transactions involving the stockholders' equity of Meadow, Inc.:   **LO4, 6**

Cash

(1)	96,000	13,500	(4)
(2)	50,000		
(5)	6,480		

Land

| (3) | 95,000 | | |

Preferred Stock, $50 Par

| | | 80,000 | (1) |

Paid-in Capital in Excess of Par Value—Preferred Stock

| | | 16,000 | (1) |

Common Stock, $10 Par

| | | 50,000 | (2) |
| | | 60,000 | (3) |

Paid-in Capital in Excess of Par Value—Common Stock

| | | 35,000 | (3) |

Paid-in Capital from Treasury Stock

| | | 1,080 | (5) |

Treasury Stock

| (4) | (900 shares of common) 13,500 | 5,400 | (5) |

Required
Using this information, give detailed descriptions, including number of shares and price per share when applicable, for each of the five transactions.

SERIAL PROBLEM: KATE'S CARDS

(Note: This is a continuation of the Serial Problem: Kate's Cards from Chapters 1 through 10.)

SP11.   Kate's business continues to flourish. It hardly seems that just eleven months ago, in September of 2018, Kate started the business. She is especially pleased that she was able to successfully defend herself against what turned out to be a mistaken attempt to sue her for copyright infringement. She was able to clearly demonstrate that her card designs were unique and significantly different from the designs sold by Mega Cards.

Kate has decided to take on an investor. Taylor Kasey believes that Kate's Cards represents a good investment and wishes to invest money to help Kate expand the business. Kate, however, is somewhat unsure how to structure Taylor's investment. Taylor wishes to be an equity investor rather than simply providing a loan to Kate. Kate wants to know whether she should issue Taylor common stock or preferred stock for her investment.

1. Discuss the difference between the two classes of stock and suggest which type is more appropriate for Kate to issue.

2. Kate has decided that she does not want to give up voting control of Kate's Cards. Since Taylor prefers to be a passive investor, but does wish to have a steady income from dividends, the decision is made to issue 50 shares of $100 par value, six percent cumulative preferred stock.

Provide the journal entry to record the issuance of the preferred stock for cash.

3. Kate also wishes to pay dividends on both her common shares and the preferred stock. She is a little confused between cash and stock dividends.

   Explain the difference between a cash dividend and a stock dividend. Since Kate is the only stockholder of the common stock, what would be the effect of issuing a 10 percent stock dividend?

4. Kate decides to issue cash dividends on both the common stock and the preferred stock. Currently there are 50 outstanding preferred shares and 500 common shares outstanding. The dividends that Kate paid were $6 per share on the preferred shares and $2 per share on the common shares.

   Provide the journal entry for the payment of the cash dividends.

5. Kate's Cards has a net income of $1,500 for the current month of August 2019. Kate had decided that the business will have a fiscal year-end of August 31, so this is the completion of the company's first year. Kate will be preparing her annual financial statements; however, she would also like to see a monthly statement of retained earnings for August 2019. In addition, she would like to see how the stockholders' equity section of the balance sheet will look after the addition of the preferred stock. The stockholders' equity section from July 2019 is shown below:

Stockholders' Equity	
Common stock (5,000 shares authorized, 500 shares issued and outstanding)	$ 500
Paid-in capital in excess of par value—common stock	9,500
Retained earnings	15,000
Total stockholders' equity	$25,000

Prepare a statement of retained earnings for the month of August 2019 and the stockholders' equity section of the balance sheet as of August 31, 2019.

EXTENDING YOUR KNOWLEDGE

REPORTING AND ANALYSIS

COLUMBIA
SPORTSWEAR
COMPANY

EYK11-1. **Financial Reporting Problem: Columbia Sportswear Company** The financial statements for the Columbia Sportswear Company can be found in Appendix A at the end of this book.

Required
Answer the following questions:
  a.   How many shares of common stock are authorized at the end of 2017?
  b.   What percentage of the common shares authorized are outstanding at the end of 2017?
  c.   Does Columbia Sportswear have any preferred shares outstanding at the end of 2017?
  d.   How many shares of common stock did Columbia Sportswear repurchase in 2017? What was the dollar amount of this repurchase?
  e.   What amount of dividends per share did Columbia Sportswear report for 2017? 2016?

COLUMBIA
SPORTSWEAR
COMPANY

UNDER ARMOUR,
INC.

EYK11-2. **Comparative Analysis Problem: Columbia Sportswear Company vs Under Armour, Inc.** The financial statements for the Columbia Sportswear Company can be found in Appendix A at the end of this book, and the financial statements of Under Armour, Inc. can be found in Appendix B (the complete annual report is available on this book's Website).

Required
Answer the following questions:
  a.   Calculate the return on common stockholders' equity for each company for 2017.
  b.   Calculate the dividend payout ratio for each company for 2017.
  c.   Based on these ratios, which company performed better for its shareholders during 2017?

EYK11-3. **Business Decision Problem** Egghead, Inc., was a software chain that had over 100 stores across the U.S. Initially its founders and employees owned the company privately. The company eventually went public with an initial public offering (IPO) of 3.6 million shares (the company had 12 million shares prior to the IPO). The new shares were priced at $15 each. The company did not hold any treasury shares.

Required

a. Assume that the common shares had a $1 par value. Provide the journal entry to record the issuance of new shares.

b. Discuss whether you think Egghead's board of directors and existing shareholders had to approve the public issuance before it occurred.

c. Provide some reasons why Egghead wished to raise $54 million with equity rather than debt.

EYK11-4. **Financial Analysis Problem** The following data were obtained prior to the acquisition of Gillette Company by **Procter & Gamble**. Gillette Company, the Procter & Gamble Company, and **Colgate-Palmolive Company** are three firms in the personal care consumer products industry. During the prior year, the average return on common stockholders' equity for the personal care consumer products industry was 28.1 percent. In the same year, the relevant financial data for Gillette, Procter & Gamble, and Colgate-Palmolive were as follows (in millions):

GILLETTE COMPANY

PROCTER & GAMBLE

COLGATE-PALMOLIVE COMPANY

	Gillette	Procter & Gamble	Colgate-Palmolive
Preferred stockholders' equity, beginning.	$ 99.2	$1,969.0	$ 418.3
Preferred stockholders' equity, ending	99.0	1,942.0	414.3
Preferred dividends	4.7	102.0	21.6
Common stockholders' equity, beginning.	1,397.2	5,472.0	2,201.5
Common stockholders' equity, ending	1,380.0	6,890.0	1,460.7
Net income	426.9	2,211.0	548.1

Required

a. Calculate Gillette Company's return on common stockholders' equity.

b. Evaluate Gillette Company's return on common stockholders' equity by comparing it with the following:

1. The average for the personal care consumer products industry.

2. The return earned by the Procter & Gamble Company.

3. The return earned by Colgate-Palmolive Company.

4. The return earned by Gillette Company in the previous year (in the previous year, Gillette's net income was $513.4 million, preferred stock dividends were $4.8 million, and average common stockholders' equity was $1,227.3 million).

CRITICAL THINKING

EYK11-5. **Financial Analysis on the Web: General Mills, Inc.** The fiscal year 2017 annual report of **General Mills, Inc.** is available on this book's Website.

GENERAL MILLS, INC.

Required

a. How many shares of common stock is General Mills authorized to issue? How many common shares are issued as of May 28, 2017?

b. What is the par value of General Mills' common stock?

c. Does General Mills have any preferred shares? If so, how many shares of preferred stock are outstanding on May 28, 2017?

d. How many treasury shares did General Mills purchase on the open market during the 2017 fiscal year? What did General Mills pay to purchase these shares? How many common shares are in the treasury as of May 28, 2017?

e. What is General Mills' return on common stockholders' equity for the 2017 fiscal year?

f. What is the cash dividend per share declared by General Mills in fiscal year 2017? 2016?

g. What are General Mills' basic earnings per share in fiscal year 2017? 2016?

h. What is General Mills' dividend payout ratio for fiscal year 2017? 2016?

EYK11-6. **Accounting Communication Activity** Your neighbor, Norman Vetter, has always been tinkering in his garage with his inventions. He believes he has finally come up with one that could really sell well. He is a little concerned about some potential safety issues, but he believes those issues will be worked out. He wants to form a business to manufacture and sell his invention and has come to you for advice. In particular, he would like to know the advantages and disadvantages of forming a corporation, rather than simply organizing as a sole proprietor.

Required

Write a brief memorandum to your neighbor explaining the advantages and disadvantages of the corporate form of organization.

EYK11-7.   Accounting Ethics Case Colin Agee, chairperson of the board of directors and chief executive officer of Image, Inc., is pondering a recommendation to make to the firm's board of directors in response to actions taken by Sam Mecon. Mecon recently informed Agee and other board members that he (Mecon) had purchased 15 percent of the voting stock of Image at $12 per share and is considering an attempt to take control of the company. His effort to take control would include offering $16 per share to stockholders to induce them to sell shares to him. Mecon also indicated that he would abandon his takeover plans if the company would buy back his stock at a price 50 percent over its current market price of $13 per share.

Agee views the proposed takeover by Mecon as a hostile maneuver. Mecon has a reputation of identifying companies that are undervalued (that is, their underlying net assets are worth more than the price of the outstanding shares), buying enough shares to take control of the company, replacing top management, and, on occasion, breaking up the company (that is, selling off the various divisions to the highest bidder). The process has proven profitable to Mecon and his financial backers. Stockholders of the companies taken over have also benefited because Mecon paid them attractive prices to buy their shares.

Agee recognizes that Image is currently undervalued by the stock market but believes that eventually the company will significantly improve its financial performance to the long-run benefit of its stockholders.

Required

What are the ethical issues that Agee should consider in arriving at a recommendation to make to the board of directors regarding Mecon's offer to be "bought out" of his takeover plans?

EYK11-8.   Corporate Social Responsibility Problem In the corporate social responsibility highlight regarding Starbucks on page 528 in this chapter, it was stated that Starbucks believes in measuring and monitoring the company's CSR progress. The forward to Starbucks' Global Social Impact 2017 Performance Report stated:

Part 1

Our 2017 Global Social Impact Performance report marks our progress as a company, one that's performance-driven through the lens of humanity. Together with our more than 330,000 partners and organizations like Conservation International and Feeding America, we can use our scale for good.

We've made this progress by being purposeful in our decisions and our collective actions, and we have bold, new aspirations for the years ahead. Our efforts are focused in four areas where our commitment and scale can make the biggest impact:

- SUSTAINABLE COFFEE: Working to make coffee the world's first sustainable agricultural product.
- GREENER RETAIL: Building and operating the world's largest green retail business.
- CREATING OPPORTUNITIES: Investing in pathways to opportunity through employment, education and training.
- STRENGTHENING COMMUNITIES: Welcoming all and creating impact on issues that matter.

Part 2

Go to: https://www.starbucks.com/responsibility/global-report and select one of the four areas of focus and identify how the company is doing with respect to its goals.

EYK11-9.   Forensic Accounting Problem The Forensic Accounting Box on page 531 of this chapter noted that forensic accounting techniques are being used to help pick stocks for investing. How might identifying accounting concerns be useful for investors?

EYK11-10. Working With The Takeaways The following data are from a recent **General Electric Company** annual report. All amounts, except per share data, are in $ millions.

Net income	$ 8,176
Preferred stock dividends	0
Average common stockholders' equity	87,051
Dividends per share	0.93
Earnings per share	0.90
Per share market price of common stock at year-end	29.70

Required

Compute the following ratios for the General Electric Company:

a. Return on common stockholders' equity

b. Dividend yield

c. Dividend payout

EYK11-11. IFRS Financial Statements The 2017 financial statements of **LVMH Moet Hennessey-Louis Vuitton S.A.** are presented in Appendix C at the end of this book. LVMH is a Paris-based holding company and one of the world's largest and best-known luxury goods companies. As a member of the European Union, French companies are required to prepare their consolidated (group) financial statements using International Financial Reporting Standards (IFRS). Calculate LVMH's (a) return on common stockholders' equity, (b) dividend yield, and (c) dividend payout for 2017 and 2016. Additional information that you will need is below:

LVMH MOET
HENNESSEY-
LOUIS VUITTON
S.A.

	2017	2016
Earnings per share (in euros)	10.21	7.92
Dividend per share (in euros)	5.00	4.00
Market price per share (in euros)	245.40	181.40

ANSWERS TO SELF-STUDY QUESTIONS:

1. c, (p. 525)   2. a, (p. 530)   3. c, (p. 532)   4. d, (pp. 535–536)   5. d, (pp. 537–538)   6. d, (p. 534)
7. c, (p. 543)   8. d, (p. 531)   9. a, (p. 537)   10. d, (p. 541)

YOUR TURN! SOLUTIONS

Solution 11.1

1. Disadvantage
2. Advantage
3. Advantage
4. Disadvantage
5. Disadvantage
6. Advantage

Solution 11.2
b.

Solution 11.3
1. d   **2.** e   **3.** b   **4.** f   **5.** c   **6.** a

Solution 11.4

Paid-in capital in excess of par value = ($9 − $1) × 10,000 shares = $80,000

Solution 11.5

After the split Aston Enterprises would report 1,500,000 shares outstanding with a par value of $1.00. Joe Smith would own 1,500 shares of Aston.

Solution 11.6

$75,000

Solution 11.7

a. A cash dividend will lower retained earnings by $30,000 ($3 × 10,000 shares) to $470,000.
b. A ten percent stock dividend will lower retained earnings by $20,000 (.10 × 10,000 × $20) to $480,000.

Solution 11.8

	Common Stock	Paid-in Capital in Excess of Par Value	Retained Earnings	Treasury Stock	Total
DIOR COMPANY Statement of Stockholders' Equity For Year Ended December 31, 2019					
Balance, January 1, 2019.	$100,000	$900,000	$50,000	$(10,000)	$1,040,000
Net income			30,000		30,000
1,000 common shares issued. . . .	1,000	14,000			15,000
Cash dividend.			(8,000)		(8,000)
Balance, December 31, 2019. . . .	$101,000	$914,000	$72,000	$(10,000)	$1,077,000

Solution 11.9

a. Return on common stockholders' equity = ($150,000 − $15,000)/[($650,000 + $700,000)/2] = 20 percent
b. Dividend yield = $0.75/$33.00 = 2.3 percent
c. Dividend payout ratio = $0.75/$3.00 = 25 percent

Chapter 12

Statement of Cash Flows

PAST

Chapter 11 examined the accounting for stockholders' equity.

PRESENT

In this chapter we turn our attention to the statement of cash flows.

FUTURE

Chapter 13 completes our study of financial accounting by looking at the analysis and interpretation of financial statements.

Home Depot is the largest home improvement retailer in the United States. Founded in 1978 in Atlanta, Georgia, the company now operates over 2,250 stores in the United States, Canada, and Mexico.

It takes a lot of cash to build and operate a business as big as Home Depot, especially when the average size of each store is over 105,000 square feet. In fiscal year 2017 alone Home Depot spent almost $2 billion on capital expenditures.

How can a financial statement user determine where a company obtained the cash to fund such growth? In this chapter we examine the statement of cash flows and learn how a company discloses both the sources and uses of its cash. Understanding the content, format, and construction of the statement of cash flows enables a financial statement user to assess just how a company like Home Depot was able to finance its capital expenditures for new store growth.

Road Map

LO	Learning Objective	Page	eLecture	Guided Example	Assignments
LO1	Discuss the content and format of the statement of cash flows.	572	E12-1	YT12.1	SS1, SS2, SS3, SS6, SS8, SE1, SE2, SE3, E1A, E2A, E1B, E2B
LO2	Explain the preparation of a statement of cash flows using the indirect method.	578	E12-2	YT12.2	SS4, SS9, SE1, SE2, SE3, E3A, E4A, E5A, E6A, E11A, E3B, E4B, E5B, E6B, E11B, P1A, P2A, P3A, P4A, P1B, P2B, P3B, P4B
LO3	Define several ratios used to analyze the statement of cash flows and explain their use.	586	E12-3	YT12.3	SS5, SS7, SE4, SE5, SE6, E4A, E7A, E3B, E7B, P1A, P5A, P6A, P1B, P5B, P6B
LO4	Appendix 12A: Explain the preparation of a statement of cash flows using the direct method.	590	E12-4	YT12.4	SS10, SS11, SS12, SE7, SE8, SE9, SE10, E8A, E9A, E10A, E11A, E8B, E9B, E10B, E11B, P6A, P7A, P8A, P9A, P6B, P7B, P8B, P9B

CASH AND CASH EQUIVALENTS

LO1 **Discuss** the content and format of the statement of cash flows.

Do you maintain a checkbook in which you record the checks you write and the bank deposits you make? If so, you are keeping a record of your cash flows—the checks you write are your cash outflows and the bank deposits you make are your cash inflows. Businesses also experience cash inflows and outflows, but they do more than just record their cash flows because GAAP requires that businesses prepare an entirely separate financial statement explaining where their cash flow came from and how it was used.

The statement of cash flows complements the balance sheet and the income statement. While a balance sheet reports a company's financial position as of a point in time, usually the end of a fiscal period, the statement of cash flows explains the change in one component of a company's financial position—its cash—from one balance sheet date to the next. The income statement, on the other hand, reveals the results of a company's operating activities for the period, and these operating activities are a major source and use of the cash reported in a company's statement of cash flows.

In the eyes of most creditors, investors, and managers, cash is a business's most important asset. Without cash, a business would be unable to pay its employees, its lenders, its suppliers, its service providers, or its shareholders. In short, cash is the only asset that a business can't operate without.

The dilemma for most managers, however, is knowing exactly how much cash to keep on hand. Although managers know that they need to keep some cash on hand in a checking account and/or petty cash fund to pay their immediate bills, they also know that cash is the lowest return generating asset that a business has. Keeping too much cash on hand means that a business is not maximizing the value of its assets. For this reason, most managers spend considerable time assessing their cash needs—an activity called **cash management**. Because the science of cash management is inexact, managers have derived ways to help them minimize the amount of cash that they need to keep on hand while also maximizing the return on a business's assets. One such method is to invest any excess cash in alternative investments that are readily convertible back into cash and earn a higher rate of return than cash, but which do not place the invested cash at risk of loss. These alternative investments are known as cash equivalents.

Cash equivalents are short-term, highly liquid investments that are (1) easily convertible into cash and (2) close enough to maturity so that their market value is relatively insensitive to interest rate changes (generally, investments with maturities of three months or less). U.S. Treasury bills, certificates of deposit (CDs), commercial paper (short-term notes issued by corporations), and money market funds are examples of cash equivalents. Because firms may differ as to exactly which investments they consider to be cash equivalents, GAAP requires that each firm disclose in the notes to the financial statements the company's policy regarding which investments are treated as cash equivalents.

When preparing a statement of cash flows, the cash and cash equivalents are added together and treated as a single amount. This is done because the purchase and sale of investments in cash equivalents are considered to be part of a firm's overall cash management strategy rather than a source or use of cash. As financial statement users evaluate a firm's cash flows, it should not matter whether the cash is on hand, deposited in a bank account, or invested in cash equivalents. Transfers back and forth between a firm's Cash account and its investments in cash equivalents, consequently, are not treated as cash inflows or outflows in the statement of cash flows.

When discussing the statement of cash flows, accountants often just use the word *cash* rather than the term *cash and cash equivalents*. We follow that practice in this chapter.

Definition of Cash Equivalents

ACCOUNTING IN PRACTICE

There are some differences between firms regarding which investments of cash are considered to be cash equivalents. For example, **PepsiCo, Inc.**, the beverage and snack food company, states in the notes to its financial statements that "Cash equivalents are investments with original maturities of three months or less." **International Game Technology**, a manufacturer of gaming machines and proprietary gaming software systems, on the other hand, notes that "In addition to cash deposits at major banks, cash and equivalents include other marketable securities with original maturities of 90 days or less, primarily in U.S. Treasury-backed money market funds." The commonality among all firms, however, is that cash equivalents represent a temporary investment of excess cash in risk-free investments until such time as the cash is needed to support a business's operations.

ACTIVITY CLASSIFICATIONS IN THE STATEMENT OF CASH FLOWS

A statement of cash flows classifies a company's cash receipts and cash payments into three major business activity categories: operating activities, investing activities, and financing activities. Grouping cash flows into these categories identifies the effect on cash of each of the major business activities of a firm (see Chapter 1). The combined effects on cash from all three categories explain the net change in cash for the period. The net change in cash is then reconciled with the beginning and ending balances of cash from the balance sheet. **Exhibit 12-1** illustrates the basic format for a statement of cash flows.

Exhibit 12-1	**Format for the Statement of Cash Flows**

SAMPLE COMPANY
Statement of Cash Flows
For Year Ended December 31, 2019

Cash Flow from Operating Activities		
(Details of cash flow from operating activities)	$###	
Cash provided (used) by operating activities		$###
Cash Flow from Investing Activities		
(Details of investing cash inflows and outflows)	###	
Cash provided (used) by investing activities.		###
Cash Flow from Financing Activities		
(Details of financing cash inflows and outflows)	###	
Cash provided (used) by financing activities.		###
Net increase (decrease) in cash.		###
Cash at beginning of year.		###
Cash at end of year		$###

Operating Activities

A company's income statement reflects the transactions and events that constitute its operating activities. The focus of a firm's operating activities involves selling goods or rendering services. The cash flow from **operating activities** is defined broadly enough, however, to include any cash receipts or payments that are not classified as investing activities or financing activities. For example, cash received from a lawsuit settlement and cash payments to charity are treated as cash flow from operating activities. The following are examples of cash inflows and outflows relating to a firm's operating activities:

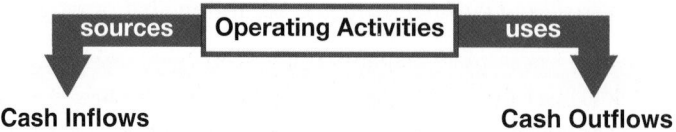

Cash Inflows

1. Receipts from customers for sales of goods or services.
2. Receipts of interest and dividends.
3. Other receipts that are not related to investing or financing activities, such as lawsuit settlements and refunds received from suppliers.

Cash Outflows

1. Payments to suppliers.
2. Payments to employees.
3. Payments of interest to creditors.
4. Payments of taxes to governmental agencies.
5. Other payments that are not related to investing or financing activities, such as contributions to charity.

Investing Activities

A firm's **investing activities** include those transactions involving (1) the acquisition or disposal of plant assets and intangible assets, (2) the purchase or sale of stocks, bonds, and other securities (that are not cash equivalents), and (3) the lending and subsequent collection of money.[1] The related cash receipts and cash payments appear in the investing activities section of the statement of cash flows. Examples of these cash flows include:

Cash Inflows

1. Receipts from the sale of plant assets and intangible assets.
2. Receipts from sales of investments in stocks, bonds, and other securities (other than cash equivalents).
3. Receipts from repayments of loans by borrowers.

Cash Outflows

1. Payments to purchase plant assets and intangible assets.
2. Payments to purchase stocks, bonds, and other securities (other than cash equivalents).
3. Payments made to lend money to borrowers.

Financing Activities

A firm engages in **financing activities** when it obtains cash from shareholders, returns cash to shareholders, borrows from creditors, and repays amounts borrowed from creditors. Cash flows related to these events are reported in the financing activities section of the statement of cash flows. Examples of these cash flows include:

---

[1] There are exceptions to the classification of these events as investing activities. For example, the purchase or sale of mortgage loans by a mortgage banker, like Bank of America, and the purchase or sale of securities in the trading account of a broker/dealer in financial securities, like Merrill Lynch, represent operating activities for these businesses.

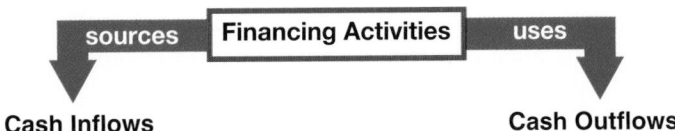

Cash Inflows

1. Receipts from the issuance of common stock and preferred stock and from sales of treasury stock.
2. Receipts from the issuance of bonds payable, mortgage notes payable, and other notes payable.

Cash Outflows

1. Payments to acquire treasury stock.
2. Payments of dividends.
3. Payments to settle outstanding bonds payable, mortgage notes payable, and other notes payable.

Observe that paying cash to settle such obligations as accounts payable, wages payable, interest payable, and income tax payable is an operating activity, not a financing activity. Also observe that cash received as interest and dividends and cash paid as interest are classified as cash flows from operating activities, although cash paid as dividends to a company's stockholders is classified as a financing activity.

IFRS ALERT

Although the statement of cash flows under U.S. GAAP has three activity categories—operations, investing, and financing—this is not the case under International Financial Reporting Standards (IFRS). Under IFRS, the statement of cash flows may have either four or five activity categories: Operations, Investing, Debt Financing, Equity Financing, and sometimes a category called the Effect of Foreign Currency Translation. In essence, IFRS segments the financing activities category into two separate categories relating to financing with debt and financing with equity. The sum of these two categories is exactly equivalent to the single category of financing activities under U.S. GAAP.

Usefulness of Activity Classification

The classification of cash flows into the three business activity categories helps financial statement users analyze and interpret a company's cash flow data. To illustrate, assume that companies D, E, and F operate in the same industry, and that each company reported a $100,000 increase in cash during the period. Information from each company's statement of cash flows is summarized below:

	Company		
	D	**E**	**F**
Cash flow from operating activities................	$100,000	$ 0	$ 0
Cash flow from investing activities:			
Sale of plant assets.........................	0	100,000	0
Cash flow from financing activities:			
Issuance of notes payable	0	0	100,000
Net increase in cash.........................	$100,000	$100,000	$100,000

Although each company's increase in cash was exactly $100,000, the source of the cash increase varied by company. This variation affects the analysis of the cash flow data, particularly for potential creditors who must evaluate the likelihood of the repayment of funds loaned to a company. Based only on this cash flow data, a potential creditor would feel more comfortable lending money to Company D than to either Company E or F. D's cash increase came from its operating activities, whereas E's cash increase came from the sale of plant assets, a source that is unlikely to recur, and F's cash increase came from borrowed funds. Company F faces additional future uncertainty when the interest and principal payments on the existing notes become due, and for this reason, a potential creditor would be less inclined to extend additional loans to Company F.

NONCASH INVESTING AND FINANCING ACTIVITIES

Although many investing and financing activities affect cash and therefore are included in the investing and financing sections of the statement of cash flows, some significant investing and financing events do not affect current cash flow. Examples of **noncash investing and financing activities** are the issuance of stock or bonds in exchange for plant assets or intangible assets, the exchange of long-term assets for other long-term assets, and the conversion of long-term debt into common stock. A common feature among each of these transactions is that no cash is exchanged between the parties involved in the transaction.

Noncash investing and financing transactions generally do, however, affect future cash flows. Issuing bonds in exchange for equipment, for example, requires future cash payments for interest and principal on the bonds. On the other hand, converting bonds into common stock eliminates the future cash payments related to the bonds' interest and principal. Knowledge of these types of events, therefore, should be helpful to financial statement users who wish to evaluate a firm's future cash flows.

Information regarding noncash investing and financing transactions is disclosed in a separate accounting schedule. The separate schedule may be placed immediately below the statement of cash flows or it may be placed among the notes to the financial statements.

PRINCIPLE ALERT	**Objectivity Principle**
	The *objectivity principle* asserts that the usefulness of financial statements is enhanced when the underlying data are objective and verifiable. Measuring cash and the changes in cash are among the most objective measurements that accountants make. The statement of cash flows, therefore, is the most objective financial statement required under generally accepted accounting principles. This characteristic of the statement of cash flows is welcomed by investors and creditors interested in evaluating the quality of a firm's net income and assets. Financial statement users often feel more confident about the quality of a company's net income and assets when there is a high correlation between, or relationship with, a company's cash flow from operating activities and its net income.

USING THE STATEMENT OF CASH FLOWS

The Financial Accounting Standards Board believes that one of the principal objectives of financial reporting is to help financial statement users assess the amount, timing, and uncertainty of a business's future cash flows. These assessments, in turn, help users evaluate prospective future cash receipts from their investments in, or loans to, a business. Although the statement of cash flows describes a company's past cash flows, the statement is also useful for assessing future cash flows since the recent past is often a very good predictor of the future.

The statement of cash flows shows the cash effects of a firm's operating, investing, and financing activities. Distinguishing among these different categories of cash flow helps financial statement users compare, evaluate, and predict a business's future cash flows. With cash flow information, creditors and investors are better able to assess a company's ability to repay its liabilities and pay dividends. A firm's need for outside financing can also be evaluated using the statement of cash flows. Further, the statement enables users to observe and analyze management's investing and financing policies, plans, and strategies.

The statement of cash flows also provides information useful in evaluating a firm's financial flexibility. **Financial flexibility** is a company's ability to generate sufficient amounts of cash to respond to unanticipated needs and opportunities. Information about past cash flows, particularly cash flow from operations, helps in assessing financial flexibility. An evaluation of a firm's ability to survive an unexpected drop in demand for its goods and services, for example, may include a review of its past cash flow from operations. The larger these past cash flows, the greater will be a firm's ability to withstand adverse changes in future economic conditions.

Some investors and creditors find the statement of cash flows useful in evaluating the "quality" of a firm's net income. As we saw in Chapter 4, determining net income under the accrual basis of accounting requires many accruals, deferrals, allocations, and valuations. These adjustment and measurement procedures introduce greater subjectivity into a company's income determination than some financial statement users are comfortable with. Consequently, these users can relate a more objective performance measure—a firm's cash flow from operations—to net income. To these users, the higher the relationship between a company's net income and the cash flow from operations, the higher is the quality of the firm's net income.

CASH FLOW FROM OPERATING ACTIVITIES

The first section of the statement of cash flows presents a firm's cash flow from operating activities. Two alternative formats are available to present the cash flow from operating activities: the indirect method and the direct method. Both methods report the same amount of cash flow from operating activities and differ only in how the cash flow from operating activities is derived.

The **indirect method** starts with net income using the accrual basis of accounting and applies a series of adjustments to convert it to net income under the cash basis of accounting, which is equivalent to the cash flow from operating activities. The adjustments to net income do not represent specific cash flows; consequently, the indirect method does not report any detail concerning individual operating cash inflows and outflows.

The **direct method** shows individual amounts of cash inflows and cash outflows for the major operating activities. The net difference between these inflows and outflows is the cash flow from operating activities.

The Financial Accounting Standards Board encourages companies to use the direct method but permits the use of the indirect method. Despite the FASB's preference for the direct method, more than 95 percent of companies preparing the statement of cash flows use the indirect method. The indirect method is popular because (1) it is easier and less expensive to prepare than the direct method and (2) the direct method requires a supplemental disclosure showing cash flow from operating activities prepared under the indirect method.

Popularity of Method for Reporting the Cash Flow from Operations	**ACCOUNTING IN PRACTICE**

Do you think a direct approach in communicating with financial statement users is best, or should your approach be more indirect? When it comes to reporting the cash flow from operations, companies appear to favor the indirect approach by a wide margin as evidenced by the responses to a survey of 600 large U.S. companies.

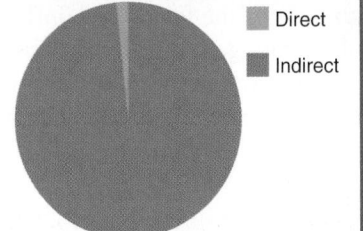

Source: Accounting Trends and Techniques

A Comparison of Accrual-Basis and Cash-Basis Amounts

Accountants calculate net income on the income statement using the accrual basis of accounting. The cash flow from operating activities, presented on the statement of cash flows, represents a company's net income using the cash basis of accounting. There is no necessary relationship between the two numbers. Compared with net income, the cash flow from operating activities may be larger, smaller, or about the same amount. Financial data from past annual reports of three well-known companies—**Chiquita Brands**, **Levi Strauss**, and **Harley-Davidson**—bear this out.

	Net Income or (Loss)	Cash Flow Provided (Used) by Operating Activities
Chiquita Brands Intl. Inc.	$(323,725,000)	$ 8,204,000
Levi Strauss & Co.	$ 229,285,000	$ 224,809,000
Harley-Davidson Inc.	$ 654,718,000	$(684,649,000)

YOUR TURN! 12.1

The solution is on page 618.

Classify each of the cash flow events listed below as either an (1) operating activity, (2) investing activity, or (3) financing activity:

1. Cash received from customers
2. Cash sale of land
3. Cash paid to suppliers
4. Cash purchase of equipment
5. Payment on note payable

6. Cash dividend payment
7. Cash wages paid
8. Purchase of treasury stock
9. Cash sale of investments

The following section on preparing the statement of cash flows uses the indirect method. Appendix 12A uses the direct method. Your instructor can choose to cover either one or both methods. If the indirect method is skipped, then read Appendix 12A and return to the section (8 pages ahead) titled "Analyzing Cash Flows."

PREPARING THE STATEMENT OF CASH FLOWS USING THE INDIRECT METHOD

LO2 **Explain** the preparation of a statement of cash flows using the indirect method.

To prepare a statement of cash flows using the indirect method, the following information is needed: a company's income statement, comparative balance sheets for the current and prior year, and possibly additional data taken from the company's financial statements. **Exhibit 12-2** presents this information for the Bennett Company. We will use these data to prepare Bennett's 2019 statement of cash flows using the indirect method. As will be seen shortly, Bennett's statement of cash flows will explain the $25,000 increase in the company's cash account that occurred during 2019 (from $10,000 at the beginning of the year to $35,000 at the end of the year) by classifying the firm's cash inflows and outflows into the three business activity categories of operating, investing, and financing.

To see that the statement of cash flows can be prepared using only a company's income statement and the changes in its balance sheet accounts, consider again the balance sheet equation that was first introduced in Chapter 1:

$$\text{Assets (A)} = \text{Liabilities (L)} + \text{Stockholders' equity (SE)} \tag{1}$$

Separating a firm's assets into its cash and noncash assets (NCA) gives:

$$\text{Cash} + \text{NCA} = \text{L} + \text{SE} \qquad (2)$$

And, rewriting the balance sheet equation in changes form yields:

$$\Delta\text{Cash} + \Delta\text{NCA} = \Delta\text{L} + \Delta\text{SE} \qquad (3)$$

Finally, rearranging the components of the equation shows that the change in cash (which is the end result of the statement of cash flows) can be computed from the change in all of the other balance sheet accounts:

$$\Delta\text{Cash} = \Delta\text{L} - \Delta\text{NCA} + \Delta\text{SE} \qquad (4)$$

Exhibit 12-2 | **Financial Data of Bennett Company**

BENNETT COMPANY Income Statement For Year Ended December 31, 2019		
Sales revenue.		$250,000
Cost of goods sold	$148,000	
Wages expense	52,000	
Insurance expense.	5,000	
Depreciation expense.	10,000	
Income tax expense	11,000	
Gain on sale of plant assets.	(8,000)	218,000
Net income		$ 32,000

BENNETT COMPANY Balance Sheets		
As of December 31	2019	2018
Assets		
Cash	$ 35,000	$ 10,000
Accounts receivable	39,000	34,000
Inventory.	54,000	60,000
Prepaid insurance.	17,000	4,000
Long-term investments.	15,000	—
Plant assets	180,000	200,000
Accumulated depreciation	(50,000)	(40,000)
Patent.	60,000	—
Total assets	$350,000	$268,000
Liabilities and Equity		
Accounts payable	$ 10,000	$ 19,000
Income tax payable	5,000	3,000
Common stock	260,000	190,000
Retained earnings	75,000	56,000
Total liabilities and equity	$350,000	$268,000

Additional Data for 2019

1. Sold plant assets costing $20,000 for $28,000 cash.
2. Declared and paid cash dividends of $13,000.

IFRS ALERT

Currently, both U.S. GAAP and IFRS permit a company to present its statement of cash flows using either the direct method or the indirect method. A topic being considered by the FASB/IASB convergence project would limit the preparation of the statement of cash flows to just the direct method. The direct method is currently preferred by both the FASB and the IASB, although most U.S. firms present their statement of cash flows using the indirect method.

Five Steps to Preparing a Statement of Cash Flows

The process to prepare a statement of cash flows using the indirect method involves five steps. The approach begins by focusing initially only on the balance sheet and then proceeds to integrate a business's income statement through a series of systematic adjustments to a preliminary statement of cash flows derived solely from balance sheet data.

Step One   Using just the beginning and ending balance sheets (see Columns 1 and 2 in **Exhibit 12-3**), calculate the change in each balance sheet account by subtracting the beginning balance sheet amount from the ending amount. The results of this step for the Bennett Company are presented in Column 3 of **Exhibit 12-3**. To simplify this step, the change in the Plant Assets account is combined with the Accumulated Depreciation account—that is, the change in the Plant Assets account is calculated on a net of accumulated depreciation basis.

To verify the accuracy of the Step One calculations, simply compare the sum of the changes in the asset accounts ($82,000) with the sum of the changes in the liability and stockholders' equity accounts ($82,000). These totals must be equal. If the totals are not equal, it indicates the presence of a subtraction error that must be identified and corrected before proceeding to Step Two.

Exhibit 12-3	Preparing a Statement of Cash Flows: The Indirect Method			
	BENNETT COMPANY **Balance Sheet** **December 31, 2019**			
	(1) **Beginning of Year**	**(2)** **End of Year**	**(3)** **Change for Year**	**(4)** **Cash Flow Classification**
Assets				
Cash.	$ 10,000	$ 35,000	**$25,000**	**Cash flow increase**
Accounts receivable	34,000	39,000	5,000	Operating
Inventory.	60,000	54,000	(6,000)	Operating
Prepaid insurance.	4,000	17,000	13,000	Operating
Long-term investments.	0	15,000	15,000	Investing
Plant assets (net)	160,000	130,000	(30,000)	Investing/Operating
Patent.	0	60,000	60,000	Investing/Operating
Total assets	$268,000	$350,000	$82,000	
Liabilities and Equity				
Accounts payable.	$ 19,000	$ 10,000	$ (9,000)	Operating
Income tax payable	3,000	5,000	2,000	Operating
Common stock	190,000	260,000	70,000	Financing
Retained earnings	56,000	75,000	19,000	Operating/Financing
Total liabilities and equity	$268,000	$350,000	$82,000	

An important figure identified during Step One is the "bottom line" of the statement of cash flows, namely the change in the cash account. **Exhibit 12-3** reveals that the cash account of the Bennett Company increased by $25,000 from the beginning of the year to the end of the year. Hence, all of the various cash inflows and outflows for the company must aggregate to this figure.

Step Two   Identify the appropriate business activity category—operating, investing, or financing—for each balance sheet account. The cash flow activity classifications are presented in Column 4 of **Exhibit 12-3**.

Although measuring the change in the balance sheet accounts in Step One is a straightforward arithmetic activity, there can be some confusion over the correct activity classification for some of the balance sheet accounts in Step Two. The change in accounts receivable, inventory, prepaid insurance, accounts payable, and income tax payable are all easily identified as operating activities because they are associated with the day-to-day operations of a business. The change in common stock, on the other hand, is clearly a financing activity because it is associated with raising capital to finance a business. The change in net plant assets, however, can be both an investing activity and an operating activity. Purchases and sales of plant assets are associated with the capital investment needed to run a business, and thus are an investing activity. However, the depreciation expense associated with plant assets is an operating activity since the depreciation of plant assets is deducted as an expense in the calculation of a company's net income. Similarly, the change in intangible assets such as patents can be both an investing activity and an operating activity because the acquisition or sale of intangibles is an investing activity, whereas the amortization of intangibles is an expense deducted in the calculation of net income, and hence, an operating activity. Finally, the change in retained earnings can be both an operating activity and a financing activity because retained earnings is increased by net income, an operating activity, but decreased by the payment of dividends, a financing activity.

As a general rule, the following cash flow activity classifications apply, although exceptions exist:

Balance Sheet Account	Cash Flow Activity Category
Current assets	Operating
Noncurrent assets	Investing/Operating
Current liabilities.	Operating
Noncurrent liabilities.	Financing
Capital stock.	Financing
Retained earnings	Operating/Financing

Examples of exceptions to the above cash flow activity classifications include the following:

- Short-term investments, a current asset, are an investing activity item.
- Short-term (current) notes payable, a current liability, are a financing activity item.
- Current maturities of long-term debt, a current liability, are a financing activity item.
- Employee pension obligations, a noncurrent liability, are an operating activity item.

Step Three   Having completed Steps One and Two, you are now ready to build a preliminary statement of cash flows using the calculated increases or decreases in the various balance sheet accounts from Step One and the identified activity classifications from Step Two. The preliminary statement of cash flows for the Bennett Company using the change values from Column 3 of **Exhibit 12-3** and the cash flow activity classifications from Column 4 is presented in **Exhibit 12-4**.

Because a statement of cash flows measures the inflows and outflows of cash for a business, it is important to note that the sign of the asset account changes calculated in Step One must be reversed for purposes of preparing the preliminary statement of cash flows in **Exhibit 12-4**. This can be seen in equation (4) above in which the change in noncash assets has a negative sign. For instance, **Exhibit 12-4** shows that the change in accounts receivable was an increase of $5,000, whereas the change in inventory was a decrease of $6,000. When preparing the indirect method statement of cash flows, a $5,000 increase in accounts receivable represents a subtraction from net income (a cash outflow), and a decline in inventory of $6,000 represents an addition to net income (a cash inflow), to arrive at the cash flow from operations. To illustrate why an increase in accounts receivable must be subtracted from net income to arrive at operating cash flow, consider how sales revenue is initially recorded. Assume that a $2,000 sale of goods is paid for with $1,200 in cash and the remaining amount recorded as an increase in accounts receivable. In this example, net income increases by $2,000, but cash is increased by only $1,200. Therefore, net income must be reduced by the $800 increase in accounts receivable in order to yield the correct cash flow from operations. Hence, when preparing the preliminary statement of cash flows in Step Three, it is important to remember to reverse the sign of the change values for the asset accounts. This is unnecessary for the liability and stockholders' equity accounts as can also be seen from equation (4) above.

Exhibit 12-4	An Illustration of a Preliminary Statement of Cash Flows: The Indirect Method

BENNETT COMPANY
Preliminary Statement of Cash Flows
For Year Ended December 31, 2019

Operating Activities	
Retained earnings	$19,000
Accounts receivable	(5,000)
Inventory	6,000
Prepaid insurance	(13,000)
Accounts payable	(9,000)
Income tax payable	2,000
Cash flow provided by operating activities	0
Investing Activities	
Long-term investments	(15,000)
Plant assets (net)	30,000
Patent	(60,000)
Cash flow used by investing activities	(45,000)
Financing Activities	
Common stock	70,000
Cash flow provided financing activities	70,000
Change in cash (from the balance sheet)	$25,000

Exhibit 12-4 presents the preliminary statement of cash flows for the Bennett Company. This preliminary statement suggests that the firm's cash flow provided by operating activities was $0, the cash flow used by investing activities was $45,000, and the cash flow provided financing activities was $70,000. As required, the cash inflows and outflows aggregate to the change in cash from the balance sheet, an increase of $25,000.

Step Four To this point we have used the balance sheet exclusively to provide the needed inputs to our statement of cash flows. For most businesses, however, cash flow will also be generated by a firm's ongoing operations. Hence, it is now appropriate to introduce the operations-related data found on the company's income statement (see **Exhibit 12-2**).

In this step, we accomplish two important actions involving the preliminary statement of cash flows in **Exhibit 12-4**. First, the change in retained earnings from the balance sheet will be replaced by net income from the income statement. For the Bennett Company, the change in retained earnings of $19,000 does not equal net income of $32,000. The difference of $13,000 ($32,000 − $19,000) represents a cash dividend paid to Bennett's shareholders (see the Additional Data in **Exhibit 12-2**). Thus, when we replace retained earnings of $19,000 with net income of $32,000, it is also necessary to report the $13,000 cash dividend payment as a cash outflow under the financing activities section in **Exhibit 12-5**. Increasing the cash flow from operations and decreasing the cash flow from financing activities by an equivalent amount ($13,000) allows the statement of cash flows to remain in balance with the net change in cash of $25,000.

Second, we adjust the Bennett Company's net income for any **noncash expenses** such as the depreciation of plant assets and the amortization of intangibles that were deducted in the process of calculating the firm's accrual basis net income.[2] These noncash expenses must be added back to net income in the operating activities section to

---

[2] Depreciation expense and amortization expense are called noncash expenses because these expenses do not involve any cash outflow. Depreciation expense, for example, represents the allocation of the purchase price of plant assets over the many periods that these assets produce sales revenue for a business. The matching principle requires that the cost of plant assets be matched with the sales revenue produced by these assets, and this is accomplished on the income statement by the deduction of the periodic depreciation charge.

correctly measure the firm's operating cash flow. However, to keep the preliminary statement of cash flows in balance with an increase in cash of $25,000, it is also necessary to subtract equivalent amounts in the investing activities section.

To summarize, the adjustments to the Bennett Company's preliminary statement of cash flows in **Exhibit 12-4** are:

1. Net income of $32,000 replaces the change in retained earnings of $19,000 in the operating activities section. This action adds $13,000 to the cash flow from operating activities. To keep the statement of cash flows in balance with the change in cash of $25,000, it is necessary to subtract $13,000 elsewhere on the statement. Since retained earnings is calculated as follows:

> Retained earnings
> (beginning)
> + Net income for the period
> − Dividends declared
> = Retained earnings (ending)

the outflow of $13,000 is also reflected as a cash dividend to shareholders under the financing activities section.

2. Depreciation expense of $10,000, a noncash deduction from net income, is added back to net income to avoid understating the cash flow from operations. However, to keep the statement of cash flows in balance with the change in cash of $25,000, a similar amount is subtracted from plant assets under the investing activities section.

Step Five   To provide the most useful cash flow data, a final step is required: Remove the financial effects of any nonrecurring or nonoperating transactions from net income. As noted above, a firm's operating cash flow should include only the cash flows from operating activities. Consequently, to calculate the cash flow from operating activities of a business, it is necessary to review a company's income statement to identify and remove the financial effects of any nonoperating transactions included in net income.[3]

To illustrate this point, note that the Bennett Company sold plant assets during the year at a gain of $8,000 ($28,000 sales price less $20,000 cost). (See the Additional Data in **Exhibit 12-2**.) This event is an investing activity and therefore properly belongs in the investing activities section. However, the gain of $8,000 is included in net income in the operating activities section. Thus, to correctly assess Bennett's cash flows, it is necessary to subtract the gain from the operating activities section and add it to the change in plant assets in the investing activities section. When combined with the adjustment for depreciation expense from Step Four, the cash flow from plant assets is $28,000 ($30,000 change in plant assets − $10,000 adjustment for depreciation expense + $8,000 adjustment for gain). The adjusted amount of $28,000 is equal to the cash received on the sale of plant assets.

Exhibit 12-5 presents the final statement of cash flows for Bennett Company and includes not only the adjustments from Step Four, but also the adjustment to remove any nonoperating gains and losses from the cash flow from operating activities (Step Five). Note that the company's statement of cash flows remains in balance with the change in cash of $25,000 after the adjustments in both of these steps. This result is possible because whatever amount was added to (or subtracted from) net income under the cash flow from operating activities, an equivalent amount was subtracted from (or added to) the investing activities or the financing activities.

---

[3] An exception is interest expense, which most investment professionals view as a financing activity. Regardless, interest payments are required to be included in the cash flow from operating activities.

Exhibit 12-5	Statement of Cash Flows—The Indirect Method

BENNETT COMPANY
Statement of Cash Flows
For Year Ended December 31, 2019

Cash Flow from Operating Activities

Net income		$32,000	
Add (deduct) items to convert net income to cash basis		
Depreciation	10,000	
Gain on sale of plant assets	(8,000)	
Accounts receivable increase	(5,000)	
Inventory decrease	6,000	
Prepaid insurance increase	(13,000)	
Accounts payable decrease	(9,000)	
Income tax payable increase	2,000	
Cash provided by operating activities		$15,000
Cash Flow from Investing Activities		
Purchase of long-term investments	(15,000)	
Sale of plant assets	28,000	
Purchase of patent	(60,000)	
Cash used by investing activities		(47,000)
Cash Flow from Financing Activities		
Issuance of common stock	70,000	
Payment of dividends	(13,000)	
Cash provided by financing activities		57,000
Net increase in cash		25,000
Cash at beginning of year		10,000
Cash at end of year		$35,000

Bennett's statement of cash flows reveals that the cash flow provided by operating activities is $15,000, the cash flow used by investing activities is $47,000, and the cash flow provided by financing activities is $57,000. The resulting total cash flow of $25,000 exactly equals the increase in cash on the balance sheet of $25,000, as required.

The following illustration summarizes the five-step process to prepare an indirect method statement of cash flows:

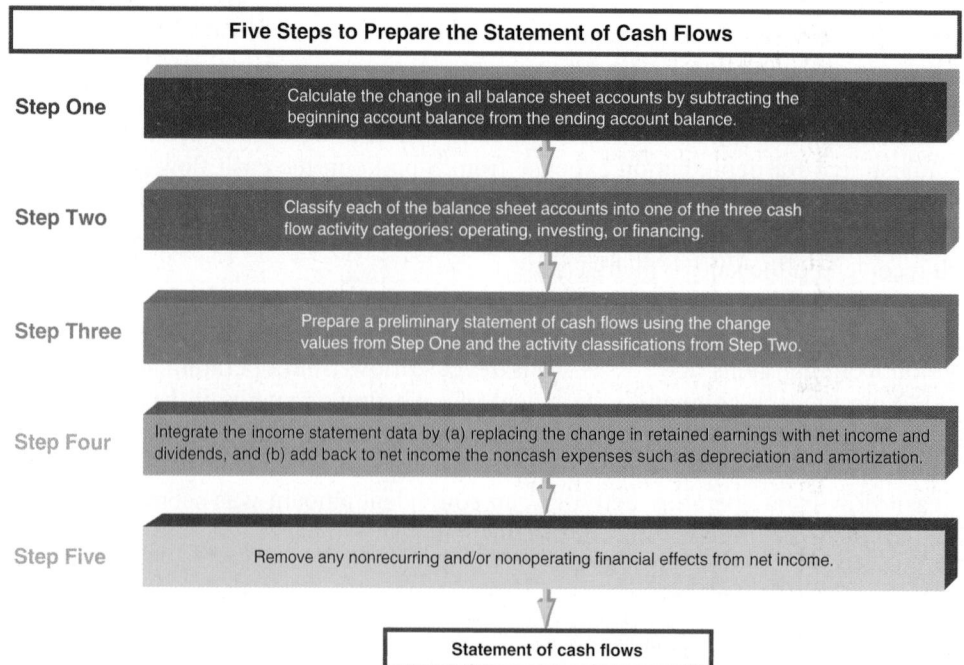

Five Steps to Prepare the Statement of Cash Flows

Step One — Calculate the change in all balance sheet accounts by subtracting the beginning account balance from the ending account balance.

Step Two — Classify each of the balance sheet accounts into one of the three cash flow activity categories: operating, investing, or financing.

Step Three — Prepare a preliminary statement of cash flows using the change values from Step One and the activity classifications from Step Two.

Step Four — Integrate the income statement data by (a) replacing the change in retained earnings with net income and dividends, and (b) add back to net income the noncash expenses such as depreciation and amortization.

Step Five — Remove any nonrecurring and/or nonoperating financial effects from net income.

Statement of cash flows

According to **Home Depot**, "Our values are our beliefs, principles and standards that do not change over time. Values are the resources we draw on when asked to make decisions. They form the groundwork for our ethical behavior. All that we do at The Home Depot must be consistent with the values of the Company. We believe in *Doing the Right Thing*, having *Respect for all People*, building *Strong Relationships*, *Taking Care of Our People*, *Giving Back*, providing *Excellent Customer Service*, *Encouraging Entrepreneurial Spirit* and providing strong *Shareholder Returns*."

Home Depot believes that "Doing the Right Thing" leads to doing well for all its stakeholders, including its shareholders. As Home Depot states, "We will conduct our business and ourselves in a way that enhances and preserves the reputation of the Company while providing our shareholders with a fair return on their investment." There seems to be a lot of truth in this as Home Depot weathered the poor U.S. economy that battered the construction industry in 2007 and 2008, reporting a profit as well as positive cash flow from operating activities in both years.

Husky Company's 2019 income statement and comparative balance sheets as of December 31 of 2019 and 2018 are shown below:

YOUR TURN! 12.2

The solution is on page 619.

HUSKY COMPANY Income Statement For Year Ended December 31, 2019		
Sales revenue.		$1,270,000
Cost of goods sold	$860,000	
Wages expense	172,000	
Insurance expense	16,000	
Depreciation expense.	34,000	
Interest expense	18,000	
Income tax expense	58,000	1,158,000
Net income		$ 112,000

HUSKY COMPANY Balance Sheets	Dec. 31, 2019	Dec. 31, 2018
Assets		
Cash.	$ 22,000	$ 10,000
Accounts receivable	82,000	64,000
Inventory.	180,000	120,000
Prepaid insurance.	10,000	14,000
Plant assets	500,000	390,000
Accumulated depreciation	(136,000)	(102,000)
Total assets	$658,000	$496,000
Liabilities and Stockholders' Equity		
Accounts payable	$ 14,000	$ 20,000
Wages payable.	18,000	12,000
Income tax payable	14,000	16,000
Bonds payable	260,000	150,000
Common stock	180,000	180,000
Retained earnings	172,000	118,000
Total liabilities and stockholders' equity	$658,000	$496,000

Cash dividends of $58,000 were declared and paid during 2019. Plant assets were purchased for cash, and bonds payable were issued for cash. Accounts payable relate to merchandise purchases.

Required

Prepare a 2019 statement of cash flows for the Husky Company using the indirect method.

For readers skipping the indirect method, please resume reading here.

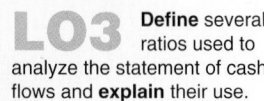

ANALYZING CASH FLOWS

LO3 Define several ratios used to analyze the statement of cash flows and **explain** their use.

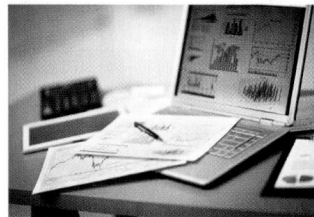

Data from the statement of cash flows are often used to calculate financial measures to evaluate a company's cash flow health. Three such measures include the company's free cash flow, the operating-cash-flow-to-current-liabilities ratio, and the operating-cash-flow-to-capital-expenditures ratio.

Free Cash Flow

Free cash flow (FCF) is often used by investment professionals and investors to evaluate a company's cash-flow strength. FCF is an important performance reference point for investment professionals because it is less subject to the accounting trickery that may characterize accrual basis net income of some firms. Free cash flow is calculated as follows:

FCF = Cash flow from operating activities − Capital expenditures

As discussed in Chapter 9, capital expenditures refer to investment in a business's plant and intangible assets necessary to enable a firm to remain a going concern. Subtracting capital expenditures from the firm's cash flow from operating activities measures the amount of excess or "free" cash flow that can be used for expansion, paying dividends, reducing debt, or other purposes. A firm with strong free cash flow will carry a higher stock value than one with weak (or no) free cash flow.

TAKEAWAY 12.1	Concept ⟶	Method ⟶	Assessment
	Does a company generate cash flows in excess of its capital expenditure needs?	Statement of cash flows. FCF = Cash flow from operating activities − Capital expenditures	The higher the free cash flow, the greater is a company's ability to generate cash for needs other than capital expenditures.

Operating-Cash-Flow-to-Current-Liabilities Ratio

Two measures previously introduced—the current ratio and the quick ratio—emphasize the relationship of a company's current or quick assets to its current liabilities in an attempt to measure the ability of a firm to pay its current liabilities. The **operating-cash-flow-to-current-liabilities ratio** is another measure of a company's ability to pay its current liabilities. While the current and quick ratios focus on a firm's ability to pay liabilities using existing current or quick assets, the operating cash flow to current liabilities ratio highlights a firm's ability to pay its current liabilities using its operating cash flow. The ratio is calculated as follows:

$$\text{Operating-cash-flow-to-current-liabilities ratio} = \frac{\text{Cash flow from operating activities}}{\text{Average current liabilities}}$$

The cash flow from operating activities is obtained from the statement of cash flows. The denominator is the average of the beginning and ending current liabilities for the year.

The following amounts were taken from the financial statements of the **Gannett Co., Inc.**, a diversified news and information company that publishes *USA Today:*

Cash flow from operating activities.	$236,468,000
Current liabilities at beginning of the year	571,987,000
Current liabilities at end of the year	510,197,000

The operating cash flow to current liabilities ratio for the Gannett Co. is calculated as follows (in millions):

$$\frac{\$236,468}{\left[\dfrac{(\$571,987 + \$510,197)}{2}\right]} = 0.44$$

The higher this ratio, the greater is a firm's ability to pay current liabilities using its operating cash flow. A ratio of 0.5 is considered a strong ratio; consequently, Gannett's ratio of 0.44 would be interpreted as a little weak. A ratio of 0.44 indicates that Gannett generates $0.44 of operating cash flow for every dollar of current liabilities.

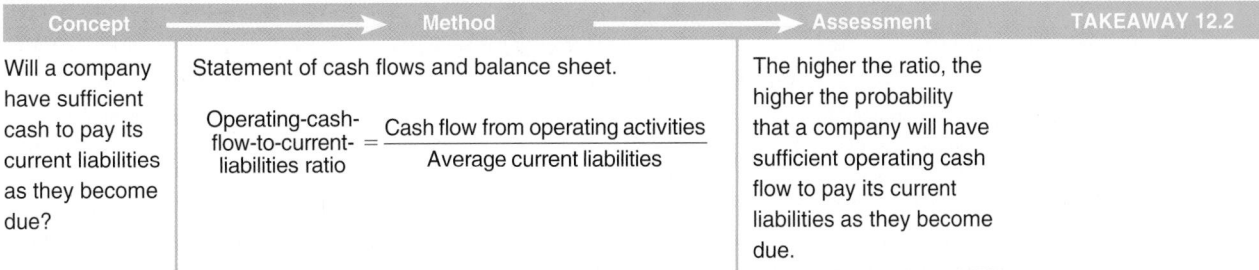

Concept	Method	Assessment	TAKEAWAY 12.2
Will a company have sufficient cash to pay its current liabilities as they become due?	Statement of cash flows and balance sheet. Operating-cash-flow-to-current-liabilities ratio $=\dfrac{\text{Cash flow from operating activities}}{\text{Average current liabilities}}$	The higher the ratio, the higher the probability that a company will have sufficient operating cash flow to pay its current liabilities as they become due.	

Operating-Cash-Flow-to-Capital-Expenditures Ratio

To remain competitive, a business must be able to replace, and expand when appropriate, its property, plant, and equipment. A ratio that evaluates a firm's ability to finance its capital investments from operating cash flow is the **operating-cash-flow-to-capital-expenditures ratio**. This ratio is calculated as follows:

$$\text{Operating-cash-flow-to-capital expenditures ratio} = \frac{\textbf{Cash flow from operating activities}}{\textbf{Annual net capital expenditures}}$$

The numerator in this ratio comes from the statement of cash flows. Information for the denominator may be found in one or more places in the financial statements. Data regarding a company's capital expenditures are presented in the investing activities section of the statement of cash flows. (When capital expenditures are reported in the statement of cash flows, the amount is often broken into two figures—(1) Proceeds from the sale of property, plant and equipment and (2) Purchases of property, plant and equipment. The appropriate "capital expenditures" figure for the purpose of calculating this ratio is the net of the two amounts.) Data on capital expenditures are also part of the required industry segment disclosures in the notes to the financial statements. Finally, management's discussion and analysis of the financial statements may identify the company's annual capital expenditures.

A ratio in excess of 1.0 indicates that a firm's current operating activities are providing sufficient cash to fund its desired investment in plant assets and would normally be considered a sign of financial strength. The interpretation of this ratio is influenced by the trend in recent years, the ratio being achieved by other firms in the same industry, and the stage of a firm's life cycle. A firm in the early stages of its life cycle—when periods of rapid expansion may occur—may be expected to experience a lower ratio than a firm in the later stage of its life cycle—when maintenance of plant capacity may be more likely than an expansion of plant capacity.

To illustrate the ratio's calculation, **Abbott Laboratories**, a manufacturer of pharmaceutical and health care products, reported capital expenditures (in thousands of dollars) of $1,135,000. Abbott's cash flow from operating activities was $5,570,000. Thus, Abbott's operating-cash-flow-to-capital-expenditures ratio for the year was 4.91, or ($5,570,000/$1,135,000). The following are operating-cash-flow-to-capital-expenditures ratios for other well-known companies:

PepsiCo Inc. (Consumer foods and beverages) 3.37
Lockheed Martin Corporation (Aerospace). 5.50
Norfolk Southern Corporation (Freight transportation services). 1.89

ACCOUNTING IN EVERYDAY LIFE	**Know Your Cash Flow**

The expression "Cash is King" certainly holds true for any small business. It is critical for entrepreneurs to understand the difference between net income and cash flow. Cash is what is needed to pay the bills. While being profitable is important, it is cash and not net income that runs the business. Many small businesses have failed because of poor cash flow management.

TAKEAWAY 12.3	Concept	Method	Assessment
	Does a company generate sufficient operating cash flows to finance its capital expenditure needs?	Statement of cash flows. Operating-cash-flow-to-capital-expenditures ratio $= \dfrac{\text{Cash flow from operating activities}}{\text{Annual net capital expenditures}}$	The higher the ratio, the higher the probability that a company will generate sufficient operating cash flow to finance its capital expenditure needs.

YOUR TURN! 12.3

The solution is on page 619.

MBC

The following selected data were obtained from the financial statements of Blake Enterprises:

Cash flow from operating activities.	$40,000
Annual net capital expenditures	12,500
Average current liabilities	30,000

Calculate the following financial measures for Blake Enterprises:

1. Free cash flow
2. Operating-cash-flow-to-current-liabilities ratio
3. Operating-cash-flow-to-capital-expenditures ratio

COMPREHENSIVE PROBLEM

MBC

Terry Company's income statement and comparative balance sheets at December 31, 2019 and 2018, are as follows:

TERRY COMPANY Income Statement For Year Ended December 31, 2019		
Sales revenue.		$385,000
Dividend income.		5,000
		390,000
Cost of goods sold	$233,000	
Wages expense	82,000	
Advertising expense.	10,000	
Depreciation expense.	11,000	
Income tax expense	17,000	
Loss on sale of investments.	1,000	354,000
Net income		$ 36,000

TERRY COMPANY Balance Sheets		
	Dec. 31, 2019	Dec. 31, 2018
Assets		
Cash.	$ 8,000	$ 12,000
Accounts receivable	22,000	28,000
Inventory.	94,000	66,000
Prepaid advertising.	12,000	9,000
Long-term investments.	30,000	40,000
Plant assets	178,000	130,000
Accumulated depreciation	(72,000)	(61,000)
Total assets	$272,000	$224,000
Liabilities and Stockholders' Equity		
Accounts payable.	$ 27,000	$ 14,000
Wages payable.	6,000	2,500
Income tax payable	3,000	4,500
Common stock	139,000	125,000
Retained earnings	97,000	78,000
Unrealized loss on investments	—	—
Total liabilities and stockholders' equity	$272,000	$224,000

Cash dividends of $17,000 were declared and paid during 2019. Plant assets were purchased for cash, and, later in the year, additional common stock was issued for cash. Investments costing $10,000 were sold for cash at a $1,000 loss.

Required

a. Calculate the change in cash that occurred during 2019.

b. Prepare a 2019 statement of cash flows using the indirect method.

Solution

a. $8,000 ending balance − $12,000 beginning balance = $4,000 decrease in cash

b. 1. Use the indirect method to determine the cash flow from operating activities.
   - The adjustments to convert Terry Company's net income of $36,000 to the cash provided by operating activities of $38,000 are shown in the following statement of cash flows.

   2. Analyze changes in remaining noncash asset (and contra asset) accounts to determine cash flows from investing activities.
   - Long-term investments: $10,000 decrease resulted from sale of investments for cash at a $1,000 loss. Cash received from sale of investments = $9,000 ($10,000 cost − $1,000 loss).
   - Plant assets: $48,000 increase resulted from purchase of plant assets for cash. Cash paid to purchase plant assets = $48,000.
   - Accumulated depreciation: $11,000 increase resulted from the recording of 2019 depreciation. No cash flow effect.

   3. Analyze changes in remaining liability and stockholders' equity accounts to determine cash flows from financing activities.
   - Common stock: $14,000 increase resulted from the issuance of stock for cash. Cash received from issuance of common stock = $14,000.
   - Retained earnings: $19,000 increase resulted from net income of $36,000 and dividend declaration of $17,000. Cash paid as dividends = $17,000.

   The statement of cash flows (indirect method) is as follows:

TERRY COMPANY
Statement of Cash Flows
For the Year Ended December 31, 2019

Cash Flow from Operating Activities		
Net income	$35,000	
Add (deduct) items to convert net income to cash basis		
Depreciation	11,000	
Loss on sale of investments	2,000	
Accounts receivable decrease.	6,000	
Inventory increase.	(28,000)	
Prepaid advertising increase.	(3,000)	
Accounts payable increase	13,000	
Wages payable increase.	3,500	
Income tax payable decrease	(1,500)	
Cash provided by operating activities		$38,000
Cash Flow from Investing Activities		
Sale of investments.	9,000	
Purchase of plant assets.	(48,000)	
Cash used by investing activities		(39,000)
Cash Flow from Financing Activities		
Issuance of common stock	14,000	
Payment of dividends	(17,000)	
Cash used by financing activities		(3,000)
Net decrease in cash		(4,000)
Cash at beginning of year.		12,000
Cash at end of year		$ 8,000

APPENDIX 12A: Preparing the Statement of Cash Flows Under the Direct Method

LO4 Explain the preparation of a statement of cash flows using the direct method.

Although it is quite straightforward to create a direct method statement of cash flows given access to a company's internal accounting records, such access is rarely available to anyone except a company's management team. All that is necessary is to pull the numbers directly off the Cash general ledger account and place them in the appropriate section of the statement of cash flows. This is why the direct method is referred to as "direct." The cash flow from operations is taken directly from the company's general ledger, rather than being indirectly computed from net income. Unfortunately, investment professionals, lenders, and stockholders rarely have access to such proprietary internal data. Thus, it is necessary to be able to create direct method cash flow information using only such publicly available data as the indirect method statement of cash flows.

The process to convert an indirect method statement of cash flows to the direct method requires two steps. First, replace net income (the first line item under the operating activities section of the indirect method statement format) with the line items appearing on a firm's income statement. For instance, Bennett Company's income statement in **Exhibit 12-2** contains the following line items:

Sales revenue.	$250,000
Cost of goods sold	(148,000)
Wages expense	(52,000)
Insurance expense.	(5,000)
Depreciation expense.	(10,000)
Income tax expense	(11,000)
Gain on sale of plant assets.	8,000
Net income	$ 32,000

Thus, for the Bennett Company, we begin by replacing the net income of $32,000 under the operating activities section in **Exhibit 12-5** with the seven income statement line items shown above, which aggregate to $32,000.

The second step involves adjusting the income statement line items identified in Step One with the remaining line items from the operating activities section of the indirect method statement of cash flows. **Exhibit**

12A-1 summarizes the procedures for converting individual income statement items to the corresponding cash flows from operating activities.

Exhibit 12A-1	Direct Method Conversion Schedule: Adjustments to Convert Income Statement Items to Operating Activity Cash Flows

Income Statement Item	Adjustment to Cash Flow	Operating Activity Cash Flow
Sales revenue	+ Decrease in accounts receivable *or* – Increase in accounts receivable	= Receipts from customers
Cost of goods sold	+ Increase in inventory *or* – Decrease in inventory **and** + Decrease in accounts payable *or* – Increase in accounts payable	= Payments for merchandise
Operating expenses Interest expense Income tax expense (excluding items listed below)	+ Increase in related prepaid expense *or* – Decrease in related prepaid expense **and** + Decrease in related accrued liability *or* – Increase in related accrued liability	= Payments for expenses
Depreciation expense Depletion expense Amortization expense	+ Depreciation expense + Depletion expense + Amortization expense	= 0
Gains (investing/financing) Losses (investing/financing)	Omit: Not related to operating activities	= 0

Using Bennett Company's data in **Exhibit 12-5**, those adjustments would appear as follows:

Income Statement Line Items		Operating Activities Line Items	Direct Method Cash Flow	
Sales revenue.	$250,000	– **$5,000 accounts receivable**	Cash received from customers.	$245,000
Cost of goods sold	(148,000)	+ **$6,000 inventory** – **$9,000 accounts payable**	Cash paid for merchandise.	(151,000)
Wage expense	(52,000)	**No adjustment**	Cash paid to employees.	(52,000)
Insurance expense.	(5,000)	– **$13,000 prepaid insurance**	Cash paid for insurance	(18,000)
Depreciation expense.	(10,000)	+ $10,000 depreciation		
Income tax expense	(11,000)	+ $2,000 income tax payable	Cash paid for income taxes	(9,000)
Gain on sale of plant assets	8,000	– **$8,000 gain on sale of plant assets**		
Net income	$ 32,000		Cash flow from operations	$ 15,000

Exhibit 12A-2 presents the Bennett Company's direct method statement of cash flows after undertaking the above two steps. As expected, the direct method cash flow from operating activities of $15,000 is exactly equivalent to the indirect method result of $15,000 as reported in **Exhibit 12-5**. Note that the cash flow from investing activities and the cash flow from financing activities sections are exactly the same in both **Exhibit 12-5** and **Exhibit 12A-2**. The only difference between the two exhibits is the manner in which the cash flow from operating activities is calculated. In **Exhibit 12-5**, the cash flow from operating activities is calculated beginning with net income and then adjusting for various noncash expenses (depreciation expense) and nonoperating transactions (gain on sale of plant assets), as well as adjusting for the changes in the various working capital accounts (accounts receivable, inventory, prepaid insurance, accounts payable, and taxes payable). In **Exhibit 12A-2**, net income is replaced with the income statement line items and the noncash expenses and working capital adjustments are disaggregated to the individual line items. But in each case, the operating cash flow is $15,000. A company using the direct method must also separately disclose the reconciliation of net income to cash flow from operating activities prepared using the indirect method.

Exhibit 12A-2	Statement of Cash Flows Under the Direct Method

BENNETT COMPANY
Statement of Cash Flows
For Year Ended December 31, 2019

Cash Flow from Operating Activities

Cash received from customers.		$245,000
Cash paid for merchandise purchased.	$(151,000)	
Cash paid to employees.	(52,000)	
Cash paid for insurance	(18,000)	
Cash paid for income taxes	(9,000)	(230,000)
Cash provided by operating activities.		15,000
Cash Flow from Investing Activities		
Purchase of long-term investments	(15,000)	
Sale of plant assets	28,000	
Purchase of patent	(60,000)	
Cash used by investing activities		(47,000)
Cash Flow from Financing Activities		
Issuance of common stock.	70,000	
Payment of dividends.	(13,000)	
Cash provided by financing activities		57,000
Net increase in cash.		25,000
Cash at beginning of year.		10,000
Cash at end of year		$ 35,000

YOUR TURN! 12A.1

The solution is on pages 619–620.

Husky Company's 2019 income statement and comparative balance sheets as of December 31 of 2019 and 2018 are shown below:

HUSKY COMPANY
Income Statement
For the Year Ended December 31, 2019

Sales revenue.		$1,270,000
Cost of goods sold	$860,000	
Wages expense	172,000	
Insurance expense.	16,000	
Depreciation expense.	34,000	
Interest expense.	18,000	
Income tax expense	58,000	1,158,000
Net income		$ 112,000

HUSKY COMPANY
Balance Sheets

	Dec. 31, 2019	Dec. 31, 2018
Assets		
Cash.	$ 22,000	$ 10,000
Accounts receivable	82,000	64,000
Inventory.	180,000	120,000
Prepaid insurance.	10,000	14,000
Plant assets	500,000	390,000
Accumulated depreciation	(136,000)	(102,000)
Total assets	$658,000	$496,000

continued

continued from previous page

HUSKY COMPANY Balance Sheets (continued)		
	Dec. 31, 2019	Dec. 31, 2018
Liabilities and Stockholders' Equity		
Accounts payable.	$ 14,000	$ 20,000
Wages payable.	18,000	12,000
Income tax payable	14,000	16,000
Bonds payable	260,000	150,000
Common stock	180,000	180,000
Retained earnings	172,000	118,000
Total liabilities and stockholders' equity	$658,000	$496,000

Cash dividends of $58,000 were declared and paid during 2019. Plant assets were purchased for cash, and bonds payable were issued for cash. Bond interest is paid semiannually on June 30 and December 31. Accounts payable relate to merchandise purchases.

Required
Prepare a 2019 statement of cash flows using the direct method.

SUMMARY OF LEARNING OBJECTIVES

Discuss the content and format of the statement of cash flows. (p. 572)   LO1

- The statement of cash flows explains the net increase or decrease in cash and cash equivalents during the period.
- The statement of cash flows separates cash flows into operating, investing, and financing activity categories.
- The statement of cash flows also provides a required supplemental disclosure reporting noncash investing and financing activities.
- The statement of cash flows helps users compare, evaluate, and predict a firm's cash flows and also helps evaluate its financial flexibility.

Explain the preparation of a statement of cash flows using the indirect method. (p. 578)   LO2

- The indirect method of preparing the cash flow from operating activities section reconciles net income to cash flow from operating activities.

Define several ratios used to analyze the statement of cash flows and explain their use. (p. 586)   LO3

- Free cash flow is defined as a company's cash flow from operations less its capital expenditures; the metric provides a measure of a firm's cash flow that can be used to fund business activities beyond the replacement of property, plant, and equipment.
- The operating-cash-flow-to-current-liabilities ratio is calculated by dividing a company's cash flow from operating activities by its average current liabilities for the year; the ratio reveals a firm's ability to repay current liabilities from operating cash flow.
- The operating-cash-flow-to-capital-expenditures ratio is calculated by dividing a firm's cash flow from operating activities by its annual net capital expenditures; the ratio evaluates a firm's ability to fund its capital investment using operating cash flow.

Appendix 12A: Explain the preparation of a statement of cash flows using the direct method. (p. 590)   LO4

- The direct method of preparing the cash flow from operating activities section shows the major categories of operating cash receipts and payments.
- The FASB encourages use of the direct method but permits use of either the direct or the indirect method.
- A firm using the direct method must separately disclose the reconciliation of net income to cash flow from operating activities.

SUMMARY	Concept	Method	Assessment
TAKEAWAY 12.1	Does a company generate cash flows in excess of its capital expenditure needs?	Statement of cash flows. FCF = Cash flow from operating activities − Capital expenditures	The higher the free cash flow, the greater is a company's ability to generate cash for needs other than capital expenditures.
TAKEAWAY 12.2	Will a company have sufficient cash to pay its current liabilities as they become due?	Statement of cash flows and balance sheet. $$\text{Operating-cash-flow-to-current-liabilities ratio} = \frac{\text{Cash flow from operating activities}}{\text{Average current liabilities}}$$	The higher the ratio, the higher the probability that a company will have sufficient operating cash flow to pay its current liabilities as they become due.
TAKEAWAY 12.3	Does a company generate sufficient operating cash flows to finance its capital expenditure needs?	Statement of cash flows. $$\text{Operating-cash-flow-to-capital-expenditures ratio} = \frac{\text{Cash flow from operating activities}}{\text{Annual net capital expenditures}}$$	The higher the ratio, the higher the probability that a company will generate sufficient operating cash flow to finance its capital expenditure needs.

KEY TERMS

Cash equivalents (p. 572)

Cash management (p. 572)

Direct method (p. 577)

Financial flexibility (p. 577)

Financing activities (p. 574)

Free cash flow (FCF) (p. 586)

Indirect method (p. 577)

Investing activities (p. 574)

Noncash expenses (p. 582)

Noncash investing and financing activities (p. 576)

Operating activities (p. 574)

Operating-cash-flow-to-capital-expenditures ratio (p. 587)

Operating-cash-flow-to-current-liabilities ratio (p. 586)

Assignments with the ⊜ logo in the margin are available in BusinessCourse.
See the Preface of the book for details.

SELF-STUDY QUESTIONS

(Answers to the Self-Study Questions are at the end of the chapter.)

LO1

1. **Which of the following is not disclosed in a statement of cash flows?**
   a. A transfer of cash to a cash equivalent investment
   b. The amount of cash at year-end
   c. Cash outflows from investing activities during the period
   d. Cash inflows from financing activities during the period

LO1

2. **Which of the following events will appear in the cash flows from investing activities section of the statement of cash flows?**
   a. Cash received as interest
   b. Cash received from issuance of common stock
   c. Cash purchase of truck
   d. Cash payment of dividends

LO1

3. **Which of the following events will appear in the cash flows from financing activities section of the statement of cash flows?**
   a. Cash purchase of equipment
   b. Cash purchase of bonds issued by another company
   c. Cash received as repayment for funds loaned
   d. Cash purchase of treasury stock

4. Tyler Company has net income of $49,000 and the following related items: **LO2**

Depreciation expense.	$ 5,000
Accounts receivable increase.	2,000
Inventory increase	10,000
Accounts payable decrease	4,000

Using the indirect method, what is Tyler's cash flow from operations?
   a. $42,000   c. $58,000
   b. $46,000   d. $38,000

5. Free cash flow is a measure of a firm's   **LO3**
   a. interest free debt.
   b. ability to generate net income.
   c. ability to generate cash and invest in new capital expenditures.
   d. ability to collect accounts receivable in a timely manner.

6. Which of the following events will not appear in the cash flows from financing activities section of the statement of cash flow?   **LO1**
   a. Borrowing cash from a bank
   b. Issuance of stock in exchange for plant assets
   c. Sales of common stock
   d. Payment of dividends on preferred stock

7. Taylor Company reports free cash flow of $15,000, total cash of $18,000, net income of $50,000, current assets of $90,000, average current liabilities of $38,400, and cash flow from operating activities of $48,000. Compute the operating-cash-flow-to-current-liabilities ratio for Taylor Company.   **LO3**
   a. 0.83
   b. 0.80
   c. 0.30
   d. 1.25

8. Which of the following is not a cash equivalent?   **LO1**
   a. Short-term U.S. Treasury bill
   b. Short-term certificate of deposit
   c. Money-market account
   d. IBM common stock

9. Which of the following expenses are not added back to net income when using the indirect method to prepare a statement of cash flows?   **LO2**
   a. Amortization expense
   b. Depletion expense
   c. Interest expense
   d. Depreciation expense

10. Smith & Sons reports interest expense of $90,000 on its income statement. The beginning and ending balances for interest payable reported on its balance sheet are $15,000 and $10,000, respectively. How much cash did Smith & Sons pay for interest expense this period?   **LO4 (Appendix 12A)**
   a. $85,000
   b. $95,000
   c. $100,000
   d. $105,000

11. Which of the following methods will disclose the cash received from customers in the statement of cash flows?   **LO4 (Appendix 12A)**
   a. Indirect method
   b. Reconciliation method
   c. Direct method
   d. Both direct and indirect methods

LO4
(Appendix 12A)

MBC

12. **Smith & Sons reports sales revenue of $1,000,000 on its income statement. Its balance sheet reveals beginning and ending accounts receivable of $92,000 and $60,000, respectively. What is the amount of cash collected from customers of the company?**
   a. $1,032,000
   b. $968,000
   c. $1,060,000
   d. $1,092,000

QUESTIONS

1. What is the definition of *cash equivalents?* Give three examples of cash equivalents.

2. Why are cash equivalents included with cash in a statement of cash flows?

3. What are the three major types of activities classified on a statement of cash flows? Give an example of a cash inflow and a cash outflow in each classification.

4. In which of the three activity categories of a statement of cash flows would each of the following items appear? Indicate for each item whether it represents a cash inflow or a cash outflow:
   a. Cash purchase of equipment
   b. Cash collection on loans
   c. Cash dividends paid
   d. Cash dividends received
   e. Cash proceeds from issuing stock
   f. Cash receipts from customers
   g. Cash interest paid
   h. Cash interest received

5. Why is a statement of cash flows a useful financial statement?

6. What is the difference between the direct method and the indirect method of presenting the cash flow from operating activities?

7. In determining the cash flow from operating activities using the indirect method, why is it necessary to add depreciation back to net income? Give an example of another item that is added back to net income under the indirect method.

8. Vista Company sold land for $98,000 cash that had originally cost $70,000. The company recorded a gain on the sale of $28,000. How is this event reported in a statement of cash flows using the indirect method?

9. A firm uses the indirect method. Using the following information, what is its cash flow from operating activities?

Net income	$88,000
Accounts receivable decrease	13,000
Inventory increase	9,000
Accounts payable decrease	3,500
Income tax payable increase	1,500
Depreciation expense	6,000

10. If a business had a net loss for the year, under what circumstances would the statement of cash flows show a positive cash flow from operating activities?

11. A firm is converting its accrual revenues to corresponding cash amounts using the direct method. Sales revenue on the income statement are $925,000. Beginning and ending accounts receivable on the balance sheet are $58,000 and $44,000, respectively. What is the amount of cash received from customers?

12. A firm reports $86,000 wages expense in its income statement. If beginning and ending wages payable are $3,900 and $2,800, respectively, what is the amount of cash paid to employees?

13. A firm reports $43,000 advertising expense in its income statement. If beginning and ending prepaid advertising are $6,000 and $7,600, respectively, what is the amount of cash paid for advertising?

14. Rusk Company sold equipment for $5,100 cash that had cost $35,000 and had $29,000 of accumulated depreciation. How is this event reported in a statement of cash flows using the direct method?

15. What separate disclosures are required for a company that reports a statement of cash flows using the direct method?

16. How is the *operating-cash-flow-to-current-liabilities ratio* calculated? Explain its use.

17. How is the *operating-cash-flow-to-capital-expenditures ratio* calculated? Explain its use.

18. The statement of cash flows provides information that may be useful in predicting future cash flows, evaluating financial flexibility, assessing liquidity, and identifying a company's financing needs. It is not, however, the best financial statement for learning about a firm's financial performance during a period. Information about a company's financial performance is provided by the income statement. Two basic principles—the revenue recognition principle and the matching concept—work to distinguish the income statement from the statement of cash flows. (a) Define the revenue recognition principle and the matching concept. (b) Briefly explain how these two principles work to make the income statement a better report regarding a firm's periodic financial performance than the statement of cash flows.

SHORT EXERCISES

Use the following information regarding the Melville Corporation to answer Short Exercises 12-1 through 12-3:

Accounts payable increase.	$12,000
Accounts receivable increase.	4,000
Accrued liabilities decrease	5,000
Amortization expense.	7,000
Cash balance, January 1	22,000
Cash balance, December 31	23,000
Cash paid as dividends	31,000
Cash paid to purchase land	90,000
Cash paid to retire bonds payable at par	60,000
Cash received from issuance of common stock.	37,000
Cash received from sale of equipment.	19,000
Depreciation expense.	29,000
Gain on sale of equipment	4,000
Inventory decrease.	13,000
Net income.	80,000
Prepaid expenses increase	2,000

SE12-1. **Cash Flow from Operating Activities** Using the information for the Melville Corporation above, calculate the cash flow from operating activities. **LO1, 2**

SE12-2. **Cash Flow from Investing Activities** Using the information for the Melville Corporation above, calculate the cash flow from investing activities. **LO1, 2**

SE12-3. **Cash Flow from Financing Activities** Using the information for the Melville Corporation above, calculate the cash flow from financing activities. **LO1, 2**

The following information for Evans & Sons relates to Short Exercises 12-4 through 12-6:

Cash flow from operating activities.	$1,600,000
Capital expenditures.	850,000
Current liabilities, beginning of year	300,000
Current liabilities, end of year.	380,000

SE12-4. **Free Cash Flow** Using the above data, calculate the free cash flow for Evans & Sons. **LO3**

SE12-5. **Operating-Cash-Flow-to-Current-Liabilities Ratio** Using the above data, calculate the operating-cash-flow-to-current-liabilities ratio for Evans & Sons. **LO3**

LO3 **SE12-6.** **Operating-Cash-Flow-to-Capital-Expenditures Ratio** Using the above data, calculate the operating-cash-flow-to-capital-expenditures ratio for Evans & Sons.

LO4 **SE12-7.** **Converting Sales Revenue to Cash** Evans & Sons is converting its sales revenues to correspond-
(Appendix ing cash amounts using the direct method. Sales revenue on the income statement are $1,025,000.
12A) Beginning and ending accounts receivable on the balance sheet are $58,000 and $38,000, respectively. Calculate the amount of cash received from customers.

LO4 **SE12-8.** **Direct Method** Using the following data for Evans & Sons, calculate the cash paid for rent:
(Appendix
12A)

Rent expense	$80,000
Prepaid rent, January 1	10,000
Prepaid rent, December 31	8,000

LO4 **SE12-9.** **Direct Method** Using the following data for Evans & Sons, calculate the cash received as interest:
(Appendix
12A)

Interest income	$30,000
Interest receivable, January 1	3,000
Interest receivable, December 31	3,700

LO4 **SE12-10.** **Direct Method** Using the following data for Evans & Sons, calculate the cash paid for merchandise
(Appendix purchased:
12A)

Cost of goods sold	$128,000
Inventory, January 1	19,000
Inventory, December 31	22,000
Accounts payable, January 1	11,000
Accounts payable, December 31	7,000

EXERCISES—SET A

LO1 **E12-1A.** **Classification of Cash Flows** For each of the items below, indicate whether the cash flow item
relates to an operating activity, an investing activity, or a financing activity:

   a. Cash receipts from customers for services rendered
   b. Sale of long-term investments for cash
   c. Acquisition of plant assets for cash
   d. Payment of income taxes
   e. Bonds payable issued for cash
   f. Payment of cash dividends declared in previous year
   g. Purchase of short-term investments (not cash equivalents) for cash

LO1 **E12-2A.** **Classification of Cash Flows** For each of the items below, indicate whether it is (1) a cash flow
from an operating activity, (2) a cash flow from an investing activity, (3) a cash flow from a financing activity, (4) a noncash investing and financing activity, or (5) none of the above:

   a. Paid cash to retire bonds payable at a loss
   b. Received cash as settlement of a lawsuit
   c. Acquired a patent in exchange for common stock
   d. Received advance payments from customers on orders for custom-made goods
   e. Gave large cash contribution to local university
   f. Invested cash in 60-day commercial paper (a cash equivalent)

LO2 **E12-3A.** **Cash Flow from Operating Activities (Indirect Method)** The Washington Company owns no
plant assets and had the following income statement for the year:

Sales revenue.		$900,000
Cost of goods sold	$470,000	
Wages expense	120,000	
Rent expense	50,000	
Insurance expense	15,000	655,000
Net income		$245,000

Additional information about the company includes:

	End of Year	Beginning of Year
Accounts receivable	$54,000	$51,000
Inventory.	60,000	76,000
Prepaid insurance.	8,000	7,000
Accounts payable	24,000	18,000
Wages payable.	7,000	11,000

Use the preceding information to calculate the cash flow from operating activities using the indirect method.

E12-4A. **Statement of Cash Flows (Indirect Method)** Use the following information regarding the Surpa Corporation to (a) prepare a statement of cash flows using the indirect method and (b) compute Surpa's operating-cash-flow-to-current-liabilities ratio.

LO2, 3

Accounts payable increase.	$ 13,000
Accounts receivable increase.	4,000
Accrued liabilities decrease	6,000
Amortization expense.	7,000
Cash balance, January 1	21,000
Cash balance, December 31	17,000
Cash paid as dividends	31,000
Cash paid to purchase land	90,000
Cash paid to retire bonds payable at par	60,000
Cash received from issuance of common stock.	40,000
Cash received from sale of equipment.	17,000
Depreciation expense.	29,000
Gain on sale of equipment	7,000
Inventory decrease.	13,000
Net income	78,000
Prepaid expenses increase	3,000
Average current liabilities	140,000

E12-5A. **Cash Flow from Operating Activities (Indirect Method)** The Azuza Company owns no plant assets and had the following income statement for the year:

LO2

Sales revenue.		$930,000
Cost of goods sold	$650,000	
Wages expense	210,000	
Rent expense	42,000	
Utilities expense	12,000	914,000
Net income		$ 16,000

Additional information about the company includes:

	End of Year	Beginning of Year
Accounts receivable	$67,000	$59,000
Inventory	62,000	86,000
Prepaid rent	9,000	7,000
Accounts payable	22,000	30,000
Wages payable	9,000	7,000

Use the preceding information to calculate the cash flow from operating activities using the indirect method.

LO2 **E12-6A.** **Statement of Cash Flows (Indirect Method)** Use the following information regarding the Hamilton Corporation to prepare a statement of cash flows using the indirect method:

Accounts payable decrease	$ 3,000
Accounts receivable increase	10,000
Wages payable decrease	9,000
Amortization expense	19,000
Cash balance, January 1	31,000
Cash balance, December 31	2,000
Cash paid as dividends	6,000
Cash paid to purchase land	110,000
Cash paid to retire bonds payable at par	65,000
Cash received from issuance of common stock	45,000
Cash received from sale of equipment	13,000
Depreciation expense	39,000
Gain on sale of equipment	16,000
Inventory increase	11,000
Net income	94,000
Prepaid expenses increase	9,000

LO3 **E12-7A.** **Cash Flow Ratios** Tracy Company reports the following amounts in its annual financial statements:

Cash flow from operating activities	$90,000	Capital expenditures	$ 31,000*
Cash flow from investing activities	(70,000)	Average current assets	80,000
Cash flow from financing activities	(10,000)	Average current liabilities	60,000
Net income	44,000	Total assets	180,000

* This amount is a cash outflow.

a. Compute Tracy's free cash flow.
b. Compute Tracy's operating-cash-flow-to-current-liabilities ratio.
c. Compute Tracy's operating-cash-flow-to-capital-expenditures ratio.

LO4
(Appendix 12A) **E12-8A.** **Operating Cash Flows (Direct Method)** Calculate the cash flow in each of the following cases:

a. Cash paid for advertising:

Advertising expense	$62,000
Prepaid advertising, January 1	13,000
Prepaid advertising, December 31	15,000

b. Cash paid for income taxes:

Income tax expense	$31,000
Income tax payable, January 1	7,100
Income tax payable, December 31	5,900

    c. Cash paid for merchandise purchased:

Cost of goods sold	$180,000
Inventory, January 1	30,000
Inventory, December 31	24,000
Accounts payable, January 1	10,000
Accounts payable, December 31	11,000

E12-9A. **Statement of Cash Flows (Direct Method)** Use the following information regarding the cash flows of Dixon Corporation to prepare a statement of cash flows using the direct method: **LO4 (Appendix 12A)**

Cash balance, December 31	$ 9,000
Cash paid to employees and suppliers	158,000
Cash received from sale of land	42,000
Cash paid to acquire treasury stock	10,000
Cash balance, January 1	18,000
Cash received as interest	8,000
Cash paid as income taxes	9,000
Cash paid to purchase equipment	89,000
Cash received from customers	199,000
Cash received from issuing bonds payable	30,000
Cash paid as dividends	22,000

E12-10A. **Operating Cash Flows (Direct Method)** Refer to the information in Exercise E12-3A. Calculate the cash flow from operating activities using the direct method. Show a related cash flow for each revenue and expense.   **LO4 (Appendix 12A)**

E12-11A. **Investing and Financing Cash Flows** During the year, Paton Corporation's Long-Term Investments account (at cost) increased $20,000, the net result of purchasing stocks costing $85,000 and selling stocks costing $65,000 at a $7,000 loss. Also, the Bonds Payable account decreased by $35,000, the net result of issuing $100,000 of bonds at 102 and retiring bonds with a face value (and book value) of $135,000 at an $8,000 gain. What items and amounts will appear in the (a) cash flows from investing activities and the (b) cash flows from financing activities sections of Paton's statement of cash flows?   **LO2, 4 (Appendix 12A)**

EXERCISES—SET B

E12-1B. **Classification of Cash Flows** For each of the items below, indicate whether the cash flow item relates to an operating activity, an investing activity, or a financing activity: **LO1**

    a. Cash loaned to borrowers
    b. Cash paid as interest on bonds payable
    c. Cash received from issuance of preferred stock
    d. Cash paid as state income taxes
    e. Cash received as dividends on stock investments
    f. Cash paid to acquire treasury stock
    g. Cash paid to acquire a franchise to distribute a product line

E12-2B. **Classification of Cash Flows** For each of the items below, indicate whether it is (1) a cash flow from an operating activity, (2) a cash flow from an investing activity, (3) a cash flow from a financing activity, (4) a noncash investing and financing activity, or (5) none of the above: **LO1**

    a. Received cash as interest earned on bond investment
    b. Received cash as refund from supplier
    c. Borrowed cash from bank on six-month note payable
    d. Exchanged, at a gain, stock held as an investment for a parcel of land
    e. Invested cash in a money market fund (cash may be easily withdrawn from the fund)
    f. Loaned cash to help finance the start of a new biotechnology firm

LO2, 3 **E12-3B.** **Cash Flow from Operating Activities (Indirect Method)** The following information was obtained from Melville Company's comparative balance sheets:

	End of Year	Beginning of Year
Cash	$ 19,000	$ 9,000
Accounts receivable	50,000	35,000
Inventory.	55,000	49,000
Prepaid rent	6,000	8,000
Long-term investments.	21,000	32,000
Plant assets	140,000	106,000
Accumulated depreciation	(42,000)	(32,000)
Accounts payable.	24,000	22,000
Income tax payable	4,000	6,000
Common stock	127,000	92,000
Retained earnings	106,000	91,000
Capital expenditures.	15,200	

Assume that Melville Company's income statement showed depreciation expense of $10,000, a gain on sale of investments of $7,000, and a net income of $60,000. (a) Calculate the cash flow from operating activities using the indirect method and (b) compute Melville's operating-cash-flow-to-capital-expenditures ratio.

LO2 **E12-4B.** **Cash Flow from Operating Activities (Indirect Method)** Zaire Company had a $26,000 net loss from operations. Depreciation expense for the year was $9,600, and a dividend of $2,000 was declared and paid. The balances of the current asset and current liability accounts at the beginning and end of the year are as follows:

	End	Beginning
Cash.	$ 3,500	$ 7,000
Accounts receivable	16,000	27,000
Inventory.	51,000	53,000
Prepaid expenses.	5,000	9,000
Accounts payable.	12,000	8,000
Accrued liabilities	6,000	7,600

Did Zaire Company's operating activities provide or use cash? Use the indirect method to determine your answer.

LO2 **E12-5B.** **Cash Flow from Operating Activities (Indirect Method)** The Smith Company owns no plant assets and had the following income statement for the year:

Sales revenue.		$1,140,000
Cost of goods sold	$770,000	
Wages expense	230,000	
Rent expense	65,000	
Insurance expense.	47,000	1,112,000
Net income		$ 28,000

Additional information about the company includes:

	End of Year	Beginning of Year
Accounts receivable	$74,000	$49,000
Inventory.	70,000	74,000
Prepaid insurance.	5,000	8,000
Accounts payable.	26,000	28,000
Wages payable.	6,000	13,000

Use the preceding information to calculate the cash flow from operating activities using the indirect method.

E12-6B. **Statement of Cash Flows (Indirect Method)** Use the following information regarding the Fremont Corporation to prepare a statement of cash flows using the indirect method: **LO2**

Accounts payable increase.	$ 14,000
Accounts receivable increase.	7,000
Accrued liabilities decrease	5,000
Amortization expense.	31,000
Cash balance, January 1	21,000
Cash balance, December 31	141,000
Cash paid as dividends	41,000
Cash paid to purchase land	81,000
Cash paid to retire bonds payable at par	70,000
Cash received from issuance of common stock.	75,000
Cash received from sale of equipment.	17,000
Depreciation expense.	65,000
Gain on sale of equipment	12,000
Inventory decrease.	11,000
Net income	126,000
Prepaid expenses increase	3,000

E12-7B. **Cash Flow Ratios** Morris Company reports the following amounts in its annual financial statements: **LO3**

Cash flow from operating activities.	$75,000	Capital expenditures.	$ 47,500*
Cash flow from investing activities	(60,000)	Average current assets.	150,000
Cash flow from financing activities	(8,500)	Average current liabilities	90,000
Net income	37,500	Total assets	225,000

* This amount is a cash outflow.

a. Compute Morris's free cash flow.
b. Compute Morris's operating-cash-flow-to-current-liabilities ratio.
c. Compute Morris's operating-cash-flow-to-capital-expenditures ratio.

E12-8B. **Operating Cash Flows (Direct Method)** Calculate the cash flow in each of the following cases: **LO4 (Appendix 12A)**

a. Cash paid for rent:

Rent expense	$62,000
Prepaid rent, January 1	10,000
Prepaid rent, December 31	6,000

b. Cash received as interest:

Interest income.	$16,000
Interest receivable, January 1	6,000
Interest receivable, December 31.	3,700

c. Cash paid for merchandise purchased:

Cost of goods sold	$98,000
Inventory, January 1.	19,000
Inventory, December 31.	22,000
Accounts payable, January 1.	11,000
Accounts payable, December 31	6,000

E12-9B. **Statement of Cash Flows (Direct Method)** Use the following information regarding the cash flows of Jack Corporation to prepare a statement of cash flows using the direct method:

Cash balance, December 31	$ 26,000
Cash paid to employees and suppliers	151,000
Cash received from sale of equipment	91,000
Cash paid to retire bonds payable	70,000
Cash balance, January 1	20,000
Cash paid as interest	4,000
Cash paid as income taxes	24,000
Cash paid to purchase patent	76,000
Cash received from customers	221,000
Cash received from issuing common stock	35,000
Cash paid as dividends	16,000

E12-10B. **Operating Cash Flows (Direct Method)** The Thurston Company's current year income statement contains the following data:

Sales revenue	$790,000
Cost of goods sold	550,000
Gross profit	$240,000

Thurston's comparative balance sheets show the following data (accounts payable relate to merchandise purchases):

	End of Year	Beginning of Year
Accounts receivable	$ 71,000	$61,000
Inventory	120,000	96,000
Prepaid expenses	3,000	10,000
Accounts payable	31,000	35,000

Compute Thurston's current-year cash received from customers and cash paid for merchandise purchased.

E12-11B. **Investing and Financing Cash Flows** Refer to the information in Exercise 12-3B. During the year, Melville Company purchased plant assets for cash, sold investments for cash (the entire $7,000 gain developed during the year), and issued common stock for cash. The firm also declared and paid cash dividends. What items and amounts will appear in (a) the cash flow from investing activities and (b) the cash flow from financing activities sections of a statement of cash flows?

PROBLEMS—SET A

P12-1A. **Statement of Cash Flows (Indirect Method)** The Artic Company's income statement and comparative balance sheets at December 31 of 2019 and 2018 are shown below:

ARTIC COMPANY Income Statement For the Year Ended December 31, 2019		
Sales revenue		$645,000
Cost of goods sold	$430,000	
Wages expense	91,000	
Insurance expense	12,000	
Depreciation expense	13,000	
Interest expense	15,000	
Income tax expense	29,000	590,000
Net income		$ 55,000

ARTIC COMPANY Balance Sheets		
	Dec. 31, 2019	Dec. 31, 2018
Assets		
Cash.	$ 41,000	$ 8,000
Accounts receivable	41,000	32,000
Inventory.	90,000	65,000
Prepaid insurance.	5,000	7,000
Plant assets	219,000	202,000
Accumulated depreciation	(68,000)	(55,000)
Total assets	$328,000	$259,000
Liabilities and Stockholders' Equity		
Accounts payable	$ 7,000	$ 10,000
Wages payable.	10,000	6,000
Income tax payable	6,000	7,000
Bonds payable	141,000	87,000
Common stock	90,000	90,000
Retained earnings	74,000	59,000
Total liabilities and stockholders' equity	$328,000	$259,000

Cash dividends of $40,000 were declared and paid during 2019. Plant assets were purchased for cash and bonds payable were issued for cash. Bond interest is paid semi-annually on June 30 and December 31. Accounts payable relate to merchandise purchases.

Required
a. Calculate the change in cash that occurred during 2019.
b. Prepare a statement of cash flows using the indirect method.
c. Compute free cash flow.
d. Compute the operating-cash-flow-to-current-liabilities ratio.
e. Compute the operating-cash-flow-to-capital-expenditures ratio.

P12-2A. **Statement of Cash Flows (Indirect Method)** North Company's income statement and comparative balance sheets as of December 31 of 2019 and 2018 follow:

LO2

NORTH COMPANY Income Statement For the Year Ended December 31, 2019		
Sales revenue.		$770,000
Cost of goods sold	$550,000	
Wages expense	195,000	
Advertising expense.	31,000	
Depreciation expense.	24,000	
Interest expense.	20,000	
Gain on sale of land	(25,000)	795,000
Net loss.		$ (25,000)

NORTH COMPANY Balance Sheets	Dec. 31, 2019	Dec. 31, 2018
Assets		
Cash.	$ 80,000	$ 32,000
Accounts receivable	42,000	49,000
Inventory.	107,000	115,000
Prepaid advertising.	10,000	14,000
Plant assets	360,000	210,000
Accumulated depreciation	(80,000)	(56,000)
Total assets	$519,000	$364,000
Liabilities and Stockholders' Equity		
Accounts payable.	$ 19,000	$ 25,000
Interest payable	6,000	—
Bonds payable	210,000	—
Common stock	245,000	245,000
Retained earnings	69,000	94,000
Treasury stock	(30,000)	—
Total liabilities and stockholders' equity	$519,000	$364,000

During 2019, North sold land for $70,000 cash that had originally cost $45,000. North also purchased equipment for cash, acquired treasury stock for cash, and issued bonds payable for cash. Accounts payable relate to merchandise purchases.

Required
a. Calculate the change in cash that occurred during 2019.
b. Prepare a statement of cash flows using the indirect method.

LO2 **P12-3A.** **Statement of Cash Flows (Indirect Method)** The Pruitt Company's income statement and comparative balance sheets as of December 31 of 2019 and 2018 follow:

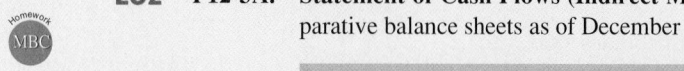

PRUITT COMPANY Income Statement For the Year Ended December 31, 2019		
Sales revenue.		$770,000
Cost of goods sold	$450,000	
Wages and other operating expenses	195,000	
Depreciation expense.	22,000	
Goodwill amortization expense.	7,000	
Interest expense.	5,000	
Income tax expense	36,000	
Loss on bond retirement.	5,000	720,000
Net income		$ 50,000

PRUITT COMPANY Balance Sheets	Dec. 31, 2019	Dec. 31, 2018
Assets		
Cash.	$ 8,000	$ 19,000
Accounts receivable	43,000	28,000
Inventory.	101,000	131,000
Prepaid expenses.	12,000	11,000
Plant assets	360,000	334,000
Accumulated depreciation	(87,000)	(84,000)
Goodwill	43,000	50,000
Total assets	$480,000	$489,000

continued

continued from previous page

PRUITT COMPANY Balance Sheets	Dec. 31, 2019	Dec. 31, 2018
Liabilities and Stockholders' Equity		
Accounts payable	$ 32,000	$ 28,000
Interest payable	3,000	7,000
Income tax payable	6,000	8,000
Bonds payable	60,000	100,000
Common stock	252,000	248,000
Retained earnings	127,000	98,000
Total liabilities and stockholders' equity	$480,000	$489,000

During the year, the company sold for $15,000 cash old equipment that had cost $34,000 and had $19,000 accumulated depreciation. New equipment worth $60,000 was acquired in exchange for $60,000 of bonds payable. Bonds payable of $100,000 were retired for cash at a loss. A $21,000 cash dividend was declared and paid. All stock issuances were for cash.

Required
a. Compute the change in cash that occurred in 2019.
b. Prepare a statement of cash flows using the indirect method.

P12-4A. **Statement of Cash Flows (Indirect Method)** The Sky Company's income statement and comparative balance sheets as of December 31 of 2019 and 2018 follow:

LO2

SKY COMPANY Income Statement For Year Ended December 31, 2019		
Sales revenue.		$800,000
Dividend income.		19,000
		819,000
Cost of goods sold	$440,000	
Wages and other operating expenses	130,000	
Depreciation expense.	39,000	
Patent amortization expense	7,000	
Interest expense.	13,000	
Income tax expense	30,000	
Loss on sale of equipment	5,000	
Gain on sale of investments	(10,000)	654,000
Net income		$165,000

SKY COMPANY Balance Sheets	Dec. 31, 2019	Dec. 31, 2018
Assets		
Cash and cash equivalents	$ 63,000	$ 29,000
Accounts receivable	45,000	35,000
Inventory.	100,000	77,000
Prepaid expenses.	10,000	6,000
Long-term investments—available for sale	—	50,000
Fair value adjustment to investments.	—	7,000
Land	190,000	100,000
Buildings.	445,000	350,000
Accumulated depreciation—Buildings	(91,000)	(75,000)
Equipment	179,000	225,000
Accumulated depreciation—Equipment	(42,000)	(46,000)
Patents.	50,000	32,000
Total assets	$949,000	$790,000

continued

continued from previous page

SKY COMPANY Balance Sheets	Dec. 31, 2019	Dec. 31, 2018
Liabilities and Stockholders' Equity		
Accounts payable.	$ 21,000	$ 18,000
Interest payable	6,000	5,000
Income tax payable	8,000	12,000
Bonds payable	135,000	130,000
Preferred stock ($100 par value)	100,000	75,000
Common stock ($5 par value)	379,000	364,000
Paid-in-capital in excess of par value—Common.	133,000	124,000
Retained earnings	167,000	55,000
Unrealized gain on investments	—	7,000
Total liabilities and stockholders' equity	$949,000	$790,000

During the year, the following transactions occurred:

1. Sold long-term investments costing $50,000 for $60,000 cash. Unrealized gains totaling $7,000 related to these investments had been recorded in earlier years. At year-end, the fair value adjustment and unrealized gain account balances were eliminated.
2. Purchased land for cash.
3. Capitalized an expenditure made to improve the building.
4. Sold equipment for $14,000 cash that originally cost $46,000 and had $27,000 accumulated depreciation.
5. Issued bonds payable at face value for cash.
6. Acquired a patent with a fair value of $25,000 by issuing 250 shares of preferred stock at par value.
7. Declared and paid a $53,000 cash dividend.
8. Issued 3,000 shares of common stock for cash at $8 per share.
9. Recorded depreciation of $16,000 on buildings and $23,000 on equipment.

Required

a.   Calculate the change in cash and cash equivalents that occurred during 2019.
b.   Prepare a statement of cash flows using the indirect method.

LO3   **P12-5A.**   **Analyzing Cash Flow Ratios**   Pearce Enterprises reported the following information for the past year of operations:

Transaction	Free Cash Flow $250,000	Operating-Cash- Flow-to-Current- Liabilities Ratio 1.0 times	Operating-Cash- Flow-to-Capital- Expenditures Ratio 3.0 times
a. Recorded credit sales of $9,000			
b. Collected $4,000 owed from customers			
c. Purchased $28,000 of equipment on long-term credit			
d. Purchased $16,000 of equipment for cash			
e. Paid $10,000 of wages with cash			
f. Recorded utility bill of $1,750 that has not been paid			

For each transaction, indicate whether the ratio will (I) increase, (D) decrease, or (N) have no effect.

LO3, 4
(Appendix
12A)   **P12-6A.**   **Statement of Cash Flows (Direct Method)**   Refer to the data given for the Artic Company in Problem P12-1A.

Required

a. Calculate the change in cash that occurred during 2019.
b. Prepare a statement of cash flows using the direct method.
c. Compute free cash flow.
d. Compute the operating-cash-flow-to-current-liabilities ratio.
e. Compute the operating-cash-flow-to-capital-expenditures ratio.

P12-7A. **Statement of Cash Flows (Direct Method)** Refer to the data given for the North Company in Problem P12-2A.

LO4
(Appendix 12A)

Required

a. Calculate the change in cash that occurred during 2019.
b. Prepare a statement of cash flows using the direct method.

P12-8A. **Statement of Cash Flows (Direct Method)** Refer to the data given for the Pruitt Company in Problem P12-3A.

LO4
(Appendix 12A)

Required

a. Compute the change in cash that occurred in 2019.
b. Prepare a statement of cash flows using the direct method. Use one cash outflow for "cash paid for wages and other operating expenses." Accounts payable relate to inventory purchases only.

P12-9A. **Statement of Cash Flows (Direct Method)** Refer to the data given for the Sky Company in Problem P12-4A.

LO4
(Appendix 12A)

Required

a. Calculate the change in cash that occurred in 2019.
b. Prepare a statement of cash flows using the direct method. Use one cash outflow for "cash paid for wages and other operating expenses." Accounts payable relate to inventory purchases only.

PROBLEMS—SET B

P12-1B. **Statement of Cash Flows (Indirect Method)** The Forrester Company's income statement and comparative balance sheets as of December 31 of 2019 and 2018 are shown below:

LO2, 3

FORRESTER COMPANY Income Statement For the Year Ended December 31, 2019		
Sales revenue.		$660,000
Cost of goods sold	$376,000	
Wages expense	107,000	
Depreciation expense.	22,000	
Rent expense	28,000	
Income tax expense	24,000	557,000
Net income		$103,000

FORRESTER COMPANY Balance Sheets	Dec. 31, 2019	Dec. 31, 2018
Assets		
Cash.	$ 58,000	$ 30,000
Accounts receivable	52,000	60,000
Inventory.	142,000	120,000
Prepaid rent	16,000	10,000
Plant assets	420,000	301,000
Accumulated depreciation	(127,000)	(105,000)
Total assets	$561,000	$416,000

continued

continued from previous page

FORRESTER COMPANY Balance Sheets	Dec. 31, 2019	Dec. 31, 2018
Liabilities and Stockholders' Equity		
Accounts payable.	$ 29,000	$ 17,000
Wages payable.	14,000	9,000
Income tax payable	7,000	8,000
Common stock	295,000	252,000
Paid-in-capital in excess of par value.	72,000	58,000
Retained earnings	144,000	72,000
Total liabilities and stockholders' equity	$561,000	$416,000

Cash dividends of $31,000 were declared and paid during 2019. Plant assets were purchased for cash and additional common stock was issued for cash. Accounts payable relate to merchandise purchases.

Required
a. Calculate the change in cash that occurred during 2019.
b. Prepare a statement of cash flows using the indirect method.
c. Compute free cash flow.
d. Compute the operating-cash-flow-to-current-liabilities ratio.
e. Compute the operating-cash-flows-to-capital-expenditures ratio.

LO2 **P12-2B.** **Statement of Cash Flows (Indirect Method)** The Lowe Company's income statement and comparative balance sheets as of December 31 of 2019 and 2018 are presented below:

LOWE COMPANY Income Statement For the Year Ended December 31, 2019		
Sales revenue.		$925,000
Cost of goods sold	$490,000	
Wages expense	207,000	
Depreciation expense.	62,000	
Insurance expense.	17,000	
Interest expense.	12,000	
Income tax expense	57,000	
Gain on sale of equipment	(16,000)	829,000
Net income		$ 96,000

LOWE COMPANY Balance Sheets	Dec. 31, 2019	Dec. 31, 2018
Assets		
Cash.	$ 25,000	$ 33,000
Accounts receivable.	68,000	51,000
Inventory.	177,000	126,000
Prepaid insurance.	8,000	11,000
Plant assets	887,000	763,000
Accumulated depreciation	(191,000)	(175,000)
Total assets	$974,000	$809,000

continued

continued from previous page

LOWE COMPANY Balance Sheets		
	Dec. 31, 2019	Dec. 31, 2018
Liabilities and Stockholders' Equity		
Accounts payable..	$ 37,000	$ 27,000
Interest payable...	7,000	—
Income tax payable	11,000	19,000
Bonds payable	145,000	80,000
Common stock...	660,000	585,000
Retained earnings	166,000	98,000
Treasury stock	(52,000)	—
Total liabilities and stockholders' equity	$974,000	$809,000

During the year, Lowe Company sold equipment for $27,000 cash that originally cost $57,000 and had $46,000 accumulated depreciation. New equipment was purchased for cash. Bonds payable and common stock were issued for cash. Cash dividends of $28,000 were declared and paid. At the end of the year, shares of treasury stock were purchased for cash. Accounts payable relate to merchandise purchases.

Required
a. Compute the change in cash that occurred during 2019.
b. Prepare a statement of cash flows using the indirect method.

P12-3B. Statement of Cash Flows (Indirect Method) The Madison Company's income statement and comparative balance sheets as of December 31 of 2019 and 2018 follow:

LO2

MADISON COMPANY Income Statement For the Year Ended December 31, 2019		
Sales revenue..		$825,000
Cost of goods sold	$530,000	
Wages and other operating expenses	179,000	
Depreciation expense..	29,000	
Patent amortization expense	6,000	
Interest expense...	18,000	
Income tax expense	25,000	
Gain on exchange of land for patent	(37,000)	750,000
Net income...		$ 75,000

MADISON COMPANY Balance Sheets		
	Dec. 31, 2019	Dec. 31, 2018
Assets		
Cash...	$ 67,000	$ 25,000
Accounts receivable	64,000	49,000
Inventory..	85,000	66,000
Land..	117,000	160,000
Building and equipment	441,000	353,000
Accumulated depreciation	(122,000)	(100,000)
Patent..	74,000	—
Total assets	$726,000	$553,000

continued

continued from previous page

MADISON COMPANY
Balance Sheets

	Dec. 31, 2019	Dec. 31, 2018
Liabilities and Stockholders' Equity		
Accounts payable	$ 36,000	$ 26,000
Interest payable	13,000	8,000
Income tax payable	7,000	12,000
Bonds payable	190,000	75,000
Common stock	350,000	350,000
Retained earnings	130,000	82,000
Total liabilities and stockholders' equity	$726,000	$553,000

During 2019, $27,000 of cash dividends were declared and paid. A patent valued at $80,000 was obtained in exchange for land. Equipment that originally cost $20,000 and had $7,000 accumulated depreciation was sold for $13,000 cash. Bonds payable were sold for cash and cash was used to pay for structural improvements to the building.

Required

a. Compute the change in cash that occurred during 2019.

b. Prepare a statement of cash flows using the indirect method.

LO2   P12-4B.   Statement of Cash Flows (Indirect Method) The Geary Company's income statement and comparative balance sheets as of December 31 of 2019 and 2018 follow:

GEARY COMPANY
Income Statement
For the Year Ended December 31, 2019

Service fees earned		$320,000
Dividend and interest income		16,000
		$336,000
Wages and other operating expenses	$288,000	
Depreciation expense	55,000	
Franchise amortization expense	10,000	
Loss on sale of equipment	7,000	
Gain on sale of investments	(17,000)	343,000
Net loss		$ (7,000)

GEARY COMPANY
Balance Sheets

	Dec. 31, 2019	Dec. 31, 2018
Assets		
Cash	$ 21,000	$ 33,000
Accounts receivable	14,000	18,000
Interest receivable	—	4,000
Prepaid expenses	16,000	10,000
Long-term investments—available for sale	—	70,000
Fair value adjustment to investments	—	10,000
Plant assets	656,000	655,000
Accumulated depreciation	(237,000)	(185,000)
Franchise	91,000	29,000
Total assets	$561,000	$644,000

continued

continued from previous page

GEARY COMPANY Balance Sheets		
	Dec. 31, 2019	**Dec. 31, 2018**
Liabilities and Stockholders' Equity		
Accrued liabilities	$ 12,000	$ 14,000
Notes payable	—	26,000
Common stock ($10 par value)	535,000	535,000
Retained earnings	34,000	59,000
Unrealized gain on investments	—	10,000
Treasury stock	(20,000)	—
Total liabilities and stockholders' equity	$561,000	$644,000

During the year, the following transactions occurred:

1. Sold equipment for $9,000 cash that originally cost $19,000 and had $3,000 accumulated depreciation.
2. Sold long-term investments that had cost $70,000 for $87,000 cash. Unrealized gains totaling $10,000 related to these investments had been recorded in earlier years. At year-end, the fair value adjustment and unrealized gain account balances were eliminated.
3. Paid cash to extend the company's exclusive franchise for another three years.
4. Paid off a note payable at the bank on January 1.
5. Declared and paid an $18,000 dividend.
6. Purchased treasury stock for cash.
7. Purchased land valued at $20,000.

Required
a. Compute the change in cash that occurred in 2019.
b. Prepare a statement of cash flows using the indirect method.

P12-5B. **Analyzing Cash Flow Ratios** Meagan Enterprises reported the following information for the past year of operations:

LO3

Transaction	Free Cash Flow $400,000	Operating-Cash-Flow-to-Current-Liabilities Ratio 1.1 times	Operating-Cash-Flow-to-Capital-Expenditures Ratio 5.0 times
a. Recorded credit sales of $17,000			
b. Collected $6,000 owed from customers			
c. Purchased $50,000 of equipment on long-term credit			
d. Purchased $70,000 of equipment for cash			
e. Paid $17,000 of wages with cash			
f. Recorded utility bill of $14,750 that has not been paid			

For each transaction, indicate whether the ratio will (I) increase, (D) decrease, or (N) have no effect.

P12-6B. **Statement of Cash Flows (Direct Method)** Refer to the data given for the Forrester Company in Problem P12-1B.

LO3, 4 (Appendix 12A)

Required
a. Compute the change in cash that occurred during 2019.
b. Prepare a statement of cash flows using the direct method.
c. Compute free cash flow.
d. Compute the operating-cash-flow-to-current-liabilities ratio.
e. Compute the operating-cash-flow-to-capital-expenditures ratio.

LO4
(Appendix 12A)

P12-7B. **Statement of Cash Flows (Direct Method)** Refer to the data given for the Lowe Company in Problem P12-2B.

Required
a. Compute the change in cash that occurred during 2019.
b. Prepare a statement of cash flows using the direct method.

LO4
(Appendix 12A)

P12-8B. **Statement of Cash Flows (Direct Method)** Refer to the data given for the Madison Company in Problem P12-3B.

Required
a. Compute the change in cash that occurred during 2019.
b. Prepare a statement of cash flows using the direct method. Use one cash outflow for "cash paid for wages and other operating expenses." Accounts payable relate to inventory purchases only.

LO4
(Appendix 12A)

P12-9B. **Statement of Cash Flows (Direct Method)** Refer to the data given for the Geary Company in Problem P12-4B.

Required
a. Compute the change in cash that occurred during 2019.
b. Prepare a statement of cash flows using the direct method. Use one cash outflow for "cash paid for wages and other operating expenses."

SERIAL PROBLEM: KATE'S CARDS

(Note: This is a continuation of the Serial Problem: Kate's Cards from Chapter 1 through Chapter 11.)

SP12. Kate has just completed her first year running Kate's Cards. She has been preparing monthly income statements and balance sheets, so she knows that her company has been profitable and that there is cash in the bank. She has not, however, prepared a statement of cash flows. Kate provides you with the year-end income statement and balance sheet and asks that you prepare a statement of cash flows for Kate's Cards.

Additional information:

1. There were no disposals of equipment during the year.
2. Dividends in the amount of $1,300 were paid in cash during the year.
3. Prepaid expenses relate to operating expenses.

Required
a. Prepare a statement of cash flows for Kate's Cards for the year ended August 31, 2019, using the indirect method. Hint: Since this was Kate's first year of operations, the beginning balance sheet account balances were zero.
b. Prepare a statement of cash flows for Kate's Cards for the year ended August 31, 2019, using the direct method. (Appendix 12A)

KATE'S CARDS Income Statement Year Ended August 31, 2019	
Sales revenue.	$185,000
Cost of goods sold	106,000
Gross profit.	79,000
Operating expenses	
Wages	18,000
Consulting.	11,850
Insurance	1,200
Utilities	2,400
Rent	14,400
Depreciation	3,250
Total operating expenses	51,100
Income from operations	27,900
Interest expense.	900
Income before income tax	27,000
Income tax expense	5,400
Net income	$ 21,600

KATE'S CARDS Balance Sheet As of August 31, 2019	
Assets	
Current assets	
Cash.	$17,400
Accounts receivable	11,000
Inventory.	16,000
Prepaid insurance.	1,000
Total current assets	45,400
Equipment	17,500
Accumulated depreciation	(3,250)
Total assets	$59,650
Liabilities	
Current liabilities	
Accounts payable.	$ 6,200
Unearned revenue	1,250
Other current liabilities	1,900
Total current liabilities.	9,350
Note payable	15,000
Total liabilities.	24,350
Stockholders' equity	
Common stock	500
Additional paid-in-capital	9,500
Preferred stock.	5,000
Retained earnings	20,300
Total stockholders' equity	35,300
Total liabilities and stockholders' equity	$59,650

EXTENDING YOUR KNOWLEDGE

REPORTING AND ANALYSIS

COLUMBIA
SPORTSWEAR
COMPANY

EYK12-1. **Financial Reporting Problem: Columbia Sportswear Company** The financial statements for the **Columbia Sportswear Company** can be found in Appendix A at the end of this book.

Required
Answer the following questions:

a. How much did Columbia Sportswear's cash and cash equivalents increase in 2017?
b. What was the largest source of cash and cash equivalents in 2017?
c. What was the single largest use of cash and cash equivalents in 2017?
d. How much dividends were paid in 2017?
e. Why do depreciation and amortization, both noncash items, appear on Columbia's statement of cash flows?

COLUMBIA
SPORTSWEAR
COMPANY

UNDER ARMOUR,
INC.

EYK12-2. **Comparative Analysis Problem: Columbia Sportswear Company vs Under Armour, Inc.** The financial statements for the Columbia Sportswear Company can be found in Appendix A at the end of this book, and the financial statements of Under Armour, Inc. can be found in Appendix B (the complete annual report is available on this book's Website).

Required
Answer the following questions:

a. Compute the free cash flow in 2017 for both Columbia Sportswear and Under Armour, Inc.
b. Compute the operating cash flows to capital expenditures for both Columbia Sportswear and Under Armour, Inc.
c. Comment on the ability of each company to finance its capital expenditures.

EYK12-3. **Business Decision Problem** Recently hired as assistant controller for Finite, Inc., you are sitting next to the controller as she responds to questions at the annual stockholders' meeting. The firm's financial statements contain a statement of cash flows prepared using the indirect method. A stockholder raises his hand.

Stockholder: "I notice that depreciation expense is shown as an addition in the calculation of the cash flow from operating activities."

Controller: "That's correct."

Stockholder: "What depreciation method do you use?"

Controller: "We use the straight-line method for all plant assets."

Stockholder: "Well, why don't you switch to an accelerated depreciation method, such as double-declining balance, increase the annual depreciation amount, and thus increase the cash flow from operating activities?"

The controller pauses, turns to you, and replies, "My assistant will answer your question."

Required
Prepare an answer to the stockholder's question.

PARKER HANNIFIN
CORPORATION

EYK12-4. **Financial Analysis Problem** **Parker Hannifin Corporation**, headquartered in Cleveland, Ohio, manufactures motion control and fluid system components for a variety of industrial users. The firm's financial statements contain the following data (Year 3 is the most recent year; dollar amounts are in thousands):

	Year 3	Year 2	Year 1
Current assets at year-end............................	$1,018,354	$1,056,443	$1,055,776
Current liabilities at year-end	504,444	468,254	358,729
Current liabilities at beginning of year	468,254	358,729	345,594
Cash provided by operating activities................	259,204	229,382	235,186
Capital expenditures.............................	99,914	91,484	84,955

a. Calculate Parker Hannifin's current ratio (current assets/current liabilities) for Years 1, 2, and 3.
b. Calculate Parker Hannifin's operating-cash-flow-to-current-liabilities ratio for Years 1, 2, and 3.

    c. Comment on the three-year trend in Parker Hannifin's current ratio and operating-cash-flow-to-current-liabilities ratio. Do the trends in these two ratios reinforce each other or contradict each other as indicators of Parker Hannifin's ability to pay its current liabilities?

    d. Calculate Parker Hannifin's operating-cash-flow-to-capital-expenditures ratio for Years 1, 2, and 3. Comment on the strength of this ratio over the three-year period.

CRITICAL THINKING

EYK12-5. **Accounting Research Problem:** General Mills, Inc. The fiscal year 2017 annual report of General Mills, Inc. is available on this book's Website.

GENERAL MILLS, INC.

Required

    a. Refer to Note 2. How does General Mills define its cash equivalents?

    b. What method does General Mills use to report its cash provided by operating activities?

    c. What is the change in cash and cash equivalents experienced by General Mills during fiscal 2017? What is the amount of cash and cash equivalents as of May 28, 2017?

    d. What is General Mills' operating-cash-flow-to-capital-expenditures ratio for fiscal year 2017?

    e. Calculate General Mills' 2017 operating-cash-flow-to-current-liabilities ratio.

EYK12-6. **Accounting Communication Activity** Susan Henderson, the vice president of marketing, was told by the CEO that she needs to understand the numbers because the company's existence depends on making money. It has been a long time since Susan took a class in accounting. She recalls that companies report net income and cash flows in two separate statements. She feels pretty comfortable with the income statement, but is somewhat lost looking at the statement of cash flows. She asks you to help explain this statement.

Required

Write a brief memo to Susan explaining the form and content of the statement of cash flows, along with a short discussion of how to analyze the statement.

EYK12-7. **Accounting Ethics Case** Due to an economic recession, Anton Corporation faces severe cash flow problems. Management forecasts that payments to some suppliers will have to be delayed for several months. Jay Newton, controller, has asked his staff for suggestions on selecting the suppliers for which payments will be delayed.

    "That's a fairly easy decision," observes Tim Haslem. "Some suppliers charge interest if our payment is late, but others do not. We should pay those suppliers that charge interest and delay payments to the ones that do not charge interest. If we do this, the savings in interest charges will be quite substantial."

    "I disagree," states Tara Wirth. "That position is too 'bottom line' oriented. It's not fair to delay payments only to suppliers who don't charge interest for late payments. Most suppliers in that category are ones we have dealt with for years; selecting these suppliers would be taking advantage of the excellent relationships we have developed over the years. The fair thing to do is to make pro-rata payments to each supplier."

    "Well, making pro-rata payments to each supplier means that *all* our suppliers will be upset because no one receives full payment," comments Sue Myling. "I believe it is most important to maintain good relations with our long-term suppliers; we should pay them currently and delay payments to our newer suppliers. The interest costs we end up paying these newer suppliers are the price we must pay to keep our long-term relationships solid."

Required

Which suppliers should Jay Newton select for delayed payments? Discuss.

EYK12-8. **Corporate Social Responsibility Problem** The corporate social responsibility highlighted in this chapter (see page 585) mentions that **Home Depot** believes in giving back. One of the ways the company has done this is through its Team Depot program of employee volunteerism. Under this program, Home Depot employees volunteer their own time to work together on projects that benefit communities in which the company does business. Each year the program provides millions of hours of employee volunteerism.

THE HOME DEPOT, INC.

    One of the many programs that benefits from Team Depot is Habitat for Humanity. Do a computer search and report how Team Depot has helped Habitat for Humanity.

EYK12-9. **Forensic Accounting Problem** Cash larceny involves the fraudulent stealing of an employer's cash. These schemes often target the company's bank deposits. The fraudster steals the money after the deposit has been prepared, but before the deposit is taken to the bank. Most often these schemes involve a deficiency in the internal control system where segregation of duties is not present. The perpetrator is often in charge of recording receipts, preparing the deposit, delivering the deposit to the bank, and verifying the receipted deposit slip. Without proper segregation of duties, the fraudster is able to cover up the theft.

In addition to segregation of duties, what internal control procedures might help deter and detect cash larceny?

EYK12-10. **Working with the Takeaways** For the fiscal year ended January 28, 2018, Home Depot reports (in millions) cash provided by operating activities of $12,031. For the same period, average current liabilities were reported to be $16,194, and annual capital expenditures were $1,897. Calculate the free cash flow, operating-cash-flow-to-current-liabilities ratio, and the operating-cash-flow-to-capital-expenditures ratio for Home Depot and comment on the results.

EYK12-11. **Analyzing IFRS Financial Statements** The 2017 financial statements of LVMH Moet Hennessey-Louis Vuitton S.A. are presented in Appendix C at the end of this book. LVMH is a Paris-based holding company and one of the world's largest and best-known luxury goods companies. As a member of the European Union, French companies are required to prepare their consolidated (group) financial statements using International Financial Reporting Standards (IFRS). After reviewing LVMH's consolidated financial statements, calculate LVMH's (a) free cash flow, (b) operating-cash-flow-to-current-liabilities ratio (use the year-end current liabilities instead of the average current liabilities), and (c) operating-cash-flow-to-capital-expenditures ratio for 2016 and 2017. What do the ratio results reveal about LVMH? *Hint:* Capital expenditures are classified as "Operating investments" on LVMH Consolidated cash flow statement.

ANSWERS TO SELF-STUDY QUESTIONS:

1. a, (p. 573)   2. c, (p. 574)   3. d, (p. 575)   4. d, (pp. 579–584)   5. c, (p. 586)   6. b, (pp. 575–576)
7. d, (pp. 586–587)   8. (d, p. 572)   9. c, (pp. 582–583)   10. b, (p. 591)   11. c, (p. 591)   12. a, (p. 591)

YOUR TURN! SOLUTIONS

Solution 12.1

1. Operating
2. Investing
3. Operating
4. Investing
5. Financing
6. Financing
7. Operating
8. Financing
9. Investing

Solution 12.2

HUSKY COMPANY **Statement of Cash Flows** **For the Year Ended December 31, 2019**		
Cash Flow from Operating Activities		
Net income	$112,000	
Add (deduct) items to convert net income to cash basis		
Depreciation	34,000	
Accounts receivable increase.	(18,000)	
Inventory increase	(60,000)	
Prepaid insurance decrease.	4,000	
Accounts payable decrease	(6,000)	
Wages payable increase	6,000	
Income tax payable decrease.	(2,000)	
Cash provided by operating activities.		$ 70,000
Cash Flow from Investing Activities		
Purchase of plant assets		(110,000)
Cash Flow from Financing Activities		
Issuance of bonds payable.	110,000	
Payment of dividends	(58,000)	
Cash provided by financing activities		52,000
Net increase in cash.		12,000
Cash at beginning of year.		10,000
Cash at end of year		$ 22,000

Solution 12.3

Free cash flow: $40,000 − $12,500 = $27,500

Operating-cash-flow-to-current-liabilities-ratio: $40,000/$30,000 = 1.33

Operating-cash-flow-to-capital-expenditures-ratio: $40,000/$12,500 = 3.20

Solution 12A.1

Supporting Calculations:

Cash received from customers:

$1,270,000 Sales revenue − $18,000 Accounts receivable increase = $1,252,000

Cash paid for merchandise purchased:

$860,000 Cost of goods sold + $60,000 Inventory increase + $6,000 Accounts payable decrease = $926,000

Cash paid to employees:

$172,000 Wages expense − $6,000 Wages payable increase = $166,000

Cash paid for insurance:

$16,000 Insurance expense − $4,000 Prepaid insurance decrease = $12,000

Cash paid for interest:

Equal to the $18,000 balance in interest expense

Cash paid for income taxes:

$58,000 Income tax expense + $2,000 Income tax payable decrease = $60,000

Purchase of plant assets:

$500,000 Ending plant assets − $390,000 Beginning plant assets = $110,000

Issuance of bonds payable:

$260,000 Ending bonds payable − $150,000 Beginning bonds payable = $110,000

Payment of dividends

$58,000 given in problem data

Other Analysis

Accumulated depreciation increased by $34,000, which is the amount of depreciation expense.

Common stock account balance did not change.

Retained earnings increased by $54,000, which is the difference between the net income of $112,000 and the dividends declared of $58,000.

HUSKY COMPANY Statement of Cash Flows (Direct Method) For the Year Ended December 31, 2019		
Cash Flow from Operating Activities		
Cash received from customers		$1,252,000
Cash paid for merchandise purchased	$(926,000)	
Cash paid to employees	(166,000)	
Cash paid for insurance	(12,000)	
Cash paid for interest	(18,000)	
Cash paid for income taxes	(60,000)	(1,182,000)
Cash provided by operating activities		70,000
Cash Flow from Investing Activities		
Purchase of plant assets		(110,000)
Cash Flow from Financing Activities		
Issuance of bonds payable	110,000	
Payment of dividends	(58,000)	
Cash provided by financing activities		52,000
Net increase in cash		12,000
Cash at beginning of year		10,000
Cash at end of year		$ 22,000

Chapter **13**

Analysis and Interpretation of Financial Statements

PAST

In Chapter 12, we examined the statement of cash flows.

PRESENT

In this chapter we complete our study of financial accounting by looking at the analysis and interpretation of financial statements.

The **Procter & Gamble Company (P&G)** is one of America's oldest companies, dating back to 1837 when candle maker William Procter and soap maker James Gamble combined their small businesses. Over the next few decades the company introduced such well-known products as Ivory soap and Crisco shortening that are still sold today.

P&G has continued to grow, with annual sales of over $65 billion. Not all of the company's growth, however, is the result of internally developed products like Crest toothpaste, Head & Shoulders shampoo, and Pampers diapers. A significant part of P&G's growth has come from mergers and acquisitions. P&G's largest acquisition occurred in 2005 when it acquired Gillette for $57 billion.

Acquisitions, such as the one involving Gillette, are complex transactions. Perhaps the hardest part of any merger or acquisition is to determine the appropriate price to pay. How did P&G determine how much to pay for Gillette? Many factors go into such an analysis, but it often comes down to how much a company like Gillette will be able to add to P&G's future persistent earnings.

In this chapter we explore some of the ways that investment professionals determine how much a company is worth. The process involves analyzing a company's persistent earnings potential as well as the various risks associated with a company's day-to-day operations.

Road Map

LO	Learning Objective	Page	eLecture	Guided Example	Assignments
LO1	Identify persistent earnings and discuss the content and format of the income statement.	624	E13-1	YT13.1	SS1, SE11, E1A, E1B, P1A, P3A, P1B, P3B
LO2	Identify the sources of financial information used by investment professionals and explain horizontal financial statement analysis.	628	E13-2	YT13.2	SS10, SE12, E3A, E3B, P4A, P6A, P10A, P4B, P6B, P10B
LO3	Explain vertical financial statement analysis.	633	E13-3	YT13.3	SS2, SE13, E4A, E4B, P6A, P6B
LO4	Define and discuss financial ratios for analyzing a firm.	634	E13-4	YT13.4	SS3, SS4, SS5, SS6, SS7, SS8, SS9, SE1, SE2, SE3, SE4, SE5, SE6, SE7, SE8, SE9, SE10, E2A, E5A, E6A, E7A, E8A, E9A, E2B, E5B, E6B, E7B, E8B, P2A, P3A, P5A, P6A, P7A, P8A, P9A, P2B, P3B, P5B, P6B, P7B, P8B, P9B
LO5	Discuss the limitations of financial statement analysis.	649	E13-5	YT13.5	SS11, SE14, E10A, E10B
LO6	Appendix 13A: Describe financial statement disclosures.	651	E13-6	YT13.6	SS12, SE15, E11A, E11B

PERSISTENT EARNINGS AND THE INCOME STATEMENT

LO1 **Identify** persistent earnings and **discuss** the content and format of the income statement.

Net income is the "bottom line" measure of firm performance. It is a measure that depends on such accrual accounting procedures as the revenue recognition and expense matching policies selected by a firm's management. Generally accepted accounting principles have historically emphasized the importance of accounting earnings because past accounting earnings have been found to be a good predictor of a firm's future operating cash flow. Modern valuation theory tells us that the economic value of a company is the present value of the company's future operating cash flows. Thus, an important role for accounting numbers is their use by investment professionals when assessing the economic value of a company.

One of the determinants of the ability of historical accounting earnings to predict future cash flow is the extent to which earnings recur over time, or what is known as *earnings persistence*. Since the value of a share of common stock today is a function of a firm's ability to consistently generate earnings year in and year out, the persistence (or sustainability) of a company's operating earnings is closely linked to its economic value. **Persistent earnings** are also sometimes referred to as *sustainable earnings* or *permanent earnings*, whereas non-persistent earnings are often referred to as **transitory earnings**. In general, transitory earnings include such single-period events as special items, restructuring charges, changes in accounting principle, and discontinued operations.

Companies are required under GAAP to classify income statement accounts in a manner that aids a financial statement user in assessing persistent earnings, and hence in assessing a firm's economic value. In Chapter 4, we discussed the classified income statement. In this chapter, we discuss a refinement of the classified income statement called the multiple-step or multi-step income statement.

Exhibit 13-1 illustrates the basic format of the multi-step income statement. While a **single-step income statement** derives the net income of a business in one step by subtracting total expenses from total revenues, a **multiple-step income statement** derives one or more intermediate performance measures before net income is reported. Examples of such intermediate performance measures are gross profit, net operating income, and net income from continuing operations before taxes.

The income statement is organized in such a way that items with greater persistence are reported higher up in the income statement, whereas items considered more transitory are reported further down in the statement. Thus, accounts representing financial events that are both usual and frequent are reported first. Usual refers to whether an item is central to a firm's core operations, whereas **unusual items** display a high degree of abnormality and/or are unrelated, or only incidentally related, to the normal activities

Exhibit 13-1	The Multi-Step Income Statement

KALI COMPANY
Income Statement
For Year Ended December 31, 2019

Sales revenue.		$ 500	Usual and frequent
Cost of goods sold		200	Usual and frequent
Gross profit		300	
Operating expenses		250	Usual and frequent
Net operating income		50	
Other income and expense			
Interest income	25		**Unusual**
Interest expense	(35)		**Unusual**
Gain on sale of equipment	15	5	**Unusual**
Net income from continuing operations before tax		55	
Income tax		20	Usual and frequent
Net income from continuing operations		35	
Gain from operations of discontinued division (net of tax)	15		**Infrequent**
Loss on disposal of discontinued division (net of tax)	(5)	10	
Net income		$ 45	
Earning per share (100 shares outstanding)		$0.45	

of a business. Frequent refers to how often an item is expected to occur, with infrequent items not reasonably expected to recur in the foreseeable future. Usual and frequent items typically consist of such income statement accounts as sales revenue, cost of goods sold, and other operating expenses. Just below these usual and frequent items are items that are either unusual or infrequent, but not both. Income statement accounts such as interest expense, interest income, and gains on sales of equipment are often frequently recurring items; however, they are not considered part of a firm's central operations and therefore are considered unusual. Examples of infrequent items include such financial events as asset write-downs and restructuring charges. These items are not expected to occur regularly, but are not considered unusual in nature.

Each of the above items is reported as part of a company's continuing operations and is shown before any income tax expense. GAAP, however, requires certain single-period items, or one-time events, to be reported on an after-tax basis. For example, income from discontinued operations, or the part of a business which is being shuttered or sold, are shown net of the financial effect of any applicable income taxes. Reporting discontinued operations on a net-of-tax basis allows the income tax expense reported on the income statement to reflect only the income taxes associated with a firm's continuing operations.

Most believe that the income statement is more useful when certain types of transactions and events are reported in separate sections. For this reason, information about discontinued operations is disclosed separately in the income statement. Segregating these categories of information from the results of continuing operations makes it easier for financial statement users to identify a company's persistent earnings.

The creation of sections within the income statement, however, complicates the reporting of a company's income tax expense. Items affecting the overall amount of income tax expense may appear in more than one section. If this is the case, accountants allocate a company's total income tax expense among those sections of the income statement in which the items affecting the tax expense appear.

Regardless of the format used for the income statement, companies are required to report net income on a per common share basis, called **earnings per share (EPS)**, on the income statement immediately following net income.

IFRS ALERT

Like U.S. GAAP, IFRS encourages companies to use a multi-step income statement when presenting a company's periodic performance. Appendix C at the end of this book presents an IFRS income statement for LVMH Moet Hennessy-Louis Vuitton, a global luxury products company. Examining LVMH's income statement reveals that the retailer presents four measures of firm performance: gross margin, operating profit, net financial income, and net profit for the year. These indicators correspond closely to the four performance measures reported by the Kali Company in Exhibit 13.1: gross profit, net operating income, net income from continuing operations before tax, and net income. The income statements under U.S. GAAP and IFRS are very similar, with only minor labeling differences—like using "profit" instead of "income."

Discontinued Operations

Discontinued Operations

When a company sells, abandons, or otherwise disposes of a segment of its operations, a **discontinued operations** section of the income statement reports information about the discontinued business segment. The discontinued operations section presents two categories of information:

1. The income or loss from the segment's operations for the portion of the year before its discontinuance.

2. Any gain or loss from the disposal of the segment.

This section is reported on the income statement immediately after information regarding a firm's continuing operations.

To illustrate the reporting of discontinued operations, assume that on July 1, 2019, Kali Company, a diversified manufacturing company, sold its pet food division. **Exhibit 13-1** illustrates the income statement for Kali Company, including information regarding its pet food division in the discontinued operations section. From January 1 through June 30, Kali's pet food division operated at a profit, net of income taxes, of $15. The loss, net of income taxes, from the sale of the division's assets and liabilities was $5. Note that when there is a discontinued operations section, the difference between a firm's continuing sales revenues and expenses is labeled net income from continuing operations.

Changes in Accounting Principles

Occasionally a company may implement a **change in accounting principle**—that is, a switch from one generally accepted method to another. For example, a company may change its inventory costing method, such as from FIFO to weighted-average cost. These changes are permitted when a business can demonstrate that the reported financial results under the new accounting method are superior to the results reported under the replaced method.

PRINCIPLE ALERT   **Consistency Principle**

The *consistency principle* states that, unless otherwise disclosed, financial statements use the same accounting methods from one period to the next. A consistent use of accounting methods enhances the comparability of financial data across time. The consistency principle impacts the accounting for a change in accounting principles in several ways. First, to change an accounting principle, a company must be able to justify that the reported results under the new principle are preferable. Second, a company must present its prior year financial statements as though the new principle had been in use all along. In actual practice, only the prior year financial statements presented with the current year financial statements must be presented using the new accounting method. For all financial statements prior to those presented with the current statements, a lump sum adjustment is made to retained earnings on the statement of retained earnings and the statement of stockholders' equity.

Changing accounting principles can present a problem for financial statement users analyzing a company's performance over time because different accounting principles are likely to produce different financial statement results. Consequently, financial statements of prior years, issued in comparative form with current year financial statements, must also be presented using the new accounting principles as if the new method had been used all along.

Comprehensive Income

Most items that generate wealth changes in a business are required to be shown on the income statement. There are, however, a few items that do not appear as part of the regular content of the income statement and instead are classified under a category labeled **comprehensive income**. A business's comprehensive income includes its net income, any changes in the market value of certain marketable securities (see Appendix D at the end of this book), and any unrealized gains and losses from translating foreign currency denominated financial statements into U.S. dollars. This latter topic is covered in more advanced accounting textbooks.

Companies are given some flexibility as to how they report their comprehensive income. They are allowed to utilize two alternative formats under GAAP: (1) appending comprehensive income to the bottom of the income statement; or (2) creating a separate statement of comprehensive income. In addition to comprehensive income for the current period, GAAP requires a company to report accumulated other comprehensive income as part of stockholders' equity on the balance sheet. Accumulated other comprehensive income serves the same role for comprehensive income as retained earnings serves for regular net income—it reports the cumulative amount of comprehensive income as of the balance sheet date.

Pampers and UNICEF	**CORPORATE SOCIAL RESPONSIBILITY**

Maternal and neonatal tetanus is a disease that kills 59,000 people annually. **P&G**, through its Pampers product, has teamed up with UNICEF to fight this completely preventable disease. For every purchase of a pack of Pampers, P&G donates one dose of the tetanus vaccine. Pampers' funding has helped protect 100 million women and their babies against maternal and neonatal tetanus (MNT) and has helped eliminate this disease in Myanmar and Uganda. P&G and UNICEF are committed to the elimination of MNT from the face of the earth.

P&G and UNICEF have gone even further in their teamwork. P&G offers its employees in Europe, the Middle East, and Africa, a three-month paid sabbatical to work with UNICEF. The program is aimed at employees who have always wanted to perform humanitarian work but have lacked the financial resources to do so.

Conner Company, a retail company, entered into the following transactions during the year:

1. Sold merchandise to customers
2. Settled a major lawsuit
3. Wrote down the book value of a closed warehouse
4. Paid employee wages
5. Disposed of a line of discount stores
6. Paid income taxes

Required
Classify each of the above items as either persistent earnings or transitory earnings.

YOUR TURN! 13.1

The solution is on page 685.

SOURCES OF INFORMATION

LO2 **Identify** the sources of financial information used by investment professionals and **explain** horizontal financial statement analysis

Except for closely-held companies, businesses publish their financial statements at least annually. Most large companies also issue quarterly financial data. Normally, annual financial statements are attested to by a certified public accountant, and investment professionals carefully review the independent accountant's opinion to assess the reliability of the published financial data.

Companies listed on stock exchanges must also submit financial statements, called a 10-K for the annual report and 10-Q for the quarterly report, to the U.S. Securities and Exchange Commission (SEC). These statements are available to any interested party and are generally more useful than annual reports because they contain greater detail.

Investment professionals may also want to compare the performance of a particular firm with that of the other firms in the same industry. Data on industry norms, median financial ratios by industry, and other relationships are available from such data collection services as Dun & Bradstreet, Moody's, and Standard and Poor's. In addition, some brokerage firms compile industry norms and financial ratios from their own computer databases.

ACCOUNTING IN PRACTICE

SEC EDGAR Database

An example of a financial database is **EDGAR**, the Electronic Data Gathering, Analysis, and Retrieval system, maintained by the U.S. SEC (www.sec.gov/edgar.shtml). This computer database aids financial statement analysis by performing automated data collection, validation, indexing, acceptance, and forwarding of submissions by companies and others who are required by law to file forms with the U.S. Securities and Exchange Commission. The primary intent of the SEC in creating EDGAR was to increase the efficiency of the securities market for the benefit of investors, corporations, and the economy, by accelerating the receipt, acceptance, dissemination, and analysis of corporate information filed with the agency. An "efficient" securities market means that investors are able to make the best possible decisions regarding where and when to invest their funds.

Analytical Techniques

The dollar amounts of net income, sales revenue, total assets, and other key data are usually not meaningful when analyzed in isolation. For example, knowing that a company's annual net income is $1 million is of little informational value unless the amount of the income can be related to other factors. A $1 million profit might represent excellent performance for a company with less than $10 million in invested capital. On the other hand, $1 million in net income would be considered meager for a firm that had several hundred million dollars in invested capital. Thus, significant information can be derived by examining the relationship between two or more accounting variables, such as net income and total assets, net income and sales revenue, or net income and stockholders' equity. To describe these relationships clearly and to make comparisons easy, the relationships are often expressed in terms of ratios or percentages.

For example, we might express the relationship of $15,000 in net income to $150,000 in sales revenue as a ten percent ($15,000/$150,000) rate of return on sales. To describe the relationship between sales revenue of $150,000 and inventory of $20,000, we might use a ratio or a percentage; ($150,000/$20,000) may be expressed as 7.5, 7.5:1, or 750 percent.

Changes in selected financial statement items compared in successive financial statements are often expressed as percentages. For example, if a firm's net income increased from $40,000 last year to $48,000 this year, the $8,000 increase related to last year (the base year) is expressed as a 20 percent increase ($8,000/$40,000) in net income. To express a dollar increase or decrease as a percentage, however, the base year amount must be a positive figure. If, for example, a firm had a net loss of $4,000 in one year and net income of $20,000 in the next, the $24,000 increase cannot be meaningfully expressed as a percentage. Similarly, if a firm reported no debt securities in last year's balance sheet but showed $15,000 of such securities in this year's statement, the $15,000 increase cannot be expressed as a meaningful percentage.

When evaluating a firm's financial statements for two or more years, analysts often use **horizontal analysis**. Horizontal analysis is a technique that can be useful for detecting an improvement or deterioration in a firm's performance and for spotting trends regarding a firm's financial well-being. The term **vertical analysis** is used to describe the analysis of a single year of financial data.

HORIZONTAL ANALYSIS

The type of horizontal analysis most often used by investment professionals is **comparative financial statement analysis** for two or more years, showing dollar and/or percentage changes for important financial statement items and totals. Dollar increases and decreases are divided by data from the base year to obtain percentage changes. To illustrate, the 2017 and 2016 financial statements of Procter & Gamble (P&G) are presented in **Exhibits 13-2**, **13-3**, and **13-4**. We will use the data in these statements throughout this chapter to illustrate various analytical techniques.

Exhibit 13-2	Procter & Gamble Income Statement

THE PROCTER & GAMBLE COMPANY Consolidated Income Statements						
(in millions)	Year Ended 2017	Common-Size	Year Ended 2016	Common-Size	$ Change	% Change
Net sales.	$65,058	100.0 %	$65,299	100.0%	$ (241)	(0.4)%
Cost of goods sold	32,535	50.0 %	32,909	50.4%	(374)	(1.1)%
Gross profit.	32,523	50.0 %	32,390	49.6%	133	0.4 %
Selling, general, and administrative expense.	18,568	28.5 %	18,949	29.0%	(381)	(2.0)%
Operating income	13,955	21.5 %	13,441	20.6%	514	3.8 %
Interest expense.	465	0.7 %	579	0.9%	(144)	(19.7)%
Other non-operating income (expense)	(233)	(0.4)%	507	0.8%	(740)	(146.0)%
Earnings from continuing operations before taxes	13,257	20.4%	13,369	20.5%	(112)	(0.8)%
Income taxes on continuing operations.	3,063	4.7%	3,342	5.1%	(279)	(8.3)%
Net earnings from continuing operations.	10,194	15.7%	10,027	15.4%	167	1.7 %
Net earnings from discontinued operations, net of taxes	5,217	8.0%	577	0.9%	4,640	804.2 %
Net earnings	15,411	23.7%	10,604	16.2%	4,807	45.3 %
Earnings per share	5.80		3.80			
Dividends per share	2.70		2.66			

When analyzing financial statements, the investment professional is likely to focus his or her immediate attention on those financial statement items or percentages that are significant in amount. Although percentage changes are helpful in identifying significant items, they can sometimes be misleading. An unusually large percentage change may occur simply because the dollar amount of the base year is small. For example, P&G had a decrease in other non-operating income of $740, from $507 in 2016 to ($233) in 2017.

This represents a decrease of (146.0) percent, yet the dollar amount of this line item is quite small and insignificant relative to the other reported dollar amounts on P&G's income statement. The financial statement user's attention should be directed first to changes in key financial statement totals: sales revenue, operating income, net income, total assets, total liabilities, and so on. Next, the changes in significant individual items, such as accounts receivable, inventory, and property, plant and equipment should be examined.

P&G's total assets decreased 5.3 percent from 2016 to 2017 (see **Exhibit 13-3**), and net sales decreased 0.4 percent over the same time period (see **Exhibit 13-2**). (Recall from Chapter 5 that net sales equals gross sales revenue less any sales returns and allowances and sales discounts.) A small percentage decrease in net sales coincided with a larger decrease in total assets, reflecting a challenging environment for P&G in 2017, and indicates that P&G undertook certain business strategies to decrease capacity in light of decreasing demand. One potential note of optimism is the relationship between cost of goods sold and net sales. While net sales decreased by 0.4 percent, cost of goods sold decreased by 1.1 percent, leading to an improvement in P&G's gross profit margin percentage. P&G was also able to reduce selling, general, and administrative expense by 2.0 percent which ultimately helped contribute to an overall increase in operating income of 3.8 percent in 2017.

Exhibit 13-3	**Procter & Gamble Balance Sheet**					
THE PROCTER & GAMBLE COMPANY **Consolidated Balance Sheets**						
(in millions)	2017	Common-Size	2016	Common-Size	$ Change	% Change
Assets						
Current assets						
Cash and cash equivalents.	$ 5,569	4.6 %	$ 7,102	5.6 %	$(1,533)	(21.6)%
Short-term investments.	9,568	7.9 %	6,246	4.9 %	3,322	53.2 %
Accounts receivable	4,594	3.8 %	4,373	3.4 %	221	5.1 %
Inventories	4,624	3.8 %	4,716	3.7 %	(92)	(2.0)%
Other current assets	2,139	1.8 %	11,345	8.9 %	(9,206)	(81.1)%
Total current assets	26,494	22.0 %	33,782	26.6 %	(7,288)	(21.6)%
Property, plant, and equipment, net	19,893	16.5 %	19,385	15.2 %	508	2.6 %
Intangible assets.	68,886	57.2 %	68,877	54.2 %	9	0.0%
Other noncurrent assets.	5,133	4.3 %	5,092	4.0 %	41	0.8%
Total assets	$120,406	100.0 %	$127,136	100.0 %	$(6,730)	(5.3)%
Liabilities and Stockholders' Equity						
Current liabilities						
Accounts payable	$ 9,632	8.0 %	$ 9,325	7.3 %	$ 307	3.3 %
Other current liabilities	20,578	17.1 %	21,445	16.9 %	(867)	(4.0)%
Total current liabilities	30,210	25.1 %	30,770	24.2 %	(560)	(1.8)%
Long-term debt.	18,038	15.0 %	18,945	14.9 %	(907)	(4.8)%
Other noncurrent liabilities	16,380	13.6 %	19,438	15.3 %	(3,058)	(15.7)%
Total liabilities	64,628	53.7 %	69,153	54.4 %	(4,525)	(6.5)%
Preferred stock.	1,006	0.8 %	1,038	0.8 %	(32)	(3.1)%
Common stock	4,009	3.3 %	4,009	3.2 %	—	0.0 %
Additional paid-in capital.	63,641	52.9 %	63,714	50.1 %	(73)	(0.1)%
Treasury stock	(93,715)	(77.8)%	(82,176)	(64.6)%	(11,539)	14.0 %
Retained earnings	96,124	79.8 %	87,953	69.2 %	8,171	9.3 %
Other stockholders' equity	(15,287)	(12.7)%	(16,555)	(13.0)%	1,268	(7.7)%
Total stockholders' equity	55,778	46.3 %	57,983	45.6 %	(2,205)	(3.8)%
Total liabilities and stockholders' equity. . . .	$120,406	100.0 %	$127,136	100.0 %	$(6,730)	(5.3)%

We can see from P&G's statement of cash flows (**Exhibit 13-4**) that a decline in cash flow from operations from 2016 to 2017 resulted in a decrease in end-of-year cash over this period. Also, **Exhibit 13-4** reveals that P&G continued to repurchase its common stock (treasury stock) and to pay cash dividends in both 2016 and 2017, both of which increased the amount of the cash it returned to shareholders during this period of slow growth.

Exhibit 13-4	Procter & Gamble Statement of Cash Flows			
THE PROCTER & GAMBLE COMPANY				
Consolidated Statements of Cash Flows				
(in millions)	**Year Ended 2017**	**Year Ended 2016**	**$ Change**	**% Change**
Operating activities				
Net earnings.	$15,411	$10,604		
Depreciation and amortization	2,820	3,078		
Other adjustments to net income	(5,197)	(71)		
Changes in accounts receivable.	(322)	35		
Changes in inventories.	71	116		
Change liabilities	(149)	1,285		
Change in other operating activities.	119	388		
Net cash flow provided by operating activities	12,753	15,435	$(2,682)	(17.4)%
Investing activities				
Capital expenditures.	(2,813)	(2,882)		
Investments	(3,371)	(1,647)		
Other cash flows from investing activities.	495	(1,046)		
Net cash flow used by investing activities.	(5,689)	(5,575)	114	2.0%
Financing activities				
Dividends	(7,236)	(7,436)		
Net stock purchases.	(5,204)	(5,734)		
Net borrowings	1,399	1,285		
Other cash flows from financing activities	2,473	2,672		
Net cash used by financing activities	(8,568)	(9,213)	$ 645	(7.0)%
Effect of exchange rate changes	(29)	(381)		
Change in cash and cash equivalents	(1,533)	266		
Beginning cash and cash equivalents	7,102	6,836		
Ending cash and cash equivalents.	$ 5,569	$ 7,102		

From this limited analysis of comparative financial statements, an investment professional might conclude that P&G's operating performance for 2017 was consistent when compared with that of 2016, mostly the result of cost controls in 2017. Further analysis using some of the techniques summarized later in the chapter, however, may cause that opinion to be either affirmed or modified. The foregoing analysis did reveal some concerns, in particular, a deteriorating sales trend and a shrinking cash flow provided by operating activities.

PRINCIPLE ALERT

Consistency Principle

Horizontal analysis is a process of analyzing a firm's financial data across two or more years by examining dollar changes, percentage changes, and/or trend percentages. The utility of horizontal analysis, however, is dependent upon the effective implementation of the *consistency principle*. This accounting principle requires that a firm use the same accounting methods from one period to the next or, if a firm finds it necessary (or required) to change an accounting method, that the financial effects of any change be fully disclosed in the financial statements. The consistency principle assures financial analysts that, unless otherwise noted, changes in the accounts over time represent underlying economic changes in a business, and not the result of an accounting method change.

TREND ANALYSIS

To observe percentage changes over time in selected financial data, investment professionals often calculate **trend percentages**. Most companies provide summaries of their key financial data for the past five or ten years in their annual reports. With such information, the financial statement user can examine changes over periods longer than just the past two years. For example, suppose an analyst is interested in the trend in sales and net income for P&G for the past five years. The following are P&G's sales revenue and net income figures for 2013 through 2017:

PROCTER & GAMBLE COMPANY Annual Performance									
2013		**2014**		**2015**		**2016**		**2017**	
Millions of Dollars	Percentage of Base Year	Millions of Dollars	Percentage of Base Year	Millions of Dollars	Percentage of Base Year	Millions of Dollars	Percentage of Base Year	Millions of Dollars	Percentage of Base Year
Net sales.............. $73,138	100	$74,401	102	$70,749	97	$65,299	89	$65,058	89
Net income from continuing operations............ 10,346	100	10,658	103	8,287	80	10,027	97	10,194	99

The pattern of changes from year to year can be determined more precisely by calculating trend percentages. To do this, we select a base year and then divide the data for each of the remaining years by the base-year data. The result is an index of the changes occurring throughout the period. If, for example, 2013 is selected as the base year, all data for 2014 through 2017 will be related to 2013, which is represented as 100 percent.

To create the table of data displayed above, we divide each year's net sales—from 2013 through 2017 by $73,138, P&G's 2013 net sales (in millions of dollars). Similarly, P&G's net income for 2013 through 2017 is divided by $10,346, the company's 2013 net income (in millions of dollars).

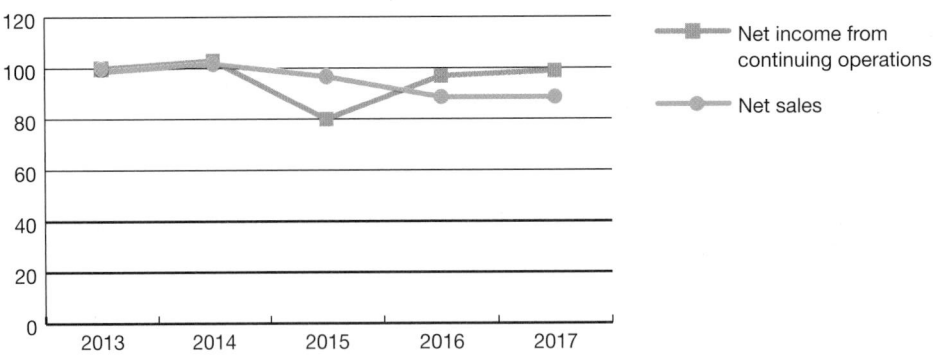

P&G's trend percentages above reveal that the company's growth in net income from continuing operations decreased in 2015 before recovering in the final two years. In contrast, the company's net sales showed a declining trend throughout the five-year period.

It is important to exercise care when interpreting trend percentages. Since all index percentages are related to a base year, it is important to select a good representative base year. For example, if 2016 was an unusual period for the firm, perhaps because of some large transitory items, its use in the trend analysis would be of limited value.

Other data items that an investment professional may relate to sales revenue and net income over multiple years include total assets, a company's investment in plant assets, and its cash flow from operations, among others.

The following data pertain to the Farrow Company:

	2019	2018
Sales revenue.	$800,000	$750,000
Net income	120,000	100,000
Total assets	300,000	290,000

Calculate both the amount in dollars and the percentage change in 2019 using horizontal analysis and 2018 as the base year.

YOUR TURN! 13.2

The solution is on page 685.

Concept →	Method →	Assessment	TAKEAWAY 13.1
How does a company's current performance compare with the prior year?	Income statement and balance sheet for current and prior year. The income statement and balance sheet should be compared using the prior year as the base. Percentage changes in financial statement amounts can be computed as the change between years divided by the base year amount.	Significant changes should be analyzed to determine the reason for any change.	

VERTICAL ANALYSIS

The relative importance of various accounts in a company's financial statements for a single year can be highlighted by showing them as a percentage of a key financial statement figure. A financial statement that presents the various account balances as a percentage of a key figure is called a **common-size financial statement**. Sales revenue (or net sales) is the key figure used to construct a common-size income statement, whereas total assets is the key figure used to construct a common-size balance sheet.

LO3 Explain vertical financial statement analysis.

A financial statement may present both the dollar amounts and common-size percentages. For example, **Exhibit 13-2** presents P&G's 2017 income statement in dollars and common-size percentages. The common-size percentages show each item in the income statement as a percentage of the company's net sales.

The common-size income statement allows financial statement users to readily compare P&G's ability to manage and control its various expenses while the level of its sales revenue changes over time. For example, P&G's net earnings increased from 16.2 percent of sales in 2016 to 23.7 percent of sales in 2017. We can also observe that there are only small changes in almost all of the line items as a percentage of net sales with the exception of net earnings from discontinued operations, which increased from 0.9 percent of net sales in 2016, to 8.0 percent of net sales in 2017. Common-size income statements are also useful when comparing across firms, especially when the firms are significantly different in size. We would expect firms of different sizes to report different levels of sales revenues and expenses on a dollar basis. But, we would expect far more similarities when the comparison is done on a common-size basis.

Common-size percentages can also be used to analyze balance sheet data. For example, by examining a firm's current assets and long-term assets as a percentage of total assets, we can determine whether a company is becoming more or less liquid over time. Another use of common-size percentages with balance sheet data is to evaluate the changing sources of financing used by a business. For example, the proportion of total assets supplied by short-term creditors, long-term creditors, preferred stockholders, and common stockholders of P&G are shown in **Exhibit 13-3**.

P&G's common-size balance sheets reveal that P&G is relying slightly less on debt financing than equity financing in 2017 compared to 2016. The primary means that P&G

used to make this shift in financing appears to be through an increase in the repurchase of its common shares as treasury stock, from 64.6 percent of total assets in 2016 to 77.8 percent of total assets in 2017. We also see that although P&G experienced a decrease in the dollar amount of total assets, the relative composition of those assets remained quite stable between 2016 and 2017.

YOUR TURN! 13.3

The solution is on page 685.

MBC

Hint: When preparing common-size income statements, expenses are expressed as a positive percentage of net sales even though they are subtractions on the income statement.

The Sanford Company reported the following income statement in 2018:

SANFORD COMPANY Income Statement For the Year Ended December 31, 2018	
Sales revenue.	$13,500
Cost of goods sold	5,400
Gross profit.	8,100
Selling and administrative expenses	1,350
Income from operations	6,750
Interest expense.	675
Other expense	135
Income before income taxes	5,940
Income tax expense	2,295
Net income	$ 3,645

Required

Prepare a 2018 common-size income statement for Sanford Company.

TAKEAWAY 13.2	Concept	Method	Assessment
	How do the relationships within a company's income statement and balance sheet compare to those of prior years?	Income statement and balance sheet for current and prior year. Each income statement item should be presented as a percentage of sales revenue and each balance sheet item should be presented as a percentage of total assets. Financial statements in this form are called common-size statements.	The percentages should be analyzed for differences between years and significant changes should be analyzed to determine the reason for any change.

THINKING GLOBALLY

Financial statement analysis is executed, worldwide, in exactly the same way. Common-size financial statements and the financial ratios discussed below are currency neutral and can be effectively used anywhere in the world. Not all ratios are relevant, however, in all countries. For example, in emerging countries that lack the financial infrastructure to support a credit system, ratios involving accounts receivable and accounts payable are likely to be irrelevant since sales transactions in those countries are only executed on a cash basis. Similarly, solvency ratios like the times-interest-earned ratio (discussed shortly) are irrelevant since bank financing in lesser-developed countries is rare (although it is becoming more prevalent with the advent of micro-finance in these countries).

RATIO ANALYSIS

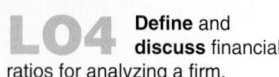

LO4 **Define** and **discuss** financial ratios for analyzing a firm.

In prior chapters, a number of financial ratios were introduced. At this juncture, we classify those ratios by their analytical objective and review their analysis and interpretation by calculating them for a single company. P&G's financial statements in **Exhibit 13-2**, **Exhibit 13-3**, and **Exhibit 13-4** provide the data for these calculations (all amounts are in millions). Also, representative industry averages are presented for comparison purposes where available. Some of the financial ratios that are commonly calculated by investment professionals, lenders, and managers are presented and explained in **Exhibit 13-5**.

Exhibit 13-5	Key Financial Ratios	
Ratio	**Definition**	**Explanation**
Analyzing Firm Profitability		
• Gross profit percentage	$$\frac{\text{Gross profit on sales}}{\text{Net sales}}$$	Percentage of income generated from sales after deducting the cost of goods sold.
• Return on sales	$$\frac{\text{Net income}}{\text{Net sales}}$$	Percentage of net income remaining from a dollar of sales after subtracting all expenses.
• Asset turnover	$$\frac{\text{Net sales}}{\text{Average total assets}}$$	Amount of sales generated from each dollar invested in assets.
• Return on assets	$$\frac{\text{Net income}}{\text{Average total assets}}$$	Rate of return generated on a company's investment in assets from all sources.
• Return on common stockholders' equity	$$\frac{(\text{Net income} - \text{Preferred stock dividends})}{\text{Average common stockholders' equity}}$$	Rate of return generated by a business for its common shareholders.
Analyzing Short-Term Firm Liquidity		
• Working capital	Current assets − Current liabilities	The difference between a firm's current assets and its current liabilities.
• Current ratio	$$\frac{\text{Current assets}}{\text{Current liabilities}}$$	Amount of current assets available to service current liabilities.
• Quick ratio	$$\frac{(\text{Cash and cash equivalents} + \text{Short-term investments} + \text{Accounts receivable})}{\text{Current liabilities}}$$	Amount of liquid assets available to service current liabilities.
• Operating-cash-flow-to-current-liabilities ratio	$$\frac{\text{Cash flow from operating activities}}{\text{Average current liabilities}}$$	Amount of cash flow from operating activities available to service current liabilities.
• Accounts receivable turnover	$$\frac{\text{Net sales}}{\text{Average accounts receivable (net)}}$$	Number of sales/collection cycles experienced by a firm.
• Average collection period	$$\frac{365}{\text{Accounts receivable turnover (net)}}$$	Number of days required, on average, to collect an outstanding accounts receivable.
• Inventory turnover	$$\frac{\text{Cost of goods sold}}{\text{Average inventory}}$$	Number of production/sales cycles experienced by a firm.
• Days' sales in inventory	$$\frac{365}{\text{Inventory turnover}}$$	Number of days, on average, required to sell the inventory currently on hand.
Analyzing Long-Term Firm Solvency		
• Debt-to-equity ratio	$$\frac{\text{Total liabilities}}{\text{Total stockholders' equity}}$$	Percentage of total assets provided by creditors.
• Times-interest-earned ratio	$$\frac{\text{Income before interest expense and income taxes}}{\text{Interest expense}}$$	Extent to which current operating income covers current debt service charges.
• Operating-cash-flow-to-capital-expenditures ratio	$$\frac{\text{Cash flow from operating activities}}{\text{Annual net capital expenditures}}$$	The ability of a firm's operations to provide sufficient cash to replace and expand its property, plant, and equipment.
Financial Ratios for Common Stockholders		
• Earnings per share	$$\frac{(\text{Net income} - \text{Preferred stock dividends})}{\text{Weighted-average number of common shares outstanding}}$$	The net income available to common shareholders calculated on a per share basis.
• Price-earnings ratio	$$\frac{\text{Market price per share}}{\text{Earnings per share}}$$	A measure of the price of a share of common stock relative to the share's annual earnings.
• Dividend yield	$$\frac{\text{Annual dividend per share}}{\text{Market price per share}}$$	The earnings on an investment in stock coming from dividends.
• Dividend payout ratio	$$\frac{\text{Annual dividend per share}}{\text{Earnings per share}}$$	The percentage of net income paid out to shareholders as dividends.

Analyzing Firm Profitability

Several ratios assist in evaluating how efficiently a firm has performed in its quest for profits, or what is referred to as firm profitability. These ratios include (1) the gross profit percentage, (2) the return on sales, (3) asset turnover, (4) the return on assets, and (5) the return on common stockholders' equity.

Gross Profit Percentage

The **gross profit percentage** is a closely watched ratio for both retailers and manufacturers, among other industries. The ratio is calculated as:

A.K.A Gross profit is often referred to as *gross margin*.

$$\text{Gross profit percentage} = \frac{\text{Gross profit on sales}}{\text{Net sales}}$$

This ratio shows the effect on firm profitability of changes in a firm's product pricing structure, sales mix, and merchandise costs. **Gross profit**, or **gross profit on sales**, is defined as the difference between net sales and cost of goods sold and reveals the amount of sales revenue remaining after subtracting the cost of products sold.

P&G's common-size income statements (see **Exhibit 13-2**) reveal that its gross profit percentage increased from 49.6 percent in 2016 to 50.0 percent in 2017. These percentages are derived using the following figures:

	2017	2016
Gross profit.	$32,523	$32,390
Net sales.	65,058	65,299
Gross profit percentage.	50.0%	49.6%
Industry average.	55.9%	

In contrast to the positive trend in P&G's gross profit percentage, we also note that P&G's ratio is below the industry average of 55.9 percent.[1]

Return on Sales (Profit Margin)

A.K.A Return on sales is often referred to as *profit margin*.

Another important measure of firm profitability is the **return on sales**. This ratio reveals the percentage of each dollar of net sales that remains as profit after subtracting all operating and nonoperating expenses. The return on sales is calculated as follows:

$$\text{Return on sales} = \frac{\text{Net income}}{\text{Net sales}}$$

When common-size income statements are available, the return on sales equals the net income percentage. P&G's common-size income statements in **Exhibit 13-2** reveal that its return on sales increased from 16.2 percent in 2016 to 23.7 percent in 2017. These percentages are calculated using the following figures:

	2017	2016
Net income.	$15,411	$10,604
Net sales.	65,058	65,299
Return on sales.	23.7%	16.2%
Industry average.	10.3%	

[1] Industry data are obtained from Reuters.com.

The increase in the return on sales for P&G is encouraging, and as noted above, P&G's increase in its return on sales is mostly attributable to the company's cost control and earnings from discontinued operations. Additionally, P&G's 2017 return on sales exceeds the industry average.

The return on sales and gross profit percentages should be used only when analyzing companies from the same industry or when comparing a firm's performance across multiple time periods (as we did above) since the ratio may vary widely across industries. Retail jewelers, for example, have much larger gross profit percentages (an industry average of 45.0 percent) than do retail grocers (an industry average of 23.0 percent). Industry averages for the asset turnover ratio, discussed next, also would be expected to vary significantly from one industry to another.

Asset Turnover

The **asset turnover ratio** measures how efficiently a firm uses its assets to generate sales revenue by calculating the amount of sales dollars generated annually for each dollar of assets invested in the company. This ratio is calculated as follows:

$$\text{Asset turnover} = \frac{\text{Net sales}}{\text{Average total assets}}$$

P&G's asset turnover is calculated as (total assets were $129,495 at year-end 2015):

		2017	2016
Net sales.		$ 65,058	$ 65,299
Total assets			
Beginning of year	(a)	127,136	129,495
End of year	(b)	120,406	127,136
Average [(a + b)/2]		123,771	128,316
Asset turnover		**0.53**	**0.51**
Industry average.		0.74	

P&G's asset turnover increased slightly from 2016 to 2017, indicating that the company is more effective in using its assets to generate sales revenue. Specifically, the company generated $0.53 in net sales for every dollar invested in total assets in 2017, compared to $0.51 in 2016. This ratio result is, however, below the industry average of $0.74.

Industries that are characterized by low gross profit percentages generally have relatively high asset turnover ratios. Retail grocery chains, for example, typically turn over their assets five to six times per year. By way of contrast, retail jewelers average only one to two asset turnovers per year. These industry differences largely reflect the high cost of products sold by jewelers versus the low cost of products sold by retail grocers.

Return on Assets

The rate of return on total assets, called the **return on assets**, is an overall measure of a firm's profitability. It reveals the rate of profit earned per dollar of assets under a firm's control. The return on assets is calculated as follows:

$$\text{Return on assets} = \frac{\text{Net income}}{\text{Average total assets}}$$

P&G's return on assets is calculated as:

	2017	2016
Net income	$ 15,411	$ 10,604
Average total assets	123,771	128,316
Return on assets	**12.5%**	**8.3%**
Industry average.	6.6%	

P&G's return on assets increased from 8.3 percent in 2016 to 12.5 percent in 2017; in addition the percentage is above the industry average.

The return on assets ratio summarizes the financial impact of two component ratios: the return on sales and asset turnover; that is, the return on assets is the multiplicative product of these latter two ratios, as follows:

Ratio:	Return on sales	×	Asset turnover	=	Return on assets
Ratio calculation:	$\dfrac{\text{Net income}}{\text{Net sales}}$	×	$\dfrac{\text{Net sales}}{\text{Average total assets}}$	=	$\dfrac{\text{Net income}}{\text{Average total assets}}$
P&G:	23.7 percent	×	0.53	=	12.5 percent

Return on Common Stockholders' Equity

The **return on common stockholders' equity** measures the profitability of the ownership interest held by a company's common stockholders. The ratio shows the percentage of income available to common stockholders—that is, net income less any preferred stock dividends—for each dollar of common stockholder equity invested in a business, as follows:

$$\text{Return on common stockholders' equity} = \frac{(\text{Net income} - \text{Preferred stock dividends})}{\text{Average common stockholders' equity}}$$

The return on common stockholders' equity for P&G is calculated as (common stockholders' equity was $62,149 at year-end 2015):

		2017	2016
Net income		$15,411	$10,604
Less: Preferred stock dividends		247	255
Common stock earnings.		15,164	10,349
Common stockholders' equity:			
Beginning of year	(a)	57,983	62,149
End of year	(b)	55,778	57,983
Average [(a + b)/2]		56,881	60,066
Return on common stockholders' equity.		**26.7%**	**17.2%**
Industry average.		12.1%	

P&G's return on common stockholders' equity increased by 9.5 percent, from 17.2 percent in 2016 to 26.7 percent in 2017. Like the return on assets, P&G's return on common stockholders' equity is well above the industry average.

YOUR TURN! 13.4

The solution is on
page 685.

The following data were obtained from the current financial statements for Kelly Corporation:

Net sales.	$30,000
Cost of goods sold	10,500
Net income	4,500
Average total assets	50,000
Average common stockholders' equity	35,000
Preferred dividends	500

Required
Calculate the following ratios for Kelly Corporation:

- a. Gross profit percentage
- b. Return on sales
- c. Asset turnover
- d. Return on assets
- e. Return on common stockholders' equity

Concept ⟶	Method ⟶	Assessment	TAKEAWAY 13.3
How much profit is a company generating relative to the amount of assets invested in the company?	Income statement and balance sheet. Calculate the return on assets by dividing net income by the average total assets for the year.	The higher the return on assets, the better a company is doing in terms of generating profits utilizing the assets under its control.	

Analyzing Short-Term Firm Liquidity

A firm's **working capital** is the difference between its current assets and current liabilities. Maintaining an adequate working capital enables a firm to repay its current obligations on a timely basis and to take advantage of any available purchase discounts associated with the timely payment of accounts payable. Shortages of working capital, on the other hand, can force a company into borrowing at inopportune times and unfavorable interest rates. As a consequence, many long-term debt contracts contain provisions that require the borrowing firm to maintain an adequate working capital position. A firm's working capital is calculated as follows:

$$\text{Working capital} = \text{Current assets} - \text{Current liabilities}$$

Analysis of a firm's short-term liquidity utilizes several financial ratios that relate to various aspects of a company's working capital. These ratios are (1) the current ratio, (2) the quick ratio, (3) operating-cash-flow-to-current-liabilities ratio, (4) accounts receivable turnover and average collection period, and (5) inventory turnover and days' sales in inventory.

Current Ratio

The **current ratio** is calculated as a firm's current assets divided by its current liabilities:

$$\text{Current ratio} = \frac{\text{Current assets}}{\text{Current liabilities}}$$

This ratio is a widely used measure of a firm's ability to meet its current obligations and to have funds available for use in daily operations. The following calculations reveal that P&G's current ratio declined from 1.10 in 2016 to 0.88 (or 0.88:1) in 2017:

	2017	2016
Current assets	$26,494	$33,782
Current liabilities...	30,210	30,770
Current ratio	**0.88**	**1.10**
Industry average...	1.23	

In essence, P&G had $0.88 in current assets for every $1 in current liabilities at the end of 2017.

In the past, a generally accepted rule of thumb was that a firm's current ratio should be approximately 2:1, indicating that a company should maintain twice the dollar amount of current assets as was needed to satisfy its current liabilities. Improved cash flow management techniques and alternate forms of short-term financing (such as bank lines of credit) have reduced the need for businesses to maintain such a high current ratio. Still, many creditors prefer to see a higher current ratio and consider a low ratio as a potential warning sign of short-term liquidity problems.

Evaluating the adequacy of a firm's current ratio may involve comparing it with the recent past (P&G's current ratio declined slightly from 2016 to 2017) or with an industry average (P&G's ratio is below the industry average of 1.23). What is considered an appropriate current ratio varies by industry. A service firm with little or no inventory, such as a car wash service, would be expected to have a smaller current ratio than would a firm carrying a large inventory, such as a hardware retailer. The composition (or mix) of a firm's current assets significantly influences any evaluation of a firm's short-term liquidity. The quick ratio, discussed next, explicitly considers the composition of a firm's current assets when evaluating short-term liquidity.

Quick Ratio

A.K.A. The quick ratio is also referred to as the *acid-test ratio.*

The **quick ratio** reveals the relationship between a firm's liquid, or quick, assets and its current liabilities. Quick assets include cash and cash equivalents, short-term investments, and accounts receivable. The quick ratio omits a company's inventory and prepaid assets, which may not be particularly liquid. Consequently, the quick ratio may give a more accurate picture of a company's ability to meet its current obligations.

Comparing the quick ratio and the current ratio indicates the financial impact of a company's inventory on its working capital. For example, a company might have an acceptable current ratio, but if its quick ratio falls to an unacceptable level, a financial analyst is likely to be concerned about the amount of inventory on hand, and consequently, analyze the company's inventory position more thoroughly.

The quick ratio is calculated as follows:

$$\text{Quick ratio} = \frac{(\text{Cash and cash equivalents} + \text{Short-term investments} + \text{Accounts receivable})}{\text{Current liabilities}}$$

The quick ratio for P&G is calculated as:

	2017	2016
Cash and cash equivalents, short-term investments, and accounts receivable....................................	$19,731	$17,721
Current liabilities...	30,210	30,770
Quick ratio...	**0.65**	**0.58**
Industry average...	0.95	

P&G's quick ratio increased from 0.58 in 2016 to 0.65 in 2017; however its 2017 quick ratio is below the industry average of 0.95. P&G's increased quick ratio is mainly due to a large increase in short-term investments in 2017.

Operating-Cash-Flow-to-Current-Liabilities Ratio

Ultimately, cash will be needed to settle a business's current liabilities. Another ratio indicating a firm's ability to pay its current liabilities as they come due focuses on a company's operating cash flow. The operating-cash-flow-to-current-liabilities ratio is calculated as follows:

$$\text{Operating-cash-flow-to-current-liabilities ratio} = \frac{\text{Cash flow from operating activities}}{\text{Average current liabilities}}$$

The operating-cash-flow-to-current-liabilities ratio relates the net cash available as a result of operating activities to the average current liabilities outstanding during the period. A higher ratio indicates that a firm has a greater ability to settle its current liabilities using its operating cash flow.

P&G's operating-cash-flow-to-current-liabilities ratio is calculated as (current liabilities at the end of 2015 was $29,790; no industry average is available):

		2017	2016
Cash flow from operating activities.		$12,753	$15,435
Current liabilities			
Beginning of year	(a)	30,770	29,790
End of year	(b)	30,210	30,770
Average [(a + b)/2]		30,490	30,280
Operating-cash-flow-to-current-liabilities ratio		**0.42**	**0.51**

P&G's operating-cash-flow-to-current-liabilities ratio declined from 2016 to 2017, primarily because of a decline in cash provided by operating activities and a slight increase in average current liabilities.

Accounts Receivable Turnover

The speed with which accounts receivable are collected is of considerable interest to investment professionals when evaluating a firm's short-term liquidity. Accounts receivable turnover indicates how many times a year a firm collects its average outstanding accounts receivable, and thus, measures how fast a firm converts its accounts receivable into cash. The quicker a firm is able to convert its accounts receivables into cash, the less cash the company needs to keep on hand to satisfy its current liabilities. Accounts receivable turnover is calculated as follows:

$$\text{Accounts receivable turnover} = \frac{\text{Net sales}}{\text{Average accounts receivable}}$$

Recall from Chapter 8 that accounts receivable less the allowance for doubtful accounts— that is, the net balance of accounts receivable—is the amount of receivables that the company expects to collect from customers. The accounts receivable turnover for P&G is calculated as (accounts receivable, net at the end of 2015 were $5,924):

	2017	2016
Net sales...		$65,058	$65,299
Average accounts receivable (net)			
Beginning of year .... (a)	4,373	5,924
End of year .... (b)	4,594	4,373
Average [(a + b)/2]	4,484	5,149
Accounts receivable turnover...........................	**14.51**	**12.68**
Industry average......................................	7.51	

The higher the accounts receivable turnover, the faster a company is able to convert its accounts receivable into cash. P&G's accounts receivable turnover increased from 12.68 in 2016 to 14.51 in 2017. In addition, P&G's 2017 accounts receivable turnover is well above the industry average of 7.51 for the year.

Average Collection Period

A.K.A. The average collection period is also referred to as the *days' sales outstanding,* or *DSO.*

An extension of the accounts receivable turnover is the **average collection period**. The average collection period reveals how many days it takes, on average, for a company to collect an account receivable. The ratio is calculated as follows:

$$\text{Average collection period} = \frac{365}{\text{Accounts receivable turnover (net)}}$$

P&G's average collection period is calculated as:

	2017	2016
Average collection period		
2017: 365/14.51; 2016: 365/12.68	**25.2 days**	**28.8 days**
Industry average......................................	48.6 days	

P&G's average collection period decreased in 2017. This may have resulted from such actions as P&G tightening the credit standards it applies to its customers or by reducing the allowed credit period. Alternatively, it may reflect that P&G's customers have experienced improving cash flows, and thus they are able to pay their accounts more promptly. Knowledge of P&G's credit terms would permit a more complete analysis of these results. If, for example, P&G's credit terms are n/20, then an average collection period of 25.2 days indicates that the company has a problem with slow-paying customers. If, on the other hand, P&G's credit terms are n/30, then the 2017 average collection period shows no particular problem with the company's speed of receivable collection.

Inventory Turnover

An analyst concerned about a company's inventory position is likely to evaluate the company's **inventory turnover**. This ratio indicates whether the inventory on hand is disproportionate to the amount of sales revenue. Excessive inventories not only tie up company funds and increase storage costs but may also lead to subsequent losses if the goods become outdated or unsalable. In general, a higher turnover is preferred to a lower turnover. The calculation of inventory turnover is as follows:

$$\text{Inventory turnover} = \frac{\text{Cost of goods sold}}{\text{Average inventory}}$$

P&G's inventory turnover is calculated as (inventory at the end of 2015 was $4,979):

		2017	2016
Cost of goods sold		$32,535	$32,909
Inventory			
Beginning of year	(a)	4,716	4,979
End of year	(b)	4,624	4,716
Average [(a + b)/2]		4,670	4,848
Inventory turnover		**6.97**	**6.79**
Industry average.		2.68	

P&G's inventory turnover increased from 6.79 in 2016 to 6.97 in 2017. In addition, the company's 2017 inventory turnover of 6.97 is above the industry average of 2.68.

The cost of goods sold is used in the calculation of inventory turnover because the inventory measure in the denominator is a *cost* figure; consequently, it is appropriate to also use a cost figure in the numerator. By way of contrast, accounts receivable turnover uses net sales in the calculation because accounts receivable is based on sales revenue, which includes a markup for the company's expected profit.

A low inventory turnover can result from an overextended inventory position or from inadequate sales volume. For this reason, an appraisal of a firm's inventory turnover should be accompanied by a review of the quick ratio and an analysis of trends in both inventory and sales revenue.

Days' Sales in Inventory

The **days' sales in inventory** ratio is derived from a firm's inventory turnover ratio and reveals how many days it takes, on average, for a firm to sell its inventory on hand. The ratio is calculated as follows:

$$\text{Days' sales in inventory} = \frac{365}{\text{Inventory turnover}}$$

P&G's days' sales in inventory is calculated as:

	2017	2016
2017: 365/6.97; 2016: 365/6.79.	52.4 days	53.8 days
Industry average.	136.2 days	

P&G's days' sales in inventory reveals that the average amount of time required to sell its inventory decreased by 1.4 days from 53.8 days in 2016 to 52.4 days in 2017. Also, P&G's average length of time to sell its inventory is much lower than the industry average of 136.2 days. The improvement in P&G's days' sales in inventory will positively impact the company's profitability due to the related decrease in inventory storage costs and a decrease in its inventory financing costs.

By combining the days' sales in inventory with the average collection period, it is possible to estimate the average time period from the acquisition of inventory, to the sale of inventory, to the eventual collection of cash. The sum of the days' sales in inventory plus the average collection period measures the length of the company's **operating cycle**. Although operating cycles will naturally vary across different industries, a shorter operating cycle is preferred as it is an indicator of the operating efficiency and working capital management of the company. In 2017, for example, it took P&G 77.6 days (52.4 days' sales in inventory + 25.2 days average collection period) to sell its average inventory and collect the related cash from its customers. This operating cycle is significantly better than the industry average of 184.8 days and slightly better than P&G's 2016 period of 82.6 days (53.8 days + 28.8 days).

YOUR TURN! 13.5

The solution is on page 686.

The following selected data were obtained from the financial statements of Justin Corporation:

Current assets	$ 60,000
Current liabilities for both current and prior year	40,000
Cash flow from operating activities.	55,000
Net sales.	100,000
Average accounts receivable	15,000
Cost of goods sold	70,000
Average inventory.	9,000

Required

Calculate the following financial measures and ratios for Justin Corporation:

a. Working capital

b. Current ratio

c. Operating-cash-flow-to-current-liabilities ratio

d. Accounts receivable turnover

e. Days' sales in inventory

TAKEAWAY 13.4	Concept ⟶	Method ⟶	Assessment
	How financially capable is a company to pay its current liabilities as they come due?	Income statement, balance sheet, and statement of cash flows. Calculate the current ratio, the quick ratio, and the operating-cash-flow-to-current-liabilities ratio.	The higher the ratios, the higher the probability that a company will have the ability to pay its current liabilities as they become due.

Analyzing Long-Term Firm Solvency

The preceding set of ratios examined a firm's short-term liquidity. A separate set of ratios analyzes a firm's long-term solvency, or its long-term debt repayment capability. Ratios in this latter group include (1) the debt-to-equity ratio, (2) the times-interest-earned ratio, and (3) the operating-cash-flow-to-capital-expenditures ratio.

Debt-to-Equity Ratio

The **debt-to-equity ratio** evaluates the financial structure of a firm by relating a company's total liabilities to its total stockholders' equity. This ratio considers the extent to which a company relies on creditors versus stockholders to provide financing. The debt-to-equity ratio is calculated as follows:

$$\text{Debt-to-equity ratio} = \frac{\text{Total liabilities}}{\text{Total stockholders' equity}}$$

This ratio uses year-end balances for the ratio's components, rather than averages, since we are interested in the firm's capital structure as of a particular point in time. The total stockholders' equity for a business is its total assets minus its total liabilities.

The debt-to-equity ratio gives creditors an indication of the margin of protection available to them (creditors' claims to assets have priority over stockholders' claims). The lower the ratio, the greater the protection being provided to creditors. A firm with a low ratio also has greater flexibility when seeking additional borrowed funds at a low rate of interest than does a firm with a high ratio.

P&G's debt-to-equity ratio is calculated as:

	2017	2016
Total liabilities (year-end)	$64,628	$69,153
Total stockholders' equity (year-end)	55,778	57,983
Debt-to-equity ratio	**1.16**	**1.19**
Industry average.	0.42	

P&G's debt-to-equity ratio decreased slightly from 1.19 in 2016 to 1.16 in 2017, indicating a small decrease in reliance on debt to finance its operations. However, the company's 2017 ratio is well above the industry average, suggesting an increased risk of insolvency. Still, this ratio is far from a point where it would represent a major concern.

Times-Interest-Earned Ratio

To evaluate the ability of a company to pay its current interest charges, an analyst may investigate the relationship between the company's current interest charges and its operating income available to meet interest charges. For example, an extremely high debt-to-equity ratio for a company may indicate extensive borrowing by the company; however, if its operating earnings are sufficient to meet the interest charges on the debt several times over, an analyst may regard the situation quite favorably.

A.K.A. The times-interest-earned ratio is also referred to as the *interest coverage ratio.*

Analysts, particularly long-term credit analysts, almost always consider the **times-interest-earned ratio** of a company with interest-bearing debt. This ratio is calculated by dividing the income before interest expense and income taxes by the annual interest expense:

$$\text{Times-interest-earned ratio} = \frac{\text{Income before interest expense and income taxes}}{\text{Interest expense}}$$

P&G's times-interest-earned ratio is calculated as:

	2017	2016
Income before interest expense and income taxes	$13,722	$13,948
Interest expense.	465	579
Times-interest-earned ratio.	**29.5**	**24.1**
Industry average.	40.1	

P&G's operating income available to meet its interest charges increased from 24.1 times in 2016 to 29.5 times in 2017. This ratio is below the industry average of 40.1, but still indicates that P&G exhibits an exceptionally good margin of safety for creditors. Generally speaking, a company that earns its interest charges several times over is regarded as a satisfactory risk by long-term creditors.

Operating-Cash-Flow-to-Capital-Expenditures Ratio

The ability of a firm's operations to provide sufficient cash to replace and expand its property, plant, and equipment is revealed by the **operating-cash-flow-to-capital-expenditures ratio**. To the extent that acquisitions of plant assets can be financed using cash provided by operating activities, a firm does not have to use other financing sources, such as long-term debt. This ratio is calculated as follows:

$$\text{Operating-cash-flow-to-capital-expenditures ratio} = \frac{\text{Cash flow from operating activities}}{\text{Annual net capital expenditures}}$$

A ratio of 1.0 indicates that a firm's current operating activities provide sufficient cash to fully fund any investment in plant capacity. A ratio in excess of 1.0 indicates that a company has sufficient operating cash flow to fund expansion in its plant capacity.

The operating-cash-flow-to-capital-expenditures ratio for P&G is:

	2017	2016
Cash flow from operating activities.	$12,753	$15,435
Annual net capital expenditures	2,813	2,882
Operating-cash-flow-to-capital-expenditures ratio	**4.5**	**5.4**

In 2017, P&G's operating-cash-flow-to capital-expenditures ratio was 4.5, a slight decrease from 5.4 in 2016. It appears that P&G is generating plenty of operating cash flow to cover its net capital expenditures in each year.

YOUR TURN! 13.6

The solution is on page 686.

The following selected data were obtained from the financial statements for the Hartford Corporation:

Total liabilities	$180,000
Total stockholders' equity	600,000
Cash flow from operating activities.	100,000
Annual capital expenditures	30,000
Net income	55,000
Interest expense.	5,000
Income tax expense	25,000

Required

Calculate the following ratios for Hartford Corporation:

a. Debt-to-equity ratio

b. Times-interest-earned ratio

c. Operating-cash-flow-to-capital-expenditures ratio

TAKEAWAY 13.5	Concept	→	Method	→	Assessment
	How solvent is a company?		Income statement, balance sheet, and statement of cash flows. Calculate the debt-to-equity ratio, the times-interest-earned ratio, and the operating-cash-flow-to-capital-expenditures ratio.		The higher the times-interest-earned and the operating-cash-flow-to-capital-expenditures ratios, and the lower the debt-to-equity ratio, the greater is a company's solvency.

Financial Ratios for Common Stockholders

Present and potential common stockholders share an interest with a business's creditors in analyzing the profitability, short-term liquidity, and long-term solvency of a company. There are also other financial ratios that are primarily of interest to common stockholders. These ratios include (1) earnings per share, (2) the price-earnings ratio, (3) dividend yield, and (4) the dividend payout ratio.

Earnings per Share

Because stock market prices are quoted on a per-share basis, the reporting of earnings per share of common stock is useful to investors. **Earnings per share (EPS)** is calculated by dividing the net income available to common stockholders by the weighted average number of common shares outstanding during a year. The net income available to common stockholders is a company's net income less any preferred stock dividends. Preferred stock dividends are subtracted from net income to arrive at the net income available exclusively to a company's common stock stockholders. Thus, earnings per share is calculated as follows:

$$\frac{\text{Earnings}}{\text{per share}} = \frac{\text{(Net income} - \text{Preferred stock dividends)}}{\text{Weighted-average number of common shares outstanding}}$$

Since earnings per share are a required disclosure on a company's income statement, investment professionals do not have to calculate this financial metric. P&G's income statements reveal the following earnings per share (see **Exhibit 13-2**):

	2017	2016
Earnings per share.	$5.80	$3.80

P&G's earnings per share increased from $3.80 in 2016 to $5.80 in 2017, an increase of 52.6 percent. This is slightly higher than the 45.3 percent increase in P&G's net income over the same period. The result is due to the increase in P&G's treasury stock, which reduces the number of common shares outstanding.

Price-Earnings Ratio

The **price-earnings ratio** is calculated by dividing the market price per share of common stock by a company's earnings per share:

A.K.A. The price-earnings ratio is also referred to as the *P/E multiple.*

$$\text{Price-earnings ratio} = \frac{\text{Market price per share}}{\text{Earnings per share}}$$

For many analysts and investors, this ratio is an important tool for assessing a stock's valuation. For example, after evaluating the financial strengths of several comparable companies, an analyst may decide which company to invest in by comparing the price-earnings ratio of each company. Assuming that the companies have equivalent persistent earnings and financial risk profiles, the company with the lowest price-earnings ratio may represent the best investment opportunity.

When calculating the price-earnings ratio, it is customary to use the latest market price per share and the earnings per share for the last four quarters of a company's operations. P&G's price-earnings ratios as of the end of fiscal years 2016 and 2017 are:

	2017	2016
Market price per share (at year-end)	$87.18	$84.78
Earnings per share.	5.80	3.80
Price-earnings ratio	15.0	22.3
Industry average.	83.5	

The market price of a share of P&G's common stock at year-end 2017 was 15.0 times the company's 2017 earnings per share. Since P&G's price-earnings ratio at the end of 2017 is below industry average, this may indicate that the company's shares are undervalued, and thus, that its stock may represent a good investment.

Dividend Yield

Investor expectations vary greatly with personal economic circumstances and with the overall economic outlook. Some investors are more interested in the potential share price appreciation of a stock than in any dividends that a company may pay on its outstanding shares. Other investors are more concerned with dividends than with stock price appreciation. These investors desire a high **dividend yield** on their investments. Dividend yield is calculated by dividing a company's current annual dividend per share by the current market price per share:

$$\text{Dividend yield} = \frac{\textbf{Annual dividend per share}}{\textbf{Market price per share}}$$

P&G's dividend yield per common share is calculated as (the dividend per share is disclosed in **Exhibit 13-2**):

	2017	2016
Annual dividend per share	$ 2.70	$ 2.66
Market price per share (at year-end)	87.18	84.78
Dividend yield	3.1%	3.1%
Industry average	0.96%	

P&G's dividend yield remained constant at 3.1 percent in both 2016 and 2017, and is well above the industry average of 0.96 percent.

Dividend Payout Ratio

Investors who emphasize the yield on their investments may also be interested in a firm's **dividend payout ratio**—that is, the percentage of net income paid out as dividends to stockholders. The payout ratio indicates whether a firm has a conservative or a liberal dividend policy, and may also indicate whether a firm is conserving funds for internal financing of its growth. The dividend payout ratio is calculated as follows:

$$\text{Dividend payout ratio} = \frac{\textbf{Annual dividend per share}}{\textbf{Earnings per share}}$$

P&G's dividend payout ratio is calculated as:

	2017	2016
Annual dividends per share	$2.70	$2.66
Earnings per share	5.80	3.80
Dividend payout ratio	46.6%	70.0%
Industry average	43.1%	

P&G's dividend payout ratio decreased from 70 percent in 2016 to 46.6 percent in 2017. This payout ratio is consistent with the payout ratio for most comparable mature U.S. industrial corporations, and is slightly higher than the industry average for P&G.

Payout ratios for mature industrial corporations vary between 40 percent and 60 percent of net income. Many corporations, however, need funds for internal financing of growth and pay out little (if any) of their net income as dividends. At the other extreme, some companies—principally utility companies—may pay out as much as 70 percent of their net income as dividends.

The following selected data were obtained from financial statements for Baylor Corporation:

Earnings per share	$ 4.50
Market price per share of common stock	54.00
Dividends per share of common stock	1.50

Required

Calculate the following ratios for Baylor Corporation:

a. Dividend yield

b. Dividend payout ratio

c. Price-earnings ratio

Concept →	Method →	Assessment	TAKEAWAY 13.6
How much dividends are common stockholders likely to receive?	Earnings per share, dividends per share, and market price of common stock. Calculate the dividend yield and dividend payout ratio.	The higher the dividend yield and the dividend payout ratio, the greater the company's dividend distribution policy.	

Accounting as an Aid to Investing   **ACCOUNTING IN EVERYDAY LIFE**

Many employers offer pension plans such as a 401(k) where the employee is responsible for deciding how to invest their contributions. Having a knowledge of the accounting techniques demonstrated in this chapter can certainly provide a better understanding of the risks and rewards of investing.

LIMITATIONS OF FINANCIAL STATEMENT ANALYSIS

The ratios, percentages, and other relationships described in this chapter reflect the analytical techniques used by investment professionals and experienced investors. Nonetheless, they must be interpreted with due consideration of the general economic conditions, the conditions of the industry in which a company operates, and the relative position of individual companies within an industry.

LO5 Discuss the limitations of financial statement analysis.

     Financial statement users must also be aware of the inherent limitations of financial statement data. Problems of comparability are frequently encountered. Companies within the same industry may use different accounting methods that can cause problems in comparing certain key relationships. For instance, inventory turnover is likely to be quite different for a company using LIFO than for one using FIFO. Inflation may also distort certain financial data and ratios, especially those resulting from horizontal analysis. For example, trend percentages calculated from data unadjusted for inflation may be deceptive.

     Financial statement users must also be careful when comparing companies within a particular industry. Factors such as firm size, diversity of product line, and mode of operations can make firms within the same industry dissimilar in their reported results. Moreover, some firms, particularly conglomerates, are difficult to classify by industry. If segment information is available, the financial statement user may compare the statistics for several industries. Often, trade associations prepare industry statistics that are stratified by size of firm or type of product, facilitating financial statement analysis.

FORENSIC ACCOUNTING

It is generally considered more difficult to deter financial statement fraud than it is to deter other types of fraud such as embezzlement. The best approach to fraud deterrence is to put into place a strong set of internal controls. Unfortunately, senior management, such as a firm's CEO and CFO, are the most likely employees to commit financial statement fraud. These individuals are able to use their position of authority to override most internal controls. Thus, it is important to consider alternative approaches to fraud deterrence. Potential alternative approaches are based on the fraud triangle concept, in which fraud is related to the interaction of three factors: (1) pressure, (2) opportunity, and (3) rationalization.

The fraud element of pressure can be reduced by avoiding the practice of setting unachievable financial goals and utilizing compensation systems that are considered fair but which do not create excessive incentives to commit fraud. Although internal controls may be circumvented by senior management, it is still important to maintain a strong system of internal controls and to establish clear and uniform accounting procedures with no exception clauses. In addition, a strong internal control department reporting to the board of directors provides further deterrence. Finally, the creation and promotion of a culture of honesty and integrity throughout an organization make the rationalization of financial statement fraud much more difficult.

COMPREHENSIVE PROBLEM

Knox Instruments, Inc., is a manufacturer of various medical and dental instruments. Financial statement data for the firm follow:

(thousands of dollars, except per-share amount)	2019
Sales revenue.	$200,000
Cost of goods sold	98,000
Net income	10,750
Dividends	4,200
Cash provided by operating activities.	7,800
Earnings per share	3.07

KNOX INSTRUMENTS, INC.
Balance Sheets

(thousands of dollars)	Dec. 31, 2019	Dec. 31, 2018
Assets		
Cash.	$ 3,000	$ 2,900
Accounts receivable (net).	28,000	28,800
Inventory.	64,000	44,000
Total current assets.	95,000	75,700
Plant assets (net) .	76,000	67,300
Total assets	$171,000	$143,000
Liabilities and Stockholders' Equity		
Current liabilities.	$ 45,200	$ 39,750
10% bonds payable	20,000	14,000
Total liabilities .	65,200	53,750
Common stock, $10 par value	40,000	30,000
Retained earnings	65,800	59,250
Total stockholders' equity.	105,800	89,250
Total liabilities and stockholders' equity	$171,000	$143,000

Required

a. Using the given data, calculate the nine financial ratios below for 2019. Compare the ratio results for Knox Instruments, Inc., with the following industry averages and comment on its operations.

Median Ratios for the Industry

1. Current ratio	2.7
2. Quick ratio	1.6
3. Average collection period	73 days
4. Inventory turnover	2.3
5. Operating-cash-flow-to-current-liabilities ratio	0.22
6. Debt-to-equity ratio	0.50
7. Return on assets	4.9 percent
8. Return on common stockholders' equity	10.2 percent
9. Return on sales	4.1 percent

b. Calculate the dividends paid per share of common stock. (Use the average number of shares outstanding during the year.) What was the dividend payout ratio?

c. If the 2019 year-end market price per share of Knox's common stock is $25, what is the company's (1) price-earnings ratio and (2) dividend yield?

Solution

a.

1. Current ratio = $95,000/$45,200 = 2.10
2. Quick ratio = $31,000/$45,200 = 0.69
3. Average collection period:
   Accounts receivable turnover = $200,000/($28,800 + $28,000)/2 = 7.04
   Average collection period = 365/7.04 = 51.8 days
4. Inventory turnover = $98,000/($44,000 + $64,000)/2 = 1.81
5. Operating-cash-flow-to-current-liabilities ratio = $7,800/($39,750 + $45,200)/2 = 0.18
6. Debt-to-equity ratio = $65,200/$105,800 = 0.62
7. Return on assets = $10,750/($143,000 + $171,000)/2 = 6.8 percent
8. Return on common stockholders' equity = $10,750/($89,250 + $105,800)/2 = 11.0 percent
9. Return on sales = $10,750/$200,000 = 5.4 percent

Although the firm's current ratio of 2.10 is below the industry median, it is still acceptable; however, the quick ratio of 0.69 is well below the industry median. This indicates that Knox's inventory (which is omitted from this calculation) is excessive. This is also borne out by the firm's inventory turnover of 1.81 times, which compares with the industry median of 2.3 times. The firm's average collection period of 51.8 days is significantly better than the industry median of 73 days, while the operating-cash-flow-to-current-liabilities ratio is close to the industry median. Knox's debt-to-equity ratio of 0.62 indicates that the firm has proportionately more debt in its capital structure than the median industry firm, which has a debt-to-equity ratio of 0.50. Knox's operations appear efficient as its return on assets, return on common stockholders' equity, and return on sales all exceed the industry medians.

b. Average number of shares outstanding = (4,000,000 + 3,000,000)/2 = 3,500,000 shares.
   $4,200,000 dividends/3,500,000 shares = $1.20 dividend per share.
   Dividend payout ratio = $1.20/$3.07 = 39.1 percent.

c. Price-earnings ratio = $25/$3.07 = 8.1.
   Dividend yield = $1.20/$25 = 4.8 percent.

APPENDIX 13A: Financial Statement Disclosures

Disclosures related to a company's financial statements fall into one of three categories: (1) parenthetical disclosures on the face of the financial statements, (2) notes to the financial statements, and (3) supplementary information. Most disclosures amplify or explain aggregated information contained in the financial statements. Some disclosures, however, provide additional information.

Parenthetical Disclosures

LO6 Describe financial statement disclosures.

Parenthetical disclosures are placed next to an account title or other descriptive label in the financial statements. Their purpose is to provide additional detail regarding the item or account.

An example of parenthetical disclosures indicating the amount of the allowance for doubtful accounts follows:

	2019	2018
Accounts receivable, less allowances for doubtful accounts (2019—$7,545; 2018—$7,098)	$351,538	$300,181

Instead of using a parenthetical disclosure, companies may choose to present the additional detail in the notes to the financial statements.

Notes to the Financial Statements

Although much information is gathered, summarized, and reported in a company's financial statements, the financial statements alone are limited in their ability to convey a complete picture of a company's financial status. *Notes* are added to the financial statements to help fill in these gaps. In fact, over time, accountants have given so much attention to the financial statement notes that the notes now consume more page space in the annual report than the financial statements themselves. Notes may cover a wide variety of topics. Typically, they deal with significant accounting policies, explanations of complex or special transactions, details of reported amounts, commitments, contingencies, business segments, quarterly data, and subsequent material events.

Significant Accounting Policies

GAAP contains a number of instances for which alternative accounting procedures are equally acceptable. For example, there are several generally accepted depreciation and inventory valuation methods. The particular accounting policies selected by a company affect the financial data presented. Knowledge of a firm's specific accounting principles and methods of applying these principles helps users more fully understand a company's financial statements. Accordingly, these principles and methods are disclosed in a **summary of significant accounting policies**, which is typically the first note to the financial statements.

For example, the annual report of the **Columbia Sportswear Company** contains the following description of its inventory policy:

> Inventories are carried at the lower of cost or market. Cost is determined using the first-in, first-out method. The Company periodically reviews its inventories for excess, close-out or slow moving items and makes provisions as necessary to properly reflect inventory value.

Explanations of Complex or Special Transactions

The complexity of certain transactions means that not all important aspects are likely to be reflected in the accounts. Financial statement notes, therefore, report additional relevant details about such transactions. Typical examples include notes discussing the financial aspects of pension plans, profit-sharing plans, acquisitions of other companies, borrowing agreements, stock option and other incentive plans, and income taxes.

Transactions with related parties are special transactions requiring disclosure in the financial statement notes. Related party transactions include transactions between a firm and its (1) principal owners, (2) members of management, (3) subsidiary companies, or (4) affiliate companies.

Details of Reported Amounts

Financial statements often summarize several groups of accounts into a single aggregate dollar amount. For example, a balance sheet may show one asset account labeled *Property, Plant, and Equipment,* or it may list *Long-Term Debt* as a single amount among the liabilities. Notes report more detail, presenting schedules that list the types and amounts of property, plant, and equipment and long-term debt. Other items that may be summarized in the financial statements and detailed in the notes include inventories, other current assets, notes payable, accrued liabilities, stockholders' equity, and a company's income tax expense.

The notes to Columbia Sportswear Company's 2017 annual report contain several examples of financial statement items that are detailed, including accounts receivable (**Note 5**), property, plant, and equipment (**Note 6**), short-term borrowing and credit lines (**Note 8**), accrued liabilities (**Note 9**), other long-term liabilities (**Note 11**), and income taxes (**Note 10**).

Commitments

A firm may have contractual arrangements existing as of a balance sheet date in which both parties to the contract still have acts yet to be completed. If performance under these **commitments** will have a significant financial impact on a firm, the existence and nature of the commitments should be disclosed in the notes to the financial statements. Examples of commitments reported in the notes include contracts to purchase materials or equipment, contracts to construct facilities, salary commitments to executives, commitments to retire or redeem stock, and commitments to deliver goods.

Columbia Sportswear Company reports the following commitments in its annual report:

> During its normal course of business, the Company has made certain indemnities, commitments and guarantees under which it may be required to make payments in relation to certain transactions. These include (i) intellectual property indemnities to the Company's customers and licensees in connection with the use, sale and/or license of Company products, (ii) indemnities to various lessors in connection with facility leases for certain claims arising from such facility or lease, (iii) indemnities to customers, vendors and service providers pertaining to claims based on the negligence or willful misconduct of the Company, (iv) executive severance arrangements and (v) indemnities involving the accuracy of representations and warranties in certain contracts. The duration of these indemnities, commitments and guarantees varies, and in certain cases, may be indefinite. The majority of these indemnities, commitments and guarantees do not provide for any limitation of the maximum potential for future payments the Company could be obligated to make. The Company has not recorded any liability for these indemnities, commitments and guarantees in the accompanying Consolidated Balance Sheets.

Contingencies

Contingent liabilities were discussed in Chapter 10. As noted there, if the future event that would turn a contingency into an obligation is not likely to occur, or if the liability cannot be reasonably estimated, the **contingency** is disclosed in a note to the financial statements. Typical contingencies disclosed in the notes include pending lawsuits, environmental cleanup costs, possible income tax assessments, credit guarantees, and discounted notes receivable.

Under Armour, Inc. reports the following regarding contingencies in its annual report:

> The company is, from time to time, involved in routine legal matters incidental to its business. The company believes that the ultimate resolution of any such current proceedings and claims will not have a material adverse effect on its consolidated financial position, results of operations or cash flows.

Segments

Many firms diversify their business activities and operate in several different industries. A firm's financial statements often combine information from all of a company's operations into aggregate amounts. This complicates the financial statement user's ability to analyze the statements because the interpretation of financial data is influenced by the industry in which a firm operates. Different industries face different types of risk and have different rates of profitability. In making investment and lending decisions, financial statement users evaluate risk and required rates of return. Having financial data available by industry segment is helpful to such evaluations.

The FASB recognizes the usefulness of industry data to investors and lenders. Public companies with significant operations in more than one industry must report certain financial information by industry **segment**. Typically, these disclosures are in the financial statement notes. The major disclosures by industry segment are sales revenue, operating profit or loss, identifiable assets (the assets used by the segment), capital expenditures, and depreciation.

Other types of segment data may also be disclosed. Business operations in different parts of the world are subject to different risks and opportunities for growth. Thus, public companies with significant operations in foreign countries must report selected financial data by foreign geographic area. The required data disclosures include sales revenue, operating profit or loss (or other profitability measure), and identifiable assets. Also, if a firm has export sales or sales revenue to a single customer that are ten percent or more of total sales revenue, the amount of such sales revenue must be separately disclosed.

Note 18 to **Columbia Sportswear's** financial statements in its annual report illustrates segment disclosures by foreign versus domestic segments.

Quarterly Data

Interim financial reports cover periods shorter than one year. Companies that issue interim reports generally do so quarterly. These reports provide financial statement users with timely information on a firm's progress and are useful in predicting a company's annual financial results. The SEC requires that certain companies disclose selected quarterly financial data in their annual reports to stockholders. Included among the notes, the data reported for each quarter include sales revenue, gross profit, net income, and earnings per share. **Quarterly data** permit financial statement users to analyze such things as the seasonal nature of operations, the impact of diversification on quarterly activity, and whether the firm's activities lead or lag general economic trends.

The Columbia Sportswear Company provides quarterly financial information as supplemental data in its annual report.

Subsequent Events

If a company issues a large amount of securities or suffers a casualty loss after the balance sheet date, this information should be reported in a note, even though the situation arose subsequent to the balance sheet date. Firms are responsible for disclosing any significant events that occur between the balance sheet date and the date the financial statements are issued. This guideline recognizes that it takes several weeks for financial statements to be prepared and audited before they are issued. Events occurring during this period may have a material effect on a firm's operations and should be disclosed. Other examples of **subsequent events** requiring disclosure are sales of assets, significant changes in long-term debt, and acquisitions of other companies.

Supplementary Information

Supplementing the financial statements are several additional disclosures—management's discussion and analysis of the financial statements and selected financial data covering a five- to ten-year period along with possible other supplementary disclosures that are either required of certain companies by the SEC or recommended (but not required) by the FASB.

Management Discussion and Analysis

A.K.A. The management discussion and analysis are also referred to simply as the *MD&A*.

Management may increase the usefulness of financial statements by sharing some of their knowledge about a company's financial condition and operations. This is the purpose of the disclosure devoted to the management discussion and analysis. In this supplement to the financial statements, management identifies and comments on events and trends influencing a company's liquidity, operating results, and financial resources. Management's position within a company not only provides it with insights unavailable to outsiders, but also may introduce certain biases into the analysis. Nonetheless, management's comments, interpretations, and explanations should contribute to a better understanding of a company's financial statements.

Comparative Selected Financial Data

The analysis of a company's financial performance is enhanced when financial data for several years are available. By analyzing trends over time, it is possible for a financial statement user to learn much more about a company than would be possible by analyzing only a single year of data. Year-to-year changes may give clues as to a firm's future growth or may highlight areas for concern. Corporate annual reports to stockholders present complete financial statements in comparative form, showing the current year and one or two preceding years. Beyond this, however, the financial statements are supplemented by a summary of selected key financial statistics for a five- or ten-year period. The financial data presented in this historical summary usually include sales revenue, net income, dividends, earnings per share, working capital, and total assets.

SUMMARY OF LEARNING OBJECTIVES

LO1 **Identify persistent earnings and discuss the content and format of the income statement. (p. 624)**

- Persistent earnings are earnings that are likely to recur, while transitory earnings are unlikely to recur.
- The continuing income of a business may be reported in a single-step format or in a multiple-step format.
- Gains and losses from discontinued operations are reported in a special income statement section following income from continuing operations.
- The effect of most changes in accounting principle requires restatement of prior financial statements as if the new method had been applied all along.
- Companies are required to report other comprehensive income in addition to regular income in their financial statements.

Identify the sources of financial information used by investment professionals and explain horizontal financial statements analysis. (p. 628)   **LO2**

- Data sources for investment professionals include published financial statements, filings with the U.S. Securities and Exchange Commission, and statistics available from financial data services.
- A common form of horizontal analysis involves analyzing dollar and percentage changes in comparative financial statements for two or more years.
- Analyzing trend percentages of key figures, such as sales revenue, net income, and total assets for a number of years, related to a base year, is often useful.

Explain vertical financial statement analysis. (p. 633)   **LO3**

- Vertical analysis deals with the relationship of financial statement data for a single year.
- Common-size statements express financial statement items as a percentage of another key item, such as expressing income statement items as a percentage of sales revenue and balance sheet items as a percentage of total assets.

Define and discuss financial ratios for analyzing a firm. (p. 634)   **LO4**

- Ratios for analyzing firm profitability include the gross profit percentage, the return on sales, asset turnover, the return on assets, and the return on common stockholders' equity.
- Ratios for analyzing short-term firm liquidity include the current ratio, quick ratio, operating-cash-flow-to-current-liabilities ratio, accounts receivable turnover, average collection period, inventory turnover, and days' sales in inventory.
- Ratios for analyzing long-term firm solvency include the debt-to-equity ratio, the times-interest-earned ratio, and the operating-cash-flow-to-capital-expenditures ratio.
- Ratios of particular interest to common stockholders include a company's earnings per share, the price-earnings ratio, dividend yield, and the dividend payout ratio.

Discuss the limitations of financial statement analysis. (p. 649)   **LO5**

- When analyzing financial statements, financial statement users must be aware of a firm's accounting methods, the effects of inflation, and the difficulty of currently identifying a firm's industry classification.

Appendix 13A: Describe financial statement disclosures. (p. 651)   **LO6**

- Parenthetical disclosures on the face of the financial statements provide additional detail regarding the item or account.
- Notes to the financial statements provide information on significant accounting policies, explanations of complex or special transactions, details of reported amounts, commitments, contingencies, segments, quarterly data, and subsequent events.
- Supplemental information includes the management discussion and analysis, and comparable selected financial information.

SUMMARY OF FINANCIAL STATEMENT RATIOS

Analyzing Firm Profitability

$$\text{Gross profit percentage} = \frac{\text{Gross profit on sales}}{\text{Net sales}}$$

$$\text{Return on sales} = \frac{\text{Net income}}{\text{Net sales}}$$

$$\text{Asset turnover} = \frac{\text{Net sales}}{\text{Average total assets}}$$

$$\text{Return on assets} = \frac{\text{Net income}}{\text{Average total assets}}$$

$$\text{Return on common stockholders' equity} = \frac{(\text{Net income} - \text{Preferred stock dividends})}{\text{Average common stockholders' equity}}$$

Analyzing Short-Term Firm Liquidity

$$\text{Current ratio} = \frac{\text{Current assets}}{\text{Current liabilities}}$$

$$\text{Quick ratio} = \frac{(\text{Cash and cash equivalents} + \text{Short-term investments} + \text{Accounts receivable})}{\text{Current liabilities}}$$

$$\text{Operating-cash-flow-to-current-liabilities ratio} = \frac{\text{Cash flow from operating activities}}{\text{Average current liabilities}}$$

$$\text{Accounts receivable turnover} = \frac{\text{Net sales}}{\text{Average accounts receivable (net)}}$$

$$\text{Average collection period} = \frac{365}{\text{Accounts receivable turnover (net)}}$$

$$\text{Inventory turnover} = \frac{\text{Cost of goods sold}}{\text{Average inventory}}$$

$$\text{Days' sales in inventory} = \frac{365}{\text{Inventory turnover}}$$

Analyzing Long-Term Firm Solvency

$$\text{Debt-to-equity ratio} = \frac{\text{Total liabilities}}{\text{Total stockholders' equity}}$$

$$\text{Times-interest-earned ratio} = \frac{\text{Income before interest expense and income taxes}}{\text{Interest expense}}$$

$$\text{Operating-cash-flow-to-capital-expenditures ratio} = \frac{\text{Cash flow from operating activities}}{\text{Annual net capital expenditures}}$$

Financial Ratios for Common Stockholders

$$\text{Earnings per share} = \frac{(\text{Net income} - \text{Preferred stock dividends})}{\text{Weighted average common shares outstanding}}$$

$$\text{Price-earnings ratio} = \frac{\text{Market price per share}}{\text{Earnings per share}}$$

$$\text{Dividend yield} = \frac{\text{Annual dividend per share}}{\text{Market price per share}}$$

$$\text{Dividend payout ratio} = \frac{\text{Annual dividend per share}}{\text{Earnings per share}}$$

SUMMARY	Concept ⟶	Method ⟶	Assessment
TAKEAWAY 13.1	How does a company's current performance compare with the prior year?	Income statement and balance sheet for current and prior year. The income statement and balance sheet should be compared using the prior year as the base. Percentage changes in financial statement amounts can be computed as the change between years divided by the base year amount.	Significant changes should be analyzed to determine the reason for any change.

continued

Concept →	Method →	Assessment	SUMMARY
How do the relationships within a company's income statement and balance sheet compare to those of prior years?	Income statement and balance sheet for current and prior year. Each income statement item should be presented as a percentage of sales revenue and each balance sheet item should be presented as a percentage of total assets. Financial statements in this form are called common-size statements.	The percentages should be analyzed for differences between years and significant changes should be analyzed to determine the reason for any change.	TAKEAWAY 13.2
How much profit is a company generating relative to the amount of assets invested in the company?	Income statement and balance sheet. Calculate the return on assets by dividing net income by the average total assets for the year.	The higher the return on assets, the better a company is doing with respect to generating profits utilizing the assets under its control.	TAKEAWAY 13.3
How financially capable is a company to pay its current liabilities as they come due?	Income statement, balance sheet, and statement of cash flows. Calculate the current ratio, the quick ratio, and the operating-cash-flow-to-current-liabilities ratio.	The higher the ratios, the higher the probability that a company will have the ability to pay its current liabilities as they come due.	TAKEAWAY 13.4
How solvent is a company?	Income statement, balance sheet, and statement of cash flows. Calculate the debt-to-equity ratio, the times-interest-earned ratio, and the operating-cash-flow-to-capital-expenditures ratio.	The higher the times-interest-earned and the operating-cash-flow-to-capital-expenditures ratios, and the lower the debt-to-equity ratio, the greater is a company's solvency.	TAKEAWAY 13.5
How much dividends are common stockholders likely to receive?	Earnings per share, dividends per share, and market price of common stock. Calculate the dividend yield and dividend payout ratio.	The higher the dividend yield and the dividend payout ratio, the greater the company's dividend distribution policy.	TAKEAWAY 13.6

KEY TERMS

Accounts receivable turnover (p. 641)

Asset turnover ratio (p. 637)

Average collection period (days' sales outstanding, or DSO) (p. 642)

Change in accounting principle (p. 626)

Commitments (p. 652)

Common-size financial statement (p. 633)

Comparative financial statement analysis (p. 629)

Comprehensive income (p. 627)

Contingency (p. 653)

Current ratio (p. 639)

Days' sales in inventory (p. 643)

Debt-to-equity ratio (p. 644)

Discontinued operations (p. 626)

Dividend payout ratio (p. 648)

Dividend yield (p. 648)

Earnings per share (EPS) (p. 625, 647)

Gross profit (Gross margin) (p. 636)

Gross profit on sales (p. 636)

Gross profit percentage (p. 636)

Horizontal analysis (p. 629)

Inventory turnover (p. 642)

MD&A (p. 654)

Multiple-step income statement (p. 624)

Operating-cash-flow-to-capital-expenditures ratio (p. 645)

Operating-cash-flow-to-current-liabilities ratio (p. 641)

Operating cycle (p. 643)

Persistent earnings (p. 624)

Price-earnings ratio (P/E multiple) (p. 647)

Quarterly data (p. 654)

Quick ratio (acid-test ratio) (p. 640)

Return on assets (p. 637)

Return on common stockholders' equity (p. 638)

Return on sales profit margin (p. 636)

Segment (p. 653)

Single-step income statement (p. 624)

Subsequent events (p. 654)

Summary of significant accounting policies (p. 652)

Times-interest-earned ratio (interest coverage ratio) (p. 645)

Transitory earnings (p. 624)

Trend percentages (p. 632)

Unusual items (p. 624)

Vertical analysis (p. 629)

Working capital (p. 639)

Assignments with the ⓂⒷⒸ logo in the margin are available in $\overset{my}{\text{BusinessCourse}}$.
See the Preface of the book for details.

SELF-STUDY QUESTIONS

(Answers to the Self-Study Questions are at the end of this chapter.)

LO1 1. Assume that an income statement contains each of the three sections listed below. Which will be the last section presented in the income statement?
 a. Gross profit
 b. Income from continuing operations
 c. Discontinued operations

LO3 2. When constructing a common-sized income statement, all amounts are expressed as a percentage of:
 a. net income. *c.* net sales.
 b. gross profit. *d.* income from operations.

Questions 3–9 of the Self-Study Questions are based on the following data:

HYDRO COMPANY Balance Sheet December 31, 2018			
Cash..............................	$ 40,000	Current liabilities.........................	$ 80,000
Accounts receivable (net)............	80,000	10% bonds payable	120,000
Inventory.........................	130,000	Common stock	200,000
Plant and equipment (net)	250,000	Retained earnings	100,000
Total assets	$500,000	Total liabilities and stockholders' equity	$500,000

Sales revenues for 2018 were $800,000, gross profit was $320,000, and net income was $36,000. The income tax rate was 40 percent. One year ago, accounts receivable (net) were $76,000, inventory was $110,000, total assets were $460,000, and stockholders' equity was $260,000. The bonds payable were outstanding all year and the 2018 interest expense was $12,000.

LO4 3. The current ratio of Hydro Company at December 31, 2018, calculated using the above data, was 3.13 and the company's working capital was $170,000. Which of the following would happen if the firm paid off $20,000 of its current liabilities on January 1, 2019?
 a. Both the current ratio and working capital would decrease.
 b. Both the current ratio and working capital would increase.
 c. The current ratio would increase, but working capital would remain the same.
 d. The current ratio would increase, but working capital would decrease.

LO4 4. What was the firm's inventory turnover for 2018?
 a. 6.67 *c.* 6
 b. 4 *d.* 3.69

LO4 5. What was the firm's return on common stockholders' equity for 2018?
 a. 25.7 percent *c.* 17.1 percent
 b. 12.9 percent *d.* 21.4 percent

LO4 6. What was the firm's average collection period for 2018?
 a. 36.5 days *c.* 35.6 days
 b. 37.4 days *d.* 18.3 days

LO4 7. What was the firm's times-interest-earned ratio for 2018?
 a. 4 *c.* 5
 b. 3 *d.* 6

LO4 8. What was the firm's return on sales for 2018?
 a. 4.0 percent *c.* 5.0 percent
 b. 4.5 percent *d.* 5.5 percent

LO4 9. What was the firm's return on assets for 2018?
 a. 6.0 percent *c.* 7.5 percent
 b. 7.0 percent *d.* 8.0 percent

10. **When performing trend analysis, each line item is expressed as a percentage of:**   **LO2**
    - *a.* net income.
    - *b.* the base year amount.
    - *c.* the prior year amount.
    - *d.* total assets.

11. **Recognized limitations of financial statement analysis include each of the following except:**   **LO5**
    - *a.* companies in the same industry using different accounting methods.
    - *b.* inflation.
    - *c.* different levels of profitability between companies.
    - *d.* difficulty of classifying by industry conglomerates.

12. **Financial statement disclosures include each of the following except:**   **LO6 (Appendix 13A)**
    - *a.* notes to the financial statements.
    - *b.* parenthetical disclosures.
    - *c.* supplementary information.
    - *d.* promotional giveaways.

QUESTIONS

1. What is the difference between a single-step income statement and a multiple-step income statement?

2. Which of the following amounts would appear only in a multiple-step income statement?
   - *a.* Income from continuing operations.
   - *b.* Income from discontinued operations.
   - *c.* Gross profit on sales.
   - *d.* Net income.

3. What is a business segment? Why are gains and losses from a discontinued segment reported in a separate section of the income statement?

4. How do horizontal analysis and vertical analysis of financial statements differ?

5. "Financial statement users should focus attention on each item showing a large percentage change from one year to the next." Is this statement correct? Why?

6. What are trend percentages and how are they calculated? What pitfalls must financial statement users avoid when preparing trend percentages?

7. What are common-size financial statements and how are they used?

8. What item is the key figure (that is, 100 percent) in a common-size income statement? A common-size balance sheet?

9. During the past year, Lite Company had net income of $5 million, and Scanlon Company had net income of $8 million. Both companies manufacture electrical components for the construction industry. What additional information would you need to compare the profitability of the two companies?

10. Under what circumstances can the return on sales be used to assess the profitability of a company? Can this ratio be used to compare the profitability of companies from different industries? Explain.

11. What is the relationship between asset turnover, return on assets, and return on sales?

12. Blare Company had a return on sales of 6.5 percent and an asset turnover of 2.40. What is Blare's return on assets?

13. What does the return on common stockholders' equity measure?

14. How does the quick ratio differ from the current ratio?

15. For each of the following ratios, is a high ratio or low ratio considered, in general, a positive sign?
    - *a.* Current ratio
    - *b.* Quick ratio
    - *c.* Operating-cash-flow-to-current-liabilities ratio
    - *d.* Accounts receivable turnover
    - *e.* Average collection period
    - *f.* Inventory turnover
    - *g.* Days' sales in inventory

16. What is the significance of the debt-to-equity ratio and how is it computed?

17. What does the times-interest-earned ratio indicate and how is it calculated?

18. What does the operating-cash-flow-to-capital-expenditures ratio measure?

19. Clair, Inc., earned $4.50 per share of common stock in the current year and paid dividends of $2.34 per share. The most recent market price per share of the common stock is $46.80. What is the company's (a) price-earnings ratio, (b) dividend yield, and (c) dividend payout ratio?

20. What are two inherent limitations of financial statement data?

SHORT EXERCISES

Use the following financial data for Brenner Instruments to answer Short Exercises 13-1 through 13-10:

2019 (Thousands of Dollars, except Earnings per Share)	
Sales revenue.	$210,000
Cost of goods sold	125,000
Net income	8,300
Dividends	2,600
Earnings per share	4.15

BRENNER INSTRUMENTS, INC. Balance Sheets		
(Thousands of Dollars)	Dec. 31, 2019	Dec. 31, 2018
Assets		
Cash	$ 18,300	$ 18,000
Accounts receivable (net)	46,000	41,000
Inventory	39,500	43,700
Total current assets	103,800	102,700
Plant assets (net)	52,600	50,500
Other assets	15,600	13,800
Total assets	$172,000	$167,000
Liabilities and Stockholders' Equity		
Notes payable—banks	$ 6,000	$ 6,000
Accounts payable	22,500	18,700
Accrued liabilities	16,500	21,000
Total current liabilities	45,000	45,700
9% bonds payable	40,000	40,000
Total liabilities	85,000	85,700
Common stock, $25 par value (2,000,000 shares)	50,000	50,000
Retained earnings	37,000	31,300
Total stockholders' equity	87,000	81,300
Total liabilities and stockholders' equity	$172,000	$167,000

Industry Average Ratios for Competitors	
Quick ratio	1.3
Current ratio	2.4
Accounts receivable turnover	5.9 times
Inventory turnover	3.5 times
Debt-to-equity ratio	0.73
Gross profit percentage	42.8 percent
Return on sales	4.5 percent
Return on assets	7.6 percent

LO4   **SE13-1.**   **Quick Ratio** Calculate the company's quick ratio for 2019 and compare the result to the industry average.

LO4   **SE13-2.**   **Current Ratio** Calculate the company's current ratio for 2019 and compare the result to the industry average.

LO4   **SE13-3.**   **Accounts Receivable Turnover** Calculate the company's accounts receivable turnover for 2019 and compare the result to the industry average.

LO4   **SE13-4.**   **Inventory Turnover** Calculate the company's inventory turnover for 2019 and compare the result to the industry average.

LO4   **SE13-5.**   **Debit-to-Equity Ratio** Calculate the company's 2019 debt-to-equity ratio and compare the result to the industry average.

SE13-6. Gross Profit Percentage Calculate the company's 2019 gross profit percentage and compare the result to the industry average.   **LO4**

SE13-7. Return on Sales Calculate the company's return on sales for 2019 and compare the result to the industry average.   **LO4**

SE13-8. Return on Assets Calculate the company's return on assets for 2019 and compare the result to the industry average.   **LO4**

SE13-9. Dividends per Share Calculate the company's dividend paid per share of common stock. What was the dividend payout ratio?   **LO4**

SE13-10. Earnings per Share If the company's most recent price per share of common stock is $62.25, what is the company's price-earnings ratio and dividend yield?   **LO4**

SE13-11. Persistent Earnings Identify each of the following items as either (P) persistent, or (T) transitory.   **LO1**

    a. Sale of merchandise.
    b. Settlement of a lawsuit.
    c. Interest income.
    d. Payment to vendors.
    e. Loss from expropriations of property by a foreign government.

SE13-12. Horizontal Analysis Total assets were $1,000,000 in 2019, $900,000 in 2018, and $950,000 in 2017. What was the percentage change from 2017 to 2018 and from 2018 to 2019? Was the change an increase or a decrease?   **LO2**

SE13-13. Common-Size Income Statement A partial common-size income statement for Jag Company for three years is shown below.   **LO3**

Item	2019	2018	2017
Net sales.	100.0	100.0	100.0
Cost of goods sold	60.5	63.0	62.5
Other expenses	21.0	19.0	20.5

Did Jag's net income as a percentage of net sales increase, remain the same, or decrease over the three-year period?

SE13-14. Financial Statement Analysis Limitations Which of the following is not considered a limitation of financial statement analysis?   **LO5**

    a. Firms may use different accounting methods.
    b. Firms may be audited by different auditing firms.
    c. Inflation may distort trend analysis.
    d. It may be difficult to classify large conglomerate firms by industry.

SE13-15. Financial Statement Disclosures Which of the following is not a common form of financial statement disclosure?   **LO6 (Appendix 13A)**

    a. Notes to financial statements.
    b. Supplemental information.
    c. Parenthetical disclosure.
    d. Bullet points.

EXERCISES—SET A

E13-1A. Income Statement Sections During the current year, David Corporation sold a segment of its business at a gain of $210,000. Until it was sold, the segment had a current period operating loss of $75,000. The company had $700,000 income from continuing operations for the current year. Prepare the lower part of the income statement, beginning with the $700,000 income from continuing operations. Follow tax allocation procedures, assuming that all changes in income are subject to a 20 percent income tax rate. Disregard earnings per share disclosures.   **LO1**

LO4 **E13-2A.** **Earnings per Share** Myrtle Corporation began the year with a simple capital structure consisting of 480,000 shares of outstanding common stock. On April 1, 10,000 additional common shares were issued, and another 60,000 common shares were issued on August 1. The company had net income for the year of $589,375. Calculate the earnings per share of common stock.

LO2 **E13-3A.** **Comparative Income Statements** Consider the following income statement data from the Mono Company:

	2019	2018
Sales revenue.	$600,000	$450,000
Cost of goods sold	336,000	279,000
Selling expenses	105,000	99,000
Administrative expenses.	60,000	50,000
Income tax expense	4,000	3,000

 a. Prepare a comparative income statement, showing increases and decreases in dollars and in percentages.
 b. Comment briefly on the changes between the two years.

LO3 **E13-4A.** **Common-Size Income Statements** Refer to the income statement data given in Exercise E13-3A.

 a. Prepare common-size income statements for each year.
 b. Compare the common-size income statements and comment briefly.

LO4 **E13-5A.** **Ratios Analyzing Firm Profitability** The following information is available for Jay Company:

Annual Data	2019	2018
Net sales.	$9,000,000	$8,200,000
Gross profit on sales.	3,050,000	2,736,000
Net income	567,600	500,000

Year-End Data	Dec. 31, 2019	Dec. 31, 2018
Total assets	$6,500,000	$6,000,000
Stockholders' equity	5,000,000	3,200,000

Calculate the following ratios for 2019:

 a. Gross profit percentage
 b. Return on sales
 c. Asset turnover
 d. Return on assets
 e. Return on common stockholders' equity (Jay Company has no preferred stock.)

LO4 **E13-6A.** **Working Capital and Short-Term Liquidity Ratios** Ritter Company has a current ratio of 3.00 on December 31. On that date the company's current assets are as follows:

Cash.	$ 32,000
Short-term investments	49,300
Accounts receivable (net).	170,000
Inventory.	200,000
Prepaid expenses.	11,600
Current assets	$462,900

Ritter Company's current liabilities at the beginning of the year were $150,000 and during the year its operating activities provided a cash flow of $60,000.

 a. What are the firm's current liabilities on December 31?
 b. What is the firm's working capital on December 31?
 c. What is the quick ratio on December 31?
 d. What is Bell's operating-cash-flow-to-current-liabilities ratio?

E13-7A. **Accounts Receivable and Inventory Ratios** Ritter Company, whose current assets at December   **LO4**
31 are shown in Exercise E13-6A, had net sales for the year of $850,000 and cost of goods sold of
$550,000. At the beginning of the year, Ritter's accounts receivable (net) were $160,000 and its
inventory was $175,000.

    a. What is the company's accounts receivable turnover for the year?

    b. What is the company's average collection period for the year?

    c. What is the company's inventory turnover for the year?

    d. What is the company's days' sales in inventory for the year?

E13-8A. **Ratios Analyzing Long-Term Firm Solvency** The following information is available for Banner   **LO4**
Company:

Annual Data	2019	2018
Interest expense.	$ 85,000	$ 82,000
Income tax expense	203,500	185,000
Net income	496,500	425,000
Capital expenditures.	320,000	380,000
Cash provided by operating activities.	450,000	390,000

Year-End Data	Dec. 31, 2019	Dec. 31, 2018
Total liabilities	$2,400,000	$1,900,000
Total stockholders' equity	4,200,000	3,800,000

Calculate the following:

    a. 2019 debt-to-equity ratio.

    b. 2019 times-interest-earned ratio.

    c. 2019 operating-cash-flow-to-capital-expenditures ratio.

E13-9A. **Financial Ratios for Common Stockholders** Morgan Corporation has only common stock out-   **LO4**
standing. The firm reported earnings per share of $6.00 for the year. During the year, Morgan paid
dividends of $2.10 per share. At year end the current market price of the stock was $72 per share.
Calculate the following:

    a. Price-earnings ratio

    b. Dividend yield

    c. Dividend payout ratio

E13-10A. **Financial Statement Limitations** You have been asked to perform financial statement analysis   **LO5**
on the Rush Company. The Rush Company is a large chain of retail outlets that sells a wide range
of household items. Last year the company introduced its own credit card and is pleased that profit
from this financing activity now accounts for over 20 percent of the company's total profit. As part
of your analysis you have chosen to compare the Rush Company to Johnson Stores, a much larger
chain of stores. Johnson Stores sells household items and groceries, but it does not have its own
credit card. Your analysis includes both trend analysis and vertical analysis. Identify some of the
limitations from the description above.

E13-11A. **Financial Statement Notes** The notes to financial statements present information on significant ac-   **LO6**
counting policies, complex or special transactions, details of reported amounts, commitments, con-   **(Appendix**
tingencies, segments, quarterly data, and subsequent events. Indicate which type of note disclosure   **13A)**
is illustrated by each of the following notes:

    a. The company has agreed to purchase seven EMB-120 aircraft and related spare parts. The ag-
gregate cost of these aircraft is approximately $52,000,150, subject to a cost escalation provi-
sion. The aircraft are scheduled to be delivered over the next two fiscal years.

    b. The company has deferred certain costs related to major accounting and information systems
enhancements that are anticipated to benefit future years. Upon completion, the related cost is
amortized over a period not exceeding five years.

    c. The company has guaranteed loans and leases of independent distributors approximating
$27,500,000 as of December 31 of the current year.

    d. An officer of the company is also a director of a major raw material supplier of the company. The
amount of raw material purchases from this supplier approximated $595,000 in the current year.

EXERCISES—SET B

LO1 **E13-1B.** **Income Statement Sections** During the current year, Ediza Corporation sold a segment of its business at a loss of $175,000. Until it was sold, the segment had a current period operating loss of $200,000. The company has $750,000 income from continuing operations for the current year. Prepare the lower part of the income statement, beginning with the $750,000 income from continuing operations. Follow tax allocation procedures, assuming that all changes in income are subject to a 20 percent income tax rate. Disregard earnings per share disclosures.

LO4 **E13-2B.** **Earnings per Share** Heart Corporation began the year with a simple capital structure consisting of 35,000 shares of common stock outstanding. On May 1, 5,000 additional common shares were issued, and another 20,000 common shares were issued on September 1. The company had a net income for the year of $468,000. Calculate the earnings per share of common stock.

LO2 **E13-3B.** **Comparative Balance Sheets** Consider the following balance sheet data for Davis Co., Inc., an electronics and major appliance retailer, at February 26, 2019 and February 27, 2018 (amounts in thousands):

	Feb. 26, 2019	Feb. 27, 2018
Cash and cash equivalents	$ 60,872	$ 7,138
Accounts receivables	52,944	37,968
Merchandise inventories	637,950	249,991
Other current assets	13,844	9,729
Current assets	765,610	304,826
Property and equipment (net)	172,724	126,442
Other assets	15,160	7,774
Total assets	$953,494	$439,042
Current liabilities	$402,028	$186,005
Long-term liabilities	239,022	70,854
Total liabilities	641,050	256,859
Common stock	3,087	1,149
Additional paid-in-capital	224,089	137,151
Retained earnings	85,268	43,883
Total stockholders' equity	312,444	182,183
Total liabilities and stockholders' equity	$953,494	$439,042

   a. Prepare a comparative balance sheet, showing increases in dollars and percentages.
   b. Comment briefly on the changes between the two years.

LO3 **E13-4B.** **Common-Size Balance Sheets** Refer to the balance sheet data given in Exercise E13-3B.

   a. Prepare common-size balance sheets for each year (use total assets as the base amount for computing percentages).
   b. Compare the common-size balance sheets and comment briefly.

LO4 **E13-5B.** **Ratios Analyzing Firm Profitability** The following information is available for Virginia Company:

Annual Data	2019	2018
Sales revenue	$6,600,000	$6,000,000
Cost of goods sold	4,006,400	3,800,000
Net income	325,000	264,000

Year-End Data	Dec. 31, 2019	Dec. 31, 2018
Total assets	$2,850,000	$2,500,000
Common stockholders' equity	1,900,000	1,700,000

Calculate the following ratios for 2019:

a.   Gross profit percentage

b.   Return on sales

c.   Asset turnover

d.   Return on assets

e.   Return on common stockholders' equity (Virginia Company declared and paid preferred stock dividends of $20,000 in 2019.)

E13-6B.   Working Capital and Short-Term Firm Liquidity Ratios   Purple Company has a current ratio of 2.2 on December 31. On that date its current assets are as follows: **LO4**

Cash and cash equivalents	$ 13,000
Short-term investments	90,000
Accounts receivable (net)	125,000
Inventory	178,500
Prepaid expenses	11,500
Current assets	$418,000

Purple Company's current liabilities at the beginning of the year were $195,000 and during the year its operating activities provided a cash flow of $35,000.

a.   What are the firm's current liabilities at December 31?

b.   What is the firm's working capital on December 31?

c.   What is the quick ratio on December 31?

d.   What is the firm's operating-cash-flow-to-current-liabilities ratio?

E13-7B.   Accounts Receivable and Inventory Ratios   Purple Company, whose current assets at December 31 are shown in Exercise E13-6B, had net sales for the year of $580,000 and cost of goods sold of $339,000. At the beginning of the year, accounts receivable (net) were $121,000 and inventory was $160,500.   **LO4**

a.   What is the company's accounts receivable turnover?

b.   What is the company's average collection period?

c.   What is the company's inventory turnover?

d.   What is the company's days' sales in inventory?

E13-8B.   Ratios Analyzing Long-Term Firm Solvency   The following information is available for Rae Company: **LO4**

Annual Data	2019	2018
Interest expense	$170,000	$166,000
Income tax expense	126,000	117,000
Net income	310,000	275,000
Capital expenditures	435,000	350,000
Cash provided by operating activities	247,000	220,000

Year-End Data	Dec. 31, 2019	Dec. 31, 2018
Total liabilities	$3,400,000	$2,900,000
Total stockholders' equity	2,200,000	2,000,000

Calculate the following:

a.   2019 debt-to-equity ratio

b.   2019 times-interest-earned ratio

c.   2019 operating-cash-flow-to-capital-expenditures ratio

LO4 **E13-9B.** **Financial Ratios for Common Stockholders** Jason Corporation has only common stock outstanding. The firm reported earnings per share of $4.00 for the year. During the year, Jason paid dividends of $0.85 per share. At year end, the current market price of the stock was $70.30 per share.

Calculate the following:

a. Price-earnings ratio
b. Dividend yield
c. Dividend payout ratio

LO5 **E13-10B.** **Financial Statement Limitations** You have been asked to perform financial statement analysis on the Ian Company. The Ian Company is a large manufacturer of construction machinery and vehicles. Last year the company closed down a segment of the business that produced mining equipment because it was not providing an adequate return on assets. This segment represented 15 percent of the company's total assets. As part of your analysis you have chosen to compare the Ian Company to Bertran, Inc., a much smaller manufacturer of equipment, although Bertran, Inc. also performs contract repairs for many other brands of equipment. Your analysis includes both trend analysis and vertical analysis. Identify some of the limitations from the description above.

LO6
(Appendix 13A)

E13-11B. **Financial Statement Notes** Notes to the financial statements present information on significant accounting policies, complex or special transactions, details of reported amounts, commitments, contingencies, segments, quarterly data, and subsequent events. Indicate the type of note disclosure that is illustrated by each of the following notes:

a. Sales by the Farm and Equipment segment to independent dealers are recorded at the time of shipment to those dealers. Sales through company-owned retail stores are recorded at the time of sale to retail customers.
b. Members of the board of directors, the advisory board, and employees are not charged the vendor's commission on property sold at auction for their benefit. (From the notes of an auctioneer company.)
c. Sales to an airline company accounted for approximately 48 percent of the company's net sales in the current year.
d. The company's product liability insurance coverage with respect to insured events occurring after January 1 of the current year is substantially less than the amount of that insurance available in the recent past. The company is now predominantly self-insured in this area. The reduction in insurance coverage reflects trends in the liability insurance field generally and is not unique to the company.

PROBLEMS—SET A

LO1 **P13-1A.** **Income Statement Format** The following information from Buchanan Company's current operations is available:

Administrative expenses.	$ 73,000
Cost of goods sold	470,000
Sales revenue.	772,000
Selling expenses	87,000
Interest expense.	10,000
Loss from operations of discontinued segment	60,000
Gain on disposal of discontinued segment.	40,000
Income taxes:	
Amount applicable to ordinary operations.	40,000
Reduction applicable to loss from operations of discontinued segment	14,000
Amount applicable to gain on disposal of discontinued segment	8,000

Required
a. Prepare a multiple-step income statement. (Disregard earnings per share.)
b. Prepare a single-step income statement. (Disregard earnings per share.)

P13-2A. **Earnings per Share** Stanford Corporation began the year with 150,000 shares of common stock out-standing. On March 1, an additional 10,000 shares of common stock were issued. On August 1, another 16,000 shares of common stock were issued. On November 1, 12,000 shares of common stock were acquired as Treasury Stock. Stanford Corporation's net income for the calendar year is $489,000.

LO4

Required
Calculate the company's earnings per share.

P13-3A. **Earnings per Share and Multiple-Step Income Statement** The following summarized data relate to Robert Corporation's current operations:

LO1, 4

Sales revenue.	$800,000
Cost of goods sold	460,000
Selling expenses	65,000
Administrative expenses.	72,000
Loss on sale of equipment	4,000
Income tax expense	42,000
Shares of common stock	
Outstanding at January 1	20,000 shares
Additional issued at May 1	7,000 shares
Additional issued at November 1	2,000 shares

Required
Prepare a multiple-step income statement for Robert Corporation for the year. Include earnings per share disclosure at the bottom of the income statement.

P13-4A. **Trend Percentages** Net sales, net income, and total asset figures for Janice Controls, Inc., for five consecutive years are given below (Janice manufactures pollution controls):

LO2, 4

	Annual Amounts (Thousands of Dollars)				
	Year 1	Year 2	Year 3	Year 4	Year 5
Net sales.	$72,000	$79,800	$85,275	$88,400	$94,700
Net income	3,200	3,650	4,000	4,250	4,790
Total assets	42,500	45,000	48,700	51,000	54,900

Required
a. Calculate trend percentages, using Year 1 as the base year.
b. Calculate the return on sales for each year. (Rates above 2.8 percent are considered good for manufacturers of pollution controls; rates above 6.5 percent are considered very good.)
c. Comment on the results of your analysis.

P13-5A. **Changes in Various Ratios** Presented below is selected information for Turner Company:

LO4

	2019	2018
Sales revenue.	$950,000	$850,000
Cost of goods sold	575,000	545,000
Interest expense.	20,000	20,000
Income tax expense	27,000	30,000
Net income	65,000	55,000
Cash flow from operating activities.	70,000	60,000
Capital expenditures.	45,000	45,000
Accounts receivable (net), December 31	126,000	120,000
Inventory, December 31	196,000	160,000
Stockholders' equity, December 31	450,000	400,000
Total assets, December 31.	750,000	675,000

Required
a. Calculate the following ratios for 2019. The 2018 results are given for comparative purposes.

		2018
1.	Gross profit percentage	35.9 percent
2.	Return on assets	8.3 percent
3.	Return on sales	6.5 percent
4.	Return on common stockholders' equity (no preferred stock was outstanding)	13.9 percent
5.	Accounts receivable turnover	8.00
6.	Average collection period	45.6 days
7.	Inventory turnover	3.61
8.	Times-interest-earned ratio	5.25
9.	Operating-cash-flow-to-capital-expenditures ratio	1.33

b. Comment on the changes between the two years.

LO2, 3, 4 **P13-6A.** **Ratios from Comparative and Common-Size Data** Consider the following financial statements for Benjamin Company.

During 2019, management obtained additional bond financing to enlarge its production facilities. The company faced higher production costs during the year for such things as fuel, materials, and freight. Because of temporary government price controls, a planned price increase on products was delayed several months.

As a holder of both common and preferred stock, you decide to analyze the financial statements:

BENJAMIN COMPANY Balance Sheets (Thousands of Dollars)	Dec. 31, 2019	Dec. 31, 2018
Assets		
Cash and cash equivalents	$ 21,000	$ 12,000
Accounts receivable (net)	55,000	43,000
Inventory	120,000	105,000
Prepaid expenses	20,000	14,000
Plant and other assets (net)	471,000	411,000
Total assets	$687,000	$585,000
Liabilities and Stockholders' Equity		
Current liabilities	$ 93,000	$ 82,000
10% bonds payable	225,000	160,000
9% Preferred stock, $50 par value	75,000	75,000
Common stock, $10 par value	200,000	200,000
Retained earnings	94,000	68,000
Total liabilities and stockholders' equity	$687,000	$585,000

BENJAMIN COMPANY Income Statements (Thousands of Dollars)	2019	2018
Sales revenue	$820,000	$680,000
Cost of goods sold	545,000	433,920
Gross profit on sales	275,000	246,080
Selling and administrative expenses	175,000	149,200
Income before interest expense and income taxes	100,000	96,880
Interest expense	23,000	16,000
Income before income taxes	77,000	80,880
Income tax expense	15,000	19,000
Net income	$ 62,000	$ 61,880
Other financial data (thousands of dollars)		
Cash provided by operating activities	$ 65,200	$ 60,500
Preferred stock dividends	6,750	6,750

Required

a. Calculate the following for each year: current ratio, quick ratio, operating-cash-flow-to-current-liabilities ratio (current liabilities were $77,000,000 at January 1, 2018), inventory turnover (inventory was $87,000,000 at January 1, 2018), debt-to-equity ratio, times-interest-earned ratio, return on assets (total assets were $490,000,000 at January 1, 2018), and return on common stockholders' equity (common stockholders' equity was $235,000,000 at January 1, 2018).

b. Calculate common-size percentages for each year's income statement.

c. Comment on the results of your analysis.

P13-7A. Constructing Statements from Ratio Data The following are the 2018 financial statements for   **LO4**
Omni Company, with almost all dollar amounts missing:

		OMNI COMPANY Balance Sheet December 31, 2018		
Cash..........................	$	?	Current liabilities...............	$	?
Accounts receivable (net).........		?	8% bonds payable		?
Inventory.....................		?	Common stock		?
Equipment (net)		?	Retained earnings		950,000
			Total liabilities and		
Total assets	$6,500,000		stockholders' equity	$6,500,000	

	OMNI COMPANY Income Statement For the Year Ended December 31, 2018	
Sales revenue.	$	?
Cost of goods sold		?
Gross profit		?
Selling and administrative expenses		?
Income before interest expense and income taxes		?
Interest expense.		80,000
Income before income taxes		?
Income tax expense (20%).		?
Net income		$580,000

The following information is available about Omni Company's financial statements:

1. Quick ratio, 0.95.
2. Inventory turnover (inventory at January 1 was $924,000), 5 times.
3. Return on sales, 8.0 percent.
4. Accounts receivable turnover (accounts receivable (net) at January 1 were $860,000), 8 times.
5. Gross profit percentage, 32 percent.
6. Return on common stockholders' equity (common stockholders' equity at January 1 was $3,300,000), 16 percent.
7. The interest expense relates to the bonds payable that were outstanding all year.

Required
Compute the missing amounts, and complete the financial statements of Omni Company. *Hint:* Complete the income statement first.

P13-8A. Ratios Compared with Industry Averages Because you own the common stock of Jacob Corpo-   **LO4**
ration, a paper manufacturer, you decide to analyze the firm's performance for the most recent year.
The following data are taken from the firm's latest annual report:

	Dec. 31, 2019	Dec. 31, 2018
Quick assets.	$ 700,000	$ 552,000
Inventory and prepaid expenses	372,000	312,000
Other assets.	4,788,000	4,200,000
Total assets	$5,860,000	$5,064,000
Current liabilities.	$ 724,000	$ 564,000
10% bonds payable	1,440,000	1,440,000
8% Preferred stock, $100 par value.	480,000	480,000
Common stock, $10 par value	2,700,000	2,160,000
Retained earnings	516,000	420,000
Total liabilities and stockholders' equity	$5,860,000	$5,064,000

For 2019, net sales amount to $12,500,000, net income is $550,000, and preferred stock dividends paid are $50,000.

Required

a. Calculate the following ratios for 2019:
1. Return on sales
2. Return on assets
3. Return on common stockholders' equity
4. Quick ratio
5. Current ratio
6. Debt-to-equity ratio

b. Trade association statistics and information provided by credit agencies reveal the following data on industry norms:

	Median	Upper Quartile
Return on sales	4.2 percent	8.6 percent
Return on assets	6.5 percent	11.2 percent
Return on common stockholders' equity	10.6 percent	17.3 percent
Quick ratio	1.0	1.8
Current ratio	1.8	3.0
Debt-to-equity-ratio.	1.08	0.66

Compare Jacob Corporation's performance with industry performance.

LO4 **P13-9A.** **Ratios Compared with Industry Averages** Adams Plastics, Inc., manufactures various plastic and synthetic products. Financial statement data for the firm follow:

	2019 (Thousands of Dollars, except Earnings per Share)
Sales revenue.	$825,000
Cost of goods sold	550,000
Net income	50,500
Dividends	17,500
Earnings per share	4.04

ADAMS PLASTICS, INC. Balance Sheets (Thousands of Dollars)	Dec. 31, 2019	Dec. 31, 2018
Assets		
Cash..	$ 2,100	$ 2,700
Accounts receivable (net)........................	66,900	60,900
Inventory.......................................	148,000	140,000
Total current assets...........................	217,000	203,600
Plant assets (net)	215,000	194,000
Other assets....................................	13,900	4,000
Total assets	$445,900	$401,600
Liabilities and Stockholders' Equity		
Notes payable—banks............................	$ 31,400	$ 25,000
Accounts payable...............................	27,600	23,000
Accrued liabilities	25,100	24,800
Total current liabilities	84,100	72,800
10% bonds payable	150,000	150,000
Total liabilities	234,100	222,800
Common stock, $10 par value (12,500,000 shares).............	125,000	125,000
Retained earnings	86,800	53,800
Total stockholders' equity	211,800	178,800
Total liabilities and stockholders' equity	$445,900	$401,600

Required

a. Using the given data, calculate items 1 through 8 below for 2019. Compare the performance of Adams Plastics, Inc., with the following industry averages and comment on its operations.

		Median Ratios for Manufacturers of Plastic and Synthetic Products
1.	Quick ratio	1.2
2.	Current ratio	1.9
3.	Accounts receivable turnover......................	7.9 times
4.	Inventory turnover...............................	7.8 times
5.	Debt-to-equity ratio..............................	0.95
6.	Gross profit percentage	32.7 percent
7.	Return on sales	3.5 percent
8.	Return on assets	6.3 percent

b. Calculate the dividends paid per share of common stock. What was the dividend payout ratio?

c. If the most recent price per share of common stock is $51.00, what is the price-earnings ratio? The dividend yield?

P13-10A. **Financial Statement Notes: Quarterly Data** Quarterly data are presented below for Company A and Company B. One of these companies is Gibson Greetings, Inc., which manufactures and sells greeting cards. The other company is Hon Industries, Inc., which manufactures and sells office furniture. Both companies are on a calendar year basis.

LO2

	(Amounts in Thousands)				
	First Quarter	Second Quarter	Third Quarter	Fourth Quarter	Year
Company A					
Net sales.	$186,111	$177,537	$203,070	$213,608	$780,326
Gross profit	55,457	53,643	64,024	69,374	242,498
Company B					
Net sales.	$ 84,896	$ 83,796	$142,137	$235,336	$546,165
Gross profit	53,900	52,983	66,018	104,961	277,862

Required

a. Compute the percent of annual net sales generated each quarter by Company A. Round to the nearest percent.

b. Compute the percent of annual net sales generated each quarter by Company B. Round to the nearest percent.

c. Which company has the most seasonal business? Briefly explain.

d. Which company is Gibson Greetings, Inc.? Hon Industries, Inc.? Briefly explain.

e. Which company's interim quarterly data are probably most useful for predicting annual results? Briefly explain.

PROBLEMS—SET B

LO1 **P13-1B.** **Income Statement Format** The following information from Jefferson Company's operations is available:

Administrative expenses.	$ 145,000
Cost of goods sold	928,000
Sales revenue.	1,850,000
Selling expenses	174,000
Interest expense.	14,000
Loss from operations of discontinued segment	120,000
Gain on disposal of discontinued segment.	90,000
Income taxes	
Amount applicable to ordinary operations.	125,000
Reduction applicable to loss from operations of discontinued segment	22,000
Amount applicable to gain on disposal of discontinued segment	15,000

Required

a. Prepare a multiple-step income statement. (Disregard earnings per share amounts.)

b. Prepare a single-step income statement. (Disregard earnings per share amounts.)

LO4 **P13-2B.** **Earnings per Share** Lincoln Corporation began the year with 50,000 shares of common stock outstanding. On May 1, an additional 18,000 shares of common stock were issued. On July 1, 20,000 shares of common stock were acquired as treasury stock. On September 1, the 6,000 treasury shares of common stock were reissued. Lincoln Corporation's net income for the calendar year is $229,500.

Required

Compute earnings per share.

LO1, 4 **P13-3B.** **Earnings per Share and Multiple-Step Income Statement** The following summarized data are related to Kennedy Corporation's operations:

Sales revenue.	$2,216,000
Cost of goods sold	1,290,000
Selling expenses	180,000
Administrative expenses.	142,800
Loss from plant strike	95,000
Income tax expense	204,000
Shares of common stock	
Outstanding at January 1	65,000 shares
Additional issued at April 1	17,000 shares
Additional issued at August 1	3,000 shares

Required

Prepare a multiple-step income statement for Kennedy Corporation. Include earnings per share disclosure at the bottom of the income statement. Kennedy Corporation has no preferred stock.

P13-4B. **Trend Percentages** Sales of automotive products for **Ford Motor Company** and **General Motors Corporation** for a five-year period are:

LO2, 4

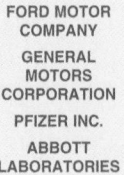

	Net Sales of Automotive Products (Millions of Dollars)				
	Year 1	Year 2	Year 3	Year 4	Year 5
Ford Motor Company	$82,879	$81,844	$72,051	$ 84,407	$ 91,568
General Motors Corporation.	99,106	97,312	94,828	103,005	108,027

Net sales for **Pfizer Inc.** and **Abbott Laboratories** for the same five years follow:

	Net Sales (Millions of Dollars)				
	Year 1	Year 2	Year 3	Year 4	Year 5
Pfizer Inc.	$5,672	$6,406	$6,950	$7,230	$7,478
Abbott Laboratories	5,380	6,159	6,877	7,852	8,408

FORD MOTOR
COMPANY

GENERAL
MOTORS
CORPORATION

PFIZER INC.

ABBOTT
LABORATORIES

Required

a. Calculate trend percentages for all four companies, using Year 1 as the base year.

b. Comment on the trend percentages of Ford Motor Company and General Motors Corporation.

c. Comment on the trend percentages of Pfizer Inc. and Abbott Laboratories.

P13-5B. **Changes in Various Ratios** Selected information follow for Bush Company:

LO4

	2019	2018
Sales revenue.	$700,000	$520,000
Cost of goods sold	407,700	310,000
Interest expense.	22,000	14,000
Income tax expense	6,500	5,100
Net income	30,000	20,300
Cash flow from operating activities.	29,500	26,500
Capital expenditures.	42,000	25,000
Accounts receivable (net), December 31	182,000	128,000
Inventory, December 31	225,000	180,000
Stockholders' equity, December 31	205,000	165,000
Total assets, December 31.	460,000	350,000

Required

a. Calculate the following ratios for 2019. The 2018 results are given for comparative purposes.

		2018
1.	Gross profit percentage	40.4 percent
2.	Return on assets	6.5 percent
3.	Return on sales	3.9 percent
4.	Return on common stockholders' equity (no preferred stock was outstanding)	14.2 percent
5.	Accounts receivable turnover	4.77
6.	Average collection period	76.5 days
7.	Inventory turnover	2.07
8.	Times-interest-earned ratio	2.81
9.	Operating-cash-flow-to-capital-expenditures ratio	1.06

b. Comment on the changes between the two years.

LO2, 3, 4 **P13-6B.** **Ratios from Comparative and Common-Size Data** Consider the following financial statements for Nixon Company.

During the year, management obtained additional bond financing to enlarge its production facilities. The plant addition produced a new high-margin product, which is supposed to improve the average rate of gross profit and return on sales.

As a potential investor, you decide to analyze the financial statements:

NIXON COMPANY Balance Sheets (Thousands of Dollars)	Dec. 31, 2019	Dec. 31, 2018
Assets		
Cash	$ 25,000	$ 18,100
Accounts receivable (net)	39,000	21,400
Inventory	105,000	72,000
Prepaid expenses	1,500	4,000
Plant and other assets (net)	463,500	427,500
Total assets	$634,000	$543,000
Liabilities and Stockholders' Equity		
Current liabilities	$ 80,000	$ 48,000
9% bonds payable	187,500	150,000
8% preferred stock, $50 par value	60,000	60,000
Common stock, $10 par value	225,000	225,000
Retained earnings	81,500	60,000
Total liabilities and stockholders' equity	$634,000	$543,000

NIXON COMPANY Income Statements (Thousands of Dollars)	2019	2018
Sales revenue	$850,000	$697,500
Cost of goods sold	552,000	465,000
Gross profit on sales	298,000	232,500
Selling and administrative expenses	231,000	174,000
Income before interest expense and income taxes	67,000	58,500
Interest expense	17,000	13,500
Income before income taxes	50,000	45,000
Income tax expense	10,000	9,000
Net income	$ 40,000	$ 36,000
Other financial data (thousands of dollars):		
Cash provided by operating activities	$ 28,000	$ 24,000
Preferred stock dividends	5,000	4,800

Required

a. Calculate the following for each year: current ratio, quick ratio, operating-cash-flow-to-current-liabilities ratio (current liabilities were $40,000,000 at January 1, 2018), inventory turnover (inventory was $68,000,000 at January 1, 2018), debt-to-equity ratio, times-interest-earned ratio, return on assets (total assets were $490,000,000 at January 1, 2018), and return on common stockholders' equity (common stockholders' equity was $265,000,000 at January 1, 2018).

b. Calculate common-size percentage for each year's income statement.

c. Comment on the results of your analysis.

P13-7B. Constructing Statements from Ratio Data The following are the financial statements for Truman   **LO4**
Company, with almost all dollar amounts missing:

TRUMAN COMPANY Balance Sheet December 31			
Cash..........................	$?	Current liabilities.................	$?
Accounts receivable (net)...........	?	10% bonds payable	144,000
Inventory......................	?	Common stock	?
Equipment (net)	?	Retained earnings	50,000
		Total liabilities and	
Total assets	$576,000	stockholders' equity	$576,000

TRUMAN COMPANY Income Statement For the Year Ended December 31	
Sales revenue.	$?
Cost of goods sold	?
Gross profit on sales.	?
Selling and administrative expenses	?
Income before interest expense and income taxes	?
Interest expense.	?
Income before income taxes	?
Income tax expense (20%).	?
Net income	$70,200

The following information is available about Truman Company's financial statements:

1. Quick ratio, 2.5.
2. Current ratio, 3.0.
3. Return on sales, 8.0 percent.
4. Return on common stockholders' equity (common stockholders' equity at January 1 was $340,000), 20 percent.
5. Gross profit percentage, 40 percent.
6. Accounts receivable turnover (accounts receivable (net) at January 1 were $97,200), 12 times.
7. The interest expense relates to the bonds payable that were outstanding all year.

Required

Compute the missing amounts, and complete the financial statements of Truman Company. (*Hint:* Complete the income statement first.)

P13-8B. Ratios Compared with Industry Averages You are analyzing the performance of Jackson Corporation, a manufacturer of personal care products, for the most recent year. The following data are   **LO4**
taken from the firm's latest annual report:

	Dec. 31, 2019	Dec. 31, 2018
Quick assets.	$ 385,000	$ 350,000
Inventory and prepaid expenses	975,000	820,000
Other assets.	4,165,000	3,700,000
Total assets	$5,525,000	$4,870,000
Current liabilities.	$ 600,000	$ 500,000
10% bonds payable	1,300,000	1,300,000
7% preferred stock.	900,000	900,000
Common stock, $5 par value	1,925,000	1,800,000
Retained earnings	800,000	370,000
Total liabilities and stockholders' equity	$5,525,000	$4,870,000

In 2019, net sales amount to $8,800,000, net income is $700,000, and preferred stock dividends paid are $70,000.

Required

a. Calculate the following for 2019:
   1. Return on sales
   2. Return on assets
   3. Return on common stockholders' equity
   4. Quick ratio
   5. Current ratio
   6. Debt-to-equity ratio

b. Trade association statistics and information provided by credit agencies reveal the following data on industry norms:

	Median	Upper Quartile
Return on sales	3.7 percent	10.6 percent
Return on assets	5.8 percent	14.2 percent
Return on common stockholders' equity	18.5 percent	34.2 percent
Quick ratio	1.0	1.8
Current ratio	2.2	3.7
Debt-to-equity ratio.	1.07	0.37

Compare Jackson Corporation's performance with industry performance.

LO4 **P13-9B.** **Ratios Compared with Industry Averages** Hardy Instruments, Inc., is a manufacturer of various measuring and controlling instruments. Financial statement data for the firm are as follows:

	2019 (Thousands of Dollars, except Earnings per Share)
Sales revenue.	$220,000
Cost of goods sold	125,000
Net income	10,000
Dividends	4,300
Earnings per share.	5.00

HARDY INSTRUMENTS, INC. Balance Sheets (Thousands of Dollars)	Dec. 31, 2019	Dec. 31, 2018
Assets		
Cash..	$ 20,000	$ 19,000
Accounts receivable (net)......................	46,000	43,000
Inventory......................................	39,500	43,700
Total current assets.........................	105,500	105,700
Plant assets (net)	52,600	51,500
Other assets.....................................	15,600	12,800
Total assets	$173,700	$170,000
Liabilities and Stockholders' Equity		
Notes payable—banks..........................	$ 6,000	$ 6,000
Accounts payable................................	22,700	18,700
Accrued liabilities	18,000	24,000
Total current liabilities	46,700	48,700
9% bonds payable	40,000	40,000
Total liabilities	86,700	88,700
Common stock, $25 par value (2,000,000 shares)............	50,000	50,000
Retained earnings	37,000	31,300
Total stockholders' equity	87,000	81,300
Total liabilities and stockholders' equity	$173,700	$170,000

Required

a. Using the given data, calculate ratios 1 through 8 for 2019. Compare the performance of Hardy Instruments, Inc., with the following industry averages and comment on its operations.

		Median Ratios for Manufacturers of Measuring and Controlling Instruments
1.	Quick ratio	1.3
2.	Current ratio	2.4
3.	Accounts receivable turnover...............	5.9 times
4.	Inventory turnover........................	3.5 times
5.	Debt-to-equity ratio......................	0.73
6.	Gross profit percentage	44.3 percent
7.	Return on sales	4.7 percent
8.	Return on assets	7.6 percent

b. Calculate the dividends paid per share of common stock. What was the dividend payout ratio?

c. If the most recent price per share of common stock is $65, what is the price-earnings ratio? The dividend yield?

P13-10B. Financial Statement Notes: Quarterly Data Past quarterly data are presented below for Company C and Company D. One of these companies is Toys "R" Us, a children's specialty retail chain. The company's fiscal year ends on the Saturday nearest to January 31. The other company is the Gillette Company prior to its acquisition by Procter & Gamble. Gillette manufactures and sells blades, razors, and toiletries. Gillette was on a calendar year basis.

LO2

TOYS "R" US

GILLETTE
COMPANY

PROCTER &
GAMBLE

	(Amounts in Millions)				
	First Quarter	**Second Quarter**	**Third Quarter**	**Fourth Quarter**	**Year**
Company C					
Net Sales	$1,216.6	$1,237.3	$1,339.7	$1,617.2	$5,410.8
Gross profit	753.1	773.6	839.0	1,000.8	3,366.5
Company D					
Net Sales	$1,172.5	$1,249.1	$1,345.8	$3,401.8	$7,169.2
Gross profit	362.5	384.6	423.2	1,030.3	2,200.6

Required

a.   Compute the percentage of annual net sales generated each quarter by Company C. Round to the nearest percent.

b.   Compute the percentage of annual net sales generated each quarter by Company D. Round to the nearest percent.

c.   Which company has the most seasonal business? Briefly explain.

d.   Which company is Toys "R" Us? The Gillette Company? Briefly explain.

SERIAL PROBLEM: KATE'S CARDS

(Note: This is a continuation of the Serial Problem: Kate's Cards from Chapter 1 through Chapter 12.)

SP13.   Kate is very pleased with the results of the first year of operations for Kate's Cards. She ended the year on a high note, with the company's reputation for producing quality cards leading to more business than she can currently manage. Kate is considering expanding and bringing in several employees. In order to do this, she will need to find a larger location and also purchase more equipment. All this means additional financing. Kate has asked you to look at her year-end financial statements as if you were a banker considering giving Kate a loan. Comment on your findings and provide calculations to support your comments.

KATE'S CARDS Income Statement Year Ended August 31, 2019	
Sales revenue.	$185,000
Cost of goods sold	106,000
Gross profit.	79,000
Operating expenses	
Wages	18,000
Consulting.	11,850
Insurance	1,200
Utilities	2,400
Rent	14,400
Depreciation	3,250
Total operating expenses	51,100
Income from operations	27,900
Interest expense.	900
Income before income tax	27,000
Income tax expense	5,400
Net income	$ 21,600

KATE'S CARDS
Balance Sheet
August 31, 2019

Assets

Current assets

Cash.	$17,400
Accounts receivable	11,000
Inventory.	16,000
Prepaid insurance.	1,000
Total current assets	45,400
Equipment	17,500
Accumulated depreciation	3,250
Total assets	$59,650

Liabilities

Current liabilities

Accounts payable.	$ 6,200
Unearned revenue	1,250
Other current liabilities	1,900
Total current liabilities.	9,350
Note payable	15,000
Total liabilities.	24,350

Stockholders' equity

Common stock.	500
Additional paid-in-capital	9,500
Preferred stock.	5,000
Retained earnings	20,300
Total stockholders' equity	35,300
Total liabilities and stockholders' equity	$59,650

KATE'S CARDS
Statement of Cash Flows
Year Ended August 31, 2019

Cash flow from operating activities

Net income	$21,600
Add depreciation	3,250
Increase in accounts receivable	(11,000)
Increase in inventory.	(16,000)
Increase in prepaid expenses.	(1,000)
Increase in accounts payable	6,200
Increase in unearned revenue	1,250
Increase in other current liabilities	1,900
Cash provided by operating activities.	6,200

Cash flow from investing activities

Purchase of equipment.	(17,500)
Cash used by investing activities	(17,500)

Cash flow from financing activities

Proceeds from bank note	15,000
Issuance of common stock	10,000
Issuance of preferred stock.	5,000
Cash dividends	(1,300)*
Cash provided by financing activities	28,700
Net increase in cash.	17,400
Cash at beginning of year.	0
Cash at end of year	$17,400

*Kate issued cash dividends on both the common stock and the preferred stock. There are 50 preferred shares outstanding and 500 common shares outstanding. The dividends that Kate paid were $6 per share on the preferred shares and $2 per share on the common shares.

EXTENDING YOUR KNOWLEDGE

REPORTING AND ANALYSIS

COLUMBIA
SPORTSWEAR
COMPANY

EYK13-1. Financial Reporting Problem: Columbia Sportswear Company The financial statements for the Columbia Sportswear Company can be found in Appendix A at the end of this book.

You are considering an investment in Columbia Sportswear after a recent outdoor trip in which you really liked some of the clothes you purchased from the company. You decide to do an analysis of the company's financial statements in order to help you make an informed decision.

Required
a. Using the five-year selected financial data reported in the annual report, produce a five-year trend analysis, using 2013 as a base year, of (1) net sales, (2) net income, and (3) total assets. Comment on your findings.
b. Calculate the (1) gross profit percentage, (2) return on sales, and (3) return on assets for 2016 and 2017. Comment on Columbia Sportswear's profitability. (2015 total assets = $1,846,153,000)
c. Calculate the (1) current ratio, (2) quick ratio, and (3) operating-cash-flow-to-current liabilities ratio for 2016 and 2017. (2015 current liabilities = $355,070,000) Comment on Columbia Sportswear's liquidity.
d. Calculate the debt-to-equity ratio for 2016 and 2017. Comment on Columbia Sportswear's solvency.

COLUMBIA
SPORTSWEAR
COMPANY

UNDER ARMOUR,
INC.

EYK13-2. Comparative Analysis Problem: Columbia Sportswear Company vs Under Armour, Inc. The financial statements for the Columbia Sportswear Company can be found in Appendix A at the end of this book, and the financial statements of Under Armour, Inc. can be found in Appendix B (the complete annual report is available on this book's Website).

Required
Based on the information from the financial statements of each company, do the following.
a. Calculate the percentage change in (1) net sales, (2) net income, (3) cash flow from operating activities, and (4) total assets from 2016 to 2017.
b. What conclusions can you draw from this analysis?

EYK13-3. Business Decision Problem Crescent Paints, Inc., a paint manufacturer, has been in business for five years. The company has had modest profits and has experienced few operating difficulties until this year, 2019, when president Alice Becknell discussed her company's working capital problems with you, a loan officer at Granite Bank. Becknell explained that expanding her firm has created difficulties in meeting obligations when they come due and in taking advantage of cash discounts offered by manufacturers for the timely payment of the company's accounts payable. She would like to borrow $50,000 from Granite Bank. At your request, Becknell submits the following financial data for the past two years:

	2019	2018
Sales revenue.	$2,000,000	$1,750,000
Cost of goods sold	1,320,000	1,170,000
Net income	42,000	33,600
Dividends	22,000	18,000
December 31, 2017, data.		
Total assets	1,100,000	
Accounts receivable (net).	205,000	
Inventory.	350,000	

CRESCENT PAINTS, INC. Balance Sheets	Dec. 31, 2019	Dec. 31, 2018
Assets		
Cash.	$ 31,000	$ 50,000
Accounts receivable (net).	345,000	250,000
Inventory.	525,000	425,000
Prepaid expenses.	11,000	6,000
Total current assets.	912,000	731,000
Plant assets (net)	483,000	444,000
Total assets	$1,395,000	$ 1,175,000
Liabilities and Stockholders' Equity		
Notes payable—banks	$ 100,000	$ 35,000
Accounts payable	244,000	190,000
Accrued liabilities	96,000	85,000
Total current liabilities	440,000	310,000
10% mortgage payable.	190,000	250,000
Total liabilities	630,000	560,000
Common stock	665,000	535,000
Retained earnings	100,000	80,000
Total stockholders' equity	765,000	615,000
Total liabilities and stockholders' equity	$1,395,000	$1,175,000

Calculate the following items for both years from the given data and then compare them with the median ratios for paint manufacturers provided by a commercial credit firm:

		Median Ratios for Paint Manufacturers
1.	Current ratio	2.5
2.	Quick ratio	1.3
3.	Accounts receivable turnover	8.1
4.	Average collection period	44.9 days
5.	Inventory turnover.	4.9
6.	Debt-to-equity ratio.	0.78
7.	Return on assets	4.8%
8.	Return on sales	2.4%

Required

Based on your analysis, decide whether and under what circumstances you would grant Becknell's request for a loan. Explain the reasons for your decision.

EYK13-4. Financial Analysis Problem Listed below are selected financial data for three corporations: Honeywell International, Inc. (environmental controls), The Dow Chemical Company (chemicals and plastic products), and Abbott Laboratories (health care products). These data cover five years (Year 5 is the most recent year; net income in thousands):

HONEYWELL INTERNATIONAL, INC.

THE DOW CHEMICAL COMPANY

ABBOTT LABORATORIES

	Year 5	Year 4	Year 3	Year 2	Year 1
Honeywell International, Inc.					
Net income	$278,900	$322,200	$246,800	$331,100	$381,900
Earnings per common share	$2.15	$2.40	$1.78	$2.35	$2.52
Dividend per common share	$1.00	$0.91	$0.84	$0.77	$0.70
The Dow Chemical Company					
Net income	$938,000	$644,000	$276,000	$942,000	$1,384,000
Earnings per common share	$3.88	$2.33	$0.99	$3.46	$5.10
Dividend per common share	$2.60	$2.60	$2.60	$2.60	$2.60
Abbott Laboratories					
Net income*	$1,399,100	$1,239,100	$1,088,700	$965,800	$859,800
Earnings per common share*	$1.69	$1.47	$1.27	$1.11	$0.96
Dividend per common share	$0.68	$0.60	$0.50	$0.42	$0.35

*Before accounting change

Required

a. Calculate the dividend payout ratio for each company for each of the five years.
b. Companies may differ in their dividend policy; that is, they may differ in whether they emphasize a constant dividend amount per share, a steady growth in dividend amount per share, a target or constant dividend payout ratio, or some other criterion. Based on the data available, identify what appears to be each of the above firm's dividend policy over the five-year period.

CRITICAL THINKING

GENERAL MILLS, INC.

EYK13-5.   Accounting Research Problem: General Mills, Inc. The fiscal year 2017 annual report of General Mills, Inc. is available on this book's Website.

Required

a. Calculate (or identify) the following financial ratios for 2016 and 2017:
    1. Gross profit percentage
    2. Return on sales
    3. Asset turnover (2015, total assets = $21,832.0 million)
    4. Return on assets (2015, total assets = $21,832.0 million)
    5. Return on common stockholders' equity (2015, total stockholders' equity = $4,996.7 million)
    6. Current ratio
    7. Quick ratio
    8. Operating-cash-flow-to-current-liabilities ratio (2015, current liabilities = $4,890.1 million)
    9. Accounts receivable turnover (2015, accounts receivable = $1,386.7 million)
    10. Average collection period
    11. Inventory turnover (2015, inventory = $1,540.9 million)
    12. Days' sales in inventory
    13. Debt-to-equity ratio
    14. Times-interest-earned ratio
    15. Operating-cash-flow-to-capital-expenditures ratio
    16. Earnings per share
    17. Price-earnings ratio (Use year-end adjusted closing stock price of $57.32 for 2017 and $63.69 for 2016.)
    18. Dividend yield
    19. Dividend payout ratio
b. Comment briefly on the changes from fiscal 2016 to fiscal 2017 in the ratios computed above.

EYK13-6.   Accounting Communication Activity Pete Hollingsworth is currently taking an accounting course and is confused about what his professor told the class about analyzing financial statements. Pete would like you to lead a study session on the topic. In order to help everyone out, you decide to write a short memo describing some of the key points.

Required

Include the following items in your memo:

a. What is meant by trend analysis and how is it helpful?

b. How are common-size statements constructed and what are their uses?

c. What are a few common profitability, liquidity, and solvency ratios and how are they interpreted?

d. What are some limitations of financial statement analysis?

EYK13-7. Accounting Ethics Case Chris Nelson, the new assistant controller for Grand Company, is preparing for the firm's year-end closing procedures. On December 30, 2019, a memorandum from the controller directed Nelson to make a journal entry debiting Cash and crediting Long-Term Advances to Officers for $1,000,000. Not finding the $1,000,000 in the cash deposit prepared for the bank that day, Nelson went to the controller for a further explanation. In response, the controller took from her desk drawer a check for $1,000,000 payable to Grand Company from Jason Grand, chief executive officer of the firm. Attached to the check was a note from Jason Grand saying that if this check were not needed to return it to him next week.

"This check is paying off a $1,000,000 advance the firm made to Jason Grand six years ago," stated the controller. "Mr. Grand has done this every year since the advance; each time we have returned the check to him in January of the following year. We plan to do so again this time. In fact, when Mr. Grand retires in four years, I expect the board of directors will forgive this advance. However, if the firm really needed the cash, we would deposit the check."

"Then why go through this charade each year?" inquired Nelson.

"It dresses up our year-end balance sheet," replied the controller. "Certain financial statement ratios are improved significantly. Further, the notes to the financial statements don't have to reveal a related-party loan. Lots of firms engage in year-end transactions designed to dress up their financial statements."

Required

a. What financial statement ratios are improved by making the journal entry contained in the controller's memorandum?

b. Is the year-end handling of Jason Grand's advance an ethical practice? Discuss.

EYK13-8. Corporate Social Responsibility Problem The chapter highlighted one way in which the **Procter & Gamble Company** demonstrates its commitment to being a good corporate citizen (see page 627). Go to Procter & Gamble's Website and navigate to the section on sustainability. From there you can download its annual sustainability report. The report contains a section on social responsibility. In addition to the joint effort with UNICEF, what are some other ways that P&G demonstrates its commitment to being a good corporate citizen?

PROCTER
& GAMBLE
COMPANY

EYK13-9. Forensic Accounting Problem Accrual accounting is based on the principle that revenue should be reported when earned and that expenses associated with that revenue should be matched against the revenue in the same period. Some financial statement frauds violate this fundamental concept in order to overstate net income in the current year. Provide an example of how this may be accomplished.

EYK13-10. Working with the Takeaways Below are income statements and balance sheets for the Peyton Company for 2019 and 2018:

PEYTON COMPANY Income Statement For the Years Ended December 31, 2019 and 2018		
(in millions)	2019	2018
Sales revenue.	$10,000	$9,500
Cost of goods sold	5,500	5,200
Gross profit.	4,500	4,300
Selling and administrative expenses	2,800	2,700
Income from operations	1,700	1,600
Interest expense.	300	250
Income before income taxes	1,400	1,350
Income tax expense.	420	400
Net income.	$ 980	$ 950

PEYTON COMPANY
Balance Sheet
December 31, 2019 and 2018

(in millions)	2019	2018
Assets		
Current assets		
Cash and cash equivalents	$ 200	$ 400
Accounts receivable	900	800
Inventory	700	650
Other current assets	400	250
Total current assets	2,200	2,100
Property, plant, & equipment (net)	2,600	2,500
Other assets	5,700	5,900
Total assets	$10,500	$10,500
Liabilities and Stockholders' Equity		
Current liabilities	$ 3,000	$ 2,900
Long-term liabilities	5,000	5,400
Total liabilities	8,000	8,300
Stockholders' equity—common	2,500	2,200
Total liabilities and stockholders' equity	$10,500	$10,500

Required

Calculate the following ratios for the Peyton Company for 2019 and 2018 and discuss your findings:

1. Profitability
   a. Return on sales
   b. Return on common stockholders' equity (common stockholders' equity was $2,000 on December 31, 2017)
2. Liquidity
   a. Current ratio
   b. Accounts receivable turnover (accounts receivable was $780 on December 31, 2017)
   c. Inventory turnover (inventory was $620 on December 31, 2017)
3. Solvency
   a. Debt-to-equity ratio
   b. Times-interest-earned ratio

LVMH MOET
HENNESSEY-
LOUIS VUITTON
S.A.

EYK13-11. Analyzing IFRS Financial Statements The 2017 financial statements of **LVMH Moet Hennessey-Louis Vuitton S.A.** are presented in Appendix C at the end of this book. LVMH is a Paris-based holding company and one of the world's largest and best-known luxury goods companies. As a member of the European Union, French companies are required to prepare their consolidated (group) financial statements using International Financial Reporting Standards (IFRS). After reviewing LVMH's consolidated financial statements, calculate the following for 2017 and 2016:

a. Current ratio
b. Quick ratio
c. Accounts receivable turnover
d. Inventory turnover
e. Debt-to-equity ratio
f. Times-interest-earned ratio *(Hint: interest expense is called "Cost of net financial debt.")*
g. Return on sales
h. Return on assets
i. Return on common stockholders' equity

ANSWERS TO SELF-STUDY QUESTIONS:

1. c, (pp. 624–625) 2. c, (p. 633) 3. c, (p. 642) 4. b, (p. 642) 5. b, (p. 638) 6. c, (p. 642)
7. d, (p. 645) 8. b, (p. 636) 9. c, (p. 637) 10. b, (p. 632) 11. c, (p. 649) 12. d, (pp. 651–654)

YOUR TURN! SOLUTIONS

Solution 13.1
1. Persistent
2. Transitory
3. Transitory
4. Persistent
5. Transitory
6. Persistent

Solution 13.2

	Change in 2019	
	Amount	Percent
Sales revenue.	$50,000	6.7 percent [($800,000 − $750,000)/$750,000]
Net income	20,000	20.0 percent [($120,000 − $100,000)/$100,000]
Total assets	10,000	3.4 percent [($300,000 − $290,000)/$290,000]

Solution 13.3

SANFORD COMPANY
Income Statement
For the Year Ended December 31, 2018

	Amount	Percent
Sales revenue.	$13,500	100.0
Cost of goods sold	5,400	40.0
Gross profit.	8,100	60.0
Selling and administrative expenses	1,350	10.0
Income from operations	6,750	50.0
Interest expense.	675	5.0
Other expense	135	1.0
Income before income taxes	5,940	44.0
Income tax expense	2,295	17.0
Net income.	$ 3,645	27.0

Solution 13.4
a. Gross profit percentage = ($30,000 − $10,500)/$30,000 = 65.0 percent
b. Return on sales = $4,500/$30,000 = 15.0 percent
c. Asset turnover = $30,000/$50,000 = 0.60
d. Return on assets = $4,500/$50,000 = 9.0 percent
e. Return on common stockholders' equity = ($4,500 − $500)/$35,000 = 11.4 percent

Solution 13.5

a. Working capital = $60,000 − $40,000 = $20,000
b. Current ratio = $60,000/$40,000 = 1.5
c. Operating-cash-flow-to-current-liabilities ratio = $55,000/$40,000 = 1.375
d. Accounts receivable turnover = $100,000/$15,000 = 6.67 times
e. Days' sales in inventory = 365/($70,000/$9,000) = 46.9 days

Solution 13.6

a. Debt-to-equity ratio = $180,000/$600,000 = 0.30
b. Times-interest-earned ratio = ($55,000 + $5,000 + $25,000)/$5,000 = 17.0 times
c. Operating-cash-flow-to-capital-expenditures ratio = $100,000/$30,000 = 3.33 times

Solution 13.7

a. Dividend yield = $1.50/$54.00 = 2.8 percent
b. Dividend payout ratio = $1.50/$4.50 = 33.3 percent
c. Price-earnings ratio = $54.00/$4.50 = 12.0

Chapter 14

Overview of Managerial Accounting

PAST

The second half of this book builds upon many of the concepts introduced in the preceding financial accounting chapters.

PRESENT

Chapter 14 introduces managerial accounting. Moreover, it presents an overview of two companies used throughout the managerial accounting chapters of this text to illustrate various concepts and procedures common to managerial accounting and decision-making.

FUTURE

Chapter 15 defines basic costing terminology and introduces different types of manufacturing inventories. It illustrates how costs flow through the inventories and explains the schedule of cost of goods manufactured.

Amazon.com (Amazon) is the world's largest online retailer. Amazon claims to offer "Earth's Biggest Selection," offering millions of unique products through its website. With the acquisition of Whole Foods, these products now include groceries. If you have ever purchased something online, you have most likely visited Amazon's retail website.

What you may not know is that Amazon offers much more than retail consumer products. For example, it is a major provider of cloud computing services, known as "Amazon Web Services." In addition to being a retailer and a service provider, Amazon is also a manufacturer. It produces an e-book reader, the Amazon Kindle; a tablet computer, the Kindle Fire HD; and, a smartphone, the Fire Phone.

This chapter introduces managerial accounting and how management accounting information is used to help business managers in all types of businesses (retail, services, and manufacturing) make better decisions regarding future performance.

© Shutterstock.com

Road Map

LO	Learning Objective	Page	eLecture	Guided Example	Assignments
LO1	Define managerial accounting and describe its objectives.	690	E14-1	YT14.1	SS1, Q1, Q2, Q3
LO2	Describe the three types of business entities.	692	E14-2	YT14.2	SS2, Q4, Q5, Q6
LO3	Discuss major trends in business and managerial accounting.	693	E14-3	YT14.3	SS3, Q7, Q8, Q9, Q10
LO4	Describe important characteristics of two companies used throughout the managerial accounting chapters of this book to illustrate key concepts and processes.	697	E14-4		SS4, Q11, Q12, Q13
LO5	Describe career options in managerial accounting.	699	E14-5	YT14.4	SS5, Q14, Q15, Q16
LO6	Understand differences between various professional certifications available to managerial accountants.	700	E14-6	YT14.5	SS6, Q17, Q18, Q19

INTRODUCTION TO MANAGERIAL ACCOUNTING

LO1 **Define** managerial accounting and **describe** its objectives.

Businesses make decisions every day that impact their competitiveness in the market. What is our target market? What products or services should we offer? How should we price our goods or services to compete effectively with our competitors? How much should we pay our employees to attract and retain great talent? Where should we locate our office or fulfillment center to minimize delivery time and cost? How do we build awareness of our firm and products or services within our target market? How do we achieve our objectives with limited resources? How many employees do we need to hire in the coming year to meet anticipated demand for our products or services? Which employees should we assign to work on this project?

These questions, and many others, require an understanding of broad business disciplines, including finance, marketing, organizational behavior, supply chain management, operations management, and strategy. However, a common element to all of these questions is the need to have a clear understanding of the financial implications of each alternative course of action. For example, in setting the price of a good or service, management needs to not only understand the customers' needs and expectations, competitors' positions in the marketplace, and the anticipated demand for the product or service, but also the business's costs of providing them.

Managerial Accounting versus Financial Accounting

The second half of this text focuses on managerial accounting, which plays a vital role in *internal* decision-making. The first half of this text discussed financial accounting concepts, which focused on reporting a company's financial performance to *external* parties. Financial accountants are typically engaged in measuring and reporting the financial results of a business's *past* actions and activities. They report the results of past transactions in accordance with a set of standards known as generally accepted accounting principles (GAAP). Financial accountants typically produce reports such as 10-Qs and 10-Ks (for regulators of publicly traded companies); Annual Reports (for investors and creditors); and, periodic income statements, balance sheets, and cash flow statements (for management).

	Financial Accounting	Management Accounting
Guiding standard	Generally accepted accounting principles (FASB Accounting Standards Codification)	None. Company management's prescribed format.
Purpose	Demonstrate compliance with reporting standards	Help management make informed business decisions
Users of the information	Regulators, investors, creditors, management	Internal management
Types of reports	Annual statements (10-Ks) and quarterly statements (10-Qs) for regulators, audited financial statements for investors and creditors, periodic financial reports for management	Financial and operating budgets, reports on variances from standards, capital budgeting/resource investment
Reporting periods	Recently concluded quarter or year, often compared to previous quarters or years	Future periods (next year's budget, 10-year capital projection, etc.)
Focus	Financial results of past performance	Financial projections of future performance

Management accountants utilize data from many different sources, such as financial operations, sales, and human resources, to help top management make decisions regarding *future* performance. They provide information to management in a form that is timely, relevant, decision-useful, and in a format that is easily accessible to management but not determined by any external organization. Management accountants might use data gathered from production, marketing, and human resources to prepare a budget for the next operating period; calculate differences between expected and actual results of operations (aka variances) to evaluate production results and revise production standards; or, prepare a net present value or internal rate of return analysis to assist management in selecting from among competing proposed capital investments.

Objectives of Managerial Accounting

Management accountants are professionals who work in business, across all areas of an organization, in decision support, planning, and control functions. They partner with personnel from their firm's executive management to its line employees to make strategic business decisions. Management accountants must capture, analyze, and report critical data in a timely manner. To address important strategic questions like those mentioned previously, management accountants will identify data needed to answer those questions. Such data will usually include financial information, but often include non-financial information from both inside and outside the company. If the necessary data aren't readily available, management accountants may help design systems to capture the data. Sometimes, the data are available, but must be summarized in a form that is useful to management. Management accountants can help develop reports that allow management to make sense of the data. They are also proactive in identifying relevant information to help recommend needed improvements in all aspects of their firm's business.

Hint: Because the information management accountants provide managers is so important, they must ensure that it is both accurate and relevant.

Would the following activities be associated with financial accounting or managerial accounting?

1. Issuing a quarterly earnings report to investors.
2. Determining the cost of producing a product.
3. Calculating the breakeven point.
4. Preparing a report for the Securities and Exchange Commission (SEC).
5. Preparing a sales budget.
6. Preparing a Statement of Cash Flows in accordance with generally accepted accounting principles (GAAP).
7. Choosing among competing capital projects using net present value analysis.

YOUR TURN! 14.1

The solution is on page 706.

TYPES OF BUSINESS ENTITIES

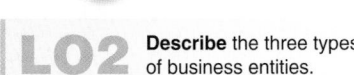

Describe the three types of business entities.

Manufacturing firms are companies that convert materials such as sheets of steel and coils of wire and components such as electric motors and microprocessors into finished products. The manufacturer utilizes human labor; utilities such as electricity, natural gas, and water; and factory assets such as buildings, machinery, and computers to convert the materials and components into sellable products. Manufacturers will normally report three types of inventory on their balance sheets: raw materials inventory, work-in-process inventory, and finished goods inventory.

Merchandising firms are companies that purchase finished products from manufacturers for warehousing, display, and sale to consumers. Wholesalers typically buy finished products in large quantities and store them in large warehouses until they can be sold and shipped in smaller quantities to local retailers. The retailer utilizes human labor or electronic advertising to sell products from a "brick-and-mortar" store or through an online store available through a website. Because merchandising firms purchase finished products for sale, they typically report a single type of inventory on their balance sheets: finished goods or merchandise inventory.

Service firms are companies that provide services to customers. Examples include companies in health care, legal, and accounting services. The types of costs incurred by these firms are generally similar to those of other types of firms except they don't sell a product. Hence, they normally do not carry a raw materials and finished goods inventory. However, if the services provided take many months or years to complete, i.e., project-based services, a service firm could report work-in-process inventory on its balance sheet.

Accounting for manufacturing operations is usually more complex because more activities are involved in producing a product than in purchasing and selling merchandise or providing a service.

Each year, *Forbes* magazine reports the world's "most reputable" companies. The 2018 ranking[1] indicates that roughly 75% of the world's most reputable, and presumably best known, companies are manufacturing firms. You probably recognize most of them and are likely familiar with their products. For example, Rolex, Lego Group, Canon, Sony, Adidas, BMW, Microsoft, Intel, Nestle, and Apple are among the most reputable manufacturing firms in the world. Interestingly, less than 10% of the most reputable firms are retailers. You are familiar with retailers like Amazon, Giorgio Armani, and eBay. Notably missing from this list are some of the world's largest retailers, such as Walmart, Target, Costco, Home Depot, and Lowes. A slightly higher percentage, about 15%, are service companies. This list contains well-known companies like Google, Marriott International, FedEx, UPS, and several airlines (Lufthansa Group, Air France/KLM, Emirates, and British Airways), whereas the U.S.-based airlines are all noticeably absent.

YOUR TURN! 14.2

The solution is on page 706.

For each of the following companies, identify whether they are a manufacturing, merchandising, or service firm.

Exxon Mobil Co.	Walmart
Southwest Airlines	Hershey Co.
Costco	Boston Consulting Group

---

[1] Vicky Valet, "The World's Most Reputable Companies 2018," *Forbes*, March 15, 2018.

Concept →	Method →	Assessment	TAKEAWAY 14.1
Can you determine a company's business entity type by looking at its financial statements?	Look at the company's balance sheet or financial statement footnotes for reported inventory accounts.	• If the company reports raw materials, work-in-process, and finished goods inventory, it is a manufacturer. • If the company reports only finished goods inventory, it is a merchandiser. • If the company reports only work-in-process inventory (or no inventory), it is a service firm.	

Choosing a Cost Accounting System

CORPORATE SOCIAL RESPONSIBILITY

Being a good corporate citizen means more than just providing large returns to a company's shareholders; it means considering all the company's stakeholders. In addition to shareholders, other stakeholders include employees, customers, suppliers, the environment, and the community—essentially, all of society. But does a company have to sacrifice shareholder returns in order to provide for these other stakeholders? Enlightened companies are learning that the answer is no. In fact, providing for all stakeholders can enhance shareholder returns.

Amazon.com, one of the top retailers on Forbes' list of the world's 100 most reputable companies, has learned that being a good corporate citizen is good for business. One example of this is Amazon's Frustration-Free Packaging program that eliminates hard plastic clamshell cases that prove so difficult to open and replaces the plastic cases with 100% recyclable packaging that is not only less frustrating but also better for the planet and less costly to the manufacturer.

As Amazon explains on its website:

At Amazon, if we do our job right, our greatest contribution to the good of society will come from our core business activities: lowering prices, expanding selection, driving convenience, driving frustration-free packaging, creating Kindle, innovating in web services, and other initiatives we'll work hard on in the future.

We also contribute to the communities where our employees and customers live. Our contributions can be seen in many ways—through our donations to dozens of nonprofits across the United States, through the disaster relief campaigns that we host on our homepage, through our employees' volunteer efforts, through the grants that we make to the writing community, and through the Amazon Web Services credits that we provide to educators.

MAJOR TRENDS IN BUSINESS AND MANAGERIAL ACCOUNTING

Outsourcing

Many companies have ceased trying to maintain a general focus. Instead, they have increasingly tried to identify their strengths and focus on these activities. **Outsourcing** occurs when a business hires or contracts with another business to provide a product or service that had previously been provided within the business. Examples might include the hiring of a third party to handle a company's customer service call center, hiring a landscaping service, and hiring an expert to develop and maintain the company website. One advantage is that it allows the company to focus on its core competency (e.g., the manufacturing of a product or provision of a service). Also, it may allow the company to pay for only the level of service that it needs, without having to worry about hiring and training staff, paying for excess capacity, or staffing to meet seasonal demand.

LO3 Discuss major trends in business and managerial accounting.

The growth and development of the Internet have allowed companies to provide specialized business services virtually from anywhere in the world. For example, many firms outsourced their customer service centers to India and other countries around the world. A call to your Internet service provider for technical support may be answered by someone in India, who is able to test your Internet connection and even reprogram your modem remotely over the Internet.

The anticipated cost savings that result from outsourcing do not always materialize as expected, however. KPMG found in a 2017 study that only 36% of those who had used outsourcing thought that it had been very effective at lowering costs. Less than one-third of the respondents to the study thought that outsourcing had been very effective at providing increased flexibility to scale operations, access to new technologies or strategic talent, or improved automated or cognitive processes.[2] There are many reasons for this, including miscommunication, lower quality of intermediate products or services, and unexpected delays in the production process.

Factory Automation

Factory automation is a widely recognized trend in modern manufacturing facilities. Factory automation exists in many forms. **Stand-alone automation** incorporates a robot or computer-controlled machine into an existing manufacturing process to perform a single function, such as welding. Stand-alone automation is usually undertaken to reduce both labor and material costs.

© Adobe Stock

Flexible-manufacturing-system automation involves multiple cells of two or more automated machines. All of the machines in each cell are controlled by a computer. The machines in each cell are interconnected to allow an automated flow of product through the **manufacturing cell**. This type of automated system produces the product from start to finish. The functions performed within the cell can be changed quickly by changing the program in the computer that controls the process.

When deciding whether to automate all or part of a manufacturing process, a manufacturer must compare the costs associated with the automation with the benefits to be derived from the automation. The costs may include the cost of the automated equipment, the costs of eliminating direct labor workers, and the costs of reorganizing the manufacturing operation. The benefits may include lower direct labor costs, better product quality, and fewer defective units. In general, automation should reduce direct labor costs and increase factory overhead costs. However, the increase in factory overhead should be less than the decrease in direct labor costs.

Just-in-Time Inventory Systems

Manufacturing firms typically maintain inventories (materials, work in process, and finished goods) as buffers against unforeseen delays. For example, a manufacturer would keep a supply of various materials on hand to protect against a supplier's being late in the delivery of materials needed to produce a particular product. This approach is sometimes referred to as maintaining **just-in-case inventories** (just-in-case the supplier does not deliver when scheduled), or **safety stocks**. Safety stocks create carrying costs for the manufacturer, including casualty insurance, warehousing costs, and the cost of capital on the investment in the inventory. Higher levels of inventory create higher levels of carrying costs.

Just-in-time (JIT) inventory systems seek to eliminate the safety stock balances. A company operating under a complete just-in-time philosophy would have no inventories at the end of each day of operations, that is, zero balances of materials, work in process, and finished goods. Materials would be ordered so that only the materials needed for production each day would be received each morning. Production would be scheduled

---

[2] "State of the outsourcing, shared services, and operations industry 2017," *KPMG and HfS Research*, April 2017.

so that all products started during the day would be completed by the end of the day (resulting in no work in process inventory) and shipped to customers by the end of the day (resulting in no finished goods inventory). Just-in-time means that materials are received just in time to be placed into production and that products are completed just in time to be shipped to customers.

Most manufacturing companies have been unable to reach the ideal zero balance level of all three manufacturing inventories. To guard against delayed shipments due to inclement weather or other problems, manufacturers may order materials so they arrive one or two days before they are actually needed. Even with this approach, the true just-in-case quantities are still minimized. In addition, manufacturers may be subject to seasonal demand for their products, so that they may be required to build finished goods inventory during low-demand periods of the year so they can meet customer demand during high-demand periods of the year.

Lean Manufacturing

Henry Ford is credited with integrating an entire production process by combining interchangeable parts with a moving conveyance system to produce the Model T Ford. His approach allowed the Ford Company to significantly reduce the production time and cost of producing an automobile. However, initially he was only able to provide one model in one color—black. Even when additional body styles became available, they were drop-on features from outside suppliers that were added at the very end of the production line. All models used the same chassis.

As demand for more variety increased, U.S. car manufacturers responded, but production times increased. Attempts to reduce the time to deliver an automobile meant larger and faster fabrication machines, larger parts inventories, and more complex operational and accounting information systems.

© Shutterstock.com

Mr. Kiichiro Toyoda studied the U.S. car manufacturing process and identified innovations that would improve the process flow and the variety of model offerings. He called this approach the Toyota Production System. By focusing on the flow of product through the entire manufacturing process, Toyota reduced the number of fabrication machines, lined up the machines in process sequence, reduced setup times, and introduced a system whereby a product was "pulled" through the process by demand from the subsequent step in the process.[3] This is the basis of **lean manufacturing**.

Lean manufacturing concepts have been adopted by manufacturers all over the world and have begun to be applied to other disciplines, including logistics and distribution, services, retail, health care, and construction. Lean manufacturing has also impacted companies' business information systems, performance measures, reports, and decisions.

Customer Profitability

In the past, companies focused their efforts on the development and standardization of products and services. As discussed previously, management attention was given to wringing all reasonable cost savings from the production process through the automation of manufacturing processes, the modification of product flow to improve efficiencies, the improvement of product quality, and the streamlining of production and delivery systems to minimize inventory on hand.

---

[3] http://www.sae.org/manufacturing/lean/

As markets have become more competitive and available products more homogeneous, companies have shifted to trying to differentiate themselves from their competitors through service. Customers have access to a tremendous amount of information about product features, prices, and quality via the Internet and have become more demanding of quality customer service.

Likewise, companies have a tremendous amount of information about their customers, including the frequency and volume of product purchases by type, their history of change orders, special handling and delivery requests, product returns, and customer service calls. Companies have begun to distinguish among their high-demand and low-demand customers relative to the cost of service to the customer and to focus on ways to increase customer profitability, not just product margin.

Big Data and Predictive Analytics

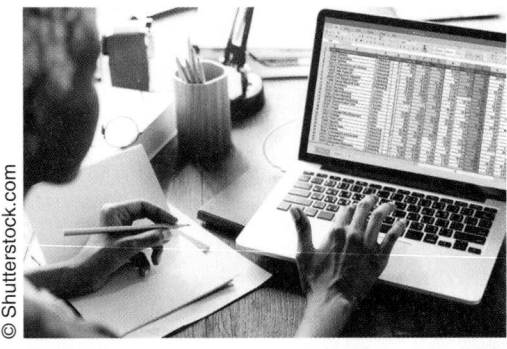

© Shutterstock.com

Bernard Marr, CEO and Director of Research at Advanced Performance Institute, posted an article in the blog "The Big Data Guru"[4] on Amazon.com's use of customer data to predict who will order what and when. In the article, he notes that Amazon has obtained a patent for what it calls "Anticipatory Shipping." The concept is that Amazon believes that its customer data will allow it to predict what you want and ship it to your door even before you order it. Already, Amazon customizes your online shopping experience by remembering what you bought previously, what you have on your wish list, what you have previously rated and reviewed, and what other customers who searched for similar items bought.

Amazon is not the only company trying to read your mind. The development of new and faster ways of analyzing the data trail that you leave behind following every online search, purchase, and social media interaction is allowing companies of all sizes to anticipate your desires and customize their products and services to better meet those needs. See Appendix F at the end of this book for further discussion of data analytics.

YOUR TURN! 14.3

The solution is on page 706.

GuidedExamples
MBC

Match each term to the appropriate description:

1. Outsourcing
2. Factory automation
3. Just-in-time inventory systems
4. Lean manufacturing
5. Customer profitability
6. Predictive analytics

a. A sportswear manufacturer takes steps to improve water efficiency by 15% per unit in apparel materials dyeing and finishing and to reduce waste from finished goods manufacturing by 10%.

b. A regional bakery contracts with a distribution company for delivery of its products to customers.

c. A business with a limited marketing budget uses customer data to forecast which customers have the highest probability of buying its products and sends a 10% discount coupon to only those customers.

d. A car manufacturer installs robots to perform welding and other dangerous tasks previously performed by humans.

e. A company uses a software package to perform algorithmic calculations to determine how to split customers into subcategories based on average order size, number of shipments per order, and number of customer returns for purposes of creating a customer income statement.

f. A computer company orders parts for a laptop from its suppliers only after an order has been received from a customer.

---

[4] http://smartdatacollective.com/bernardmarr/182796/amazon-using-big-data-analytics-read-your-mind.

INTRODUCING TWO NEW COMPANIES

Throughout the managerial accounting chapters of this textbook we will highlight two companies to explain key concepts and illustrate how real companies implement different managerial accounting practices. To provide a real-world view of manufacturing and retail sales, we frequently highlight Fezzari Performance Bicycles. Although it is important to understand the manufacture and sale of inventory, the U.S. economy has evolved into a much more service-oriented network of businesses. Hence, we will focus significant attention on how managerial accounting practices are used in the service sector and provide illustrations based on a consulting business, Environmental Business Consultants, LLC. Both of these companies will become very familiar to you throughout the various managerial accounting chapters of the book.

LO4   **Describe** important characteristics of two companies used throughout the managerial accounting chapters of this book to illustrate key concepts and processes.

Fezzari—A U.S. Bicycle Manufacturer and Distributor

Fezzari is a manufacturer and distributor located in Lindon, Utah, that designs, engineers, manufactures, and builds both mountain and road bikes. Fezzari's business model uses primarily a consumer-direct approach, with the vast majority of its sales completed through web-based, direct orders. This direct-order approach allows Fezzari to cut out the middleman (the local bike shop) and provide its customers with a higher-quality product at a lower cost than the brand-name bike manufacturers. Fezzari provides a 23-point custom setup with each bike sold, allowing the company to provide customers with a custom fit.

Fezzari's business model is not without risk. Most cyclists, particularly those who want to purchase a higher-end bike for several thousand dollars, want to be able to see, touch, and even ride the bike before purchase. Almost three-quarters of all bikes are sold in the United States through mass merchandisers (department, discount, and chain toy stores), and local bike shops account for an additional 15% of bike sales. However, according to the National Bicycle Dealers Association, the local bike shops' 13% unit sales is equivalent to 50% of the dollar value of bikes sold in 2015. Fezzari competes primarily with the local bike dealers for sales. By using a consumer-direct, web-based sales model, most Fezzari customers are unable to "kick the tires" before purchase like they can in a mass merchandiser or local bike shop.

Nevertheless, Fezzari's growth has been impressive. Fezzari sold its first bike in 2006 and now sells thousands of bikes each year. The company achieved a 20% year-over-year annual growth rate and is looking to expand its current facility to better service its growing customer base.

Although transactions are typically begun through the company's website, virtually all transactions involve one or more phone calls to gather information from the customer that is needed in the custom-build process. Not only does Fezzari gather body measurements (e.g., height, weight, inseam length, torso length, arm length, etc.), it also asks about the customer's age, the type of riding that the customer plans to do, and injuries that the customer may have experienced that might impact range of motion or flexibility.

Once the specific bike model and components are selected, Fezzari orders the required parts from its suppliers. A minimal quantity of parts is kept in inventory so that the bike assembly can be started without waiting for the parts to arrive. A technician assembles the bike to the customer's specifications, tunes it up, and then test rides it to ensure that it works properly. A second technician then checks the assembly, testing every screw and component, then checks the tune, and performs a second test ride. The bike is then sent to packing to be prepared for shipment by a packer. A second packer checks the pack for completeness. The bike is then sent to the shipping bay, where a final check is performed. The assembly and packaging process can take up to 8 to 12 hours for one of Fezzari's high-end bikes, depending on the degree of customization.

The bicycle manufacturing business is seasonal, with sales picking up in the early spring and not slowing down until the early fall. As a result, Fezzari's employee headcount varies from winter to summer, almost doubling from its low point to its high point.[5]

Environmental Business Consultants, LLC—A U.S. Service Firm

Environmental Business Consultants, LLC (EBC) is a fictitious management consulting firm headquartered in Los Angeles, California, based on an actual company. It was formed

in 1984 by three individuals who had worked together at one of the large international accounting firms. EBC provides consulting services to the local government market, including cities, counties, and special districts, in the areas of recycling and solid waste and water/wastewater management services.

In the western United States, most local governments contract with private companies for garbage, recycling, and water services. Wastewater, or sewer, services are often provided by a regional sewer district created by the local governments utilizing the service. In many cases, the local governments do not have the necessary personnel resources or expertise to manage these services effectively. They frequently turn to outside consultants to assist them. These outside consultants include engineering firms, large international and regional accounting firms, and local consulting firms. Competition is fierce and success is largely based on relationships and reputation.

EBC has performed thousands of consulting projects for hundreds of municipal agencies, assisting them with the procurement, management, and delivery of solid waste, water, and wastewater services. With a focus on west coast agencies, EBC offers its clients a breadth of experience coupled with responsiveness, accountability, and personal commitment. EBC has an excellent reputation within its chosen market.

EBC has grown from the three founders and an administrative assistant in 1984 to six owners located in offices in both northern and southern California with a staff of over 30 accountants, economists, engineers, and management consultants.

EBC obtains its client work primarily through requests from clients for whom the firm has worked for many years and also by responding to competitive requests for proposals issued by other municipal agencies. In most instances, EBC will meet with the client to discuss the project and gain an understanding of the client's needs. EBC will then prepare a written proposal outlining a scope of work to be performed for a specified fee. Competitive proposals typically require a presentation of the proposal to the client, where the client has the opportunity to ask questions and discuss the details of the proposed approach.

---

[5] We are grateful to Fezzari Performance Bicycles for providing significant access to its business model and management philosophy. Moreover, the company has given us access to management and many company resources.

CAREERS IN MANAGERIAL ACCOUNTING

Alternative Career Paths

LO5 **Describe** career options in managerial accounting.

Some college students believe that graduating with a degree in accounting leads to one thing: a career in public accounting, often with one of the "Big 4" accounting firms. This may be particularly true at one of the top 5 or 10 college accounting programs in the United States, because the Big 4 spend considerable time and money recruiting students from these schools. A 2017 study published by the Association of International Certified Public Accountants reported that just over 57,000 bachelor's and 22,000 master's students graduated from accounting degree programs in the United States. Approximately 35,000, or 44%, of these students began their careers in public accounting.[6] Regardless of where they begin their careers, it is clear that most accountants will eventually work as management accountants in industry. The U.S. Bureau of Labor Statistics reports that approximately 75% of all U.S. accountants and auditors work in management accounting and academic roles.[7]

A start in public accounting can be advantageous for some students because of the ongoing training and experience that can be obtained as these graduates are exposed to different companies and business functions. Audit or tax attestation experience is often required to be licensed as a certified public accountant (CPA), as discussed further in the next section. Many students want to be certified as CPAs because they believe this professional designation can open doors for future job opportunities. However, upwards of 90% of those who begin their careers in public accounting will leave public accounting and join a company in business or industry within a few years of graduation. Thus, the study of managerial accounting is critical for the success of virtually all accountants.

One of the reasons for this migration from public accounting to private industry is the myriad of opportunities for accountants. Accounting careers may be forged in government, public accounting, private business, and academia. Every business, from the small "mom-and-pop" store to the multinational conglomerate, needs the skills and expertise of an accountant. Accountants fill many roles, with titles such as accounting manager, controller, chief financial officer, treasurer, budget analyst, finance director, internal auditor, forensic accountant, environmental accountant, trustee in bankruptcy, Internal Revenue Service (IRS) criminal investigation special agent, tax consultant, small business owner, and management accountant. A management accountant might:

- be involved in evaluating the relative costs and benefits of outsourcing certain elements of a business;
- be involved in evaluating whether to "insource" services that have previously been outsourced;
- conduct an analysis and help management decide whether or not to automate a manufacturing process;
- be part of the team that determines the appropriate level of safety stock and seasonal inventory required to ensure that the company can meet customer demand;
- be part of the team that helps to implement lean manufacturing at the company;
- be charged with analyzing customer profitability by determining which customers should be offered special incentives to increase the size and reduce the frequency of their orders and which customers are unprofitable and should either be dropped or receive a reduced level of customer service, or

---

[6] Association of International Certified Public Accountants, "2017 Trends in the Supply of Accounting Graduates and the Demand for Public Accounting Recruits," 2017, https://www.aicpa.org/InterestAreas/AccountingEducation/NewsAndPublications/DownloadableDocuments/2017-trends-report.pdf

[7] American Institute of Certified Public Accountants, Inc., "2013 Trends in the Supply of Accounting Graduates and the Demand for Public Accounting Recruits," 2013, http://www.aicpa.org/InterestAreas/AccountingEducation/NewsAndPublications/DownloadableDocuments/2013_TrendsReport.pdf.

- help to develop a program that implements anticipatory shipping, similar to that which is under development by Amazon.

Work/Life Balance

Beginning a career in accounting entails a commitment to client service—although the "clients" may be either internal management or external entities. Because accounting typically involves the reporting of results of operations, accountants are regularly working under a deadline—reports are due by a certain date or within a certain number of days of the end of a period. To make the deadline often requires accountants to work whatever hours are needed, resulting in periods of late nights and weekends from time to time. Certain positions or career choices tend to require more overtime than others, although all accountants should expect to work more than a 40-hour work week on a regular basis. Employees of large accounting firms that audit publicly traded companies typically work an average of 55–60 hours per week. Management-level finance professionals, including management accountants, work an average of 47 hours per week, and non-management finance professionals work an average of 41 hours per week.[8] Government accountants probably have the most reliable work schedules, typically working 40 hours per week.

YOUR TURN! 14.4

The solution is on page 706.

MBC

According to the text, what percentage of accounting students begin their careers in public accounting and what percentage eventually leave for positions outside public accounting?

	Begin in public accounting	Leave public accounting
a.	75%	50%
b.	100%	90%
c.	44%	90%
d.	49%	75%

TAKEAWAY 14.2

Concept	→ Method →	Assessment
What can I do with a degree in accounting?	• Talk to career counselors, professors, professionals, and recruiters about different career options. • Visit your college or university career center to identify firms seeking graduates with an accounting degree.	Consider your career goals in light of available employment opportunities. Evaluate which opportunity provides the best start for where you see yourself in 10 years, recognizing that you will likely change employers once or twice during that time.

eLectures

MBC

PROFESSIONAL CERTIFICATIONS

LO6 Understand differences between various professional certifications available to managerial accountants.

Chapter 1 of this text briefly introduced a few of the certifications relevant to the accounting profession. Here we discuss in further detail some of their requirements and benefits.

Certified Public Accountant (CPA)

The CPA is the most widely recognized and respected professional accounting certification in the United States. The CPA professional certification has been administered by the American Institute of Certified Public Accountants (AICPA) or its predecessors since

---

[8] Thomas Thompson, Jr. and Paul MacDonald, *2017 Benchmarking the Accounting and Finance Function*, Financial Executives Research Foundation and Robert Half, 2017.

1887. The AICPA is the largest member association representing the accounting profession. It has more than 650,000 members worldwide. The AICPA administers the CPA exam, a four-part exam that covers Auditing and Attestation, Business Environment and Concepts, Financial Accounting and Reporting, and Regulation.

Passing the CPA exam is only the first step to obtaining a CPA license. Licensure is handled by each of the 55 State/Territory Boards of Accountancy. Licensure requirements vary slightly from state to state; however, most states require 150 hours of college credit plus a year or more of real-world work experience. Once licensed, CPAs are required to follow a strict Professional Code of Conduct and to complete a certain number of hours of continuing professional education.

Hint: To find out more about the AICPA's Professional Code of Conduct, see https: //www.aicpa.org /research/standards /codeofconduct.html

Certified Management Accountant (CMA)

The CMA is a professional certification administered by the Institute of Management Accountants (IMA) intended to indicate a level of knowledge and proficiency with accounting and financial management skills, including financial planning, analysis, control, decision support, and professional ethics. CMA candidates are required to hold a bachelor's degree from an accredited college or university, hold membership in the IMA, pass a two-part exam, and have at least two continuous years of professional experience in management accounting or financial management. The exam consists of two four-hour parts, with Part 1 covering Financial Reporting, Planning, Performance, and Control and Part 2 covering Financial Decision-making. Members of the IMA are required to adhere to the IMA Statement of Ethical Professional Practice.

The IMA reports that in 2017 more than 41,000 professionals held the CMA certificate. According to a 2016 IMA salary survey, professionals who have earned the CMA earn an average of over $30,000 more than noncertified peers.

Hint: To find out more about the CMA's Statement of Ethical Professional Practice, see https://www .imanet.org/insights -and-trends/business -leadership-and-ethics /ima-statement-of -ethical-professional -practice?ssopc=1

Other Professional Certifications

There are numerous other professional certifications that indicate specialized skill or experience. These include certified fraud examiner, certified financial planner, certified internal auditor, and enrolled agent.

Exhibit 14-1 shows the URL where you can find additional information regarding each of these professional certifications.

Exhibit 14-1	Information Regarding Professional Certifications
Certified Public Accountant	www.aicpa.org
Certified Management Accountant	www.imanet.org
Certified Fraud Examiner	www.acfe.com
Certified Financial Planner	www.cfp.net
Certified Internal Auditor	https://na.theiia.org
Enrolled Agent	https://www.irs.gov/tax-professionals/enrolled-agents /become-an-enrolled-agent

YOUR TURN! 14.5

Visit the website of at least two organizations from Exhibit 14-1, or another organization that provides a professional certification, and learn the minimum education requirement to take the exam.

The solution is on page 706.

SUMMARY OF LEARNING OBJECTIVES

LO1 **Define managerial accounting and describe its objectives. (p. 690)**
- Managerial accounting focuses on internal decision-making.
- Managerial accounting utilizes both financial and operational information.
- Managerial accounting provides information that is timely, relevant, decision-useful, and in a format that is easily accessible to management.
- Management accountants partner with personnel to plan, manage, and make strategic business decisions.

LO2 **Describe the three types of business entities. (p. 692)**
- Manufacturing firms convert materials into finished products.
- Merchandising firms purchase finished products from manufacturers for warehousing, display, and sale to consumers.
- Service firms are companies that perform services for customers.

LO3 **Discuss major trends in business and managerial accounting. (p. 693)**
- Outsourcing occurs when a business hires or contracts with another business to provide a product or service that had previously been provided within the business with the objective of reducing cost and allowing the business to focus on its core competencies.
- Stand-alone automation of a factory incorporates a robot or computer-controlled machine into an existing manufacturing process. Flexible-manufacturing-system automation of a factory operation involves the use of multiple cells of two or more automated machines. Each cell produces a product from start to finish.
- Traditional manufacturing inventories are used as buffers against unforeseen delays.
- Just-in-time inventory systems (rather than just-in-case inventory systems) minimize the amount of inventory that is on hand.
- Lean manufacturing focuses on the flow of the entire production process and uses customer demand to "pull" the product through production, thereby reducing setup times and inventory costs.
- Managerial accounting can help companies distinguish between high-demand and low-demand customers relative to their cost of service. This allows them to focus on ways to increase customer profitability.
- The development of new and faster ways of analyzing the data trail that customers leave behind following every online search, purchase, and social media interaction is allowing companies of all sizes to anticipate customers' desires and customize company products and services to better meet those needs.

LO4 **Describe the important characteristics of two companies used throughout the managerial accounting chapters of this book to illustrate key concepts and processes. (p. 697)**
- Fezzari is a manufacturer and distributor of bikes.
- Fezzari primarily sells direct to the customer through web-based transactions.
- Environmental Business Consultants (EBC) is a fictitious management consulting firm.
- EBC provides services to local government clients in California.

LO5 **Describe career options in managerial accounting. (p. 699)**
- Careers in managerial accounting might lead to or include titles such as management accountant, accounting manager, controller, chief financial officer, treasurer, budget analyst, finance director, internal auditor, forensic accountant, environmental accountant, trustee in bankruptcy, IRS criminal investigation special agent, tax consultant, and small business owner.
- Almost 90% of those accountants who begin their careers in public accounting will leave for a position in business or industry.

LO6 **Understand differences between various professional certifications available to managerial accountants. (p. 700)**
- The CPA is the most widely recognized and respected professional accounting certification in the United States.
- The CPA is administered by the American Institute of Certified Public Accountants (AICPA).
- The CMA is a professional certification intended to indicate a level of knowledge and proficiency with accounting and financial management skills, including financial planning, analysis, control, decision support, and professional ethics.
- The CMA is administered by the Institute of Management Accountants (IMA).
- There are numerous other professional certifications that indicate specialized skill or experience.

Concept	➔ Method	➔ Assessment	SUMMARY
Can you determine a company's business entity type by looking at its financial statements?	Look at the company's balance sheet or financial statement footnotes for reported inventory accounts.	• If the company reports raw materials, work-in-process, and finished goods inventory, it is a manufacturer. • If the company reports only finished goods inventory, it is a merchandiser. • If the company reports only work-in-process inventory (or no inventory), it is a service firm.	TAKEAWAY 14.1
What can I do with a degree in accounting?	• Talk to career counselors, professors, professionals, and recruiters about different career options. • Visit your college or university career center to identify firms seeking graduates with an accounting degree.	Consider your career goals in light of available employment opportunities. Evaluate which opportunity provides the best start for where you see yourself in 10 years, recognizing that you will likely change employers once or twice during that time.	TAKEAWAY 14.2

KEY TERMS

Financial accounting (p. 690)

Flexible-manufacturing-system automation (p. 694)

Just-in-case inventories (p. 694)

Just-in-time (JIT) inventory systems (p. 694)

Lean manufacturing (p. 695)

Managerial accounting (p. 690)

Manufacturing cell (p. 694)

Manufacturing firms (p. 692)

Merchandising firms (p. 692)

Outsourcing (p. 693)

Safety stocks (p. 694)

Service firms (p. 692)

Stand-alone automation (p. 694)

Assignments with the ⓜ logo in the margin are available in 𝐁usiness𝐂ourse.
See the Preface of the book for details.

SELF-STUDY QUESTIONS

(Answers to Self-Study Questions are at the end of this chapter.)

1. **Which of the following group of terms best describes the role of managerial accounting?**   LO1
   a. Internal decision-making, future-focused
   b. Internal decision-making, past-focused
   c. External reporting, future-focused
   d. External reporting, past-focused

2. **A company that sells finished products that it has acquired from a manufacturer to consumers is a**   LO2
   a. Manufacturer
   b. Merchandiser
   c. Service firm

3. **A manufacturer engages a company in India to respond to customer questions received online or by phone. This is an example of**   LO3
   a. lean manufacturing
   b. factory automation
   c. outsourcing
   d. on-shoring

LO4 4. **What business model does Fezzari follow to sell its products to its customers?**
  a. Sales through local bike shops.
  b. Sales through large mass merchandisers.
  c. Sales direct to customers through web-based orders.
  d. Sales of bike components to other bike manufacturers.

LO5 5. **Approximately what percentage of accountants who begin their careers in public accounting will leave for positions in businesses and corporations?**
  a. 50%
  b. 75%
  c. 90%
  d. 95%

LO6 6. **Which of the following is the professional certification intended to indicate a level of knowledge and proficiency with accounting and financial management skills, including financial planning, analysis, control, decision support, and professional ethics?**
  a. CPA
  b. CMA
  c. CFE
  d. CIA

QUESTIONS

LO1 1. How does managerial accounting differ from financial accounting?

LO1 2. Which type of accounting would produce reports relevant to stockholders?

LO1 3. A business owner plans to introduce a new product in the next year and needs to prepare a budget that reflects the increased sales, production costs, equipment, and personnel that will be required. Which of her two accountants, the financial accountant or the management accountant, would she most likely ask to help with the budget and why?

LO2 4. Name the three types of business entities and briefly describe the nature of each.

LO2 5. In what way do manufacturing firms and merchandising firms work together to provide end consumers with products?

LO2 6. Pick any large company and identify which type of business entity it is.

LO3 7. Describe a manufacturing cell and contrast a cell to the equipment arrangement in a traditional manufacturing operation.

LO3 8. Describe and contrast stand-alone automation and flexible-manufacturing-system automation.

LO3 9. Explain the relationship between safety stock and just-in-time inventory systems.

LO3 10. What is lean manufacturing?

LO4 11. Which type of business model does Fezzari use?

LO4 12. What are the advantages of Fezzari's business model?

LO4 13. From where does Environmental Business Consultants, LLC, primarily obtain its client work?

LO5 14. List five job titles that an individual with an accounting degree may have during a career.

LO5 15. Why is managerial accounting relevant to accounting majors and their future careers?

LO5 16. Do most accountants work in public accounting or in industry, and why?

LO6 17. Describe the process an accounting graduate takes to obtain the CPA certification.

LO6 18. Can an individual with an accounting degree obtain only one professional certification?

LO6 19. Use the Internet to explore different career paths that an individual with the CMA certification can take.

EXTENDING YOUR KNOWLEDGE

  EYK14-1. **Model Manufacturing** is a company that specializes in producing model cars, trains, and airplanes for customers of all ages. Model has been in business for over 50 years, and has provided generations of detailed models which can be customized by color, type of metal, size, and numerous other features. The company sells its completed models to merchandising companies, which then advertise and sell the products to the end consumer. Because Model produces mass quantities of models, it requires efficient operations to ensure timely delivery of quality products to merchandisers.

a.   Model can obtain varying qualities of metal and other materials that it uses to produce models. Why would the company choose to spend more for materials of higher quality when it can produce cheaper, similar models with lower-quality materials?

b.   Model's customers are mainly merchandising companies. Is Model more or less likely to enter into long-term contracts with these companies than Model would with an end consumer? Why?

EYK14-2.   Masterful Merchandising is a company that specializes in obtaining large quantities of products from multiple manufacturing companies and sells these products to end consumers. Its products include clothing, athletic equipment, electronics, home and kitchen products, groceries, and many other products. It prides itself in being a one-stop-shop where consumers can fill all their shopping needs without having to travel to multiple stores.

SERVICE AND MERCHANDISING

a.   Masterful receives daily shipments of goods from manufacturers to stock its shelves. From a cost perspective, is it cheaper to buy manufactured goods in small or large quantities? What incentives would a manufacturer provide in order to facilitate ordering large quantities?

b.   Why would a merchandiser choose to operate online instead of through a brick-and-mortar store? Do you think an online presence eliminates the need to have a physical store for consumer shopping?

EYK14-3.   Superior Services is a firm that provides audit, tax, and advisory services to over 100 companies in the western United States. It employs thousands of professionals who have obtained accounting, finance, economics, and business degrees, and who focus on providing value and enhancing the operations of their clients. The firm has been in existence for nearly 70 years, and many of its clients are loyal to Superior and look nowhere else for services.

SERVICE AND MERCHANDISING

a.   Superior does not sell physical products, but it does need to consider how to price its services in order to make a profit. What costs will the company consider when deciding how much to charge clients for its services?

b.   How is accounting for Superior's operations different from accounting for Model's (see EYK14-1) and Masterful's (see EYK14-2) operations? Are there costs that Superior will incur that the other two will not?

EYK14-4.   Peach Inc. is a manufacturer of consumer electronic devices, including computers, tablets, and phones. Peach has earned a reputation of providing reliable high-quality products at affordable prices. The company has also earned a reputation of being a good corporate citizen with many environmental and social initiatives. For example, the company uses far more recycled materials in its products than any of its competitors. The company is also known for its charity work with educational institutions.

In an effort to control costs, Peach outsources manufacturing of its hardware to many overseas factories; however, it closely monitors each facility to make sure quality is maintained. Tom Peach, the company CEO, was recently approached by Young, Inc., a company that asserts it can significantly reduce Peach's manufacturing costs by overseeing Peach's manufacturing. Young will find factories that it claims can maintain the same level of quality at lower costs. In addition, Young will do all the monitoring so that Peach can save the costs of monitoring and auditing the manufacturing facilities.

Jorge Workman, Peach's director of accounting, became quite concerned when he learned of the potential deal with Young. Jorge immediately went to Tom with his concerns. In particular, Jorge did not want to turn over the responsibility of monitoring the facilities to another company. Tom, however, feels that the quality control testing done locally is enough to assure that quality can be maintained, and the cost savings are very important to the company's efforts to keep its prices affordable. In addition, Tom felt that under this arrangement, anything that might go wrong at one of the facilities would be Young's responsibility and not the responsibility of Peach.

Jorge was still not convinced. He knew how labor problems in the supply chain of Nike in the 1990s had caused significant reputational and financial damage to Nike, and he did not want to risk the same thing happening to Peach.

What do you think Peach should do?

ANSWERS TO SELF-STUDY QUESTIONS:

1. a, (pp. 690–691)   2. b, (p. 692)   3. c, (pp. 693–694)   4. c, (p. 697)   5. c, (p. 699)   6. b, (pp. 700–701)

YOUR TURN! SOLUTIONS

Solution 14.1
1. Financial
2. Managerial
3. Managerial
4. Financial
5. Managerial
6. Financial
7. Managerial

Solution 14.2
Exxon Mobil Co.	Manufacturing
Walmart	Merchandising
Southwest Airlines	Service
Hershey Co.	Manufacturing
Costco	Merchandising
Boston Consulting Group	Service

Solution 14.3
1. *b.*
2. *d.*
3. *f.*
4. *a.*
5. *e.*
6. *c.*

Solution 14.4
c.

Solution 14.5
CPA: Bachelor's degree (equivalent of 120 credit hours) plus 30 additional credit hours

CMA: Bachelor's degree or professional accounting certification

CFE: Bachelor's degree or two years of fraud-related professional experience for each year of academic study

CFP: College-level program of study in personal financial planning

CIA: Associate's degree or seven years of verified experience in internal audit

EA: None

Chapter 15

Managerial Accounting Concepts and Cost Flows

PAST

Chapter 14 introduced managerial accounting. It explored career opportunities in managerial accounting, its objectives, and professional certifications for managerial accountants.

PRESENT

Chapter 15 defines basic costing terminology and introduces different types of manufacturing inventories. It illustrates how costs flow through the inventories and explains the schedule of cost of goods manufactured.

FUTURE

Chapter 16 introduces and explains job costing in more detail for both manufacturing and service industries. It also explains overhead allocation.

In chapter 4, we reviewed the classified financial statements and key ratios for Apple Inc. In this chapter, we will revisit Apple from the perspective of a manager and think about basic costing terminology and cost flows throughout the company.

At 42 years old, **Apple Inc.** is the world's largest information technology company by sales revenue ($229 billion in 2017)[1] and the largest publicly traded corporation by market capitalization ($931 billion in 2018).[2] Although it started as a seller of personal computers (PCs), it has expanded its products to include consumer electronics, consumer software, and commercial servers.

How did Apple grow from a garage-based start-up to overtake companies like Commodore, Tandy, IBM, Microsoft, Sun Microsystems, and Xerox? Perhaps as important as talented employees, innovative products, and strategic alliances, one key was the development of managerial accounting systems to capture, summarize, and report critical data to be used in making strategic business decisions.

This chapter discusses the types of cost data used in management accounting and how these costs flow through the accounting records.

---

[1] 2017 Apple Form 10-K.
[2] https://ycharts.com/companies/AAPL/market_cap

Road Map

LO	Learning Objective	Page	eLecture	Guided Example	Assignments
LO1	Identify the key objectives of a managerial accounting system and define product costs and period costs; variable, fixed, and mixed costs; direct and indirect costs; and cost control.	710	E15-1	YT15.1	SS1, SS2, Q1, Q2, Q3, SE1, SE2, SE3, SE4, E1A, E2A, E1B, E2B
LO2	Describe the three manufacturing inventories—materials, work-in-process, and finished goods—and discuss the categories of manufacturing costs and how these costs flow among the inventories and cost of goods sold.	715	E15-2	YT15.2	SS2, Q4, Q5, Q6, Q7, SE5, SE6, E3A, E4A, E5A, E3B, E4B, E5B
LO3	Define total manufacturing costs, cost of goods manufactured, and cost of goods sold, and illustrate the schedule of cost of goods manufactured and sold and the income statement.	721	E15-3	YT15.3	SS3, SS4, Q8, Q9, Q10, Q11, SE7, SE8, SE9, E3A, E5A, E6A, E7A, E8A, E9A, E10A, E3B, E5B, E6B, E7B, E8B, E9B, E10B, P1A, P2A, P3A, P1B, P2B, P3B
LO4	Illustrate the journal entries to record product cost flows using a perpetual inventory system.	725	E15-4	YT15.4	SS5, Q12, Q13, Q14, Q15, SE10, E11A, E12A, E11B, E12B, P4A, P5A, P4B, P5B

MANAGERIAL ACCOUNTING CONCEPTS AND COST FLOWS

Objectives of a Managerial Accounting System	**Inventories and Cost Categories**	**Product Cost Flows**	**Illustration of Product Cost Accumulation**
• Product costing in a manufacturing environment • Product costing in a service and merchandising environment • Cost control	• Inventories • Manufacturing product cost categories	• Raw materials • Labor • Manufacturing overhead • Cost of goods manufactured • Cost of goods sold	• Introduction of T-accounts • Schedule of cost of goods manufactured • Calculating cost of goods sold • Income statement for a manufacturing firm • Illustration of product cost journal entries

KEY OBJECTIVES OF A MANAGERIAL ACCOUNTING SYSTEM

Business operations vary widely in complexity. However, all managerial accounting systems have the objective of providing management with financial and other business information that is useful in analyzing and making business decisions.

LO1 **Identify** the key objectives of a managerial accounting system and **define** product costs and period costs; variable, fixed, and mixed costs; direct and indirect costs; and cost control.

Hint: A cost object is anything to which costs may be traced. Examples for Apple include everything from an mp3 file to a tablet PC to a service department.

Product Costing in a Manufacturing Environment

Business managers need information about the cost of their products and services in order to control costs and set prices that will result in a profit to the owners and provide the ability to grow the business. For example, Apple is clearly interested in knowing its costs and market share for its manufactured products (e.g., the iPhone and the iPad) for determining merchandise prices.

Product costing involves gathering and assigning the costs of all inputs in the manufacturing or acquisition process to individual products. The individual products represent a type of **cost object**, which may be anything for which business managers must determine a cost. The manufacturer must know its product costs in order to measure inventory values and calculate the profitability of its products for reporting on its financial statements. Using product costing information, management can also determine which products to continue producing and which products to drop. This chapter introduces product costing.

Product versus Period Costs

Exhibit 15-1 indicates that costs can be classified into two broad categories for companies that sell products. **Product costs** include all costs necessary to bring a product to completion, regardless of the period in which they are incurred. For a manufacturer, product costs include materials and components, human labor, utilities, and the use of factory assets. These costs are all recorded initially in inventory accounts.

Period costs are recognized as an expense on the income statement in the period incurred and not assigned to products. The

Exhibit 15-1	**Cost Classifications**

Costs

Product
• Sheet metal in an automobile
• Lumber for a furniture manufacturer
• Factory worker hourly wages
• Factory equipment depreciation
• Factory utilities

Period
• Sales force salaries
• General liability insurance premiums
• Advertising expenses
• Legal expenses
• CEO's salary and benefits

benefits associated with these costs are assumed to expire in the period incurred rather than in the period in which the product is sold. For manufacturers, selling expenses and non-factory administrative expenses are considered period costs. Some departments in a manufacturing firm, such as personnel, may benefit both factory and non-factory activities. The costs of these departments are therefore partly product cost and partly period cost. In summary, product costs are matched with the associated sales revenue in the period of the sale and period costs are matched with the period in which the cost is incurred.

Exhibit 15-2 presents Apple's partial income statement for its 2017 fiscal year, illustrating its product and period costs:

Exhibit 15-2	Apple's Partial Income Statement

APPLE INC.
Income Statement
For the Year Ended September 30, 2017
(in $millions)

This is a product cost.

Net sales		$229,234
Less cost of goods sold		141,048
Gross profit on sales		88,186
Operating expenses		
Research and development	$11,581	
Selling, general and administrative	15,261	26,842
Operating income		61,344

These are period costs.

A.K.A. Cost of sales is another term for cost of goods sold.

A.K.A. Gross margin is also referred to as gross profit.

Concept ⟶	Method ⟶	Assessment ⟶	TAKEAWAY 15.1
A founder of a new consulting firm is trying to determine the firm's cost of service.	• Identify the cost object. • Classify the firm's expenses as product costs vs. period costs relative to that cost object. • Sum the product costs.	• Costs associated with completion of specific consulting projects, such as consultant labor and project supplies, would be considered product costs. • Costs not directly related to projects but related to operating the business, such as general liability insurance premiums, office rent, and marketing costs, would be considered period costs.	

Variable, Fixed, and Mixed Costs

Another way to classify costs that can be helpful to decision makers is to classify them based on their behavior (see **Exhibit 15-3**). A **variable cost** is a cost that *varies in total but is fixed per unit* for a certain period of time and range of activity. In total, variable costs change proportionately with changes in the volume of activity. The cost of a microprocessor chip used in an iPad and the hourly wage paid to the iPad assembly employees are variable costs. To illustrate, assume the cost of the microprocessor chip used in producing one Apple iPad is approximately $30. If Apple produces 100,000 iPads during a period, the total cost of the chips used would be $3,000,000. Alternatively, if Apple produces 1,000,000 iPads, the total cost of the chips would be $30,000,000, still $30 per

Exhibit 15-3	Cost Classifications

Costs

Variable	Fixed	Mixed
• iPad microprocessor chips • Sheet metal in an automobile • Factory worker hourly wages	• Factory equipment depreciation • General liability insurance premiums • Factory property taxes	• Factory utilities (assuming a flat monthly charge plus a usage charge) • Pension administrative costs (fixed monthly fee plus an amount based on assets managed)

Hint: The classification of costs into these three distinct groups can often be more difficult than it may appear at first glance.

iPad. In **Exhibit 15-4**, total variable costs increase by $30 for each additional iPad produced. Yet, the cost per iPad is a constant $30 per unit.

A **fixed cost** is *fixed in total but variable on a per-unit basis* for a particular period of time and range of activity. Fixed costs do not change when the volume of activity changes. Examples are depreciation on buildings and property taxes. Assume that the depreciation on the iPad manufacturing facility is $5 million per month, as shown in **Exhibit 15-4**. If only 100,000 iPads are produced in a month, the depreciation per unit is $50. If 1,000,000 iPads are produced, the depreciation per unit is $5. As we will discuss later, making decisions based on fixed costs per unit can be problematic.

| Exhibit 15-4 | Comparison of Variable, Fixed, and Mixed Costs* |

*Assumes all costs are linear; All numbers, except per-unit, are in thousands.

A.K.A. Mixed costs are sometimes called semi-variable costs as they have both fixed and variable components.

Mixed costs—sometimes called **semi-variable costs**—have both fixed and variable components. A mixed cost changes linearly with changes in activity, but there is still a positive cost when the activity level is zero, as shown in **Exhibit 15-4**. As an example of a mixed cost, consider Apple's utility expense at the factory that produces the iPad. Assume that even if Apple shuts down production for one month, it still incurs a minimum amount for utilities, say $200,000. When production resumes, the costs of heating, air conditioning, lighting, and water increase with usage as production increases. We discuss how to determine the variable and fixed portions of a mixed cost in Chapter 19. **Exhibit 15-4** presents a graphic illustration of these three different types of costs.

Concept ➝	Method ➝	Assessment	TAKEAWAY 15.2
How can one determine whether a cost is variable, fixed, or mixed?	• Observe cost behavior as production levels change. • Use the high-low method or least squares regression analysis (see Chapter 19).	• If costs increase proportionately with production, the cost is variable. • If costs remain unchanged as production changes, the cost is fixed. • If costs change, but not proportionately, as production changes, the cost is mixed.	

Direct and Indirect Costs

Finally, costs can also be classified as *direct* or *indirect* (see **Exhibit 15-5**). A **direct cost** is a cost that can be easily and cost-effectively traced to a specific cost object, such as a unit of product. In a manufacturing company, two obvious direct costs are the main materials and labor used to produce a unit of product. However, other costs may be directly traced as well. For example, in determining the cost of an iPad, Apple would attempt to trace as many costs as possible directly to each iPad unit. Clearly, the main materials, such as the liquid crystal display (LCD) screen and the microprocessor, and the labor involved in assembly would be traced directly to each iPad. However, in a highly automated process, it is possible that Apple could also trace some robotic assembly costs directly to each iPad.

Exhibit 15-5 Cost Classifications

Classification is dependent on the definition of the cost object.

Costs

Direct
• iPad microprocessor chips
• Factory worker hourly wages
• Shipping costs

Indirect
• Factory equipment depreciation
• Factory property taxes
• Raw materials warehouse supervisor salary

An **indirect cost**, therefore, is a cost that cannot be easily and cost-effectively traced to a specific cost object. If Apple were interested in the cost of one of the thousands of products shipped from one of its warehouses, the depreciation expense for that warehouse would be an indirect cost, because it is not easily traced to any one unit of product that passes through the warehouse. It would be considered a common cost for all products of the warehouse. As noted in the previous examples, a particular cost may be considered direct or indirect, depending on the cost object.

Concept ➝	Method ➝	Assessment	TAKEAWAY 15.3
The CEO of a local medical center has asked you to identify the costs of the urgent care, family medicine, and orthopedic practices for purposes of evaluating each area's performance.	• Identify the cost object. • Classify expenses as either direct or indirect relative to that cost object. • Sum the direct costs by cost object.	• Expenses that are specific and limited to one practice (i.e., can be traced to an individual practice) are direct costs. • Expenses that are incurred for the benefit of or are used by more than one practice (i.e., cannot be easily traced to an individual practice) are indirect costs.	

SERVICE AND MERCHANDISING

Product Costing in a Service and Merchandising Environment

Product versus Period Costs

Like manufacturers, service firms need to understand the cost of providing their services to customers. Although these firms do not produce a tangible product, they must know the cost of their services to determine the proper fee for those services and ensure a return to their owners. Service firms may include labor and other directly traceable costs in determining the cost of jobs or projects. Merchandising companies record the cost of acquired inventory as a product cost, whereas items such as salaries and wages, utilities, and depreciation are recorded immediately as operating expenses.

Service firms expense period costs in the period the costs are incurred. The benefits associated with these costs are assumed to expire in the period incurred rather than in the period in which the product is sold. Like manufacturers, selling expenses and non-factory administrative expenses are considered period costs.

Variable, Fixed, and Mixed Costs

The definitions of variable, fixed, and mixed costs are the same for service and merchandise firms as those given previously for manufacturers. An example of a variable cost in a consulting firm would be office supplies expense, which would increase with the number of consulting projects performed. The consulting firm's office lease expense would be considered a fixed cost because it would not vary with the number of projects performed. The firm's contribution to the employee 401(k) profit-sharing retirement plan would be a mixed cost assuming that the plan required a minimum contribution of 3% and that additional contributions would be made based on the level of profit earned in a year.

Direct and Indirect Costs

Again, the definitions of direct and indirect costs are the same as given previously for a manufacturing firm. In a service company, wages or salaries are the most common direct cost. However, costs such as photocopying, postage, and travel can be traced to a particular job. Service companies would typically consider marketing costs and costs associated with employee continuing education classes as indirect costs.

Cost Control

Business managers also need information that will assist them in competing effectively in their chosen market. As information becomes more easily available to customers in a global market, price competition can become more intense. For example, because customers can instantly compare prices for products and services on their smartphones, tablets, and computers, businesses might have little or no control over the prices that they can charge. Therefore, business managers must control their costs to ensure a reasonable profit. Cost control involves the accumulation of information to measure management performance and evaluate operational efficiency. Subsequent chapters present cost control approaches and techniques that are used by businesses of all types. For example, Chapter 22 illustrates how business managers use budgets to evaluate actual versus expected performance. Chapter 23 introduces the use of standard costs as a way of identifying where and why operations deviate from management's expectations.

Classify each of the following costs relative to the cost object "Apple iPad":

	Product or Period	Variable, Fixed, or Mixed	Direct or Indirect
Assembly labor..................................			
iPad case			
CEO salary.....................................			
Microprocessor..................................			
Depreciation on Apple corporate headquarters			
Health insurance for factory workers			
Touch screen			
Adhesive on the serial number label			

YOUR TURN! 15.1

The solution is on page 751.

INVENTORIES AND COST CATEGORIES

Inventories

Manufacturing Firms

At any point in time, manufacturing operations typically have units of product at various stages of completion. Three inventories are usually maintained on a perpetual basis to reflect these stages—materials, work-in-process, and finished goods.

The **materials inventory** includes factory materials and components that have been purchased but not yet placed into production. Some of the items in the materials inventory, such as sheets of steel or microprocessors, were finished products to the supplying company but are materials and components to the purchasing company. All items in the materials inventory account are recorded at their net delivered cost (i.e., product cost plus inbound shipping).

The **work-in-process inventory** of a manufacturing firm includes units of product that have been placed in production but have not yet been completed. All the costs of materials and components, direct human labor, utilities, and use of factory assets (overhead costs) are included in the work-in-process inventory. All items in the work-in-process inventory account are recorded at cost.

The **finished goods inventory** of a manufacturing firm includes all units of product that have been completed but have not been sold. All items in the finished goods inventory account were recorded at cost in the work-in-process inventory account and transferred to the finished goods inventory account.

Many manufacturing firms also maintain an inventory of factory and office supplies for the manufacturing operation. **Factory supplies** are consumable items, such as cleaning supplies and machinery lubricants, used in the factory but not incorporated into the product; **office supplies** include copy paper, toner, and paper clips, items used in the office but not charged to a particular job. The inventory of factory and office supplies is usually maintained on a periodic basis, so the cost of factory and office supplies used during a period is determined at period-end after the supplies on hand are counted.

LO2 Describe the three manufacturing inventories—materials, work-in-process, and finished goods—and **discuss** the categories of manufacturing costs and how these costs flow among the inventories and cost of goods sold.

Merchandising and Service Firms

Merchandising firms have only one inventory account—merchandise inventory. This is similar to the finished goods inventory account at a manufacturer because it contains finished products that are available for immediate sale. As discussed previously,

SERVICE AND MERCHANDISING

manufacturing firms usually have three primary inventory accounts: materials, work-in-process, and finished goods.

Service firms typically have only one inventory account—work-in-process inventory. This account represents the service firm's partially completed projects. Service firms would include the cost of direct labor and overhead in work-in-process inventory. Although service firms may utilize office supplies on their projects, these costs are usually immaterial and not considered a materials inventory. Because completed projects are billed to the customer immediately upon completion, there is no need for a finished goods inventory. These inventories are reported in the current assets section of the balance sheet, as illustrated in **Exhibit 15-6**.

Exhibit 15-6	Comparison of Merchandising, Service, and Manufacturing Inventories	
Merchandising Firm	**Service Firm**	**Manufacturing Firm**
Cash .... $ 10,000	Cash .... $ 10,000	Cash .... $ 10,000
Short-term investments .. 20,000	Short-term investments .. 20,000	Short-term investments .. 20,000
Receivables 45,000	Receivables 45,000	Receivables 45,000
Merchandise inventory ... 80,000	Work-in-process inventory 80,000	Inventories:
Prepaid expenses 15,000	Prepaid expenses 15,000	Materials 35,000
Total current assets $170,000	Office supplies 5,000	Work-in-process 55,000
	Total current assets $175,000	Finished goods 25,000
		Prepaid expenses 15,000
		Factory supplies 5,000
		Total current assets $210,000

> Inventory accounts include all costs necessary to bring the inventory to completion—all product costs.

Factory Supplies versus Indirect Materials

Factory supplies are different from indirect materials. Factory supplies are used in the factory but are not part of the product itself. Lubricant used on the machine that stamps the sheet metal used in a laptop computer would be a factory supply. Indirect materials are part of the product but are difficult to trace to each individual product. Solder used to attach computer chips to a motherboard would be an indirect material. Both factory supplies and indirect materials can become part of manufacturing overhead.

Manufacturing Product Cost Categories

Product costs in a manufacturing setting can be classified into three subcategories (see **Exhibit 15-7**):

1. **Direct materials** include all the important materials and components that physically make up the product (such as sheets of steel and electric motors). Incidental material items, such as glue and fasteners, are considered **indirect materials** and are included in manufacturing overhead. Both direct material items and indirect material items are included in the materials inventory. Therefore, all items in the materials inventory will be used as either direct materials or indirect materials.

Hint: "Manufacturing product costs" include all direct materials, direct labor, and manufacturing overhead for a period of time and represent the additions to work-in-process inventory. "Manufacturing costs" should not be confused with "manufacturing overhead costs," although both terms have the word "manufacturing" in them.

Exhibit 15-7	Product Costs

Costs

Product   Period

Direct Materials   Direct Labor   Manufacturing Overhead

2. **Direct labor** includes the salary and wage cost of factory employees who work directly on the product (such as machine operators, assemblers, and painters). The sal-

ary and wage cost of factory employees who do not work directly on the product (e.g., supervisors, inspectors, and material handlers) is considered **indirect labor**, which is included in manufacturing overhead. The total amount of factory labor (direct and indirect) is identified on a manufacturing firm's factory payroll.

Apple Inc. Corporate Headquarters

iPad Factory

3. **Manufacturing overhead** consists of all manufacturing costs not included in direct materials and direct labor. Manufacturing overhead includes indirect materials, indirect labor, factory supplies used, factory payroll tax and fringe benefits costs, factory utilities, and factory building and machinery costs (such as depreciation, insurance, property taxes, and repairs and maintenance). Manufacturing overhead specifically *excludes* selling and non-factory administrative expenses because these expenses are not incurred in the manufacturing process.

A.K.A. Manufacturing overhead has several other names that are commonly used in practice, such as **factory overhead**, factory burden, and indirect manufacturing costs.

Combined Costs

Manufacturing Firms

Manufacturing cost categories are frequently combined for convenience. As illustrated in **Exhibit 15-8**, the sum of direct materials and direct labor for a particular product is known as prime cost. **Prime cost** is made up of the elements of product cost that are easily and directly traceable to individual products. **Conversion cost** is the sum of direct labor and manufacturing overhead. Conversion cost represents the elements of product cost necessary to convert the materials and components to the final finished products.

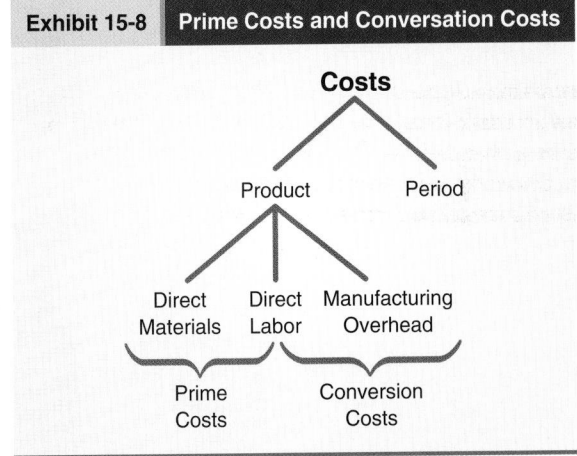

| Exhibit 15-8 | Prime Costs and Conversation Costs |

Service Firms

Prime cost and conversion cost can also apply to a service firm. A service firm's prime cost is limited to direct labor cost (because no direct materials are typically used). A service firm's conversion cost is the sum of direct labor and applied general overhead.

Although Apple is not primarily a service firm, it has a technical support department that assists customers with hardware and software questions that arise in the normal operation of Apple products. Prime costs for the technical support department would simply include the wages and salaries of support personnel because the service department would have no direct materials. Conversion costs for the technical support department would include both the wages and salaries of support personnel in addition to overhead costs, such as depreciation on office equipment, employee health insurance premiums, the costs associated with janitorial services, and utilities.

SERVICE AND MERCHANDISING

PRODUCT COST FLOWS

Raw Materials

The materials inventory frequently contains both direct and indirect materials. As direct materials are used in production, they are traced directly to specific units of product. Thus, the cost of direct materials flows from raw materials inventory directly into work-in-process inventory. On the other hand, indirect materials cannot be traced to particular units of product. As a result, as they are used in the production process, their cost is transferred from raw materials inventory to manufacturing overhead. For example, it may not be cost effective for Apple to trace the cost of screws to each iPad. As a result, screws are likely classified as indirect materials and their cost would be transferred from raw materials inventory to manufacturing overhead as they are used in production. Overhead costs are then allocated (applied) to particular jobs. **Exhibit 15-9a** illustrates the flow of both direct and indirect materials from raw materials inventory to the work-in-process and manufacturing overhead, respectively.

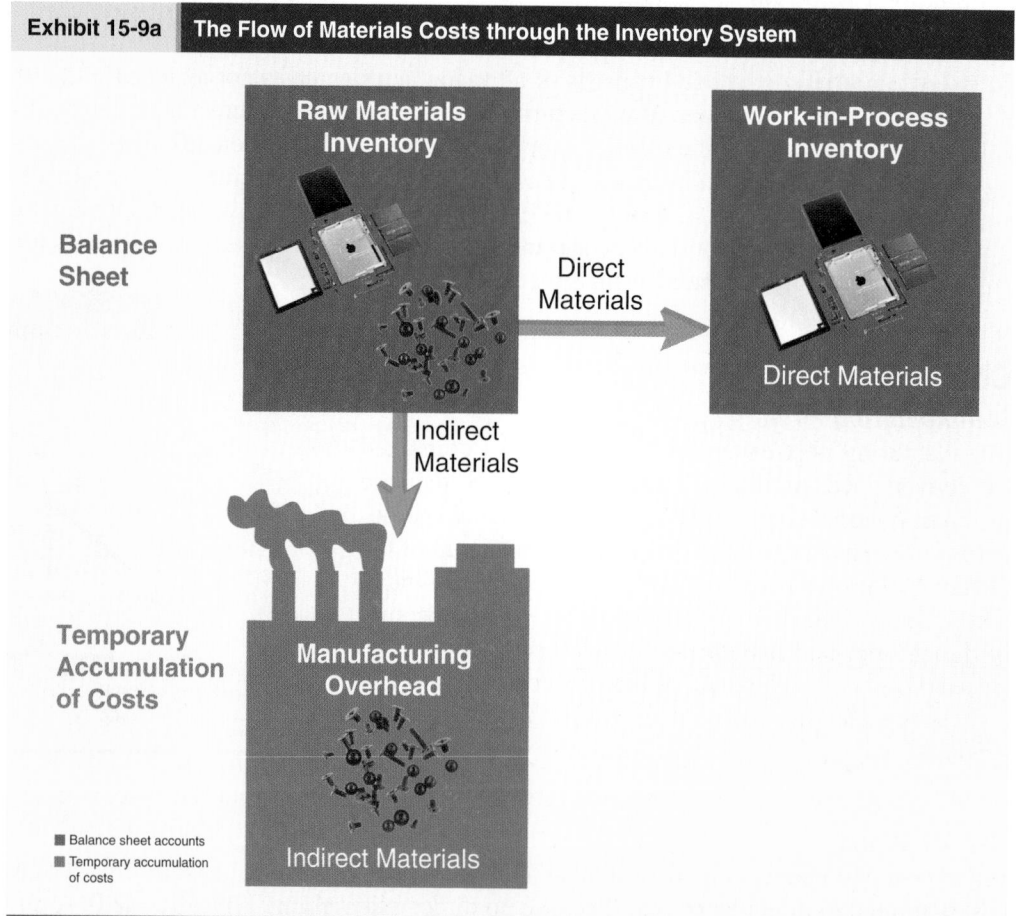

| Exhibit 15-9a | The Flow of Materials Costs through the Inventory System |

Labor

Both direct and indirect labor costs are incurred in the manufacturing process. The wages of employees who work directly on units of product are traced directly to specific units. Therefore, when these labor costs are incurred, they are recorded in work-in-process inventory. On the other hand, the wages of factory employees not working directly on the product cannot be traced directly to particular units. They are recorded as manufacturing overhead and allocated to jobs based on a predetermined overhead application rate. In the iPad manufacturing facility, the costs of employees directly involved in the assembly of iPads are recorded directly in work-in-process inventory. On the other hand, the salaries and wages of supervisors, maintenance personnel, and quality inspectors in the iPad factory would be classified as indirect labor and recorded as manufacturing overhead. **Exhibit 15-9b** illustrates how both direct and indirect labor flow into work-in-process and manufacturing overhead, respectively.

Exhibit 15-9b	The Flow of Labor Costs through the Inventory System

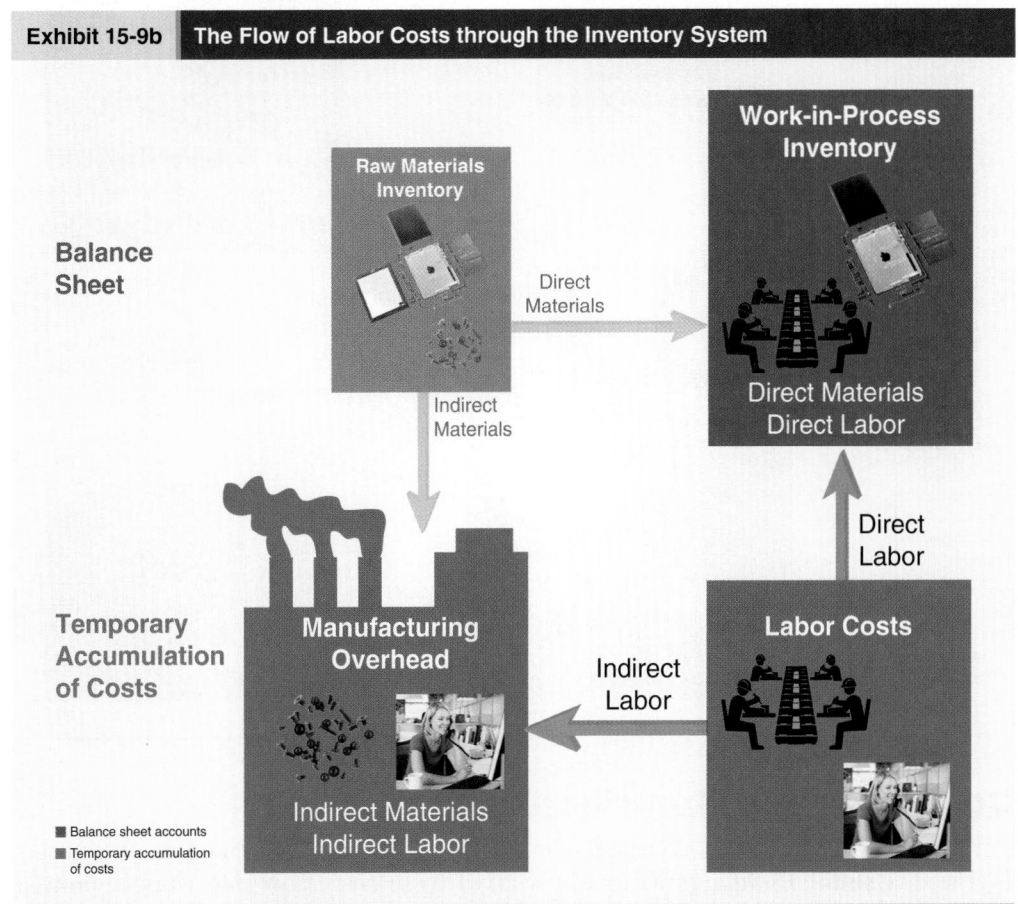

Manufacturing Overhead

Because overhead costs are, by definition, indirect costs that cannot be traced to a particular unit of product, they are accumulated in manufacturing overhead during the accounting period. Indirect materials and indirect labor are just two examples of indirect costs accumulated in manufacturing overhead. Other examples include costs that cannot be traced to a particular unit of product, such as depreciation on the factory and factory equipment, factory utilities, insurance on production facilities, property taxes related to the factory, and so forth. The problem accountants face is that it is impossible to know with certainty how much manufacturing overhead will accumulate during a particular period. Rather than waiting until the end of the period to divide the actual manufacturing overhead costs by the number of units actually produced to allocate the costs to jobs passing through the production process, accountants use their knowledge from past periods to calculate an estimated overhead rate at the beginning of the period to allocate overhead to jobs as they pass through the production process. We discuss the process for estimating and allocating manufacturing overhead in more detail in Chapter 16. However, **Exhibit 15-9c** illustrates the flow of overhead costs from manufacturing overhead to the work-in-process inventory.

Hint: Actual indirect costs are recorded on the debit side of the manufacturing overhead account, whereas overhead applied to units produced is recorded on the credit side because overhead is allocated to jobs (in the work-in-process inventory account).

Exhibit 15-9c	The Flow of Manufacturing Overhead Costs through the Inventory System

Cost of Goods Manufactured

Total manufacturing costs consist of direct materials, direct labor, and manufacturing overhead. **Exhibit 15-9d** summarizes how all of these costs flow into work-in-process inventory.

Exhibit 15-9d	The Flow of Total Manufacturing Costs through the Inventory System

The product costs that flow from work-in-process to the finished goods during an accounting period are known as **cost of goods manufactured (COGM)**. The schedule of cost of goods manufactured (which we demonstrate in the next section) summarizes all of the different costs incurred in the production of inventory: (1) direct materials, (2) labor costs, and (3) manufacturing overhead. All of these costs flow into work-in-process inventory. The total cost of goods manufactured is transferred to finished goods inventory, as illustrated in **Exhibit 15-9d**.

Cost of Goods Sold

Exhibit 15-9e illustrates the flow of all product costs through the inventory system of a manufacturing firm. All costs that are accumulated in work-in-process eventually flow to finished goods and, when the products are sold, are recognized as **cost of goods sold (COGS)**.

| Exhibit 15-9e | The Flow of Total Manufacturing Costs through the Inventory System |

■ Temporary accumulation of costs
■ Balance sheet accounts
■ Income statement account

Which of the following represents the correct sequence of the flow of costs in a typical manufacturing company?

a. Direct materials, cost of goods sold, work-in-process inventory, finished goods inventory
b. Direct materials, work-in-process inventory, cost of goods sold, finished goods inventory
c. Direct materials, work-in-process inventory, finished goods inventory, cost of goods sold
d. Work-in-process inventory, direct materials, finished goods inventory, cost of goods sold

YOUR TURN! 15.2

The solution is on page 751.

ILLUSTRATION OF PRODUCT COST ACCUMULATION

Introduction of T-Accounts

Exhibit 15-9e illustrates the flow of all product costs through the inventory accounts. As you learn in financial accounting, each account can be represented by a T-account, which is a visual illustration of the flow of dollars into and out of the account. **Exhibit 15-10** illustrates the T-accounts associated with each item in **Exhibit 15-9e**.

LO3 **Define** total manufacturing costs, cost of goods manufactured, and cost of goods sold, and **illustrate** the schedule of cost of goods manufactured and sold and the income statement.

Exhibit 15-10 | **The Flow of Total Manufacturing Costs through the Inventory Accounts**

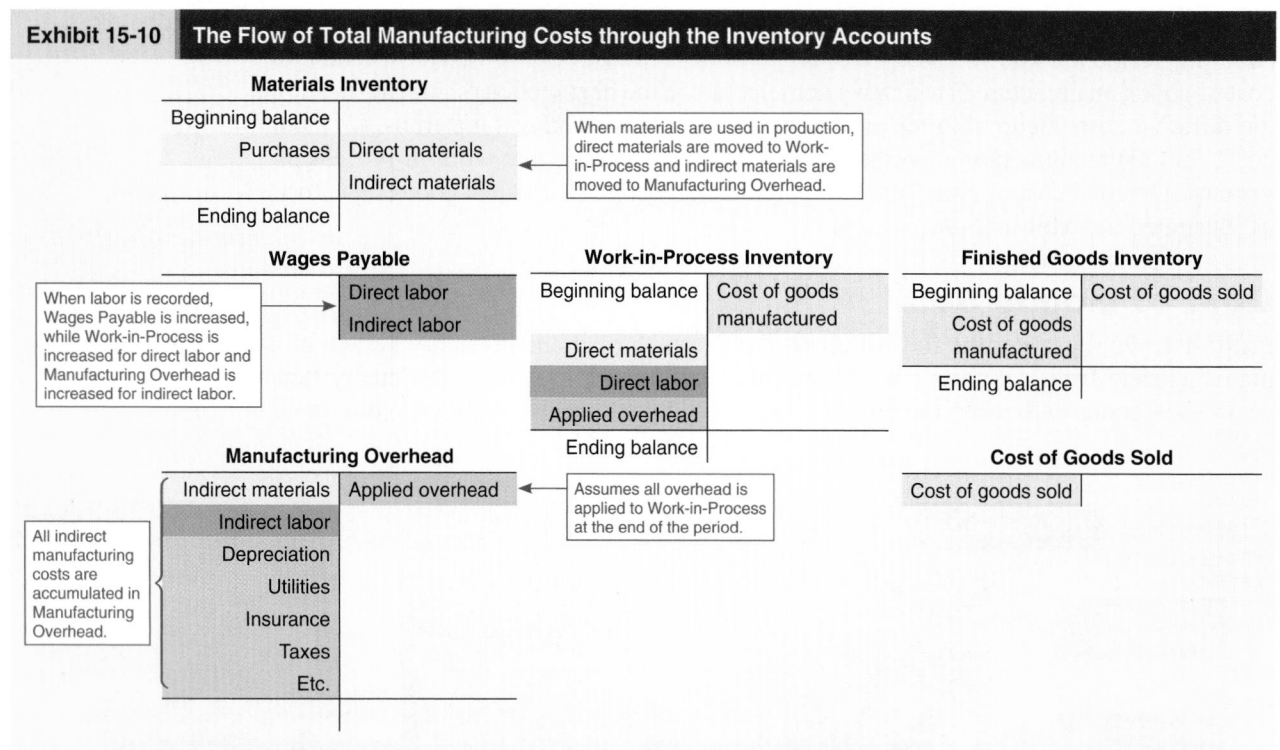

Real-World Manufacturing Example

We introduced Fezzari Performance Bicycles in Chapter 14. Fezzari is a manufacturer of road and mountain bikes. Using estimates of sales and manufacturing costs at Fezzari, **Exhibit 15-11** shows how the costs of manufacturing bikes flow through the inventory accounts.

Schedule of Cost of Goods Manufactured

Although **Exhibit 15-11** is helpful in visualizing the flow of costs through Fezzari's accounts, it is not very useful for management decision making. The schedule of cost of goods manufactured presents information about an entity's product cost for a particular accounting period in a format that is more suitable for decision making. **Exhibit 15-12** presents Fezzari's 2019 schedule of cost of goods manufactured. The schedule has two sections. The first section summarizes the **total manufacturing costs** for the year: direct materials, direct labor, and manufacturing overhead incurred in the manufacturing process during the year. These are all of the costs that flow into the work-in-process inventory account during the year. In the calculation of direct materials used during the year, the net delivered cost of materials purchased is added to the beginning materials inventory to determine the cost of materials available during the year. The cost of materials not used (ending materials inventory) is then subtracted to identify the cost of all materials used during the year. This total represents both direct materials used and indirect materials used. We subtract indirect materials used to determine the direct materials used. Direct labor is presented on a single line. The detail of manufacturing overhead is calculated by summing all of the individual components of manufacturing overhead.

Exhibit 15-11 shows how the costs of manufacturing bikes flow through the inventory accounts on the balance sheet and into the cost of goods sold account on the income statement. Review each transaction in the exhibit, then trace its impact through the related T-accounts. The balances at the beginning of the period are as follows (all numbers are in thousands): Materials Inventory, $25; Work-in-Process Inventory, $10; and Finished Goods Inventory, $12.

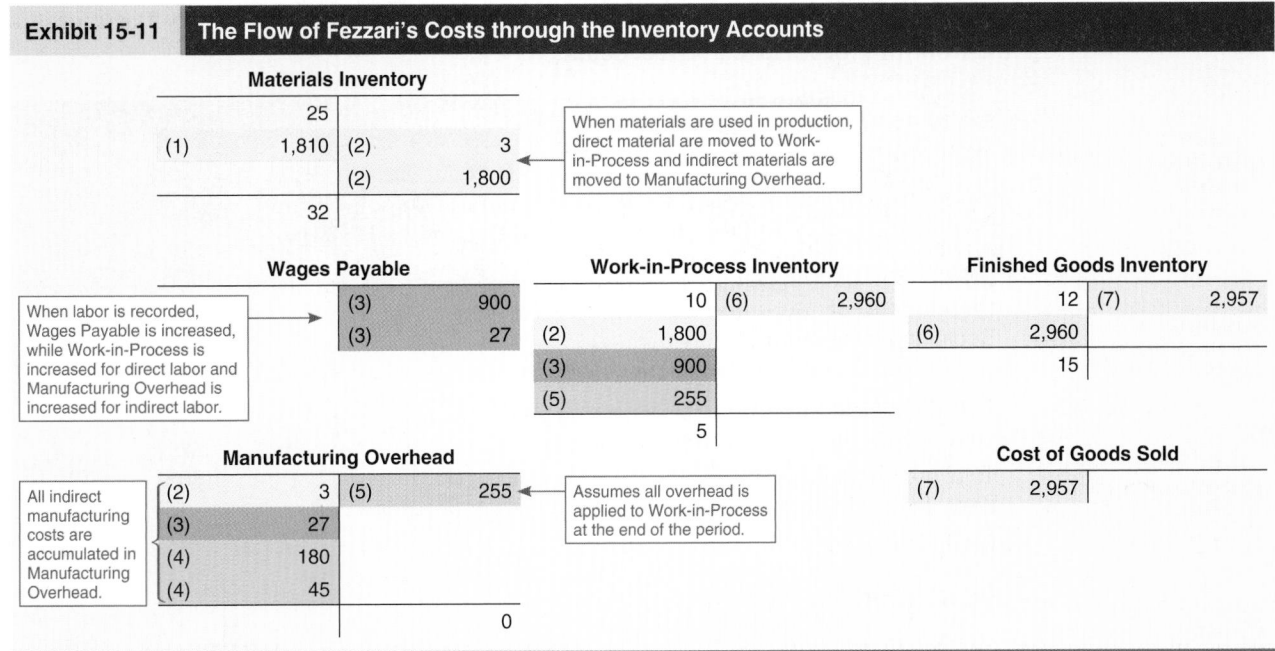

Exhibit 15-11   The Flow of Fezzari's Costs through the Inventory Accounts

Accounting for Materials

(1) Materials inventory of $1,810 are purchased and received.

(2) Materials inventory is used in the production process. Direct materials of $1,800 are used and transferred to Work-in-Process Inventory. Indirect materials of $3 are used and transferred to and accumulated in Manufacturing Overhead.

Accounting for Labor

(3) Manufacturing wages are incurred in the production process. Direct labor of $900 is incurred and recorded in both Work-in-Process Inventory and Wages Payable. Indirect labor of $27 is incurred and recorded in both Manufacturing Overhead and Wages Payable.

Accounting for Manufacturing Overhead

(4) Additional indirect manufacturing costs are incurred during the production process and accumulated in Manufacturing Overhead. These costs include the lease on the factory of $180 and depreciation on factory machinery of $45.

(5) At the end of the period, the $255 of costs accumulated in Manufacturing Overhead is applied to Work-in-Process Inventory.

Accounting for Finished Goods and Cost of Goods Sold

(6) As bikes are completed, their total manufacturing costs of $2,960 are transferred from Work-in-Process Inventory to Finished Goods Inventory.

(7) When bikes are sold, their total manufacturing costs of $2,957 are transferred out of Finished Goods Inventory and recognized as a cost of goods sold expense. This entry is recorded along with the related sales entry.

The second section of the schedule of cost of goods manufactured determines the cost of goods manufactured—the cost of goods completed during the year and transferred to finished goods. In this section, total manufacturing costs for the year are added to the amount representing the work-in-process at the beginning of the year to determine the total cost of work-in-process during the year. The cost of incomplete units (ending work-in-process inventory) is then subtracted to determine the cost associated with the completed units (cost of goods manufactured). These are all of the numbers that appear in the work-in-process inventory account.

Exhibit 15-12	Schedule of Cost of Goods Manufactured

FEZZARI PERFORMANCE BICYCLES
Schedule of Cost of Goods Manufactured
For the Year Ended December 31, 2019
(000s)

Direct Material		
Beginning materials inventory	$ 25	
Net delivered cost of materials purchased	1,810	
Cost of materials available	1,835	
Less: Ending materials inventory	(32)	
Total materials used	1,803	
Less: Indirect materials used	(3)	
Direct materials used		$1,800
Direct labor		900
Factory Overhead		
Indirect materials	3	
Indirect labor	27	
Lease—factory	180	
Depreciation—factory machinery	45	
Total factory overhead		255
Total manufacturing costs for the year		2,955
Add: Beginning work-in-process inventory		10
Total cost of work-in-process during the year		2,965
Less: Ending work-in-process inventory		(5)
Cost of goods manufactured		$2,960

Total manufacturing costs include the amounts of direct materials used, direct labor, and applied overhead for the period reported.

Cost of goods manufactured is total manufacturing costs plus or minus the change in the work-in-process inventory balance.

Calculating Cost of Goods Sold

Exhibit 15-13 presents Fezzari's cost of goods sold summary for 2019. The calculation of cost of goods manufactured is an important step in determining cost of goods sold. The cost of the beginning finished goods inventory is added to cost of goods manufactured to report the cost of goods available for sale during the year. The cost of unsold units (ending finished goods inventory) is then subtracted to identify the cost associated with the units that were sold during the year (cost of goods sold).

Exhibit 15-13	Cost of Goods Sold Calculation

FEZZARI PERFORMANCE BICYCLES
Schedule of Cost of Goods Sold
For the Year Ended December 31, 2019
(000s)

Cost of goods manufactured	$2,960
Add: Beginning finished goods inventory	12
Cost of goods available for sale	$2,972
Less: Ending finished goods inventory	(15)
Cost of goods sold	$2,957

This amount will be reported on Fezzari's income statement and matched against the related sales revenue.

The schedule of cost of goods manufactured and the calculation of cost of goods sold provide useful information about product costs in support of the income statement. They are not, however, required financial statements.

Income Statement for a Manufacturing Firm

Exhibit 15-14 presents the income statement for 2019 for Fezzari. Fezzari uses the perpetual inventory system for finished goods, so its cost of goods sold amount is reported in the general ledger account. The schedule of cost of goods manufactured (see **Exhibit 15-12**) and the cost of goods sold calculation (see **Exhibit 15-13**) tie to the cost of goods sold amount in the income statement.

Exhibit 15-14	Income Statement

FEZZARI PERFORMANCE BICYCLES
Income Statement
For the Year Ended December 31, 2019
(000s)

Sales.		$4,500
Cost of goods sold		2,957
Gross profit on sales.		$1,543
Operating expenses:		
Selling expenses.	$ 400	
Non-factory administrative expenses	340	740
Income from operations		$ 803
Other income and expense:		
Interest expense		5
Income before income tax		$ 798
Income tax expense		279
Net income		$ 519

> Represents all product costs of products sold during the period identified in the summary of costs of goods sold in Exhibit 15-13.

YOUR TURN! 15.3

The solution is on page 751.

Shea Company reported raw material purchases of $1,400, paid $1,200 in factory labor, and incurred and applied $900 in factory overhead for March. The March 1 inventory balances were $200 for raw materials, $600 for work-in-process inventory, and $400 for finished goods inventory. On March 31, inventory balances were $300 for raw materials, $500 for work-in-process inventory, and $600 for finished goods inventory. What was Shea's cost of goods manufactured for March?

ILLUSTRATION OF PRODUCT COST JOURNAL ENTRIES

The following illustration for **Apple Inc.** presents hypothetical summary transactions and adjustment entries for 2017 related to the accounts used to accumulate product costs. Assume that Apple Inc. uses the perpetual inventory system and had the following manufacturing inventory account balances (in millions) at September 24, 2016 (the beginning of its 2017 fiscal year):

LO4 **Illustrate** the journal entries to record product cost flows using a perpetual inventory system.

Materials inventory	$ 400
Work-in-process inventory	600
Finished goods inventory	1,000

When a manufacturing firm uses the perpetual inventory system for Materials Inventory, Work-in-Process Inventory, and Finished Goods Inventory, cost of goods sold can be determined directly by reference to the Cost of Goods Sold account in the general ledger.

Total manufacturing costs and cost of goods manufactured, however, are not directly available in a general ledger account. Assume Apple's subsidiary records for 2017 contain the following data:

1. Net delivered cost of materials purchased was $50,000.
2. The cost of direct materials used in production was $44,400.
3. Direct labor totaled $17,500.
4. Manufacturing overhead consists of the following:

Indirect materials	$ 5,000
Indirect labor.	4,000
Various costs	62,500
Year-end adjustments.	10,000*
	$81,500

*This is composed of $2,000 for manufacturing supplies and $8,000 for depreciation on factory machinery.

Based on this information, assume Apple records the following entries for 2017:

1. Acquisition of materials

Materials inventory	50,000	
Accounts payable		50,000
To record the delivered cost of materials purchased.		

2. Use of direct materials and indirect materials

Work-in-process inventory	44,400	
Manufacturing overhead	5,000	
Materials inventory		49,400
To record the transfer of direct materials ($44,400) to the work-in-process inventory and the transfer of indirect materials ($5,000) to manufacturing overhead.		

3. Incurrence of factory payroll

Work-in-process inventory	17,500	
Manufacturing overhead	4,000	
Wages payable		21,500
To record the factory payroll as direct labor ($17,500) to the work-in-process inventory and as indirect labor ($4,000) to manufacturing overhead.		

4. Incurrence of manufacturing overhead costs during year

Manufacturing overhead	62,500	
Accounts payable or cash		62,500
To record various factory costs incurred during the year as manufacturing overhead.		

5. Recognition of certain manufacturing overhead costs with year-end adjustments

Manufacturing overhead	10,000	
Manufacturing supplies		2,000
Accumulated depreciation—factory machinery		8,000
To record cost of supplies used for and depreciation on factory machinery.		

6. Application of manufacturing overhead

Work-in-process inventory	81,500	
Manufacturing overhead		81,500

To record the application of manufacturing overhead to the work-in-process inventory. (The procedures for determining this application will be described in a subsequent chapter.)

Cost Flows

Exhibit 15-15 presents T-accounts to which these summary entries have been posted. The arrows in **Exhibit 15-15** indicate the flows of product cost. Direct material flows from Materials Inventory to Work-in-Process Inventory, whereas indirect material flows from Materials Inventory to Manufacturing Overhead. Direct labor flows from Wages Expense to Work-in-Process Inventory, whereas indirect labor flows from Wages Payable to Manufacturing Overhead. Actual manufacturing overhead comes from several sources, and manufacturing overhead applied flows to Work-in-Process Inventory.

Hint: In practice, applied manufacturing overhead rarely equals the actual manufacturing overhead incurred during a period, as illustrated in this example. Chapter 16 explains how to deal with over- or underapplied overhead.

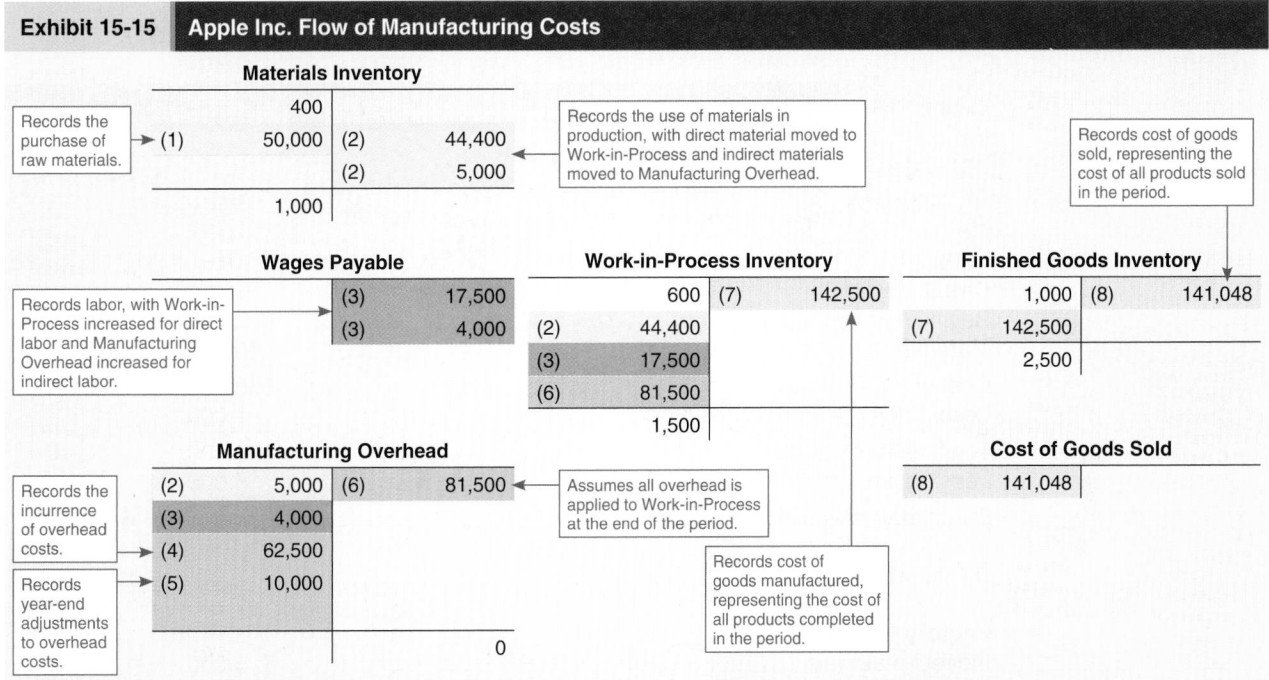

Exhibit 15-15   **Apple Inc. Flow of Manufacturing Costs**

Cost of goods manufactured (the product cost of goods completed during the accounting period) flows from Work-in-Process Inventory to Finished Goods Inventory. The cost of goods sold flows from Finished Goods Inventory to the Cost of Goods Sold account. These cost flows are represented by the following journal entries:

7. Recognition of cost of goods manufactured

Finished goods inventory	142,500	
Work-in-process inventory		142,500

To record the transfer of the cost associated with goods completed from the work-in-process inventory to the finished goods inventory.

8. Recognition of cost of goods sold

Cost of goods sold	141,048	
Finished goods inventory		141,048

To record the transfer of the cost associated with goods sold to customers from the finished goods inventory to cost of goods sold— recorded with the related sales entry.

TAKEAWAY 15.4	Concept ———————➤	Method ———————➤	Assessment
	What amount should be reported as cost of goods sold in the annual financial statements?	• Accumulate the costs of direct materials, direct labor, and manufacturing overhead for all products produced in a period. • Report the cost of goods sold in the period of the sale.	• If the ending balance in finished goods inventory is less than the beginning balance, then cost of goods sold will be greater than cost of goods manufactured. • If the ending balance in finished goods inventory is greater than the beginning balance, then cost of goods sold will be less than cost of goods manufactured.

Based on the information in these journal entries and as summarized in the T-accounts in **Exhibit 15-15**, **Exhibit 15-16** presents Apple Inc.'s schedule of cost of goods manufactured for 2017.

Exhibit 15-16	Schedule of Costs of Goods Manufactured

APPLE INC.
Schedule of Cost of Goods Manufactured
For the Year Ended September 30, 2017
(in $millions)

Direct Material

Beginning materials inventory	$ 400	
Materials purchased.....................................	50,000	
Cost of materials available.............................	$50,400	
Less: Ending materials inventory	1,000	
Total materials used	$49,400	
Less: Indirect materials used	5,000	
Direct materials used		$ 44,400
Direct labor		$ 17,500

Factory Overhead

Indirect materials	$ 5,000	
Indirect labor..	4,000	
Various costs	62,500	
Year-end adjustments....................................	10,000	
Total factory overhead		$ 81,500
Total manufacturing costs for the year		$143,400
Add: Beginning work-in-process inventory................		$ 600
Total cost of work-in-process during the year............		144,000
Less: Ending work-in-process inventory..................		(1,500)
Cost of goods manufactured...........................		$142,500

Total Manufacturing Cost includes all direct materials, direct labor, and applied overhead for **work done** during the period.

Cost of Goods Manufactured reflects the total manufacturing costs for the **products completed** during the period.

Financial Statements

Exhibit 15-17 presents Apple Inc.'s 2017 income statement.

Exhibit 15-17	Income Statement

APPLE INC.
Income Statement
For Year Ended September 30, 2017

> Cost of Goods Sold reflects the total manufacturing costs for the **products sold** during the period.

(in millions)	2017
Net sales.	$229,234
Less cost of goods sold	141,048
Gross profit on sales	88,186
Operating expenses	
Research and development expenses	11,581
Selling, general and administrative	15,261
Total operating expenses	26,842
Income from operations	61,344
Other income and expenses.	2,745
Income before income taxes	64,089
Income tax expense	15,738
Net income	$ 48,351

Exhibit 15-18 presents the September 30, 2017, balance sheet for Apple, Inc. Note that the multiple inventory accounts are combined into a single line in the current assets section for presentation purposes.

Exhibit 15-18	Balance Sheet

APPLE INC.
Balance Sheet
September 30, 2017

> All inventory accounts are combined into one line item for presentation purposes.

(in millions)	2017
Assets	
Current assets:	
Cash	$ 20,289
Short-term investments.	53,892
Accounts receivable	35,673
Inventory.	4,855
Other current assets	13,936
Total current assets	128,645
Long-term assets:	
Property, plant and equipment	33,783
Intangible assets.	8,015
Other noncurrent assets	204,876
Total long-term assets	246,674
Total assets	$375,319
Liabilities	
Current liabilities:	
Accounts payable	$ 49,049
Other current liabilities	51,765
Total current liabilities	100,814
Long-term liabilities:	140,458
Total liabilities	241,272

continued

continued from previous page

Exhibit 15-18	Balance Sheet

APPLE INC.
Balance Sheet
September 30, 2017

(in millions)	2017
Stockholders' Equity	
Common stock	35,867
Retained earnings	98,330
Other equity	(150)
Total stockholders' equity	134,047
Total liabilities and stockholders' equity	$375,319

YOUR TURN! 15.4

The solution is on page 752.

Shea Company reported raw material purchases of $1,400, paid $1,200 in factory labor, and incurred and applied $900 in factory overhead for March. The March 1 inventory balances were $200 for raw materials, $600 for work-in-process inventory, and $400 for finished goods inventory. On March 31, inventory balances were $300 for raw materials, $500 for work-in-process inventory, and $600 for finished goods inventory. What are the March journal entries to record Shea's

a. Raw materials purchase

b. Raw materials usage

c. Direct labor

d. Application of manufacturing overhead

e. Cost of goods manufactured

f. Cost of goods sold

CORPORATE SOCIAL RESPONSIBILITY

Environmental Performance Reporting at Apple

There are probably few companies as secretive as Apple. The company is very careful to control any leaks on its upcoming products. Apple uses this strategy of keeping things secret in order to increase the anticipation before new product announcements. The strategy seems to be working well, based on the excitement surrounding these new product events.

One area that Apple is not secretive about is its environmental responsibility. Apple uses its detailed managerial accounting system to measure the environmental impact of how every product is manufactured. Unlike the secrecy surrounding what the next new product will be, Apple believes in full transparency regarding its environmental performance and reports on this performance in its comprehensive *Product Environmental Reports*. Every Apple product is measured and rated in four categories: climate change, restricted substances, energy efficiency, and material efficiency.

As stated on Apple's website, "We strive to create products that are the best they can be in every way. . . . The same passion for innovation goes into how we think about environmental responsibility. It's why we work tirelessly to reduce our impact on climate change, find ways to use greener materials, and conserve the resources we all need to thrive."

A famous expression in business is that you can't manage what you can't measure. For Apple to be a leader in both product development and environmental responsibility, the company depends on its managerial accounting systems to provide the information needed to properly manage everything the company does.

SERVICE INDUSTRY IN FOCUS

Environmental Business Consultants, LLC (EBC), is a consulting firm that specializes in the areas of recycling and solid waste and water/wastewater management services. The firm has offices located in northern and southern California. EBC has serviced hundreds of municipal agencies since 1984. Both the firm's executives and consultants work on client projects. EBC's 2019 adjusted trial balance is shown below.

SERVICE AND MERCHANDISING

Description	Trial Balance	
	Debit	Credit
Cash.	390,000	
Accounts receivable	474,000	
Allowance for uncollectible accounts		—
Work-in-process inventory	247,000	
Other current assets.	32,000	
Furniture and fixtures	150,000	
Accumulated depreciation—furniture		150,000
Office equipment	277,000	
Accumulated depreciation—equipment		198,000
Accounts payable.		—
Other current liabilities		37,500
Noncurrent liabilities.		3,000
Owners' capital.		90,000
Retained earnings		573,000
Sales.		4,146,000
Reimbursable costs	431,000	
Executive salaries.	844,500	
Clerical salaries	217,500	
Consultant salaries.	1,050,000	
Employee benefits	145,500	
Payroll taxes.	123,000	
Employee bonuses.	126,000	
Marketing expenses	48,000	
Employee continuing education expenses.	27,000	
Office lease expense	202,500	
Office supplies expense	64,500	
Other general administrative expenses	355,500	
Other income/(expense).		7,500
	5,205,000	5,205,000

Required

1. Classify each of the expense line items in the trial balance as:

   a. Direct or indirect. Assume that the cost object is a consulting project.

   b. Fixed or variable. Assume that the cost object is one of EBC's two offices.

   c. Product or period. Assume that the cost object is a consulting project.

2. Prepare a schedule of cost of services for EBC for the year ended December 31, 2019. Assume that the beginning Work-in-Process Inventory balance was $223,000. Regardless of your classification in requirement 1, assume that all executive and consultant salaries, benefits, and taxes are product costs and that EBC treats all bonuses and continuing education expenses as period costs.

3. Prepare an income statement for EBC for the year ended December 31, 2019.

Solution

1a.

Line Item	Direct Cost	Indirect Cost
Reimbursable costs	X	
Executive salaries.	X	X
Clerical salaries		X
Consultant salaries.	X	
Employee benefits	X	X
Payroll taxes.	X	X
Employee bonuses.	X	X
Marketing expenses		X
Employee continuing education expenses		X
Office lease expense		X
Office supplies expense		X
Other general administrative expenses		X

1b.

Line Item	Fixed Cost	Variable Cost
Reimbursable costs		X
Executive salaries.	X	
Clerical salaries	X	
Consultant salaries.	X	
Employee benefits	X	
Payroll taxes.	X	
Employee bonuses.		X
Marketing expenses		X
Employee continuing education expenses		X
Office lease expense	X	
Office supplies expense		X
Other general administrative expenses	X	X

1c.

Line Item	Product Cost	Period Cost
Reimbursable costs	X	
Executive salaries.	X	
Clerical salaries		X
Consultant salaries.	X	
Employee benefits	X	X
Payroll taxes.	X	X
Employee bonuses.		X
Marketing expenses		X
Employee continuing education expenses		X
Office lease expense	X	
Office supplies expense	X	X
Other general administrative expenses	X	X

2.

Environmental Business Consultants, LLC Schedule of Cost Services As of December 31, 2019		
Direct labor.		$2,380,500
General Overhead:		
Office lease expense	$202,500	
Office supplies expense	64,500	
Total general overhead.		267,000
Total manufacturing costs for the year		2,647,500
Add: Beginning work-in-process inventory		223,000
Total cost of work-in-process during the year.		2,870,500
Less: Ending work-in-process inventory.		(247,000)
Cost of services		$2,623,500

3.

Environmental Business Consultants, LLC Income Statement For the Year Ended December 31, 2019		
Gross sales.		$4,146,000
Less: Reimbursable costs		$ (431,000)
Net sales.		$3,715,000
Cost of services		2,623,500
Gross profit on sales.		1,091,500
Operating Expenses:		
Employee bonuses	126,000	
Marketing expenses	48,000	
Employee continuing education expenses	27,000	
Other general administrative expenses	355,500	
Total operating expenses		556,500
Income from operations		535,000
Other income/(expense).		7,500
Net income		$ 542,500

COMPREHENSIVE PROBLEM

At December 31, 2019, the end of its fiscal year, Perez Manufacturing Corporation collected the following data for 2019:

Materials inventory, January 1	$ 80,000
Materials inventory, December 31	60,000
Work-in-process inventory, January 1	100,000
Work-in-process inventory, December 31	140,000
Finished goods inventory, January 1	120,000
Finished goods inventory, December 31	110,000
Net delivered cost of materials purchased	180,000
Direct labor	280,000
Indirect materials	15,000
Indirect labor	75,000
Factory supplies used	16,000
Factory depreciation	30,000
Factory repairs and maintenance	22,000
Selling expenses	64,000
Non-factory administrative expenses	58,000

Required
Prepare a schedule of cost of goods manufactured and sold for Perez Manufacturing Corporation for the year ended December 31, 2019, assuming that there were no other manufacturing overhead items than those listed above.

Solution

PEREZ MANUFACTURING CORPORATION
Schedule of Cost of Goods Manufactured and Sold
For the Year Ended December 31, 2019

Direct materials:		
Beginning materials inventory	$ 80,000	
Net delivered cost of materials purchased	180,000	
Cost of materials available	$260,000	
Less: Ending materials inventory	60,000	
Total materials used	$200,000	
Less: Indirect materials used	15,000	
Direct materials used		$185,000
Direct labor		280,000
Manufacturing overhead:		
Indirect materials	$ 15,000	
Indirect labor	75,000	
Manufacturing supplies used	16,000	
Manufacturing depreciation	30,000	
Manufacturing repairs and maintenance	22,000	
Total manufacturing overhead		158,000
Total manufacturing costs for the year		**$623,000**
Add: Beginning work-in-process inventory		100,000
Total Cost of work-in-process during the year		$723,000
Less: Ending work-in-process inventory		140,000
Cost of goods manufactured		**$583,000**
Add: Beginning finished goods inventory		120,000
Cost of goods available for sale		$703,000
Less: Ending finished goods inventory		110,000
Cost of goods sold		**$593,000**

SUMMARY OF LEARNING OBJECTIVES

Identify the key objectives of a managerial accounting system and define product costs and period costs; variable, fixed, and mixed costs; and direct and indirect costs; and cost control. (p. 710)   **LO1**

- The primary objectives of managerial accounting systems are to provide management with financial and other business information that is useful in analyzing and making business decisions.
- Product costs include all costs necessary to bring a product to completion.
- Period costs are expensed in the period incurred and not assigned to products.
- A variable cost varies in total but is fixed per unit for a certain range of activity. A fixed cost is fixed in total but varies per unit for a certain range of activity. Mixed costs have both fixed and variable cost components.
- A direct cost can easily be traced to a cost object. An indirect cost cannot be easily traced to a cost object.

Describe the three manufacturing inventories—materials, work-in-process, and finished goods—and discuss the categories of manufacturing costs and how these costs flow among the inventories and cost of goods sold. (p. 715)   **LO2**

- Materials inventory includes all factory materials and components that have been purchased but not yet placed into production.
- Work-in-process inventory includes all units of product that have been placed into production but not yet completed.
- Finished goods inventory includes all units of product that have been completed but not yet sold.
- Total product costs consist of direct materials, direct labor, and manufacturing overhead (which includes indirect materials and indirect labor).
- Prime cost is direct materials plus direct labor. Product costs are easily and directly traceable to individual products. Conversion cost is direct labor plus manufacturing overhead. Conversion cost represents the elements of product cost necessary to convert the materials and components to the final finished products.
- Product cost flows from the Materials Inventory account to the Work-in-Process Inventory account to the Finished Goods Inventory account and finally to the Cost of Goods Sold account.

Define total manufacturing costs, cost of goods manufactured, and cost of goods sold, and illustrate the schedule of cost of goods manufactured and sold and the income statement. (p. 721)   **LO3**

- Total manufacturing costs is the sum of direct materials, direct labor, and manufacturing overhead incurred during the accounting period.
- Cost of goods manufactured (cost of product transferred to finished goods inventory during the accounting period) is total manufacturing costs plus beginning work-in-process inventory minus ending work-in-process inventory.
- Cost of goods sold is cost of goods manufactured plus beginning finished goods inventory minus ending finished goods inventory.
- The schedule of cost of goods manufactured and sold has subtotals that reveal total manufacturing costs, cost of goods manufactured, and cost of goods sold.

Illustrate the journal entries to record product cost flows using a perpetual inventory system. (p. 725)   **LO4**

- Direct materials, direct labor, and manufacturing overhead costs are accumulated in the Work-in-Process Inventory account.
- When manufacturing is completed, product costs are transferred from the Work-in-Process Inventory account to the Finished Goods Inventory account.
- When goods are sold, product costs are transferred from the Finished Goods Inventory account to Cost of Goods Sold.

SUMMARY	Concept ⟶	Method ⟶	Assessment
TAKEAWAY 15.1	A founder of a new consulting firm is trying to determine the firm's cost of service.	• Identify the cost object. • Classify the firm's expenses as product costs vs. period costs relative to that cost object. • Sum the product costs.	• Costs associated with completion of specific consulting projects, such as consultant labor and project supplies, would be considered product costs. • Costs not directly related to projects but related to operating the business, such as general liability insurance premiums, office rent, and marketing costs, would be considered period costs.
TAKEAWAY 15.2	How can one determine whether a cost is variable, fixed, or mixed?	• Observe cost behavior as production levels change. • Use the high-low method or least squares regression analysis (see Chapter 19).	• If costs increase proportionately with production, the cost is variable. • If costs remain unchanged as production changes, the cost is fixed. • If costs change, but not proportionately, as production changes, the cost is mixed.
TAKEAWAY 15.3	The CEO of a local medical center has asked you to identify the costs of the urgent care, family medicine, and orthopedic practices for purposes of evaluating each area's performance.	• Identify the cost object. • Classify expenses as either direct or indirect relative to that cost object. • Sum the direct costs by cost object.	• Expenses that are specific and limited to one practice (i.e., can be traced to an individual practice) are direct costs. • Expenses that are incurred for the benefit of or are used by more than one practice (i.e., cannot be easily traced to an individual practice) are indirect costs.
TAKEAWAY 15.4	What amount should be reported as cost of goods sold in the annual financial statements?	• Accumulate the costs of direct materials, direct labor, and manufacturing overhead for all products produced in a period. • Report the cost of goods sold in the period of the sale.	• If the ending balance in finished goods inventory is less than the beginning balance, then cost of goods sold will be greater than cost of goods manufactured. • If the ending balance in finished goods inventory is greater than the beginning balance, then cost of goods sold will be less than cost of goods manufactured.

KEY TERMS

Conversion cost (p. 717)

Cost control (p. 714)

Cost object (p. 710)

Cost of goods manufactured
  (COGM) (p. 721)

Cost of goods sold
  (COGS) (p. 721)

Cost of jobs or projects (p. 714)

Direct cost (p. 713)

Direct labor (p. 716)

Direct materials (p. 716)

Factory overhead (p. 717)

Factory supplies (p. 715)

Finished goods inventory (p. 715)

Fixed cost (p. 712)

Indirect cost (p. 713)

Indirect labor (p. 717)

Indirect materials (p. 716)

Manufacturing overhead (p. 717)

Materials inventory (p. 715)

Mixed costs (p. 712)

Office supplies (p. 715)   Product costs (p. 710, 716)   Variable cost (p. 711)

Period costs (p. 710, 714)   Semi-variable costs (p. 712)   Work-in-process

Prime cost (p. 717)   Total manufacturing   inventory (p. 715)

Product costing (p. 710)   costs (p. 720, 722)

Assignments with the ⓂⒷⒸ logo in the margin are available in ᵐʸBusinessCourse.
See the Preface of the book for details.

SELF-STUDY QUESTIONS

(Answers to Self-Study Questions are at the end of this chapter.)

1. **Which of the following is never an element of product cost?**   **LO1**
    a.   Insurance   *c.*   Advertising
    b.   Utilities   *d.*   Supplies

2. **Which of the following is not an element of manufacturing overhead?**   **LO1, 2**
    a.   Factory office salaries   *c.*   Product inspector's salary
    b.   Plant manager's salary   *d.*   Company president's salary

3. **The sum of direct materials, direct labor, and manufacturing overhead plus beginning work-in-**   **LO3**
    process inventory minus ending work-in-process inventory computes
    a.   total manufacturing costs.   *c.*   cost of goods sold.
    b.   cost of goods manufactured.   *d.*   total cost of work-in-process.

4. **A manufacturer incurred $20,000 of direct material, $10,000 of direct labor, and $15,000 of**   **LO3**
    manufacturing overhead during 2019. Beginning work-in-process inventory was $8,000. If cost of
    goods manufactured was $47,000, what was the amount of the ending work-in-process inventory?
    a. $55,000   *c.* $10,000
    b. $6,000   *d.* $53,000

5. **The journal entry to record the distribution of the factory payroll requires**   **LO4**
    a.   a debit to Work-in-Process Inventory for direct labor.
    b.   a debit to Work-in-Process Inventory for indirect labor.
    c.   a debit to Manufacturing Overhead for direct labor.
    d.   a credit to Manufacturing Overhead for direct labor.

QUESTIONS

1. Describe how the per-unit amount of a variable and fixed cost changes as production increases over time.   **LO1**
2. Explain the difference between a direct cost and an indirect cost of production.   **LO1**
3. How are product costs accounted for differently from period costs? Give examples of each.   **LO1**
4. Name the three inventory accounts maintained by manufacturing firms and briefly describe the nature of   **LO2**
    each.
5. Name and briefly describe the three major categories used to account for manufacturing costs.   **LO2**
6. Define prime cost and conversion cost.   **LO2**
7. List six examples of manufacturing overhead costs.   **LO2**
8. What is the basic format of the income statement of a manufacturing firm?   **LO3**
9. In what way is total manufacturing cost different from cost of goods manufactured?   **LO3**
10. If the cost of work-in-process during the year is $480,000 and ending work-in-process inventory is   **LO3**
    $50,000, what is the amount of cost of goods manufactured?
11. If beginning and ending finished goods inventories are $55,000 and $45,000, respectively, and the cost of   **LO3**
    goods sold is $420,000, what is the cost of goods manufactured?
12. What journal entry would be made to record the transfer of $12,000 of direct materials and $2,500 of indi-   **LO4**
    rect materials from the materials inventory?
13. What journal entry would be made to record the distribution of a factory payroll consisting of $11,000 of   **LO4**
    direct labor and $4,000 of indirect labor?
14. What journal entry would be made to record the payment of $1,500 cash for factory utilities?   **LO4**
15. What journal entry would be required to record the transfer of completed products costing $15,000?   **LO4**

SHORT EXERCISES

LO1

SE15-1. Which one of the following refers to a cost that remains the same as the volume of activity decreases within the relevant range?

    a. Average cost per unit

    b. Variable cost per unit

    c. Unit fixed cost

    d. Total variable cost

LO1

SE15-2. Taylor Corporation is determining the cost behavior of several items in order to budget for the upcoming year. Past trends have indicated the following dollars were spent at three different levels of output.

	Unit Levels		
	10,000	12,000	15,000
Cost A.....................	$25,000	$29,000	$35,000
Cost B.....................	10,000	15,000	15,000
Cost C.....................	15,000	18,000	22,500

In establishing a budget for 14,000 units, Taylor should treat Costs A, B, and C, respectively, as

    a. mixed, fixed, and variable.

    b. variable, fixed, and variable.

    c. mixed, mixed, and mixed.

    d. variable, mixed, and mixed.

LO1

SE15-3. Claire Corporation's trial balance includes the following expenses:

Raw materials used in production	$ 5,500
Raw materials purchased.............................	6,500
General manager salary..............................	50,000
Sales manager salary................................	30,000
Direct labor incurred................................	130,000
General liability insurance premium	3,000
Factory rent	24,000
Office lease.......................................	18,000
Factory utilities	12,000
Depreciation on factory equipment.....................	14,000

Assuming that this list represents all expenses for the year, what amount should Claire report as a period (non-product) expense?

    a. $74,000

    b. $83,000

    c. $101,000

    d. $107,500

LO1

SE15-4. Claire Corporation's trial balance includes the following expenses:

Raw materials used in production	$ 5,500
Raw materials purchased.............................	6,500
General manager salary..............................	50,000
Sales manager salary................................	30,000
Direct labor incurred................................	130,000
General liability insurance premium	3,000
Factory rent	24,000
Office lease.......................................	18,000
Factory utilities	12,000
Depreciation on factory equipment.....................	14,000

Assuming no change in the work-in-process and finished goods inventory balances for the year, what total amount should Claire report as a product expense?

 a. $171,500
 b. $185,500
 c. $186,500
 d. $236,500

SE15-5. Which one of the following items would not be considered a manufacturing cost?

 a. Cream for an ice cream maker
 b. Sales commissions for a car manufacturer
 c. Plant property taxes for an ice cream maker
 d. Tires for an automobile manufacturer

SE15-6. Carson Company reported the following amounts for December:

Beginning raw materials inventory	$10,000
Beginning work-in-process inventory	20,000
Beginning finished goods inventory	45,000
Raw materials purchases	75,000
Wages paid	13,000
Applied manufacturing overhead	92,000
Ending raw materials inventory	8,000
Ending work-in-process inventory	14,000
Ending finished good inventory	50,000

What amount of raw materials was used in production in December?

 a. $71,000
 b. $73,000
 c. $77,000
 d. $85,000

SE15-7. All of the following would appear on a schedule of cost of goods manufactured except for

 a. ending work-in-process inventory.
 b. beginning finished goods inventory.
 c. the cost of raw materials used.
 d. applied manufacturing overhead.

SE15-8. Given the following data for Scurry Company, what is the cost of goods sold?

Beginning inventory of finished goods	$100,000
Cost of goods manufactured	700,000
Ending inventory of finished goods	200,000
Beginning work-in-process inventory	300,000
Ending work-in-process inventory	50,000

 a. $500,000
 b. $600,000
 c. $800,000
 d. $950,000

SE15-9. Carson Company reported the following amounts for December:

Beginning raw materials inventory	$10,000
Beginning work-in-process inventory	20,000
Beginning finished goods inventory	45,000
Raw materials purchases	75,000
Wages paid	13,000
Applied manufacturing overhead	92,000
Ending raw materials inventory	8,000
Ending work-in-process inventory	14,000
Ending finished good inventory	50,000

What is cost of goods manufactured for December?

a. $176,000
b. $182,000
c. $186,000
d. $188,000

LO4 **SE15-10.** The journal entry to record the application of manufacturing overhead to production would include a debit to which account?

a. Cost of goods sold
b. Manufacturing overhead
c. Work-in-process inventory
d. Cost of goods manufactured

EXERCISES—SET A

LO1 **E15-1A. Cost Classification** Classify each of the following costs relative to the cost object "client project" for a CPA firm that specializes in audit:

	Product or Period	Variable, Fixed, or Mixed	Direct or Indirect
Staff auditor salaries............................			
Receptionist salary.............................			
Depreciation on staff auditor laptop computers..........			
Health insurance for administrative staff			
Subscription to cloud backup service for project files......			
Office lease expense			
Travel to client location.........................			

LO1 **E15-2A. Cost Classification** Classify each of the following costs relative to the cost object "customer" for a clothing retailer:

	Product or Period	Variable, Fixed, or Mixed	Direct or Indirect
Salesperson wages			
Store manager salary...........................			
Depreciation on furniture and fixtures................			
Cost of merchandise			
Online advertising.............................			
Cost of discount coupon.........................			
Store lease expense............................			

LO2, 3 **E15-3A. Product Cost Flows** Complete the following T-accounts:

Materials Inventory

320	
?	?
	18,120
250	

Wages Payable	**Work-in-Process Inventory**	**Finished Goods Inventory**
9,000	1,000 ?	1,500 ?
300	?	?
	9,000	1,200
	?	
	500	

Manufacturing Overhead		Cost of Goods Sold	
50	?	?	
?			
18,000			
4,500			
	0		

E15-4A.   Prime Cost and Conversion Cost Piper Consulting Company incurred the following during 2019:   **LO2**

Direct labor.	$ 45,000
Overhead	90,000
Selling expenses	40,000
Administrative expenses.	100,000

Calculate prime cost and conversion cost for Piper Consulting Company during 2019.

E15-5A.   Product Cost Flows Number the following activities from 1 to 5 in the order corresponding to the   **LO2, 3**
typical flow of cost in a manufacturing company:

___ Record the transfer of raw materials into production.
___ Record cost of goods sold.
___ Record the completion of production of inventory.
___ Record the application of manufacturing overhead.
___ Record the purchase of raw materials.

E15-6A.   Schedule of Cost of Goods Manufactured and Sold At December 31, 2019, the end of its fiscal   **LO3**
year, Lederman Manufacturing Corporation collected the following data for 2019:

Materials inventory, January 1	$ 25,000
Materials inventory, December 31	15,000
Work-in-process inventory, January 1	30,000
Work-in-process inventory, December 31	41,000
Finished goods inventory, January 1	51,000
Finished goods inventory, December 31	36,000
Net delivered cost of materials purchased	150,000
Direct labor.	148,000
Indirect materials	12,000
Indirect labor.	37,000
Factory supplies used.	10,000
Factory depreciation.	65,000
Factory repairs and maintenance.	21,000
Selling expenses (total)	62,000
Non-factory administrative expenses (total)	58,000

Prepare a schedule of cost of goods manufactured and sold for Lederman Manufacturing Corporation
for the year ended December 31, 2019, assuming that there were no other manufacturing overhead
items than those listed above.

E15-7A.   Schedule of Cost of Goods Manufactured Sydney Company reported the following amounts for   **LO3**
October:

Beginning raw materials inventory	$ 80,000
Beginning work-in-process inventory	140,000
Beginning finished goods inventory	500,000
Raw materials purchases.	570,000
Wages paid.	310,000
Applied manufacturing overhead	900,000
Ending raw materials inventory	100,000
Ending work-in-process inventory	200,000
Ending finished good inventory	450,000

Use Excel to prepare a schedule of cost of goods manufactured for October.

E15-8A. **Schedule of Cost of Goods Sold** Sydney Company reported the following amounts for October:

Beginning raw materials inventory	$ 80,000
Beginning work-in-process inventory	140,000
Beginning finished goods inventory	500,000
Raw materials purchases	570,000
Wages paid	310,000
Applied manufacturing overhead	900,000
Ending raw materials inventory	100,000
Ending work-in-process inventory	200,000
Ending finished good inventory	450,000

Use Excel to prepare a schedule of cost of goods sold for October.

LO3

E15-9A. **Cost of Goods Manufactured and Cost of Goods Sold** For each of the following unrelated companies, compute the cost of goods manufactured and the cost of goods sold:

	A	B	C
Selling expenses	$ 500	$ 800	$ 600
Factory insurance	260	245	140
Ending finished goods inventory	810	750	515
Non-factory administrative expenses	250	450	350
Direct labor	2,560	2,760	2,120
Beginning materials inventory	520	670	350
Beginning work-in-process inventory	1,120	840	1,070
Indirect materials used	390	420	230
Factory utilities	240	275	150
Factory depreciation	730	760	380
Ending work-in-process inventory	1,360	790	950
Ending materials inventory	440	710	410
Indirect labor	425	280	160
Beginning finished goods inventory	850	725	480
Factory repairs and maintenance	215	230	175
Net delivered cost of materials purchased	3,140	4,410	2,870
Factory supplies used	330	310	210

LO3 **E15-10A.** **Income Statement** Lederman Manufacturing Corporation (see E15-6A) sold 14,000 units of product for $45 each during 2019. During the year, 5,000 shares of common stock were outstanding. Prepare an income statement for the year (ignore income taxes). Calculate earnings per share.

LO4 **E15-11A.** **Entries for Product Cost Flow** The following transactions occurred during January 2019 for Richards Manufacturing Company:

Jan. 5 Acquired $4,500 of materials on account that will be used to produce product for resale.

11 Requisitioned $3,750 of materials for use as direct materials in the factory.

16 Completed the manufacturing of products with a total product cost of $15,000 and transferred them to the warehouse.

Record these transactions in general journal form. Assume that Richards Manufacturing Company uses the perpetual inventory system.

LO4 **E15-12A.** **Entries for Product Cost Flow** Record the following transactions that occurred during March 2019 for Harris Manufacturing Company, which uses the perpetual inventory system:

Mar. 12 Transferred $5,000 of completed goods from the factory to the warehouse.

15 Requisitioned $3,000 of materials for use in the factory as direct materials and $500 for indirect materials.

18 Sold goods costing $4,000 for $6,000 on account.

EXERCISES—SET B

E15-1B.   **Cost Classification**   Classify each of the following costs relative to the cost object "patient" for a medical office: **LO1**

	Product or Period	Variable, Fixed, or Mixed	Direct or Indirect
Nurse salaries.			
Receptionist salary			
Depreciation on exam room computers			
Health insurance for administrative staff			
Subscription to patient management software service			
Office lease expense			
Gloves, swabs, and other medical supplies			

E15-2B.   **Cost Classification**   Classify each of the following costs relative to the cost object "customer" for a new car dealer: **LO1**

	Product or Period	Variable, Fixed, or Mixed	Direct or Indirect
Salesperson wages			
Dealership manager salary.			
Depreciation on showroom furniture.			
Cost of automobiles			
Online advertising.			
Cost of new car prep			
Showroom lease expense			

E15-3B.   **Product Cost Flows**   Complete the following T-accounts: **LO2, 3**

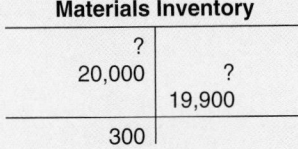

Materials Inventory

?	
20,000	?
	19,900
300	

Wages Payable

	15,000
	?

Work-in-Process Inventory

2,000	?
?	
?	
32,000	
5,000	

Finished Goods Inventory

5,000	?
?	
3,000	

Manufacturing Overhead

300	?
?	
27,000	
3,900	
0	

Cost of Goods Sold

65,900	

E15-4B.   **Prime Cost and Conversion Cost**   Benton Engineering Services Company incurred the following during 2019:   **LO2**

SERVICE AND MERCHANDISING

Direct labor	$ 60,000
Overhead	110,000
Selling expenses	56,000
Administrative expenses.	95,000

Calculate prime cost and conversion cost for Benton Engineering Services Company during 2019.

LO2, 3 **E15-5B.** **Service Cost Flows** Number the following activities from 1 to 3 in the order corresponding to the typical flow of cost in a CPA firm.

____ Record the time worked on a client project by professional staff.
____ Record the completion of a client project.
____ Record the application of office overhead.

LO3 **E15-6B.** **Schedule of Cost of Goods Manufactured and Sold** At December 31, 2019, the end of its fiscal year, Kelly Metal Products Corporation collected the following data for 2019:

Materials inventory, January 1	$ 32,000
Materials inventory, December 31	22,000
Work-in-process inventory, January 1	34,000
Work-in-process inventory, December 31	45,000
Finished goods inventory, January 1	21,000
Finished goods inventory, December 31	18,000
Net delivered cost of materials purchased	210,000
Direct labor	190,000
Indirect materials	13,000
Indirect labor	25,000
Factory supplies used	12,000
Factory depreciation	78,000
Factory repairs and maintenance	28,000
Selling expenses (total)	63,000
Non-factory administrative expenses (total)	57,000

Required

Prepare a schedule of cost of goods manufactured and sold for Kelly Metal Products Corporation for the year ended December 31, 2019, assuming that there were no other manufacturing overhead items than those listed above.

LO3 **E15-7B.** **Schedule of Cost of Goods Manufactured** Brooklyn Company reported the following amounts for October:

Beginning raw materials inventory	$ 40,000
Beginning work-in-process inventory	70,000
Beginning finished goods inventory	250,000
Raw materials purchases	285,000
Wages paid	155,000
Applied manufacturing overhead	450,000
Ending raw materials inventory	50,000
Ending work-in-process inventory	100,000
Ending finished goods inventory	225,000

Use Excel to prepare a schedule of cost of goods manufactured for October.

LO3 **E15-8B.** **Schedule of Cost of Goods Sold** Brooklyn Company reported the following amounts for October:

Beginning raw materials inventory	$ 40,000
Beginning work-in-process inventory	70,000
Beginning finished goods inventory	250,000
Raw materials purchases	285,000
Wages paid	155,000
Applied manufacturing overhead	450,000
Ending raw materials inventory	50,000
Ending work-in-process inventory	100,000
Ending finished goods inventory	225,000

Use Excel to prepare a schedule of cost of goods sold for October.

E15-9B. **Cost of Goods Manufactured and Cost of Goods Sold** For each of the following unrelated columns of data for the year, compute the cost of goods manufactured and the cost of goods sold:

	A	B	C
Selling expenses	$ 600	$ 700	$ 900
Factory insurance	180	270	300
Ending finished goods inventory	620	660	930
Non-factory administrative expenses	300	400	800
Direct labor	2,130	2,850	3,160
Beginning materials inventory	425	575	850
Beginning work-in-process inventory	840	920	1,290
Indirect materials used	270	325	520
Factory utilities	350	360	500
Factory depreciation	820	740	965
Ending work-in-process inventory	790	985	1,425
Ending materials inventory	385	610	820
Indirect labor	225	410	365
Beginning finished goods inventory	565	680	950
Factory repairs and maintenance	330	250	415
Net delivered cost of materials purchased	2,780	3,620	8,170
Factory supplies used	210	230	260

E15-10B. **Income Statement** Kelly Metal Products Corporation (see E15-6B) sold 18,000 units of product for $40 each during 2019. During the year, 10,000 shares of common stock were outstanding. Prepare an income statement for the year (ignore income taxes). Calculate earnings per share.

E15-11B. **Entries for Product Cost Flow** The following transactions occurred during February 2019 for Thompson Manufacturing Company:

Feb. 10 Acquired $10,000 of materials on account that will be used to produce product for resale.

11 Requisitioned $8,000 of materials for use as direct materials in the factory.

16 Completed the manufacturing of products with a total product cost of $48,000 and transferred them to the warehouse.

Record these transactions in general journal form. Assume that Thompson Manufacturing Company uses the perpetual inventory system.

E15-12B. **Entries for Product Cost Flow** Record the following transactions that occurred during April 2019 for Boyd Manufacturing Corporation, which uses the perpetual inventory system:

Apr. 21 Transferred $160,000 of completed goods from the factory to the warehouse.

25 Requisitioned $90,000 of materials for use in the factory as direct materials and $20,000 for indirect materials.

28 Sold goods costing $60,000 for $100,000 on account.

PROBLEMS—SET A

P15-1A. **Schedule of Cost of Goods Manufactured and Sold** The following amounts are available for 2019 for Bourne Manufacturing Company:

Administrative salaries (non-factory)	$ 70,000
Administrative rent (non-factory)	35,000
Advertising and promotion expense	41,000
Depreciation—administrative	22,000
Depreciation—factory	30,000
Depreciation—selling	17,000
Direct labor	175,000
Factory rent	18,000
Factory supplies used	12,000
Finished goods inventory (January 1)	57,000
Finished goods inventory (December 31)	50,000
Indirect materials used	14,000
Indirect labor	19,000
Materials inventory (January 1)	15,000
Materials inventory (December 31)	20,000
Net delivered cost of materials purchased	138,000
Other factory overhead	26,000
Sales	845,000
Sales salaries expense	72,000
Work-in-process inventory (January 1)	18,000
Work-in-process inventory (December 31)	20,000

Required

Using the above data, prepare a schedule of cost of goods manufactured and sold.

LO3   **P15-2A.**   **Cost of Goods Manufactured and Sold** The following data relate to three independent production periods of Riverside Manufacturing Company. Missing data are indicated by question marks.

	A	B	C
Materials:			
Beginning inventory	$ 52	$ 164	$110
Purchases	?	700	500
Ending inventory	74	100	?
Total materials used	330	?	440
Direct labor	580	960	800
Manufacturing overhead:			
Indirect materials	96	?	120
Indirect labor	160	150	350
Other	?	200	340
Total manufacturing overhead	520	480	?
Work-in-process inventories:			
Beginning	?	90	260
Ending	70	?	100
Finished goods inventories:			
Beginning	?	400	80
Ending	335	120	330
Cost of goods manufactured	1,384	?	?
Cost of goods sold	1,339	2,324	?

Required

Using the above data, determine the missing amounts. (You should set up a schedule of cost of goods manufactured and sold, fill in the known data, and calculate the missing amounts.)

LO3   **P15-3A.**   **Total Manufacturing Cost, Income Statement, Unit Cost, and Selling Price** Two inventors, recently organized as Innovation, Inc., consult you regarding a planned new product. They have estimates of the costs of materials, labor, overhead, and other expenses for 2019 but need to know how much to charge for each unit to earn a profit in 2019 equal to 15% of their estimated total long-term investment of $400,000 (ignore income taxes). Their plans indicate that each unit of the new product requires the following:

Direct materials	4 lbs. of a materials costing $5/lb.
Direct labor	2 hrs. of a metal former's time at $11/hr.
	0.6 hr. of an assembler's time at $8/hr.

Major items of production overhead would be annual rent of $46,460 for a factory building, $28,660 rent for machinery, and $21,700 of indirect materials. Other production overhead is estimated to be $233,280. Selling expenses are an estimated 30% of total sales, and non-factory administrative expenses are 20% of total sales.

The consensus at Innovation is that during 2019, 10,000 units of product should be produced for selling and another 2,000 units should be produced for the next year's beginning inventory. Also, an extra 3,000 pounds of materials will be purchased as beginning inventory for the next year. Because of the nature of the manufacturing process, all units started must be completed, so work-in-process inventories are negligible.

Required

a.   Incorporate the above data into a schedule of estimated total manufacturing costs and compute the unit production cost for 2019.

b.   Prepare an estimated income statement that would provide the target amount of profit for 2019.

c.   What unit sales price should Innovation charge for the new product?

P15-4A.   Journal Entries Taylor Manufacturing Company uses the perpetual inventory system to record   **LO4** transactions related to its manufacturing inventories. The following transactions occurred during March 2019:

Mar.   6   Recorded the payroll: $5,000 of direct labor and $1,000 of indirect labor.

8   Received $7,000 of materials and components that had been ordered on account.

10   Completed product costing $11,000 and transferred it to the warehouse. Requisitioned $2,500 of materials for use in the factory; $2,000 was used as direct materials and the remainder was used as indirect materials.

12   Sold on account product costing $1,500 for $2,250.

15   Applied $3,000 of manufacturing overhead cost to the product currently being worked on.

21   Paid $250 cash for a special material component that was shipped via overnight delivery.

27   Sold product costing $1,450 for $2,500 cash.

Required
Prepare general journal entries to record these transactions.

P15-5A.   Journal Entries Paulson Manufacturing Company uses the perpetual inventory system to account   **LO4** for its manufacturing inventories. The following are Paulson's transactions during July 2019:

July   5   Received materials costing $3,000 from a supplier. The materials were purchased on account.

9   Requisitioned $9,000 of materials for use in the factory, consisting of $7,500 of direct materials and $1,500 of indirect materials.

11   Recorded the factory payroll: $20,250 of direct labor and $2,250 of indirect labor.

17   Incurred various overhead costs totaling $21,000. (Credit Accounts Payable.)

20   Applied $30,000 of manufacturing overhead to the products being manufactured.

23   Completed product costing $20,000 and moved it to the warehouse.

26   Sold goods with a product cost of $4,500 on account for $7,500.

Required

a.   Set up T-accounts for the following four accounts and post the July 1, 2019, balances: Materials Inventory, $10,500; Work-in-Process Inventory, $37,500; Finished Goods Inventory, $15,000; and Cost of Goods Sold, $45,000.

b.   Record the transactions listed above in general journal form, post relevant portions to the four T-accounts, and balance the four accounts.

PROBLEMS—SET B

LO3 **P15-1B.** **Schedule of Cost of Goods Manufactured and Sold** The following amounts are available for 2019 for Bishop Manufacturing Company:

Administrative salaries (non-factory)	$ 85,000
Administrative rent (non-factory)	47,000
Advertising and promotion expense	93,000
Depreciation—administrative	77,000
Depreciation—factory	95,000
Depreciation—selling	36,000
Direct labor	325,000
Factory rent	68,000
Factory supplies used	23,000
Finished goods inventory (January 1)	61,000
Finished goods inventory (December 31)	65,000
Indirect materials used	27,000
Indirect labor	44,000
Materials inventory (January 1)	22,000
Materials inventory (December 31)	27,000
Net delivered cost of materials purchased	210,000
Other factory overhead	55,000
Sales	938,000
Sales salaries expense	71,000
Work-in-process inventory (January 1)	33,000
Work-in-process inventory (December 31)	25,000

Required

Using the above data, prepare a schedule of cost of goods manufactured and sold.

LO3 **P15-2B.** **Cost of Goods Manufactured and Sold** The following data relate to three independent production periods of Randolph Manufacturing Company. Missing data are indicated by question marks.

	A	B	C
Materials:			
Beginning inventory	$ 78	$ 410	$ 220
Purchases	?	1,750	1,000
Ending inventory	111	250	?
Total materials used	495	?	880
Direct labor	870	2,400	1,600
Manufacturing overhead:			
Indirect materials	144	?	110
Indirect labor	240	375	700
Other	?	500	680
Total manufacturing overhead	780	1,100	?
Work-in-process inventories:			
Beginning	?	225	520
Ending	105	?	200
Finished goods inventories:			
Beginning	?	1,000	160
Ending	495	300	660
Cost of goods manufactured	2,076	?	?
Cost of goods sold	2,016	5,275	?

Required

Using the above data, determine the missing amounts. (You should set up a schedule of cost of goods manufactured and sold, fill in the known data, and calculate the missing amounts.)

LO3 **P15-3B.** **Total Manufacturing Costs, Income Statement, Unit Cost, and Selling Price** You are consulted by Investors, Inc., a group of investors planning a new product. They have estimates of the costs of materials, labor, overhead, and other expenses for 2019 but need to know how much to charge for

each unit to earn a profit in 2019 equal to 10% of their estimated investment of $500,000 (ignore income taxes).

Their plans indicate that each unit of the new product requires the following:

Direct Materials	4 lbs. of a materials costing $6/lb.
Direct Labor	3 hrs. of a die cutter's time at $9/hr.
	2 hrs. of an assembler's time at $8/hr.

Major items of production overhead would be annual rent of $40,000 on the factory building and $25,000 on machinery as well as indirect materials of $21,000. Other production overhead is an estimated 60% of total direct labor costs. Selling expenses are an estimated 20% of total sales, and non-factory administrative expenses are 10% of total sales.

The consensus at Investors is that during 2019, 4,000 units of product should be produced for selling and another 1,000 units should be produced for the next year's beginning inventory. Also, an extra 6,000 pounds of materials will be purchased as beginning inventory for the next year. Because of the nature of the manufacturing process, all units started must be completed, so work-in-process inventories are negligible.

Required
a. Incorporate the above data into a schedule of estimated total manufacturing costs and compute the unit production cost for 2019.
b. Prepare an estimated income statement that would provide the target amount of profit for 2019.
c. What unit sales price should Investors charge for the new product?

P15-4B. **Journal Entries** Travis Manufacturing Company uses the perpetual inventory system to record   **LO4**
trans-actions related to its manufacturing inventories. The following transactions occurred during August 2019:

Aug. 5 Received $4,500 of materials and components that had been ordered on account.
     7 Recorded the payroll: $3,250 of direct labor and $750 of indirect labor.
   11 Sold on account product costing $1,750 for $2,600.
   16 Completed product costing $8,000 and transferred it to the warehouse.
   20 Requisitioned $3,500 of materials for use in the factory; $2,950 was used as direct materials and the remainder was used as indirect materials.
   25 Applied $5,000 of manufacturing overhead cost to the product currently being worked on.
   29 Paid $200 cash for a special material component that was shipped via overnight delivery.
   31 Sold product costing $500 for $850 cash.

Required
Prepare general journal entries to record these transactions.

P15-5B. **Journal Entries** Porter Manufacturing Company uses the perpetual inventory system to account for   **LO4**
its manufacturing inventories. The following are Porter's transactions during September 2019:

Sept. 5 Received materials costing $4,500 from a supplier. The materials were purchased on account.
    9 Requisitioned $10,500 of materials for use in the factory, consisting of $8,400 of direct materials and $2,100 of indirect materials.
   11 Recorded the factory payroll: $21,000 of direct labor and $3,000 of indirect labor.
   17 Incurred various overhead costs totaling $22,500. (Credit Accounts Payable.)
   20 Applied $31,500 of manufacturing overhead to the products being manufactured.
   23 Completed product costing $25,500 and moved it to the warehouse.
   26 Sold goods with a product cost of $6,000 on account for $8,000.

Required
a. Set up a T-account for the following four accounts and post the September 1, 2019, balance listed after the account title: Materials Inventory, $8,000; Work-in-Process Inventory, $26,000; Finished Goods Inventory, $11,000; and Cost of Goods Sold, $32,000.
b. Record the transactions listed above in general journal form, post relevant portions to the four T-accounts, and balance the four accounts.

EXTENDING YOUR KNOWLEDGE

LO3   **EYK15-1. Business Decision Case** James Alvarez, an engineer, needs some accounting advice. In their spare time during the past year, Alvarez and his college-aged son, Robert, have manufactured a small weed-trimming sickle in a rented building near their home. Robert, who has had one accounting course in college, keeps the books.

Alvarez is pleased about the results of their first year's operations. He asks you to look over the following income report prepared by Robert before they leave on a well-deserved vacation to Hawaii, after which they plan to expand their business significantly.

Sales (34,000 units at $10 each)		$340,000
Costs of producing 35,000 units:		
Materials:		
Precast blades at $1.50 each	$ 57,000	
Preturned handles at $1 each.	40,000	
Labor costs of hired assemblers.	26,600	
Labor costs of hired painters	33,000	
Rent on building	14,900	
Rent on machinery	7,100	
Utilities for production	8,000	
Other production costs	11,900	
Advertising expense	26,200	
Sales commissions.	35,700	
Delivery of products to customers	14,350	
Total costs.	$274,750	
Less: Ending inventory of 1,000 units at average production		
costs of $7.85 (or $274,750/35,000 units)	7,850	
Cost of goods sold		266,900
Net income		$ 73,100

After you examine the income report, Alvarez responds to your questions and assures you that (1) no theft or spoilage of materials has occurred, (2) no partially completed units are involved, and (3) he and son Robert have averaged 30 hours each per week in the business for 50 weeks (ignore income taxes).

Required

a.   Identify any apparent discrepancy in the income report in the cost of materials used.

b.   Recalculate the cost of goods manufactured, the average cost per unit produced, and the net income for the year.

c.   What factors should James consider regarding the profitability of his venture before deciding to expand it significantly?

LO2   **EYK15-2. Apple's 2017 Environmental Responsibility Report can be found at the following link:** http://www.images.apple.com/environment/reports/docs/apple_environmental_responsibility_report_0714.pdf Skim this report. Why do you think Apple is so transparent with regard to its environmental activity but so secretive regarding its product development?

LO2   **EYK15-3. Ethics Case** Great Cakes is a large bakery known for its quality "boxed cake" products. Its motto is "We Use Only the Best Ingredients." Ralph Sands, the purchasing supervisor, is responsible for ordering the ingredients for all the bakery products. He is being considered for a promotion based on his proven ability to purchase ingredients at the best price available.

The cost of all the ingredients has risen substantially over the past few months. Sands decides to purchase 25% of the ingredients at a lower quality than Great Cakes normally uses because the cost is significantly less. Without relying on the company's test kitchens, he believes this substitution will not be noticed by the customers and the lower cost will counterbalance the increased costs of the other ingredients.

Sands explains this decision to his friend, Lynn Pall, the company's accountant, one day at lunch. He also tells her that he does not intend to inform management of the inclusion of the lower-quality ingredients in the bakery's products.

Required
What ethical considerations arise from Ralph Sands' decisions? What problems face Lynn Pall because of his actions?

ANSWERS TO SELF-STUDY QUESTIONS:

1. c, (p. 711)   2. d, (pp. 716–717)   3. b, (pp. 720–721)   4. b, (p. 721)   5. a, (p. 726)

YOUR TURN! SOLUTIONS

Solution 15.1

	Product or Period	Variable, Fixed, or Mixed	Direct or Indirect
Assembly labor	Product	Variable	Direct
iPad case	Product	Variable	Direct
CEO salary	Period	Fixed	Indirect
Microprocessor	Product	Variable	Direct
Depreciation on Apple corporate headquarters	Period	Fixed	Indirect
Health insurance for factory workers	Product	Fixed	Indirect
Touch screen	Product	Variable	Direct
Adhesive on the serial number label	Product	Variable	Indirect

Solution 15.2
c.

Solution 15.3

Direct materials:		
Beginning balance	$ 200	
Purchases	1,400	
Cost of materials available	$1,600	
Less: Ending inventory	300	
Direct materials used		$1,300
Direct labor		1,200
Manufacturing overhead		900
Total manufacturing cost		$3,400
Add: Beginning work-in-process inventory		$ 600
Total cost of work-in-process		$4,000
Less: Ending work-in-process inventory		($500)
Cost of goods manufactured		**$3,500**

Solution 15.4

a.	Raw materials inventory	1,400	
	Cash or accounts payable		1,400
b.	Work-in-process inventory	1,300	
	Raw materials inventory		1,300
c.	Work-in-process inventory	1,200	
	Wages payable		1,200
d.	Work-in-process inventory	900	
	Manufacturing overhead		900
e.	Finished goods inventory	3,500	
	Work-in-process inventory		3,500
f.	Cost of goods sold	3,300	
	Finished goods inventory		3,300

Chapter 16

Cost Accounting Systems: Job Order Costing

PAST

Chapter 15 defined basic costing terminology and introduced different types of manufacturing inventories. It illustrated how costs flow through the inventories and explained the schedule of cost of goods manufactured.

PRESENT

Chapter 16 introduces and explains job costing in more detail for both manufacturing and service industries. It also explains overhead allocation.

FUTURE

Chapter 17 introduces process costing and how it differs from job order costing. It illustrates equivalent units and the flow of costs through the inventory accounts, as well as introduces the production cost report.

CH2M is a U.S.-based consulting, design, construction, operation, and program management service firm that provides services to clients worldwide. CH2M has performed thousands of projects on six continents and in more than 180 countries. CH2M Hill's projects are typically very large and complex. These have included the Panama Canal Expansion Program, a project to replace the entire sanitary sewer system for the country of Singapore, and the deconstruction of the Maine Yankee Atomic Power Company.

As you think about the massive scale of these projects, you might wonder how CH2M Hill keeps track of all of the costs (materials, labor, and overhead) incurred over weeks, months, and even years. To properly track the costs and customer billings associated with each of its projects, CH2M Hill must use some very sophisticated job order costing systems!

This chapter describes one of two basic types of cost accounting systems—called job order costing.

Road Map

LO	Learning Objective	Page	eLecture	Guided Example	Assignments
LO1	Describe the two basic types of cost accounting systems, discuss how they may be used in both manufacturing and nonmanufacturing environments, and explain the need for the timely determination of product costs.	756	E16-1	YT16.1	SS1, Q1, Q2, Q3, Q4, SE1
LO2	Explain the need for a predetermined overhead rate and demonstrate its calculation.	759	E16-2	YT16.2	SS2, Q5, Q6, Q7, Q8, Q9, SE2, SE3, SE4, E1A, E2A, E3A, E6A, E7A, E1B, E2B, E3B, E6B, E7B, P1A, P2A, P1B, P2B
LO3	Describe and explain a job order costing system, identify types of records used in job order costing, and demonstrate the journal entries that accompany the flow of product costs.	760	E16-3	YT16.3	SS3, SS4, Q10, Q11, Q12, E4A, E5A, E4B, E5B, P1A, P3A, P4A, P5A, P6A, P7A, P1B, P3B, P4B, P5B, P6B, P7B
LO4	Discuss the procedures and journal entries used to account for finished goods and the sale of finished goods.	766	E16-4	YT16.4	SS4, SS5, Q13, Q14, Q15, SE5, SE6, SE7, E6A, E7A, E8A, E9A, E10A, E11A, E12A, E6B, E7B, E8B, E9B, E10B, E11B, E12B, P2A, P4A, P5A, P6A, P7A, P2B, P4B, P5B, P6B, P7B
LO5	Describe the procedures for cost allocation for service departments.	771	E16-5	YT16.5	SS6, Q16, Q17, Q18, Q19, Q20, Q21, SE8, E13A, E13B, P8A, P8B
LO6	Contrast plant-wide overhead rates and departmental overhead rates.	775	E16-6	YT16.6	SS7, Q7, Q22, Q23, SE9, SE10, P8A, P8B

COST ACCOUNTING SYSTEMS: JOB ORDER COSTING

Cost Accounting Systems	**Predetermined Overhead Rate**	**Job Order Costing Systems**	**Service Departments**	**Departmental Overhead Rates**
• Job order costing • Process costing • Timely product costing	• Calculation of predetermined overhead rate	• Illustration of job order costing for a manufacturer • Accounting for finished goods • Illustration of job order costing for a service firm	• Cost centers • Product costs • Cost allocation	• Departmental rates

COST ACCOUNTING SYSTEMS

LO1 **Describe** the two basic types of cost accounting systems, **discuss** how they may be used in both manufacturing and nonmanufacturing environments, and **explain** the need for the timely determination of product costs.

Virtually all manufacturing and service firms have a cost accounting system consisting of forms, procedures, and records used to develop and report timely information about product and service costs. Any orderly method of developing product or service cost information constitutes a cost accounting system. Typically, some amount of cost is accumulated and related to some unit of activity or accomplishment. Examples include accumulating the cost of cutting and forming materials, assembling parts, and painting the final product that results in a completed unit of product such as a lawnmower, a computer, or a custom-designed executive jet aircraft, or the costs associated with CH2M Hill's overseeing the widening of the Panama Canal. Although a cost accounting system could be maintained independently of a firm's formal accounting system, most comprehensive cost accounting systems are integrated into the formal accounting system.

Cost accounting systems are usually illustrated for manufacturing situations involving product costs per unit. Note, however, that reliable cost-per-unit-of-production information is vital to managerial decision making in all types of entities, including service firms and governmental units. For example, a hospital may need to know the cost per patient of providing a specific surgical procedure, an insurance company may want to know the cost of providing health care insurance to a particular group, and a city may need to know the cost per ton of trash removal. Many of the cost accounting concepts and techniques that we discuss in this and subsequent chapters therefore apply to nonmanufacturing as well as manufacturing entities.

Two Basic Types of Cost Accounting Systems

Job order costing systems and process costing systems are designed to develop timely information about product and job costs, manufacturing inventories, and per-unit costs.

A **job order costing system** is used for *customized* products and services. Therefore, job order costing is characterized by a series of *unique products* or *jobs* undertaken either to fill specific orders from customers or to produce a general stock of products from which future customer orders are filled. In a job order costing system, the costs of direct materials, direct labor, and manufacturing overhead are accumulated separately for each job or product, as illustrated in **Exhibit 16-1**.

Job order costing is used by construction companies (to accumulate the cost of each construction project), printing companies

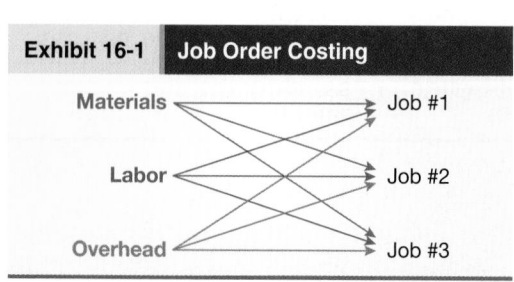

Exhibit 16-1   Job Order Costing

(to track the cost of each printing job), manufacturers of consumer products (to determine the cost per unit of each product manufactured), and hospitals (to determine the cost per patient). For example, CH2M Hill keeps track of the costs associated with its Singapore project separately from those associated with its Panama project.

A **process costing system** (**Exhibit 16-2**) lends itself to the production of a *large volume* of *homogenous products* manufactured in a continual flow operation, such as the distillation of fuels or manufacture of paint or wire. In these manufacturing contexts, the materials and operations are involved repetitively during each manufacturing period. Direct materials, direct labor, and manufacturing overhead are accumulated by a production department or process for a period and then divided by the units produced during that period to calculate a per-unit cost. Assembly-line operations of entities such as breweries or flour mills and mass-production operations such as power plants and chemical companies would use process costing.

Exhibit 16-2 Process Costing

Job order costing and process costing are two extremes along the spectrum of costing systems. A company will design its own accounting system to fit its particular needs. Many companies blend ideas from both job order costing and process costing systems.

| Choosing a Cost Accounting System | ACCOUNTING IN PRACTICE |

Both job order and process costing systems allocate materials, labor, and overhead costs to determine unit costs. In a job order system, costs are identified with specific jobs or products, but a process costing system identifies costs with production processes and averages them over all jobs completed or products made during the period. The type of cost accounting system used by a particular company depends on the nature of the company's operations. One company may, in fact, use job order costing to account for one part of its operation and use process costing to account for another part of its operation. For example, Fezzari Performance Bicycles (introduced in Chapter 14) uses job costing for each unique bike order received. Yet, the manufacture of bicycle frames is accounted for using process costing because each frame of a particular size and model is identical.

Timely Product Costing

Manufacturing Firms

A cost accounting system—either job order costing or process costing—must provide for the timely determination of product costs. Companies need to calculate product costs to determine work-in-process and finished goods inventory balances, which they report in periodic financial statements. In order to accurately calculate income, companies must develop a way to identify product costs for products sold and for products that remain on hand, either finished or unfinished.

Managers use engineering studies and cost analyses to establish budgets. They then compare actual product costs to budgets so that problems can be identified and remedial action can be taken when necessary. Managers also use product costs as one of the considerations in setting product prices.

To identify costs with a product or group of products, a manufacturer must trace production costs—direct materials, direct labor, and manufacturing overhead—to products. To account for materials used, a company may keep track of the costs of materials requisitioned for production by job, product, or department. Labor costs can similarly be accounted for based on timekeeping records or by identifying a particular product or job with total payroll costs of personnel in the factory production departments. A manufacturing firm cannot, however, directly determine the amount of manufacturing overhead that should be identified with particular products or a group of products. The reason is quite simple: Overhead costs are accumulated during a particular accounting period, but it is impossible to know exactly how much overhead cost will accumulate until the *end* of the period. The problem is that companies need to assign product costs *during* the period *before* total overhead costs can be determined for the period. It isn't feasible to wait until the end of the period to determine total product costs to bill customers for jobs completed during the period. Consequently, firms typically assign manufacturing overhead costs to products during the period based on estimates by using predetermined overhead rates.

Service Firms

SERVICE AND MERCHANDISING

The same principles apply to a service company like CH2M Hill. CH2M Hill is also interested in the timely determination of the costs of its projects (or jobs) in order to prepare periodic financial reports and determine income or loss on each project.

Because CH2M Hill's projects typically extend more than a year in length, it is likely that it will have many projects that are in process at the end of each reporting period. Project managers may help to establish budgets, compare budgets to actual results, and take action to control project costs.

© istockphoto.com

For example, the Panama Canal Expansion Program required CH2M Hill to trace labor costs for assigned project managers, engineers, and other consultants to this project over the course of several years. These individuals' salaries and benefits were assigned directly to the project for the period of their involvement on the project team. In addition, CH2M Hill traced other direct project costs to the project as well, such as team member travel, lodging, and meals incurred while working on the project. Corporate overhead was assigned to the project on a monthly basis to allow management to determine project profitability at any point in time.

CORPORATE SOCIAL RESPONSIBILITY | **Shortage of Highly Trained Engineers**

As was noted in the opening vignette, CH2M Hill manages some massive engineering projects. Projects of this size and complexity involve many highly trained engineers. A problem that companies like CH2M Hill face is the acute shortage of engineering talent, especially among women, Hispanics, and African Americans, groups that will comprise a large percentage of the future workforce. As part of its corporate responsibility initiative, CH2M Hill is doing something about this pressing problem.

CH2M Hill believes that "today's children are tomorrow's leaders" is a core tenet of sustainability. The company also understands how important it is to invest in future generations and to mentor them toward careers in engineering and science. CH2M Hill offers summer programs at no cost to the families that introduce their children to these important fields of study. As John Madia, CH2M Hill's chief human resources officer, states, "For most kids, particularly children of color and girls, STEM [Science, Technology, Engineering, and Mathematics] learning opens minds and doors where they have few role models. In helping to grow a diverse pool of future talent, our firm benefits by putting into practice our values of creating partnerships to help sustain and build better communities."

Source: CH2M Hill 2014 Sustainability and Corporate Citizenship Report

---

YOUR TURN! 16.1

The solution is on page 800.

Which costing system (job order or process) would most likely be used by the following industries?

Production of chemicals in large batches

Custom printing of wedding announcements or marketing materials

Construction of commercial aircraft

Refining of crude oil into gas and other products for retail sale

Production of exterior or interior paint for the DIY market

Production of glass windows for use in residential construction

Construction of custom furniture

Construction of large machinery used for producing integrated circuits for the computer industry

PREDETERMINED OVERHEAD RATES

Predetermined manufacturing overhead rates are so named because (1) they are calculated prior to the beginning of each accounting period; (2) they deal with production overhead, that is, all production costs other than direct materials and direct labor; and (3) they are usually stated in terms of a rate, such as $20 per direct labor hour. Recall that the purpose of calculating the predetermined overhead rate is to allow management to estimate total product costs in a timely manner to allow for the establishment of appropriate prices and the evaluation of operating results. Before the beginning of each year, management normally prepares budgets. Included in the total budget is a production budget, which estimates utilization of the firm's productive capacity in terms of a common measure of activity. Traditionally, firms have used volume measures that are already being recorded for other purposes, such as direct labor hours (recorded for payroll) and machine hours (recorded for depreciation). More recently, more sophisticated and detailed measures have been implemented by some firms, as discussed briefly later in this chapter and in more detail in Chapter 18. Also included in the total budget is an estimate of overhead costs for the year.

LO2 **Explain** the need for a predetermined overhead rate and **demonstrate** its calculation.

Multiple Predetermined Overhead Rates	ACCOUNTING IN PRACTICE

Often, companies calculate more than one predetermined manufacturing overhead rate for a given period. For example, some firms will calculate a predetermined variable overhead rate and a predetermined fixed overhead rate. Why? Doing so allows management to evaluate a production department's control of costs that are expected to vary with the level of production (often within the control of local management) separately from those costs that are related to the capacity to do work (often fixed in nature and largely out of local management's hands).

Calculation of Predetermined Overhead Rate

A **predetermined manufacturing overhead rate** is computed by dividing the budgeted or estimated total overhead cost for the year by the budgeted or estimated level of the application base. The application base is simply the activity used to assign overhead. This application base is generally the **cost driver** most closely related to the accumulation of overhead costs. This cost driver is typically the utilization of the facility's productive capacity for the year (such as total estimated direct labor hours or total estimated machine hours). Calculations of predetermined rates are typically based on one-year production periods, but they could be calculated based on shorter horizons, such as quarterly or monthly production periods. Companies should choose the application base that corresponds to the period over which activity decisions are typically made.

Assume that the most appropriate measure of activity for applying overhead at CH2M Hill is direct labor hours. If CH2M's management estimates 50 million direct labor hours for 2019 and the estimated total manufacturing overhead cost for 2019 is $2,200 million, the overhead rate for 2019 may be calculated as follows:

$$2019 \text{ Predetermined manufacturing overhead rate} = \frac{\text{Estimated overhead cost for 2019}}{\text{Estimated direct labor hours for 2019}}$$

$$= \frac{\$2,200 \text{ million}}{50 \text{ million hours}}$$

$$= \$44 \text{ per direct labor hour}$$

Hint: Applied overhead is a product of the predetermined overhead rate and actual hours for that job, not budgeted hours.

If, during March 2019, a particular project requires 1,000 direct labor hours, $44,000 of manufacturing overhead (1,000 × $44) would be assigned to this project.

Before selecting the allocation base for applying overhead to products or projects, a firm should carefully analyze the relationship between overhead incurred and various alternative measures of activity. Direct labor hours or direct labor costs would be used as the measure of activity in a service company that has labor-intensive projects. However, in a factory in which automation has replaced many of the production workers, machine hours may be a more appropriate measure.

Using a predetermined overhead rate, management can estimate the overhead costs of any job at any stage of production, computing "costs to date" both for control purposes and for inventory costing. This method also eliminates wide fluctuations in unit costs that might result if actual recorded overhead costs were assigned to products during short interim periods when production departed markedly from normal levels.

TAKEAWAY 16.1	Concept ⟶	Method ⟶	Assessment
	You have been asked to calculate the predetermined overhead rate for the next operating period.	• Forecast expected total overhead for the period. • Select an application base or cost driver. • Estimate total activity for the cost driver for the period.	Predetermined overhead rate = total estimated overhead divided by the total estimated activity level of the application base (such as machine hours or direct labor hours). Assign the predetermined overhead rate to each unit of cost driver during the period.

Assume you own a manufacturing company that budgets an estimated $250,000 in overhead for the coming year and 10,000 direct labor hours. Also assume your manufacturing overhead application base is direct labor hours. Actual overhead during the year amounts to $216,000 and employees work 9,000 actual direct labor hours. Compute the predetermined overhead rate and the amount of overhead that is applied to work-in-process inventory.

JOB ORDER COSTING SYSTEMS

LO3 Describe and explain a job order costing system, identify types of records used in job order costing, and demonstrate the journal entries that accompany the flow of product costs.

Job order costing systems are designed to accumulate product costs—direct materials, direct labor, and manufacturing overhead—by job and in total. **Exhibit 16-3** illustrates the flow of the documents in a job order costing system that might be used by Fezzari for an order of a high-end triathlon/time-trial bike.

When the customer places the order for the bike, Fezzari would create a **sales order** specifying the bike model and customer-specified options. Based on this sales order, the assembly department would create a **production order** directing the assembly employees to build the bike in accordance with the customer's specifications. Before assembly can begin, the assembly technician must gather the correct parts together. This is done based on a **bill of materials**, or list of each required part for the particular bike model. The technician creates a **materials requisition**, requesting that the bike components on the bill of materials be pulled from inventory and brought to the assembly station. As the technician assembles the bike, she would keep track of her time on a **time record**, either in written form on a timesheet or electronically through a time clock. As the job progresses, the materials used, labor expended, and overhead applied would be accumulated on a **job order cost sheet**. A job order cost sheet is a record of the materials, labor, and overhead for each job and serves as a subsidiary record or subset of the work-in-process account. When the bike is finished, the job order cost sheet would be closed.

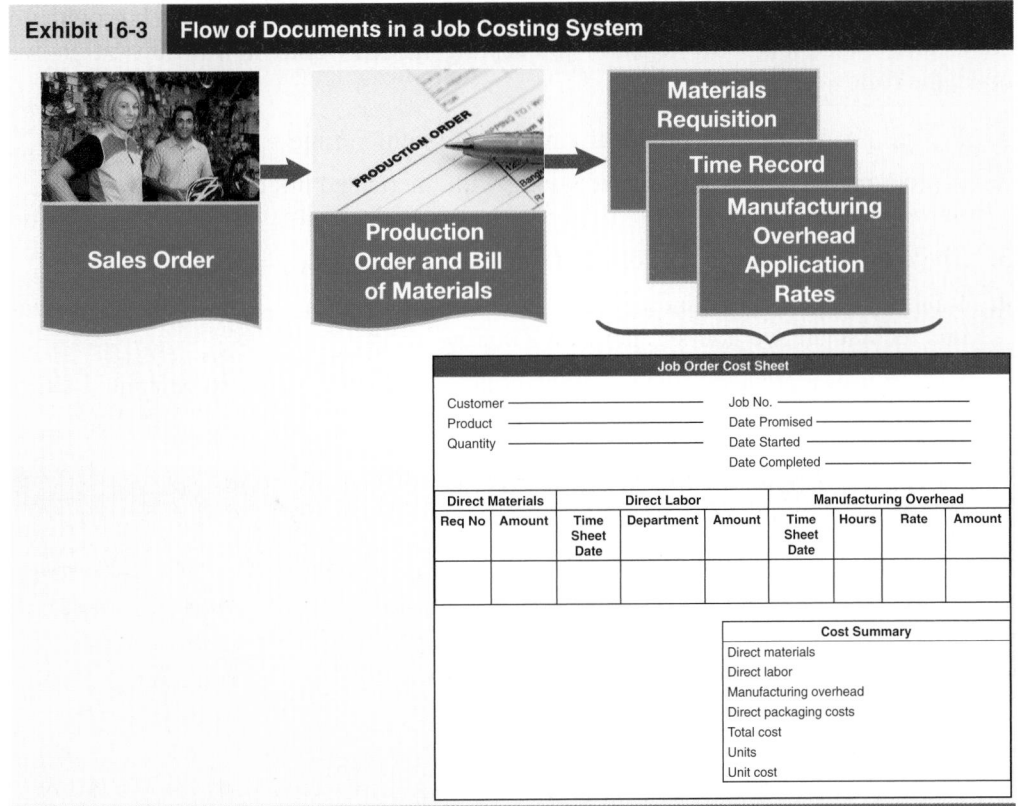

Exhibit 16-3   **Flow of Documents in a Job Costing System**

Illustration of Job Order Costing for a Manufacturer

About 36 million Americans age seven and older ride a bike six times or more in a given year. The U.S. bicycle industry has been remarkably stable at $6 billion in sales since 2003, with a slight dip in 2013 due to the U.S. recession. Approximately 12.5 million bicycles of wheel sizes over 20" were imported or produced domestically in 2015. It is estimated that 99% of these bikes were imported, mainly from China and Taiwan. Domestic bike manufacturers, over 100 in all, produce approximately 200,000 units per year. Department, discount, and chain toy stores sell approximately 74% of the bikes sold, followed by specialty local bike shops (LBSs) at 13%, chain sporting goods stores at 6%, outdoor specialty retailers at 3.5%, and "other" at 2%.[1]

Fezzari Performance Bicycles is a U.S. bike manufacturer that builds both mountain bikes and road bikes. Located in Lindon, Utah, it sells a few thousand bikes per year, from a $500 entry-level mountain and hybrid bike to a high-end full-suspension mountain bike and triathlon bike that sells for over $10,000. As described in Chapter 14, once a customer selects a specific bike model and components, Fezzari orders the required parts from its suppliers. Fezzari maintains a minimal quantity of parts in inventory so that the bike assembly can be started without waiting for ordered parts to arrive. A technician assembles the bike to the customer's specifications, tunes it up, and then test rides it to ensure that it works properly. A second technician

then checks the assembly, testing every screw and component, then checks the tune-up, and performs a second test ride. The bike is then sent to packing to be prepared for shipment.

---

[1] https://nbda.com/articles/industry-overview-2015-pg34.htm

We now turn to a comprehensive illustration of job order costing, which provides a conjectural example of how Fezzari's job costing system works. In this illustration, we make the following assumptions:

Hint: A bill of materials is a list of all parts or components needed for the manufacture of the finished product.

1. Fezzari receives a sales order for a high-end triathlon/time-trial bike, the T5.

2. A production order is then issued, along with the related bill of materials necessary to produce the T5.

3. The bill of materials, or list of parts, for the T5 is as shown in **Exhibit 16-4**.

4. It takes one Fezzari technician eight hours to assemble and test the bike and a second technician two hours to perform a quality check.

5. Fezzari uses a predetermined overhead rate of $12 per hour based on annual direct labor hours to assign overhead to products.

Exhibit 16-4	Bill of Materials—T5			
A	B	C	D	E
Item	**Description**	**Quantity**	**Cost**	**Extension**
2 Frame	Fezzari Racing Design FA1 3K Monocoque Carbon Aero TT Frame	1	$4,000	$4,000
3 Fork	Fezzari Racing XrA 3K Aero Fork, Carbon Steerer Tube	1	integrated	
4 Headset	Cane Creek Orbit IS-2 7075/T6 Crown Race, 1 1/8" Steerer Tube	1	integrated	
5 Seatpost	Fezzari Racing Design XrTT Aero 3K Carbon	1	integrated	
6 Shifters, derailleurs, cables	Shimano Dura-Ace 9000, 22 Speed	1	$ 900	$ 900
7 Cassette	Shimano Dura-Ace 9000	1	$ 170	$ 170
8 Crank	Vision Trimax Carbon	1	$ 300	$ 300
9 Chainrings	FSA BB30 Trimax 54/39t	1	$ 60	$ 60
10 Bottom bracket	FSA BB30 Ceramic	1	$ 30	$ 30
11 Chain	Shimano Dura-Ace 9000	1	$ 20	$ 20
12 Handlebars, stem, tape	Vision Trimax Carbon	1	$ 290	$ 290
13 Saddle	Fizik Arione Tri 2	1	$ 100	$ 100
14 Wheels	Reynolds 90 Areo, Carbon Clinchers	2	$1,200	$2,400
15 Tires, including tubes	Maxxis Xenith Hors Categorie M-201, 700 x 23c, race tire	2	$ 90	$ 180
16 Brakes, levers, cables	Shimano Dura-Ace 9000	2	$ 75	$ 150
17				$8,600

Accounting for Materials

For a high-end bike like the T5, Fezzari orders the frame from its Taiwanese supplier and the tires and other components from other local suppliers upon receipt of the order. Thus, the first transaction to record is the *purchase* of materials. Fezzari purchased parts listed on the bill of materials for a total cost of $8,600. Following is the entry to record this purchase:

1	Materials inventory	8,600	
	Accounts payable		8,600
	To record the purchase of materials.		

The next transaction is the *requisition* of the following materials from the materials inventory for use in the production of the T5: $4,000 for the frame, $900 for the shifters, derailleurs, and cables, $170 for the cassette, and so forth. **Exhibit 16-5** shows a sample requisition for a Fezzari T5.

Assume that in addition to the direct materials listed on the bill of materials, the assembly of the T5 requires $30 of indirect materials (lubricants, bar end plugs, etc.). The entry to record the requisitioning and use of both direct and indirect materials is as follows:

2	Work-in-process inventory	8,600	
	Manufacturing overhead	30	
	Materials inventory		8,630
	To record the requisitioning of materials—both direct and indirect.		

Exhibit 16-5	Materials Requisition Form				
	A	B	C	D	E
1	Date 8/5	Job. No. 372		Requisition No. 567	
2		Quantity			
3	Item	Authorized	Issued	Unit Price	Amount
4	Frame	1	1	$4,000	$4,000
5	Fork	1	1	integrated	
6	Headset	1	1	integrated	
7	Seatpost	1	1	integrated	
8	Shifters, derailleurs, cables	1	1	$ 900	$ 900
9	Cassette	1	1	$ 170	$ 170
10	Crank	1	1	$ 300	$ 300
11	Chainrings	1	1	$ 60	$ 60
12	Bottom Bracket	1	1	$ 30	$ 30
13	Chain	1	1	$ 20	$ 20
14	Handlebars, stem, tape	1	1	$ 290	$ 290
15	Saddle	1	1	$ 100	$ 100
16	Wheels	2	2	$1,200	$2,400
17	Tires, including tubes	2	2	$ 90	$ 180
18	Brakes, levers, cables	2	2	$ 75	$ 150
19	Total				$8,600
20	Authorized by: TC Issued by: GAP Received by: CB				

Hint: A materials requisition form is a list of items to be pulled from inventory for use in manufacturing a product.

The effect of the various postings of these transactions is shown in **Exhibit 16-6**. The amount of direct materials used would also be recorded on the job order cost sheet for Job 372 (see **Exhibit 16-10**).

Exhibit 16-6	Entries for Recording the Acquisition and Use of Materials

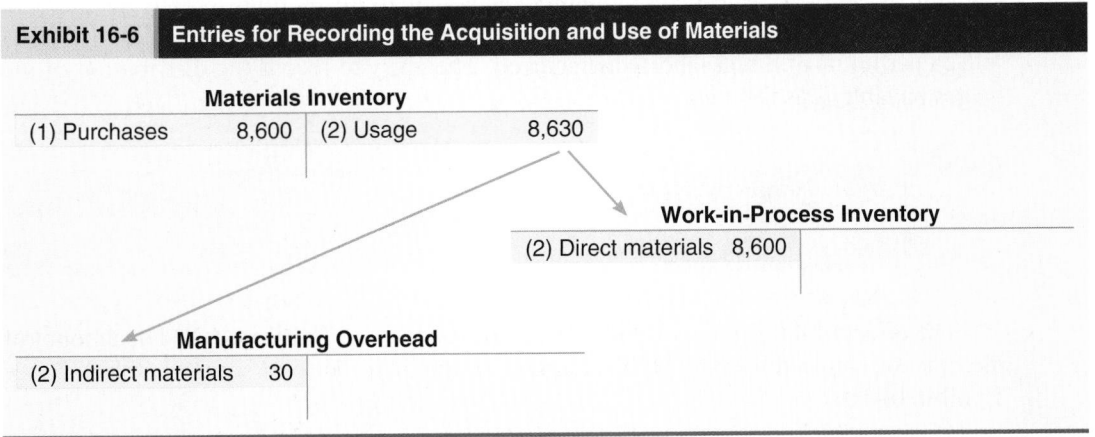

Accounting for Labor

Manufacturing firms (including Fezzari) typically use **time clocks** or time records to collect the total amount of time that each employee worked during a particular pay period. **Exhibit 16-7** shows a sample time record for a Fezzari employee.

Time clocks collect only total time worked; time records collect hours worked on particular jobs. Time clocks and computer time records are used to prepare the payroll recorded in Wages Payable.

Hint: A time record is a method of recording and organizing time spent on a product or job.

Exhibit 16-7	Time Record						
Employee Name: Robert							Employee No. 42
Skill Specification:		Technician			Date:		8/5
Time Started	**Time Stopped**	**Total Time**	**Hourly Labor Rate**	**Department**		**Job No.**	**Total Cost**
8:00	12:00	4	$25	Assembly		372	$100
1:00	5:00	4	$25	Assembly		372	$100
Total		8					$200
Approved by *LSH*							

Tracking Time

In practice, companies use various methods to track employees' time. Where employees are paid on an hourly-rate basis for hours worked, time clocks are used. In some firms, employees place a small paper card in the time clock at the beginning and end of their work shift, and the card is imprinted (or "punched") with the date and time. More commonly, employees slide or wave an employee ID card through or in front of a card reader that records the date and time information. The most recent innovation in tracking employees' time involves a device that recognizes an employee's fingerprint, iris, or face, eliminating the need for a physical card of any kind. Where employees are salaried, but there is a need to attribute hours worked to a particular job or product for costing purposes, time records are used. Employees record the amount of time that they spend each day working on a particular job or jobs so that customers can be billed the appropriate amount for labor.

Assume that Fezzari uses time records to identify labor costs with specific jobs. Hourly wage rates are used to compute the labor costs for the various products assembled. The sum of the amounts calculated using the time records should equal the total wages payable for the period. In fact, the amounts calculated from the time records are used to distribute the wages payable to the individual jobs. To assemble the T5, $200 (8 hours × $25 per hour) of direct labor was incurred. The entry to record the distribution of the wages payable is as follows:

3	Work-in-process inventory	200	
	Wages payable		200
	To distribute the wages payable.		

The effect of the posting of this transaction is shown in **Exhibit 16-8**. The amount of direct labor incurred would also be recorded on the job order cost sheet for Job 372 (see **Exhibit 16-10**).

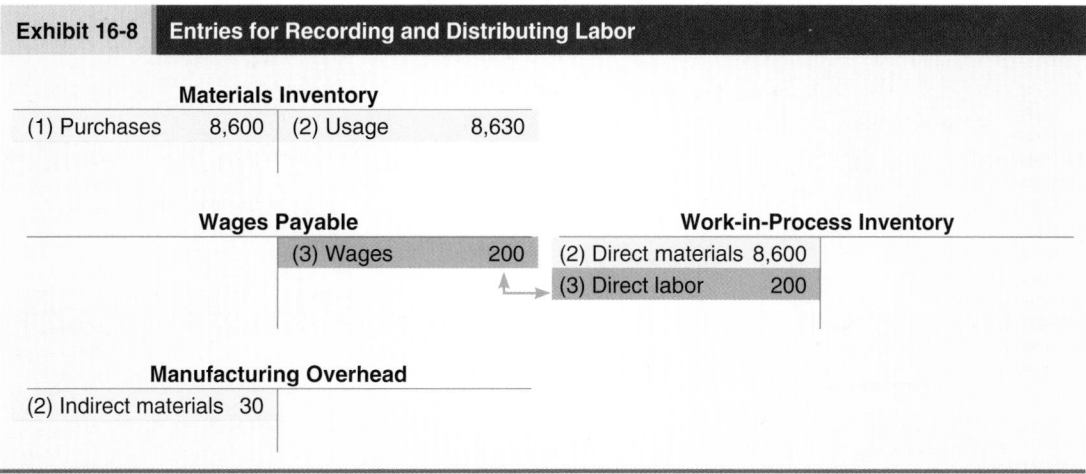

Exhibit 16-8   Entries for Recording and Distributing Labor

Accounting for Manufacturing Overhead

Factory costs are routinely charged to manufacturing overhead as incurred or through adjusting entries at the end of the accounting period. One of the elements of manufacturing overhead—indirect materials—has already been recorded through the transactions related to materials. Other general manufacturing overhead costs incurred by Fezzari during the period are recorded as they are incurred: indirect labor, $28,000; factory utilities, $31,000; factory lease, $100,000; factory insurance, $68,000; factory property taxes, $12,000; and other manufacturing overhead, $13,000. Manufacturing overhead to be recorded as a year-end adjustment is depreciation on the factory equipment of $45,000. The following are the journal entries to record these items:

4	Manufacturing overhead	252,000	
	Cash, Accounts payable, or Wages payable		252,000
	To record elements of manufacturing overhead as incurred.		

5	Manufacturing overhead	45,000	
	Accumulated depreciation—factory equipment		45,000
	To record depreciation on factory equipment.		

As explained previously, actual manufacturing overhead costs are not assigned directly to individual jobs. Instead, through the use of a predetermined overhead rate, the work-in-process inventory account is charged with manufacturing overhead applied. During the budgeting process, Fezzari determined its predetermined overhead rate to be $12 per direct labor hour. The T5 order accumulated 8 hours of direct labor. As a result, $96 of manufacturing overhead is applied to the job.

The journal entry to record the application of manufacturing overhead to Job 372 is as follows:

6	Work-in-process inventory	96	
	Manufacturing overhead		96
	To record the application of manufacturing overhead to the work-in-process inventory using the predetermined overhead rate.		

The effect of the various postings of these transactions is shown in **Exhibit 16-9**. The amount of overhead applied would also be recorded on the job order cost sheet for Job 372 (see **Exhibit 16-10**).

Exhibit 16-9	Entries for Recording and Distributing Overhead

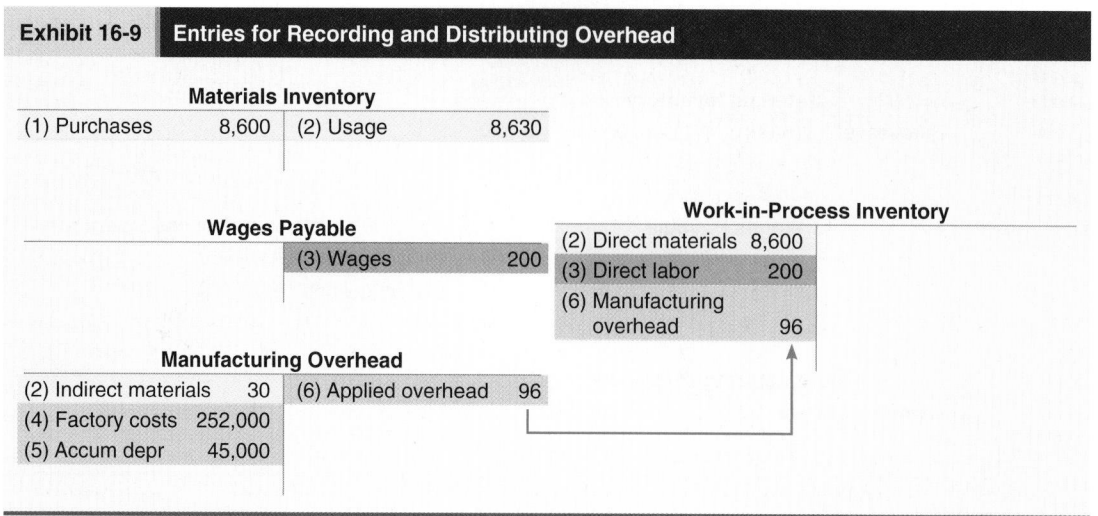

The solution is on page 800.

YOUR TURN! 16.3

Match the account that should be debited with the recorded activity (the accounts may be used more than once):

Activity	Account
____ Apply manufacturing overhead	1. Work-in-process inventory
____ Record direct labor incurred	2. Materials inventory
____ Record purchase of raw materials	3. Manufacturing overhead
____ Record indirect labor incurred	4. Wages payable
____ Record use of indirect materials	
____ Record use of direct materials	

Accounting for Packaging and Finished Goods

LO4 **Discuss** the procedures and journal entries used to account for finished goods and the sale of finished goods.

When products are finished, they are transferred from Work-in-Process Inventory to Finished Goods Inventory. The costs transferred from Work-in-Process to Finished Goods Inventory include all manufacturing costs. However, these costs also include packaging costs.

ACCOUNTING IN PRACTICE	Treatment of Packaging Costs

A product is not complete or finished until it is packaged in the container in which it will be sold. Packaging costs are part of the product cost transferred to the Finished Goods Inventory account.

Fezzari spends two hours to inspect, partially dissemble, and package the T5 for shipment to the customer. The two hours of inspecting are recorded in a time record at a pay rate of $25 per hour. Approximately $75 is required for the shipment container and packing materials. The packing materials are purchased on account and immediately placed into Work-in-Process. Remember that Fezzari applies overhead based on direct labor hours. Thus, Fezzari would also record $24 (2 hours × $12 per hour) to Work-in-Process Inventory. The total packaging costs applied to Work-in-Process are $149.

7	Work-in-process inventory	50	
	Cash and wages payable		50
	To record the packaging labor for Job 372.		

continued

continued from previous page

8	Work-in-process inventory	75	
	Accounts payable		75
	To record the cost of packing materials for Job 372.		
9	Work-in-process inventory	24	
	Manufacturing overhead		24
	To record the application of manufacturing overhead to the work-in-process inventory using the predetermined overhead rate.		

When the T5 bike order is completed, the unit cost of the T5 is obtained by summing the costs charged to the job. **Exhibit 16-10** shows the completed job cost sheet for Fezarri's Job 372. The job cost sheet accumulates all product costs for the job, including direct materials, direct labor, manufacturing overhead and packaging. The report also identifies the total unit cost of $9,045. Notice that this amount also matches the total of the debits to the work-in-process inventory account in **Exhibit 16-11**. The accountant credits Work-in-Process Inventory and debits Finished Goods Inventory for the total cost of the job completed. The journal entry to record the completion of the T5 is as follows:

10	Finished goods inventory	9,045	
	Work-in-process inventory		9,045
	To record the completion of Job 372.		

Exhibit 16-10   **Fezarri's Job Cost Sheet for Job No. 372**

Fezarri Job Cost Sheet

Customer	Ryan Hobson	Job No.	372
Product	T5	Date Promised	5/15
Quantity	1	Date Started	8/1
		Date Completed	8/6

Direct Materials		Direct Labor			Manufacturing Overhead			
Req No	Amount	Time Sheet Date	Department	Amount	Time Sheet Date	Hours	Rate	Amount
567	$8,600	8/5	Assembly	$200	8/5	8	$12/DLH	$96

Cost Summary	
Direct materials	$8,600
Direct labor	$ 200
Manufacturing overhead	$ 96
Total packaging costs	$ 149*
Total cost	**$9,045**
Units	1
Unit cost	$9,045

*Total packaging costs include materials of $75, labor of $50, and overhead of $24.

When the T5 is delivered to the customer, the cost of the bike is removed from the finished goods subaccount. Two journal entries are recorded. The first entry is a debit to Accounts Receivable and a credit to Sales for the selling price of the bike. The second entry is a debit to Cost of Goods Sold and a credit to Finished Goods Inventory for the cost of the bike. The entries to record the sale of the T5 are as follows:

11	Accounts receivable	10,500	
	Sales		10,500
	To record the sale of Job 372.		

12	Cost of goods sold	9,045	
	Finished goods inventory		9,045
	To record the cost of Job 372.		

The effect of the various postings of these transactions is shown in **Exhibit 16-11**. Note that entry 11 is not shown in this exhibit because it involves the revenue associated with the sale, not the cost of the job. The job order cost sheet for Job 372 would also be closed.

Exhibit 16-11   Entries for Completing the Job and Recording the Sale

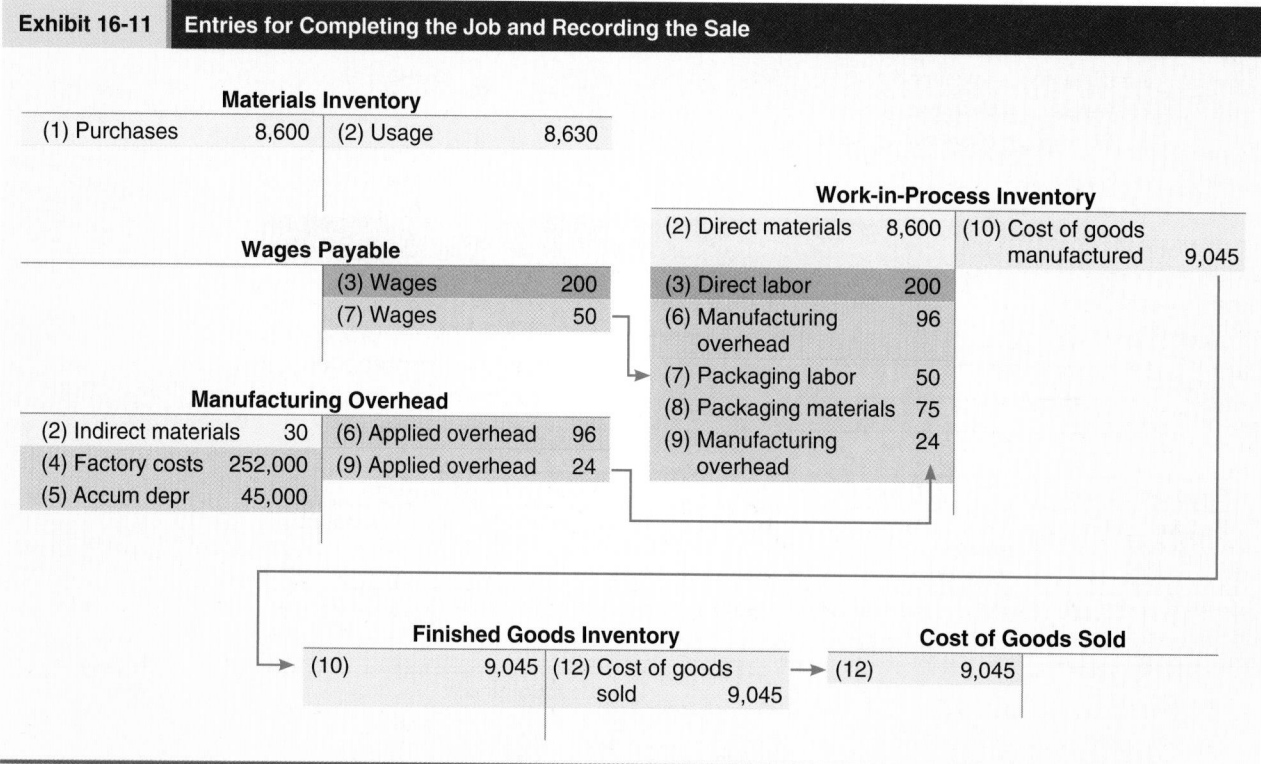

Disposition of Under- and Overapplied Overhead

As introduced in Chapter 15 and described earlier in this chapter, overhead costs are accumulated in the manufacturing overhead account during an accounting period (usually a year). During the same period, overhead costs are being applied to products or jobs based on a predetermined overhead rate. It is not until the end of the period, after all actual overhead costs have been recorded and all overhead has been applied to products and jobs, that management determines whether the amount of overhead applied to products and jobs is greater or less than the amount of actual overhead costs recorded. If more has been applied than recorded, overhead is said to be **overapplied**. If less has been applied than recorded, overhead is said to be **underapplied**.

At year-end, a journal entry is made to dispose of the underapplied or overapplied amount of manufacturing overhead. If the amount of underapplied or overapplied overhead is insignificant, an entry is made to transfer the amount to the cost of goods sold account. The under- or overapplied overhead is almost always immaterial in practice. An overapplied amount is transferred by debiting Manufacturing Overhead and crediting Cost of Goods Sold. An underapplied amount is transferred by debiting Cost of Goods Sold and crediting Manufacturing Overhead.

When the under- or overapplied amount is significant, it should be allocated to all of the jobs that were worked on during the year. This is accomplished by a journal entry that transfers the amount to Work-in-Process Inventory, Finished Goods Inventory, and Cost of Goods Sold. An overapplied amount is transferred by debiting Manufacturing Overhead and crediting Work-in-Process Inventory, Finished Goods Inventory, and Cost of Goods Sold. An underapplied amount is transferred by debiting Work-in-Process Inventory, Finished Goods Inventory, and Cost of Goods Sold sold and crediting Manufacturing Overhead. The amount transferred is allocated proportionately among Work-in-Process Inventory, Finished Goods Inventory, and Cost of Goods Sold based on the amount of Applied Overhead that is in each of the three accounts at the end of the year.

Hint: After the disposition of over- or underapplied overhead, the balance in the overhead account should be $0.

Concept ➔	Method ➔	Assessment	TAKEAWAY 16.2
Your company applies overhead based on a predetermined overhead rate. The CEO has asked you to determine actual cost of goods sold for the year just ended for an emergency management meeting. Historically, the amount of over- or underapplied overhead has not been significant.	• Determine actual overhead costs incurred for the year (sum the additions to manufacturing overhead). • Determine the amount of applied overhead for the year (sum the additions to work-in-process inventory for overhead). • Subtract applied overhead from actual overhead.	• If the difference is positive (underapplied), add the difference to the amount of cost of goods sold in the general ledger account. • If the difference is negative (overapplied), subtract the difference from the amount of cost of goods sold in the general ledger account.	

Exhibit 16-12 reflects the various postings of the journal entries related to manufacturing overhead. Items from entries 4, 5, 6, and 9 are highlighted in bold type. Assume that Fezzari has recorded a total of $3,000 of indirect materials for the period. In addition, assume that an additional $295,200 in manufacturing overhead was applied to other jobs throughout the year. Note that the sum of the debits in manufacturing overhead is $300,000 but that the sum of the credits is $295,320. In other words, actual factory costs were $300,000, but only $295,320 of manufacturing overhead was applied to the work-in-process inventory account. Therefore, overhead was underapplied by $4,680. Assume that this amount is insignificant.

The journal entry to record the transfer of the underapplied overhead is as follows:

13	Cost of goods sold	4,680	
	Manufacturing overhead		4,680
	To record the disposition of underapplied overhead.		

When perpetual inventory procedures are used in cost accounting systems, the ending balances in Materials Inventory, Work-in-Process Inventory, and Finished Goods Inventory reflect all the transactions of the accounting period that increase and decrease inventories. These ending balances are adjusted only if a discrepancy is discovered when the year-end physical counts of inventory are taken.

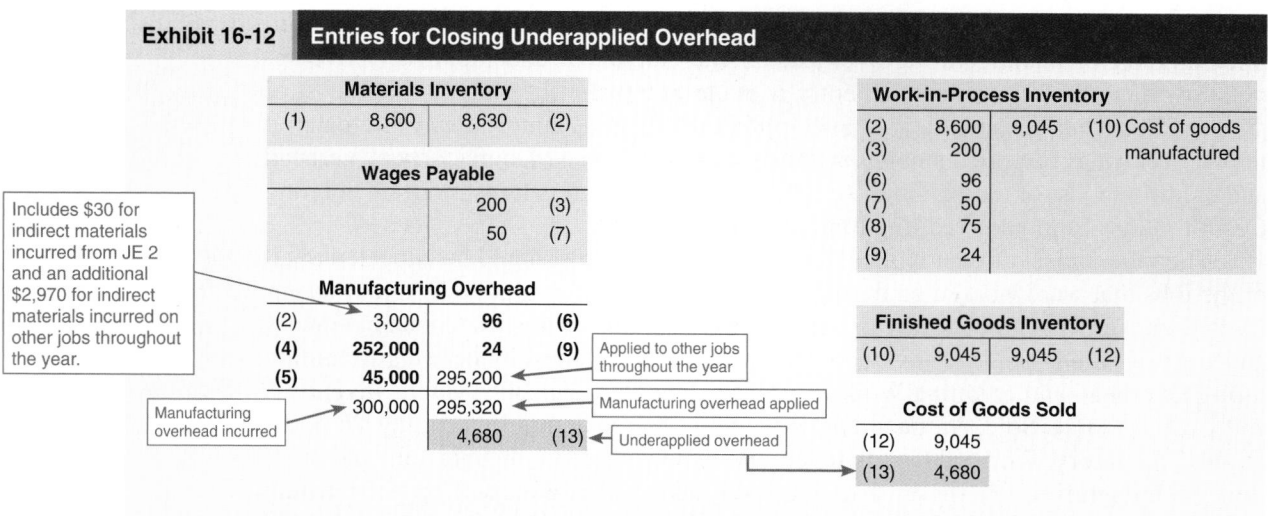

Exhibit 16-12 | **Entries for Closing Underapplied Overhead**

As illustrated in the Fezzari example in Exhibits 15-12, 13, and 14 of Chapter 15, the entries shown in the accounts in **Exhibit 16-12** could be used to create a Schedule of Cost of Goods Manufactured and a Schedule of Cost of Goods Sold for the T5. Together with other information about sales and costs of Fezzari's other products and selling and administrative expenses, Fezzari management could then prepare an Income Statement for the period.

Illustration of Job Order Costing for a Service Firm

SERVICE AND MERCHANDISING

Job order costing is also used by service companies. An abbreviated illustration using a CH2M Hill project will demonstrate the use of job order costing in a service environment.

One of the services that CH2M Hill provides to clients is assistance with implementation of lean enterprise solutions. Essentially, CH2M Hill utilizes proven approaches and methods to streamline client manufacturing and office processes. One such client was the Perrier Group of America. The objective of the CH2M Hill project was to determine the optimal location for a new bottling facility needed for projected five-year sales growth in the company's Northeast Region. CH2M Hill evaluated Perrier's entire supply chain, from the spring to the customer. The result of the project was the determination of new raw materials requirements to support projected growth, the optimal location of the bottling facility, and the number and location of additional warehouse facilities to support increased sales during peak periods of the year.

Accounting for Materials

Because this project was for services, no materials were used. This is typical of service projects.

Accounting for Labor

CH2M Hill's project manager, engineers, and consultants recorded their time working on the Perrier project on a time record or timesheet. These employees also worked on other projects during the same period and recorded the time worked on those projects separately. Assume that during one period, the assigned employees worked a total of 40 hours on the Perrier project and that the portion of their salaries associated with the time spent on the Perrier project was $5,000. This would have been recorded as follows:

Work-in-process—Perrier	5,000	
Salaries payable		5,000
To record salaries on the Perrier project.		

Accounting for Overhead

Assume that CH2M Hill uses a predetermined overhead rate for consulting engagements of $150 per hour. Because 40 hours of labor was charged to the Perrier project for the period, a total of $6,000 ($150 × 40 hours) of overhead would have been applied to the project. The entry to record the application of overhead is the same as shown earlier for Fezzari:

Work-in-process—Perrier	6,000	
Overhead		6,000
To record the application of overhead to the Perrier project using the		
predetermined overhead rate.		

Recording the Sale

Recall that with the completion of a product, the accumulated cost of the product is moved from work-in-process inventory to finished goods inventory. However, service companies do not have a finished goods inventory. Instead, when a project is completed, the accumulated cost of the service is removed from work-in-process inventory as the final project invoice is prepared. In our illustration, assume that when CH2M Hill completed the project, the Work-in-Process—Perrier account had a total balance of $245,000 and that the contract between CH2M Hill and Perrier was for $300,000. CH2M Hill would have recorded the following journal entries in its financial records:

Accounts receivable	300,000	
Sales		300,000
To record the final billing for the Perrier project.		
Cost of goods sold	245,000	
Work-in-process—Perrier		245,000
To record the cost of the Perrier project.		

YOUR TURN! 16.4

The solution is on page 800.

You are a junior accountant at Angel Manufacturing. The controller has asked you to prepare the journal entries associated with a special order (#144) recently completed for a new customer. She hands you the following information from which to prepare the journal entries, including the cost of goods sold entry:

Materials purchased.	$2,000
Direct materials used for #144	2,600
Indirect materials used for #144	350
Direct labor incurred for #144.	1,650
Overhead applied to #144	3,300

ACCOUNTING FOR SERVICE DEPARTMENTS

LO5 Describe the procedures for cost allocation for service departments.

Most factories are so large and so complex that a high degree of organizational specialization naturally exists in their operations. Production usually involves a series of specialized departments, such as cutting, reshaping, grinding, subassembly, final assembly, painting, and packaging. In addition to these production departments, a typical factory also has highly specialized service departments, which may be involved with purchasing, materials handling, personnel, warehousing, inspection, maintenance, and even food service (cafeterias). Whereas production departments work directly on products, service departments provide production departments with support services that contribute indirectly to the completion of products.

Service Departments as Cost Centers

Service departments are often viewed by management as cost centers. That is, the costs of each service department are accumulated separately so management can identify the total cost of such services. Also, unit costs for each service—such as maintenance cost per square foot of floor space—can be derived for comparison with other operating periods and/or other sources of the service such as outside contractors. Most accounting systems account for service departments as cost centers.

Service Department Costs as Product Costs

Although service departments do not perform actual work on specific products, they do provide essential services to the production departments. Thus, service department costs are appropriately considered among the related production department costs and are included in final product costs as part of manufacturing overhead.

A.K.A. This method is described as the direct method of service department allocation.

By their nature, service departments do not use direct materials or direct labor. Their costs are part of manufacturing overhead. These departments do not work directly on a product, so overhead rates, in the strict sense, are not computed for them. Instead, service department costs become part of product costs by being allocated among several production departments, according to the approximate benefits received by each production department. Service department costs become part of each production department's overhead to be applied to Work-in-Process.

The diagram in **Exhibit 16-13** illustrates how service department costs (1) are accumulated on a cost center basis, (2) are allocated to one or more production departments, and (3) become part of the product costs when manufacturing overhead is applied to Work-in-Process for each production department. To simplify this illustration, we assume that these amounts result in no over- or underapplied overhead.

Exhibit 16-13	Allocation of Service Department Costs to Production Departments' Overhead Accounts

(1) Service Department	(2) Production Department	(3) Work-in-Process Inventory
Maintenance Service Department	Allocate costs → Appliance Department Overhead	Apply overhead → Appliance Department
Quality Control Service Department	Electronics Department Overhead	Electronics Department

Note that service department costs are accumulated over a period of time, then allocated to the producing departments, before being applied to product in inventory.

Method of Cost Allocation

Costs are allocated among various departments on a basis that reflects the proportion of the service or activity that benefits each department. Some examples of allocated costs and their possible allocation bases are as follows:

Service Cost	Possible Allocation Basis
Personnel salaries	Number of employees in each department
Building depreciation	Square feet of floor space used
Utilities	Machine hours used
Building maintenance	Square feet of floor space used
Machine maintenance	Machine hours used
Heat and light	Cubic feet of building space used

Choosing an Allocation Basis

Once an allocation basis is chosen, it could remain unchanged for a long period of time. The selection of an allocation basis represents a policy decision that is typically reviewed only when major inequities exist.

The concern for cost control may justify the use of elaborate devices and schemes to measure service benefits. Some examples are departmental electric meters, timekeeping systems reflecting actual hours of service requested and used, and weighting techniques in which requests for rush or peak-hour services are assigned higher costs than requests honored at the convenience of the service department.

To allocate a particular cost, we simply divide the total cost among a series of departments in proportion to departmental shares of the appropriate base activity. For example, suppose that $8,000 of personnel department cost is allocated between the Appliance Department (manufacturing department) with 15 employees and the Electronics Department (manufacturing department) with 25 employees. The number of production employees is the allocation basis. The two distinct steps involved and illustrative calculations are shown in **Exhibit 16-14**.

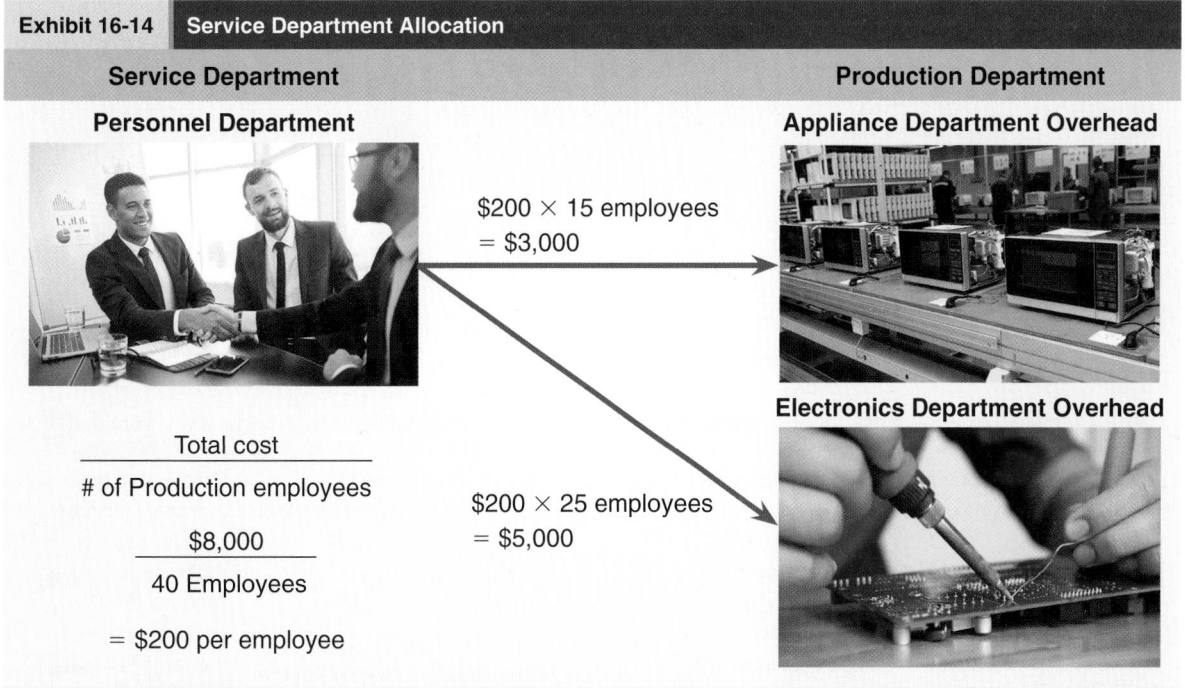

Exhibit 16-14	Service Department Allocation

Service Department

Personnel Department

$200 × 15 employees = $3,000

Production Department

Appliance Department Overhead

Electronics Department Overhead

$200 × 25 employees = $5,000

$$\frac{\text{Total cost}}{\text{\# of Production employees}}$$

$$\frac{\$8,000}{40 \text{ Employees}}$$

$$= \$200 \text{ per employee}$$

Service Department Allocation

The allocation procedure should be simple and easily understood by all involved. If the allocation computations become too complex, their cost may exceed any benefits.

As a final step, we should check allocations and verify that the sum of allocated amounts equals the total amount allocated.

Exhibit 16-15 illustrates a worksheet that could be used to accumulate and allocate manufacturing overhead in a multidepartment manufacturing operation that includes service departments. Note the following:

1. Three categories of costs are involved:
    a. Those directly identifiable with departments
    b. Those requiring allocations to production and service departments
    c. Service department costs allocated to production departments

2. A total overhead amount is first accumulated for each service department and each production department.

3. After service department costs are allocated, the total overhead is assigned to the production departments only.

We might ask why service department costs are not allocated to other service departments. More sophisticated allocation techniques may involve allocations of some service department costs to other service departments and even mutual assignment of all of one or more service department costs to all other service departments. Discussions of these techniques are for a more advanced text.

| Exhibit 16-15 | Overhead Distribution Worksheet for the Year Ended December 31, 2019 |

A		Service Depts.			Production Depts.		G
		Maint.	Engin.		Appl.	Elect.	**Allocation Basis**
(a) Directly identifiable overhead							
Indirect labor		$ 8,000	$20,000		$38,500	$18,500	Wages payable analysis
Factory supplies used		3,000	2,000		9,000	10,000	Requisition forms
(b) Allocated overhead							
Building depreciation		600	1,200		3,000	1,200	Square feet of floor space
Personal property taxes		400	800		1,500	1,300	Assessed value of equipment used
Totals		$12,000	$24,000		$52,000	$31,000	
(c) Allocation of service departments							
Maintenance		(12,000)			8,000	4,000	Square feet of factory area used
Utilities			(24,000)		4,000	20,000	Machine hours
Totals		—	—		$64,000	$55,000	

These are overhead costs that can be directly attributed to service and production departments.

These are overhead costs that cannot be directly attributed to service and production departments, but are allocated on some basis.

The service department overhead costs (both direct and allocated) are allocated to the production departments.

The appliances department occupies twice the space of the electronics department.

The electronics department uses five times the machine hours of the appliances department.

Concept	Method	Assessment
Your growing legal firm has created a new information technology (IT) department to assist the attorneys with the firm's software, hardware, and IT security issues. Management wants to allocate the cost of the IT department to each of its six offices.	• Accumulate the cost of the IT department for each reporting period. • Select an allocation base (e.g., number of computers in each office or number of service requests). • Allocate the total IT cost to each office proportionate to its share of the allocation base.	Offices that have a greater number of computers or make more frequent requests for IT services will receive the larger allocation of cost.

KRH Enterprises has two service departments (S1 and S2) and two production departments (P1 and P2). Information from the most recent year shows the following for each department:

	S1	S2	P1	P2
Direct overhead	$50,000	$40,000	$75,000	$65,000
Allocated overhead. . .	10,000	5,000	25,000	20,000
Machine hours			2,000	4,000
Square feet.			10,000	5,000

KRH allocates S1 to the production departments based on square feet and S2 based on machine hours.

What is the total overhead in the two production departments after the service department allocations?

DEPARTMENTAL OVERHEAD RATES

LO6 Contrast plant-wide overhead rates and departmental overhead rates.

Manufacturing companies that use traditional overhead rates typically use either a plant-wide (or company-wide) overhead rate or departmental overhead rates. A **plant-wide (or company-wide) overhead rate** is determined by dividing estimated total plant (or company) overhead for the year by estimated utilization of the total plant (or company) productive capacity for the year. The discussions and illustration in this chapter have incorporated a plant-wide overhead rate. When a plant-wide overhead rate is adopted, the cost accounting system uses a single predetermined rate for applying overhead to work done in all the producing departments, such as bending, drilling, welding, assembling, and painting.

Departmental Overhead Rates

Some manufacturing companies have adopted a cost accounting system that uses **departmental overhead rates**. When departmental overhead rates are used, a separate overhead rate is predetermined for each producing department in the factory by dividing the estimated overhead associated with each department by the estimated utilization of the capacity of that department.

A manufacturer would use departmental overhead rates for two primary reasons. First, the predetermined overhead rate in one department may be significantly different from the rate in another department. For instance, in department 1, the overhead rate might be $5 per direct labor hour, whereas the overhead rate in department 2 might be $20 per direct labor hour. Second, the capacity measure in one department may be different from the capacity measure in another department. For example, if department 1 is highly automated, then machine hours would be an appropriate measure of capacity for department 1. However, if department 2 is direct-labor intensive, then direct labor hours would be an appropriate measure of capacity for department 2.

When departmental overhead rates are used, the manufacturer accumulates the appropriate measure of capacity for each department for each job so that the appropriate overhead rates can be applied. Assume that a particular manufacturer has three producing departments: machining, painting, and assembling.

The capacity measure for machining and painting is machine hours, whereas the capacity measure for assembly is direct labor hours. For Job 368, the factory accumulated 30 machine hours of machining, 20 machine hours of painting, and 40 direct labor hours of assembling. Machining has a predetermined overhead rate of $4 per machine hour, painting has a predetermined overhead rate of $3 per machine hour, and assembling has a predetermined overhead rate of $2 per direct labor hour. Manufacturing overhead would be applied to Job 368 as follows:

Machining (30 machine hours × $4)	$120
Painting (20 machine hours × $3)	60
Assembling (40 direct labor hours × $2)	80
Total manufacturing overhead applied to Job 368	$260

Departmental overhead rates usually provide a more equitable application of manufacturing overhead to individual jobs than do plant-wide rates. However, when there are significant variations in volume or complexity among the individual jobs, neither plant-wide nor departmental overhead rates may provide an equitable application of manufacturing overhead among the individual jobs. Instead, **activity-based costing** may be more appropriate. Activity-based costing is discussed in detail in Chapter 18.

YOUR TURN! 16.6

The solution is on page 801.

Assume that a manufacturer has three producing departments: molding, machining, and painting. The capacity measure for molding and machining is machine hours, whereas the capacity measure for painting is direct labor hours. For Job #59, the factory accumulated 20 machine hours of molding, 10 machine hours of machining, and 5 direct labor hours of painting. Molding has a predetermined overhead rate of $10 per machine hour, machining has a predetermined overhead rate of $8 per machine hour, and painting has a predetermined overhead rate of $4 per direct labor hour. How much overhead should be applied to Job #59?

SERVICE INDUSTRY IN FOCUS

SERVICE AND MERCHANDISING

Environmental Business Consultants, LLC (EBC) worked on and completed two projects during June 2019: a review of appropriate rates for solid waste and recycling collection within Klamath County, and a competitive procurement of landfill disposal services for the City of Redding. The following information relates to these two projects:

	Rate Review Project—Klamath	Procurement Project—Redding
WIP Inventory balance at June 1, 2019	$46,320	$85,318
Hours worked during June	100	74
Payroll cost per hour:		
Partner	$ 60	$ 60
Manager	$ 38	$ 38
Staff.	$ 24	$ 24
Overhead rate per labor hour	$ 25	$ 25

During June, the partner charged 10 hours to the rate review project and 20 hours to the procurement project; the manager charged 30 hours to the rate review project and 24 hours to the procurement project; and the staff charged 60 hours to the rate review project and 30 hours to the procurement project.

On June 30, EBC billed its clients for the completed projects. The invoice for the rate review project was for $60,000 and for the procurement project was $105,000.

Required

1. Prepare the journal entry to distribute the payroll to the projects during June. (Assume that the correct entry was made when the payroll was paid.)

2. Prepare the journal entry to apply the overhead to the projects during June.

3. Prepare the journal entry(ies) to record the completion of the projects as of the end of June. (*Hint:* Don't forget the work that was performed on the jobs prior to June,

which is reflected in the beginning WIP balance. Also, don't forget that there is no finished goods inventory in a service firm—once the project is complete, it is billed to the client.)

4. Determine the amount of profit or loss that EBC earned on each of the two projects.

Solution

1.

WIP—Klamath	3,180	
WIP—Redding	2,832	
Payroll expense		6,012

Klamath: ($60 × 10 hours) + ($38 × 30 hours) + ($24 × 60 hours) = $3,180
Redding: ($60 × 20 hours) + ($38 × 24 hours) + ($24 × 30 hours) = $2,832

2.

WIP—Klamath	2,500	
WIP—Redding	1,850	
Overhead		4,350

Klamath: (10 + 30 + 60) × $25 = 2,500
Redding: (20 + 24 + 30) × $25 = 1,850

3.

Accounts receivable—Klamath	60,000	
Sales revenue		60,000
Cost of sales	52,000	
WIP—Klamath		52,000
(46,320 + 3,180 + 2,500)		
Accounts receivable—Redding	105,000	
Sales revenue		105,000
Cost of sales	90,000	
WIP—Klamath		90,000
(85,318 + 2,832 + 1,850)		

4.

Klamath:	Sales revenue	$ 60,000
	Cost of goods sold	52,000
	Gross profit	$ 8,000

Redding:	Sales revenue	$105,000
	Cost of goods sold	90,000
	Gross profit	$ 15,000

COMPREHENSIVE PROBLEM

The annual budget for Diamond Corporation for 2019 included the following costs and expenses:

Direct materials	$ 30,000
Direct labor ($8 per hour)	120,000
Sales commissions	28,000
Factory supervision	16,000
Indirect labor	27,000
Factory depreciation	25,000
Factory taxes	7,000
Factory insurance	6,000
Factory utilities	9,000

Required

a. Compute the plant-wide predetermined manufacturing overhead rate for 2019 using direct labor hours as the activity measure.

b. Determine the amount of manufacturing overhead that would be applied to jobs during March 2019 when 1,100 direct labor hours were actually incurred.

Solution

a. Budgeted manufacturing overhead:

Factory supervision	$16,000
Indirect labor.	27,000
Factory depreciation.	25,000
Factory taxes	7,000
Factory insurance.	6,000
Factory utilities	9,000
Budgeted manufacturing overhead	$90,000

Budgeted direct labor hours:

$$\frac{\$120,000}{\$8/\text{hour}} = 15,000 \text{ budgeted direct labor hours}$$

Predetermined overhead rate:

$$\frac{\text{Budgeted manufacturing overhead}}{\text{Budgeted direct labor hours}} = \frac{\$90,000}{15,000} = \$6 \text{ per direct labor hour}$$

b. 1,100 hours × $6 = $6,600 applied manufacturing overhead

SUMMARY OF LEARNING OBJECTIVES

LO1 **Describe the two basic types of cost accounting systems, discuss how they may be used in both manufacturing and nonmanufacturing environments, and explain the need for the timely determination of product costs. (p. 756)**

- A costing system is an orderly process for tracking product or service cost information.
- In a manufacturing environment, materials, labor, and overhead costs are accumulated and assigned to specific jobs and products.
- In a nonmanufacturing (service) setting, labor and overhead costs are accumulated and assigned to specific customers.
- A job order costing system is used when production is characterized by a series of unique products or jobs undertaken either to fill specific orders from customers or to produce a general stock from which future orders will be filled.
- A process costing system lends itself to the production of a large volume of homogeneous products manufactured in a continual flow operation.
- A cost accounting system must trace, on a timely basis, direct materials, direct labor, and manufacturing overhead to products or jobs.

LO2 **Explain the need for a predetermined overhead rate and demonstrate its calculation. (p. 759)**

- The predetermined overhead rate is calculated by dividing the estimated total manufacturing overhead cost for the year by the estimated utilization of the factory productive capacity during the upcoming year.
- Companies should choose the application base that corresponds to the period over which activity decisions are typically made.

LO3 **Describe and explain a job order costing system, identify types of records used in job order costing, and demonstrate the journal entries that accompany the flow of product costs. (p. 760)**

- Materials requisitions authorize issuance from the materials inventory.
- Time records document the labor time by job.

- The *job order cost sheet* summarizes the product costs—direct materials, direct labor, and manufacturing overhead applied—for one job; the predetermined overhead rate is used to apply manufacturing overhead.
- When material is requisitioned from the materials inventory, the Work-in-Process Inventory account is debited for the cost of direct materials and the Manufacturing Overhead account is debited for the cost of indirect materials.
- When the wages payable is distributed, the Work-in-Process Inventory account is debited for the cost of direct labor and the Manufacturing Overhead account is debited for the cost of indirect labor.
- Actual manufacturing overhead costs are recorded by debiting the Manufacturing Overhead account.
- Manufacturing overhead is applied to jobs by debiting the Work-in-Process Inventory account and crediting the Manufacturing Overhead account.

Discuss the procedures and journal entries used to account for finished goods and the sale of finished goods. (p. 766)   LO4

- A product is not complete or finished until it is packaged in the container in which it will be sold. Packaging costs are part of the product cost transferred to the Finished Goods Inventory account.
- The cost of finished goods is recorded by debiting the Finished Goods Inventory account and crediting the Work-in-Process Inventory account.
- The sale of finished goods is recorded by debiting the Cost of Goods Sold account and crediting the Finished Goods Inventory account for the cost of the goods sold and by debiting the Accounts Receivable account and crediting the Sales account for the selling price.
- At year end, a journal entry is made to dispose of the **underapplied** or **overapplied** amount of manufacturing overhead. If the amount of underapplied or overapplied overhead is insignificant, an entry is made to transfer the amount to the cost of goods sold account. When the amount is significant, it should be allocated to all of the jobs that were worked on during the year. This is accomplished by a journal entry that transfers the amount to Work-in-Process Inventory, Finished Goods Inventory, and Cost of Goods Sold.

Describe the procedures for cost allocation for service departments. (p. 771)   LO5

- Service department costs are overhead costs that are allocated to production departments and eventually assigned to products as part of the production department's overhead.
- Each different service cost may be allocated using a different allocation basis.
- Departments can be divided into two broad classes: operating or production departments where the main purpose of the organization is carried out, and service departments that assist the activities of operating or production departments.

Contrast plant-wide overhead rates and departmental overhead rates. (p. 775)   LO6

- When departmental overhead rates are used, a separate rate is calculated for each producing department in the factory.
- A plant-wide (or company-wide) overhead rate is determined by dividing estimated total plant (or company) overhead for the year by estimated utilization of the total plant (or company) productive capacity for the year.

Concept ⟶	Method ⟶	Assessment	SUMMARY
You have been asked to calculate the predetermined overhead rate for the next operating period.	• Forecast expected total overhead for the period. • Select an application base or cost driver. • Estimate total activity for the cost driver for the period.	Predetermined overhead rate = total estimated overhead divided by the total estimated activity level of the application base (such as machine hours or direct labor hours). Assign the predetermined overhead rate to each unit of cost driver during the period.	TAKEAWAY 16.1

continued

continued from previous page

SUMMARY	Concept ⟶	Method ⟶	Assessment
TAKEAWAY 16.2	Your company applies overhead based on a pre-determined overhead rate. The CEO has asked you to determine actual cost of goods sold for the year just ended for an emergency management meeting. Historically, the amount of over- or underapplied overhead has not been significant.	• Determine actual overhead costs incurred for the year (sum the additions to manufacturing overhead) • Determine the amount of applied overhead for the year (sum the additions to work-in-process inventory for overhead) • Subtract applied overhead from actual overhead	• If the difference is positive (under-applied), add the difference to the amount of cost of goods sold in the general ledger account. • If the difference is negative (over-applied), subtract the difference from the amount of cost of goods sold in the general ledger account.
TAKEAWAY 16.3	Your growing legal firm has created a new information technology (IT) department to assist the attorneys with the firm's software, hardware, and IT security issues. Management wants to allocate the cost of the IT department to each of its six offices.	• Accumulate the cost of the IT department for each reporting period • Select an allocation base (e.g., number of computers in each office or number of service requests) • Allocate the total IT cost to each office proportionate to its share of the allocation base	Offices that have a greater number of computers or make more frequent requests for IT services will receive the larger allocation of cost.

KEY TERMS

Activity-based costing (p. 776)

Bill of materials (p. 760)

Cost driver (p. 759)

Departmental overhead rates (p. 775)

Job order costing system (p. 756)

Job order cost sheet (p. 760)

Materials requisition (p. 760)

Overapplied (p. 768)

Plant-wide (or company-wide) overhead rate (p. 775)

Predetermined manufacturing overhead rate (p. 759)

Process costing system (p. 757)

Production order (p. 760)

Sales order (p. 760)

Time clocks (p. 764)

Time record (p. 760)

Underapplied (p. 768)

Assignments with the 🔵 logo in the margin are available in 𝐵𝑢𝑠𝑖𝑛𝑒𝑠𝑠Course.
See the Preface of the book for details.

SELF-STUDY QUESTIONS

(Answers to Self-Study Questions are at the end of this chapter.)

LO1   1. **Which product costing system would most likely be used to account for a home builder building custom homes for its customers?**
  a.   Job order costing
  b.   Process costing
  c.   Normal costing
  d.   Standard costing

LO2   2. **Predetermined manufacturing overhead rates should be**
  a.   higher than actual manufacturing overhead rates.
  b.   lower than actual manufacturing overhead rates.
  c.   based on monthly budgets.
  d.   based on annual budgets.

LO3   3. **Which account is debited to record the issuance of material to production for incorporation into the product?**
  a.   Direct Materials
  b.   Materials Inventory
  c.   Work-in-Process Inventory
  d.   Factory Supplies

4. Which of the following is usually *not* found on a job order cost sheet?   **LO3, 4**

    a. Manufacturing overhead   *c.* Direct materials

    b. Finished units currently on hand   *d.* Unit cost

5. When should the balance of the manufacturing overhead account be zero?   **LO4**

    a. At the end of each month   *c.* Never

    b. After year-end closing   *d.* Each time a job is completed

6. Which of the following is *not* one of the categories of cost involved in the allocation of service   **LO5**
department costs?

    a. Service department costs allocated to production departments

    b. Costs directly identifiable with departments

    c. Costs requiring allocation to departments

    d. Selling department costs

7. Which of the following would be a reason for choosing to use departmental overhead rates instead   **LO6**
of a single company-wide overhead rate?

    a. Each department's overhead is structured very different from other departments, resulting in very
different rates.

    b. The logical capacity measure of each department is different from the other departments.

    c. Neither a nor b

    d. Both a and b

QUESTIONS

1. Briefly describe a cost accounting system.   **LO1**

2. What types of entities, other than manufacturers, use cost accounting systems?   **LO1**

3. Contrast a job order costing system and a process costing system.   **LO1**

4. Give three examples of types of companies that would use job order costing.   **LO1**

5. Why do we name it a *predetermined* manufacturing overhead rate?   **LO2**

6. How is a predetermined manufacturing overhead rate determined?   **LO2**

7. Briefly justify the use of an annual predetermined manufacturing overhead rate as opposed to actual   **LO2**
monthly manufacturing overhead.

8. Wesley Manufacturing Company uses a predetermined plant-wide manufacturing overhead rate of $25 per   **LO2**
direct labor hour. During April, Job 541 had $3,000 of direct materials assigned to it; 60 hours of direct labor
at $10 per hour were incurred for the job. What is the total product cost accumulated on Job 541 during April?

9. Parker Manufacturing, Inc., employs an overhead rate of 140% of direct labor cost. The Job 783 cost sheet   **LO2**
shows that $5,000 in direct materials has been used and that $8,000 in direct labor has been incurred. If
1,000 units of product have been produced on Job 783, what is the unit cost of the product?

10. Briefly explain the sequential flow of product costs through a cost accounting system.   **LO3**

11. What type of records would be used or maintained for the following manufacturing activities?   **LO3**

    a. Determining the amount of a specific material on hand

    b. Issuing direct materials for production

    c. Assigning the direct labor costs for a particular worker

    d. Accumulating the cost of a particular product or batch of products

12. Explain the general format and give examples of the data that would appear on (a) a sales order, (b) a bill   **LO3**
of materials, and (c) a job order cost sheet.

13. Why can we say that the sale of a manufactured product is recorded at two different amounts?   **LO4**

14. Slaton Company records both actual overhead and applied overhead in one account, Manufacturing Over-   **LO4**
head. On January 31, the account has a credit balance. Has overhead been under- or overapplied during
January?

15. Lyle Manufacturing Company applies manufacturing overhead at the rate of 150% of direct labor cost.   **LO4**
During October 2019, Lyle incurred $82,000 of direct labor costs and $120,000 of manufacturing overhead
costs. What is the amount of over- or underapplied manufacturing overhead for October 2019?

16. Contrast service departments with production departments. Give three examples of a service department.   **LO5**

17. Why might service departments be treated as cost centers?   **LO5**

18. Explain what each of the following statements means: **LO5**

a. Service departments do not work directly on products.

b. Service department costs are manufacturing overhead costs.

c. Overhead rates are not used for service departments.

d. In spite of part (c), service department costs become part of product costs.

LO5   **19.** How do we choose a basis for allocating a cost to several departments?

LO5   **20.** How is an allocation rate calculated? How is the specific amount allocated to a department calculated?

LO5   **21.** Briefly describe the general format, data, and calculations that would appear on an overhead distribution worksheet for a company with a number of production and service departments.

LO6   **22.** Why would a company use a departmental overhead rate rather than a plant-wide overhead rate?

LO6   **23.** A company with four production departments that had been using a plant-wide overhead rate based on direct labor hours changes to a departmental overhead rate. Product A's total allocated overhead increases as a result. Why might this have happened?

SHORT EXERCISES

LO1   **SE16-1.**   A process costing system would most likely be used for all of the following except

    a. a manufacturer of plywood sheets.   *c.* a tailor.

    b. a men's barbershop.   *d.* a hay farmer.

LO2   **SE16-2.**   Henry Manufacturing, which uses direct labor hours to apply overhead to its product line, undertook an extensive renovation and modernization program two years ago. Manufacturing processes were reengineered, considerable automated equipment was acquired, and 60% of the company's nonunion factory workers were terminated.

    Which of the following statements would apply to the situation at Henry?

    I. The company's factory overhead rate has likely increased.

    II. The use of direct labor hours seems to be appropriate.

    III. Henry will lack the ability to properly determine labor variances.

    IV. Henry has likely reduced its ability to quickly cut costs in order to respond to economic downturns.

    a. I, II, III, and IV.   *c.* II and IV only.

    b. I and IV only.   *d.* I and III only.

LO2   **SE16-3.**   Using the following budget data for Valley Corporation, which produces only one product, calculate the company's predetermined manufacturing overhead application rate for variable overhead. *Hint:* The factory supervisor's salary is direct labor, since it is incurred regardless of production. SG&A expenses relate to the entire operations of Valley Corporation and not just related to manufacturing.

Units to be produced	11,000
Units to be sold	10,000
Indirect materials, varying with production	$ 1,000
Indirect labor, varying with production	10,000
Factory supervisor's salary, incurred regardless of production	20,000
Depreciation on factory building and equipment	30,000
Utilities to operate factory machines	12,000
Security lighting for factory	2,000
Selling, general and administrative (SG&A) expenses	5,000

    a. $2.09   *c.* $4.73

    b. $2.30   *d.* $5.00

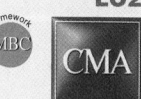

LO2   **SE16-4.**   Baldwin Printing Company uses a job order costing system and applies overhead based on machine hours. A total of 150,000 machine hours have been budgeted for the year. During the year, an order for 1,000 units was completed and incurred the following:

Direct materials costs	$1,000
Direct labor costs	1,500
Actual overhead	1,980
Machine hours	450

The accountant calculated the inventory cost of this order to be $4.30 per unit. The annual budgeted overhead in dollars was

a. $577,500.

c. $645,000.

b. $600,000.

d. $660,000.

SE16-5. As the staff accountant at Diablo Manufacturing, you have been asked to prepare the journal entries associated with a recently completed custom order (#720). You have the following information from which to prepare the journal entries: **LO4**

Materials purchased..	$1,500
Direct materials used for #720....................................	1,200
Indirect labor used for #720.......................................	250
Direct labor incurred for #720....................................	850
Overhead applied to #720..	1,000

What would be the account and amount of the debit in the journal entry to record Cost of Goods Manufactured for order #720?

a. Work-in-process inventory, $3,050

c. Work-in-process inventory, $3,300

b. Finished goods inventory, $3,050

d. Finished goods inventory, $3,300

SE16-6. Sanchez Consulting applies overhead to consulting projects based on the direct labor hours charged by employees to each job. Selected data for the firm follow: **LO4**

Budgeted overhead for the year..	$150,000
Budgeted direct labor cost for the year (@ $25/hour)	375,000
Actual overhead for November..	10,000
Actual direct labor cost for November (1,100 hours)	28,000

What is the amount of over- or underapplied overhead for the month of November?

a. $1,000 underapplied

c. $1,200 underapplied

b. $1,000 overapplied

d. $1,200 overapplied

SE16-7. Given the following data for Scurry Company, what is the cost of goods sold? **LO4**

Beginning inventory of finished goods	$100,000
Cost of goods manufactured	700,000
Ending inventory of finished goods.....................................	200,000
Beginning work-in-process inventory	300,000
Ending work-in-process inventory	50,000

a. $500,000

c. $800,000

b. $600,000

d. $950,000

SE16-8. Boston Furniture Company manufactures several steel products. It has three production departments: Fabricating, Assembly, and Finishing. The service departments include Maintenance, Material Handling, and Designing. Currently, the company does not allocate service department costs to the production departments. John Baker, who has recently joined the company as the new cost accountant, believes that service department rates should be developed and charged to the production departments for services requested. If the company adopts this new policy, the production department managers would be **least** likely to **LO5**

a. request an excessive amount of service.

b. replace outdated and inefficient systems.

c. refrain from using necessary services.

d. be encouraged to control costs.

SE16-9. John Sheng, cost accountant at Starlet Company, is developing departmental manufacturing overhead application rates for the company's tooling and fabricating departments. The budgeted overhead for each department and the data for one job are shown below. **LO6**

		Departments	
		Tooling	Fabricating
Supplies		$ 850	$ 200
Supervisors' salaries		1,500	2,000
Indirect labor.		1,200	4,880
Depreciation		1,000	5,500
Repairs		4,075	3,540
Total budgeted manufacturing overhead		$8,625	$16,120
Total direct labor hours.		460	620
Direct labor hours on Job #231		12	3

Using the departmental overhead application rates, total overhead applied to Job #231 in the Tooling and Fabricating Departments will be

a. $225. c. $537.
b. $303. d. $671.

LO6 **SE16-10.** KAB, Inc. has two service departments (S1 and S2) and two production departments (P1 and P2). Information from the most recent year shows the following for each department:

	S1	S2	P1	P2
Direct overhead	$30,000	$20,000	$55,000	$45,000
Allocated overhead. . .	5,000	2,500	12,500	10,000
Machine hours			2,00	800
Square feet.			3,000	1,000

KAB allocates S1 to the production departments based on square feet and S2 based on machine hours. How much of S1's overhead is allocated to P2?

a. $7,500 c. $11,667
b. $8,750 d. $28,000

EXERCISES—SET A

LO2 **E16-1A.** **Calculate and Use Overhead Rate** Bagley Corporation expects to incur $450,000 of factory overhead and $600,000 of general and administrative costs next year. Direct labor costs at $20 per hour are expected to total $200,000. If factory overhead is to be applied per direct labor hour, how much overhead will be applied to a job incurring 40 hours of direct labor?

LO2 **E16-2A.** **Calculate and Use Overhead Rate** Bagley Corporation expects to incur $450,000 of factory overhead and $600,000 of general and administrative costs next year. Direct labor costs at $20 per hour are expected to total $200,000. If factory overhead is to be applied per direct labor dollar, how much overhead will be applied to a job incurring $1,000 of direct labor?

LO2 **E16-3A.** **Calculate and Use Overhead Rate** During the coming accounting year, Baker Manufacturing, Inc., anticipates the following costs, expenses, and operating data:

Direct material (16,000 lb.).	$ 80,000
Direct labor (@ $10/hr.)	200,000
Indirect materials	12,000
Indirect labor.	22,000
Sales commissions.	34,000
Factory administration	16,000
Nonfactory administrative expenses.	20,000
Other manufacturing overhead*	80,000

*Provides for operating 40,000 machine hours.

a. Calculate the predetermined manufacturing overhead rate for the coming year for each of the following application bases: (1) direct labor hours, (2) direct labor costs, and (3) machine hours.

b. For each item in requirement a, determine the proper application of manufacturing overhead to Job 63, to which 16 direct labor hours, $150 of direct labor cost, and 40 machine hours have been charged.

E16-4A. **Flow of Product Costs through Accounts** Assuming a routine manufacturing activity, present   **LO3**
journal entries (account titles only) for each of the following transactions:

   a. Purchased materials on account.
   b. Recorded wages payable (for indirect labor) earned but not paid.
   c. Requisitioned both direct materials and indirect materials.
   d. Assigned direct and indirect labor costs.
   e. Recorded factory depreciation and accrued factory property tax.
   f. Applied manufacturing overhead to production.
   g. Completed work on products.
   h. Sold finished goods on account.
   i. Paid wages

E16-5A. **Job Order Cost Sheets** For each of the manufacturing transactions or activities indicated in Exer-   **LO3**
cise E16-4A, briefly identify the detailed forms, records, or documents (if any) that would probably
underlie each journal entry.

E16-6A. **Calculate and Use Overhead Rate** Selected data for the consulting department of Austin Consult-   **LO2, 4**
ing, Inc., follow:

Estimated consulting overhead cost for the year	$360,000
Estimated direct labor cost for the year (@ $9/hr.)	180,000
Actual manufacturing overhead cost for January	19,500
Actual direct labor cost for January (1,200 hours)	11,000

Assuming that direct labor cost is the basis for applying consulting overhead,

   a. Calculate the predetermined overhead rate.
   b. Prepare a journal entry that applies consulting overhead for January.
   c. By what amount is consulting overhead over- or underapplied in January?

E16-7A. **Calculate and Use Overhead Rate** Using the data in Exercise 16-6A, but assuming that the basis   **LO2, 4**
for applying consulting overhead is direct labor hours, complete requirements (a) through (c).

E16-8A. **Applied vs. Actual Manufacturing Overhead** Kubal Inc. applies overhead based on machine   **LO4**
hours. Kubal reports the following for the year just ended:

Budgeted overhead for the year	$250,000
Budgeted machine hours	2,000
Actual overhead for the year	275,000
Actual machine hours	2,400

What is the amount of over- or underapplied overhead for the year?

E16-9A. **Applied vs. Actual Manufacturing Overhead** Davis Manufacturing Corporation applies manu-   **LO4**
facturing overhead on the basis of 140% of direct labor cost. An analysis of the related accounts
and job order cost sheet indicates that during the year total manufacturing overhead incurred was
$315,000 and that at year-end Work-in-Process Inventory, Finished Goods Inventory, and Cost of
Goods Sold included $40,000, $20,000, and $140,000, respectively, of direct labor incurred during
the current year.

   a. Determine the underapplied manufacturing overhead at year-end (assume it is significant).
   b. Prepare a journal entry to record the disposition of the underapplied manufacturing overhead.

E16-10A. **Perpetual Inventories** The following summary data are from the job order cost sheets of Hampton   **LO4**
Company:

	Dates			Total Costs Assigned	Total Production
Job	Started	Finished	Shipped	at April 30	Costs Added in May
1	4/10	4/20	5/9	$7,300	
2	4/18	4/30	5/20	5,400	
3	4/24	5/10	5/25	2,900	$5,700
4	4/28	5/20	6/3	3,600	4,800
5	5/15	6/10	6/20		2,600
6	5/22	6/18	6/28		3,800

Using the above data, compute (a) the finished goods inventory at May 1 and May 31, (b) the work-in-process inventory at May 1 and May 31, and (c) the cost of goods sold for May. Hampton began operations with Job 1.

LO4

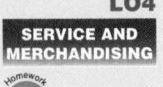

E16-11A. Finished Goods and Cost of Goods Sold Before the completed production for June is recorded, the work-in-process inventory account for James Company appears as follows:

Work-in-Process Inventory	
Balance June 1.	20,000
Direct materials.	45,000
Direct labor.	32,000
Manufacturing overhead applied	34,000

Assume that completed production for June includes Jobs 107, 108, and 109 with total costs of $28,000, $55,000, and $25,000, respectively.

a. Determine the cost of unfinished jobs at June 30 and prepare a journal entry to record completed production.

b. Using general journal entries, record the sale of Job 107 for $40,000 on account.

LO4

SERVICE AND MERCHANDISING

E16-12A. Preparing a Job Order Cost Sheet Riverwood Accounting Company has the following account in its cost records:

Work-in-Process—Jones Audit			
Direct labor	20,000	Services completed	42,253
Project overhead	27,000		

Riverwood applies overhead to projects at a predetermined rate based on direct labor costs. Assume that Riverwood uses a job order costing system and that Jones Audit is the only job in process at the end of the period. Complete the following cost sheet for services still in process for Jones Audit.

Job Order Cost Sheet—Jones Audit (Services in Process)	
Direct labor	_____
Project overhead	_____
Total cost	_____

LO5

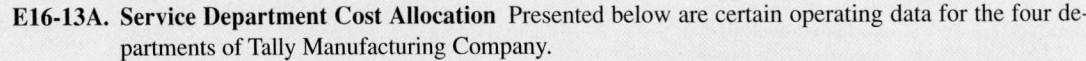

E16-13A. Service Department Cost Allocation Presented below are certain operating data for the four departments of Tally Manufacturing Company.

	Service		Production	
	1	2	1	2
Total manufacturing overhead costs either identifiable with or allocated to each department	$60,000	$72,000	$90,000	$98,000
Square feet of factory floor space.			40,000	80,000
Number of factory workers			50	10
Planned direct labor hours for the year			20,000	30,000

Allocate to the two production departments the costs of service departments 1 and 2 using factory floor space and number of workers, respectively, as bases.

What is the apparent overhead rate for each production department if planned direct labor hours are the overhead application base?

EXERCISES—SET B

LO2

E16-1B. Calculate and Use Overhead Rate Chipman Corporation expects to incur $300,000 of factory overhead and $500,000 of general and administrative costs next year. Direct labor costs at $25 per hour are expected to total $500,000. If factory overhead is to be applied per direct labor hour, how much overhead will be applied to a job incurring 100 hours of direct labor?

E16-2B. **Calculate and Use Overhead Rate** Chipman Corporation expects to incur $300,000 of factory overhead and $500,000 of general and administrative costs next year. Direct labor costs at $25 per hour are expected to total $500,000. If factory overhead is to be applied per direct labor dollar, how much overhead will be applied to a job incurring $3,000 of direct labor? **LO2**

E16-3B. **Calculate and Use Manufacturing Overhead Rate** During the coming accounting year, Ester Manufacturing, Inc., anticipates the following costs, expenses, and operating data: **LO2**

Direct materials (15,000 lb.)	$45,000
Direct labor (@ $12/hr.)	120,000
Indirect materials	7,000
Indirect labor.	12,000
Sales commissions.	18,000
Factory administration	13,000
Nonfactory administrative expenses. . . .	14,000
Other manufacturing overhead*	28,000

*Machine hours are 30,000 hours.

     a.   Calculate the predetermined manufacturing overhead rate for the coming year for each of the following application bases: (1) direct labor hours, (2) direct labor costs, and (3) machine hours.

     b.   For each item in requirement (a), determine the proper application of manufacturing overhead to Job 128, to which 9 direct labor hours, $100 of direct labor cost, and 32 machine hours have been charged.

E16-4B. **Flow of Product Costs through Accounts** The following T accounts present a cost flow in which all or part of typical manufacturing transactions are indicated by parenthetical letters on the debit or credit side of each account. **LO3**

Materials Inventory		Wages Payable		Manufacturing Overhead	
(a)	(c)	(i)	(b)	(b)	(f)
			(d)	(c)	
				(d)	
				(e)	

Work-in-Process Inventory		Finished Goods Inventory		Cost of Goods Sold	
(c)	(g)			(h)	
(d)		(g)	(h)		
(f)					

For each parenthetical letter, present a general journal entry with explanation indicating the apparent transaction or procedure that has occurred (disregard amounts).

E16-5B. **Job Order Cost Sheets** For each of the manufacturing transactions or activities indicated by the parenthetical letters in Exercise E16-4B, briefly identify the detailed forms or documents (if any) that would probably underlie each journal entry. **LO3**

E16-6B. **Calculate and Use Overhead Rate** Selected data for the consulting department of Kingman Consulting, Inc., follow: **LO2, 4**

Estimated consulting overhead cost for the year	$486,000
Estimated direct labor cost for the year (@ $9/hr.)	324,000
Actual consulting overhead cost for May	29,000
Actual direct labor cost for May (2,400 hrs.).	22,000

Assuming that direct labor cost is the basis for applying consulting overhead,

     a.   Calculate the predetermined overhead rate.

     b.   Prepare a journal entry that applies consulting overhead for May.

     c.   By what amount is consulting overhead over- or underapplied in May?

E16-7B. **Calculate and Use Overhead Rate** Using the data in Exercise E16-6B, but assuming that the basis for applying consulting overhead is direct labor hours, complete requirements (a) through (c). **LO2, 4**

LO4 **E16-8B. Applied vs. Actual Manufacturing Overhead** Harrison Inc. applies overhead based on machine hours. Harrison reports the following for the year just ended:

Budgeted overhead for the year.......	$500,000
Budgeted machine hours	25,000
Actual overhead for the year	$505,000
Actual machine hours..............	24,000

What is the amount of over- or underapplied overhead for the year?

LO4 **E16-9B. Applied vs. Actual Manufacturing Overhead** Sloan Manufacturing Corporation applies manufacturing overhead on the basis of 130% of direct labor cost. An analysis of the related accounts and job order cost sheets indicates that during the year total manufacturing overhead incurred was $210,000 and that at year-end Work-in-Process Inventory, Finished Goods Inventory, and Cost of Goods Sold included $30,000, $20,000, and $150,000, respectively, of direct labor incurred during the current year.

a. Determine the manufacturing overapplied overhead at year-end (assume it is significant).
b. Prepare a journal entry to record the disposition of the overapplied overhead.

LO4 **E16-10B. Perpetual Inventories** The following summary data are from the job order cost sheets of Castle Company:

	Dates			Total Assigned Costs at September 30	Total Production Costs Added in October
Job	Started	Finished	Shipped		
1.........	9/10	9/20	10/11	$9,000	
2.........	9/17	9/29	10/22	6,600	
3.........	9/25	10/11	10/27	3,500	$7,100
4.........	9/27	10/19	11/4	4,400	5,700
5.........	10/14	11/10	11/18		3,200
6.........	10/23	11/17	11/29		4,900

Using the data provided, compute (a) the finished goods inventory at October 1 and October 31, (b) the work-in-process inventory at October 1 and October 31, and (c) the cost of goods sold for October. Castle began operations with Job 1.

LO4 **E16-11B. Finished Goods and Cost of Goods Sold** Before the completed production for August is recorded, the work-in-process inventory account for Bayfield Company appears as follows:

Work-in-Process Inventory	
Balance, August 1	17,000
Direct materials...	33,000
Direct labor..	20,000
Manufacturing overhead applied	20,000

Assume that completed production for August includes Jobs 317, 318, and 319 with total costs of $31,000, $18,000, and $29,000, respectively.

a. Determine the cost of unfinished jobs at August 31 and prepare a journal entry to record completed production.
b. Using general journal entries, record the sale of Job 317 for $45,000 on account.

LO4 **E16-12B. Job Order Cost Sheet** Everglade Accounting Company has the following account in its cost records:

Work-in-Process—Davis Audit			
Direct labor..............	38,400	Services completed	84,000
Project overhead	57,600		

Everglade applies overhead to projects at a predetermined rate based on direct labor costs. Assume that Everglade uses a job order costing system and that Davis Audit is the only job in process at the end of the period. Complete the following cost sheet for services still in process for Davis Audit.

Job Order Cost Sheet—Davis Audit (Services in Process)	
Direct labor.............................	_____
Project overhead	_____
Total cost	_____

E16-13B. Service Department Cost Allocation Presented below are certain operating data for the four departments of Modern Manufacturing Company.

LO5

	Service		Production	
	1	**2**	**1**	**2**
Total overhead cost either identifiable with or to each department.....................	$45,000	$60,000	$55,000	$116,000
Square feet of factory floor space..............			90,000	45,000
Number of factory workers....................			20	60
Planned direct labor hours for the year			25,000	32,000

Allocate, to the two production departments, the costs of service departments 1 and 2, using factory floor space and number of workers, respectively, as bases.

What is the apparent manufacturing overhead rate for each production department if planned direct labor hours are the overhead application base?

PROBLEMS—SET A

Note: In both problem sets, assume perpetual inventory procedures, a single Manufacturing Overhead account, first-in, first-out (FIFO) costing of inventories, and that the Materials Inventory account is the control account for both direct materials and indirect materials.

P16-1A. Determine and Use Overhead Rate Cortez Consulting, Inc., expects the following costs and expenses during the coming year:

LO2, 3

SERVICE AND
MERCHANDISING

Direct labor (@ $12/hr.).......................................	$162,000
Sales commissions..	37,000
Overhead	202,500

Required

a. Compute a predetermined overhead rate applied on the basis of direct labor hours.
b. Prepare a general journal entry to apply overhead during an interim period when 1,500 direct labor hours were worked.
c. What amount of overhead would be assigned to Job 466, to which $180 in direct labor had been charged?

P16-2A. Determine and Use Overhead Rate The following selected ledger accounts of Cameron Company are for February (the second month of its accounting year):

LO2, 4

MATERIALS INVENTORY

Feb. 1 balance	31,500	Feb. credits	105,000
Feb. debits	104,000		

MANUFACTURING OVERHEAD

Feb. debits	163,350	Feb. 1 balance	11,600
		Feb. credits	166,650

WORK-IN-PROCESS INVENTORY

Feb. 1 balance	22,400	Feb. credits	375,000
Feb. debits:			
Direct materials	95,000		
Direct labor	151,500		
Manufacturing overhead	166,650		

continued

continued from previous page

WAGES PAYABLE

Feb. debits	193,500	Feb. 1 balance	45,000
		Feb. credits	185,000

FINISHED GOODS INVENTORY

Feb. 1 balance	76,500	Feb. credits	386,000
Feb. debits	375,000		

Required

a. Determine the amount of indirect materials requisitioned for production during February.

b. How much indirect labor cost was apparently incurred during February?

c. Calculate the manufacturing overhead rate based on direct labor cost.

d. Was manufacturing overhead for February under- or overapplied, and by what amount?

e. Was manufacturing overhead for the first two months of the year under- or overapplied, and by what amount?

f. What is the cost of production completed in February?

g. What is the cost of goods sold in February?

LO3   **P16-3A.**   **Job Cost Journal Entries** Holiday Manufacturing had the following inventories at December 31, 2018, the end of its fiscal year:

Materials inventory	$19,000
Work-in-process inventory	20,000
Finished goods inventory	13,000

During January 2019, the following transactions occurred:

1. Purchased materials on account, $126,000.

2. Requisitioned direct materials of $110,000 and indirect materials of $20,000.

3. Incurred wages payable, $61,000.

4. Assigned total wages payable, of which $11,000 was considered indirect labor.

5. Incurred other manufacturing overhead, $32,800. (Credit Accounts Payable.)

6. Applied manufacturing overhead on the basis of 120% of direct labor costs.

7. Determined completed production, $206,000. Use this information to determine the amount of WIP transferred to finished goods inventory.

8. Determined cost of goods sold, $203,000. Use this information to determine the reduction to finished goods inventory.

Required

a. Prepare general journal entries to record these transactions.

b. If the above transactions covered a full year's operations, prepare a journal entry to dispose of the overhead account balance. Assume that the balance is significant. Also assume that the following accounts contained the indicated amounts of manufacturing overhead applied during 2019:

Work-in-process inventory	$ 6,000
Finished goods	4,000
Cost of goods sold	50,000

LO3, 4   **P16-4A.**   **Job Cost Journal Entries** Prior to the beginning of 2019, Lowe Company estimated that it would incur $176,000 of manufacturing overhead cost during 2019, using 16,000 direct labor hours to produce the desired volume of goods. On January 1, 2019, beginning balances of Materials Inventory, Work-in-Process Inventory, and Finished Goods Inventory were $28,000, $-0-, and $43,000, respectively.

Required

Prepare general journal entries to record the following for 2019:

a. Purchased materials on account, $39,000.

b. Of the total dollar value of materials used, $31,000 represented direct materials and $11,000 indirect materials.

    c.   Determined total factory labor, $135,000 (15,000 hrs. @ $9/hr.).

    d.   Of the factory labor, 80% was direct and 20% indirect.

    e.   Applied manufacturing overhead based on direct labor hours to work-in-process.

    f.   Determined actual manufacturing overhead other than those items already recorded, $92,000. (Credit Accounts Payable.)

    g.   Ending inventories of work-in-process and finished goods were $32,000 and $57,000, respectively. Determine the cost of finished goods (credit WIP) and the cost of goods sold (credit FG inventory). Make separate entries.

    h.   Transferred the balance in Manufacturing Overhead to Cost of Goods Sold.

P16-5A.   **Job Cost Journal Entries and T Accounts**   Following are certain operating data for Durango Manufacturing Company for January 2019:   **LO3, 4**

	Materials Inventory	Work-in-Process Inventory	Finished Goods Inventory
Beginning inventory	$57,000	$24,000	$75,000
Ending inventory	33,000	40,500	48,000

Total sales were $1,800,000, on which the company earned a 40% gross profit. Durango uses a predetermined manufacturing overhead rate of 120% of direct labor costs. Manufacturing overhead applied was $360,000. Exclusive of indirect materials used, total manufacturing overhead incurred was $243,000; it was overapplied by $22,500.

Required

Compute the following items. (Set up T accounts for Materials Inventory, Work-in-Process Inventory, Finished Goods Inventory, and Manufacturing Overhead; fill in the known amounts; and then use the normal relationships among the various accounts to compute the unknown amounts.)

    a.   Cost of goods sold.   *d.*   Direct materials used.

    b.   Cost of goods manufactured.   *e.*   Indirect materials used.

    c.   Direct labor incurred.   *f.*   Total materials purchased.

P16-6A.   **Job Cost Journal Entries and T Accounts**   Summarized data for the first month's operations of   **LO3, 4** Dobson Welding Foundry during 2019 are presented below. A job order costing system is used.

    1.   Materials purchased on account, $58,000

    2.   Amounts of materials requisitioned and foundry labor used:

Job	Materials	Foundry Labor
1	$ 4,400	$2,600
2	7,000	5,000
3	3,200	2,400
4	12,000	4,600
5	4,800	2,800
6	1,400	1,200
Indirect materials	6,200	
Indirect labor.		3,400

    3.   Foundry overhead is applied at the rate of 200% of direct labor costs.

    4.   Miscellaneous foundry overhead incurred:

Prepaid foundry insurance written off.	$ 1,480
Property taxes on foundry building accrued.	2,360
Foundry utilities payable accrued.	5,280
Depreciation on foundry equipment	7,440
Other costs incurred on account.	10,320

    5.   Ending work-in-process consisted of Jobs 4 and 6.

    6.   Jobs 1 and 3 and one-half of Job 2 were sold on account for $20,000, $17,400, and $14,400, respectively.

Required

a. Open general ledger T accounts for Materials Inventory, Wages Payable, Foundry Overhead, Work-in-Process Inventory, Finished Goods Inventory, and Cost of Goods Sold. Also set up subsidiary T accounts as job order cost sheets for each job.

b. Prepare general journal entries to record the summarized transactions for the month, and post appropriate entries to any accounts listed in requirement (a). Key each entry parenthetically to the related number in the problem data.

c. Determine the balances of any accounts necessary and prepare schedules of jobs in ending work-in-process and jobs in ending finished goods to confirm that they agree with the related control accounts.

LO3, 4 **P16-7A.** **Complex Job Cost Journal Entries and Analysis** During June 2019, its first month of operations, Weston Manufacturing Company completed the transactions listed below. Weston uses a job order costing system. Materials requisitions and the wages payable summary are analyzed on the 15th and the last day of each month, and charges for direct materials and direct labor are entered directly on specific job order cost sheets. Manufacturing overhead at the rate of 140% of direct labor costs is recorded on individual job order cost sheets when a job is completed and at month-end for any job then in process. At month-end, entries to the general ledger accounts summarize materials requisitions, distribution of wages, payable costs, and the application of manufacturing overhead for the month. All other entries to general ledger accounts are made as they occur.

1. Purchased materials on account, $130,000.
2. Paid miscellaneous manufacturing overhead costs, $32,600.
3. An analysis of materials requisitions and the wages payable summary for June 1–15 indicates the following cost distribution:

Job	Materials	Factory Labor
1.........	$21,600	$36,800
2.........	10,400	16,000
3.........	4,400	10,800
Indirect materials	7,600	
Indirect labor.........		35,400
	$44,000	$99,000

4. Jobs 1 and 2 were completed on June 15 and transferred to finished goods inventory on the next day. (Enter the appropriate manufacturing overhead amounts on the job order cost sheets, mark them completed, and make a general journal entry transferring the appropriate amount of cost to the Finished Goods Inventory account.)
5. Paid miscellaneous manufacturing overhead costs, $23,400.
6. Sold Job 1 on account, $185,600 (recognized its cost of sales in the general journal).
7. An analysis of materials requisitions and wages payable summary for June 16–30 indicates the following cost distribution:

Job	Materials	Factory Labor
3.........	$22,800	$16,800
4.........	18,000	32,400
5.........	7,800	13,000
6.........	3,000	4,600
Indirect materials	6,800	
Indirect labor.........		29,400
	$58,400	$96,200

8. Jobs 3 and 4 were completed on June 30 and transferred to finished goods inventory on the same day. (See transaction 4.)
9. Sold Job 3 on account, $155,600 (recognized its cost of sales in the general journal).
10. Recorded the following additional manufacturing overhead:

Depreciation on factory building.	$26,000
Depreciation on factory equipment.	15,200
Expiration of prepaid factory insurance	4,200
Accrual of factory property taxes payable	7,000
	$52,400

11. Recorded monthly general journal entry for the costs of all materials used.

12. Recorded monthly general journal entry for the distribution of wages payable costs.

13. Recorded manufacturing overhead on the job order cost sheets for jobs in ending work-in-process and in the general journal for all manufacturing overhead applied during the month.

Required

a. Set up the following general ledger T accounts: Materials Inventory, Wages Payable, Manufacturing Overhead, Work-in-Process Inventory, Finished Goods Inventory, Cost of Goods Sold, and Sales.

b. Set up T accounts for each of Jobs 1–6 as job order cost sheets.

c. Noting the accounting procedures described in the first paragraph of the problem, do the following:

    i. Record general journal entries for all transactions. Note that general journal entries are not required in transactions 3 and 7. Post only those portions of these entries affecting the general ledger accounts set up in requirement (a).

    ii. Enter the applicable amounts directly on the appropriate job order cost sheets for transactions 3, 4, 7, 8, and 13. Note parenthetically the nature of each amount entered.

d. Present a brief analysis showing that the general ledger accounts for Work-in-Process Inventory and for Finished Goods Inventory agree with the related job order cost sheets.

e. Explain in one sentence each what the balance of each general ledger account established in requirement (a) represents.

P16-8A. **Manufacturing Overhead Distribution Worksheet** The following are selected operating data for the production and service departments of Bluestone Company for 2019.

LO5, 6

	Departments			
	Service		Production	
	1	2	1	2
Overhead costs (identified by department).				
Indirect materials.	$48,400	$ 82,200	$ 25,440	$ 516,000
Indirect labor.	$97,200	$144,000	$ 32,584	$1,439,000
Square feet of building floor space used	4,800	7,200	12,000	24,000
Assessed value of equipment used	$21,000	$ 63,000	$126,000	$ 210,000
Cubic yards of factory space used			88,000	132,000
Machine hours			51,200	204,800
Direct labor.			$ 20,000	$ 400,000

Building depreciation of $110,000 is allocated on the basis of square feet of floor space. Personal property taxes of $30,000 are allocated on the basis of assessed values of equipment used. Costs for service departments 1 and 2 are allocated to production departments on the basis of cubic yards of factory space and machine hours, respectively.

Required

a. Prepare a 2019 overhead distribution worksheet for Bluestone Company similar to the one prepared for **Exhibit 16-15**.

b. Compute the manufacturing overhead rates for production departments 1 and 2 using machine hours and direct labor costs, respectively, for allocation bases. Round your answer to two decimal places.

PROBLEMS—SET B

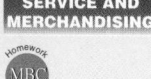

LO2, 3   **P16-1B.**   **Determine and Use Consulting Rate** Oxford Consulting, Inc., expects the following costs and expenses during the coming year:

Direct labor (@ $14/hr.)	$336,000
Sales commissions	72,000
Overhead	312,000

Required

a.   Compute a predetermined overhead rate applied on the basis of direct labor hours.

b.   Prepare a general journal entry to apply overhead during an interim period when 3,500 direct labor hours were worked.

c.   What amount of overhead would be assigned to Job 325, to which $532 in direct labor had been charged?

LO2, 4   **P16-2B.**   **Determine and Use Manufacturing Overhead Rate** The following selected ledger accounts of the Lakewood Manufacturing Company are for May (the fifth month of its accounting year):

Materials Inventory			
May 1 balance	40,000	May credits	145,000
May debits	125,000		

Factory Overhead			
May debits	160,000	May 1 balance	14,000
		May credits	171,000

Work-in-Process Inventory			
May 1 balance	28,000	May credits	480,000
May debits:			
Direct materials	129,000		
Direct labor	180,000		
Manufacturing overhead	171,000		

Factory Payroll Payable			
May debits	200,000	May 1 balance	50,000
		May credits	196,000

Finished Goods Inventory			
May 1 balance	102,000	May credits	500,000
May debits	480,000		

Required

a.   Determine the amount of indirect materials requisitioned for production during May.

b.   How much indirect labor cost was apparently incurred during May?

c.   Calculate the manufacturing overhead rate based on direct labor cost.

d.   Was manufacturing overhead for May under- or overapplied, and by what amount?

e.   Was manufacturing overhead for the first five months of the year under- or overapplied, and by what amount?

f.   What is the cost of production completed in May?

g.   What is the cost of goods sold in May?

LO3   **P16-3B.**   **Job Cost Journal Entries** Dillon Manufacturing had the following inventories at December 31, 2018, the end of its fiscal year:

Materials inventory	$15,000
Work-in-process inventory	17,000
Finished goods inventory	30,000

During January 2019, the following transactions occurred:

1. Purchased materials on account, $125,000.
2. Requisitioned total materials of $130,000, of which $8,000 was considered indirect materials.
3. Incurred wages payable, $105,000.
4. Assigned total wages payable, of which $15,000 was considered indirect labor.
5. Incurred other manufacturing overhead, $57,000. (Credit Accounts Payable.)
6. Applied manufacturing overhead on the basis of 100% of direct labor costs.
7. Determined ending work-in-process, $14,000. Use this information to calculate the amount of WIP transferred to finished goods inventory (credit WIP).
8. Determined ending finished goods, $26,000. Use this information to calculate the cost of goods sold (credit FG inventory).

Required

a. Prepare general journal entries to record these transactions.
b. If the above transactions covered a full year's operations, prepare a journal entry to dispose of the overhead account balance. Assume that the balance is significant. Also assume that the following accounts contained the indicated amounts of manufacturing overhead applied during 2019:

Work-in-process inventory	$ 3,000
Finished goods inventory	7,000
Cost of goods sold	80,000

P16-4B. **Job Cost Journal Entries** Prior to the beginning of 2019, Stapleton Company estimated that it would incur $153,000 of manufacturing overhead cost during 2019, using 17,000 direct labor hours to produce the desired volume of goods. On January 1, 2019, beginning balances of Materials Inventory, Work-in-Process Inventory, and Finished Goods Inventory were $48,000, $-0-, and $87,000, respectively.

LO3, 4

Required

Prepare general journal entries to record the following for 2019:

a. Purchased materials on account, $316,000.
b. Of the total dollar value of materials used, $284,000 represented direct materials and $35,000 indirect materials.
c. Determined total factory labor, $189,000 (18,000 hrs. @ $10.50/hr.).
d. Of the factory labor, 15,800 were direct labor hours.
e. Applied manufacturing overhead based on direct labor hours to work-in-process.
f. Determined actual manufacturing overhead other than those items already recorded, $83,000. (Credit Accounts Payable.)
g. Ending inventories of work-in-process and finished goods were $57,000 and $71,800, respectively. Determine the cost of finished goods (credit WIP) and the cost of goods sold (credit FG inventory). Make separate entries.
h. Transferred the balance in Manufacturing Overhead to Cost of Goods Sold.

P16-5B. **Job Cost Journal Entries and T Accounts** Following are certain operating data for Redwood Manufacturing Company for January 2019:

LO3, 4

	Materials Inventory	Work-in-Process Inventory	Finished Goods Inventory
Beginning inventory	$40,000	$50,000	$80,000
Ending inventory.	70,000	60,000	56,000

Total sales were $2,000,000, on which the company earned a 40% gross profit. Redwood uses a predetermined manufacturing overhead rate of 110% of direct labor costs. Manufacturing overhead applied was $396,000. Exclusive of indirect materials used, total manufacturing overhead incurred was $300,000; it was underapplied by $24,000.

Required

Compute the following items. (Set up T accounts for Materials Inventory, Work-in-Process Inventory, Finished Goods Inventory, and Manufacturing Overhead; fill in the known amounts; and then use the normal relationships among the various accounts to compute the unknown amounts.)

a. Cost of goods sold.

b. Cost of goods manufactured.

c. Direct labor incurred.

d. Direct materials used.

e. Indirect materials used.

f. Total materials purchased.

LO3, 4 P16-6B. **Job Cost Journal Entries and T Accounts** Summarized data for the first month's operations of Slater Foundry during 2019 are presented below. A job order costing system is used.

1. Materials purchased on account, $88,000.

2. Amounts of materials requisitioned and foundry labor used:

Job	Materials	Foundry Labor
1	$ 4,600	$ 3,600
2	5,200	6,000
3	3,800	8,800
4	13,400	12,000
5	6,400	7,200
6	4,000	2,000
Indirect materials	11,000	
Indirect labor		18,000

3. Foundry overhead is applied at the rate of 150% of direct labor costs.

4. Miscellaneous foundry overhead incurred:

Prepaid foundry insurance written off	$ 1,880
Property taxes on foundry building accrued	3,760
Foundry utilities payable accrued	4,400
Depreciation on foundry equipment	8,400
Other costs incurred on account	14,640

5. Ending work-in-process consisted of Jobs 4 and 6. Jobs 1 and 3 and one-half of Job 2 were sold on account for $25,200, $31,600, and $18,920, respectively.

Required

a. Open general ledger T accounts for Materials Inventory, Wages Payable, Foundry Overhead, Work-in-Process Inventory, Finished Goods Inventory, and Cost of Goods Sold. Also set up subsidiary T accounts as job order cost sheets for each job.

b. Prepare general journal entries to record the summarized transactions for the month, and post appropriate entries to any accounts listed in requirement (a). Key each entry parenthetically to the related number in the problem data.

c. Determine the balances of any accounts necessary and prepare schedules of jobs in ending work-in-process and jobs in ending finished goods to confirm that they agree with the related control accounts.

LO3, 4 P16-7B. **Complex Job Cost Journal Entries and Analysis** During June 2019, its first month of operations, Logan Manufacturing Company completed the transactions listed below. Logan uses a job order costing system. Materials requisitions and the wages payable summary are analyzed on the 15th and the last day of each month, and charges for direct materials and direct labor are entered directly on specific job order cost sheets. Manufacturing overhead at the rate of 160% of direct labor costs is recorded on individual job order cost sheets when a job is completed and at month-end for any job then in process. At month-end, entries to the general ledger accounts summarize materials requisitions, distribution of wages payable costs, and the application of manufacturing overhead for the month. All other entries to general ledger accounts are made as they occur.

1. Purchased materials on account, $210,000.
2. Paid miscellaneous manufacturing overhead costs, $52,000.
3. An analysis of materials requisitions and the wages payable summary for June 1–15 indicates the following cost distribution:

Job	Materials	Factory Labor
1	$34,000	$60,000
2	16,000	26,000
3	8,000	18,000
Indirect materials	14,000	
Indirect labor.		56,000
Total	$72,000	$160,000

4. Jobs 1 and 2 were completed on June 15 and transferred to finished goods inventory on the next day. (Enter the appropriate manufacturing overhead amounts on the job order cost sheets, mark them completed, and make a general journal entry transferring the appropriate amount of cost to the Finished Goods Inventory account.)
5. Paid miscellaneous manufacturing overhead costs, $38,000.
6. Sold Job 1 on account, $300,000 (recognized its cost of sales in the general journal).
7. An analysis of materials requisitions and wages payable summary for June 16–30 indicates the following cost distribution:

Job	Materials	Factory Labor
3	$36,000	$28,000
4	30,000	54,000
5	12,000	20,000
6	6,000	8,000
Indirect materials	10,000	
Indirect labor.		46,000
Total	$94,000	$156,000

8. Jobs 3 and 4 were completed on June 30 and transferred to finished goods inventory on the same day. (See transaction 4.)
9. Sold Job 3 on account, $250,000 (recognized its cost of sales in the general journal).
10. Recorded the following additional manufacturing overhead:

Depreciation on factory building	$42,000
Depreciation on factory equipment.	24,000
Expiration of prepaid factory insurance	7,000
Payable.	13,000
	$86,000

11. Recorded monthly general journal entry for the costs of all materials used.
12. Recorded monthly general journal entry for the distribution of wages payable costs.
13. Recorded manufacturing overhead on the job order cost sheets for jobs in ending work-in-process and in the general journal for all manufacturing overhead applied during the month.

Required

a. Set up the following general ledger T accounts: Materials Inventory, Wages Payable, Manufacturing Overhead, Work-in-Process Inventory, Finished Goods Inventory, Cost of Goods Sold, and Sales.
b. Set up T accounts for each of Jobs 1–6 as job order cost sheets.
c. Noting the accounting procedures described in the first paragraph of the problem, do the following:

1. Record general journal entries for all transactions. Note that general journal entries are not required in transactions 3 and 7. Post only those portions of these entries affecting the general ledger accounts set up in requirement (a).

2. Enter the applicable amounts directly on the appropriate job order cost sheets for transactions 3, 4, 7, 8, and 13. Note parenthetically the nature of each amount entered.

d. Present a brief analysis showing that the general ledger accounts for work-in-process inventory and for finished goods inventory agree with the related job order cost sheets.

e. Explain in one sentence each what the balance of each general ledger account established in requirement (a) represents.

LO5, 6

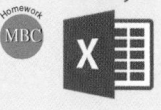

P16-8B. Manufacturing Overhead Distribution Worksheet The following are selected operating data for the production and service departments of Danville Company for 2019.

| | Departments | | | |
| | Service | | Production | |
	1	2	1	2
Manufacturing overhead costs (identified by department)				
Factory supplies used.	$12,800	$21,440	$ 67,840	$137,600
Indirect labor.	$25,920	$38,400	$ 86,400	$384,000
Square feet of building floor space used	7,200	10,800	18,000	36,000
Assessed value of equipment used	$28,000	$84,000	$168,000	$280,000
Cubic yards of factory space used			132,000	198,000
Machine hours			51,200	204,800
Direct labor ($10 per hour)			$250,000	$500,000

Building depreciation of $75,000 is allocated on the basis of square feet of floor space. Personal property taxes of $25,200 are allocated on the basis of assessed values of equipment used. Costs for service departments 1 and 2 are allocated to production departments on the basis of cubic yards of factory space and machine hours, respectively.

Required

a. Prepare a 2019 manufacturing overhead distribution worksheet for Danville Company similar to the one prepared for **Exhibit 16-15**.

b. Compute the manufacturing overhead rates for production departments 1 and 2 using machine hours and direct labor hours, respectively, for allocation bases. Round your answer to two decimal places.

EXTENDING YOUR KNOWLEDGE

EYK16-1. Business Decision Case Elizabeth Flanigan and Associates is an engineering and design firm that specializes in developing plans for recycling plants for municipalities. The firm uses a job costing system to accumulate the cost associated with each design project. Flanigan employs three levels of employee: senior engineers, associate engineers, and clerical staff. The salary cost of the senior engineers and the associate engineers is assigned to each project as direct labor. The salary cost of the clerical staff is included in overhead, along with the cost of engineering supplies, automobile travel, and equipment depreciation. The cost of airline travel, motels, building permits, and fees from other consultants is charged to each project as direct materials. Overhead is applied to projects using a predetermined overhead rate based on total engineering hours. The rate for 20X0 is $5 per hour.

The six different salary levels for 20X1 for the employees of Elizabeth Flanigan and Associates are listed below. The hourly rate is determined by dividing the yearly salary by 2,000 hours per year.

Senior engineer
Level 1: $44,000 per year ($22 per hour)
Level 2: $36,000 per year ($18 per hour)
Associate engineer
Level 3: $30,000 per year ($15 per hour)
Level 4: $24,000 per year ($12 per hour)
Clerical staff
Level 5: $16,000 per year ($8 per hour)
Level 6: $14,500 per year ($7.25 per hour)

The billings that are sent to the municipalities for engineering services utilize cost-plus billing. Typically, the total costs accumulated for a project (direct materials, direct labor, and overhead) are multiplied by 140% to determine the amount of the billing. The difference between the billed amount and the accumulated cost is the "plus" in cost plus.

During March 20X1, Flanigan accumulated the following information related to Job 295 for Johnson Creek City:

Senior engineer hours	
Level 1	52
Level 2	84
Associate engineer hours	
Level 3	106
Level 4	44
Clerical hours	
Level 5	20
Level 6	66
Building permits	$1,500
Airline travel and motel	$865

Required
a. What amount should be billed to Johnson Creek City for March 20X1?
b. How much profit was earned on Job 295 during March 20X1?

EYK16-2.   **Corporate Social Responsibility Problem**   The CSR box in this chapter discusses CH2M Hill's efforts to offer summer programs at no cost introducing underrepresented groups to STEM education. The company's stated goal is twofold: to increase the pool of future engineering talent and to build better communities.

Some would look at these efforts as costly programs with no tangible financial benefit. There is certainly no guarantee that these children will work for CH2M Hill in the future, or even that they will choose careers in engineering. In fact, these efforts may end up supplying talent for CH2M Hill's competitors and driving up future engineering wages.

What do you think?

EYK16-3.   **Ethics Case**   Metal Creations, Inc., is a custom manufacturer that uses a job order costing system. Currently, Metal Creations has 35% excess capacity in its factory. Charlie Rollins, the president, has instituted a campaign to obtain new customers. Rollins has offered the salespeople a bonus equal to 25% of the gross profit on work for new customers. The average gross profit rate has been 30% of the contract price.

Steve Starling, the sales manager for Metal Creations, wants to submit a proposal to a new customer that undercuts the usual pricing structure by 30%. As a result, this job would have no gross profit using the regular job order costing system. Instead, Starling suggests that the overhead rate applied to this job should be only 40% of the normal overhead rate, resulting in a gross profit of 28%. Starling suggests that the controller should handle this contract herself, and that no one else in the organization should know about it, especially the other salespeople, because the creative approach to overhead application might create problems.

Required
Does taking an order at a significantly reduced price create an ethical problem? Does altering the accounting for a particular order create an ethical problem? Does asking the controller to handle the contract and keep the accounting confidential create an ethical problem?

ANSWERS TO SELF-STUDY QUESTIONS:

1. a, (p. 756)   2. d, (p. 759)   3. c, (pp. 762–763)   4. b, (pp. 760–761)   5. b, (pp. 768–769)
6. d, (pp. 771–772)   7. d, (p. 775)

YOUR TURN! SOLUTIONS

Solution 16.1

Industry	Cost System
Chemicals	Process
Printing	Job order
Aircraft	Job order
Oil refining	Process
Paints	Process
Glass	Process
Furniture	Job order
Machinery	Job order

Solution 16.2

Estimated manufacturing overhead	$250,000
Divided by budgeted direct labor hours	10,000
Predetermined overhead rate per direct labor hour	$ 25
Actual direct labor hours.	$ 9,000
Multiplied by predetermined overhead rate	× 25
Applied overhead	$225,000

Solution 16.3

1, 1, 2, 3, 3, 1

Solution 16.4

Materials inventory	2,000	
Cash or Accounts Payable		2,000
WIP inventory—#144	2,600	
Materials inventory		2,600
Manufacturing overhead	350	
Materials inventory		350
WIP inventory—#144	1,650	
Wages payable or cash		1,650
WIP inventory—#144	3,300	
Manufacturing overhead		3,300
Finished goods inventory	7,550	
WIP inventory—#144		7,550
Cost of goods sold	7,550	
Finished goods inventory		7,550

Solution 16.5

	Service Depts.		Production Depts.		
	S1	S2	P1	P2	Allocation Basis
Directly identifiable overhead	$50,000	$40,000	$ 75,000	$ 65,000	
Allocated overhead.	10,000	5,000	25,000	20,000	
Total overhead cost to be allocated	$60,000	$45,000	$100,000	$85,000	
Allocation of service departments					
S1	(60,000)		20,000	40,000	Square feet
S2		(45,000)	30,000	15,000	Machine hours
Totals	—	—	$150,000	$140,000	

Solution 16.6

Molding (20 hours × $10).	$200
Machining (10 hours × $8).	80
Painting (5 hours × $4)	20
Total	$300

Chapter 17

Cost Accounting Systems: Process Costing

PAST

Chapter 16 introduced and explained job costing in more detail for both manufacturing and service industries. It also explained overhead allocation.

PRESENT

Chapter 17 introduces process costing and how it differs from job order costing. It illustrates equivalent units and the flow of costs through the inventory accounts, as well as introduces the product cost report.

FUTURE

Chapter 18 explores activity-based costing and its benefits relative to traditional plant-wide and departmental overhead allocation, and contrasts it with activity-based management.

General Mills Inc. is a Fortune 500 company based in Golden Valley, Minnesota. Consumers know General Mills best for its ready-to-eat cereal products, of which they consume 60 million servings per day. The quality of these cereal products can be traced back to Gold Medal flour in 1880, which today remains the number-one-selling brand of flour in the United States. General Mills' brand portfolio includes more than 100 leading U.S. brands and numerous category leaders around the world. Some of the top-selling brands include Betty Crocker, Yoplait, Totinos, Pillsbury, Cheerios, Trix, and Lucky Charms. One unique manufacturing feature these brands share is that they are produced in mass quantities, with little to distinguish one cupful of cereal or yogurt from another.

Manufacturers like General Mills that produce massive quantities of inventory that are indistinguishable from one another rely on process costing to track inventory costs. Rather than track the cost of each piece of cereal, General Mills tracks the total costs of inventory produced over a given period and divides these total costs by the pounds of inventory produced to obtain an average price per pound for each product. This costing system stands in stark contrast to industries such as custom cabinet manufacturing, in which costs are tallied on a job cost record for each unique custom cabinet rather than spreading them over multiple identical units of inventory.

This chapter examines how companies like General Mills utilize process costing in order to properly value their inventory. We focus on how the weighted average method of process costing provides useful information to managers and illustrates the journal entries required throughout the manufacturing process. We also introduce the concept of equivalent units and their application to process costing.

Road Map

LO	Learning Objective	Page	eLecture	Guided Example	Assignments
LO1	Compare and contrast job order costing and process costing.	804	E17-1		Q1, Q2
LO2	Describe the basic concepts of process costing.	806	E17-2		SS1, SS2, Q2, Q3
LO3	Explain the techniques for determining unit costs when process costing is used.	808	E17-3	YT17.1, YT17.2, YT17.3, YT17.4, YT17.5	SS1, Q3, Q4, Q5, Q6, Q7, Q8, SE1, SE2, SE3, SE4, SE5, E1A, E2A, E3A, E4A, E5A, E1B, E2B, E3B, E4B, E5B, P1A, P2A, P3A, P4A, P5A, P1B, P2B, P3B, P4B, P5B
LO4	Explain the procedures used to prepare the product cost report using the weighted average method in a process costing system.	816	E17-4		SE1, SE2, SE5, E3A, E4A, E5A, E3B, E4B, E5B, P1A, P2A, P3A, P4A, P5A, P1B, P2B, P3B, P4B, P5B
LO5	Illustrate the journal entries used with process costing.	817	E17-5	YT17.6	E6A, E6B, P5A, P5B
LO6	Appendix 17A: Explain the techniques for determining unit costs when the FIFO method for process costing is used.	822	E17-6	YT17.7, YT17.8, YT17.9, YT17.10, YT17.11	SS3, Q9, SE6, SE7, E7A, E8A, E9A, E10A, E11A, E7B, E8B, E9B, E10B, E11B, P6A, P7A, P6B, P7B
LO7	Appendix 17A: Explain the procedures used to prepare the product cost report using the FIFO method in a process costing system.	829	E17-7		Q9, E8A, E9A, E10A, E11A, E9B, E10B, E11B, P6A, P7A, P8A, P6B, P7B, P8B
LO8	Appendix 17A: Illustrate the journal entries used with FIFO process costing.	831	E17-8	YT17.12	Q9

INTRODUCTION TO PROCESS COSTING

LO1 **Compare** and **contrast** job order costing and process costing.

The early sections of this chapter explain and illustrate the concepts and procedures that are typical in a process costing system that involves only one processing department using the weighted average cost flow assumption. Appendix 17A illustrates the procedures and differences under the first-in, first-out (FIFO) cost flow assumption.

Job Order Costing Review

Prior chapters have introduced and discussed the concepts used in job order costing. Recall that job order costing accumulates costs for each specific job in a separate work-in-process inventory account dedicated to that unique job. **Exhibit 17-1** presents the typical flow of product costs in a job order costing system for Job 372. Direct materials and direct labor are traced to each specific job, whereas indirect overhead costs are allocated to each job.

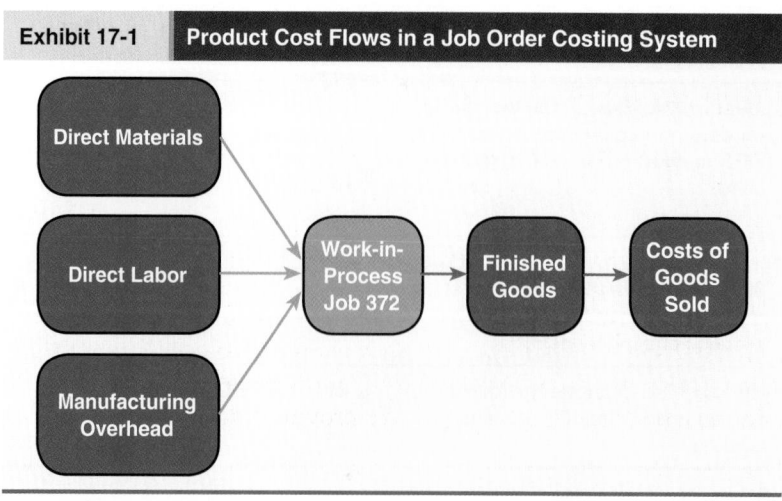

| Exhibit 17-1 | Product Cost Flows in a Job Order Costing System |

Although production costs are tracked separately for each job, companies also need to understand their total costs. Hence, costs for all of the individual jobs are accumulated in the work-in-process control account, which represents the overall cost summary of all jobs currently in production. For example, **Exhibit 17-2** lists four individual jobs that are currently in process. The work-in-process inventory control account represents the sum of all jobs that are currently in process. Overhead costs are accumulated and applied to the work-in-process inventory control account based on an annual predetermined overhead rate. Specifically, actual overhead costs, including indirect materials and indirect labor, are accumulated in the manufacturing overhead account as debits, and the applied overhead is transferred to Work-in-Process Inventory with a credit. Perpetual inventory techniques are typically used to move product cost from Work-in-Process Inventory to Finished Goods Inventory and finally to Cost of Goods Sold, as illustrated in **Exhibit 17-2**.

Exhibit 17-2	Job Order Costing Summary (Accumulating Costs by Job)

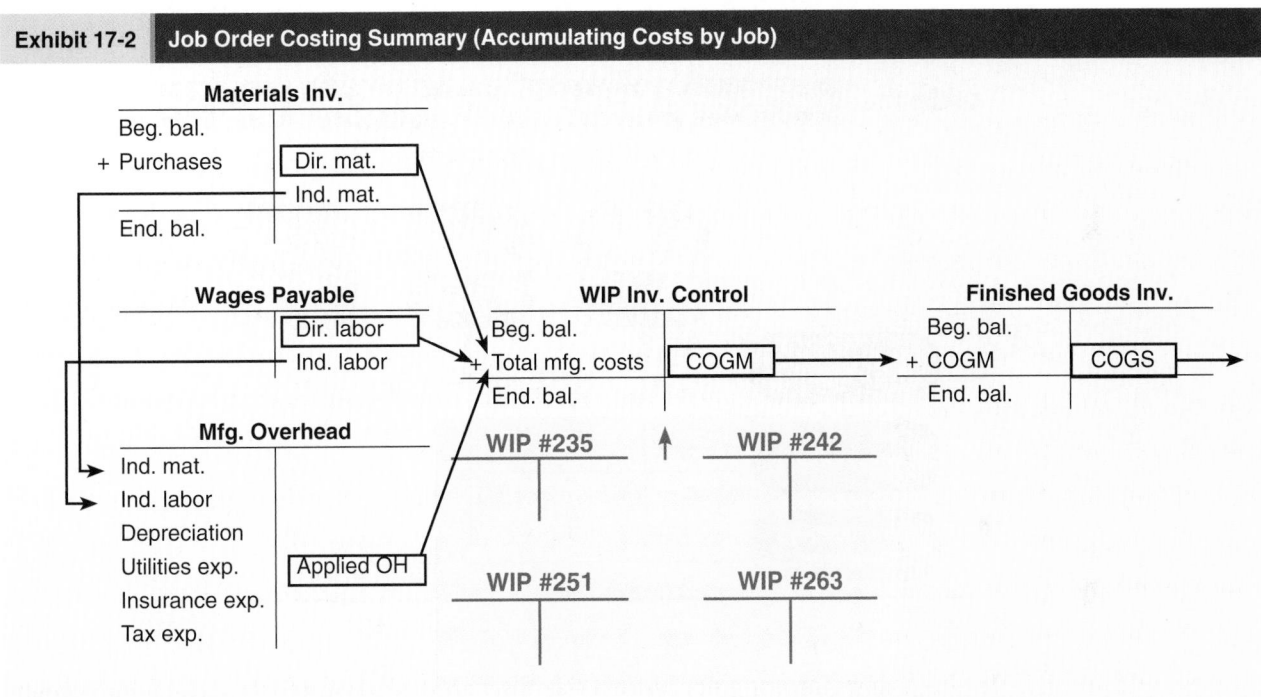

Job order costing is appropriate when products or services are characterized by customization to meet the customer's specifications. Job order costing can result when products are produced or jobs are undertaken to (1) fill specific customer orders or (2) produce a stock of products from which future orders can be filled.

Process Costing

Process costing, however, is used when large volumes of identical (homogeneous) products are manufactured in a continuous-flow operation, such as the production of fuels, chemicals, small appliances, building materials, and electricity. In process costing, product costs are accumulated by department, not by job or product. We note at the outset that although it is possible to use process costing in a service environment, it is not common. For example, a service agency that provides identical services to each customer could calculate an average cost per customer. However, most of the examples in this chapter focus on manufacturing companies because process costing is much more common in a manufacturing setting. We provide a detailed service example at the end of the chapter.

CHARACTERISTICS OF PROCESS COSTING

LO2 **Describe** the basic concepts of process costing.

Exhibit 17-3 presents the typical flow of product cost in a **process costing system**. The following process costing characteristics are evident in **Exhibit 17-3**:

Exhibit 17-3	Product Cost Flows in a Process Costing System

1. Each manufacturing department has a separate work-in-process inventory account. **Exhibit 17-3** assumes a company with two manufacturing departments: production and packaging. Costs are accumulated for each department in a separate work-in-process inventory account.

Hint: A process can be defined as a step in the manufacture of a product. In a process costing system, materials, labor, and overhead are charged to processing departments rather than to specific jobs.

2. **Exhibit 17-4** shows how the costs in this process flow through the accounts. Direct materials, direct labor, and manufacturing overhead costs can be added to the work-in-process inventory account in each department. **Exhibit 17-4** shows all three elements of product cost being added to both work-in-process inventory accounts.

3. Products physically move through the process on a first-in, first-out (FIFO) basis. That is, the unfinished units in work-in-process are assumed to be completed first in the subsequent period before new units are started.

A.K.A. The product cost report is also known as a "cost of production report" or a "process cost summary."

4. Under process costing, managers use a **product cost report** to accumulate costs by process or department. These costs are then allocated to specific units of product that pass through that process or department using either the weighted average or FIFO allocation method. In this chapter, we focus on the weighted average costing method, and Appendix 17A explains the FIFO costing method.

Exhibit 17-4	Process Costing Summary (Accumulating Costs by Process or Department)

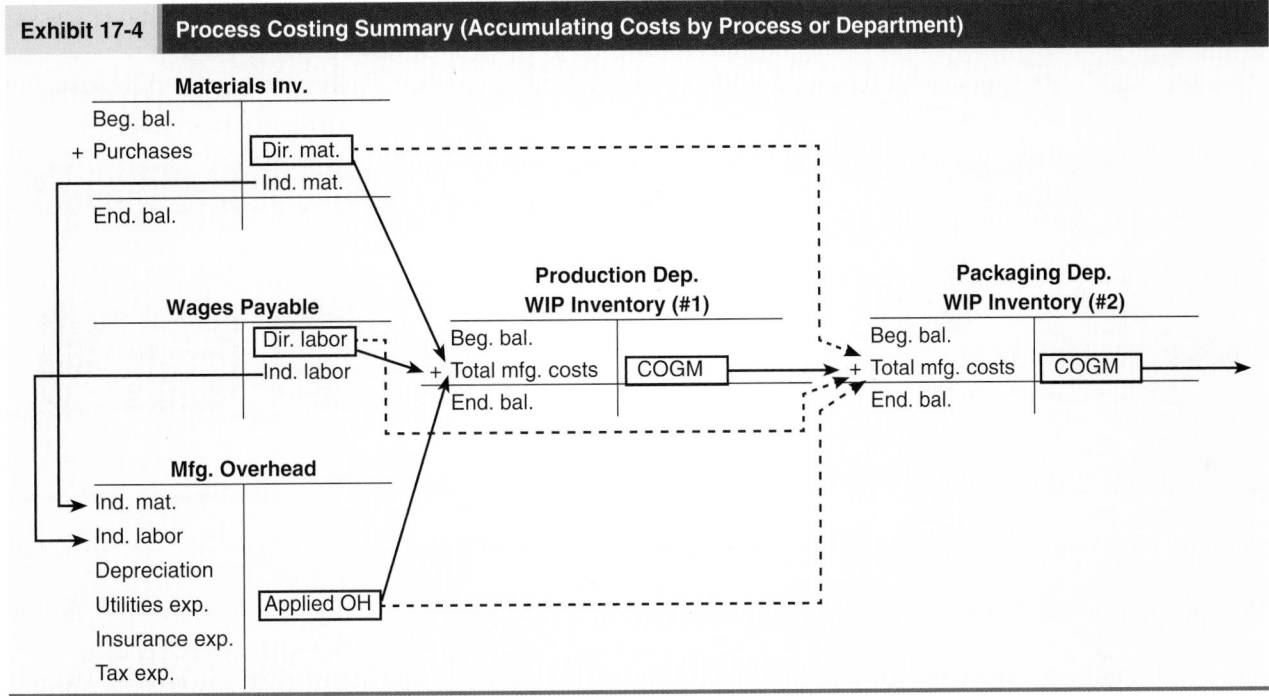

Manufacturing Departments

Typically, multiple manufacturing departments are identified when process costing is used. Products will flow through these departments at different stages of the manufacturing process. For example, a baked good product might be processed through three departments: mixing, baking, and packaging. In a particular bakery, some products may go through many departments or processes, and other products may go through only a few departments or processes, depending on the nature of the product being baked. Regardless, the work in any department must be performed uniformly on all units, and the output of the department must be uniform in nature.

Basic Processing Patterns

There are two basic patterns for arranging the departments in a process costing setting: sequential and parallel processing. **Exhibit 17-5** presents a sequential product processing pattern, in which all baked products follow a single path through the manufacturing process to finished goods inventory.

Exhibit 17-5	Sequential Product Processing

Work-in-Process Mixing → **Work-in-Process Baking** → **Work-in-Process Packaging** → **Finished Goods Inventory**

Exhibit 17-6 presents a simple example of **parallel product processing**. Numerous variations of parallel processing are possible, but similar products may begin with the same raw materials or processing in one department and then follow slightly different processes to arrive in finished goods inventory. In this example, cakes and donuts both begin in the mixing department. However, they undergo different parallel processes prior to packaging. Whereas the cake goes through baking and frosting processes, the donut goes through deep frying and glazing processes. Finally, both go to the packaging department.

Exhibit 17-6	Parallel Product Processing for Cakes and Donuts

TAKEAWAY 17.2	Concept	Method	Assessment
	How are departments that use process costing different from those that use job order costing?	Think about the work that is being performed in each department.	When process costing is appropriate, each processing department has two essential features: 1. The activity is performed uniformly on all products passing through it. 2. The output is homogeneous.

PROCESS COSTING STEPS

LO3 Explain the techniques for determining unit costs when process costing is used.

The techniques described in this chapter require the calculation of unit costs to facilitate the end-of-period transfer of product cost from one work-in-process inventory account to another, from the final work-in-process inventory account to the finished goods inventory account, and from the finished goods inventory account to the cost of goods sold account. In process costing, unit costs are usually calculated on a monthly basis. These unit costs can be compared to unit costs of prior accounting periods to determine when additional cost control measures are necessary.

Process costing requires five steps or calculations:

1. Visualize or chart the physical flow of the units through the system.
2. Determine the equivalent whole units of work completed (or **equivalent units** of production) during the period. This calculation is usually performed separately for materials and **conversion costs** (i.e., labor and overhead) because conversion costs are usually added uniformly throughout the process, whereas materials are often added at a particular point in the process.
3. Compute the per-unit cost of production for the period for materials and conversion costs by dividing the total costs incurred in each category by the equivalent units of production for that cost category.
4. Using the per-unit costs for materials and conversion costs, compute the dollar value of the units completed and transferred (Cost of Goods Manufactured) to the next department.
5. Using the same per-unit costs, compute the dollar value of the unfinished units that remain in the department (these ending work-in-process units will usually be completed in the following period).

The objective of each step is the same for both the weighted average and FIFO methods of cost allocation. However, the execution of the steps is slightly different between the two methods. We discuss these steps in more detail for the weighted average method in the following sections. For illustration purposes, assume that the Big G division of General Mills uses process costing to account for its cereal production (measured in tons) and that it has the results for January as illustrated in **Exhibit 17-7**.

Exhibit 17-7	Big G Process Costing Example

Work-in-process, January 1:
Direct materials. . . . . $ 166,413
Direct labor.   37,812
Manufacturing overhead.   76,120
Total beginning work-in-process. . . . . $ 280,345

> Inventory costs incurred prior to January.

Work done during January:
Direct materials (grain) added $19,237,725
Direct labor incurred.   3,210,425
Manufacturing overhead applied   9,602,543
Total costs incurred during January $32,050,693

> Inventory costs incurred during the month of January.

Units in process at January 1 (20% complete). . . . .   2,600 tons
Units started during January. . . . . 58,500 tons
Units in process at January 31 (40% complete). . . . .   3,500 tons

> At the beginning of January some 2,600 tons of cereal were still in process.
> Big G started 58,500 tons during the month of January.
> As of January 31, 3,500 tons were incomplete.

Further, assume that all materials are added at the beginning of the process, whereas labor and manufacturing overhead costs are added evenly throughout the process. The T-account in **Exhibit 17-8** illustrates the purpose of process costing: to allocate actual costs incurred between units completed and transferred out, and partially completed units remaining in ending inventory.

Exhibit 17-8	The Objective: Allocate Costs between Ending Inventory and Those Transferred Out

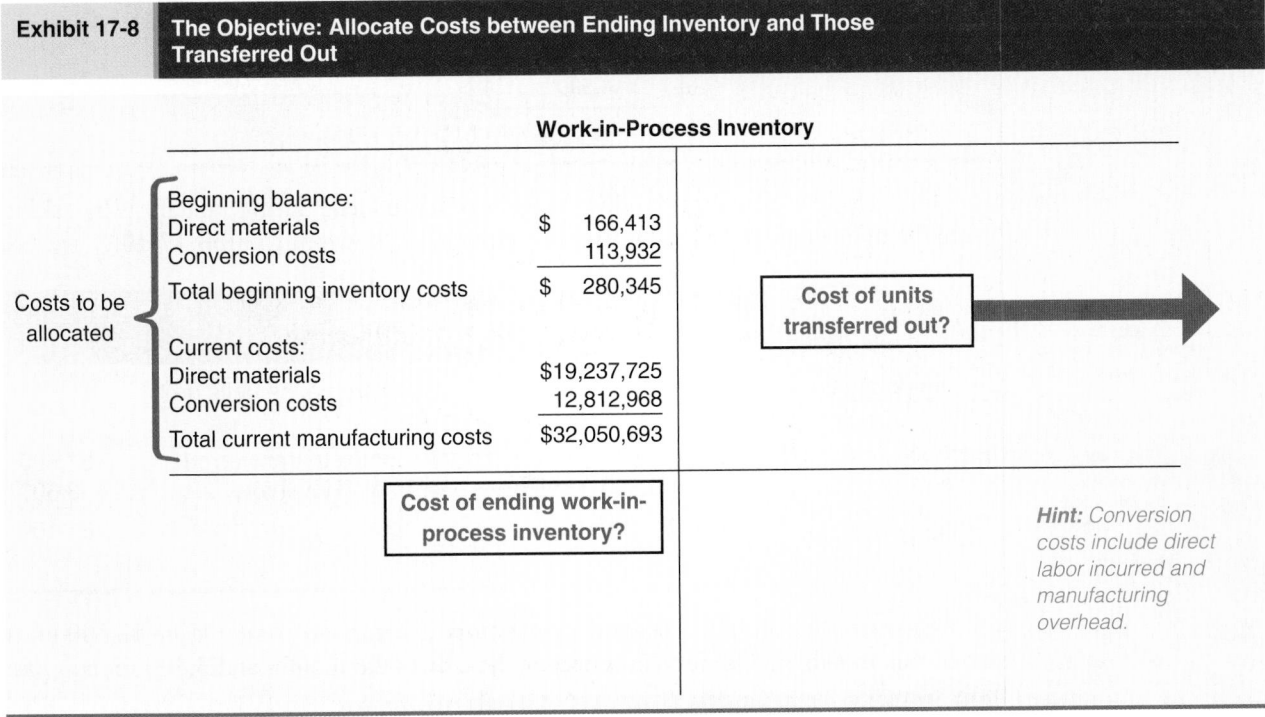

We know the costs associated with the beginning work-in-process inventory on January 1 ($280,345). We also know the costs incurred during the month of January for direct materials ($19,237,725), direct labor ($3,210,425), and manufacturing overhead ($9,602,543). For simplicity, because we assume both direct labor and manufacturing overhead costs are applied uniformly during the production process, we combine them and simply refer to them as "conversion costs." Because we started the period with partially completed inventory, during the period we will first finish the previously started units and then begin work on new units. We also end the period with partially completed units. We don't know how much of these costs should be applied to units transferred out at the end of the period and how much should remain with the partially complete ending inventory. Process costing helps us calculate an average cost per unit to apply to (1) the units completed and transferred out at the end of the period and (2) the units remaining in ending inventory.

Step 1: Visualize the Physical Flow of the Units

The starting point in process costing is to visualize how the units flow through the production process, as illustrated in **Exhibit 17-9**. In the General Mills Big G example, the quantity produced is measured in tons of cereal processed during the month of January. Sometimes it is useful to visualize how the units correspond to the dollars in the T-account in **Exhibit 17-8**.

Exhibit 17-9	T-account to Summarize the Physical Flow of Units

Another way to visualize the flow of the cereal produced during January is by asking where the units come from and where they end up, as shown in **Exhibit 17-10**.

Exhibit 17-10	Step 1: Visualize the Physical Flow of the Units

The complete/transferred inventory is composed of the 2,600 units in the beginning inventory (which were completed first) as well as 55,000 of the units that were started this period (leaving 3,500 unfinished units in the ending inventory).

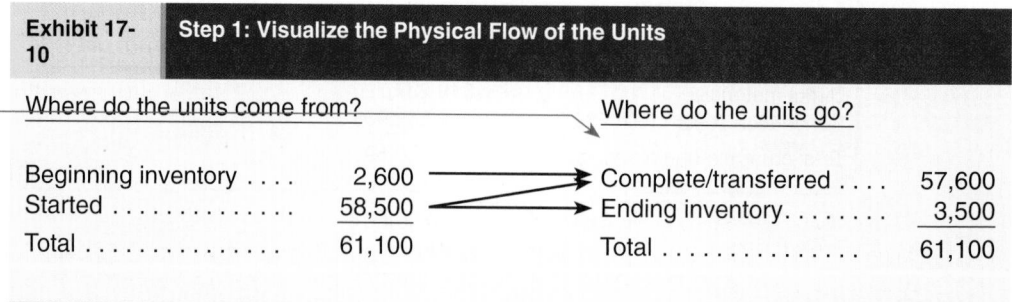

We assume that all of the beginning inventory is completed first. Of the 58,500 units started this month, 55,000 are complete by the end of the month, and 3,500 remain partially complete.

YOUR TURN! 17.1

The solution is on page 850.

Beginning work-in-process is composed of 100 units. Also assume that 700 units are started and completed during the period, and ending work-in-process includes 90 units. Summarize "Where do the units come from" and "Where do the units go."

Step 2: Calculate the Equivalent Units

Introduction to Equivalent Units

The average cost per unit is calculated by dividing total costs by the total number of units produced. The work-in-process accounts described in **Exhibits 17-5** and **17-6** illustrate how total costs are accumulated and tracked through the system. Accountants are good at keeping track of costs. However, cost accountants face a major problem in allocating costs in continuous-flow manufacturing processes. At any given point in time, units of product are at various stages of completion. Hence, it is difficult to determine the number of units to use in the average cost per unit calculation:

Hint: Instead of tracking specific costs incurred to produce each unit of product as in job order costing, process costing accumulates costs by department and then calculates an average cost per unit to be assigned to all units of product produced during that period.

$$\text{Average cost per unit} = \frac{\text{Total costs incurred}}{\text{\# of equivalent units}} \qquad \begin{array}{l}\text{We know this.} \\ \text{We don't know this.}\end{array}$$

The notion of equivalent units of production is a key concept in process costing. When units of product are produced in a continuous process, engineers and manufacturing supervisors must estimate the average percentage completion of units in a given department at the end of each period. Accountants use this information to estimate the number of equivalent *complete* units of product. For example, the following illustration shows eight glasses of water that are *half* full. How many *full* glasses of water is this equivalent to?

8 Glasses ½ Full = 4 Full Glasses

The eight half-full glasses are approximately equivalent to four full glasses. This example illustrates what accountants do each period in determining the average cost per unit in a given department.

To properly determine per-unit costs, we must first calculate equivalent units of production to be used in the denominator of the average cost per unit calculation. **Equivalent units** are the equivalent number of *whole units* completed during the period. In the previous illustration, the eight partially full glasses of water are equivalent to four full glasses (similar to four equivalent complete units of production). The calculation of equivalent units of production requires accountants to (1) track the *actual quantity* of products at each stage of production and (2) estimate the *average amount of work completed* on each unit of product in terms of conversion costs and direct material costs.

Engineers or production experts estimate the percentage of work completed in terms of conversion costs, on average. As illustrated in **Exhibit 17-11**, because the 2,600 tons of cereal on hand on January 1 is 20% complete (based on work completed during December), Big G only has to complete the remaining 80% of the processing during the month of January. During January, Big G begins work on 55,000 tons of cereal that is both started and completed during the month of January. Finally, Big G begins work on an additional 3,500 tons of cereal that is not completed by the end of the month. Engineers determine that only 40% of the processing is complete on this batch of cereal by January 31.

Exhibit 17-11	Illustration of Conversion Costs Incurred

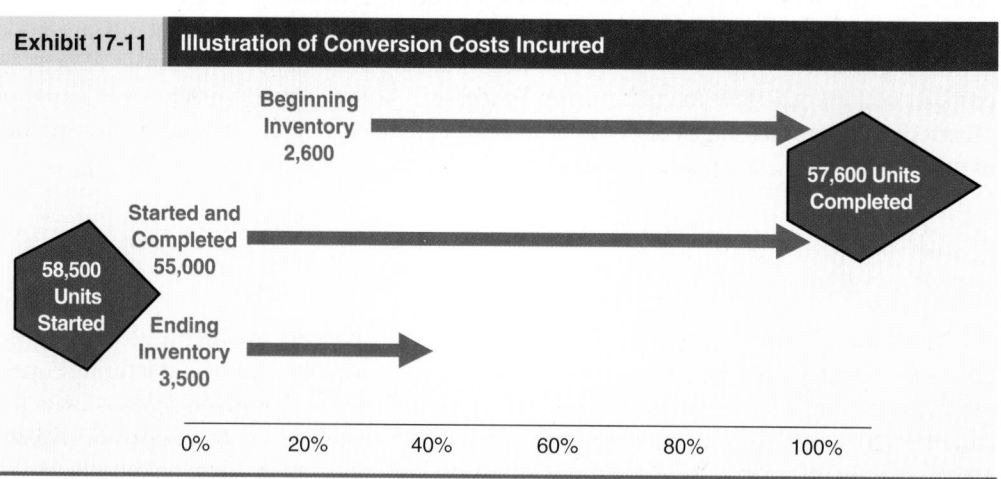

We assume that all direct materials are added at the beginning of the process; therefore, the average amount of work completed on each unit of product related to direct materials is 100%.

Calculating equivalent units can be performed using either the weighted average or the FIFO cost flow assumption. We illustrate the **weighted average method** here and the FIFO method in **Appendix 17A**. A key difference between the two methods is that the weighted average method mixes inventory layers, whereas the **FIFO method** keeps inventory layers separate. To keep these layers separate, the FIFO method tracks costs incurred during December separate from those incurred during January, the weighted average method averages all costs incurred in the production of a batch of units, regardless of when those costs were incurred. Thus, the FIFO method asks "What costs were incurred during THIS PERIOD?" whereas the weighted average method simply asks "How much work is complete (regardless of when the work was done)?"

Hint: The weighted average method is called a "rollback" method because the average includes all work done in the current period plus work done on beginning inventory in the prior period.

Equivalent Unit Calculation for Direct Materials—Weighted Average

Because materials are added at the beginning of the process, all units that have been started (61,100) are 100% complete with respect to materials. **Exhibit 17-12** illustrates the calculation of equivalent units in terms of direct materials based on the weighted average cost flow assumption.

Exhibit 17-12	Step 2: Calculate the Equivalent Units—Direct Materials

	Physical Units (tons)		Proportion Completed		Equivalent Units (tons)
Complete and transferred.......	57,600	×	100%	=	57,600
Ending inventory..............	3,500	×	100%	=	3,500
Total	61,100				61,100

Equivalent Unit Calculation for Conversion Costs—Weighted Average

When considering conversion costs (direct labor and manufacturing overhead), it is often useful to visualize the amount of work done during the period on each unique set of inventory passing through the production process, as previously illustrated in **Exhibit 17-11**. Despite the fact that some of the units were started during December, the weighted average method simply asks what percentage of the work has been completed by the end of January, as illustrated in **Exhibit 17-13**.

Exhibit 17-13	Step 2: Calculate the Equivalent Units—Conversion Costs				
	Physical Units (tons)		**Proportion Completed**		**Equivalent Units (tons)**
Complete and transferred.......	57,600	×	100%	=	57,600
Ending inventory..............	3,500	×	40%	=	1,400
Total	61,100				59,000

We can summarize the flow of the units worked on during the period and how the amount of work completed translates them into equivalent units, as illustrated in **Exhibit 17-14**.

Exhibit 17-14	Summary of Steps 1 and 2: Unit Flows and Equivalent Units Calculations

Step 1: Visualize the Physical Flow of the Units

Step 2: Calculate the Equivalent Units

Where do the units come from?		Where do the units go?			Equivalent Units			
					% Work Done?	Dir. Mat.	% Work Done?	Conv. Costs
Beginning inventory	2,600	Complete/transferred ...	57,600		100%	57,600	100%	57,600
Started	58,500	Ending inventory.......	3,500		100%	3,500	40%	1,400
Total	61,100	Total	61,100			61,100		59,000

Concept →	Method →	Assessment	TAKEAWAY 17.3
How many full glasses of water are equivalent to this number of partially full glasses?	Multiply the percentage of completion by the number of units being worked on.	An equivalent unit is the amount of work necessary to produce one complete physical unit of product.	

YOUR TURN! 17.2

Assume all materials are added at the beginning of the production process, and conversion costs are added uniformly throughout the process. Beginning work-in-process is composed of 100 units, which are 35% complete with respect to conversion costs. Also assume that 700 units are started and completed during the period, and ending work-in-process includes 90 units that are 70% complete with respect to conversion costs. Compute equivalent units of production for direct materials and conversion costs under the weighted average cost flow assumption.

The solution is on page 851.

Step 3: Determine the Per-Unit Costs

The product cost report summarizes where the costs come from and where they go (i.e., where they are allocated). In order to calculate an average cost per unit of direct materials and conversion costs, we first need to summarize the total costs incurred for direct materials and conversion costs. These numbers were illustrated in the T-account in **Exhibit 17-8**. The top part of our product cost report simply asks where the costs come from and organizes them into categories: Direct Materials and Conversion Costs, as illustrated in **Exhibit 17-15**.

Exhibit 17-15	Product Cost Report: Where Do the Costs Come From?		
Product Cost Report **General Mills Big G Division** **January Production**			
Where do the costs come from?	**Total**	**Direct Materials**	**Conversion Costs**
Beginning inventory	$ 280,345	$ 166,413	$ 113,932
Current	32,050,693	19,237,725	12,812,968
Total costs to account for	$32,331,038	$19,404,138	$12,926,900

We then calculate the average cost per unit by dividing total costs in each category by total equivalent units in each category from Step 2. In other words, we divide total materials costs by total equivalent units of materials ($19,404,138/61,100 equivalent units) to get an average cost per unit of $317.58. Similarly, we divide total conversion costs by total equivalent units of conversion costs ($12,926,900/59,000 equivalent units) to get an average cost per unit of $219.10. **Exhibit 17-16** summarizes this calculation.

Exhibit 17-16	Step 3: Product Cost Report: Determine Per-Unit Costs		
Product Cost Report **General Mills Big G Division** **January Production**			
Where do the costs come from?	**Total**	**Direct Materials**	**Conversion Costs**
Beginning inventory	$ 280,345	$ 166,413	$ 113,932
Current	32,050,693	19,237,725	12,812,968
Total costs to account for	$32,331,038	$19,404,138	$12,926,900
÷ Total equivalent units		**61,100**	**59,000**
Average cost per unit		$ **317.58**	$ **219.10**

Note that the weighted average method includes *all* costs incurred on units worked on during the month, whereas the FIFO method only includes costs incurred during the *current* period. Hence, both the numerator (costs incurred) and the denominator (equivalent units) will differ between the weighted average and FIFO methods.

YOUR TURN! 17.3

The solution is on page 851.

Assume that you have 890 total equivalent units of materials and 863 total equivalent units of conversion costs. Also assume that your beginning inventory is composed of $3,390 of materials and $1,493 of conversion costs and that you use $19,750 of materials and incur $14,904 of conversion costs during the current period. Calculate the average cost per unit of materials and conversion costs assuming the weighted average cost flow assumption.

Step 4: Calculate the Cost of Goods Manufactured

At the end of each month and for each department, we calculate the cost of goods manufactured (illustrated in **Exhibit 17-17**), which is composed of the cost of the goods that are completed and transferred to the finished goods inventory. Under the weighted average cost flow assumption, the Big G division's cost of goods manufactured during January consists of 57,600 equivalent units of materials and conversion costs (shown in **red** in

Exhibit 17-14) multiplied by their respective per-unit costs computed in Step 3 (shown in **green** in **Exhibit 17-16**).

Exhibit 17-17	Step 4: Cost of Goods Manufactured Calculation	
Materials...............................	[57,600 EU × $317.58]	18,292,608
Conversion costs	[57,600 EU × $219.10]	12,620,160
Total cost of goods manufactured		$30,912,768

YOUR TURN! 17.4

The solution is on page 851.

Assume that you have completed and transferred 800 units out of your department during the period and that you have determined your average cost per equivalent unit of direct materials to be $26.00 and your average cost per equivalent unit of conversion costs to be $19.00. Determine your cost of goods manufactured.

Step 5: Calculate the Cost of Ending Work-in-Process Inventory

Exhibit 17-18 illustrates the final step, which is to calculate the **cost of goods remaining** in ending work-in-process. Assuming all materials are added at the beginning and conversion costs are added evenly throughout the process, we multiply the equivalent units of materials and conversion costs in ending inventory (denoted in **red** in **Exhibit 17-14**) by their respective unit costs (shown in **green** in **Exhibit 17-16**) computed in Step 3, as shown in **Exhibit 17-18**.

Exhibit 17-18	Step 5: Calculate Cost of Ending Work-in-Process Inventory	
Materials...............................	[3,500 EU × $317.58]	1,111,530
Conversion costs	[1,400 EU × $219.10]	306,740
Total cost of ending inventory...........		$1,418,270

YOUR TURN! 17.5

The solution is on page 851.

Assume that your ending inventory is composed of 90 equivalent units of materials and 63 equivalent units of conversions costs and that you have determined your average cost per equivalent unit of direct materials to be $26.00 and your average cost per equivalent unit of conversion costs to be $19.00. Determine the cost of your ending inventory.

CORPORATE SOCIAL RESPONSIBILITY

General Mills Tries to Make a Difference

If you read the current popular media reports, you are likely to get the idea that the only stakeholders a corporation cares about are its shareholders. General Mills thinks differently. The goal of General Mills is to stand among the world's most socially responsible food companies. The company believes that being a good corporate citizen means considering all its stakeholders. To do this, General Mills seeks to create long-term economic, social, and environmental value.

General Mills recognizes that its customers depend on the company to provide healthy food choices. One example of what General Mills is doing in this area is an improvement in the health profile of 80% of its retail U.S. sales volume since 2005. To improve the health profile of their products, the company has increased R&D spending on health and wellness by 75% since 2004. General Mills is also committed to sustainable sourcing, with a goal of 50% of its annual raw materials purchases to be from sustainable sources by 2020. General Mills strives to create a culture of ethics with 95% of employees stating that General Mills leaders demonstrate a commitment to ethical business. Finally, General Mills' commitment to community included over $139 million of donations to charitable causes in 2017 and over $2.25 billion since the General Mills Foundation was established in 1954.

Source: https://www.generalmills.com/en/Responsibility/Overview

THE PRODUCT COST REPORT

LO4 **Explain** the procedures used to prepare the product cost report using the weighted average method in a process costing system.

Using the Big G example, the product cost report illustrated in **Exhibit 17-19** summarizes all of the steps in the total cost allocation process from (1) visualizing the physical flow of the units, to (2) calculating equivalent units, to (3) calculating unit costs, to (4) calculating cost of goods manufactured, to (5) calculating the cost of ending work-in-process inventory. Moreover, **Exhibit 17-19** also provides Big G's product cost report. Note that in this illustration, the equivalent units of production for materials and conversion costs (the numbers in **red**) are multiplied by the corresponding cost per unit figures for materials and conversion costs (the numbers in **green**) to calculate the cost allocation to cost of goods manufactured and ending inventory.

Exhibit 17-19	Summary of the Five Process Costing Steps

Flow of the Units and Equivalent Units Calculation

Step 1: Visualize the Physical Flow of the Units

			Step 2: Calculate the Equivalent Units			
				Equivalent Units		
Where do the units come from?		Where do the units go?	% Work Done?	Dir. Mat.	% Work Done?	Conv. Costs
Beginning inventory. . .	2,600	Compl./transferred . . 57,600	100%	57,600	100%	57,600
Started	58,500	Ending inventory. . . . 3,500	100%	3,500	40%	1,400
Total	61,100	Total 61,100		61,100		59,000

Product Cost Report
General Mills Big G Division
January Production

Step 3: Determine Per-Unit Costs

Where do the costs come from?	Total		Dir. Mat.	Conv. Costs
Beginning inventory	$ 280,345		$ 166,413	$ 113,932
Current	32,050,693		19,237,725	12,812,968
Total costs to account for	$32,331,038		$19,404,138	$12,926,900
÷ Total equivalent units			61,100	59,000
Average cost per equivalent unit			$ 317.58	$ 219.10

Where do the costs go?

Step 4: Calculate the Cost of Goods Manufactured

Complete/transferred:		
Materials	$18,292,608	[57,600 × $317.58]
Conversion costs	12,620,160	[57,600 × $219.10]
Cost of goods manuactured	$30,912,768

Step 5: Calculate the Cost of the Ending Work-in-Process Inventory

Ending inventory:		
Materials	$ 1,111,530	[3,500 × $317.58]
Conversion costs	306,740	[1,400 × $219.10]
Cost of ending inventory	1,418,270
Total costs allocated	$32,331,038

As a final check to see that we have performed all of the calculations correctly, the sum of the Cost of Goods Manufactured ($30,912,768) and the ending Working Process Inventory balance ($1,418,270) should equal the total costs that we determined at the outset needed to be allocated (Beginning balance $280,345 + Current costs $32,050,693 = $32,331,038). Specifically, the T-account in **Exhibit 17-20** summarizes the process costing allocation of costs between costs transferred out and costs remaining in ending inventory.

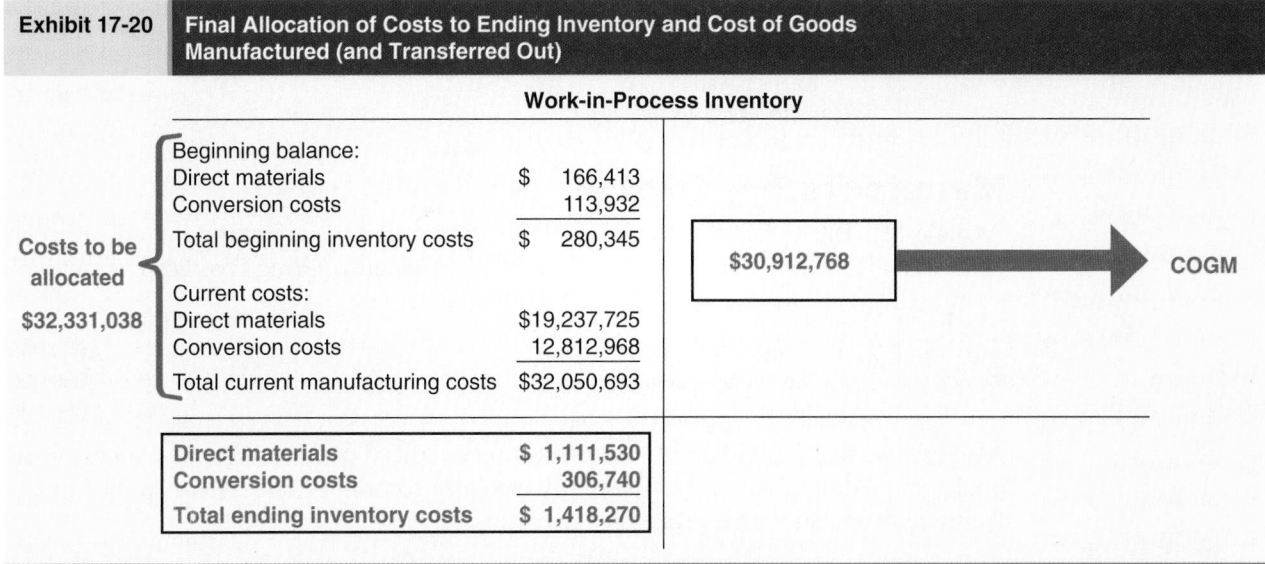

Exhibit 17-20 | **Final Allocation of Costs to Ending Inventory and Cost of Goods Manufactured (and Transferred Out)**

Work-in-Process Inventory

Costs to be allocated
$32,331,038

Beginning balance:		
Direct materials	$	166,413
Conversion costs		113,932
Total beginning inventory costs	$	280,345
Current costs:		
Direct materials		$19,237,725
Conversion costs		12,812,968
Total current manufacturing costs		$32,050,693

$30,912,768 → COGM

Direct materials	$	1,111,530
Conversion costs		306,740
Total ending inventory costs	$	1,418,270

Companies with Multiple Production Processes

At the outset of this chapter, we described situations in which a company produces its products through a long series of production processes. So far, we have illustrated process costing in a single department. When a company's production process involves a series of different departments, costs are accumulated by production process. The costs transferred out of one department are transferred into the next department. Hence, as units of product move from one department or process to the next, they carry the costs from all prior processes with them. From a practical perspective, the only thing that changes in the product costing process is that an extra column is added for transferred-in costs. For example, the $30,912,768 transferred out of the production process described in the previous section would become the transferred-in costs for the next department.

Hint: For companies with multiple production processes, their product costing process will include transferred-in costs. These costs will be part of their cost of goods manufactured and ending inventory.

JOURNAL ENTRIES ILLUSTRATED

After computing these amounts, Big G would record the following journal entries related to January production. *These entries assume that materials are added at the beginning of the process, and that labor and overhead are added evenly over the month of January.*

LO5
Illustrate the journal entries used with process costing.

Materials

During January, assume that Big G purchased $20,000,000 of grain on account. The following is a summary journal entry for the January purchases:

1	Materials inventory	20,000,000	
	Accounts payable		20,000,000
	To record January materials purchases.		

The direct materials requisitioned during January for the processing department are shown in the following entry:

2	Work-in-process	19,237,725	
	Materials inventory		19,237,725
	To record direct materials used during January.		

Labor

During January, Big G accrued $3,210,425 of direct labor expense. The journal entry to record this payroll would be as follows:

3	Work-in-process	3,210,425	
	Wages payable		3,210,425
	To record the payroll for January.		

Manufacturing Overhead

Assume that Big G has recorded $10,000,000 of actual manufacturing overhead costs (such as maintenance, depreciation, and utilities) in Manufacturing Overhead as incurred.

4	Manufacturing overhead	10,000,000	
	Maintenance wages payable		2,000,000
	Accumulated depreciation		7,000,000
	Utilities payable		1,000,000

Also assume that Big G applies manufacturing overhead costs to Work-in-Process using predetermined overhead rates. The following entry records $9,602,543 of applied manufacturing overhead for the processing department:

5	Work-in-process	9,602,543	
	Manufacturing overhead		9,602,543
	To apply manufacturing overhead to work-in-process		
	inventory.		

As a result of the journal entries recorded during the month, the Work-in-Process account contains the following balance as of the end of the month:

	Work-in-Process
Beginning balance	$ 280,345
Direct materials.	19,237,725
Direct labor	3,210,425
Manufacturing overhead.	9,602,543
Balance before month-end adjustments.	$32,331,038

At the end of the month, an additional journal entry is needed to transfer product costs from the processing department to Finished Goods (the amount of Cost of Goods Manufactured). The following entry records the Cost of Goods Manufactured:

6	Finished goods	30,912,768	
	Work-in-process		30,912,768
	To transfer the cost of completed product from work-in-		
	process inventory.		

YOUR TURN! 17.6

The solution is on page 852.

Assume the following cost information related to May production, and only one manufacturing department. What journal entries would be made to capture May production?

Direct materials.	$19,750
Direct labor	9,500
Manufacturing overhead applied	5,404

SERVICE INDUSTRY IN FOCUS

Environmental Business Consultants, LLC (EBC) has a contract with Terrabean Coffee, a large retail coffee company with 5,000 shops across North America, to manage the company's waste disposal and recycling services. Under the contract with Terrabean, EBC is responsible for negotiating, monitoring, and servicing contracts with dozens of garbage and recycling collection companies in major cities throughout the United States and Canada. These contracts generally require the garbage and recycling collection companies to collect both garbage and recyclables on a daily basis from between 10 and 30 shops, 365 days per year. When collection is missed, invoices are questioned, service is changed, new shops are opened, or other issues arise, the shop managers call EBC for assistance.

EBC maintains a call center to receive these calls and coordinate the appropriate response. The call center employees record each call and refer the issue to the EBC manager responsible for that location for follow-up. Locations are assigned to one of five geographic regions: Northeast (includes major metropolitan areas in eastern Canada), Southeast, Midwest, Southwest, and Northwest (includes major metropolitan areas in western Canada). EBC uses process costing with a weighted average cost flow assumption to assign the call center cost to each geographic region on a per-call unit cost. Overhead is applied per labor hour worked. Thus, the percentage complete can be applied to both labor and overhead. Because some questions or complaints take more than a day or two to resolve, there are typically some "unfinished" calls at the end of each period.

For the fiscal year ended September 30, 2019, the EBC call center reported the following information regarding calls handled:

Work-in-process, October 1, 2018:.	$350
Work done during fiscal year 2019:	
Direct labor incurred	$262,480
Overhead applied	247,947
Total costs incurred during fiscal year 2019	$510,427
Calls in process at October 1, 2018 (30% complete)	50 calls
Calls started and finished during fiscal year 2019	35,200 calls
Calls in process at September 30, 2019 (40% complete)	40 calls

Required

1. Determine the equivalent number of calls completed during fiscal year 2019.

2. Determine the per-unit cost of each call.

3. Determine the cost of the calls completed.

4. Determine the cost of ending work-in-process inventory at September 30, 2019.

Solution: **Exhibit 17-21** shows the solution.

> The first 50 calls (on October 1, 2018) were all completed. Plus, 35,160 of the calls started during the year (35,200 − 40) were also completed, leaving 40 unfinished calls at the end of the year.

Exhibit 17-21	Service Industry In Focus Solution

Flow of the Units and Equivalent Units Calculation

Where do the units come from?		Where do the units go?		% Work Done?	Conv. Costs
Calls in process (10/1/2018) .	50	Calls complete	35,210	100%	**35,210**
Calls started and finished . . .	35,200	Calls in process (9/30/2019) . .	40	40%	16
Total	35,250	Total	35,250		35,226

continued

continued from previous page

Product Cost Report Environmental Business Consultants, LLC Fiscal 2019 Service Calls		Conv. Costs
Where do the costs come from?		
Beginning WIP	$ 350	$ 350
Current period costs	510,427	510,427
Total costs to account for...	$510,777	$510,777
÷ Total equivalent units		35,226
Average cost per equivalent unit		**$14.50**
Where do the costs go?		
Cost of calls completed...	510,545	[35,210 × $14.50]
Cost of ending inventory..	232	[16 × $14.50]
Total costs allocated	$510,777	

COMPREHENSIVE PROBLEM (INCLUDING TRANSFERRED-IN COSTS)

Kensington Corp. makes gourmet brownies. Brownies are produced in a three-stage process. In the Baking Department, the raw materials for the brownies are mixed, poured into large trays, and baked. In the Finishing Department, frosting is applied to the brownies and they are sliced while still in the baking trays. Finally, in the Packing Department, the brownies are divided into smaller packages containing 12 brownies per package and prepared for shipping. Kensington has tracked the following information for the Baking and Finishing Departments during October 2019:

	Baking	Finishing
Trays in beginning inventory	200	100
Trays started/transferred in	5,100	?
Trays in ending inventory	100	300
Total cost of brownies transferred out in October	$18,200	?

The beginning inventory in the Finishing Department included $350 of transferred-in costs from the Baking Department incurred during September, $25 of materials, and $80 of conversion costs. During October, the Finishing Department incurred $1,075 for materials and $4,221 for conversion costs. The Finishing Department's beginning inventory was estimated to be 60% complete, and the ending inventory was estimated to be 20% complete. The frosting (the only new materials added in the Finishing Department) is added when the brownies are 25% through the production process.

One purpose of this comprehensive problem is to illustrate a more realistic example of how costs flow through a process with multiple departments or processes. Therefore, because this problem focuses on the second of three departments (the Finishing Department), we must consider transferred-in costs in addition to the direct materials costs and conversion costs incurred in the current department. Transferred-in costs merely represent the costs transferred from one department to the next and are therefore considered 100% complete as they are carried forward to the next department. In this problem, the costs incurred in the Baking Department stay with the trays of baked brownies as they come into the Finishing Department. The 100 trays in the beginning inventory (transferred in during September) carried $350 of costs from the Baking department, whereas the units transferred in during October carried $18,200 of costs from the Baking Department.

Required

1. Assuming Kensington uses the weighted average cost flow assumption, prepare the October product cost report for the Finishing Department. Be sure to include your equivalent units calculations.
2. Give the journal entry to transfer completed brownies from the Finishing Department to the Packing Department.

Solution to Comprehensive Problem

Before preparing the solution for the Finishing Department, it is important to first determine the number of trays transferred out of the Baking Department. The 5,200 trays transferred OUT of the Baking Department are the trays transferred IN to the Finishing Department. Obviously, Kensington would need to prepare a product cost report to determine the cost of the brownie trays transferred out. Because this problem focuses on the second department in the production process, the costs incurred to bake these 5,200 trays is simply given ($18,200). This number is used in the Finishing Department as the cost of trays transferred in.

1. We first illustrate the percentage complete and T-accounts (in units and dollars) that are helpful in preparing the product cost report. Note that each arrow in the timeline represents the conversion costs incurred in the Finishing Department during October for each inventory group: (1) the beginning inventory balance, (2) the trays transferred in and finished during the period, and (3) the trays transferred in and remaining in ending inventory.

We then calculate equivalent units and prepare the product cost report.

Finishing Department				Equivalent Units			
Where do the units come from?		Where do the units go?	% Trans-in	Trans-in	% Work Done?	Dir. Mat.	% Work Done?	Conv. Costs
Beg. inv.	100	Compl./transf.	5,000	100%	5,000	100%	5,000	100%	5,000
Started	5,200	End. inv.	300	100%	300	0%	0	20%	60
Total	5,300	Total	5,300		5,300		5,000		5,060

Product Cost Report			
Where do the costs come from?	Trans-in	Dir. Mat.	Conv. Costs
Beg. inv.	$ 455	$ 350	$ 25	$ 80
Current	23,496	18,200	1,075	4,221
Total costs to account for	$23,951	$18,550	$ 1,100	$ 4,301
÷ Total equivalent units		5,300	5,000	5,060
Average cost/equiv. unit		$3.5000	$0.2200	$ 0.850

continued

continued from previous page

Where do the costs go?				
Compl./transf.:				
Trans-in.	$17,500	[5,000 × $3.500]		
Direct materials.	1,100		[5,000 × $0.2200]	
Conversion costs	4,250			[5,000 × $0.85]
COGM	$22,850			
End. inv.:				
Trans-in.	1,050	[300 × $3.500]		
Direct materials.	—			
Conversion costs	51			[60 × $0.85]
Cost of ending inv.	1,101			
Total costs allocated.	$23,951			

2.

	WIP—Packing Department	22,850	
	WIP—Finishing Department		22,850

APPENDIX 17A: Process Costing Using FIFO Method

This appendix illustrates the use of process costing and the first-in, first-out method, or FIFO method, to assign product costs to the goods transferred out and to the ending work-in-process inventories. In this appendix, we will continue the Big G example introduced in the chapter.

PROCESS COSTING STEPS

LO6 **Explain** the techniques for determining unit costs when the FIFO method for process costing is used.

In this chapter, we discussed process costing and the use of the weighted average cost allocation method to transfer product costs from one work-in-process inventory account to another, from the final work-in-process inventory account to the finished goods inventory account, and from the finished goods inventory account to the cost of goods sold account. In this appendix, we will accomplish the same task, but we will use the FIFO cost allocation method to assign and transfer product costs. The following steps are the same as those used for the weighted average method. However, the execution of these steps is slightly different.

Recall, process costing requires five steps or calculations:

1. Visualize or chart the physical flow of the units through the system.
2. Determine the equivalent whole units of work completed (or equivalent units of production) during the period. This calculation is usually performed separately for materials and conversion costs (i.e., labor and overhead) because conversion costs are usually added uniformly throughout the process, whereas materials are often added at a particular point in the process.
3. Compute the per-unit cost of production for the period for materials and conversion costs by dividing the total costs incurred in each category by the equivalent units of production for that cost category.
4. Using the per-unit costs for materials and conversion costs, compute the dollar value of the units completed and transferred (Cost of Goods Manufactured) to the next department.
5. Using the same per-unit costs, compute the dollar value of the unfinished units that remain in the department (these ending work-in-process units will usually be completed in the following period).

We discuss these steps in more detail with respect to the FIFO cost allocation method in the following sections. Recall that the Big G division of General Mills uses process costing to account for its cereal production and that it had the results for January as illustrated in **Exhibit 17-1A**.

Exhibit 17-1A	Big G Process Costing Example

Work-in-process, January 1:

Direct materials.	$ 166,413
Direct labor.	37,812
Manufacturing overhead.	76,120
Total beginning work-in-process.	$ 280,345

Inventory costs incurred prior to January.

Work done during January:

Direct materials (grain) added	$19,237,725
Direct labor incurred.	3,210,425
Manufacturing overhead applied	9,602,543
Total costs incurred during January	$32,050,693

Inventory costs incurred during the month of January.

Units in process at January 1 (20% complete).	2,600 tons
Units started during January.	58,500 tons
Units in process at January 31 (40% complete).	3,500 tons

At the beginning of January some 2,600 tons of cereal were still in process.

Big G started 58,500 tons during the month of January.

As of January 31, 3,500 tons were incomplete.

Further, assume that all materials are added at the beginning of the process, whereas labor and manufacturing overhead costs are added evenly throughout the process. The T-account in **Exhibit 17-2A** illustrates the purpose of process costing, to allocate actual costs incurred between units completed and transferred out and partially completed units remaining in ending inventory.

Exhibit 17-2A	The Objective: Allocate Costs between Ending Inventory and Those Transferred Out

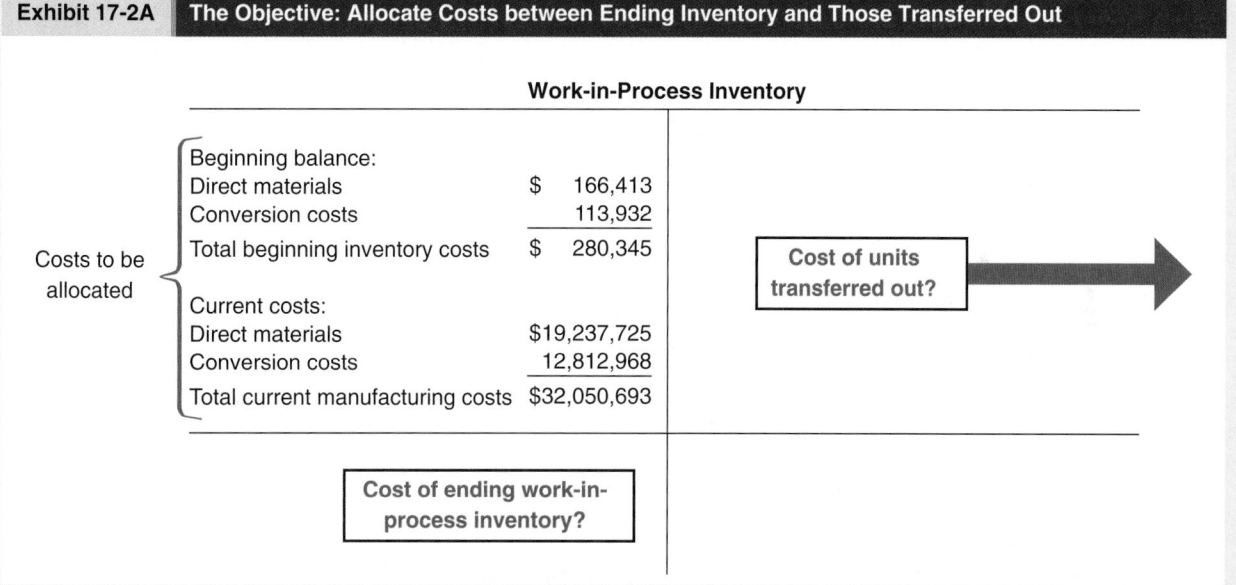

We know the costs associated with the beginning work-in-process inventory on January 1 ($280,345). We also know the costs incurred during the month of January for direct materials ($19,237,725), direct labor ($3,210,425), and manufacturing overhead ($9,602,543). For simplicity, because we assume both direct labor and manufacturing overhead costs are applied uniformly during the production process, we combine them and simply refer to them as "conversion costs." Because we started the period with partially completed inventory, during the period we will finish the previously started units and also begin work on new units. We also end the period with partially completed units. We don't know how much of these costs should be applied to units transferred out at the end of the period and how much should remain with the partially complete ending inventory. Process costing helps us calculate an average cost per unit to apply to (1) the units completed and transferred out at the end of the period and (2) the units remaining in ending inventory.

Step 1: Visualize the Physical Flow of the Units

The starting point in process costing is to visualize how the units flow through the production process, as illustrated in **Exhibit 17-3A**. In the General Mills Big G example, the quantity produced is measured in tons of cereal processed during the month of January. Sometimes it is useful to visualize how the units correspond to the dollars in the T-account in **Exhibit 17-2A**.

Exhibit 17-3A	T-account to Summarize the Physical Flow of Units

Work-in-Process Inventory (in units)

Units to be accounted for (61,100)

Beginning units: 2,600

Units started: 58,500

Units transferred: 57,600

Ending units: 3,500

Another way to visualize the flow of the cereal produced during January is by asking where the units come from and where they end up, as shown in **Exhibit 17-4A**.

Hint: Under the weighted average cost flow assumption, the costs of beginning inventory and costs incurred in the current period are "averaged" together. However, under the FIFO method, the inventory "layers" are kept separate. Thus, we do not mix costs incurred in different periods.

Exhibit 17-4A	Step 1: Visualize the Physical Flow of the Units

Where do the units come from?		Where do the units go?	
		Complete/transferred:	
Beginning inventory	2,600	Beginning inventory	2,600
		Started and complete	55,000
Started	58,500	Ending inventory	3,500
Total	61,100	Total	61,100

We assume that all 2,600 units in beginning inventory are completed first. Then, of the 58,500 units started this month, 55,000 are complete by the end of the month, and 3,500 remain partially complete. Unlike the weighted average method, which mixes inventory layers (i.e., not distinguishing between work done in each period), the FIFO method keeps the beginning inventory separate from units started during the period and accounts for each inventory layer separately. Whereas the weighted average method does not distinguish between work done in different periods, the FIFO method does not mix costs incurred in different periods.

YOUR TURN! 17.7

The solution is on page 853.

Beginning work-in-process is composed of 100 units. Also assume that 700 units are started and completed during the period, and ending work-in-process includes 90 units. Summarize "Where do the units come from" and "Where do the units go."

Step 2: Calculate the Equivalent Units

Introduction to Equivalent Units

The average cost per unit is calculated by dividing total costs by the total number of units produced. The work-in-process accounts previously described in **Exhibits 17-5** and **17-6** illustrate how total costs are accumulated and tracked through the system. Accountants are good at keeping track of costs. However, cost accountants face a major problem in allocating costs in continuous-flow manufacturing processes. At any given point in time, units of product are at various stages of completion. Hence, it is difficult to determine the number of units to use in the average cost per unit calculation:

Hint: Instead of tracking specific costs incurred to produce each unit of product as in job order costing, process costing accumulates costs by department and then calculates an average cost per unit to be assigned to all units of product produced during that period.

$$\text{Average cost per unit} = \frac{\text{Total costs incurred}}{\text{\# of equivalent units}}$$

⟵ We know this.
⟵ We don't know this.

The notion of equivalent units of production is a key concept in process costing. When units of product are produced in a continuous process, engineers and manufacturing supervisors must estimate the average percentage completion of units in a given department at the end of each period. Accountants use this information to estimate the number of equivalent *complete* units of product. For example, the following illustration shows eight glasses of water that are *half* full. How many *full* glasses of water is this equivalent to?

8 Glasses ½ Full = 4 Full Glasses

The eight half-full glasses are approximately equivalent to four full glasses. This example illustrates what accountants do each period in determining the average cost per unit in a given department.

To properly determine per-unit costs, we must first calculate equivalent units of production to be used in the denominator of the average cost per unit calculation. **Equivalent units** are the equivalent number of *whole units* completed during the period. In the previous illustration, the eight partially full glasses of water are equivalent to four full glasses (similar to four equivalent complete units of production). The calculation of equivalent units of production requires accountants to (1) track the *actual quantity* of products at each stage of production and (2) estimate the *average amount of work completed* on each unit of product in terms of conversion costs and direct material costs.

Engineers or production experts estimate the percentage of work completed in terms of conversion costs, on average. As illustrated in **Exhibit 17-5A**, because the 2,600 tons of cereal on hand on January 1 is 20% complete (based on work completed during December), Big G only has to complete the remaining 80% of the processing during the month of January. During January, Big G begins work on 55,000 tons of cereal that is both started and completed during the month of January. Finally, Big G begins work on an additional 3,500 tons of cereal that is not completed by the end of the month. Engineers determine that only 40% of the processing is complete on this batch of cereal by January 31. We assume that all direct materials are added at the beginning of the process; therefore, the average amount of work completed on each unit of product related to direct materials is 100%.

Exhibit 17-5A	Illustration of Conversion Costs Incurred

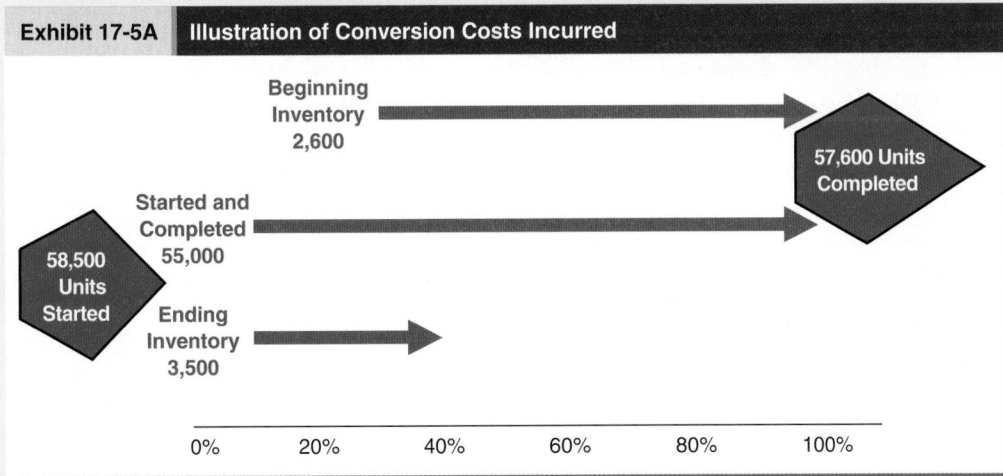

A key difference between the weighted average method and the FIFO method is that the weighted average mixes costs across inventory layers, whereas the FIFO method keeps costs incurred across inventory layers (i.e., incurred in different periods) separate. Whereas the weighted average method averages all costs incurred in the production of a batch of units, regardless of when those costs were incurred, the FIFO method keeps costs incurred during December separate from those incurred during January. Thus, the weighted average method asks "How much work is complete (regardless of when the work was done)?" whereas the FIFO method asks "What costs were incurred during THIS PERIOD?" A critical feature of the FIFO method is that because materials are added at the *beginning* of the process in this example, the beginning inventory

Hint: An item that is 20% complete at the beginning of the period means 80% of the work is done this period, not 20%.

units moved beyond the point of adding materials during the last period. Thus, NO materials are added THIS PERIOD. Because the beginning inventory was started last month, the materials for the beginning inventory were actually added during December. Thus, no new materials are added to these 2,600 units during January.

Equivalent Unit Calculation for Direct Materials—FIFO

The materials for the units started and completed during the month and for the ending inventory are added during this period. **Exhibit 17-6A** illustrates the calculation of equivalent units based on the FIFO cost flow assumption. The units in each "layer" of inventory are multiplied by the percentage of materials added during the CURRENT period (January) to calculate the equivalent units of materials added during THIS PERIOD, as shown in **Exhibit 17-6A**.

Hint: The 2,600 units of direct materials inventory were started last month. Thus, they will not be counted during the current period.

Exhibit 17-6A	**Step 2: Calculate the Equivalent Units—Direct Materials**					
		Physical Units (tons)		**Proportion Completed**		**Equivalent Units (tons)**
Beginning inventory		2,600	×	0%	=	0
Started and finished during January.		55,000	×	100%	=	55,000
Ending inventory.		3,500	×	100%	=	3,500
Total		61,100				58,500

Hint: Notice that the equivalent units for direct materials are lower under the FIFO cost flow assumption than they were under the weighted average method. The difference is due to the fact that the FIFO method only allocates CURRENT costs. This is why the equivalent units for beginning inventory are zero (under the FIFO method) because these costs were incurred last period.

Equivalent Unit Calculation for Conversion Costs—FIFO

When considering conversion costs (direct labor and manufacturing overhead), it is often useful to visualize the amount of work done during the period on each unique set of inventory passing through the production process, as previously illustrated in **Exhibit 17-5A**, which summarizes the work performed in the Big G division during the month of January. Because materials are added at the beginning of the period, the arrows only represent the amount of conversion costs applied to the process during the *current* period. We can then calculate the number of equivalent units with respect to conversion costs incurred during January, as illustrated in **Exhibit 17-7A**.

Exhibit 17-7A	**Step 2: Calculate the Equivalent Units—Conversion Costs**					
		Physical Units (tons)		**Proportion Completed This Month**		**Equivalent Units (tons)**
Beginning inventory		2,600	×	80%	=	2,080
Started and finished during January.		55,000	×	100%	=	55,000
Ending inventory.		3,500	×	40%	=	1,400
Total		61,100				58,480

Again, we calculate equivalent units of production by multiplying the number of units in each "layer" of inventory by the percentage of conversion costs added during the current period.

We can then summarize the flow of the units worked on during the period and how the amount of work completed during the period translates them into equivalent units, as illustrated in **Exhibit 17-8A**.

Exhibit 17-8A	Summary of Steps 1 and 2: Unit Flows and Equivalent Units Calculations

Step 1: Visualize the Physical Flow of the Units

Step 2: Calculate the Equivalent Units

Where do the units come from?		Where do the units go?		% in Jan.?	Materials	% in Jan.?	Conv. Costs
					Equivalent Units		
Beginning inventory . . .	2,600	Complete/transferred:					
		Beginning inventory	2,600	0%	0	80%	2,080
		Started and completed	55,000	100%	55,000	100%	55,000
Started	58,500	Ending inventory.	3,500	100%	3,500	40%	1,400
Total	61,100	Total	61,100		58,500		58,480

Concept ⟶	Method ⟶	Assessment	TAKEAWAY 17.3A
How many full glasses of water are equivalent to this number of partially full glasses?	Multiply the percentage of completion by the number of units being worked on.	An equivalent unit is the amount of work necessary to produce one complete physical unit of product.	

YOUR TURN! 17.8

The solution is on page 853.

Assume all materials are added at the beginning of the production process, and conversion costs are added uniformly throughout the process. Beginning work-in-process is composed of 100 units, which are 35% complete with respect to conversion costs. Also assume that 700 units are started and completed during the period, and ending work-in-process includes 90 units that are 70% complete with respect to conversion costs. Compute equivalent units of production for direct materials and conversion costs under the FIFO cost flow assumption.

Step 3: Determine the Per-Unit Costs

The product cost report summarizes where the costs come from and where they go (i.e., where they are allocated). The FIFO method differs from the weighted average method in an important way. The FIFO method does not mix "layers" of costs incurred during different periods. The $280,345 of costs in beginning inventory at the start of the month were incurred during December. When we calculate the average cost per unit, we calculate the average cost per unit of costs incurred during the CURRENT PERIOD. Hence, the costs incurred last month to help the inventory to reach the 20% point stay with those beginning inventory units and are NOT ALLOCATED across the units started during THIS PERIOD. In order to calculate an average cost per unit of materials and conversion costs incurred during THIS PERIOD, we first need to separate the current-period costs into their materials and conversion cost components. These numbers were illustrated in the T-account in **Exhibit 17-2A**. **Exhibit 17-9A** illustrates two important points. First, the beginning inventory costs incurred in the prior period are carried down and assigned to stay with the beginning inventory units. Second, only the costs incurred during the current period are allocated and used subsequently in the average cost per unit calculation.

Exhibit 17-9A	Product Cost Report: Where Do the Costs Come From?

Product Cost Report
General Mills Big G Division
January Production

Where do the costs come from? Total		Direct Materials	Conversion Costs
Beginning inventory	$ 280,345		
Current	32,050,693	$19,237,725	$12,812,968
Total costs to account for	$32,331,038		

Carry to Step 4

We then calculate the average cost per unit by dividing current-period costs in each category by total equivalent units in each category from Step 2. In other words, we divide current materials costs by total equivalent units of materials ($19,237,725/58,500 equivalent units) to get an average cost per unit of $328.85. Similarly, we divide current conversion costs by total equivalent units of conversion costs ($12,812,968/58,480 equivalent units) to get an average cost per unit of $219.10. **Exhibit 17-10A** summarizes this calculation.

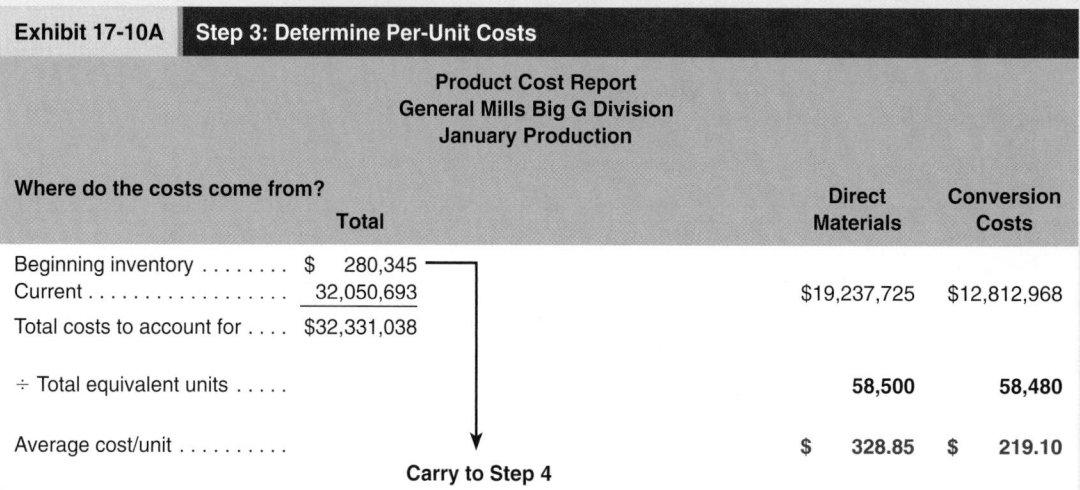

Exhibit 17-10A	Step 3: Determine Per-Unit Costs		
Product Cost Report			
General Mills Big G Division			
January Production			
Where do the costs come from?		**Direct Materials**	**Conversion Costs**
	Total		
Beginning inventory	$ 280,345		
Current	32,050,693	$19,237,725	$12,812,968
Total costs to account for	$32,331,038		
÷ Total equivalent units		**58,500**	**58,480**
Average cost/unit		$ 328.85	$ 219.10
	Carry to Step 4		

Note that under the FIFO cost flow assumption, the costs from the prior period associated with the beginning inventory stay with the beginning inventory and are not allocated to any other units. The costs incurred during the current period are allocated across all work incurred during the current period. Hence, under the FIFO cost flow assumption, the accountant keeps the "layers" of inventory separate. In the Big G example, note that the per-unit costs of materials and conversions costs only include costs incurred during January.

YOUR TURN! 17.9

The solution is on page 853.

Assume that you have 790 total equivalent units of materials and 828 total equivalent units of conversion costs. Also assume that your beginning inventory is composed of $3,390 of materials and $1,493 of conversion costs and that you use $19,750 of materials and incur $14,904 of conversion costs during the current period. Calculate the average cost per unit of materials and conversion costs assuming the FIFO cost flow assumption.

Step 4: Calculate the Cost of Goods Manufactured

At the end of each month and for each department, we calculate the cost of goods manufactured and transferred out (illustrated in **Exhibit 17-11A**). Under the FIFO cost flow assumption, the Big G division's product completed and transferred out during January consists of (1) the product in beginning work-in-process (2,080 equivalent tons) and (2) the product started and completed during the period (55,000 equivalent tons). Specifically, it is composed of all costs to manufacture the beginning inventory (both this period and last period) and the cost of units started and finished this period. To determine the dollar cost value of the product transferred to finished goods (called Cost of Goods Manufactured), we multiply the equivalent units of materials and conversion costs transferred (shown in **red** in **Exhibit 17-8A**) by their respective per-unit costs computed in Step 3 (shown in **green** in **Exhibit 17-10A**) and add these costs to the cost value of the beginning work-in-process, as shown in **Exhibit 17-11A**.

Exhibit 17-11A	Step 4: Cost of Goods Manufactured Calculation	
		Carry from Step 3
Beginning inventory:		
Costs incurred in December		$ 280,345
Conversion costs incurred in January.	[2,080 EU × $219.10]	455,728
Started and finished:		
Materials	[55,000 EU × $328.85]	18,086,750
Conversion costs	[55,000 EU × $219.10]	12,050,500
Total cost of goods manufactured.		$30,873,323

Assume that you had beginning inventory costs incurred last period of $14,883 and that you added 65 equivalent units of conversion costs to complete your beginning inventory. Moreover, you started and completed 700 units during the current period. Finally, assume you have determined your average cost per equivalent unit of direct materials to be $25.00 and your average cost per equivalent unit of conversion costs to be $18.00. Determine your cost of goods manufactured assuming the FIFO cost flow assumption.

YOUR TURN! 17.10

The solution is on page 854.

Step 5: Calculate the Cost of Ending Work-in-Process Inventory

Exhibit 17-12A illustrates the final step, which is to calculate the cost of goods remaining in ending work-in-process inventory. Assuming all materials are added at the beginning and conversion costs are added evenly through the process, we multiply the equivalent units of materials and conversion costs in ending inventory (denoted in **red** in **Exhibit 17-8A**) by their respective unit costs (shown in **green** in **Exhibit 17-10A**) computed in Step 2, as follows:

Exhibit 17-12A	Step 5: Calculate Cost of Ending Work-in-Process Inventory	
Materials..	[3,500 EU × **$328.85**]	$1,150,975
Conversion costs	[1,400 EU × **$219.10**]	306,740
Total cost of goods remaining in ending inventory		$1,457,715

Cost of goods manufactured and transferred out (**Exhibit 17-11A**)....	$30,873,323
Cost of ending inventory (**Exhibit 17-12A**)......................	1,457,715
Total cost to account for (**Exhibit 17-10A**)......................	$32,331,038

Assume that your ending inventory is composed of 90 equivalent units of materials and 63 equivalent units of conversions costs and that you have determined your average cost per equivalent unit of direct materials to be $25.00 and your average cost per equivalent unit of conversion costs to be $18.00. Determine the cost of your ending inventory assuming the FIFO cost flow assumption.

YOUR TURN! 17.11

The solution is on page 854.

THE PRODUCT COST REPORT

The product cost report in **Exhibit 17-13A** summarizes the last three steps in the cost allocation process. The report calculates the cost of goods manufactured and transferred out of work-in-process and into finished goods. The report also calculates the cost of the remaining ending balance in work-in-process. Using the Big G example, **Exhibit 17-13A** also summarizes all of the steps in the total cost allocation process from (1) visualizing the physical flow of the units, to (2) calculating equivalent units, to (3) calculating per-unit costs, to (4) calculating cost of goods manufactured, to (5) calculating the cost of ending work-in-process inventory. Finally, **Exhibit 17-13A** provides Big G's product cost report. Note that in this illustration, the equivalent units of production for materials and conversion costs (the numbers in **red**) are multiplied by the corresponding cost per unit figures for materials and conversion costs (the numbers in **green**) to calculate the cost allocation amounts used to assign costs to cost of goods manufactured and ending inventory.

LO7 **Explain** the procedures used to prepare the product cost report using the FIFO method in a process costing system.

Exhibit 17-13A	Summary of the Five Process Costing Steps

Flow of the Units and Equivalent Units Calculation

Step 1: Visualize the Physical Flow of the Units

Step 2: Calculate the Equivalent Units

Where do the units come from?		Where do the units go?		% in Jan.?	Materials	% in Jan.?	Conversion Costs
						Equivalent Units	
		Complete/transferred:					
Beginning inventory .... 2,600 →		Beginning inventory	2,600	0%	0	80%	2,080
		Started and completed ..	55,000	100%	55,000	100%	55,000
Started .... 58,500 →		Ending inventory	3,500	100%	3,500	40%	1,400
Total 61,100		Total	61,100		58,500		58,480

Product Cost Report
General Mills Big G Division
January Production

Step 3: Determine Per-Unit Costs

Where do the costs come from?	Total		Direct Materials	Conversion Costs
Beginning inventory .... $ 280,345				
Current 32,050,693			$19,237,725	$12,812,968
Total costs to account for $32,331,038				
÷ Total equivalent units			58,500	58,480
Average cost/unit			**$328.85**	**$219.10**

Where do the costs go?

Step 4: Calculate the Cost of Goods Manufactured

Beginning inventory:				
Costs incurred in December ..... $ 280,345				
Costs incurred in January 455,728		[0 × **$328.85**] +	[2,080 × **$219.10**]	
Started and finished 30,137,250		[55,000 × **$328.85**] +	[55,000 × **$219.10**]	
Cost of goods manufactured	$30,873,323			

Step 5: Calculate the Cost of the Ending Work-in-Process Inventory

Ending inventory:			
Materials .... $ 1,150,975		[3,500 × **$328.85**]	
Conversion costs 306,740			[1,400 × **$219.10**]
Cost of ending inventory	1,457,715		
Total costs allocated	$32,331,038		

As a final check to see that we have performed all of the calculations correctly, the sum of Cost of Goods Manufactured ($30,873,323) and the ending work-in-process balance ($1,457,715) should equal the total costs that we determined at the outset needed to be allocated (Beginning Balance $280,345 + Current Costs $32,050,693 = $32,331,038). Specifically, the T-account in **Exhibit 17-14A** summarizes the process costing allocation of costs between costs transferred out and costs remaining in ending inventory.

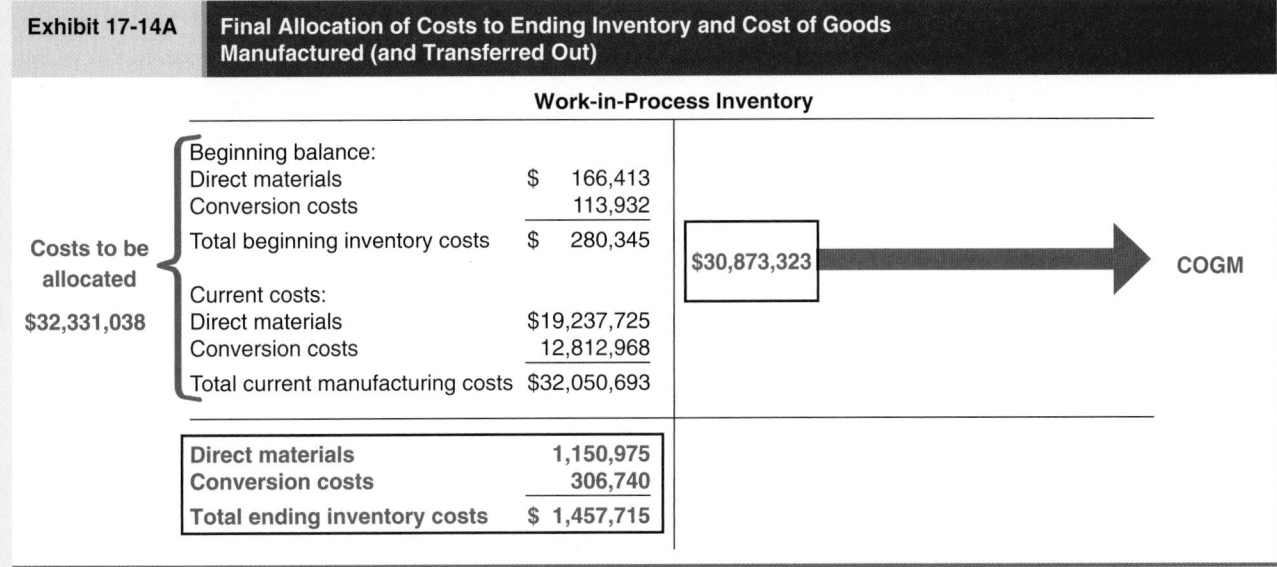

Exhibit 17-14A	Final Allocation of Costs to Ending Inventory and Cost of Goods Manufactured (and Transferred Out)

Work-in-Process Inventory

Costs to be allocated $32,331,038

Beginning balance:
Direct materials .... $ 166,413
Conversion costs 113,932
Total beginning inventory costs ...... $ 280,345

Current costs:
Direct materials $19,237,725
Conversion costs 12,812,968
Total current manufacturing costs ... $32,050,693

$30,873,323 → COGM

Direct materials 1,150,975
Conversion costs 306,740
Total ending inventory costs .... $ 1,457,715

Companies with Multiple Production Processes

At the outset of this chapter, we described situations in which a company produces its products through a long series of production processes. So far, we have illustrated process costing in a single department. When a company's production process involves a series of different departments, costs are accumulated by production process. The costs transferred out of one department are transferred into the next department. Hence, as units of product move from one department or process to the next, they carry the costs from all prior processes with them. From a practical perspective, the only thing that changes in the product costing process is that an extra column is added for transferred-in costs. For example, the $30,873,323 transferred out of the production process described in the previous section would become the transferred-in costs for the next department.

Hint: If a company has multiple production processes, all of them (except for the first process) will have transferred-in costs, whether they use the weighted average or the FIFO cost flow assumption.

JOURNAL ENTRIES ILLUSTRATED

After computing these amounts, Big G would record the following journal entries related to January production. *These entries assume that materials are added at the beginning of the process, and that labor and overhead are added evenly over the month of January.*

LO8 Illustrate the journal entries used with FIFO process costing.

Materials

During January, assume that Big G purchased $20,000,000 of grain on account. The following is a summary journal entry for the January purchases:

1	Materials inventory	20,000,000	
	Accounts payable		20,000,000
	To record January materials purchases.		

The direct materials requisitioned during January for the processing department is shown in the following entry:

2	Work-in-process	19,237,725	
	Materials inventory		19,237,725
	To record direct materials used during January.		

Labor

During January, Big G accrued $3,210,425 of direct labor expense. The journal entry to record this payroll would be as follows:

3	Work-in-process	3,210,425	
	Wages payable		3,210,425
	To record the payroll for January.		

Manufacturing Overhead

Assume that Big G has recorded its manufacturing overhead costs (such as maintenance, depreciation, and utilities) in Manufacturing Overhead as incurred. Also assume that Big G applies manufacturing overhead costs to Work-in-Process using predetermined overhead rates. The following entry records the amount of applied manufacturing overhead for the processing department:

4	Work-in-process	9,602,543	
	Manufacturing overhead		9,602,543
	To apply manufacturing overhead to work-in-process		
	inventory.		

As a result of the journal entries recorded during the month, the Work-in-Process account contains the following balance as of the end of the month:

	Work-in-Process
Beginning balance	$ 280,345
Direct materials	19,237,725
Direct labor	3,210,425
Manufacturing overhead	9,602,543
Balance before month-end adjustments	$32,331,038

At the end of the month, an additional journal entry is needed to transfer product costs from the processing department to Finished Goods (the amount of Cost of Goods Manufactured). The following entry records the Cost of Goods Manufactured:

5	Finished goods	30,873,323	
	Work-in-process		30,873,323
	To transfer the cost of completed product from work-in-process		
	inventory.		

YOUR TURN!
17.12

The solution is on
page 855.

Assume the following cost information for May production and only one manufacturing department. What journal entries would be made to capture May production?

Direct materials	$19,750
Direct labor	9,500
Manufacturing overhead applied	5,404

SUMMARY OF LEARNING OBJECTIVES

LO1   Compare and contrast job order costing and process costing. (p. 804)

- Job order costing is used when production consists of a variety of different products or unique customer orders.

- Process costing is used when production consists of a large volume of the same (homogeneous) product produced in a continual flow.

Describe the basic concepts of process costing. (p. 806)   **LO2**

■   There is a separate work-in-process account for each department under a process costing system, whereas there is only one work-in-process control account in a job order costing system.

■   In a process costing environment, products flow through multiple departments that are arranged in either a sequential pattern or a parallel pattern.

Explain the techniques for determining unit costs when process costing is used. (p. 808)   **LO3**

■   Visualize or chart the physical flow of the units through the system.

■   Determine the equivalent whole units of work completed (or equivalent units of production) during the period. This calculation is usually performed separately for materials and conversion costs (i.e., labor and overhead) because conversion costs are usually added uniformly throughout the process, whereas materials are often added at a particular point in the process.

■   Compute the per-unit cost of production for the period for materials and conversion costs by dividing the total costs incurred in each category by the equivalent units of production for that cost category.

■   Using the per-unit costs for materials and conversion costs, compute the dollar value of the units completed and transferred (cost of goods manufactured) to the next department.

■   Using the same per-unit costs, compute the dollar value of the unfinished units that remain in the department (these ending work-in-process units will usually be completed in the following period).

Explain the procedures used to prepare the product cost report using the weighted average method in a process costing system. (p. 816)   **LO4**

■   The product cost report and its supporting calculations include all of the five steps in the process costing procedure.

■   The weighted average method mixes inventory layers and asks the question "how much work has been completed?" in calculating equivalent units of production.

Illustrate the journal entries used with process costing. (p. 817)   **LO5**

■   At each stage of the manufacturing process, costs are added to the work-in-process account of the department where the work is completed. The journal entries are identical to those illustrated under a job order costing system.

■   Direct materials are added to the materials inventory account when they are purchased.

■   Materials used in the manufacturing process are transferred from the materials inventory account with a credit and debited to the appropriate work-in-process account.

■   Labor and overhead are recorded as debits to the appropriate work-in-process account.

Appendix 17A: Explain the techniques for determining unit costs when the FIFO method for process costing is used. (p. 822)   **LO6**

■   The five process costing steps are the same under the FIFO method as under the weighted average method.

■   In assigning manufacturing costs, one must consider three batches (or layers) of product: units from beginning work-in-process, units started and finished during this period, and units remaining in the ending work-in-process. Instead of mixing the layers (as in the weighted average method), the FIFO method keeps these three layers of inventory separate.

■   The key difference between the weighted average and FIFO methods is that under the FIFO method, costs per equivalent unit are calculated by dividing current costs by current equivalent units; prior period costs and equivalent units are excluded from these calculations but are included in the total costs to be accounted for.

Appendix 17A: Explain the procedures used to prepare the product cost report using the FIFO method in a process costing system. (p. 829)   **LO7**

■   When work-in-process inventories exist at the beginning and the end of the accounting period, the measurement of work accomplished requires that partially finished units be converted to equivalent units for accounting purposes.

■   When materials are added at a different rate than conversion work is accomplished, equivalent units must be computed separately for materials and conversion.

■   The product cost report and its supporting calculations include all of the five steps in the process costing procedure.

■ The FIFO method keeps inventory layers separate and asks the question "how much work was completed during THIS PERIOD?" in calculating equivalent units of production.

LO8 **Appendix 17A: Illustrate the journal entries used with FIFO process costing. (p. 831)**

■ At each stage of the manufacturing process, costs are added to the work-in-process account of the department where the work is completed. The journal entries are identical to those illustrated under a job order costing system.

■ Direct materials are added to the materials inventory account when they are purchased.

■ Materials used in the manufacturing process are transferred from the materials inventory account with a credit and debited to the appropriate work-in-process account.

■ Labor and overhead are recorded as debits to the appropriate work-in-process account.

SUMMARY	Concept ⟶	Method ⟶	Assessment
TAKEAWAY 17.1	How to distinguish between situations when job order and product costing would be more appropriate?	Think about the nature of the manufacturing process.	Job order costing is used for unique products or orders, whereas process costing is used for uniform products.
TAKEAWAY 17.2	How are departments that use process costing different from those that use job order costing?	Think about the work that is being performed in each department.	When process costing is appropriate, each processing department has two essential features: 1. The activity is performed uniformly on all products passing through it. 2. The output is homogeneous.
TAKEAWAY 17.3A	How many full glasses of water are equivalent to this number of partially full glasses?	Multiply the percentage of completion by the number of units being worked on.	An equivalent unit is the amount of work necessary to produce one complete physical unit of product.

KEY TERMS

Conversion costs (p. 808)
Cost of goods
   remaining (p. 815)
Equivalent units (p. 808, 811,
   825)
FIFO method (p. 812)

Parallel product
   processing (p. 807)
Process costing (p. 805)
Process costing system (p. 806)
Product cost report (p. 806)

Sequential product
   processing (p. 807)
Transferred-in costs (p. 831)
Weighted average
   method (p. 812)

Assignments with the logo in the margin are available in BusinessCourse.
See the Preface of the book for details.

SELF-STUDY QUESTIONS

(Answers to Self-Study Questions are at the end of this chapter.)

LO2, 3 **1. Which of the following costs will not be part of product cost when using a process costing system?**
   a. Prior department cost   *c.* Byproduct cost
   b. Conversion cost   *d.* Materials cost

LO2 **2. For which of the following will there be multiple accounts in the general ledger when using process costing?**
   a. Finished goods   *c.* Materials
   b. Work-in-process   *d.* Wages payable

3. **Which of the following will not influence the calculation of equivalent units when the FIFO cost flow assumption is used?**

   a. Units processed in prior departments
   b. Ending inventory units
   c. Beginning inventory units
   d. Units sold

LO6
(Appendix 17A)

QUESTIONS

1. What are the important differences between job order and process costing systems? **LO1**

2. How are all manufacturing costs for a series of processing departments accumulated into finished goods inventory? **LO1, 2**

3. Why do unit cost computations in a manufacturing process require equivalent unit computations? **LO2, 3**

4. Why do we say that process cost accounting is basically an averaging computation? **LO3**

5. What is meant by the term *equivalent unit*? **LO3**

6. What are conversion costs? **LO3**

7. Why must we sometimes compute equivalent units separately for materials and for conversion costs? **LO3**

8. Why is it true that in each department's work-in-process inventory account all beginning inventory and current-period costs must end up either being transferred out or in ending work-in-process inventory? **LO3**

9. Describe the three "layers" of inventory that are typically involved in a period's production under the FIFO accounting method. In what special situation are there only two layers? **LO6, 7, 8**
(Appendix 17A)

SHORT EXERCISES

SE17-1. During December, Krause Chemical Company had the following selected data concerning the manufacture of Xyzine, an industrial cleaner.

LO3, 4

Production Flow	Physical Units	
Completed and transferred to the next department	100	
Add: Ending work-in-process inventory	10	(40% complete as to conversion)
Total units to account for	110	
Less: Beginning work-in-process inventory	20	(60% complete as to conversion)
Units started during December.....................	90	

All materials are added at the beginning of processing in this department, and conversion costs are added uniformly during the process. The beginning work-in-process inventory had $120 of raw materials and $180 of conversion costs incurred. Materials added during December was $540 and conversion costs of $1,484 were incurred. Krause uses the weighted-average process-costing method. The total raw materials costs in the ending work-in-process inventory for December are

   a. $120.
   b. $72.
   c. $60.
   d. $36.

SE17-2. Mack Inc. uses a weighted-average process costing system. Direct materials and conversion costs are incurred evenly during the production process. During the month of October, the following costs were incurred:

LO3, 4

Direct materials.	$39,700
Conversion costs	70,000

The work-in-process inventory as of October 1 consisted of 5,000 units, valued at $4,300, that were 20% complete. During October, 27,000 units were transferred out. Inventory as of October 31 consisted of 3,000 units that were 50% complete. The weighted-average inventory cost per unit completed in October was

a. $3.51.
b. $3.88.
c. $3.99.
d. $4.00.

LO3   **SE17-3.**   Colt Company uses a weighted-average process cost system to account for the cost of producing a

chemical compound. As part of production, Material B is added when the goods are 80% complete. Beginning work-in-process inventory for the current month was 20,000 units, 90% complete. During the month, 70,000 units were started in process, and 65,000 units were completed. There were no lost or spoiled units. If the ending inventory was 60% complete, the total equivalent units for Material B for the month were

a. 65,000 units.
b. 70,000 units.
c. 85,000 units.
d. 90,000 units.

LO3   **SE17-4.**   San Jose Inc. uses a weighted-average process costing system. All materials are introduced at the

start of manufacturing, and conversion costs are incurred evenly throughout production. The company started 70,000 units during May and had the following work-in-process inventories at the beginning and end of the month:

May 1	30,000 units, 40% complete
May 31	24,000 units, 25% complete

Assuming no spoilage or defective units, the total equivalent units used to assign costs for May are

	Materials	**Conversion Cost**
a.	70,000	70,000.
b.	82,000	82,000.
c.	100,000	70,000.
d.	100,000	82,000.

LO3, 4   **SE17-5.**   During December, Krause Chemical Company had the following selected data concerning the manufacture of Xyzine, an industrial cleaner:

Production Flow	**Physical Units**	
Completed and transferred to the next department	100	
Add: Ending work-in-process inventory	10	(40% complete as to conversion)
Total units to account for	110	
Less: Beginning work-in-process inventory	20	(60% complete as to conversion)
Units started during December.	90	

All materials are added at the beginning of processing in this department, and conversion costs are added uniformly during the process. The beginning work-in-process inventory had $120 of raw materials and $180 of conversion costs incurred. Materials added during December was $540 and conversion costs of $1,484 were incurred. Krause uses the weighted-average process-costing method. The total conversion costs assigned to units transferred to the next department in December were

a. $1,664.
b. $1,600.
c. $1,513.
d. $1,484.

LO6
(Appendix 17A)   **SE17-6.**   During December, Krause Chemical Company had the following selected data concerning the manufacture of Xyzine, an industrial cleaner:

Production Flow	Physical Units	
Completed and transferred to the next department	100	
Add: Ending work-in-process inventory	10	(40% complete as to conversion)
Total units to account for	110	
Less: Beginning work-in-process inventory	20	(60% complete as to conversion)
Units started during December.	90	

All materials are added at the beginning of processing in this department, and conversion costs are added uniformly during the process. The beginning work-in-process inventory had $120 of raw materials and $180 of conversion costs incurred. Materials added during December was $540 and conversion costs of $1,484 were incurred. Krause uses the first-in, first-out (FIFO) process-costing method. The equivalent units of production used to calculate conversion costs for December were

a.   110 units.
b.   104 units.
c.   100 units.
d.   92 units.

SE17-7.   Jones Corporation uses a first-in, first-out (FIFO) process costing system. Jones has the following unit information for the month of August:

LO6
(Appendix 17A)

	Units
Beginning work-in-process inventory, 100% complete	
for materials, 75% complete for conversion cost	10,000
Units completed and transferred out	90,000
Ending work-in-process inventory, 100% complete	
for materials, 60% complete for conversion costs	8,000

The number of equivalent units of production for conversion costs for the month of August is

a.   87,300.
b.   88,000.
c.   92,300.
d.   92,700.

EXERCISES—SET A

E17-1A.   **Equivalent Units Calculations—Weighted Average Method**   Ferris Corporation makes a powdered rug shampoo in two sequential departments, Compounding and Drying. Materials are added at the beginning of the process in the Compounding Department. Conversion costs are added evenly throughout each process. Ferris uses the weighted average method of process costing. In the Compounding Department, beginning work-in-process was 6,000 pounds (70% processed), 38,000 pounds were started in process, 36,000 pounds transferred out, and ending work-in-process was 60% processed.
     Calculate equivalent units for March 2019 for the Compounding Department.

LO3

E17-2A.   **Equivalent Units Calculations—Weighted Average Method**   The following are selected operating data for Jackson Company's Blending Department for April 2019. Tinting and packaging operations are carried out subsequently in other departments.

LO3

Beginning inventory	4,000 units, 60% complete
Started and completed	68,000 units
Ending inventory.	6,000 units, 30% complete

Calculate the equivalent units completed using the weighted average method, assuming that the materials are added at the beginning of the process and conversion costs are incurred evenly throughout.

LO3, 4 **E17-3A.** **Equivalent Units and Product Cost Report—Weighted Average Method** In its first month's operations (January 2019), Schramski Company's Department 1 incurred charges of $120,000 for direct materials (10,000 units), $29,875 for direct labor, and $58,000 for manufacturing overhead. At month-end, 9,000 units had been finished and transferred out. The remaining units were finished with respect to materials but only 25% complete with respect to conversion costs.

Assuming Schramski uses the weighted average method and that materials are added at the beginning of the process and conversion costs occur evenly, compute the following:

a. The equivalent units of materials and conversion costs.
b. The cost per equivalent unit of materials and conversion costs.
c. The total cost assigned to the units transferred out.
d. The total cost assigned to the ending inventory.
e. Prove that your solutions to requirements (c) and (d) sum to the total costs to be accounted for.

LO3, 4 **E17-4A.** **Equivalent Units and Product Cost Report—Weighted Average Method** The following data (and annotations) are for the work-in-process account of the first of Johnson Company's four departments used in manufacturing its only product for October 2019.

Work-in-Process—Department 1	
Beginning balance (2,000 units, 70% complete)	
Direct materials.	$ 15,500
Conversion costs	9,600
Transferred to Department 2: (20,000 units)	(a)
Direct materials (21,000 units)	157,000
Direct labor.	145,200
Manufacturing overhead.	48,135
Ending balance [(b) units, 25% complete]	(c)

Assuming that Johnson uses the weighted average method and that materials are added at the beginning of the process and conversion costs are incurred evenly throughout, solve for the three missing numbers.

LO3, 4 **E17-5A.** **Equivalent Units and Product Cost Report—Weighted Average Method** The following data (and annotations) are for Joyner Company's processing department work-in-process account for the month of June 2019:

Beginning inventory (700 units, 40% complete)	
Direct materials.	$ 2,905
Conversion costs	7,942
Current period	
Direct materials (5,000 units)	35,000
Direct labor.	59,600
Manufacturing overhead applied.	37,800

Joyner uses the weighted average method. Materials are added at the beginning of the process and conversion costs are incurred evenly throughout. Ending work-in-process is composed of 900 units, 70% complete. Compute the following:

a. Equivalent units for materials and conversion.
b. Cost per equivalent unit for materials and conversion.
c. Total cost assigned to the units transferred out.

LO5 **E17-6A.** **Cost Flows Through Journal Entries** The Mixing Department performs a series of processes in which a fluid chemical is concentrated. Records indicate that the Mixing Department has been charged with $64,000 of direct labor costs. The manufacturing overhead rate is 150% of direct labor costs. Beginning work-in-process was $224,000, and ending work-in-process totaled $34,000. One-half of this period's completed products is sold on account at a price equal to 160% of its cost.

Prepare journal entries to record (1) various costs charged to the Mixing Department this period, (2) transfer of this period's completed product, and (3) sale of one-half of this period's production.

E17-7A. **Equivalent Units Calculations—FIFO Method** Ferris Corporation makes a powdered rug shampoo in two sequential departments, Compounding and Drying. Materials are added at the beginning of the process in the Compounding Department. Conversion costs are added evenly throughout each process. Ferris uses the FIFO method of process costing. In the Compounding Department, beginning work-in-process was 6,000 pounds (70% processed), 38,000 pounds were started in process, 36,000 pounds transferred out, and ending work-in-process was 60% processed.

LO6
(Appendix 17A)

Calculate equivalent units for March 2019 for the Compounding Department.

E17-8A. **Equivalent Units Calculations—FIFO Method** The following selected operating data are for Jackson Company's Blending Department for the month of April 2019. Tinting and packaging operations are carried out subsequently in other departments.

LO6
(Appendix 17A)

Beginning inventory	4,000 units, 60% complete
Started and completed	68,000 units
Ending inventory	6,000 units, 30% complete

Calculate the equivalent units accomplished using the FIFO method, assuming that the materials are added at the beginning of the process and conversion costs are incurred evenly throughout.

E17-9A. **Equivalent Units and Product Cost Report—FIFO Method** In its first month's operations (January 2019), Allred Company's Department 1 incurred charges of $120,000 for direct materials (10,000 units), $33,000 for direct labor, and $58,000 for manufacturing overhead. At month-end, 8,800 units had been finished and transferred out. The remaining units were finished with respect to materials but only 25% complete with respect to conversion costs.

LO6, 7
(Appendix 17A)

Assuming Allred uses the FIFO method and that materials are added at the beginning of the process and conversion costs occur evenly, compute the following:

a. The equivalent units for material and conversion.
b. The cost per equivalent unit for materials and conversion.
c. The total cost assigned to the units transferred out.
d. The total cost assigned to the ending inventory.
e. Prove that your solutions to requirements (c) and (d) sum to the total costs to be accounted for.

E17-10A. **Equivalent Units and Product Cost Report—FIFO Method** The following data (and annotations) are for the work-in-process account of the first of Crocker Company's four departments used in manufacturing its only product for October 2019.

LO6, 7
(Appendix 17A)

Work-in-Process—Department 1	
Beginning balance (2,000 units, 70% complete)	$ 25,100
Transferred to Department 2: (20,000 units)	(a)
Direct materials (21,000 units)	157,500
Direct labor	145,200
Manufacturing overhead	48,300
Ending balance [(b) units, 25% complete]	(c)

Assuming that Crocker uses the FIFO method and that materials are added at the beginning of the process and conversion costs are incurred evenly throughout, solve for the three missing numbers.

E17-11A. **Equivalent Units and Product Cost Assignment—FIFO Method** The following data (and annotations) are related to the June 2019 charges appearing in the work-in-process account for Sutter Company's first processing department:

LO6, 7
(Appendix 17A)

Beginning inventory (700 units, 40% complete)	
Direct materials	$ 5,780
Conversion costs	5,000
Current period	
Direct materials (5,000 units)	50,000
Direct labor	59,600
Manufacturing overhead applied	22,800

Sutter uses the FIFO method. Direct materials are added at the beginning of the process and conversion costs are incurred evenly throughout. Ending work-in-process totals 900 units, 70% complete. Compute the following:

a. Equivalent units for direct materials and conversion costs.
b. Cost per equivalent unit for direct materials and conversion costs.
c. Total cost assigned to the units transferred out.

EXERCISES—SET B

LO3 **E17-1B. Equivalent Units Calculations—Weighted Average Method** Terrace Corporation makes an industrial cleaner in two sequential departments, Compounding and Drying. All materials are added at the beginning of the process in the Compounding Department. Conversion costs are added evenly throughout each process. Terrace uses the weighted average method of process costing. In the Compounding Department, beginning work-in-process was 2,000 pounds (60% processed), 36,000 pounds were started, 34,000 pounds were transferred out, and ending work-in-process was 70% processed.

Calculate equivalent units for the Compounding Department for August 2019.

LO3 **E17-2B. Equivalent Units Calculations—Weighted Average Method** The following are selected operating data for Jackson Company's Blending Department for November 2019. Painting and packaging operations are carried out subsequently in other departments.

Beginning inventory	5,000 units, 70% complete
Started and completed	62,000 units
Ending inventory.	3,000 units, 40% complete

Calculate the equivalent units finished for the month of November using the weighted average method, assuming that the materials are added at the beginning of the process and conversion costs are incurred evenly throughout.

LO3, 4 **E17-3B. Equivalent Units and Product Cost Assignment—Weighted Average Method** In its first month of operations (May 2019), Holland Company's Department 1 incurred charges of $72,000 for direct materials (9,000 units), $38,700 for direct labor, and $13,950 for manufacturing overhead. At month-end, 7,500 units had been finished and transferred out. Those remaining were finished with respect to materials but only 40% finished with respect to conversion.

Assuming Holland uses the weighted average method and that materials are added at the beginning of the process and conversion occurs evenly, compute the following:

a. The equivalent units for materials and conversion.
b. The cost per equivalent unit for materials and conversion.
c. The total cost assigned to the units transferred out.
d. The total cost assigned to the ending inventory.
e. Prove that your solutions to requirements (c) and (d) sum to the total costs to be accounted for.

LO3, 4 **E17-4B. Equivalent Units and Product Cost Report—Weighted Average Method** The following data (and annotations) for March 2019 are for the work-in-process account of the first of Eyring Company's four departments used in manufacturing its only product.

Work-in-Process—Department 1	
Beginning balance (3,000 units, 40% complete)	
Direct materials.	$13,350
Conversion costs	5,600
Transferred to Department 2: (23,000 units)	(a)
Direct materials (24,000 units)	96,000
Direct labor.	77,300
Manufacturing overhead.	34,700
Ending balance [(b) units, 25% complete]	(c)

Assuming that Eyring uses the weighted average method, that materials are added at the beginning of the process and that conversion costs are incurred evenly throughout, solve for the three missing numbers.

E17-5B. **Equivalent Units and Product Cost Report—Weighted Average Method** The following data (and annotations) are for Nelson Company's processing department work-in-process account for the month of September 2019:

Beginning inventory (1,500 units, 70% complete)	
Direct materials.	$22,000
Conversion costs	10,000
Current period	
Direct materials (6,000 units)	50,000
Direct labor	41,000
Manufacturing overhead applied.	65,440

Nelson uses the weighted average method. Materials are added at the beginning of the process and conversion costs are incurred evenly throughout. Ending work-in-process is composed of 1,000 units, 60% complete. Compute the following:

a.   Equivalent units for direct materials and conversion.
b.   Cost per equivalent unit for direct materials and conversion.
c.   Total cost assigned to the units transferred out.

E17-6B. **Cost Flows Through Journal Entries** The Mixing Department performs a series of processes in which a fluid chemical is concentrated. Records indicate that the Mixing Department has been charged with $50,000 of direct labor costs. The manufacturing overhead rate is 170% of direct labor costs. Beginning work-in-process was $170,000, and ending work-in-process totaled $36,000. One-half of this period's completed products is sold on account at a price equal to 150% of its cost.

    Prepare journal entries to record (1) various costs charged to the Mixing Department this period, (2) transfer of this period's completed product, and (3) sale of one-half of this period's production.

E17-7B. **Equivalent Units Calculations—FIFO Method** Terrace Corporation makes an industrial cleaner in two sequential departments, Compounding and Drying. All materials are added at the beginning of the process in the Compounding Department. Conversion costs are added evenly throughout each process. Terrace uses the FIFO method of process costing. In the Compounding Department, beginning work-in-process was 2,000 pounds (60% processed), 36,000 pounds were started, 34,000 pounds were transferred out, and ending work-in-process was 70% processed.

    Calculate equivalent units for the Compounding Department for August 2019.

E17-8B. **Equivalent Units Calculations—FIFO Method** The following are selected operating data for Jackson Company's Blending Department for November 2019. Painting and packaging operations are carried out subsequently in other departments.

Beginning inventory	5,000 units, 70% complete
Started and completed	62,000 units
Ending inventory.	3,000 units, 40% complete

    Calculate the equivalent units finished for the month of November using the FIFO method, assuming that the materials are added at the beginning of the process and conversion costs are incurred evenly throughout.

E17-9B. **Equivalent Units and Product Cost Report—FIFO Method** In its first month of operations (May 2019), Allred Company's Department 1 incurred charges of $72,000 for direct materials (9,000 units), $38,700 for direct labor, and $13,500 for manufacturing overhead. At month-end, 8,500 units had been finished and transferred out. Those units remaining were finished with respect to materials but only 40% finished with respect to conversion.

    Assuming Allred uses the FIFO method and that materials are added at the beginning of the process and conversion costs are incurred evenly throughout the period, compute the following:

a.   The equivalent units for materials and conversion costs.
b.   The cost per equivalent unit for materials and conversion costs.
c.   The total cost assigned to the units transferred out.

d. The total cost assigned to the ending inventory.

e. Prove that your solutions to requirements (c) and (d) sum to the total costs to be accounted for.

LO6, 7
(Appendix 17A)

E17-10B. Equivalent Units and Product Cost Report—FIFO Method The following data (and annotations) for March 2019 are for the work-in-process account of the first of Olympus Company's four departments used in manufacturing its only product.

Work-in-Process—Department 1	
Beginning balance (3,000 units, 40% complete)	$18,200
Transferred to Department 2: (23,000 units)	(a)
Direct materials (24,000 units)	96,000
Direct labor.	77,300
Manufacturing overhead.	36,700
Ending balance [___(b)___ units, 25% complete]	(c)

Assuming that Olympus uses the FIFO method, that materials are added at the beginning of the process and that conversion costs are incurred evenly throughout, solve for the three missing numbers.

LO6, 7
(Appendix 17A)

E17-11B. Equivalent Units and Product Cost Report—FIFO Method Following are the September 2019 charges (and certain annotations) appearing in the work-in-process account for Empire Company's processing department:

Beginning inventory (1,500 units, 70% complete)	
Direct materials.	$21,950
Conversion costs	10,000
Current period	
Direct materials (6,000 units)	72,000
Direct labor	32,500
Manufacturing overhead applied.	52,200

Empire uses the FIFO method. Materials are added at the beginning of the process and conversion costs are incurred evenly throughout. Ending work-in-process is composed of 1,000 units, 60% complete. Compute the following:

a. Equivalent units for direct materials and conversion.

b. Cost per equivalent unit or units transferred in and conversion.

c. Total cost assigned to the units transferred out.

PROBLEMS—SET A

LO3, 4

P17-1A. Calculate Equivalent Units, Unit Costs, and Transferred Costs—Weighted Average Method Canfield Manufacturing, Inc., operates a plant that produces its own regionally marketed Spicy Steak Sauce. The sauce is produced in two processes, blending and bottling. In the Blending Department, all materials are added at the start of the process, and labor and overhead are incurred evenly throughout the process. Canfield uses the weighted average method. The following data from the Work-in-Process—Blending Department account for January 2019 are missing a few items:

Work-in-Process—Blending Department	
January 1 inventory (5,000 gallons, 60% processed)	
Direct materials.	$ 12,000
Conversion costs	5,900
Transferred to Bottling Department (60,000 gallons)	
January charges:	
Direct materials (61,000 gallons)	153,000
Direct labor.	73,600
Manufacturing overhead.	42,480
January 31 inventory (_____ gallons, 70% processed)	

Required

Assuming Canfield uses the weighted average method in process costing, calculate the following amounts for the Blending Department:

a.   Number of units in the January 31 inventory.
b.   Equivalent units for materials and conversion costs.
c.   January cost per equivalent unit for materials and conversion costs.
d.   Cost of the units transferred to the Bottling Department.
e.   Cost of the incomplete units in the January 31 inventory.

P17-2A.   Calculate Equivalent Units, Unit Costs, and Transferred Costs—Weighted Average Method   Monroe Company processes a food seasoning powder through its Compounding and Packaging departments. In the Compounding Department, direct materials are added at the beginning of the process, and direct labor and manufacturing overhead are incurred evenly throughout the process. Monroe uses the weighted average method. Costs in the Compounding Department can be summarized as follows:

LO3, 4

Inventory, August 1, 2019 (2,000 units, 40% complete)	
Direct materials.	$ 980
Conversion costs	4,100
Current period (31,000 units started)	
Direct materials.	33,010
Direct labor	62,560
Manufacturing overhead.	75,789
	$171,359

At August 31, 2019, 3,000 units were in process, 30% complete with respect to conversion costs.

Required

Calculate the following for the Compounding Department:

a.   Equivalent units for materials and conversion costs during August.
b.   Costs per equivalent unit for materials and conversion costs.
c.   Total cost of units transferred to the Packaging Department.
d.   Inventory cost at August 31, 2019.

P17-3A.   Product Cost Report—Weighted Average Method   Riley Manufacturing Corporation produces a cosmetic product in three consecutive processes. The costs of Department 1 for May 2019 were as follows:

LO3, 4

Cost of beginning inventory		
Direct materials.		$ 9,800
Conversion costs		16,480
Costs added in Department 1:		
Direct materials.	$295,120	
Direct labor	298,550	
Manufacturing overhead.	203,130	796,800

Department 1 handled the following units during May:

Units in process, May 1, 2019	2,000
Units started in Department 1.	40,000
Units transferred to Department 2	39,000
Units in process, May 31, 2019	3,000

On average, the May 1 units were 30% complete. The May 31 units were 60% complete. Materials are added at the beginning of the process, and conversion costs occur evenly throughout the process in Department 1. Riley uses the weighted average method for process costing.

Required

Prepare the product cost report for Department 1 for May.

LO3, 4   P17-4A.   Product Cost Report—Weighted Average Method Bath Manufacturing Company uses the weighted average method for process costing. Bath produces processed food products that pass through three sequential departments. The costs for Department 1 for September 2019 were as follows:

Cost of beginning inventory:	
Materials	$ 11,850
Conversion	20,544
	$ 32,394
Costs added in Department 1 during September:	
Direct materials	$340,150
Direct labor	341,370
Manufacturing overhead	245,990
	$927,510
Department 2 handled the following units during September:	
Units in process, September 1	2,000
Units started in Department 1	48,000
Units transferred out to Department 2	46,000
Units in process, September 30	4,000

On average, the September 1 units were 30% complete, and the September 30 units were 60% complete. Materials are added at the beginning of the process and conversion costs occur evenly throughout the process in Department 1.

Required

Prepare the product cost report for September for Department 1.

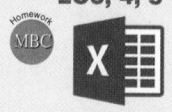

LO3, 4, 5   P17-5A.   Two Departments, Journal Entries with Supporting Calculations—Weighted Average Method (Note: This problem includes two departments. The second department may be beyond the scope of most classes. Instructors may choose to assign only the requirements related to Department 1.)

Patterson Laboratories, Inc., produces one of its products in two successive departments. All materials are added at the beginning of the process in Department 1; no materials are used in Department 2. Conversion costs are incurred evenly in both departments. Patterson uses the weighted average method for process costing. January 1, 2019, inventory account balances are as follows:

Materials inventory	$30,000
Work-in-process—Department 1 (3,000 units, 30% complete)	
Direct materials	4,560
Conversion costs	10,640
Work-in-process—Department 2 (3,550 units, 40% complete)	43,439
Finished goods inventory (2,000 units @ $16)	32,000

During January, the following transactions occurred:

1. Purchased materials on account, $90,000.
2. Placed $84,000 of materials into process in Department 1. This $84,000 represents 24,000 units of materials.
3. Distributed total payroll costs: $108,116 of direct labor to Department 1, $62,700 of direct labor to Department 2, and $51,000 of indirect labor to Manufacturing Overhead.
4. Incurred other actual manufacturing overhead costs, $81,000. (Credit Other Accounts.)
5. Applied overhead to the two processing departments: $88,000 to Department 1 and $43,900 to Department 2.
6. Transferred 25,000 completed units from Department 1 to Department 2. The 2,000 units remaining in Department 1 were 20% completed with respect to conversion costs.
7. Transferred 26,000 completed units from Department 2 to finished goods inventory. The 2,550 units remaining in Department 2 were 70% completed with respect to conversion costs.
8. Sold 20,000 units on account at $27 per unit. Patterson uses weighted average inventory costing procedures for the finished goods inventory.

Required

a. Record the January transactions in general journal form for Department 1 and Department 2.
b. Prepare a product cost report (with its supporting calculations) for Department 1.
c. Prepare a product cost report (with its supporting calculations) for Department 2.
d. Determine the balances remaining in the Materials Inventory account, in each work-in-process account, and in the Finished Goods Inventory account.

P17-6A.   Calculate Equivalent Units, Unit Costs, and Transferred Costs—FIFO Method Gaston Manu- facturing, Inc., operates a plant that produces its own regionally marketed Spicy Steak Sauce. The sauce is produced in two processes, blending and bottling. In the Blending Department, all materi- als are added at the start of the process, and labor and overhead are incurred evenly throughout the process. Gaston uses the FIFO method. The following data from the Work-in-Process—Blending Department account for January 2019 are missing a few items:

LO6, 7
(Appendix 17A)

Work-in-Process—Blending Department	
January 1 inventory (5,000 gallons, 60% processed)	$17,900
Transferred to Bottling Department (65,000 gallons)	————
January charges:	
Direct materials (66,000 gallons)	161,700
Direct labor.	79,400
Manufacturing overhead.	53,000
January 31 inventory (———— gallons, 70% processed)	————

Required

Assuming Gaston uses the FIFO method in process costing, calculate the following amounts for the Blending Department:

a. Number of units in the January 31 inventory.
b. Equivalent units for materials and conversion costs.
c. January cost per equivalent unit for materials and conversion costs.
d. Cost of the units transferred to the Bottling Department.
e. Cost of the incomplete units in the January 31 inventory

P17-7A.   Calculate Equivalent Units, Unit Costs, and Transferred Costs—FIFO Method Commodore Company processes a food seasoning powder through its Compounding and Packaging departments. In the Compounding Department, direct materials are added at the beginning of the process, and direct labor and manufacturing overhead are incurred evenly throughout the process. Arrow uses the FIFO method. August 2019 costs in the Compounding Department can be summarized as follows:

LO6, 7
(Appendix 17A)

Inventory, August 1 (2,000 units, 40% complete)	$ 5,080
Direct materials (31,000 units)	32,550
Direct labor.	62,560
Manufacturing overhead.	75,900
	$176,090

At August 31, 3,000 units were in process, 30% complete with respect to conversion costs.

Required

Calculate the following for the Compounding Department:

a. Equivalent units during August.
b. Costs per equivalent unit.
c. Total cost of units transferred to finished goods inventory.
d. Inventory cost at August 31.

LO7
(Appendix 17A)

P17-8A. Product Cost Report—FIFO Method Reston Manufacturing Corporation produces a cosmetic product in three consecutive processes. The costs of Department 1 for May 2019 were as follows:

Cost of beginning inventory		$606,390
Costs added in Department 1:		
Direct materials.	$80,400	
Direct labor	81,550	
Manufacturing overhead	55,130	217,080

Department 1 handled the following units during May:

Units in process, May 1	2,000
Units started in Department 1.	40,000
Units transferred to Department 2	39,000
Units in process, May 31	3,000

On average, the May 1 units were 30% complete; the May 31 units were 60% complete. Materials are added at the beginning of the process and conversion costs occur evenly throughout the process in Department 1. Reston uses the FIFO method for process costing.

Required

Prepare the product cost report for Department 1 for May.

PROBLEMS—SET B

LO3, 4

P17-1B. Calculate Equivalent Units, Unit Costs, and Transferred Costs—Weighted Average Method Chelsea Manufacturing, Inc., operates a plant that produces its own regionally marketed Super Salad Dressing. The dressing is produced in two processes, blending and bottling. In the Blending Department, all materials are added at the beginning of the process, and labor and overhead are incurred evenly throughout the process. Chelsea uses the weighted average method. The Work-in-Process—Blending Department account for January 2019 follows:

Work-in-Process—Blending Department	
January 1 inventory (4,000 gallons, 75% finished)	
Direct materials.	$ 31,200
Conversion costs	8,800
Transferred to Bottling Department (70,000 gallons)	
January charges:	
Direct materials (71,000 gallons)	568,800
Direct labor	164,000
Manufacturing overhead.	184,900
January 31 inventory (_____ gallons, 60% processed)	

Required

Calculate the following amounts for the Blending Department:

a. Number of units in the January 31 inventory.

b. Equivalent units for materials cost and conversion costs.

c. January cost per equivalent unit for materials and conversion costs.

d. Cost of the units transferred to the Bottling Department.

e. Cost of the incomplete units in the January 31 inventory.

LO3, 4

P17-2B. Calculate Equivalent Units, Unit Costs, and Transferred Costs—Weighted Average Method Evans Company processes a scouring powder through its Compounding Department and Packaging Department. In the Compounding Department, direct materials are added at the beginning of the process, and direct labor and manufacturing overhead are incurred evenly throughout the process. Evans uses the weighted average method. Costs charged to the Compounding Department in October 2019 follow:

Inventory, October 1 (5,000 units, 25% complete)		
Direct materials.		$ 2,400
Conversion costs		1,850
Current period (82,000 units started):		
Direct materials.		171,600
Direct labor		67,440
Manufacturing overhead.		71,470
		$310,510

At October 31, 7,000 units were in process, 40% completed.

Required

Calculate the following for the Compounding Department:

a. Equivalent units during October.
b. Costs per equivalent unit.
c. Total cost of units transferred to the Packaging Department.
d. Inventory cost at October 31.

P17-3B. Product Cost Report—Weighted Average Method Salanger Manufacturing Corporation produces a dandruff shampoo in three consecutive processes. The costs of Department 1 for June 2019 were as follows:

LO3, 4

Cost of beginning inventory		
Direct materials.		$ 5,500
Conversion costs		12,740
Costs added in Department 1:		
Direct materials.	$223,390	
Direct labor	358,300	
Manufacturing overhead.	155,269	736,959

Department 1 handled the following units during June:

Units in process, June 1.	2,000
Units started in Department 1.	45,000
Units transferred to Department 2	46,000
Units in process, June 30.	1,000

On average, the June 1 units were 40% complete; the June 30 units were 70% complete. Direct materials are added at the beginning of the process, and conversion costs occur evenly throughout the process in Department 1. Salanger uses the weighted average method for process costing.

Required

Prepare the product cost report for Department 1 for June.

P17-4B. Equivalent Units and Product Cost Report—Weighted Average Method Summers Manufacturing Corporation produces chemical products using a continual process. Summers uses the weighted average method for process costing. All manufacturing is accomplished in one department. Materials are added at the beginning of the process while conversion costs are incurred evenly throughout the process.

LO3, 4

The work-in-process inventory at the beginning of February 2019 consisted of 10,000 gallons that were 20% complete. The work-in-process at the end of February consisted of 15,000 gallons that were 40% complete. During February 195,000 gallons were transferred to finished goods.

The beginning inventory contained $90,000 of materials and $30,000 of conversion costs. Product costs incurred during February consisted of $2,010,000 of materials and $3,186,000 of conversion costs.

Required

Calculate equivalent units, cost per equivalent unit, and prepare the product cost report for Summers Manufacturing Corporation for the month of February.

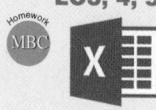

LO3, 4, 5

P17-5B. **Two Departments, Journal Entries with Supporting Calculations—Weighted Average Method** (Note: This problem includes two departments. The second department may be beyond the scope of most classes. Instructors may choose to assign only the requirements related to Department 1.)

Parker Laboratories, Inc., produces one of its products in two successive departments. All materials are added at the beginning of the process in Department 1. No materials are used in Department 2. Conversion costs are incurred evenly in both departments. August 1, 2019, inventory account balances are as follows:

Materials inventory	$15,000
Work-in-process—Department 1 (6,000 units, 25% finished)	
Direct materials	11,500
Conversion costs	18,750
Work-in-process—Department 2 (3,500 units, 35% finished)	41,000
Finished goods inventory (4,000 units @ $12.50)	50,000

During August, the following transactions occurred:

1. Purchased materials on account, $58,000.
2. Placed $63,300 (16,000 units) of materials into process in Department 1.
3. Distributed total payroll costs: $83,770 of direct labor to Department 1, $42,300 of direct labor to Department 2, and $19,100 of indirect labor to Manufacturing Overhead.
4. Incurred other actual manufacturing overhead costs, $21,200. (Credit Other Accounts.)
5. Applied overhead to the two processing departments: Department 1, $21,080, Department 2, $17,900.
6. Transferred 20,000 completed units from Department 1 to Department 2. The 2,000 units remaining in Department 1 were 30% completed with respect to conversion costs.
7. Transferred 15,000 completed units from Department 2 to Finished Goods Inventory. The 8,500 units remaining in Department 2 were 40% completed with respect to conversion costs.
8. Sold 13,000 units on account at $24 per unit. Parker uses weighted average inventory costing for finished goods inventory.

Required

a. Record the August transactions in general journal form for Department 1 and Department 2.
b. Prepare a product cost report (with its supporting calculations) for Department 1.
c. Prepare a product cost report (with its supporting calculations) for Department 2.
d. Determine the balances remaining in the Materials Inventory account, in each work-in-process account, and in the Finished Goods Inventory account.

LO6, 7
(Appendix 17A)

P17-6B. **Calculate Equivalent Units, Unit Costs, and Transferred Costs—FIFO Method** Kipling Manufacturing, Inc., operates a plant that produces its own regionally marketed Super Salad Dressing. The dressing is produced in two processes, blending and bottling. In the Blending Department, all materials are added at the beginning of the process, and labor and overhead are incurred evenly throughout the process. Kipling uses the FIFO method. The Work-in-Process—Blending Department account for January 2019 follows:

Work-in-Process—Blending Department	
January 1 inventory (4,000 gallons, 75% finished)	$ 40,000
Transferred to Bottling Department (70,000 gallons)	
January charges:	
Direct materials (71,000 gallons)	568,000
Direct labor	164,000
Manufacturing overhead	186,000
January 31 inventory (_____ gallons, 60% processed)	

Required

Calculate the following amounts for the Blending Department:

a. Number of units in the January 31 inventory.
b. Equivalent units for materials cost and conversion costs.

c.   January cost per equivalent unit for materials and conversion costs.
d.   Cost of the units transferred to the Bottling Department.
e.   Cost of the incomplete units in the January 31 inventory.

P17-7B.   Calculate Equivalent Units, Unit Costs, and Transferred Costs—FIFO Method Kipper Company
processes a scouring powder through its Compounding Department and Packaging Department. In
the Compounding Department, direct materials are added at the beginning of the process, and direct
labor and manufacturing overhead are incurred evenly throughout the process. Kipper uses the FIFO
method. Costs charged to the Compounding Department in October 2019 follow:

LO6, 7
(Appendix 17A)

Inventory, October 1 (5,000 units, 25% complete)	$ 4,250
Direct material (82,000 units)	246,000
Direct labor	31,770
Manufacturing overhead	33,470
	$315,490

At October 31, 7,000 units were in process, 40% completed.

Required
Calculate the following for the Compounding Department:

a.   Equivalent units during October.
b.   Costs per equivalent unit.
c.   Total cost of units transferred to the Packaging Department.
d.   Inventory cost at October 31.

P17-8B.   Product Cost Report—FIFO Method Chauncer Manufacturing Corporation produces a dandruff
shampoo in three consecutive processes. The costs of Department 1 for June 2019 were as follows:

LO7
(Appendix 17A)

Cost of beginning inventory		$ 18,240
Costs added in Department 1:		
Direct material	$219,600	
Direct labor	361,300	
Manufacturing overhead	155,993	736,893

Department 1 handled the following units during June:

Units in process, June 1	2,000
Units started in Department 1	45,000
Units transferred to Department 2	46,000
Units in process, June 30	1,000

On average, the June 1 units were 40% complete. The June 30 units were 70% complete. Materials
are added at the beginning of the process and conversion costs occur evenly throughout the process
in Department 1. Chauncer uses the FIFO method for process costing.

Required
Prepare the product cost report for Department 1 for June.

EXTENDING YOUR KNOWLEDGE

EYK17-1.   Ethics Case Sweet Fragrances Company uses process costing to account for the manufacture of
its perfume. The factory consists of three departments: Blending, Bottling, and Packaging.

   The production manager of the Bottling department, Janine Post, has recommended that her
department not be charged for new labels that are more elaborate and expensive than those used
in previous years. The new labels were designed as a tie-in for the marketing and advertising campaigns. Post recommends that the costs of the labels be charged to advertising expense. This would
result in slightly lower product costs charged to the Bottling department than last year.

   The company has instituted a bonus plan for all managers based on keeping costs within a range
of previous years' costs.

Sam Block, the accounting manager, reviews all recommendations by all managers before they are presented to top management.

Required

What ethical considerations may arise from Janine Post's recommendation? What alternative recommendations might be made?

ANSWERS TO SELF-STUDY QUESTIONS:

1. c, (pp. 806–807)   2. b, (p. 807)   3. a, (pp. 825–827)

YOUR TURN! SOLUTIONS

Solution 17.1

Where do the units come from?		Where do the units go?	
Beginning inventory . . .	100	Complete/transferred . . .	800
Started	790	Ending inventory	90
Total	890	Total	890

Solution 17.2

Remember that when using the weighted average method, the question is "what percentage of the work has been completed?"

Where do the units come from?		Where do the units go?		% Work Done?	Direct Materials	% Work Done?	Conversion Costs
					Equivalent Units		
Beginning inventory . . .	100	Complete/transferred . . .	800	100%	800	100%	800
Started	790	Ending inventory.	90	100%	90	70%	63
Total	890	Total	890		890		863

Solution 17.3

Where do the costs come from?	Total	Direct Materials	Conversion Costs
Beginning inventory	$ 4,883	$ 3,390	$ 1,493
Current	34,654	19,750	14,904
Total costs to account for	$39,537	$23,140	$16,397
÷ Total equivalent units		890	863
Average cost/unit		$ 26.00	$ 19.00

Solution 17.4

Materials.	[800 EU × $26.00]	20,800
Conversion costs	[800 EU × $19.00]	15,200
Total cost of goods manufactured		$36,000

Solution 17.5

Materials.	[90 EU × $26.00]	2,340
Conversion costs	[63 EU × $19.00]	1,197
Total cost of goods manufactured		$3,537

Comprehensive Solution to Your Turn 17.1–17.5

Flow of the Units and Equivalent Units Calculation

Step 2: Calculate the Equivalent Units

Step 1: Visualize the Physical Flow of the Units

Where do the units come from?		Where do the units go?		% Work Done?	Direct Materials	% Work Done?	Conversion Costs
					Equivalent Units		
Beginning inventory...	100	Compl./transferred ...	800	100%	800	100%	800
Started	790	Ending inventory.	90	100%	90	70%	63
Total	890	Total	890		890		863

Product Cost Report
January Production

Step 3: Determine Per-Unit Costs

Where do the costs come from?	Total	Dir. Mat.	Conv. Costs
Beginning inventory	$ 4,883	$ 3,390	$ 1.493
Current	34,654	19,750	14,904
Total costs to account for	$39,537	$23,140	$16,397
÷ Total equivalent units..............		890	863
Average cost/equivalent unit		**$ 26.00**	**$ 19.00**

Where do the costs go?

Step 4: Calculate the Cost of Goods Manufactured

Complete/transferred:			
Materials.......................	$20,800	**[800 EU × $26.00]**	
Conversion costs	15,200		**[800 EU × $19.00]**
Cost of goods manuactured	$36,000		

Step 5: Calculate the Cost of the Ending Work-in-Process Inventory

Ending inventory:			
Materials.......................	$ 2,340	**[90 EU × $26.00]**	
Conversion costs	1,197		**[63 EU × $19.00]**
Cost of ending inventory...........	3,537		
Total costs allocated................	$39,537		

Solution 17.6

Work-in-process.....................................	19,750	
Materials inventory		19,750
Work-in-process.....................................	9,500	
Wages payable.................................		9,500
Work-in-process.....................................	5,404	
Manufacturing overhead		5,404

Solution 17.7

Where do the units come from?		Where do the units go?	
		Complete/transferred . . .	
Beginning inventory . . .	100	Beginning inventory . .	100
		Started and compl. . . .	700
Started	790	Ending inventory	90
Total	890	Total	890

Solution 17.8

Remember that when using the FIFO method, the question is "what percentage of the work was completed during THIS PERIOD?"

Where do the units come from?		Where do the units go?		% in Jan.?	Direct Materials	% in Jan.?	Conversion Costs
					Equivalent Units		
		Complete/transferred:					
Beginning inventory	100	Beginning inventory	100	0%	0	65%	65
		Started and completed . . .	700	100%	700	100%	700
Started	790	Ending inventory	90	100%	90	70%	63
Total	890	Total	890		790		828

Solution 17.9

Where do the costs come from?	Total	Direct Materials	Conversion Costs
Beginning inventory	$ 4,883		
Current	34,654	$19,750	$14,904
Total costs to account for	$39,537		
÷ Total equivalent units		790	828
Average cost/unit		$ 25.00	$ 18.00

Solution 17.10

Beginning inventory:		
Costs incurred last period		$ 4,883
Costs incurred this period	[65 EU × $18.00]	1,170
Started and finished:		
Materials	[700 EU × $25.00]	17,500
Conversion costs	[700 EU × $18.00]	12,600
Total cost of goods manufactured		$36,153

Solution 17.11

Materials	[90 EU × $25.00]	2,250
Conversion costs	[63 EU × $18.00]	1,134
Total cost of goods manufactured		$3,384

Comprehensive Solution to Your Turn 17.7–17.11

Flow of the Units and Equivalent Units Calculation

Step 1: Visualize the Physical Flow of the Units

Step 2: Calculate the Equivalent Units

Where do the units come from?		Where do the units go? Compl./transferred		Equivalent Units			
				% in Jan.?	Materials	% in Jan.?	Conversion Costs
Beginning inventory. . .	100	Beginning inventory . .	100	0%	0	65%	65
		Started and compl. . . .	700	100%	700	100%	700
Started	790	Ending inventory.	90	100%	90	70%	63
Total	890	Total	890		790		828

Product Cost Report
January Production

Step 3: Determine Per-Unit Costs

Where do the costs come from?	Total	Dir. Mat.	Conv. Costs
Beginning inventory	$ 4,883		
Current	34,654	$19,750	$14,904
Total costs to account for	$39,537		
÷ Total equivalent units		790	828
Average cost/equivalent unit		$ 25.00	$ 18.00

Where do the costs go?

Step 4: Calculate the Cost of Goods Manufactured

Beginning inventory:			
Costs incurred last period	$4,883		
Costs incurred this period	1,170	[0 × $329.06]	[65 EU × $18.00]
Started and finished	30,100	[700 EU × $25.00]	[700 EU × $18.00]
Cost of goods manufactured		$36,153	

Step 5: Calculate the Cost of the Ending Work-in-Process Inventory

Ending inventory:			
Materials	$ 2,250	[90 EU × $25.00]	
Conversion costs	1,134		[63 EU × $18.00]
Cost of ending inventory		3,384	
Total costs allocated		$39,537	

Solution 17.12

Work-in-process	19,750	
Materials inventory		19,750
Work-in-process	9,500	
Wages payable		9,500
Work-in-process	5,404	
Manufacturing overhead		5,404

Chapter 18
Activity-Based Costing

Among its several responsibilities, the **California State Bar Association** regulates the professional conduct of the state's lawyers. The State Bar's discipline system is designed to protect the public from lawyers who violate the state's ethical code of professional conduct. The state's Business and Professions Code authorizes the State Bar to recover a portion of the costs of pursuing action against disciplined lawyers, including "charges determined by the State Bar to be 'reasonable costs' of investigation, hearing, and review." What constitutes "reasonable costs?"

To answer this question, the State Bar used activity-based costing (ABC) to determine the amount of "reasonable costs." Each of the State Bar offices (Office of Investigation, Office of Trials, etc.) is a "cost pool" that is allocated to a "product" (a type of case) based on a "cost driver" (a task performed). Although ABC is traditionally used to determine the cost of products, it can have application in a service setting as well.

This chapter explains how ABC can be used as a more precise method of measuring the overhead cost of products and services.

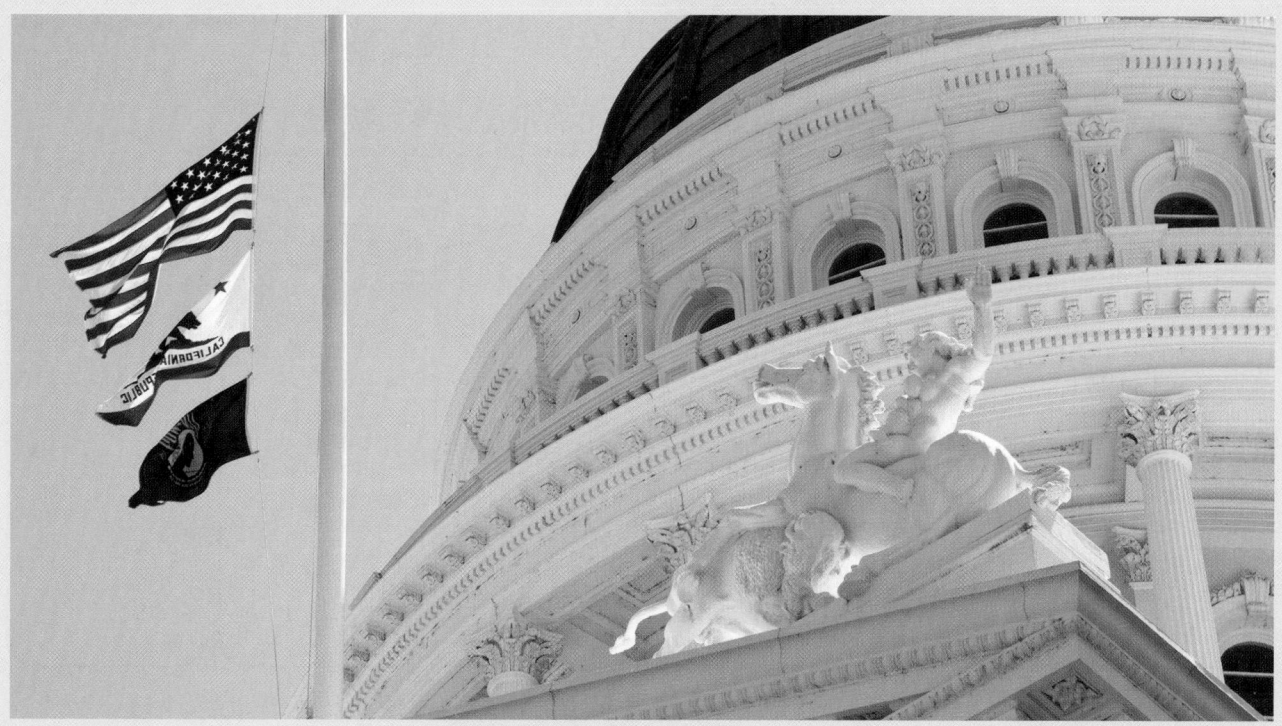

Road Map

LO	Learning Objective	Page	eLecture	Guided Example	Assignments
LO1	Explain the changes in the modern production environment that have affected cost structures.	858	E18-1		SS1, SE1
LO2	Understand the concept of activity-based costing (ABC) and how it is applied.	860	E18-2	YT18.1	SS2, Q1, Q2, Q3, Q4, Q5, SE2, E1A, E2A, E3A, E4A, E5A, E1B, E2B, E3B, E4B, E5B, P3A, P4A, P5A, P6A, P1B, P2B, P3B, P4B, P5B, P6B, P7B
LO3	Explain the difference between traditional company-wide and departmental overhead methods and ABC.	863	E18-3	YT18.2	SS3, Q6, SE3, SE4, SE5, SE6, SE7, SE8, SE9, E5A, E5B, P1A, P2A, P5A, P6A, P7A, P1B, P2B, P3B, P5B, P6B, P7B
LO4	Describe the implementation of an ABC system.	868	E18-4	YT18.3	SS4, Q7, P7A
LO5	Explain customer profitability analysis based on ABC.	869	E18-5	YT18.4	SS5, Q8, SE10, E6A, E6B, P8A, P9A, P8B
LO6	Explain the difference between ABC and activity-based management.	872	E18-6	YT18.5	SS6, Q9

UNDERSTANDING INDIRECT COSTS USING ACTIVITY-BASED COSTING

LO1 **Explain** the changes in the modern production environment that have affected cost structures.

Effective management of costs is a hallmark of sound financial management, and indirect costs (commonly referred to as overhead) are the most challenging costs to measure and manage. Direct costs, including direct materials and direct labor, can be readily traced to a job, product, or other unit of work. Indirect costs, which are typically incurred for the benefit of several different products or cost objects, are not as easily traced to specific units or projects. Managing indirect costs is a major concern of managers because this broad category of costs has become increasingly more significant over time.

Many companies that once thrived have failed, arguably, because they did not manage effectively a growing pool of indirect costs. You might say they failed because they did not fully understand their business or their business model. If a business's actual cost of producing and selling products is more than the revenues generated by those products, the business will not succeed in the long term.

It is well documented that for many years the **U.S. Postal Service (USPS)**, a service entity, has struggled with mounting losses while its competitors, **UPS** and **FedEx**, have thrived in a highly competitive marketplace. At a meeting of the President's Commission on the United States Postal Service (created to examine the problems of the USPS), the discussion focused on differences in the cost systems at the USPS and UPS. It was reported that the USPS cost system attributes only 58% of its operating costs to it various products, whereas UPS attributes 100% of its costs to its products. The UPS representative on the panel stated that UPS does not price any product below its full cost. With only 58% of its costs attributed to products, the USPS cannot know whether any of its products, individually, is making a profit.[1]

As global competition puts increasing pressure on companies to price products more competitively, cost management is increasingly important. Organizations and entities

---

[1] James A. Johnson and Harry J. Pearce, Co-chairs, "Minutes of Meeting of the President's Commission on the U.S. Postal Service," May 28, 2003, p3, http://www.ustreas.gov/offices/domestic-finance/usps/pdf/may_28_minutes.pdf.

such as UPS, Coca-Cola, IBM, the City of Indianapolis, and Toronto's Hospital for Sick Children have benefited greatly from a type of cost system referred to as **activity-based costing (ABC)**. In this chapter, we will define and discuss ABC systems, compare ABC with traditional costing systems, and demonstrate how ABC can be used to analyze customer profitability. Finally, we will introduce the notion of **activity-based management (ABM)**, which uses ABC information to better manage processes and activities within an organization.

Changing Cost Environment

As technology has advanced over the last century, there has been a fundamental shift in manufacturing organizations from labor-intensive to automated assembly processes. These changes have had a profound influence on the activities performed to meet customer needs and, consequently, the costs of producing goods and services.

At the beginning of the twentieth century, products had long life cycles, production procedures were relatively straightforward, production was labor intensive, and only limited numbers of related products were produced in a single plant. It was said of the Model T Ford that "you could have any color you wanted, as long as it was black." The largest cost elements of most manufactured goods were the cost of raw materials and the wages paid to production employees. Manufacturing overhead was a relatively small portion of the overall cost of manufacturing products.

The twentieth century saw an accelerating shift from traditional labor-based activities to production procedures requiring large investments in automated equipment. In the past, production employees used equipment to assist them in performing their jobs. Now employees spend considerable time scheduling, setting up, maintaining, and moving materials to and from equipment. They spend relatively little time on actual production. The equipment does the work, and the employees keep it running efficiently. Increased complexity of production procedures and an increase in the variety of products produced in a single facility have also caused a shift toward more support person-

nel and fewer production employees. The result is a significant increase in manufacturing overhead as a percentage of total product cost. This change in the typical production cost structure over the past century is illustrated in **Exhibit 18-1**.

In the "low-tech," labor-intensive manufacturing environment, factors related to direct labor were often the primary drivers of manufacturing overhead costs; however, in today's "high-tech" automated environment there are many other factors that drive manufacturing overhead costs, and the specific set of cost drivers differs from organization to organization.

Chapter 16 on product costing illustrates a simplified traditional system for allocating manufacturing overhead to products using a single, volume-based cost driver, such as direct labor hours. The following section introduces ABC, which recognizes the multiple activities that drive manufacturing overhead costs in today's production environment.

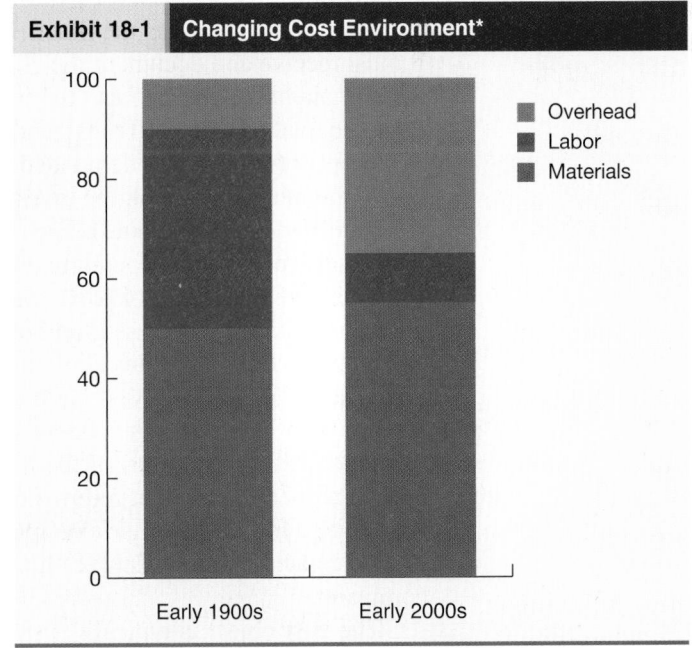

Exhibit 18-1 Changing Cost Environment*

* James F. Cox, III and Michael S. Spencer, *The Constraints Management Handbook* (CRC Press, 1997), p. 54.

ACTIVITY-BASED COSTING

The manufacturing overhead cost account has been referred to as a "bucket" of common costs. The constant growth of costs classified as overhead has forced us to search for increasingly detailed methods to analyze these costs. If overhead costs are low in comparison with materials and labor costs and if factories produce few products in large production runs, the use of a single overhead rate based on direct labor hours or machine hours may be adequate. However, as the amount of overhead costs grows, as manufacturing facilities produce a wider variety of products, and as competition intensifies, the inadequacies of a single overhead rate based on a single cost driver such as direct labor hours become evident.

Fortunately, advances in information technology and the declining costs of computerized information systems have facilitated the development and maintenance of increasingly detailed databases. The increased complexity of the production environment, coupled with faster and cheaper computing technology, gave rise to the emergence and development of activity-based costing during the 1980s and 1990s.

ABC involves determining the cost of **activities** (discrete tasks or steps in a manufacturing or service process) and tracing those costs to cost objects based on their proportionate usage of the activities.

It might be helpful to review a few terms used in the discussion of activity-based costing. A **resource** is simply a cost or expense incurred by a company. These expenses are recorded in the company's general ledger of accounts. A **cost pool** represents the sum of resources related to a particular activity undertaken in response to a customer request or need. A cost pool might contain the sum of several different resources that are incurred as a result of the activity. A **cost object** is typically a product or customer service supplied by the company in response to a customer demand or need.

The California State Bar vignette from the beginning of the chapter can be used to illustrate these concepts. As illustrated in **Exhibit 18-2**, the State Bar incurs various costs in response to customer needs. For example, a client may complain that a lawyer has broken his fiduciary responsibility to the client in mismanaging the client's trust fund. The client's complaint causes the State Bar to incur costs (or use resources) in several ways. It must receive and document the client's complaint (referred to as "intake"), investigate the complaint (referred to as "the investigation"), prepare and prosecute the complaint (handled by the Office of Trials), and conduct a trial in a courtroom (the State Bar Court). The costs of (or resources demanded by) each of these activities are accumulated into cost pools (the intake cost pool, the investigation cost pool, the Office of Trials cost pool, and the State Bar Court cost pool). Each client complaint may differ significantly in terms of total resource demand, depending on the type of complaint and the lawyer's response.

There are two stages of ABC costing: Stage 1—the assigning of resources to the cost pools; and Stage 2—the assigning of the cost pools to the cost objects. In Stage 1, there should be a logical and causal relationship between the resource and the cost pool. In our State Bar example, the investigation cost pool would logically include the salaries of the lawyers who investigate the clients' claims. In Stage 2, the cost pools should be assigned to cost objects on the basis of the units of activity (machine hours, number of purchase orders, number of product returns, number of invoice line items, etc.) consumed by the cost object. In the State Bar example, if a typical malpractice complaint takes 20 hours to investigate, the equivalent 20-hour cost of the investigator should be assigned to the complaint.

The cost object is typically a product or service provided to a customer. In our example, the cost object is the client's complaint—that is, we want to know what it costs to follow up on each client complaint so that we can recover the appropriate cost from the wayward attorney. Depending on the information needs of decision makers, as we will discuss later in this chapter, the cost object could be the customer.

To summarize, ABC is a system of analysis that identifies and summarizes the cost of key activities into cost pools, and then traces these cost pools to products or other cost objects based on the quantity of the cost pools consumed by the cost objects. ABC is based on the premise that activities drive costs and that costs should be assigned to products (or other cost objects) in proportion to the volume of activities they consume. Although activity cost analysis is most often associated with product costing, it offers many benefits for controlling and managing costs, as we will see later in this chapter. As the Accounting in Practice box, (page 862) explains, ABC was actually used first to improve cost management before it was used for product costing.

Exhibit 18-2	Activity-Based Costing Illustration

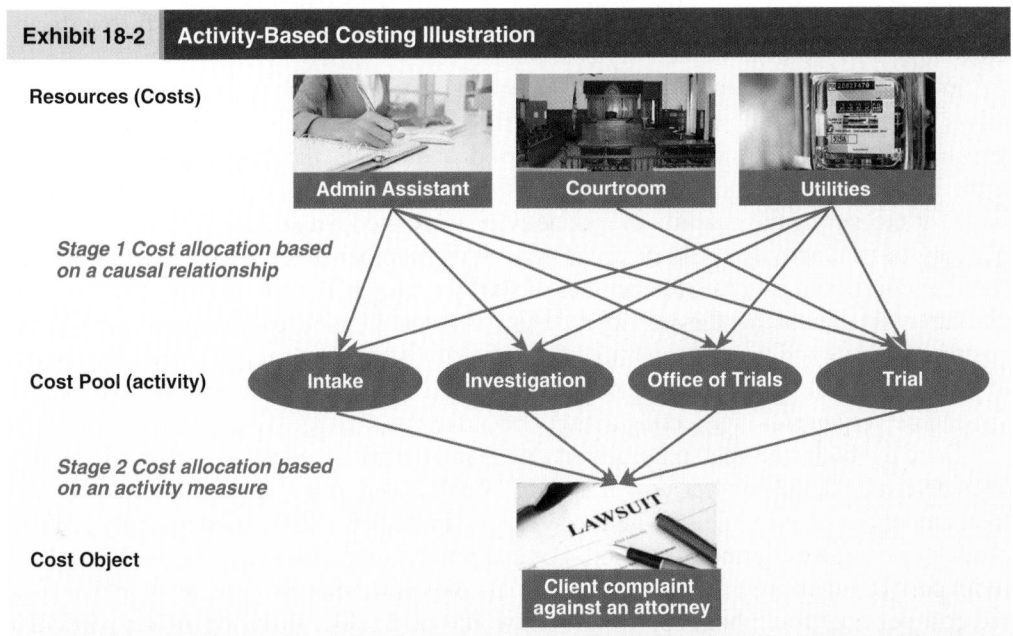

Standards of Professionalism

CORPORATE SOCIAL RESPONSIBILITY

The opening vignette of this chapter discusses how the California State Bar Association determines the reasonable costs of pursuing action against disciplined lawyers. Because of the extraordinary responsibility society places upon the attorneys within our democracy, it is critical that groups such as the California State Bar Association maintain the highest ethical standards for its members. Just how does the Association see this responsibility? The following is quoted from the California Attorney Guidelines of Civility and Professionalism:

> As officers of the court with responsibilities to the administration of justice, attorneys have an obligation to be professional with clients, other parties and counsel, the courts and the public. This obligation includes civility, professional integrity, personal dignity, candor, diligence, respect, courtesy, and cooperation, all of which are essential to the fair administration of justice and conflict resolution.

ABC Product Costing Model

Traditional costing considers the cost of a product to be its direct costs for materials and labor plus some allocated portion of manufacturing overhead, using overhead rates typically based on direct labor or machine hours. ABC is based on the notion that companies incur costs because of the activities they conduct in pursuit of their goals and objectives. For example, various activities take place to produce a particular product, such as setting up, maintaining, or monitoring the machines to make the product, physically moving raw materials and work-in-process, and so forth. Each of these activities has a cost; therefore, the total cost of producing a product using ABC is the sum of the direct materials and direct labor costs of that product, plus the cost of other activities conducted to produce that product.

Exhibit 18-2 illustrates the general two-stage ABC product cost model. The first stage includes the assignment of overhead resource costs, such as indirect labor, depreciation, and utilities, to activity cost pools for the key activities identified. Typical activity cost pools in a manufacturing environment include pools for machine setup, material movement, and engineering. The second stage assigns those activity cost pools to cost objects.

Remember that **Exhibit 18-2** is focused solely on overhead costs—the direct product or service costs, such as direct materials and direct labor, are directly assigned to cost objects and are excluded from the activity cost pools. Only indirect product costs (overhead) are assigned to products via activity cost pools.

Probably the most critical step in ABC is identifying **cost drivers**. The activity cost driver for a particular cost (or cost pool) is the characteristic selected for measuring the quantity of the activity for a particular period of time. In the example shown in **Exhibit 18-2**, if an activity cost pool is established for a trial, it is necessary to select some basis for measuring the quantity of trial activity associated with the costs in the pool. The quantity of trial activity could be measured by the number of trials held, the amount of time the courtroom is in use, the number of staff working in the courtroom, or some other measure. It is critical that the activity measure used has a logical causal relationship to the costs in the pool and that the quantity of the activity is highly correlated with the amount of cost in the pool. Statistical methods, such as regression analysis and correlation analysis, can be very useful in selecting activity cost drivers.

Once the budgeted cost in the activity pool and the budgeted activity cost driver have been determined, the cost per unit of activity is calculated as the total cost divided by the total amount of activity. This is the predetermined rate that will be used to apply costs to products or services during the period. For example, if total costs assigned to the trial activity pool in July were $100,000 and 100 hours of courtroom time were available in July, the cost per courtroom hour for the month would be $1,000. If during July a particular trial took eight hours of courtroom time, the total courtroom cost that would be assigned to the trial would be $8,000 ($1,000 $\times$ 8 hours).

ACCOUNTING IN PRACTICE   **Development of ABC**

ABC came to the forefront in the 1980s and 1990s; however, it was beginning to evolve as early as the 1960s when finance and accounting staff at **General Electric** (GE) attempted to improve the usefulness of accounting information in controlling ever-increasing indirect costs. The GE staff noted that indirect costs were often the result of "upstream" decisions, such as engineering design and change orders, which were made long before the costs were actually incurred. Frequently, the engineering department was not informed of the consequences its actions had on the other parts of the organization.

The second phase of the development of ABC was accomplished by business consultants, professors, and manufacturing companies during the 1970s and early 1980s. By generating more accurate cost and profitability measures for the various products offered by companies, these consultants and professors hoped to improve product cost information used in pricing and product mix decisions. ABC has since been extended to assess customer profitability.

In the late 1980s and 1990s, ABC was being promoted by many of the leading consulting firms, and it almost became a fad, much as total quality management (TQM) and just-in-time (JIT) systems had before it. Consequently, many companies that jumped on the ABC bandwagon early in its life later determined that it was not for them. Most of the companies that abandoned ABC probably adopted it initially for the wrong reasons.

Knowledge of the historical development of ABC is important in order to clearly understand what ABC analysis was intended to accomplish, as well as what it was not intended to accomplish.

Concept	→ Method →	Assessment	TAKEAWAY 18.1
Can a company that has traditionally allocated overhead on a single, company-wide rate improve its understanding of its product costs by using a different approach?	• Choose a cost object (typically a product or service). • Identify the activities required to complete and deliver that cost object. • Determine the costs incurred for each activity. • Assign the costs to the activity cost pool(s). • Choose an activity driver for each cost pool. • Allocate the cost pools to each cost object based on the proportion of the activity driver used by each cost object.	Cost objects that require more of a particular activity will receive a greater portion of that activity's costs, leading to a better understanding of the cost object's real cost.	

Only Chips specializes in making two types of chip cookies, semi-sweet and butterscotch, and delivering them to customers while they are still warm from the oven. The butterscotch cookies tend to be preferred by those living downtown while the semi-sweet cookies are more popular in the suburbs. Most bakers assess a product's profitability by comparing revenues to the cost of goods sold. However, due to its unique business model, Jessy Baker, the firm's new accountant, wants to use an activity-based costing system that takes into consideration the cost of the delivery person. Listed below are activity and cost information for Only Chips' two products.

YOUR TURN! 18.1

The solution is on page 899.

	Semi-Sweet	Butterscotch
Revenue.	$200,000	$140,000
Cost of goods sold	$112,000	$ 84,000
Delivery activity:		
Number of deliveries.	15,000	10,500
Average length of delivery	18 Minutes	12 Minutes
Cost per hour for delivery	$15.00	$15.00

Using activity-based costing, which one of the products is more profitable?

TRADITIONAL PRODUCT COSTING AND ABC COMPARED

Recall that in Chapter 16, Fezzari Performance Bicycles applied overhead using a company-wide overhead rate of $12.00 per direct labor hour. This may seem to be a very low overhead rate until you remember that Fezzari is primarily assembling parts that have been manufactured by other suppliers. Fezzari's factory doesn't have large, expensive manufacturing equipment that you might associate with other types of manufacturers.

LO3 **Explain** the difference between traditional company-wide and departmental overhead methods and ABC.

We assumed that each hour of labor worked on a project caused $12.00 of overhead to be incurred. In that case, all overhead costs were associated with one factor, direct labor hours. As discussed at the beginning of this chapter, such an assumption is often not appropriate with modern methods of producing goods or services where manufacturing overhead is related to a diverse set of activities and cost drivers.

Where overhead costs or capacity measures vary significantly from one department to the next, a separate overhead rate may be calculated for each department. Chapter 16 introduced the concept of departmental overhead rates, where a separate overhead rate is predetermined for each producing department in a factory. In most multiproduct manufacturing environments, this approach represents a cost system improvement over using a single, company-wide overhead rate, and it reduces the likelihood of cost cross-subsidization, which occurs when one product is assigned too much cost as a result of another being assigned too little cost.

Assume that Fezzari has two production departments, Assembly and Packaging, and that these departments have overhead costs of $240,000 and $60,000, respectively. Assume, further, that Fezzari management determined that the Assembly Department overhead costs should be allocated to bicycles on the basis of direct labor hours and that the Packaging Department overhead costs should be allocated to bicycles on the basis of units produced. **Exhibit 18-3** shows that the resulting department predetermined overhead rates would be $9.60 per direct labor hour for the Assembly Department and $12.63 per unit for the Packaging Department.

Exhibit 18-3	Computing Department Overhead Rates		
	A	B	C
1	**Overhead costs per unit**	**Assembly**	**Packaging**
2	Total department manufacturing overhead (direct department costs plus allocated costs)	$240,000	$60,000
3	Quantity of overhead application base		
4	Direct labor hours	25,000	
5	Units produced		4,750
6	Department manufacturing overhead rates	$ 9.60	$ 12.63
7		*per direct labor hour*	*per unit*

Department overhead rates may improve product costing results for many organizations, and in fact may be satisfactory. However, this method does not attempt to reflect the actual activities used in producing the different products.

Applying Overhead with Activity-Based Costing

An even more precise method of measuring the cost of products than company-wide or departmental rates is the ABC method. As stated earlier, ABC typically involves two stages of cost allocation. The first stage is identifying and measuring the cost of activities used to produce the various products. The second stage is summing the cost of those activities to determine the ultimate cost of the products.

The overhead rates for each Fezzari department were determined in the last section as $9.60 and $12.63, respectively. The easiest way to assign these costs to products is by using one base and one rate for all products going through a given process (e.g., assembly). However, different products typically use different amounts of resources from a given process and using the same base and overhead rate for all may distort the cost for some or all products.

Overhead costs in the Assembly and Packaging Departments consisted of two types of costs: **production department costs** and support department costs. Production department overhead costs are costs that are incurred by the production department, such as indirect labor, indirect materials, depreciation on equipment, supervisory wages, and so forth. Support department costs are costs allocated from other departments (for the Fezzari example, the support departments include Design, Receiving/Inventory, and Building) that provide services to both Assembly and Packaging. Fezzari's accountant determined that the production department overhead costs in Assembly were driven primarily by labor hours, whereas support department overhead costs in Packaging were driven primarily

According to a presentation entitled "Activity Based Costing at UPS," UPS developed its ABC system to link its operating behavior to its business segment costs, support pricing decisions, and report consistent and reliable profitability by product. The UPS ABC system was created by cross-functional teams from Finance and Accounting, Engineering, IT, and Operations.

UPS operations are extremely complex, involving numerous service options, operating conditions, and supporting activities. However, because UPS has an extensive database of work measurement and package movement information, it is able to precisely measure a package's movement from location to location and measure product cost. UPS uses data mining techniques to analyze tens of millions of records to determine profits by package and by customer.

The UPS ABC system produces reports at multiple levels (corporate, operational business unit, customer, and product). Reports are generated monthly in an electronic format that can be viewed across periods. The information in the ABC system is updated continuously.

Using their ABC system allows UPS to focus on improving operations in high-impact areas, change shipping behavior, modify their distribution network, and integrate logistic solutions over the entire value chain. By measuring their financial performance more accurately, UPS is able to make better decisions about pricing, cost control, quality improvement, reengineering, forecasting, and customer relationship management.

Source: http://govinfo.library.unt.edu/usps/offices/domestic-finance/usps/pdf/Holsen.pdf

by units produced. It was also determined that each component of design, receiving/inventory, and building represents a separate activity cost pool, and that these costs should be assigned to the products based on specific cost drivers rather than a single cost driver for the entire department.

Exhibit 18-4 presents a detailed analysis of overhead cost data for July's operations.

Exhibit 18-4	ABC Stage One: Assign Costs to Cost Pools (Activities)				
	A	B	C	D	E	F
1	**Overhead Cost Pool**	**Total Cost**		**Cost Pool Driver (number of)**	**Driver Quantity**	**Unit Rates***
2	Direct departmental overhead costs:					
3	Assembly	$200,000		Direct labor hours	25,000	$8.00
4	Packaging	21,500		Units produced	4,750	$4.53
5	Allocated support costs:					
6	Receiving/Inventory	28,500		Units produced	4,750	$6.00
7	Design	50,000		Change orders	20,000	$2.50
8	Total	$300,000				
9						
10	* Rounded					

The total cost is divided by the driver quantity to compute the per-unit rate.

Each cost is taken from the general ledger.

The selected driver should have a causal relationship to the cost pool such that changes in the driver would cause changes in the cost.

Data for each driver should be readily available from the financial or operational systems.

Assume that Fezzari management wants to compare the use of a company-wide, departmental, and ABC overhead allocation method on the cost of two road bikes, the top-end T5 (from Chapter 16) and the entry-level Catania. The T5 is typically purchased by serious triathletes who are very particular about the setup and customization of their bikes, whereas the Catania is typically purchased by fitness newbies who know little about bike components and fit and are primarily driven by price in the selection of their bikes. For simplicity, assume that these are the only two bikes produced by Fezzari. The amounts of activity attributed to the T5 and Catania and the overhead cost per unit based on ABC costs are shown in **Exhibit 18-5**.

Exhibit 18-5	ABC Stage Two: Assign Activities to Cost Objects							
	A	B	C	D	E	F	G	H
1 **Bicycle Model**					T5		Catania	
2 Activity	Cost Driver	Cost per unit of activity	Quantity of Activity	Cost of Activity		Quantity of Activity	Cost of Activity
3 Assembly	Direct labor hours	$8.00	12,000	$ 96,000.00		13,000	$104,000.00
4 Packaging	Units produced	4.53	1,500	6,795.00		3,250	14,722.50
5 Receiving/Inventory	Units produced	6.00	1,500	9,000.00		3,250	19,500.00
6 Design	Change orders	2.50	18,000	45,000.00		2,000	5,000.00
7 Total overhead product cost				$156,795.00			$143,222.50
8 Units produced				1,500.00			3,250.00
9 Overhead per unit of product				$ 104.53			$ 44.07
10							
11							

> These rates were calculated in Exhibit 18-4.

> The sum of each driver quantity line should equal the total driver quantity on Exhibit 18-4.

Exhibit 18-6 summarizes the allocated overhead costs for Fezzari's two products using the three different overhead cost assignment methods.

Exhibit 18-6	Overhead Cost per Unit Using Various Overhead Methods		
		T5	**Catania**
Company-wide overhead rate*		$ 96.00	$48.00
Departmental overhead rates**		89.43	51.03
ABC		104.53	44.07

> The ABC method is more precise and more accurately reflects the T5 overhead cost. This is important for determining pricing and inventory valuation.

*Direct labor hours per unit × $12.00 = (12,000/1,500) × $12 = $96 (T5); = (13,000/3,250) × $12 = $48 (Catania)

**(Direct labor hours per unit × $9.60) + $12.63 per unit = ((12,000/1,500) × $9.60) + $12.63 = $89.43 (T5); = ((13,000/3,250) × $9.60) + $12.63 = $51.03 (Catania)

ABC product costing reveals a different cost picture. Using either a company-wide overhead rate or departmental rates, the Catania bike is bearing more than its share of total overhead costs.

Using either of these methods could lead the company into pricing the Catania too high in the market. With a more accurate overhead cost of $44.07, rather than $51.03 or $48.00, the company clearly has the ability to compete on price with other companies in this market. In Fezzari's case, overhead is a relatively minor cost relative to the cost of the direct materials, as shown in Chapter 16. This is due to the fact that Fezzari is mainly an assembler of parts, rather than a manufacturer of those parts. However, in other industries, the effect of adopting ABC may be much more significant.

However, regardless of the differences among the various cost methods, inaccurate costing can affect management's assessment of product profitability and its decisions regarding which products to continue to produce and which products to discontinue. Flawed product costing information can cause management mistakenly to decide to keep products that are losing money, while deciding to discontinue products that are profitable. Using a company-wide or departmental overhead allocation method could have led Fezzari management to shift its emphasis from the low-end bike to the high-end bike market, a decision that could have been damaging to the company.

Limitations of ABC Illustration

Several limitations of the Fezzari illustration should be mentioned. For the sake of simplicity, the example was limited to manufacturing cost considerations. A complete analysis would also require considerations of nonmanufacturing costs, such as marketing, distribution, and customer service, before a final determination of product profitability could be made. Finally, in calculating the activity cost per unit of activity, it is necessary to decide how to measure the total quantity of activity. For example, for Fezzari, the receiving/inventory cost per unit was calculated as $6.00 based on the actual quantity of 4,750 bicycles produced for the period. Alternatively, the receiving cost could have been calculated based on **practical capacity**, which is the maximum possible volume of activity, while allowing for normal downtime for repairs and maintenance. If the plant has a practical capacity to produce 5,000 bicycles per period, the cost per bike based on the practical capacity is $5.70 per purchase order. Using this overhead rate in costing products, only $27,075 would have been assigned to the two products, which required only 4,750 bicycles, and the remaining $1,425 for the 250 bicycles of excess (or idle) capacity not used would be written off as an operating expense of the period as underapplied overhead. Practical capacity is generally regarded as better than actual capacity for calculating activity costs because it does not hide the cost of idle capacity within product costs, and it gives a truer cost of the activities used to produce the product.

Comparing Traditional and Activity-Based Costing

Procedurally, ABC is not a new method for assigning costs to cost objectives. Traditional costing systems have used a two-stage allocation model (similar to the ABC model) to assign costs to cost pools (such as departments) and subsequently assign those cost pools to products using an allocation base. In most traditional costing systems, overhead is assigned to one or more cost pools based on departments and functional characteristics (such as labor-related, machine-related, and space-related costs) and then reassigned to products using a general allocation base such as direct labor hours or machine hours. ABC is different in that it divides the overall manufacturing processes into activities. ABC accumulates costs in cost pools for the major activities and then assigns the costs of these activities to products or other cost objectives that benefit from these activities. *Conceptually,* ABC is different because of the way it views the operations of the company; *procedurally,* it uses a methodology that has been around for a long time.

The challenge in using ABC is specifying the model—that is, determining how many activity pools should be established for a given cost measurement purpose, which costs should be assigned to each activity pool, and the appropriate activity driver for each pool. Specifying the model also includes determining the resource cost drivers for assigning indirect resource costs to the various activity cost pools.

Concept ⟶	Method ⟶	Assessment	TAKEAWAY 18.2
Why might a company choose to calculate its overhead rates based on practical capacity instead of budgeted capacity?	• Total overhead cost pool/ **budgeted** activity driver = predetermined overhead rate • Total overhead cost pool/ **practical** activity driver = predetermined overhead rate	If budgeted (and actual) activity is less than practical activity, the company has excess capacity. Using practical capacity to calculate overhead rates will highlight this idle capacity in the form of under-applied overhead.	

YOUR TURN! 18.2

Assume you are a controller for a manufacturing company that uses a traditional product costing system, but is looking to transition to ABC. The CEO has asked you why this would be a useful transition. What would you tell him regarding the benefits of activity-based costing?

The solution is on page 899.

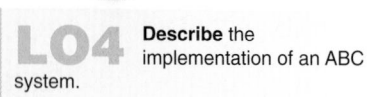

ABC IMPLEMENTATION ISSUES

LO4
Describe the implementation of an ABC system.

The distortion in product costs for Fezzari from using traditional cost systems based on company-wide or departmental rates, although hypothetical, is not uncommon. Studies have shown that distortions of this type occur regularly in traditional systems in which a significant variation exists in the volume and complexity of products and services produced. Traditional systems tend to over-cost high-volume, low-complexity products, and they tend to under-cost low-volume, high-complexity products. These studies indicate that the typical amount of over-costing is up to 200% for high-volume products with low complexity and that the typical under-costing can be more than 1,000% for low-volume, highly complex products. In companies with a large number of different products, traditional costing can show that most products are profitable. After changing to ABC, however, these companies might find that 10% to 15% of the products are profitable while the remainder are unprofitable. Adopting ABC often leads to increased profits merely by changing the product mix to minimize the number of unprofitable products.[2]

Most companies initially do not abandon their traditional cost system and move to a system that uses ABC for management and financial reporting purposes because financial statements must withstand the scrutiny of auditors and tax authorities. This scrutiny typically implies more demands on the cost accounting system for consistency, objectivity, and uniformity than required when the system is used only for management purposes. In addition, ABC systems must be built facility by facility rather than being embedded in a software program that can be used by all facilities within the company.[3] Often, companies maintain traditional costing for external reporting purposes and ABC for pricing and other internal decision-making purposes.

Once an ABC system has been developed for a production facility, including an activities list (sometimes called an activities dictionary), identification of activity cost drivers, and calculation of cost per unit of driver activity, the activity costs of a current or proposed product can be readily determined. In ABC, as illustrated for Fezzari, manufacturing a product is viewed simply as the combination of activities selected to make it; therefore, the activity cost of a product or service is the sum of the costs of those activities. This approach to viewing a product enables management to evaluate the importance of each of the activities consumed in making a product. Possibly some activities can be eliminated or a lower-cost activity substituted for a more costly one without reducing the quality or performance of the product.

ACCOUNTING IN PRACTICE | **Results of ABC**

In the 1980s, the **Coca-Cola Company** used ABC to determine that it was less costly—and thus more profitable—to deliver soft drink concentrate to some fountain drink retailers (such as fast-food restaurants) in nonreturnable, disposable containers rather than in returnable stainless steel containers, which had been standard in the industry for many years.

Although an ABC system may be complex, it merely mirrors the complexity of an organization's design, manufacturing, and distribution systems. If a firm's products are diverse and its production and distribution procedures complex, the ABC system will also be complex; however, if its products are homogeneous and its production environment relatively simple, its ABC system should also be relatively simple. Even in highly complex manufacturing environments, ABC systems usually have no more than 10 to 20 cost pools. Many ABC experts in practice have observed that creating a large number of

---

[2] Gary Cokins, Alan Stratton, and Jack Helbling, *An ABC Manager's Primer* (Montvale, NJ: Institute of Management-Based Accountants, 1993).

[3] Robert S. Kaplan and Robin Cooper, *Cost and Effect* (Boston: Harvard Business School Press, 1998), p. 105.

activity cost pools for a given costing application normally does not significantly improve cost accuracy above that of a smaller number of cost pools. As with any information system design, the costs of developing and maintaining the system must not exceed its benefits; hence, although adding more activity cost pools may result in some small amount of increased accuracy, it may be so small as not to be cost effective.

In addition to using ABC for product costing purposes, other important uses for ABC have also been found. One of the most useful applications for ABC discussed in the next section is in evaluating customer costs and distribution channel costs. Other applications include costing administrative functions such as processing accounts receivable or accounts payable; costing the process of hiring and training employees; and costing such menial tasks as processing a letter or copying a document. As illustrated by the California State Bar illustration at the beginning of the chapter, any process, function, or activity performed in an organization, whether it is related to production, marketing and sales, finance and accounting, human resources, or even research and development, is a candidate for ABC analysis. In short, almost any cost objective that has more than an insignificant amount of indirect costs can be more effectively measured using ABC.

A company has a significantly varied product and service mix, with many high-volume, homogeneous products and many low-volume, complex products. Historically, the company has used a single, company-wide overhead rate. After implementing an activity-based costing system, the company is likely to find?

  a. The high-volume products were under-costed previously.
  b. The high-volume products were over-costed previously.
  c. The low-volume products were over-costed previously.
  d. The costs of both low- and high-volume products will be unchanged.

YOUR TURN! 18.3

The solution is on page 899.

ABC AND CUSTOMER PROFITABILITY ANALYSIS

One of the most beneficial applications of activity-based costing is in the analysis of the profitability of customers. Companies that have a large number of diverse customers also usually have widely varied profits from serving those customers. Many companies never attempt to calculate the profit earned from individual customers. They merely assume that if they are selling products above their costs, and that overall the company is earning a profit, then each of the customers must be profitable. Unfortunately, the cost incurred to sell goods and services, and to provide services, to individual customers is not usually proportionate with the gross profits generated by those sales. Customers with high sales volume are not necessarily the most profitable. Profitability of individual customers depends on whether the gross profits from sales to those customers exceed the customer-specific costs of serving those customers. Some customers are simply more costly than others, and some may even be unprofitable, and the unprofitable customers are eating away at the total profits of the company. In an ideal world, only profitable customers would be retained, and unprofitable customers would be either converted to a profitable status or they would be dropped as customers.

LO5 Explain customer profitability analysis based on ABC.

Customer Profitability Profile

If a company knows the amount of profits (or losses) generated by each of its customers, a customer profitability profile can be prepared, as illustrated in the following section.

ABC Customer Profitability Analysis Illustrated

Let's assume that Pure Water Company is a "green" company located in the West that manufactures and sells all-natural compounds for purifying water distributed through large public water systems. Let's also assume that Ron James, the CEO and founder of Pure Water, personally developed the compounds using natural materials obtained from remote regions of the world. He knows that he has a product that is far superior to the traditional processes based on synthetic chemicals that have been used for generations to purify water. After five years in business, Pure Water has built a solid and growing customer base, but it has to invest significant time and expense servicing customers, especially those that have recently embraced its approach to water purification. Some customers require a lot of "hand-holding," with frequent visits and telephone calls, and they tend to purchase frequently in small amounts, often requiring repackaging. Other customers require little attention and support, and many of them purchase in large amounts once a year.

Although the company is making money, there is concern that profits could be higher if sales and other customer-related costs could be decreased. Ron James decided to ask Environmental Business Consultants (EBC; introduced in Chapter 14) to conduct a customer profitability analysis using activity-based costing. As a first step, EBC determined that there were five primary activities related to serving customers: visits of customers by sales representatives, remote contacts (phone, email, fax), processing and shipping of customer orders, repackaging, and billing and collection. After extensive analysis, including numerous interviews and statistical analyses of activity and cost data, EBC determined the cost drivers and cost per unit of activity for the five customer-related activities, shown in **Exhibit 18-7**.

Exhibit 18-7	Pure Water's Customer Service Activity Per-Unit Costs	
Activity	**Activity Cost Driver**	**Cost per Unit of Driver Activity**
Visits to customers	Number of visits	$800
Remote contacts.	Number of contacts	75
Processing & shipping	Number of customer orders	450
Repackaging.	Number of requests	250
Billing and collection.	Number of invoices.	90

After collecting activity driver data on each of these activities for Pure Water's major customers, EBC prepared the customer activity cost and profitability analysis presented in **Exhibit 18-8** for its five largest customers (in terms of sales dollars) in the order of greatest to least profit for the most recent year.

Because Pure Water is selling only one product to all of its customers, and has the same pricing policy for all customers, there is a constant 40% gross profit ratio across all customers, and the combined net profitability of these customers is 11.6% of sales. However, all customers are not equally profitable. The high level of support required by Manhattan and Great Lakes resulted in a net customer loss from sales to Great Lakes and only a 6.8% customer profitability ratio for Manhattan.

Armed with the information in the customer activity cost and profitability analysis, Pure Water can take proactive steps to increase its overall profitability ratio. An obvious option would be to try to terminate its relationship with Great Lakes because the company is clearly losing money on that customer. If Great Lakes were terminated as a customer, and assuming that all of the activity costs associated with Great Lakes could be avoided by the termination, Pure Water's total sales would drop to $68,750 (or $80,750 minus $12,000), but its total profit would increase to $11,785 (or $9,335 plus $2,450), resulting in a profitability ratio on the remaining four customers of 17.1%.

A more proactive approach would be to work with Great Lakes and Manhattan, which have high support requirements, such as repackaging, frequent visits, and phone contacts, to try to lower the level of high-cost support activities without reducing sales to those

Exhibit 18-8	Pure Water Customer Activity Cost and Profitability Analysis						
	A	B	C	D	E	F	G
1	These activity counts would come from Pure Water's customer management, operations, and financial systems.	Consolidated Water, Inc.	West Coast Utilities	Seattle Water District	Manhattan Water Authority	Great Lakes Utility	Total
2	**Customer Activity Cost Analysis:**						
3	*Activity Cost Driver Data*						
4	Visits to customers	1	1	3	5	4	
5	Remote contacts	3	2	5	7	8	
6	Processing & shipping	1	4	3	3	5	
7	Repackaging	0	0	0	2	3	
8	Billing & collection	1	4	3	3	5	
9	*Customer Activity Cost*						
10	Visits to customers	$ 800	$ 800	$ 2,400	$ 4,000	$ 3,200	
11	Remote contacts	225	150	375	525	600	
12	Processing & shipping	450	1,800	1,350	1,350	2,250	
13	Repackaging	0	0	0	500	750	
14	Billing & collection	90	360	270	270	450	
15	Total activity cost	$ 1,565	$ 3,110	$ 4,395	$ 6,645	$ 7,250	
16							
17	**Customer Profitability Analysis**						
18	Customer sales	$16,250	$15,000	$17,500	$20,000	$12,000	$80,750
19	Less cost of goods sold	9,750	9,000	10,500	12,000	7,200	48,450
20	Gross profit on sales	$ 6,500	$ 6,000	$ 7,000	$ 8,000	$ 4,800	$32,300
21	Less activity cost	1,565	3,110	4,395	6,645	7,250	22,965
22	Customer profitability	$ 4,935	$ 2,890	$ 2,605	$ 1,355	$(2,450)	$ 9,335
23	Customer profitability ratio*	30.4%	19.3%	14.9%	6.8%	−20.4%	11.6%
24							
25	** Customer profitability ÷ Sales*						

These amounts are computed by multiplying the activity counts by the per-unit costs computed in Exhibit 18-7.

Customer activity costs are subtracted from customer gross profit to determine customer profitability.

Customer gross profit percentage (gross profit/sales) is the same for all customers at 40%.

customers. This could result in maintaining the current level of gross profit, but generating a significantly higher level of total net customer profitability.

Once a company has profitability data on each of its customers (or categories of customers), only then can it proceed to try to convert them to profitability, or seek to terminate the relationships with those customers. Just as we saw that ABC provided a model for producing more accurate product cost data, ABC is also a valuable tool for generating customer profitability data.

Two caveats should be considered when using activity cost data to manage customer profitability. First, there may be justifiable reasons (such as having a new customer that requires a high level of early-stage support, trying to penetrate a new geographic market, or existing relationships with other more profitable customers) for keeping customers that have lower profitability, or even customers that are not profitable. If so, these customers should be managed intensely to attempt to reduce the activities devoted to their support. Second, eliminating a customer may not immediately translate into an immediate reduction of activity costs. Some activity costs may not have a variable cost behavior pattern, and eliminating customers may merely create excess capacity in the short term.

TAKEAWAY 18.3	Concept	→	Method	→	Assessment
	Which customers are a company's most profitable?		Use ABC analysis to allocate customer service costs to each customer based on each customer's demand on the company's customer service activities.		Customers that have a customer profitability ratio that is less than the company average should be evaluated to determine how to decrease the cost of servicing them.

YOUR TURN! 18.4

The solution is on page 899.

Quality Meats provides standard cuts of beef, lamb, and pork to restaurant chains for use in preparing customer meals. The price and cost of the beef, lamb, and pork is the same for all customers, with an average gross profit of 15%. However, the sales manager has recently been complaining that a particular customer is too "picky" and would like to drop them as a customer. As the corporate controller, you have gathered the following information about this customer and the costs of performing certain activities. The cost of these activities would be avoided if they were dropped as a customer.

Total sales	$100,000
Total cost of meat	$ 85,000
Number of returns	50
Number of visits	25
Number of calls	120
Cost per return	$100
Cost per visit	$150
Cost per call	$30

Based on this information, should Quality Meats drop this customer?

ACTIVITY-BASED MANAGEMENT

LO6 Explain the difference between ABC and activity-based management.

Activity-based costing has been highly touted as a technique for improving the measurement of the cost and profitability of products, customers, and other cost objectives. In the early development of ABC, it was discovered that a by-product of accurately measuring costs using ABC is that management invariably gains a much better understanding of the processes and activities that are used to create cost objects, such as products. Although ABC could be justified on the basis of its value as a tool in helping produce more accurate cost measurements for various cost objectives, its greatest potential value may be in its by-products. The access to ABC data enables managers to engage in **activity-based management (ABM)**, defined as the identification and selection of activities to maximize the value of the activities while minimizing their cost from the perspective of the final consumer. In other words, ABM is concerned with how to efficiently and effectively manage activities and processes to provide value to the final consumer.

Defining processes and identifying key activities help management better understand the business and evaluate whether activities being performed add value to the customer. ABM focuses managerial attention on what is most important among the activities performed to create value for customers.

Hint: It is often not feasible to perform a cost analysis on every activity, so management must exercise judgment in choosing activities to track costs for.

A helpful analogy in understanding what ABC can do for a company is to compare a company's operations with a large retail store, such as a **Home Depot** store. In a Home Depot store, there is a clearly marked price on each of the tens of thousands of individual items that customers may decide to purchase. Similarly, every activity that takes place in any organization has a cost that can be determined and that management can use to make a judgment about the activity's value. In an ideal world, a manager could walk through the business and evaluate the cost of every activity being performed—maybe thousands of different activities—and then decide which ones are worth the cost and which ones are not adding value. But because generating ABC data has a cost, management must decide which ABC data are likely to be useful and cost beneficial. Our discussion here is only an introduction to activity-based costing and some of its applications. As the following Accounting in Practice points out, over the past quarter of a century, ABC has matured well beyond merely accurately measuring costs of products and customers. More advanced ABC topics and methods are covered in advanced managerial accounting (or cost accounting) courses.

Current Status of ABC | **ACCOUNTING IN PRACTICE**

One of the leading thinkers and authors on the topic of activity-based costing over the past 25 years has been Peter B. B. Turney. He recently traced the evolution of ABC within the context of a product life cycle, showing how ABC functionality has expanded since it was first introduced in the 1980s. Turney asserts that ABC is now in its fourth generation, where it has become "an integral part of business performance management solutions, including profitability management, performance measurement, financial management, sustainability, and human capital management." In its current state of development, a single ABC model can support a number of needs, including historical cost measurement, resource planning, performance measurement, and other analyses.

In using activity-based management techniques, management would be most likely to try to eliminate or reduce which of the following activities? (Hint: Which activity adds the least value from the customer's perspective?)

a. Inspection of the final product before transfer to finished goods inventory.

b. Engineering design to improve product ergonomics.

c. Movement of materials from the raw materials storeroom to the production floor.

d. Operation of robots in the manufacturing process.

YOUR TURN! 18.5

The solution is on page 899.

SERVICES INDUSTRY IN FOCUS

Customer Profitability Analysis

SERVICE AND MERCHANDISING

Environmental Business Consultants (EBC) serves three different sizes of clients (large, medium, and small). EBC's solid waste rate review projects are fairly standardized and routine; hence, the pricing is also standardized for all clients. Although the company is profitable overall, the CFO thinks the net margins should be higher. She is concerned that customer support costs are eating up some of the margin and has decided to do a customer profitability analysis based on the three different sizes of clients to see if some of the client groups may actually be less profitable than others. The following data for the most recent period have been collected to support the analysis:

Support Activity	Driver	Cost per Driver Unit
A. Scope change requests.	Number of requests	$150
B. Visits to client.	Number of visits	$200
C. Communication	Number of calls	$ 50

Customer Group	Activity A	Activity B	Activity C	Profit Before Support Costs
Large	36	72	180	$390,000
Medium..................	75	150	205	100,500
Small....................	21	42	80	52,000

Required

1. Calculate the customer profitability for each customer group, taking into account the support activity required for each customer group.

2. Comment on the usefulness of this type of analysis. What reasonable actions might the CEO take as a result of this analysis?

Solution

1. Activity A—Scope change requests

    Activity B—Visits to client

    Activity C—Communication

Activity	Large	Medium	Small
A (@ $150).....................................	$ 5,400	$ 11,250	$ 3,150
B (@ $200).....................................	14,400	30,000	8,400
C (@ $50)......................................	9,000	10,250	4,000
Total support costs	$ 28,800	$ 51,500	$15,550
Profit before support costs	390,000	100,500	52,000
Customer profits...............................	$361,200	$ 49,000	$36,450
Ratio of support costs to profit before support costs:..	7.4%	51.2%	29.9%

2. This analysis is beneficial to EBC because it shows that large clients consume the lowest amount in terms of support services required. Medium clients are a significantly larger consumer of activities for all three of the support activities. Calculating the ratio of total support costs to profit before support costs provides additional insight into the relative profitability of the client groups. All three client groups are profitable; however, this analysis provides useful information for improving profits by working with the medium and small client groups to control support activities and related costs and attempt to bring their support costs in line with the large client group.

SUMMARY OF LEARNING OBJECTIVES

LO1   **Explain the changes in the modern production environment that have affected cost structures. (p. 858)**

- Manufacturing organizations have shifted from labor-intensive to automated assembly processes.
- Activity-based costing recognizes that multiple activities drive manufacturing overhead costs in today's production environment.

LO2   **Understand the concept of activity-based costing (ABC) and how it is applied. (p. 860)**

- ABC involves determining the cost of activities and tracing those costs to cost objects based on their proportionate usage of the activities.
- ABC is based on the premise that activities drive costs and that costs should be assigned to products in proportion to the volume of activities they consume.

Explain the difference between traditional company-wide and departmental overhead methods and ABC. (p. 863) LO3

- Company-wide and departmental overhead methods base overhead costs on one cost driver, whereas ABC allocates overhead based on a diverse set of activities and cost drivers.

- ABC divides the overall manufacturing processes into activities, accumulates costs in cost pools for the major activities, and then assigns the costs of these activities to products or other cost objectives that benefit from these activities.

- The challenge in using ABC is determining how many activity pools should be established for a given cost measurement purpose, which costs should be assigned to each activity pool, and the appropriate activity driver for each pool.

- A complete ABC analysis would require considerations of nonmanufacturing costs, such as marketing, distribution, and customer service, before a final determination of product profitability could be made.

- Practical capacity, the maximum possible volume of activity, is generally regarded as better than actual capacity for calculating activity costs because it does not hide the cost of idle capacity within product costs, and it gives a truer cost of the activities used to produce the product.

- Procedurally, ABC is not a new method for assigning costs to objects. Traditional costing systems have used a two-stage allocation model similar to ABC to assign costs to cost pools and subsequently assign those cost pools to products using an allocation base.

Describe the implementation of an ABC system. (p. 868) LO4

- Most companies initially do not abandon their traditional cost system and move to a system that uses ABC for management and financial reporting purposes because financial statements must withstand the scrutiny of auditors and tax authorities.

- Often, companies maintain traditional costing for external reporting purposes and ABC for pricing and other internal decision-making purposes.

- Although an ABC system may be complex, it merely mirrors the complexity of an organization's design, manufacturing, and distribution systems. If a firm's products are diverse and its production and distribution procedures complex, the ABC system will also be complex; however, if its products are homogeneous and its production environment relatively simple, its ABC system should also be relatively simple.

- One of the most useful applications for ABC is evaluating customer costs and distribution channel costs.

Explain customer profitability analysis based on ABC. (p. 869) LO5

- A customer profitability profile can be prepared if a company knows the amount of profits (or losses) generated by each of its customers.

- Even if the company is making a profit overall, individual customers may be sold to at a loss.

- If customers have low profitability, there may be justifiable reasons for keeping them, but they should be managed intensely to attempt to reduce the activities devoted to their support.

Explain the difference between ABC and activity-based management. (p. 872) LO6

- The access to ABC data enables managers to engage in activity-based management (ABM), which is the identification and selection of activities to maximize the value of the activities while minimizing their cost from the perspective of the final consumer.

- ABM focuses managerial attention on what is most important among the activities performed to create value for customers.

SUMMARY	Concept	Method	Assessment
TAKEAWAY 18.1	Can a company that has traditionally allocated overhead on a single, company-wide rate improve its understanding of its product costs by using a different approach?	• Choose a cost object (typically a product or service). • Identify the activities required to complete and deliver that cost object. • Determine the costs incurred for each activity. • Assign the costs to the activity cost pool(s). • Choose an activity driver for each cost pool. • Allocate the cost pools to each cost object based on the proportion of the activity driver used by each cost object.	Cost objects that require more of a particular activity will receive a greater portion of that activity's costs, leading to a better understanding of the cost object's real cost.
TAKEAWAY 18.2	Why might a company choose to calculate its overhead rates based on practical capacity instead of budgeted capacity?	• Total overhead cost pool/**budgeted** activity driver = predetermined overhead rate • Total overhead cost pool/**practical** activity driver = predetermined overhead rate	If budgeted (and actual) activity is less than practical activity, the company has excess capacity. Using practical capacity to calculate overhead rates will highlight this idle capacity in the form of under-applied overhead.
TAKEAWAY 18.3	Which customers are a company's most profitable?	Use ABC analysis to allocate customer service costs to each customer based on each customer's demand on the company's customer service activities.	Customers that have a customer profitability ratio that is less than the company average should be evaluated to determine how to decrease the cost of servicing them.

KEY TERMS

Activities (p. 860)

Activity-based costing (ABC) (p. 859)

Activity-based management (ABM) (p. 859, 872)

Cost drivers (p. 862)

Cost object (p. 860)

Cost pool (p. 860)

Practical capacity (p. 867)

Production department costs (p. 864)

Resource (p. 860)

Assignments with the ⓂⒷⒸ logo in the margin are available in 𝐁𝐮𝐬𝐢𝐧𝐞𝐬𝐬Course.
See the Preface of the book for details.

SELF-STUDY QUESTIONS

(Answers to Self-Study Questions are at the end of this chapter.)

LO1
1. **Which of the following statements most accurately describes the current production environment and its effect on manufacturers' cost structures?**
   a. Due to the relatively high cost of technology and normal resistance to change by employees, production remains relatively labor-intensive.
   b. As more and more of the earth's resources are consumed, some raw materials are growing scarce, driving up their cost and making raw materials cost the most significant production cost for most companies.
   c. Technological advances have led to a shift from labor-intensive operations to automated operations, reducing the need for production employees while increasing the level of support, or overhead costs, as a percentage of manufacturing costs.
   d. None of the above.

2. Which of the following is not an element of ABC?   **LO2**

   a. Tracing costs to cost objects   *c.* Identifying the cost drivers

   b. Calculating a predetermined rate   *d.* All are elements of ABC.

3. ABC differs from traditional product costing in which of the following ways?   **LO3**

   a. Overhead is allocated to products in ABC.   *c.* Diverse cost drivers are used.

   b. Estimated costs are used.   *d.* It is completely accurate.

4. Implementation of ABC costing in a company that has been using a plant-wide overhead rate   **LO4**
would typically be expected to result in all of the following except what?

   a. More accurate product costing

   b. Elimination of traditional cost accounting systems used for financial reporting purposes

   c. Increased profitability from the elimination or reduction of unprofitable products or services

   d. Greater insight into the production activities that add value to the company's products

5. Which of the following is not a benefit of customer profitability analysis?   **LO5**

   a. Identifies unprofitable customers

   b. Helps track cost spent on customers

   c. Helps managers identify actions to improve specific customer profitability

   d. Speeds up production process

6. Activity-based management (ABM) is defined as what?   **LO6**

   a. The implementation of an activity-based costing system in a service company, such as a management consulting firm.

   b. The identification and selection of activities to minimize the value of the activities while maximizing their cost from the perspective of the final consumer of the product or service.

   c. The process of identifying the cost drivers to be used in calculating the per-activity rate for each cost pool in an activity-based costing system.

   d. The identification and selection of activities to maximize the value of the activities while minimizing their cost from the perspective of the final consumer of the product or service.

QUESTIONS

1. Summarize the concepts underlying activity-based costing in two sentences.   **LO2**
2. What steps are required to implement the two-stage activity-based costing model?   **LO2**
3. Define activity cost pool, activity cost driver, and cost per unit of activity.   **LO2**
4. Name two possible activity cost drivers for each of the following activities: maintenance, materials movement, machine setup, inspection, materials purchases, and customer service.   **LO2**
5. What is the premise of activity-based costing for product costing purposes?   **LO2**
6. In what ways does ABC product costing differ from traditional product cost methods?   **LO3**
7. Explain why ABC often reveals that low-volume products are over-costed and high-volume products are under-costed.   **LO4**
8. How can ABC be used to improve customer profitability analysis?   **LO5**
9. Explain activity-based management and how it differs from activity-based costing.   **LO6**

SHORT EXERCISES

SE18-1. Product costs in a complex organization are likely to be distorted if a traditional volume-based cost   **LO1**
driver is used and

   a. raw materials costs are a significant percentage of total production costs.

   b. direct labor costs are a significant percentage of total production costs.

   c. manufacturing overhead costs are a significant percentage of total production costs.

   d. direct costs are a significant percentage of total production costs.

SE18-2. All of the following are likely to be used as a cost allocation base in activity-based costing **except** the   **LO2**

   a. number of different materials used to manufacture the product.

   b. units of materials used to manufacture the product.

   c. number of vendors supplying the materials used to manufacture the product.

   d. cost of materials used to manufacture the product.

LO3   **SE18-3.**   A profitable company with five departments uses plant-wide overhead rates for its highly diversified operation. The firm is studying a change to either allocating overhead by using departmental rates or using activity-based costing (ABC). Which one of these two methods will likely result in the use of a greater number of cost allocation bases and more accurate costing results?

	Greater Number of Allocation Bases	More Accurate Costing Results
a.	Departmental	Departmental
b.	Departmental	ABC
c.	ABC	Departmental
d.	ABC	ABC

LO3   **SE18-4.**   Pelder Products Company manufactures two types of engineering diagnostic equipment used in construction. The two products are based upon different technologies, x-ray and ultra-sound, but are manufactured in the same factory. Pelder has computed the manufacturing cost of the x-ray and ultra-sound products by adding together direct materials, direct labor, and overhead cost applied based on the number of direct labor hours. The factory has three overhead departments that support the single production line that makes both products. Budgeted overhead spending for the departments is as follows:

Department			
Engineering Design	Materials Handling	Setup	Total
$6,000	$5,000	$3,000	$14,000

Pelder's budgeted manufacturing activities and costs for the period are as follows:

	Product	
Activity	X-Ray	Ultra-Sound
Units produced and sold.	50	100
Direct materials used	$5,000	$ 8,000
Direct labor hours used	100	300
Direct labor cost	$4,000	$12,000
Number of parts used.	400	600
Number of engineering changes	2	1
Number of product setups	8	7

The budgeted cost to manufacture one ultra-sound machine using the activity-based costing method is

a. $225.
b. $264.
c. $293.
d. $305.

LO3   **SE18-5.**   The Chocolate Baker specializes in chocolate baked goods. The firm has long assessed the profitability of a product line by comparing revenues to the cost of goods sold. However, Barry White, the firm's new accountant, wants to use an activity-based costing system that takes into consideration the cost of the delivery person. Listed below are activity and cost information relating to two of Chocolate Baker's major products.

	Muffins	Cheesecake
Revenue.	$53,000	$46,000
Cost of goods sold	26,000	21,000
Delivery activity:		
Number of deliveries.	150	85
Average length of delivery	10 Minutes	15 Minutes
Cost per hour for delivery.	$20.00	$20.00

Using activity-based costing, which one of the following statements is correct?

a.   The muffins are $2,000 more profitable.
b.   The cheesecakes are $75 more profitable.
c.   The muffins are $1,925 more profitable.
d.   The muffins have a higher profitability as a percentage of sales and, therefore, are more advantageous.

SE18-6.   Atmel Inc. manufactures and sells two products. Data with regard to these products are given below.

	Product A	Product B
Units produced and sold.	30,000	12,000
Machine hours required per unit.	2	3
Receiving orders per product line.	50	150
Production orders per product line	12	18
Production runs	8	12
Inspections	20	30

Total budgeted machine hours are 100,000. The budgeted overhead costs are shown below.

Receiving costs	$ 450,000
Engineering costs.	300,000
Machine setup costs.	25,000
Inspection costs	200,000
Total budgeted overhead costs.	$ 975,000

Using activity-based costing, the per unit overhead cost allocation of receiving costs for product A is

a. $3.75.
b. $10.75.
c. $19.50.
d. $28.13.

SE18-7.   TC Company makes four types of patio sets: wood, plastic, wicker, and aluminum. Data regarding the four products follows:

	DLHs/Unit	Annual Production
Wood	2.0	1,000 units
Plastic.	1.0	2,000 units
Wicker.	5.0	5,000 units
Aluminum	3.0	10,000 units

Additional information about the company follows:

- Wood sets require $40 in direct materials per unit, plastic sets require $20, wicker sets require $60 and aluminum sets require $50.
- The direct labor wage rate for all production except for the aluminum sets is $15 per hour. Aluminum sets are more difficult to produce, so the wage rate for direct labor is $20 per hour.
- Wood and wicker sets go through a special painting process.
- Wood, plastic, and wicker sets all go through the sanding process.

The ABC system used for allocating Manufacturing Overhead Costs has the following activity pools:

			Level of Activity			
Activity Cost Pool	**Activity Measure**	**Estimated Cost**	**Wood**	**Plastic**	**Wicker**	**Aluminum**
Mach setups.	# of setups	$136,000	100	100	500	1,000
Painting.	# pints used	$ 30,000	250	—	1,250	—
Sanding	# machine hrs.	$ 17,500	250	500	1,000	—
Gen. factory	# DLHs	$354,000	2,000	2,000	25,000	30,000

What is the total cost per unit under the ABC system for wicker patio sets?

a. $45.00
b. $135.00
c. $147.50
d. $180.00

LO3   **SE18-8.**   Curry Company has two divisions, Eastern Division and Western Division. Curry Company has been allocating overhead based on direct labor hours. For the most recent year, the predetermined overhead rate was $70 per direct labor hour.

An activity-based costing analysis of Curry's operations has identified three different cost pools. Data about the cost drivers for each pool for the most recent year given below.

Cost Pool	Number of Events per Year	Cost Pool
A..............	2,000	$100,000
B..............	1,000	200,000
C..............	50	50,000
Total		$350,000

The following data relate to cost driver event activity within the two divisions during the most recent year:

	Eastern Division	Western Division	Total
Cost Driver A events......	1,500	500	2,000
Cost Driver B events......	200	800	1,000
Cost Driver C events	30	20	50
Direct labor hours........	2,000	3,000	5,000

Which of the following statements is *correct*?

If the activity-based costing system had been used in the most recent year in place of the traditional overhead allocation technique,

a. profit for Eastern Division would have increased by $5,000.
b. profit for Western Division would have increased by $5,000.
c. profit for Eastern Division would have decreased by $145,000.
d. profit for Western Division would have decreased by $205,000.

LO3   **SE18-9.**   The controller for Tamale Cooking Oil Co. established the following overhead cost pools and cost drivers:

Overhead Cost Pool	Budgeted Overhead	Cost Driver	Estimated Cost Driver Level
Machine setup	$14,300	# of setups	11 setups
Materials handling	$12,480	# of barrels	780 barrels
Quality control...............	$31,620	# of inspections......	102 inspections
Machine utilities/maintenance ...	$17,250	# of machine hours...	1,150 machine hours

An order of 80 finished barrels of cooking oil used:

Machine setups	1 setup
Materials handling	82 barrels
Quality inspections	10 inspections
Machine hours	??? machine hours

If the company uses activity-based costing and the total overhead charged to the order was $7,182, how many machine hours were used to complete the order?

a. 98   c. 118
b. 109   d. 479

SE18-10. ClearView Inc. provides quarterly commercial window cleaning services for three high-rise com-   **LO5**
mercial buildings, Sequoia, Tower Plaza, and Cornwall, and it uses a job costing system for determining the costs for completing each job. ClearView guarantees its customers' satisfaction and will
return to reclean windows that do not meet the customer's requirements at no additional charge to
the customer. The job cost system does not capture any cost incurred by ClearView for return touch-
ups. ClearView cleans each building on a square footage contract price, which includes the initial
cleaning as well as all required touch-ups. Each year, the company generates about one-third of its
total revenues and gross profits from each of the three buildings. The ClearView owner has observed
that the buildings, however, require substantially different levels of support following the initial
completion of jobs. The following data have been gathered:

Support Activity	Driver	Cost per Driver Unit
Major touch-ups	Hours on jobs	$ 40
Minor touch-ups	Number of visits . . .	$160
Communication.	Number of calls. . . .	$ 20

Customer	Major Touch-ups	Minor Touch-ups	Communication
Sequoia	48	12	50
Tower Plaza	16	24	48
Cornwall	0	40	120

Assuming that each of the three customers produces gross profits of $50,000, which customer is the
most profitable, after taking into account the support activity required for each building?

a. Sequoia
b. Tower Plaza
c. Cornwall
d. Can't determine from the information given

EXERCISES—SET A

E18-1A. Activities and Cost Drivers For each of the following activities, select the most appropriate cost   **LO2**
driver. Each cost driver may be used only once.

Activity	Cost Driver
1. Pay vendors	a. Number of different kinds of raw materials
2. Evaluate vendors	b. Number of classes offered
3. Inspect raw materials	c. Number of tables
4. Plan for purchases of raw materials	d. Number of employees
5. Packaging	e. Number of operating hours
6. Supervision	f. Number of units of raw materials received
7. Employee training	g. Number of moves
8. Clean tables	h. Number of vendors
9. Machine maintenance	i. Number of checks issued
10. Move in-process product from one work station to the next	j. Number of customer orders

E18-2A. Stage 1 ABC for Machine Shop: Assigning Costs to Activity As the chief engineer of a small   **LO2**
fabrication shop, Brenda Tolliver refers to herself as a "jack-of-all-trades." When an order for a new
product comes in, Brenda must do the following:

1. Design the product to meet customer requirements.
2. Prepare a bill of materials (a list of materials required to produce the product).
3. Prepare an operations list (a sequential list of the steps involved in manufacturing the product).

Each time the foundry manufactures a batch of the product, Brenda must perform these activities:

1. Schedule the job.
2. Supervise the setup of machines that will work on the job.
3. Inspect the first unit produced to verify that it meets specifications.

Brenda supervises the production employees who perform the actual work on individual units of product. She is also responsible for employee training, ensuring that production facilities are in proper operating condition, and attending professional meetings. Brenda's estimates (in percent) of time spent on each of these activities last year are as follows:

Unit-level activities:	
Supervising production	25%
Batch-level activities:	
Scheduling jobs	18%
Supervising setups	7%
Inspecting first units	1%
Product-level activities:	
Designing product	15%
Preparing bills of materials	5%
Preparing operations lists	8%
Facility-level activities:	
Training employees	14%
Maintaining facility	5%
Attending professional meetings	2%
	100%

Required
Assuming Brenda salary is $132,000 per year, determine the dollar amount of her salary assigned to unit-, batch-, product-, and facility-level activities.

LO2   **E18-3A.**   **Stage 2 ABC for Manufacturing: Reassigning Costs to Cost Objectives** National Technology, Ltd. has developed the following activity cost information for its manufacturing activities:

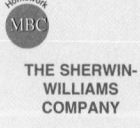

Activity	Activity Cost
Machine setup	$60.00 per batch
Movement	15.00 per batch
	0.10 per pound
Drilling	3.00 per hole
Welding	4.00 per inch
Shaping	25.00 per hour
Assembly	18.00 per hour
Inspection	2.00 per unit

Filling an order for a batch of 50 fireplace inserts that weighed 100 pounds each required the following:

- Four batch moves
- Two sets of inspections
- Drilling ten holes in each unit
- Completing 100 inches of welds on each unit
- Forty-five minutes of shaping for each unit
- One hour of assembly per unit

Required
Determine the activity cost of converting the raw materials into 50 fireplace inserts.

LO2   **E18-4A.**   **Stage 2 ABC for Manufacturing** Assume **The Sherwin-Williams Company**, a large paint manufacturer, has determined the following activity cost pools and cost driver levels for the latest period:

THE SHERWIN-
WILLIAMS
COMPANY

Activity Cost Pool	Activity Cost	Activity Cost Driver
Machine setup	$900,000	2,500 setup hours
Materials handling	820,000	4,000 materials moves
Machine operation	400,000	20,000 machine hours

The following data are for the production of single batches of two products, Mirlite and Subdue:

	Mirlite	Subdue
Gallons produced	60,000	25,000
Direct labor hours	400	250
Machine hours	800	250
Direct labor cost	$ 10,000	$ 7,500
Direct materials cost	$360,000	$150,000
Setup hours	15	12
Materials moves	60	35

Required

Determine the batch and unit costs per gallon of Mirlite and Subdue using ABC.

E18-5A.   Activity-Based Costing   Steampunk Corporation has the following predicted indirect costs and cost drivers for 2019 for the given activity cost pools:

LO2, 3

	Fabrication Department	Finishing Department	Cost Driver
Maintenance	$ 30,000	$15,000	Machine hours
Materials handling	45,000	22,500	Material moves
Machine	105,000	7,500	Machine setups
Inspections	—	37,500	Inspection hours
Total	$180,000	$82,500	

The following activity predictions were also made for the year:

	Fabrication Department	Finishing Department
Machine hours	5,000	2,500
Materials moves	1,500	750
Machine setups	350	25
Inspection hours	—	500

It is assumed that the cost per unit of activity for a given activity does not vary between departments.

Steampunk's president, Abner Punk, is trying to evaluate the company's product mix strategy regarding two of its product models, SW100 and SG150. The company has been using a company-wide overhead rate based on machine hours but is considering switching to either department rates or activity-based rates. The production manager has provided the following data for the production of a batch of 100 units for each of these models:

	SW100	SG150
Direct materials cost	$10,000	$15,000
Direct labor cost	$ 4,000	$ 3,000
Machine hours (Fabrication)	250	350
Machine hours (Finishing)	100	50
Materials moves	20	40
Machine setups	5	10
Inspection hours	15	30

Required

a.   Determine the cost of one unit each of SW100 and SG150, assuming a company-wide overhead rate is used based on total machine hours.

b.   Determine the cost of one unit of SW100 and SG150, assuming department overhead rates are used. Overhead is assigned based on machine hours in both departments.

c.   Determine the cost of one unit of SW100 and SG150, assuming activity-based overhead rates are used for maintenance, materials handling, machine setup, and inspection activities.

d.   Comment on the results of these cost calculations.

E18-6A. **Customer Profitability Analysis** HyStandard Services, Inc. provides residential painting services for three home building companies, Alpine, Blue Ridge, and Pineola, and it uses a job costing system for determining the costs for completing each job. The job cost system does not capture any cost incurred by HyStandard for return touch-ups and refinishes after the homeowner occupies the home. HyStandard paints each house on a square footage contract price, which includes painting as well as all refinishes and touch-ups required after the homes are occupied. Each year, the company generates about one-third of its total revenues and gross profits from each of the three builders. The HyStandard owner has observed that the builders, however, require substantially different levels of support following the completion of jobs. The following data have been gathered:

Support Activity	Driver	Cost per Driver Unit
Major refinishes	Hours on jobs	$ 60
Touch-ups.	Number of visits	$100
Communication.	Number of calls	$ 40

Builder	Major Refinishes	Touch-ups	Communication
Alpine	80	150	260
Blue Ridge	35	110	105
Pineola	42	115	90

Required
Assuming that each of the three customers produces gross profits of $100,000, calculate the profitability from each builder after taking into account the support activity required for each builder.

EXERCISES—SET B

E18-1B. **Developing List of Activities for Baggage Handling at an Airport** As part of a continuous improvement program, you have been asked to determine the activities involved in the baggage-handling process of a major airline at one of the airline's hubs. Prior to conducting observations and interviews, you decide that a list of possible activities would help you to better observe key activities and ask meaningful questions.

Required
For incoming aircraft only, develop a sequential list of baggage-handling activities. Your list should contain between 8 and 10 activities.

E18-2B. **Stage 1 ABC at a College: Assigning Costs to Activities** An economics professor at Prince Town University devotes 60% of her time to teaching, 35% of her time to research and writing, and 5% of her time to service activities such as committee work and student advising. The professor teaches two semesters per year. During each semester, she teaches one section of an introductory economics course (with a maximum enrollment of 50 students) and one section of a graduate economics course (with a maximum enrollment of 30 students). Including course preparation, classroom instruction, and appointments with students, each course requires an equal amount of time. The economics professor is paid $250,000 per year.

Required
Determine the activity cost of instruction per student in both the introductory and the graduate economics courses.

E18-3B. **Stage 2 ABC for a Wholesale Company** Information is presented for the activity costs of Oxford Wholesale Company:

Activity Cost per Unit of Activity Driver	
Customer relations per month	$100.00 per customer
Selling.	0.06 per sales dollar
Accounting	5.00 per order
Warehousing	0.50 per unit shipped
Packing.	0.25 per unit shipped
Shipping	0.20 per pound shipped

The following information pertains to Oxford Wholesale Company's activities in Massachusetts for the month of March 2019:

Number of orders	200
Sales revenue.	$160,000
Cost of goods sold	$95,000
Number of customers.	25
Units shipped	5,400
Pounds shipped	90,000

Required
Determine the profitability of sales in Massachusetts for March 2019.

E18-4B.   Stage 2 ABC for Manufacturing   Detroit Foundry, a large manufacturer of heavy equipment components, has determined the following activity cost pools and cost driver levels for the year: **LO2**

Activity Cost Pool	Activity Cost	Activity Cost Driver
Machine setup	$720,000	12,000 setup hours
Materials handling	120,000	3,000 tons of materials
Machine operation	680,000	10,000 machine hours

The following data are for the production of single batches of two products, C23 Cams and U2 Shafts, during the month of August:

	C23 Cams	U2 Shafts
Units produced	500	300
Machine hours	4	5
Direct labor hours	200	400
Direct labor cost	$ 5,000	$10,000
Direct materials cost.	$20,000	$15,000
Tons of materials	13	8
Setup hours	3	7

Required
Determine the unit costs of C23 Cams and U2 Shafts using ABC.

E18-5B.   Activity-Based Costing   Slack Corporation has the following predicted indirect costs and cost drivers for 2019 for the given activity cost pools: **LO2, 3**

	Fabrication Department	Finishing Department	Cost Driver
Maintenance.	$ 20,000	$10,000	Machine hours
Materials handling	30,000	15,000	Material moves
Machine setups	70,000	5,000	Machine setups
Inspections	—	25,000	Inspection hours
	$120,000	$55,000	

The following activity predictions were also made for the year:

	Fabrication Department	Finishing Department
Machine hours	10,000	5,000
Materials moves	3,000	1,500
Machine setups	700	50
Inspection hours	—	1,000

It is assumed that the cost per unit of activity for a given activity does not vary between departments.

Slack's president, Charles Slack, is trying to evaluate the company's product mix strategy regarding two of its five product models, ZX300 and SL500. The company has been using a company-wide overhead rate based on machine hours but is considering switching to either department rates or activity-based rates. The production manager has provided the following data for the production of a batch of 100 units for each of these models:

	ZX300	SL500
Direct materials cost	$12,000	$18,000
Direct labor cost	$ 5,000	$ 4,000
Machine hours (Fabrication)	500	700
Machine hours (Finishing)	200	100
Materials moves	30	50
Machine setups	5	9
Inspection hours	30	60

Required

a. Determine the cost of one unit each of ZX300 and SL500, assuming a company-wide overhead rate is used based on total machine hours.

b. Determine the cost of one unit of ZX300 and SL500, assuming department overhead rates are used. Overhead is assigned based on machine hours in both departments.

c. Determine the cost of one unit of ZX300 and SL500, assuming activity-based overhead rates are used for maintenance, materials handling, machine setup, and inspection activities.

d. Comment on the results of these cost calculations.

LO5   E18-6B.   Customer Profitability Analysis FanGear Inc. produces metal products for universities and colleges, including items such as trailer hitch covers and license plate holders with the institutions' logos and mascot likenesses, for sale by the institutions to their alumni and sports fans. FanGear produces these products in batches and uses a job costing system for determining the costs for completing each job. Each new batch requires a unique design, reconfiguring of dies and machinery to produce the product, and cleaning and maintenance of the machinery following the production run in preparation for the next batch. FanGear's CFO wants to implement an activity-based costing system for allocating overhead costs to each job. The accounting department staff have gathered the following activity cost pools and per-activity rates for the latest period:

Support Activity	Driver	Cost per Driver Unit
Product design	Change orders	$100
Batch setup.	Setup hours	$ 50
Machine maintenance	Machine hours	$ 40

For the latest period, FanGear produced products for three new major university customers:

Customer	Change Orders	Setup Hours	Machine hours
Southern Utah	10	4	32
Utah Valley	6	8	48
Utah State.	4	6	40

Assuming that the production run for each of the three universities results in gross profits of $10,000, calculate the profitability from each university customer after taking into account the support activity required for each university customer.

PROBLEMS—SET A

P18-1A.   Calculating Manufacturing Overhead Rates Glassman Company accumulated the following data   **LO3**
for 2019:

Milling Department manufacturing overhead	$484,000
Finishing Department manufacturing overhead	$260,000
Machine hours used	
Milling Department	10,000 hours
Finishing Department	2,000 hours
Labor hours used	
Milling Department	1,000 hours
Finishing Department	1,000 hours

Required

a.   Calculate the company-wide manufacturing overhead rate using machine hours as the allocation base.

b.   Calculate the company-wide manufacturing overhead rate using direct labor hours as the allocation base.

c.   Calculate department overhead rates using machine hours in Milling and direct labor hours in
Finishing as the allocation bases.

d.   Calculate department overhead rates using direct labor hours in Milling and machine hours in
Finishing as the allocation bases.

e.   Which of these allocation systems seems to be more appropriate? Explain.

P18-2A.   Calculating Activity-Based Costing Overhead Rates Assume that manufacturing overhead for   **LO3**
Glassman Company in the previous exercise consisted of the following activities and costs:

Setup (1,000 setup hours)	$288,000
Production scheduling (400 batches)	60,000
Production engineering (60 change orders)	180,000
Supervision (2,000 direct labor hours)	56,000
Machine maintenance (12,000 machine hours)	168,000
Total activity costs	$752,000

The following additional data were provided for Job 845:

Direct materials costs	$7,000
Direct labor cost (5 Milling direct labor hours;	
35 Finishing direct labor hours)	$1,000
Setup hours	5 hours
Production scheduling	1 batch
Machine hours used (25 Milling machine hours;	
5 Finishing machine hours)	30 hours
Production engineering	3 change orders

Required

a.   Calculate the cost per unit of activity driver for each activity cost category.

b.   Calculate the cost of Job 845 using ABC to assign the overhead costs.

c.   Calculate the cost of Job 845 using the company-wide overhead rate based on machine hours
calculated in P18-1A(a).

d.   Calculate the cost of Job 845 using a machine hour departmental overhead rate for the Milling
Department and a direct labor hour overhead rate for the Finishing Department (see P18-1A
(c)).

P18-3A.   ABC—A Service Application Grand Haven is a senior living community that offers a full range of   **LO2**
services including independent living, assisted living, and skilled nursing care. The assisted living
division provides residential space, meals, and medical services (MS) to its residents. The current
costing system adds the cost of all of these services (space, meals, and MS) and divides by total
resident days to get a cost per resident day for each month. Recognizing that MS tends to vary

significantly among the residents, Grand Haven's accountant recommended that an ABC system be designed to calculate more accurately the cost of MS provided to residents. She decided that residents should be classified into four categories (A, B, C, D) based on the level of services received, with group A representing the lowest level of service and D representing the highest level of service. Two cost drivers being considered for measuring MS costs are number of assistance calls and number of assistant contacts. A contact is registered each time an assistance professional provides medical services or aid to a resident. The accountant has gathered the following data for the most recent annual period:

Resident Classification	Annual Resident Days	Annual Assistance Hours	Number of Assistance Contacts
A.............	8,760	15,000	60,000
B.............	6,570	20,000	52,000
C.............	4,380	22,500	52,000
D.............	2,190	32,500	52,000
	21,900	90,000	216,000

Other Data:

Total cost of medical services for the period......................	$5,000,000
Total cost of meals and residential space........................	$3,280,000

Required (Round Answers and Intermediate Calculations to the Nearest Dollar)

a. Determine the ABC cost of a resident day for each category of residents using assistance hours as the cost driver.

b. Determine the ABC cost of a resident day for each category of residents using assistance contacts as the cost driver.

c. Which cost driver do you think provides the more accurate measure of the cost per day for a Grand Haven resident?

LO2   **P18-4A.**   **Stage 2 ABC for Manufacturing** Merlot Company has determined its activity cost pools and cost drivers to be the following:

Cost Pools	
Setup..	$ 59,500
Materials handling....................................	16,000
Machine operation	300,000
Packing...	60,000
Total indirect manufacturing costs....................	$435,500

Cost drivers	
Setups..	350
Materials moves	640
Machine hours	20,000
Packing orders	1,000

One product made by Merlot, metal casements, used the following activities during the period to produce 500 units:

Setups	20
Materials moves......................................	80
Machine hours	1,900
Packing orders	150

Required

a. Calculate the cost per unit of activity for each activity cost pool for Merlot Company.

b. Calculate the manufacturing overhead cost per metal casement manufactured during the period.

P18-5A. **Traditional Product Costing versus Activity-Based Costing** Assume that **Panasonic Company** has determined its estimated total manufacturing overhead cost for one of its plants to be $204,000, consisting of the following activity cost pools for the current month:

LO2, 3

Activity Centers	Activity Costs	Cost Drivers	Activity Level
Assembly setups	$ 45,000	Setup hours	1,500
Materials handling	15,000	Number of moves	300
Assembly	120,000	Assembly hours	12,000
Maintenance.	24,000	Maintenance hours.	1,200
Total	$204,000		

PANASONIC COMPANY

Total direct labor hours used during the month were 8,000. Panasonic produces many different electronic products, including the following two products produced during the current month:

	Model X301	Model Z205
Units produced	1,000	1,000
Direct materials costs	$15,000	$15,000
Direct labor costs	$12,500	$12,500
Direct labor hours	500	500
Setup hours	50	100
Materials moves	25	50
Assembly hours	800	800
Maintenance hours.	10	40

Required
a. Calculate the total per-unit cost of each model using direct labor hours to assign manufacturing overhead to products.
b. Calculate the total per-unit cost of each model using activity-based costing to assign manufacturing overhead to products.
c. Comment on the accuracy of the two methods for determining product costs.
d. Discuss some of the strategic implications of your answers to the previous requirements.

P18-6A. **Activity-Based Costing in a Service Organization** Red River Banking Company has ten automatic teller machines (ATMs) spread throughout the city maintained by the ATM Department. You have been assigned the task of determining the cost of operating each machine. Management will use the information you develop, along with other information pertaining to the volume and type of transactions at each machine, to evaluate the desirability of continuing to operate each machine and/or changing security arrangements for a particular machine.

LO2, 3

SERVICE AND MERCHANDISING

The ATM Department consists of a total of six employees: a supervisor, a head cashier, two associate cashiers, and two maintenance personnel. The associate cashiers make between two and four daily trips to each machine to collect and replenish cash and to replenish supplies, deposit tickets, and so forth. Each machine contains a small computer that automatically summarizes and reports transactions to the head cashier. The head cashier reconciles the activities of the two associate cashiers to the computerized reports. The supervisor, who does not handle cash, reviews the reconciliation. When an automatic teller's computer, a customer, or a cashier reports a problem, the two maintenance employees and one cashier are dispatched immediately. The cashier removes all cash and transaction records, and the maintenance employees repair the machine.

Maintenance employees spend all of their time on maintenance-related activities. The associate cashiers spend approximately 50% of their time on maintenance-related activities and 50% on daily trips. The head cashier's time is divided, with 75% directly related to daily trips to each machine and 25% related to supervising cashiers on maintenance calls. The supervisor devotes 20% of the time to daily trips to each machine and 80% to the equal supervision of each employee. Cost information for a recent month follows:

Salaries	
Supervisor.	$ 4,000
Head cashier.	3,000
Other ($1,800 each)	7,200
Lease and operating costs	
Cashiers' service vehicle	1,200
Maintenance service vehicle.	1,400
Office rent and utilities	2,300
Machine lease, space rent, and utilities ($1,500 each).	15,000
Total	$34,100

Related monthly activity information for this month follows:

Machine	Routine Trips	Maintenance Hours
1	30	5
2	90	17
3	60	15
4	60	30
5	120	15
6	30	10
7	90	25
8	120	5
9	60	20
10	60	18
Total	720	160

Additional information follows:

- The office is centrally located with about equal travel time to each machine.
- Maintenance hours include travel time.
- The cashiers' service vehicle is used exclusively for routine visits.
- The office space is divided equally between the supervisor and the head cashier.

Required

a. Determine the monthly operating costs of machines 7 and 8 when cost assignments are based on the number of machines.

b. Determine the activity cost of a routine trip and a maintenance hour for the month given. Round answers to the nearest cent.

c. Determine the operating costs assigned and reassigned to machines 7 and 8 when activity-based costing is used.

d. How can ABC cost information be used by Red River Banking Company to improve the overall management of monthly operating costs?

LO3, 4   **P18-7A.**   **Product Costing: Company-wide Overhead versus ABC** LaMesa produces machine parts as a contract provider for a large manufacturing company. LaMesa produces two particular parts, shafts and gears. The competition is keen among contract producers, and LaMesa's top management realizes how vulnerable its market is to cost-cutting competitors. Hence, having a very accurate understanding of costs is important to LaMesa's survival.

LaMesa's president, Jose Rodriguez, has observed that the company's current cost to produce shafts is $21.35, and the current cost to produce gears is $12.36. He indicated to the controller that he suspects some problems with the cost system because LaMesa is suddenly experiencing extraordinary competition on shafts, but it seems to have a virtual corner on the gears market. He is even considering dropping the shaft line and converting the company to a one-product manufacturer of gears. He asked the controller, Felix Bernhardt, to conduct a thorough cost study and to consider whether changes in the cost system are necessary. The controller collected the following data about the company's costs and various manufacturing activities for the most recent month:

	Shafts	Gears
Production units	50,000	10,500
Selling price	$31.86	$24.00
Overhead per unit (based on direct labor hours)	$12.82	$ 6.10
Materials and direct labor cost per unit.	$ 8.53	$ 6.26
Number of production runs.	10	20
Number of purchasing and receiving orders processed.	40	100
Number of machine hours	12,750	6,000
Number of direct labor hours	25,000	2,500
Number of engineering hours.	5,000	5,000
Number of material moves	50	40

The controller was able to summarize the company's total manufacturing overhead into the following pools:

Setup costs.	$ 30,000
Machine cost	175,000
Purchasing and receiving costs	210,000
Engineering costs.	200,000
Materials handling costs.	90,000
Total	$705,000

Required

a. Calculate LaMesa's current company-wide overhead rate based on direct labor hours.

b. Verify LaMesa's calculation of overhead cost per unit of $12.82 for shafts and $6.10 for gears.

c. Calculate the manufacturing overhead cost per unit for shafts and gears using activity-based costing, assuming each of the five cost pools represents a separate activity pool. Use the most appropriate activity driver for assigning activity costs to the two products.

d. Comment on LaMesa's current cost system and the reason the company is facing fierce competition for shafts but little competition for gears.

P18-8A.   Customer Profitability Analysis Gonalong, Inc., has ten customers that account for all of its $4,500,000 of net income. Its activity-based costing system is able to assign all costs, except for $650,000 of general administrative costs, to key activities incurred in connection with serving its customers. A customer profitability analysis based on activity costing produced the following customer profits and losses:

LO5

Customer #1.	$ 346,000
#2	624,000
#3	(257,000)
#4	969,000
#5	1,040,000
#6	872,000
#7	628,000
#8	322,000
#9	(105,000)
#10	711,000
Total	$5,150,000

Required

Prepare a customer profitability profile graph. Sort the customers in order of profitability from most profitable to least profitable, then plot the cumulative profit with total profits along the y-axis and customers along the x-axis. What is the maximum amount of profit that Gonalong could achieve if it were to eliminate its unprofitable customers?

LO5 **P18-9A.** **Customer Profitability Analysis** Refer to the previous exercise P18-8A for Gonalong, Inc.

Required

a. If Gonalong were to notify customers 3 and 9 that it will no longer be able to provide them services in the future, will that increase company profits by $362,000? Why or why not?

b. What is the primary benefit of preparing a customer profitability analysis?

PROBLEMS—SET B

LO2, 3 **P18-1B.** **Activity-Based Costing and Conventional Costs Compared** Hickory Grill Company manufactures two types of cooking grills: the Gas Cooker and the Charcoal Smoker. The cooker is a premium product sold in upscale outdoor shops; the smoker is sold in major discount stores. Following is information pertaining to the manufacturing costs for the current month:

	Gas Cooker	Charcoal Smoker
Units	1,000	4,000
Number of batches	50	10
Number of batch moves	80	20
Direct materials	$40,000	$90,000
Direct labor	$20,000	$25,000

Manufacturing overhead follows:

Activity	Cost	Cost Driver
Materials acquisition and inspection	$52,000	Amount of direct materials cost
Materials movement	17,450	Number of batch moves
Scheduling	30,000	Number of batches
	$99,450	

Required

a. Determine the total and per-unit costs of manufacturing the Gas Cooker and Charcoal Smoker for the month, assuming all manufacturing overhead is assigned on the basis of direct labor dollars.

b. Determine the total and per-unit costs of manufacturing the Gas Cooker and Charcoal Smoker for the month, assuming manufacturing overhead is assigned using activity-based costing.

LO2, 3 **P18-2B.** **Activity-Based Costing versus Conventional Costing** Refer to the previous exercise in P18-1B for Hickory Grill.

Required

a. Comment on the differences between the solutions to requirements (a) and (b). Which is more accurate? What errors might managers make if all manufacturing overhead costs are assigned on the basis of direct labor dollars?

b. Comment on the adequacy of the preceding data to meet management's needs.

LO2, 3 **P18-3B.** **Traditional Product Costing versus Activity-Based Costing** High Country Outfitters, Inc., makes backpacks for large sporting goods chains that are sold under the customers' store brand names. The accounting department has identified the following overhead costs and cost drivers for next year:

Overhead Item	Expected Costs	Cost Driver	Maximum Quantity
Setup costs	$ 828,000	Number of setups	7,200
Ordering costs	252,000	Number of orders	60,000
Maintenance	1,360,000	Number of machine hours	80,000
Power	210,000	Number of kilowatt hours	600,000

Total predicted direct labor hours for next year is 60,000. The following data are for two recently completed jobs:

	Job 201	Job 202
Cost of direct materials.	$13,500	$15,000
Cost of direct labor	$19,125	$71,250
Number of units completed.	1,125	915
Number of direct labor hours	270	330
Number of setups.	18	22
Number of orders	24	45
Number of machine hours	540	450
Number of kilowatt hours	270	360

Required

a. Determine the unit cost for each job using a traditional company-wide overhead rate based on direct labor hours.

b. Determine the unit cost for each job using ABC. (Round answers to two decimal places.)

c. As the manager of High Country, is there additional information that you would want to help you evaluate the pricing and profitability of Jobs 201 and 202?

d. Assuming the company has been using the method required in part *a,* how should management react to the findings in part *b*?

P18-4B.   Stage 2 ABC for Manufacturing with Variances Montreat Manufacturing has developed the following activity cost pool information for its 2019 manufacturing activities:

	Budgeted Activity Cost	Activity Cost Driver at Practical Capacity
Purchasing and materials handling	$675,000	900,000 kilograms
Setup	700,000	1,120 setups
Machine operations	954,000	12,000 hours
First unit inspection.	50,000	1,000 batches
Packaging.	250,000	312,500 units

Actual 2019 production information is as follows:

	Standard Product A	Standard Product B	Specialty Products
Units	150,000	100,000	50,000
Batches.	100	80	600
Setups*.	300	160	900
Machine operations (hours)	6,000	3,000	2,000
Kilograms of raw materials.	400,000	300,000	200,000
Direct materials costs.	$900,000	$600,000	$820,000

*Some products require setups on two or more machines.

Required

a. Determine the unit cost of each product for Montreat Manufacturing.

b. Explain why the unit cost of the specialty products is so much higher than the unit cost of Standard Product A or Standard Product B.

P18-5B.   ABC Costing for a Service Organization Fairfield Mortgage Company is a full-service residential mortgage company in the Atlanta area that operates in a very competitive market. The CEO, Richard Sissom, is concerned about operating costs associated with processing mortgage applications and has decided to install an ABC costing system to help him get a handle on costs. Although labor hours seem to be the primary driver of the cost of processing a new mortgage, the labor cost for the different activities involved in processing new loans varies widely. The Accounting Department has provided the following data for the company's five major cost pools for 2019:

Activity Cost Pools		Activity Drivers	
Taking customer applications. . . .	$ 300,000	Time—assistant managers.	12,000 hours
Conducting credit investigations. .	450,000	Time—credit managers	16,500 hours
Underwriting	525,000	Time—Underwriting Department . . .	10,000 hours
Preparing loan packages	200,000	Time—Processing Department	8,000 hours
Closing loans	600,000	Time—Legal Department hours	6,000 hours
	$2,075,000		52,500 hours

During 2019, the company processed and issued 5,000 new mortgages, two of which are summarized here with regard to activities used to process the mortgages:

	Loan 5066	Loan 5429
Application processing hours	1.50	2.75
Credit investigating hours.	4.00	3.00
Underwriting hours	2.50	4.75
Processing hours	3.50	3.00
Legal processing hours	1.50	1.50
Total hours	13.00	15.00

Required

a. Determine the cost per unit of activity for each activity cost pool.

b. Determine the cost of processing loans 5066 and 5429.

c. Determine the cost of preparing loans 5066 and 5429 assuming that an average cost per hour for all activities is used.

d. Compare and discuss your answers to requirements (*b*) and (*c*).

LO2, 3 **P18-6B.** **Product Costing: Department versus ABC for Overhead** Advertising Technologies Inc. (ATI) specializes in providing both published and online advertising services for the business marketplace. The company monitors its costs based on the cost per column inch of published space printed in print advertising media and based on the cost per minute of telephone advertising time delivered on "The AD Line," a computer-based, online advertising service. ATI has one new competitor, Tel-a-Ad, in its local teleadvertising market; and with increased competition, ATI has seen a decline in sales of online advertising in recent years. ATI's president, Robert Beard, believes that predatory pricing by Tel-a-Ad has caused the problem. The following is a recent conversation between Robert and Jane Minnear, director of marketing for ATI:

Jane: I just received a call from one of our major customers concerning our advertising rates on "The AD Line" who said that a sales rep from another firm (it had to be Tel-a-Ad) had offered the same service at $1 per minute, which is $1.50 per minute less than our price.

Robert: It's costing about $1.27 per minute to produce that product. I don't see how they can afford to sell it so cheaply. I'm not convinced that we should meet the price. Perhaps the better strategy is to emphasize producing and selling more published ads, which we're more experienced with and where our margins are high and we have virtually no competition.

Jane: You may be right. Based on a recent survey of our customers, I think we can raise the price significantly for published advertising and still not lose business.

Robert: That sounds promising; however, before we make a major recommitment to publishing, let's explore other possible explanations. I want to know how our costs compare with our competitors. Maybe we could be more efficient and find a way to earn a good return on teleadvertising.

After this meeting, Robert and Jane requested an investigation of production costs and comparative efficiency of producing published versus online advertising services. The controller, Tim Gentry, indicated that ATI's efficiency was comparable to that of its competitors and prepared the following cost data:

	Published Advertising	Online Advertising
Estimated number of production units	200,000	10,000,000
Selling price	$200	$2.50
Direct product costs	$21,000,000	$5,000,000
Overhead allocation*	$9,800,000	$7,700,000
Overhead per unit.	$49	$0.77
Direct costs per unit	$105	$0.50
Number of customers.	180,000	25,000
Number of salesperson days	32,000	5,500
Number of art and design hours.	35,000	5,000
Number of creative services subcontract hours	100,000	25,000
Number of customer service calls	72,000	8,000

*Based on direct labor costs

Upon examining the data, Robert decided that he wanted to know more about the overhead costs because they were such a high proportion of total production costs. He was provided the following list of overhead costs and told that they were currently being assigned to products in proportion to direct labor costs:

Selling costs	$7,500,000
Visual and audio design costs	3,000,000
Creative services costs.	5,000,000
Customer service costs	2,000,000

Required

Using the data provided by the controller, prepare analyses to help Robert and Jane in making their decisions. (*Hint:* Prepare cost calculations for both product lines using ABC to see whether there is any significant difference in their unit costs). Should ATI switch from the fast-growing, online advertising market back into the well-established published advertising market? Does the charge of predatory pricing seem valid? Why are customers likely to be willing to pay a higher price to get published services? Do traditional costing and activity-based costing lead to the same conclusions?

P18-7B. **Unit-Level and Multiple-Level Cost Assignments** CarryAll Company produces briefcases from leather, fabric, and synthetic materials in a single production department. The basic product is a standard briefcase made from leather and lined with fabric. CarryAll has a good reputation in the market because the standard briefcase is a high-quality item that has been produced for many years.

LO2, 3

Last year, the company decided to expand its product line and produce specialty briefcases for special orders. These briefcases differ from the standard in that they vary in size, contain both leather and synthetic materials, and are imprinted with the buyer's logo (the standard briefcase is simply imprinted with the CarryAll name in small letters). The decision to use some synthetic materials in the briefcase was made to hold down the materials cost. To reduce the labor costs per unit, most of the cutting and stitching on the specialty briefcases is done by automated machines, which are used to a much lesser degree in the production of the standard briefcases. Because of these changes in the design and production of the specialty briefcases, CarryAll management believed that they would cost less to produce than the standard briefcases. However, because they are specialty items, they were priced slightly higher; standards are priced at $30 and specialty briefcases at $32.

After reviewing last month's results of operations, CarryAll's president became concerned about the profitability of the two product lines because the standard briefcase showed a loss while the specialty briefcase showed a greater profit margin than expected. The president is wondering whether the company should drop the standard briefcase and focus entirely on specialty items. Units and cost data for last month's operations as reported to the president are as follows:

	Standard	Specialty
Units produced	10,000	2,500
Direct materials		
Leather (1 sq. yd. × $15.00; ½ sq. yd. × $15.00)	$15.00	$ 7.50
Fabric (1 sq. yd. × $5.00; 1 sq. yd. × $5.00)	5.00	5.00
Synthetic.		5.00
Total Materials	20.00	17.50
Direct Labor (½ hr. × $12.00; ¼ hr. × $12.00).	6.00	3.00
Manufacturing Overhead (½ hr. × $8.98; ¼ hr. × $8.98).	4.49	2.25
Cost per unit	$30.49	$22.75

Manufacturing overhead is applied on the basis of direct labor hours. The rate of $8.98 per direct labor hour was calculated by dividing the total overhead ($50,500) by the direct labor hours (5,625). As shown in the table, the cost of a standard briefcase is $0.49 higher than its $30 sales price; the specialty briefcase has a cost of only $22.75, for a gross profit per unit of $9.25. The problem with these costs is that they do not accurately reflect the activities involved in manufacturing each product. Determining the costs using ABC should provide better product costing data to help gauge the actual profitability of each product line.

     The manufacturing overhead costs must be analyzed to determine the activities driving the costs. Assume that the following costs and cost drivers have been identified:

- The Purchasing Department's cost is $6,000. The major activity driving these costs is the number of purchase orders processed. During the month, the Purchasing Department prepared the following number of purchase orders for the materials indicated:

Leather	20
Fabric	30
Synthetic materials	50

- The cost of receiving and inspecting materials is $7,500. These costs are driven by the number of deliveries. During the month, the following number of deliveries were made:

Leather	30
Fabric	40
Synthetic materials	80

- Production line setup cost is $10,000. Setup activities involve changing the machines to produce the different types of briefcases. Each setup for production of the standard briefcases requires one hour; each setup for specialty briefcases requires two hours. Standard briefcases are produced in batches of 200, and specialty briefcases are produced in batches of 25. During the last month, there were 50 setups for the standard item and 100 setups for the specialty item.
- The cost of inspecting finished goods is $8,000. All briefcases are inspected to ensure that quality standards are met. However, the final inspection of standard briefcases takes very little time because the employees identify and correct quality problems as they do the hand cutting and stitching. A survey of the personnel responsible for inspecting the final products showed that 150 hours were spent on standard briefcases and 250 hours on specialty briefcases during the month.
- Equipment-related costs are $6,000. Equipment-related costs include repairs, depreciation, and utilities. Management has determined that a logical basis for assigning these costs to products is machine hours. A standard briefcase requires 1/2 hour of machine time, and a specialty briefcase requires two hours. Thus, during the last month, 5,000 hours of machine time relate to the standard line and 5,000 hours relate to the specialty line.
- Plant-related costs are $13,000. These costs include property taxes, insurance, administration, and others. For the purpose of determining average unit costs, they are to be assigned to products using machine hours.

Required

a.   Using activity-based costing concepts, what overhead costs should be assigned to the two products?

b. What is the unit cost of each product using activity-based costing concepts?
c. Reevaluate the president's concern about the profitability of the two product lines.
d. Discuss the merits of activity-based management as it relates to CarryAll's ABC cost system.

P18-8B. Customer Profitability Analysis Rogers Aeronautics Ltd., is a British aeronautics subcontract company that designs and manufactures electronic control systems for commercial airlines. The vast majority of all commercial aircraft are manufactured by Boeing in the U.S. and Airbus in Europe; however, there is a relatively small group of companies that manufacture narrow-body commercial jets. Assume for this exercise that Rogers does contract work for the two major manufacturers plus three companies in the second tier.

LO5

Because competition is intense in the industry, Rogers has always operated on a fairly thin 20% gross profit margin; hence, it is crucial that it manage non-manufacturing overhead costs effectively in order to achieve an acceptable net profit margin. With declining profit margins in recent years, Rogers Aeronautics' CEO, Len Rogers, has become concerned that the cost of obtaining contracts and maintaining relations with its five major customers may be getting out of hand. You have been hired to conduct a customer profitability analysis.

Rogers Aeronautics' non-manufacturing overhead consists of $2.5 million of general and administrative (G&A) expense (including, among other expenses, the CEO's salary and bonus and the cost of operating the company's corporate jet) and selling and customer support expenses of $3 million (including 5% sales commissions and $1,050,000 of additional costs).

The accounting staff determined that the $1,050,000 of additional selling and customer support expenses related to the following four activity cost pools:

Activity	Activity Cost Driver	Cost per Unit of Activity
1. Sales visits	Number of visit days	$ 800
2. Product adjustments.	Number of adjustments	1,300
3. Phone and email contacts	Number of calls/contacts	50
4. Promotion and entertainment events	Number of events	2,000

Financial and activity data on the five customers follows (Sales and Gross Profit data in millions):

Customer	Sales	Gross Profit	Quantity of Sales and Support Activity			
			Activity 1	Activity 2	Activity 3	Activity 4
#1	$17	$3.40	106	23	220	82
#2	12	2.4	130	36	354	66
#3	3	0.6	52	10	180	74
#4	4	0.8	34	6	138	18
#5	3	0.6	16	5	104	10
	$39	$7.80	338	80	996	250

In addition to the above, the sales staff used the corporate jet at a cost of $800 per hour for trips to customers as follows:

Customer #1.	24 hours
Customer #2.	36 hours
Customer #3.	5 hours
Customer #4.	0 hours
Customer #5.	6 hours

The total cost of operating the airplane is included in general and administrative expense; none is included in selling and customer support costs.

Required
a. Prepare a customer profitability analysis for Rogers Aeronautics that shows the gross profits less all expenses that can reasonably be assigned to the five customers.
b. Now assuming that the remaining general and administrative costs are assigned to the five customers based on relative sales dollars, calculate net profit for each customer.
c. Discuss the merits of the analysis in part *a* versus part *b*.

EXTENDING YOUR KNOWLEDGE

EYK18-1. Business Decision Case The Reserve Club is a traditional private golf and country club that has three different categories of memberships: golf, tennis & swimming, and social. Golf members have access to all amenities and programs in the club, Tennis & Swimming members have access to all amenities and programs except use of the golf course, and Social members have access to only the social activities of the club, excluding golf, tennis, and swimming. All members have clubhouse privileges, including use of the bar and restaurant, which is operated by an outside contractor. During the past year, the average membership in each category, along with the number of club visits during the year, was as follows:

	Members	Visits
Golf.	260	9,360
Tennis and swimming.	50	1,500
Social	120	2,160

Some members of the club have been complaining that heavy users of the club are not bearing their share of the costs through their membership fees. Dess Rosmond, General Manager of the Reserve Club, agrees that monthly fees paid by the various member groups should be based on the annual average amount of cost-related activities provided by the club for the three groups, and he intends to set fees on that basis for the coming year. The annual direct costs of operating the golf course, tennis courts, and swimming pool have been calculated by the club's controller as follows:

Golf course.	$900,000
Swimming pool.	50,000
Tennis courts.	25,000

The operation of the bar and restaurant and all related costs, including depreciation on the bar and restaurant facilities, are excluded from this analysis. In addition to the above costs, the club incurs general overhead costs in the following amounts for the most recent (and typical) year:

General Ledger Overhead Accounts	**Amounts**
Indirect labor for the club management staff (the general manager, assistant general manager, membership manager, and club controller).	$250,000
Utilities (other than those directly related to golf, swimming, and tennis).	24,000
Website maintenance.	2,000
Postage	5,000
Computers and information systems maintenance	7,500
Clubhouse maintenance and depreciation.	30,000
Liability insurance.	4,000
Security contract.	12,000
	$334,500

Dess believes that the best way to assign most of the overhead costs to the three membership categories is with an activity-based system that recognizes four key activities that occur regularly in the club:

1. Recruiting and providing orientation for new members
2. Maintaining the membership roster and communicating with members
3. Planning, scheduling, and managing club events
4. Maintaining the financial records and reporting for the club

Required

a. Identify and explain which overhead costs can reasonably be assigned to one or more of the four key activities, and suggest a basis for making the assignment.

b. Identify a cost driver for each activity cost pool that would seem to be suitable for assigning the activity cost pool to the three membership categories.

c. Suggest a method for assigning any overhead costs to the three membership categories that cannot reasonably be assigned to activity pools.

d. Comment on the suitability of ABC to this cost assignment situation.

ANSWERS TO SELF-STUDY QUESTIONS:

1. c, (p. 859) 2. d, (p. 862) 3. c, (p. 867) 4. d, (p. 868) 5. d, (p. 871) 6. d, (p. 872)

YOUR TURN! SOLUTIONS

Solution 18.1

The butterscotch cookies are $4,000 more profitable, as shown below:
- Cost of semi-sweet cookie delivery: [(15,000 × 18) ÷ 60] × $15 = $67,500
- Cost of butterscotch cookie delivery: [(10,500 × 12) ÷ 60] × $15 = $31,500
- Semi-sweet cookie profit: $200,000 − $112,000 − $67,500 = $20,500
- Butterscotch cookie profit: $140,000 − $84,000 − $31,500 = $24,500
- Profit difference: $4,000

Solution 18.2

Your response might include the following major points:

1. An ABC costing system would help the company to more completely identify all of the activities that cause the company to incur the overhead cost in the first place.
2. An ABC costing system would provide for more accurate tracing of overhead costs to products because the overhead costs are more closely associated with the related activity (or cost driver).
3. Having a better understanding of the costs of each product will help management set production priorities, sales targets, and prices to maximize company profits.

Solution 18.3

b. Traditional cost systems that utilize a single overhead rate tend to over-cost high volume products.

Solution 18.4

No. Despite the customer's large number of returns and high demand for visits and calls, a customer profitability analysis shows that they are still profitable:
- Sales − cost of sales − (cost of returns + cost of visits + cost of calls) = customer profit
- $100,000 − $85,000 − (50*$100 + 25*$150 + 120*$30) = $2,650

Solution 18.5

c. Movement of materials does not add value from the customer's perspective. The company might arrange for the vendor to deliver the raw materials directly to the production floor as needed, eliminating or reducing the need for a raw materials storehouse.

Chapter 19

Cost-Volume-Profit Relationships

PAST

Chapter 18 explored activity-based costing and its benefits relative to traditional company-wide and departmental overhead allocation, and contrasted it with activity-based management.

PRESENT

Chapter 19 advances our understanding of cost behaviors (introduced in Chapter 15) to assist in the development of cost formulas. We also use cost behaviors to determine break-even points, target profit volumes, and make planning and budgeting decisions.

FUTURE

Chapter 20 will use the cost formula approach and contribution margin statement developed in Chapter 19 to prepare a variable income statement. We will also discuss reporting for segments of businesses.

iTunes, the original Apple music platform, celebrated its 15th Anniversary in early 2018.[1] In 2003, iTunes was originally conceived as a "break-even" business to drive sales of Apple's hardware products, principally the iPod which had been introduced in 2001. Apple's business strategy was to provide individual songs at "cost" that could be downloaded to the iPod as part of the customer's music library to be played on demand. Apple planned to make its profit on the sale of the iPod. The strategy worked! In its first week, iTunes sold over 1 million songs, making it the largest online music company in the world. In that same week, Apple sold over 130,000 iPods too.

Now, 15 years later, iTunes has close to 600 million active accounts, has sold over 25 billion music downloads, has over 40 million subscribers to its streaming music service, and by some estimates is selling 50,000 movies per day.[2] iTunes is no longer a "break-even" business, but a highly profitable one, generating an estimated $34 billion in annual sales.[3]

This chapter explores how cost-volume-profit analysis can help a company such as Apple determine the number of songs it would need to sell to break even on its business or help Fezzari predict the number of bikes it must produce and sell to achieve a particular profit level.

---

[1] https://www.standard.co.uk/tech/itunes-15th-anniversary-15-facts-a3825741.html

[2] http://fortune.com/2008/06/19/itunes-store-5-billion-songs-50000-movies-per-day/

[3] https://www.billboard.com/articles/business/8023006/apples-itunes-division-touts-record-85b-revenue

Road Map

LO	Learning Objective	Page	eLecture	Guided Example	Assignments
LO1	Develop an understanding of how specific types of costs change in response to volume changes.	902	E19-1	YT19.1	SS1, Q1, Q2, Q3, Q4, Q7, SE2, E1A, E18A, E18B, P2A, P7A, P2B, P7B
LO2	Define the concept of relevant range.	905	E19-2	YT19.2	SS2, Q1, Q6, E3A, P2A, P3A, P4A, P7A, P2B, P3B, P4B, P7B
LO3	Outline the approach to developing cost formulas.	906	E19-3	YT19.3	SS3, Q4, Q5, Q7, Q8, SE2, E2A, E3A, E4A, E5A, E6A, E1B, E2B, E3B, E4B, E5B, E6B, P2A, P3A, P4A, P5A, P6A, P7A, P2B, P3B, P4B, P5B, P6B, P7B
LO4	Present a discussion of and a formula for calculating the break-even point.	912	E19-4	YT19.4	SS4, Q9, Q10, Q11, Q12, SE2, E7A, E13A, E14A, E7B, E8B, E9B, E10B, E12B, E13B, E14B, E15B, P8A, P9A, P10A, P11A, P1B, P8B, P9B, P10B, P11B
LO5	Define contribution margin and contribution margin ratio and present alternate break-even formulas and examples of their application.	914	E19-5	YT19.5	SS5, Q13, E8A, E9A, E10A, E11A, E13A, E14A, E15A, E8B, E9B, E10B, E11B, E12B, E13B, E14B, E15B, P1A, P8A, P9A, P10A, P11A, P1B, P8B, P9B, P10B, P11B
LO6	Discuss approaches to planning net income using cost-volume-profit analyses.	917	E19-6	YT19.6	SS6, Q14, Q15, Q16, SE3, SE5, E12A, E13A, E14A, E16A, E17A, E9B, E10B, E12B, E13B, E14B, E15B, E16B, E17B, P3A, P8A, P9A, P10A, P11A, P3B, P8B, P9B, P10B, P11B

"We lose money on every sale—but make up the difference in volume."

ANONYMOUS

Management must study a number of factors when planning the future course for an organization. One of the most important factors is the relationships among sales (revenue), costs (expenses), and profit (net income). **Cost-volume-profit (CVP) analysis** is used to study these relationships.

CVP analysis is appropriately used by for-profit organizations as well as not-for-profit (NFP) organizations. NFPs use the analysis with a target profit of zero. All of the relationships studied in the analysis are equally valid for both types of organizations.

COST BEHAVIOR ANALYSIS

LO1 **Develop an** understanding of how specific types of costs change in response to volume changes.

Recall from Chapter 15 that classifying costs based on their behavior is incredibly useful to decision makers. We briefly revisit these concepts in Chapter 19 because the foundation for CVP analysis is a thorough understanding of cost behavior. **Cost behavior analysis** is the study of how specific costs respond to changes in the volume of business activity. Each specific cost incurred by an organization may be affected differently by changes in the volume of business activity. Some costs will increase proportionately as volume increases, some costs will change disproportionately, and some costs will remain the same. Other factors besides volume can also cause changes in specific costs. For example, an increase in the assessment rate can increase property tax expense, whereas a decrease in electricity rates can lower total utility expense. These types of changes, however, are not typically caused by changes in business activity volume.

Selecting the Activity Basis

For meaningful managerial analysis, costs must be related to some measure of business activity. As we introduced in Chapter 16 and discussed further in Chapter 18, this measure of business activity is referred to as a cost driver. Cost drivers can include units of product, direct labor hours, machine hours, or percentage of capacity. A critical aspect is that the activity measure used must have a logical causal relation with costs, and the quantity of the activity must be highly correlated with the level of costs. Management must consider the objective of the analysis when selecting the most relevant and useful cost driver. For example, if iTunes managers want to analyze the cost of iTunes servers for budgeting purposes, they might choose the number of song downloads as the business activity or cost driver. CVP analysis can often use several bases, depending on the objectives of the analysis.

To help demonstrate various cost behaviors, we'll return to the Fezzari example. Fezzari produces a carbon water bottle cage that can be used on both road and mountain bikes. In the first part of this chapter, we explore several examples related to the various costs associated with producing Fezzari's water bottle cages. We discuss various types of cost behaviors and graph those behaviors in cost-volume graphs. Later in the chapter, we further analyze those costs and how they relate to profits.

Cost-Volume Graphs

One of the most useful tools for analyzing the relationship between changes in cost and volume is the **cost-volume graph**. A cost-volume graph illustrates the relationship between costs and volume. These graphs typically plot total costs on the vertical axis and either volume or activity level on the horizontal axis. Recall from Chapter 15 that companies typically have both variable and fixed costs. **Exhibits 19-1** and **19-2** are examples of cost-volume graphs, plotting total cost on the *y*-axis and the number of water bottle cages on the *x*-axis. Keep in mind that the total cost line in **Exhibits 19-1** and **19-2** is composed of both fixed and variable costs. Point A in **Exhibit 19-1** indicates that at a volume level of 5,000 units the associated cost is $7,500. Similarly, point B in **Exhibit 19-1** represents a cost of $22,500 for a volume level of 35,000 units.

Cost-volume graphs are particularly valuable when available cost-volume data are plotted on the same graph and other cost-volume relationships are estimated by fitting a line to the known points. In **Exhibit 19-1**, for example, we use three known data points (an increased number of known data points should be used to develop a more reliable graph). The known data points, represented by solid points, are as follows:

| Exhibit 19-1 | Graphic Presentation of Cost-Volume Relationships |

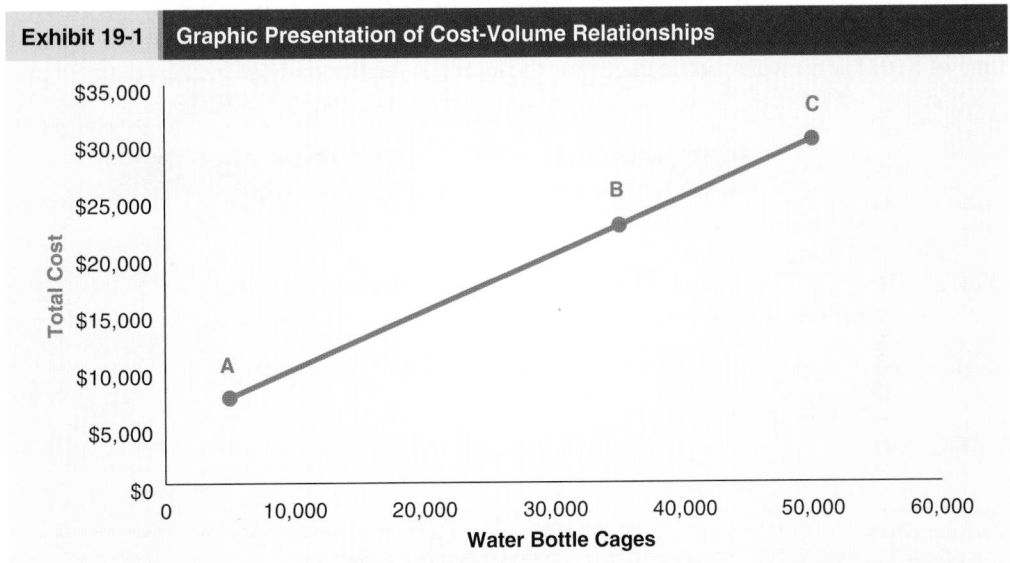

By connecting the known data points with a straight line, we can estimate the costs associated with other volume levels. For example, as illustrated in **Exhibit 19-2**, the open points indicate that for volumes of 22,500, 42,500, and 59,000 units, the related costs would be $16,250, $26,250, and $34,500, respectively. We discuss important limitations to using the cost-volume relationship to estimate costs later in the chapter.

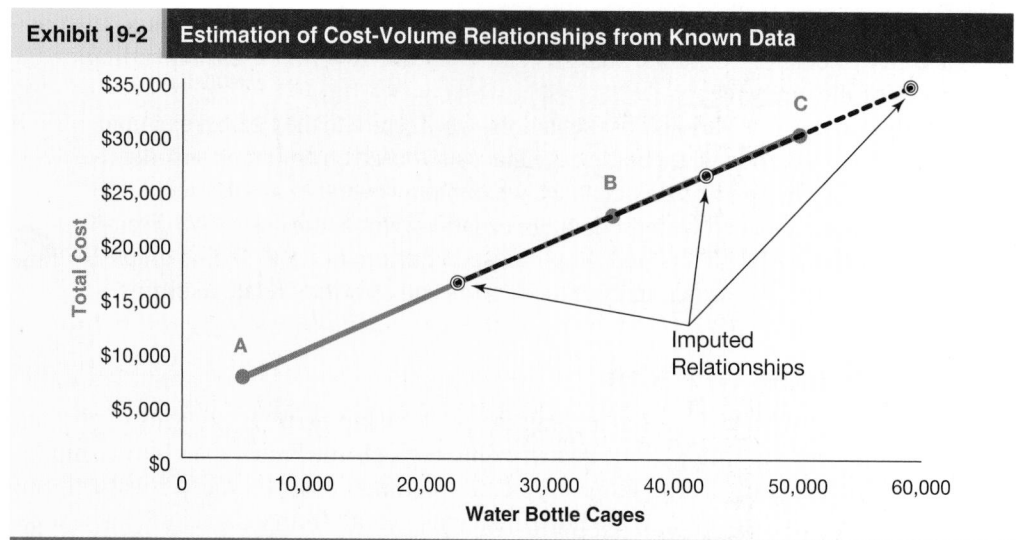

Exhibit 19-2 Estimation of Cost-Volume Relationships from Known Data

Classifications of Cost Behavior Patterns

To better analyze cost behavior patterns, we typically classify costs (based on the definitions discussed in Chapter 15) as *variable, fixed,* or *mixed.*

Hint: The variable cost per unit is the slope of the line, commonly referred to as "rise over run."

Total variable costs change proportionately with changes in the volume of activity. For example, the cost of each water bottle cage is a variable cost in producing either a road or mountain bike. **Exhibit 19-3** is a typical variable cost graph. As illustrated here, a purely variable cost pattern always passes through the origin, because zero cost is associated with zero volume. Also, because variable costs respond in direct proportion to changes in volume, a variable cost line always slopes upward to the right. The steepness of the slope depends on the amount of cost associated with each unit of volume—the greater the unit cost, the steeper the slope. Assume the variable cost associated with each water bottle cage is $0.50 per unit. **Exhibit 19-3** shows that if Fezzari produces 20,000 bikes, it will spend a total of $10,000 on water bottle cages for those bikes. Additionally, if Fezzari doubles production to 40,000 bikes, the cost of water bottle cages also doubles to $20,000.

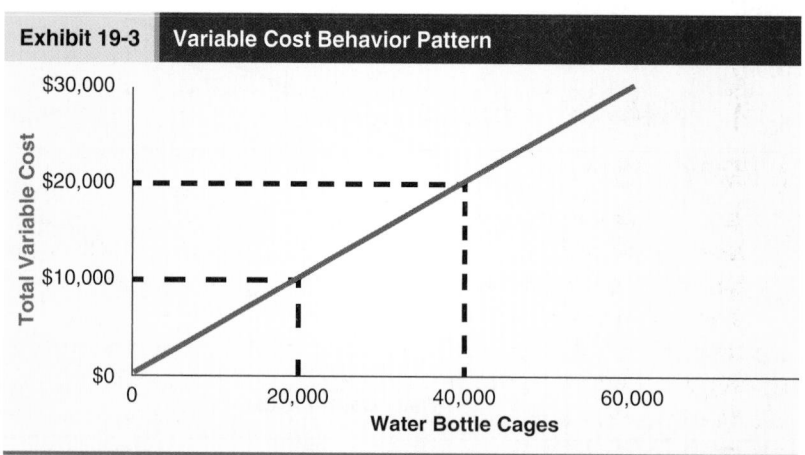

Exhibit 19-3 Variable Cost Behavior Pattern

Fixed costs do not change when the volume of activity changes. Depreciation on manufacturing machinery is an example of a fixed cost.

Because fixed costs do not respond to changes in volume, they are represented by horizontal lines on a cost-volume graph. In **Exhibit 19-4**, fixed costs are $5,000 regardless of the volume level considered. Note in **Exhibit 19-4** that whether Fezzari uses zero, 20,000, or 40,000 water bottle cages in the production of bikes, total fixed costs remain $5,000.

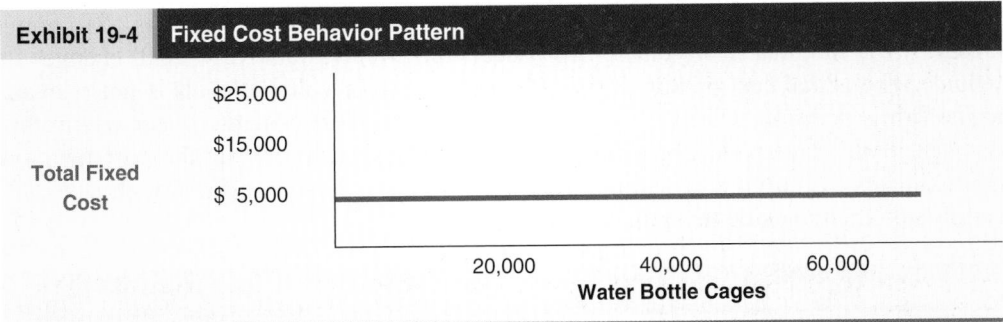

Exhibit 19-4   Fixed Cost Behavior Pattern

Mixed costs—sometimes called *semi-variable costs*—can be described as having both fixed and variable components. Mixed costs respond to volume changes but less than proportionately. For example, assume that Fezzari's process for installing a water bottle cage on each bike manufactured uses the labor of an employee. The employee is paid a fixed monthly salary, but is also paid a monthly bonus for each water bottle cage installed beyond some base level (e.g., a monthly base salary of $1,500 for the first 500 water bottle cages installed but an additional $5 for every water bottle cage installed beyond 500). Because the cost of installing a water bottle cage is composed of both a fixed and a variable component, the cost would be considered a mixed cost.

Hint: The fixed portion of a mixed service cost represents the basic charge for a service. The variable portion represents the charge for the use of the service.

A mixed cost is a single cost containing both a fixed and variable component. For analysis and planning purposes, mixed costs are typically broken down into their fixed and variable components. Total costs are then the sum of all of a company's fixed and variable costs over a period of time. As shown in **Exhibit 19-5**, total costs are composed of both fixed and variable costs.

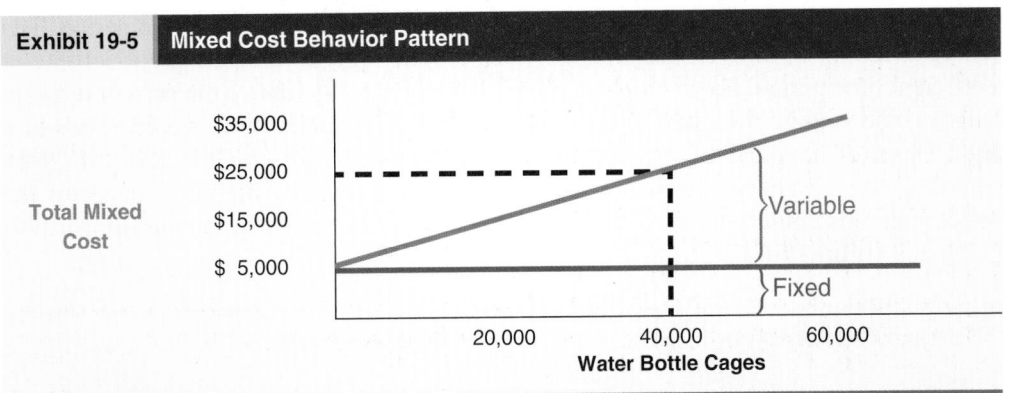

Exhibit 19-5   Mixed Cost Behavior Pattern

Using the cost assumptions in **Exhibit 19-5**, what are the total costs Fezzari will incur to mount water bottle cages on 40,000 bikes?

YOUR TURN! 19.1

The solution is on page 951.

RELEVANT RANGE

The cost behavior illustrations provided thus far are oversimplified because they portray linear cost behavior over the entire range of possible activity. Actually, plotting costs against volume may not always produce a single straight line. For example, certain costs may increase abruptly at intervals in a "step" pattern. Others may exhibit a curvilinear pattern when plotted over a wide range of activity. We present examples graphically of these cost patterns in **Exhibit 19-6**.

The **relevant range** is the range of activity over which the behavior of a cost behaves consistently. Clearly, an assumption of linear costs over the entire scale on either axis in

LO2   Define the concept of *relevant range*.

these two cases causes some degree of error. The significance of this error is often minimized by the fact that many of the firm's decisions involve relatively small changes in volume. The actual cost pattern at extremely low or high volume levels is not relevant to the firm's decisions. The cost pattern only needs to be reasonably linear within this relevant range of activity. For example, **Exhibit 19-6** illustrates that the cost function approximates a straight line within the relevant range indicated, even though costs are clearly not linear outside this range.

Exhibit 19-6 | **Illustrations of Relevant Ranges**

Total Cost

Relevant Range

Within the relevant range, the cost is variable. That is, changes in volume cause a proportional change in total cost.

Total Cost

Water Bottle Cages
Step Cost

Within the relevant range, the cost remains fixed. That is, changes in volume do not result in a change in cost.

Relevant Range

Water Bottle Cages
Curvilinear Cost

The cost-volume relationships for fixed cost, variable cost, and mixed cost typically remain the same for only one range of activity and for only one time period (frequently 1 year). Therefore fixed, variable, and mixed costs are assumed to have a consistent relationship in terms of volume within this relevant range during the given time period. The cost relationships, however, may change when moving to a different range of activity or a different time period. For example, a higher level of activity (above the current relevant range) could require a higher level of supervisory personnel, which would result in a higher level of fixed salary expense (as shown in the step cost graph in **Exhibit 19-6**). Alternatively, a higher direct materials cost due to significantly higher demand for the direct materials could lead to a different relationship (as shown in the curvilinear cost graph in **Exhibit 19-6**).

YOUR TURN! 19.2

The solution is on page 952.

Can the concept of relevant range be applied to mixed costs, fixed costs, and variable costs?

ANALYZING COST BEHAVIOR

LO3 Outline the approach to developing cost formulas.

Managers often have detailed information about costs. Nevertheless, in order to perform CVP analysis to make better decisions, they need to break total costs into fixed and variable components. Although some costs are easy to classify as variable or fixed costs, it isn't always easy to split mixed (semivariable) costs into variable and fixed components. We illustrate three approaches for better understanding the nature of a company's costs: (1) the scattergraph method, (2) the high-low method, and (3) the least squares regression method. We note at the outset that these methods differ both in their ease of application and in their accuracy. For example, the scattergraph method is fast and easy, but it isn't very accurate. On the other extreme, the least squares regression method may take a little more effort, but it is much more accurate. Managers need to weigh costs and benefits in determining which approach is most useful.

Scattergraph Method

For purposes of cost analysis, a mixed cost is divided into its fixed and variable components. We accomplish this by any one of several approaches that vary in their degree of sophistication. One simple method entails plotting the observed cost at several levels of volume on a graph. If cost behavior in actual situations were perfectly correlated, the observations (points) would form a straight line (see **Exhibit 19-1** for an example). More realistically, however, we expect only a discernible pattern.

Assume that Fezzari purchases its carbon water bottle cages from a company in Taiwan that produces similar products for companies around the world. **Exhibit 19-7** reports the supplier's manufacturing costs for various levels of production over the past eight months (sorted by production volume):

Cost	Water Bottle Cages
$27,000	44,000
29,500	48,000
30,000	51,000
31,500	52,000
32,500	54,000
32,000	55,000
36,000	63,000
38,000	66,000

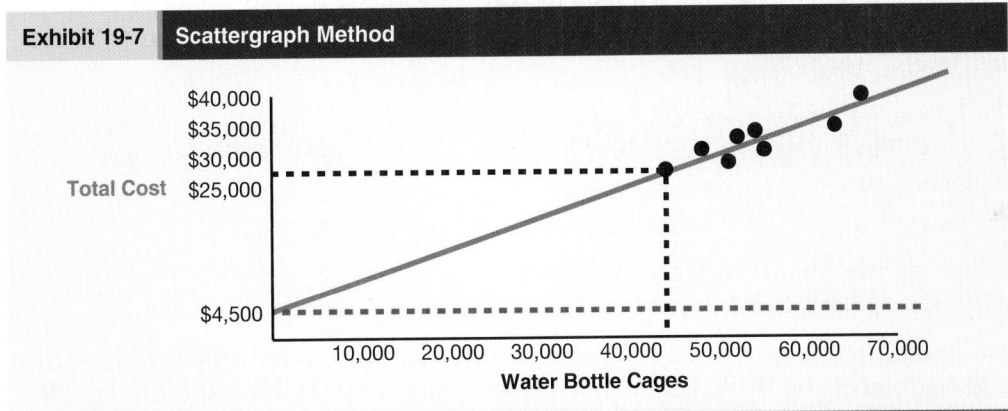

Exhibit 19-7   **Scattergraph Method**

HINT: Where the scattergraph plot line intersects the y-axis represents the fixed cost component (i.e., the cost level at an activity level of zero).

After plotting the actual costs relative to volume over the past eight months, the individual performing the analysis would simply draw a line that places approximately half of the dots above and half below the line. The line in **Exhibit 19-7** has been subjectively determined to approximate the pattern of data points on this scattergraph. Extending this line to the y-axis intercept indicates that $4,500 of total costs are fixed costs. To determine the approximate formula for the total cost line at a volume level of 44,000 water bottle cages, we subtract the $4,500 in fixed costs from the approximate total cost of $27,000 at 44,000 water bottle cages to get total variable costs of $22,500. Therefore, the variable cost per water bottle cage is $22,500/44,000 cages, or approximately $0.51 per water bottle cage. In summary, we describe the mixed cost as $4,500 in fixed costs plus variable costs of $0.51 per water bottle cage and quantify the mixed cost using the following cost formula:

Total cost = $4,500 + ($0.51 × Number of water bottle cages)

High-Low Method

When too few cost observations are available to plot a graph, or when the analyst wishes to avoid visually fitting a subjective line to the data points, the high-low method can be used to approximate the position and slope of the cost line. This relatively simple method compares costs at the highest and lowest levels of activity for which representative cost data are available. The line is drawn between the highest- and lowest-volume data points, as shown in **Exhibit 19-8**. The variable cost per activity unit (here, per water bottle cage) is determined by dividing the difference in costs at these two levels by the difference in activity. The fixed element of cost is then isolated by multiplying the variable cost per unit by either the top or bottom level of activity and then subtracting the resulting product from the total cost at the selected activity level.

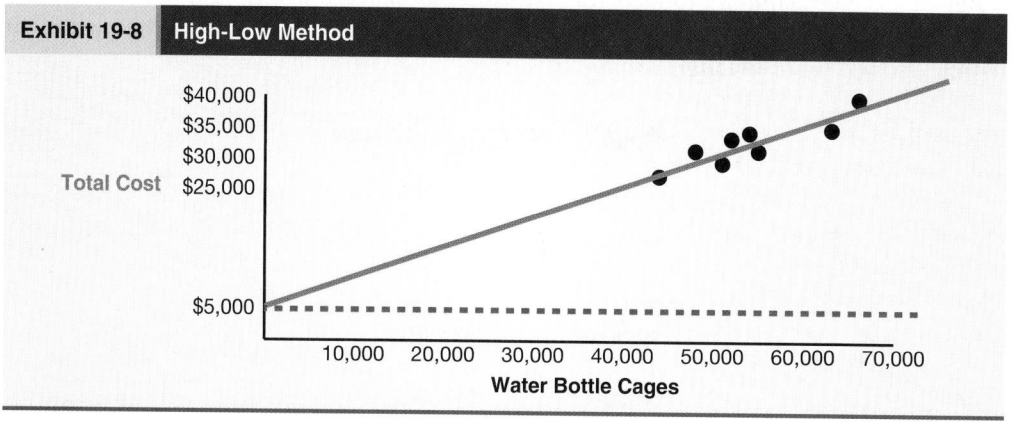

Exhibit 19-8 | **High-Low Method**

Using the same data from our prior example, the lowest and highest levels of activity are 44,000 and 66,000 cages, respectively, and the following are the total costs for these two levels:

Level of Activity		Total Cost
High	66,000 Water bottle cages	$38,000
Low	44,000 Water bottle cages	$27,000
Difference	22,000 (increase)	$11,000 (increase)

Because an increase of 22,000 cages is associated with an $11,000 increase in total cost (remember that by definition only the variable portion of the cost could increase), the variable portion of the total mixed cost must be $11,000/22,000 water bottle cages, or $0.50 per water bottle cage. Subtracting the total variable portion from the total mixed cost at the high- and low-activity levels gives us the fixed portion of total cost as follows:

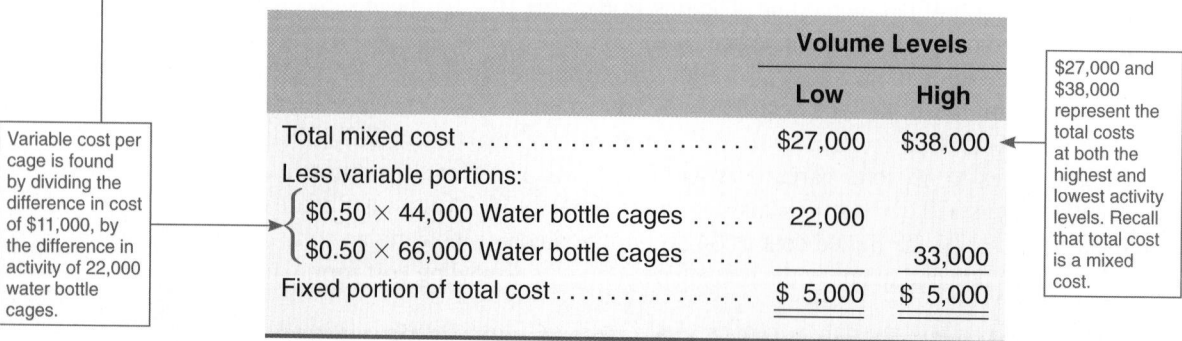

	Volume Levels	
	Low	High
Total mixed cost	$27,000	$38,000
Less variable portions:		
$0.50 × 44,000 Water bottle cages	22,000	
$0.50 × 66,000 Water bottle cages		33,000
Fixed portion of total cost	$ 5,000	$ 5,000

Variable cost per cage is found by dividing the difference in cost of $11,000, by the difference in activity of 22,000 water bottle cages.

$27,000 and $38,000 represent the total costs at both the highest and lowest activity levels. Recall that total cost is a mixed cost.

The high-low analysis tells us that any volume level has $5,000 of fixed cost plus a variable portion of $0.50 per water bottle cage, which can be formulated as follows:

Total cost = $5,000 + ($0.50 × Water bottle cages)

In other words, we can now easily compute the total cost for varying levels of production. However, if either the high or low value used in this method is not representative of the actual cost behavior (that is, the value is an outlier), the resulting cost formula lacks precision.

Least Squares Regression Method

The most accurate method of fitting a line to the cost data points is the least squares regression method, or regression analysis. The least squares regression method is a statistical tool that uses all of the data points to separate a mixed cost into its variable and fixed components. A regression line is fitted to the data points so that the distance from each point to the line is minimized for all points. Although regression analysis can be relatively challenging to do by hand, it is a very simple task to complete using Microsoft Excel. Using the same data used for the scattergraph and high-low methods, **Exhibit 19-9** illustrates the regression analysis output provided by Microsoft Excel.

In an Excel spreadsheet, type in your data as pictured in the table above **Exhibit 19-7**. Put the volume data in one column and the associated cost data in the adjacent column. Click on the "Data" tab on the menu bar. Next, click on "Data Analysis" (if you do not see the Data Analysis option, it will need to be added, see HINT in the margin). From the list of data analysis tools, select "Regression," then "OK." Follow the two instructions on the screen:

   i.   Highlight (or type in) the y-axis data range (this is your cost data).

   ii.   Highlight (or type in) the x-axis data (this is your volume data).

   iii.   click "OK."

Excel provides the output shown in **Exhibit 19-9**.

HINT: If you don't see "Data Analysis" in your Excel menu bar, follow these directions for add-ins:

i. Click on the "File" tab on the menu bar. Then select "Options" on the left-hand side of the screen.

ii. Click "Add-ins."

iii. In the "Manage" selection box at the bottom of the screen, select "Excel Add-ins" and click "GO."

iv. In the "Add-ins available" box, select the "Analysis Toolpak" check box and then click "OK."

v. If asked, click "Yes" to install.

vi. Excel may need to be closed and relaunched for the Analysis Toolpak to become active.

Exhibit 19-9   Least Squares Regression Excel Output

	A	B	C	D	E	F	G
1	SUMMARY OUTPUT						
2							
3	*Regression Statistics*						
4	Multiple R	0.99228					
5	**R Square**	**0.98461**					
6	Adjusted R Square	0.98205					
7	Standard Error	474.33286					
8	Observations	8					
9							
10	ANOVA						
11		*df*	*SS*	*MS*	*F*	*Significance F*	
12	Regression	1	86368800.017	86368800.017	383.8755558	1.14564E-06	
13	Residual	6	1349949.983	224991.664			
14	Total	7	87718750				
15							
16		*Coefficients*	*Standard Error*	*t Stat*	*P-value*	*Lower 95%*	*Upper 95%*
17	**Intercept**	**6082.86**	1336.546	4.551	0.004	2812.452	9353.270
18	**Water Bottle Cages**	**0.48**	0.024	19.593	0.000	0.420	0.540

The intercept represents the total fixed cost component of the mixed cost.

The X-variable, Water Bottle Cages, represents the variable cost per water bottle cage component of the mixed cost.

Although **Exhibit 19-9** may seem overwhelming, only three figures from the Microsoft Excel output are needed to develop and evaluate the cost formula estimated by the least squares regression method:

1. The coefficient for "Intercept" (Y-intercept) represents fixed costs of $6,082.86.

2. The coefficient for "Water Bottle Cages" (X-variable) is the slope of the line and represents variable costs per unit of $0.48 per cage.

3. The R-Square value measures how well the least square line fits the data points = 0.985 (rounded)

The resulting cost equation would be written as:

Total cost = **$6,082.86 + ($0.48 × Number of water bottle cages produced)**

Further explanation of these three figures provides valuable insight into the cost formula.

- First, the "Intercept" coefficient represents where the mixed cost line intercepts the y-axis. This intercept is the fixed cost component of the mixed cost. Thus, the fixed cost component of the mixed cost is approximately $6,083. Note that this amount is different than the $5,000 we found using the high-low method and $4,500 we approximated using the scattergraph method. As opposed to the high-low method, which only uses two data points, regression analysis uses every data point to fit the line. Additionally, instead of subjectively fitting a line using the scattergraph method, regression analysis mathematically minimizes the distances of each point from the line to calculate the "line of best fit."

- Second, the "Water Bottle Cages" coefficient is the slope of the line and represents the variable cost per unit. Thus the manufacturer incurs $0.48 in variable costs on each water bottle cage that it installs. This is slightly lower than the $0.50 per water bottle cage that we calculated using the high-low method.

- Last, the R-Square value is a statistic that can range in value from zero to one, and is often referred to as a "goodness of fit" measure. The R-Square measures how well the x-values predict the y-values. That is, how well do the number of water bottle cages predict total costs? If the x-values perfectly predict the y-values, then the R-Square value would be one. In our case, the number of water bottle cages explains approximately 98.5% of the total cost, which is a very strong relationship. An R-Square over 0.80 generally means that the cost equation provided by the regression analysis can reliably predict costs within the relevant range.

  Looking back, we can see how each method arrives at a somewhat different result:

Scattergraph equation:	Total cost = **$4,500 + ($0.51 × Water bottle cages)**
High-low equation:	Total cost = **$5,000 + ($0.50 × Water bottle cages)**
Least squares equation:	Total cost = **$6,083 + ($0.48 × Water bottle cages)**

Although the scattergraph and high-low methods are the easiest to implement, they are also less accurate. They work well for quick estimates. However, with the availability of desktop computers and programs that can compute least squares regressions, and given the limitations of the scattergraph and high-low methods, managers generally prefer to use the least squares regression method to estimate the fixed and variable portions of a mixed cost.

Analyzing Costs in Practice

SERVICE AND MERCHANDISING

How might we use this understanding of cost behavior as business managers? The budget for a business, which is discussed in detail in Chapter 22, is a financial plan that reflects anticipated or planned amounts of such items as revenue, costs, cash balances, and net income. Underlying most aspects of budgeting is some assumed number of units or dollars of sales, as well as an analysis of the total cost incurred for that level of operation.

For an example, assume that iTunes management is preparing the budget for the next fiscal year. Because of uncertainty regarding the continued economic recovery from a recent recession, management wants to prepare a budget that will allow it to quickly determine expected costs if iTunes sales vary significantly from anticipated levels. Based on the previous year, total fixed costs are $2.0 billion, mixed costs have a fixed portion of $250 million and a variable portion of $0.05 per song, and variable costs are $0.35 per song. The formula for budgeting the total cost is as follows:

Total cost = Total fixed cost + (Variable cost per song × # of songs sold)

Total cost = $2.25 billion fixed cost + ($0.40 Variable cost × # of songs sold)

By using this formula, iTunes management can forecast costs at different levels of activity. **Exhibit 19-10** illustrates how each type of cost behavior pattern is considered in the formula.

Exhibit 19-10	iTunes Cost Factors Example				
Type of Cost	**Total Cost (in millions)**		**Total Fixed Cost (in millions)**	**Variable Cost per Song**	**Number of Songs (in millions)**
Variable costs.......	$10,500	=	$ 0	+ $0.35	× 30,000
Mixed costs:					
Variable portion....	1,500	=	0	+ 0.05	× 30,000
Fixed portion......	250	=	250	+ 0	× 30,000
Fixed costs........	2,000	=	2,000	+ 0	× 30,000
Total cost	$14,250	=	$2,250	+ $0.40	× 30,000

Notice in **Exhibit 19-10** that by combining the various cost factors into the aggregate formula, iTunes management can determine expected costs not only at the 30-billion-song level but also at other levels simply by inserting the appropriate volume figure in the final formula. For example, total budgeted cost at 45 billion songs is $20.250 billion ($2.25 billion + [$0.40 × 45 billion songs]) and at 62 billion songs, total budgeted cost is $27.05 billion ($2.25 billion + [$0.40 × 62 billion songs]).

A word of caution is appropriate here. Because the cost formula relies so heavily on cost analysis, all of the limitations of cost analysis (assumed linearity, relevant ranges, and so on) apply. Also, categorizing many costs into fixed and variable components is often quite complex and inexact. All of these limitations to some degree affect the potential usefulness of managerial cost analysis. It is important to note that these models provide data that can be used to help managers make decisions. However, managers should not blindly follow the outputs from their models. Managers ultimately need to evaluate all relevant information to make sound decisions. In some cases, the simple analytical approach presented here is sufficient, but it cannot be followed blindly.

Concept →	Method →	Assessment	TAKEAWAY 19.1
Can a firm determine the variable and fixed components of a mixed cost?	Three different techniques used to determine the variable and fixed elements of mixed costs: • Scattergraph method • High-low method • Least squares regression method	Each method provides an estimated cost function formula with the variable cost per unit and total fixed cost. Both the scattergraph and high-low methods rely on just two observations to estimate the cost function. Least square regression analysis uses all available data and does not rely on subjective judgment to draw a cost line.	

YOUR TURN! 19.3

The solution is on page 952.

Given the following cost and volume levels, calculate the variable cost per unit and fixed cost within this relevant range using

a. the high-low method and

b. least squares regression method.

Cost	Volume	Cost	Volume
$15,000	5,000 units	$24,500	9,750 units
$13,000	4,000 units	$18,000	6,500 units
$19,300	7,150 units	$21,000	8,000 units

COST-VOLUME-PROFIT (CVP) ANALYSIS

Break-Even Analysis

LO4 **Present** a discussion of and a formula for calculating the break-even point.

Management frequently wants to know the sales level (in dollars) or the number of units that must be sold in order to cover its costs. The level at which total revenues equal total costs is called the **break-even point**. The break-even point can be expressed in dollars or in units sold. As an example, we illustrate several important calculations for one of Fezzari's medium-range road bikes, the Foré CR1, using the condensed income statement data shown in **Exhibit 19-11**.

Exhibit 19-11	Fezzari Foré CR1 Operating Income		
Sales (3,000 units @ $1,500)			$4,500,000
Costs:			
Variable cost (3,000 units @ $1,138)	$3,414,000		
Fixed cost	595,000		
Total cost.			$4,009,000
Net operating income			$ 491,000

Any mixed costs are divided into their fixed or variable component.

Revenue   Cost

This information assumes that all mixed costs have been accurately divided into their fixed and variable components and combined with other fixed and variable costs. We now examine some of the uses of this information.

The Cost-Volume-Profit Chart

To prepare a cost-volume-profit (CVP) chart for the Foré CR1, we use the same basic graph employed previously to explain and portray cost behavior patterns. In **Exhibit 19-12** the vertical axis measures both total revenues and total costs. As in previous exhibits, volume is measured along the horizontal axis. In this Fezzari product line, the activity basis is the number of Foré CR1s manufactured and sold. Total revenues and total costs are measured in thousands of dollars along the vertical axis.

With zero revenue for zero units sold, the graph of total revenues always passes through the origin. We draw the total revenue line by connecting the origin with any other point that represents total revenue for some volume amount. For Fezzari's CR1, total revenue for 3,000 units is $4,500,000, point **A** in **Exhibit 19-12**. To construct the total revenue line, we simply draw a straight line from the origin to **A** and extend it beyond **A**.

We now construct the total cost line in the same manner. With fixed costs of $595,000, the total cost line must intersect the vertical axis at the fixed costs level, $595,000. To produce 3,000 bicycles, Fezzari incurs total costs of $4,009,000. Given this information, we can plot point **B** and draw the total cost line connecting the intersection of the fixed cost line and the vertical axis with **B** as shown in **Exhibit 19-12**. After constructing the total cost line, its intersection with the total revenue line marks the break-even point.

Extending the dashed horizontal and vertical lines from the break-even point, we find that Fezzari's break-even point can be described as either (1) 1,644 units of production or (2) $2,466,000 of total sales revenue. (We explain the calculation of these numbers next.) Note that all levels of sales below the break-even point indicate a loss, and levels of sales above the break-even point result in a profit. In other words, Fezzari earns a profit from its CR1 product line when the total revenue line is above the total cost line, and it incurs a loss when the reverse is true. **Exhibit 19-12** indicates the profit and loss areas. The amount of profit or loss at any volume level is determined by measuring the vertical distance between the total cost and total revenue lines. For example, the difference between points **A** and **B** indicates the profit of $491,000 for selling 3,000 CR1 road bikes.

Exhibit 19-12	Fezzari Foré CR1 Cost-Volume-Profit Chart

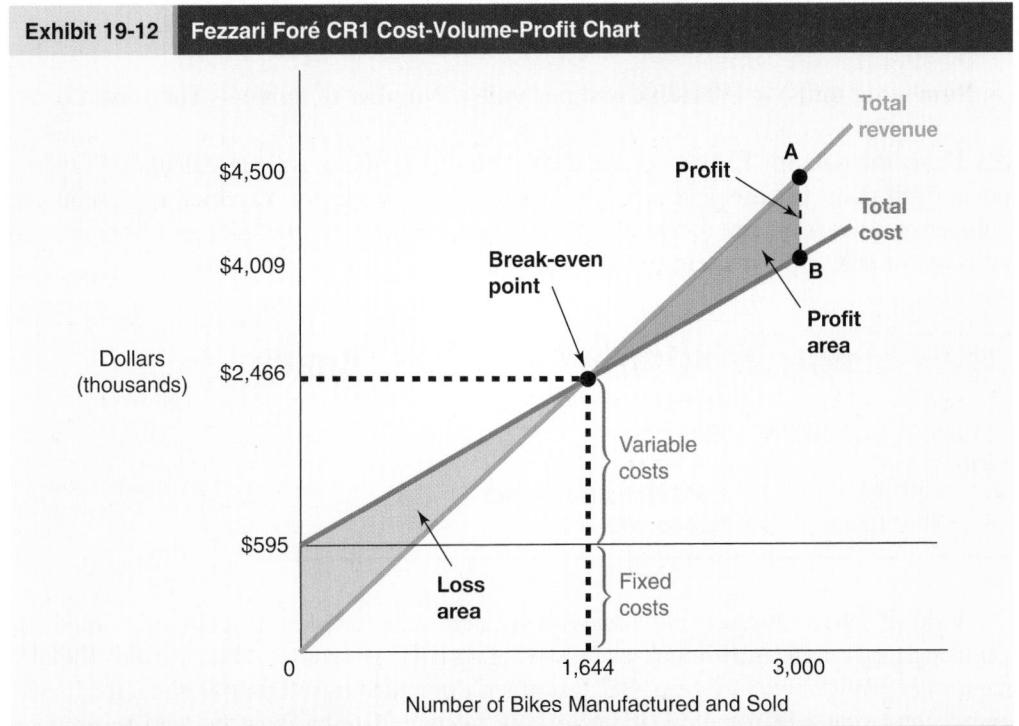

Number of Bikes Manufactured and Sold

Tesla Breaks Even!

In a quarterly letter to investors in May 2018, CEO Elon Musk and CFO Deepak Ahuja claimed that the luxury electric car maker, Tesla, would be in the green in the second half of 2018. However, for Q1 2018, Tesla generated $3.4 billion in car revenues and posted a loss of $785 million. The company says it needs to "reach the 5,000–6,000 per week production mark" for the Model 3 car and target a gross margin of 25% in order to reach its "profitability" goal and post positive operating cash flows. The letter stressed that Tesla's strategy was "all about having automated factories that are producing the world's highest quality cars as quickly and as cost-effectively as possible."

The Basic Assumptions of Break-Even Analysis

In our construction of a break-even chart, we assumed linear relationships over a wide range of activity. This approach implies the following:

1. Total fixed cost and total variable cost per unit are constant over the entire range of analysis.
2. Selling price per unit remains the same regardless of the volume of sales.
3. When more than one product is involved and sales volume varies, each product's percentage of total sales (i.e., the sales mix) does not change.

Even though these assumptions somewhat limit the usefulness of break-even analysis, it is still a convenient method of measuring the effect of changes in sales, costs, volumes, and profits.

Break-Even Formula

The following formula reflects the basic relationship between the break-even point and costs; the break-even point is that point at which total revenue equals total cost:

$$\textbf{Break-even sales = Total variable costs + Total fixed costs}$$

Break-even sales and total variable costs can be expressed as follows:

> **(Selling price per unit × Number of units) = (Variable cost per unit × Number of units) + Total fixed costs**

Using the data for Fezzari's Foré CR1 with this formula, we can calculate Fezzari's break-even point in units and sales dollars. First, we solve for Y, which represents the number of units at the break-even level. We can then multiply the number of break-even units by the sales price to determine break-even sales.

Hint: When total sales are approximately $2,466,000, Fezzari is generating just enough sales dollars to cover its variable and fixed operating costs. Therefore, operating income will be very close to $0.

Break-even sales	= Total variable costs + Total fixed costs
$1,500 Y	= $1,138 Y + $595,000
$1,500 Y − $1,138 Y	= $595,000
$362 Y	= $595,000
Y	= **1,644 units (rounded)**
$1,500 × 1,644	= **$2,466,000** ◄

> When unit sales are 1,644, revenue equals $2,466,000. At this level, sales dollars are just enough to cover all variable and fixed operating costs. Therefore, operating income approximates $0.

Exhibit 19-13 illustrates the break-even calculation based on Fezzari's flexible budget using 1,644 units as the break-even level of activity. Obviously, "break-even" literally means net profit of exactly zero. Because it isn't practical to sell partial units, the break-even calculation will normally indicate how many full units must be sold to produce enough contribution margin to cover fixed costs. In this example, 1,644 CR1 road bikes sold allows the company to "break-even," with $128 left over, whereas selling 1,643 units would have resulted in a small loss. Hence, we round to the number of complete units that allows the company to just exceed the zero-profit threshold.

Exhibit 19-13	Fezzari Performance Bicycles	
	A	B
1	Sales (1,644 units @ $1,500)	$2,466,000 ◄
2	Variable cost (1,644 units @ $1,138)	1,870,872
3	Contribution margin	$ 595,128
4	Fixed cost	595,000
5	Net operating income	$ 128

YOUR TURN! 19.4

The solution is on page 952.

Sam runs his own sandwich truck on the U of C campus. The monthly cost of the truck and necessary campus permit is $595. Sam spends $2.10 on each sandwich sold, including all of the ingredients, condiments, and paper products. He sells each sandwich for $3.50.

  a. How many sandwiches does Sam have to sell each month to break even?
  b. Predict operating income for a month in which Sam sell 1,200 sandwiches.

Contribution Margin Analysis

LO5 **Define** *contribution margin* and *contribution margin ratio* and **present** alternate break-even formulas and examples of their application.

Because total variable costs change proportionately with changes in total revenue, each time additional revenue is generated, additional variable costs are also generated. The difference between the revenue generated and the variable costs generated is called the **contribution margin**. The restructured

variable operating income statement for Fezzari's CR1 shown in **Exhibit 19-14** illustrates the importance of contribution margin.

Exhibit 19-14	Fezzari Foré CR1 Operating Income	
	A	B
1	Sales (3,000 units @ $1,500)	$4,500,000
2	Variable cost (3,000 units @ $1,138)	3,414,000
3	**Contribution margin**	**$1,086,000**
4	Fixed cost	595,000
5	Net operating income	$ 491,000

The contribution margin tells us how much money is left over after subtracting out variable costs.

The contribution margin of $1,086,000 "contributes" to covering fixed costs of $595,000 and earning operating income of $491,000.

When using the variable format for the income statement, we first deduct all variable costs from sales to calculate the contribution margin. We then deduct fixed costs from the contribution margin to calculate operating income. Thus, contribution margin can be viewed as a measure of what is left over after covering variable costs to go toward covering fixed costs and generating profits. At 3,000 units, the total contribution margin is $1,086,000. The contribution margin per unit is calculated as the selling price per unit minus the variable cost per unit. In the Fezzari CR1 example, the contribution margin per unit of $362 would be calculated as the selling price per unit of $1,500 minus the $1,138 variable cost per unit. The contribution margin per unit means that for each additional CR1 sold beyond the break-even point, $362 of additional contribution margin is generated to help produce additional profit.

Contribution Margin Ratio

A related concept often used in break-even analysis is the **contribution margin ratio**, which is the ratio of the contribution margin to sales. The formula to calculate the contribution margin ratio can use either *total* amounts:

$$\text{Contribution margin ratio} = \frac{\text{Contribution margin}}{\text{Sales}}$$

or *per-unit* amounts:

$$\text{Contribution margin ratio} = \frac{\text{Unit contribution margin}}{\text{Unit sales price}}$$

In the Fezzari CR1 example:

$$\text{Contribution margin ratio} = \frac{\$1,086,000}{\$4,500,000} = 0.24 \text{ (rounded)}$$

or

$$\text{Contribution margin ratio} = \frac{\$362}{\$1,500} = 0.24 \text{ (rounded)}$$

The contribution margin ratio is easier to work with than the unit contribution margin if a company has more than one product line. The contribution margin ratio allows comparisons among product lines, which we illustrate later in the chapter.

Hint: The contribution margin is defined as the amount of sales revenue after variable expenses are deducted that is used to cover fixed costs and provide a profit. At the break-even point, the contribution margin equals fixed costs (i.e., profit is zero).

Alternative Break-Even Formulas

Two alternative break-even formulas[4] can be directly derived from our previous break-even formula. To calculate the break-even point either in *units:*

$$\text{Break-even units} = \frac{\text{Total fixed cost}}{\text{Unit contribution margin}}$$

or in *sales dollars:*

$$\text{Break-even sales dollars} = \frac{\text{Total fixed cost}}{\text{Contribution margin ratio}}$$

In the Fezzari CR1 example, we can calculate the break-even point using these two formulas. Using the first formula (expressed in units):

$$\text{Break-even units} = \frac{\$595,000}{\$362} = 1,644 \text{ units}$$

Using the second formula (expressed in sales dollars):

$$\text{Break-even sales} = \frac{\$595,000}{0.24} = \$2,479,167 \text{ }^{5}$$

The results obtained from any of the break-even formulas can be verified by placing the amounts in an income statement format and verifying that net income equals zero.

TAKEAWAY 19.2	Concept ➞	Method ➞	Assessment
	Can management determine how many units or how many sales dollars must be generated to break even?	• Break-even point in units = Total fixed costs/Unit contribution margin • Break-even point in sales dollars = Total fixed costs/Contribution margin ratio	Knowing the point at which unit sales or sales dollars result in zero income provides managers valuable information. For example, if the break-even point in units is higher than the projected demand, managers could either increase the sales price or reduce variable costs per unit, or both. This would increase the contribution margin and decrease the break-even point in units.

---

[4] These formulas can be derived from the general break-even formula provided previously:

Break-even sales = Total variable cost + Total fixed cost

(Selling price per unit × Number of units) = (Variable cost per unit × Number of units) + Total fixed costs

(Selling price per unit × Number of units) – (Variable cost per unit × Number of units) = Total fixed costs

(Selling price per unit − Variable cost per unit) × Number of units = Total fixed costs

(Contribution margin per unit) × Number of units = Total fixed costs

$$\text{Number of units} = \frac{\text{Total fixed costs}}{\text{Contribution margin per unit}}$$

The second formula can be derived simply by multiplying both sides of this equation by the selling price per unit.

[5] This solution differs from the sales revenue computed previously because the contribution margin used has been rounded to the nearest hundredth.

Sam runs his own sandwich truck on the U of C campus. The monthly cost of the truck and necessary campus permit is $595. Sam's contribution margin per unit is $1.40, and the contribution margin ratio is 40%.

  a. How many sandwiches does Sam have to sell each month to break even?
  b. Predict total variable costs for a month in which Sam sell 1,400 sandwiches.

PLANNING FOR PROFIT

Desired Profit
Target Profits without Taxes

LO6 Discuss approaches to planning net income using cost-volume-profit analyses.

With an understanding of the cost-volume-profit relationship, business managers can develop plans for desired levels of profit. Rather than making the calculations for break-even, where profit is equal to zero, they use formulas that include a *desired profit*. These formulas are similar to the previous CVP break-even formula and take into consideration the additional desired net income (or profit):

$$\text{Desired sales} = \text{Total variable costs} + \text{Total fixed costs} + \text{Desired profit}^{\,6}$$

Recall that the definition of contribution margin is what is left over from sales, after covering variable costs, to cover fixed costs and generate profits. Using the contribution margin approach, we can then rearrange our CVP formula to solve for the level of units and sales to achieve our desired net income:

A.K.A. The desired profit is also referred to as desired net income. These terms are also referred to as target profit or target income.

$$\text{Desired units} = \frac{\text{Total fixed costs} + \text{Desired net income}}{\text{Unit contribution margin}}$$

And

$$\text{Desired sales} = \frac{\text{Total fixed costs} + \text{Desired net income}}{\text{Contribution margin ratio}}$$

Assume that Fezzari wants to attain a net income of $1,000,000 before income tax on its CR1 line. Using these formulas, we can determine the level of output in sales dollars or units as follows:

Using the CVP equation:

$1,500 × Y	= $1,138Y + $595,000 + $1,000,000
$1,500Y − $1,138Y	= $1,595,000
$362Y	= $1,595,000
Y	= **4,406 units**
4,406 units × $1,500	= **$6,609,000**

---

[6] Note that the desired net income in these formulas is pre-tax net income. When taxes are applicable, managers need to adjust the formulas to account for taxes in order to determine a desired after-tax net income.

Using the contribution margin approach:

$$\text{Desired units} = \frac{\$595{,}000 + \$1{,}000{,}000}{\$362}$$

$$= 4{,}406 \text{ units}$$

$$\text{Desired sales} = \frac{\$595{,}000 + \$1{,}000{,}000}{0.24}$$

$$= \$6{,}645{,}833^{7}$$

Target Profits with Taxes

Fezzari's management might want to develop plans using net income (after tax) rather than net income before income taxes. In this case, net income (after tax) must be converted to net income before income tax so the formulas presented previously can be used:

$$\textbf{Net income before income tax} = \frac{\textbf{Net income}}{\textbf{1 – Income tax rate}}$$

Assume that Fezzari's management wants to attain an after-tax net income of $700,000 when the income tax rate is 30%. Net income before income tax can be calculated as follows:

$$\textbf{Net income before income tax} = \frac{\textbf{\$700{,}000}}{\textbf{1 – 0.3}} = \frac{\textbf{\$700{,}000}}{\textbf{0.7}} = \textbf{\$1{,}000{,}000}$$

A brief income statement verifies the calculations made in the preceding sections:

Sales (4,406 units × $1,500)	$6,609,000
Less: Variable cost (4,406 units × $1,138)	5,014,028
Contribution margin	$1,594,972
Less: Fixed cost	595,000
Net operating income	$ 999,972
Income tax ($999,972 × 0.30)	299,992
Net income	$ 699,980[8]

ACCOUNTING IN PRACTICE   **CVP Disclosure**

The Securities and Exchange Commission requires all publicly held companies to include a "management discussion and analysis (MD&A) of the results of operations" in quarterly and annual reports. This analysis may include cost-volume-profit data. For example, in Amazon's 2017 annual report, the MD&A section addresses several items that impact its target profitability—including variations in the sales mix of its products and services, increases in the cost of packing materials, shipping costs incurred, that rate of vendor returns, and its significant capital investments that result in future fixed costs. Management's focus on these items indicates extensive use of CVP analysis and its sensitivity to their impact on profitability.

---

[7] This calculation differs from the sales revenue computed using the first formula because the contribution margin used has been rounded to the nearest hundredth.

[8] Difference from target net income after tax of $700,000 due to rounding.

Concept	Method	Assessment	TAKEAWAY 19.3
Do income taxes impact the break-even and desired profit calculations?	Income taxes have no impact on the break-even calculations because at the break-even point, operating income is equal to zero. Income taxes are only paid when operating income is greater than $0. Income taxes impact both the desired sales and the desired units calculations. The desired income figure must be converted to a pre-tax figure using the following formula: • Net income before income tax = Net income after income tax/(1 − income tax rate) • Once net income before income tax has been calculated, the formulas for desired sales and desired units can be used. • Desired units = (Total fixed costs + Desired net income before income tax)/Unit contribution margin • Desired sales = (Total fixed costs + Desired net income before income tax)/Contribution margin ratio	Income taxes are an important expense for all for-profit companies and the expense impacts the desired units and desired sales calculations. Regardless of the tax rate faced by a company, income taxes will increase the desired unit and desired sales figures.	

Margin of Safety

The **margin of safety** is the amount by which the actual sales level of a company exceeds the break-even sales level. It represents the company's "breathing room" in which it will remain profitable. If sales decrease by more than the margin of safety, then the company will incur an operating loss. The formula for calculating the margin of safety follows:

$$\text{Margin of safety} = \text{Actual sales} - \text{Break-even sales}$$

In the Fezzari CR1 example, **Exhibit 19-13** indicates that Fezzari needs sales of $2,466,000 (i.e., 1,644 CR1s) to break even. Assume Fezzari achieves sales of $3,000,000 in a given year. Its margin of safety for that year would be calculated as:

$$\text{Margin of safety} = \$3,000,000 - \$2,466,000 = \$534,000$$

In other words, Fezzari could decrease sales by up to $534,000 and still achieve a profit.

Another way of looking at the "breathing room" beyond break-even sales is on a ratio (or percentage) basis, referred to as the margin-of-safety ratio. It is calculated as follows:

$$\text{Margin-of-safety ratio} = \frac{\text{Margin of safety}}{\text{Actual sales}}$$

For example, continuing the previous Fezzari example (and assuming sales of $3,000,000), the margin-of-safety ratio would be calculated as:

$$\text{Margin-of-safety ratio} = \frac{\$534,000}{\$3,000,000} = 17.8\%$$

In other words, Fezzari could decrease CR1 sales by up to 17.8% and still achieve a profit.

Operating Leverage

Apple's iTunes division and Fezzari have relatively low fixed costs. On the other hand, other companies or industries are characterized by relatively high fixed costs, including utilities (e.g., Pacific Gas and Electric Co. and Florida Power & Light) and auto manufacturers (e.g., General Motors Company and Toyota Motor Corporation). One measure of a firm's relative level of fixed costs is **operating leverage**. Operating leverage is computed as follows:

$$\text{Operating leverage} = \frac{\textbf{Contribution margin}}{\textbf{Net operating income}}$$

Note that the difference between the numerator (contribution margin) and the denominator (net operating income) is the amount of fixed costs (look back at the variable income statement in **Exhibit 19-14** to confirm this). Thus, this ratio is really a measure of a company's operating cost structure, or its level of fixed costs (relative to variable costs). If two companies have the same level of sales and costs, but the cost structure (i.e., the mix between variable and fixed costs) is different, the company with relatively higher fixed costs will have the higher operating leverage. At one extreme, a company that has no fixed costs (i.e., all costs are variable) will have an operating leverage of 1.0 because its contribution margin and net operating income will be the same. **Exhibit 19-15** illustrates graphically a company with an operating leverage of 1.0. Note that because there are no fixed costs, as long as the per-unit sales price of the product is greater than the cost of the product, each sale generates an operating profit equal to the unit contribution margin.

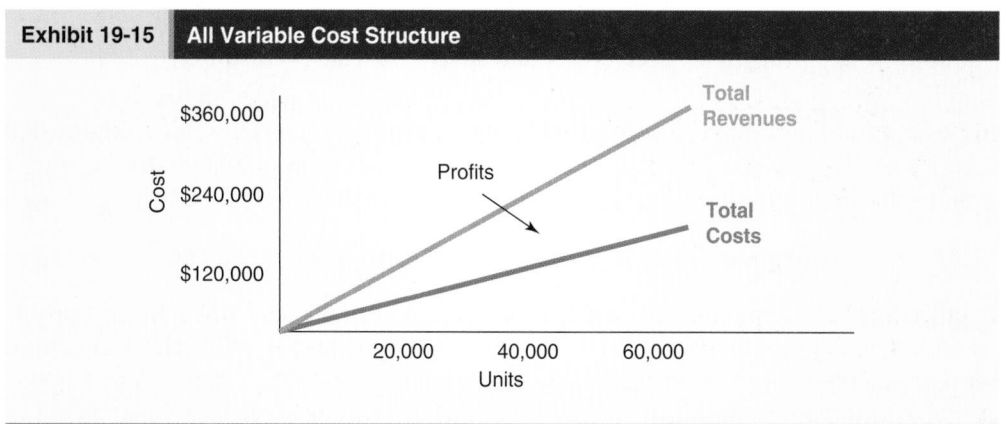

Exhibit 19-15   **All Variable Cost Structure**

The company illustrated in **Exhibit 19-15** sells its products for $6 per unit, and the variable costs to produce a unit of product amount to $2 per unit. Thus, the contribution margin per unit is $4 ($6 − $2). Because the company has no fixed costs, when it sells its first unit of product to a customer, it will generate $4 of operating profit. Each additional unit of product sold will likewise result in additional operating profits of $4 per unit.

Because a world without fixed costs isn't reasonable, operating leverage is an important measure to help managers assess how their cost structure (their unique mix of variable and fixed costs) influences their break-even point. The higher a company's fixed costs, the more units it will need to sell in order to break even. Hence, a company struggling to break even would want to avoid fixed costs in order to lower its break-even point.

As a company's relative mix of costs shifts more toward fixed costs, its operating leverage increases, suggesting greater risk. **Exhibit 19-16** graphically illustrates a company with an operating leverage greater than 1.0 (i.e., with both fixed and variable costs). Assume the company has fixed costs of $120,000, variable costs of $2 per unit, and a selling price of $6 per unit.

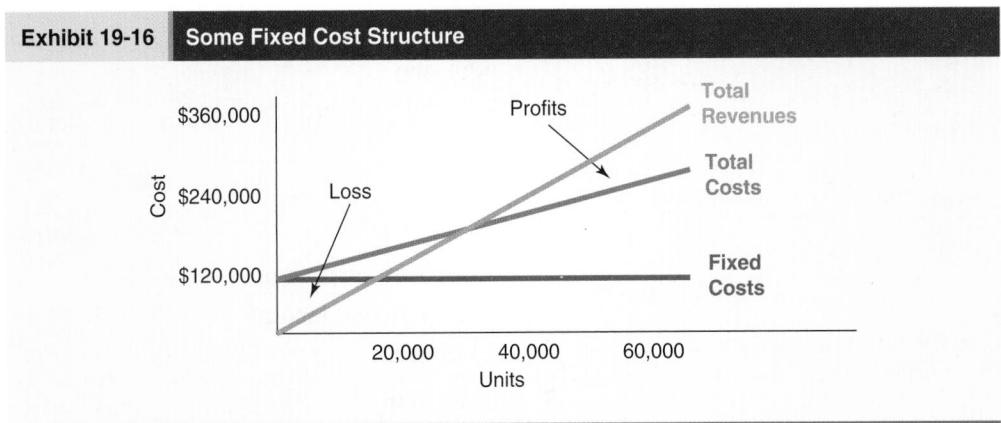

Exhibit 19-16   Some Fixed Cost Structure

Break-even for this company would be computed as follows:

$$\textbf{Break-even units} = \frac{\textbf{Total fixed cost}}{\textbf{Unit contribution margin}}$$

$$\textbf{Break-even units} = \frac{\$120,000}{\$4 \,/\, \textbf{unit}} = \textbf{30,000 units}$$

Note that because the company has $120,000 of fixed costs, it must sell 30,000 units before making a profit. What happens as a company's fixed costs increase? It will need to sell more units to break even. For example, if the company in this example were to increase its fixed costs to $160,000, its break-even point would shift up to 40,000 units. Because it would be harder for the company to break even with this higher level of fixed costs, its risk would increase. Operating leverage can be a useful metric to help managers assess the risk associated with their fixed costs.

An important thing to remember about operating leverage is that a firm's operating leverage changes with its level of output and sales. For example, assume that the company in **Exhibit 19-16** is operating at a level of sales above break-even where it achieves a profit. Compare the company's performance if the company sells 50,000 units or 60,000 units; its operating income would be calculated as follows:

	Sales Volume	
	50,000	60,000
Sales ($6/unit)	$300,000	$360,000
Less: Variable cost ($2/unit)	(100,000)	(120,000)
Contribution margin	200,000	240,000
Less: Fixed cost	(120,000)	(120,000)
Net operating income	$ 80,000	$120,000

Operating leverage at the 50,000 level of sales would be 2.5, computed as follows:

$$\text{Operating leverage} = \frac{\text{Contribution margin}}{\text{Net operating income}}$$

$$= \frac{\$200,000}{\$80,000}$$

$$= 2.5$$

and operating leverage at the 60,000 level would change to 2.0:

$$\text{Operating leverage} = \frac{\text{Contribution margin}}{\text{Net operating income}}$$

$$= \frac{\$240,000}{\$120,000}$$

$$= 2.0$$

Thus, for a given level of fixed costs, the operating leverage ratio decreases as the levels of output and sales increase. Another way of thinking about this concept is that for a given level of fixed costs, if the company can barely maintain a positive operating profit (i.e., it can barely cover its fixed costs), it is constantly operating under a high degree of uncertainty about whether or not it will be able to cover its fixed costs and turn a profit. Hence, its operating leverage would be high. To the extent that the company can comfortably sell more than the number of units required to break even (i.e., it has a high margin of safety), it has less risk of falling short and reporting a loss. Hence, for a given level of fixed costs, as output and sales increase, operating leverage (and the associated risk of reporting a loss) will decrease. The degree of operating leverage can be used to determine, at a given level of sales, how a percentage change in the level of sales will impact net operating profit:

% Increase in operating income = % Increase in sales × Operating leverage

Fezzari's CR1 example illustrates this concept. Assume that Fezzari's management anticipates a 20% increase in sales in the coming year. What should the resulting operating income be? From **Exhibit 19-17**, we can calculate Fezzari's operating leverage as follows:

$$\text{Operating leverage} = \frac{\text{Contribution margin}}{\text{Net operating income}}$$

$$\text{Operating leverage} = \frac{\$1,086,000}{\$491,000} = 2.2118 \text{ (rounded)}$$

If sales increase by 20%, operating income should be $708,200, calculated as follows:

% Increase in operating income = % Increase in sales × Operating leverage

$$44.236\% = 20\% \times 2.2118$$

$$\$708,200^* = \$491,000 \times (1 + 0.44236)$$

* Difference due to rounding.

Exhibit 19-17 proves this calculation.

Exhibit 19-17	Fezzari Foré CR1 Operating Income Comparison			
	A	B	C	D
1			Sales Increase	
2	Sales (3,000 units @ $1,500)	$4,500,000	20%	$5,400,000
3	Variable cost (3,000 units @ $1,138)	3,414,000	20%	$4,096,800
4	Contribution margin	$1,086,000		$1,303,200
5	Fixed cost	595,000		595,000
6	Net operating income	$ 491,000		$ 708,200

Note that operating leverage for the CR1 product line is not a constant, but is computed for each level of sales. For example, Fezzari's new operating leverage (following the 20% increase in sales) would be:

$$\text{Operating leverage} = \frac{\$1,303,200}{\$708,200} = 1.8402 \text{ (rounded)}$$

True Innovation

Anyone who pays monthly water bills for a home, condo, business, or anything else knows that water is becomingly increasingly scarce. Apple recognizes this, and has constructed manufacturing processes that reuse as much water as possible. When it comes to Apple's relationship with suppliers, the company does not simply criticize inefficient suppliers but rather works "with suppliers that don't meet our standards for water reuse" and "help[s] them improve until they do."

Water use is not the only environmental impact Apple considers in its manufacturing processes; as highlighted on Apple's environmental responsibility web page, "We believe true innovation must consider everything." This all-inclusive approach to environmental consideration includes a partnership with the Conservation Fund to "protect and create the type of forests we use in our packaging," develop "a renewable micro-hydro project to power our data center in Prineville, Oregon," and construct "a solar farm in China to offset energy used by our offices and retail stores." While environmental impact is a necessary aspect of Apple's operations, the company has implemented processes that reduce the environmental impact and improve the company's relationship with its various stakeholders and with the general public.

Using Cost-Volume-Profit Relationships

Cost-volume-profit relationships can be used in a number of ways during planning and budgeting sessions to test possible courses of action. The following three independent situations, based on Fezzari's operating income presented in **Exhibit 19-11**, reveal ways that Fezzari might use cost-volume-profit relationships to make business decisions.

Situation 1

Assume that Fezzari's managers are considering reducing the average price of the CR1 (on a per-unit basis) from $1,500 to $1,300. *How would this change affect the break-even point in units?*

$$\text{Break-even units} = \frac{\text{Total fixed cost}}{\text{Unit contribution margin}}$$

$$= \frac{\$595,000}{(\$1,300 - \$1,138)}$$

$$= 3,673 \text{ units}$$

The $200 price decrease would cause the break-even point to increase from 1,644 units (previously calculated) to 3,673 units.

Situation 2

Assume that Fezzari's managers are considering an advertising campaign that would increase the CR1's fixed costs by $50,000 to $645,000 and allow a price increase from $1,500 to $1,600 per unit. *How would this change affect the break-even point in units* for the CR1 product line?

$$\text{Break-even units} = \frac{\text{Total fixed cost}}{\text{Unit contribution margin}}$$

$$= \frac{\$645,000}{(\$1,600 - \$1,138)}$$

$$= 1,396 \text{ units}$$

The $50,000 advertising campaign and the related $100 price increase would cause the CR1 break-even point to decrease from 1,644 units to 1,396 units.

Situation 3

Assume that Fezzari's managers are considering eliminating the sales commission program and increasing the sales force base salaries. This change would decrease the CR1 unit variable cost from $1,138 to $1,088 and would increase fixed costs from $595,000 to $695,000. Average unit sales price would remain at $1,500. If the company wants to achieve an after-tax net income for the CR1 product line of $700,000 and if the income tax rate is 30%, *what would the impact be on desired units sold of eliminating the sales commission program?*

$$\text{Desired units} = \frac{\text{Total fixed cost} + \text{Desired net income before income tax}}{\text{Unit contribution margin}}$$

With the current sales commissions program:

$$\text{Desired units} = \frac{\$595,000 + \dfrac{\$700,000}{(1 - 0.30)}}{\$1,500 - \$1,138} = 4,406 \text{ units}$$

Without the current sales commissions program:

$$\text{Desired units} = \frac{\$695,000 + \dfrac{\$700,000}{(1 - 0.30)}}{\$1,500 - \$1,088} = 4,114 \text{ units}$$

The elimination of the sales commission program would decrease the desired CR1 volume from 4,406 units to 4,114 units. As a result, Fezzari would be able to sell 292 fewer CR1s at the same price and still attain the same desired after-tax net income.

Break-Even Analysis and Multiple Products

As indicated previously, we must assume in break-even analysis that only one product is involved or that the product mix (the ratio of units of each product sold to the total units sold) is constant. Break-even sales can be computed for a sales mix of two or more products by calculating the weighted average unit contribution margin.

Assume that a company sells three units of product A for every unit of B (note that this information indicates that the sales mix is 75% A and 25% B) and has fixed costs of $88,000. Also assume the following relationships between selling price and variable costs:

	Product A	Product B
Unit selling price	$14.00	$7.00
Less: Unit variable cost	8.00	3.00
Unit contribution margin	$ 6.00	$4.00

The weighted average unit contribution margin can be calculated as follows:

Product A: $6.00 × 0.75 =	$4.50
Product B: $4.00 × 0.25 =	1.00
Weighted average unit contribution margin	$5.50

The break-even volume can then be calculated:

$$\text{Break-even units} = \frac{\textbf{Total fixed cost}}{\textbf{Weighted average contribution margin}}$$

$$= \frac{\$88,000}{\$5.50}$$

$$= 16,000 \text{ Weighted average units}$$

The 16,000 weighted average units include a mix of units A and B, based on their relative sales mix. The exact mix and related contribution margin are calculated as illustrated in **Exhibit 19-18**.

Exhibit 19-18	Multiple Product Break-Even Analysis				
	A	B	C	D	E
1	Product	Product Mix	Units Sold	Unit Contribution Margin	Total Contribution Margin
2	A	0.75	12,000	$6.00	$72,000
3	B	0.25	4,000	$4.00	16,000
4	Total		16,000		$88,000

Recall that the sales mix was 75% of unit A and 25% of unit B.
16,000 × 75% = 12,000 units of A
16,000 × 25% = 4,000 units of B

These concepts could be applied to any product mix or number of products.

Cost-Volume-Profit Analysis for Retail Businesses

Most retailing industries have developed relationships between product costs and retail price that need to be maintained in order to be profitable. Each segment of each industry has its own ideal relationship. For example, a men's clothing store would typically have a lower ratio of retail price to product cost than a custom tailor, whereas a downhill ski shop would typically have a higher ratio than a general sports retail store.

SERVICE AND MERCHANDISING

Many restaurants strive to have the price of their meals set at 2.5 times the cost of the food used in the meal. Portion control is a key element in applying this ratio. For each food item or ingredient to be included in one portion or meal, a standard quantity (weight or volume) must be established. This standard recipe can be used to determine the food cost of a meal. For example, if a restaurant serves 8 ounces of ingredient A (costing 35 cents per ounce) plus 2 ounces of ingredient B (costing 25 cents per ounce), this would yield a food cost of $3.30 per portion and a target price of $8.25 (based on the 2.5 rule).

Retail establishments also have varying staffing needs. The number of employees on duty will change, for example, depending on the time of day. For instance, assume Joe's Food Shack, located on a southern California beach, has one cook and one cashier working from 11:00 a.m. to 2:00 p.m., two cooks and three cashiers working from 2:00 p.m. to 5:00 p.m., and two cooks and two cashiers working from 5:00 p.m. to 9:00 p.m. The number and type of employees on duty must be predetermined. Therefore, the cost to employ these servers and cooks is fixed over a given shift. They are typically paid the same amount regardless of how many meals are served. Customer tips (which are not an expense of the company) would vary, depending in part on the number of meals served.

These concepts should be incorporated in cost-volume-profit analysis for a restaurant. Assume Joe's Food Shack serves only three food choices: hamburgers, hot dogs, and nachos, with food costs per item of $5.00, $4.00, and $3.00, respectively. Because Joe's is the only establishment on the entire beach, Joe's can charge monopoly prices for its food items. Using the 2.5 ratio, the related prices are $12.50, $10.00, and $7.50, respectively. If 20% of the items sold are hamburgers, 50% are hot dogs, and 30% are nachos, then the average revenue per food item sold would be $9.75 and the average food cost would be $3.90, as illustrated in **Exhibit 19-19**.

Exhibit 19-19	Cost and Pricing Analysis for Joe's Food Shack				
	A	B	C	D	E	F
1	Food Type	Proportion	Cost per Unit	Weighted Average Cost	Price per Unit	Weighted Average Price
2	Hamburger	20%	$5.00	$1.00	$12.50	$2.50
3	Hot dog	50%	4.00	2.00	10.00	5.00
4	Nachos	30%	3.00	0.90	7.50	2.25
5	Total			$3.90		$9.75

The weighted average unit contribution margin, therefore, is $9.75 − $3.90 = $5.85.

If the total fixed costs, including personnel, are $64,350 for a typical 30-day month when the restaurant is open every day for the scheduled hours, the break-even volume would be calculated as follows:

$$\frac{\$64,350}{\$5.85} = 11,000 \text{ food items per month}$$

Thus, this sales mix is composed of 2,200 hamburgers (11,000 × 0.20), 5,500 hot dogs (11,000 × 0.50), and 3,300 nachos (11,000 × 0.30).

Managing costs is a prevailing concern for managers. The concepts introduced in this chapter underlie most efforts to analyze and project cost in a variety of decision situations. In practice, because projections of future costs are subject to many complicating factors, for most companies they are *estimates of probable costs* rather than precise determinations. Properly used—with full recognition of their limitations—cost behavior analyses can be highly useful to management.

YOUR TURN! 19.6

The solution is on page 952.

Hungry Hikers buys nutrition bars for $1.25 each and sells them for $5.00. Management budgets monthly fixed expenses of $12,675 for sales volumes between 0 and 10,000 bars.

Requirements:

1. Use the contribution margin ratio approach to compute monthly break-even sales in revenue (dollars).
2. Use the unit contribution margin approach to compute monthly break-even sales in units.
3. Compute the monthly sales level (in units) required to earn a pre-tax target operating profit of $15,000.
4. Assume Hungry Hikers wants to earn an after-tax monthly net income of $18,000 when the income tax rate is 25%. Compute the monthly sales level (in units) to achieve the after-tax net income target.
5. Assuming a no-tax environment, calculate the margin of safety in dollars at sales level of 7,400 units.

SERVICE INDUSTRY IN FOCUS

Environmental Business Consultants (EBC) has two offices, one in northern California and one in southern California. EBC provides three basic services to its clients: rate reviews, contract procurement and negotiations, and operational studies. EBC management wants to determine how many projects of each service would need to be performed in 2020 to achieve a before-tax profit of $650,000. EBC managers have gathered the following information from 2018 for the analysis.

SERVICE AND MERCHANDISING

The proportion of projects done in each office was as follows:

	Northern California	Southern California
Rate reviews.	30%	50%
Contract procurements. . .	60%	30%
Operational studies.	10%	20%

The average contribution margin for each project type was as follows:

	Northern California	Southern California
Rate reviews.	$ 5,100	$24,124
Contract procurements. . .	28,000	37,000
Operational studies.	10,035	20,000

EBC has budgeted 2018 fixed expenses to be $2,251,159 and $644,341 in the northern and southern California offices, respectively.

Required

1. How many projects of each type must EBC perform in the northern California office if managers expect the office to generate $450,000 of the desired total income?

2. How many projects of each type must EBC perform in the southern California office if managers expect the office to generate $200,000 of the desired total income?

Solution

1. The weighted average contribution margin for the northern California office is:

$ 5,100 × 0.30 =	$ 1,530
$28,000 × 0.60 =	16,800
$10,035 × 0.10 =	1,004
Weighted average contribution margin	$19,334

The number of total projects needed is:

$$\textbf{Needed projects} = \frac{\$2,251,159 + \$450,000}{\$19,334}$$

$$= \textbf{140 projects (rounded)}$$

The number of projects by type is:

Rate reviews............	(140 × 0.30)	42
Contract procurements....	(140 × 0.60)	84
Operational studies.......	(140 × 0.10)	14

2. The weighted average contribution margin for the southern California office is:

$24,124 × 0.50 =	$12,062
$37,000 × 0.30 =	11,100
$20,000 × 0.20 =	4,000
Weighted average contribution margin	$27,162

The number of total projects needed is:

$$\textbf{Needed projects} = \frac{\$644,341 + \$200,000}{\$27,162}$$

$$= \textbf{31 projects (rounded)}$$

The number of projects by type is:

Rate reviews............	(31 × 0.50)	16 (rounded)
Contract procurements....	(31 × 0.30)	9 (rounded)
Operational studies.......	(31 × 0.20)	6 (rounded)

Maricopa Corporation has developed the budget for its next year of operations. The budget included the following:

Sales of 100,000 units at $5	
Units sold will equal units produced	
Variable costs for 100,000 units:	
Direct materials....................	$125,000
Direct labor	100,000
Variable overhead................	30,000
Selling and administrative expense ...	45,000
Total fixed cost	120,000
Income tax rate of 30%	

Required

a. What is Maricopa's break-even point, in units and in dollars, for next year?

b. Demonstrate that the unit amount reconciles with the dollar amount.

c. What amount of sales revenue would Maricopa need to realize next year in order to generate a net income of $63,000 after tax?

d. Demonstrate the correctness of the calculations in requirement (c) by constructing an income statement.

Solution

a.   Variable costs:

Direct materials.....................	$125,000
Direct labor.......................	100,000
Variable overhead	30,000
Selling and administrative............	45,000
Total variable cost at 100,000 units ...	$300,000

$$\$300{,}000 \,/\, 100{,}000 \text{ units } = \$3 \text{ per unit}$$

$$\text{Unit contribution margin } = \$5 - \$3 = \$2$$

$$\text{Contribution margin ratio } = \frac{\$2}{\$5} = 0.4$$

$$\text{Break-even units} = \frac{\text{Total fixed cost}}{\text{Unit contribution margin}}$$

$$= \frac{\$120{,}000}{\$2}$$

$$= 60{,}000 \text{ units}$$

$$\text{Break-even sales} = \frac{\text{Total fixed cost}}{\text{Contribution margin ratio}}$$

$$= \frac{\$120{,}000}{0.4}$$

$$= \$300{,}000$$

b.   60,000 units × $5 unit selling price = $300,000

c.

$$\text{Desired sales} = \frac{\text{Total fixed cost} + \dfrac{\text{Net income}}{1 - \text{Income tax}}}{\text{Contribution margin ratio}}$$

$$= \frac{\$120{,}000 + \dfrac{\$63{,}000}{1 - 0.3}}{0.4}$$

$$= \$525{,}000$$

d.

Sales.	$525,000
Variable cost ([1 − 0.4] × $525,000) . . .	315,000
Contribution margin	$210,000
Fixed cost	120,000
Net income before income tax	$ 90,000
Income tax at 30%	27,000
Net income	$ 63,000

SUMMARY OF LEARNING OBJECTIVES

LO1 **Develop an understanding of how specific types of costs change in response to volume changes. (p. 902)**

- For meaningful managerial analysis, costs must be related to some measure of business activity or cost driver. A critical aspect is that the activity measure used must have a logical causal relation with costs, and the quantity of the activity must be highly correlated with the level of costs.

- One of the most useful tools for analyzing the relationship between changes in cost and volume is the *cost-volume graph*. Such graphs typically plot total costs on the vertical axis and either volume or activity level on the horizontal axis. Cost-volume graphs are particularly valuable when available cost-volume data are plotted on the same graph and other cost-volume relationships are estimated by fitting a line to the known points.

- The behavior of total cost in response to volume changes is divided into three basic categories within a relevant range:
  - ❑ Variable, which responds proportionately, with zero cost at zero volume
  - ❑ Fixed, which is constant
  - ❑ Mixed, which responds, but less than proportionately, due to the fixed component

- Total cost for most entities is best represented by the mixed cost pattern.

LO2 **Define the concept of *relevant range*. (p. 905)**

- We can assume linearity of cost because it is approximately true within the range of volume relevant to the analysis.

- The relevant range is the range of activity over which the behavior of a cost behaves consistently.

- Within the relevant range, *per-unit* costs behave as follows when volume is increased:
  - ❑ Variable costs remain constant.
  - ❑ Fixed costs decrease proportionately.
  - ❑ Variable plus fixed cost decreases, but not proportionately.

LO3 **Outline the approach to developing cost formulas. (p. 906)**

- In order to perform CVP analysis to make better decisions, total costs need to be broken into fixed and variable components. We illustrate three approaches for accomplishing this: (1) the scattergraph method, (2) the high-low method, and (3) the least squares regression method.

- The scattergraph method entails plotting the observed cost at several levels of volume on a graph, then drawing a line that places approximately half of the dots above and half below the line.

- The high-low method is relatively simple and compares costs at the highest and lowest levels of activity for which representative cost data are available. A line is then drawn between the highest- and lowest-volume data points.

- The least squares regression method is a statistical tool that uses all of the data points to separate a mixed cost into its variable and fixed components. A regression line is fitted to the data points so that the distance from each point to the line is minimized for all points. Although regression analysis can be relatively challenging to do by hand, it is a very simple task to complete using Microsoft Excel.
- A general formula for planning total cost is as follows: Total cost = Total fixed cost + (Variable cost per unit × Number of units).

Present a discussion of and a formula for calculating the break-even point. (p. 912)   **LO4**

- The break-even point (where Revenues = Costs) can be derived by graph, formula, or contribution margin analysis.
- Assumptions underlying break-even analysis include the following:
  - ❏ Total fixed cost and per-unit variable cost are constant over the entire relevant range.
  - ❏ Selling price per unit remains the same regardless of the volume of sales.
  - ❏ When more than one product is involved and sales volume varies, each product's percentage of total sales (sales mix) does not change.

Define *contribution margin* and *contribution margin ratio* and present alternate break-even formulas and examples of their application. (p. 914)   **LO5**

- Contribution margin = Revenue − Variable cost

- $\text{Contribution margin ratio} = \dfrac{\text{Contribution margin}}{\text{Sales}}$

  or

- $\text{Contribution margin ratio} = \dfrac{\text{Unit contribution margin}}{\text{Unit selling price}}$

- Formulas used in break-even analysis include the following:

  - ❏ $\text{Break-even units} = \dfrac{\text{Total fixed cost}}{\text{Unit contribution margin}}$

  - ❏ $\text{Break-even sales} = \dfrac{\text{Total fixed cost}}{\text{Contribution margin ratio}}$

Discuss approaches to planning net income using cost-volume-profit analyses. (p. 917)   **LO6**

- Formulas used in planning net income include the following:
  - ❏ Desired sales = Total variable cost + Total fixed cost + Desired net income

  - ❏ $\text{Desired units} = \dfrac{\text{Total fixed cost} + \text{Desired net income}}{\text{Unit contribution margin}}$

  - ❏ $\text{Desired sales} = \dfrac{\text{Total fixed cost} + \text{Desired net income}}{\text{Contribution margin ratio}}$

- Often management wants to develop plans using net income after tax instead of net income. The relationship between net income before income tax and net after-tax income is demonstrated by the following formula:

  - ❏ $\text{Net income before income tax} = \dfrac{\text{Net after-tax income}}{1 - \text{Income tax rate}}$

- Margin of safety = Actual sales − Break-even sales
- One measure of a firm's relative level of fixed costs is operating leverage. Operating leverage is computed as follows:

  - ❏ $\text{Operating leverage} = \dfrac{\text{Contribution margin}}{\text{Net operating income}}$

- Break-even and net income planning computations involving multiple products incorporate the concept of weighted average unit contribution margin.

SUMMARY	Concept	Method	Assessment
TAKEAWAY 19.1	Can a firm determine the variable and fixed components of a mixed cost?	Three different techniques used to determine the variable and fixed elements of mixed costs: • Scattergraph method • High-low method • Least squares regression method	Each method provides an estimated cost function formula with the variable cost per unit and total fixed cost. Both the scattergraph and high-low methods rely on just two observations to estimate the cost function. Least square regression analysis uses all available data and does not rely on subjective judgment to draw a cost line.
TAKEAWAY 19.2	Can management determine how many units or how many sales dollars must be generated to break even?	• Break-even point in units = Total fixed costs/Unit contribution margin • Break-even point in sales dollars = Total fixed costs/Contribution margin ratio	Knowing the point at which unit sales or sales dollars result in zero income provides managers valuable information. For example, if the break-even point in units is higher than the projected demand, managers could either increase the sales price or reduce variable costs per unit, or both. This would increase the contribution margin and decrease the break-even point in units.
TAKEAWAY 19.3	Do income taxes impact the break-even and desired profit calculations?	Income taxes have no impact on the break-even calculations because at the break-even point, operating income is equal to zero. Income taxes are only paid when operating income is greater than $0. Income taxes impact both the desired sales and the desired units calculations. The desired income figure must be converted to a pre-tax figure using the following formula: • Net income before income tax = Net income after income tax/(1 − income tax rate) • Once net income before income tax has been calculated, the formulas for desired sales and desired units can be used. • Desired units = (Total fixed costs + Desired net income before income tax)/Unit contribution margin • Desired sales = (Total fixed costs + Desired net income before income tax)/Contribution margin ratio	Income taxes are an important expense for all for-profit companies and the expense impacts the desired units and desired sales calculations. Regardless of the tax rate faced by a company, income taxes will increase the desired unit and desired sales figures.

KEY TERMS

Break-even point (p. 912)

Contribution margin (p. 914)

Contribution margin ratio (p. 915)

Cost behavior analysis (p. 902)

Cost-volume graph (p. 903)

Cost-volume-profit (CVP) analysis (p. 902)

Fixed costs (p. 904)

Margin of safety (p. 919)

Mixed costs (p. 905)

Operating leverage (p. 920)

Relevant range (p. 905)

Total variable costs (p. 904)

Variable operating income statement (p. 915)

SELF-STUDY QUESTIONS

(Answers to Self-Study Questions are at the end of this chapter.)

1. A(n) _____ cost is a cost whose total amount changes in direct proportion to a change in volume.   **LO1**
   a. variable
   b. fixed
   c. mixed
   d. irrelevant

2. When moving from the low end to the high end of a relevant range, straight-line depreciation expense per unit   **LO2**
   a. increases.
   b. decreases.
   c. remains the same.
   d. changes unpredictably.

3. In a typical cost formula,   **LO3**
   a. fixed costs are per unit and variable costs are per unit.
   b. fixed costs are per unit and variable costs are in total.
   c. fixed costs are in total and variable costs are in total.
   d. fixed costs are in total and variable costs are per unit.

4. At the break-even point,   **LO4**
   a. Contribution margin = fixed costs.
   b. Variable costs = fixed costs.
   c. Sales = contribution margin.
   d. Contribution margin = 0.

5. Contribution margin ratio is   **LO5**
   a. Unit sales price/unit contribution margin.
   b. 1/margin of safety.
   c. Total contribution margin/sales.
   d. Variable cost/fixed cost.

6. Net income before income tax is   **LO6**
   a. Net income/(1 – Income tax rate).
   b. Income tax rate/Net income.
   c. Net income + Contribution margin.
   d. Net income/Income tax rate.

QUESTIONS

1. Define the terms *cost behavior* and *relevant range*.   **LO1, 2**

2. Identify some common activity bases in terms of which the volume of a manufacturing operation might be stated. What general criterion might be used in choosing an activity base?   **LO1**

3. Name and define briefly the three most widely recognized cost behavior patterns.   **LO1**

4. Explain (a) how a mixed cost can be considered "partly fixed and partly variable," and (b) why a firm's total cost is best represented by the mixed cost pattern.   **LO1, 3**

5. Briefly describe the two most straightforward techniques for dividing a mixed cost into its fixed and variable components.   **LO3**

6. "Actual costs often behave in a nonlinear fashion. Therefore, assumptions of linearity invalidate most cost behavior analyses." Do you agree or disagree with this statement? Briefly defend your position.   **LO2**

7. Describe how fixed and variable costs per unit respond to volume increases.   **LO1, 3**

8. Present a formula based on units for planning total cost, and explain how mixed costs are incorporated into the formula.   **LO3**
    LO4

9. Define and briefly explain three approaches to break-even analysis.

LO4 **10.** Patrick's Bakery Shop has fixed costs per month of $3,600, and variable costs are 55% of sales. What amount of monthly sales allows the shop to break even?

LO4 **11.** Quality Car Wash has fixed costs per month of $16,800, and variable costs are 20% of sales. The average amount collected per car washed during the past year has been $5. How many cars must be washed per month to break even?

LO4 **12.** You have graphed the cost-volume-profit relationships for a company on a break-even chart after being informed of certain assumptions. Explain how the lines on the chart would change if (a) fixed costs increased over the entire range of activity, (b) selling price per unit decreased, and (c) variable costs per unit increased.

LO5 **13.** Define *contribution margin*. Is it best expressed as a total amount or as a per-unit amount? In what way is the term descriptive of the concept it represents?

LO6 **14.** Explain the approach to break-even analysis that is used for a mix of two or more products.

LO6 **15.** Explain how break-even formulas can provide income-planning analyses.

LO6 **16.** In planning net income, how can (post tax) net income be incorporated into the planning formula?

SHORT EXERCISES

LO1, 3 **SE19-1.** All of the following are assumptions of cost-volume-profit analysis **except**

    a. total fixed costs do not change with a change in volume.
    b. revenues change proportionately with volume.
    c. variable costs per unit change proportionately with volume.
    d. sales mix for multi-product situations do not vary with volume changes.

LO4 **SE19-2.** Break-even quantity is defined as the volume of output at which revenues are equal to

    a. marginal costs.
    b. total costs.
    c. variable costs.
    d. fixed costs.

LO6 **SE19-3.** Bolger and Co. manufactures large gaskets for the turbine industry. Bolger's per unit sales price and variable costs for the current year are as follows:

Sales price per unit $300
Variable costs per unit   210

Bolger's total fixed costs aggregate $360,000. As Bolger's labor agreement is expiring at the end of the year, management is concerned about the effect a new agreement will have on its unit break-even point. The controller performed a sensitivity analysis to ascertain the estimated effect of a $10 per unit direct labor increase and a $10,000 reduction in fixed costs. Based on these data, it was determined that the break-even point would

    a. decrease by 1,000 units.
    b. decrease by 125 units.
    c. increase by 375 units.
    d. increase by 500 units.

LO6 **SE19-4.** Carson Inc. manufactures only one product and is preparing its budget for next year based on the following information:

Selling price per unit	$100
Variable costs per unit	75
Fixed costs	250,000
Effective tax rate	35%

If Carson wants to achieve a net income of $1.3 million next year, its sales must be

    a. 62,000 units.
    b. 70,200 units.
    c. 80,000 units.
    d. 90,000 units.

SE19-5. Ticker Company sells two products. Product A provides a contribution margin of $3 per unit, and Product B provides a contribution margin of $4 per unit. If Ticker's sales mix shifts toward Product A, which one of the following statements is **correct**?

a. The total number of units necessary to break even will decrease.

b. The overall contribution margin ratio will increase.

c. Operating income will decrease if the total number of units sold remains constant.

d. The contribution margin ratios for Products A and B will change.

EXERCISES—SET A

E19-1A. Cost-Volume Graphs Set up a cost-volume graph. Volume should range from zero to 24,000 units (in 4,000-unit increments), and cost should range from zero to $35,000 (in $5,000 increments). Plot each of the following groups of cost data using different marks for each group. After completing the graph, indicate the type of cost behavior exhibited by each group.

LO1

Volume (applicable to each group)	Group A Costs	Group B Costs	Group C Costs
2,000	$ 2,600	$ 1,000	$2,400
12,000	12,600	6,000	2,400
16,000	16,600	8,000	2,400
20,000	20,600	10,000	2,400

E19-2A. High-Low Method Apply the high-low method of cost analysis to the three cost data groups in E19-1A. What cost behavior patterns are apparent? Express each as a cost formula.

LO3

E19-3A. Relevant Range and High-Low Method The following selected data relate to the major cost categories experienced by Shaw Company at varying levels of operating volumes. Assuming that all operating volumes are within the relevant range, calculate the appropriate costs in each column in which blanks appear.

LO2, 3

	Total Cost (@ 3,000 units)	Total Cost (@ 4,000 units)	Variable Cost per Unit	Total Fixed Cost	Total Cost (@ 5,000 units)
Direct labor (variable)	$90,000	$120,000	_____	_____	_____
Factory supervision (semivariable)	60,000	72,000	_____	_____	_____
Factory depreciation (fixed)	40,000	40,000	_____	_____	_____

E19-4A. Total Cost Formula Davis Company has analyzed its overhead costs and derived a general formula for their behavior: $65,000 + $16 per direct labor hour employed. The company expects to use 80,000 direct labor hours during the next accounting period. What overhead rate per direct labor hour should be applied to jobs worked during the period?

LO3

E19-5A. Interpreting Cost Formula Wylie Enterprises' controller, Josh Senior, estimated the following formula, based on monthly data, for total overhead cost:

LO3

$$\text{Overhead costs} = \$167,500 + (\$42.50 \times \text{Direct labor hours})$$

Required

1. Link each term in Column A to the corresponding term in Column B.

Column A	Column B
Overhead cost	Fixed cost (intercept)
$167,500	Y-axis variable
$42.50	X-axis variable
Direct labor hours	Variable rate (slope)

2. If next month's budgeted direct labor hours equal 8,000, and are within the relevant range, what is the budgeted overhead cost?

3. If next quarter's budgeted direct labor hours equal 26,000, and are within the relevant range, what is the budgeted overhead cost?

4. If next year's budgeted direct labor hours equal 101,250, and are within the relevant range, what is the budgeted overhead cost?

LO3 **E19-6A.** **Interpreting Regression Output** Rikki Bake, the controller for XYZ Incorporated, suspects that factory overhead costs are driven by the number of machine hours used. Using Excel, Ms. Bake input twelve months of historical data for total factory overhead costs and machine hours used. The summary output information is provided below. Use the output information provided to develop a cost formula for overhead cost. Round the fixed and variable costs to the nearest penny.

	A	B	C	D	E	F	G	H	I
1	SUMMARY OUTPUT								
2									
3	*Regression Statistics*								
4	Multiple R	0.963809718							
5	R Square	0.928929173							
6	Adjusted R Square	0.92182209							
7	Standard Error	56.42709871							
8	Observations	12							
9									
10	ANOVA								
11		*df*	*SS*	*MS*	*F*	*Significance F*			
12	Regression	1	416166.0753	416166.0753	130.7047086	4.6008E-07			
13	Residual	10	31840.17469	3184.017469					
14	Total	11	448006.25						
15									
16		*Coefficients*	*Standard Error*	*t Stat*	*P-value*	*Lower 95%*	*Upper 95%*	*Lower 95%*	*Upper 95%*
17	Intercept	$970.12	415.4592475	2.335045169	0.0416902	44.41521808	1895.816999	44.41521808	1895.816999
18	Machine Hours	36.138	3.160962926	11.432616	4.6008E-07	29.09501101	43.18113962	29.09501101	43.18113962

LO4 **E19-7A.** **Break-Even Chart** Set up a break-even chart similar to the one in **Exhibit 19-12** with proportional scales from zero to $72,000 (in $12,000 increments) on the vertical axis and from zero to 12,000 units of production (in 2,000-unit increments) on the horizontal axis. Prepare the break-even chart for Morton Company, assuming total fixed costs of $24,000 and unit selling price and unit variable cost for the company's one product of $8 and $5, respectively. Label the total revenue line and the total cost line. Indicate the break-even point in units and dollars.

LO5 **E19-8A.** **Cost-Volume Profit Analysis** Incline Company generated $1,400,000 in revenue selling 800 units of its only product. Each unit has a contribution margin of $280. The company has fixed costs of $125/unit at the current production volume (assume unit production volume equals unit sales volume).

a. What is the contribution margin ratio for Incline's product?

b. Calculate the break-even point in revenue for Incline?

LO5 **E19-9A.** **Cost-Volume Profit Analysis** Recline Company is planning to produce and sell 11,250 units of its only product at a unit price of $106. At this sales level, Recline Company will generate $405,000 in total contribution margin and incur fixed costs of $25/unit.

a. Calculate Recline's contribution margin ratio.

b. Calculate the break-even point in sales dollars for Recline?

E19-10A. Break-Even (Units) Parker & Associates LLC has budgeted the following amounts for its next fis-   **LO5**
cal year:

Total fixed expenses.	$980,000
Selling price per unit.	$ 48
Variable expenses per unit.	$ 23

If fixed expenses increase by 10%, the selling price per unit would need to increase by what percentage
in order to maintain the original break-even sales in units (round to the nearest tenth of a percent)?

E19-11A. Break-Even (Sales Dollars) Fixed expenses total $28,678, the break-even sales in dollars is   **LO5**
$92,512, and the selling price per unit is $98. Calculate the variable expense per unit (round to the
nearest cent).

E19-12A. Net Income Planning Nolden Company has charged a selling price of $24 per unit, incurred vari-   **LO6**
able costs of $15 per unit, and total fixed costs of $108,000. What unit sales volume is necessary to
earn the following related amounts of net income before income tax?
a. $18,000.
b. $27,000.
c.   Equal to 20% of sales revenue.

E19-13A. Cost-Volume Profit Analysis Hailstorm Company sells a single product for $28 per unit. Variable   **LO4, 5, 6**
costs are $22 per unit, and fixed costs are $60,000 at an operating level of 7,000 to 15,000 units.
a.   What is Hailstorm Company's break-even point in units?
b.   How many units must be sold to earn $12,000 before income tax?
c.   How many units must be sold to earn $14,500 after income tax, assuming a 35% tax rate?

E19-14A. Break-Even with Multiple Products Wagner Enterprise sells two products, large tractors and   **LO4, 5, 6**
small tractors. A large tractor sells for $62,000 per unit with variable costs of $28,520 per unit. Small
tractors sell for $34,000 per unit with variable costs of $16,320 per unit. Total fixed costs for the
company are $1,560,000. Wagner Enterprises typically sells two large tractors for every three small
tractors. Assuming the sales mix remains constant, how many large and small tractors are sold (in
units) at Wagner's break-even point?

E19-15A. Break-Even with Multiple Products McDoogle Farms has $240,340 of total fixed costs and sells   **LO5**
products A and B with a product mix of 30% A and 70% B. Selling prices and variable costs for A
and B result in contribution margins per unit of $8 and $14, respectively. Compute the break-even
point.

E19-16A. Margin of Safety Yellow Sticker Company's variable expenses are 40% of sales. The company   **LO6**
has monthly fixed expenses of $15,000 and sells each unit for $0.50. The monthly target operating
income is $3,750.
a.   What is the monthly margin of safety in dollars if Yellow Sticker Company achieves its operating income goal?
b.   What is the monthly margin of safety in units if Yellow Sticker Company achieves its operating
income goal?

E19-17A. Operating Leverage PB&J Eatery has a monthly target operating income of $8,400. Variable ex-   **LO6**
penses are 60% of sales and monthly fixed expenses are $12,600. What is PB&J Eatery's operating
leverage factor at the target level of operating income?

E19-18A. Cost Patterns The graphs below represent approximations of cost behavior patterns. The horizontal   **LO1**
axis of each graph represents units and the vertical axis represents dollars of total cost.

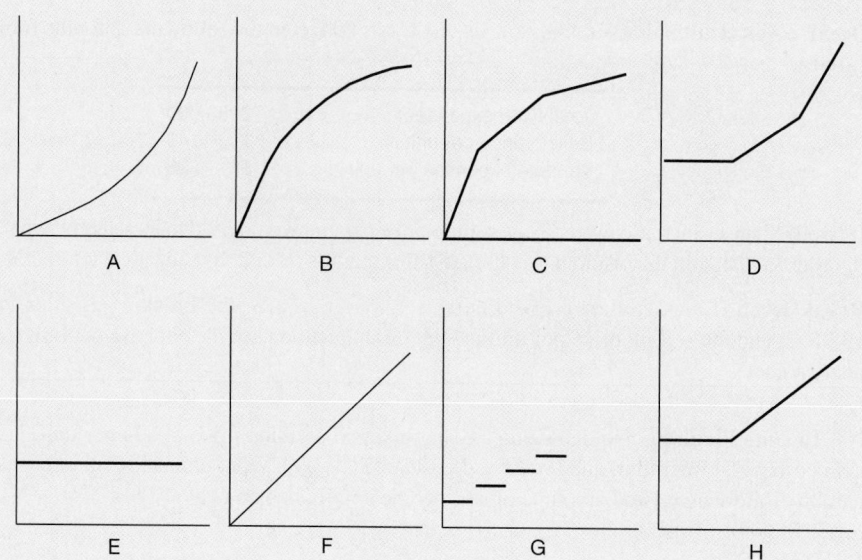

A   B   C   D

E   F   G   H

Select the graph that best matches each of the situations described below. Each graph may be selected more than once.

a. Straight-line depreciation of a factory building.

b. Utility bill for electricity that includes a fixed charge per month plus a constant usage rate per hour for hours in excess of 100.

c. Cost of microchip incorporated into a product.

d. Labor cost of machine operators who become more productive as they gain experience.

e. Water bill that includes a flat fee for the first 10,000 gallons used plus an increasing usage charge for each additional 10,000 gallons used.

f. Cost of factory supplies when increasing quantities bring cost discounts as each price break level is attained.

g. Salaries of quality inspectors when one additional inspector is hired for each 20,000 units produced.

h. Cost of an advertising campaign.

EXERCISES—SET B

LO3

E19-1B. High-Low Method The highest and lowest levels of activity for the Felton Company were 58,000 direct labor hours and 42,000 direct labor hours, respectively. If maintenance costs were $420,000 at the 58,000-hour level and $380,000 at the 42,000-hour level, what cost might we expect at an operating level of 52,000 direct labor hours?

LO3

E19-2B. High-Low Method During the past year, Gutter Corp., operated within the relevant range of its fixed costs. Monthly production volume during the year ranged from 30,000 to 50,000 units of product and corresponding total manufacturing costs ranged from $5.75 to $4.75 per unit. Determine the total cost behavior pattern experienced by Gutter Corp.

LO3

E19-3B. Relevant Range and High-Low Method The following selected data relate to the major cost categories experienced by Silver & Company at varying levels of operating volumes. Assuming that all operating volumes are within the relevant range, calculate the appropriate costs in each column in which blanks appear (some blanks can be $0):

	Total Cost (@ 2,000 units)	Total Cost (@ 3,000 units)	Variable Cost per Unit	Total Fixed Cost	Total Cost (@ 4,000 units)
Direct labor (variable)............	$120,000	$150,000	—	—	—
Factory supervision (semivariable)...	54,000	66,000	—	—	—
Factory depreciation (fixed)........	35,000	35,000	—	—	—

E19-4B. **Cost Formula** The following amounts of various cost categories are experienced by Patton Manufacturing in producing and selling its only product:

Direct materials.	$14 per unit of product
Direct labor.	$12 per direct labor hour*
Manufacturing overhead.	$15,000 + $3.50 per direct labor hour
Selling expenses	$17,000 + $2.75 per unit of product
Administrative.	$9,000 + $0.40 per unit of product

*Each unit of product requires 1.5 direct labor hours.

Combine the various cost factors into a general total cost formula for Patton Manufacturing and determine the total cost of producing and selling 25,000 units.

E19-5B. **Least Squares Regression Analysis** Bogota Corporation has gathered data on its overhead activities and associated costs for the past 12 months. Josh Hopper, from the accounting department, has convinced management that overhead costs can be better estimated and controlled if the fixed and variable components of each overhead activity are known. One such activity is the purchasing department (receiving and reviewing purchase requisitions, issuing purchase orders, and managing vendor relationships), which he believes is driven by the number of purchase orders issued. Twelve months of data have been gathered for the purchasing activity and are as follows:

Month	Purchase Orders Issued	Purchasing Cost
1.	1,050	$18,100
2.	750	$15,100
3.	1,550	$28,100
4.	1,250	$17,100
5.	1,350	$25,100
6.	1,150	$21,100
7.	1,650	$29,100
8.	1,450	$24,100
9.	1,750	$27,100
10.	950	$16,100
11.	1,250	$18,100
12.	1,500	$18,600

Assume Josh has used the method of least squares (i.e., regression analysis) on the purchasing data and has gotten the following results:

Intercept	$3,231
Slope	$13.99

Required

a. Using the results from the method of least squares, prepare a cost formula for the purchasing activity.

b. Using the formula for Requirement A, what is the predicted cost of purchasing for a month in which 1,525 purchase orders are processed? (Note: Round your answer to the nearest dollar.)

E19-6B. **Least Squares Regression Analysis** Bogota Corporation has gathered data on its overhead activities and associated costs for the past 12 months. Josh Hopper, from the accounting department, has convinced management that overhead costs can be better estimated and controlled if the fixed and variable components of each overhead activity are known. One such activity is the purchasing department (receiving and reviewing purchase requisitions, issuing purchase orders, and managing vendor relationships), which he believes is driven by the number of purchase orders issued. Twelve months of data have been gathered for the purchasing activity and are as follows:

Month	Purchase Orders Issued	Purchasing Cost
1	1,050	$23,738
2	750	16,788
3	1,550	35,113
4	1,250	27,263
5	1,350	27,463
6	1,150	27,988
7	1,650	34,388
8	1,450	29,213
9	1,750	38,663
10	950	21,938
11	1,250	25,688
12	1,500	34,200

    a.   Run a regression using Excel or a similar computer spreadsheet program. Provide the intercept, slope, and R^2 for the regression.

    b.   Using the results from requirement *a*, prepare a cost formula for the purchasing activity.

    c.   Using the formula from requirement *b*, what is the predicted cost of purchasing for a month in which 1,375 purchase orders are issued? (Note: Round your answer to the nearest dollar.)

LO4   **E19-7B.**   **Break-Even Calculations**   Compute the break-even point in units for each of the following independent situations:

	Unit Selling Price	Unit Variable Cost	Total Fixed Cost
a.	$12.00	$8.00	$ 87,000
b.	15.00	11.00	146,000
c.	8.75	2.50	52,000

Using the break-even point in units, calculate the break-even point in revenue. Confirm the break-even point in revenue using the contribution margin ratio.

LO4, 5   **E19-8B.**   **Break-Even Analysis**   Feet-First Industries plans to sell 7,750 sleds at $80 each in the coming year. Variable cost is 60 percent of the sales price. Fixed factory overhead equals $49,540 and fixed selling and administrative expense equals $34,780.

    a.   Calculate the units that Feet-First must sell in order to break even.

    b.   Calculate the sales revenue that Feet-First must earn to break even by using the contribution margin.

    c.   Confirm your answer in requirement *b*, by multiplying the number of break-even units in requirement *a* by the unit sales price.

LO4, 5, 6   **E19-9B.**   **Net Income Planning**   Holland Corporation earned an after-tax net income of $182,000 last year. Fixed costs were $750,000. The selling price per unit of its product was $130, of which $60 was a contribution to fixed cost and net income. The income tax rate was 35%.

    a.   How many units of product were sold last year?

    b.   What was the break-even point in units last year?

    c.   The company wishes to increase its after-tax net income by 20% this year. If selling prices and the income tax rate remain unchanged, how many units must be sold?

LO4, 5, 6   **E19-10B.**   **Cost-Volume-Profit Analysis**   Gannon Company sells a single product for $18.75 per unit. Variable costs are $9 per unit and fixed costs are $134,940 at an operating level of 12,000 to 25,000 units.

    a.   What is Gannon Company's break-even point in units?

    b.   How many units must be sold to earn $20,000 before income tax?

    c.   How many units must be sold to earn $30,000 after income tax, assuming a 40% tax rate?

LO5   **E19-11B.**   **Break-Even Analysis**   Pinnacle Party Inflatables, a supplier of inflatable bouncy houses, has budgeted the following amounts for its next fiscal year:

Total fixed expenses..........	$236,250
Selling price per unit..........	$ 300
Variable expenses per unit......	$ 125

If Pinnacle Party Inflatables can reduce fixed expenses by $47,250, by how much can variable expenses per unit increase and still allow the company to maintain the original break-even sales in units?

E19-12B. Multiple Product Break-Even Analysis Wynn Company has $141,360 total fixed cost and sells products A and B with a product mix of 70% A and 30% B. Selling prices and variable costs for A and B result in contribution margins per unit of $9 and $7, respectively. Compute the break-even point in units of A and B.

E19-13B. Break-Even with Multiple Products We Scream For Ice Cream sells ice cream in three flavors: Chocolate, Strawberry, and Vanilla. It sold 28,000 gallons last year, but it is still losing money. For every five gallons of ice cream sold, one gallon is Strawberry and the remainder is split evenly between Chocolate and Vanilla. Fixed costs for We Scream For Ice Cream are $55,056 and additional information follows:

	Chocolate	Vanilla	Strawberry
Sales price per gallon.........	$5.25	$5.25	$5.25
Variable cost per gallon	$2.75	$3.75	$3.95

    a.   Assuming the sales mix remains constant, how many total gallons of ice cream must be sold to break even?

    b.   How many gallons of strawberry ice cream will be sold at the break-even point?

    c.   What will total revenue equal at the break-even point?

E19-14B. Break-Even with Multiple Products Wylie's Watering Hole sells fruit smoothies. Last year, Wylie sold a total of 24,000 fruit smoothies. Pineapple smoothies outsold Coconut smoothies 2 to 1. Sales of Mango smoothies were the same as sales of pineapple. Fixed costs for the company are $18,189 and additional information follows:

Product	Unit Sales Prices	Unit Variable Cost
Pineapple	$2.50	$0.80
Coconut	$3.75	$1.35
Mango....................	$3.20	$1.40

    a.   Calculate the sales mix percentage of all three products (based upon the number of smoothies).

    b.   Calculate the weighted average contribution margin for all three types of drinks.

    c.   Calculate the break-even volume in number of total smoothies.

    d.   Calculate the break-even point in revenue.

E19-15B. Break-Even with Multiple Products Pippy's Tasty Treats sells muffins, scones, and cookies. It sold a total of 19,000 dozens last year. Cookies and muffins each represent 40% of unit sales. Scones represent the remaining 20% of unit sales. Fixed costs for Pippy's Tasty Treats are $154,601 and additional information follows:

Product	Sales Prices	Variable Cost
1 dozen muffins	$36.00	$28.00
1 dozen scones	$45.00	$32.00
1 dozen cookies	$33.00	$21.00

    a.   Calculate the weighted average contribution margin for all three types of dozens.

    b.   Calculate the break-even volume in number of dozens.

    c.   Calculate the break-even sales in dollars.

E19-16B. Margin of Safety Jake's Sub Shop sells large sub sandwiches for $8.75. Unit variable expenses total $3.85. The break-even sales in units is 5,250 and budgeted sales in units is 9,500. What is the margin of safety in dollars? What are Jake's fixed costs?

LO6 **E19-17B.** **Operating Leverage** Jordan's Bake Shop has a monthly target operating income of $10,500. Variable expenses are 50% of sales and the bakery must sell 3,500 units to break even. Jordan sells her product for $4.50 per unit. What is the operating leverage factor for Jordan's Bake Shop at the target level of operating income?

LO1 **E19-18B.** **Cost Patterns** The following graph depicts cost-volume relationships for Tallmadge Company:

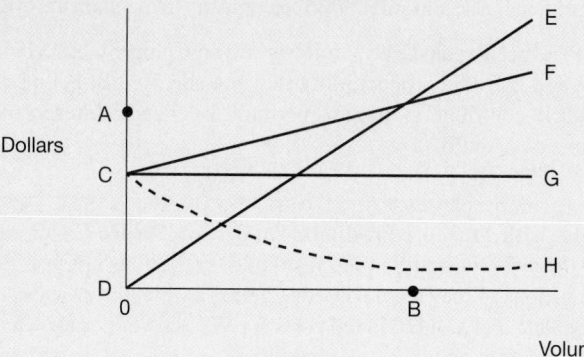

Choose a labeled point *or* line on the graph that *best* represents the behavior of each of the following items as operating volume is increased. Answers may be the same for more than one item. Answer each item independently.

a. Total sales revenue.
b. Total costs.
c. Total variable costs.
d. Total fixed costs.
e. Total mixed cost.
f. Break-even point.

PROBLEMS—SET A

LO5 **P19-1A.** **Net Income Planning** Selected operating data for Oakbrook Company in four independent situations are as follows:

SERVICE AND MERCHANDISING

	A	B	C	D
Sales.	$525,000	$ c.	$ e.	$300,000
Variable expense	$ a.	$405,000	$ f.	$ g.
Fixed expense	$ b.	$98,000	$47,000	$140,000
Net income before tax (loss).	$ 22,000	$307,000	$28,000	$ (20,000)
Units sold	35,000	d.		
Unit contribution margin	$ 8.25	$ 9.00		
Contribution margin ratio			0.25	h.

Required
Fill in the blanks for each independent situation. Show your calculations.

LO1, 2, 3 **P19-2A.** **Graphing Mixed Cost** During a recent six-month period, Wade Corporation had the following monthly production volume and total monthly maintenance expense:

	Units Produced	Maintenance Expense
March	21,000	$140,000
April	15,000	112,000
May	30,000	184,000
June	27,000	172,000
July	35,000	208,000
August	25,000	160,000

Required

Assume that all volumes are in the relevant range.

a. Explain why the data indicate that the maintenance expense is neither a fixed nor a variable expense.
b. Construct a graph similar to the one in **Exhibit 19-7** and plot the maintenance expense data.
c. Fit a line (by sight) to the cost observation points and estimate the cost formula.
d. Confirm your answer in requirement (c) with high-low analysis.

P19-3A. Cost Formulas Longboat Manufacturing produces a single product requiring the following direct materials and direct labor: LO2, 3, 6

Description	Cost per Unit of Input	Required Amount per Unit of Product
Material A	$ 9/pound	20 ounces
Material B	7/pound	4 ounces
Material C	25/gallon	0.4 gallon
Cutting labor	12/hour	45 minutes
Shaping labor	15/hour	15 minutes
Finishing labor	14/hour	75 minutes

Manufacturing overhead consists of indirect materials, $0.60 per unit of product; indirect labor, $1,000 per month plus $0.75 per unit of product; factory maintenance, $17,000 per year plus $0.65 per unit of product; factory depreciation, $18,000 per year; and annual factory property taxes, $10,000. Selling and administrative expenses include the salaries of a sales manager, $40,000 per year; an office manager, $22,000 per year; and two salespersons, each of whom is paid a base salary of $15,000 per year and a commission of $4 per unit sold. Advertising and promotion of the product are done through a year-round media package program costing $1,500 per week.

Required

a. Analyze all cost and expense factors to determine a general formula (based on units of production) for total cost.
b. Assuming a relevant range of 10,000 to 30,000 units, what is the estimated unit cost for producing and selling 10,000 units? 25,000 units? Explain the variation in unit cost at the two levels of production.
c. If 22,000 units are produced and sold in a year, what selling price results in a net income before income tax of $75,000?

P19-4A. High-Low and Cost Formula Harrison Company has accumulated the following total manufacturing overhead costs for two levels of activity (within the relevant range): LO2, 3

	Low	High
Activity (direct labor hours)	90,000	130,000
Total manufacturing overhead	$484,000	$628,000

The total overhead cost includes variable, fixed, and mixed costs. At 130,000 direct labor hours, the total cost breakdown is as follows:

Variable cost	$286,000
Fixed cost	85,000
Semi-mixed cost	257,000

Required

a. Using the high-low method of cost analysis, determine the variable portion of the semi-variable cost per direct labor hour. Determine the total fixed cost component of the mixed cost.

b. What should the total planned overhead cost be at 115,000 direct labor hours?

LO3 **P19-5A. Least Squares Regression Analysis** The controller for TG Enterprises is trying to determine whether direct labor hours or machine hours is driving the company's overhead cost. He collected the following data on the number of direct labor hours, the number of machine hours, and the associated factory overhead cost for the year 2018:

Month	Machine Hours	Direct Labor Hours	Overhead Cost
January..........	132	724	$5,750
February.........	130	730	5,685
March	131	715	5,790
April	126	685	5,480
May.............	128	695	5,590
June	123	585	5,430
July.............	135	775	5,790
August	130	680	5,705
September	132	725	5,804
October..........	138	840	5,976
November........	128	775	5,487
December........	143	825	6,108

Required

a. Using Excel, run a regression on these data using machine hours as the independent variable. Provide the cost formula for overhead cost. Round fixed and variable costs to the nearest cent.

b. Using Excel, run a regression on these data using direct labor hours as the independent variable. Provide the cost formula for overhead cost. Round the fixed and variable costs to the nearest cent.

c. What is the R^2 for the regression in requirement a? What is the R^2 for the regression in requirement b? Which independent variable, direct labor hours or machine hours, is a better predictor of factory overhead cost?

d. Assuming that expected January 2019 machine hours are 150, what is expected factory overhead cost using the cost formula in requirement a? (*Note:* Round to the nearest dollar.)

LO3 **P19-6A. Least Squares Regression Analysis** The management of Digger Inc., is trying to develop a cost formula for its major manufacturing overhead activities. Digger's manufacturing process is highly automated and power costs are a significant manufacturing cost. Cost analysts have decided that power costs are mixed. The costs must be separated into their fixed and variable components so that the cost behavior of the power usage activity can be better understood. Analysts have determined that machine hours drive power usage; thus machine hours are the cost driver for power costs. Nine months of data have been collected and are presented in the chart below:

Period	Machine Hours	Power Cost
January..............	24,000	$32,500
February.............	30,000	47,500
March	36,000	53,125
April	26,400	46,250
May.................	25,200	42,500
June	21,600	36,250
July.................	28,800	45,000
August	33,600	50,000
September	31,200	40,000

Note: For the following requirements, round the variable cost per unit to the nearest cent and the total fixed cost to the nearest dollar.

Required

a. Use the high and low points to estimate a power cost formula.

b. Use the method of least squares in Excel or a similar computer program to estimate a power cost formula.

    c. Evaluate R^2 from requirement *b.* Are machine hours a good predictor of power costs?

P19-7A. **Cost Formula** Princeton Manufacturing Company summarizes the following total cost data for the month of March. Princeton has a normal capacity per month of 25,000 units of product that sell for $40 each. For the foreseeable future, sales volume should equal normal capacity of production.   **LO1, 2, 3**

Direct materials.	$295,000
Direct labor	165,000
Variable overhead	85,000
Fixed overhead (Note 1).	140,000
Selling expense (Note 2)	80,000
Administrative expense (fixed)	56,000
	$821,000

Notes:

    1. Beyond normal capacity, fixed overhead cost increases $6,350 for each 1,000 units *or fraction thereof until* a maximum capacity of 30,000 units is reached.

    2. Selling expenses are a 5% sales commission plus shipping costs of $1.20 per unit.

Required

    a. Using the information available, prepare a formula to estimate Princeton's total cost at various production volumes up to normal capacity.

    b. Prove your answer in requirement (a) relative to the total cost figure for 25,000 units.

    c. Calculate the planned total cost at 20,000 units, and explain why total cost did not decrease in proportion to the reduced volume.

    d. If Princeton were operating at normal capacity and accepted an order for 500 more units, what would it have to charge for the order to earn a net income before income tax of $8 per unit on the new sale?

P19-8A. **Net Income Planning** Superior Corporation sells a single product for $75 per unit, of which $42 is contribution margin. Fixed costs total $100,800 and net income before income tax is $28,800.   **LO4, 5, 6**

Required

Determine the following (show key computations):

    a. The present sales volume in dollars.

    b. The break-even point in units.

    c. The sales volume in units necessary to attain a net income before income tax of $39,000.

    d. The sales volume in units necessary to attain a net income before income tax equal to 20% of sales revenue.

    e. The sales volume in units necessary to attain an after-tax net income of $43,720 if the tax rate is 40%.

P19-9A. **Break-Even and Net Income Planning** The controller of Grafton Company is preparing data for a conference call concerning certain *independent* aspects of its operations.   **LO4, 5, 6**

Required

Prepare answers to the following questions for the controller:

    a. Total fixed cost is $1,440,000 and a unit of product is sold for $12 in excess of its unit variable cost. What is the break-even in units?

    b. The company will sell 60,000 units of product—each having a unit variable cost of $22—at a price that will enable the product to absorb $600,000 of fixed cost. What minimum unit sales price must be charged to break even?

    c. Net income before income tax of $320,000 is desired after covering $1,200,000 of fixed costs. What minimum contribution margin ratio must be maintained if total sales revenue is to be $3,800,000?

    d. Net income before income tax is 10% of sales revenue, the contribution margin ratio is 30%, and the break-even dollar sales is $640,000. What is the amount of total revenue?

    e. Fixed costs total $1,000,000, the variable cost per unit is $30, and selling price per unit is $80. What dollar sales volume will generate an after-tax net income of $84,000 when the income tax rate is 40%?

LO4, 5, 6   P19-10A.   Break-Even and Net Income Planning Hank Company has recently leased facilities for the manufacture of a new product. Based on studies made by its accounting personnel, the following data are
available:

Estimated annual sales: 20,000 units.

Estimated Costs	Amount	Unit Cost
Direct materials.	$345,000	$17.25
Direct labor	328,000	16.40
Manufacturing overhead.	196,000	9.80
Administrative expenses.	124,000	6.20
	$993,000	$49.65

Selling expenses are expected to be 10% of sales, and the selling price is $71 per unit. Ignore income
tax in this problem.

Required

a. Compute a break-even point in dollars and in units. Assume that manufacturing overhead and
administrative expenses are fixed but that other costs are variable. (Round contribution margin
ratio computation to three decimal places.)

b. What would net income before income tax be if 30,000 units were sold?

c. How many units must be sold to earn a net income before income tax of 10% of sales?

LO4, 5, 6   P19-11A.   Multiple Product Break-Even and Net Income Planning Grand Company manufactures and
sells the following three products:

	Economy	Standard	Deluxe
Unit sales	10,000	6,000	4,000
Unit sales price.	$48	$56	$68
Unit variable cost	$30	$32	$36

Required
Assume that total fixed cost is $339,000.

a. Compute the net income before income tax based on the sales volumes shown above.

b. Compute the break-even point in total dollars of revenue and in units for each product.

c. Prove your break-even calculations by computing the total contribution margin related to your
answer in requirement (b).

PROBLEMS—SET B

LO4, 5   P19-1B.   Net Income Planning Selected operating data for Verona Company in four independent situations
are shown below.

	A	B	C	D
Sales.	$320,000	$ c.	$ e.	$280,000
Variable expense	$ a.	$48,000	$ f.	$ g.
Fixed expense	$ b.	$56,000	$240,000	$120,000
Net income before tax	$ 40,000	$16,000	$ 96,000	$ (8,000)
Units sold	7,000	d.		
Unit contribution margin	$ 20	$ 9		
Contribution margin ratio			0.70	h.

Required
Fill in the blanks for each independent situation. Show your calculations.

LO1, 2, 3   P19-2B.   Graphing Mixed Cost During the past operating year, Davenport Corporation had the following
monthly volume of production and total monthly maintenance expense:

	Units Produced	Maintenance Expense		Units Produced	Maintenance Expense
January.........	123,000	$28,600	July............	127,000	$29,000
February........	147,000	31,600	August	157,000	32,800
March..........	159,000	33,000	September	131,000	29,600
April	133,000	29,400	October.........	163,000	33,400
May............	143,000	31,200	November.......	155,000	32,600
June	153,000	32,600	December.......	159,000	33,000

Required

Assume that all volumes are in the relevant range.

a. Explain why the data indicate that the maintenance expense is neither a fixed nor a variable expense.

b. Construct a graph similar to the one in **Exhibit 19-7** and plot the maintenance expense data.

c. Fit a line (by sight) to the cost observation points, and estimate the cost formula.

d. Confirm your answer in requirement (c) with high-low analysis.

P19-3B.   **Cost Formulas** Colonial Manufacturing produces a single product requiring the following direct materials and direct labor:

LO2, 3, 6

Description	Cost per Unit of Input	Required Amount per Unit of Product
Material A.....................................	$12/pound	24 ounces
Material B.....................................	8/pound	8 ounces
Material C.....................................	15/gallon	0.6 gallon
Cutting labor..................................	14/hour	45 minutes
Shaping labor.................................	12/hour	30 minutes
Finishing labor	16/hour	90 minutes

Manufacturing overhead consists of indirect materials, $0.40 per unit of product; indirect labor, $900 per month plus $0.80 per unit of product; factory maintenance, $18,000 per year plus $0.75 per unit of product; factory depreciation, $22,000 per year; and annual factory property taxes, $12,000. Selling and administrative expenses include the salaries of a sales manager, $45,000 per year, an office manager, $24,000 per year, and two salespersons, each of whom is paid a base salary of $18,000 per year and a commission of $3 per unit sold. Advertising and promotion of the product are done through a year-round media package program costing $1,000 per week.

Required

a. Analyze all cost and expense factors to determine a general formula (based on units of production) for total cost.

b. Assuming a relevant range of 10,000 to 30,000 units, what is the estimated unit cost for producing and selling 12,000 units? 24,000 units? Explain the variation in unit cost at the two levels of production.

c. If 28,000 units are produced and sold in a year, what selling price results in a net income before taxes of $75,000?

P19-4B.   **High-Low and Cost Formula** Harrison Company has accumulated the following total manufacturing overhead costs for two levels of activity (within the relevant range):

LO2, 3

	Low	High
Activity (direct labor hours)......................................	120,000	180,000
Total manufacturing overhead	$963,500	$1,251,500

The total overhead cost includes variable, fixed, and mixed costs. At 120,000 direct labor hours, the total cost breakdown is as follows:

Variable cost.	$318,000
Fixed cost.	260,500
Semi-variable cost	385,000

Required

a.   Using the high-low method of cost analysis, determine the variable portion of the mixed cost per direct labor hour. Determine the total fixed cost component of the mixed cost.

b.   What should the total planned overhead cost be at 140,000 direct labor hours?

LO3   P19-5B.   Least Squares Regression Analysis The controller for TG Enterprises is trying to determine whether direct labor hours or machine hours is driving the company's overhead cost. He collected the following data on the number of direct labor hours, the number of machine hours, and the associated factory overhead cost for the year 2018:

Month	Machine Hours	Direct Labor Hours	Overhead Cost
January.	198	1810	$17,610
February.	195	1825	17,410
March	197	1788	17,735
April	189	1713	16,780
May.	192	1738	17,240
June	185	1463	16,635
July.	203	1938	17,700
August	195	1700	17,500
September	198	1813	17,775
October.	207	2100	18,400
November.	192	1938	16,805
December.	215	2063	18,895

Required

a.   Using Excel, run a regression on these data using machine hours as the independent variable. Provide the cost formula for overhead cost. Round fixed and variable costs to the nearest cent.

b.   Using Excel, run a regression on these data using direct labor hours as the independent variable. Provide the cost formula for overhead cost. Round the fixed and variable costs to the nearest cent.

c.   What is the R^2 for the regression in requirement a? What is the R^2 for the regression in requirement b? Which independent variable, direct labor hours or machine hours, is a better predictor of factory overhead cost?

d.   Assuming that expected January 2019 machine hours are 212, what is expected factory overhead cost using the cost formula in requirement a? (Note: Round to the nearest dollar.)

LO3   P19-6B.   Least Squares Regression Analysis The management of Digger Inc., is trying to develop a cost formula for its major manufacturing overhead activities. Digger's manufacturing process is highly automated and power costs are a significant manufacturing cost. Cost analysts have decided that power costs are mixed. The costs must be separated into their fixed and variable components so that the cost behavior of the power usage activity can be better understood. Analysts have determined that machine hours drive power usage, thus machine hours are the cost driver for power costs. Nine months of data have been collected and are presented in the chart below:

Period	Machine Hours	Power Cost
January.	36,000	$45,000
February.	45,000	60,300
March	54,000	67,500
April	39,600	53,064
May.	37,800	47,250
June	32,400	43,416
July.	43,200	54,000
August	50,400	67,536
September	46,800	58,500

Note: For the following requirements, round the variable cost per unit to the nearest cent and the total fixed cost to the nearest dollar.

Required

a.   Use the high and low points to estimate a power cost formula.

b.   Use the method of least squares in Excel or a similar computer program to estimate a power cost formula.

c.   Evaluate R^2 from requirement *b*. Are machine hours a good predictor of power costs?

d.   Using the cost formula from requirement *b*, estimate power costs when 55,800 machine hours are used.

P19-7B.   **Cost Formula** The following total cost data are for Phoenix Manufacturing Company, which has a normal capacity per period of 40,000 units of product that sell for $60 each. For the foreseeable future, sales volume should equal normal capacity of production.

LO1, 2, 3

Direct materials.	$ 640,000
Direct labor.	400,000
Variable overhead	200,000
Fixed overhead (Note 1).	216,000
Selling expense (Note 2)	280,000
Administrative expense (fixed)	88,000
	$1,824,000

Notes:

1.   Beyond normal capacity, fixed overhead cost increases $6,240 for each 2,000 units *or fraction thereof* until a maximum capacity of 50,000 units is reached.

2.   Selling expenses are a 10% sales commission plus shipping costs of $1 per unit.

Required

a.   Using the information available, prepare a formula to estimate Phoenix's total cost at various production volumes up to normal capacity.

b.   Prove your answer in requirement (a) against the above total cost figure at 40,000 units.

c.   Calculate the planned total cost at 30,000 units, and explain why total cost did not decrease in proportion to the reduced volume.

d.   If Phoenix were operating at normal capacity and accepted an order for 600 more units, what would it have to charge for the order to earn a net income before tax of $8 per unit on the new sale?

P19-8B.   **Net Income Planning** Night Hawk Corporation sells a single product for $150 per unit, of which $60 is contribution margin. Total fixed cost is $240,000, and net income before income tax is $54,000.

LO4, 5, 6

Required

Determine the following (show key computations):

a.   The present sales volume in dollars.

b.   The break-even point in units.

c.   The sales volume in units necessary to attain a net income before income tax of $75,000.

d.   The sales volume in units necessary to attain a net income before income tax equal to 10% of sales revenue.

e.   The sales volume in units necessary to attain a net income of $54,000 if the tax rate is 20%.

P19-9B.   **Break-Even and Net Income Planning** The controller of Wright Company is preparing data for a conference concerning certain *independent* aspects of its operations.

LO4, 5, 6

Required

Prepare answers to the following questions for the controller:

a.   Total fixed cost is $720,000, and a unit of product is sold for $10 in excess of its unit variable cost. What is the break-even unit volume?

b.   The company will sell 30,000 units of product—each having a unit variable cost of $14—at a price that will enable the product to absorb $360,000 of fixed cost. What minimum unit sales price must be charged to break even?

c.   Net income before income tax of $150,000 is desired after covering $410,000 of fixed cost. What minimum contribution margin ratio must be maintained if total sales revenue is to be $1,600,000?

d.   Net income before income tax is 20% of sales revenue, the contribution margin ratio is 60%, and the break-even dollar sales is $200,000. What is the amount of total revenue?

e.   Total fixed cost is $350,000, variable cost per unit is $26, and unit sales price is $50. What dollar sales volume will generate an after-tax net income of $60,000 when the income tax rate is 40%?

LO4, 5, 6   **P19-10B. Break-Even and Net Income Planning**   Venice Company has recently leased facilities for the manufacture of a new product. Based on studies made by its accounting personnel, the following data are available:

Estimated annual sales	60,000 units

Estimated Costs	Amount	Unit Cost
Direct materials.	$ 870,000	$14.50
Direct labor	750,000	12.50
Manufacturing overhead.	384,000	6.40
Administrative expenses.	228,000	3.80
	$2,232,000	$37.20

Selling expenses are expected to be 20% of sales, and the selling price is $82 per unit. Ignore income tax in this problem.

Required

a.   Compute a break-even point in dollars and in units. Assume that manufacturing overhead and administrative expenses are fixed but that other costs are variable.

b.   What would net income before income tax be if 40,000 units were sold?

c.   How many units must be sold to earn a net income before income tax of 10% of sales?

LO4, 5, 6   **P19-11B. Multiple Product Break-Even and Net Income Planning**   Madison Company manufactures and sells the following three products:

	Red	Blue	Green
Unit sales	20,000	30,000	50,000
Unit sales price.	$30	$62	$18
Unit variable cost	$18	$38	$14

Required

Assume that total fixed cost is $324,800.

a.   Compute the net income before income tax based on the sales volumes shown above.

b.   Compute the break-even point in total dollars of revenue and in specific unit sales volume for each product.

c.   Prove your break-even calculations by computing the total contribution margin related to your answer in requirement (b).

EXTENDING YOUR KNOWLEDGE

LO6   **EYK19-1. Business Decision Case**   The following total cost data are for Ralston Manufacturing Company, which has a normal capacity per period of 400,000 units of product that sell for $18 each. For the foreseeable future, regular sales volume should continue at normal capacity of production.

Direct materials.	$1,720,000
Direct labor	1,120,000
Variable overhead	560,000
Fixed overhead (Note 1).	880,000
Selling expense (Note 2)	720,000
Administrative expense (fixed)	200,000
	$5,200,000

Notes:

1. Beyond normal capacity, fixed overhead cost increases $30,000 for each 20,000 units *or fraction thereof* until a maximum capacity of 640,000 units is reached.
2. Selling expenses are a 10% sales commission. Ralston pays only one-half of the regular sales commission rates on any sale of 20,000 or more units.

Ralston's sales manager has received a special order for 48,000 units from a large discount chain at a special price of $16 each, F.O.B. factory. The controller's office has furnished the following additional cost data related to the special order:

1. Changes in the product's construction will reduce direct materials $1.80 per unit.
2. Special processing will add 25% to the per-unit direct labor costs.
3. Variable overhead will continue at the same proportion of direct labor costs.
4. Other costs should not be affected.

Required

a. Present an analysis supporting a decision to accept or reject the special order. Assume Ralston's regular sales are not affected by this special order.
b. What is the lowest unit sales price Ralston could receive and still make a before-tax profit of $39,600 on the special order?

EYK19-2. Ethics Case Gina DeMarc, a partner in a large CPA firm, has been approached by Bruce Jonas, a manager, with the following recommendation for incentive bonuses for staff members. Jonas recommends that the firm continue to pay each staff member a straight annual salary (which has been traditionally the only payment made) plus a bonus based on the staff member's ability to achieve a 10% reduction in time spent on each client's work. The firm would also pay a 5% finder's fee for any new client the staff member brings into the firm.

Jonas believes this will motivate the staff to work more efficiently, to sell the firm to new clients, and to service more clients in any given time period. This should also generate more revenue for the firm.

Required
How would you advise Gina DeMarc? What ethical issues should she consider?

ANSWERS TO SELF-STUDY QUESTIONS:

1. a, (p. 904)   2. b, (p. 906)   3. d, (p. 907)   4. a, (p. 912)   5. c, (p. 915)   6. a, (p. 918)

YOUR TURN! SOLUTIONS

Solution 19.1
y-intercept = Total fixed costs of $5.000
Slope = Variable cost per unit of approximately $0.50 per water bottle cage
Total cost = ($0.50 × # of water bottle cages) + $5,000
$25,000 = $0.50 × 40,000 + $5,000

Solution 19.2

The concept of relevant range can be applied to variable, fixed, and mixed costs. The assumption of a linear pattern is sufficiently accurate within a range of probable operations (i.e., the relevant range) where fixed costs remain unchanged and the addition of each additional unit is accompanied by a proportional increase in total cost.

Solution 19.3

a. Mixed cost: $2 per unit plus $5,000

$$\frac{\$24,500 - \$15,000}{9,750 - 5,000} = \$2 \text{ per unit}$$

$24,500 − ($2 × 9,750) = $5,000 fixed cost
Or
$15,000 − ($2 × 5,000) = $5,000 fixed cost

b. From the Excel output:
Intercept = $5,000
X-variable (Volume) = $2.00
Mixed cost = ($2 × volume) + $5,000

Solution 19.4

Contribution margin = $3.50 − $2.10 = $1.40 per sandwich
Fixed cost = $595

a. Break-even point = $595/$1.40 per sandwich = 425 sandwiches
b. Total CM = 1,200 sandwiches × $1.40 = $1,680
Operating income = $1,680 − $595 in fixed cost = $1,085

Solution 19.5

Sales price = $1.40/40% = $3.50 per sandwich

a. BEP in sales dollars = $595/40% = $1,487.50
$1,487.50/$3.50 per sandwich = 425 sandwiches must be sold to break even
b. Variable cost per unit = $3.50 − $1.40 = $2.10 per unit
1,400 sandwiches × $2.10 = $2,940 OR
VC % = 1 − CM% so 1 − 40% = 60%
$3.50 × 60% = $2.10 in variable cost per unit
1,400 sandwiches × $2.10 = $2,940

Solution 19.6

CM per unit = $5.00 − $1.25 = $3.75 per unit
CM % = $3.75/$5.00 = 75%
Total fixed costs = $12,675

1. $12,675/75% = $16,900
2. From part (1) $16,900 in BEP revenue. $16,900/$5.00 per unit = 3,380 units to break even
3. [$12,675 + $15,000]/$3.75 unit contribution margin = 7,380 desired units
4. Pre-tax operating profit = $18,000/(1 − 25%) = $24,000
[$12,675 + $24,000]/$3.75 unit contribution margin = 36,675 desired units
5. At 7,400 units, sales dollars = 7,400 × $5 per unit = $37,000
From part (1), at break-even sales dollars are $16,900
Margin of safety = $37,000 − $16,900 = $20,100
Check: 7,400 units − 3,380 units at break-even = 4,020 units
4,020 units × $5 per unit = $20,100

Chapter 20

Variable Costing: A Tool for Decision Making

PAST

Chapter 19 utilized our understanding of cost behavior to determine break-even and make planning and budgeting decisions.

PRESENT

Chapter 20 discusses the preparation of a variable income statement.

FUTURE

Chapter 21 describes some of the tools and techniques that management can use in making strategic business decisions.

General Motors (GM) designs, manufactures, and sells cars, trucks, and automobile parts worldwide. In North America, they are recognized by their Buick, Cadillac, Chevrolet, and GMC brands. GM operates in a highly competitive global marketplace.

The automotive industry has relatively high fixed costs and significant limitations on their ability to reduce these costs. Automobile manufacturers typically respond to these relatively high fixed costs by attempting to sell more vehicles by adding vehicle options, providing financing programs, offering marketing incentives, or reducing vehicle prices. In 2014, GM reported that its inventories declined from $14.0 billion to $13.6 billion.[1] Because a significant portion of GM's costs are fixed, this means that fixed manufacturing costs incurred in previous years (that had been recorded as part of inventories) were expensed in 2014, reducing GAAP income from what it would have been had GM sold fewer vehicles!

This chapter describes the difference in treatment of product costs between variable costing (useful for internal reporting) and absorption costing (required by GAAP).

---

[1] General Motors 10-K Report dated February 4, 2015.

Road Map

LO	Learning Objective	Page	eLecture	Guided Example	Assignments
LO1	Describe the difference in the treatment of product costs between variable costing and absorption costing.	956	E20-1	YT20.1	SS1, SS6, Q1, Q2, SE1, SE2
LO2	Prepare an income statement under both variable costing and absorption costing methods.	958	E20-2	YT20.2	SS2, SS3, SE3, SE4, E1A, E2A, E1B, E2B, P1A, P2A, P3A, P1B, P2B, P3B
LO3	Explain why net income differs between absorption costing and variable costing. Reconcile the two different income amounts.	961	E20-3	YT20.3	SS3, SS4, SS5, Q3, Q4, SE5, SE6, SE7, SE8, SE9, E2A, E3A, E4A, E2B, E3B, E4B, P3A, P4A, P3B, P4B
LO4	Describe the advantages and disadvantages of the variable costing method.	963	E20-4	YT20.4	SS6, Q5, SE10

TREATMENT OF PRODUCT COSTS

Absorption Costing

LO1 **Describe** the difference in the treatment of product costs between variable costing and absorption costing.

In Chapter 15, we define product costs as **all** manufacturing costs: direct materials, direct labor, and variable and fixed manufacturing overhead. These costs are capitalized as inventory during the production period and recognized as expense (cost of goods sold) only when the related merchandise is sold. This method of attaching all manufacturing costs to the product is known as **absorption costing**. When using absorption costing, and production is greater than sales, a portion of the current period's fixed costs is attached to the inventory that is added to the balance sheet. As a result, a company can defer recognition of fixed costs as an expense by merely producing more inventory than it sells in a period. **Exhibit 20-1a** presents the absorption costing income statement for Fezzari.

A.K.A. Absorption costing is also referred to as *full costing* because it includes both variable and fixed components of product costs.

Exhibit 20-1a	Absorption Costing Income Statement for Fezzari

FEZZARI PERFORMANCE BICYCLES **Absorption Costing Income Statement** **For the Year Ended December 31, 2019** **(000's)**		
Sales.		$4,500
Cost of goods sold		2,957
Gross profit on sales.		$1,543
Operating expenses:		
Selling expenses.	$400	
Non-factory administrative expenses	340	740
Income from operations		$ 803
Other Income and Expense:		
Interest expense		5
Income before income tax		$ 798
Income tax expense		279
Net income		$ 519

Includes fixed manufacturing overhead costs associated with the units sold, associating all manufacturing costs with the related sales revenue.

A.K.A. Variable costing is also referred to as *direct costing*. The latter is a misnomer, however, because variable costs—not direct costs—are capitalized under direct costing.

Variable Costing

In contrast, for internal reporting purposes, some companies use **variable costing** to determine the cost of their manufactured products. Under variable costing, only *variable* manufacturing costs are capitalized as inventory. This includes direct materials, direct labor, and the variable portion of manufacturing overhead. All fixed manufacturing overhead costs are expensed in the period incurred. These fixed manufacturing costs are treated as a period cost in the same manner as selling, general, and administrative expenses. As a result, under variable costing, costs of goods sold amounts do not include the fixed portion of manufacturing overhead. **Exhibit 20-1b** presents the variable costing income statement for Fezzari.

Exhibit 20-1b	Variable Costing Income Statement for Fezzari

FEZZARI PERFORMANCE BICYCLES
Variable Costing Income Statement
For the Year Ended December 31, 2019
(000's)

Sales.		$4,500
Variable cost of goods sold.	$2,732	
Variable selling expenses	300	
Variable non-factory administrative expenses	50	3,082
Contribution margin		$1,418
Fixed Expenses:		
Fixed manufacturing costs	$ 225	
Fixed selling expenses	100	
Fixed non-factory administrative expenses.	290	615
Income from operations		$ 803
Other Income and Expense:		
Interest expense		5
Income before income tax		$ 798
Income tax expense		279
Net income		$ 519

> Includes only variable costs of production (direct materials, direct labor, and variable manufacturing overhead costs) associated with the units sold.

> All fixed manufacturing overhead costs are expensed in the period incurred.

The only difference between absorption and variable costing is that when production exceeds sales, a portion of fixed manufacturing overhead is capitalized under absorption costing, whereas it is fully expensed under variable costing. **Exhibit 20-2** illustrates this difference.

Exhibit 20-2	Illustration of Absorption vs. Variable Costing

Appropriate Use of Absorption Costing and Variable Costing

In general, variable costing (carrying only variable costs in the inventory accounts) is considered a departure from generally accepted accounting standards. These standards require that published financial reports attested to by CPAs be prepared on an absorption costing basis. In these reports, all manufacturing costs should be attributed to products, and inventories of work-in-process and finished goods should contain their allocable shares of manufacturing costs, both fixed and variable. Likewise, the Internal Revenue Service has generally insisted on the use of absorption costing in determining net income for tax purposes, with some adjustments.

Although variable costing should not be used to prepare financial statements for external use, management may use variable costing statements for internal decision making. A principal benefit is that variable costing usually causes net income figures to move in the same direction as sales.

With absorption costing, net income may increase in periods when production volume exceeds sales (increasing inventory on the balance sheet) and decrease when sales volume exceeds production (decreasing inventory on the balance sheet). Why is this important to understand? This is important knowledge because it may be possible for managers to increase reported net income to meet analysts' expectations by increasing production of product during the last few weeks of a reporting period. Of course, this short-term "fix" could result in excess inventory levels that lead to obsolescence and inventory write-offs in subsequent periods.

YOUR TURN! 20.1	How are fixed overhead production costs treated under absorption and variable costing methods?

The solution is on page 977.

	Absorption	Variable Costing
a.	Period	Period
b.	Product	Product
c.	Period	Product
d.	Product	Period

TAKEAWAY 20.1	Concept	➡	Method	➡	Assessment
	How should a firm report its inventory in accordance with generally accepted accounting principles?		Firms are required to use the absorption costing method, which requires that all production costs, including fixed overhead costs, be included in the inventory valuation reported on the balance sheet.		• Absorption costing for external reporting purposes. • Variable costing for internal decision making.

VARIABLE COSTING INCOME STATEMENT

LO2 **Prepare** an income statement under both variable costing and absorption costing methods.

Income Statement Preparation

Exhibit 20-3a provides comparative production and sales information for Fezzari for three consecutive periods. For purposes of this illustration, we assume that Period 1 was the first year of operation (therefore, there is no beginning inventory balance). Notice that we assume that unit sales are the same in all three years, 4,500 units each year. However, production varies over time— 4,500 units in the first period, 5,000 units in the second period, and 4,000 units in the third period. As a result of this production schedule, 500 units are left in ending inventory in the second period. These units are then sold during the third period.

Exhibit 20-3a	Production Data				
	A	B	C	D	E
1	FEZZARI PERFORMANCE BICYCLES				
2		Period 1	Period 2	Period 3	Total
3	Beginning Inventory (units)	—	—	500	—
4	Production (units)	4,500	5,000	4,000	13,500
5	Sales (units)	4,500	4,500	4,500	13,500
6	Ending Inventory (units)	—	500	—	—

Exhibit 20-3b shows the absorption income statement that would be prepared for the three periods. Assume that Fezzari sells each bicycle for $1,000 per unit, that variable product costs are $618 per unit, and that fixed manufacturing costs are $225,000 per period. In the absorption income statement, the cost of goods manufactured includes both fixed and variable product costs. The inventory balance presented at the end of Period 2 consists of $309,000 of variable production costs (500 units × $618 per unit) and $22,500 in fixed production costs (because 10% of the units produced in Period 2 remain in inventory, 10% of the $225,000 in fixed production costs is assigned to the units in inventory).

Exhibit 20-3b	Partial Absorption Income Statement					
	A	B	C	D	E	F
1		FEZZARI PERFORMANCE BICYCLES				
2			Period 1	Period 2	Period 3	Total
3		Beginning Inventory (units)	—	—	500	—
4		Production (units)	4,500	5,000	4,000	13,500
5		Sales (units)	4,500	4,500	4,500	13,500
6		Ending Inventory (units)	—	500	—	—
7		Absorption Costing Income Statement ($000s)				
8			Period 1	Period 2	Period 3	Total
9	(1)	Sales	$4,500	$4,500	$4,500	$13,500
10	(2)	Beginning Inventory	—	—	332	—
11	(3)	Cost of Goods Manufactured	3,006	3,315	2,697	9,018
12	(4)	Less Ending Inventory	—	332	—	—
13	(5)	Cost of Goods Sold [(2) + (3) − (4)]	$(3,006)	$(2,983)	$(3,029)	$ (9,018)
14	(6)	Gross Profit on Sales [(1) + (5)]	$ 1,494	$ 1,517	$ 1,471	$ 4,482

Note that although sales were steady over the three periods, gross profit changed with production (as production increased, so did profit; as production decreased, so did profit).

Variable cost: 500 units × $618 = $309,000
Fixed cost: 500 units/5,000 units × $225,000 =   22,500
Total cost: $331,500

Exhibit 20-3c shows the variable costing income statement for the periods. The variable cost of goods sold includes only the variable costs of production at $618 per unit. The inventory balance presented at the end of Period 2 consists of only the variable costs of production (500 units × $618 per unit, or $309,000).

Exhibit 20-3c	Partial Variable Income Statement					
	A	B	C	D	E	F
1		FEZZARI PERFORMANCE BICYCLES				
2			Period 1	Period 2	Period 3	Total
3		Beginning Inventory (units)	—	—	500	—
4		Production (units)	4,500	5,000	4,000	13,500
5		Sales (units)	4,500	4,500	4,500	13,500
6		Ending Inventory (units)	—	500	—	—
7			Variable Costing Income Statement ($000's)			
8			Period 1	Period 2	Period 3	Total
9	(1)	Sales	$4,500	$4,500	$4,500	$13,500
10	(2)	Beginning Inventory	—	—	309	—
11	(3)	Variable Cost of Goods Manufactured	2,781	3,090	2,472	8,343
12	(4)	Less Ending Inventory	—	309	—	—
13	(5)	Variable Cost of Goods Sold [(2) + (3) − (4)]	$(2,781)	$(2,781)	$(2,781)	$ (8,343)
14	(6)	Contribution Margin [(1) + (5)]	$ 1,719	$ 1,719	$ 1,719	$ 5,157
15	(7)	Fixed Manufacturing Costs	(225)	(225)	(225)	(675)
16	(8)	Income from Operations [(6) + (7)]	$ 1,494	$1,494	$ 1,494	$ 4,482

Variable cost: 500 units × $618 = $309,000
Fixed cost: 0
Total cost: $309,000

Note that, unlike absorption costing, income from operations follows sales, not production.

TAKEAWAY 20.2	Concept ⟶	Method ⟶	Assessment
	How do cost of goods sold and inventory values differ between absorption and variable costing income statements?	• Absorption costing: Includes all production costs (direct materials, direct labor, variable and fixed manufacturing overhead) • Variable costing: Includes only variable production costs (direct materials, direct labor, variable manufacturing overhead)	Under variable costing, both cost of goods sold and inventory valuation will be less than under absorption costing.

A total of $4,482,000 gross profit/income from operations is reported for the three periods under both methods. However, the variable costing method indicates the same income from operations figures in each period ($1,494,000), which are correlated with the constant sales volume over the three periods. On the other hand, under the absorption costing method, gross profit moves up and down with production (from $1,494,000 to $1,517,000 to $1,471,000). The reason, of course, is that the fixed costs are added to the inventory (and therefore not included in cost of goods sold) when production exceeds sales in period 2 and are released (through cost of goods sold) when the company sells more than it produces in period 3.

CORPORATE SOCIAL RESPONSIBILITY

Triple Bottom Line Reporting

This chapter has introduced an internal reporting approach called variable costing, which allows management to more easily focus on the contribution of customers, products, product lines, business segments, and other business units to the overall profitability of the company. Another type of reporting has

continued

continued from previous page

also gained in importance. That other type of reporting, called triple-bottom-line reporting, considers not just financial results, but also environmental and social results as well. GM is committed to acting in a socially responsible manner, behavior that earns high marks in a triple bottom line. As stated on GM's web site, "Through the lens of sustainability, we view industry challenges and change as new business opportunities that can drive additional value for our customers. We call this Customer-Driven Sustainability. From designing more fuel-efficient vehicles and deploying advanced-safety technologies to being the workplace of choice for employees and the neighbor of choice for communities, we make strategic decisions based on how the outcome of those decisions ultimately translates into value for our customers." An example of this behavior is illustrated by GM's greening of the General Motors Baltimore Operations complex. The LEED Silver building exceeds the voluntary U.S. Environmental Protection Agency's ENERGY STAR® Challenge for Industry, which requires a 10% reduction in energy intensity within 5 years. "We believe reducing our environmental footprint is good for the climate and good for our business," said Greg Martin, executive director of Global Public Policy. "Wherever we can, we are reducing our energy use, powering our plants with renewable energy and conserving resources."

YOUR TURN! 20.2

The solution is on page 977.

Tilley Manufacturing Company produces one product, which sells for $100. Product costs at the normal level of manufacturing operations (100,000 units) are the following:

Direct materials.	$25 per unit
Direct labor	$20 per unit
Variable overhead	$10 per unit
Fixed overhead.	$495,000

During its first year of operations, Tilley produced 100,000 units and sold 90,000 units. Determine:
1. Gross profit using absorption costing.
2. Income from operations using variable costing.

Income Reconciliation

Once the relationship between variable costing and absorption costing is understood, it is possible to determine the differences between variable income and absorption income using a "short-cut" calculation without having to prepare separate financial statements. Remember that the only difference between variable income and absorption income is the treatment of the fixed costs of production—under absorption costing, some of these fixed production costs are included in inventory on the balance sheet, whereas they are all expensed under variable costing. So, if inventory increases by 500 units from one period to the next (as illustrated previously in **Exhibit 20-3b**), each unit in inventory will have $45.00 ($22,500/500 units) of fixed manufacturing costs. Because all fixed manufacturing costs have been expensed under the variable costing approach, absorption income should be $22,500 more than variable income, as shown:

LO3   **Explain** why net income differs between absorption costing and variable costing. **Reconcile** the two different income amounts.

$$\text{\$45.00 fixed manufacturing cost per unit} \times \text{500 units added to inventory} = \text{\$22,500 (or \$23,000 as rounded in the Excel exhibit)}$$

$$\underset{\text{(absorption income)}}{\$1,517,000} - \underset{\substack{\text{(fixed manufacturing cost} \\ \text{added to inventory)}}}{\$23,000} = \underset{\text{(variable income)}}{\$1,494,000}$$

The impact of differences between production and sales under both absorption and variable costing is summarized in **Exhibit 20-4**.

Exhibit 20-4	Impact of Varying Levels of Production		
	Income Statement	**Balance Sheet**	**Explanation**
Production = Sales	No difference in reported income	No change in inventory values	Current period fixed costs expensed under both absorption and variable costing methods
Production > Sales	Absorption net income is greater than variable net income	Absorption balance sheet inventory increases by more than variable balance sheet inventory	Some current period fixed costs are added to inventory under absorption costing method, but all are expensed under variable costing method
Production < Sales	Absorption net income is less than variable net income	Absorption balance sheet inventory decreases by more than variable balance sheet inventory	Some prior period fixed costs that are in the beginning inventory balance under absorption costing method are expensed in the current period as cost of goods sold, but only current period fixed costs are expensed under variable costing method

To highlight the effect of variable costing on inventories and income in the foregoing illustration, we consider only manufacturing costs. When detailed income statements are prepared under the variable costing method, fixed and variable costs of all types—including selling and administrative expenses—must be properly segregated. **Exhibit 20-5** presents an example of a complete and detailed income statement prepared in accordance with the variable costing concept. As illustrated in **Exhibit 20-5**, absorption net income changes with the level of production and variable net income changes with the level of sales. Because unit sales does not change over the three periods, reported variable net income does not change. The reason is that, as noted previously, fixed costs are not included in the inventory account on the balance sheet, but are expensed in the period that they are incurred under variable costing.

Contribution margin can be determined by deducting all variable expenses (cost of goods sold, selling, and administrative expenses) from sales. (This concept was previously introduced in Chapter 19.) All types of fixed expenses (manufacturing, selling, and administrative) are deducted to arrive at net income.

YOUR TURN! 20.3

The solution is on page 977.

Assume that Fezzari's reported absorption costing income was $1,600,000 in 2019. What would variable costing income be if Fezzari's inventory increased by 100 units during 2019 and fixed manufacturing cost was equal to $50 per unit?

Exhibit 20-5	Absorption vs. Variable Costing Income Statements				
	A	B	C	D	E	F

	A	B	C	D	E	F
1		**FEZZARI PERFORMANCE BICYCLES**				
2			**Period 1**	**Period 2**	**Period 3**	**Total**
3		Beginning Inventory (units)	—	—	500	—
4		Production (units)	4,500	5,000	4,000	13,500
5		Sales (units)	4,500	4,500	4,500	13,500
6		Ending Inventory (units)	—	500	—	—
7			**Absorption Costing Income Statement ($000s)**			
8			**Period 1**	**Period 2**	**Period 3**	**Total**
9	(1)	Sales	$ 4,500	$ 4,500	$ 4,500	$13,500
10	(2)	Beginning Inventory	—	—	332	—
11	(3)	Cost of Goods Manufactured	3,006	3,315	2,697	9,018
12	(4)	Less Ending Inventory	—	332	—	—
13	(5)	Cost of Goods Sold [(2) + (3) − (4)]	$(3,006)	$(2,983)	$(3,029)	$ (9,018)
14	(6)	Gross Profit on Sales [(1) + (5)]	$ 1,494	$ 1,517	$ 1,471	$ 4,482
15		Operating Expenses:				
16	(7)	Selling Expenses	(400)	(400)	(400)	(1,200)
17	(8)	Administrative Expenses	(340)	(340)	(340)	(1,020)
18	(9)	Income from Operations [(6) + (7) + (8)]	$ 754	$ 777	$ 731	$ 2,262
19			**Variable Costing Income Statement ($000s)**			
20			**Period 1**	**Period 2**	**Period 3**	**Total**
21	(1)	Sales	$ 4,500	$ 4,500	$ 4,500	$13,500
22	(2)	Beginning Inventory	—	—	309	—
23	(3)	Variable Cost of Goods Manufactured	2,781	3,090	2,472	8,343
24	(4)	Less Ending Inventory	—	309	—	—
25	(5)	Variable Cost of Goods Sold [(2) + (3) − (4)]	$(2,781)	$(2,781)	$(2,781)	$ (8,343)
26	(6)	Variable Selling Expenses	(300)	(300)	(300)	(900)
27	(7)	Variable Administrative Expenses	(50)	(50)	(50)	(150)
28	(8)	Contribution Margin [(1) + (5) + (6) + (7)]	$ 1,369	$ 1,369	$ 1,369	$ 4,107
29		Fixed Expenses:				
30	(9)	Fixed Manufacturing Costs	(225)	(225)	(225)	(675)
31	(10)	Fixed Selling Expenses	(100)	(100)	(100)	(300)
32	(11)	Fixed Administrative Expenses	(290)	(290)	(290)	(870)
33	(12)	Income from Operations [(8) + (9) + (10) + (11)]	$ 754	$ 754	$ 754	$ 2,262

All production costs, including fixed overhead, are included in cost of goods sold under absorption costing.

Only variable production costs are included in cost of goods sold under variable costing.

All variable costs (including selling and administrative) are subtracted to determine contribution margin under absorption costing.

Fixed overhead costs are treated as period costs and expensed in the period incurred under variable costing.

ADVANTAGES AND DISADVANTAGES OF VARIABLE COSTING

The following advantages and disadvantages of using variable costing result from the fact that under variable costing no fixed overhead costs are assigned to inventory carrying values.

LO4 **Describe** the advantages and disadvantages of the variable costing methods.

Advantages

1. Variable costing assigns only variable costs to inventory. Reporting inventory values in this manner helps managers avoid making "death spiral" decisions.

2. Under variable costing, because all fixed costs are reported separately, managers are able to see how much fixed cost must be covered before a profit will be generated.

3. Reported net income tends to follow sales volume, eliminating the incentive to temporarily boost income by producing more product than can be sold in the short term.

4. Cost-volume-profit (CVP) relationships are more easily discerned from variable costing income statements than from conventional absorption costing statements. The cost information needed for CVP analysis (which was discussed in **Chapter 19**) is readily available from variable cost financial statements.

5. Variable costing statements make it easier to determine the contribution of customers, products, product lines, business segments, and other business units to the overall profitability of the company. This is typically obscured by the allocation of fixed costs under absorption costing.

Hint: A "death spiral" decision is one in which management eliminates a product or division that has a positive contribution margin, but shows a loss when other non-controllable costs are allocated to it. By eliminating the product or division, the positive contribution margin is lost so that other products or divisions now have to cover all of the fixed costs. This may cause another product or division to appear unprofitable, leading to additional decisions to eliminate products or divisions that have positive contribution margins.

Disadvantages

1. Accounting measures derived under variable costing are not in conformity with generally accepted accounting principles, nor are they acceptable for reporting purposes under the Internal Revenue Code.

2. Inventories (and therefore working capital and owners' equity) tend to be understated.

3. Carrying inventories at only their variable costs may lead to long-run pricing decisions that provide for recovery of variable cost only rather than total cost, which will not produce net income in the long run.

4. Variable costing generally requires that a "second set" of accounting records be kept, increasing the cost of the required accounting systems and possible confusion among managers.

YOUR TURN! 20.4

The solution is on page 977.

Which of the following is a disadvantage of using the variable costing method to value inventory?

a. Managers are able to determine the amount of revenue needed to cover fixed costs.

b. Because net income follows production, incentives to increase profit by boosting production are eliminated.

c. Variable costing is not allowed under generally accepted accounting principles.

d. Cost-volume-profit relationships are more easily discerned.

SERVICES INDUSTRY IN FOCUS

SERVICE AND MERCHANDISING

Environmental Business Consultants (EBC) compensates all of its employees as salaried workers. Thus, EBC considers its labor cost as fixed—that is, EBC consultants are paid their full salary and benefits regardless of the number of consulting projects that they perform during a year. The only other fixed cost is the office lease expense. A partial trial balance for 2019 is provided below.

Description	Trial Balance		Variable or Fixed	Direct Service or SGA
	Debit	Credit		
Sales.		4,146,000		
Reimbursable costs	431,000		V	D
Executive salaries.	844,500		F	D
Clerical salaries	217,500		F	D
Consultant salaries.	1,050,000		F	D
Employee benefits	145,500		F	D
Payroll taxes.	123,000		F	D
Employee bonuses.	126,000		V	SGA
Marketing expenses	48,000		V	SGA
Employee continuing education expenses. . . .	27,000		V	SGA
Office lease expense	202,500		F	D
Office supplies expense	64,500		V	D
Other general administrative expense	355,500		V	SGA

Assume that EBC's beginning absorption Work-in-Process Inventory is $223,000 and its ending absorption Work-in-Process (WIP) Inventory is $247,000. Further, assume that EBC's beginning variable WIP inventory is $5,400 and its ending variable WIP inventory is $6,000.

Required

   a. Determine income from operations using

      1. Absorption costing.

      2. Variable costing.

   b. Compare the income from operations derived under the two methods.

Solution

   a. 1.

ENVIRONMENTAL BUSINESS CONSULTANTS, LLC		
Absorption Income Statement		
For the Year Ended December 31, 2019		
Gross sales.		$4,146,000
Less reimbursable costs.		(431,000)
Net sales.		$3,715,000
Direct labor.		$2,380,500
General overhead:		
Office lease expense	$202,500	
Office supplies expense	64,500	
Total general overhead.		267,000
Total service costs for the year.		$2,647,500
Add: beginning work-in-process inventory		223,000
Total cost of work-in-process during the year.		$2,870,500
Less: ending work-in-process inventory		(247,000)
Cost of services		2,623,500
Gross profit on sales.		$1,091,500
Operating expenses:		
Employee bonuses	$126,000	
Marketing expenses	48,000	
Employee continuing education expenses	27,000	
Other general administrative expenses	355,500	
Total operating expenses		556,500
Income from operations		$ 535,000

2.

ENVIRONMENTAL BUSINESS CONSULTANTS, LLC		
Variable Income Statement		
For the Year Ended December 31, 2019		
Gross sales.		$4,146,000
Less reimbursable costs.		$ (431,000)
Net sales.		$3,715,000
Beginning variable WIP		$ 5,400
Variable costs		
Office supplies expense		64,500
Less ending variable WIP.		(6,000)
Variable cost of service		$ 63,900
Other variable expenses		
Employee bonuses	$ 126,000	
Marketing expenses	48,000	
Employee continuing education expenses	27,000	
Other general administrative expenses	355,500	
Total other variable cost		556,500
Total variable costs.		$ 620,400
Contribution margin		$3,094,600
Fixed costs		
Direct labor	$2,380,500	
Office lease expense	202,500	
Total fixed costs		2,583,000
Income from operations		$ 511,600

b.

Absorption income from operations		$535,000
Less:		
Increase in fixed costs in WIP inventory:		
Ending (247,000 − 6,000)	241,000	
Beginning (223,000 − 5,400)	217,600	
		(23,400)
Variable income from operations		$511,600

COMPREHENSIVE PROBLEM

Tuttle Manufacturing Company produces only one product, which sells for $50. Product costs at the normal level of manufacturing operations (10,000 units) are the following:

Direct materials.	$14 per unit
Direct labor.	$12 per unit
Variable overhead	$ 4 per unit
Fixed overhead.	$49,500

Selling expenses (100% variable) are $3 per unit; administrative expenses (100% fixed) are $30,000. During the year, Tuttle produced 11,000 units and sold 9,000 units. Tuttle had no beginning inventory of product.

Required

a. Determine net income (ignoring income taxes) using
   1. Absorption costing.
   2. Variable costing.
b. Compare the total net income derived under the two methods.

Solution

a.

Absorption Costing		
Sales (9,000 units × $50).		$450,000
Cost of goods sold:		
Direct materials (11,000 × $14)	$154,000	
Direct labor (11,000 × $12)	132,000	
Variable overhead (11,000 × $4)	44,000	
Fixed overhead.	49,500	
	379,500	
Less: Ending inventory [($379,500/11,000) × 2,000] . . .	69,000	
Cost of goods sold		310,500
Gross profit.		$139,500
Selling expense (9,000 units × $3).	27,000	
Administrative expense.	30,000	57,000
Net income		$ 82,500

Variable Costing		
Sales (9,000 units × $50).		$450,000
Variable expenses:		
Direct materials (11,000 × $14)	$154,000	
Direct labor (11,000 × $12)	132,000	
Variable overhead (11,000 × $4)	44,000	
	330,000	
Less: Ending inventory [($330,000/11,000) × 2,000] . . .	60,000	
Variable cost of goods sold		270,000
Variable selling expense (9,000 × $3).		27,000
Contribution margin		153,000
Fixed expenses:		
Fixed overhead.	49,500	
Administrative expense.	30,000	79,500
Net income		$ 73,500

b.

Comparison	
Absorption costing net income	$82,500
Variable costing net income	73,500
Difference (explained below)	$ 9,000

The amount of fixed overhead contained in the absorption costing ending inventory is $9,000 [($49,500/11,000) × 2,000].

The amount of fixed overhead contained in the variable costing ending inventory is 0. The different treatment of fixed overhead fully explains the difference.

SUMMARY OF LEARNING OBJECTIVES

Describe the difference in the treatment of product costs between variable costing and absorption costing. (p. 956)

LO1

- Absorption costing capitalizes all manufacturing costs as inventory during the production period and recognizes them as expense (cost of goods sold) only when the related merchandise is sold.

- Variable costing does not assign fixed manufacturing overhead as a product cost but expenses it in the period incurred.
- Accounting measures derived under variable costing are not in accord with generally accepted accounting principles, nor are they acceptable for tax reporting.

LO2   **Prepare an income statement under both variable costing and absorption costing methods. (p. 958)**

- For absorption costing, include the fixed costs and variable costs of manufacturing in the computation of cost of goods sold.
- For variable costing, only include the variable costs of manufacturing in the computation of cost of goods sold. Expense all fixed costs, including fixed manufacturing costs, in the period.

LO3   **Explain why net income differs between absorption costing and variable costing. Reconcile the two different income amounts. (p. 961)**

- The difference between absorption income and variable income will be the amount of fixed manufacturing costs either added to or subtracted from work-in-process inventory during the period.
- When production volume exceeds sales volume, absorption income will be greater than variable income.
- When production volume is less than sales volume, absorption income will be less than variable income.

LO4   **Describe the advantages and disadvantages of the variable costing methods. (p. 963)**

- The primary advantage of variable costing is that reported income follows changes in production volume, reducing the risk of "death spiral" decisions.
- Variable costing provides all of the information required for CVP analysis.
- The primary disadvantage of variable costing is that it is not acceptable for financial statement reporting or tax reporting.
- Because variable costing requires the maintenance of a "second set" of books, it is more costly.

SUMMARY	Concept ➡	Method ➡	Assessment
TAKEAWAY 20.1	How should a firm report its inventory in accordance with generally accepted accounting principles?	Firms are required to use the absorption costing method, which requires that all production costs, including fixed overhead costs, be included in the inventory valuation reported on the balance sheet.	• Absorption costing for external reporting purposes. • Variable costing for internal decision making.
TAKEAWAY 20.2	How do cost of goods sold and inventory values differ between absorption and variable costing income statements?	• Absorption costing: Includes all production costs (direct materials, direct labor, variable and fixed manufacturing overhead) • Variable costing: Includes only variable production costs (direct materials, direct labor, variable manufacturing overhead)	Under variable costing, both cost of goods sold and inventory valuation will be less than under absorption costing.

KEY TERMS

Absorption costing (p. 956)   Variable costing (p. 956)

Contribution margin (p. 962)

Assignments with the ⊕ logo in the margin are available in my BusinessCourse.
See the Preface of the book for details.

SELF-STUDY QUESTIONS

(Answers to Self-Study Questions are at the end of this chapter.)

1. **In determining inventory costs, which of the following cost elements is included when using absorption costing but excluded when using variable costing?**
   LO1
   - *a.* Selling costs
   - *b.* Direct labor cost
   - *c.* Non-factory administrative costs
   - *d.* Fixed overhead

2. **Under which costing method are fixed overhead production costs excluded from cost of goods sold and inventory?**
   LO2
   - *a.* Full costing
   - *b.* Absorption costing
   - *c.* Variable costing
   - *d.* Normal costing

3. **If unit production exceeds unit sales during the period, absorption income will be**
   LO2, 3
   - *a.* less than variable income.
   - *b.* more than variable income.
   - *c.* equal to variable income.

4. **If unit production is less than unit sales during the period, absorption income will be**
   LO3
   - *a.* less than variable income.
   - *b.* more than variable income.
   - *c.* equal to variable income.

5. **If unit production is equal to unit sales during the period, absorption income will be**
   LO3
   - *a.* less than variable income.
   - *b.* more than variable income.
   - *c.* equal to variable income.

6. **True or false: Variable costing may be used by management in preparing audited financial statements.**
   LO1, 4
   - *a.* True
   - *b.* False

QUESTIONS

1. Which method, absorption or variable costing, is used for external reporting purposes in accordance with generally accepted accounting principles?
   LO1

2. Which method, absorption or variable costing, is used for internal management reporting purposes?
   LO1

3. When inventories are increasing, will absorption income be higher or lower than variable income?
   LO3

4. What generalizations can be made about the difference in income reported under variable and absorption costing?
   LO3

5. What is variable costing? List its advantages and disadvantages.
   LO4

SHORT EXERCISES

SE20-1. If a manufacturing company uses variable costing to cost inventories, which of the following costs are considered inventoriable costs?
   LO1

   - *a.* Only raw materials, direct labor, and variable manufacturing overhead costs
   - *b.* Only raw materials, direct labor, and variable and fixed manufacturing overhead costs
   - *c.* Only raw materials, direct labor, variable manufacturing overhead, and variable selling and administrative costs
   - *d.* Only raw materials and direct labor costs

LO1 **SE20-2.** Which one of the following is true with respect to variable and absorption costing systems?

a. Variable costing systems include fixed manufacturing overhead as period costs.
b. Absorption costing systems include fixed manufacturing overhead as period costs.
c. Variable costing systems include variable manufacturing overhead as period costs.
d. Absorption costing systems include variable manufacturing overhead as period costs.

LO2 **SE20-3.** Operating income under variable costing is contribution margin minus

a. cost of goods sold and administrative expenses.
b. fixed manufacturing overhead and fixed selling and administrative expenses.
c. fixed manufacturing overhead and variable manufacturing overhead.
d. variable selling and administrative expenses and fixed selling and administrative expenses.

LO2 **SE20-4.** The following data relate to Smurf Corporation for the year just ended:

Sales revenue.	$550,000
Cost of goods sold:	
Variable portion	170,000
Fixed portion.	110,000
Variable selling and administrative cost	50,000
Fixed selling and administrative cost	125,000

Which of the following statements is correct?

a. Smurf's variable costing income statement would reveal a gross margin of $270,000.
b. Smurf's variable costing income statement would reveal a contribution margin of $330,000.
c. Smurf's absorption costing income statement would reveal a contribution margin of $220,000.
d. Smurf's absorption costing income statement would reveal a gross margin of $330,000.

LO3 **SE20-5.** When comparing absorption costing with variable costing, the difference in operating income can be explained by the difference between the

a. units sold and the units produced, multiplied by the unit sales price.
b. ending inventory in units and the beginning inventory in units, multiplied by the budgeted fixed manufacturing cost per unit.
c. ending inventory in units and the beginning inventory in units, multiplied by the unit sales price.
d. units sold and the units produced, multiplied by the budgeted variable manufacturing cost per unit.

LO3 **SE20-6.** Mill Corporation had the following unit costs for the recently concluded calendar year:

	Variable	Fixed
Manufacturing.	$8.00	$3.00
Non-manufacturing.	$2.00	$5.50

Inventory for Mill's sole product totaled 6,000 units on January 1 and 5,200 units on December 31. When compared to variable costing income, Mill's absorption costing income is

a. $2,400 lower.   c. $6,800 lower.
b. $2,400 higher.   d. $6,800 higher.

LO3 **SE20-7.** During the month of May, Robinson Corporation sold 1,000 units. The cost per unit for May was as follows:

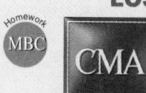

	Cost Per Unit
Direct materials.	$ 5.50
Direct labor.	3.00
Variable manufacturing overhead.	1.00
Fixed manufacturing overhead.	1.50
Variable administrative costs	.50
Fixed administrative costs	3.50
Total	$15.00

May's income using absorption costing was $9,500. The income for May, if variable costing had been used, would have been $9,125. The number of units Robinson produced during May was

a. 750 units.
b. 925 units.

c. 1,075 units.
d. 1,250 units.

SE20-8. Jorgensen Company has 10,000 units in its ending inventory. During the year, the company's variable production costs were $10 per unit and its fixed manufacturing overhead application rate was $5 per unit. The company's net income for the year was $15,000 lower under absorption costing than it was under variable costing. Given these facts, what was the number of units in the beginning inventory? (Assume the company uses normal costing and closes over- and under-applied overhead directly to COGS, and that the fixed manufacturing overhead application rate is constant from year to year.)

a. 7,000 units
b. 8,500 units

c. 11,500 units
d. 13,000 units

SE20-9. Drake Company has the following information:

LO3

Variable production costs	$10 per unit
Fixed OH production costs	$100,000 per year
Variable selling & admin.	$5 per unit
Fixed selling & admin.	$80,000 per year
Normal annual production	20,000 units
Budgeted annual production	19,000 units
Actual annual production	15,000 units
Actual annual sales	19,000 units
Beginning inventory	5,000 units

The company uses the FIFO inventory method. Over- and under-applied overhead is closed directly to cost of goods sold.

If income under absorption costing for the year is $100,000, what was the net income under the variable costing method assuming that overhead was applied to production using a rate based on normal production?

a. $80,000
b. $100,000

c. $120,000
d. $125,000

SE20-10. Which one of the following is the **best** reason for using variable costing?

LO4

a. Fixed factory overhead is more closely related to the capacity to produce than to the production of specific units.
b. All costs are variable in the long term.
c. Variable costing is acceptable for income tax reporting purposes.
d. Variable costing usually results in higher operating income than if a company uses absorption costing.

EXERCISES—SET A

E20-1A. Variable and Absorption Costing Chandler Company sells its product for $100 per unit. Variable manufacturing costs per unit are $40, and fixed manufacturing costs at the normal operating level of 10,000 units are $240,000. Variable selling expenses are $16 per unit sold. Fixed administrative expenses total $104,000. Chandler had no beginning inventory in 2019. During 2019, the company produced 10,000 units and sold 8,000. Would net income for Chandler Company in 2019 be higher if calculated using variable costing or using absorption costing? Calculate reported income using each method.

LO2

E20-2A. Variable and Absorption Costing—Service Company Lawn RX, Inc. prepares a variable costing income statement for internal management and an absorption costing income statement for its bank. Lawn RX provides a quarterly lawn care service that is sold for $140. The variable and fixed cost data are as follows:

LO2, 3

Direct labor.	$ 80.00
Overhead:	
Variable cost per unit	$ 5.00
Fixed cost	$100,000
Marketing, general, and administrative:	
Variable cost (per contract completed).	$ 6.00
Administrative expense (fixed) (per month)	$ 42,000

During 2019, 10,000 service contracts were signed and 9,800 service contracts were completed. Lawn RX had no service contracts at the beginning of the year.

Required
a. Calculate reported income for management.
b. Calculate reported income for the bank.
c. Reconcile the two income amounts.

LO3 **E20-3A. Variable and Absorption Costing** During its first year, Walnut, Inc., showed a $14 per-unit profit under absorption costing but would have reported a total profit $16,000 less under variable costing. If production exceeded sales by 1,000 units and an average contribution margin of 62.5% was maintained, what is the apparent:

a. Fixed cost per unit?
b. Sales price per unit?
c. Variable cost per unit?
d. Unit sales volume if total profit under absorption costing was $168,000?

LO3 **E20-4A. Variable and Absorption Costing** Pyne Company produces a single product. The company has 50,000 units in its ending inventory. Pyne's variable production costs during the year were $10 per unit and fixed manufacturing overhead costs were applied at $25 per unit (which was the same as last year). The company's net operating income is $120,000 higher under variable costing than it is under absorption costing; and the company uses FIFO and closes any over- or under-applied overhead directly to cost of goods sold. Given these facts, what was the number of units of product in beginning inventory?

EXERCISES—SET B

LO2 **E20-1B. Variable and Absorption Costing** Grant Company sells its product for $50 per unit. Variable manufacturing costs per unit are $30, and fixed manufacturing costs at the normal operating level of 15,000 units are $90,000. Variable selling expenses are $4 per unit sold. Fixed administrative expenses total $155,000. Grant had 7,000 units at a per-unit cost of $35 in beginning inventory in 2019. During 2019, the company produced 15,000 units and sold 20,000. Would net income for Grant Company in 2019 be higher if calculated using variable costing or using absorption costing? Calculate reported income using each method.

LO2, 3 **E20-2B. Variable and Absorption Costing—Service Company** Tech Helpers Company prepares a variable costing income statement for internal management and an absorption costing income statement for its bank. Tech Helpers provides a personal computer maintenance service that is sold for $100. The variable and fixed cost data are as follows:

Direct labor.	$ 25.00
Overhead:	
Variable cost per unit	$ 5.00
Fixed cost	$240,000
Marketing, general, and administrative:	
Variable cost (per service contract completed).	$ 5.00
Fixed cost (per month)	$ 20,000

During 2019, 4,500 service contracts were started and 5,000 service contracts were completed. At the beginning of 2019, Tech Helpers had 500 service contracts in process at a per-unit cost of $90 in beginning work-in-process inventory.

Required

   a. Calculate reported income for management.

   b. Calculate reported income for the bank.

   c. Reconcile the two income amounts.

E20-3B. **Variable and Absorption Costing** During its first year, Concord, Inc., showed a $20 per-unit profit under absorption costing but would have reported a total profit $16,800 less under variable costing. If production exceeded sales by 600 units and an average contribution margin of 60% was maintained, what is the apparent:

   a. Fixed cost per unit?

   b. Sales price per unit?

   c. Variable cost per unit?

   d. Unit sales volume if total profit under absorption costing was $189,000?

E20-4B. **Variable and Absorption Costing** Beech Company produces a single product. The company has 50,000 units in its beginning inventory. Beech's variable production costs during the year were $10 per unit and fixed manufacturing overhead costs were applied at $30 per unit (which was the same as last year). The company's net operating income is $120,000 lower under variable costing than it is under absorption costing; and the company uses FIFO and closes any over- or under-applied overhead directly to cost of goods sold. Given these facts, what was the number of units of product in beginning inventory?

PROBLEMS—SET A

P20-1A. **Variable and Absorption Costing** Summarized data for 2019 (the first year of operations) for Gorman Products, Inc., are as follows:

Sales (70,000 units)	$2,800,000
Production costs (80,000 units):	
Direct materials.	880,000
Direct labor	720,000
Manufacturing overhead:	
Variable.	544,000
Fixed.	320,000
Operating expenses:	
Variable.	175,000
Fixed.	240,000
Depreciation on equipment.	60,000
Real estate taxes	18,000
Personal property taxes (on inventory and equipment)	28,800
Personnel department expenses	30,000

Required

   a. Prepare an income statement based on full absorption costing.

   b. Prepare an income statement based on variable costing.

   c. Assume that you must decide quickly whether to accept a special one-time order for 1,000 units for $25 per unit. Which income statement presents the most relevant data? Determine the apparent profit or loss on the special order based solely on these data.

   d. If the ending inventory is destroyed by fire, which costing approach would you use as a basis for filing an insurance claim for the fire loss? Why?

LO2   P20-2A.   Variable and Absorption Costing—Service Company Jensen's Tailoring provides custom tailoring services. After the company's first year of operations, its owner prepared the following summarized data report for 2019:

Sales (500 completed jobs)	$100,000
Tailoring costs (550 jobs):	
Direct labor	47,000
Manufacturing overhead:	
Variable	12,000
Fixed	9,000
Operating expenses:	
Variable	5,600
Fixed	5,800

Required

a. Prepare an income statement based on full absorption costing. (Round ending inventory to the nearest $.)

b. Prepare an income statement based on variable costing. (Round ending inventory to the nearest $.)

c. Assume that you must decide quickly whether to accept a special one-time order to alter 50 band costumes for $125 per costume. Which income statement presents the most relevant data? Determine the apparent profit or loss on the special order based solely on these data.

LO2, 3   P20-3A.   Variable and Absorption Costing Scott Manufacturing makes only one product with total unit manufacturing costs of $54, of which $40 is variable. No units were on hand at the beginning of 2019. During 2019 and 2020, the only product manufactured was sold for $65 per unit, and the cost structure did not change. Scott uses the first-in, first-out inventory method and has the following production and sales for 2019 and 2020:

	Units Manufactured	Units Sold
2019	110,000	90,000
2020	110,000	120,000

Required

a. Prepare gross profit computations for 2019 and 2020 using absorption costing.

b. Prepare gross profit computations for 2019 and 2020 using variable costing.

c. Explain how your answers illustrate the impact of differences between production and sales volumes on the gross profits reported each year under absorption and variable costing.

LO3   P20-4A.   Variable and Absorption Costing The following information shows the expected client invoice work-in-process levels for the staff group at Smith & Smith, LLP, a local CPA firm. Fixed overhead is applied based on labor hours.

Units in WIP	Percent Complete	Fixed Overhead Rate
Beginning Inventory: 10 units	40%	$200 per unit
Ending Inventory: 20 units	30%	

How is absorption costing income expected to compare to variable costing income?

PROBLEMS—SET B

P20-1B. Variable and Absorption Costing Summarized data for 2019 (the first year of operations) for   **LO2**
Trenton Products, Inc., are as follows:

Sales (100,000 units)	$8,000,000
Production costs (105,000 units):	
Direct materials.	2,100,000
Direct labor	1,680,000
Manufacturing overhead:	
Variable.	1,260,000
Fixed.	1,050,000
Operating expenses:	
Variable.	560,000
Fixed.	640,000

Required

a.   Prepare an income statement based on full absorption costing.

b.   Prepare an income statement based on variable costing.

c.   Assume that you must decide quickly whether to accept a special one-time order for 1,000 units
for $56 per unit. Which income statement presents the most relevant data? Determine the appar-
ent profit or loss on the special order based solely on these data.

d.   If the ending inventory is destroyed by fire, which costing approach would you use as a basis
for filing an insurance claim for the fire loss? Why?

P20-2B. Variable and Absorption Costing—Service Company Rocky's Automotive specializes in per-   **LO2**
forming automobile safety checks. After the company's first year of operations, its accountant pre-   **SERVICE AND**
pared the following summarized data report for the safety checks for 2019:   **MERCHANDISING**

Sales (7,000 safety checks)	$700,000
Production costs (7,010 safety checks):	
Direct labor	490,700
Shop overhead:	
Variable.	112,160
Fixed.	70,100
Operating expenses:	
Variable.	21,030
Fixed.	16,000

Required

a.   Prepare an income statement based on full absorption costing.

b.   Prepare an income statement based on variable costing.

c.   Assume that you must decide quickly whether to accept a special one-time order for 20 safety
checks on local police cars for $85 per safety check. Determine the apparent profit or loss on
the special order based solely on these data.

P20-3B. Variable and Absorption Costing Frances Manufacturing makes a product with total unit manu-   **LO2, 3**
facturing cost of $64, of which $36 is variable. No units were on hand at the beginning of 2019. During 2019 and 2020, the only product manufactured was sold for $96 per unit, and the cost structure
did not change. Frances uses the first-in, first-out inventory method and has the following production and sales for 2019 and 2020:

	Units Manufactured	Units Sold
2019	90,000	70,000
2020	90,000	100,000

Required

a.   Prepare gross profit computations for 2019 and 2020 using absorption costing.

    b. Prepare gross profit computations for 2019 and 2020 using variable costing.

    c. Explain how your answers illustrate the impact of differences between production and sales volumes on the gross profits reported each year under absorption and variable costing.

LO3 **P20-4B.** **Variable and Absorption Costing** The following information shows the expected client invoice work-in-process levels for the staff group at Tayler & Swain, LLP, a local CPA firm. Fixed overhead is applied based on labor hours.

Units in WIP	Percent Complete	Fixed Overhead Rate
Beginning Inventory: 30 units.	20%	$150 per unit
Ending Inventory: 10 units.	60%	

How is absorption costing income expected to compare to variable costing income?

EXTENDING YOUR KNOWLEDGE

EYK20-1. **Business Decision Case** Ben and Chris have been lifelong friends. They are engineer-minded and have always dreamed of starting a manufacturing company. They want to manufacture tires, but realize that this industry is heavily regulated and that achieving profitable operations will require skillful management. Despite the odds, they form Smooth Ride, Inc., and resolve to only stay in business if they report a positive net income after the company's first year of operations. At the end of 2019, its first year of operations, Smooth Ride reported the following summarized data:

Sales (105,000 tires)	$13,125,000
Production costs (120,000 tires):	
Direct materials.	4,750,000
Direct labor	3,675,000
Manufacturing overhead:	
Variable.	2,300,000
Fixed.	950,000
Operating expenses:	
Variable.	1,050,000
Fixed.	800,000
Depreciation on machinery.	455,000
Property taxes	330,000
Personnel department expenses	140,000

Required

    a. Prepare income statements based on full absorption costing and based on variable costing. Based on the reported incomes using these methods, did Smooth Ride exceed the expectations of Ben and Chris?

    b. Smooth Ride follows generally accepted accounting standards. Which method, full absorption or variable costing, will the company use to report its net income?

ANSWERS TO SELF-STUDY QUESTIONS:

1. d, (p. 957)   2. c, (p. 959)   3. b, (p. 962)   4. a, (p. 962)   5. c, (p. 962)   6. b, (pp. 958, 964)

YOUR TURN! SOLUTIONS

Solution 20.1
d.

Solution 20.2

	Absorption Costing	Variable Costing
Sales.	$9,000,000	$9,000,000
Cost of goods sold		
Cost of goods manufactured		
100,000 units × ($25 + $20 + $10 + $495,000/100,000). . . .	5,995,000	
100,000 units × ($25 + $20 + $10).		5,500,000
Less ending inventory		
10,000 units × ($25 + $20 + $10 + $495,000/100,000).	599,500	
10,000 units × ($25 + $20 + $10).		550,000
Cost of goods sold	$5,395,500	$4,950,000
Gross profit.	$3,604,500	
Contribution margin		$4,050,000
Less fixed overhead costs		495,000
Income from operations		$3,555,000

Solution 20.3
$1,600,000 − (100 × $50) = $1,595,000

Solution 20.4
c.

Chapter 21

Relevant Costs and Short-Term Decision Making

PAST

Chapter 20 discussed the preparation of a variable income statement.

PRESENT

Chapter 21 describes some of the tools and techniques that management can use in making short-term business decisions.

FUTURE

Chapter 22 discusses the budgeting process, the components of the master budget, and the interrelationships of the individual budgets, and presents an illustration of a budget for a manufacturer and a service company.

What did you have for dinner last night? If it included fresh produce, grains, dairy, or meat from U.S. farms, there is a 60% chance that it was planted, fertilized, irrigated, harvested, or fed with a **John Deere** product. John Deere didn't start out with the intent of becoming the world's largest manufacturer of agriculture and construction equipment. In 1837, John Deere, a blacksmith in Illinois, was simply looking for a way to help the local farmers plow their fields without frequently stopping to clean sticky prairie soil off their wooden or cast-iron plows. Today, the company he founded has become the world's largest producer and seller of farm and industrial tractors and equipment.

Along the way, the company's management faced many challenges and questions, including

- Whether to introduce new products and product lines;
- Whether to produce or purchase new technology (e.g., steam tractors);
- Whether to drop products and product lines (e.g., bicycles and snowmobiles); and,
- How to deal with restricted production capacity during World War II.

In this chapter, we examine some of the decision tools and techniques that managers may use in answering these strategic questions.

Road Map

LO	Learning Objective	Page	eLecture	Guided Example	Assignments
LO1	Describe management's use of accounting information in the decision-making process. Define relevant costs and describe the use of differential analysis.	980	E21-1	YT21.1	SS1, Q1, Q2, Q3, Q4, Q5, Q6, SE1, E1A, E2A, E3A, E1B, E2B, E3B, PA1, P1B
LO2	Demonstrate when to accept a special order.	985	E21-2	YT21.2	SS2, Q7, SE2, SE3, E4A, E5A, E6A, E4B, E5B, E6B, P2A, P2B
LO3	Demonstrate when to make or buy needed parts.	987	E21-3	YT21.3	SS3, Q7, SE4, SE5, SE6, E7A, E8A, E9A, E7B, E8B, E9B, P3A, P3B
LO4	Demonstrate when to drop an unprofitable product or segment.	989	E21-4	YT21.4	SS4, Q7, SE7, E10A, E10B, P4A, P4B
LO5	Demonstrate when to sell a product or process it further.	990	E21-5	YT21.5	SS5, Q7, Q8, SE8, E11A, E12A, E11B, P5A
LO6	Demonstrate how to determine which product to produce when a resource is constrained.	994	E21-6	YT21.6	SS6, Q7, Q9, SE9, SE10, E13A, E12B, P6A, P5B

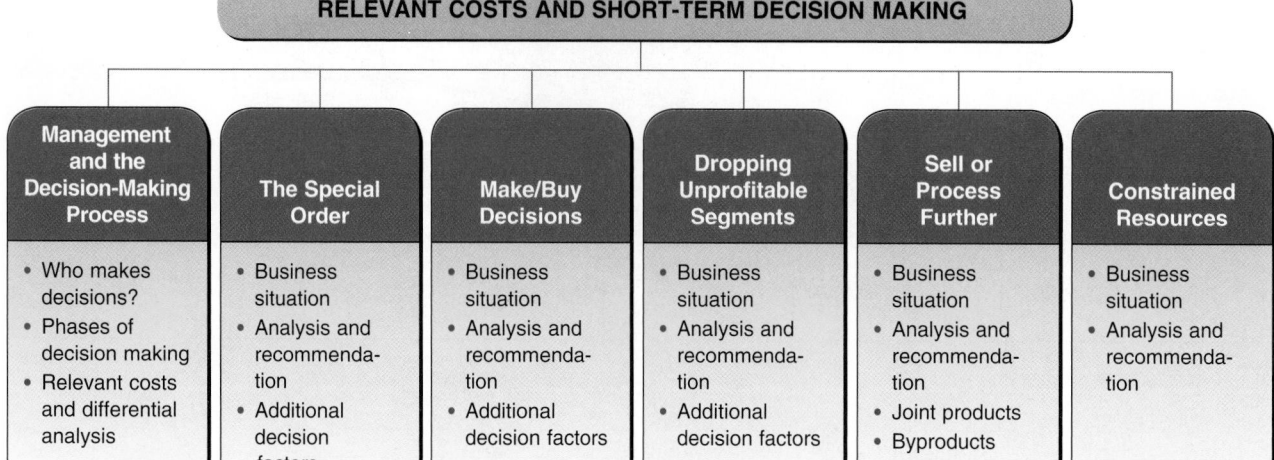

The traditional measurement is not the right measurement; if it were, there would be no need for decisions.

PETER DRUCKER

A well-developed accounting system is a continuing source of operational information for management. The quality of information available to management will influence the success of the operating decisions based on that information. In this chapter, we consider the management decision-making process and some cost concepts that are used in managerial analyses.

There are many definitions of **management**. In the broad sense, anyone who directs the activities of others is a manager. For a manufacturing firm like John Deere, this includes shop supervisors, department heads, plant supervisors, division managers, and the company president. A large, complex firm may have many management levels.

MANAGEMENT AND THE DECISION-MAKING PROCESS

Who Makes Decisions?

LO1 **Describe** management's use of accounting information in the decision-making process. **Define** relevant costs and **describe** the use of differential analysis.

As **Exhibit 21-1** illustrates, upper-level management is responsible for establishing long-range goals and policies, including major financing, expansion into new markets (foreign and domestic), and acquisitions of or mergers with other firms. Middle-level management may deal with the strategies and tactics related to the automation of a department, the establishment of new product lines, and the direction of the marketing plan. Such matters as daily production quotas, compliance with planned costs, and other detailed operating concerns are the responsibility of lower-level management. To varying degrees, therefore, all levels of management are involved in decision making.

Exhibit 21-1   Management Responsibilities

Upper Management → **Long-Term Goals** (vision, major financing, expansion, acquisitions/mergers, return on investment)

Middle Management → **Intermediate Goals** (product development, market plans, product profitability)

Lower Management → **Short-Term Goals** (production targets, cost management, quality control)

Decision making requires that a choice be made among alternatives. The business decision process is analogous to the play of a well-organized football team. Virtually all elements of decision making are present in football: the establishment of the objectives and goals that lead to winning; the development of organization, strategy, and tactics in a competitive environment; the creation of plays with the hope of achieving particular results; the period of execution; and, finally, the informal evaluation of performance on the field followed by a formal evaluation when game films are analyzed.

CORPORATE SOCIAL RESPONSIBILITY

This chapter discusses the concept of decision making. One of the decisions a company like John Deere must make is how many resources it should invest in items benefiting non-shareholder stakeholders, and whether these investments will benefit shareholders in the long run. John Deere has been making these types of decisions for well over a century. Some of the early decisions, noted on its web site, include

- 1901—Deere implements voluntary workers' compensation program. This is 10 years before the first U.S. workers' compensation statutes.
- 1920—Deere designs and builds its own cloth-screen filtering system to clean exhaust from plow-grinding operations.
- 1936—First foundry equipped with air-pollution-controlled molding equipment.
- 1938—Product safety committee formed; warning decals placed on corn pickers; shielding for power take-offs introduced.
- 1940—Power take-off shields installed on tractors and made available in retrofit programs for tractors produced after 1932.
- 1947—Corporate industrial safety department established.
- 1949—First boiler equipped with a device to control fly-ash emission at Waterloo Tractor Works. Planter Works, Moline, Illinois, installs a wetcap to control cupola emissions.

These investments in its employees' welfare and in the environment appear to have been wise ones, as John Deere is still around more than a hundred years later, delivering billions of dollars of annual net income to its shareholders.

Phases of Decision Making

Decision making may be divided roughly into a planning phase, an execution phase, and an evaluation phase incorporating some form of remedial feedback. **Exhibit 21-2** illustrates the sequential nature of the elements of most decision processes.

| Exhibit 21-2 | Decision-Making Phases |

The **planning phase** begins with *goal identification,* the specification of objectives to be sought or accomplished. One of the most common business goals is the long-run optimization of net income, often expressed in terms of return on assets. Other goals include target growth rates in sales revenue or total assets, target market shares in various markets, or leadership in product research, innovation, and quality.

The next steps in planning are identifying feasible alternative courses of action for achieving desired goals and estimating their qualitative and quantitative effects on the specified goals. Because planning involves the future, data related to the alternative courses of action must be estimated and projected in an environment of uncertainty.

The **execution phase** begins with the actual moment of decision: management commits to a specific plan of action. Because of the complexity of modern business, some elaborate plans may need lead times of several years. Poor planning, or the absence of planning, may lead to operating crises that carry significant penalties for the firm in terms of extra costs, lost opportunities, and—in extreme cases—bankruptcy.

Once a decision has been made, the plan is implemented, which usually involves the acquisition and commitment of materials, labor, and long-lived assets such as machinery and buildings. Management is kept informed through periodic accounting reports on the acquisition and use of these facilities during the execution phase.

In the **evaluation phase**, steps are taken to control the outcome of a specific plan of action. Virtually every important aspect of business—costs, product quality, inventory levels, and sales revenue—must be reasonably well controlled if a firm is to operate successfully. Measuring performance is an essential element of control. Performance measurement must compare actual operations with planned operations to allow management to take remedial action when significant unfavorable variations exist. Managerial accounting data and reports play a key role in informing management about performance in various areas during the evaluation phase of decision making.

Decision processes do not, however, fall into three neatly divided phases. Changes in competition, technology, and customer demand must be considered. Furthermore, most management teams are engaged in all three decision-making phases at any given time. They may be planning decisions in one area, executing them in a second, and evaluating them in a third.

What is the role of management accountants in decision making?	• Planning phase—estimating and projecting data for alternative courses of action • Execution phase—measuring the acquisition and use of resources during execution of selected plan • Evaluation phase—measuring and comparing planned and actual performance	• During planning, some courses of action may not be pursued because they do not meet management's criteria. • During execution, measurement may lead to mid-course corrections to the plan. • Unfavorable variances between planned and actual results may lead to remedial action.

RELEVANT COSTS AND DIFFERENTIAL ANALYSIS

Decision making involves choosing among different alternatives. In business, managers make decisions by evaluating the costs and benefits associated with each alternative. However, not all costs and benefits should be considered. Sound decision making is based on the widely accepted decision rule that only the aspects of a choice that differ among alternatives are relevant to a decision.

For example, imagine that you want to see an action movie in the theater. There are two theaters in your local community that are showing the movie. As a college student on a limited budget, you are careful with your money and want to choose the least-cost alternative, so you assemble the following information:

Cost/benefit	Theater #1	Theater #2
Ticket price.	$ 9.25	$ 9.25
Parking.	$ 3.00	$ 4.00
Popcorn and drink	$10.00	$10.00
Concessions coupon	N/A	50% off
Gas for car	$0.10/mile	$0.10/mile
Car insurance (based on 10,000 miles per year)	$0.06/mile	$0.06/mile
Depreciation on car (based on 10,000 miles per year). . .	$0.30/mile	$0.30/mile
Distance to theater.	5 miles	10 miles

When you are deciding which theater to attend, the admission price is irrelevant if both theaters charge the same price. However, if the cost to park is $4 at one and $3 at the other, then the $1 differential parking cost is relevant to the choice. Likewise, if the popcorn and drink are $10 at both theaters, but you have a coupon for half off at one theater, the $5 savings is also relevant to the choice. If you plan to drive to the theater, the cost of the gas that would be consumed would be relevant if the theaters are different distances away, but the cost that you paid for your car (reflected in the annual depreciation cost) would not be because it was incurred in the past and is considered a **sunk cost**. Finally, the cost of insurance will be incurred regardless of which theater you choose, so it is not relevant to the decision. The decision process is simplified by concentrating only on the factors that are different between the alternatives the manager is evaluating. Thus, **relevant costs** in making a decision are defined as those that differ between alternatives.

In choosing between alternatives, managers must exercise care to avoid including irrelevant data that could lead to a poor decision. In the theater example, two categories of irrelevant costs were identified: costs that do not differ among the alternatives and sunk costs. Sunk costs are costs that have been incurred in the past and cannot be avoided regardless of the decision made.

Finally, managers should consider **opportunity costs**. Opportunity cost is the future benefit that is given up when a choice is made. In our theater example, assume that a third alternative is to stay home and study for an upcoming exam. A potential opportunity cost of choosing to go to the theater is the higher score that might result from the additional three hours of study.

ACCOUNTING IN PRACTICE

Quantitative vs. Qualitative Factors in Decision Making

Differential analysis considers revenues and expenses that differ among alternatives. However, it does not include qualitative factors, such as impact on labor force or customer base. Thus, the results of differential analysis are only one input into the decision-making process—successful managers must also consider qualitative factors.

Suppose that by 1860 John Deere had determined that he could use his blacksmith shop to produce and sell either plows or hayforks. His decision would have been in favor of the product promising the higher net income based on the estimated operating data shown in **Exhibit 21-3**.

Exhibit 21-3	John Deere Estimated Operating Data		
	A	B	C
1		Alternatives	
		Plows	Hayforks
2	Units that can be produced and sold	14,000	20,000
3	Unit selling price	$ 12.00	$ 7.00
4	Manufacturing costs:		
5	Variable (per unit)	$ 4.00	$ 2.00
6	Fixed (total)	$44,400	
7	Selling and administrative expenses:		
8	Variable (per unit)	$ 1.00	$ 1.00
9	Fixed (total)	$ 3,000	

These amounts would be based on the productive capacity of the blacksmith shop.

These prices would be based on the market for similar items.

The manufacturing and selling costs would typically be projected based on John Deere's experience.

We may compare the alternatives by preparing comparative income statements, as shown in **Exhibit 21-4**, from these data.

Exhibit 21-4	Product Choice Differential Analysis			
1		Alternatives		
		Plows	Hayforks	Difference
2	Revenue	$168,000	$140,000	$28,000
3	Cost of goods sold (manufacturing costs):			
4	Variable	56,000	40,000	16,000
5	Fixed (total)	44,400	44,400	—
6	Selling and administrative expenses:			
7	Variable	14,000	20,000	(6,000)
8	Fixed (total)	3,000	3,000	—
9	Total expenses	$117,400	$107,400	$10,000
10	Net income	$ 50,600	$ 32,600	$18,000

Plows: (14,000 units @ $12 each) Hayforks: (20,000 units @ $7 each)

Plows: (14,000 units @ $4 each) Hayforks: (20,000 units @ $2 each)

Plows: (14,000 units @ $1 each) Hayforks: (20,000 units @ $1 each)

This analysis shows an $18,000 increase in net income associated with plows as a result of a $28,000 increase in total revenue that is partially offset by a $10,000 net increase in cost of goods sold and variable selling and administrative expenses.

   A simple differential analysis of the same situation is as follows, where consideration is limited to the revenue and expense factors that differ if plows are produced rather than hayforks:

Differential analysis if plows are produced rather than hayforks		
Revenue forgone on 6,000 hayforks	[$7 × 6,000 units]	$(42,000)
Additional revenue from increased sales		
price over hayforks	[($12 − $7) × 14,000 units]	70,000
Net additional revenue		$ 28,000
Differential costs:		
Additional cost of goods sold	[($4 − $2) × 14,000 units]	$(28,000)
Savings on last 6,000 hayforks	[$2 × 6,000 units]	12,000
Savings on variable selling and		
administrative expenses	[$1 × 6,000 units]	6,000
Net differential income in favor of plows		$ 18,000

> If plows are sold, 6,000 fewer hayforks will be produced and sold.

> If plows are sold, each unit sold will generate $12, or $5 more than hayforks.

> Each plow costs $2 more to produce than a hayfork.

> The variable production and selling costs will not be incurred on 6,000 hayforks.

   Note that the cost of John Deere's blacksmith shop would be considered a sunk cost, and not relevant to the choice between producing plows or hayforks.

   Clearly, the differential approach indicates the same net advantage for plows as the income statements but it does so more concisely. In reality, a company's income statement is much more complex than that presented in **Exhibit 21-4**. In addition, analyzing the incremental differences among alternatives allows management to focus on the critical elements of the decision and is less prone to making errors than creating a complete set of income statements. Therefore, management uses the more efficient differential analysis in decision making.

A.K.A. A *differential cost*, also called an *incremental cost*, is any cost present in one alternative but absent in whole or part in another alternative.

A yard tool manufacturer can produce either metal shovels or rakes. Given the following estimated operating data, use differential analysis to determine which product would result in the highest net income?

	Shovels	Rakes
Units produced and sold	200,000	250,000
Unit selling price	$ 30.00	$ 20.00
Manufacturing costs:		
Variable (per unit)	$ 18.00	$ 9.00
Fixed (total)	$600,000	
Selling and administrative expenses:		
Variable (per unit)	$ 2.00	$ 2.00
Fixed (total)	$140,000	

YOUR TURN! 21.1

The solution is on page 1017.

ILLUSTRATIONS OF DIFFERENTIAL ANALYSIS

The Special Order

Businesses occasionally receive special orders from purchasers who request a price concession. The prospective buyer may suggest a price or ask for a bid. Sometimes the buyer may request that the firm produce a special version of a product to be identified with the buyer's private brand. As long as no overriding qualitative considerations exist, management should evaluate such propositions and accept the special order if incremental revenues exceed incremental costs.

LO2   **Demonstrate** when to accept a special order.

Business Situation

Assume that Fezzari Bicycles makes an entry-level mountain bike, the Lone Peak, which it sells to retail customers for $549. A bike share company has proposed that Fezzari supply 300 bikes for $400 per bike for a new bike share program in Salt Lake City, Utah. The bikes would carry the brand name of the bike share company. If Fezzari were to accept the order, a special machine attachment would be needed in production to differentiate the bike and affix the private brand logo. This attachment, which costs $1,500, would be discarded after the completion of this order. Also assume that Fezzari has unused production capacity, and thus anticipates no change in fixed capacity costs. The following unit cost data are available for the regular production of the Lone Peak bike:

Direct materials.	$233
Direct labor	100
Variable manufacturing overhead.	20
Fixed manufacturing overhead (allocated)	47
Total cost per unit	$400

Analysis and Recommendation

At first glance, the proposal seems unprofitable because the unit cost figure is $400, which is exactly equal to the buyer's offered price, and an additional one-time cost of $1,500 must be incurred to process the order. However, the fixed overhead of $47 included in the $400 total unit cost is not relevant to the decision and should not be considered because Fezzari's total fixed costs will be incurred whether or not the special order is accepted. The differential cost and revenue analysis in **Exhibit 21-5** demonstrates that the special order should be accepted.

Exhibit 21-5	Special Order Differential Analysis			
	A	B	C	D
1	Increase in sales revenue (300 units × $400)			$120,000
2	Increase in variable production costs:			
3	Direct materials (300 units × $233)	$(69,900)		
4	Direct labor (300 units × $100)	(30,000)		
5	Variable manufacturing overhead (300 units × $20)	(6,000)		
6	Total increase in production costs (300 units × $353)		$(105,900)	
7	Cost of special attachment		(1,500)	
8	Total differential cost			(107,400)
9	Net advantage in accepting special order			$ 12,600

The differential costs of accepting the order consist of the variable production costs and the additional cost of the attachment needed to affix the private brand. Actually, with any price higher than $358 ($107,400 total differential costs ÷ 300 units), Fezzari would earn a profit on the order.

Note that excess production capacity is significant to the special order decision. Without sufficient excess capacity, the additional production would probably cause additional amounts of fixed costs to be incurred or the loss of productive capacity for Fezzari's normal bike production. In addition, Fezzari management would also want to consider the opportunity cost of utilizing the available production capacity for this special order, because accepting the order would limit Fezzari's ability to meet increased demand for a higher-margin bike. Also note that although the $1,500 special attachment in this example is a fixed cost, it is relevant to this decision because it differs between alternatives.

Concept ──────▶	Method ──────▶	Assessment	TAKEAWAY 21.2
Should a company accept a special order at a reduced price?	Compare incremental revenues to incremental costs for the order.	Accept the order if incremental revenues exceed incremental costs (assuming there are no qualitative factors deemed to outweigh the quantitative analysis).	

Additional Decision Factors

Specific qualitative factors that should be considered here include ascertaining that (1) the special price does not constitute unfair price discrimination; (2) the special order does not negatively impact the actual or perceived quality of the retail bikes; and (3) the long-term price structure for the product is not adversely affected by the special order. Significant concern in any of these, or other areas, might be a basis for rejecting the special order despite the potential $12,600 profit.

Current sales are 50,000 units at $25 per unit. Production capacity is 80,000 units. Variable costs are $14 per unit. Fixed costs are $400,000. A special order for 10,000 units at $20 each is received. It will require the purchase of new equipment for $40,000. The equipment will have a salvage value of $5,000 at the end of the contract. Should the offer be accepted?

YOUR TURN! 21.2

The solution is on page 1018.

GuidedExamples
MBC

Make or Buy?

Many manufacturing situations require the assembly of large numbers of specially designed components and subassemblies. Usually, the manufacturer must choose between making these components and subassemblies and buying them from outside suppliers. In each situation, management should evaluate the relative costs of the two choices and buy from outside if the differential cost of buying is less than the differential cost of making the components or subassemblies. Because making a component uses some portion of the firm's manufacturing capacity, we assume that no more attractive use of that capacity is available.

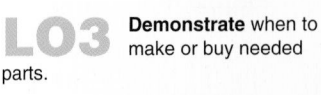

LO3

Demonstrate when to make or buy needed parts.

eLectures
MBC

Business Situation

To illustrate the make-or-buy decision, we assume that John Deere manufactures a loader-backhoe with the following costs:

Manufactured Cab:		
Direct materials.	$3,000	
Direct labor.	1,190	
Variable manufacturing overhead.	750	
Fixed manufacturing overhead.	650	
Total cost.	$5,590	

Make ◀ ▶ Buy

Investigations by John Deere's purchasing department indicate that the loader-backhoe cab assembly can be purchased in sufficient quantities at a unit price of $5,031, an indicated savings of 10% per unit. At first glance, the opportunity to purchase seems attractive.

Analysis and Recommendation

A review of operations indicates that by purchasing the component, John Deere can reduce its variable costs of production, but the fixed overhead costs will remain. The fixed overhead costs related to equipment used to manufacture the cabs are an example of a sunk cost. The differential analysis in **Exhibit 21-6** indicates that by purchasing the cab, John Deere's overall costs would increase by $91 per unit. Thus, John Deere should continue to manufacture the cab.

Exhibit 21-6	Make or Buy Differential Analysis			
	A	B	C	D
1		Manufacture Cab	Purchase Cab	Incr/(Decr) in Cost if Cab Is Purchased
2	Cost per unit:			
3	Direct materials	$3,000		$(3,000)
4	Direct labor	1,190		(1,190)
5	Variable manufacturing overhead	750		(750)
6	Fixed manufacturing overhead	650	$ 650	—
7	Purchase price of components		5,031	5,031
8		$5,590	$5,681	$ 91
9				
10	The following differential analysis confirms the more comprehensive one above:			
11	Cost to purchase cab			$ 5,031
12	Less costs avoided by purchasing:			
13	Direct materials		$3,000	
14	Direct labor		1,190	
15	Variable manufacturing overhead		750	$ 4,940
16	Increase in acquisition cost by purchasing			$ 91

> The fixed manufacturing cost is irrelevant to the decision because it does not differ between the alternatives.

> Represents incremental cost to purchase the cab assembly.

> Represents the incremental cost avoided by purchasing the cab assembly.

Additional Decision Factors

These analyses assume that the manufacturing capacity released by the decision to purchase would not be used. However, should an opportunity arise to use this capacity to generate another product with more than $91 of contribution margin per unit, then the opportunity to purchase the components would be more attractive. However, qualitative factors, such as the effects on employee morale, product quality, and dependability of the supply chain, are also very important. Once a decision is reached based on the quantitative analyses, it should be weighed against these and other qualitative factors that may be important to management.

TAKEAWAY 21.3	Concept →	Method →	Assessment
	Should a company continue to make a component of a product or buy from an outside supplier?	Compare incremental costs to make the component to incremental costs to buy the product from outside.	Buy from the outside supplier if the differential cost of buying is less than the differential cost of making (assuming there are no qualitative factors deemed to outweigh the quantitative analysis).

YOUR TURN! 21.3

The solution is on page 1018.

Scott Corporation produces a part for use in the production of one of its products. The per-unit costs associated with the annual production of 1,000 units of this part are as follows:

Direct materials.	$10.50
Direct labor.	24.00
Variable factory overhead.	5.50
Fixed factory overhead.	12.00
Total costs	$52.00

Larson Company has offered to sell 1,000 units of the same part to Scott Corporation for $42 per unit. Should Scott accept Larson's offer?

Dropping Unprofitable Segments

Occasionally, a company's financial reporting system provides its management with segment information that suggests that a particular division, department, office, product, or product line is losing money. In these situations, management should compare the direct segment cost saved to the revenue lost if the segment were to be dropped. The company should drop the segment if the cost saved is greater than the revenue lost.

LO4 Demonstrate when to drop an unprofitable product or segment.

Business Situation

Assume that EBC's segment financial statements show that the Water/Wastewater segment lost $5,298 for 2018. It would appear that dropping the segment would increase EBC's profit by $5,298, or almost 1% (see **Exhibit 21-7**).

SERVICE AND MERCHANDISING

Exhibit 21-7	Segment Income Statement

ENVIRONMENTAL BUSINESS CONSULTANTS, LLC
Line of Business Statement
For the Year Ended December 31, 2018

	Solid Waste	Water/ Wastewater	Firm Total
Gross sales.	$3,676,000	$470,000	$ 4,146,000
Less reimbursable costs.	(366,350)	(64,650)	(431,000)
Net sales.	$3,309,650	$405,350	$ 3,715,000
Cost of services	(2,238,787)	(384,713)	(2,623,500)
Gross profit on sales.	$1,070,863	$ 20,637	$ 1,091,500
Direct operating expenses	(166,065)	(25,935)	(192,000)
Line of business contribution	$ 904,798	$ (5,298)	$ 899,500
Common operating expenses.			(364,500)
Interest revenue			7,500
Income before tax.			$ 542,500

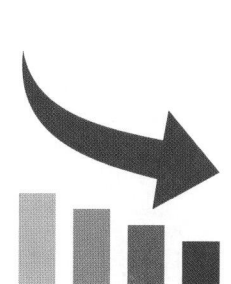

Assume that the Water/Wastewater cost of services includes an office lease expense of $38,625 that would continue even if the business line were discontinued. The rest of the Water/Wastewater cost of services and direct operating expenses are variable in nature and would be eliminated with the dropping of the segment.

Analysis and Recommendation

The differential analysis in **Exhibit 21-8** indicates that EBC's overall income would decrease, rather than increase, by discontinuing the Water/Wastewater.

Exhibit 21-8	Dropping Unprofitable Segment Differential Analysis

	A	B	C
1	Decrease in net revenue		$(405,350)
2	Decrease in expenses:		
3	Variable cost of goods sold*	$346,088	
4	Variable direct operating expenses	25,935	$ 372,023
5	Decrease in total contribution margin (and net income) from discontinuing Water/Wastewater		$ (33,327)
6	*$384,713 − $38,625		

Even though Water/Wastewater reports a $5,298 annual loss, it does generate a contribution margin of $33,327 toward the absorption of fixed costs and expenses. If Water/Wastewater is discontinued, there would be no contribution margin, although $38,625 of fixed cost would remain. This would result in a loss of $38,625, which is $33,327 worse than the current $5,298 loss. Thus, EBC should maintain its Water/Wastewater segment and look for ways to either increase revenue or decrease costs.

Additional Decision Factors

Management must often consider other factors in decisions of this type. Among these are (1) the potential termination of employees and subsequent effects on non-terminated employee morale, and (2) the possible effects on customer patronage (for example, customers of the Solid Waste line of business may go to other firms for all of their consulting services if Water/Wastewater's services are no longer available from the same source). On the other hand, EBC management might also begin to explore other potential services that might generate greater profits than the Water/Wastewater segment.

TAKEAWAY 21.4	Concept ⟶	Method ⟶	Assessment
	Should a company drop an unprofitable segment?	Compare the direct cost savings to the lost revenue from dropping the segment.	Drop the segment if the direct cost savings is greater than the revenue lost from dropping the segment (assuming there are no qualitative factors deemed to outweigh the quantitative analysis).

YOUR TURN! 21.4

The solution is on page 1018.

GPS Corporation, a manufacturer of global positioning system devices, is considering eliminating the Oceania Model from its line of devices because of losses over the past year. The past year's information on the Oceania Model is provided below:

Sales (10,000 units)	$1,000,000
Manufacturing costs:	
Direct materials.	450,000
Direct labor	250,000
Overhead	400,000
Gross Margin	$ (100,000)

Overhead costs are 80% variable, and the remaining 20% is an allocation of the general manager's salary (the general manager is over multiple product lines). If the Oceania Model is dropped, what will be the most likely impact on gross margin for the firm in the next year?

Sell or Process Further?

LO5   Demonstrate when to sell a product or process it further.

Firms sometimes face the decision of either selling products at one point in the production sequence or processing them further and selling them at a higher price. Examples are finished versus unfinished furniture, crude oil versus gasoline, and unassembled kits versus assembled units of product. In these process-further decision situations, management should compare the incremental revenue to the additional processing costs and process the products further if the incremental revenue exceeds the incremental processing costs.

Business Situation

Assume that Sunrise Landscape sells screened topsoil with the following values per yard:

Current sales price (per cubic yard)		$20.00
Costs:		
Direct materials	$5.00	
Direct labor	5.00	
Variable overhead	1.00	
Fixed overhead*	2.50	13.50
Gross margin per unit		$ 6.50

*Applied at 50% of direct labor costs.

Sunrise has excess productive capacity, which should remain available in the foreseeable future. Consequently, management believes that part of this excess capacity could be used to create a garden mix blended soil (topsoil that has been amended with compost and peat) and sell it at $30.00 per cubic yard to homeowners for their vegetable gardens and planting beds. A study carried out by the company's management indicates that the additional processing will add $5.00 to the direct materials cost and $2.00 to the direct labor cost of each unit and that variable overhead will continue to be incurred at 20% of direct labor cost. See **Exhibit 21-9** for the specific steps involved.

Exhibit 21-9   Sell or Process Further?

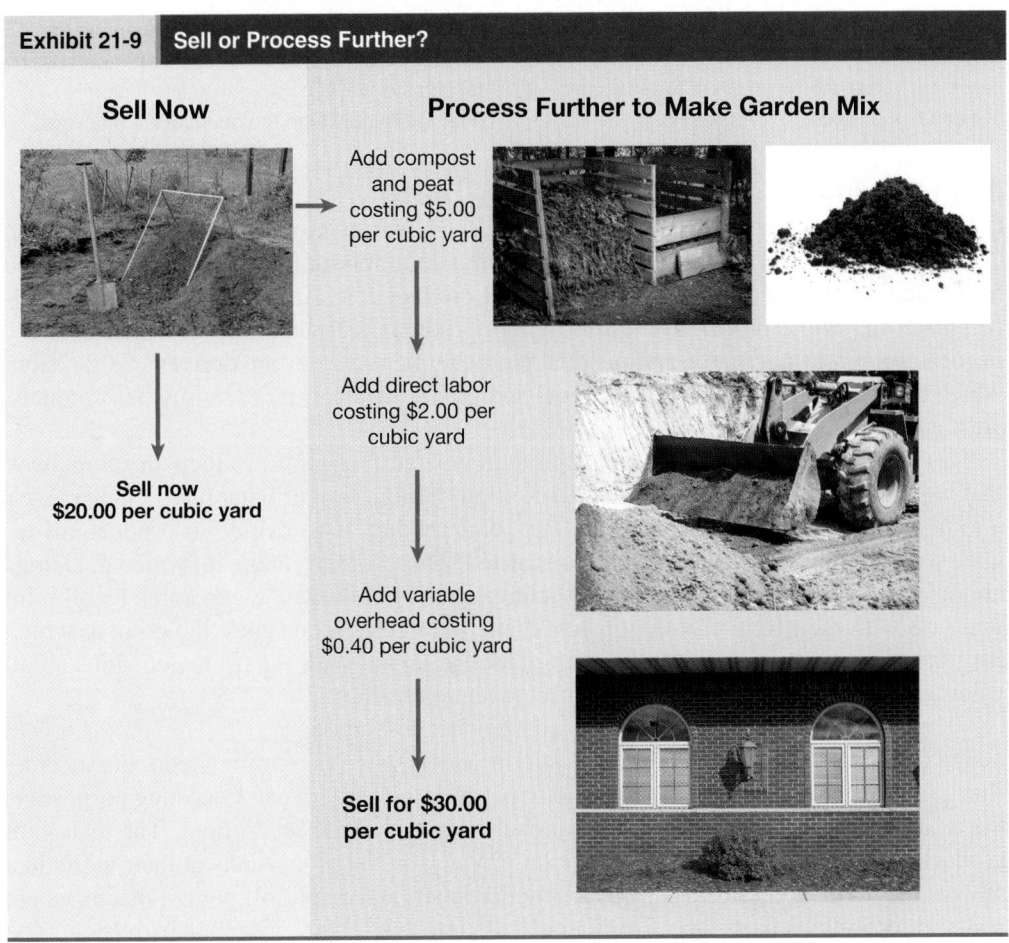

Sell Now

Process Further to Make Garden Mix

Add compost and peat costing $5.00 per cubic yard

Add direct labor costing $2.00 per cubic yard

Add variable overhead costing $0.40 per cubic yard

Sell now $20.00 per cubic yard

Sell for $30.00 per cubic yard

Analysis and Recommendation

The differential analysis in **Exhibit 21-10** supports the proposal to process further:

Exhibit 21-10	Sell or Process Further Differential Analysis		
	A	B	C
1			**Per Cubic Yard**
2	Differential revenue ($30.00 − $20.00)		$10.00
3	Differential cost:		
4	Direct materials	$5.00	
5	Direct labor	2.00	
6	Variable manufacturing overhead (20% of direct labor)	0.40	
7	Fixed manufacturing overhead	—	
8	Total differential cost		7.40
9	Excess of differential revenue over differential cost		$ 2.60

The per-unit differential analyses indicate that Sunrise will earn an additional $2.60 per cubic yard for every yard of garden mix processed and sold.

TAKEAWAY 21.5	Concept ⟶	Method ⟶	Assessment
	Should a company sell a product or process it further to sell at a higher price?	Compare the differential revenues after processing to the differential costs of processing.	Process further if the differential revenues are greater than the differential costs after processing (assuming there are no qualitative factors deemed to outweigh the quantitative analysis).

Joint Products

A.K.A. *Joint product costs* are manufacturing costs incurred in producing joint products up to the split-off point.

Often, the processing of direct materials results in two or more products of significant commercial value. Such products derived from a common input are **joint products**, and the related cost of the direct materials is a joint product cost. An obvious example of a direct materials whose processing results in joint products is crude oil, from which a variety of fuels, solvents, lubricants, and residual petrochemical pitches are derived. Cattle, from which the meat packer obtains many cuts and grades of meat, hides, and other products, are another example.

It is impossible to allocate a joint product cost among joint products in such a way that management can decide whether to continue production or what price to charge for a joint product. To decide to produce one joint product is to decide to produce all related joint products, even if some are discarded. Therefore, to make informed decisions about joint products, management must compare the total revenue generated by all joint products with their total production costs. The joint costs incurred to the point at which the joint products are separately identified are irrelevant with regard to decisions about whether to sell or process any of the joint products further.

The primary reason for allocating a joint product cost among two or more products is to assign cost to the ending inventories of joint products when determining periodic income. The most popular method of allocating joint product costs for inventory costing purposes is the relative sales value method. This approach uses arithmetic proportions. The total joint product cost is allocated to the various joint products in the proportions of their individual sales values to the total sales value of all joint products at the split-off point—that is, where physical separation takes place. For example, assume that 50,000 55-gallon barrels of crude oil costing $5,000,000 are processed into 800,000 gallons of fuel selling for $3.00 per gallon, 400,000 gallons of lubricants selling for $5.00 per gallon, and 1,000,000 gallons of petrochemical residues selling for $1.50 per gallon. The following calculations illustrate the joint product cost allocation using the relative sales value approach:

Joint Product	Quantity Produced (gallons)	Unit Sales Value	Product Sales Value	Proportion of Total Product Sales Value	Allocated Cost	Quantity Produced (gallons)	Cost per Unit
Fuel........	800,000	$3.00	$2,400,000	40.68%	$2,034,000	800,000	$2.54
Lubricants...	400,000	$5.00	2,000,000	33.90%	1,695,000	400,000	$4.24
Residues....	1,000,000	$1.50	1,500,000	25.42%	1,271,000	1,000,000	$1.27
			$5,900,000	100.00%	$5,000,000		

Note that the relative sales value approach results in assigned unit costs that are the same percentage of the selling price for each product. In our illustration, the cost per unit equals approximately 85% of the sales value per unit.

Exhibit 21-11 illustrates the allocation of the $5,000,000 joint product cost to the three joint products. Note also that each product may then incur additional manufacturing costs before it is completed and ready for sale. For example, in **Exhibit 21-11**, an additional $206,000 of costs are incurred after the split-off point to finish the production of the fuel. When added to the allocated joint costs, the total cost of the fuel is $2,240,000, or $2.80 per gallon.

Exhibit 21-11   Joint Product Costs

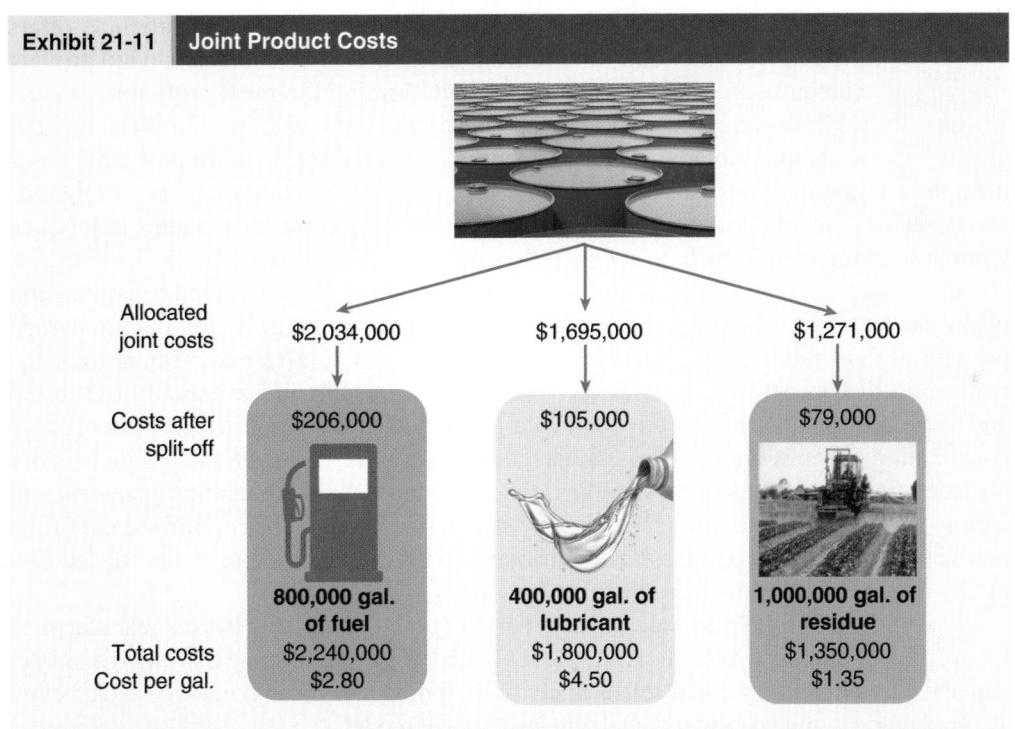

Allocated joint costs	$2,034,000	$1,695,000	$1,271,000
Costs after split-off	$206,000	$105,000	$79,000
	800,000 gal. of fuel	400,000 gal. of lubricant	1,000,000 gal. of residue
Total costs	$2,240,000	$1,800,000	$1,350,000
Cost per gal.	$2.80	$4.50	$1.35

Byproducts

Byproducts have relatively little sales value compared with the other products derived from a particular process. Byproducts are considered incidental to the manufacture of the more important products. For example, the sawdust and shavings generated in a lumber mill or in a furniture manufacturer's cutting department are byproducts.

We may account for byproducts by assigning them a cost equal to their sales value less any disposal costs. This net amount is charged to an inventory account for the byproduct and credited to the work-in-process account that was charged with the original materials. For example, consider a furniture factory in which walnut boards are processed through a cutting and shaping department. In processing $40,000 worth of lumber, 800 bushels of sawdust and shavings are generated, which, after treatment costing $80, can be sold for $1 per bushel. The amount to be charged to the Sawdust and Shavings Inventory account would be $720 [(800 bushels × $1) − $80].

This procedure reduces the costs of the main products by the net amount recovered from byproducts.

YOUR TURN! 21.5

The solution is on page 1018.

MBC

Wright Company produces two products from a joint batch process. Both products are processed further before they are sold. Joint costs per batch are $350,000. Information for each product includes:

	Product X	Product Y
Units produced per batch	10,000	20,000
Further processing and marketing cost per unit	$2.50	$1.75
Final sales value per unit	5.00	3.00

If Wright uses the net realizable value method of allocating joint costs, how much of the joint costs should be allocated to Product Y?

eLectures
MBC

Constrained Resources

LO6 **Demonstrate** how to determine which product to produce when a resource is constrained.

Because most firms produce several products, management must continually examine operating data and decide which combination of products offers the greatest total long-term profit potential. The decisions related to product emphasis are seldom as simple as determining the most profitable product and confining production to that one product. For example, John Deere faces such operational constraints as limited demand for the most profitable products, the competitive necessity of offering a line of products with a variety of qualities and capacities, and, in seeking better utilization of existing capacity, the need to produce other, less profitable products.

A.K.A. Constrained resources are commonly referred to as *bottlenecks*.

In a **constrained resource** analysis, an important and widely accepted generalization is that the firm optimizes its income when it maximizes the contribution margin earned per unit of constraining resource. The concept of constraining resource stems from the realization that as a firm increases its volume, some resource is eventually exhausted and thus constrains, or limits, the continued expansion of the firm. Which resources are constraining depends on the firm, the operating conditions, and even the products under consideration. Typical examples are key materials, labor skills, machine capacities, and factory floor space or storage space. Simply stated, management has optimized the firm's product mix when it maximizes the contribution margin earned on each unit of the particular resource that limits increased production.

An example will help explain the concept. Suppose that Larry's Brakes manufactures three different brake models: Model A, Model B, and Model C. Assume that enough market demand exists that Larry could sell as many of each model as it can build. The table below shows the prices and costs associated with each brake model.

	Model A	Model B	Model C
Selling price	$150	$200	$300
Direct materials cost.	40	50	100
Direct labor cost ($30 per hour)	60	60	90
Variable support cost ($10 per machine hour)	10	20	40
Fixed support cost	10	10	10

Also assume that the number of machine hours is limited (i.e., machine hours represent a constrained resource). Which brake model should Larry produce? Larry would want to produce the model that generates the largest contribution margin per machine hour. **Exhibit 21-12** shows the calculation of the contribution margin per machine hour for each brake model. As shown in the exhibit, Model A generates the largest contribution margin per machine hour at $40 per hour. With unlimited demand for Model A, Larry should devote all of its production capacity to producing Model A.

Exhibit 21-12	Constrained Resource Example			
	A	B	C	D
1		Model A	Model B	Model C
2	Selling price	$150.00	$200.00	$300.00
3	Less variable costs			
4	Direct materials	40.00	50.00	100.00
5	Direct labor	60.00	60.00	90.00
6	Variable support	10.00	20.00	40.00
7	Total variable costs	$110.00	$130.00	$230.00
8	Contribution margin per unit	$ 40.00	$ 70.00	$ 70.00
9	Machine hours per unit	1	2	4
10	Contribution margin per machine hour	$ 40.00	$ 35.00	$ 17.50

> Variable support cost/Cost per machine hour = # of machine hours
> A: $10/$10 = 1 hour
> B: $20/$10 = 2 hours
> C: $40/$10 = 4 hours

How can we be sure that this is the correct solution? Assume that the maximum number of hours that Larry can run his machine is 2,000 hours. **Exhibit 21-13** shows the contribution margin for each brake model, assuming that Larry produces only that model. Model A generates the largest contribution margin at $80,000, which could also be calculated as the product of the number of machine hours available (2,000 hours) and the contribution margin per machine hour ($40; see **Exhibit 21-12**).

Exhibit 21-13	Contribution Margin by Model Under Constraint			
	A	B	C	D
1		Model A	Model B	Model C
2	Constrained resource:			
3	Machine hours available	2,000	2,000	2,000
4	Machine hours per unit	1	2	4
5	Total units of production	2,000	1,000	500
6				
7	Sales revenue	$300,000	$200,000	$150,000
8	Less variable costs			
9	Direct materials	80,000	50,000	50,000
10	Direct labor	120,000	60,000	45,000
11	Variable support	20,000	20,000	20,000
12	Total variable costs	220,000	130,000	115,000
13	Contribution margin	$ 80,000	$ 70,000	$ 35,000

Most companies do not enjoy unlimited demand for their products. How does this analysis change if there is limited demand for one or more products? Assume that Larry can sell 1,000 units of Model A, 400 units of Model B, and 300 units of Model C. In this case, Larry should make

- all 1,000 units of Model A, which would use 1,000 of the available machine hours;
- all 400 units of Model B, which would use 800 of the remaining available machine hours; and,

■ use the remaining 200 machine hours to produce 50 units of Model C. **Exhibit 21-14** shows the calculation of the resulting contribution margin.

Exhibit 21-14	Contribution Margin by Model Under Constraint with Limited Demand				
A	B	C	D	E	F
1		Model A	Model B	Model C	Total
2	(1) Market demand	1,000	400	300	
3	(2) Machine hours per unit	1	2	4	
4	(3) Total machine hours required to meet demand [(1) × (2)]	1,000	800	1,200	3,000
5	(4) Total machine hours available	1,000	800	200	2,000
6	(5) Total units produced and sold [(4)/(2)]	1,000	400	50	1,450
7					
8	Sales revenue	$150,000	$80,000	$15,000	$245,000
9	Less variable costs				
10	Direct materials	40,000	20,000	5,000	65,000
11	Direct labor	60,000	24,000	4,500	88,500
12	Variable support	10,000	8,000	2,000	20,000
13	Total variable costs	$110,000	$52,000	$11,500	$173,500
14	Contribution margin	$ 40,000	$28,000	$ 3,500	$ 71,500

Hours are assigned to produce as many of each model as possible beginning with the largest contribution margin per machine hour (see **Exhibit 21-12**) until the total of 2,000 machine hours is reached.

Business Situation

To illustrate constrained resource decisions, assume that John Deere's Waterloo Works Tractor, Cab, and Assembly Operations in Waterloo, Illinois, produces three 6R Series row-crop tractors, the 6140R, the 6150R, and the 6170R. Also assume the operation's constraining resource is its factory machine capacity. John Deere operates at 90% capacity, and management wants to devote the unused capacity to one of the three products. The following data represent John Deere's current operations:

	Products		
	6140R	**6150R**	**6170R**
Per-unit data:			
Sales price	$130,000	$143,000	$150,000
Variable costs	99,450	109,000	117,000
Contribution margin	$ 30,550	$ 34,000	$ 33,000
Fixed costs*	16,150	18,700	17,850
Net income	$ 14,400	$ 15,300	$ 15,150
Machine hours required	38	44	42

*Allocated on basis of machine hours at $425 per hour.

Analysis and Recommendation

Intuition suggests that the extra capacity should be devoted either to the 6170R, which has the highest sales price, or to the 6150R, which has the highest per-unit contribution margin and net income. However, an analysis of the contribution margin of each product per unit of constraining resource (machine hour) reveals that the 6140R should receive the added capacity.

Note that fixed costs are allocated among products on the basis of machine hours—the constraining resource in our example. Furthermore, the unit allocations of fixed costs, noted previously, indicate that the 6170R requires 2 fewer machine hours than the 6150R and 4 more than the 6140R. The contribution per unit of machine capacity for each product is shown in **Exhibit 21-15**.

Exhibit 21-15	Constrained Resource Differential Analysis		
	Products		
	6140R	**6150R**	**6170R**
Contribution margin per unit....................	$30,550	$34,000	$33,000
Divided by machine hours required	38	44	42
Contribution margin per machine hour (the constraining resource).....................	$ 804	$ 773	$ 786

Use of the remaining capacity generates a greater contribution margin if devoted to the 6140R. As this example illustrates, in deciding how to utilize the constraining resource, management should use contribution margin per unit of constraining resource, rather than the relative sales prices, unit contribution margins, or even unit profit of various products.

Concept →	Method →	Assessment	TAKEAWAY 21.6
When resource constraints exist, which product(s) should a company manufacture and sell to maximize profits?	Calculate the contribution margin per constrained resource for each product.	Produce as much of the product with the highest contribution margin per constrained resource as possible, then the next highest, and so forth (assuming there are no qualitative factors deemed to outweigh the quantitative analysis).	

YOUR TURN! 21.6

Product A requires 2 machine hours per unit, has a unit contribution margin of $15, and has a contribution margin ratio of 60%. Product B requires 1 machine hour per unit, has a unit contribution margin of $12, and has a contribution margin ratio of 40%. Which product should be emphasized if machine hours are limited?

The solution is on page 1018.

SERVICE INDUSTRY IN FOCUS

SERVICE AND MERCHANDISING

Environmental Business Consultants, LLC (EBC) has been approached by Terrabean Coffee, a large retail coffee company with 5,000 shops across North America, to manage Terrabean Coffee's waste disposal and recycling services under a 3-year contract. It is unlikely that the contract would be extended beyond the initial 3-year term. Terrabean has asked EBC to provide these services at a discounted average hourly billing rate of $60 per hour.

In order to take on this major new contract, EBC would need to establish a call center to receive calls from the 5,000 shops and coordinate the appropriate response. The call center would be in a leased office space at a cost of $3,000 per month, including utilities. Additional capital, including office furniture, computers, and phones, would be purchased at a total cost of $35,000. The office furniture, computers, and phones are expected to have a value of $5,000 at the end of the contract and would not be of use to EBC in its regular business. The call center would be managed by a current EBC consultant that normally bills 1,800 hours per year at a rate of $125 per hour. An additional ten call center employees would be hired at an average hourly wage of $25, plus benefits equal to 50% of the hourly wage. Each employee would be expected to work 2,000 hours per year. EBC expects to bill Terrabean 20,000 hours per year for the call center under the contract.

Required

1. Determine whether EBC should accept this new contract offer from Terrabean. Calculate the differential net revenue or cost associated with the contract. (Hint: Don't forget that the call center manager is a current EBC employee and would not be available for any other work.)

2. What other factors should EBC management consider in making the decision?

Solution

1.

Solution	Service Industry in Focus	
Increase in annual revenue (20,000 hours × $60).		$1,200,000
Lost revenue from call center manager (1,800 × $125). . .		(225,000)
Total differential billing revenue		$ 975,000
Increase in costs:		
Direct labor (10 employees × 2,000 hours × $37.50) . . .	$750,000	
Office lease ($3,000 × 12 months).	36,000	
Other capital costs [($35,000 − 5,000)/3 years)]	10,000	
Total differential cost.		$ 796,000
Net advantage in accepting contract offer		$ 179,000

2. EBC management should consider the impact on the ten employees who will need to be hired for the call center. At the end of the contract term, these employees will need to be terminated unless other work can be found.

SUMMARY OF LEARNING OBJECTIVES

LO1   **Describe management's use of accounting information in the decision-making process. Define relevant costs and describe the use of differential analysis. (p. 980)**

- Top management establishes long-range goals, middle management deals with intermediate goals, and lower management focuses on short-range goals.
- Decision making, which is essentially choosing among alternatives, usually comprises three phases: planning, execution, and evaluation.
- Relevant costs are those that differ between alternatives.
- Differential analysis is the study of those amounts that are expected to differ among alternatives.

LO2   **Demonstrate when to accept a special order. (p. 985)**

- Management should evaluate special order propositions and accept the special order if incremental revenues exceed incremental costs.
- Management should also consider qualitative factors that could be the basis of rejecting a special order despite a net increase in revenues, such as unfair pricing, impact on quality, and long-term pricing impact.

LO3   **Demonstrate when to make or buy needed parts. (p. 987)**

- Management should evaluate the relative costs of the two choices and buy from outside if the differential cost of buying is less than the differential cost of making the components or subassemblies.
- Management should also consider qualitative factors such as the effects on employee morale, product quality, and dependability of the supply chain.

LO4   **Demonstrate when to drop an unprofitable product or segment. (p. 989)**

- Management should compare the direct segment cost saved to the revenue lost if the segment were to be dropped. The company should drop the segment if the cost saved is greater than the revenue lost.
- Management should also consider the potential termination of employees and subsequent effects on non-terminated employee morale, and the possible effects on customer patronage.

Demonstrate when to sell a product or process it further. (p. 990)   **LO5**

- Management should compare the incremental revenue to the additional processing costs and process the products further if the incremental revenue exceeds the incremental processing costs.
- The joint costs incurred to the point at which the joint products are separately identified are irrelevant with regard to decisions about whether to sell or process any of the joint products further.

Demonstrate how to determine which product to produce when a resource is constrained. (p. 994)   **LO6**

- Management should maximize the contribution margin earned on each unit of the particular resource that limits increased production.

Concept	Method	Assessment	SUMMARY
What is the role of management accountants in decision making?	• Planning phase—estimating and projecting data for alternative courses of action • Execution phase—measuring the acquisition and use of resources during execution of selected plan • Evaluation phase—measuring and comparing planned and actual performance	• During planning, some courses of action may not be pursued because they do not meet management's criteria. • During execution, measurement may lead to mid-course corrections to the plan. • Unfavorable variances between planned and actual results may lead to remedial action.	TAKEAWAY 21.1
Should a company accept a special order at a reduced price?	Compare incremental revenues to incremental costs for the order.	Accept the order if incremental revenues exceed incremental costs (assuming there are no qualitative factors deemed to outweigh the quantitative analysis).	TAKEAWAY 21.2
Should a company continue to make a component of a product or buy from an outside supplier?	Compare incremental costs to make the component to incremental costs to buy the product from outside.	Buy from the outside supplier if the differential cost of buying is less than the differential cost of making (assuming there are no qualitative factors deemed to outweigh the quantitative analysis).	TAKEAWAY 21.3
Should a company drop an unprofitable segment?	Compare the direct cost savings to the lost revenue from dropping the segment.	Drop the segment if the direct cost savings is greater than the revenue lost from dropping the segment (assuming there are no qualitative factors deemed to outweigh the quantitative analysis).	TAKEAWAY 21.4
Should a company sell a product or process it further to sell at a higher price?	Compare the differential revenues after processing to the differential costs of processing.	Process further if the differential revenues are greater than the differential costs after processing (assuming there are no qualitative factors deemed to outweigh the quantitative analysis).	TAKEAWAY 21.5
When resource constraints exist, which product(s) should a company manufacture and sell to maximize profits?	Calculate the contribution margin per constrained resource for each product.	Produce as much of the product with the highest contribution margin per constrained resource as possible, then the next highest, and so forth (assuming there are no qualitative factors deemed to outweigh the quantitative analysis).	TAKEAWAY 21.6

KEY TERMS

Constrained resource (p. 994)

Decision making (p. 981)

Differential analysis (p. 984)

Differential cost (p. 985)

Evaluation phase (p. 982)

Execution phase (p. 982)

Incremental cost (p. 985)

Joint product costs (p. 992)

Joint products (p. 992)

Management (p. 980)

Opportunity costs (p. 983)

Planning phase (p. 982)

Relevant costs (p. 983)

Sunk cost (p. 983)

Assignments with the ⬤ logo in the margin are available in 𝐁𝐮𝐬𝐢𝐧𝐞𝐬𝐬𝐂𝐨𝐮𝐫𝐬𝐞.
See the Preface of the book for details.

SELF-STUDY QUESTIONS

(Answers to Self-Study Questions are at the end of this chapter.)

LO1 1. **When using differential analysis to analyze two alternatives to the current operation, what factors should *not* be considered?**
   a. Direct materials costs that are different
   b. Direct labor costs that exist for only one alternative
   c. Overhead costs that are the same for both alternatives
   d. Sales commissions that apply to only one alternative

LO2 2. **When considering a special order, management should accept the order if which of the following conditions is met?**
   a. Incremental costs are greater than incremental revenues.
   b. There is excess production capacity.
   c. Incremental costs are less than incremental revenues.
   d. Employees are willing to work overtime.

LO3 3. **When considering whether to continue to manufacture a part or buy it from an outside supplier, management should buy the part if the**
   a. incremental cost to buy is less than the incremental cost to manufacture the part.
   b. equipment used for making the part is fully depreciated.
   c. equipment used for making the part could be sold.
   d. incremental cost to buy is less than the total cost to manufacture the part.

LO4 4. **A business segment reports segment revenues of $1.2 million, segment costs of $1.0 million, and allocated corporate overhead costs of $300,000. If management were to drop the segment, overall corporate profits would**
   a. increase by $100,000.
   b. decrease by $100,000.
   c. increase by $200,000.
   d. decrease by $200,000.

LO5 5. **True or false: Costs incurred to the split-off point in the manufacture of joint products are always relevant to the decision of whether to sell the joint products or process them further.**
   a. True
   b. False

LO6 6. **Smith Construction typically struggles to complete the plumbing work on schedule and within budget on new residential homes that it constructs because of a shortage of local plumbing subcontractors. In selecting among several floorplans for new homes that it plans to construct, which measurement tool should Smith select?**
   a. Contribution margin
   b. Gross profit
   c. Contribution margin ratio
   d. Contribution margin per plumbing hour

QUESTIONS

LO1 1. Identify three phases of decision making and briefly discuss the role of each phase in the decision process.

LO1 2. Although separate phases of decision making are identifiable, management is usually involved in all phases at the same time. Explain.

LO1 3. In the chapter we discuss quantitative methods to assist management in making business decisions. Discuss other common aspects of decision making that are not often subject to quantification.

LO1 4. Explain what is meant by the term *differential analysis*.

LO1 5. "In differential analysis, we can generally count on variable cost being relevant and fixed cost being irrelevant." Comment.

LO1 6. If both approaches to a decision lead to the same conclusion, why might differential analysis be considered superior to a comprehensive analysis that reflects all revenue and costs?

7. Explain how differential analysis can be applied to the following types of decisions:
      a. Accepting special orders
      b. Making or buying product components
      c. Dropping unprofitable segments of the firm
      d. Selling or processing further
      e. Product emphasis

   LO2, 3, 4, 5, 6

8. Delton Company produces unassembled picture frames at the following average per-unit costs: direct materials, $X; direct labor, $Y; and manufacturing overhead, $Z. Delton can assemble the frames at a unit cost of $2.50 and raise the selling price from $11 to $15. What is the apparent advantage or disadvantage of assembling the frames?

   LO5

9. Explain the concept of *constraining resource*, and present a general rule for optimizing product mixes.

   LO6

SHORT EXERCISES

SE21-1. With respect to relevant information for decision making, which of the following is TRUE?
   a. Fixed costs are never relevant costs.
   b. Managers should pay little attention to bottleneck operations since they have limited capacity for producing output.
   c. Customer satisfaction and quality concerns are not relevant for management accounting decision making.
   d. Relevant costs will include opportunity costs if current production is at capacity.

LO1

SE21-2. Johnson Company manufactures a variety of shoes, and has received a special one-time-only order directly from a wholesaler. Johnson has sufficient idle capacity to accept the special order to manufacture 15,000 pairs of sneakers at a price of $7.50 per pair. Johnson's normal selling price is $11.50 per pair of sneakers. Variable manufacturing costs are $5.00 per pair and fixed manufacturing costs are $3.00 a pair. Johnson's variable selling expense for its normal line of sneakers is $1.00 per pair. What would the effect on Johnson's operating income be if the company accepted the special order?

   a. Decrease by $60,000
   b. Increase by $22,500
   c. Increase by $37,500
   d. Increase by $52,500

LO2

SE21-3. The loss of a key customer has temporarily caused Bedford Machining to have some excess manufacturing capacity. Bedford is considering the acceptance of a special order, one that involves Bedford's most popular product. Consider the following types of costs:

   I. Variable costs of the product
   II. Fixed costs of the product
   III. Direct fixed costs associated with the order
   IV. Opportunity cost of the temporarily idle capacity

Which one of the following combinations of cost types should be considered in the special order acceptance decision?

   a. I and II
   b. I and IV
   c. II and III
   d. I, III, and IV

LO2

SE21-4. Refrigerator Company manufactures ice-makers for installation in refrigerators. The costs per unit, for 20,000 units of ice-makers, are as follows:

LO3

Direct materials	$ 7
Direct labor	12
Variable overhead	5
Fixed overhead	10
Total costs	$34

Cool Compartments Inc. has offered to sell 20,000 ice-makers to Refrigerator Company for $28 per unit. If Refrigerator accepts Cool Compartments' offer, the facilities used to manufacture ice-makers could be used to produce water filtration units. Revenues from the sale of water filtration units are estimated at $80,000, with variable costs amounting to 60% of sales. In addition, $6 per unit of the fixed overhead associated with the manufacture of ice-makers could be eliminated.

For Refrigerator Company to determine the **most** appropriate action to take in this situation, the total relevant costs of make vs. buy, respectively, are

a. $600,000 vs. $560,000.
b. $648,000 vs. $528,000.
c. $600,000 vs. $528,000.
d. $680,000 vs. $440,000.

LO3 **SE21-5.** Scott Corporation produces a part for use in the production of one of its products. The per-unit costs associated with the annual production of 1,000 units of this part are as follows:

Direct materials.	$10.50
Direct labor	$24.00
Variable factory overhead.	$ 5.50
Fixed factory overhead.	$12.00
Total costs.	$52.00

$5,000 of the fixed factory overhead costs associated with the production of this product are common fixed costs.

Larson Company has offered to sell 1,000 units of the same part to Scott Corporation for $42 per unit. Scott should:

a. buy the part, because this would save $10.00 per unit.
b. buy the part, because this would save the company $5,000 annually.
c. make the part, because this would save $2.00 per unit.
d. make the part, because this would save the company $5,000 annually.

LO3 **SE21-6.** A company currently sells 6,000 units per month and has received a special order from an international customer. The international customer would like to purchase 1,500 units for a price of $80 per unit. The company currently sells the product to regular customers for $95 per unit. The company has excess capacity to produce the special order. The product unit cost is shown below.

Direct materials.	$49.50
Direct labor	16.50
Variable overhead	9.50
Fixed overhead.	3.50

Fixed manufacturing overhead totals $35,000 per month. Management has determined that the additional shipping costs for the international delivery would be $4 per unit. Should the company accept the special order?

a. Yes, because operating income will increase by $750.
b. Yes, because operating income will increase by $6,750.
c. No, because operating income will decrease by $4,500.
d. No, because operating income will decrease by $21,000.

LO4 **SE21-7.** Current business segment operations for Whitman, a mass retailer, are presented below.

	Merchandise	Automotive	Restaurant	Total
Sales.	$500,000	$400,000	$100,000	$1,000,000
Variable costs	300,000	200,000	70,000	570,000
Fixed costs	100,000	100,000	50,000	250,000
Operating income (loss) . . .	$100,000	$100,000	$ (20,000)	$ 180,000

Management is contemplating the discontinuance of the Restaurant segment because "it is losing money." If this segment is discontinued, $30,000 of its fixed costs will be eliminated. In addition, Merchandise and Automotive sales will decrease 5% from their current levels. What will Whitman's total contribution margin be if the Restaurant segment is discontinued?

     a. $160,000

     b. $220,000

     c. $367,650

     d. $380,000

SE21-8.   Tucariz Company processes Duo into two joint products, Big and Mini. Duo is purchased in 1,000-gallon drums for $2,000. Processing costs are $3,000 to process the 1,000 gallons of Duo into 800 gallons of Big and 200 gallons of Mini. The selling price is $9 per gallon for Big and $4 per gallon for Mini. If the sales value at split-off method is used to allocate joint costs to the final products, the per-gallon cost (rounded to the nearest cent) of producing Big is

     a. $5.63 per gallon.

     b. $5.00 per gallon.

     c. $4.50 per gallon.

     d. $3.38 per gallon.

SE21-9.   Cervine Corporation makes two types of motors for use in various products. Operating data and unit cost information for its products are presented below.

	Product A	Product B
Annual unit capacity	10,000	20,000
Annual unit demand	10,000	20,000
Selling price	$100	$80
Variable manufacturing cost	53	45
Fixed manufacturing cost	10	10
Variable selling & administrative	10	11
Fixed selling & administrative	5	4
Fixed other administrative	2	0
Unit operating profit	$ 20	$10
Machine hours per unit	2.0	1.5

Cervine has 40,000 productive machine hours available. The relevant contribution margins, per machine hour for each product, to be utilized in making a decision on product priorities for the coming year, are

	Product A	Product B
a.	$17.00	$14.00.
b.	$18.50	$16.00.
c.	$20.00	$10.00.
d.	$37.00	$24.00.

SE21-10.   Paul's Pumps manufactures three different product lines: Model A, Model B, and Model C. Plenty of market demand exists for all models. The table below reports the prices and costs per unit of each product.

	Model A	Model B	Model C
Selling price	$50	$60	$70
Direct materials costs	$ 6	$ 6	$ 6
Direct labor costs ($12 per labor hour)	$12	$12	$24
Variable support costs ($4 per machine hour)	$ 4	$ 8	$ 8
Fixed support costs	$10	$10	$10

Assuming that machine hours are limited (i.e., this is the constrained resource), which model is the most profitable to produce?

     a.   Model A

     b.   Model B

     c.   Model C

     d.   Model A and B would be equally profitable

EXERCISES—SET A

LO1   **E21-1A.**   **Analyzing Operational Changes**   Operating results for department B of Delta Company during 2019 are as follows:

Sales.	$540,000
Cost of goods sold	378,000
Gross profit.	$162,000
Direct expenses	$120,000
Common expenses.	66,000
Total expenses	$186,000
Net loss.	$ (24,000)

If department B could maintain the same physical volume of product sold while raising selling prices an average of 5% and making an additional advertising expenditure of $30,000, what would be the effect on the department's net income or net loss? (Ignore income tax in your calculations.)

LO1   **E21-2A.**   **Analyzing Operational Changes**   Suppose that department B in Exercise E21-1A could increase physical volume of product sold by 10% if it spent an additional $40,000 on advertising while leaving selling prices unchanged. What effect would this have on the department's net income or net loss? (Ignore income tax in your calculations.)

LO1   **E21-3A.**   **Differential Analysis**   In each of four independent cases, the amount of differential revenue or differential cost is as follows (parentheses indicate decreases):

	1	2	3	4
Increases (decreases) in:				
Revenue	$18,000	$-0-	?	?
Costs.	?	?	($12,000)	$-0-

For each case, determine the missing amount that would be necessary for the net differential amount to be

a. $8,000
b.   ($4,000)

Indicate whether your answers reflect increases or decreases.

LO2   **E21-4A.**   **Special Order**   Carson Manufacturing, Inc., sells a single product for $36 per unit. At an operating level of 8,000 units, variable costs are $18 per unit and fixed costs $10 per unit.

Carson has been offered a price of $20 per unit on a special order of 2,000 units by Big Mart Discount Stores, which would use its own brand name on the item. If Carson accepts the order, materials cost will be $3 less per unit than for regular production. However, special stamping equipment costing $4,000 would be needed to process the order; the equipment would then be discarded.

Assuming that volume remains within the relevant range, prepare an analysis of differential revenue and costs to determine whether Carson should accept the special order.

LO2   **E21-5A.**   **Special Order**   Pope Company manufactures a variety of hiking boots and has received a special one-time-only order from a new customer. Pope has sufficient idle capacity to accept the special order to manufacture 1,000 pairs of boots at a price of $50.00 per pair. Pope's normal selling price is $65.00 per pair of sneakers. Variable manufacturing costs are $35.00 per pair and fixed manufacturing costs are $12.00 a pair. Pope's variable selling expense for its normal line of sneakers is $1.00 per pair. What would be the effect on Pope's operating income be if the company accepted the special order?

LO2   **E21-6A.**   **Special Order**   Roy & Roy, CPAs currently provides tax return preparation services to individuals in the local community. Roy has received a one-time only request to prepare 100 tax returns for clients of another CPA firm in the community while the owner recovers from major surgery. Roy has the capacity to prepare 700 returns. Roy has an effective income tax rate of 40%. Roy's income statement, before consideration of the one-time-only request, is as follows:

Sales (500 returns at $300 per return)............	$150,000
Variable preparation costs....................	20,000
Contribution margin.........................	130,000
Fixed preparation costs.....................	80,000
Operating income...........................	50,000
Income taxes..............................	20,000
Net income................................	$ 30,000

In negotiating a price for the special request, at what amount should Roy & Roy set the minimum per-return price?

E21-7A. **Make or Buy** Eastside Company incurs a total cost of $120,000 in producing 10,000 units of a component needed in the assembly of its major product. The component can be purchased from an outside supplier for $11 per unit. A related cost study indicates that the total cost of the component includes fixed costs equal to 25% of the variable costs involved. **LO3**

    a.   Should Eastside buy the component if it cannot otherwise use the released capacity? Present your answer in the form of differential analysis.

    b.   What would be your answer to requirement (a) if the released capacity could be used in a project that would generate $20,000 of contribution margin?

E21-8A. **Make or Buy** Filtration, Inc. manufactures filters for use in secondary water irrigation systems. The costs per unit, for 20,000 filters, are as follows. **LO3**

Direct materials.............................	$5.00
Direct labor................................	6.00
Variable overhead...........................	1.00
Fixed overhead.............................	2.00
Total costs.................................	$14.00

Irrigation Products has offered to sell 20,000 filters to Filtration for $14 per filter. If Filtration accepts Irrigation Products' offer, the facilities used to manufacture filters could be used to produce refrigerator filtration units. Revenues from the sale of refrigerator filtration units are estimated at $50,000, with variable costs amounting to 50% of sales. In addition, $1 per unit of the fixed overhead associated with the manufacture of secondary water irrigation filters could be eliminated.

    Should Filtration, Inc. accept Irrigation Product's offer?

E21-9A. **Make or Buy** Desert Industries manufactures 5,000 units of Part X300 each month for use in production. The facilities now being used to produce Part X300 have fixed monthly overhead costs of $40,000, and a theoretical capacity to produce 7,000 units per month. If Desert were to buy Part X300 from an outside supplier, the facilities would be idle and 80% of the fixed costs would continue to be incurred. There are no alternative uses for the production facilities. The variable production costs of Part X300 are $24 per unit. Fixed overhead is allocated based on planned production levels. **LO3**

    If Desert Industries continues to use 5,000 units of Part X300 each month, it would realize a net benefit by purchasing Part X300 from an outside supplier only if the supplier's unit price is less than what amount?

E21-10A. **Dropping Unprofitable Department** Thomas Corporation has four departments, all of which appear to be profitable except department 4. Operating data for 2019 are as follows: **LO4**

	Total	Departments 1–3	Department 4
Sales.....................	$950,000	$800,000	$150,000
Cost of sales..............	626,000	512,000	114,000
Gross profit...............	$324,000	$288,000	$ 36,000
Direct expenses	$144,000	$120,000	$ 24,000
Common expenses..........	125,000	105,000	20,000
Total expenses	$269,000	$225,000	$ 44,000
Net income (Loss)	$ 55,000	$ 63,000	$ (8,000)

Required

  a.   Calculate the gross profit percentage for departments 1–3 combined and for department 4.
  b.   What effect would elimination of department 4 have had on total firm net income? (Ignore the effect of income tax.)

LO5   **E21-11A. Sell or Process Further** Jensen Manufacturing Company makes a partially completed assembly unit that it sells for $36 per unit. Normally, 42,000 units are sold each year. Variable unit cost data on the assembly are as follows:

Direct materials.	$10
Direct labor.	8
Variable manufacturing overhead.	4

The company is now using only 70% of its normal capacity; it could fully use its normal capacity by processing the assembly further and selling it for $41 per unit. If the company does this, materials and labor costs will each increase by $2 per unit and variable overhead will go up by $1 per unit. Fixed costs will increase from the current level of $160,000 to $180,000.

Prepare an analysis showing whether Jensen should process the assemblies further.

LO5   **E21-12A. Joint Cost** Cheyenne, Inc. produces three products from a common input. The joint costs for a typical quarter follow:

Direct materials.	$45,000
Direct labor.	55,000
Overhead	60,000

The revenues from each product are as follows:

Product A	$75,000
Product B	80,000
Product C	30,000

Management is considering processing Product A beyond the split-off point, which would increase the sales value of Product A to $116,000. However, to process Product A further means that the company must rent some special equipment costing $17,500 per quarter. Additional materials and labor also needed would cost $12,650 per quarter.

Required

  a.   What is the gross profit currently being earned by the three products for one quarter?
  b.   What is the effect on quarterly profits if the company decides to process Product A further?

LO6   **E21-13A. Service Emphasis** The following analysis of selected data is for each of the two services Gates Corporation provides.

	Service A	Service B
Per-service data at 10,000 services		
Sales price	$26	$22
Service costs:		
Variable.	9	9
Fixed.	6	4
Selling and administrative expenses:		
Variable.	5	3
Fixed.	3	1

In the Gates operation, labor capacity is the company's constraining resource. Each unit of A requires 3 hours of labor, and each unit of B requires 2 hours of labor. Assuming that all services can be sold at a normal price, prepare an analysis showing which of the two services should be provided with any unused productive capacity that Gates might have.

EXERCISES—SET B

E21-1B. Analyzing Operational Changes Operating results for department B of Shaw Company during 2019 are as follows:

Sales.	$800,000
Cost of goods sold	480,000
Gross profit.	$320,000
Direct expenses	$200,000
Common expenses.	123,000
Total expenses	$323,000
Net loss.	$ (3,000)

If department B could maintain the same physical volume of product sold while raising selling prices an average of 6% and making an additional advertising expenditure of $40,000, what would be the effect on the department's net income or net loss? (Ignore income tax in your calculations.)

E21-2B. Analyzing Operational Changes Suppose that department B in Exercise E21-1B could increase physical volume of product sold by 10% if it spent an additional $50,000 on advertising while leaving selling prices unchanged. What effect would this have on the department's net income or net loss? (Ignore income tax in your calculations.)

E21-3B. Differential Analysis In each of four independent cases, the amount of differential revenue or differential cost is as follows (parentheses indicate decreases):

	1	2	3	4
Increases (decreases) in:				
Revenue	$36,000	$-0-	?	?
Costs.	?	?	$(20,000)	$-0-

For each case, determine the missing amount that would be necessary for the net differential amount to be

a. $22,000
b. ($9,000)

Indicate whether your answers reflect increases or decreases.

E21-4B. Special Order Northern Company regularly sells its only product for $34 per unit and has a 25% profit on each sale. The company has accepted a special order for a number of units, the production of which would use part of its unused capacity. The special order sales price is 50% of the normal price, and the profit margin is only 60% of the regular dollar profit. What, apparently, is

a. Northern's profit per unit on the special order?
b. Northern's variable cost per unit?
c. Northern's average fixed cost per unit on regular sales?

E21-5B. Special Order Plastic Pipe Company manufactures a variety of pipes, and has received a special one-time-only order from a new customer. Plastic Pipe has sufficient idle capacity to accept the special order to manufacture 2,000 16-foot lengths of pipe at a price of $8.00 per pipe. Plastic Pipe's normal selling price is $12.00 per 16-foot length. Variable manufacturing costs are $7.00 per pipe and fixed manufacturing costs are $1.00 per pipe. Plastic Pipe's variable selling expense for its normal line of pipes is $0.50 per pipe. What would be the effect on Plastic Pipe's operating income be if the company accepted the special order?

E21-6B. Special Order William A. Smith Pest Control, Inc. (WASP) currently provides pest control services to households in the local community. WASP has an opportunity to service 250 customers of another pest control firm that has also been selling in the community. WASP has the capacity to service 1,000 homes. WASP has an effective income tax rate of 30%. WASP's income statement, before consideration of the new opportunity, is as follows.

Sales (750 homes at $250 per home)	$187,500
Variable service costs.	135,000
Contribution margin	52,500
Fixed service costs.	30,000
Operating income	22,500
Income taxes	6,750
Net income	$ 15,750

In negotiating a price for the special opportunity, at what amount should WASP set the minimum per-home price?

LO3   **E21-7B.**   **Make or Buy** Harper Company incurs a total cost of $252,000 in producing 20,000 units of a component needed in the assembly of its major product. The component can be purchased from an outside supplier for $7 per unit. A related cost study indicates that the total cost of the component includes fixed costs equal to 75% of the variable costs involved.

     a.   Should Harper buy the component if it cannot otherwise use the released capacity? Present your answer in the form of differential analysis.

     b.   What would be your answer to requirement (a) if the released capacity could be used in a project that would generate $5,000 of contribution margin?

LO3   **E21-8B.**   **Make or Buy** Specialty Metal Products, Inc. manufactures filters for use in custom over-the-range hoods. The costs per unit, for a batch of 10,000 filters, are as follows.

Direct materials.	$ 5.00
Direct labor	3.00
Variable overhead	1.00
Fixed overhead.	4.00
Total costs	$13.00

Custom Kitchens has offered to sell 10,000 filters to Specialty Metal Products for $14 per filter. If Specialty Metal Products accepts Custom Kitchens' offer, the facilities used to manufacture filters could be used to produce BBQ grates. Revenues from the sale of BBQ grates are estimated at $20,000, with variable costs amounting to 80% of sales. In addition, $1 per unit of the fixed overhead associated with the manufacture of filters could be eliminated.

Should Specialty Metal Products accept Custom Kitchens' offer?

LO3   **E21-9B.**   **Make or Buy** RKR Consultants produces a monthly report on the semiconductor chip manufacturing industry for use by its consultants in serving RKR clients. The research office now being used to produce the report has fixed monthly overhead costs of $2,000. The research staff have a theoretical capacity to prepare another report on a second industry each month.

RKR has learned that a semiconductor industry trade group produces a similar industry report that is available on a subscription basis. If RKR were to subscribe to the report from the industry trade group, the research office would be idle and 90% of the fixed costs would continue to be incurred. There are no alternative uses for the research office. The variable costs associated with preparing the monthly research report are $500 per report. Fixed overhead is allocated based on planned production levels.

If RKR Consultants continues to use the monthly research report, it would realize a net benefit by purchasing the report from the semiconductor industry trade group only if the monthly subscription price is less than what amount?

LO4   **E21-10B.**   **Dropping Unprofitable Department** Penn Corporation has four departments, all of which appear to be profitable except department 4. Operating data for 2019 are as follows:

	Total	Departments 1-3	Department 4
Sales.	$1,052,000	$900,000	$152,000
Cost of sales.	654,000	540,000	114,000
Gross profit.	$ 398,000	$360,000	$ 38,000
Direct expenses	$ 177,000	$150,000	$ 27,000
Common expenses.	140,000	120,000	20,000
Total expenses	$ 317,000	$270,000	$ 47,000
Net income (loss)	$ 81,000	$ 90,000	$ (9,000)

a. Calculate the gross profit percentage for departments 1–3 combined and for department 4.

b. What effect would elimination of department 4 have had on total firm net income? (Ignore the effect of income tax.)

E21-11B. Sell or Process Further Turner Manufacturing Company makes a partially completed assembly unit that it sells for $50 per unit. Normally, 35,000 units are sold each year. Variable unit cost data on the assembly are as follows:

Direct materials.	$12
Direct labor	7
Variable manufacturing overhead.	9

The company is now using only 75% of its normal capacity; it could fully use its normal capacity by processing the assembly further and selling it for $58 per unit. If the company does this, materials and labor costs will each increase by $2 per unit and variable overhead will go up by $1 per unit. Fixed costs will increase from the current level of $125,000 to $165,000.

Prepare an analysis showing whether Turner should process the assemblies further.

E21-12B. Service Emphasis The following analysis of selected data is for each of the two services Rockville Corporation provides.

	Service G	Service H
Per-unit data @ 10,000 services		
Sales price	$29	$16
Service costs:		
Variable.	9	7
Fixed.	6	4
Selling and administrative expenses:		
Variable.	5	2
Fixed.	3	1

In Rockville's operation, labor capacity is the company's constraining resource. Each unit of G requires 3 hours of labor, and each unit of H requires 1 hour of labor. Assuming that all services can be sold at a normal price, prepare an analysis showing which of the two services should be provided with any unused productive capacity that Rockville might have.

PROBLEMS—SET A

P21-1A. Analyze Operational Changes Richmond's is a retail store with eight departments, including a garden department that has been operating at a loss. The following condensed income statement gives the latest year's operating results:

	Garden Department	All Other Departments
Sales.	$336,000	$2,400,000
Cost of sales.	201,600	1,560,000
Gross profit.	$134,400	$ 840,000
Direct expenses	$108,000	$ 273,000
Common expenses.	48,000	312,000
Total expenses	$156,000	$ 585,000
Net income (Loss)	$ (21,600)	$ 255,000

Required

a. Calculate the gross profit percentage for the garden department and for the other departments as a group.

b. Suppose that if the garden department were discontinued, the space occupied could be rented to an outside firm for $18,000 per year, and the common expenses of the firm would be reduced by $4,500. What effect would this action have on Richmond's net income? (Ignore income tax in your calculations.)

c. It is estimated that if an additional $6,000 were spent on advertising, prices in the garden center could be raised an average of 5% without a change in physical volume of products sold. What effect would this have on the operating results of the garden department? (Again, ignore income tax in your calculations.)

LO2   P21-2A.   Special Order Total cost data follow for Glendale Manufacturing Company, which has a normal capacity per period of 8,000 units of product that sell for $60 each. For the foreseeable future, regular sales volume should continue to equal normal capacity.

Direct materials.	$100,800
Direct labor.	62,400
Variable manufacturing overhead.	46,800
Fixed manufacturing overhead (Note 1).	38,400
Selling expense (Note 2)	35,200
Administrative expense (fixed)	15,000
	$298,600

Notes:

1. Beyond normal capacity, fixed overhead costs increase $1,800 for each 500 units *or fraction thereof* until a maximum capacity of 10,000 units is reached.

2. Selling expenses consist of a 6% sales commission and shipping costs of 80 cents per unit. Glendale pays only three-fourths of the regular sales commission on sales totaling 501 to 1,000 units and only two-thirds the regular commission on sales totaling 1,000 units or more.

   Glendale's sales manager has received a special order for 1,200 units from a large discount chain at a price of $36 each, F.O.B. factory. The controller's office has furnished the following additional cost data related to the special order:

1. Changes in the product's design will reduce direct materials costs $1.50 per unit.
2. Special processing will add 20% to the per-unit direct labor costs.
3. Variable overhead will continue at the same proportion of direct labor costs.
4. Other costs should not be affected.

Required

a. Present an analysis supporting a decision to accept or reject the special order. (Round computations to the nearest cent.)

b. What is the lowest price Glendale could receive and still make a $3,600 profit before income taxes on the special order?

c. What general qualitative factors should Glendale consider?

P21-3A. **Make or Buy** Allen Corporation currently makes the nylon convertible top for its main product, a fiberglass boat designed especially for water skiing. The costs of producing the 1,500 tops needed each year follow:

Nylon fabric.	$270,000
Aluminum tubing.	96,000
Frame fittings	24,000
Direct labor.	162,000
Variable manufacturing overhead.	30,000
Fixed manufacturing overhead.	180,000

Dustin Company, a specialty fabricator of synthetic materials, can make the needed tops of comparable quality for $390 each, F.O.B. shipping point. Allen would furnish its own trademark insignia at a unit cost of $12. Transportation would be $18 per unit, paid by Allen Corporation.

Allen's chief accountant has prepared a cost analysis that shows that only 20% of fixed overhead could be avoided if the tops are purchased. The tops have been made in a remote section of Allen's factory building, using equipment for which no alternate use is apparent in the foreseeable future.

Required

a. Prepare a differential analysis showing whether or not you would recommend that the convertible tops be purchased from Dustin Company.

b. Assuming that the production capacity released by purchasing the tops could be devoted to a subcontracting job for another company that netted a contribution margin of $42,000, what maximum purchase price could Allen Corporation pay for the tops?

c. Identify two important qualitative factors that Allen Corporation should consider in deciding whether to purchase the needed tops.

P21-4A. **Dropping Unprofitable Division** Based on the following analysis of last year's operations of Bingham, Inc., a financial vice president of the company believes that the firm's total net income could be increased by $400,000 if its engineering division were discontinued. (Amounts are given in thousands of dollars.)

	Totals	All Other Divisions	Engineering Division
Sales.	$11,000	$8,000	$ 3,000
Cost of services:			
Variable.	(3,880)	(2,600)	(1,280)
Fixed.	(2,120)	(1,400)	(720)
Gross profit.	$ 5,000	$4,000	$ 1,000
Operating expenses:			
Variable.	(3,000)	(2,000)	(1,000)
Fixed.	(1,600)	(1,200)	(400)
Net income (loss)	$ 400	$ 800	$ (400)

Required

Provide answers for each of the following independent situations:

a. Assuming that total fixed costs and expenses would not be affected by discontinuing the engineering division, prepare an analysis showing why you agree or disagree with the vice president.

b. Assume that discontinuance of the engineering division will enable the company to avoid 40% of the fixed portion of cost of services and 25% of the fixed operating expenses allocated to the engineering division. Calculate the resulting effect on net income.

c. Assume that in addition to the cost avoidance in requirement (b), the capacity released by discontinuance of the engineering division can be used to provide 6,000 new services that would have a variable cost per service of $36 and would require additional fixed costs totaling $72,000. At what unit price must the new service be sold if Bingham is to increase its total net income by $120,000?

LO5 **P21-5A.** **Joint Cost** The Sun-Kissed Company manufactures two skin-care lotions, Soft Skin and Silken Skin, out of a joint process. The joint (common) costs incurred are $420,000 for a standard production run that generates 180,000 gallons of Soft Skin and 120,000 gallons of Silken Skin. Additional processing costs beyond the split-off point are $1.40 per gallon for Soft Skin and $0.90 per gallon for Silken Skin. Soft Skin sells for $2.40 per gallon while Silken Skin sells for $3.90 per gallon.

The Best Eastern Hotel chain has asked the Sun-Kissed Company to supply it with 240,000 gallons of Silken Skin at a price of $3.65 per gallon. Best Eastern plans to have the Silken Skin bottled in 1.5-ounce personal-use containers that are supplied in each of its hotel rooms as part of the complimentary personal products for guest use.

If Sun-Kissed accepts the order, it will save $0.05 per gallon in packaging of Silken Skin. There is sufficient excess capacity in Sun-Kissed's production system to handle just one more production run in order to have sufficient Silken Skin for this special order. However, the nature of the joint process always results in 180,000 gallons of Soft Skin and 120,000 gallons of Silken Skin. Also, the market for Soft Skin is saturated; hence, any additional sales of Soft Skin would take place at a price of $1.60 per gallon.

Required

a. What is the profit normally earned on one production run of Soft Skin and Silken Skin?
b. What is the incremental effect on overall income if the Sun-Kissed Company accepts the special order for Silken Skin?

LO6 **P21-6A.** **Product Emphasis** Lowell Corporation manufactures both a deluxe and a standard model of a household food blender. Because of limited demand, for several years production has been at 80% of estimated capacity, which is thought to be limited by the number of machine hours available. At current operation levels, a profit analysis for each product line shows the following data:

	Per-Unit Data			
	Deluxe		**Standard**	
Sales price		$216		$84
Production costs:				
Direct materials.	$89		$12	
Direct labor	36		23	
Variable manufacturing overhead	15		11	
Fixed manufacturing overhead*	25	$165	10	$56
Variable operating expenses		18		10
Fixed operating expenses		8		5
Total cost		$191		$71
Operating income		$ 25		$13

* Assigned on the basis of machine hours at normal capacity.

Management wants to utilize the company's current excess capacity by increasing production.

Required

a. What general decision guideline applies in this situation?
b. Assuming that sufficient units of either product can be sold at current prices to use existing capacity fully and that total fixed cost will not be affected, prepare an analysis showing which product line should be emphasized if net income for the firm is the decision basis.

PROBLEMS—SET B

LO1 **P21-1B.** **Analyze Operational Changes** The management of Manchester's Department Store is concerned about the operation of its sporting goods department, which has not been very successful. The following condensed income statement gives the latest year's results:

	Sporting Goods Department	All Other Departments
Sales.	$480,000	$2,400,000
Cost of goods sold	360,000	1,560,000
Gross profit.	$120,000	$ 840,000
Direct expenses	$ 67,500	$ 336,000
Indirect expenses	48,000	240,000
Total expenses	$115,500	$ 576,000
Net income	$ 4,500	$ 264,000

Required

a. Calculate the gross profit percentage for the sporting goods department and for the other departments as a group.

b. It is estimated that if an additional $10,500 were spent on promotion of sporting goods, average prices can be raised 5% without affecting physical volume of goods sold. What effect would this have on the operating results of the sporting goods department? (Ignore the effect of income tax.)

c. Alternatively, it is estimated that physical volume of goods sold could be increased 8% if an additional $15,000 were spent on promotion of sporting goods and prices were not increased. Assuming that operating expenses remain the same, what effect would this have on the operating results of the sporting goods department? (Ignore the effect of income tax.)

P21-2B. **Special Order** Total cost data follow for Greenfield Manufacturing Company, which has a normal capacity per period of 20,000 units of product that sell for $54 each. For the foreseeable future, regular sales volume should continue to equal normal capacity. **LO2**

Direct materials.	$266,800
Direct labor.	200,000
Variable manufacturing overhead.	152,000
Fixed manufacturing overhead (Note 1).	118,800
Selling expense (Note 2)	129,600
Administrative expense (fixed)	50,000
	$917,200

Notes:

1. Beyond normal capacity, fixed overhead costs increase $4,500 for each 1,000 units *or fraction thereof* until a maximum capacity of 24,000 units is reached.

2. Selling expenses consist of a 10% sales commission and shipping costs of $1 per unit. Greenfield pays only one-half of the regular sales commission rates on sales amounting to $3,000 or more.

Greenfield's sales manager has received a special order for 2,500 units from a large discount chain at a price of $44 each, F.O.B. factory. The controller's office has furnished the following additional cost data related to the special order:

1. Changes in the product's design will reduce direct materials costs by $4 per unit.
2. Special processing will add 10% to the per-unit direct labor costs.
3. Variable overhead will continue at the same proportion of direct labor costs.
4. Other costs should not be affected.

Required

a. Present an analysis supporting a decision to accept or reject the special order.

b. What is the lowest price Greenfield could receive and still make a profit of $5,000 before income taxes on the special order?

c. What general qualitative factors should Greenfield consider?

P21-3B. **Make or Buy** Walsh Corporation currently makes the nylon mooring cover for its main product, a fiberglass boat designed for tournament bass fishing. The costs of producing the 2,000 covers needed each year follow: **LO3**

Nylon fabric.	$320,000
Wood battens	64,000
Brass fittings.	32,000
Direct labor	128,000
Variable manufacturing overhead.	96,000
Fixed manufacturing overhead.	170,000

Calvin Company, a specialty fabricator of synthetic materials, can make the needed covers of comparable quality for $290 each, F.O.B. shipping point. Walsh would furnish its own trademark insignia at a unit cost of $20. Transportation would be $15 per unit, paid by Walsh Corporation.

Walsh's chief accountant has prepared a cost analysis that shows that only 30% of fixed overhead could be avoided if the covers are purchased. The covers have been made in a remote section of Walsh's factory building, using equipment for which no alternate use is apparent in the foreseeable future.

Required

a. Prepare a differential analysis showing whether or not you would recommend that the mooring covers be purchased from Calvin Company.

b. Assuming that the production capacity released by purchasing the covers could be devoted to a subcontracting job for another company that netted a contribution margin of $64,000, what maximum purchase price could Walsh pay for the covers?

c. Identify two important qualitative factors that Walsh Corporation should consider in deciding whether to purchase the needed covers.

LO4

P21-4B. **Dropping Unprofitable Division** Based on the following analysis of last year's operations of Groves, Inc., a financial vice president of the company believes that the firm's total net income could be increased by $(560,000) if its design division were discontinued. (Amounts are given in thousands of dollars.)

	Totals	All Other Divisions	Design Division
Sales.	$18,400	$14,400	$4,000
Cost of services:			
Variable.	(7,600)	(5,600)	(2,000)
Fixed	(4,800)	(4,000)	(800)
Gross profit	$ 6,000	$ 4,800	$1,200
Operating expenses:			
Variable.	(3,360)	(2,000)	(1,360)
Fixed	(1,600)	(1,200)	(400)
Net income (loss)	$ 1,040	$ 1,600	$ (560)

Required

Provide answers for each of the following independent situations:

a. Assuming that total fixed costs and expenses would not be affected by discontinuing the design division, prepare an analysis showing why you agree or disagree with the vice president.

b. Assume that discontinuance of the design division will enable the company to avoid 30% of the fixed portion of cost of services and 40% of the fixed operating expenses allocated to the design division. Calculate the resulting effect on net income.

c. Assume that in addition to the cost avoidance in requirement (b), the capacity released by discontinuance of the design division can be used to provide 6,000 new services that would have a variable cost per service of $60 and would require additional fixed costs totaling $80,000. At what unit price must the new service be sold if Groves is to increase its total net income by $180,000?

LO6

P21-5B. **Product Emphasis** McDermott Corporation manufactures both automatic and manual residential water treatment units. Because of limited demand, for several years production has been at 90% of estimated capacity, which is thought to be limited by the number of machine hours available. At current operation levels, a profit analysis for each product line shows the following:

	Per-Unit Data			
	Automatic		**Manual**	
Sales price		$800		$416
Production costs:				
Direct materials.	$144		$80	
Direct labor	128		64	
Variable manufacturing overhead.	64		32	
Fixed manufacturing overhead*	144	$480	72	$248
Variable operating expenses		80		16
Fixed operating expenses		144		96
Total cost		$704		$360
Operating income.		$ 96		$ 56

*Assigned on the basis of machine hours at normal capacity.

Management wants to utilize the company's current excess capacity by increasing production.

Required

a. What general decision guideline applies in this situation?
b. Assuming that sufficient units of either product can be sold at current prices to use existing capacity fully and that total fixed cost will not be affected, prepare an analysis showing which product line should be emphasized if net income for the firm is the decision basis.

EXTENDING YOUR KNOWLEDGE

EKY21-1. Business Decision Case Marvin Corporation manufactures both an automatic and a manual household dehumidifier. Because of limited demand, for several years production has been at 80% of estimated capacity, which is thought to be limited by the number of machine hours available. At current operation levels, a profit analysis for each product line shows the following:

	Per-unit Data			
	Automatic		**Manual**	
Sales price		$350		$150
Production costs:				
Direct materials.	$65		$32	
Direct labor	35		25	
Variable manufacturing overhead.	68		16	
Fixed manufacturing overhead	50	$218	18	$ 91
Variable operating expenses		52		21
Fixed operating expenses		30		13
Total cost		$300		$125
Operating income.		$ 50		$ 25

Management wants to make use of the company's current excess capacity by increasing production. Each unit of the automatic model requires 2.5 machine hours; the manual model requires 1 machine hour per unit.

Required

Present answers for the following questions in each independent situation:

a. Assume that sufficient units of either product can be sold at current prices to utilize existing capacity fully and that fixed costs will not be affected.
    1. To which product should the excess capacity be devoted if the decision basis is maximization of contribution margin per unit of product?

2. Prepare an analysis showing which product line should be emphasized if the firm's net income is the decision basis.

3. What general decision guideline applies in this situation?

b. Suppose the excess capacity represents 10,000 machine hours, which can be used to make 4,000 automatic units or 10,000 manual units or any proportionate combination. The only market available for these extra units is a foreign market in which the sales prices must be reduced by 20% and in which no more than 6,000 units of either model can be sold. All costs will remain the same except that the sales commission of 10% (included in the variable operating expenses) will be avoided. Prepare an analysis showing which product should be emphasized and the effect on the firm's net income.

c. Assume that the excess capacity can be used as indicated in requirement (b) and that the firm's market research department believes that the production available from using the excess capacity exclusively on either model can be sold in the domestic market at regular prices if a promotion campaign costing $225,000 is undertaken for the automatic model or $235,000 for the manual model. Prepare an analysis indicating for which product the campaign should be undertaken.

EKY21-2. Business Decision Case Hall Manufacturing Corporation makes a new high-tech adhesive in a single process that blends and bottles die product, which currently sells for $20 per gallon. Market demand for the product seems good, but management is not satisfied with the product's seemingly low profit margin and has sought your advice.

Because of its concern, management has allocated a $60,000 fund for a program of product promotion or cost reduction, or both. Members of the firm's controller's office and marketing staff have identified the following three possible plans:

1. Plan A: Devote all funds to product promotion, which allows all costs and the sales volume to remain the same, but permits a sales price increase of $3.50 per gallon.

2. Plan B: Spend $32,000 on product promotion and $28,000 on cost reduction techniques, which maintains sales volume, permits a price increase of $2 per gallon, and reduces conversion costs by 10% per gallon.

3. Plan C: Devote all funds to cost reduction efforts. Sales volume and price do not change. For each gallon produced, however, direct materials cost decreases 10%, and conversion cost decreases 20%.

The controller's office also provides you with the following operating data for a typical period (all materials are added initially; conversion costs occur evenly throughout the process; the weighted average method is used for process costing):

Beginning work in process (2,500 gallons, 60% processed)	$ 32,250
Units started in process (34,000 gallons)	
Ending work in process (3,500 gallons, 60% processed)	
Costs charged to the department:	
Direct materials.	275,400
Direct labor	186,390
Manufacturing overhead.	156,330
	$650,370

Required

Using the data from this representative production period, analyze the apparent relative benefits derived from each plan and make a recommendation supported by relevant calculations. Assume that sales for each period will equal units completed in that period. *Hint:* You will need to prepare a Production Report, Cost per Equivalent Unit Report, and Production Cost Report to analyze the three plans. These reports were discussed in Chapter 17.

EKY21-3. **Ethics Case** Swan Sports manufactures golfing equipment. Traditionally, the company has been busy all year but has noticed that over the past few years business has fallen off in October and November. If new business does not come in this year, the company will have to lay off some long-time employees for those 2 months. Rob Patell, a sales representative, received an order from Better Equipment Co., a competitor. Better Equipment cannot meet a customer's rush order on time and is willing to subcontract the work to Swan Sports on the condition that the Better Equipment Co. name—not Swan Sports' name—appear on all products. The order is at a price substantially below Swan Sports' usual selling price. The only way this order can be produced is to use lower-quality materials than Swan Sports normally uses in its own products.

     Rob Patell has recommended to his supervisor that this order be accepted and that lower-quality materials be used. Patell's reasoning includes the following points:

  a.   It is clearly a one-time order.

  b.   Swan Sports' name will not appear on it.

  c.   Workers will not have to be laid off during October and November.

A differential analysis shows that Swan Sports will lose $1,000 on the order.

Required

What should the sales supervisor consider before making a decision?

EKY21-4. **Corporate Social Responsibility** The "Corporate Social Responsibility" box in this chapter highlights some early citizenship milestones of John Deere. Go to John Deere's web site (https://www.deere.com) and search under the "Company Information" tab for "Citizenship & Sustainability." Under the Citizenship & Sustainability page, review one of John Deere's Citizenship Focus Areas. Read about one of the reported focus areas and briefly summarize your findings. Can you think of a good business purpose for these reported achievements, or are they simply things that make John Deere a good corporate citizen?

ANSWERS TO SELF-STUDY QUESTIONS:

1. c, (p. 983)   2. c, (p. 985)   3. a, (pp. 987–988)   4. d, (pp. 989–990)   5. b, (p. 992)   6. d, (p. 994)

YOUR TURN! SOLUTIONS

Solution 21.1

Assume that rakes are produced. What are the incremental revenues and costs if shovels are produced instead?

Incremental revenue:		
Revenue forgone on 50,000 rakes	[$20 × 50,000 units]	$(1,000,000)
Additional revenue from shovels price	[($30 − $20) × 200,000 units]	2,000,000
Incremental revenue		$ 1,000,000
Incremental costs:		
Additional cost of goods sold	[($18 − $9) × 200,000 units]	$(1,800,000)
Savings on 50,000 rakes not produced	[$9 × 50,000]	450,000
Savings on selling and administrative	[$2 × 50,000]	100,000
Incremental costs		$(1,250,000)
Net differential cost of producing shovels		$ (250,000)

So, the manufacturer should produce rakes.

Solution 21.2
Yes.

Differential revenue	$200,000
Differential cost (10,000 × $14) + ($40,000 − $5,000). . .	175,000
Net increase in profit.	$ 25,000

Solution 21.3

Relevant per-unit costs to manufacture:	
Direct materials.	$10.50
Direct labor.	24.00
Variable factory overhead.	5.50
Total	$40.00
Relevant per-unit cost to purchase.	42.00
Net cost to purchase.	($ 2.00)

Scott should continue to manufacture the part.

Solution 21.4

Differential analysis:	
Lost revenue.	$1,000,000
Expenses eliminated:	
Direct materials.	$ 450,000
Direct labor.	250,000
Variable overhead [80% × 400,000]	320,000
Decreased expenses	1,020,000
Incremental increase in gross profit	$ 20,000

Solution 21.5

Product X	[10,000 units × ($5.00 − $2.50)] . .	$ 25,000
Product Y	[20,000 units × ($3.00 − $1.75)] . .	25,000
Total		$ 50,000
Product Y allocation	[$25,000/$50,000].	50%
	[$350,000 × 50%]	$175,000

Solution 21.6
Product B. ($12/1 hour is greater than $15/2 hours)

Chapter 22

Planning and Budgeting

PAST

Chapter 21 described some of the tools and techniques that management can use in making short-term business decisions.

PRESENT

Chapter 22 discusses the budgeting process, the components of the master budget, and the interrelationships of the individual budgets and presents an illustration of a budget for a manufacturer and a service company.

FUTURE

Chapter 23 provides an overview of standard costing and variance analysis. Moreover, it describes how standard costs influence financial statements.

Monsanto manufactures agricultural products for farmers throughout the world. Monsanto's business is highly seasonal, with approximately three-fourths of its seed sales occurring during the second and third quarters of its fiscal year. Its business is also influenced by weather. With climate shifts becoming more volatile, planting time may vary by several weeks in a specific location. Because Monsanto must produce its products well in advance of the season, even a small error in forecasting demand for its products can result in either (1) significant leftover inventory or (2) product shortages.

Monsanto has attempted to address its demand uncertainties by employing local sales employees to develop more frequent (as often as weekly) forecasts of the local market demand. These forecasts are aggregated into weekly demand forecasts that are used to develop production and distribution plans. Nevertheless, demand uncertainty will always make the budgeting process a challenge to manage!

This chapter discusses the planning and budgeting process and describes the major components of a master budget.

Road Map

LO	Learning Objective	Page	eLecture	Guided Example	Assignments
LO1	Describe the planning process, including strategic planning and operational planning.	1022	E22-1	YT22.1	SS1, Q1, Q2, Q3
LO2	Discuss the budgeting process and summarize its advantages. Define the key elements of effective budgeting.	1025	E22-2	YT22.2	SS2, Q4, Q5, Q6, Q7, Q8, SE1, SE2, SE3, SE4
LO3	Define the components of a master budget and illustrate the interrelationships of the individual budgets that comprise the master budget.	1029	E22-3	YT22.3	SS3, Q9, Q10, SE5
LO4	Prepare individual budgets for a manufacturing and a service company, including the cash budget.	1030	E22-4	YT22.4	SS4, SS5, SS6, Q11, Q12, Q13, Q14, Q15, SE6, SE7, SE8, SE9, SE10, E1A, E2A, E3A, E4A, E5A, E6A, E7A, E8A, E9A, E1B, E2B, E3B, E4B, E5B, E6B, E7B, E8B, E9B, P1A, P2A, P4A, P1B, P2B, P4B
LO5	Prepare budgeted financial statements.	1040	E22-5	YT22.5	SS7, Q16, P3A, P4A, P5A, P3B, P4B, P5B

Prediction is very difficult, especially about the future.

NIELS BOHR

Your ability to live within your means over the long term and meet your financial obligations from paycheck to paycheck depends in large part on your ability to accurately identify your income and manage your expenses. If you consistently overestimate your income or underestimate your expenses, you may find yourself getting deeper and deeper into debt. Without a financial plan, or budget, you run the risk of financial hardship or ruin.

Likewise, to be successful, every business needs to produce products or provide services at competitive costs for a growing customer base to ensure that reasonable profits are made to continue to grow the business. Management has a basic responsibility to plan, control, and measure performance and to make decisions. To carry out these responsibilities, management must develop plans and budgets, determine actual operating results, compare actual results to planned results, evaluate differences, and take corrective action to improve operations. This chapter focuses on managerial planning and budgeting.

THE PLANNING PROCESS

LO1 **Describe** the planning process, including strategic planning and operational planning.

All types of organizations—service organizations, merchandising firms, manufacturing companies, government agencies, and not-for-profit entities—can benefit from formalized planning. A formal planning process usually includes strategic planning and operational planning.

A **planning horizon** is the future time span, usually expressed in years, for which a particular plan is developed. Different types of plans have different planning horizons. Typically, longer planning horizons are associated with higher-level planning (e.g., strategic planning), whereas shorter planning horizons are associated with lower-level planning (e.g., annual operational planning.) **Exhibit 22-1** is an example of a formal planning process. As illustrated, the planning process begins with the definition of a vision or mission statement. This statement defines what the company is and provides a focus for its strategy and operational planning. The best vision statements are succinct and clear. Monsanto states that it is a sustainable agriculture company that supports farmers, enabling them to produce more from their land while conserving the world's natural resources, such as water and energy.

Exhibit 22-1 **Planning Process**

Strategic Planning
======

Strategic Planning

Strategic planning is a formal process that addresses and documents the overall mission and long-term goals of the organization based on the vision statement. Management must evaluate and decide in what directions the organization should go in the future. Issues to be decided include what basic lines of business to pursue, which geographic markets to establish, what organizational structure to develop, where to locate facilities, which means of sales and distribution to use, and how aggressively the organization should grow. For example, Monsanto's strategic plan is to provide healthy and nutritious food for a world population that is growing faster than food production. In keeping with this strategy, Monsanto's management sold its animal agricultural products business (its dairy business) in 2008 to focus on seeds and improving crop productivity.

Management must accumulate and analyze a great deal of information to create an appropriate strategic plan incorporating these decisions. Many companies use a technique such as a **strengths, weaknesses, opportunities, and threats (SWOT) analysis** to begin this accumulation and analysis process. **Exhibit 22-2** illustrates this process in the form of a 2 × 2 matrix.

Management uses SWOT analysis to analyze and document those internal and external factors that both help and harm the company's ability to achieve its strategy. The SWOT analysis will specifically address management, employees, products, services, physical facilities, customers, competitors, distribution channels, and systems. It is very important to recognize and document the current strengths and weaknesses of the firm as well as the future opportunities and threats facing it when formulating the firm's future strategic directions.

Exhibit 22-2	SWOT Matrix	
	Helpful	Harmful
Internal	Strengths	Weaknesses
External	Opportunities	Threats

Management takes the information accumulated during the SWOT analysis, makes assumptions about the economy and the future competitive environment, and formulates management strategies for the entity. A 5- or 10-year planning horizon is typical. These strategies are documented in the strategic plan, which is typically updated and revised annually for changing conditions. Frequently, elements of a SWOT analysis can be seen in the "Management's Discussion and Analysis" section of a public company's Form 10-K filing with the Securities and Exchange Commission.

Operational Planning

Management also prepares operating plans consistent with the strategic plan. **Operational planning** is the process of developing specific goals and objectives for the entity as a whole and its individual departments, formulating an operating plan to accomplish the goals and objectives, and preparing written documentation of the goals and objectives as well as the operating plan. Firms frequently develop a long-term operating plan that covers a 3- to 5-year planning horizon as well as an annual operating plan that covers a 1-year planning horizon. The annual operating plan is typically more detailed than the long-term operating plan.

The annual operating plan projects some of the current operations as they exist and provides for changes in others to reflect management's desires for improvements in the operations. The annual operating plan reflects the strategies, goals, objectives, and action plan documented in the strategic plan and the long-term operating plan. Further, the annual operating plan is usually not in a format that enables management to determine whether the plans are economically feasible. Management tests the economic feasibility of the annual operating plan through the development of the annual operating budget.

For example, Monsanto's 2017 Annual Report[1] identifies plans to improve its vegetable seeds business, in part through strategic acquisitions and continued investment in seeds, genomics, and biotechnology.

---

[1] https://monsanto.com/app/uploads/2017/12/2017_Monsanto_Annual_Report.pdf, page 31.

Progress Measurement and Reporting

No planning process is complete without an accounting of the progress achieved in pursuing the plans made. A periodic accounting is helpful in measuring progress, holding individuals accountable for aspects of the plan that are within their area of responsibility, and evaluating whether changes need to be made to future plans based on changes in the internal or external environment in which the company operates. This accounting takes many forms, including internal management reports and external reports to owners, creditors, and other stakeholders. For example, Monsanto's external reports include quarterly earnings releases, numerous Securities and Exchange Commission reports, and a corporate sustainability report. Each of these reports highlights different results of Monsanto's operations.

Monsanto's Employee Volunteer Program—Monsanto Together	**CORPORATE SOCIAL RESPONSIBILITY**

This chapter discusses the importance of budgeting to a company's financial performance. A 2012 *Forbes* article discusses the importance of budgeting for corporate social responsibility success.* The article discusses how doing good through employee volunteering programs leads to the company doing well through increased employee engagement, employee retention, and employee recruitment.

Monsanto appears to agree with what the article's author writes. As noted in Monsanto's 2017 Sustainability report, Monsanto employees are fighting rural hunger as part of a coordinated volunteer effort in areas where Monsanto employees live and work across the United States. In 2016, 3,700 Monsanto employees worked more than 90,000 volunteer hours across many countries. The effort is part of an employee volunteer program called Monsanto Together, which is focused on enriching the communities where Monsanto employees live and work. Employees are encouraged to volunteer with nonprofits focused on social causes such as food and nutrition, STEM education, and veteran concerns. In 2016, Monsanto awarded more than $600,000 in grants to non-profit organizations based on nearly 90,000 employee volunteer hours. Since 2010, over $2.5 million in grants have been awarded based on 490,000 volunteer hours by Monsanto employees.

*Ryan Scott, "'Tis the Season to Budget for CSR Success," *Forbes*, November 19, 2012.

Assume that you are performing a SWOT analysis for the retail company Target. List at least two strengths, weaknesses, opportunities, and threats that might apply to the company in the coming years.

YOUR TURN! 22.1

The solution is on page 1065.

THE BUDGETING PROCESS

A **budget** is a detailed plan for the acquisition and use of financial resources during a specific period of time. A budget serves as a plan for how a firm will achieve its quantifiable goals and a basis for measuring performance against those goals.

Budgeting is the process of developing a formal, written operating plan that presents management's planned actions in financial terms. Budgeting should reflect the conclusions reached in the strategic plan and the operating plan. Two budgets usually result from the budgeting process: the annual operating budget and the capital expenditures budget. We present and discuss the annual operating budget in this chapter and the capital expenditures budget in Chapter 25. **Exhibit 22-1** presents the sequence for preparing the various types of plans and budgets.

LO2 Discuss the budgeting process and **summarize** its advantages. **Define** the key elements of effective budgeting.

A.K.A. The annual operating budget is also called the **master budget**.

All types of entities can derive benefits from the budgeting process. Although the basic concepts of budgeting apply to all types of entities, the precise budget form will vary among those entities. Budgeting typically incorporates many accounting concepts discussed in previous chapters. In fact, some components of the annual operating budget have familiar accounting formats.

TAKEAWAY 22.1	Concept ⟶	Method ⟶	Assessment
	How can management best ensure that the efforts of all employees are congruent with the company's strategy?	Develop multi-year operating plans and budgets (both operating and capital) linked to the company's strategy.	Compare actual results with operating plans and budgets to evaluate company performance.

Advantages of Budgeting

The use of budgets to manage and control a firm's activities is known as **budgetary control.** Budgetary control involves the steps taken by management to ensure that the goals and objectives established during the planning stage are attained, and to ensure that all segments of the firm operate in a manner consistent with organizational policies. Used properly, a budget can sharpen management's focus, ensure that operating activities will help achieve management's overall strategy, and be useful in evaluating performance.

The annual planning and budgeting process forces management to step back from the daily operations of the entity, examine current operations, decide what improvements are necessary, and formulate plans and budgets that implement the established goals and objectives for the entity. The annual operating budget represents a specific plan for accomplishing these goals and objectives.

A budget can be used to control operations. When a business is large enough to be divided into departments, management needs to ensure that the operation of each department is consistent with the overall plans for the entity as a whole. The budget provides guidance for the departmental managers so their decisions will be consistent with decisions in other departments. For example, the budget provides guidance so the purchasing department buys quantities of material consistent with the factory's budget of units to be manufactured; that budget, in turn, is consistent with the sales department's budget of units to be sold.

Budgets serve as guides and targets to managers when they make decisions and as one basis for performance evaluation. Performance evaluations could be based on comparison of actual results to prior-period results. However, comparison to prior-period results fails to take into account the changes and improvements that have been incorporated into the budget. As a result, the budget is frequently the basis for evaluating performance. Because the budget is used as a basis for evaluating performance, it can also be a motivating factor for individual managers. Assuming that the budget is realistic, it provides a target that each manager will try to attain.

Elements of Effective Budgeting

Even though specific budgeting procedures vary widely among business firms, all entities engaged in comprehensive budgeting should consider the following elements of effective budgeting.

Identifying a **budget director** is vital to effective budgeting. Budget director may be a full-time or part-time position, depending on the size and complexity of the business. The budget director must be well organized and a good communicator, since he or she is responsible for organizing the budgeting process, communicating with the people involved in budgeting, and monitoring the process to ensure that it proceeds on a timely basis.

The **budget committee** generally consists of representatives from all major areas of the firm, such as sales, manufacturing, purchasing, and accounting, and is usually headed by the budget director. The primary functions of the budget committee are to provide central guidance to the budget preparation process, ensure that all departments participate in the process, and evaluate the proposed budget segments for reasonableness.

The task of developing the detailed amounts for the budget is usually not done by the budget director or the budget committee. **Participative budgeting** requires that detailed budget amounts be formulated "from the bottom up." That is, all departments should participate in the development and refinement of the budget amounts so they will be accepted by the departments as reasonable standards of performance. The participants in this process are illustrated in **Exhibit 22-3**.

Exhibit 22-3 | **Participants in a Participative Budgeting Process**

There are advantages to participative budgeting:

1. Individuals at all levels are part of a team.

2. The person in direct contact with the activity is in the best position to make the estimates.

3. A person has ownership of and is therefore more motivated to work at fulfilling a budget that he or she has helped establish.

The **budget period,** the future time span for which the budget is prepared, varies according to the nature of the specific activity involved. Most companies, however, prepare annual operating budgets, which are segmented into quarterly or monthly budgets. Short-term operating budgets covering a month or a quarter may be useful benchmarks as one element of performance evaluations, enabling management to compare budgeted amounts to actual results and initiate corrective action as required.

The capital expenditures budget usually covers a multiyear period, often 3 to 5 years. This longer budget period is necessary because of the long time period required to construct or acquire long-term assets of a unique nature.

Many businesses use **continuous budgeting** techniques for the operating budget. As each monthly or quarterly budget period passes, the oldest month or quarter is removed from the budget and another month or quarter is added to extend the budget to a full year in the future. With this approach, regardless of the time of the year, the budget always covers 12 months or four quarters.

A.K.A. Continuous budgets are also known as **perpetual** and **rolling** budgets.

Zero-Based Budgeting

Traditional budgeting procedures typically use an incremental approach to the development of the annual operating budget. For example, the level of each expense for the prior year is used as the starting point for determining the budgeted level for the next year. The person preparing the budget then either adds to or subtracts from the amount in the previous budget. During the budget process, only the increase or decrease is justified to the managers reviewing the proposed budget drafts. The prior year base amount is assumed to be reasonable. For example, the simple traditional budget example in **Exhibit 22-4** shows a budget based on a 10% increase from the current year.

Many organizations—manufacturing companies, merchandising firms, service organizations, governmental agencies, and not-for-profit entities—have experienced increases in their annual operating budgets that they deem to be unacceptable. Some of these organizations have decided to use zero-based budgeting techniques to address this problem. **Zero-based budgeting** requires budget preparers to start at a zero level for every item in the budget and justify every dollar, not just the increases or decreases. In effect, the budget is prepared "from the ground up" as if the entity had just been formed. The simple zero-base budget example in **Exhibit 22-4** shows that the budget is created without reference to the previous year's budgets.

Exhibit 22-4	Traditional Budgeting versus Zero-Based Budgeting				
	A	B	C	D	E
1		Prior Year	Current Year	Adjustment	Budget Year
2	**Traditional Budgeting**				
3	Sales revenue	$10,000	$12,000	10%	$13,200
4	Cost of goods sold	7,000	8,400	10%	9,240
5	Gross profit	$ 3,000	$ 3,600		$ 3,960
6	Sales, general, & administrative expenses	2,000	2,400	10%	2,640
7	Operating income	$ 1,000	$ 1,200		$ 1,320
8					
9	**Zero-Based Budgeting**				
10	Sales revenue	$ —	$ —	$13,200	$13,200
11	Cost of goods sold	—	—	9,240	9,240
12	Gross profit	—	—	$ 3,960	$ 3,960
13	Sales, general, & administrative expenses	—	—	2,640	2,640
14	Operating income	$ —	$ —	$ 1,320	$ 1,320

With traditional budgeting, the budget is typically based on the prior year's budget, adjusted for inflation or other incremental changes.

With zero-based budgeting, each budget is created from scratch, without reference to prior year amounts.

Organizations that have adopted zero-based budgeting use a variety of specific procedures. A common approach is to segment the budget into "decision packages" in which the preparer ranks all of the activities according to their relative importance for each activity. The preparer might note the consequences of not performing the activity, possible alternative activities, and whether there is an external mandate to perform the activity. This approach enables various levels of management to eliminate low-ranking activities until a desired budget level is reached.

Note that zero-based budgeting is a time-consuming and costly process. As a result, many entities that employ the technique usually do not apply it to all portions of the operating budget each year. Some use zero-based budgeting every year but apply the technique to only selected segments of the budget so that all segments will be subjected to the technique once during each 5-year period. Others apply the technique to all segments periodically (e.g., every third year). As a result, traditional budgeting techniques might be used to prepare budgets for years 1 and 2, with zero-based budgeting used to prepare the budget for year 3.

Concept	⟶	Method	⟶	Assessment	TAKEAWAY 22.2
How should a company implement a zero-based budgeting approach?		1. Determine goals, operations, and costs for all activities. 2. Determine alternative means of conducting each activity. 3. Evaluate the implications of changes in the level of each activity. 4. Establish workload. 5. Rank activities in order of importance. 6. Select activities necessary to accomplish goals at the minimum cost.		Although costly and time-consuming, zero-based budgeting results in a careful examination and justification of all critical activities, rooting out inefficient and ineffective activities.	

All of the following are advantages of budgeting except:

   a. Helps management ensure that operating activities will help achieve the overall corporate strategy.

   b. Provides guidance to mid-level department managers so that their decisions are consistent with other departments.

   c. Allows individual managers to act independently of other managers within the organization.

   d. Provides a basis for evaluating performance.

YOUR TURN! 22.2

The solution is on page 1065.

THE FRAMEWORK OF THE MASTER BUDGET

Master budget is the name given to the comprehensive annual operating budget. The master budget combines and integrates all of the individual, detailed operating budgets for all of the firm's various activities for the year. All amounts in the master budget are usually based on the expected level of operations. The exact structure of the master budget varies according to whether the firm's operations are manufacturing, merchandising, service, or government oriented. In this chapter, we illustrate budgeting and a master budget for Fezzari, the small bicycle manufacturer introduced in Chapter 14. The following budgets constitute Fezzari's master budget:

LO3   **Define** the components of a master budget and **illustrate** the interrelationships of the individual budgets that comprise the master budget.

1. Sales budget
2. Production budget
3. Direct materials budget
4. Direct labor budget
5. Manufacturing overhead budget
6. Selling and administrative expense budget
7. Capital expenditures budget
8. Cash budget
9. Budgeted income statement
10. Budgeted balance sheet
11. Budgeted statement of cash flows

    Fezzari's master budget includes budgets that are interdependent and must be prepared in a specific sequence. **Exhibit 22-5** presents Fezzari's master budget and the data flows that are necessary between the individual budgets during their preparation.

The sales budget is prepared first. It is based on the sales forecast and typically includes both sales dollars and quantities. As the sales budget feeds into each of the succeeding budgets, the quality of the sales forecast determines the success of the remaining process. Then the production budget is prepared to identify the number of units of each product to be manufactured. Then the direct materials budget, the direct labor budget, and the manufacturing overhead budget determine the levels of product cost to be incurred based on the units to be manufactured. The selling and administrative expense budget determines the level of selling and general administrative expense necessary to support the sales budget.

The cash budget receives input from the budgets established previously as well as the capital expenditures budget and the budgeted income statement. In turn, the cash budget provides inputs to the budgeted balance sheet and the budgeted statement of cash flows. The budgeted balance sheet also receives input from the budgeted income statement, and the capital expenditures budget and supplies input to the budgeted income statement. We illustrate these interrelationships in the following example.

Exhibit 22-5 **Budgets and Data Flows in Fezzari's Master Budget**

YOUR TURN! 22.3

The solution is on page 1065.

Place the following budgets in the order that they would normally be prepared:

1. Direct materials budget
2. Production budget
3. Manufacturing overhead budget
4. Capital expenditures budget
5. Cash budget
6. Direct labor budget
7. Sales budget

ILLUSTRATION OF A MASTER BUDGET AND ITS COMPONENTS

Sales Budget

LO4 **Prepare** individual budgets for a manufacturing and a service company, including the cash budget.

The **sales budget** provides the basis for all subsequent budgets. Anticipated unit sales volume is based on the **sales forecast**. The sales forecast is the sales department's best estimate of what sales will be for the company and the industry in which it operates. Factors that are evaluated in preparing the sales forecast include prior company sales levels, future pricing policies, market research studies, general economic conditions, specific economic indicators, advertising and promotion plans, and anticipated activities of the competition. Overestimating sales volume can lead to large unwanted inventories, which in turn result in extra storage costs and possibly sales price reductions when liquidating the excess inventory. Underestimating sales can lead to loss of sales revenue and customer ill will stemming from unfilled orders.

Assume that Fezzari managers are preparing their budget for the upcoming fiscal year. As we have discussed in earlier chapters, Fezzari sells two types of bikes, road and mountain, with several different models of each type. For purposes of this illustration, we will assume that the budget is prepared at the bike-type level, although in reality the budget would be prepared at the model level. Further, assume that Fezzari's management anticipates a 20% growth in sales in the next year.

The estimated unit sales volume of each product is multiplied by planned average unit sales prices to estimate total sales revenue. We present an example of a sales budget in **Exhibit 22-6**. To simplify the presentation of the cash budget, assume all Fezzari's sales are on a cash basis; therefore, Fezzari carries no accounts receivable balances. This assumption is consistent with a bike manufacturer selling customized bikes to customers via e-commerce. We will demonstrate a sales budget for a service firm with credit sales later in the chapter.

Exhibit 22-6	Sales Budget Illustration

FEZZARI PERFORMANCE BICYCLES
Sales Budget
For the Year Ended December 31, 2019

> The sales budget forms the basis of all other budgets, so it is usually created first.

	Forecast Unit Sales Volume	Average Unit Sales Price	Budgeted Total Sales
Road bicycles.............	2,160	$1,250	$2,700,000
Mountain bicycles..........	3,240	$1,000	3,240,000
Total bicycles	5,400		$5,940,000
Other bicycle accessories.....			297,000
Total sales revenue			$6,237,000

Production Budget

The **production budget** reflects the quantity of each product to be produced during the budget period. Scheduled production should specifically provide for anticipated sales and desired ending inventories and, of course, consider the beginning inventories of each product. Assume that Fezzari wants to increase its inventory of road bikes from 8 to 12 units and its inventory of mountain bikes from 14 to 18 units. Fezzari's production budget appears in **Exhibit 22-7**. Note that the desired change in inventory of each product is accomplished by scheduling the appropriate production volumes. Because bicycle accessories are not manufactured by Fezzari, but simply purchased from vendors for resale, they are not included in the production budget.

Hint: Companies that do not use the just-in-time inventory method often determine required inventory levels based on a percentage of unit sales.

Like Fezzari, many manufacturing companies use the just-in-time approach for finished goods inventory to reduce their inventory carrying costs. When the **just-in-time inventory** approach is used, finished goods are not produced until they are needed for shipment to customers. As a result, the planned ending inventory of finished goods is zero or nearly zero.

Exhibit 22-7	Production Budget Illustration

FEZZARI PERFORMANCE BICYCLES
Production Budget
For the Year Ended December 31, 2019

	Units of Finished Product	
	Road Bikes	Mountain Bikes
Forecast unit sales	2,160	3,240
Desired ending finished goods inventories	12	18
Quantities to be available	2,172	3,258
Less: Beginning finished goods inventories	8	14
Total production to be scheduled	2,164	3,244

> The production budget reflects the quantity of each product to be produced during the budget period.

> The forecasted unit sales numbers come from the sales budget (Exhibit 22-6).

Hint: Running out of an item of inventory not only results in the loss of a current sale but could also cause the loss of future sales due to negative publicity.

This approach is practical only for companies that can forecast their sales very accurately, that do not have highly seasonal demand, and that have highly reliable suppliers of the materials and components needed to manufacture the finished goods. Many companies prefer to maintain a **safety stock** of finished goods inventory so they minimize the risk of running out of stock. Safety stock is defined as a quantity of inventory maintained to supply unexpected demand or to provide stock when manufacturing is slowed through delays in receipt of materials and components from suppliers.

Direct Materials Budget

The quantities of materials to be purchased to meet scheduled production and desired ending materials inventory requirements are presented in the **direct materials budget**. Any beginning materials inventory must be considered in estimating purchases for the budget period. Because Fezzari assembles its bikes only after receiving a customer order, it does not maintain a large inventory of direct materials. The quantities to be acquired are multiplied by the anticipated unit prices to calculate the total dollar amounts of materials purchases. In the direct materials budget illustrated in **Exhibit 22-8**, we assume that Fezzari uses only two direct materials, a frame and a build kit containing all of the other components, in producing road and mountain bikes. Further, Fezzari targets to have sufficient frames and build kits in ending inventory for 6 road bikes and 10 mountain bikes.

The just-in-time inventory philosophy may also apply to the materials inventory of manufacturing firms. Under this philosophy, materials and components needed to manufacture finished products would not be received from the suppliers until immediately before they are needed for manufacturing. As a result, the materials inventory would be zero or nearly zero. Many firms prefer to carry safety stocks of materials and components to ensure that the manufacturing facility is not slowed or stopped by a supplier missing a scheduled delivery.

The direct materials budget in **Exhibit 22-8** shows the total purchases that are budgeted for the year. However, because Fezzari purchases these materials on credit from its suppliers, the dollar amount of purchases may not equal the cash that will be expended for materials during the year. Thus, in preparing the cash budget, an adjustment must be made for the change in the accounts payable balance during the year. **Exhibit 22-8** illustrates how the cash expended for direct materials might be calculated assuming that the balance in accounts payable was expected to increase from $50,000 to $75,000.

The increase in the accounts payable balance of $25,000 over the year means that Fezzari will spend $25,000 less than the total materials purchases in cash.

Exhibit 22-8 **Direct Materials Budget Illustration**

The direct materials budget presents the quantities of materials to be purchased to meet scheduled production and desired ending materials inventory requirements.

FEZZARI PERFORMANCE BICYCLES
Direct Materials Budget
For the Year Ended December 31, 2019

	Frame	Build Kit	Total
Direct materials required:			
Road bicycles	2,164	2,164	
Desired ending materials inventory	6	6	
Total units of materials to be available	2,170	2,170	
Less: Beginning materials inventory	8	8	
Total units of materials to be purchased	2,162	2,162	
Average unit purchase price	$ 325	$ 275	
Total road bike materials purchases	$ 702,650	$ 594,550	$1,297,200
Direct materials required:			
Mountain bicycles	3,244	3,244	
Desired ending materials inventory	10	10	
Total units of materials to be available	3,254	3,254	
Less: Beginning materials inventory	14	14	
Total units of materials to be purchased	3,240	3,240	
Average unit purchase price	$ 350	$ 290	
Total mountain bike materials purchases	$1,134,000	$ 939,600	$2,073,600
Total materials purchases	$1,836,650	$1,534,150	$3,370,800
Add: Beginning accounts payable balance			50,000
Less: Ending accounts payable balance			(75,000)
Cash budgeted for materials purchases			$3,345,800

The forecasted unit production numbers come from the production budget (Exhibit 22-7).

Direct Labor Budget

The **direct labor budget** presents the number of direct labor hours necessary for the production volume planned for the budget period. These hours are multiplied by the applicable hourly labor rates to determine the total dollar amounts of direct labor costs to be budgeted. In the direct labor budget for Fezzari in **Exhibit 22-9**, we have assumed that both road and mountain bikes require the following average hours in the assembly and quality control and packaging departments:

	Assembly Hours	Quality Control and Packaging Hours
Road bikes	5.5	2.0
Mountain bikes	7.0	2.0

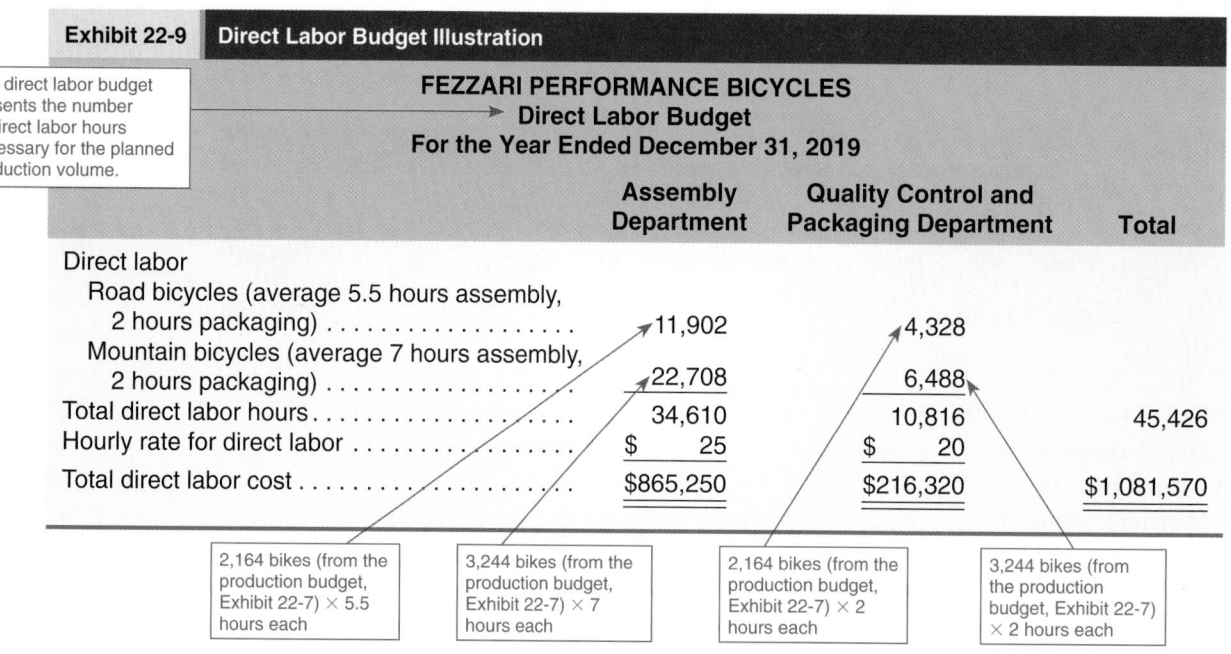

| Exhibit 22-9 | Direct Labor Budget Illustration |

The direct labor budget presents the number of direct labor hours necessary for the planned production volume.

FEZZARI PERFORMANCE BICYCLES
Direct Labor Budget
For the Year Ended December 31, 2019

	Assembly Department	Quality Control and Packaging Department	Total
Direct labor			
Road bicycles (average 5.5 hours assembly, 2 hours packaging)	11,902	4,328	
Mountain bicycles (average 7 hours assembly, 2 hours packaging)	22,708	6,488	
Total direct labor hours	34,610	10,816	45,426
Hourly rate for direct labor	$ 25	$ 20	
Total direct labor cost	$865,250	$216,320	$1,081,570

2,164 bikes (from the production budget, Exhibit 22-7) × 5.5 hours each

3,244 bikes (from the production budget, Exhibit 22-7) × 7 hours each

2,164 bikes (from the production budget, Exhibit 22-7) × 2 hours each

3,244 bikes (from the production budget, Exhibit 22-7) × 2 hours each

Manufacturing Overhead Budget

Hint: Manufacturing overhead is any cost incurred within the factory that is not direct in nature. Hence, factory costs – direct costs = indirect costs.

Recall from earlier chapters that manufacturing overhead comprises all manufacturing costs that are not direct materials or direct labor. Examples of manufacturing overhead are indirect materials, indirect labor, supervisory salaries, utilities, depreciation, maintenance, property taxes, and insurance. Because of the variety of cost factors, manufacturing overhead includes both variable and fixed cost elements.

The **manufacturing overhead budget** for Fezzari's Assembly and Packaging departments is shown in **Exhibit 22-10**. Note that the format separates variable and fixed overhead cost elements and presents budgeted overhead costs for the 45,426 direct labor hours expected to be incurred.

Management would determine the budgeted variable costs based on purchase agreements with its vendors (indirect materials), labor agreements with its employees (indirect labor), and contracted rates for other services (utilities). Management would determine the budgeted fixed costs based on lease agreements, insurance contracts, local government tax notices, and current levels of equipment. These amounts would not be expected to vary from year to year. Usually, lease agreements are multiyear agreements with fixed rates for each year of the agreement and insurance coverage is adjusted only as manufacturing facilities are expanded. To simplify the presentation of the cash budget, assume that all overhead expenses, except depreciation, are paid in the month they are incurred.

As we discussed in Chapter 16, the predetermined overhead rate is determined by dividing the total budgeted manufacturing overhead by the budgeted activity level, or direct labor hours in this example. For the year ended December 31, 2019, the total cost formula for overhead at the planned operating volume of 45,426 direct labor hours (DLH) would be as follows:

$$\text{Total manufacturing overhead cost} = \$1.66 \times \text{DLH} + \$225,000$$

Exhibit 22-10	Manufacturing Overhead Budget Illustration

FEZZARI PERFORMANCE BICYCLES
Overhead Budget
For the Year Ended December 31, 2019

The manufacturing overhead budget includes all production costs that are not direct materials and direct labor.

	Variable Cost per Direct Labor Hour	Total Costs at 45,426 Direct Labor Hours
Variable manufacturing costs		
Indirect materials.	$0.07	$ 3,180
Indirect labor	0.62	28,164
Factory utilities	0.68	30,890
Other.	0.29	13,174
Total variable manufacturing overhead	$1.66	$ 75,408
Fixed manufacturing costs		
Lease expense		$100,000
Insurance		68,000
Property taxes.		12,000
Depreciation		45,000
Total fixed manufacturing overhead		$225,000
Total manufacturing overhead		$300,408
Less: Depreciation		(45,000)
Cash budgeted for manufacturing overhead		$255,408
Direct labor hours.		45,426
Budgeted predetermined manufacturing overhead rate (rounded)		$ 6.61

Note that variable and fixed overhead elements are presented separately.

Noncash expenses are deducted to determine cash expenditures for the cash budget.

The direct labor hours come from the direct labor budget, Exhibit 22-9.

Selling and Administrative Expense Budget

The **selling and administrative expense budget** will consist of variable and fixed expenses. The variable selling expenses will typically vary with dollars of sales. To simplify the presentation of the cash budget, assume that selling and administrative expenses, except depreciation, are paid in the month incurred. **Exhibit 22-11** presents Fezzari's selling and administrative expense budget.

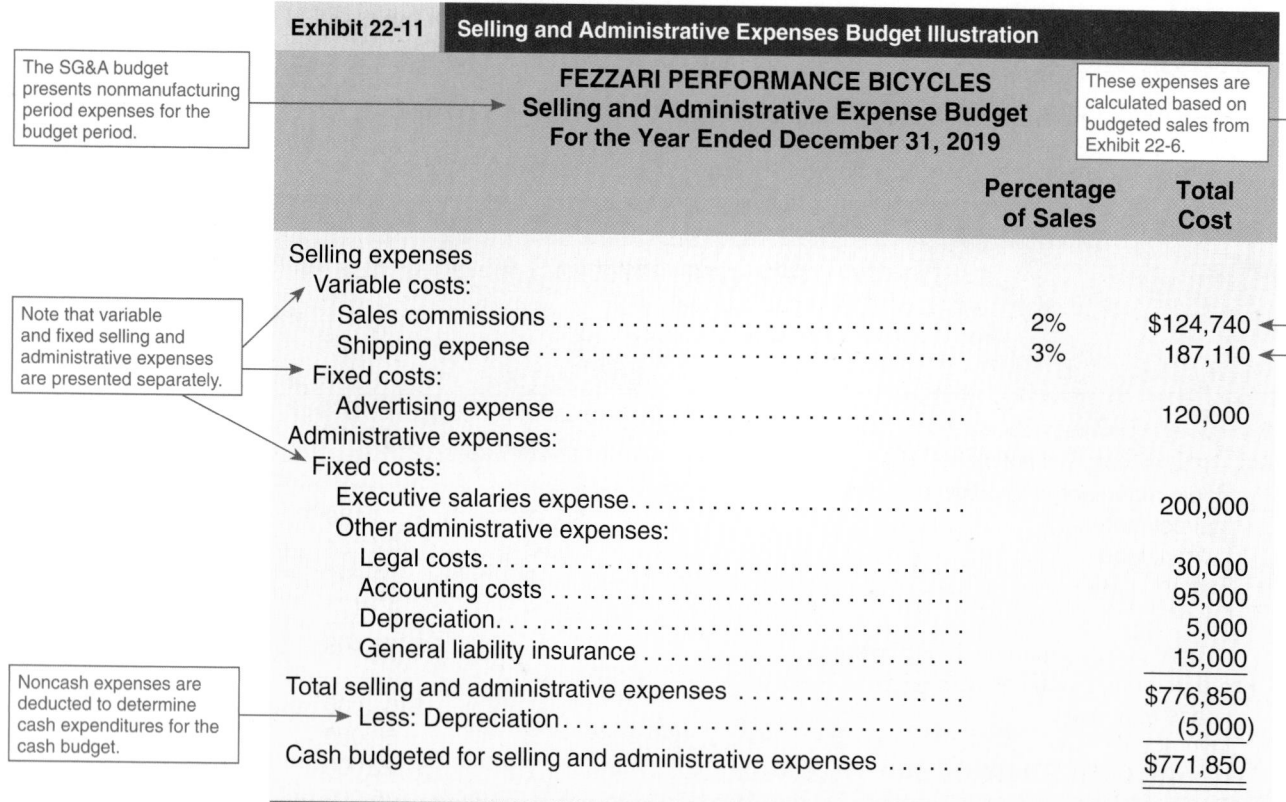

The SG&A budget presents nonmanufacturing period expenses for the budget period.

These expenses are calculated based on budgeted sales from Exhibit 22-6.

Note that variable and fixed selling and administrative expenses are presented separately.

Noncash expenses are deducted to determine cash expenditures for the cash budget.

Exhibit 22-11 **Selling and Administrative Expenses Budget Illustration**

FEZZARI PERFORMANCE BICYCLES
Selling and Administrative Expense Budget
For the Year Ended December 31, 2019

	Percentage of Sales	Total Cost
Selling expenses		
Variable costs:		
Sales commissions	2%	$124,740
Shipping expense	3%	187,110
Fixed costs:		
Advertising expense		120,000
Administrative expenses:		
Fixed costs:		
Executive salaries expense		200,000
Other administrative expenses:		
Legal costs		30,000
Accounting costs		95,000
Depreciation		5,000
General liability insurance		15,000
Total selling and administrative expenses		$776,850
Less: Depreciation		(5,000)
Cash budgeted for selling and administrative expenses		$771,850

Capital Expenditures Budget

Expenditures for property, plant, and equipment are among a firm's most important transactions. The type of analysis that is undertaken to determine whether a particular item should be acquired is known as capital budgeting and is discussed in detail in Chapter 25. The **capital expenditures budget** lists long-term assets that are planned to be acquired over a multiyear period. **Exhibit 22-12** presents an illustration for Fezzari. We will assume that it is abstracted from the complete capital expenditures budget.

Exhibit 22-12 **Capital Expenditures Budget Illustration**

FEZZARI PERFORMANCE BICYCLES
Capital Expenditures Budget
For the Year Ended December 31, 2019

The capital expenditures budget lists investments in assets that are expected to be used over a multiyear period.

	1st Quarter	2nd Quarter	3rd Quarter	4th Quarter	Total
Assembly equipment	$25,000		$25,000		$50,000
Packaging equipment		$10,000			$10,000
Administrative computers				$5,000	$ 5,000
Total	$25,000	$10,000	$25,000	$5,000	$65,000

The capital expenditures budget has an impact on many other budgets. The plant and equipment available at any point in time determine the productive capacity of the firm. Further, depreciation expense in both the overhead budgets and the selling and administrative expense budget is affected by the capital expenditures budget, as are the cash expenditures in the cash budget and the property, plant, and equipment assets on the balance sheet.

Cash Budget

The **cash budget** presents the projected cash flows during the budget period. The budgeted cash flows are separated into two groups, *cash receipts* (inflows of cash) and *cash disbursements* (outflows of cash). *Cash receipts* include cash sales, collections of accounts receivable, sale of investments and unneeded assets, and proceeds from borrowings and stock sales. *Cash disbursements* include payments for manufacturing costs (direct materials, direct labor, and manufacturing overhead), payments for selling and administrative expenses, interest expense, capital expenditures (land, buildings, and equipment), income tax payments, and cash dividends.

Financing Cash Flows	**ACCOUNTING IN PRACTICE**

In practice, the cash budget often includes a separate section for financing activities. This section would provide details of borrowings and repayments, including interest payments.

Much of the information needed to prepare the cash budget is available in the previously prepared budgets. However, because of characteristic time lags between transactions and their related effects on cash, cash budgeting often requires the analysis of other data as well. For example, sales precede collections from customers, purchases precede payments on account, depreciation is not a cash outflow, and prepayments call for cash outlays before the related expenses are recognized. **Exhibit 22-13** shows the cash budget for Fezzari. For simplicity, the cash budget assumes that all sales are made in cash and that all expenses, with the exception of depreciation and direct materials, are paid in cash. We demonstrate the determination of cash from sales when sales are made on account in the following section.

Exhibit 22-13	**Cash Budget Illustration**

FEZZARI PERFORMANCE BICYCLES
Cash Budget
For the Year Ended December 31, 2019

> The cash budget presents the projected cash inflows and outflows for the budget period.

	Amount	Source
Cash receipts:		
Sales.	$6,237,000	Exhibit 22-6
Cash disbursements:		
Direct materials.	(3,345,800)	Exhibit 22-8
Direct labor	(1,081,570)	Exhibit 22-9
Manufacturing overhead	(255,408)	Exhibit 22-10 (excluding depreciation)
Selling and administrative costs . . .	(771,850)	Exhibit 22-11
Capital expenditures	(65,000)	Exhibit 22-12
Interest	(5,000)	Financing budget (not shown)
Income taxes.	(176,395)	Exhibit 22-16
Net change in cash.	$ 535,977	
Beginning cash.	550,905	
Ending cash	$1,086,882	

Illustration of a Service Firm's Budgets

Assume that Environmental Business Consultants (EBC) has collected the following actual data for February and March 2019 and developed the following forecasted data for the quarter ended June 30, 2019:

SERVICE AND MERCHANDISING

1. Actual sales for February and March 2019 were the following:

	Actual Credit Sales
February	$310,000
March	290,000

2. Forecast sales for the quarter ended June 30, 2019, are as follows:

	Forecast Credit Sales
April	$400,000
May	350,000
June	380,000

3. The collection of cash from credit sales during the quarter ended June 30, 2019, will follow the same pattern as the previous quarter:

   a. In the month of sale, 10% is collected.

   b. In the month following sale, 50% is collected.

   c. In the second month following sale, 38% is collected. The remaining 2% of accounts receivable are written off as uncollectible.

   Based on the information in items 1–3, the cash collections can be computed as follows:

	A	B	C	D	E
1		Cash Collections from Customers			
	Month of Credit Sale	April	May	June	Quarter Total
2	February	$117,800			
3	March	145,000	$110,200		
4	April	40,000	200,000	$152,000	
5	May		35,000	175,000	
6	June			38,000	
7	Month total	$302,800	$345,200	$365,000	$1,013,000

4. Forecast cash disbursements for the quarter ended June 30, 2019, are as follows:

	A	B	C	D
1		Forecast Cash Disbursements		
		April	May	June
2	Labor	$195,000	$195,000	$195,000
3	Office lease	16,875	16,875	16,875
4	Office supplies	2,000	5,000	3,000
5	Selling and administrative expenses	31,000	32,000	62,000
6	Interest expense (on existing debt)	417	417	417
7	Cash distributions to owners	—	—	100,000

The increase in the selling and administrative expense in June is due to the anticipated payment of employee midyear bonuses.

5. EBC has a policy of maintaining a cash balance of $500,000. All borrowings and repayments are made at the end of the month and the short-term loan carries an annual interest rate of 6%.

The cash budget for EBC is shown in **Exhibit 22-14**. A three-column format is used so the cash flow of each month of the quarter can be analyzed separately. The starting point in preparing this cash budget is a beginning cash balance for April of $400,000. The cash receipts and cash disbursements for April are then added to the budget. Note that interest is assumed to be paid in the period in which it is incurred. The preliminary ending cash balance of $457,508 is then calculated.

Remember that EBC has a policy of maintaining a cash balance of $500,000. As shown in **Exhibit 22-14**, EBC starts and ends the month of April with a cash balance below this target. To meet its target by the end of April, EBC could budget to borrow $42,492 ($500,000 – $457,508) on a short-term basis. In May, EBC would have sufficient cash to repay this short-term borrowing.

The budgeted ending cash balance for April becomes the budgeted beginning cash balance for May. The procedure described earlier is then repeated for May.

Exhibit 22-14	Service Firm Cash Budget Illustration		

ENVIRONMENTAL BUSINESS CONSULTANTS
Cash Budget
For the Quarter Ended June 30, 2019

	April	May	June
Beginning cash balance	$400,000	$500,000	$553,204
Cash receipts:			
Collections from customers	302,800	345,200	365,000
Cash available	$702,800	$845,200	$918,204
Cash disbursements:			
Labor	$195,000	$195,000	$195,000
Office lease	16,875	16,875	16,875
Office supplies	2,000	5,000	3,000
Selling and administrative costs	31,000	32,000	62,000
Interest (on existing debt)	417	629	417
Cash distributions to owners	—	—	100,000
Total disbursements	$245,292	$249,504	$377,292
Preliminary ending cash balance	$457,508	$595,696	$540,912
Target cash balance	$500,000	$500,000	$500,000
Required short-term borrowing (repayment)	42,492	(42,492)	—
Final ending cash balance	$500,000	$553,204	$540,912

Interest on existing debt	$417
Interest on short-term borrowing	212 [$42,492 × (6.0%/12)]
Total interest	$629

The budgeted ending cash balance for May then becomes the budgeted beginning cash balance for June and the process is repeated again. One additional cash disbursement appears in June: the $100,000 quarterly cash distribution to the owners.

Zinc Company's management team is preparing a cash budget for the coming quarter. They have prepared the following budgeted information for the first quarter:

	January	February	March
Revenue..............	$500,000	$600,000	$700,000
Inventory purchases.......	400,000	500,000	550,000
Other expenses	200,000	225,000	225,000

The company expects to collect 60% of its monthly sales in the month of sale and 40% in the following month. Seventy percent of inventory purchases are paid in the month of purchase and the other 30% in the following month. All payments for other expenses are made in the month incurred.
Zinc forecasts the following account balances at the beginning of the quarter:

Cash.....................................	$200,000
Accounts receivable.........................	200,000
Accounts payable (Inventory)....................	150,000

Given the above information, what is the projected change in cash during the coming quarter?

Budgeted Financial Statements

Budgeted Income Statement

LO5 Prepare budgeted financial statements.

The development of the master budget is completed with the preparation of the budgeted financial statements: the budgeted income statement, the budgeted balance sheet, and the budgeted statement of cash flows. The **budgeted income statement** is usually prepared first. In addition to the budgets that were previously prepared, supplemental schedules and worksheets may be needed to prepare the budgeted income statement. Returning to the Fezzari example, one of these supplementary schedules is the schedule of estimated product cost per unit, which is presented in **Exhibit 22-15**. We then use the estimated cost per unit to calculate our budgeted cost of goods sold, which is included in our budgeted income statement (**Exhibit 22-16**).

Exhibit 22-15	**Estimated Product Cost per Unit Illustration**

FEZZARI PERFORMANCE BICYCLES
Estimated Product Cost per Unit
For the Year Ended December 31, 2019

		Cost			
	Quantity	Road Bicycle	Mountain Bicycle	Road Bicycle	Mountain Bicycle
Direct materials:					
Frame	1.0	× $325.00	$350.00	= $325.00	$350.00
Build kit	1.0	× 275.00	290.00	= 275.00	290.00
	Cost per unit	**Quantity**			
Direct labor:					
Assembly	$ 25.00	× 5.5	7.0	= 137.50	175.00
QC and packaging ..	$ 20.00	× 2.0	2.0	= 40.00	40.00
Manufacturing overhead:					
Combined	$ 6.61	× 7.5	9.0	= 49.58	59.49
Product cost per unit. . .				$827.08	$914.49

See Exhibit 22-8

See Exhibit 22-10

See Exhibit 22-9

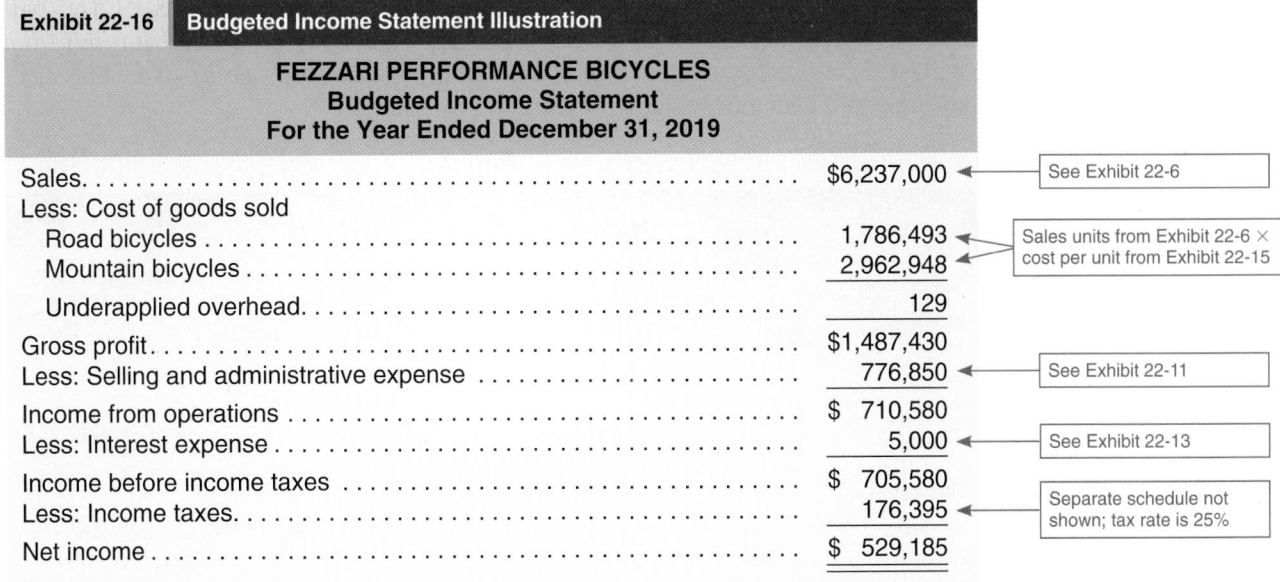

Exhibit 22-16	Budgeted Income Statement Illustration

FEZZARI PERFORMANCE BICYCLES
Budgeted Income Statement
For the Year Ended December 31, 2019

Sales.	$6,237,000	See Exhibit 22-6
Less: Cost of goods sold		
Road bicycles	1,786,493	Sales units from Exhibit 22-6 × cost per unit from Exhibit 22-15
Mountain bicycles	2,962,948	
Underapplied overhead.	129	
Gross profit.	$1,487,430	
Less: Selling and administrative expense	776,850	See Exhibit 22-11
Income from operations	$ 710,580	
Less: Interest expense	5,000	See Exhibit 22-13
Income before income taxes	$ 705,580	
Less: Income taxes.	176,395	Separate schedule not shown; tax rate is 25%
Net income	$ 529,185	

Budgeted Balance Sheet

The preparation of the **budgeted balance sheet** usually follows the preparation of the budgeted income statement. It is important to note that the budgeted balance sheet is based on the ending balance sheet from the prior year adjusted for budgeted changes. **Exhibit 22-17** presents Fezzari's beginning balance sheet as of December 31, 2018.

Exhibit 22-17	Actual Balance Sheet

FEZZARI PERFORMANCE BICYCLES
Balance Sheet
As of December 31, 2018

Assets

Current assets:		
Cash.		$550,905
Inventories		33,178
Total current assets		$584,083
Plant assets:		
Equipment	$135,000	
Less: Accumulated depreciation.	(45,000)	90,000
Total assets		$674,083

Liabilities

Current liabilities:		
Accounts payable		50,000
Long-term liabilities:		
Long-term borrowing.		83,333
Total liabilities		$133,333

Stockholders' Equity

Common stock ($1 par value; 10,000 shares authorized and issued) . . .	$10,000	
Paid-in capital—excess of par—common stock	90,000	
Total paid-in capital.		$100,000
Retained earnings		440,750
Total stockholders' equity		$540,750
Total liabilities and stockholders' equity		$674,083

Exhibit 22-18 presents the budgeted balance sheet for December 31, 2019. This balance sheet reflects the changes in the asset, liability, and equity accounts that result from the budgeted activity for the year. For 2019, Fezzari management has assumed that there will be no additional borrowings or stock sales.

Exhibit 22-18	Budgeted Balance Sheet Illustration

FEZZARI PERFORMANCE BICYCLES
Budgeted Balance Sheet
As of December 31, 2019

Assets

Current assets:			
Cash		$1,086,882	a
Inventories			
Direct materials	$ 10,000		b
Finished goods	26,387	36,387	c
Total current assets		$1,123,269	
Plant assets:			
Equipment	$200,000		d
Less: Accumulated depreciation	(95,000)	105,000	e
Total assets		$1,228,269	

Liabilities

Current liabilities:			
Accounts payable		75,000	
Long-term liabilities:			
Long-term borrowing		83,333	f
Total liabilities		$ 158,333	

Stockholders' Equity

Common stock ($1 par value; 10,000 shares authorized and issued)	$ 10,000		f
Paid-in capital—excess of par—common stock	90,000		f
Total paid-in capital		$ 100,000	
Retained earnings		969,936	g
Total stockholders' equity		$1,069,936	
Total liabilities and stockholders' equity		$1,228,269	

[a] Beginning cash balance from Exhibit 22-17 plus net cash increase from Exhibit 22-13.

[b] (6 road bike units × [$325 + $275]) + (10 mountain bike units × [$350 + $290]) = $10,000

[c] (12 road bike units × $827.08) + (18 mountain bike units × $914.49) = $26,387. Difference due to rounding.

[d] Beginning equipment ($135,000) plus budgeted capital purchases from Exhibit 22-12 ($65,000).

[e] Beginning accumulated depreciation ($45,000) plus current year depreciation from Exhibit 22-10 ($45,000) and Exhibit 22-11($5,000).

[f] No change.

[g] Beginning retained earnings ($440,750) plus net income from Exhibit 22-16 ($529,185). Difference due to rounding.

Budgeted Statement of Cash Flows

The **budgeted statement of cash flows** follows directly from the cash budget. The dollar amounts will be the same, but the grouping and sequence will usually be different. **Exhibit 22-19** presents Fezzari's budgeted statement of cash flows. Note that this statement groups the cash flows into three sections: cash flows from operating activities, cash flows from investing activities, and cash flows from financing activities.

Exhibit 22-19	Budgeted Statement of Cash Flows Illustration

FEZZARI PERFORMANCE BICYCLES
Budgeted Statement of Cash Flows—Direct Method
For the Period Ended December 31, 2019

Cash flows from operating activities

Cash receipts from customers	$6,237,000	
Cash payments for inventory	(4,682,778)	
Cash paid for selling and administrative expenses	(771,850)	
Cash paid for interest	(5,000)	
Income tax payment	(176,395)	
Net cash provided by operating activities		$ 600,977

Cash flows from investing activities

Capital expenditures.	(65,000)	
Net cash used by investing activities		(65,000)

Cash flows from financing activities

Net cash provided by financing activities		—
Net increase (decrease) in cash.		$ 535,977
Beginning cash balance		550,905
Ending cash balance		$1,086,882

YOUR TURN! 22.5

The solution is on page 1065.

What is the proper order for the preparation of the budgeted financial statements?

a. Budgeted income statement, budgeted balance sheet, budgeted statement of cash flows

b. Budgeted statement of cash flows, budgeted balance sheet, budgeted income statement

c. Budgeted balance sheet, budgeted income statement, budgeted statement of cash flows

d. Budgeted cost of goods sold statement, budgeted income statement, budgeted statement of cash flows

SERVICES INDUSTRY IN FOCUS

SERVICE AND MERCHANDISING

Refer to the Environmental Business Consultants (EBC) illustration on page 1037 in the chapter. Assume that local governments (EBC's target market) are experiencing a sharp reduction in the collection of tax revenues due to a recession in the general economy. EBC anticipates that this will impact the timeliness of payments made by its clients *beginning in April* as shown below:

a. In the month of sale, 10% is collected.

b. In the month following sale, 30% is collected.

c. In the second month following sale, 30% is collected.

d. In the third month following sale, 20% is collected. The remaining 10% of accounts receivable will be written off as uncollectible.

Note that payments related to the February and March sales that have yet to be collected will be impacted by the recession also. For example, 10% of the February sales were collected in February, 50% were collected in March, but only 30% will be collected in April (not 38%), and the remaining 10% will be written off. Further, 10% of the March sales were collected in March, but only 30% will be collected in April (not 50%), 30% will be collected in May, and 20% will be collected in June. Assume that all other forecasted data remain the same.

Assume that because of the recession, EBC has temporarily eliminated its policy of maintaining a cash balance of $500,000.

Required

1. Recompute the forecasted cash collections for the quarter ended June 30, 2019.
2. Prepare a new cash budget reflecting these new cash collections.

Solution

1.

Month of Credit Sale	Cash Collections from Customers			
	April	May	June	Quarter Total
February...............	$ 93,000			
March	87,000	$ 87,000	$ 58,000	
April	40,000	120,000	120,000	
May....................		35,000	105,000	
June			38,000	
Month total	$220,000	$242,000	$321,000	$783,000

2.

ENVIRONMENTAL BUSINESS CONSULTANTS
Cash Budget
For the Quarter Ended June 30, 2019

	April	May	June
Beginning cash balance	$400,000	$374,708	$367,416
Cash receipts			
Collections from customers.	220,000	242,000	321,000
Cash available	$620,000	$616,708	$688,416
Cash disbursements			
Labor......................................	$195,000	$195,000	$195,000
Office lease...........................	16,875	16,875	16,875
Office supplies	2,000	5,000	3,000
Selling and administrative expenses.........	31,000	32,000	62,000
Interest expense (on existing debt)..........	417	417	417
Cash distributions to owners...............	—	—	100,000
Total disbursements	$245,292	$249,292	$377,292
Ending cash balance	$374,708	$367,416	$311,124

COMPREHENSIVE PROBLEM

The sales department of Jackson Manufacturing, Inc. has completed the following sales forecast for the months of January through March 20X5 for its only two products: 40,000 units of X1 to be sold at $110 each and 20,000 units of X2 to be sold at $85 each. The desired unit inventories at March 31, 20X5, are 10% of the next quarter's unit sales forecast, which are 50,000 units of X1 and 25,000 units of X2. The January 1, 20X5, unit inventories were 7,000 units of X1 and 1,500 units of X2.

Each unit of X1 requires 4 pounds of material R and 2 pounds of material S for its manufacture; X2 requires 2 pounds of R and 3 pounds of S. The purchase cost of R is $10 per pound and of S is $5 per pound. Materials on hand at January 1, 20X5, were 20,000 pounds of R and 8,000 pounds of S. Desired inventories at March 31, 20X5, are 15,000 pounds of R and 6,000 pounds of S.

Each unit of X1 requires 0.5 hours of direct labor in the factory; each unit of X2 requires 1.0 hour of direct labor. The average hourly rate for direct labor is $12 per hour. Estimated manufacturing overhead cost is $8 per direct labor hour plus $100,000 per month. Selling and administrative expenses are estimated to be 10% of sales revenue plus $200,000 per month.

Cash sales in December 20X4 were $250,000 and credit sales were $2,000,000. Cash sales for the first quarter are estimated to be $200,000 per month. It is forecast that 40% of the credit sales for the quarter ended March 31, 20X5, will occur in January, 30% in February, and 30% in March. Of credit sales (December through March), 40% will be collected as cash in the month of sale and 50% will be collected in the following month. The remainder will be uncollectible.

The January 1, 20X5, cash balance was $60,000. The minimum acceptable cash balance at the end of each month is $50,000. Short-term borrowings are made in multiples of $10,000, with interest charged at the rate of 1% per month. The first interest payment is made the month following the borrowing. Cash disbursements (excluding interest on short-term borrowings) are estimated as follows:

	January	February	March
Manufacturing costs	$1,200,000	$1,100,000	$1,000,000
Selling and administrative expenses	$ 380,000	$ 400,000	$ 340,000
Interest expense	$ 100,000	$ 100,000	$ 100,000
Income tax payment	—	—	200,000
Capital expenditures	100,000	340,000	60,000
Cash dividends	400,000	—	—

Required

a. Prepare the sales budget for the quarter ended March 31, 20X5.
b. Prepare the production budget for the quarter ended March 31, 20X5.
c. Prepare the direct materials budget for the quarter ended March 31, 20X5.
d. Prepare the direct labor budget for the quarter ended March 31, 20X5.
e. Prepare the overhead budget for the quarter ended March 31, 20X5.
f. Prepare a schedule of estimated product cost per unit for the quarter ended March 31, 20X5.
g. Prepare a schedule of cash collected from customers for the quarter ended March 31, 20X5.
h. Prepare the cash budget for the quarter ended March 31, 20X5.

SOLUTION TO COMPREHENSIVE PROBLEM

a.

JACKSON MANUFACTURING, INC.
Sales Budget
For the Quarter Ended March 31, 20X5

Product	Forecasted Unit Sales Volume	Planned Unit Sales Price	Budgeted Total Sales
X1	40,000	$110.00	$4,400,000
X2	20,000	$ 85.00	1,700,000
Total sales revenue			$6,100,000

b.

JACKSON MANUFACTURING, INC.
Production Budget
For the Quarter Ended March 31, 20X5

	Units of Finished Product	
	X1	X2
Forecast unit sales	40,000	20,000
Desired ending inventories:		
10% × 50,000	5,000	
10% × 25,000		2,500
Quantities to be available	45,000	22,500
Less: Beginning inventories	7,000	1,500
Total production to be scheduled	38,000	21,000

c.

JACKSON MANUFACTURING, INC.
Direct Material Budget
For the Quarter Ended March 31, 20X5

	Material R	Material S
Direct materials required:		
Product X1:.....................................38,000 × 4	152,000	
....38,000 × 2		76,000
Product X2:.....................................21,000 × 2	42,000	
....21,000 × 3		63,000
Desired ending materials inventories..............................	15,000	6,000
Total pounds of materials to be available.........................	209,000	145,000
Less: Beginning materials inventories	20,000	8,000
Total pounds of materials to be purchased.........................	189,000	137,000
Unit purchase price...	$ 10.00	$ 5.00
Total materials purchases......................................	$1,890,000	$685,000

d.

JACKSON MANUFACTURING, INC.
Direct Labor Budget
For the Quarter Ended March 31, 20X5

Direct labor hours required for production:	
Product X1: 38,000 × 0.5 hours	19,000
Product X2: 21,000 × 1.0 hours	21,000
Total direct labor hours required	40,000
Hourly rate for direct labor	$ 12.00
Total direct labor cost	$480,000

e.

JACKSON MANUFACTURING, INC.
Overhead Budget
For the Quarter Ended March 31, 20X5

Total direct labor hours..	40,000
Variable manufacturing overhead rate	$ 8.00
Variable manufacturing overhead cost...	$320,000
Fixed manufacturing overhead cost ($100,000 × 3 months).........................	$300,000
Total manufacturing overhead cost	$620,000

f.

JACKSON MANUFACTURING, INC.
Schedule of Estimated Product Cost Per Unit
For the Quarter Ended March 31, 20X5

	Quantity				
	Product X1	Product X2	Cost	Product X1	Product X2
Direct materials:					
Material R...................	4	2	$10.00	$40.00	$20.00
Material S...................	2	3	$ 5.00	$10.00	$15.00
Direct labor..................	0.5	1	$12.00	$ 6.00	$12.00
Manufacturing overhead.........	0.5	1	$15.50*	$ 7.75	$15.50
Product cost per unit............				$63.75	$62.50

*$620,000/40,000 = $15.50 per direct labor hour

g.

JACKSON MANUFACTURING, INC.
Schedule of Cash Collected From Customers
For the Quarter Ended March 31, 20X5

	January	February	March
Cash sales	$ 200,000	$ 200,000	$ 200,000
Credit sales			
December: . . . . $2,000,000 × 50%	1,000,000		
January: . . . . $2,200,000* × 40%	880,000		
. . . . $2,200,000* × 50%		1,100,000	
February:. . . . .$1,650,000** × 40%		660,000	
. . . .$1,650,000** × 50%			825,000
March:. . . . .$1,650,000** × 40%			660,000
	$1,880,000	$1,760,000	$1,485,000
Total cash collected	$2,080,000	$1,960,000	$1,685,000

*($6,100,000 total sales − $600,000 cash sales) × 40% = $2,200,000
**($6,100,000 total sales − $600,000 cash sales) × 30% = $1,650,000

h.

JACKSON MANUFACTURING, INC.
Cash Budget
For the Quarter Ended March 31, 20X5

	January	February	March
Beginning cash balance	$ 60,000	$ 50,000	$ 69,100
Cash receipts:			
Cash sales	200,000	200,000	200,000
Collections from credit customers.	1,880,000	1,760,000	1,485,000
Short-term borrowing	90,000	—	—
Cash available	$2,230,000	$2,010,000	$1,754,100
Cash disbursements:			
Manufacturing costs	$1,200,000	$1,100,000	$1,000,000
Selling and administrative expenses.	380,000	400,000	340,000
Interest expense*	100,000	100,900	100,900
Income tax payments	—	—	200,000
Capital expenditures.	100,000	340,000	60,000
Cash dividends	400,000	—	—
Total disbursements	$2,180,000	$1,940,900	$1,700,900
Ending cash balance	$ 50,000	$ 69,100	$ 53,200

* For February and March: $100,000 + ($90,000 × 1%) = $100,900

SUMMARY OF LEARNING OBJECTIVES

Describe the planning process, including strategic planning and operational planning. (p. 1022)   **LO1**

- Strategic planning is a formal process that addresses and documents the mission and long-term goals of the organization. SWOT analysis is used to develop and analyze the data needed for this type of planning.

- Operational planning is the development of specific goals and objectives for the entity as a whole and its individual departments, the formulation of a plan of attack to accomplish the goals and objectives, and the written documentation of the goals and objectives and the plan of attack.

LO2   **Discuss the budgeting process and summarize its advantages. Define the key elements of effective budgeting. (p. 1025)**

- Budgeting is the process of developing a formal, written operational plan that presents management's planned actions in financial terms.
- Two budgets result from the budgeting process: the annual operating budget that covers a 1-year budget period and the capital expenditures budget that covers a multiple-year budget period.
- Budgets represent a plan for accomplishing goals and objectives. They provide operational guidance to the department managers so they make decisions that are consistent with decisions made in other departments.
- Because the budget is used as a basis for evaluating performance, it serves as a target for individual managers.
- A budget director should be identified to organize the budgeting process, communicate with people involved in budgeting, and monitor the budgeting process.
- A budget committee, consisting of representatives from all major areas of the company, should provide general guidance to the budgeting process and evaluate proposed budget segments for reasonableness.
- Participative budgeting requires that all departments participate in the development and refinement of the budget amounts so that departmental managers will accept the budget as a reasonable standard of performance.
- The future time span, for which the budget is prepared, known as the budget period, varies according to the activity involved.
- The use of budgets to manage and control a firm's activities is known as budgetary control.
- Zero-based budgeting requires budget preparers to start at a zero level for every item in the budget and justify every dollar, not just the increases or decreases.

LO3   **Define the components of the master budget and illustrate the interrelationships of the individual budgets that comprise the master budget. (p. 1029)**

- The master budget for a manufacturing firm consists of at least the following individual budgets:
  - Sales budget
  - Production budget
  - Direct materials budget
  - Direct labor budget
  - Manufacturing overhead budget
  - Selling and administrative expense budget
  - Capital expenditures budget
  - Cash budget
  - Budgeted income statement
  - Budgeted balance sheet
  - Budgeted statement of cash flows
- The individual budgets must be prepared in a specific sequence, beginning with the sales budget, to properly reflect the interrelationships among the individual budgets.

LO4   **Prepare individual budgets for a manufacturing and a service company, including the cash budget. (p. 1030)**

- The sales budget is based on the sales forecast.
- The production budget determines the number of units of each product that should be manufactured during the budget period.
- The direct materials budget displays the amount of each direct materials item that should be purchased to supply the budgeted production.
- The direct labor budget presents the amount of direct labor, by department, that is required to accomplish the budgeted production.
- The manufacturing overhead budget determines, for each factory department, the amount of variable overhead and the amount of fixed overhead needed to complete the budgeted production.
- The selling and administrative expense budget accumulates the variable and fixed selling and administrative expenses for the entity. Some of the expenses may vary with sales; others may vary with production.
- The capital expenditures budget presents the planned expenditures for property, plant, and equipment over an extended budget period, possibly 5 years.

- The cash budget, usually segmented by month, presents all of the cash receipts and cash disbursements planned for the budget period.
- Much of the information needed to prepare the cash budget comes from previously prepared budgets. However, additional schedules and worksheets are usually needed to place required information in proper form.
- Cash collected from customers from prior credit sales needs careful analysis to take into account timing, cash discounts, and uncollectible accounts.

Prepare budgeted financial statements. (p. 1040)   **LO5**

- The budgeted income statement is prepared for the budget period.
- The budgeted balance sheet is prepared as of the ending date of the budget period.
- The budgeted statement of cash flows is prepared for the budget period, based primarily on data from the cash budget.

Concept	Method	Assessment	SUMMARY
How can management best ensure that the efforts of all employees are congruent with the company's strategy?	Develop multiyear operating plans and budgets (both operating and capital) linked to the company's strategy.	Compare actual results with operating plans and budgets to evaluate company performance.	TAKEAWAY 22.1
How should a company implement a zero-based budgeting approach?	1. Determine goals, operations, and costs for all activities. 2. Determine alternative means of conducting each activity. 3. Evaluate the implications of changes in the level of each activity. 4. Establish workload. 5. Rank activities in order of importance. 6. Select activities necessary to accomplish goals at the minimum cost.	Although costly and time-consuming, zero-based budgeting results in a careful examination and justification of all critical activities, rooting out inefficient and ineffective activities.	TAKEAWAY 22.2

KEY TERMS

Budget (p. 1025)

Budgetary control (p. 1026)

Budget committee (p. 1026)

Budget director (p. 1026)

Budgeted balance sheet (p. 1041)

Budgeted income statement (p. 1040)

Budgeted statement of cash flows (p. 1042)

Budgeting (p. 1025)

Budget period (p. 1027)

Capital expenditures budget (p. 1036)

Cash budget (p. 1037)

Continuous budgeting (p. 1027)

Direct labor budget (p. 1033)

Direct materials budget (p. 1032)

Just-in-time inventory (p. 1031)

Manufacturing overhead budget (p. 1034)

Master budget (p. 1029)

Operational planning (p. 1024)

Participative budgeting (p. 1027)

Planning horizon (p. 1022)

Production budget (p. 1031)

Safety stock (p. 1032)

Sales budget (p. 1030)

Sales forecast (p. 1030)

Selling and administrative expense budget (p. 1035)

Strategic planning (p. 1023)

Strengths, weaknesses, opportunities, and threats (SWOT) analysis (p. 1023)

Zero-based budgeting (p. 1028)

Assignments with the ⊙ logo in the margin are available in 𝑚𝑦BusinessCourse.
See the Preface of the book for details.

SELF-STUDY QUESTIONS

(Answers to Self-Study Questions are at the end of this chapter.)

LO1 **1.** Analyzing a company's technological capabilities, employee skills, and sales team performance will provide
   a. external factors that identify the company's strengths and threats.
   b. internal factors that identify the company's strengths and opportunities.
   c. external factors that identify the company's strengths and weaknesses.
   d. internal factors that identify the company's strengths and weaknesses.

LO2 **2.** If a company uses participative budgeting, which group should prepare the initial set of budget dollar amounts?
   a. Budget committee
   c. Top management
   b. Operating department managers
   d. Accounting department

LO3 **3.** Which of the following budgets should be prepared before all of the others listed below?
   a. Cash budget
   c. Manufacturing overhead budget
   b. Direct materials budget
   d. Production budget

LO4 **4.** Which of the following budgets will typically have the longest budget period?
   a. Capital expenditures budget
   c. Sales budget
   b. Cash budget
   d. Budgeted income statement

LO4 **5.** If the beginning inventory of a company that manufactures only one product is 5,000 units, the sales forecast is 34,000 units sold, and the desired ending inventory is 6,000 units, how many units should be produced?
   a. 35,000
   c. 40,000
   b. 33,000
   d. 39,000

LO4 **6.** Smith Company started business on September 1. Smith had credit sales of $200,000 in September and $300,000 in October. The pattern for collection of cash from customers is expected to be 40% in the month of sale (subject to a 2% cash discount), 50% in the month following the month of sale, and 7% in the second month following the month of sale, with 3% uncollectible. How much cash did Smith Company receive from customers on account during October?
   a. $120,000
   c. $217,600
   b. $117,600
   d. $220,000

LO5 **7.** The budgeted statement of cash flows is most closely related to
   a. the sales budget.
   c. the cash budget.
   b. the capital expenditures budget.
   d. the budgeted balance sheet.

QUESTIONS

LO1 **1.** What is a planning horizon? How will it differ between strategic planning and operational planning?

LO1 **2.** Describe strategic planning.

LO1 **3.** Describe operational planning.

LO2 **4.** Define budgeting.

LO2 **5.** List and briefly explain four advantages of budgeting.

LO2 **6.** Describe the budget committee.

LO2 **7.** Why is participative budgeting important to the success of the budgeting process?

LO2 **8.** What is meant by continuous budgeting?

LO3 **9.** What is the master budget? List, in the order of preparation, the various budgets that the master budget for a small manufacturing company might comprise.

LO3 **10.** Why do most firms prepare the sales budget first?

LO4 **11.** Beginning finished goods inventory is 10,000 units, anticipated sales volume is 60,000 units, and the desired ending finished goods inventory is 12,000 units. What number of units should be produced?

12. Three pounds of material R (costing $5 per pound) and 4 pounds of material S (costing $7 per pound) are required to make one unit of product T. If management plans to increase the inventory of material R by 500 pounds and reduce the inventory of material S by 800 pounds during a period when 3,000 units of product T are to be produced, what are the budgeted purchase costs of material R and material S? **LO4**

13. Carroll Manufacturing Company has two labor operations in its factory: machining and assembly. Workers in the machining department are paid $14 per hour; workers in the assembly department are paid $12 per hour. During January, 10,000 units of product A and 20,000 units of product B are to be manufactured. Each unit of A requires 1 hour of machining and 2 hours of assembly; each unit of B requires 3 hours of machining and 1 hour of assembly. What is the total direct labor budget for January? **LO4**

14. Johnson Manufacturing Company has budgeted 30,000 direct labor hours for March. The budgeted cost formula for monthly manufacturing overhead is $4 per direct labor hour plus $65,000. What is the manufacturing overhead budget for March? **LO4**

15. A company collects cash from its credit sales in the following pattern: 30% in the month of sale, 50% in the month following the month of sale, and 20% in the second month following the month of sale. What percentage of which months' credit sales will be collected during October? **LO4**

16. What are the three major groupings of cash flows in the budgeted statement of cash flows? **LO5**

SHORT EXERCISES

SE22-1. All of the following are advantages of the use of budgets in a management control system, *except* that budgets **LO2**

    a. force management planning.

    b. provide performance criteria.

    c. promote communication and coordination within the organization.

    d. limit unauthorized expenditures.

SE22-2. Which one of the following items would most likely cause the planning and budgeting system to fail? **LO2**

    a. Lack of historical financial data

    b. Lack of input from several levels of management

    c. Lack of top management support

    d. Lack of adherence to rigid budgets during the year

SE22-3. Which one of the following statements concerning approaches for the budget development process is **correct**? **LO2**

    a. The authoritative approach to budgeting discourages strict adherence to strategic organizational goals.

    b. To prevent ambiguity, once departmental budgeted goals have been developed, they should remain fixed even if the sales forecast upon which they are based proves to be wrong in the middle of the fiscal year.

    c. With the information technology available, the role of budgets as an organizational communication device has declined.

    d. Because department managers have the most detailed knowledge about organizational operations, they should use this information as the building blocks of the operating budget.

SE22-4. Cerawell Products Company is a ceramics manufacturer that is facing several challenges in its operations due to economic and industry conditions. The company is currently preparing its annual plan and budget. Which one of the following is subject to the **least** control by the management of Cerawell in the current fiscal year? **LO2**

    a. A new machine that was purchased this year has not helped reduce Cerawell's unfavorable labor efficiency variances.

    b. A competitor has achieved an unexpected technological breakthrough that has given them a significant quality advantage and has caused Cerawell to lose market share.

    c. Vendors have asked that the contract price for the goods they supply to Cerawell be renegotiated and adjusted for inflation.

    d. Experienced employees have decided to terminate their employment with Cerawell and go to work for the competition.

LO3 **SE22-5.** What would be the correct chronological order of preparation for the following budgets?

     I. Cost of goods sold budget

    II. Production budget

   III. Purchases budget

   IV. Administrative budget

   a. I, II, III, IV

   b. III, II, IV, I

   c. IV, II, III, I

   d. II, III, I, IV

LO4 **SE22-6.** Hannon Retailing Company prices its products by adding 30% to its cost. Hannon anticipates sales of $715,000 in July, $728,000 in August, and $624,000 in September. Hannon's policy is to have on hand enough inventory at the end of the month to cover 25% of the next month's sales. What will be the cost of the inventory that Hannon should budget for purchase in August?

   a. $509,600

   b. $540,000

   c. $560,000

   d. $680,000

LO4   **SE22-7.** Netco's sales budget for the coming year is as follows:

Item	Volume in Units	Sales Price	Sales Revenue
1	200,000	$50	$10,000,000
2	150,000	10	1,500,000
3	300,000	30	9,000,000
Total sales revenue			$20,500,000

Items 1 and 3 are different models of the same product. Item 2 is a complement to Item 1. Past experience indicates that the sales volume of Item 2 relative to the sales volume of Item 1 is fairly constant. Netco is considering a 10% price increase for the coming year for Item 1, which will cause sales of Item 1 to decline by 20% while simultaneously causing sales of Item 3 to increase by 5%. If Netco institutes the price increase for Item 1, total sales revenue will decrease by

   a. $1,050,000.

   b. $850,000.

   c. $750,000.

   d. $550,000.

LO4 **SE22-8.** Streeter Company produces plastic microwave turntables. Sales for the next year are expected to be 65,000 units in the first quarter, 72,000 units in the second quarter, 84,000 units in the third quarter, and 66,000 units in the fourth quarter. Streeter maintains a finished goods inventory at the end of each quarter equal to one half of the units expected to be sold in the next quarter. How many units should Streeter produce in the second quarter?

   a. 72,000 units

   b. 75,000 units

   c. 78,000 units

   d. 84,000 units

LO4   **SE22-9.** Stevens Company manufactures electronic components used in automobile manufacturing. Each component uses two raw materials, Geo and Clio. Standard usage of the two materials required to produce one finished electronic component, as well as the current inventory, are shown below.

	Standard		
Material	Per Unit	Price	Current Inventory
Geo	2.0 pounds	$15/lb.	5,000 pounds
Clio	1.5 pounds	$10/lb.	7,500 pounds

Stevens forecasts sales of 20,000 components for each of the next two production periods. Company policy dictates that 25% of the raw materials needed to produce the next period's projected sales be maintained in ending direct materials inventory.

Based on this information, what would the budgeted direct materials purchases for the coming period be?

	Geo	Clio
a.	$450,000	$450,000
b.	$675,000	$300,000
c.	$675,000	$400,000
d.	$825,000	$450,000

SE22-10. Petersons Planters Inc. budgeted the following amounts for the coming year:

Beginning inventory, finished goods.................	$ 10,000
Cost of goods sold	400,000
Direct materials used in production	100,000
Ending inventory, finished goods	25,000
Beginning and ending work-in-process inventory.........	0

Overhead is estimated to be two times the amount of direct labor dollars. What amount that should be budgeted for direct labor for the coming year?

a. $315,000
b. $210,000
c. $157,500
d. $105,000

EXERCISES—SET A

E22-1A. Budgeting Inventories For each independent situation below, determine the amounts indicated by the question marks:

	A	B	C	D
Beginning inventory	12,000	?	7,000	?
Produced	40,000	27,000	?	56,000
Available....................................	?	?	32,000	64,000
Sold	45,000	28,000	?	?
Ending inventory.............................	?	12,000	6,000	2,000

E22-2A. Budget Preparation Collins Company is preparing its master budget for April. Use the given estimates to determine the amounts necessary for each of the following requirements. (Estimates may be related to more than one requirement.)

a. What should total sales revenue be if territories A and B estimate sales of 10,000 and 12,000 units, respectively, and the unit selling price is $46?

b. If the beginning finished goods inventory is an estimated 3,000 units and the desired ending inventory is 2,000 units, how many units should be produced?

c. What dollar amount of materials should be purchased at $4 per pound if each unit of product requires 3 pounds and beginning and ending materials inventories should be 4,000 and 5,000 pounds, respectively?

d. How much direct labor cost should be incurred if each unit produced requires 1.5 hours at an hourly rate of $20?

e. How much manufacturing overhead should be incurred if fixed manufacturing overhead is $50,000 and variable manufacturing overhead is $3 per direct labor hour?

E22-3A. Budget Preparation Westport Company is preparing its master budget for May. Use the estimates provided to determine the amounts necessary for each of the following requirements. (Estimates may be related to more than one requirement.)

LO4

LO4

LO4

LO4

a. What should total sales revenue be if territories E and W estimate sales of 50,000 and 100,000 units, respectively, and the unit selling price is $30?

b. If the beginning finished goods inventory is an estimated 6,000 units and the desired ending inventory is 7,000 units, how many units should be produced?

c. What dollar amount of materials should be purchased at $2 per pound if each unit of product requires 2.5 pounds and beginning and ending materials inventories should be 12,000 and 13,500 pounds, respectively?

d. How much direct labor cost should be incurred if each unit produced requires 0.5 hours at an hourly rate of $15?

e. How much manufacturing overhead should be incurred if fixed manufacturing overhead is $45,000 and variable manufacturing overhead is $1.50 per direct labor hour?

LO4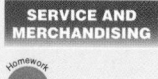

E22-4A. **Budgeting Cash Collections** Spencer Consulting, which invoices its clients on terms 2/10, n/30, had credit sales for May and June of $150,000 and $170,000, respectively. Analysis of Spencer's operations indicates that the pattern of customers' payments on account is as follows (percentages are of total monthly credit sales):

	Receiving Discount	Beyond Discount Period	Totals
In month of sale	50%	25%	75%
In month following sale	10%	10%	20%
Uncollectible accounts, returns, and allowances			5%
			100%

Determine the estimated cash collected on customers' accounts in June.

LO4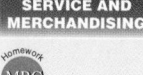

E22-5A. **Budgeting Cash Flow** The following various elements relate to Whitfield, Inc.'s cash budget for April of the current year. For each item, determine the amount of cash that Whitfield should receive or pay in April.

a. At $28 each, unit sales are 5,000 and 6,000 for March and April, respectively. Total sales are typically 40% for cash and 60% on credit; 30% of credit sales are collected in the month of sale, with the balance collected in the following month. Uncollectible accounts are negligible.

b. Merchandise purchases were $45,000 and $78,000 for March and April, respectively. Typically, 20% of total purchases are paid for in the month of purchase with a 5% cash discount. The balance of purchases is paid for (without discount) in the following month.

c. Fixed administrative expenses, which total $11,000 per month, are paid in the month incurred. Variable administrative expenses amount to 20% of total monthly sales revenue, one-half of which is paid in the month incurred, with the balance paid in the following month.

d. A store asset originally costing $8,000, on which $6,000 depreciation has been taken, is sold for cash at a loss of $400.

LO4

E22-6A. **Prepare Cash Budget for 3 Months** Brewster Corporation expects the following cash receipts and disbursements during the first quarter of 2019 (receipts exclude new borrowings and disbursements exclude interest payments on borrowings since January 1, 2019):

	January	February	March
Cash receipts	$260,000	$280,000	$250,000
Cash disbursements	240,000	320,000	260,000

The expected cash balance at January 1, 2019, is $42,000. Brewster wants to maintain a cash balance at the end of each month of at least $40,000. Short-term borrowings at 1% interest per month will be used to accomplish this, if necessary. Borrowings (in multiples of $1,000) will be made at the beginning of the month in which they are needed, with interest for that month paid at the end of the month. Prepare a cash budget for the quarter ended March 31, 2019.

LO4

E22-7A. **Prepare Cash Budget from Budgeted Transactions** Prepare a cash budget for the month ended May 31, 2019. Campton Company anticipates a cash balance of $84,000 on May 1, 2019. The following budgeted transactions for May 2019 present data related to anticipated cash receipts and cash disbursements:

1. For May, budgeted cash sales are $60,000 and budgeted credit sales are $500,000. (Credit sales for April were $450,000.) In the month of sale, 40% of credit sales are collected, with the balance collected in the month following sale.

2. Budgeted merchandise purchases for May are $280,000. (Merchandise purchases in April were $240,000.) In the month of purchase, 70% of merchandise purchases are paid for, and the balance is paid for in the following month.

3. Budgeted cash disbursements for salaries and operating expenses for May total $165,000.

4. During May, $25,000 of principal repayment and $4,000 of interest payment are due to the bank.

5. A $20,000 income tax deposit is due to the federal government during May.

6. A new delivery truck will be purchased during May for $6,000 cash and an $8,000 note payable. Depreciation for May will be $500.

Prepare a cash budget for Campton Company for the month of May 2019.

E22-8A. Budgeted Cash Collection In an effort to improve cash collection, Suburban Medical Clinic offers terms of 2/10, n/30, with a 5% discount on patient payments made with cash. Suburban estimates its total billings for the second calendar quarter of the year as follows: April, $200,000; May, $240,000; and June, $290,000. Historically, Suburban has had the following patient collection patterns:

	Portions of Total Sales
In month of sale:	
Cash at time of sale	25%
On account during the discount period.	20%
On account after the discount period	10%
In month following sale:	
On account after the discount period	25%
In second month following sale:	
On account after discount period	15%
Average portion uncollectible	5%
	100%

What would be Suburban's budgeted total cash collection for June?

E22-9A. Purchases Budget Rest Inn provides four-star accommodations for the vacation traveler. It is located just off a major interstate freeway. There are three other competing motels at the same exit. Hotel management is preparing its budget for the busiest three-month period of the year, June through August. To differentiate themselves from the competition, Rest Inn provides a complimentary spa package for each guest stay that includes specialty shampoo, conditioner, soap, lotion, toothpaste, lavender essential oil, slippers, earplugs, and a sleep mask. Rest Inn purchases the spa package from a local vendor that puts the Rest Inn private label on the products. The hotel follows a policy of purchasing enough spa packages to ensure that 40% of next month's bookings are in the current month's ending inventory. Rest Inn's sales budget for guest stays for the next quarter is as follows:

June	2,300 guest stays
July.	2,500 guest stays
August	2,100 guest stays

How many spa packages should Rest Inn budget for purchase in July?

EXERCISES—SET B

E22-1B. Budgeting Inventories For each independent situation below, determine the amounts indicated by the question marks.

Number of Units	A	B	C	D
Beginning inventory	7,500	?	6,000	?
Produced	15,000	27,000	?	70,000
Available.	?	?	46,000	85,000
Sold	18,000	31,000	?	?
Ending inventory.	?	3,000	5,000	11,000

LO4

LO4

LO4

LO4   **E22-2B.**   **Budget Preparation**   Reeves Company is preparing its master budget for July. Use the given esti-mates to determine the amounts necessary for each of the following requirements. (Estimates may be related to more than one requirement.)

    a. What should total sales revenue be if territories A and B estimate sales of 8,000 and 20,000 units, respectively, and the unit selling price is $55?

    b. If the beginning finished goods inventory is an estimated 2,500 units and the desired ending in-ventory is 1,000 units, how many units should be produced?

    c. What dollar amount of materials should be purchased at $3 per pound if each unit of product requires 2 pounds and beginning and ending materials inventories should be 3,000 and 4,000 pounds, respectively?

    d. How much direct labor cost should be incurred if each unit produced requires 1.5 hours at an hourly rate of $16?

    e. How much manufacturing overhead should be incurred if fixed manufacturing overhead is $60,000 and variable manufacturing overhead is $2 per direct labor hour?

LO4   **E22-3B.**   **Budget Preparation**   Tuttle Company is preparing its master budget for November. Use the esti-mates provided to determine the necessary amounts for each of the following requirements. (Esti-mates may be related to more than one requirement.)

    a. What should total sales revenue be if territories N and S estimate sales of 40,000 and 80,000 units, respectively, and the unit selling price is $20?

    b. If the beginning finished goods inventory is an estimated 5,000 units and the desired ending in-ventory is 6,000 units, how many units should be produced?

    c. What dollar amount of materials should be purchased at $2 per pound if each unit of product requires 3 pounds and beginning and ending materials inventories should be 10,000 and 12,000 pounds, respectively?

    d. How much direct labor cost should be incurred if each unit produced requires 0.5 hours at an hourly rate of $14?

    e. How much manufacturing overhead should be incurred if fixed manufacturing overhead is $32,000 and variable manufacturing overhead is $2 per direct labor hour?

LO4   **E22-4B.**   **Budgeting Cash Collections**   Lowell Consulting, which sells on terms 2/10, n/30, had credit sales for March and April of $200,000 and $180,000, respectively. Analysis of Lowell's operations in-dicates that the pattern of customers' payments on account is as follows (percentages are of total monthly credit sales):

	Receiving Discount	Beyond Discount Period	Totals
In month of sale	40%	25%	65%
In month following sale.	20%	10%	30%
Uncollectible accounts, returns, and allowances			5%
			100%

Determine the estimated cash collected on customers' accounts in April.

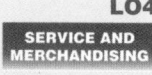

LO4   **E22-5B.**   **Budgeting Cash Flow**   The following various elements relate to Murphy, Inc.'s cash budget for October of the current year. For each item, determine the amount of cash that Murphy should receive or pay in October.

    a. At $24 each, unit sales are 10,000 and 12,000 for September and October, respectively. Total sales are typically 30% for cash and 70% on credit; 40% of credit sales are collected in the month of sale, with the balance collected in the following month. Uncollectible accounts are negligible.

    b. Merchandise purchases were $43,000 and $76,000 for September and October, respectively. Typ-ically, 20% of total purchases are paid for in the month of purchase with a 5% cash discount. The balance of purchases is paid for (without discount) in the following month.

    c. Fixed administrative expenses, which total $15,000 per month, are paid in the month incurred. Variable administrative expenses amount to 20% of total monthly sales revenue, 65% of which is paid in the month incurred, with the balance paid in the following month.

d. Fixed selling expenses, which total $4,200 per month, are paid in the month incurred. Variable selling expenses, which are 5% of total sales revenue, are paid in the month following their incurrence.

E22-6B. **Prepare Cash Budget for 3 Months** Windsor Corporation expects the following cash receipts and disbursements during the first quarter of 2019 (receipts exclude new borrowings and disbursements exclude interest payments on borrowings since January 1, 2019):

	January	February	March
Cash receipts	$430,000	$440,000	$400,000
Cash disbursements.	390,000	520,000	420,000

The expected cash balance at January 1, 2019, is $75,000. Windsor wants to maintain a cash balance at the end of each month of at least $60,000. Short-term borrowings at 1% interest per month will be used to accomplish this, if necessary. Borrowings (in multiples of $1,000) will be made at the beginning of the month in which they are needed, with interest for that month paid at the end of the month. Prepare a cash budget for the quarter ended March 31, 2019.

E22-7B. **Prepare Cash Budget from Budgeted Transactions** McCall Company anticipates a cash balance of $100,000 on July 1, 2019. The following budgeted transactions for July 2019 present data related to anticipated cash receipts and cash disbursements:

1. For July, budgeted cash sales are $72,000 and budgeted credit sales are $600,000. (Credit sales for June were $550,000.) In the month of sale, 40% of credit sales are collected, with the balance collected in the month following sale.
2. Budgeted merchandise purchases for July are $340,000. (Merchandise purchases in June were $290,000.) In the month of purchase, 70% of merchandise purchases are paid for, and the balance is paid for in the following month.
3. Budgeted cash disbursements for salaries and operating expenses for July total $200,000.
4. During July, $30,000 of principal repayment and $5,000 of interest payment are due to the bank.
5. A $25,000 income tax deposit is due to the federal government during July.
6. A new delivery truck will be purchased during July for $7,000 cash and a $10,000 note payable. Depreciation for July will be $600.

Prepare a cash budget for McCall Company for the month of July 2019.

E22-8B. **Budgeted Cash Collection** The Smile Doctor offers terms of 3/10, n/30, with a 10% discount on patient payments made with cash. The Smile Doctor estimates its total billings for the first calendar quarter of the year as follows: January, $125,000; February, $110,000; and March, $130,000. Historically, the Smile Doctor has had the following patient collection patterns:

	Portions of Total Sales
In month of sale:	
Cash at time of sale	25%
On account during the discount period	15%
On account after the discount period	10%
In month following sale:	
On account after the discount period	30%
In second month following sale:	
On account after discount period	15%
Average portion uncollectible	5%
	100%

What would the Smile Doctor's budgeted total cash collection be for March?

E22-9B. **Sales Budget** Hawaiian Style supplies island-inspired clothing to hotel gift shops, golf shops, and specialty boutiques throughout the Hawaiian islands. The clothing distributor purchases its inventory from a Chinese clothing manufacturer that uses the latest designs provided by Hawaiian Style.

Due to manufacturing lead times, Hawaiian Style must provide the final designs no later than 90 days before it receives the completed clothing. Due to the costs of retooling and the risks associated with consumers' changing tastes for clothing styles and colors, the Chinese clothing manufacturer requires Hawaiian Style to order its clothing in large batches, effectively resulting in Hawaiian Style ordering its entire annual inventory at the beginning of each year.

Hawaiian Style attempts to balance its concerns about stockouts of popular styles with its concerns about excess inventory from season to season by carefully budgeting its purchases for the next fashion year. Based on its analysis, Hawaiian Style has developed the following probabilities for sales for the coming year:

Sales Level	Probability
$ 750,000	20%
900,000	30%
1,100,000	30%
1,250,000	15%
1,300,000	5%

What amount should Hawaiian Style budget for sales for the coming year?

PROBLEMS—SET A

LO4   **P22-1A.**   **Budgeting Cash** Whitney's, Inc., sells on terms of 5% discount for "cash and carry" or 2/10, n/30 and estimates its total sales for the second calendar quarter of next year as follows: April, $300,000; May, $240,000; and June, $360,000. An analysis of operations indicates the following customer collection patterns:

	Portions of Total Sales
In month of sale:	
Cash at time of sale	30%
On account during discount period	15%
On account after discount period	10%
In month following sale:	
On account during discount period	15%
On account after discount period	10%
In second month following sale:	
On account after discount period	15%
Average portion uncollectible	5%
	100%

Prepare an estimate of the cash to be collected from customers during June.

LO4   **P22-2A.**   **Monthly Cash Budget** Grove, Inc. is a wholesaler for its only product, deluxe wireless electric drills, which sell for $90 each and cost Grove $54 each. On December 1, 2019, Grove's management requested a cash budget for December. The following selected account balances at November 30, 2019, were gathered by the accounting department:

Cash..	$ 135,000
Marketable securities (at cost)	210,000
Accounts receivable (all trade)...	1,710,000
Inventories (15,000 units)...	810,000
Operating expenses payable	140,400
Accounts payable (all merchandise)...	583,200
Note payable (due 12/31/2019)	393,000

Actual sales for the months of October and November were 20,000 and 30,000 units, respectively. Projected unit sales for December and January are 50,000 and 40,000, respectively. Experience indicates that 50% of sales should be collected in the month of sale, 30% in the month following sale, and the balance in the second month following sale. Uncollectible accounts, returns, and allowances are negligible.

Planned purchases should provide ending inventories equal to 30% of next month's unit sales volume. Approximately 70% of the purchases are paid for in the month of purchase and the balance in the following month.

Monthly operating expenses are budgeted at $8.10 per unit sold plus a fixed amount of $189,000, including depreciation of $81,000. Except for depreciation, 60% of operating expenses are paid in the month incurred and the balance in the following month. Interest expense is included in operating expenses.

Special anticipated year-end transactions include the following:

1. Declaration of a $22,500 cash dividend to be paid 2 weeks after the December 20 date of record.
2. Sale of one-half of the marketable securities held on November 30; a gain of $21,000 is anticipated.
3. Pay off the note payable due December 31, 2019.
4. Trade-in of an old computer originally costing $675,000 and now having accumulated depreciation of $540,000 at a gain of $157,500 on a new computer costing $1,350,000. Sufficient cash will be paid at the time of trade-in so that only 50% of the total price will have to be financed.
5. Grove's treasurer has a policy of maintaining a minimum month-end cash balance of $135,000 but wants to raise this to $225,000 at December 31. She has a standing arrangement with the bank to borrow any amount up to a limit of $450,000.

Required

Prepare a cash budget for Grove, Inc., for December 2019.

P22-3A. Budgeting Production and Purchases and Just-in-Time Materials Inventory Hancock Manufacturing, Inc. is preparing budgets for the third quarter of 2019. Hancock produces only one product in its factory. This product requires 5 pounds of material B, 2 pounds of material G, and a component, K, that is purchased from another manufacturer. Hancock operates on a just-in-time basis for material B. As a result, Hancock maintains no inventory of material B. On July 1, 2019, the inventory of material G is expected to be 2,000 pounds and the inventory of component K is expected to be 500 units. Hancock wants the inventories of G and K at September 30, 2019, to be 20% less than the inventories at July 1, 2019. The inventory of finished products at June 30, 2019, is expected to be 1,000 units; the desired inventory at September 30, 2019, is 3,000 units to allow a buildup for heavy sales in the fourth quarter. The sales forecast for the third quarter is 12,000 units at $300 each. Budgeted purchase costs are $10 per pound for B, $7 per pound for G, and $40 per component for K.

Required

a. Prepare the production budget for Hancock Manufacturing, Inc., for the third quarter of 2019.

b. Prepare the direct materials budget for Hancock Manufacturing, Inc., for the third quarter of 2019.

P22-4A. Preparation of Individual Budgets During the first calendar quarter of 2019, Clinton Corporation is planning to manufacture a new product and introduce it in two regions. Market research indicates that sales will be 6,000 units in the urban region at a unit price of $53 and 5,000 units in the rural region at $48 each. Because the sales manager expects the product to catch on, he has asked for production sufficient to generate a 4,000-unit ending inventory. The production manager has furnished the following estimates related to manufacturing costs and operating expenses:

	Variable (per unit)	Fixed (total)
Manufacturing costs:		
Direct materials:		
A (4 lbs. @ $3.15/lb.)	$12.60	—
B (2 lbs. @ $4.65/lb.)	9.30	—
Direct labor (0.5 hrs./unit)	7.50	—
Manufacturing overhead:		
Depreciation	—	$ 7,650
Factory supplies	0.90	4,500
Supervisory salaries	—	28,800
Other	0.75	22,950
Operating expenses:		
Selling:		
Advertising	—	22,500
Sales salaries and commissions*	1.50	15,000
Other*	0.90	3,000
Administrative:		
Office salaries	—	2,700
Supplies	0.15	1,050
Other	0.08	1,950

*Varies per unit sold, not per unit produced.

Required

a. Assuming that the desired ending inventories of materials A and B are 4,000 and 6,000 pounds, respectively, and that work-in-process inventories are immaterial, prepare budgets for the calendar quarter in which the new product will be introduced for each of the following operating factors:
1.   Total sales
2.   Production
3.   Material purchases cost
4.   Direct labor costs
5.   Manufacturing overhead costs
6.   Selling and administrative expenses

b. Using data generated in requirement (a), prepare a budgeted income statement for the calendar quarter. Assume an overall effective income tax rate of 30%.

LO5   **P22-5A.**   **Prepare and Evaluate Budgeted Income Statement** Fairfield Stores, a retailer in a shopping mall, prepared the following income statement for its operations for the month just ended:

SERVICE AND
MERCHANDISING

FAIRFIELD STORES		
Income Statement		
For the Month Ended April 30, 2019		
Sales.		$500,000
Cost of goods sold		240,000
Gross profit.		$260,000
Operating expenses:		
Sales commissions expense.	$25,000	
Advertising expense	60,000	
Lease expense	20,000	
Depreciation expense.	10,000	
Salaries expense	30,000	
Other operating expenses.	15,000	160,000
Income before income taxes		$100,000
Income tax expense		30,000
Net income		$ 70,000

Sales commissions were 5% of sales. Income taxes were 30% of income before income taxes. Both should continue at the same rate for the remainder of the year.

Fairfield Stores is preparing the budget for the month of May 2019. If no basic changes are made, Fairfield's management expects that the income statement would be virtually identical to the one for April. However, Fairfield's management has decided to make some changes in the operations. The plans include the following:

1. Increase advertising expense by 40%.
2. Decrease all selling prices by 10%.
3. Increase the number of units sold by 25% as a result of the first two changes.

Required

a. Prepare a budgeted income statement for the month of May 2019. (Round all amounts on the income statement to the nearest dollar.)

b. Should Fairfield's management make the planned changes?

PROBLEMS—SET B

LO4   **P22-1B.**   **Budgeting Cash** Judson, Inc., sells on terms of 5% discount for "cash and carry" or 2/10, n/30 and estimates its total sales for the second calendar quarter of next year as follows: July, $225,000; August, $150,000; and September, $180,000. An analysis of operations indicates the following customer collection patterns:

	Portions of Total Sales
In month of sale:	
Cash at time of sale	30%
On account during discount period	20%
On account after discount period	5%
In month following sale:	
On account during discount period	20%
On account after discount period	15%
In second month following sale:	
On account after discount period	7%
Average portion uncollectible	3%
	100%

Required

Prepare an estimate of the cash to be collected from customers during September.

P22-2B. **Monthly Cash Budget** Sutter, Inc. is a wholesaler for its only product, deluxe wireless recharge-able electric shavers, which sell for $70 each and cost Sutter $48 each. On June 1, 2019, Sutter's management requested a cash budget for June. The following selected account balances at May 31, 2019, were gathered by the accounting department: **LO4**

Cash	$ 56,000
Marketable securities (at cost)	160,000
Accounts receivable (all trade)	2,170,000
Inventories (12,000 units)	576,000
Operating expenses payable	196,800
Accounts payable (all merchandise)	902,400
Note payable	600,000

Actual sales for April and May were 30,000 and 50,000 units, respectively. Projected unit sales for June and July are 40,000 and 20,000, respectively. Experience indicates that 50% of sales should be collected in the month of sale, 30% in the month following sale, and the balance in the second month following sale. Uncollectible accounts, returns, and allowances are negligible.

Planned purchases should provide ending inventories equal to 30% of next month's unit sales volume. Approximately 60% of the purchases are paid for in the month of purchase and the balance in the following month.

Monthly operating expenses are budgeted at $9.60 per unit sold plus a fixed amount of $288,000, including depreciation of $112,000. Except for depreciation, 70% of operating expenses are paid in the month incurred and the balance in the following month. Interest expense is included in operating expenses.

Special anticipated June transactions include the following:

1. Declaration of a $60,000 cash dividend to be paid 2 weeks after the June 20 date of record.
2. Sale of all but $40,000 of the marketable securities held on May 31; a gain of $18,000 is anticipated.
3. Payment of $50,000 installment on the note payable.
4. Trade-in of an old company plane originally costing $300,000 and now having accumulated de-preciation of $200,000 at a gain of $160,000 on a new plane costing $2,000,000. Sufficient cash will be paid at the time of trade-in so that only 50% of the total price will have to be financed.
5. Sutter's treasurer has a policy of maintaining a minimum month-end cash balance of $40,000 and has a standing arrangement with the bank to borrow any amount up to a limit of $400,000.

Required

Prepare a cash budget for Sutter, Inc., for June 2019.

P22-3B. **Budgeting Production and Purchases and Just-in-Time Materials Inventory** Central Manufac-turing, Inc. is preparing budgets for the second quarter of 2019. Central produces only one product in its factory. This product requires 4 pounds of material C, 3 pounds of material H, and a compo-nent, M, that is purchased from another manufacturer. Central operates on a just-in-time basis for **LO5**

material C. As a result, Central maintains no inventory of material C. On April 1, 2019, the inventory of material H is expected to be 3,000 pounds and the inventory of component M is expected to be 600 units. Central wants the inventories of H and M at June 30, 2019, to be 20% less than the inventories at April 1, 2019. The inventory of finished products at March 31, 2019, is expected to be 2,000 units; the desired inventory at June 30, 2019, is 4,000 units to allow a buildup for heavy sales in the third quarter. The sales forecast for the second quarter is 14,000 units at $200 each. Budgeted purchase costs are $5 per pound for C, $6 per pound for H, and $50 per component for M.

Required

a. Prepare the production budget for the second quarter of 2019.

b. Prepare the direct materials budget for the second quarter of 2019.

LO4, 5

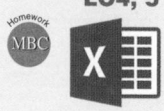

P22-4B. Preparation of Individual Budgets During the first calendar quarter of 2019, Williams Corporation is planning to manufacture a new product and introduce it in two regions. Market research indicates that sales will be 8,000 units in the urban region at a unit price of $65 and 6,000 units in the rural region at $55 each. Because the sales manager expects the product to catch on, she has asked for production sufficient to generate a 4,000-unit ending inventory. The production manager has furnished the following estimates related to manufacturing costs and operating expenses:

	Variable (per Unit)	Fixed (Total)
Manufacturing costs:		
Direct materials:		
A (2 lbs. @ $2.50/lb.)	$ 5.00	—
B (5 lbs. @ $1.40/lb.)	7.00	—
Direct labor (2 hrs./unit)	10.00	—
Manufacturing overhead:		
Depreciation	—	$22,500
Factory supplies	0.55	2,500
Supervisory salaries	—	16,250
Other	0.65	9,200
Operating expenses:		
Selling:		
Advertising	—	12,500
Sales salaries and commissions*	1.25	20,000
Other*	0.50	4,200
Administrative:		
Office salaries	—	15,000
Supplies	0.40	1,200
Other	0.25	5,000

*Varies per unit sold, not per unit produced.

Required

a. Assuming that the desired ending inventories of materials A and B are 4,000 and 20,000 pounds, respectively, and that work-in-process inventories are immaterial, prepare budgets for the calendar quarter in which the new product will be introduced for each of the following operating factors:

1. Total sales
2. Production
3. Material purchases cost
4. Direct labor costs
5. Manufacturing overhead costs
6. Selling and administrative expenses

b. Using data generated in requirement (a), prepare a budgeted income statement for the calendar quarter. Assume an overall effective income tax rate of 35%. (Round income statement amounts to the nearest dollar.)

LO5

SERVICE AND MERCHANDISING

P22-5B. Prepare and Evaluate Budgeted Income Statement Medford Stores, a retailer in a shopping mall, prepared the following income statement for its operations for the month just ended:

MEDFORD STORES Income Statement for the Month Ended April 30, 2019		
Sales.		$700,000
Cost of goods sold		330,000
Gross profit.		$370,000
Operating expenses:		
Sales commissions expense.	$35,000	
Advertising expense	90,000	
Lease expense	50,000	
Depreciation expense.	20,000	
Salaries expense	40,000	
Other operating expenses.	25,000	260,000
Income before income taxes		$110,000
Income tax expense		33,000
Net income		$ 77,000

Sales commissions were 5% of sales. Income taxes were 30% of income before income taxes. Both should continue at the same rate for the remainder of the year.

Medford Stores is preparing the budget for the month of May 2019. If no basic changes are made, Medford's management expects that the income statement would be virtually identical to the one for April. However, Medford's management has decided to make some changes in the operations. The plans include the following:

1. Increase advertising expense by 20%.
2. Decrease all selling prices by 10%.
3. Increase the number of units sold by 25% as a result of the first two changes.

Required

a. Prepare a budgeted income statement for the month of May 2019. (Round all amounts on the income statement to the nearest dollar.)
b. Should Medford's management make the planned changes?

EXTENDING YOUR KNOWLEDGE

EYK22-1. Business Decision Case The sales department of Donovan Manufacturing, Inc. has completed the following sales forecast for the months of January through March 20X1 for its only two products: 50,000 units of J to be sold at $90 each and 30,000 units of K to be sold at $70 each. The desired unit inventories at March 31, 20X1, are 10% of the next quarter's unit sales forecast, which are 60,000 units of J and 30,000 units of K. The January 1, 20X1, unit inventories were 5,000 units of J and 2,000 units of K.

Each unit of J requires 3 pounds of material A and 2 pounds of material B for its manufacture; K requires 2 pounds of A and 4 pounds of B. The purchase cost of A is $9 per pound and the purchase cost of B is $5 per pound. Materials A and B on hand at January 1, 20X1, were 19,000 pounds of A and 7,000 pounds of B. Desired inventories at March 31, 20X1, are 14,000 pounds of A and 8,000 pounds of B.

Each unit of J requires 0.5 hours of direct labor in the factory; each unit of K requires 1.0 hour of direct labor. The average hourly rate for direct labor is $12 per hour. Estimated manufacturing overhead cost is $6 per direct labor hour plus $90,000 per month. Selling and administrative expenses are estimated to be 10% of sales revenue plus $180,000 per month.

Cash sales for the first quarter are estimated to be $300,000 per month. It is forecast that 30% of the credit sales for the quarter ended March 31, 20X1, will occur in January, 30% in February, and 40% in March. Of credit sales (December through March), 40% will be collected as cash in the month of sale and 55% will be collected in the following month. The remainder will be uncollectible. Cash collected in January 20X1 from December 20X0 sales will be $1,050,000.

The January 1, 20X1, cash balance was $70,000. The minimum acceptable cash balance at the end of each month is $60,000. Short-term borrowings (6-month term) are made in multiples of $10,000. Interest is charged at the rate of 1% per month on short-term borrowings. The first interest payment is made the month following the borrowing. Cash disbursements (excluding interest on short-term borrowings) are estimated as follows:

	January	February	March
Manufacturing costs	$1,500,000	$1,300,000	$1,400,000
Selling and administrative expenses	390,000	410,000	400,000
Interest expense.	90,000	90,000	90,000
Income tax payment.	0	0	210,000
Capital expenditures.	124,000	110,000	50,000
Cash dividends.	300,000	0	0

Required

a. Prepare the sales budget for the quarter ended March 31, 20X1.
b. Prepare the production budget for the quarter ended March 31, 20X1.
c. Prepare the direct materials budget for the quarter ended March 31, 20X1.
d. Prepare the direct labor budget for the quarter ended March 31, 20X1.
e. Prepare the manufacturing overhead budget for the quarter ended March 31, 20X1.
f. Prepare the selling and administrative expense budget for the quarter ended March 31, 20X1.
g. Prepare a schedule of cash collected from customers for the quarter ended March 31, 20X1.
h. Prepare the cash budget for the quarter ended March 31, 20X1.

EYK22-2. **Ethics Case** Steve Waller is the corporate accounting manager for Giant Video Stores. As part of the budgeting process for the entire corporation, he has asked the manager of each video store to prepare a store master budget.

The manager of one of the largest stores, Jeff Miller, decides to understate the sales budget and overstate all the budgets related to expenses. Jeff believes this is a more conservative approach than using the estimated numbers he honestly believes will be achieved for the year. He also thinks that the corporate office will look more favorably on his store's actual achievements when they are subsequently compared to this budget.

Jeff has asked Lisa Dorton, his assistant manager, to review the budget before it is submitted. Lisa is aware of the real estimates that Jeff made.

Required

What is the impact of Jeff Miller's budget for the corporation? What ethical issues face Lisa Dorton?

ANSWERS TO SELF-STUDY QUESTIONS:

1. d, (p. 1024) 2. b, (p. 1027) 3. d, (p. 1030) 4. a, (p. 1036) 5. a, (p. 1032) 6. c, (p. 1039)
7. c, (pp. 1037, 1043)

YOUR TURN! SOLUTIONS

Solution 22.1

Items might include but not be limited to the following:

Strengths: Perception of quality products, strong brand loyalty, appeal to younger customers, move to online retail sales, diversification beyond fashion and housewares

Weaknesses: Dependence on U.S. consumers (virtually no international sales), in-store pickup of online orders

Opportunities: Smaller neighborhood stores, capitalize on urban brand expertise among increasingly urbanized country, continued modernization of stores

Threats: Amazon.com's e-commerce shopping experience intense competition from Walmart, and other similar retailers an economic slowdown in the United States

Solution 22.2

c. Budgeting requires coordination among departments to ensure that all are working toward a common goal.

Solution 22.3

7, 2, 1, 6, 3, 4, 5

Solution 22.4

Change in cash:

Collection of beginning A/R . . .	$ 200,000	Given
January sales	300,000	$500,000 × 60%
February sales	560,000	($500,000 × 40%) + ($600,000 × 60%)
March sales	660,000	($600,000 × 40%) + ($700,000 × 60%)
Payment of beginning A/P	(150,000)	Given
January purchases	(280,000)	$400,000 × 70%
February purchases	(470,000)	($400,000 × 30%) + ($500,000 × 70%)
March purchases	(535,000)	($500,000 × 30%) + ($550,000 × 70%)
January other	(200,000)	$200,000 × 100%
February other	(225,000)	$225,000 × 100%
March other	(225,000)	$225,000 × 100%
Change in cash.	$(365,000)	

Solution 22.5

a.

Chapter 23

Standard Costing and Variance Analysis

PAST

Chapter 22 discussed the budgeting process, the components of the master budget and interrelationships of the individual budgets, and presented an illustration of a budget for a manufacturer and a service company.

PRESENT

Chapter 23 defines standard costs and standard cost variances: direct materials, direct labor, and variable overhead variances.

FUTURE

Chapter 24 introduces flexible budgets and performance evaluation of business segments. In addition, it explores both performance and variance analysis.

Boeing is the world's largest aerospace company and a leading manufacturer of commercial jetliners and defense, space, and security systems. Its products include commercial and military aircraft, satellites, weapons, electronic and defense systems, launch systems, and advanced information and communication systems. As the largest American manufacturing exporter, Boeing employs more than 140,000 employees in the U.S. and in more than 65 other countries. Nearly half of the world's fleet of commercial jetliners currently in service (more than 10,000 jets), were made by Boeing. The main commercial jetliner products include the familiar 737, 747, 767, 777, and 787 families of airplanes. New jetliner products include the 787-10 Dreamliner, 737 MAX, and the 777X.

In an industry where safety is a critical concern, the company is under constant scrutiny. Balancing intense regulatory constraints and increasing competition requires a delicate balance in maintaining extremely high quality standards and monitoring costs. This chapter introduces standard costing and variance analysis, tools that are critical for companies like Boeing.

Road Map

LO	Learning Objective	Page	eLecture	Guided Example	Assignments
LO1	Define standard costs and describe their use in standard cost accounting.	1068	E23-1	YT23.1	SS1, Q1, Q2, Q3, Q4
LO2	Develop an overall understanding of the determination of standard costs for direct materials, direct labor, and variable overhead.	1070	E23-2	YT23.2	SS2, Q5, Q6, Q7, Q8, Q9, SE1, SE2, E1A, E1B
LO3	Understand and calculate direct materials variances.	1074	E23-3	YT23.3	SS3, Q10, Q11, SE3, SE4, SE5, E2A, E4A, E5A, E2B, E4B, E5B, P1A, P2A, P3A, P4A, P1B, P2B, P3B, P4B
LO4	Understand and calculate direct labor variances.	1078	E23-4	YT23.4	Q12, Q13, SE5, SE6, SE7, SE8, E2A, E4A, E5A, E2B, E4B, E5B, P1A, P2A, P3A, P4A, P1B, P2B, P3B, P4B
LO5	Understand and calculate variable overhead variances.	1081	E23-5	YT23.5	SS4, Q14, SE9, SE10, E3A, E4A, E5A, E3B, E4B, E5B, P1A, P2A, P3A, P4A, P1B, P2B, P3B, P4B
LO6	Present and illustrate the use of standard costs in financial statements.	1083	E23-6	YT23.6	SS5, Q15, P2A, P2B
LO7	Appendix 23A: Present journal entries associated with standard costs.	1085	E23-7	YT23.7	Q16, P2A, P3A, P2B, P3B

STANDARD COSTING AND VARIANCE ANALYSIS

Standard Costs	Determining Standard Costs	Direct Materials Variances	Direct Labor Variances	Variable Overhead Variances	Financial Statements	Cost Variance Journal Entries (Appendix 23A)
• Definition • Uses	• Direct materials standards • Direct labor standards • Variable overhead standards • Total standard costs	• Cost variances • Materials price variance • Materials efficiency variance • Fezzari's direct materials variances	• Labor rate variance • Labor efficiency variance • Fezzari direct labor variances	• Spending variances • Efficiency variances • Fezzari variable overhead variances	• Standard costs in financial statements	• Raw materials variances • Direct labor variances • Variable overhead variances

STANDARD COSTS

L01 **Define** standard costs and **describe** their use in standard cost accounting.

Managers follow a cycle of planning (budgeting) before each accounting period and then following up with performance evaluation after the period ends. An important tool that managers use in both the pre-planning phase and in the post-evaluation phase is standard costing. Standard costing consists of setting targets, benchmarks, or goals for performance. In other words, managers define standards or expectations of what they consider to be efficient quantities, costs, and rates they expect to achieve in the production process. After setting these objectives at the beginning of the period (during the budgeting phase), they use them to evaluate performance after the period ends. Specifically, in order to budget expected costs for a period, managers determine how much they "should" spend to produce products or services. Thus, **standard costs** are the costs that should be incurred under normal, efficient operating conditions to produce specific products or to perform specific services. Standards should be attainable through efficient efforts by the typical worker at a task. A complex process, involving engineering specifications, time and motion studies, estimates of supply and demand, and analyses of historical trends, is used to develop standard costs. Standard costs are usually stated per unit of product or service and are useful for a number of purposes, including preparing flexible budgets and master budgets, establishing selling prices, and preparing performance reports.

Standard costs are budgeted costs, the costs that should be incurred during the upcoming year. Obviously, managers use past performance to set standards, but these standards are not intended to simply be a description of past performance, but are intended to be their best projection of *future* performance. In other words, managers want to spend their time looking through the windshield to see where they are going rather than looking at the rearview mirror. Nevertheless, the past is often the best way to project the firm's trajectory for the future. Reasonably attainable levels of efficiency and productivity are used to establish standard costs, so they can serve as a motivating factor and a standard of performance. Typically, standard costs are revised no more frequently than once each year.

Standard costs are usually established prior to the beginning of each year as part of the budgeting process. They should not be updated during the year unless there are major, unexpected changes in vendor costs, wage rates, technology, or product design. One of the important uses of standard costs is to compare them to actual costs to identify significant differences. This comparison process will be most meaningful when the standards used represent the level of efficiency and productivity that was planned during the budgeting process.

Uses of Standard Cost Accounting

Many companies, especially manufacturing firms, adopt **standard cost accounting** for product costs. Although we focus on manufacturing firms in this chapter, it is important to note that standard costing concepts also apply in service companies. The concepts discussed in this chapter relative to labor and overhead apply equally in service and manufacturing environments. When this approach is taken in a manufacturing setting, all inventory accounts—materials, work-in-process, and finished goods—and the cost of goods sold account are stated in terms of standard or predetermined costs rather than actual costs incurred. Specifically, standard costs are used for direct materials, direct labor, variable overhead, and fixed overhead. (Fixed overhead standard costs and variances are beyond the scope of this textbook. We will limit our discussion to variable production costs and assume that in each example, actual fixed overhead costs are equal to standard fixed overhead costs for the period.)

Standard cost accounting can be used with either job order costing or process costing. When standard cost accounting is used, standard costs are carried in the inventory accounts and the cost of goods sold account and the differences between the standard costs and actual costs are recorded as **variances**. Essentially, variances are the deviations from the company's predetermined standards. Thus, variances serve as an important evaluation tool to help managers assess how realistic their budgeted costs determined at the beginning of the period were. Moreover, they allow managers to pinpoint areas for improvement in future periods. **Exhibit 23-1** illustrates how standard costs are set at the beginning of the period. Managers rely on many sources to determine the costs they "should" incur under efficient operating conditions by consulting with engineers regarding historical and projected production rates, past purchase contracts for materials, historical labor rates, and so forth. These standard costs become the basis for the current-period budget. At the end of the period, managers compare the actual costs to the previously defined standard costs to evaluate performance and to help them identify areas for improvement.

Exhibit 23-1	Comparing Standard Cost Budgets to Actual Results

Nelson Electronics Inc. began a new standard cost accounting system after monitoring costs over the past several years. Based on expected production of 8,000 units, Nelson's new standard costing system would have predicted the following costs for the month of January for its main product line:

Direct materials.	$32,000
Direct labor.	11,500
Variable overhead	2,900

Assume that the company achieved the expected output of 8,000 units, but the actual costs for the month were as follows:

Direct materials.	$34,600
Direct labor.	11,200
Variable overhead	2,400

How would you evaluate the company's performance during January?

eLectures
MBC

DETERMINING STANDARD COSTS

LO2 **Develop** an overall understanding of the determination of standard costs for direct materials, direct labor, and variable overhead.

The development of standard costs per unit of product for all variable inputs requires the use of six components: (1) direct materials standard price, (2) direct materials standard quantity, (3) direct labor standard rate, (4) direct labor standard time allowed, (5) standard variable overhead rate, and (6) variable overhead standard capacity. The cost-related components are developed and updated as part of the budgeting process, and quantity and capacity standards are usually developed as part of the product design and engineering process. We describe the six standard costing components in the following sections.

Direct Materials Standards

Hint: The product of direct materials standard price and direct materials standard quantity is part of a static budget.

The standard direct materials cost to produce a unit of a particular finished product is determined by multiplying the direct materials standard quantity (SQ) per unit by the direct materials standard price (SP) per unit:

Standard direct materials cost per unit = Standard quantity × Standard price = SQ × SP

To illustrate this calculation, consider the fact that each of Boeing's 787 jetliners requires seat-back tray tables. Assume that the standard quantity of seat-back tray tables per 787 is 232. Moreover, assume that Boeing has a supplier that produces the tray tables and that the standard purchase price per tray table is $50. Given this information, the standard direct materials cost to provide seat-back tray tables for a Boeing 787 would be calculated as follows:

Standard tray table cost per 787 airplane =	SQ × SP
=	232 tables per 787 × $50 per table
=	$11,600 per 787

A number of factors affect the direct materials standard quantity, including materials quality, engineering specifications, the skill of the direct labor workers, and the capabilities of the equipment used to process the materials. Factors affecting the direct materials standard price include the quality of the materials, its availability, and discounts for volume purchases.

The standard materials cost should be the expected cost of materials including delivery costs and net of any discounts.

Direct Labor Standards

The standard cost of direct labor required to produce one unit of a particular product is determined by multiplying the direct labor standard time allowed, usually specified in hours (SH), by the direct labor standard wage rate (SR):

Standard direct labor cost per unit = Standard hours × Standard wage rate = SH × SR

Continuing the Boeing illustration, assume that the standard amount of direct labor needed to install the seat-back tray tables is 8 hours per 787 and that the standard hourly wage rate for direct labor is $30. The resulting standard direct labor cost per 787 is $240:

Standard direct labor cost per 787 =	SH × SR
	= 8 Direct labor hours per 787 × $30 per direct labor hour
	= $240 per 787

The direct labor standard wage rate represents the expected weighted average of labor rates for all levels of workers who undertake direct labor tasks on the product. The rates for the various levels of workers are set by the company or prescribed by labor contract. Direct labor standard times are based primarily on prior employee performance and current time and motion studies. Moreover, these wage rates include all compensation components guaranteed to employees (such as health insurance, payroll taxes, retirement plans, etc.).

The direct labor standard time should include an allowance for breaks, personal needs, cleanup, and so on.

Variable Overhead Standards

The standard cost of variable overhead needed to manufacture one unit of a particular product is determined by multiplying the variable overhead standard capacity (SC) by the standard (or predetermined) variable overhead application rate (SR):

Standard variable overhead cost per unit = **Variable overhead standard capacity** × **Variable overhead application rate** = SC × SR

Traditionally we separate overhead costs into fixed and variable components. This is necessary because fixed costs hold constant within all production levels within our relevant range. Only the variable component fluctuates in response to changes in volume. Therefore our variable overhead application rate (SR) is the variable portion of the predetermined overhead application rate that was explained in the discussion of job order costing in Chapter 16. Recall that the basis for determining the rate can be direct labor hours, direct labor dollars, machine hours, or some other overhead application base. The basis selected should be the best common measure of variable overhead capacity utilized during production.

The variable overhead standard capacity (SC) should be stated in the same terms as the rate (SR). For instance, if the basis for the variable overhead application rate is direct labor hours, then the variable overhead standard capacity allowed will be the number of direct labor hours expected to produce one unit. This will also typically be the same application base used to apply the overhead application rate to production.

In the Boeing illustration, assume that Boeing allocates variable overhead based on direct labor hours and that the standard variable overhead application rate (SR) is calculated to be $50 per direct labor hour and that the variable overhead standard capacity (SC) for installing the seat-back tray tables is 8 direct labor hours per 787 (i.e., the same as the direct labor standard time or SH allowed). The resulting standard variable overhead cost per 787 associated with the tray installation is calculated as follows:

$$
\begin{aligned}
\text{Standard variable overhead cost per 787} \;=\;\; & \text{SC} \times \text{SR} \\
=\;\; & 8 \text{ Direct labor hours per 787} \times \$50 \text{ per direct labor hour} \\
=\;\; & \$400 \text{ per 787}
\end{aligned}
$$

A.K.A. The standard variable overhead rate is also known as the predetermined variable overhead rate.

The standard variable overhead rate is based on the expected level of operations. Because a wide variety of cost items is included in variable overhead, many different factors affect the rate. The variable overhead standard capacity is influenced by such factors as prior employee performance, prior machine performance, and current time and motion studies.

TAKEAWAY 23.1	Concept ⟶	Method ⟶	Assessment ⟶
	Management needs to understand and utilize standard costs and variances.	Establishing standards helps managers track actual results and compare them to standards.	The process of comparing actual to budgeted results guides management to better understand factors that cause cost fluctuations.

Total Standard Costs

Exhibit 23-2 summarizes the relationships described so far. Most firms that use standard costs prepare a summary of the standard product costs for each product that they produce.

Exhibit 23-2	Standard Cost Summary
Standard direct materials cost per unit . . . . . . =	SQ × SP
Standard direct labor cost per unit . . . . =	SH × SR
Standard variable overhead cost per unit. . . . =	SC × SR

Where: SQ = Standard Quantity
SP = Standard Price
SH = Standard Hours
SR = Standard Rate
SC = Standard Capacity

Based on the preceding concepts, Boeing's standard cost summary for seat-back tray tables in a 787 would appear as in **Exhibit 23-3**.

Exhibit 23-3	Standard Cost Summary

BOEING 787
Seat-Back Tray Tables

Direct materials.	(232 tables × $50 per table) =	$11,600
Direct labor.	(8 DLH × $30 per DLH) =	240
Variable overhead	(8 DLH × $50 per DLH) =	400
Total standard product cost per 787		$12,240

Where: DLH = Direct labor hours

Standard costs are also used in determining product cost variances. The remaining sections of this chapter deal with the calculation and use of product cost variances.

Use of Standard Costs in Setting Selling Prices	ACCOUNTING IN PRACTICE

Standard costs of products are an important consideration in setting selling prices, but are certainly not the only, or even the most important, consideration. Prices of competitors' products and prices of substitute products must also be considered when determining product selling prices.

COST VARIANCES

Standard costs are extremely helpful in budgeting prior to the start of a fiscal period. Moreover, they can also be very useful in evaluating performance at the end of a period. Even in well-managed companies with carefully established and currently maintained cost standards, actual costs will differ from standard costs. The differences, often called *variances*, should be analyzed for indications of their cause so that appropriate action may be taken to prevent them in future periods.

We first provide an overview of each type of variance and then illustrate the calculation of these variances based on the production data for an important Fezzari product. Suppose that during June 2019, Fezzari Bicycles produced 100 Fore CR2 road bikes for which it incurred the following actual costs (assume no beginning or ending work-in-process inventories):

Direct materials:	
Frame	$33,600
Build kit	31,500
Direct labor:	
Assembly	15,000
Quality control and packaging.	5,000
Variable overhead	1,525
Total actual variable production costs	$86,625

Exhibit 23-4 compares the actual costs with standard costs to produce 100 bikes, and calculates the differences, or variances, for each cost category. We multiply the standard costs by the actual quantity of 100 bikes produced in June. Note that both favorable and unfavorable variances exist and that the overall net variance of $7,315 is unfavorable. To initiate remedial action, management must analyze the variance for each manufacturing cost element to determine the underlying causal factors related to prices paid, quantities used, and productive capacity used.

Exhibit 23-4	Comparison of Standard and Actual Costs

FEZZARI PERFORMANCE BICYCLES
Variance Analysis
June 30, 2019

	Actual Costs	Standard Costs	Total Flexible Budget Variances	
Direct materials.	$65,100	$60,000	$5,100	Unfavorable*
Direct labor	20,000	17,750	2,250	Unfavorable
Variable overhead	1,525	1,560	(35)	Favorable
Total	$86,625	$79,310	$7,315	Unfavorable

*The total materials variance calculated in the next section is not equal to the difference between the total standard costs and total actual costs because the amount purchased is different from the amount used in production. See the chapter discussion for a detailed explanation.

YOUR TURN! 23.2

The solution is on page 1101.

Feagin Company planned to produce 22,000 units of product during the current month. In order to produce this level of output, the standard costing system predicts the use of 88,000 feet of material at a standard rate of $3.00 per foot. The standard costing system would anticipate 33,000 direct labor hours at a standard rate is $7.00 per hour. Finally, the standard (predetermined) variable overhead rate is $2.00 per direct labor hour based on the standard number of direct labor hours for this production level. Assume Feagin achieved the projected output of 22,000 units by incurring the following actual costs for the month:

Direct materials.	$261,000
Direct labor	262,500
Variable overhead	63,000

Determine Feagin Company's total flexible budget variance for the month.

Direct Materials Variances

We begin our discussion with direct materials variances. Direct materials variances are often slightly more complicated than the other variable manufacturing cost variances simply because the quantity of materials purchased often differs from the quantity used in production during the period. To aid in (1) understanding how variances work, (2) remembering how they are calculated, and (3) visualizing each type of variance, we present each type of variable manufacturing cost variance using a simple "fork diagram." **Exhibit 23-5** provides a simple diagram for materials (assuming the quantity purchased is equal to the quantity used in production).

LO3 **Understand** and **calculate** direct materials variances.

Exhibit 23-5	Direct Materials Variances

Actual Cost	Split Cost	Standard Cost
(AQ × AP)	(AQ × SP)	(SQ × SP)
	Price variance	Efficiency variance
	AQ (AP − SP)	SP (AQ − SQ)

Total Materials Flexible Budget Variance

Variance analysis simply compares actual costs with standard costs. We place the actual materials cost on the left. How much did we spend to purchase materials? Actual materials purchased equals the actual quantity (AQ) purchased times the actual price per unit (AP). We place the standard cost of materials allowed for this level of production on the far right of the diagram. How much should we have spent on raw materials at this level of production? As explained previously, standard materials cost equals the standard quantity allowed (SQ) for this level of output times the standard price per unit (SP). The total difference between actual and standard costs (as explained in more detail in Chapter 24) is called the total materials flexible budget variance. However, there are two reasons we may spend more or less than our standards would indicate. First, we may pay too much or too little when we purchase the materials. Second, we may not use the materials efficiently in the production process. Hence, it is useful to split the total materials flexible budget variance into its two main components: (1) the **materials price variance** and (2) the **materials efficiency variance**. In order to facilitate this analysis, we place a new number in the middle of the diagram (the split cost), which takes the actual quantity purchased (AQ) from the far left of the diagram and multiplies it by the standard price (SP) from the far right of the diagram. This number represents the standard price we should have spent to buy the actual quantity purchased (AQ × SP).

We calculate the materials price variance by subtracting the standard price we should have paid for the actual quantity purchased from our actual purchase price:

$$\text{Materials price variance} = (\text{AQ} \times \text{AP}) - (\text{AQ} \times \text{SP})$$

Using simple algebra, we can factor out the common element in each number (AQ) and rewrite the materials price variance as follows:

$$\text{Materials price variance} = \text{AQ} (\text{AP} - \text{SP})$$

Written this way, we see that the *cause* of this variance is the difference between the actual price paid to purchase materials compared to the standard price management had budgeted at the beginning of the period. If the actual price exceeds the standard price (i.e., we paid too much), the materials price variance will appear as a positive number. Thus, positive price variance is "unfavorable" because it would indicate that we paid too much per unit when we purchased the materials. On the other hand, if the materials price variance is a negative number (i.e., we paid less than our standards had predicted), the variance is "favorable."

We calculate the materials efficiency variance by subtracting the standard materials cost (SQ × SP) from what we should have paid for the actual quantity purchased according to our standards (AQ × SP):

$$\text{Materials efficiency variance} = (\text{AQ} \times \text{SP}) - (\text{SQ} \times \text{SP})$$

Again, we can use basic algebra to factor out the common element (SP) to rewrite the materials efficiency variance to better illustrate what causes the variance:

$$\text{Materials efficiency variance} = \text{SP} (\text{AQ} - \text{SQ})$$

When expressed this way, it is clear that, holding the standard price constant, what *causes* the variance is the quantity used. If we do not use the materials efficiently in production, we may spend too much or too little. Similar to what we observe for the materials price variance, if the actual quantity exceeds the standard quantity (i.e., we used too much of the material in producing products during this period), the materials efficiency variance will appear as a positive number, suggesting that we did not use our materials efficiently (thus the variance will be "unfavorable"). On the other hand, if we use less than our budgeted standards would dictate (i.e., the materials efficiency variance is negative), we conclude that we used less than we expected (and we would label this negative number as a "favorable" materials efficiency variance).

When the quantity of materials purchased is exactly equal to the quantity used in production, this simple diagram indicates that the total materials flexible budget variance is equal to the sum of the materials price variance and the materials efficiency variance. However, it is common in practice that companies purchase more or less than they actually use in production. To account for these common differences, **Exhibit 23-6** illustrates how we modify the "fork diagram" for materials to better differentiate between these two quantities because the materials price variance is based on the quantity of materials *purchased*, whereas the materials efficiency variance depends on the amount of materials *used* in the production process. In other words, the split cost number (AQ × SP), the actual quantity at the standard price, must actually be shown twice because the price variance is based on the quantity *purchased*, whereas the efficiency variance is calculated using the actual quantity *used* in the production process. It is easy to make mistakes in calculating variances if you don't pay close attention to which quantity you are referring to! The version of the materials "fork diagram" in **Exhibit 23-6** can help you to avoid these careless errors. We illustrate these calculations next.

ACCOUNTING IN PRACTICE	**Managing Variances**

Managers may trade off one variance for another. For example, a manager may decide to use a pre-cut material rather than a bulk material. This usually will result in higher cost (unfavorable price variance) and lower quantities (favorable quantity variance) than budgeted.

Exhibit 23-6 Direct Materials Variances

Fezzari's Direct Materials Variances

We first calculate the materials price variance for frames. Fezzari actually ***purchased*** 105 frames at a price of $320 per frame and ***used*** 101 in production during the month. Assume that the standard price is $325 per frame.

The calculations in **Exhibit 23-7** indicate a favorable price variance for frames of $525. This is calculated as the difference between the actual and budgeted price for frames ($320 − $325) multiplied by the number of frames purchased (105). The variance is favorable because Fezzari spent $5 less per frame than anticipated in the budget. However, these calculations also indicate an unfavorable efficiency variance of $325. This is calculated as the budgeted price per frame ($325) multiplied by the difference between the actual number of frames used and the budgeted number of frames used (101 − 100).

Fezzari used one more frame than anticipated for this level of production because one bike was damaged beyond repair during production.

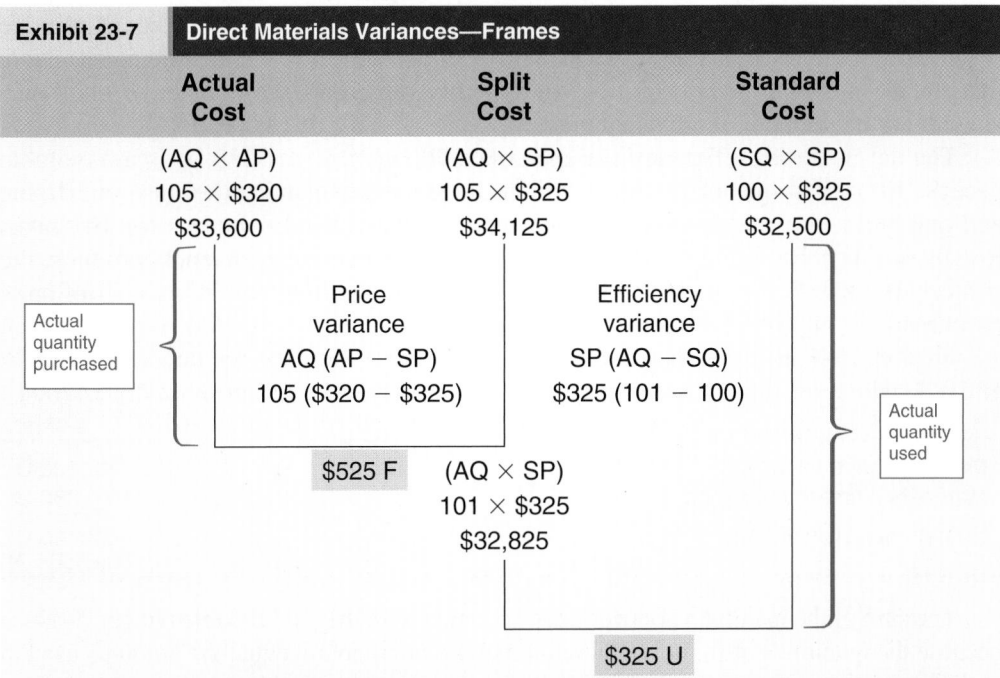

Exhibit 23-7 Direct Materials Variances—Frames

Next, we use the same process to calculate the materials price variance for build kits. Fezzari actually ***purchased*** 105 build kits at a price of $300 per build kit and ***used*** 101 in production during the month. Assume that the standard price is $275 per build kit.

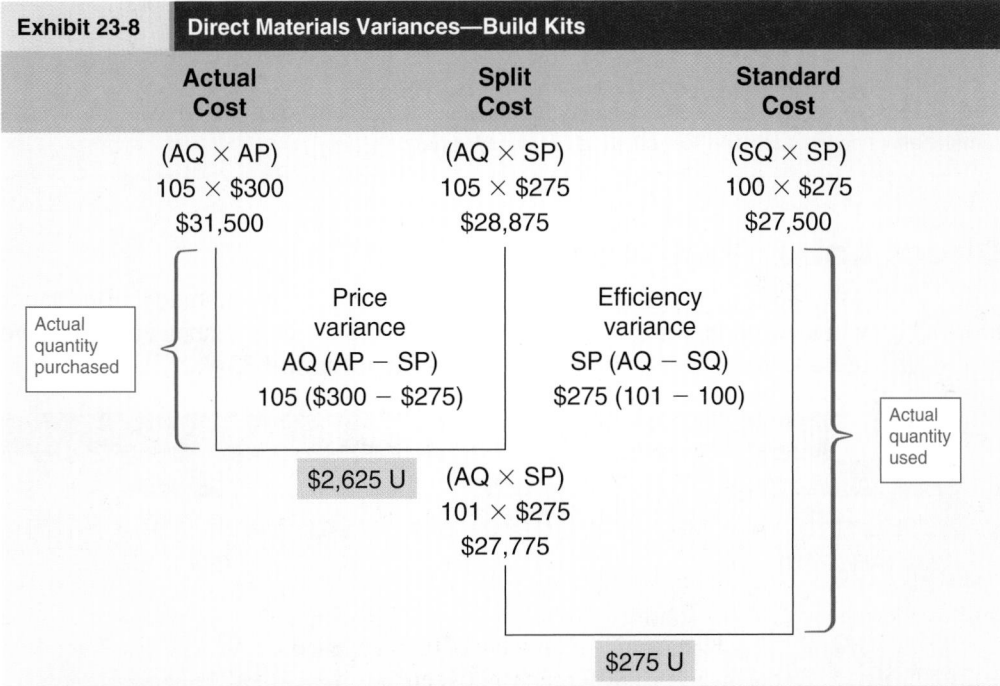

Exhibit 23-8 Direct Materials Variances—Build Kits

The calculations in **Exhibit 23-8** indicate an unfavorable price variance for build kits of $2,625 (105 build kits × $25 per build kit) because Fezzari spent $25 more per build kit than anticipated in the budget. These calculations also indicate an unfavorable efficiency variance of $275 ($275 × 1 extra build kit). Fezzari used one more build kit than would normally be anticipated for this level of production because one bike was damaged beyond repair during production.

The net materials price variance of $2,100 ($2,625 U − $525 F) is unfavorable because the actual price for build kits was $25 per unit greater than the standard price (even though the price of frames was actually $5 per unit lower than anticipated). Note that for the materials price variance, the quantity represents the number of units purchased, not the number of units manufactured.

The net materials efficiency variance of $600 ($325 U + $275 U) is unfavorable because the actual quantity is greater than the standard quantity (because one frame and one build kit were damaged beyond repair, Fezzari used materials for 101 bikes to only produce 100 usable bikes). Note that for the materials efficiency variance, the quantity represents the number of units issued into production, not the number of units purchased.

Exhibit 23-4 indicates that the total flexible budget variance for direct materials is $5,100 U. However, the sum of the materials price and efficiency variances is only $2,700 U:

Materials price variance	$2,100 U
Materials efficiency variance	600 U
Sum of materials variances	$2,700 U

The sum of the material variances does not agree with the total flexible budget variance because the quantities of frames and build kits purchased do not equal the amounts used in production. Although the sums of individual variances always add up to the total flexible budget variance for labor and variable overhead variances, this relationship only holds for materials if the quantity purchased equals the quantity used in production during the period.

The unfavorable price variance may have been caused by increases in supplier prices, improper purchasing, or other factors. The unfavorable efficiency variance may have been caused by inefficient workers, inferior-quality materials, or other factors.

YOUR TURN! 23.3

The solution is on page 1101.

Feagin Company purchased and used 90,000 feet of material at $2.90 per foot to make 22,000 units of a finished product. The per-unit standard for material is 4 feet @ $3.00 = $12.00. What were the materials price variance and the materials efficiency variance?

Direct Labor Variances

LO4   **Understand** and **calculate** direct labor variances.

After gaining experience with materials variances, most students find labor variances to be much easier. In order to visualize direct labor variances, we use a similar "fork diagram," as illustrated in **Exhibit 23-9**.

Similar to materials variances, we place the actual direct labor cost on the left. How much did we pay our labor force? Actual labor costs equal the actual number of hours worked (AH) times the actual wage rate (AR). We place the standard direct labor cost on the far right of the diagram. How much should we have paid our employees to produce this level of output? As explained previously, standard labor costs equal the standard number of hours to produce this many units (SH) times the standard hourly wage rate (SR). The total difference between actual and standard costs (as explained in more detail in Chapter 24) is called the total labor flexible budget variance. However, there are two reasons we may spend more or less than our standards would indicate. First, we may pay our employees too much or too little relative to what we expected when we prepared our budget at the beginning of the period. Second, we may not use our workforce efficiently in producing inventory. Similar to what we observed for materials, it is useful to split the total labor flexible budget variance into its two main components: (1) the **labor rate variance** and (2) the **labor efficiency variance**. In order to facilitate this analysis, we place a split cost number in the middle of the diagram, which takes the actual hours worked (AH) from the far left of the diagram and multiplies it by the standard wage rate (SR) from the far right of the diagram. This number represents the standard amount we should have spent to pay our workforce (AH × SR) to produce this level of output.

We calculate the labor rate variance by subtracting the standard price we should have paid our employees for the actual level of production from our actual labor costs:

$$\text{Labor rate variance} = (\text{AH} \times \text{AR}) - (\text{AH} \times \text{SR})$$

Using simple algebra, we can factor out the common element in each number (AH) and rewrite the labor rate variance as follows:

$$\text{Labor rate variance} = \text{AH}\,(\text{AR} - \text{SR})$$

When the equation is written this way, we see that the *cause* of this variance is the difference between the actual wage rate as compared with the standard wage rate management had forecasted at the beginning of the period. If the actual rate exceeds the standard rate (i.e., we paid employees more than expected), the labor rate variance will appear as a positive number. Thus, a positive price variance is "unfavorable" because we paid more than we had budgeted. On the other hand, if the labor rate variance is a negative number (i.e., we paid less than our standards had predicted), the variance is "favorable."

We calculate the labor efficiency variance by subtracting the standard labor cost (SH × SR) from what we should have paid for the actual hours worked according to our standards (AH × SR):

$$\text{Labor efficiency variance} = (\text{AH} \times \text{SR}) - (\text{SH} \times \text{SR})$$

Again, we can use basic algebra to factor out the common element (SR) to rewrite the labor efficiency variance to better illustrate what causes the variance:

$$\text{Labor efficiency variance} = \text{SR}\,(\text{AH} - \text{SH})$$

After factoring the variance formula this way, it is clear that holding the standard wage rate constant, what *causes* the variance is the number of hours used. If we do not use our employees efficiently in production, we may spend too much or too little. If the actual number of hours worked exceeds the standard number of hours (i.e., we used too many employee hours), the labor efficiency variance will appear as a positive number, suggesting that we did not use our labor force efficiently (thus the variance will be "unfavorable"). On the other hand, if we use fewer hours than our standards would have predicted (i.e., the labor efficiency variance is negative), we conclude that we were able to use our workers less than we expected (and we would label this negative number as a "favorable" labor efficiency variance).

Fezzari's Direct Labor Variances

We illustrate the calculation of direct labor variances using the Fezzari data presented previously. Specifically, we use the data for the assembly department. Assembly personnel actually worked 750 hours during June at an average rate of $20 per hour. However, the standard number of hours to produce 100 CR2 bikes is 550 hours and the standard wage rate in this department is $25 per hour. Using this information, we can calculate assembly labor variances as illustrated in **Exhibit 23-10**. These calculations indicate a favorable rate variance in the assembly department of $3,750, calculated as 750 hours multiplied by the $5-per-hour difference between the actual and standard rate. The variance is favorable because Fezzari paid an average of $5 less per hour than anticipated in the budget. However, these calculations also indicate an unfavorable efficiency variance of $5,000 ($25 standard rate × 200 extra hours) because Fezzari's assembly crew worked 200 hours more than anticipated for this level of production.

Exhibit 23-10	Assembly Labor Variances	
Actual Cost	**Split Cost**	**Standard Cost**
(AH × AR)	(AH × SR)	(SH × SR)
750 × $20	750 × $25	550 × $25
$15,000	$18,750	$13,750

	Rate variance	Efficiency variance
	AH (AR − SR)	SR (AH − SH)
	750 ($20 − $25)	$25 (750 − 550)
	$3,750 F	$5,000 U

Total Labor Flexible Budget Variance = $1,250 U

Next, **Exhibit 23-11** calculates the labor variances for the quality control (QC) and packaging department. Employees in this department actually worked 250 hours during June at an average rate of $20 per hour. Assume that the standard number of hours at this production level is 200 and the standard wage rate is exactly $20 per hour.

Exhibit 23-11	QC and Packaging Labor Variances	
Actual Cost	**Split Cost**	**Standard Cost**
(AH × AR)	(AH × SR)	(SH × SR)
250 × $20	250 × $20	200 × $20
$5,000	$5,000	$4,000

	Rate variance	Efficiency variance
	AH (AR − SR)	SR (AH − SH)
	250 ($20 − $20)	$20 (250 − 200)
	$0	$1,000 U

Total Labor Flexible Budget Variance = $1,000 U

Because the actual wage rate coincides perfectly with the standard wage rate, there is no labor rate variance. However, these calculations indicate an unfavorable efficiency variance of $1,000 ($20 standard rate × 50 extra hours) because Fezzari's QC and packaging employees worked 50 hours more than anticipated for this level of production.

Combining the results for the assembly and the QC and packaging departments, we calculate the following total variances:

Labor rate variance.	$3,750 F
Labor efficiency variance	6,000 U
Total flexible budget variance for labor.	$2,250 U

Notice that the sum of the labor rate and efficiency variances equals the total flexible budget variance for labor in **Exhibit 23-4**.

Feagin Company's actual hours worked were 35,000 at a rate of $7.50 per hour to make 22,000 units of a finished product. The per-unit standard for labor is 1.5 hours @ $7.00 per hour = $10.50. What were the labor rate variance and the labor efficiency variance?

YOUR TURN! 23.4

The solution is on page 1101.

Variable Overhead Variances

Variable overhead variances are virtually identical to labor variances. Therefore we can visualize variable overhead variances using the **Exhibit 23-12** "fork diagram" that is very similar to the direct labor diagram. As explained previously, overhead may be applied to product cost based on any application base that represents the "cost driver." Therefore the standard cost of variable overhead needed to manufacture one unit of a particular product, shown on the far right of the diagram, is determined by multiplying the variable overhead standard capacity (SC) of that "cost driver" by the standard (or predetermined) variable overhead application rate (SR). Note that variable overhead items are recorded as "actual" debits to the manufacturing overhead account as they occur. There is no "rate" applied to these actual amounts. The "actual" amount spent, shown on the far left of the diagram, is simply the sum of all indirect variable items (such as indirect materials, indirect labor, etc.). For simplicity, assume that a company uses direct labor hours as that cost driver in developing a predetermined variable overhead application rate.

LO5 Understand and calculate variable overhead variances.

Exhibit 23-12	Variable Overhead Variances

Actual Cost	Split Cost	Standard Cost
	(AH × SR)	(SH × SR)
Spending variance	Efficiency variance	
(Actual − Split)	SR (AH − SH)	

Total Variable Overhead Flexible Budget Variance

In this diagram, the predetermined variable overhead application rate (i.e., the standard rate, SR) is based on direct labor hours. The variable overhead spending variance (i.e., the rate variance) determines whether that predetermined overhead application rate is higher or lower than the standard rate determined by managers in the budgeting process. Similarly, variable overhead efficiency variance is attributable to the use of that overhead application base or "driver." In this diagram, we list the number of direct labor hours as the "cause" of the efficiency variance. Obviously, if some other application base were used to calculate the predetermined overhead application rate, such as machine hours, direct labor dollars, or quality inspections, the efficiency variance would be based on that factor. For example, if we had used the number of inspections as our variable overhead application base, the formula for the variable overhead efficiency variance would be SR (AI − SI), where "AI" would represent the actual number of quality inspections and "SI" would represent the standard number of quality inspections for that production run.

FEZZARI'S VARIABLE OVERHEAD VARIANCES

Fezzari's variable overhead variances result from paying more or less than planned for items that comprise variable overhead (the **variable overhead spending variance**) and from using more or less than the standard amount of capacity (the **variable overhead efficiency variance**).

ACCOUNTING IN PRACTICE

Standard Capacity

The standard capacity allowed for variable overhead and fixed overhead will be stated in terms of a common measure of plant capacity, such as direct labor hours or machine hours. A different measure may be used for variable overhead and fixed overhead.

Assume that Fezzari incurs actual variable overhead during the month of June of $1,525, comprised of the following items:

Indirect materials	$ 55
Indirect labor	550
Factory utilities	645
Other	275
Total	$1,525

These items would be recorded as debits to the manufacturing overhead account as incurred:

Manufacturing overhead	1,525	
Raw materials inventory		55
Wages payable		550
Utilities payable		645
Other payables (or cash)		275

Also assume that during its budgeting process for the year, Fezzari decided to allocate variable overhead based on estimated labor hours in the QC and packaging department and that the predetermined overhead application rate is $7.80 per hour. Therefore, the variable overhead variances for Fezzari are computed and recorded as shown in **Exhibit 23-13**. The calculations are similar to those for materials and labor, which, like variable overhead, are variable product cost components.

The actual variable overhead costs are less than would be projected, based on the actual number of hours worked in this department multiplied by the predetermined (standard) variable overhead application rate. Therefore, the variable overhead spending variance is $425 favorable. The variable overhead efficiency variance is $390 unfavorable simply because employees in the QC and packaging department worked 50 hours more than was anticipated for this level of projection.

Exhibit 23-13	Variable Overhead Variances

Actual Cost	Split Cost	Standard Cost
	(AH × SR)	(SH × SR)
	250 × $7.80	200 × $7.80
$1,525	$1,950	$1,560

Spending variance

(Actual − Split)
$1,525 − $1,950

Efficiency variance

SR (AH − SH)
$7.80 (250 − 200)

$425 F $390 U

Total Variable Overhead Flexible Budget Variance = $35 F

The total variable overhead variance would be as follows:

Variable overhead spending variance	$425 F
Variable overhead efficiency variance	390 U
Total variable overhead variance	$ 35 F

Notice that the total variable overhead variance agrees with the amount in **Exhibit 23-4**.

Feagin Company's actual variable overhead was $63,000. Actual hours were 35,000 to make 22,000 finished products. The per-unit standard for variable overhead is 1.5 hours @ $2.00, or $3.00. What were the variable overhead spending variance and the variable overhead efficiency variance?

YOUR TURN! 23.5

The solution is on page 1101.

STANDARD COSTS IN FINANCIAL STATEMENTS

When the standard costs and related variances for direct materials, direct labor, and variable overhead are recorded as previously illustrated, the work-in-process account is debited for each in amounts representing standard quantities and standard prices. All variances—favorable and unfavorable—are carried in separate accounts with appropriate titles. Fezzari records completed production for June in the following entry (assume no beginning or ending work-in-process inventories):

LO6 Present and Illustrate the use of standard costs in financial statements.

Finished goods inventory (at standard cost)	79,310	
Work-in-process inventory (at standard cost)		79,310
To record completion of June's production of 100 units at a standard variable unit cost of $793.10 ($60,000 materials, $17,750 labor, and $1,560 variable overhead).		

As each month's production is sold, the related amounts of standard costs are transferred from Finished Goods Inventory to Cost of Goods Sold.

Standard costs and related variances are usually reported in financial reports intended only for management's use. **Exhibit 23-14** contains a partial income statement that illustrates how variances might appear on interim financial statements for Fezzari's internal use (amounts are assumed).

Exhibit 23-14	Summary

FEZZARI PERFORMANCE BICYCLES
Partial Income Statement
For the Month Ended June 30, 2019

Sales.	$375,000
Cost of goods sold at standard cost	250,000
Gross profit at standard cost	$125,000
Less: Net unfavorable cost variance	6,500
Gross profit.	$118,500

> The "net" cost variance is simply the net of all individual materials, labor, and overhead variances.

The total net variance could be broken down into sub-variances or detailed in a schedule of variances accompanying the financial statements.

At year-end, firms commonly close the variance accounts by transferring their balances to Cost of Goods Sold. In effect, this transfer converts Cost of Goods Sold from standard costs to be accurate costs. If large variances exist at year-end and there is evidence that the standards may not be accurate, a firm may be justified in allocating all or part of the variances to Work-in-Process Inventory, Finished Goods Inventory, and Cost of Goods Sold.

YOUR TURN! 23.6

The solution is on page 1102.

Assume Paterson Company reports sales of $500,000, cost of goods sold (based on standard costs) of $460,000 for 2019. However, during the year the company also reports the following variances:

Materials price variance	6,000
Materials efficiency variance	(2,000)
Labor rate variance.	(9,000)
Labor efficiency variance	(1,500)
Variable overhead spending variance	11,000
Variable overhead efficiency variance	(2,000)

Note that positive numbers denote unfavorable variances. How would Paterson incorporate these variances in the income statement?

SERVICES INDUSTRY IN FOCUS

SERVICE AND MERCHANDISING

Environmental Business Consultants, Inc. (EBC) has hired several new staff members in the last year and has invested considerable effort in training these new employees in the EBC approach to conducting rate review projects. Due to the unique market in which EBC operates, there are not commercial training conferences or online training materials available to provide the necessary training. Therefore, the training is done primarily on the job by EBC managers, resulting in extra hours over what is typically incurred in completing this type of project. EBC management is interested in estimating the cost of this on-the-job training in terms of "lost billings," that is, the billing value of the extra hours incurred by both managers and staff as compared with normal budgeted hours. This is equivalent to the labor efficiency variance.

Assume that for the year just ended, EBC completed 25 rate review projects. The following table shows the normal hourly budget for managers and staff on a rate review project. EBC managers billed a total of 1,200 hours and staff billed a total of 3,500 hours on rate review projects during the year. For the year, managers were billed at a standard rate of $200 per hour and staff were billed at a standard rate of $120 per hour.

	Managers	Staff
Budgeted hours per rate review project	40	120

Required:
Determine the total labor efficiency variance for both managers and staff for the year.

Solution

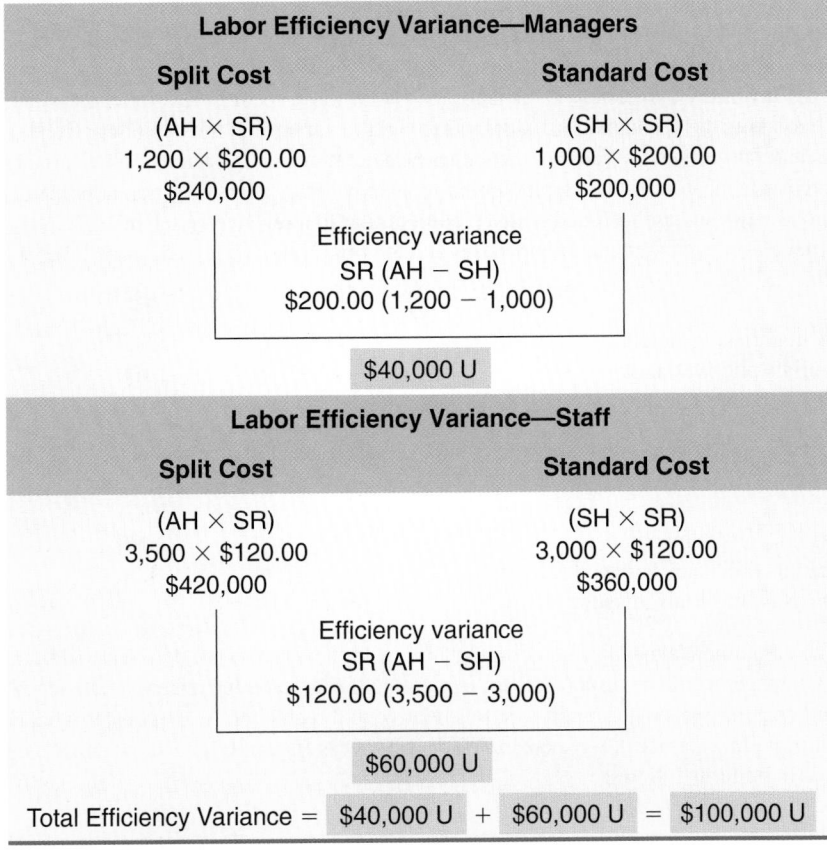

Labor Efficiency Variance—Managers

Split Cost	Standard Cost
(AH × SR)	(SH × SR)
1,200 × $200.00	1,000 × $200.00
$240,000	$200,000

Efficiency variance
SR (AH − SH)
$200.00 (1,200 − 1,000)

$40,000 U

Labor Efficiency Variance—Staff

Split Cost	Standard Cost
(AH × SR)	(SH × SR)
3,500 × $120.00	3,000 × $120.00
$420,000	$360,000

Efficiency variance
SR (AH − SH)
$120.00 (3,500 − 3,000)

$60,000 U

Total Efficiency Variance = $40,000 U   + $60,000 U   = $100,000 U

APPENDIX 23A: Cost Variance Journal Entries Illustrated

This appendix illustrates the journal entries used in a standard costing system to record materials, labor, and variable overhead variances based on the Fezzari example used throughout the chapter.

JOURNAL ENTRIES ILLUSTRATED

LO7   **Present** journal entries associated with standard costs.

The materials price variance is recorded in the accounting system at the time materials are purchased. Although the amount paid to suppliers is always the "actual" invoice price, we enter materials into the raw materials inventory account at the standard price:

Raw materials inventory	(AQ × SP)	
Materials price variance	U	or F
Accounts payable (or cash)		(AQ × AP)

Thus, the credit to Accounts Payable (or Cash) is for the actual amount (AQ × AP), whereas the debit to Raw Materials Inventory is for the standard price to purchase the actual quantity acquired (AQ × SP). We record the difference as the raw materials price variance to allow the manager of the purchasing department to explain the variance at the end of the fiscal period. Note that the materials price variance can either be a debit or a credit. Unfavorable variances (U) are bad news. Hence, they are recorded with a debit (similar to an expense or a loss). On the other hand, favorable variances (F) are good news and are recorded with a credit (similar to a revenue or a gain).

The materials efficiency variance is recorded in the accounting records when raw materials are used in production:

Work-in-process inventory	(SQ × SP)	
Materials efficiency variance	U	or F
Raw materials inventory		(AQ × SP)

We note that when raw materials were purchased, they were recorded at the actual quantity purchased times the standard price per unit. When we use materials in the production process, we take them out of Raw Materials Inventory as the actual quantity used times the standard price per unit (AQ × SP). However, we enter materials into Work-in-Process Inventory completely at standard (SQ × SP). We record the difference as the materials efficiency variance to allow the production manager to explain the variance at the end of the fiscal period. We again note that the materials efficiency variance can either be a debit or a credit. Unfavorable variances (U) are bad news. Hence, they are recorded with a debit (similar to an expense or a loss). On the other hand, favorable variances (F) are good news and are recorded with a credit (similar to a revenue or a gain).

Fezzari's journal entry to record material purchases and the price variance for CR2 road bikes would be as follows (see **Exhibits 23-7** and **23-8**):

Raw materials inventory	63,000	
Materials price variance	2,100	
Accounts payable (or cash)		65,100

Moreover, Fezzari's journal entry to record the materials that are used in production for CR2s would be as follows:

Work-in-process inventory	60,000	
Materials efficiency variance	600	
Raw materials inventory		60,600

The purchasing department's manager can best explain the higher-than-expected prices paid for materials and the production manager would be responsible for explaining the unfavorable materials efficiency variance.

We only record one entry in the accounting records relative to direct labor. As employees work directly on our products (or in providing services), we increase Work-in-Process Inventory and show either a decrease to cash or an increased liability, as follows:

Work-in-process inventory	(SH × SR)	
Labor rate variance	U	or F
Labor efficiency variance	U	or F
Wages payable (or cash)		(AH × AR)

Obviously, our employees won't continue working for us if we don't pay them for their services. Moreover, they are not likely to be happy if we tell them, "We're sorry, but your wage rates are higher than our budget anticipated, so we're only going to pay you the standard wage rate." We have to pay our employees whatever wage rate we contracted with them when we hired them (or when they received their last raise). Hence, the credit to Wages Payable (or Cash) must be for the amount the employees actually earned (AH × AR). However, as explained previously, under a standard costing approach, we record manufacturing costs in Work-in-Process Inventory completely at standard (SH × SR). Thus, the difference between actual and standard costs can be explained by both the labor rate variance and the labor efficiency variance. As explained previously, positive variances are deemed to be "unfavorable" (U) and are recorded with debits, whereas negative variances are deemed to be "favorable" (F) and are recorded with a credit.

The following journal entry records these costs and variances (see **Exhibits 23-10** and **23-11**):

Work-in-process inventory	17,750	
Labor efficiency variance	6,000	
Labor rate variance		3,750
Wages payable (or cash)		20,000

The journal entry charges Work-in-Process Inventory with standard direct labor costs, records the unfavorable labor efficiency variance as a debit and the favorable labor rate variance as a credit, and records the liability for direct labor (or cash) at the amount owed, which is determined using actual hours worked and actual rates paid.

The unfavorable labor efficiency variance might be charged to the production supervisor, who presumably oversees the production teams. The favorable labor rate variance resulted from assigning lower-paid employees to perform the assembly. Other reasons for a favorable labor rate variance include using less overtime or paying decreased labor rates.

Similar to direct labor, we only record one entry in the accounting records relative to the application of variable overhead to units produced. In this example, because we use direct labor hours as the application base in our predetermined variable overhead rate, it would be driven by the actual number of direct labor hours. As employees work directly on our products (or in providing services), we apply more variable overhead to Work-in-Process Inventory and a corresponding decrease to Manufacturing Overhead, as follows:

Work-in-process inventory	(SC × SR)	
Variable overhead spending variance	U	or F
Variable overhead efficiency variance	U	or F
Manufacturing overhead		(AC × AR)

The interpretations of the variable overhead variances are identical to those for the labor variances.

For Fezzari, the general journal entry to record variable overhead costs and variances is as follows (see **Exhibit 23-13**):

Work-in-process inventory	1,560	
Variable overhead efficiency variance	390	
Variable overhead spending variance		425
Manufacturing overhead		1,525

This journal entry assumes that no overhead is applied to Work-in-Process Inventory until the end of the accounting period. When this entry is recorded at period end, all of the efficiency and spending variances are recorded simultaneously. In this example, the "applied overhead" for the entire period is actually $1,950 (250 actual hours worked × 7.80 predetermined overhead rate). If overhead were applied to Work-in-Process during the period as jobs were completed, the applied overhead for each job would be analogous to smaller pieces of the middle number in the fork diagram (i.e., the credit to Manufacturing Overhead) and a portion of the variable overhead efficiency variance would be recorded with each portion of the overhead applied. The entire variable overhead spending variance would be recorded at the end of the period as the over- or under-applied overhead amount written off to Cost of Goods sold.

This journal entry charges Work-in-Process Inventory with standard variable overhead costs, and records the unfavorable variable overhead efficiency variance as a debit and the favorable variable overhead spending variance as a credit.

D'Adduzio Company planned to produce 11,000 units of finished product during the current month. The company was able to achieve this desired level of production. During the month, D'Adduzio purchased and used 55,000 pounds of material at $5.30 per pound. The per-unit standard for material established by management was 4 pounds @ $5.10 per hour = $20.40. D'Adduzio used 23,000 actual direct labor hours at a rate of $3.00 per hour to make the 11,000 units of a finished product. The company's per-unit labor standard for each unit is 2 hours @ 3.50 per hour = $7.00. Finally, D'Adduzio actually incurred $32,500 in variable overhead costs in producing the 11,000 completed units. D'Adduzio's standard (predetermined) variable overhead rate is $1.50 per direct labor hour based on the standard number of direct labor hours for a particular production level.

1. What were the materials price and efficiency variances, and what journal entries would management make to record these variances?
2. What were the labor rate and efficiency variances, and what journal entry would management make to record these variances?
3. What were the variable overhead spending and efficiency variances, and what journal entry would management make to record these variances?

YOUR TURN! 23.7

The solution is on page 1102.

COMPREHENSIVE PROBLEM

Crenshaw Manufacturing, Inc. planned to produce 25,000 units of its only product during the year. The standard cost data for this product are as follows:

	Per Unit
Direct materials (3 lb. @ $2 per lb.)	$ 6
Direct labor (0.5 hr. @ $8 per hr.)	4
Variable overhead (0.5 hr. @ $4 per hr.)	2
Total standard cost per unit	$12

The actual level of production was 24,000 units, with the following actual total costs incurred:

	Total Cost
Direct materials (74,000 lb. @ $1.80)	$133,200
Direct labor (13,000 hr. @ $8.10)	105,300
Variable overhead	50,200
Total actual cost	$288,700

Required

a. Calculate the variances for materials, labor, and variable overhead.
b. Is the difference between total actual cost and total standard cost equal to the sum of all the variances? Why?

Solution to Comprehensive Problem

a.

Materials Variances

Actual Cost	Split Cost	Standard Cost
(AQ × AP)	(AQ × SP)	(SQ × SP)
74,000 × $1.80	74,000 × $2.00	72,000 × $2.00
$133,200	$148,000	$144,000

Price variance	Efficiency variance
AQ (AP − SP)	SP (AQ − SQ)
74,000 ($1.80 − $2.00)	$2.00 (74,000 − 72,000)
$14,800 F	$4,000 U

Labor Variances

Actual Cost	Split Cost	Standard Cost
(AH × AR)	(AH × SR)	(SH × SR)
13,000 × $8.10	13,000 × $8.00	12,000 × $8.00
$105,300	$104,000	$96,000

Rate variance	Efficiency variance
AH (AR − SR)	SR (AH − SH)
13,000 ($8.10 − $8.00)	$8.00 (13,000 − 12,000)
$1,300 U	$8,000 U

continued

continued from previous page

	Variable Overhead Variances	
Actual Cost	**Split Cost**	**Standard Cost**
(AH × AR)	(AH × SR) (13,000 × $4.00)	(SH × SR) (12,000 × $4.00)
$50,200	$52,000	$48,000

Spending variance
(Actual − Split)
($50,200 − $52,000)

Efficiency variance
SR (AH − SH)
$4.00 (13,000 −12,000)

$1,800 F

$4,000 U

b.

Total actual cost	$288,700
Total standard cost ($12 X 24,000)	288,000
Total variance	$ 700 U
Materials price variance	$ 14,800 F
Materials quantity variance.	4,000 U
Labor rate variance.	1,300 U
Labor efficiency variance	8,000 U
Variable overhead spending variance	1,800 F
Variable overhead efficiency variance	4,000 U
Sum of all variances	$ 700 U

In this example, the difference between total actual cost and total standard cost is equal to the sum of all variances. However, this is only true because, in this example, the amount of direct materials *purchased* is equal to the direct materials *used* in production. If this were not the case, the materials price variance plus the materials efficiency variance would not be equal to the total flexible budget variance for materials. Hence, in a broader sense, it is also true that if the amount of direct materials *purchased* had not been equal to the direct materials *used* in production, the difference between total actual costs and total standard costs would not have been equal to the sum of all of the variances. This is a key concept to remember.

SUMMARY OF LEARNING OBJECTIVES

Define standard costs and their use in standard cost accounting. (p. 1068)   LO1

- Standard costs represent the costs per unit that should be incurred during the upcoming year. They are established as part of the budgeting process.
- When standard cost accounting is used, all inventory accounts—materials, work-in-process, and finished goods—and the cost of goods sold account are stated in terms of standard costs. Actual costs are accumulated separately.

Develop an overall understanding of the determination of standard costs for direct materials, direct labor, and variable overhead. (p. 1070)   LO2

- Six components are required to develop standard variable product costs:
  - Direct materials standard price
  - Direct materials standard quantity
  - Direct labor standard rate
  - Direct labor standard time allowed
  - Standard variable overhead rate
  - Variable overhead standard capacity
- The standard direct materials cost to produce a unit of a particular finished product is determined by multiplying the direct materials standard quantity per unit by the direct materials standard price per unit.

- The standard cost of direct labor required to produce one unit of a particular product is determined by multiplying the direct labor standard time allowed, usually specified in hours, by the direct labor standard wage rate.

- The standard cost of variable overhead needed to manufacture one unit of a particular product is determined by multiplying the variable overhead standard capacity by the standard (or predetermined) variable overhead application rate.

- A standard cost summary is usually prepared for each product that is manufactured. Standard costs are extremely helpful in budgeting prior to the start of a fiscal period. Moreover, they can also be very useful in evaluating performance at the end of a period.

LO3 **Understand and calculate direct materials variances. (p. 1074)**

- We calculate the materials price variance by subtracting the standard price we should have paid for the actual quantity purchased from our actual purchase price.

- We calculate the materials efficiency variance by subtracting the standard materials cost from what we should have paid according to our standards for the actual quantity purchased.

- Each variance can be either favorable or unfavorable.

LO4 **Understand and calculate direct labor variances. (p. 1078)**

- We calculate the labor rate variance by subtracting the standard price we should have paid our employees for the actual level of production from our actual labor costs.

- We calculate the labor efficiency variance by subtracting the standard labor cost from what we should have paid according to our standards for the actual hours worked.

- Each variance can be either favorable or unfavorable.

LO5 **Understand and calculate variable overhead variances. (p. 1081)**

- The variable overhead "rate" variance (i.e., the spending variance) determines whether the predetermined overhead application rate is higher or lower than the standard rate determined by managers in the budgeting process.

- Similarly, variable overhead efficiency variance is attributable to the use of that overhead application base or "driver."

- Each variance can be either favorable or unfavorable.

LO6 **Present and illustrate the use of standard costs in financial statements. (p. 1083)**

- When the standard costs and related variances for direct materials, direct labor, and variable overhead are recorded, the work-in-process account is debited for each in amounts representing standard quantities and standard prices.

- All variances—favorable and unfavorable—are carried in separate accounts with appropriate titles.

- Standard costs are typically used in financial statements for internal use only by management.

- At year-end, firms commonly close the variance accounts by transferring their balances to Cost of Goods Sold.

- If large variances exist at year-end and there is evidence that the standards may not apply, a firm may be justified in allocating all or part of the variances to Work-in-Process Inventory, Finished Goods Inventory, and Cost of Goods Sold.

LO7 **Appendix 23A: Present journal entries associated with standard costs. (p. 1085)**

- Illustration of journal entries related to raw materials

- Illustration of journal entries related to direct labor

- Illustration of journal entries related to variable overhead

SUMMARY	Concept ⟶	Method ⟶	Assessment
TAKEAWAY 23.1	Management needs to understand and utilize standard costs and variances.	Establishing standards helps managers track actual results and compare them to standards.	The process of comparing actual to budgeted results guides management to better understand factors that cause cost fluctuations.

KEY TERMS

Labor efficiency
    variance (p. 1079)
Labor rate variance (p. 1079)
Materials efficiency
    variance (p. 1075)

Materials price
    variance (p. 1075)
Standard cost
    accounting (p. 1069)
Standard costs (p. 1068)

Variable overhead efficiency
    variance (p. 1082)
Variable overhead spending
    variance (p. 1082)
Variances (p. 1069)

Assignments with the Ⓜ logo in the margin are available in ᵐʸ BusinessCourse.
See the Preface of the book for details.

SELF-STUDY QUESTIONS

(Answers to Self-Study Questions are at the end of this chapter.)

1. **When a standard costing system is used, which of the following accounts will be reported at standard costs?**   **LO1**
   - *a.* Accounts payable
   - *b.* Wages payable
   - *c.* Work-in-process inventory
   - *d.* Accounts receivable

2. **In what terms are standard variable overhead application rates (SR) usually stated?**   **LO2**
   - *a.* Per dollar
   - *b.* Per direct labor hour
   - *c.* Per unit of product
   - *d.* Per month

3. **The formula [(Actual Price − Standard Price) × Actual Quantity] can be used to calculate which cost variance?**   **LO3**
   - *a.* Variable overhead volume
   - *b.* Labor efficiency
   - *c.* Materials efficiency
   - *d.* Materials price

4. **Which variance considers production capacity not used?**   **LO5**
   - *a.* Variable overhead efficiency
   - *b.* Labor efficiency
   - *c.* Variable overhead spending
   - *d.* Materials efficiency

5. **The gross profit on the interim income statement of a firm using standard costs is computed as:**   **LO6**
   - *a.* Sales less cost of goods sold at standard
   - *b.* Sales less cost of goods sold at standard plus net unfavorable variances
   - *c.* Sales less cost of goods sold at standard less net unfavorable variances
   - *d.* Sales less cost of goods sold at actual

QUESTIONS

1. What is the difference between budgeted costs and standard costs?   **LO1**
2. When should standard costs be established and how often should such standards be changed?   **LO1**
3. "Standard costs can be set too high or too low for motivational purposes." Comment.   **LO1**
4. "Total actual cost exactly equals total standard cost, so everything must be okay." Comment.   **LO1**
5. What is standard cost accounting?   **LO2**
6. Define standard costs and describe how they are developed.   **LO2**
7. A finished product requires 2 pounds of materials costing $6 per pound. What is the standard cost of direct materials per unit of product?   **LO2**
8. A finished product requires 20 minutes of direct labor to complete each unit. Factory workers are paid $12 per hour. What is the standard cost of direct labor per unit of product?   **LO2**
9. Assume that the variable overhead rate for the product described in Question 8 is $9 per hour. What is the standard cost of variable overhead per unit of product?   **LO2**
10. Name and briefly describe the two direct materials variances.   **LO3**
11. Garcia Company used 6,300 pounds of direct materials costing $7.80 per pound for a batch of products that should have consumed 6,000 pounds costing $8 per pound. What are the materials variances?   **LO3**
12. Name and briefly describe the two direct labor variances.   **LO4**
13. Wong Lee used 1,200 direct labor hours at an average wage rate of $8.70 to manufacture products that should have used 1,300 direct labor hours at an average wage rate of $8.50 per hour. What are the labor variances?   **LO4**

LO5   **14.** The variable overhead rate is $5 per direct labor hour; 31,000 direct labor hours were used to produce 7,500 units of product. The standard is 4 direct labor hours per unit. Actual, variable overhead cost was $153,000. Determine the variable overhead variances.

LO6   **15.** Briefly explain how standard cost variances are reported on financial statements.

LO7   **16.** Who in the firm might be responsible for each of the following variances?
(Appendix 23A)
    a. Materials price and efficiency variances
    b. Labor rate and efficiency variances
    c. Variable overhead spending and efficiency variances

SHORT EXERCISES

LO2   **SE23-1.**   Which one of the following statements is correct concerning a flexible budget cost formula? Variable costs are stated

    a. per unit and fixed costs are stated in total.
    b. in total and fixed costs are stated per unit.
    c. in total and fixed costs are stated in total.
    d. per unit and fixed costs are stated per unit.

LO2   **SE23-2.**   Marten Company has a cost-benefit policy to investigate any variance that is greater than $1,000 or 10% of budget, whichever is larger. Actual results for the previous month indicate the following.

	Budget	Actual
Raw materials.	$100,000	$89,000
Direct labor	50,000	54,000

The company should investigate

    a. neither the materials variance nor the labor variance.
    b. the materials variance only.
    c. the labor variance only.
    d. both the materials variance and the labor variance.

LO3   **SE23-3.**   Frisco Company recently purchased 108,000 units of raw materials for $583,200. Three units of raw materials are budgeted for use in each finished good manufactured, with the raw materials standard set at $16.50 for each completed product. Frisco manufactured 32,700 finished units during the period just ended and used 99,200 units of raw materials. If management is concerned about the timely reporting of variances in an effort to improve cost control and bottom-line performance, the materials purchase price variance should be reported as

    a. $6,050 unfavorable.
    b. $9,920 favorable.
    c. $10,800 unfavorable.
    d. $10,800 favorable.

LO3   **SE23-4.**   Micah Corporation purchased 3,800 pounds of raw materials on March 1 at a price of $5.20 per pound to use in production during March. Micah produced 2,000 units during March though the production budget anticipated production of 2,200 units. The company's standards recommend 2 pounds of materials per unit and dictate a standard price of $5.05 per pound. Which of the following is correct with respect to Micah's materials variances for the month of March?

    a. The materials price variance is $570 favorable.
    b. The materials efficiency variance is $1,010 unfavorable.
    c. The materials price variance is $570 unfavorable.
    d. The materials efficiency variance is $3,030 favorable.

LO3, 4   **SE23-5.**   Of the following pairs of variances found in a flexible budget report, which pair is most likely to be related?

    a. Materials price variance and variable overhead efficiency variance.
    b. Labor rate variance and variable overhead efficiency variance.
    c. Materials usage variance and labor efficiency variance.
    d. Labor efficiency variance and fixed overhead volume variance.

SE23-6. A company budgets to sell 4,000 units of its product. Actual sales are 4,200 units. The product has a standard price of $43. When analyzing its direct labor flexible-budget variance for the period, the company determined that its direct labor efficiency variance was an unfavorable variance of $8,600. Which one of the following is closest to the actual price for direct labor if the total direct labor flexible-budget variance was an unfavorable variance of $4,000? LO4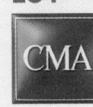

    a. $39
    b. $40
    c. $41
    d. $42

SE23-7. Randall Company uses standard costing and flexible budgeting and is evaluating its direct labor. The total budget variance can usually be broken down into two other variances identified as the LO4

    a. direct labor rate variance and direct labor efficiency variance.
    b. direct labor cost variance and the direct labor volume variance.
    c. direct labor rate variance and direct labor volume variance.
    d. direct labor cost variance and direct labor labor efficiency variance.

SE23-8. Caleb manufacturing produced 3,000 units during June even though the company had anticipated producing 2,800 units. The company's employees actually logged 3,200 hours during the month and were paid $8.40 per hour. The company's standard costing system indicates 1 direct labor hour per unit at a standard wage rate of $8.70. Which of the following is incorrect? LO4

    a. The labor rate variance is $960 favorable.
    b. The labor efficiency variance is $3,480 unfavorable.
    c. The labor efficiency variance is $1,740 unfavorable.
    d. The actual amount paid to employees for their labor during the month is $26,880.

SE23-9. Lee manufacturing uses a standard cost system with overhead applied based on direct labor hours. The manufacturing budget for the production of 5,000 units for the month of June included 10,000 hours of direct labor at $15 per hour, $150,000. During June, 4,500 units were produced, using 9,600 direct labor hours, incurring $39,360 of variable overhead, and showing a variable overhead efficiency variance of $2,400 unfavorable. The standard variable overhead rate per direct labor hour was LO5

    a. $3.85.
    b. $4.00.
    c. $4.10.
    d. $6.00.

SE23-10. James manufacturing produced 3,000 units during June even though the company had anticipated producing 2,800 units. The company's employees actually logged 3,200 hours during the month. The company's standard costing system allocates variable overhead at a rate of $6.00 per direct labor hour. Standards also dictate 1 direct labor hour per unit produced. Assume that James actually incurred $19,500 of variable overhead costs. Which of the following is true? LO5

    a. The variable overhead rate variance is $300 favorable.
    b. The variable overhead efficiency variance is is $1,400 unfavorable.
    c. The variable overhead efficiency variance is $1,000 unfavorable.
    d. The variable overhead rate variance is $300 unfavorable.

EXERCISES—SET A

E23-1A. Standard Product Costs Deerfield Company manufactures product M in its factory. Production of M requires 2 pounds of material P, costing $4 per pound and 0.5 hour of direct labor costing $10 per hour. The variable overhead rate is $8 per direct labor hour, and the fixed overhead rate is $12 per direct labor hour. What is the standard product cost for product M? LO2

E23-2A. Materials and Labor Variances The following actual and standard cost data for direct materials and direct labor relate to Hadley Company's production of 2,000 units of a product: LO3, 4

	Actual costs	Standard costs
Direct materials.	3,900 lb. @ $5.20	4,000 lb. @ $5.10
Direct labor	6,200 hr. @ $8.40	6,000 hr. @ $8.60

Determine the following variances:

a.   Materials price   c.   Labor rate
b.   Materials efficiency   d.   Labor efficiency

LO5

E23-3A. Variable Overhead Variances Smith Tax Company considers 6,000 direct labor hours or 300 tax returns its normal monthly capacity. Its standard variable overhead rate is $50 per direct labor hour. During the current month, $250,400 of variable overhead cost was incurred in working 5,500 direct labor hours to prepare 270 tax returns. Determine the following variances, and indicate whether each is favorable or unfavorable:

a.   Variable overhead spending
b.   Variable overhead efficiency

LO3, 4, 5

E23-4A. Materials, Labor, and Variable Overhead Variances The following summarized manufacturing data relate to Steffan Corporation's April operations, during which 2,000 finished units of product were produced. Normal monthly capacity is 1,100 direct labor hours.

	Standard Unit Costs	Total Actual Costs
Direct materials:		
Standard (2 lb. @ $9.50/lb.)	$19	
Actual (4,200 lb. @ $10.20/lb.)		$42,840
Direct labor:		
Standard (0.5 hr. @ $24/hr.)	12	
Actual (970 hr. @ $23.40/hr.)		22,698
Variable overhead:		
Standard (0.5 hr. @ $6/hr.)	3	
Actual		6,200
Total.	$34	$71,738

Assume that the 4,200 lb. of materials purchased were all used in producing the 2,000 completed units. Determine the materials price and efficiency variances, labor rate and efficiency variances, and variable overhead spending and efficiency variances.

LO3, 4, 5

E23-5A. Working with Variances From the following data, determine the total actual costs incurred for direct materials, direct labor, and variable overhead.

	Standard Costs	Variances
Direct materials.	$120,000	
Price variance.		$3,000 U
Quantity variance		4,000 F
Direct labor.	100,000	
Rate variance		1,400 U
Efficiency variance		1,800 U
Variable overhead	44,000	
Spending variance		1,000 F
Efficiency variance		600 U

EXERCISES—SET B

LO2

E23-1B. Standard Product Costs Harrison Company manufactures product Q in its factory. Production of Q requires 3 pounds of material T, costing $7 per pound and 2 hours of direct labor, costing $10 per hour. The variable overhead rate is $6 per direct labor hour, and the fixed overhead rate is $9 per direct labor hour. What is the standard product cost for product Q?

E23-2B. Materials and Labor Variances The following actual and standard cost data for direct materials and direct labor relate to Jones Company's production of 2,000 units of a product:

	Actual Costs	Standard Costs
Direct materials.	4,200 lb. @ $4.90	4,000 lb. @ $5.10
Direct labor.	5,800 hr. @ $9.30	6,000 hr. @ $9.50

Determine the following variances:

a.   Materials price   c.   Labor rate
b.   Materials efficiency   d.   Labor efficiency

E23-3B. Variable Overhead Variances Dallin Tax Company considers 8,000 direct labor hours or 400 tax returns its normal monthly capacity. Its standard variable overhead rate is $40 per direct labor hour. During the current month, $308,500 of variable overhead cost was incurred in working 7,400 direct labor hours to produce 360 units of product. Determine the following variances, and indicate whether each is favorable or unfavorable:

a.   Variable overhead spending
b.   Variable overhead efficiency

E23-4B. Materials, Labor, and Variable Overhead Variances The following summarized manufacturing data relate to Kiosse Corporation's May operations, during which 2,000 finished units of product were produced. Normal monthly capacity is 1,100 direct labor hours.

	Standard Unit Costs	Total Actual Costs
Direct materials:		
Standard (3 lb. @ $2.00/lb.)	$ 6	
Actual (6,200 lb. @ $2.20/lb.)		$13,640
Direct labor:		
Standard (0.5 hr. @ $14/hr.)	7	
Actual (980 hr. @ $13.70/hr.)		13,426
Variable overhead:		
Standard (0.5 hr. @ $4/hr.)	2	
Actual		4,200
Total.	$15	$31,266

Assume that the 6,200 lb. of materials purchased were all used in producing the 2,000 completed units. Determine the materials price and efficiency variances, labor rate and efficiency variances, and variable overhead spending and efficiency variances.

E23-5B. Working with Variances From the following data, determine the total actual costs incurred for direct materials, direct labor, and variable overhead.

	Standard Costs	Variances
Direct materials.	$55,000	
Price variance.		$1,200 U
Quantity variance.		2,200 F
Direct labor.	46,000	
Rate variance.		500 U
Efficiency variance.		800 U
Variable overhead	18,000	
Spending variance.		400 F
Efficiency variance.		700 U

PROBLEMS—SET A

P23-1A. Calculate Variances The following summary data relate to the operations of Dobson Company for April, during which 9,000 finished units were produced. Normal monthly capacity was 20,000 direct labor hours.

	Standard Unit Costs	Total Actual Costs
Direct materials:		
Standard (4 lb. @ $2.20/lb.)	$ 8.80	
Actual (38,000 lb. @ $2.00/lb.)		$ 76,000
Direct labor:		
Standard (2 hr. @ $11.00/hr.)	22.00	
Actual (18,500 hr. @ $11.30/hr.)		209,050
Variable overhead:		
Standard (2 hr. @ $3.00/hr.)	6.00	
Actual		54,900
Total.	$36.80	$339,950

Required

Determine the following variances and indicate whether each is favorable or unfavorable:

a. Materials price and efficiency variances
b. Labor rate and efficiency variances
c. Variable overhead spending and efficiency variances

P23-2A. Variances, Entries, and Income Statement A summary of Martindale Company's manufacturing variance report for May 2019 follows:

	Total Standard Costs (9,200 units)	Total Actual Costs (9,200 units)	Variances
Direct materials.	$ 38,640	$ 41,760	$3,120 U
Direct labor	193,200	191,760	1,440 F
Variable overhead	22,080	23,230	1,150 U
Fixed overhead.	9,660	9,660	
Total	$263,580	$266,410	$2,830 U

Standard materials cost per unit of product is 0.5 pounds at $8.40 per pound, and standard direct labor cost is 1.5 hours at $14.00 per hour. The total actual materials cost represents 4,800 pounds purchased at $8.70 per pound. Total actual labor cost represents 14,100 hours at $13.60 per hour. According to standards, variable overhead rate is applied at $1.60 per direct labor hour (based on a normal capacity of 15,000 direct labor hours or 10,000 units of product). Assume that all fixed overhead is applied to work-in-progress inventory.

Required

a. Calculate variances for materials price and efficiency, labor rate and efficiency, and variable overhead spending and efficiency.
b. Prepare general journal entries to record standard costs, actual costs, and related variances for materials, labor, and overhead.
c. Prepare journal entries to record the transfer of all completed units to Finished Goods Inventory and the subsequent sale of 8,400 units on account at $54 each (assume no beginning finished goods inventory).
d. Prepare a partial income statement (through gross profit on sales) showing gross profit based on standard costs, the incorporation of variances, and gross profit based on actual costs.

P23-3A. Variances and Journal Entries Jacobs Company manufactures a single product and uses a standard costing system. The nature of its product dictates that it be sold in the period it is produced. Thus, no ending work-in-process or finished goods inventories remain at the end of the period. However, raw materials can be stored and are purchased in bulk when prices are favorable. Per-unit standard product costs are materials, $8 (4 pounds); labor, $6 (0.5 hour); and variable overhead, $4 (based on direct labor hours). Budgeted fixed overhead is $54,000.

      Jacobs accounts for all inventories and cost of goods sold at standard cost and records each variance in a separate account. The following data relate to May 2019 when 17,700 finished units were produced.

LO3, 4, 5, 7

Required

a.   Assume Jacobs purchased 69,000 pounds of raw materials on account at $2.20 per pound and used 67,000 pounds in May's production, prepare a journal entry to record the purchase of raw materials and a separate journal entry to record the use of raw materials in production. Record these entries using standard costs and include the appropriate materials variances.

b.   Assuming employees worked 8,900 direct labor hours at an average hourly rate of $11.70, prepare a journal entry to record actual costs, standard costs, and any labor variances.

c.   Assuming Jacobs' actual and applied variable overhead was $74,200 and that budgeted and actual fixed overhead incurred was $54,000, prepare a journal entry to record actual and standard overhead costs and any overhead variances.

P23-4A. Variances, Total Overhead Variances, and Variance Reconciliation Milton Company planned to produce 21,000 units of its only product during the year. Milton established the following standard cost data for this product prior to the beginning of the year:

LO3, 4, 5

	Per Unit
Direct materials (3 lb. @ $5.00 per lb.).	$15.00
Direct labor (2 hr. @ $17.50 per hr.).	35.00
Variable overhead (2 hr. @ $6 per hr.).	12.00
Total standard cost per unit	$62.00

Total budgeted fixed overhead is $400,000.

Assume that Milton (1) actually produced 22,000 units, (2) used 68,000 pounds of direct materials in production, (3) and incurred the following actual total costs:

	Total Cost
Direct materials purchased (70,000 lb. @ 4.80).	$ 336,000
Direct labor (43,000 hr. @ $18.00).	774,000
Variable overhead	262,320
Fixed overhead.	400,000
Total actual costs	$1,772,320

Required

a.   Calculate the variances for materials, labor, and variable overhead.

b.   Does the difference between total actual costs and total standard costs equal the sum of all of the variances? Explain.

PROBLEMS—SET B

P23-1B. Calculate Variances The following summary data relate to the operations of Randolph Company for July, during which 4,500 finished units were produced:

LO3, 4, 5

	Standard Total Unit Costs	Total Actual Costs
Direct materials:		
Standard (0.6 lb. @ $9.00/lb.)..........................	$ 5.40	
Actual (3,000 lb. @ $9.40/lb.)............................		$ 28,200
Direct labor:		
Standard (0.8 hr. @ $12.80/hr.).........................	10.24	
Actual (3,800 hr. @ $12.50/hr.).........................		47,500
Variable overhead:		
Standard (0.8 hr. @ $7.50/hr.).........................	6.00	
Actual..		30,100
Total..	$21.64	$105,800

Required

Determine the following variances and indicate whether each is favorable or unfavorable:

a. Materials price variance and efficiency variance
b. Labor rate variance and efficiency variance
c. Variable overhead spending variance and efficiency variance

LO3, 4, 5, 6, 7

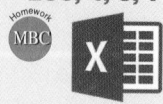

P23-2B. Variances, Entries, and Income Statement A summary of Flaker Company's manufacturing variance report for June 2019 follows.

	Total Standard Costs (7,600 units)	Total Actual Costs (7,600 units)	Variances
Direct materials.....................	$ 66,880	$ 66,150	$ 730 F
Direct labor........................	77,520	81,420	3,900 U
Variable overhead	33,060	33,000	60 F
Fixed overhead.....................	102,600	102,600	
Total	$280,060	$283,170	$3,110 U

Standard materials cost per unit of product is 4 pounds at $2.20 per pound, and standard direct labor cost is 0.75 hour at $13.60 per hour. Total actual materials cost represents 31,500 pounds purchased at $2.10 per pound. Total actual labor cost represents 5,900 hours at $13.80 per hour. According to standards, variable overhead rate is applied at $5.80 per direct labor hour (based on a normal capacity of 6,000 direct labor hours or 8,000 units of product). Assume that all fixed overhead is applied to work-in-progress inventory.

Required

a. Calculate variances for materials price and efficiency, labor rate and efficiency, and variable overhead spending and efficiency.
b. Prepare general journal entries to record standard costs, actual costs, and related variances for materials, labor, and overhead.
c. Prepare journal entries to record the transfer of all completed units to Finished Goods Inventory and the subsequent sale of 6,400 units on account at $60 each (assume no beginning finished goods inventory).
d. Prepare a partial income statement (through gross profit on sales) showing gross profit based on standard costs, the incorporation of variances, and gross profit based on actual costs.

LO3, 4, 5, 7

P23-3B. Variances and Journal Entries Kent Company manufactures a single product and uses a standard costing system. The nature of its product dictates that it be sold in the period it is produced. Thus, no ending work-in-process or finished goods inventories remain at the end of the period. However, raw materials can be stored and are purchased in bulk when prices are favorable. Per-unit, standard product costs are materials, $6 (0.5 pound); labor, $15 (1.5 hours); and variable overhead, $3 (based on direct labor hours). Budgeted fixed overhead is $96,000.

Kent Company accounts for all inventories and cost of goods sold at standard cost and records each variance in a separate account. The following data relate to June 2019 when 7,800 finished units were produced.

Required

a. Assume Kent purchased 4,500 pounds of raw materials on account at $11.60 per pound and used 4,200 pounds in June's production, prepare a journal entry to record the purchase of raw materials and a separate journal entry to record the use of raw materials in production. Record these entries using standard costs and include the appropriate materials variances.

b. Assuming Kent's employees worked 12,000 direct labor hours at an average hourly rate of $10.50, prepare a journal entry to record actual costs, standard costs, and any labor variances.

c. Assuming Kent's actual and applied variable overhead was $23,100 and that budgeted and actual fixed overhead incurred was $96,000, prepare a journal entry to record actual and standard overhead costs and any overhead variances.

P23-4B. Variances, Total Overhead Variances, and Variance Reconciliation Sanchez Company planned to produce 10,000 units of its only product during the year. Sanchez established the following standard cost data for this product prior to the beginning of the year:

LO3, 4, 5

	Per Unit
Direct materials (2 lb. @ $7.50 per lb.)	$15.00
Direct labor (1.5 hr. @ $13.50 per hr.)	20.25
Variable overhead (1.5 hr. @ $6 per hr.)	9.00
Total standard cost per unit	$44.25
Total budgeted fixed overhead is $144,000.	

Assume that Sanchez (1) actually produced 9,000 units, (2) used 17,000 pounds of direct materials in production, (3) and incurred the following actual total costs:

	Total Cost
Direct materials purchased (19,000 lb. @ 7.80)	$148,200
Direct labor (14,000 hr. @ $13.35)	186,900
Variable overhead	80,250
Fixed overhead	144,000
Total actual costs	$559,350

Required

a. Calculate the variances for materials, labor, and variable overhead.

b. Does the difference between total actual costs and total standard costs equal the sum of all of the variances? Explain.

EXTENDING YOUR KNOWLEDGE

EYK23-1. Business Decision Case Porter Corporation has just hired Bill Harlow as its new controller. Although Harlow has had little formal accounting training, he professes to be highly experienced, having learned accounting "the hard way" in the field. At the end of his first month's work, Harlow prepared the following performance report:

PORTER CORPORATION
Performance Report
for the Month of June, 2018

	Total Actual Costs	Total Budgeted Costs	Variances
Direct materials.	$216,630	$237,600	$20,970 F
Direct labor.	119,340	132,000	12,660 F
Variable overhead	63,000	66,000	3,000 F
Fixed overhead.	184,000	184,000	
	$582,970	$619,600	$36,630 F

In his presentation at Porter's month-end management meeting, Harlow indicated that things were going "fantastically." "The figures indicate," he said, "that the firm is beating its budget in all cost categories." This good news made everyone at the meeting happy and furthered Harlow's acceptance as a member of the management team.

After the management meeting, Susan Jones, Porter's general manager, asked you, as an independent consultant, to review Harlow's report. Jones' concern stemmed from the fact that Porter has never operated as favorably as Harlow's report seems to imply, and she cannot explain the apparent significant improvement.

While reviewing Harlow's report, you are provided the following cost and operating data for June: Porter has a monthly normal capacity of 11,000 direct labor hours or 8,800 units of product. Standard costs per unit for its only product are direct materials 3 pounds at $9 per pound; direct labor, 1.25 hours at $12 per hour; and variable overhead rate per direct labor hour of $6. During June, Porter produced 8,000 units of product, using 24,900 pounds of materials costing $8.70 each, 10,200 direct labor hours at an average rate of $11.70 each, and incurred variable overhead costs of $63,000 and fixed overhead costs of $184,000.

After reviewing Porter's June cost data, you tell Harlow that his cost report contains a classic budgeting error, and you explain how he can remedy it. In response to your suggestion, Harlow revises his report as follows:

	Total Actual Costs	Total Budgeted Costs	Variances
Direct materials.	$216,630	$216,000	$ 630 U
Direct labor.	119,340	120,000	660 F
Variable overhead	63,000	60,000	3,000 U
Fixed overhead.	184,000	184,000	
	$582,970	$580,000	$2,970 U

Harlow's revised report is accompanied by remarks expressing regret at the oversight in the original report.

Required

In your role as consultant,

a. Verify that Harlow's actual cost figures are correct.

b. Identify and explain the classic budgeting error that Harlow apparently incorporated into his original cost report.

c. Explain why Harlow's revised figures could be considered deficient.

d. Further analyze Harlow's revised variances, isolating underlying potential causal factors. How do your analyses indicate bases for concern to management?

EYK23-2. Ethics Case Custom Furniture, manufacturer of handmade furniture, uses standard cost accounting for the company. Standards are developed annually based on input from production workers and supervisors.

The supervisor of the table department has approached several employees that work for him and suggested that the employees overestimate the amount of materials (by 20%) and labor (by 30%) involved in producing certain new tables. He states that it is better to overestimate than underestimate costs as the product has never been manufactured in quantity before and it is uncertain what the actual materials and labor will be. In addition, he states that this would result in any variances being favorable to the department.

The employees are not sure what estimates they should discuss with the accounting department. The accounting department wants accurate input that it will adjust for uncertainty.

Required
How would you advise the employees? What ethical issues are involved?

ANSWERS TO SELF-STUDY QUESTIONS:

1. c, (p. 1069)   2. b, (p. 1072)   3. d, (p. 1075)   4. a, (pp. 1081–1082)   5. c, (p. 1084)

YOUR TURN! SOLUTIONS

Solution 23.1

Nelson spent $2,600 more than expected for materials. The company would have to investigate the extent to which this unfavorable variance is attributable to higher materials prices or inefficient operations. Nelson actually spent $300 less on labor than would be expected based on the new standard costing system. The company would need to explore the extent to which this favorable variance relates to a difference in the expected wage rates of employees or their efficiency. Finally, Nelson also spent $500 less than expected for variable overhead. The company would need to determine the extent to which this favorable variance resulted from actual spending was less than standard rates would predict or whether efficiencies in the process resulted in the use of lower quantities of overhead drivers.

Solution 23.2

	Actual Costs	Standard Costs	Total Flexible Budget Variances
Direct materials	$261,000	$264,000	($ 3,000)
Direct labor	262,500	231,000	31,500
Variable overhead	63,000	66,000	(3,000)
Total	$586,500	$561,000	$25,500

Solution 23.3
Materials price variance: AQ (AP − SP) = 90,000 ($2.90 − $3.00) = $9,000 F
Materials efficiency variance: SP (AQ − SQ) = $3.00 [90,000 − (4 × 22,000)] = $6,000 U

Solution 23.4
Labor rate variance: AH (AR − SR) = 35,000 × ($7.50 − $7.00) = $17,500 U
Labor efficiency variance: SR (AH − SH) = $7.00 [35,000 − (1.5 × 22,000)] = $14,000 U

Solution 23.5
Variable overhead spending variance: Actual VOH − (AQ × SR) = $63,000 − (35,000 × $2.00) = $7,000 F
Variable overhead efficiency variance: SR (AH − SH) = $2.00 [35,000 − (1.5 × 22,000)] = $4,000 U

Solution 23.6

Sales.	$500,000
Cost of goods sold at standard cost	460,000
Gross profit at standard cost	40,000
Less: Net unfavorable cost variance	(2,500)
Gross profit	$ 37,500

Solution 23.7

1. What were the materials price and efficiency variances, and what journal entries would management make to record these variances?

   Materials price variance: AQ (AP − SP) = 55,000 ($5.30 − $5.10) = $11,000 U

Raw Materials Inventory	280,500	
Materials Price Variance	11,000	
Accounts Payable (or Cash)		291,500

   Materials efficiency variance: SP (AQ − SQ) = $5.10 [55,000 − (4 × 11,000)] = $56,100 U

Work-in-Process Inventory	224,400	
Materials Efficiency Variance	56,100	
Raw Materials Inventory		280,500

2. What were the labor rate and efficiency variances, and what journal entry would management make to record these variances?

   Labor rate variance: AH (AR − SR) = 23,000 ($3.00 − $3.50) = $11,500 F

   Labor efficiency variance: SR (AH − SH) = $3.50 [23,000 − (2 × 11,000)] = $3,500 U

Work-in-Process Inventory	77,000	
Labor Efficiency Variance	3,500	
Labor Rate Variance		11,500
Wages Payable		69,000

3. What were the variable overhead spending and efficiency variances, and what journal entry would management make to record these variances?

   VOH spending variance: Actual spending − (AH × SR) = $32,500 − (23,000 × $1.50) = $2,000 F

   VOH efficiency variance: SR (AH − SH) = $1.50 [23,000 − (2 × 11,000)] = $1,500 U

Work-in-Process Inventory	33,000	
VOH Efficiency Variance	1,500	
VOH spending Variance		2,000
Manufacturing Overhead		32,500

Flexible Budgets, Segment Reporting, and Performance Analysis

PAST

Chapter 23 defined standard costs and standard cost variances: direct material, direct labor, and variable overhead variances.

PRESENT

Chapter 24 introduces flexible budgets and performance evaluation of business segments. In addition, it explores both performance and variance analysis.

FUTURE

Chapter 25 introduces capital budgeting and illustrates how capital budgeting is used to make capital investment decisions.

Chances are the software you use on your computer was produced by **Microsoft Corporation**. In chapter 10 we introduced Microsoft as one of the world's most well-recognized companies. As the global leader in software production, it is also one of the world's most valuable companies.

Microsoft has maintained an edge in the software industry through the careful application of managerial accounting concepts. In budgeting sales and production needs for future periods, Microsoft is never 100% accurate in its forecasts. To accommodate the fluctuation in sales, the company uses a budgeting approach called "flexible budgeting."

In this chapter, we will introduce flexible budgeting, segment reporting, and performance analysis, and explain performance measures that are helpful in assessing the health of a company. Segment reporting allows managers to compare and assess the performance of individual segments of the company by evaluating key performance indicators, such as return on investment, profit margin, asset turnover, and residual income. Another tool used to assess performance is the balanced scorecard, which includes both financial and nonfinancial measures of performance.

Road Map

LO	Learning Objective	Page	eLecture	Guided Example	Assignments
LO1	Describe a static budget, illustrate its use, and present an example of a static budget performance report.	1106	E24-1	YT24.1	SS1, Q1, Q2, SE1, E1A
LO2	Introduce the flexible budget and present an example of a flexible budget performance report. Explain how flexible budgeting helps in variance analysis.	1107	E24-2	YT24.2	SS2, Q1, Q2, Q3, SE2, SE3, SE4, E1A, E2A, E1B, P1A, P1B
LO3	Present an overview of reporting operations for segments of a business.	1114	E24-3	YT24.3	SS3, Q4, Q5, SE5
LO4	Construct a segmented contribution margin income statement. Identify the difference between traceable and common fixed costs.	1117	E24-4	YT24.4	SS4, SS5, Q6, Q7, Q8, Q9, Q10, Q11, E3A, E2B, P2A, P3A, P4A, P2B, P3B, P4B
LO5	Compute return on investment, return on sales, return on assets, and residual income for business segments. Discuss the importance of each indicator in assessing a company's performance.	1123	E24-5	YT24.5, YT24.6	SS6, SS7, Q12, Q13, Q14, SE6, SE7, SE8, SE9, E4A, E3B, E4B, P5A, P6A, P5B, P6B
LO6	Appendix 24A: Determine the proper transfer price to maximize company profit with and without excess productive capacity.	1130	E24-6	YT24.7	SS8, Q15, SE10, P7A, P7B

It is critically important that management have a means of measuring and evaluating the performance of employees, departments, segments, and the overall company to ensure that all are working toward the achievement of the company's strategic vision. In this chapter, we discuss several tools available to assist managers in evaluating performance: flexible budgets, segment reporting, and performance analysis and reporting.

STATIC BUDGETS

LO1 **Describe** a static budget, **illustrate** its use, and **present** an example of a static budget performance report.

The master budget is made up of budgets known as static budgets. A **static budget** is a financial plan developed for a fixed level of operating activity, typically the expected or most likely level. The static budget is the budgeted amount used to calculate the standard costs that we discussed in Chapter 23.

If actual results are compared to a static budget, the calculated differences that result are of little use to management, because the budget is often based on a different level of activity than the actual operations. The following example illustrates this point.

A.K.A. Static budgets are also called nonmoving or stationary budgets.

Exhibit 24-1 presents a simple static budget for Fezzari's Foré CR1 product line for the 2019 fiscal year. Although Fezzari's management has a target production of 500 Foré CR1 road bikes during the year, it anticipates that this may be an aggressive projection.

Exhibit 24-1	Static Budget Illustration

FEZZARI FORÉ CR1 PRODUCT LINE **Static Budget for Product Costs** **For the Year Ended December 31, 2019**	
Budgeted units of production	500
Budgeted costs:	
Direct material.	$300,000
Direct labor	88,750
Manufacturing overhead	24,750
Total.	$413,500

500 units x $600 per unit → Direct material

500 units x $177.50 per unit → Direct labor

500 units x $49.50 per unit → Manufacturing overhead

Exhibit 24-2 presents a static budget performance report for the CR1 product line for 2019. The static budget performance report compares the *actual* costs to produce 480 units with the *budgeted* costs to produce 500 units. The performance report accurately reveals that actual units of CR1 production were 20 less than management had budgeted. In a performance report comparing actual costs to budgeted costs, "F" indicates a favorable difference, or **variance**, and "U" identifies an unfavorable difference.

Exhibit 24-2	Static Budget Performance Report Illustration

FEZZARI FORÉ CR1 PRODUCT LINE
Static Budget Performance Report
For the Year Ended December 31, 2019

Budgeted units of production		500	
Actual units of production		480	
Units of production variance		20	U

	Actual Cost Incurred for 480 Units	Budget Based on 500 Units	Cost Variances	
Direct material	$292,800	$300,000	($7,200)	F
Direct labor	91,200	88,750	2,450	U
Manufacturing overhead	21,600	24,750	(3,150)	F
Total	$405,600	$413,500	$(7,900)	F

These are the actual costs of producing 480 units.

This is the static budget from Exhibit 24-1.

Revenue variances are favorable if actual revenues exceed budgeted revenues.

Cost variances are unfavorable if actual costs exceed budgeted costs, and favorable if actual costs are less than budgeted costs.

U = Unfavorable
F = Favorable

The static budget performance report, however, provides misleading cost variances. For example, the direct material variance is $7,200 favorable (i.e., the actual cost is less than budgeted cost). This comparison is misleading because the actual cost to produce 480 units is being compared to the budgeted cost to produce 500 units, not 480 units. Moreover, although the total variance is $7,900 favorable, the actual cost per unit is about $845 per unit ($405,600/480 CR1s), and the budgeted cost per CR1 is only $827($413,500/500 CR1s). Hence, although the cost per unit is actually higher than the budgeted cost per unit, the total static budget variance appears to be favorable simply because the company produced 20 fewer CR1s than it anticipated.

YOUR TURN! 24.1

The solution is on page 1156.

Carson CPAs specializes in preparing 1040EZ returns for low-income clients. The firm charged $100 per return this year and budgeted $100 per return. Additional information for the firm includes:

	Actual	Budgeted
Returns processed	800	750
Variable costs	$36,000	$37,500
Fixed costs	12,500	12,000

Prepare Carson's static budget and the static budget performance report.

FLEXIBLE BUDGETS

A **flexible budget** is a financial plan in the form of a cost formula or a multiple-column presentation that makes cost projections for various activity levels within a relevant range.

LO2 Introduce the flexible budget and **present** an example of a flexible budget performance report. **Explain** how flexible budgeting helps in variance analysis.

Flexible Budgets in a Manufacturing Environment

Exhibit 24-3 presents a 2019 flexible budget for Fezzari's Foré CR1 product line. The first two columns show the CR1 budgeted per-unit variable costs and budgeted total fixed costs of production. The last three columns present the budget for different levels of production. The middle column is the budget for 500 units of production that would be comparable to the static budget in **Exhibit 24-1**. Knowing the per-unit variable costs and the fixed costs of production allows Fezzari management to prepare a budget for any level of production within the relevant range.

| Exhibit 24-3 | Flexible Budget for Fezzari Foré CR1 |

FEZZARI FORÉ CR1 PRODUCT LINE
Flexible Budget for Product Costs
For the Year Ended December 31, 2019

> This is the static budget from Exhibit 24-1.

	Variable Cost per Unit	Total Fixed Cost	480 Units	500 Units	520 Units
Variable costs					
Direct material	$600.00		$288,000	$300,000	$312,000
Direct labor	177.50		85,200	88,750	92,300
Variable overhead . . .	12.45		5,976	6,225	6,474
	$789.95		$379,176	$394,975	$410,774
Fixed costs					
Fixed overhead.		18,525	$ 18,525	$ 18,525	$ 18,525
Total.			$397,701	$413,500	$429,299

> The manufacturing overhead has been split into variable and fixed components.

Exhibit 24-3 demonstrates a number of the characteristics about flexible budgets. First, the flexible budget usually divides costs and expenses into two groups: variable and fixed. Second, the flexible budget typically presents the variable costs and expenses on a per-unit basis and the fixed costs and expenses in total. Third, in using a columnar format, all of the columns are based on levels of activity within the relevant range. It is important to remember that the flexible budget formula is valid only for the range of activity for which it is formulated.

| ACCOUNTING IN PRACTICE | **Relevant Range** |

To illustrate the concept of relevant range, assume that XYZ Company has one manufacturing building in which it manufactures toys. As long as no more than 10,000 toys are produced, the fixed costs associated with this building belong to one relevant range, 0–10,000 toys. If more than 10,000 toys are produced, XYZ will need an additional building, thus incurring additional fixed costs. The costs will be in a new relevant range.

A flexible budget, prepared with columns representing different projected levels of activity, provides managers with targets for various activity levels. Hence, during the period, a flexible budget can help managers assess the reasonableness of the firm's performance as the period progresses. However, one of the most important uses of the flexible budget comes not during, but *after* the end of the period. The flexible budget formula also allows managers to compare actual costs to budgeted costs based on the actual production level achieved. Specifically, the flexible budget performance report compares actual costs at the actual level of activity to the budgeted costs at the actual level of activity.

Exhibit 24-4 presents Fezzari's 2019 flexible budget performance report for the Foré CR1 product line. This performance report allows managers to evaluate how the company's actual performance compares to budgeted performance (based on the actual level of production) for different products. Specifically, the flexible budget performance report compares actual performance in column A to budgeted performance in column B with a flexible budget (rate or price) variance, as discussed in Chapter 23, for each component of product cost (direct materials, direct labor, variable overhead, and fixed overhead). Further, it compares the flexible budget in column A (based on 480 actual units) to the static budget in column C (based on 500 budgeted units). These differences are the efficiency variances, as discussed in Chapter 23.

Exhibit 24-4	Flexible Budget Performance Report Illustration

FEZZARI FORÉ CR1 PRODUCT LINE
Flexible Budget Performance Report
For the Year Ended December 31, 2019

Budgeted units of production		500			
Actual units of production		480			
Units of production variance		20 U			

	A Actual Costs Incurred for 480 Units	B Flexible Budget Based on 480 Units	(A-B) Flexible Budget Variance	C Static Budget Based on 500 Units	(A-C) Static Budget Variance
Variable costs:					
Direct material.	$292,800	$288,000	$ 4,800 U	$300,000	$(7,200) F
Direct labor	91,200	85,200	6,000 U	88,750	2,450 U
Variable overhead.	5,400	5,976	(576) F	6,225	(825) F
	$389,400	$379,176	$10,224 U	$394,975	$(5,575) F
Fixed costs:					
Fixed overhead	$ 16,200	$ 18,525	$(2,325) F	$ 18,525	$(2,325) F
Total	$405,600	$397,701	$ 7,899 U	$413,500	$(7,900) F

U = Unfavorable

F = Favorable

In essence, the flexible budget performance report compares "what we actually spent" to "what we should have spent" for the final production level. The flexible performance report is prepared by simply using the flexible budget formula to budget what the company "should have spent" based on the actual level of production (i.e., inserting the actual number of CR1 units produced, 480, into the flexible product costs budget).

A comparison of cost variances in the static budget performance report (**Exhibit 24-2**) and the flexible budget performance report (**Exhibit 24-4**) reveals a very different result. The static budget performance report indicates a total favorable cost variance of $7,900, whereas the flexible budget performance report reveals a total unfavorable flexible budget variance of $7,899. As explained previously, one reason the budget projections in **Exhibit 24-2** do not provide an accurate depiction of budgeted costs is that the static budget is based on the projected production level (500 CR1s) when actual production fell short (480 CR1s). Thus, part of the difference in the two comparisons is related to the volume differential (i.e., actual production came up 20 units short of the static budget production level). Clearly, the variances from the flexible budget performance report provide a more complete explanation because they are based on a comparison of what the costs actually were to what the costs should have been at the actual level of activity.

As discussed in Chapter 23, management can delve further into the causes for the overall flexible budget variance (columns A and B) by breaking each component of the variance down into individual price/and efficiency variances. For example, to explain the $4,800 unfavorable flexible budget variance for direct materials, price and efficiency variances could be calculated for *each* direct material used in producing a Foré CR1.

Similarly, labor rate and efficiency variances would be computed to explain the overall $6,000 unfavorable labor flexible budget variance and the overall $576 favorable variable overhead flexible budget variance.

ACCOUNTING IN PRACTICE	**Management by Exception**
	Performance reports should incorporate the management-by-exception concept. Variances outside acceptable ranges should be identified so management attention can be directed to those exceptional items.

Flexible Budgets in a Service Environment

SERVICE AND MERCHANDISING

Flexible budgets can be used in a service company just like in a manufacturing firm. For example, Old Rosebud is a 400-acre farm on the outskirts of the Kentucky Bluegrass region that specializes in boarding broodmares and their foals. An economic downturn in the thoroughbred industry has led to a decline in breeding activities. As a consequence, the demand for thoroughbred boarding has decreased, making the boarding business extremely competitive. To meet the competition, in 2019 Old Rosebud planned to entertain clients, advertise, and absorb expenses formerly borne by clients (for example, the company would pay for both veterinary and blacksmith's fees).

Exhibit 24-5 presents the variances between Old Rosebud's actual operating results in 2019 and amounts budgeted for the year. Its budget—like those of most service organizations—was a static budget (i.e., it forecast an expected level of activity). Old Rosebud expected to log 21,900 boarding days, and it budgeted boarding rates at $25 per day per mare.

The variable expenses per mare per day were budgeted as follows:

Feed	$5.00
Veterinary fees	$3.00
Blacksmith fees	$0.30
Supplies	$0.40

All other budgeted expenses were either semi-fixed or fixed.

The static budget in **Exhibit 24-5** can be used to explain only two factors: sales and fixed expenses. As sales volume problems arose during the year, Old Rosebud decided not to replace a farm worker who quit in March. It also developed a new farm brochure and entertained more potential clients. These strategies generated the fixed-expense variances—that is, the differences between the budgeted and actual line item amounts in the income statement.

No sound conclusions can be drawn about either the effect of price changes on the decrease in net income or the expense variances. When sales volume declines, sales revenue and variable expenses may be expected to decrease proportionately. However, the rate of Old Rosebud's decline in the number of boarding days (13%) differs from the rate of decrease in sales revenue (31%) and the rate of decrease in variable expenses (7%).

A plausible interpretation of the variances in **Exhibit 24-5** is that the large variance in net income is caused by a decrease in sales volume. This interpretation follows from the large unfavorable sales revenue variance and the generally favorable expense variances.

Indeed, at first glance, it appears as though expenses are well under control. All variable-expense variances are favorable, and the total of the two unfavorable fixed-expense variances is insignificant in relation to the total sales-revenue variance. The unfavorable advertising and entertainment variances may be interpreted as having pre-vented the unfavorable net income variance from being even greater. More business might have been lost had Old Rosebud not overspent its budgeted amounts for those items.

Because sales are down and expenses are well under control, this analysis suggests an obvious but faulty remedy: Do more advertising and entertaining.

Exhibit 24-5	Static Budget Illustration—Service

OLD ROSEBUD
Static Budget Income Statement
Year Ended December 31, 2019

	Actual	Static Budget	Variance
Number of mares	52	60	(8) U
Number of boarding days	18,980	21,900	(2,920) U
Sales.	$379,600	$547,500	$(167,900) U
Less variable expenses:			
Feed	104,390	109,500	(5,110) F
Veterinary fees	58,838	65,700	(6,862) F
Blacksmith fees.	6,074	6,570	(496) F
Supplies	7,402	8,760	(1,358) F
Total variable expenses	$176,704	$190,530	(13,826) F
Contribution margin	$202,896	$356,970	$(154,074) U
Less fixed expenses:			
Depreciation	$ 45,000	$ 45,000	$ —
Insurance	11,000	11,000	—
Utilities	12,000	14,000	(2,000) F
Repairs and maintenance.	10,000	11,000	(1,000) F
Labor.	88,000	96,000	(8,000) F
Advertisement	11,000	8,000	3,000 U
Entertainment	8,000	5,000	3,000 U
Total fixed expenses.	$185,000	$190,000	$ (5,000) F
Net income	$ 17,896	$166,970	$(149,074) U

U = Unfavorable
F = Favorable

Exhibit 24-6 compares Old Rosebud's actual operating results with those in a flexible budget for 2019. The flexible budget takes the same budgeted per-unit amounts for sales and variable expenses and applies them to the actual number of boarding days achieved in 2019. Because, by definition, fixed expenses don't vary with volume, they're the same as in the static budget. A budget constructed in this way removes the distortion in the sales-revenue and variable-expense variances of a static budget.

Two surprises are immediately apparent. First, when the unfavorable sales-revenue variance of $167,900 is separated into the unfavorable sales-price ($94,900) and unfavor-able sales-volume ($73,000) variances, it becomes clear that the sales-price variance is larger. Further investigation of the sales-price variance revealed that Old Rosebud lost a major client in 2019. Moreover, because of fierce competition, the farm reduced its boarding charges well below $25 per day per mare as the year progressed. As a result, the average boarding rate declined for the year.

The second surprise in **Exhibit 24-6** is that expense control was far worse than analysis of the static budget variance had indicated. All variable-expense variances, except supplies, were unfavorable. The unfavorable feed variance of $9,490 alone accounted for nearly 82% of the net unfavorable variable-expense variances of $11,578. The large feed variance was explained by the drought that hit Kentucky and most of the rest of the nation in 2019. In addition, several recent studies had indicated that copper feed supplements may be necessary to minimize skeletal bone disease in young horses. Old Rosebud incorporated the supplement at an increased cost and continued to feed first-class hay despite the drought.

Exhibit 24-6	Flexible Budget Illustration—Service			
	OLD ROSEBUD Flexible Budget Income Statement Year Ended December 31, 2019			
Budgeted number of boarding days . . .	21,900			
Actual number of boarding days	18,980			
	Budget (per mare per day)	**Actual**	**Flexible Budget**	**Variance**
Number of mares		52	52	0
Number of boarding days		18,980	18,980	0
Sales.	$25.00	$379,600	$474,500	$ (94,900) U
Less variable expenses:				
Feed	5.00	104,390	94,900	9,490 U
Veterinary fees	3.00	58,838	56,940	1,898 U
Blacksmith fees.	0.30	6,074	5,694	380 U
Supplies	0.40	7,402	7,592	(190) F
Total variable expenses	$ 8.70	$176,704	$165,126	$ 11,578 U
Contribution margin	$16.30	$202,896	$309,374	$(106,478) U
Less fixed expenses:				
Depreciation		$ 45,000	$ 45,000	$ —
Insurance		11,000	11,000	—
Utilities		12,000	14,000	(2,000) F
Repairs and maintenance.		10,000	11,000	(1,000) F
Labor.		88,000	96,000	(8,000) F
Advertisement.		11,000	8,000	3,000 U
Entertainment		8,000	5,000	3,000 U
Total fixed expenses.		$185,000	$190,000	(5,000) F
Net income		$ 17,896	$119,374	$(101,478) U

U = Unfavorable

F = Favorable

Accurate information about what causes the differences between actual and expected results is a precondition for corrective action. Variance analysis can lead to an accurate analysis. In contrast, a static budget can focus only on sales and fixed expenses that differ from budgeted figures, and not realizing this may lead to faulty analysis of the results. Flexible budget variances aren't misleading because they incorporate actual levels of activity if different from those expected.

For Old Rosebud, the main problem is price—not volume. Had the farm been able to maintain its boarding rates but not the number of boarding days, its actual net income would have been:

Sales revenue.	$474,500
Less total variable expenses	(176,704)
Less total fixed expenses.	(185,000)
Net income.	$112,796

This amount is six times greater than the net income of $17,896 actually achieved. The farm needs to develop a strategy that restores boarding rates more than it needs to replace the eight horses it lost.[1]

Concept	→	Method	→	Assessment	TAKEAWAY 24.1
How can management evaluate the company's performance relative to the budget?		• Prepare a flexible budget based on actual output achieved. • Compare the actual results to the flexible budget.		• Actual costs for materials, labor, or variable overhead that are less than the flexible budget amounts result in favorable variances. • Actual costs that are greater than the flexible budget amounts result in unfavorable variances.	

YOUR TURN! 24.2

The solution is on page 1156.

The following static budget performance report was prepared for Chip Manufacturing for July.

	Actual Results	Static Budget	Variance
Sales units	100,000	90,000	10,000 F
Sales dollars.	$190,000	$180,000	$10,000 F
Variable costs	125,000	108,000	17,000 U
Fixed costs	50,000	45,000	5,000 U
Operating income	$ 15,000	$ 27,000	$12,000 U

Using a flexible budget, calculate Chip's total flexible budget variance for variable costs.

CORPORATE SOCIAL RESPONSIBILITY

Microsoft's Corporate Citizenship "Budget"

The opening vignette discussed the importance of budgeting to Microsoft's operations, in particular financial measures such as sales. The process of budgeting as discussed in this chapter is applicable to far more than just financial results. Microsoft uses budgets to track revenues and expenses that are eventually communicated to interested parties in its annual financial report. In addition, Microsoft sets goals and tracks these goals with budgeting techniques outlined in this chapter for its annual Citizenship Report. In this report Microsoft highlights its performance in such areas as Ethical Business Conduct and Governance, People, Serving Communities, Human Rights, Responsible Sourcing, and Environmental Sustainability. The report can be found at and downloaded from Microsoft's website under the Corporate Citizenship section at the following link: https://www.microsoft.com/about/corporatecitizenship/en-us/

[1] SOURCE: Adapted from Hans Sprohge and John Talbott, "New Applications for Variance Analysis," *Journal of Accountancy*, April 1989, pp. 137, 138, 140, 141. Reprinted with permission from the *Journal of Public Accountancy*, copyright © 1989 by the American Institute of Certified Public Accountants, Inc. Opinions of the authors are their own and do not necessarily reflect the policies of the AICPA.

INTERNAL REPORTING OF SEGMENT OPERATIONS

LO3 Present an overview of reporting operations for segments of a business.

Decentralized Organizations

As businesses grow, management of the organization becomes more and more difficult. Most large businesses are decentralized, meaning that the authority to make decisions is spread throughout the business.

Although decentralization occurs almost out of necessity as businesses grow, there are significant advantages to involving lower-level management in the decision-making process of the business:

1. Delegation of day-to-day operational decisions frees up upper management to focus on strategy and business development.

2. Involvement of lower-level management in running the business provides excellent on-the-job training for those who will eventually become the upper management of the business.

3. Empowering lower-level managers may increase their job satisfaction and motivation to work hard.

4. Because lower-level managers are more familiar with the day-to-day operation of the business, they are more likely to identify and react more quickly to trends in the marketplace.

On the other hand, decentralization can lead to less desirable consequences:

1. Lower-level managers may not be privy to the larger business strategy.

2. Decisions made by lower-level managers may not be consistent with and supportive of goals and objectives of other departments or divisions within the business.

3. Largely autonomous departments or divisions may lead to "silos" within the business, resulting in important operating information or innovative ideas not being shared with other departments or divisions, to the detriment of the business overall.

Segment Reporting

Many business entities are very complex, with diverse divisions and departments in multiple locations. Managers of this type of entity often find it useful to divide the entity into segments to enhance managerial planning and control. Segments usually are based on organizational units (divisions or departments) or areas of economic activity (geographic regions or product lines). Many large companies have found that segmentation by organizational unit is the approach that proves most useful. It is important that the managerial accounting systems and procedures that develop information for planning and control decisions be structured to reflect the segmentation.

Internal reporting of segment operations deals primarily with the measurement of operating performance. As a result, segmented reports usually take the format of a contribution margin income statement. These statements may provide information to answer the following types of questions:

1. What amount does each segment contribute to the sales and operating income of the entity as a whole?

2. How do revenues and expenses for each segment compare to planned or budgeted amounts?

3. What is the rate of profitability of each segment? Should any segment be expanded, reduced, or eliminated?

4. Which areas need corrective action, and what should be done?

5. Where should promotional efforts be directed?

Types of Business Segments

With delegated authority comes accountability. In a decentralized organization, segment managers must demonstrate that the results of their decisions support and are congruent with the overall business strategy of the organization. Portions of a business for which a manager has been given a measure of authority and accountability are often referred to as **responsibility centers**. Depending on the authority delegated, these responsibility centers may be described as cost centers, profit centers, and investment centers. An example of these responsibility centers may be seen in PACCAR, a heavy-duty truck manufacturer.

PACCAR is a Fortune 200 company that designs, manufactures, and distributes trucks and related aftermarket parts that are sold worldwide under the Kenworth, Peterbilt, and DAF nameplates. It ranked as the third-largest manu-facturer of medium- and heavy-duty trucks in the world in 2012.

The company has its headquarters in Bellevue, Washington. It began in 1905 as Seattle Car Manufac-turing Company, at which time it produced railway and logging equipment. Over time, it expanded through acquisitions of commercial truck manufacturers and parts suppliers. As it grew and became more complex, management organized various business segments or responsibility centers. As described in the following discussion, some of PACCAR's responsibility centers might be considered cost centers, profit centers, or in-vestment centers.

The manager of a **cost center** is responsible for the costs and expenses of only that segment of the business. He or she has no responsibility for

revenue generation. An example of a PACCAR cost center is its Technical Centers, which provide re-search, development, and testing for new products. The output of these Technical Centers is a service to other PACCAR divisions or segments that is not sold to consumers outside the company. As a result, no revenue is generated directly by these centers.

The manager of a **profit center** is responsible for revenue generation as well as for cost and ex-pense control. An example of a PACCAR profit cen-ter is its PACCAR Parts business, which operates a network of parts distribution centers that offer af-termarket support to its truck dealerships and cus-tomers throughout the world. PACCAR evaluates the performance of PACCAR Parts on its operating profit or segment contribution margin.

The manager of an **investment center** is responsible for the use of capital (productive assets), along with revenues and costs. The manager is typically evaluated on a measure of return on assets or return on investment. An example of a PACCAR investment center is its PACCAR Mexico (KENMEX) division, which manufactures trucks for Mexico and exports to other countries in a 590,000-square-foot facility.

Managerial reports that measure the operating performance of a business entity and its segments reflect whether the segments are investment, profit, or cost centers. Return on investment, revenue, expenses, and profits are reported for investment centers; revenue, expenses, and profits are reported for profit centers; and only expenses are reported for cost centers. **Exhibit 24-7** illustrates the relationship among the different reporting segments.

Exhibit 24-7	Reporting Segments

Segment Reporting

In June 2013, the Securities and Exchange Commission (SEC) charged PACCAR for various accounting deficiencies that obscured the company's financial reporting to investors and regulators from 2008 through 2012. Among the charges was that PACCAR failed to report the operating results of its aftermarket parts business separately from its truck sales business as required under segment reporting requirements. These requirements are intended to allow investors to gain the same insight into the company's operations as its executives.

How significant was this violation of generally accepted accounting principles (GAAP)? In its 2009 annual report, PACCAR reported $68 million in income before taxes for its truck segment. However, had it followed GAAP, it would have reported a $474 million loss in the truck segment and a $542 million profit in its parts segment.

The SEC and PACCAR agreed to a settlement under which, without admitting or denying the charges, PACCAR agreed to the entry of a permanent injunction and the payment of a $225,000 penalty. Michael S. Dicke, associate regional director of the SEC's San Francisco Regional Office said, "Companies must continually and diligently monitor their internal accounting systems to ensure that the information they are providing investors is accurate and consistent with relevant accounting guidance. The deficient controls and procedures at PACCAR caused inconsistencies in its financial reporting and kept investors and regulators from seeing the company through the eyes of management." http://www.sec.gov/News/PressRelease/Detail/PressRelease/1365171575142#.VATK9_IdV8E

TAKEAWAY 24.2	Concept ———————▶	Method ———————————▶	Assessment ————————▶
	How might firm management measure and evaluate the performance of its responsibility centers?	• Cost center: cost variances, measuring differences between actual and budgeted costs • Profit center: revenue and cost variances, return on sales, and segment contribution margin • Investment center: return on investment and residual income	• Variances help managers identify explanations for differences between actual and expected performance. • Financial ratios are compared to targets and benchmarks to determine whether the firm met its goals and evaluate its performance relative to its competitors.

YOUR TURN! 24.3

The solution is on page 1156.

Access the most recent 10-K filing of PACCAR at edgar.sec.gov. What operating segments does PACCAR report (search for the term "segment" under Item 1 of the 10-K filing)?

PERFORMANCE REPORTING

Performance reports are usually constructed periodically for each investment, profit, and cost center. They contain different levels of detail for different levels of managerial responsibility. Whereas top managers need highly summarized information, lower-level managers require more detailed, specialized reports.

LO4 **Construct** a segmented contribution margin income statement. **Identify** the difference between traceable and common fixed costs.

Hint: Direct expenses do not need to be allocated.

Exhibit 24-8 presents multilevel performance reports for three successively higher levels of management. The arrows show how the totals from the lower-level reports flow to and are included in the higher-level reports.

Note that in this illustration, all costs from the lower level are included in the upper level. In practice, this may not always be the case—for proper decision-making purposes, only those costs that are directly traceable (see Chapter 15 for a discussion of direct versus indirect costs) to each department should be assigned to that department. Common costs would not be assigned for purposes of performance evaluation.

Also note that the reports in Panels B and C are for cost centers, so these reports only contain cost information. The manager of machining operations and the vice president of operations do not have responsibility for revenue, so revenues are not allocated to their reports. The divisions shown in Panel A are profit centers, so the report shows revenues, traceable variable costs, contribution margin, traceable fixed costs, allocated segment costs, and segment contribution margin in a contribution margin income statement format.

Departmental Operations

Departmentalization is a common and logical type of segmentation for many firms. In many companies, departments are classified by processes performed. In the previous example, the Kitchen Cutlery division is composed of three segments, or departments: machining, fabricating, and assembly. These departments represent the primary processes performed in making the knives, forks, and spoons that comprise a set of kitchen cutlery.

In other companies, departments might be classified by products sold. The very term *department store* signifies a type of merchandising by product (men's clothing, women's clothing, home furnishings, etc.). Grocery stores are also commonly departmentalized by product groups such as meat, produce, groceries, bakery, and delicatessen. Sometimes departments are classified by type of customer. For example, home improvement centers selling such products as floor coverings, lighting fixtures, and heating and air-conditioning units may separate commercial sales operations from residential sales operations.

The methods of accounting and reporting departmental operating activities depend on the performance measures used and the degree of analysis desired by management. Some firms may desire to identify only contribution margin by department. Others may adopt a more detailed performance measure, such as contribution margin less those fixed costs directly incurred by the department (segment or department income).

Contribution Margin Income Statement

The main reason for analyzing segment contribution margin is that it permits management to review pricing policies and supplier costs. Comparisons can be made among segments to determine areas with high segment contribution margin and areas that may need major promotional efforts. For example, in the Metal Works, Inc. example in **Exhibit 24-8**, the segment report permits a comparison of the Cutlery and Hand Tools divisions (or segments) of the company. Comparisons can also be made with contribution margin achieved in previous periods or with statistics for other firms selling similar

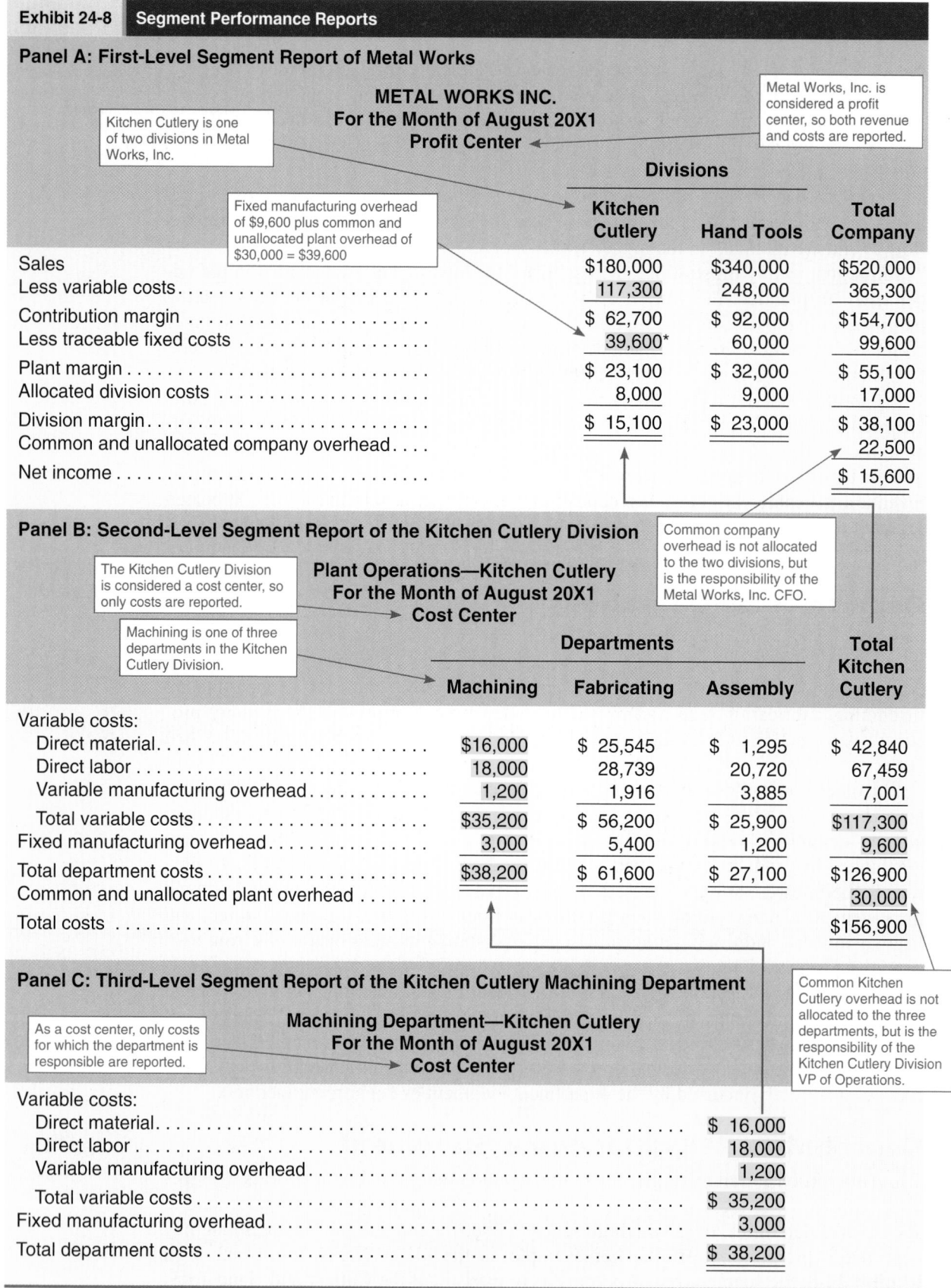

Exhibit 24-8 | Segment Performance Reports

Panel A: First-Level Segment Report of Metal Works

Kitchen Cutlery is one of two divisions in Metal Works, Inc.

METAL WORKS INC.
For the Month of August 20X1
Profit Center

Metal Works, Inc. is considered a profit center, so both revenue and costs are reported.

Fixed manufacturing overhead of $9,600 plus common and unallocated plant overhead of $30,000 = $39,600

| | Divisions | | |
	Kitchen Cutlery	Hand Tools	Total Company
Sales	$180,000	$340,000	$520,000
Less variable costs	117,300	248,000	365,300
Contribution margin	$ 62,700	$ 92,000	$154,700
Less traceable fixed costs	39,600*	60,000	99,600
Plant margin	$ 23,100	$ 32,000	$ 55,100
Allocated division costs	8,000	9,000	17,000
Division margin	$ 15,100	$ 23,000	$ 38,100
Common and unallocated company overhead			22,500
Net income			$ 15,600

Panel B: Second-Level Segment Report of the Kitchen Cutlery Division

Common company overhead is not allocated to the two divisions, but is the responsibility of the Metal Works, Inc. CFO.

The Kitchen Cutlery Division is considered a cost center, so only costs are reported.

Plant Operations—Kitchen Cutlery
For the Month of August 20X1
Cost Center

Machining is one of three departments in the Kitchen Cutlery Division.

| | Departments | | | Total Kitchen Cutlery |
	Machining	Fabricating	Assembly	
Variable costs:				
Direct material	$16,000	$ 25,545	$ 1,295	$ 42,840
Direct labor	18,000	28,739	20,720	67,459
Variable manufacturing overhead	1,200	1,916	3,885	7,001
Total variable costs	$35,200	$ 56,200	$ 25,900	$117,300
Fixed manufacturing overhead	3,000	5,400	1,200	9,600
Total department costs	$38,200	$ 61,600	$ 27,100	$126,900
Common and unallocated plant overhead				30,000
Total costs				$156,900

Panel C: Third-Level Segment Report of the Kitchen Cutlery Machining Department

Common Kitchen Cutlery overhead is not allocated to the three departments, but is the responsibility of the Kitchen Cutlery Division VP of Operations.

As a cost center, only costs for which the department is responsible are reported.

Machining Department—Kitchen Cutlery
For the Month of August 20X1
Cost Center

Variable costs:	
Direct material	$ 16,000
Direct labor	18,000
Variable manufacturing overhead	1,200
Total variable costs	$ 35,200
Fixed manufacturing overhead	3,000
Total department costs	$ 38,200

products. (These statistics may be obtained from trade association publications and credit agencies.[2]) A very low segment contribution margin may signal a need to investigate purchasing policies or to revise prices.

To obtain contribution margin figures by segment or department, a firm customarily creates a contribution margin income statement. A contribution margin income statement allows managers to identify those costs that are controllable by the segment and for which the segment manager should be held accountable. The use of a contribution margin income statement requires management to segregate those costs that are attributable to the segment from those costs that are attributable to other segments. As shown in Panel A of **Exhibit 24-8**, the attributable costs must be further classified as variable and fixed costs (both traceable to the department and common). Recall that in a contribution margin income statement, cost of goods sold consists of only variable manufacturing costs, all variable costs (both production and selling and administrative) are deducted from sales revenue to compute the contribution margin, and all fixed costs are deducted from contribution margin to compute the division margin. Note that in creating a segment contribution margin income statement, only fixed costs that are traceable to the segment are deducted to arrive at the segment contribution margin.

Segment Performance Evaluation

Department managers should be held responsible only for costs and expenses that they control. Therefore in segment reporting, costs are commonly classified and reported as traceable (controlled by the segment) or common (not controlled by the segment). **Traceable expenses** are those operating expenses or costs traceable to and incurred for the benefit of a single department and thus ordinarily controllable by the department. **Common expenses** are those operating expenses or costs incurred for the benefit of multiple departments and thus neither traceable to nor controllable by a specific department. In Panel A of **Exhibit 24-8**, $22,500 of company expenses is determined to be common and unallocated to the Kitchen Cutlery and Hand Tools divisions.

Frequently, costs are considered controllable at one level of management but not at other levels. For example, the vice president of marketing for Metal Works, Inc. may be responsible for decisions related to advertising. Even though the cost of advertising is incurred at the division level (Kitchen Cutlery and Hand Tools), the manager of these divisions should not be held responsible for that expense if the vice president of marketing makes all the decisions relative to that cost or expense. These costs would be included in the common and unallocated company overhead costs shown in Panel A of **Exhibit 24-8**.

Concept ⟶	Method ⟶	Assessment ⟶	TAKEAWAY 24.3
How can a firm hold segment managers responsible for revenues and costs?	Prepare periodic performance reports for each segment.	• Cost center managers are responsible for directly traceable variable and fixed costs. • Profit center managers are responsible for directly traceable revenues and variable and fixed costs. • Investment center managers are responsible for invested capital, revenues, and variable and fixed costs.	

SERVICE COMPANY SEGMENT REPORTING ILLUSTRATION

Let's review an example of segment reporting with Environmental Business Consultants (EBC). EBC, which has two offices in northern and southern California, was introduced

---

[2] For example, the Risk Management Association publishes the RMA Annual Statement Studies, which is a source of comparative data drawn from the financial statements of the small- and medium-sized business customers of RMA's member institutions.

to you in earlier chapters. Within EBC, each office is considered a department—the word *department* is used interchangeably with *office* in the following discussion.

Office Margin

EBC maintains its accounting records to produce absorption income statements in accordance with GAAP as required by its bank. However, assume that EBC's management desires a better measure of operating performance. It is then faced with the problem of assigning or *allocating* operating expenses to the offices. If managers desire a measure of office margin, it is necessary to trace the operating expenses to the offices.

Some expenses may be readily identified with the operation of particular offices, but others cannot be. To identify expenses with offices, it is helpful to classify them into traceable and common expenses. For example, payroll expense related to personnel who work exclusively in one office is a traceable expense of that office. Payroll expense related to administrative personnel whose work benefits all offices is a common expense of the offices. EBC also has several common expenses, incurred for the benefit of both offices. Some examples are marketing expenses, some administrative salaries, and a variety of other administrative expenses. These expenses must be fairly assigned, where traceable, to the offices if the measure of office net income is to be meaningful. Note that some general administrative costs such as executive salaries, general accounting expenses, and general legal expenses should not be allocated for purposes of evaluating an office's performance because the office manager has no control over those items.

Assume that EBC management classifies its operating costs as variable or fixed as follows:

Variable Expenses	Amount
Employee bonuses	$126,000
Marketing expenses	48,000
Office supplies expense	64,500
Other general administrative expenses	70,000
Total variable operating expenses	$308,500

Fixed Expenses	Amount
Executive salaries	$ 844,500
Clerical salaries	217,500
Consultant salaries	1,050,000
Employee benefits	145,500
Payroll taxes	123,000
Employee continuing education expenses	27,000
Office lease expense	202,500
Other general administrative expenses	285,500
Total fixed operating expenses	$2,895,500

In preparing an office income statement, EBC might analyze and assign these expenses as described in the following subsections.

Employee Bonuses

All EBC employees are eligible for bonuses based on the profits earned during the year. Because each employee is assigned to an office, the bonuses for each office can be directly determined from payroll records, which show $96,178 for northern California and $29,822 for southern California.

Marketing Expenses

Of EBC's $48,000 marketing expenses, $28,000 was spent on proposal preparation in northern California, $11,000 on proposal preparation in southern California, $4,000 on attendance at industry trade shows that benefit both markets, and $5,000 on general professional journal advertisements directed at both markets. The latter two amounts are not assigned to the offices because they are considered common expenses, as shown in **Exhibit 24-9**.

Exhibit 24-9	Marketing Expenses Allocation			
		Northern California	Southern California	Firm Total
Proposal preparation		$28,000*	$11,000*	$39,000
Trade shows				4,000
Advertising				5,000
				$48,000

* Directly identified

Office Supplies Expenses

Office supplies are purchased by each office as needed, so they are easily traceable to each office. EBC records show that $51,600 and $12,900 of office supplies were purchased by the northern and southern California offices, respectively, during the year.

Other General Administrative Expenses

Other general administrative expenses include the salaries and benefits for the office manager and bookkeeper and other costs associated with billings, collections, and customer inquiries. These costs, both the variable and fixed portions, are considered common costs and are not assigned to the individual offices.

Salaries and Related Benefits

Executive, clerical, and consultant salaries and related employee benefits and taxes are traceable to the office in which the employee works. EBC payroll records show that the total salaries, benefits, and taxes for each office are $1,876,200 and $504,300 for the northern and southern California offices, respectively.

Employee Continuing Education Expenses

All professional consultants are required to complete 40 hours of continuing education (CE) credits each year. As with salaries and related benefits, these costs can be determined directly for each office. The firm's time records show CE expenses of $20,828 for northern California consultants and $6,172 for southern California consultants.

Office Lease Expense

Each of the EBC offices negotiates and pays for its own office space. EBC records show that $154,500 in lease expense was paid by the northern California office and $48,000 was paid by the southern California office.

Exhibit 24-10 presents a summary of the operating expenses, showing the traceable variable and traceable fixed expenses of each department and common expenses for the firm.

Exhibit 24-10	Operating Expense Assignment				
	A	B	C	D	E
1		Northern California	Southern California	Common	Firm Total
2	Variable costs				
3	Employee bonuses	$ 96,178	$ 29,822		$ 126,000
4	Marketing expenses	28,000	11,000	9,000	48,000
5	Office supplies expense	51,600	12,900		64,500
6	Other general administrative expenses			70,000	70,000
7	Total variable costs	$ 175,778	$ 53,722	$ 79,000	$ 308,500
8	Fixed costs				
9	Salaries and benefits	$1,876,200	$504,300		$2,380,500
10	Employee continuing education expenses	20,828	6,172		27,000
11	Office lease expense	154,500	48,000		202,500
12	Other general administrative expenses			$285,500	285,500
13	Total fixed costs	$2,051,528	$558,472	$285,500	$2,895,500
14	Total costs	$2,227,306	$612,194	$364,500	$3,204,000

The traceable variable and fixed costs are used to prepare the office margin statement in Exhibit 24-11.

The common costs are NOT allocated to the offices in the office margin statement in Exhibit 24-11.

ACCOUNTING IN
PRACTICE

Expense Allocation for Federal Government Grants and Contracts

Organizations, such as universities, that do business with the federal government under grants and contracts must use federal-government-specified allocation methods. The guidelines, known as OMB Circular A-87, establish the principles and standards for determining allowable costs for federal awards carried out through grants, cost reimbursement contracts, and other agreements with state and local governments. Allowable costs must meet certain criteria, including being necessary and reasonable, legally incurred under state or local law, consistent with federal policies and regulations, consistently applied, and adequately documented.

This departmental expense distribution is used to prepare the variable income statement for EBC shown in **Exhibit 24-11**, which extends the departmental operating results through office margin. Note that in this presentation, traceable variable costs are deducted to compute office contribution margin, from which traceable fixed costs are subtracted to compute office margin. Common expenses are not allocated to the individual offices.

Operating statements that extend departmental results to operating or net income measures are often criticized on the grounds that the indirect or common expenses are not controllable at the departmental level and therefore should not be assigned to departments when measuring performance. An additional criticism is that the bases for assignment of common expenses are frequently arbitrary.

In the EBC example, the other general administrative costs, although necessary expenses for the firm overall, are not controllable by the individual office managers. Thus, they should not be allocated to the offices at all. To allocate these costs on some arbitrary basis could lead management to draw incorrect conclusions and make poor business decisions.

Exhibit 24-11	Office Margin Statement		
	A	B	C	D

		Northern California	Southern California	Firm Total
	ENVIRONMENTAL BUSINESS CONSULTANTS, LLC **Office Margin Statement** **For the Year Ended December 31, 2019**			
3	Gross sales	$2,900,000	$1,246,000	$4,146,000
4	Less reimbursable costs	(344,800)	(86,200)	(431,000)
5	Net sales	2,555,200	1,159,800	3,715,000
6	Traceable variable costs	(175,778)	(53,722)	(229,500)
7	Office contribution margin	2,379,422	1,106,078	3,485,500
8	Traceable fixed costs	(2,051,528)	(558,472)	(2,610,000)
9	**Office margin**	**$ 327,894**	**$ 547,606**	875,500
10	Common expenses			(364,500)
11	Operating income			511,000
12	Interest revenue			7,500
13	Income before tax			$ 518,500

> The traceable variable and fixed costs were assigned to each office in Exhibit 24-10.

> The common costs are not allocated to the offices because they are not controllable by the office managers.

Departmental revenue is $600,000 for Department X, and departmental operating income is $350,000. Traceable expenses for this department are as follows:

Direct labor	$25,000
Other traceable costs	$40,000
Direct materials	$30,000

Compute common expenses for this department.

YOUR TURN! 24.4

The solution is on page 1156.

PERFORMANCE ANALYSIS

The contribution margin income statement that was discussed in the previous section may be used to evaluate the performance of a profit center. This section addresses evaluation of investment centers.

LO5 **Compute** return on investment, return on sales, return on assets, and residual income for business segments. **Discuss** the importance of each indicator in assessing a company's performance.

Managers use a number of methods for evaluating the performance of investment centers. We explore several performance evaluation methods and discuss their relative strengths and weaknesses. To illustrate these different performance methods, we compare hypothetical data for Fezzari's mountain bike and road bike divisions. **Exhibit 24-12** indicates that the mountain bike division earned $2.5 million during 2019, and the road bike division earned $1.7 million. It also shows that the mountain bike division's investment in operating assets is $18.3 million, and the road bike division's investment is $11 million. We use this information to demonstrate the relative pros and cons of the various performance methods.

We note that one might be tempted to simply compare the operating income numbers of the two divisions and conclude that the mountain bike division is outperforming the road bike division because it has a higher operating income for the period. However, some of the other performance metrics we discuss here may provide different insights.

Exhibit 24-12	Performance Analysis

FEZZARI PERFORMANCE BICYCLES
Division Performance
For the Year Ended December 31, 2019

	Divisions	
(in thousands)	Mountain	Road
Sales.	$14,400	$ 7,900
Expenses	(11,900)	(6,200)
Operating income.	$ 2,500	$ 1,700
Asset investment	$18,300	$11,000

Return on Investment

One of the problems with simply comparing the net income figures of the two divisions is that they differ in size. One way to "level the playing field" of two divisions of different sizes is to compare the divisions on a relative basis based on a ratio.

One ratio that is useful in comparing the profitability of two divisions is the **return on investment** (ROI) ratio, which is calculated as the operating income number divided by the investment in operating assets:

$$ROI = \frac{\text{Operating income}}{\text{Operating asset investment}}$$

ROI examines the division's operating income as a percentage of the asset base used to generate that income.

Given the information in **Exhibit 24-12**, Fezzari's mountain bike division has an ROI of 13.7% ($2,500/$18,300), and the road bike division has an ROI of 15.5% ($1,700/$11,000). Therefore, the ROI ratio indicates that the road bike division earns a higher rate of return on its investment in assets than the mountain bike division earns on its investment. Thus, Fezzari's division ROI measures indicate that the mountain bike division generates 13.7 cents of profit for every dollar invested in assets, and the road bike division earns 15.5 cents of profit on every dollar invested in its asset base. Therefore, the ROI ratio provides evidence that the road bike division is more profitable on a relative basis, given its investment in assets.

In the 1920s, the DuPont brothers recognized that ROI could be further divided into two ratios, profit margin and asset turnover, which provided managers additional levers to improve the overall ROI. This has come to be referred to as the **DuPont formula**. The formula for ROI can be expressed as:

$$ROI = \text{Profit margin} \times \text{Asset turnover} = \frac{\text{Operating income}}{\text{Sales}} \times \frac{\text{Sales}}{\text{Investment}}$$

Exhibit 24-13 summarizes the calculation of ROI based on the DuPont formula for Fezzari's mountain and road bike divisions. The calculations of Fezzari's return on sales and asset utilization are discussed in the following sections.

Exhibit 24-13	ROI Analysis

FEZZARI PERFORMANCE BICYCLES
DuPont ROI Analysis
For the Year Ended December 31, 2019

	ROI	=	Profit Margin	×	Asset Utilization
Mountain.	13.7%	=	17.4%	×	78.7%
Road.	15.5%	=	21.5%	×	71.8%*

* Difference due to rounding

Profit Margin

The **profit margin** ratio (the first component of the DuPont ROI formula) is useful in comparing the profitability of two divisions, which is simply calculated as the operating income number divided by sales:

AKA Profit margin is also known as return on sales.

$$\text{Profit margin} = \frac{\text{Operating income}}{\text{Sales}}$$

As shown in **Exhibit 24-13**, Fezzari's mountain bike division has a profit margin of 17.4% ($2,500/$14,400), whereas the road bike division has a profit margin of 21.5% ($1,700/$7,900). Thus, even though the road bike division has a lower net income than the mountain bike division, it is higher as a percentage of sales. One way of interpreting the profit margin ratio is the number of pennies left over from each dollar of sales after covering all costs. Thus, Fezzari's division profit margin measures indicate that although the mountain bike division may have a greater operating income number, it does not manage expenses as efficiently as the road bike division, because only 17.4 cents of every sales dollar is left over after covering operating costs, whereas the road bike division generates 21.5 cents of operating income for every sales dollar generated. At least based on this profitability measure, the road bike division is actually relatively more profitable.

Asset Turnover

The **asset turnover** ratio (the second component of the DuPont ROI formula) is used to compare the efficiency with which the divisions are using their operating assets to generate sales. It is calculated as sales divided by the investment in operating assets:

$$\text{Asset turnover} = \frac{\text{Sales}}{\text{Investment}}$$

As shown in **Exhibit 24-13**, Fezzari's mountain bike division has an asset turnover ratio of 78.7% ($14,400/$18,300), and the road bike division has an asset turnover ratio of 71.8% ($7,900/$11,000). This means that the mountain bike division generates 78.7 cents in sales for every dollar of operating assets, whereas the road bike division generates only 71.8 cents in sales for every dollar of operating assets. The mountain bike division uses its operating assets more efficiently.

Interestingly, the DuPont analysis indicates that the road bike division has higher core profitability but the mountain bike division uses its assets more efficiently. Nevertheless, the result of multiplying the profit margin ratio by the asset turnover ratio is that the road bike division has a higher ROI.

Residual Income

Another method for comparing two subsidiary companies or operating divisions is based on **residual income**. Similar to ROI, residual income takes the size of the division into account. However, unlike ROI, residual income is not a ratio; it is defined as the income that is left over after the company or division earns some minimum return on investment. Residual income is based on the idea that owners or investors expect a company to provide a reasonable rate of return on their investment. Investors could invest their money in other types of investments, so they likely have some minimum rate of return (called a hurdle rate) they would like to earn on their investment in the company. Another way of looking at residual income is to calculate the amount of extra income after a division earns a minimum ROI. The formula for residual income is:

Residual income = Net operating income − (Average operating assets × Minimum ROI)

Exhibit 24-14 first assumes that managers or owners expect each division to earn a hurdle rate of 5%. Given the mountain bike division's investment in assets of $18.3 million and the company's desired ROI of $915,000 ($18.3 million × 0.05), it has residual income of $1.59 million. Similarly, the road bike division has a desired ROI of $550,000 ($11.0 million × 0.05) and residual income of $1.15 million. Thus, we would conclude that the mountain bike division generates more residual income than the road bike division.

Exhibit 24-14	Residual Income Analysis	
	A	B	C
1	FEZZARI PERFORMANCE BICYCLES Residual Income Analysis For the Year Ended December 31, 2019		
2		Divisions	
3	(in thousands)	Mountain	Road
4	Net income	$2,500	$1,700
5	Required return (5% rate)	(915)	(550)
6	Residual income	$1,585	$1,150
7			
8	Net income	$2,500	$1,700
9	Required return (12% rate)	(2,196)	(1,320)
10	Residual income	$ 304	$ 380

On the other hand, what if managers or owners expect each division to earn a hurdle rate of 12%? Given the mountain bike division's investment in assets of $18.3 million and the company's desired ROI of $2.20 million ($18.3 million × 0.12), it has residual income of $304,000. Similarly, the road bike division has a desired ROI of $1.32 million ($11.0 million × 0.12) and residual income of $380,000. Thus, we would conclude that the road bike division's $380,000 of residual income exceeds the mountain bike division's $304,000 of residual income.

How is it possible that the mountain bike division has higher residual income if the required ROI is 5% and the road bike division has a higher residual income when the desired ROI is 12%? The answer is in the size of the asset base. When interest rates are low, it is relatively inexpensive to borrow money to buy assets. However, when interest rates are high, it becomes more costly to borrow money to buy assets. Hence, when the required ROI is low, larger divisions are favored, but when the desired ROI is high, smaller divisions have an advantage.

Balanced Scorecard

One drawback to the performance measures discussed so far is that they focus solely on financial measures. Over time, managers have become more aware of the fact that there are also many *nonfinancial* measures that influence both performance and other major corporate decisions. Thus, in recent years, many companies have begun evaluating performance using the balanced scorecard.[3] The **balanced scorecard** seeks to provide a "balanced view" of company performance by evaluating a company's subunits based on both financial and nonfinancial measures in each of the following areas:

1. Financial performance
2. Customer satisfaction
3. Internal business processes
4. Learning and growth

Obviously, financial performance remains perhaps the most important area of focus for most managers, because if a business isn't profitable and if it doesn't generate positive cash flows, it won't survive for long. Examples of financial measures include ratios and other financial statement measures. However, the long-term health of a company depends largely on its ability to attract and retain customers. Hence, the second focus area relates to customer satisfaction. Customer-related performance measures include such factors as the number of customer complaints. A well-run company seeks to achieve the highest level of efficiency. In their quest to maximize financial goals and maintain customer satisfaction, companies constantly seek to improve internal operations to achieve highly efficient processes. Evaluation of internal processes can measure factors such as throughput time and the number of quality inspection failures. Finally, effective organizations recognize that their greatest asset doesn't appear on the balance sheet. A company's employees bring perhaps the greatest value in determining the organization's continued success. Attracting and developing the best people is a constant struggle for any organization and is directly associated with an organization's capacity to grow and improve. Thus, the learning and growth aspect of a business can measure factors such as training and employee development efforts.

Exhibit 24-15 illustrates how Fezzari might evaluate itself based on the objectives it has defined in each of the four areas of focus.

Company X has a profit margin of 8% and a return on investment of 10%, with a net profit for the year of $50,000. The required return for the company investments has been set at 8%. The company plans to purchase a new machine worth $100,000 and expects sales and net profit to rise by an additional $150,000 and $15,000, respectively. The new purchase decision will increase profit margin, asset turnover, return on investment, and residual income to what amounts?	**YOUR TURN! 24.5** The solution is on page 1157.
Assume that you are the managing partner of a small CPA firm. You have decided to evaluate the firm's performance using a balanced scorecard. Identify at least one measure that you might use in each of the four areas of the balanced scorecard: financial performance, customer satisfaction, internal business processes, and learning and growth.	**YOUR TURN! 24.6** The solution is on page 1157.

---

[3] The balanced scorecard originated in the 1990s with Robert Kaplan and David Norton at the Harvard Business School ("Using the Balanced Scorecard as a Strategic Management System," *Harvard Business Review*, January–February 1996, p. 76).

TAKEAWAY 24.4	Concept	⟶	Method	⟶	Assessment
	How might an investment center's performance be evaluated?		$\text{Profit margin} = \dfrac{\text{Operating income}}{\text{Sales}}$ $\text{Asset turnover} = \dfrac{\text{Sales}}{\text{Investment in operating assets}}$ $\dfrac{\text{Return on}}{\text{investment}} = \dfrac{\text{Operating income}}{\text{Investment in operating assets}}$ $\dfrac{\text{Residual}}{\text{income}} = \dfrac{\text{Net}}{\text{operating}} - \left(\dfrac{\text{Average}}{\text{operating}} \times \dfrac{\text{Required}}{\text{minimum}}\right)$ income assets return Balanced scorecard (financial performance, customer satisfaction, internal business practices, learning and growth)		• Calculated ratios can be compared to similar ratios determined over time or to ratios for similar companies in the same industry. • Balanced scorecards include nonfinancial measures that impact a company's performance and provide a more balanced view of performance.

Exhibit 24-15	Balanced Scorecard Illustration

FEZZARI PERFORMANCE BICYCLES
Balanced Scorecard
For the Year Ended December 31, 2019

	Objectives	Measures	Targets	Initiatives
Financial	Maximize returns	ROI	14%	
	Profitable growth	Revenue growth	6%	
	Manage operating costs	Operating costs/customer	$1,000	
Customer	Industry-leading customer loyalty	Customer satisfaction survey	90%	Customer loyalty program
Internal Processes	Business growth -Use alliances and joint ventures	% of customers serviced through alliances	10%	
	Customer service excellence -Educate customers	% education plans executed	90%	
	-Effective customer service	Problem resolution cycle time	6 hrs.	Customer service software integration
Learning & Growth	Leading employee satisfaction	Employee satisfaction rating	3 on 5-point scale	Performance compensation link

SERVICE INDUSTRY IN FOCUS

SERVICE AND MERCHANDISING

In addition to evaluating its operations by office as shown earlier, EBC also wishes to evaluate the performance of its two lines of business, Solid Waste and Water/ Wastewater (Water/WW). EBC management has prepared the following line of business income statement:

ENVIRONMENTAL BUSINESS CONSULTANTS, LLC
Line of Business Statement
For the Year Ended December 31, 2019

	Solid Waste	Water/WW	Firm Total
Gross sales.	$3,676,000	$470,000	$ 4,146,000
Less reimbursable costs.	(366,350)	(64,650)	(431,000)
Net sales.	$3,309,650	$405,350	$ 3,715,000
Cost of services	(2,256,787)	(390,713)	(2,647,500)
Gross profit on sales.	$1,052,863	$ 14,637	$ 1,067,500
Operating expenses			(556,500)
Operating income			$ 511,000
Interest revenue			7,500
Income before tax.			$ 518,500

EBC accountants have provided the following analysis of the cost of services, all of which are considered traceable:

Cost of Services

Solid Waste			Water/WW			
Variable	Fixed	Total	Variable	Fixed	Total	Firm Total
$51,600	$2,205,187	$2,256,787	$12,900	$377,813	$390,713	$2,647,500

In addition, EBC has accumulated the following information regarding the operating expenses. Variable costs are shown in red; fixed costs are shown in black.

	A	B	C	D	E	F	G	H	I
1				Operating Expenses Allocation					
2		Solid Waste				Water/WW			
3		Traceable	Common	Total		Traceable	Common	Total	Firm Total
4	**Employee bonuses**	$109,722	$ —	$109,722		$16,278	$ —	$16,278	$126,000
5	**Proposal preparation**	31,400	—	31,400		7,600	—	7,600	39,000
6	Trade shows	—	3,000	3,000		—	1,000	1,000	4,000
7	Advertising	—	4,000	4,000		—	1,000	1,000	5,000
8	Employee CE expenses	24,943	—	24,943		2,057	—	2,057	27,000
9	Other general admin. expenses	—	306,849	306,849		—	48,651	48,651	355,500
10		$166,065	$313,849	$479,914		$25,935	$50,651	$76,586	$556,500

Required

1. Prepare a line of business contribution margin statement for EBC (similar to **Exhibit 24-11**) that extends the line of business operating results through line of business contribution to common expenses.

2. Comment on the operating results for each line of business. What should EBC management do with regard to the Water/WW business based on these results?

Solution

1.

Solution 1	Service Industry in Focus		
ENVIRONMENTAL BUSINESS CONSULTANTS, LLC **Line of Business Statement** **For the Year Ended December 31, 2019**			
	Solid Waste	**Water/WW**	**Firm Total**
Gross sales.	$3,676,000	$470,000	$4,146,000
Less reimbursable costs.	(366,350)	(64,650)	(431,000)
Net sales.	$3,309,650	$405,350	$3,715,000
Traceable variable costs.	(192,722)*	(36,778)*	(229,500)
Contribution margin.	$3,116,928	$368,572	$3,485,500
Traceable fixed costs	(2,230,130)**	(379,870)**	(2,610,000)
Line of business contribution	$ 886,798	$ (11,298)	$ 875,500
Common operating expenses.			(364,500)***
Interest revenue			7,500
Income before tax.			$ 518,500

*Solid Waste: $51,600 + $109,722 + $31,400 = $192,722
 Water/WW: $12,900 + $16,278 + $7,600 = $36,778

**Solid Waste: $2,205,187 + $24,943 = $2,230,130
 Water/WW: $377,813 + $2,057 = $379,870

*** $313,849 + $50,651 = $364,500

2. The Water/WW line of business has a net loss at the line of business contribution level. It is not covering its own traceable operating costs, let alone contributing to the firm's common operating expenses. EBC management has several possible courses of action to consider:

   a. Determine whether revenues can be increased through higher fees for the service provided. An increase of just over 2.4% (11,298/470,000) would eliminate the loss.

   b. Carefully review the classification of expenses as cost of service and traceable operating expenses. Even a minor misclassification of an expense could make a difference in the reported results.

   c. Consider whether some of the Water/WW traceable expenses could be reduced or eliminated. For example, given these results, perhaps Water/WW employees should not be receiving bonuses.

   d. Consider whether the Water/WW line of business should be spun off or eliminated. This is a major decision with significant implications for EBC and its owners and employees. It may be that the Water/WW line of business provides cross-selling opportunities for the Solid Waste line of business that would have a greater impact on income before tax if eliminated.

APPENDIX 24A: Transfer Pricing

DOMESTIC TRANSFER PRICING

LO6 **Determine** the proper transfer price to maximize company profit with and without excess productive capacity.

Management of a large, complex company usually divides the business into a number of segments. A segment is a logical portion of a business, such as a division or department. When a segment is established as a profit center, the segment's manager is responsible for revenue generation as well as cost and expense control. If the profit center receives products or services from another profit center within the same business or provides products or services to another profit center within the same business, the two profit center managers must agree on a transfer price for the product or service. The **transfer price** is the price that the selling profit center will charge the buying profit center for the product or service provided.

Objectives for Transfer Pricing

Two objectives should be met when establishing transfer prices. First, the transfer price of the product or service transferred should allow both the selling and buying divisions to make a reasonable gross profit. Second, the contribution margin of the entire business should be maximized.

Reasonable Gross Profit

Assume that John Deere Waterloo Works has two operating divisions, the Drivetrain Operations division and the Tractor, Cab, and Assembly Operations division. Top management has decided that the Drivetrain Operations division should sell a particular component to the Tractor, Cab, and Assembly Operations division, which will incorporate the component into the 6170R tractor that it manufactures and sells for $150,000 per unit. The per-unit product costs incurred in this process are the following:

	Drivetrain Operations Division	Tractor, Cab, and Assembly Operations Division
Direct material	$6,250	$62,250
Direct labor	1,500	27,750
Variable overhead	1,000	17,000
Fixed overhead	1,250	17,850
Transfer price of component	?	

A negotiated transfer price below market price can be justified. Expenses may be less when intercompany sales are made, or volume may be large enough to justify quantity discounts.

BUSINESS SITUATION 1: Assume that the transfer price is established as $10,000, the total absorption product cost of the component in the Drivetrain Operations division ($6,250 + $1,500 + $1,000 + $1,250 = $10,000). The resulting gross profit per unit for the two divisions would be calculated as follows:

	Drivetrain Operations Division	Tractor, Cab, and Assembly Operations Division
Revenue:		
Transfer price	$10,000	
Sales price		$150,000
Cost:		
Transfer price		$10,000
Direct material	$6,250	62,250
Direct labor	1,500	27,750
Variable overhead	1,000	17,000
Fixed overhead	1,250	17,850
	10,000	$134,850
Gross profit per unit	$ —	$ 15,150

BUSINESS SITUATION 2: Assume that the transfer price is established as $12,000, the price that the Drivetrain Operations division would receive from an outside customer and the cost that the Tractor, Cab, and Assembly Operations division would incur from an outside supplier. The resulting gross profit per unit for the two divisions would be calculated as follows:

	Drivetrain Operations Division	Tractor, Cab, and Assembly Operations Division
Revenue:		
Transfer price	$12,000	
Sales price		$150,000
Cost:		
Transfer price		$12,000
Direct material.	$6,250	62,250
Direct labor	1,500	27,750
Variable overhead.	1,000	17,000
Fixed overhead.	1,250	17,850
	10,000	$136,850
Gross profit per unit	$ 2,000	$ 13,150

In situation 1, the Tractor, Cab, and Assembly Operations division generates a 10.1% gross profit ($15,150/$150,000 = 0.101), and the Drivetrain Operations division generates no gross profit. In situation 2, the Drivetrain Operations division generates a gross profit of $2,000 and the Tractor, Cab, and Assembly division generates a gross profit of $13,150. Situation 1 illustrates a full absorption product cost transfer price, and situation 2 illustrates a market price transfer price. In both situations, total John Deere gross profit per 6170R is $15,150.

Situation 2 meets the first objective—the transfer price of the product or service transferred should allow both the selling and buying divisions to make a reasonable gross profit. In general, a transfer price based on market price, not absorption product cost, will satisfy the objective of reasonable gross profits for both the selling and buying profit centers or divisions.

Maximize Contribution Margin

The second objective—that the contribution margin of the entire business should be maximized—can be met by identifying a proper minimum transfer price and allowing the manager of the buying profit center to decide whether to buy from the selling profit center or from an outside supplier. As shown in **Exhibit 24A-1**, assume the Drivetrain Operations division of John Deere is currently manufacturing and selling only component A to outside customers for $7,500 per unit.

Exhibit 24A-1   Transfer Pricing Decisions

The Tractor, Cab, and Assembly Operations division has proposed that the Drivetrain Operations division begin manufacturing and selling 2,000 units of component B per year to the Tractor, Cab, and Assembly Operations division. The formula for the minimum transfer price for component B is the following:

Product B minimum transfer price	=	Variable cost of product B, per unit	+	Contribution margin lost from not selling product A, per unit of product B

Next we will apply these objectives of transfer pricing to two situations, one in which the supplier does not have any excess capacity and one in which the supplier does have excess capacity.

No Excess Capacity

Assume the Drivetrain Operations division has no excess manufacturing capacity. Therefore, if the Drivetrain Operations division produces component B for the Tractor, Cab, and Assembly Operations division, the Drivetrain Operations division will have to reduce its production and sale of component A to outside customers. Assume that 5,000 fewer units of component A will have to be produced and sold to allow the manufacture of 2,000 units of component B.

The minimum transfer price that the Drivetrain Operations division is willing to accept is one that maintains the contribution margin of the Drivetrain Operations division at its current level. The formula given earlier will generate a transfer price that would allow this to happen. Assume that the variable cost per unit of component A is $5,000, and its selling price is $7,500. The variable cost per unit of component B is $8,750. The total contribution margin that would be given up on 5,000 units of component A is $12,500,000 (5,000 units × [$7,500 − $5,000]). Using the formula, the minimum transfer price for component B is $15,000 ($8,750 + [$12,500,000/2,000 units of B]) (see **Exhibit 24A-2**).

Exhibit 24A-2	Transfer Pricing Decisions, No Excess Capacity

The switch from the production and sale of 5,000 units of component A to 2,000 units of component B would not affect total fixed costs, would create new variable costs of $8,750 per unit, and would eliminate $12,500,000 of contribution margin. The $15,000 transfer price would reimburse the Drivetrain Operations division for the additional variable costs and the lost contribution margin. As a result, the Drivetrain Operations division would generate exactly the same contribution margin whether it produced and sold component A or component B.

Concept ➡	Method ➡	Assessment	TAKEAWAY 24.5
How do transfer prices between domestic divisions of a company affect the company's overall profit?	Division managers negotiate the transfer price to be paid and received for transactions between the two divisions.	Because the transfer price represents a cost to the buying division and a revenue to the selling division in the same amount, total company profits are unaffected by the transfer price.	

With the transfer price set at $15,000, the Tractor, Cab, and Assembly Operations division is in a position to make a decision that will maximize its contribution margin and the contribution margin of the entire business. Assume that the Tractor, Cab, and Assembly Operations division adds $107,000 of variable cost in addition to the costs of the Drivetrain Operations division and then sells the end product for $150,000. If the Tractor, Cab, and Assembly Operations division can only buy component B from an outside supplier for a price greater than $15,000, then it will choose to buy component B from the Drivetrain Operations division. However, if the product division can buy component B from an outside supplier for a price less than $15,000, then it will choose to buy the component from the outside supplier (see **Exhibit 24A-3**). In either case, the contribution margin of the company as a whole has been maximized.

Exhibit 24A-3	Transfer Pricing Decisions, No Excess Capacity

To illustrate, let us assume two situations:
(1) the outside supplier's price is $16,000; and,
(2) the outside supplier's price is $14,000.

BUSINESS SITUATION 1:   **Exhibit 24A-4** shows the calculation of the contribution margin for the first situation. If the Tractor, Cab, and Assembly Operations division purchases component B from the Drivetrain Operations division at a per-unit transfer price of $15,000, the Drivetrain Operations division would earn a contribution margin of $12,500,000 and the Tractor, Cab, and Assembly Operations division would earn a contribution margin of $56,000,000 on the sale of the 6170R to its customers, for a total contribution margin of $68,500,000.

Exhibit 24A-4	Transfer Pricing Decisions, No Excess Capacity

However, **Exhibit 24A-5** shows the calculation of the contribution margin if the Tractor, Cab, and Assembly Operations division purchases component B from outside suppliers at a price of $16,000 per unit. This would allow the Drivetrain Operations division to continue to sell component A to its outside customers at a contribution margin of $12,500,000. The Tractor, Cab, and Assembly Operations division would earn a contribution margin of $54,000,000 on the sale of the 6170R, for a total contribution margin of $66,500,000.

Exhibit 24A-5	Transfer Pricing Decisions, No Excess Capacity

A careful study of **Exhibits 24A-4** and **24A-5** shows that John Deere will earn $2,000,000 more in contribution margin by purchasing component B from the Drivetrain Operations division.

BUSINESS SITUATION 2:   **Exhibit 24A-6** shows the calculation of the contribution margin for the second situation. If the Tractor, Cab, and Assembly Operations division purchases component B from the Drivetrain Operations division at a per-unit transfer price of $15,000, the Drivetrain Operations division would earn a contribution margin of $12,500,000 and the Tractor, Cab, and Assembly Operations division would earn a contribution margin of $56,000,000 on the sale of the 6170R to its customers, for a total contribution margin of $68,500,000. This is exactly the same as the first situation.

Exhibit 24A-6	Transfer Pricing Decisions, No Excess Capacity

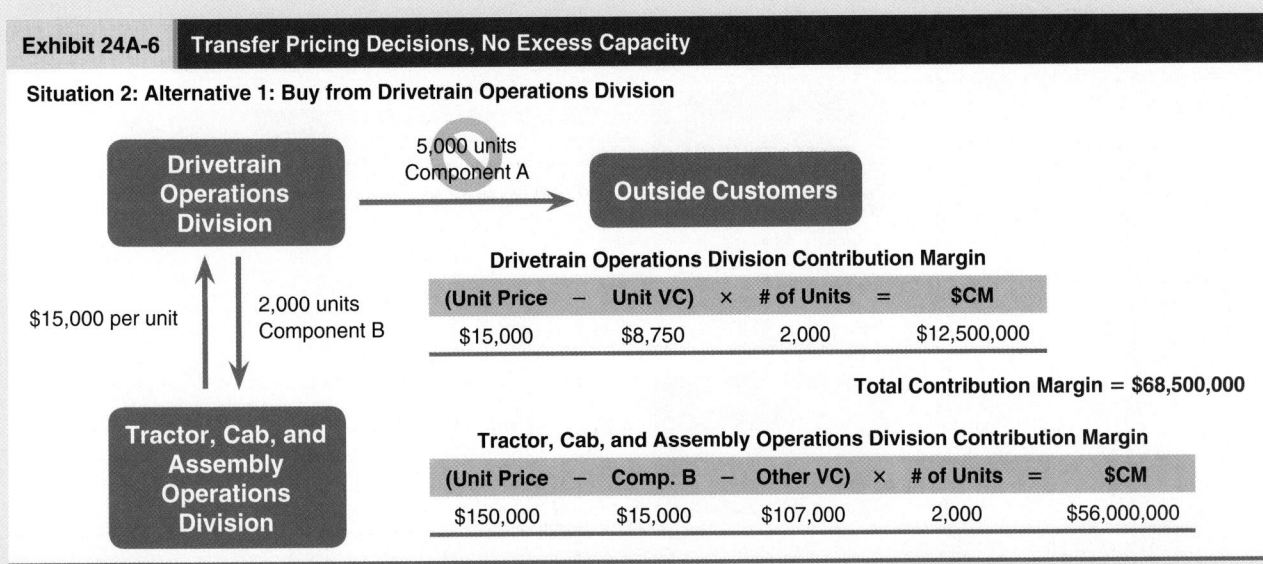

However, **Exhibit 24A-7** shows the calculation of the contribution margin if the Tractor, Cab, and Assembly Operations division purchases component B from outside suppliers at a price of $14,000 per unit. This would allow the Drivetrain Operations division to continue to sell component A to its outside customers at a contribution margin of $12,500,000. The Tractor, Cab, and Assembly Operations division would earn a contribution margin of $58,000,000 on the sale of the 6170R, for a total contribution margin of $70,500,000.

Exhibit 24A-7	Transfer Pricing Decisions, No Excess Capacity

Situation 2: Alternative 2: Buy from Outside Supplier

Drivetrain Operations Division Contribution Margin

(Unit Price	–	Unit VC)	×	# of Units	=	$CM
$7,500		$5,000		5,000		$12,500,000

Total Contribution Margin = $70,500,000

Tractor, Cab, and Assembly Operations Division Contribution Margin

(Unit Price	–	Comp. B	–	Unit VC)	×	# of Units	=	$CM
$150,000		$14,000		$107,000		2,000		$58,000,000

A comparison of **Exhibits 24A-6** and **24A-7** shows that John Deere will earn $2,000,000 more in contribution margin by purchasing component B from the outside supplier.

Excess Capacity

In the John Deere example, we assumed that the Drivetrain Operations division had no excess manufacturing capacity. If we now assume that the Drivetrain Operations division has sufficient capacity to produce and sell the 2,000 units of component B without reducing the production and sale of component A, we will determine a different minimum transfer price. Applying the previous formula for the minimum transfer price, we determine that the minimum transfer price is $8,750 ($8,750 + [$0/2,000]) (see **Exhibit 24A-8**).

Exhibit 24A-8	Transfer Pricing Decisions, Excess Capacity

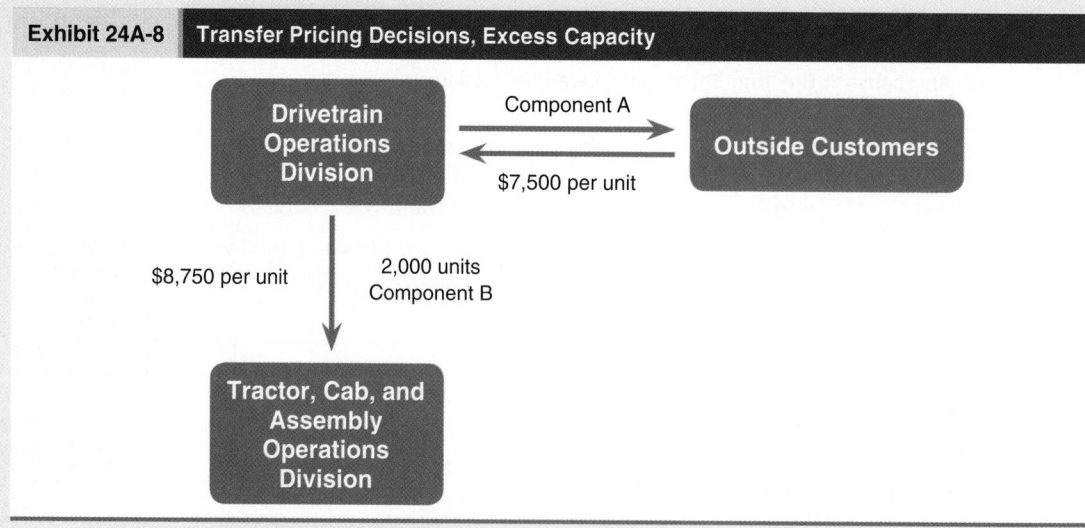

In this case, the production and sale of 2,000 units of component B would not affect total fixed costs, would create new variable costs of $8,750 per unit, and would eliminate no contribution margin from the production and sale of component A. The $8,750 transfer price would reimburse the Drivetrain Operations division for the additional variable costs. As a result, the Drivetrain Operations division would generate exactly the same contribution margin whether or not it produced and sold product B.

Negotiated Transfer Prices

The formula that determines minimum transfer price results in a transfer price that is frequently different from the market value of the product or service being transferred. If the minimum transfer price is greater than the market price, then the buying profit center will buy the product or service from an outside supplier and there will be no need for a transfer price.

If the minimum transfer price is less than the market price, however, then the buying profit center will buy the product or service from the other profit center in the same company. The exact transfer price will be negotiated by the two profit centers. The resulting amount will be greater than or equal to the minimum transfer price and less than or equal to the market price. Any negotiated transfer price within this range will result in the same total contribution margin for the firm. In the John Deere example, with a minimum transfer price of $8,750 and a market price of $15,000, any transfer price from $8,750 to $15,000 results in a contribution margin of $12,500,000 for John Deere.

INTERNATIONAL TRANSFER PRICING

Transfer pricing becomes more complex if one of the segments is in a different country than the other. When products or services are being transferred between segments in different countries, the two objectives stated earlier still apply. However, there also are additional objectives that may conflict with the two previously mentioned. The additional objectives include minimization of international income taxes and tariffs and conformance with international trade agreements. These topics are beyond the scope of this introduction to transfer pricing. Intermediate cost accounting textbooks generally provide a more in-depth coverage of these topics related to international transfer pricing.

YOUR TURN! 24.7

Able Corporation has a manufacturing division that manufactures valves and an assembly division that produces final products. Currently, the manufacturing division has sufficient capacity to manufacture an additional 400 valves. An external market exists for the valves. The market price for one valve is $100 and the cost to sell is $10. The fixed manufacturing cost per valve is $25 and the unit variable cost is $60. The assembly division plans to purchase 400 valves. Management of the assembly division thinks that it should be able to purchase from the manufacturing division at a lower price since both divisions are under common control of the corporation. What is the minimum transfer price between the manufacturing division and the assembly division?

The solution is on page 1157.

COMPREHENSIVE PROBLEM

LT Roofing Company sells roofing products through two departments, composite and steel. Operating information for 2019 is as follows:

	Composite Department	Steel Department
Inventory, January 1, 2019	$ 90,000	$ 39,000
Inventory, December 31, 2019	75,000	45,000
Net sales	1,170,000	720,000
Purchases	726,000	543,000
Purchases returns	42,000	12,000
Purchases discounts	24,000	6,000
Transportation in	27,000	21,000
Traceable department expenses	162,000	84,000

Common operating expenses of the firm were $180,000.

Required

a. Prepare a department income statement showing department contribution to common expenses and net income of the firm. Assume an overall effective income tax rate of 30%. LT uses a periodic inventory system.

b. Calculate the gross profit percentage for each department.

c. If the common expenses were allocated 55% to the composite department and 45% to the steel department, what would the net income be for each department?

Solution

LT ROOFING COMPANY
Department Income Statement
For the Year Ended December 31, 2019

a.

	Composite Department	Steel Department	Total
Net sales.	$1,170,000	$720,000	$1,890,000
Cost of goods sold:			
Inventory, January 1, 2019	90,000	39,000	129,000
Purchases.	726,000	543,000	1,269,000
Less: Purchases returns	(42,000)	(12,000)	(54,000)
Purchases discounts	(24,000)	(6,000)	(30,000)
Transportation in	27,000	21,000	48,000
Cost of goods available for sale	$ 777,000	$585,000	$1,362,000
Inventory, December 31, 2019	75,000	45,000	120,000
Cost of goods sold	$ 702,000	$540,000	$1,242,000
Gross profit.	$ 468,000	$180,000	$ 648,000
Traceable department expenses	162,000	84,000	246,000
Department margin.	$ 306,000	$ 96,000	$ 402,000
Common expenses.			180,000
Income before tax.			$ 222,000
Income tax expense (30% × $222,000).			66,600
Net income			$ 155,400

b. Gross profit percentages:
   Composite dept.: $468,000/$1,170,000 = 40%
   Steel dept.: $180,000/$720,000 = 25%

c.

	Composite	Steel	Total
Department margin.	$ 306,000	$ 96,000	$ 402,000
Common expenses*	99,000	81,000	180,000
Income before tax	$ 207,000	$ 15,000	$ 222,000
Income tax expense (30% × $207,000 and 30% × $15,000)	62,100	4,500	66,600
Net income	$ 144,900	$ 10,500	$ 155,400

* 55% × $180,000 = $99,000
  45% × $180,000 = $81,000

SUMMARY OF LEARNING OBJECTIVES

LO1 **Describe a static budget, illustrate its use, and present an example of a static budget performance report. (p. 1106)**

- A static budget is a financial plan developed for a fixed level of operating activity, typically the expected or most likely level.

- If actual results are compared to a static budget, the variances that result are of little use to management, because the budget is often based on a different level of activity than the actual operations.

Introduce the flexible budget and present an example of a flexible budget performance report. Explain how flexible budgeting helps in variance analysis. (p. 1107) **LO2**

- A flexible budget is a financial plan that makes cost projections for various activity levels within a relevant range.
- A flexible budget usually divides costs and expenses into variable and fixed costs.
- A flexible budget performance report compares actual costs to budgeted costs based on the actual production level achieved.

Present an overview of reporting operations for segments of a business. (p. 1114) **LO3**

- Business segments may consist of organizational units (departments or divisions) or areas of economic activity (product lines or markets).
- A business segment may be an investment center (where management is responsible for the efficient use of capital as well as revenues and expenses), a profit center (where management is responsible for both revenues and expenses), or a cost center (where management is responsible for expenses only).
- Internal reporting of segment operations deals primarily with the measurement of operating performance.
- Accounting and reporting by business segment are indispensable to management and very important to external groups such as investors and creditors.

Construct a segmented contribution margin income statement. Identify the difference between traceable and common fixed costs. (p. 1117) **LO4**

- Total amounts from lower-level reports flow to and are included in higher-level reports.
- A performance report is usually prepared for each accounting period for each profit center and each cost center.
- Expenses incurred by, or for the benefit of, one business segment are called traceable expenses. Expenses incurred for more than one business segment are called common expenses.
- Reporting for segments of a firm is typically extended to contribution to common expenses. Only traceable expenses are deducted.

Compute return on investment, return on sales, return on assets, and residual income for business segments. Discuss the importance of each indicator in assessing a company's performance. (p. 1123) **LO5**

- Return on investment is operating income as a percentage of the asset base used to generate that income. It illustrates the amount of profit generated for every dollar invested in the company's asset base.
- The DuPont formula recognizes that ROI can be further divided into two ratios, return on sales and asset utilization.
- Return on sales is operating income as a percentage of sales revenue. It may be interpreted as the number of pennies left over from each dollar of sales after covering all costs.
- Asset utilization is sales divided by the investment in operating assets. It is a measure of a company's efficiency in utilizing its operating assets. It represents the amount of sales per dollar of operating asset.
- Residual income is the income that is left over after the company or division earns some minimum return on investment.
- The balanced scorecard seeks to provide a "balanced view" of company performance by evaluating a company's subunits based on both financial and nonfinancial measures, including financial performance, customer satisfaction, internal business processes, and learning and growth.

Appendix 24A: Determine the proper transfer price to maximize company profit with and without excess productive capacity. (p. 1130) **LO6**

- The transfer price of the product or service transferred should allow both the selling and buying divisions to make a reasonable gross profit.
- The negotiated transfer price should maximize the contribution margin of the entire business.
- A transfer price based on market price will satisfy the objective of reasonable gross profits for both the selling and buying profit centers or divisions.

SUMMARY	Concept ⟶	Method ⟶	Assessment
TAKEAWAY 24.1	How can management evaluate the company's performance relative to the budget?	• Prepare a flexible budget based on actual output achieved. • Compare the actual results to the flexible budget.	• Actual costs for materials, labor, or variable overhead that are less than the flexible budget amounts result in favorable variances. • Actual costs that are greater than the flexible budget amounts result in unfavorable variances.
TAKEAWAY 24.2	How might firm management measure and evaluate the performance of its responsibility centers?	• Cost center: cost variances, measuring differences between actual and budgeted costs • Profit center: revenue and cost variances, return on sales, and segment contribution margin • Investment center: return on investment and residual income	• Variances help managers identify explanations for differences between actual and expected performance. • Financial ratios are compared to targets and benchmarks to determine whether the firm met its goals and evaluate its performance relative to its competitors.
TAKEAWAY 24.3	How can a firm hold segment managers responsible for revenues and costs?	Prepare periodic performance reports for each segment.	• Cost center managers are responsible for directly traceable variable and fixed costs. • Profit center managers are responsible for directly traceable revenues and variable and fixed costs. • Investment center managers are responsible for invested capital, revenues, and variable and fixed costs.
TAKEAWAY 24.4	How might an investment center's performance be evaluated?	$$\text{Profit margin} = \frac{\text{Operating income}}{\text{Sales}}$$ $$\text{Asset turnover} = \frac{\text{Sales}}{\text{Investment in operating assets}}$$ $$\text{Return on investment} = \frac{\text{Operating income}}{\text{Investment in operating assets}}$$ $$\text{Residual income} = \text{Net operating income} - \left(\text{Average operating assets} \times \text{Required minimum return}\right)$$ Balanced scorecard (financial performance, customer satisfaction, internal business practices, learning and growth)	• Calculated ratios can be compared to similar ratios determined over time or to ratios for similar companies in the same industry. • Balanced scorecards include nonfinancial measures that impact a company's performance and provide a more balanced view of performance.
TAKEAWAY 24.5	How do transfer prices between domestic divisions of a company affect the company's overall profit?	Division managers negotiate the transfer price to be paid and received for transactions between the two divisions.	Because the transfer price represents a cost to the buying division and a revenue to the selling division in the same amount, total company profits are unaffected by the transfer price.

KEY TERMS

Asset turnover (p. 1125)

Balanced scorecard (p. 1127)

Common expenses (p. 1119)

Cost center (p. 1115)

DuPont formula (p. 1124)

Flexible budget (p. 1107)

Investment center (p. 1115)

Performance reports (p. 1117)

Profit center (p. 1115)

Profit margin (p. 1125)

Residual income (p. 1126)

Responsibility centers (p. 1115)

Return on investment (p. 1124)

Static budget (p. 1106)

Traceable expenses (p. 1119)

Transfer price (p. 1131)

Variance (p. 1107)

Assignments with the ⓂⒷⒸ logo in the margin are available in 𝑚𝑦 BusinessCourse.
See the Preface of the book for details.

SELF-STUDY QUESTIONS

(Answers to Self-Study Questions are at the end of this chapter.)

1. **Mabel's Mobile Pet Grooming Service specializes in providing outrageous dog grooming services, turning the average household pet into a lion, tiger, dinosaur, or other non-canine-looking animal. The average grooming session takes several hours and is done in the back of a specially outfitted van at the client's home. Mabel budgeted $200 per grooming session for the coming year. Additional information for the company includes**

LO1

	Budgeted
Sessions...............................	250
Variable costs..........................	$31,250
Fixed costs............................	$20,000

Mabel's static budget income for the year is
   a.   a profit of $18,750.
   b.   a profit of $1,250.
   c.   a loss of $1,250.
   d.   a loss $32,500.

2. **The following static budget performance report was prepared for Chip Manufacturing for July:**

LO2

	Actual Results	Static Budget	Variance
Sales units	100,000	90,000	10,000 F
Sales dollars...........................	$190,000	$180,000	$10,000 F
Variable costs.........................	125,000	108,000	17,000 U
Fixed costs............................	50,000	45,000	5,000 U
Operating income.......................	$ 15,000	$ 27,000	[$12,000 U]

What is Chip's total flexible budget variance for operating income?
   a. $10,000 favorable
   b. $10,000 unfavorable
   c. $12,000 unfavorable
   d. $20,000 unfavorable

3. **The manager of which of the following segments of a business is responsible for revenue generation as well as for cost and expense control?**

LO3

   a.   Cost center
   b.   Accounting department
   c.   Profit center
   d.   Assembly line

LO4 4. Which of the following is not considered in determining contribution to common expenses?

    a. Income taxes   *c.* Traceable expenses

    b. Cost of goods sold   *d.* Net sales

LO4 5. In performance reporting (budgeted cost compared to actual cost), which performance report must be prepared first?

    a. Division, consisting of five departments

    b. Region, consisting of three divisions

    c. Department, consisting of four cost centers

    d. Company, consisting of two regions

LO5 6. Which of the following is the correct formula for return on sales?

    a. Income/Investment

    b. Investment/Income

    c. Income/Revenue

    d. Revenue/Investment

LO5 7. During the past twelve months, the Aaron Corporation had a net income of $50,000. What is the amount of the investment if the return on investment is 20%?

    a. $100,000

    b. $200,000

    c. $250,000

    d. $500,000

LO6

(Appendix 24A)

8. Morrison's Plastics Division, a profit center, sells its products to external customers as well as to other internal profit centers. Which one of the following circumstances would justify the Plastics Division selling a product internally to another profit center at a price that is below the market-based transfer price?

    a. The buying unit has excess capacity.

    b. The selling unit is operating at full capacity.

    c. Routine sales commissions and collection costs would be avoided.

    d. The profit centers' managers are evaluated on the basis of unit operating income.

QUESTIONS

LO1, 2 1. Explain the difference between a static budget and a flexible budget.

LO1, 2 2. Explain what is meant by a static budget variance and a flexible budget variance.

LO2 3. "The higher the management level receiving reports, the more detailed the reports should be." Comment.

LO3 4. Give examples of segments of business firms segmented by (a) organizational unit and (b) economic activity.

LO3 5. Distinguish between a profit center and a cost center.

LO4 6. Distinguish between traceable expenses and common expenses. Which are more likely to be controllable at the department level?

LO4 7. Suggest an allocation basis for each of the following traceable expenses of a departmentalized firm that uses a net income measure to determine the profitability of departments:

    a. Janitorial expense

    b. Plant manager's salary

    c. Utilities (heat, light, and air conditioning)

    d. Property taxes

LO4 8. What is meant by departmental contribution to common expenses? What advantages does this measure have over net income in measuring departmental performance?

LO4 9. Department B of the local Top Value Store shows a contribution to common expenses of $22,000 and a net loss of $9,000 (before taxes). The firm believes that discontinuing department B will not affect sales, gross profit, or traceable expenses of other departments. If total common expenses remain unchanged, what effect will discontinuing department B have on the income before taxes of the Top Value Store?

LO4 10. Department 2 of Kapp Company has a gross profit of $100,000, representing 40% of net departmental sales. Traceable departmental expenses are $75,000. Management believes that an increase of $6,500 in advertising, coupled with a 5% average increase in sales prices, will permit the physical volume of products sold to remain the same next period but will improve the department's contribution to common expenses. If management's expectations are correct, what will be the effect on this contribution?

11. Department A of Racine Company has a gross profit of $140,000, representing 35% of net departmental sales. Management believes that an increase of $36,000 in advertising will increase volume of product sold by 20%. Other traceable departmental expenses are $64,000. What effect will this decision have on department A's contribution to common expenses? **LO4**

12. If a firm wishes to compare the performance of two divisions, why might divisional operating income be a poor basis for comparison? **LO5**

13. What is the primary purpose of the balanced scorecard? **LO5**

14. What are the four key performance measures in the balanced scorecard? **LO5**

15. What is the maximum amount that one division should pay to another division of the same company for a component needed in manufacturing its product? **LO6**
(Appendix 24A)

SHORT EXERCISES

SE24-1. Rainbow Inc. recently appointed Margaret Joyce as vice president of finance and asked her to design a new budgeting system. Joyce has changed to a monthly budgeting system by dividing the company's annual budget by twelve. Joyce then prepared monthly budgets for each department and asked the managers to submit monthly reports comparing actual to budget. A sample monthly report for Department A is shown below. **LO1**

RAINBOW INC. Monthly Report for Department A			
	Actual	**Budget**	**Variance**
Units	1,000	900	100F
Variable production costs			
Direct material.	$ 2,800	$ 2,700	$ 100U
Direct labor	4,800	4,500	300U
Variable factory overhead.	4,250	4,050	200U
Fixed costs			
Depreciation	3,000	2,700	300U
Taxes	1,000	900	100U
Insurance	1,500	1,350	150U
Administration.	1,100	990	110U
Marketing	1,000	900	100U
Total costs.	$19,450	$18,090	$1,360U

This monthly budget has been imposed from the top and will create behavior problems. All of the following are causes of such problems **except**

a.   the use of a flexible budget rather than a fixed budget.
b.   top management authoritarian attitude toward the budget process.
c.   the inclusion of non-controllable costs such as depreciation.
d.   the lack of consideration for factors such as seasonality.

SE24-2. When compared to static budgets, flexible budgets **LO2**

a.   offer managers a more realistic comparison of budget and actual fixed cost items under their control.
b.   provide a better understanding of the capacity variances during the period being evaluated.
c.   encourage managers to use less fixed cost items and more variable cost items that are under their control.
d.   offer managers a more realistic comparison of budget and actual revenue and cost items under their control.

LO2 **SE24-3.** Arkin Co.'s controller has prepared a flexible budget for the year just ended, adjusting the original static budget for the unexpected large increase in the volume of sales. Arkin's costs are mostly variable. The controller is pleased to note that both actual revenues and actual costs approximated amounts shown on the flexible budget. If actual revenues and actual costs are compared with amounts shown on the original (static) budget, what variances would arise?

a. Both revenue variances and cost variances would be favorable.
b. Revenue variances would be favorable and cost variances would be unfavorable.
c. Revenue variances would be unfavorable and cost variances would be favorable.
d. Both revenue variances and cost variances would be unfavorable.

LO2 **SE24-4.** Of the following pairs of variances found in a flexible budget report, which pair is **most likely** to be related?

a. Material price variance and variable overhead efficiency variance
b. Labor rate variance and variable overhead efficiency variance.
c. Material usage variance and labor efficiency variance.
d. Labor efficiency variance and fixed overhead volume variance.

LO3 **SE24-5.** Sara Bellows, manager of the telecommunication sales team, has the following department budget.

Billings—long distance	$350,000
Billings—phone card	75,000
Billings—toll free	265,000

Her responsibility center is **best** described as a

a. cost center.
b. revenue center.
c. profit center.
d. investment center.

LO5 **SE24-6.** A company's year-end selected financial data is shown below.

	Year 2	Year 1
Current assets	$250,000	$175,000
Total assets	600,000	500,000
Total liabilities	300,000	225,000
Net sales	200,000	150,000
Net income	75,000	60,000

The company's rate of return on average assets and rate of return on average equity for Year 2 are:

a. 12% and 22%, respectively.
b. 13% and 25%, respectively.
c. 14% and 26%, respectively.
d. 36% and 25%, respectively.

LO5 **SE24-7.** Snug-fit, a maker of bowling gloves, is investigating the possibility of liberalizing its credit policy. Currently, payment is made on a cash-on-delivery basis. Under a new program, sales would increase by $80,000. The company has a gross profit margin of 40%. The estimated bad debt loss rate on the incremental sales would be 6%. Ignoring the cost of money, what would be the return on sales before taxes for the new sales?

a. 34.0%.
b. 36.2%.
c. 40.0%.
d. 42.5%.

LO5 **SE24-8.** A company had $5 million in sales, $3 million in cost of goods sold, and $1 million in selling and administrative expenses during the last fiscal year. If the company's income tax rate was 25%, what was the company's gross profit margin percentage?

a. 20%.   c. 40%.
b. 30%.   d. 50%.

SE24-9. The assets of Moreland Corporation are presented below.

LO5

	January 1	December 31
Cash..	$ 48,000	$ 62,000
Marketable securities	42,000	35,000
Accounts receivable	68,000	47,000
Inventory......................................	125,000	138,000
Plant & equipment (net of accumulated depreciation) ...	325,000	424,000

For the year just ended, Moreland had net income of $96,000 on $900,000 of sales. Moreland's total asset turnover ratio is: (Hint: Use average total assets.)

a. 1.27.
b. 1.37.
c. 1.48.
d. 1.50.

SE24-10. The Robo Division, a decentralized division of GMT Industries, has been approached to submit a bid for a potential project for the RSP Company. Robo Division has been informed by RSP that they will not consider bids over $8,000,000. Robo Division purchases its materials from the Cross Division of GMT Industries. There would be no additional fixed costs for either the Robo or Cross Divisions. Information regarding this project is as follows.

LO6
(Appendix 24A)

	Cross Division	Robo Division
Variable Costs	$1,500,000	$4,800,000
Transfer Price......................................	3,700,000	—

If Robo Division submits a bid for $8,000,000, the amount of contribution margin recognized by the Robo Division and GMT Industries, respectively, is:

a. $(500,000) and $(2,000,000).
b. $3,200,000 and $(500,000).
c. $(500,000) and $1,700,000.
d. $3,200,000 and $1,700.000.

EXERCISES—SET A

E24-1A. **Static and Flexible Budgets** Graham Corporation used the following data to evaluate its current operating system. The company sells items for $10 each and used a budgeted selling price of $10 per unit.

LO1, 2

	Actual	Budgeted
Units sold	400,000 units	430,000 units
Variable costs......................................	$1,250,000	$1,500,000
Fixed costs..	$1,500,000	$1,290,000

a. Prepare the actual income statement, flexible budget, and static budget.
b. What is the static-budget variance of revenues?
c. What is the flexible budget variance for variable costs?
d. What is the flexible budget variance for fixed costs?

E24-2A. **Using Flexible Budgets** The following summary data are from a performance report for Sterling Company for May, during which 9,600 units were produced. The budget reflects the company's normal capacity of 10,000 units.

LO2

	Actual Costs (9,600 Units)	Budget (10,000 Units)	Variances
Direct material	$136,800	$140,000	[$3,200 F]
Direct labor	277,200	280,000	[2,800 F]
Variable overhead	98,400	96,000	2,400 U
Fixed overhead	72,400	72,000	400 U
Total	$584,800	$588,000	[$3,200 F]

a. What is the general implication of the performance report? Why might Sterling question the significance of the report?

b. Revise the performance report using flexible budgeting, and comment on the general implication of the revised report.

LO4 **E24-3A. Assigning Traceable Fixed Expenses** Selected data for Miller Company, which operates three departments, follow:

	Department A	Department B	Department C
Inventory	$ 80,000	$288,000	$112,000
Equipment (average cost)	$720,000	$432,000	$288,000
Payroll	$405,000	$360,000	$135,000
Square feet of floor space	18,000	9,000	3,000

During the year, the company's fixed expenses included the following:

Depreciation on equipment	$140,000
Real estate taxes	48,000
Personal property taxes (on inventory and equipment)	28,800
Personnel department expenses	225,000

Assume that the property tax rate is the same for both inventory and equipment. Using the most causally related bases, prepare a schedule assigning the fixed expenses to the three departments. *Hint:* Not all fixed expenses are traceable to the three departments. One of these fixed costs should be considered a common cost and not traceable to the departments.

LO5 **E24-4A. Return on Investment and Residual Income** Johnson Company has two sources of funds: long-term debt and equity capital. Johnson Company has profit centers in the following locations with the following net incomes and total assets:

	Net Income	Assets
Las Vegas	$ 960,000	$ 4,000,000
Dallas	$1,200,000	$ 9,600,000
Tampa	$2,280,000	$12,000,000

a. Calculate ROI for each profit center and rank them from highest to lowest based on ROI.
b. Calculate residual income for each profit center based on a desired ROI of 12% and rank them from highest to lowest based on residual income.

EXERCISES—SET B

LO2 **E24-1B. Using Flexible Budgets** The following summary data are from a performance report for Hyland Company for June, during which 9,600 units were produced. The budget reflects the company's normal capacity of 10,000 units.

	Actual Costs (9,600 Units)	Budget (10,000 Units)	Variances
Direct material	$102,600	$105,000	[$2,400 F]
Direct labor	207,900	210,000	[2,100 F]
Variable overhead	73,800	72,000	1,800 U
Fixed overhead	54,300	54,000	300 U
Total	$438,600	$441,000	[$2,400 F]

a.   What is the general implication of the performance report? Why might Hyland question the significance of the report?

b.   Revise the performance report using flexible budgeting and comment on the general implication of the revised report.

E24-2B.   **Assigning Traceable Fixed Expenses**   Selected data for Colony Company, which operates three departments, follow:

LO4

	Department A	Department B	Department C
Inventory	$ 40,000	$144,000	$ 56,000
Equipment (average cost)	$360,000	$216,000	$144,000
Payroll	$607,500	$540,000	$202,500
Square feet of floor space	27,000	13,500	4,500

During the year, the company's fixed expenses included the following:

Depreciation on equipment	$ 90,000
Real estate taxes	112,500
Personal property taxes (on inventory and equipment)	14,400
Personnel department expenses	337,500

Assume that the property tax rate is the same for both inventory and equipment. Using the most causally related bases, prepare a schedule assigning the fixed expenses to the three departments. *Hint:* Not all fixed expenses are traceable to the three departments. One of these fixed costs should be considered a common cost and not traceable to the departments.

E24-3B.   **Return on Investment and Residual Income**   The Emergency Medical Services Company has two divisions that operate independently of one another. The financial data for the year 20X5 reported the following results:

LO5

SERVICE AND MERCHANDISING

	North	South
Sales	$3,000,000	$2,500,000
Operating income	750,000	550,000
Taxable income	650,000	375,000
Investment	5,000,000	4,400,000

The company's desired rate of return is 15%. Income is defined as operating income.

a.   What are the respective return-on-investment ratios for the North and South divisions?

b.   What are the respective residual incomes for the North and South divisions?

c.   Which division has the better return on investment and which division has the better residual income figure?

E24-4B.   **Evaluating Investment Centers**   Terry Enterprises, Inc. has two divisions—the Foods division and the Clothes division. Historically, Terry has used the division's ROI as the performance measure for the bonus determinations. Terry Foods division has gross total assets of $1,000,000, accumulated depreciation of $350,000, current liabilities of $250,000, and sales of $2,000,000. Foods' operating income is $200,000. Terry Clothes division has gross total assets of $5,000,000, accumulated depreciation of $2,100,000, current liabilities of $1,500,000, and sales of $8,000,000. Clothes' operating income is $750,000.

LO5

Required

Use the DuPont formula to compute ROI for each division and for Terry Enterprises as a whole. Use operating income and gross total assets as the measures of income and investment. *Hint:* Calculate each of the ROIs for Terry Enterprises to three decimal places.

PROBLEMS—SET A

LO2 **P24-1A.** **Flexible Budget Application** The polishing department of Taylor Manufacturing Company operated during April 2019 with the following manufacturing overhead cost budget based on 4,000 hours of monthly productive capacity:

TAYLOR MANUFACTURING COMPANY Polishing Department Overhead Budget (4,000 Hours) for the Month of April 2019		
Variable costs:		
Factory supplies	$100,000	
Indirect labor	152,000	
Utilities (usage charge)	68,000	
Patent royalties on secret process	296,000	
Total variable overhead		$ 616,000
Fixed costs:		
Supervisory salaries	$160,000	
Depreciation on factory equipment	144,000	
Factory taxes	48,000	
Factory insurance	32,000	
Utilities (base charge)	80,000	
Total fixed overhead		$ 464,000
Total manufacturing overhead		$1,080,000

The polishing department was operated for 4,600 hours during April and incurred the following manufacturing overhead costs:

Factory supplies	$ 97,520
Indirect labor	136,160
Utilities (usage factor)	82,800
Utilities (base factor)	96,000
Patent royalties	280,416
Supervisory salaries	168,000
Depreciation on factory equipment	144,000
Factory taxes	56,000
Factory insurance	32,000
Total manufacturing overhead incurred	$1,092,896

Required

Using a flexible budgeting approach, prepare a performance report for the polishing department for April 2019, comparing actual overhead costs with budgeted overhead costs for 4,600 hours. Separate overhead costs into variable and fixed components and show the amounts of any variances between actual and budgeted amounts.

LO4 **P24-2A.** **Departmental Income Statement** Elgin Flooring Company sells floor coverings through two departments, carpeting and hard covering (tile and linoleum). Operating information for 2019 appears below.

	Carpeting Department	Hard Covering Department
Inventory, January 1, 2019	$ 60,000	$ 26,000
Inventory, December 31, 2019	50,000	30,000
Net sales	500,000	800,000
Purchases	300,000	560,000
Purchases returns	28,000	8,000
Purchases discounts	16,000	4,000
Transportation in	18,000	14,000
Traceable departmental expenses	108,000	56,000

Common operating expenses of the firm were $225,000.

Required

a. Prepare a departmental income statement showing departmental contribution to common expenses and net income of the firm. Assume an overall effective income tax rate of 20%. Elgin uses a periodic inventory system.

b. Calculate the gross profit percentage for each department.

c. If the common expenses were allocated 40% to the carpeting department and 60% to the hard covering department, what would the net income be for each department?

P24-3A. Departmental Income Statement The following information was obtained from the ledger of Woodfield Candies, Inc., at the end of 2019:   **LO4**

WOODFIELD CANDIES, INC, Trial Balance December 31, 2019		
	Debit	Credit
Cash	$ 42,000	
Accounts receivable (net)	156,000	
Inventory, December 31, 2019	180,000	
Equipment and fixtures (net)	540,000	
Accounts payable		$ 108,000
Common stock		450,000
Retained earnings		180,000
Revenue—department X		840,000
Revenue—department Y		360,000
Cost of goods sold—department X	420,000	
Cost of goods sold—department Y	216,000	
Sales salaries expense	192,000	
Advertising expense	42,000	
Insurance expense	24,000	
Uncollectible accounts expense	9,000	
Occupancy expense	36,000	
Office and other administrative expense	81,000	
	$1,938,000	$1,938,000

Woodfield analyzes its operating expenses at the end of each period in order to prepare an income statement that will exhibit departmental contribution to common expenses. From payroll records, advertising copy, and other records, the following tabulation was obtained:

	Traceable Expense		Common Expense
	Dept. X	Dept. Y	
Sales salaries expense.	$147,000	$45,000	
Advertising expense	18,000	6,000	$18,000
Insurance expense	15,000	9,000	
Uncollectible accounts expense	6,000	3,000	
Occupancy expense.			36,000
Office and other administrative expense	12,000	9,000	60,000

Required

Prepare a departmental income statement for Woodfield Candies, Inc., showing departmental contribution to common expenses, assuming an overall income tax rate of 35%.

LO4

SERVICE AND MERCHANDISING

P24-4A. **Departmental Contribution to Common Expenses** Certain operating information is shown below for Palmer Department Store:

	Department A	Department B	All Other Departments
Sales.	$600,000	$900,000	$2,100,000
Traceable expenses	105,000	165,000	600,000
Common expenses.	90,000	120,000	300,000
Gross profit percentage	30%	40%	50%

The managers are disappointed with the operating results of department A. They do not believe that competition will permit raising prices; however, they believe that spending $21,000 more for promoting this department's products will increase the physical volume of products sold by 20%.

An alternative is to discontinue department A and use the space to expand department B. It is believed that department B's physical volume of products sold can thus be increased 37.5%. Special sales personnel are needed, however, and department B's traceable expenses would increase by $90,000. Neither alternative would appreciably affect the total common departmental expense.

Required

a. Calculate the contribution now being made to common expenses by department A, by department B, and by the combination of other departments.
b. Which of the two alternatives should management choose: increase promotional outlays for department A or discontinue department A and expand department B? Support your answer with calculations.

LO5 **P24-5A.** **Return on Investment and Residual Income** For many years, Miner Industries has manufactured prefabricated garden sheds where the sheds are constructed in sections to be assembled on customers' property. The company expanded into the pre-fabricated shed market in 20X1 when it acquired V-Shed Company. V-Shed pre-cuts various types of lumber into the appropriate lengths, packages them, and ships the product to customers' for assembly. Miner decided to maintain V-Shed's separate identity and, thus, established the V-Shed Division as an investment center of Miner.

Miner uses return on *average* investment (ROI) as a performance measure, with the investment defined as "operating assets employed." All investments in operating assets are expected to earn a minimum return of 12% before income taxes. V-Shed's ROI has ranged from 15% to 18% since it was acquired in 20X1.

V-Shed's operating statement for the year just ended is presented below. The division's "operating assets employed" were $5,250,000 at the end of the year, a 5% increase over the balance at the end of the previous year.

V-Shed Division Operating Statement For the Year Ended December 31 ($000 omitted)		
Sales revenue.		$10,000
Cost of goods sold		6,500
Gross profit		$ 3,500
Operating expenses		
Administrative	$1,200	
Selling	1,500	2,700
Income from operations before income taxes		$ 800

Required

Calculate the following performance measures for the year just ended for the V-Shed Division of Miner Industries:

a.   Return on *average* investment in operating assets employed (ROI).

b.   Residual income calculated on the basis of *average* operating assets employed.

P24-6A.   **Return on Investment and Residual Income**   Skyview Company has two divisions, Residential Skylights and Automotive Sunroofs. The manager of the Residential Skylights Division is evaluated based on return on investment (ROI). The manager of the Automotive Sunroofs Division is evaluated based on residual income. The required return is 12% and the return on investment has been 16% for the two divisions. Each manager is currently considering a project with the following projections (in $000s):   **LO5**

	Residential Skylights	Automotive Sunroofs
Projected operating income	$350	$560
Investment in operating assets	$2,500	$4,000

Required

a.   What is the Residential Skylights' ROI?

b.   What is Automotive Sunroofs' residual income?

c.   According to the current evaluation system for managers, which manager(s) would have incentive to undertake the project?

P24-7A.   **Transfer Price**   Sell Division makes part JS13 with the following characteristics: **LO6**
(Appendix 24A)

Production capacity	15,000 units
Selling price of JS13 to outside customers	$40 per unit
Variable cost per unit	$21
Fixed cost per unit	$5
Total fixed costs	$75,000

Buy Division, another division of the same company, wants to purchase 5,000 units of part OC53 each period from Sell Division. Parts JS13 and OC53 have the same variable cost per unit for Sell Division. Producing Part OC53 will not change Sell Division's total fixed costs. Buy Division is now purchasing Part OC53 from an outside supplier at a price of $29 each. Hence, Buy Division won't pay more than $29 to Sell Division for the same product.

Suppose that Sell Division has ample idle capacity to handle all of Buy Division's needs for Part OC53 without any increase in fixed costs and without cutting into current sales to outside customers for Part JS13.

Required

If Sell Division refuses to accept the $29 price to produce and sell Part OC53 to Buy Division, what will be the impact on the company as a whole?

PROBLEMS—SET B

LO2 **P24-1B.** **Flexible Budget Application** The cutting department of Liberty Manufacturing Company operated during September 2019 with the following manufacturing overhead cost budget based on 5,000 hours of monthly productive capacity:

LIBERTY MANUFACTURING COMPANY Cutting Department Overhead Budget (5,000 Hours) for the Month of September 2019		
Variable costs:		
Factory supplies	$ 48,000	
Indirect labor...	72,000	
Utilities (usage charge)....................................	36,000	
Patent royalties on secret process	144,000	
Total variable overhead................................		$300,000
Fixed costs:		
Supervisory salaries	$ 96,000	
Depreciation on factory equipment........................	140,000	
Factory taxes	40,000	
Factory insurance..	24,000	
Utilities (base charge)....................................	32,000	
Total fixed overhead		$332,000
Total manufacturing overhead		$632,000

The cutting department was operated for 4,500 hours during September and incurred the following manufacturing overhead costs:

Factory supplies	$ 40,400
Indirect labor...	67,200
Utilities (usage factor)...	38,100
Utilities (base factor)..	32,000
Patent royalties...	134,000
Supervisory salaries...	96,000
Depreciation on factory equipment...	140,000
Factory taxes	43,400
Factory insurance...	27,000
Total manufacturing overhead incurred	$618,100

Required

Using a flexible budgeting approach, prepare a performance report for the cutting department for September 2019, comparing actual overhead costs with budgeted overhead costs for 4,500 hours. Separate overhead costs into variable and fixed components and show the amounts of any variances between actual and budgeted amounts.

LO4 **P24-2B.** **Departmental Income Statement** Perkins Appliance & Furniture Company has two departments, appliances and furniture. Operating information for 2019 appears below.

	Appliance Department	Furniture Department
Inventory, January 1, 2019......................................	$ 120,000	$ 90,000
Inventory, December 31, 2019	75,000	50,000
Net sales..	1,120,000	760,000
Purchases...	600,000	500,000
Purchases discounts	8,000	6,000
Transportation in..	18,000	16,000
Traceable departmental expenses...............................	199,600	82,000

Common operating expenses of the firm were $180,000.

Required

a.   Prepare a departmental income statement showing departmental contribution to common expenses and net income of the firm. Assume an overall effective income tax rate of 25%. Perkins uses a periodic inventory system.

b.   Calculate the gross profit percentage for each department.

c.   If the common expenses were allocated 60% to the appliance department and 40% to the furniture department, what would the net income be for each department?

P24-3B.   Departmental Income Statement The following information was obtained from the ledger of   **LO4** Stillwell Emporium, Inc., at the end of 2019:

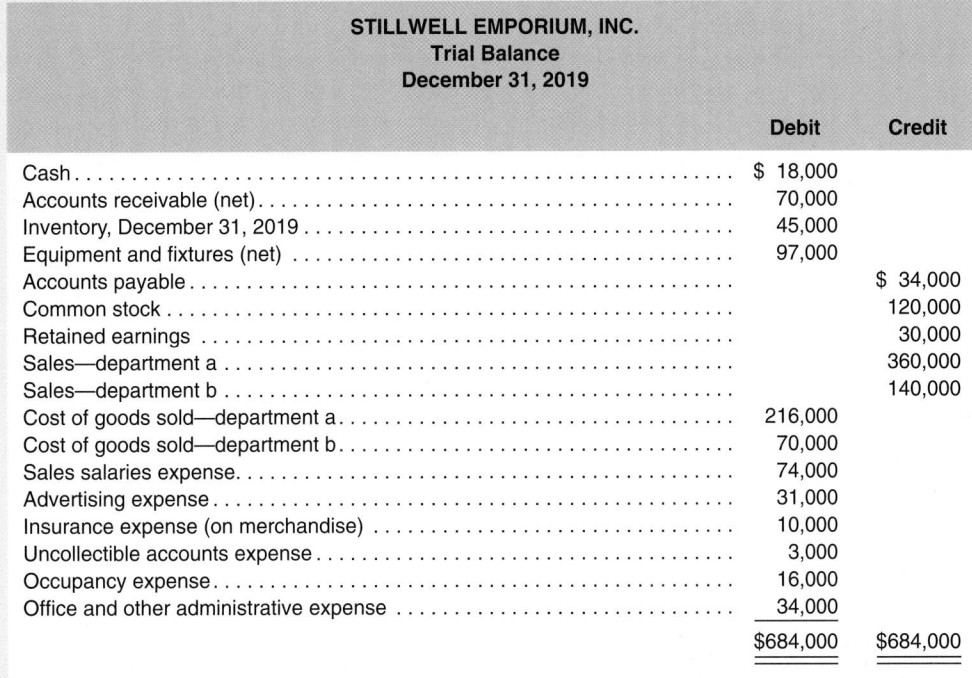

STILLWELL EMPORIUM, INC.
Trial Balance
December 31, 2019

	Debit	Credit
Cash.	$ 18,000	
Accounts receivable (net).	70,000	
Inventory, December 31, 2019.	45,000	
Equipment and fixtures (net)	97,000	
Accounts payable.		$ 34,000
Common stock.		120,000
Retained earnings		30,000
Sales—department a.		360,000
Sales—department b.		140,000
Cost of goods sold—department a.	216,000	
Cost of goods sold—department b.	70,000	
Sales salaries expense.	74,000	
Advertising expense.	31,000	
Insurance expense (on merchandise)	10,000	
Uncollectible accounts expense.	3,000	
Occupancy expense.	16,000	
Office and other administrative expense	34,000	
	$684,000	$684,000

Stillwell analyzes its operating expenses at the end of each period in order to prepare an income statement that will exhibit departmental contribution to common expenses. From payroll records, advertising copy, and other records, the following tabulation was obtained:

	Traceable Expense		Common
	Dept. A	Dept. B	Expense
Sales salaries expense.	$48,000	$20,000	$ 6,000
Advertising expense.	15,000	6,000	10,000
Insurance expense.	8,000	2,000	
Occupancy expense.			16,000
Uncollectible accounts expense.	2,000	1,000	
Office and other administrative expense	17,000	9,000	8,000

Required

Prepare a departmental income statement for Stillwell Emporium, Inc., showing departmental contribution to common expenses, assuming an overall income tax rate of 30%.

P24-4B.   Departmental Contribution to Common Expenses Certain operating information is shown below   **LO4** for Harris Department Store:

	Department R	Department S	All Other Departments
Sales	$320,000	$480,000	$1,120,000
Traceable expenses	56,000	88,000	320,000
Common expenses	48,000	64,000	160,000
Gross profit percentage	30%	40%	50%

The managers are disappointed with the operating results of department R. They do not believe that competition will permit raising prices; however, they believe that spending $10,000 more for promoting this department's products will increase the physical volume of products sold by 20%.

An alternative is to discontinue department R and use the space to expand department S. It is believed that department S's physical volume of products sold can thus be increased 35%. Special sales personnel are needed, however, and department S's traceable expenses would increase by $48,000. Neither alternative would appreciably affect the total common departmental expense.

Required

a. Calculate the contribution now being made to common expenses by department R, by department S, and by the combination of other departments.

b. Which of the two alternatives should management choose: increase promotional outlays for department R, or discontinue department R and expand department S? Support your answer with calculations.

LO5 P24-5B. Return on Investment and Residual Income Simonsen Structural Engineers provides engineering consulting services to clients engaged in major commercial construction projects. The company expanded into the wastewater treatment market in 20X1 when it acquired Scott Industries. Scott Industries fabricates equipment used in wastewater treatment plants. Simonsen decided to maintain Scott's separate identity and, thus, established the Scott Division as an investment center of Simonsen.

Simonsen uses return on *average* investment (ROI) as a performance measure, with the investment defined as "operating assets employed." All investments in operating assets are expected to earn a minimum return of 18% before income taxes. Scott's ROI has ranged from 18% to 21% since it was acquired in 20X1.

Scott's operating statement for the year just ended is presented below. The division's "operating assets employed" were $21,000,000 at the end of the year, a 5% increase over the balance at the end of the previous year.

Scott Division Operating Statement
For the Year Ended December 31
($000 omitted)

Sales revenue		$25,000
Cost of goods sold		14,000
Gross profit		$11,000
Operating expenses		
Administrative	$4,000	
Selling	3,000	7,000
Income from operations before income taxes		$ 4,000

Required

Calculate the following performance measures for the year just ended for the Scott Division of Simonsen Structural Engineers: (Service and Merchandising;

a. Return on *average* investment in operating assets employed (ROI).

b. Residual income calculated on the basis of *average* operating assets employed.

LO5 P24-6B. Return on Investment and Residual Income A company has an 10% required rate of return. It is evaluating the following four mutually exclusive projects as possible investments.

	Estimated Operating Income	Assets
Project A.	$1,750,000	$ 7,000,000
Project B.	1,900,000	9,500,000
Project C.	2,275,000	6,500,000
Project D.	825,000	11,000,000

Required

a. Calculate each project's ROI.

b. Calculate each project's residual income.

c. Using the residual income method, which one of the four projects should the company accept?

P24-7B. Transfer Price Sell Division makes part JS13 with the following characteristics:

LO6
(Appendix 24A)

Production capacity	15,000 units
Selling price of JS13 to outside customers.	$40 per unit
Variable cost per unit	$21
Fixed cost per unit	$5
Total fixed costs	$75,000

Buy Division, another division of the same company, wants to purchase 5,000 units of part OC53 each period from Sell Division. Parts JS13 and OC53 have the same variable cost per unit for Sell Division. Producing Part OC53 will not change Sell Division's total fixed costs. Buy Division is now purchasing Part OC53 from an outside supplier at a price of $29 each. Hence, Buy Division won't pay more than $29 to Sell Division for the same product.

Suppose that Sell Division is producing at capacity and would have to forego some of its current sales to outside customers to handle all of Buy Division's needs for Part OC53.

Required

If Sell Division accepts the $29 price to produce and sell Part OC53 to Buy Division, what will be the impact on the company as a whole?

EXTENDING YOUR KNOWLEDGE

EYK24-1. Business Decision Case The monthly sales volume of Shugart Corporation varies from 7,000 units to 9,800 units over the course of a year. Management is currently studying anticipated selling expenses along with the related cash resources that will be needed. Which type of budget (flexible or static) (1) should be used by Shugart in planning, and (2) will provide Shugart the best feedback in performance reports for comparing planned expenditures with actual amounts? When Shugart's CEO asks you why it is advantageous to use a flexible budget instead of a static budget, what is one example you could give him?

EYK24-2. Ethics Case CJ Corporation manufactures steel rebar for use in construction. The accounting staff is currently preparing next year's budget. Bob Johnson is new to the firm and is interested in learning how this process occurs. He has lunch with the sales manager and the production manager to discuss further the planning process. Over the course of lunch, Bob discovers that the sales manager adjusts sales projections between a flexible amount and a static amount based on which will reflect the lowest variance from actual results. The production manager does the same for cost estimates. Both managers' year-end bonus is determined based on how low of a variance is achieved. When Bob asks about why they adjust their projections between flexible and static budgets, the response is simply that everyone around here does it.

Required

a. What do the sales and production managers hope to accomplish by their methods?

b. How might this backfire and work against them?

c. Are the actions of the sales and production managers unethical?

ANSWERS TO SELF-STUDY QUESTIONS:

1. c, (p. 1106) 2. a, (p. 1109) 3. c, (p. 1115) 4. a, (p. 1123) 5. c, (p. 1118) 6. c, (p. 1125)
7. c, (p. 1124) 8. c, (p. 1131)

YOUR TURN! SOLUTIONS

Solution 24.1

Budgeted returns		750
Actual returns		800
Returns processed variance		[(50) F]

	Actual Results for 800 Returns Processed	Budget Based on 750 Returns	Variances
Revenue	$80,000	$75,000	$ 5,000 F
Variable costs	36,000	37,500	[1,500 F]
Fixed costs	12,500	12,000	[500 U
Net income	$31,500	$25,500	[$ 6,000 F]

Solution 24.2

	Actual Results	Flexible Budget	Variance
Sales units	100,000	100,000	
Sales dollars	$190,000	$200,000	[$10,000 U]
Variable costs	**125,000**	**120,000**	**5,000 U**
Fixed costs	50,000	45,000	5,000 U
Operating income	$ 15,000	$ 35,000	[$20,000 U]

Solution 24.3

PACCAR Trucks segment, Parts segment, and Financial Services segment.

Solution 24.4

Revenue	$600,000
Traceable departmental expenses:	
Direct materials	$30,000
Direct labor	25,000
Other traceable expenses	40,000
Department contribution	$505,000
Common expenses	**155,000**
Departmental operating income	$350,000

Solution 24.5

Profit margin:
Current sales = $50,000/0.08 = $625,000 + $150,000 = $775,000 new total sales
New profit margin = ($50,000 + $15,000)/$775,000 = .084 or 8.4%

Asset turnover:
Current investment in assets = $50,000/0.10 = $500,000 + $100,000 = $600,000 new total assets
Current asset turnover = $625,000/$500,000 = 1.25 or 125%
New asset turnover ratio = $775,000/$600,000 = 1.29 or 129%

Return on investment:
New return on investment = ($50,000 + $15,000)/($500,000 + $100,000) = 0.108 or 10.8%

Residual income:
New residual income = ($50,000 + $15,000) − (0.08 × $600,000) = $17,000

Solution 24.6

A CPA firm's balanced scorecard might include some of the following measures:

Financial Performance
Segment margin by practice area (tax, audit, consulting)
Average collection period by practice area
Revenue by partner

Customer Satisfaction
Summary of customer satisfaction survey results
Percentage of repeat customers
Average number of years completing customer tax returns

Internal Business Processes
Ratio of new sales to billings for the period
Ratio of chargeable hours to total available hours by staff level
Ratio of billable hours to hours (actually) charged

Learning and Growth
Average number of annual continuing education hours
Partner-to-staff ratio
Average number of community service hours per staff

Solution 24.7

Because the manufacturing division has adequate capacity to fill the assembly division's needs, it should be willing to establish a transfer price that will cover its variable cost per unit. Because it would not incur any selling cost for the internal transfer, the minimum transfer price would be $60, equal to the variable cost per unit.

Chapter 25
Capital Budgeting

PAST

Chapter 24 discussed methods used to analyze companies' performance, including flexible budgets, segment reporting, and performance analysis.

PRESENT

Chapter 25 introduces capital budgeting and illustrates how capital budgeting is used to make capital investment decisions.

Waste Management (WM) is the largest environmental solutions provider in North America.[1] At the end of 2017, the company employed approximately 42,300 people, had approximately 20 million customers, owned or operated 249 landfills and 90 material recovery facilities, managed 305 waste transfer stations, and had 127 landfill gas beneficial use projects. WM has the permitted capacity to handle approximately 4.9 billion cubic yards of solid waste and projects that it will manage over 100 million tons of waste annually for the foreseeable future.

The current facilities that WM operates require significant capital outlays to upgrade or replace old equipment and buildings and close and maintain landfills. In addition, expenditures are needed for new equipment and buildings to accommodate the company's growth opportunities. WM has a team dedicated to evaluating these seemingly continuous capital expenditure opportunities designed to maintain, supplement, or expand its current operations.

This chapter introduces the process of and analysis techniques for capital budgeting decision making.

---

[1] http://nasdaqomx.mobular.net/nasdaqomx/7/3549/5057/

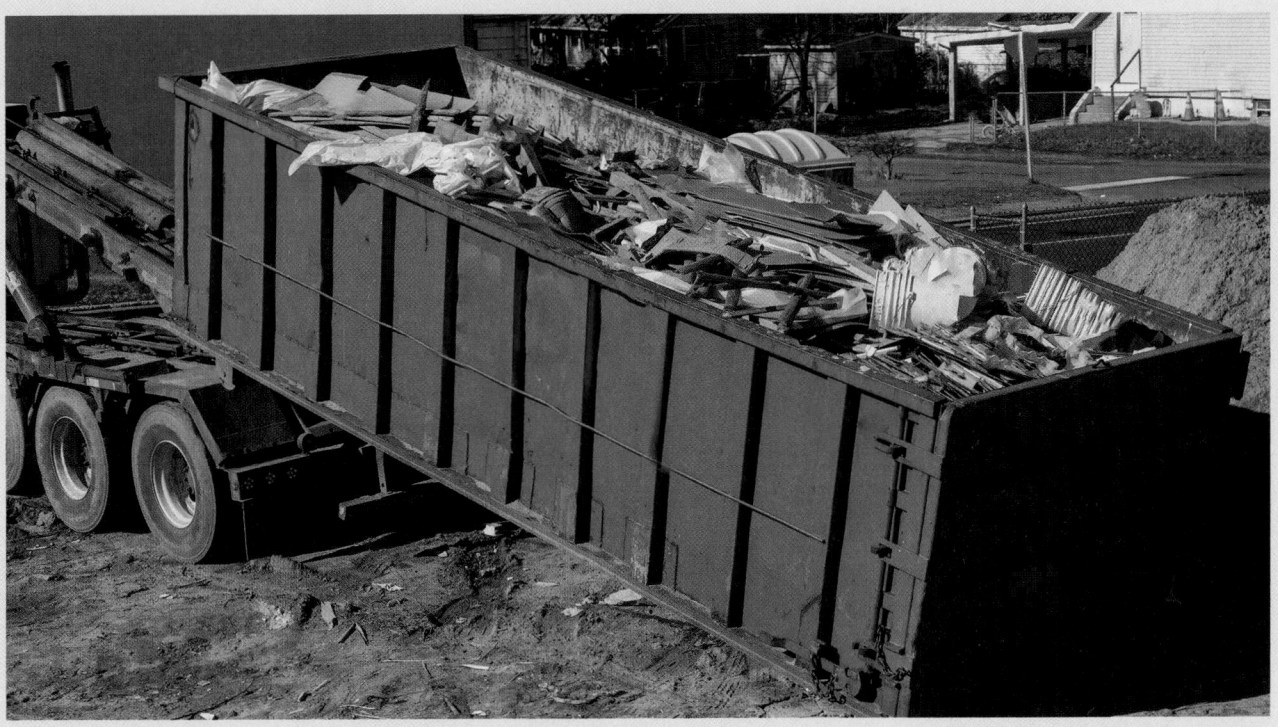

Road Map

LO	Learning Objective	Page	eLecture	Guided Example	Assignments
LO1	Introduce and illustrate the elements of capital budgeting.	1160	E25-1	YT25.1	Q1, Q2, Q3
LO2	Discuss required rates of return and the time value of money.	1162	E25-2	YT25.2	SS1, SS2, Q4, Q5, Q6, Q7, SE2, SE3, E1A, E1B, P6A, P6B
LO3	Demonstrate the use of present value factors to perform time value of money calculations.	1165	E25-3	YT25.3	Q8, Q9, Q10, Q13, SE4, SE5, E2A, E2B
LO4	Explain and illustrate the determination of after-tax cash flows.	1167	E25-4	YT25.4	SS3, Q11, Q12, SE1, SE4, SE10, E3A, E4A, E5A, E3B, E4B, E5B, P1A, P3A, P5A, P1B, P3B, P5B
LO5	Describe the net present value method of capital expenditure analysis.	1171	E25-5	YT25.5	SS4, Q13, Q14, SE6, SE10, E6A, E6B, P2A, P3A, P4A, P5A, P6A, P2B, P3B, P4B, P5B, P6B
LO6	Demonstrate the internal rate of return method of capital expenditure analysis.	1177	E25-6	YT25.6	SS5, Q15, SE7, SE8, E7A, E7B, E8B, P3A, P4A, P5A, P3B, P4B, P5B
LO7	Present the cash payback and average rate of return methods of capital expenditure analysis.	1179	E25-7	YT25.7	SS6, Q16, Q17, SE9, E8A, E9A, E9B, E10B, P3A, P4A, P5A, P3B, P4B, P5B

Planning long-term investments in productive assets is known as **capital budgeting**. The term reflects the fact that for most firms the total cost of all attractive investment opportunities exceeds the available investment capital. Thus, management must ration, or budget, investment capital among competing investment proposals. In deciding which new long-term assets to acquire, management must seek investments that promise to optimize return on the funds employed.

Capital budgeting is most valuable for organizations in which managers are responsible for the long-term profitability of their area of concern and are therefore encouraged to develop new products and more efficient production processes. Firms often make their most capable employees responsible for capital budgeting decisions, because such decisions determine how large sums of money are invested and commit the firm for extended future periods. Furthermore, investment decision errors are often difficult and costly to remedy or abandon.

Managers as well as accountants should be familiar with the special analytical techniques that evaluate the relative attractiveness of alternative uses of available capital. In this chapter, we first discuss the nature and procedures of capital budgeting, how required investment earning rates are determined, the time value of money, and the effect of income taxes on capital expenditure decisions. We conclude by illustrating three approaches to capital expenditure analysis: the net present value method, the cash payback method, and the average rate of return method.

ELEMENTS OF CAPITAL BUDGETING

LO1 Introduce and illustrate the elements of capital budgeting.

Capital Budgeting Phases

Capital budgeting has three phases:

1. Identify potential investments,
2. Select investments to be undertaken, and
3. Monitor the selected investments.

Hint: Inventory and other current asset purchases are not capital expenditures, even though they are commonly referred to as working "capital."

Many firms have a capital budgeting calendar calling for consideration of capital expenditure proposals at regular intervals, for example, every 6 months or every year. Proposals are usually examined with respect to (1) compliance with capital budget policies and procedures; (2) aspects of operational urgency, such as the need to replace critical equipment; (3) established criteria for minimum return on capital investments; and, (4) consistency with the firm's operating policies and long-term goals. Proposals for relatively small cash outlays may require the approval of low-level management only, whereas major proposals with more long-term impact are subject to approval at high management levels, perhaps including the board of directors. These major proposals and the decisions based on them profoundly affect a firm's long-term success.

Once approved, capital expenditures should be monitored to ensure that amounts and purposes are consistent with the original proposal. At appropriate intervals, the actual rates of return earned on important expenditures should be compared with projected rates. These periodic reviews encourage those responsible to formulate thorough and realistic proposals, and often provide an incentive for improving overall capital budgeting procedures.

Capital Expenditure Analysis

The scope of capital expenditures varies widely, ranging from the routine replacement of production equipment to the construction of entire manufacturing complexes. Whatever their size, most capital expenditure projects have the three stages shown in **Exhibit 25-1**.

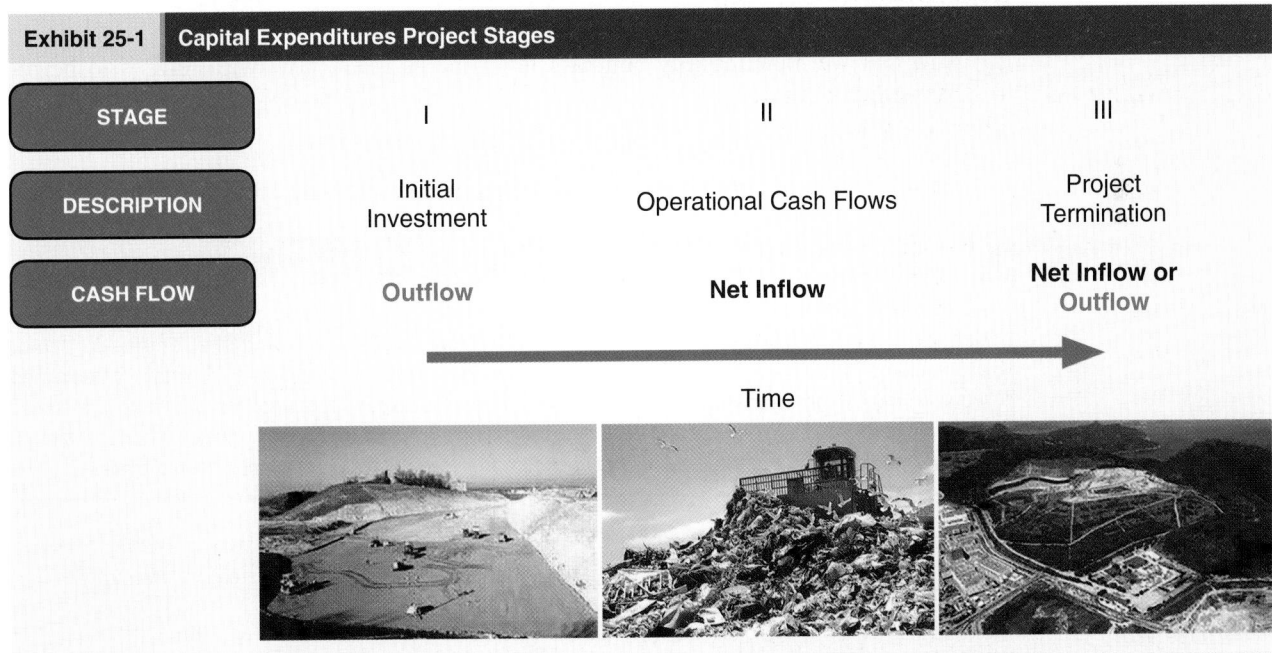

Exhibit 25-1   **Capital Expenditures Project Stages**

STAGE	I	II	III
DESCRIPTION	Initial Investment	Operational Cash Flows	Project Termination
CASH FLOW	Outflow	**Net Inflow**	**Net Inflow or** Outflow

Time

Initial investment (stage I) consists of a net cash outlay for a project or an asset. Net operational cash flows during the life of the project (stage II) may result from either an excess of periodic cash revenues over related cash expenditures or a periodic saving in some cash expenditure. Finally, the termination of a project (stage III) often results in some amount of liquidation proceeds from the sale of the project capital or could result in some cash outlay for the removal of the project or restoration of the property to its former condition.

For example, the development of a new WM municipal waste landfill (stage I) requires millions of dollars for the purchase of the property, performance of the necessary environmental studies, obtainment of land use approvals and permits, and the development of appropriate access roads, gatehouse and vehicle scales, administrative buildings, security fencing, and environmental protection systems.

Over the life of the landfill (stage II), WM will collect cash fees from users of the landfill and expend cash for the compacting and covering of the trash and the monitoring, collection, and treatment of liquids and methane gas created by the decomposing waste.

Finally, once the landfill reaches its permitted capacity, WM must close the landfill (stage III), applying a final cap on the waste, and then monitor, collect, and treat the liquids and methane gas created by the decomposing waste for a period of 30 to 40 years.

The attractiveness of a particular investment is determined in large part by the quantitative relationship between the cash investment in stage I and the net cash receipts expected in stages II and III. In its simplest form, this relationship is usually expressed as a ratio known as the **rate of return**:

$$\text{Rate of return} = \frac{\text{Returns}}{\text{Investment}}$$

All other things being equal, the higher the expected rate of return, the more attractive the investment opportunity. Proposed investments can be ranked according to their expected rates of return, and capital outlays can be allocated among the most attractive investments. Capital expenditure analysis consists of judging the attractiveness of income-producing or cost-saving opportunities in relation to required investments. The results of this analysis are among the most important input data in capital budgeting decisions.

Three questions are of considerable concern in capital budgeting:

1. How do we determine an acceptable rate of return for a given project?

2. How can we meaningfully compare investments made now with returns to be received in the future?

3. In what terms should investments and returns be measured?

These challenging problems are considered in the following sections of this chapter.

ACCOUNTING IN PRACTICE

Capital Budgeting in Growing a Company

Waste Management's 2017 annual report includes the following on page 55 of the management discussion and analysis (MD&A) section: "We used $1,509 million, $1,339 million, and $1,233 million for capital expenditures in 2017, 2016, and 2015, respectively. The Company continues to maintain a disciplined focus on capital management and fluctuations in our capital expenditures are a result of new business opportunities, growth, in our existing business, the timing of replacement of aging assets and investment in assets that support our strategy of continuous improvement through efficiency and innovation."

YOUR TURN! 25.1

The solution is on page 1201.

Provide an explanation of the capital budgeting process and the importance of capital investments.

REQUIRED RATES OF RETURN AND THE TIME VALUE OF MONEY

The mix of capital sources (i.e., available cash or proceeds from new debt or equity) that a company uses will depend on market conditions as well as the philosophies of the members of the board of directors and the management team.

LO2 Discuss required rates of return and the time value of money.

Cost of Capital

In determining an acceptable rate of return for a given project, we must consider not only the initial capital outlay, but also all of the costs associated with the acquisition of that capital. The parties providing the funds expect to be reasonably compensated for their use. When the money is borrowed from a bank or through a bond issuance, the interest paid by the firm is a cost of using the funds. When stockholder funds are used, we assume that some combination of dividend payments and increase in the value of the capital stock compensates stockholders for furnishing the investment capital. The cost to the firm of acquiring the funds used in capital investment projects—typically expressed as an annual percentage rate—is called the **cost of capital**.

A firm may acquire capital by issuing preferred or common stock, using retained earnings, borrowing, or some combination of these. Consequently, the overall cost of capital for a given project should reflect the cost rates of the several sources of funds in proportion to the amounts obtained from each source. This is called the **weighted average cost of capital**, or **WACC**.

Assume that a particular company had acquired capital through all four sources and in the proportions and with the cost of capital rates as shown here:

	A	B	C	D	E	F
1	**Source of Capital**	**Percentage of Total**	**×**	**Cost of Capital Rate**	**=**	**Weighted Average Cost of Capital Component**
2	Debt	40%	×	8%	=	3.2%
3	Preferred stock	10%	×	9%	=	0.9%
4	Common stock	20%	×	12%	=	2.4%
5	Retained earnings	30%	×	12%	=	3.6%
6	Weighted average cost of capital					10.1%

Multiplying the percentage of each capital source by its cost of capital rate provides weighted cost factors whose sum is the weighted average cost of capital. This percentage (in this case, 10.1%) can then be used to compare the attractiveness of proposed investments.

TAKEAWAY 25.1

Concept ➔	Method ➔	Assessment
Can a firm determine the cost of acquiring resources to fund capital investment decisions?	Use the weighted average cost of capital to determine the cost of aquiring capital by issuing stock, using retained earnings, borrowings, or a combination of therof.	At a minimum, capital investments should provide a rate of return at least as high as a firm's weighted average cost of capital.

Logically, for a capital investment to be considered favorably by a firm, its expected rate of return must be at least as high as the cost of capital. Therefore, the cost of capital represents a minimum required rate of return, or **hurdle rate**. In other words, a firm whose cost of capital is 10% will ordinarily want to invest only in an asset or project whose expected rate of return is more than 10%. An investment whose return is less than the cost of capital would be economically detrimental, although firms sometimes disregard their cost of capital if qualitative considerations override the quantitative aspects of the decision. Qualitative considerations might include the desire to achieve environmental goals, the desire to maintain research leadership in the industry, the need to maintain full employment of the workforce during a business slowdown, or the desire to maintain a percentage of market share or to penetrate a specific market.

Some firms consider only investments whose rates of return are at least a certain number of percentage points higher than the cost of capital. This **buffer margin** acts as a safety factor, because proposals that project estimated cash inflows and outflows years into the future have a significant amount of uncertainty regarding the amount and timing of those cash flows. Of course, in an environment of limited resources, even proposals whose expected rate of return is higher than the hurdle rate may be rejected if other investment opportunities offer still higher returns.

Time Value of Money

We have seen that in determining the desirability of a proposed capital investment, management compares the amount of investment required at the beginning of a project with its expected returns—typically a series of returns extending several years into the future.

Hint: Because the earnings retained by the firm might otherwise have been distributed to the common shareholders in the form of dividends, firms often use the same cost of capital for retained earnings as is used for common stock.

A.K.A. The minimum rate of return is also known as the hurdle rate or target rate.

This comparison, which is so important in capital budgeting decisions, cannot be made properly using the absolute amounts of the future returns because money has a time value. The **time value of money** means that the right to receive an amount of money today is worth more than the right to receive the same amount at some future date, because a current receipt can be invested to earn interest over the intervening period. Thus, if 10% annual interest can be obtained on investments, $100 received today is equal in value to $110 received 1 year from now. Assuming a 10% rate of return, $100 today will have a future value of $110 in 1 year's time. Conversely, assuming the same 10% rate of return, a $110 cash receipt expected in 1 year's time has a present value of $100 today.

The difference between present and future values is a function of interest rates and time periods. The higher the interest rate or longer the time period involved, the higher the amount by which a future value is reduced, or discounted, in deriving its present value. For example, **Exhibit 25-2** shows just how significant the time value of money can be at various interest rates and time periods. As the table indicates, five years from now $100 has a present value of $78, $62, or $50 if the applicable interest rates are 5%, 10%, and 15%, respectively. Note also that the longer the time period or higher the interest rate, the larger the difference between the future value of $100 and its present value. Comparing a current investment with its future returns without discounting the returns to their present value would substantially overstate the economic significance of the returns. We must therefore recognize the time value of money in capital budgeting procedures.

Exhibit 25-2 Time Value of Money

Years	Present Value of $100 (Rounded to Nearest Dollar)		
	Rate		
	5%	10%	15%
1	$95	$91	$87
2	91	83	76
3	86	75	66
4	82	68	57
5	78	62	50
10	61	39	25
20	38	15	6
30	23	6	2
40	14	2	0
50	9	1	0

The longer the time period, the larger the difference between the future value of $100 and its present value.

The higher the interest rate, the larger the difference between the future value of $100 and its present value.

Hint: Discounted cash flows (DCFs) are also known as the present value of future cash flows. The cash flows can either be inflows (receipts) or outflows (payments).

Techniques for discounting future cash flows to their present values apply to both cash receipts and cash outlays. In other words, the current value of the right to receive—or the current value of the obligation to pay—a sum in the future is its present value computed at an appropriate interest rate. We maximize our economic position by arranging to receive amounts as early as possible and postponing amounts to be paid as long as possible. These generalizations will be apparent in the capital budgeting illustrations later in the chapter.

TAKEAWAY 25.2

Concept	Method	Assessment
What is the time value of money?	Money available at the present time is worth more than the identical sum in the future due to its potential earning capacity. That is, the provided money can earn interest.	The time value of money explains why interest is paid or earned. Interest, whether it is on a deposit or debt, compensates the depositor or lender for the time value of money.

The following sources of financing, their proportions, and their cost of capital rates are for a merchandising company. Calculate and interpret the WACC for this company.

	Percentage of Total	Cost of Capital Rate
Bank loan	45%	12%
Equity capital	55%	9%

PERFORMING NET PRESENT VALUE CALCULATIONS

Appendix 10A introduced time value of money concepts as they relate to the pricing of bonds. Appendix 10A demonstrated present value calculations using three methods; 1) tables, 2) a financial calculator, 3) and an electronic spreadsheet. In this chapter we will perform net present value calculations using tables to measure capital investments and their related returns. Present value tables provide factors for combinations of time periods and interest rates that may be multiplied by a stream of cash flows or a one-time future cash flow to determine its present value. These tables can be found in Appendix E of the text, along with a more detailed discussion of time value of money concepts.

LO3 **Demonstrate** the use of present value factors to perform time value of money calculations.

Throughout the chapter, the following abbreviations, related to time value of money calculations, are used:

$$PV = \text{present value at time 0}$$
$$FV = \text{future value at time N}$$
$$i = \text{interest at which the amount compounds each period}$$
$$N = \text{number of periods (time)}$$
$$PMT = \text{periodic cash flow (payment)}$$

Single-Sum Cash Flows

Let us first consider how to compute the present value of a single-sum cash flow. This calculation will be used to determine the present value of sporadic cash flows when the returns expected on an investment, or the expenditures it requires, are unequal amounts or are expected at irregular intervals during or at the end of the life of the investment.

Hint: Present values should always be less than future values; otherwise, the calculation was performed incorrectly.

To illustrate, we assume that an investment project promises a return of $2,000 at the end of two years and another $1,000 at the end of five years. The desired rate of return is 10% per year. **Exhibit 25-3** illustrates the cash flows on a timeline.

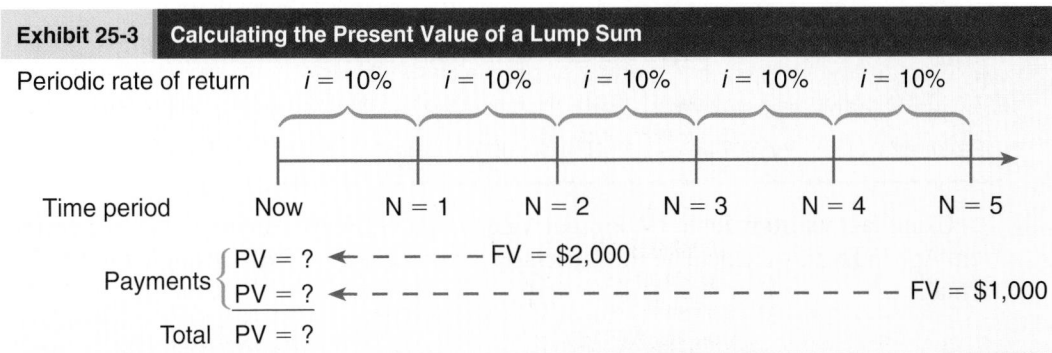

Exhibit 25-3   **Calculating the Present Value of a Lump Sum**

Using factors from Table III, Present Value of $1, from Appendix E, we calculate the present value of each cash flow separately using the following process.

First, calculate the present value of the $2,000 cash flow. The formula for calculating the present value of a future sum is as follows:

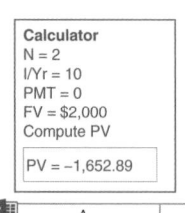

Present value (PV) = Future value (FV) × PV table factor*

$$PV = \$2,000 \times 0.82645$$
$$PV = \$1,652.90$$

*Because the $2,000 cash flow occurs at the end of Year 2, we use the factor associated with a 10% rate of return and 2 years (0.82645; see Table III in Appendix E).

This value may be interpreted as the amount that, if invested today in an account paying 10% interest, would allow for the withdrawal of $2,000 at the end of two years. This can be proved as follows: $1,652.90 invested today would earn $165.29 in interest in the first year, for a total value of $1,818.19 ($1,652.90 + $165.29). This balance would earn $181.82 in interest in the second year, for a total value of $2,000.01 ($1,818.19 + $181.82).

Next, calculate the present value of the $1,000 cash flow:

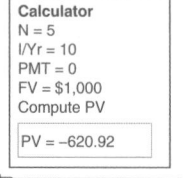

PV = FV × PV table factor*

$$PV = \$1,000 \times 0.62092$$
$$PV = \$620.92$$

*Because the $1,000 cash flow occurs at the end of Year 5, we use the factor from a present value table for a single amount associated with a 10% rate of return and 5 years (0.62092; see Table III in Appendix E).

This value may be interpreted as the amount that, if invested today in an account paying 10% interest, would allow for the withdrawal of $1,000 at the end of five years.

The total present value of the combined flows is $2,273.82 ($1,652.90 + $620.92). That is, $2,273.82 invested today in an account paying 10% interest would allow withdrawal of $2,000 at the end of two years and $1,000 at the end of five years.

Annuity Cash Flows

Let us next consider how to compute the present value of an annuity. An **annuity** is cash flows that are the same each period over two or more equal periods.

To illustrate, we assume that a project has expected cash inflows of $1,000 at the end of each of the next three periods, and 8% is the appropriate cost of capital. **Exhibit 25-4** illustrates the cash flows on a timeline.

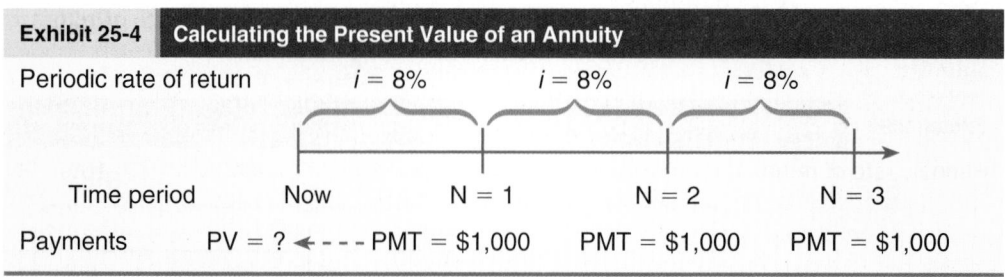

Using factors from Table IV, Present Value of an Ordinary Annuity of $1 per Period, from Appendix E, we calculate the present value of these cash flows using the following formula:

$$\textbf{PV} = \textbf{PMT} \times \textbf{PV table factor*}$$
$$\text{PV} = \$1,000 \times 2.57710$$
$$\text{PV} = \$2,577.10$$

*Because the $1,000 cash flow occurs at the end of each year for 3 years, we use the factor associated with an 8% rate of return and 3 years (2.57710; see Table IV in Appendix E).

Calculator
N = 3
I/Yr = 8
PMT = $1,000
FV = 0
Compute PV

PV = −2,577.10

X		A	B
1	Discount rate (rate)		8%
2	Number of periods (nper)		3
3	Annuity (pmt)		1,000
4	Future value (fv)		0
5	Present value(pv)		(2,577.10)
6	= PV(B1,B2,B3,B4)		
7	= (2,577.10)		

This value may be interpreted as the amount that, if invested today in an account paying 8% interest annually, would allow for the withdrawal of $1,000 at the end of each year for the next three years. This can be proved as follows: $2,577.10 invested today would earn $206.17 ($2,577.10 × 0.08) in interest in the first year, for a total value of $2,783.27 ($2,577.10 + $206.17). A withdrawal of $1,000 would leave a balance of $1,783.27. This balance would earn $142.66 ($1,783.27 × 0.08) in interest in the second year, for a total value of $1,925.93 ($1,783.27 + $142.66). A second withdrawal of $1,000 would leave a balance of $925.93. This balance would earn $74.07 ($925.93 × 0.08) in interest in the third year, for a total value of $1,000 ($925.93 + $74.07), allowing for a third and final withdrawal of $1,000.

Both illustrations assume that all cash flows occur at the end of the periods. This assumption is somewhat simplistic, because cash receipts or cost savings from most industrial investments occur in a steady stream throughout the operating periods. Nevertheless, businesses assume end-of-period cash flows for ease of use. These calculations will understate the present values of flows that are gradual throughout the period, because the present values of cash flows early in the period are higher than similar inflows or outlays at the end of the period. The difference, however, is normally not material.

JB Enterprises has a cost of capital of 12%. Calculate the present value of the following investment opportunities:

a. An investment project promises a return of $3,000 at the end of year 3 and $5,000 at the end year 4.

b. An investment project promises a return of $2,000 at the end of each of the next four years.

YOUR TURN! 25.3

The solution is on page 1201.

GuidedExamples
MBC

MEASUREMENT OF INVESTMENTS AND RETURNS

Cash Flows

eLectures
MBC

When present value analysis is used to make investment decisions, investments and returns must be stated in the form of cash flows. Present value determinations are basically interest calculations, and therefore only money amounts—cash flows—are properly used in interest calculations. Furthermore, only the *incremental* cash flows that will occur if the project is accepted should be considered in the analysis.

LO4

Explain and **illustrate** the determination of after-tax cash flows.

Typically, financial data available in the accounts are not stated in terms of cash flows because accrual-basis accounting is used. Amounts compiled on the accrual basis must be restated in terms of the appropriate cash flows for capital budgeting purposes. For example, apportioning the cost of an asset over its life through depreciation accounting is an important feature of accrual accounting. When present value analysis is used, the cost of an asset is treated as a cash outlay when the asset is paid for. In measuring future returns related to the asset, depreciation expense does not represent a cash outlay. However, depreciation expense affects cash flows indirectly by reducing cash outlays for income tax payments.

Likewise, earnings from projects should reflect the cash inflows rather than the revenue amounts computed using accrual accounting. The timing of the cash collections is important, too, because the essence of present value analysis is that cash received can be reinvested.

After-Tax Cash Flows

Both federal and state income taxes are important to investment decisions; for some companies, the combined federal and state income tax rate may approach 30%. Generally, income taxes reduce the economic significance of taxable receipts and deductible expenditures.

Exhibit 25-5	Tax Impact on Cash Flows		
	A	B	C
1		Inflow	Outflow
2	Pre-tax amount	$40,000	$(15,000)
3	Income tax rate	30%	30%
4	Tax benefit/(expense)	(12,000)	4,500
5	After-tax amount	28,000	(10,500)

As illustrated in **Exhibit 25-5**, assuming a 30% tax rate, a $40,000 before-tax gain (cash inflow) would increase taxable income by $40,000 and income taxes by $12,000 (30% × $40,000), resulting in a $28,000 after-tax cash inflow. A $15,000 before-tax expense would reduce taxable income by $15,000 and income taxes by $4,500 (30% × $15,000), resulting in a $10,500 after-tax cash outflow. In general terms, the formulas for determining after-tax cash flows are as follows:

After-tax cash inflow = Pre-tax cash inflow × (1 − Tax rate)

After-tax cash outflow = Pre-tax cash outflow × (1 − Tax rate)

After-tax cash flows are more relevant than before-tax cash flows because they represent the amounts available to retire debt, finance expansions, or pay dividends. For this reason, investment decision analyses must be formulated in terms of after-tax cash flows.

Depreciation Tax Shield

Depreciation deductions *shield* revenues from taxation and thus reduce the taxes a company must pay. Depreciation creates a tax savings. **Exhibit 25-6** illustrates how to compute the amount of tax savings created by depreciation.

Exhibit 25-6	Tax Impact of Depreciation	
	A	B
1		Inflow
2	Pre-tax amount	$30,000
3	Income tax rate	30%
4	Tax benefit/(expense)	9,000

To understand this effect, assume that a company had taxable revenues of $30,000 and no expenses. Assuming a 30% tax rate, this company would owe $9,000 in tax ($30,000 × 30%). Now, assume that the company had one deductible expense: depreciation in the amount of $30,000. In this case, the company would owe no taxes, because it can deduct the depreciation expense from its taxable revenue ($30,000 − $30,000 = $0 taxable income). Thus, the depreciation saved the company from having to pay $9,000 in tax. The formula for determining the tax shield is as follows:

After-tax depreciation tax shield = Depreciation expense × Tax rate

Illustration of After-Tax Cash Flows

Thinking in terms of after-tax cash flows represents a significant departure from the accrual-based accounting for revenue and expenses. However, remember that the pre-tax cash flows are available to us in the cash flow statement. We can use our understanding of the cash flow statement to determine the after-tax cash flows needed for capital budgeting and other time value of money analyses.

To explore the relationship between the traditional income statement and the related after-tax cash flows, let's revisit Fezzari's 2019 income statement from Chapter 22. **Exhibit 25-7** shows Fezzari's income statement in column A. Column B identifies the related cash flows from Fezzari's cash flow statement. An understanding of **Exhibit 25-7** will provide a basis for understanding the comprehensive illustration of capital budgeting later in the chapter.

Column A in **Exhibit 25-7** is the traditional income statement, showing that revenue minus operating expenses and income taxes results in a net income of $529,185. For simplicity, we assume that revenue and cash expenses involve no significant accruals and that depreciation is the same on both the books and the tax return. Ordinarily, net income does not represent after-tax cash flows because depreciation expense—a noncash expense—is deducted to derive net income. As indicated in column A of **Exhibit 25-7**, to convert the $529,185 net income to after-tax cash flow, we must add back the depreciation of $45,000, resulting in $574,185 of after-tax cash flow.

Column B of **Exhibit 25-7** confirms the $574,185 amount of after-tax cash flow determined in column A. This is accomplished by simply listing the amounts in column A that constitute cash inflows (revenue of $6,237,000) and cash outflows (cash expenses of $4,704,570, $776,850, and $5,000 and income tax payments of $176,395). Depreciation is excluded because it does not represent a cash payment.

Column C in **Exhibit 25-7** illustrates the determination of the individual amounts of after-tax cash flows for each item on the income statement. We use this approach in the comprehensive illustration of capital budgeting appearing later in the chapter. Amounts in column C are determined as follows (again, a 25% income tax rate is assumed).

Exhibit 25-7	Illustration of Determining After-Tax Cash Flows			
	A	B	C	D
1	Fezzari Performance Bicycles For the Period Ended December 31, 2019			
2		A	B	C
3		Traditional Income Statement	Income Statement Cash Inflows (Outflows)	Individual After-Tax Cash Inflow (Outflow) Effects
4	Sales	$6,237,000	$6,237,000	$ 4,677,750
5	Less: Cost of goods sold (excluding depreciation)	4,704,570	(4,704,570)	$(3,528,427)
6	Less: Depreciation expense	45,000		11,250
7	Gross profit	$1,487,430		
8	Less: Selling and administrative expense	776,850	(776,850)	$ (582,638)
9	Income from operations	$ 710,580		
10	Less: Interest expense	5,000	(5,000)	$ (3,750)
11	Income before income taxes	$ 705,580		
12	Less: Income taxes	176,395	(176,395)	
13	Net income	$ 529,185		
14	Add back depreciation expense	45,000		
15	After-tax cash flow	$ 574,185	$ 574,185	$ 574,185

Receipt of $6,237,000 cash revenue

Receipt of $6,237,000 cash revenue would, by itself, increase taxable income by $6,237,000, adding $1,559,250 ($6,237,000 × 25%) to income taxes. The $4,677,750 after-tax cash inflow is the difference between the $6,237,000 cash revenue received and the related $1,559,250 increase in income taxes (a cash outflow). Applying the previous formula for an after-tax inflow results in the same amount:

$$\text{After-tax cash inflow} = \text{Pre-tax cash inflow} \times (1 - \text{Tax rate})$$

OR

$$\$4,677,750 = \$6,237,000 \times (1 - 0.25)$$

Payment of $4,704,570 in cash operating expenses

Payment of $4,704,570 in cash operating expenses represents a deductible cash outflow that reduces taxable income by $4,704,570 and thus reduces income taxes by $1,176,143 ($4,704,570 × 25%). The $3,528,427 net cash outflow is the difference between the $4,704,570 actually paid out for expenses and the $1,176,143 of income tax payments avoided by virtue of the tax deductibility of the expenses. Applying the previous formula for an after-tax outflow results in the same amount:

$$\text{After-tax cash outflow} = \text{Pre-tax cash outflow} \times (1 - \text{Tax rate})$$

OR

$$\$3,528,427 = \$4,704,570 \times (1 - 0.25)$$

Notice that *avoiding a cash outflow* has the same effect on net cash flows as a cash inflow. In other words, total net cash inflows can be increased by adding to cash inflows or by avoiding cash outflows.

Recording $45,000 of depreciation expense

Hint: The depreciation amount that provides a tax shield is the depreciation deduction on the tax return. Tax depreciation deductions are governed by tax regulations, not by generally accepted accounting principles. Often the periodic tax depreciation will differ from depreciation expense on the income statement (in Exhibit 25-7 we assume that the amounts are equal). When identifying the depreciation tax shield in capital budgeting analysis, then, it is important to use the depreciation amount from the tax return.

Although depreciation expense is tax deductible, no related cash expenditure occurs during the period. The $45,000 deduction reduces taxable income by $45,000 and income taxes by $11,250 ($45,000 × 25%). Depreciation expense and similar noncash expense deductions are often referred to as *tax shields* because they shield an equal amount of income from whatever income tax rate is applicable.

Payment of $776,850 in cash selling and administrative expenses

Payment of $776,850 in cash selling and administrative expenses represents a deductible cash outflow that reduces taxable income by $776,850 and thus reduces income taxes by $194,212 ($776,850 × 25%). The $582,638 net cash outflow is the difference between the $776,850 actually paid out for expenses and the $194,212 of income tax payments avoided by virtue of the tax deductibility of the expenses. Applying the previous formula for an after-tax outflow results in the same amount:

$$\text{After-tax cash outflow} = \text{Pre-tax cash outflow} \times (1 - \text{Tax rate})$$

OR

$$\$582,638 = \$776,850 \times (1 - 0.25)$$

Payment of $5,000 in cash interest expense

Payment of $5,000 in cash interest expense represents a deductible cash outflow that reduces taxable income by $5,000 and thus reduces income taxes by $1,250 ($5,000 × 25%). The $3,750 net cash outflow is the difference between the $5,000 actually paid out for interest expense and the $1,250 of income tax payments avoided by virtue of the tax deductibility of the expense. Applying the previous formula for an after-tax outflow results in the same amount:

$$\text{After-tax cash outflow} = \text{Pre-tax cash outflow} \times (1 - \text{Tax rate})$$

OR

$$\$3,750 = \$5,000 \times (1 - 0.25)$$

Combining the after-tax cash flow effect of each individual amount in column C again confirms that net cash inflows total $574,185.

Summary of Concerns Underlying Capital Budgeting

1. The typical investment pattern involves a present investment of funds resulting in anticipated returns, often extending years into the future.

2. The basic question in capital budgeting is whether present investments are justified by related future returns.

3. Because money has a time value, returns that occur in the future must be discounted to their present values for a proper comparison with present investments.

4. To use discounting (interest) calculations properly, we must state amounts in capital budgeting analyses in terms of cash flows.

5. Because income tax rates are substantial, capital budgeting analyses should be formulated in terms of after-tax cash flows.

Thus far in the chapter, we have presented a number of important aspects of capital budgeting as background for the review of several approaches to capital expenditure analysis. These background materials have focused on the analytical concept known as net present value. Accountants generally concede that the net present value approach is conceptually and analytically superior to the other two approaches that we will also illustrate: cash payback and average rate of return.

Calculate the individual after-tax cash flow effect of each of the following relevant items, assuming the income tax rate is 30%:

   a. Cash revenue received of $90,000

   b. Cash operating expenses paid of $45,000

   c. Depreciation expense on tax return of $10,000

   d. Interest expense paid of $5,000

YOUR TURN! 25.4

The solution is on page 1201.

NET PRESENT VALUE ANALYSIS

Basic Steps

The basic approach to the **net present value method** is shown in **Exhibit 25-8**. Each step described here and used in the example that follows is color coded to correspond to the exhibit. Referring to the items in the exhibit, the steps in the net present value approach are to:

LO5 Describe the net present value method of capital expenditure analysis.

Step 1: Determine the amount of the **investment outlay** required in terms of incremental after-tax cash flows.

Step 2: Estimate the amounts and timing of **future operating receipts or cost savings** in terms of incremental after-tax cash flows.

Step 3: Estimate any **incremental after-tax liquidation proceeds** to be received on termination of the project.

A.K.A. The present value of cash flows is also know as discounted cash flows.

Step 4: Discount all future cash flows to their **present value** at an appropriate interest rate, usually the minimum desired rate of return on capital.

Step 5: Subtract the investment outlay from the total present value of future cash flows to determine **net present value**. If net present value is zero or positive (returns equal or exceed investment), then the project's rate of return equals or exceeds the minimum desired rate and should be accepted. Negative net present values indicate that the project's return is less than desired, and the project should be rejected.

ACCOUNTING IN PRACTICE	**Undertaking Negative-Net Present Value Projects**

There are reasons companies may follow through with a capital investment even though it has a projected negative Net Present Value. Reasons for this include projects that support other projects, hope that the investment will return more than originally expected, response to competition, and response to government regulations. These and other qualitative factors should be considered by management.

Exhibit 25-8	**Net Present Value Method Approach**

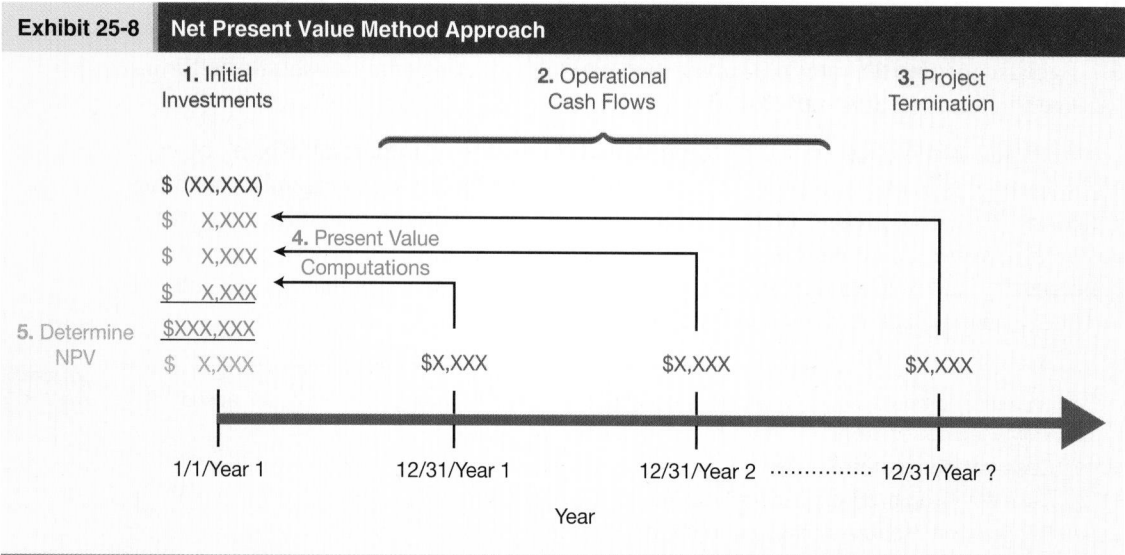

Illustration of Net Present Value (NPV) Analysis

To illustrate net present value analysis, assume that Fezzari owns its bicycle assembly facility. The building is 30 years old, and its heating, ventilating, and air-conditioning (HVAC) systems are functioning, but significantly out of date. A local HVAC contractor has told Fezzari management that new HVAC technology could significantly reduce Fezzari's monthly utility bill. The HVAC contractor has offered to replace the current HVAC system with a new, state-of-the-art system for an installed price of $150,000. The new system has an expected useful life of 20 years, at which point it will be worthless, but it will save an estimated $22,500 per year in cash utilities expenses during its useful life. Fezzari management has a minimum desired return of 10% on any capital project. Fezzari's tax rate is 25%.

To evaluate the local contractor's proposal, management decides to use a net present value analysis.

Recall that depreciation is based on the depreciation deduction from the tax return. Based on a half-year convention (one-half of the first year's depreciation is recognized in the year of acquisition and disposition), the annual depreciation (rounded to the nearest dollar) would be computed as follows:

	A	B	C	D
1	**Year**	**Capitalized Cost**	**Depreciation Rate**	**Annual Depreciation**
2	1	$150,000	3.750%	$ 5,625
3	2	150,000	7.219	10,829
4	3	150,000	6.677	10,016
5	4	150,000	6.177	9,266
6	5	150,000	5.713	8,570
7	6	150,000	5.285	7,928
8	7	150,000	4.888	7,332
9	8	150,000	4.522	6,783
10	9	150,000	4.462	6,693
11	10	150,000	4.461	6,692
12	11	150,000	4.462	6,693
13	12	150,000	4.461	6,692
14	13	150,000	4.462	6,693
15	14	150,000	4.461	6,692
16	15	150,000	4.462	6,693
17	16	150,000	4.461	6,692
18	17	150,000	4.462	6,693
19	18	150,000	4.461	6,692
20	19	150,000	4.462	6,693
21	20	150,000	4.461	6,692
22	21	150,000	2.231	3,347

Tax return depreciation, 150% declining balance, half-year convention.

Exhibit 25-9 presents a net present value analysis of the HVAC system as an investment project. Note that the format (including the color coding) follows the analysis outlined in **Exhibit 25-8**: Future returns are stated in terms of after-tax cash flows; then the present values of future cash flows are determined and compared with the investment. The computations shown in **Exhibit 25-9** are explained in the following subsections.

Step 1: Initial investment

The initial investment of $150,000 occurs at the beginning of Year 1, which we identify as Year 0. It is shown in **Exhibit 25-9** as a negative number, signifying that it represents an outflow of cash.

Step 2: Annual cash flows (expense savings)

Cash savings or expense reductions have the same effects as cash revenue, income, or gains. Thus, these amounts are shown as positive amounts, signifying that they represent an inflow of cash. They also have the same consequence of increasing income taxes. In our example, saving $22,500 in cash expenses each year raises taxable income by $22,500, which leads to an increase in taxes of $5,625 ($22,500 × 25%). Thus, the annual after-tax cash flow is $16,875—the $22,500 savings less the $5,625 tax increase.

Annual depreciation tax shield: The depreciation deduction on the tax return shields an equal amount of income from taxes. The avoided taxes are equal to the depreciation deduction multiplied by the applicable tax rate. In our illustration, the annual tax savings from the depreciation tax shield are as follows:

Exhibit 25-9   Illustration of Net Present Value Analysis: After-Tax Cash Flows (Rounded to Nearest Dollar)

	A	B Present Value	C Year 0	D Year 1	E Year 2	F Year 3	G Year 4	H Year 5	I Year 6	J Year 7	K Year 8	L Year 9	M	N Year 19	O Year 20	P Year 21
								Projected After-Tax Cash Flows								
3	Initial investment	$(150,000)	$(150,000)													
4																
5	Annual cash expenses savings			$22,500	$22,500	$22,500	$22,500	$22,500	$22,500	$22,500	$22,500	$22,500		$22,500	$22,500	—
6	Less income tax @ 25%			5,625	5,625	5,625	5,625	5,625	5,625	5,625	5,625	5,625		5,625	5,625	—
7	After-tax expenses savings	$ 143,666		$16,875	$16,875	$16,875	$16,875	$16,875	$16,875	$16,875	$16,875	$16,875		$16,875	$16,875	$ —
8																
9	Tax savings from depreciation tax shield:															
10	Year 1	$ 1,278		$ 1,406												
11	Year 2	2,237			$ 2,707											
12	Year 3	1,881				$ 2,504										
13	Year 4	1,583					$ 2,317									
14	Year 5	1,331						$ 2,143								
15	Year 6	1,119							$ 1,982							
16	Year 7	941								$ 1,833						
17	Year 8	791									$ 1,696					
18	Year 9	710										$ 1,673				
19	Year 10	645														
20	Year 11	586														
21	Year 12	533														
22	Year 13	485														
23	Year 14	440														
24	Year 15	400														
25	Year 16	364														
26	Year 17	331														
27	Year 18	301														
28	Year 19	274												$ 1,673		
29	Year 20	249													$ 1,673	
30	Year 21	113														837
31	Total PV of future cash flows	$ 160,258		$18,281	$19,582	$19,379	$19,192	$19,018	$18,857	$18,708	$18,571	$18,548		$18,548	$18,548	$ 837
32	Net present value	$ 10,258														

	A	B	C	D
1	Year	Annual Depreciation	Tax Rate	Tax Shield
2	1	$ 5,625	25%	$1,406
3	2	10,829	25	2,707
4	3	10,016	25	2,504
5	4	9,266	25	2,317
6	5	8,570	25	2,143
7	6	7,928	25	1,982
8	7	7,332	25	1,833
9	8	6,783	25	1,696
10	9	6,693	25	1,673
11	10	6,692	25	1,673
12	11	6,693	25	1,673
13	12	6,692	25	1,673
14	13	6,693	25	1,673
15	14	6,692	25	1,673
16	15	6,693	25	1,673
17	16	6,692	25	1,673
18	17	6,693	25	1,673
19	18	6,692	25	1,673
20	19	6,693	25	1,673
21	20	6,692	25	1,673
22	21	3,347	25	837

Tax return depreciation, 150% declining balance, half-year convention.

Step 3: Project termination

For purposes of this illustration, we have assumed that the HVAC system will be worthless at the end of its 20-year life. Thus, there will be no additional incremental cash flow at the end of the project. When the system is replaced, any cost of removing the old system will be added to the cost of the installation of a new HVAC system as part of the initial investment in the new system.

Step 4: Present value calculations

The present value column in **Exhibit 25-9** shows the results of the calculations of the present values of the cash flows discussed earlier. Proper consideration of the required investment involves neither an income tax nor a present value calculation. Fezzari's $150,000 investment itself is not tax deductible; the related depreciation deductions are tax deductible, and are, of course, incorporated into our previous analysis. Because the investment expenditure is immediate, no discounting for present value is required. Thus, $150,000 represents the after-tax present value of the required investment outflow.

The $16,875 saved each year for 20 years can be treated as an annuity. The present value of an annuity of $16,875 for 20 years at 10% is $143,666 (PV = $16,875 × 8.51356).

Because the tax shield amounts differ from year to year based on the tax depreciation deduction, the present value of each year's amount must be computed separately. These amounts are computed using the PV factors as shown below:

Present value of a single sum payment, over 20 periods, at a 10% discount factor. See Table III in Appendix E.			

	A	B	C	D
1	**Year**	**Depreciation**	**PV Factor**	**PV**
2	1	$1,406	0.90909	$1,278
3	2	2,707	0.82645	2,237
4	3	2,504	0.75131	1,881
5	4	2,317	0.68301	1,583
6	5	2,143	0.62092	1,331
7	6	1,982	0.56447	1,119
8	7	1,833	0.51316	941
9	8	1,696	0.46651	791
10	9	1,673	0.42410	710
11	10	1,673	0.38554	645
12	11	1,673	0.35049	586
13	12	1,673	0.31863	533
14	13	1,673	0.28966	485
15	14	1,673	0.26333	440
16	15	1,673	0.23939	400
17	16	1,673	0.21763	364
18	17	1,673	0.19784	331
19	18	1,673	0.17986	301
20	19	1,673	0.16351	274
21	20	1,673	0.14864	249
22	21	837	0.13501*	113
23	* Manually computed.			

These amounts are summed to arrive at the total present value of the future cash flows, or $160,258.

Step 5: Net present value calculation

The net present value is calculated by subtracting the initial investment from the total present value of the future cash flows. With its annual savings of cash expense and tax savings from the depreciation tax shield, the $150,000 investment results in future cash flows with a total present value of $160,258 and therefore a net present value of $10,258. This positive return on the capital invested, adjusted for the time value of money, means that the project will return more than the 10% return sought by Fezzari management.

On the basis of the net present value analysis alone, it would appear that Fezzari management should accept the proposal. However, rather than accept the project outright, this analysis may provide a basis to review the underlying assumptions of the analysis that resulted in acceptance of the project. For example, management may wish to evaluate the estimate of $22,500 in annual utility savings. If the anticipated savings are expected to decrease, then the projects becomes more risky.

Hint: Note that net present value calculations do not provide an exact rate of return provided by the capital investment decision. The net present value method only tells management whether the investment exceeds the minimum required rate of return.

Liquidation Proceeds

The amount realized when an asset is liquidated contributes to the relative attractiveness of an investment in capital equipment. Liquidation proceeds on long-lived assets are sometimes disregarded because their occurrence is so far in the future that the amounts are difficult to predict, and their present values tend to be small. When useful lives are short, however, liquidation proceeds may be a deciding factor in the analysis. In our illustration, the HVAC system has a 20-year life with no salvage value. However, assume that as a sales promotion, the manufacturer of the HVAC system guaranteed to buy back the system for $20,000 after 20 years. For tax purposes, salvage value may be ignored in computing depreciation, so the machine is fully depreciated over the 20 years to a zero book value. The HVAC's sale for $20,000, then, creates a $20,000 gain on the tax return ($20,000 sales price − $0 tax book value). The $20,000 gain increases income taxes by $5,000, which is deducted from the sales price of $20,000 to produce a net after-tax cash flow of $15,000 in Year 20. The present value of $15,000 for 20 years at 10% is $2,229.60 ($15,000 × 0.14864; see Table III in Appendix E).

Note that if an asset is sold before the end of its tax depreciation period, a loss may be generated for tax purposes. The loss operates as a tax shield because it shields an equal amount of income from taxes. The tax savings is added to the cash proceeds to determine the net after-tax cash flow.

Concept ⟶	Method ⟶	Assessment	TAKEAWAY 25.3
You have been asked to calculate the NPV of a potential investment in a new piece of machinery used in your company's manufacturing process.	Perform NPV Analysis: • Step 1: Identify the initial investment. • Step 2: Calculate the annual cash flows. • Step 3: Project any termination values. • Step 4: Perform present value calculations. • Step 5: Calculate the net present value.	The calculated NPV is then compared to the company's minimum required rate of return. However, rather than accept or reject the project outright, this may provide a basis to review the underlying assumptions of the analysis.	

Excess Present Value Index

Alternative capital expenditure proposals may be compared in terms of their **excess present value index**, defined as follows:

$$\text{Excess present value index} = \frac{\text{Total present value of future cash flows}}{\text{Initial investment}}$$

For the investment presented in **Exhibit 25-9**, the excess present value index would be

$$\frac{\$160,258}{\$150,000} = 1.068$$

The higher the ratio of return on investment, the more attractive is the proposal. A ratio below 1.00 means that the project returns less than the target rate of return, and a ratio above 1.00 means that the project return exceeds the target rate of return. Although the excess present value index may be a convenient measure for ranking various proposals, it does not reflect the amount of the investment. Two proposals, requiring initial cash investments of $5,000 and $5,000,000, respectively, could have identical excess present value indexes but could hardly be considered equal investment opportunities.

Mining Equipment Manufacturer is considering the purchase of a new building. The building would require an initial outlay of $350,000. It would be depreciated using the straight-line method over 20 years, with a $15,000 salvage value. The building would generate cash inflows of $47,200/year; the company's income tax rate is 30% and WACC is 8%. Calculate the NPV of this project and decide whether the investment should be undertaken.

YOUR TURN! 25.5

The solution is on page 1201.

OTHER CAPITAL BUDGETING ANALYSES

Internal Rate of Return Analysis

The net present value (NPV) method only tells management whether an investment exceeds (a positive NPV) or fails to exceed (a negative NPV) the

LO6 Demonstrate the internal rate of return method of capital expenditure analysis minimum required rate of return used in the NPV calculation. Managers may prefer to know the exact rate of return of the capital investment.

The **internal rate of return (IRR)** method provides the rate of return, based on the present value of all future cash flows, that a company can expect to earn on a capital investment decision. More specifically, the IRR method calculates the interest rate that makes the NPV of the capital investment exactly equal to zero. Another way of thinking about IRR is that the calculation provides the exact interest rate that makes the initial cost of the investment equal to the present value of the investment's net cash flows. The higher the IRR, the more advantageous the project.

IRR calculations are quite burdensome when done manually, as it often requires trial-and-error NPV calculations before a discount rate that yields an NPV value equal to zero can be discovered. However, IRR calculations are very simple to perform using Excel or business calculators.

Basic Steps

Exhibit 25-10 illustrates the IRR method using Excel. For simplicity and comparison purposes, we will use the same after-tax cash flows presented in **Exhibit 25-9**.

In **Exhibit 25-9** the net present value calculations indicate a positive NPV of $10,258. Again, the positive return on capital invested, adjusted for the time value of money, simply indicates that the project will return more than the 10% return sought by Fezzari management. As illustrated in **Exhibit 25-10**, the IRR method provides the actual rate of return of the project, 11.0%. Again, note that the IRR analysis returns a rate greater than the minimum required rate of return of 10%.

IRR Method Using Excel	
Step 1	Enter the initial investment as a negative number [Cell D2]. In our example, the new HVAC system has an installed price of $150,000.
Step 2	In [Cell D3], immediately under the initial investment [Cell D2], enter the sum of net cash after-tax cash flows for Year 1. In our example, Year 1 provides after-tax expense savings of $16,875 and after-tax savings from the depreciation tax shield of $1,406, for a total of $18,281 in after-tax savings.
Step 3	Continue to enter the sum of net after-tax cash flows for Years 2 through 21. Each year's cash flows should be entered in its own cell immediately under the prior year's value of cash flows.
Step 4	Click on **Formulas**.
Step 5	Choose **IRR** from the **Financial** drop-down list.
Step 6	The Formula Builder diolog box will appear. With the cursor in the Value dialog box, highlight the entire array of cells containing the sum of net after-tax cash flows. In **Exhibit 25-10**, this array would be (D2:D23).
Step 7	Hit **Enter** and the result will appear in the cell. The result is in the Internal Rate of Return (IRR) and is 11%.

	A	B	C	D
Exhibit 25-10	**Internal Rate of Return (IRR) Example**			
1	Year	After-Tax Expense Savings	Tax-Savings from Depr. Tax Shield	Sum of Net After-Tax Cash Flows
2	0			$(150,000)
3	1	$16,875	$1,406	18,281
4	2	16,875	2,707	19,582
5	3	16,875	2,504	19,379
6	4	16,875	2,317	19,192
7	5	16,875	2,143	19,018
8	6	16,875	1,982	18,857
9	7	16,875	1,833	18,708
10	8	16,875	1,696	18,571
11	9	16,875	1,673	18,548
12	10	16,875	1,673	18,548
13	11	16,875	1,673	18,548
14	12	16,875	1,673	18,548
15	13	16,875	1,673	18,548
16	14	16,875	1,673	18,548
17	15	16,875	1,673	18,548
18	16	16,875	1,673	18,548
19	17	16,875	1,673	18,548
20	18	16,875	1,673	18,548
21	19	16,875	1,673	18,548
22	20	16,875	1,673	18,548
23	21	—	837	837
24				
25	IRR			11.00%
26	Minimum required rate of return			10.00%

11% is the interest rate that makes the initial investment of $150,000 equal to the present value of the investment's net cash flows.

The IRR of 11% indicates that the project will provide a greater return than the minimum required rate of return of 10%.

The Farm Company is considering investing in solar panels to generate enough power to run its irrigation system. The local utility company has agreed to purchase any unused power generated by the Farm Company's new solar panels. Between the new source of revenue and the cost savings provided by the solar panels, the company expects to generate $225,000 per year in net after-tax cash inflows. The solar panels will cost $1,750,000 to purchase and install and have an expected useful life of 15 years with no residual value. Calculate the internal rate of return (IRR) of the capital investment.

YOUR TURN! 25.6

The solution is on page 1202.

Cash Payback Analysis

The **cash payback method** is a form of capital expenditure analysis that evaluates investment proposals in terms of the **cash payback period**. The cash payback period is the time in years that it takes net future after-tax cash inflows to equal the original investment.

Assume that Fezzari received a competing proposal for its new HVAC system. Management is considering purchasing either system A or system B, for which the following data are given:

LO7 **Present** the cash payback and average rate of return methods of capital expenditure analysis.

System	Investment Required	Annual Net After-Tax Cash Inflows	Useful Life
A..............................	$150,000	$17,250	20 years
B..............................	115,000	15,000	15 years

For this illustration, we have assumed that the systems will be depreciated on a straight-line basis for tax purposes, making the annual net cash inflows equal over time. The cash payback period is computed as follows:

$$\frac{\text{Original investment}}{\text{Annual net cash inflows}} = \text{Cash payback in years}$$

Thus, for the two systems, we obtain:

$$\text{System A: } \frac{\$150,000}{\$17,250} = 8.70\text{-year cash payback}$$

$$\text{System B: } \frac{\$115,000}{\$15,000} = 7.67\text{-year cash payback}$$

This analysis shows that system A will pay back its required investment in 8.7 years, and system B will take 7.67 years. Because the decision rule in cash payback analysis states that the shorter the payback period, the better, system B would be considered the better investment.

If annual net cash inflows are not equal, the cash payback period is computed by summing the annual cash inflows until the cumulative amount equals the initial investment. For example, refer back to **Exhibit 25-9**. The investment is expected to generate annual net after-tax cash inflows for nine years, as follows:

Year	Annual After-Tax Cash Inflows	Cumulative Cash Payback	Amount Required to Reach $150,000
1......................	$18,281	$ 18,281	$131,719
2......................	19,582	37,863	112,137
3......................	19,379	57,242	92,758
4......................	19,192	76,434	73,566
5......................	19,018	95,452	54,548
6......................	18,857	114,309	35,691
7......................	18,708	133,017	16,983
8......................	18,571	151,588	
9......................	18,548	170,136	

As shown in the amount required to reach $150,000 column, the original investment in the HVAC system will be recovered in cash partway through Year 8. The portion of the year required may be computed by dividing the remaining amount needed by the next year's inflow ($16,983/$18,571 = 0.914). The cash payback period, then, is 7.914 years.

Concern for the payback of investments is quite natural because the shorter a project's payback period, the more quickly the funds invested in that project are recovered and available for other investments. In high-risk investments, the payback period indicates how soon a firm is "bailed out" of an investment should projected cash inflows prove inaccurate.

Concept	→	Method	→	Assessment	TAKEAWAY 25.4
You work for a startup that needs to make quick cash recovery on its capital investments. You are asked to analyze a capital investment project.		The cash payback in years is computed as the original investment divided by the annual net cash flows. If annual net cash inflows are not equal, the cash payback period is determined by summing the annual cash inflows until the cumulative amount equals the initial investment.		The cash payback period is the time in years that it takes net future after-tax cash inflows to equal the original investment. The cash payback is particularly important to new companies or companies that may need a fast recovery of cash.	

The cash payback method is considered less sophisticated than net present value analysis. A primary limitation of cash payback analysis is that the relative profitability of various investments is not specifically considered. Note, for example, that in the previous illustration, system B has the better (shorter) cash payback period. However, its useful life, which is ignored in cash payback analysis, indicates that system B will stop generating cash inflows about seven years beyond payback. In contrast, although system A has a longer payback period, it will generate future cash inflows for over 11 years beyond payback and therefore promises to be more profitable.

Regardless of its failure to consider profitability, cash payback analysis is widely used, probably because of its relative simplicity. It can be useful in conjunction with other analyses or as a preliminary screening device for investment projects under consideration.

Average Rate of Return Analysis

The **average rate of return method** uses accrual accounting information in its calculation, not cash flows. This approach addresses the future impact on the income statement.

This measure is calculated as follows:

$$\text{Average rate of return} = \frac{\text{Average annual net income from investment}}{\text{Average investment}}$$

Note that the focus here is not on after-tax cash flows but on traditional accounting net income.

Assume that system A described earlier requires an initial investment of $150,000, provides $17,250 annual cash inflows from operations, and has a useful life of 20 years. Assuming no salvage value, the accounting annual straight-line depreciation on system A would be ($150,000/20), or $7,500. With an income tax rate of 25%, the average annual net income from the investment would be $7,312, computed as follows:

Cash inflow from operations.	$17,250
Depreciation expense.	7,500
Pre-tax income from investment.	$ 9,750
Income tax expense.	2,438
Net income from investment.	$ 7,312

If the annual net incomes from investment are unequal, we would compute the average annual net income from investment by (1) summing the annual net incomes and (2) dividing by the number of years.

We may calculate average investment simply by adding the beginning and ending investments and dividing by 2. The ending investment is the expected salvage value. In our illustration, system A has no salvage value, so the ending investment is zero. Average investment is therefore $75,000 [($150,000 + $0)/2].

The average rate of return on system A is

$$\frac{\$7,312}{\$75,000} = 9.75\%$$

The decision rule for average rate of return analyses states that the higher the return, the more attractive the investment.

ACCOUNTING IN PRACTICE	**U.S. Business Capital Expenditures**

What are U.S. businesses doing to keep up with their foreign rivals? According to a PwC October 2018 Trendsetter Barometer report, the mean level of investment for Q3 2018 was slightly lower than 5.2 percent of sales. Thirty three percent of respondents are planning for major new investments of capital for business growth over the next twelve months.

https://www.pwc.com/us/en/private-company-services/publications/assets/pwc-trendsetter-barometer-q3-2018-chart-pack.pdf

According to the U.S. Census Bureau's 2017 Capital Spending Report, capital spending by U.S. nonfarm businesses increased 31.8% over the five-year period from 2011 to 2015 and 2.5% (or $40.7 billion) from 2014 to 2015. Capital spending between 2014 and 2015 in the U.S. manufacturing sector was up 3.7% (or $8.5 billion), construction was up 10.6% (or $3.2 billion), educational services was up 21.7% (or $5.6 billion), and healthcare and social assistance were up 5.2% (or $4.6 billion).

https://www.census.gov/library/publications/2017/econ/2017-csr.html

As an approach to capital expenditure analysis, the average rate of return method is often defended as being most easily understood by management personnel who are accustomed to thinking in accounting terms and concepts. It has two major limitations, however. First, the calculations rely heavily on accounting computations of net income and depreciation, and are thus subject to arbitrary choices, such as the selection of a depreciation method. Second, average rate of return calculations do not consider the time value of money. Future cash flows are treated the same as current cash flows. Our discussion of net present value analysis illustrates the often substantial differences between future values and related present values discounted by even moderate interest rates.

As an example of how deceptive the average annual income figures used in average rate of return computations can be, consider three investment proposals, each of which requires a $40,000 initial investment (with a zero salvage value) and promises the annual cash inflows shown in **Exhibit 25-11**. Note that cash flows are concentrated in Year 1 in proposal A, are uniform in proposal B, and are concentrated in Year 5 in proposal C. Because average rate of return calculations fail to consider the timing of cash flows from operations, these three proposals would have identical 10% average rates of return and therefore would be considered equally attractive. Such an implication is hardly defensible in view of the substantial differences in the relative net present values of the operating cash flows. In our illustration, the difference between the present values of A and C is $12,968, an amount equal to 41% of the present value of C.

ACCOUNTING IN PRACTICE	**Sensitivity Analysis**

In practice, NPV projects often involve the use of sensitivity analysis. Sensitivity analysis provides a method of assessing the amount of risk involved in a proposed project. Sensitivity analysis also involves calculating the impact of variations on different quantifiable components of a project, helping management identify potential pitfalls. Management may also use sensitivity analysis to identify components (such as the discount rate or yearly cash inflows) of a plan that, when changed even slightly, will most impact the outcome of a project.

Exhibit 25-11	Present Value Comparison of Equal Annual Average Incomes			
	A	B	C	D
1			Proposals	
			A	B	C
2	Annual net cash inflows:			
3	Year 1	$46,000	$10,000	$ 1,000
4	Year 2	1,000	10,000	1,000
5	Year 3	1,000	10,000	1,000
6	Year 4	1,000	10,000	1,000
7	Year 5	1,000	10,000	46,000
8	Aggregate net cash inflows	$50,000	$50,000	$50,000
9	Average annual net cash inflows ($50,000/5)	$10,000	$10,000	$10,000
10	Less depreciation ($40,000/5)	8,000	8,000	8,000
11	Average annual net income	$ 2,000	$ 2,000	$ 2,000
12	Average rate of return on investment			
13	$2,000/[($40,000 + $0)/2]	10%	10%	10%
14	Present value of net cash inflows at 10%	$44,700	$37,908	$31,732

Capital Budgeting: A Complex Subject

Because it incorporates aspects of such fields as economics, finance, business management, and accounting, the subject of capital budgeting is too complex to treat comprehensively in an introductory accounting book. In this chapter, we have simply provided some insight into problem-solving techniques in capital budgeting by stating decision rules in their simplest form, showing the relevance of present value concepts and after-tax cash flows, and creating an awareness of the potentials and limitations of several widely used approaches to capital expenditure analysis. The illustrations have highlighted key relationships. The rudiments presented here should serve as a basis for further study in finance and economics courses.

The Farm Company is considering investing in solar panels to generate enough power to run its irrigation system. The local utility company has agreed to purchase any unused power generated by the Farm Company's new solar panels. Between the new source of revenue and the cost savings provided by the solar panels, the company expects to generate $225,000 per year in net after-tax cash inflows. The solar panels will cost $1,750,000 to purchase and install and have an expected useful life of 15 years with no residual value. Calculate the cash payback period.

YOUR TURN! 25.7

The solution is on page 1202.

SERVICE INDUSTRY IN FOCUS

Environmental Business Consultants (EBC) is deciding whether to purchase an office building. EBC has found a three-story Class A office building in San Jose, California, with a purchase price of $2,000,000. Only two stories are needed to operate, and as such EBC can lease out the lower story, which consists of 3,000 square feet of floor space. The average full-service market lease rate for Class A office buildings in San Jose is $40 per square foot per year. In order to prepare the lower floor for lease, EBC will need to spend $250,000 on leasehold improvements. The building will be useful for 30 years and will be depreciated on a straight-line basis. EBC's income tax rate is 25% and its cost of capital is 10%.

SERVICE AND MERCHANDISING

The following table summarizes the cash flows from purchasing the building and leasing out the lower floor:

Initial outflows:	
Building purchase	$(2,000,000)
Leasehold improvements	(250,000)
Total initial outflows	$(2,250,000)
Annual cash flows:	
Lease revenue*	$ 120,000
Total annual inflows	$ 120,000
Annual depreciation expense**	$ 75,000
Building useful life (years)	30
Income tax rate	25%
Cost of capital	10%

* 3,000 sq. ft. × $40/sq. ft. per year

** $2,250,000/30 years

Required

Perform a capital expenditure analysis to decide whether EBC should purchase the building, analyzing the net present value as well as payback period and average rate of return.

Solution

Net present value analysis:		
Annual after-tax revenues	$120,000 × (1 − 25%)	$ 90,000
Tax shield from depreciation	$75,000 × 25%	18,750
Annual net cash inflows		$ 108,750
Present value of the annual cash inflows	($108,750 × 9.42691)	$ 1,025,176
Net present value		
Initial outflows		$(2,250,000)
PV of future cash flows		1,025,176
NPV		$(1,224,824)

Cash payback analysis:	
Initial cash outflow	$2,250,000
Divided by the annual net cash inflows ...	$108,750
Payback period	20.69 years

Average rate of return analysis:		
Annual revenues		$ 120,000
Annual expenses		(75,000)
Average annual net income		45,000
Income tax @ 25%		(11,250)
Average after-tax net income		33,750
Initial investment		2,250,000
Ending investment		0
Average investment	($2,250,000 + $0)/2	$ 1,125,000
Average rate of return	$33,750/$1,125,000	3.0%

Based on the negative NPV, the long cash payback period and the small average rate of return, EBC should *not* purchase the building for $2,000,000.

Carolina Company is evaluating a possible $150,000 investment in equipment that would increase cash flows from operations for four years. The equipment will have no salvage value.

The income tax rate is 30%. Carolina uses a 15% hurdle rate when using net present value analysis. Other information regarding the proposal is as follows:

	Year 1	Year 2	Year 3	Year 4
Cash inflow from operations (pre-tax)	$60,000	$87,000	$42,000	$40,000
Depreciation on tax return	50,000	67,000	22,000	11,000
Depreciation in financial statements	37,500	37,500	37,500	37,500
Net income from investment	15,750	34,650	3,150	1,750
PV Factor @ 15%	0.86957	0.75614	0.65752	0.57175

Required

a. What are the annual net after-tax cash inflows from this proposal?
b. Compute the net present value and indicate whether it is positive or negative (round amounts to nearest dollar).
c. Compute the cash payback period.
d. Compute the average rate of return.

Solution

a. We may compute the individual after-tax cash effects by multiplying (1) the cash inflow from operations by 70% (that is, 1 – Income tax rate) and (2) the tax return depreciation by 30% (that is, the income tax rate). Combining the individual after-tax cash effects gives the annual net after-tax cash inflows:

Year 1:	$60,000 × 70% = $42,000		Year 3:	$42,000 × 70% = $29,400
	50,000 × 30% = 15,000			22,000 × 30% = 6,600
	After-tax cash flow $57,000			After-tax cash flow $36,000

Year 2:	$87,000 × 70% = $60,900		Year 4:	$40,000 × 70% = $28,000
	67,000 × 30% = 20,100			11,000 × 30% = 3,300
	After-tax cash flow $81,000			After-tax cash flow $31,300

Alternatively, we may compute the net after-tax cash inflows by subtracting the cash income tax payments from the cash inflows from operations. The annual cash income tax payments are 30% of the cash inflow from operations less the tax return depreciation.

	Year 1	Year 2	Year 3	Year 4
Cash inflow from operations	$60,000	$87,000	$42,000	$40,000
Cash payment for income taxes	3,000	6,000	6,000	8,700
After-tax cash flows	$57,000	$81,000	$36,000	$31,300

b.

Year	Annual Net After-Tax Cash Inflows	PV Factor	Present Value
1	$57,000	0.86957	$ 49,565
2	81,000	0.75614	61,247
3	36,000	0.65752	23,671
4	31,300	0.57175	17,896
	Total present value		152,379
	Investment required in equipment		150,000
	Net positive present value		$ 2,379

c. The cash payback period is 2 1/3 years, computed as follows:

Year	Annual Net After-Tax Cash Inflows	Cumulative Cash Payback	
1	$57,000	$ 57,000	
2	81,000	138,000	
3	36,000	150,000	(requires 1/3 of $36,000 to reach $150,000)
4	31,300		

d.

Annual net income from investment:	Year 1	$15,750
	Year 2	34,650
	Year 3	3,150
	Year 4	1,750
	Total	$55,300

Average annual net income from investment: $55,300/4 = $13,825
Average investment: ($150,000 + $0)/2 = $75,000
Average rate of return: $13,825/$75,000 = 18.4%

SUMMARY OF LEARNING OBJECTIVES

LO1   Introduce and illustrate the elements of capital budgeting. (p. 1160)

- Capital budgeting is the planning of long-lived asset investments. Capital expenditure analysis basically examines how well prospective future returns justify related current investments.
- Most capital expenditures have three stages: (1) initial investment, (2) operational cash flows, and (3) project termination.

LO2   Discuss required rates of return and the time value of money. (p. 1162)

- Cost of capital is a measure of the firm's cost for investment capital; it usually represents the minimum acceptable return for investment opportunities.
- The time value of money concept recognizes that the further into the future cash flows occur, the less current economic worth they have.
- The difference between present and future values is a function of interest rates and time periods.

LO3   Demonstrate the use of present value factors to perform time value of money calculations. (p. 1165)

- Present value factor tables enable us to compute the present values of future cash flows at appropriate interest rates.
- The present value calculations used most frequently in capital budgeting are those for future single-sum flows and end-of-period annuity flows.
- The present value of a single sum calculation is used to determine the present value of sporadic cash flows when the returns expected on an investment, or the expenditures it requires, are unequal amounts or are expected at irregular intervals during or at the end of the life of the investment. The formula for the present value of a single sum is PV = FV × PV table factor.
- The present value of an annuity is used to determine the present value of cash flows that are the same each period over two or more equal periods. The formula for the present value of an annuity is PV = PMT × PV table factor.

LO4   Explain and illustrate the determination of after-tax cash flows. (p. 1167)

- After-tax cash flows probably represent the most relevant measure of the prospective returns of proposed investments.
- We convert cash flows from revenues and expenses into after-tax amounts by multiplying them by (1 − Income tax rate).

- Depreciation deductions shield revenues from taxation, referred to as a tax shield. We convert depreciation deductions into their after-tax cash flow effect by multiplying the deduction by the applicable income tax rate.

Describe the net present value method of capital expenditure analysis. (p. 1171)   **LO5**

- Net present value analysis compares the present value of net future cash flow returns with the investment. Projects having zero or positive net present value are acceptable.
- Alternative investment proposals may be compared in terms of their excess present value index; the higher the index, the more attractive is the proposal.

Demonstrate the internal rate of return method of capital expenditure analysis. (p. 1177)   **LO6**

- Internal rate of return (IRR) is the interest rate that makes the net present value (NPV) of all cash flows (both positive and negative) from an investment equal to zero.
- The IRR represents the expected rate of return that will be earned on a capital investment.

Present the cash payback and average rate of return methods of capital expenditure analysis. (p. 1179)   **LO7**

- Cash payback analysis measures the time in years necessary for the net future after-tax cash flows to equal the original investment. In this type of analysis, the shorter the payback period, the more attractive is the investment.
- Average rate of return analysis compares the annual average net income with the average investment. The higher this ratio is, the more attractive is the investment.
- Cash payback analysis fails to consider the relative profitability of alternative projects. Average rate of return analysis fails to consider the time value of money.

Concept ➡	Method ➡	Assessment	SUMMARY
Can a firm determine the cost of acquiring resources to fund capital investment decisions?	Use the weighted average cost of capital to determine the cost of aquiring capital by issuing stock, using retained earnings, borrowings, or a combination of therof.	At a minimum, capital investments should provide a rate of return at least as high as a firm's weighted average cost of capital.	**TAKEAWAY 25.1**
What is the time value of money?	Money available at the present time is worth more than the identical sum in the future due to its potential earning capacity. That is, the provided money can earn interest.	The time value of money explains why interest is paid or earned. Interest, whether it is on a deposit or debt, compensates the depositor or lender for the time value of money.	**TAKEAWAY 25.2**
You have been asked to calculate the NPV of a potential investment in a new piece of machinery used in your company's manufacturing process.	Perform NPV Analysis: • Step 1: Identify the initial investment. • Step 2: Calculate the annual cash flows. • Step 3: Project any termination values. • Step 4: Perform present value calculations. • Step 5: Calculate the net present value.	The calculated NPV is then compared to the company's minimum required rate of return. However, rather than accept or reject the project outright, this may provide a basis to review the underlying assumptions of the analysis.	**TAKEAWAY 25.3**

continued

continued from previous page

SUMMARY	Concept ⟶	Method ⟶	Assessment
TAKEAWAY 25.4	You work for a startup that needs to make quick cash recovery on its capital investments. You are asked to analyze a capital investment project.	The cash payback in years is computed as the original investment divided by the annual net cash flows. If annual net cash inflows are not equal, the cash payback period is determined by summing the annual cash inflows until the cumulative amount equals the initial investment.	The cash payback period is the time in years that it takes net future after-tax cash inflows to equal the original investment. The cash payback is particularly important to new companies or companies that may need a fast recovery of cash.

KEY TERMS

Annuity (p. 1166)

Average rate of return method (p. 1181)

Buffer margin (p. 1163)

Capital budgeting (p. 1160)

Cash payback method (p. 1179)

Cash payback period (p. 1179)

Cost of capital (p. 1162)

Excess present value index (p. 1177)

Hurdle rate (p. 1163)

Internal rate of return (IRR) (p. 1178)

Net present value method (p. 1171)

Rate of return (p. 1162)

Tax shield (p. 1168)

Time value of money (p. 1164)

Weighted average cost of capital, or WACC (p. 1163)

Assignments with the 🔵 logo in the margin are available in Ḃusiness Course.
See the Preface of the book for details.

SELF-STUDY QUESTIONS

(Answers to Self-Study Questions are at the end of this chapter.)

LO2 **1.** **A firm's cost of acquiring the funds for capital investment projects is known as the**
  a. Payback period.   *c.* Cost of capital.
  b. Rate of return.   *d.* Time value of money.

LO2 **2.** **All other things remaining the same, when the interest rate used to discount future values increases, present values**
  a. Decrease.
  b. Increase in proportion to the interest rate increase.
  c. Remain the same.
  d. Increase but not in proportion to the interest rate increase.

LO4 **3.** **Although depreciation is a noncash expense, it does have an indirect effect on cash flows because it shelters an equal amount of income from income taxes. This feature is known as a**
  a. Buffer margin.   *c.* Depreciation flow.
  b. Cash payback.   *d.* Tax shield.

LO5 **4.** **Blaine Company is considering four investment proposals, each requiring the same amount of initial cash investment. The excess present value index for each proposal is listed below. Using the index as a selection criterion, identify the index of the most attractive proposal.**
  a. 90   *c.* 110
  b. 100   *d.* 115

LO6 **5.** **Using internal rate of return, a project is rejected if the IRR**
  a. Is less than the required rate of return.
  b. Is equal to the required rate of return.
  c. Is greater than the cost of capital.
  d. Is greater than the required rate of return.
  e. Produces an NPV equal to zero.

6. The primary limitation of the cash payback method is that it   LO7
   a. Uses before-tax cash flows.
   b. Identifies the length of time it will take to recover the investment outlay in cash.
   c. Ignores the profitability of one investment project as compared to another.
   d. Involves a more sophisticated analysis than the net present value method.

QUESTIONS

1. What is capital budgeting?   LO1
2. List three reasons why capital budgeting decisions are often important.   LO1
3. What are the three stages typical of most investments in plant and equipment?   LO1
4. Briefly describe the concept of weighted average cost of capital.   LO2
5. In what sense does the cost of capital limit a firm's investment considerations? LO2
6. A company plans to accumulate 75% of its needed investment capital by issuing bonds having a capital LO2
    cost percentage of 12%; the balance will be raised by issuing stock having a capital cost percentage of
    16%. What would be the weighted average cost of capital for the total amount of capital?
7. Briefly describe the concept of the time value of money.   LO2
8. You have the right to receive $30,000 at the end of each of the next four years, and money is worth 8%. LO3
    Using the PV tables, your financial calculator, or Excel, compute the present value of this annuity.
9. A rich uncle allows you to stipulate which of two ways you receive your inheritance: LO3

    a. $850,000 one year after his death or
    b. $250,000 on his death and $200,000 each year at the end of the first, second, and third years
        following his death. If money is worth 10%, what is the relative advantage of the more attractive
        alternative?

10. You can settle a debt with either a single payment now of $30,000 or with payments of $8,000 at the end LO3
    of each of the next five years. If money is worth 10%, what is the relative advantage of the most attractive
    alternative? If money is worth 12%, would your answer change? Why?

11. Explain how to convert before-tax cash operating expenses and depreciation deductions into after-tax LO4
    amounts.

12. What is meant by the term *depreciation tax shield*?   LO4
13. What amounts are compared in net present value analysis? State the related decision rule. LO3, 5
14. What is an excess present value index?   LO5
15. Briefly describe the concept of internal rate of return.   LO6
16. Define cash payback period, state the related decision rule, and specify an important limitation of this LO7
    analysis.
17. Define average rate of return, state the related decision rule, and specify an important limitation of this LO7
    analysis.

SHORT EXERCISES

SE25-1.   The following schedule reflects the incremental costs and revenues for a capital project. The com- LO4
              pany uses straight-line depreciation. The interest expense reflects an allocation of interest on the
              amount of this investment, based on the company's weighted average cost of capital.

Revenues		$650,000
Direct costs	$270,000	
Variable overhead	50,000	
Fixed overhead	20,000	
Depreciation	70,000	
General & administrative	40,000	
Interest expense	8,000	
Total costs		458,000
Net profit before taxes		$192,000

The annual cash flow from this investment, before tax considerations, would be

a. $192,000.   c. $262,000.
b. $200,000.   d. $270,000.

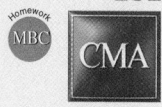

LO2   SE25-2. An accountant for Stability Inc. must calculate the weighted average cost of capital of the corporation using the following information.

		Interest Rate
Accounts payable	$35,000,000	0
Long-term debt	10,000,000	8%
Common stock	10,000,000	15%
Retained earnings	5,000,000	18%

What is the weighted average cost of capital of Stability?

a. 6.88%   c. 10.25%
b. 8.00%   d. 12.80%

LO2   SE25-3. Kielly Machines Inc. is planning an expansion program estimated to cost $100 million. Kielly is going to raise funds according to its target capital structure shown below.

Debt	0.30
Preferred stock	0.24
Equity	0.46

Kielly had net income available to common shareholders of $184 million last year of which 75% was paid out in dividends. The company has a marginal tax rate of 40%.

Additional data:

- The before-tax cost of debt is estimated to be 11%.
- The market yield of preferred stock is estimated to be 12%.
- The after-tax cost of common stock is estimated to be 16%.

What is Kielly's weighted average cost of capital?

a. 12.22%   c. 13.54%
b. 13.00%   d. 14.00%

LO3, 4   SE25-4. Which one of the following items is **least** likely to directly impact an equipment replacement capital expenditure decision?

a. The net present value of the equipment that is being replaced.
b. The depreciation rate that will be used for tax purposes on the new asset.
c. The amount of additional accounts receivable that will be generated from increased production and sales.
d. The sales value of the asset that is being replaced.

LO3   SE25-5. Wilcox Corporation won a settlement in a lawsuit and was offered four different payment alternatives by the defendant's insurance company. A review of interest rates indicates that 8% is appropriate for analyzing this situation. Ignoring any tax considerations, which one of the following four alternatives should the controller recommend to Wilcox management?

a. $135,000 now
b. $40,000 per year at the end of each of the next four years
c. $5,000 now and $20,000 per year at the end of each of the next ten years
d. $5,000 now and $5,000 per year at the end of each of the next nine years, plus a lump-sum payment of $200,000 at the end of the tenth year

LO5   SE25-6. Allstar Company invests in a project with expected cash inflows of $9,000 per year for four years. All cash flows occur at year-end. The required return on investment is 9%. If the project generates a net present value (NPV) of $3,000, what is the amount of the initial investment in the project?

a. $11,253.   c. $26,157.
b. $13,236.   d. $29,160.

SE25-7. Diane Harper, Vice President of Finance for BGN Industries, is reviewing material prepared by her staff prior to the board of directors meeting at which she must recommend one of four mutually exclusive options for a new product line. The summary information below indicates the initial investment required, the present value of cash inflows (excluding the initial investment) at BGN's hurdle rate of 16%, and the internal rate of return (IRR) for each of the four options.

Option	Investment	Present Value of Cash Inflows at 16%	IRR
X.......................................	$3,950,000	$3,800,000	15.5%
Y.......................................	3,000,000	3,750,000	19.0%
Z.......................................	2,000,000	2,825,000	17.5%
W	800,000	1,100,000	18.0%

If there are no capital rationing constraints, which option should Harper recommend?
a. Option X.   c. Option Z.
b. Option Y.   d. Option W.

SE25-8. For a given investment project, the interest rate at which the present value of the cash inflows equals the present value of the cash outflows is called the
a. hurdle rate.   c. internal rate of return.
b. payback rate.   d. cost of capital.

LO6

SE25-9. Quint Company uses the payback method as part of its analysis of capital investments. One of its projects requires a $140,000 investment and has the following projected before-tax cash flows.

LO7

Year 1...	$60,000
Year 2...	$60,000
Year 3...	$60,000
Year 4...	$80,000
Year 5...	$80,000

Quint has an effective 40% tax rate. Based on these data, the after-tax payback period is
a. 1.5.   c. 3.4.
b. 2.3.   d. 3.7.

SE25-10. A company is considering the purchase of a new production machine and is not sure whether the project fulfills its investment objective. The company requires that all investments must have a positive net present value (NPV). The machine costs $100,000 and will be depreciated for tax purposes on a straight-line basis over its useful life of five years. The machine has a $0 salvage value. The project will generate $30,000 of pretax operating cash inflow annually. The company has a 25% effective income tax rate and uses a 10% discount rate for investment projects. Which of the following represents the NPV of the project?
a. $13,724   c. $(14,707)
b. $4,246   d. $(33,661)

LO4, 5

EXERCISES—SET A

E25-1A. Weighted Average Cost of Capital Gardner, Inc., plans to finance its expansion by raising the needed investment capital from the following sources in the indicated proportions and respective capital cost rates.

LO2

Source	Capital Cost Proportion	Capital Cost Rate
Bonds	30%	13%
Preferred stock	10	9
Common stock	50	12
Retained earnings.......................................	10	9
	100%	

Calculate the weighted average cost of capital.

LO3 **E25-2A. Present Value Computations** Assuming that money is worth 8%, compute the present value of

1. $7,000 received 15 years from today.
2. The right to inherit $1,000,000 14 years from now.
3. The right to receive $1,000 at the end of each of the next six years.
4. The obligation to pay $3,000 at the end of each of the next 10 years.
5. The right to receive $5,000 at the end of the seventh, eighth, ninth, and tenth years from today.

LO4

E25-3A. After-Tax Cash Flows For each of the following independent situations, compute the net after-tax cash flow amount by subtracting cash outlays for operating expenses and income taxes from cash revenue. The cash outlay for income taxes is determined by applying the income tax rate to the cash revenue received less the cash and noncash (depreciation) expenses.

	A	B	C
Cash revenue received.	$110,000	$525,000	$275,000
Cash operating expenses paid.	64,000	385,000	165,000
Depreciation on tax return	14,000	32,000	25,000
Income tax rate.	30%	25%	20%

LO4

E25-4A. After-Tax Cash Flows Using the data in E25-3A, (a) calculate the individual after-tax cash flow effect of each relevant item in each independent situation, and (b) sum the individual after-tax cash flows in each situation to determine the overall net after-tax cash flow.

LO4 **E25-5A. Depreciation Tax Shields** Lee & Company has purchased equipment for $200,000. After it is fully depreciated, the equipment will have no salvage value. Lincoln may select either of the following depreciation schedules for tax purposes:

Year	Option 1 Depreciation	Option 2 Depreciation
1	$40,000	$20,000
2	64,000	40,000
3	38,400	40,000
4	23,040	40,000
5	23,040	40,000
6	11,520	20,000

Assuming a 40% tax rate and a 12% desired annual return, compute the total present value of the tax savings provided by these alternative depreciation tax shields. Which depreciation schedule would be more attractive to Lincoln?

LO5 **E25-6A. Net Present Value Analysis** Cooper Corporation must evaluate two capital expenditure proposals. Cooper's hurdle rate is 10%. Data for the two proposals follow.

	Proposal X	Proposal Y
Required investment.	$120,000	$120,000
Annual after-tax cash inflows	24,000	
After-tax cash inflows at the end of years 3, 6, 9, and 12.		72,000
Life of project	12 years	12 years

Using net present value analysis, which proposal is the more attractive? If Cooper has sufficient funds available, should both proposals be accepted?

LO6 **E25-7A. Internal Rate of Return Analysis** Refer to data in E25-6A. What is the internal rate of return for Proposal X? For Proposal Y?

LO7 **E25-8A. Cash Payback** Refer to the data in E25-6A. What is the cash payback period for Proposal X? For Proposal Y?

E25-9A. Average Rate of Return Lakeland Company is considering the purchase of equipment for $175,000. **LO7** The equipment will expand the company's production and increase revenue by $40,000 per year. Annual cash operating expenses will increase by $12,000. The equipment's useful life is 10 years with no salvage value. Lakeland uses straight-line depreciation. The income tax rate is 25%. What is the average rate of return on the investment?

EXERCISES—SET B

E25-1B. Weighted Average Cost of Capital Athens Manufacturing plans to finance its expansion by raising **LO2** the needed investment capital from the following sources in the indicated proportions and respective capital cost rates.

Source	Proportion	Capital Cost Rate
Bonds	45%	12%
Preferred stock	10	14
Common stock	25	8
Retained earnings	20	10
	100%	

Calculate the weighted average cost of capital.

E25-2B. Present Value Computations Assuming that money is worth 12%, compute the present value of **LO3**
1. $6,000 received 15 years from today.
2. The right to inherit $2,000,000 14 years from now.
3. The right to receive $2,000 at the end of each of the next six years.
4. The obligation to pay $1,000 at the end of each of the next 10 years.
5. The right to receive $10,000 at the end of the seventh, eighth, ninth, and tenth years from today.

E25-3B. After-Tax Cash Flows For each of the following independent situations, compute the net after-tax **LO4** cash flow amount by subtracting cash outlays for operating expenses and income taxes from cash revenue. The cash outlay for income taxes is determined by applying the income tax rate to the cash revenue received less the cash and noncash (depreciation) expenses.

SERVICE AND MERCHANDISING

	A	B	C
Cash revenue received	$74,000	$430,000	$210,000
Cash operating expenses paid	48,000	240,000	130,000
Depreciation on tax return	11,000	28,000	18,000
Income tax rate	25%	35%	30%

E25-4B. After-Tax Cash Flows Using the data in E25-3B, (a) calculate the individual after-tax cash flow **LO4** effect of each relevant item in each independent situation, and (b) sum the individual after-tax cash flows in each situation to determine the overall net after-tax cash flow.

SERVICE AND MERCHANDISING

E25-5B. Depreciation Tax Shields Mendota Company has purchased equipment for $100,000. After it is **LO4** fully depreciated, the equipment will have no salvage value. Mendota may select either of the following depreciation schedules for tax purposes:

Year	Option 1 Depreciation	Option 2 Depreciation
1	$20,000	$10,000
2	32,000	20,000
3	19,200	20,000
4	11,520	20,000
5	11,520	20,000
6	5,760	10,000

Assuming a 40% tax rate and a 12% desired annual return, compute the total present value of the tax savings provided by these alternative depreciation tax shields. Which depreciation schedule would be more attractive to Mendota?

LO5 **E25-6B.** **Net Present Value Analysis** Hermson Company must evaluate two capital expenditure proposals. Hermson's hurdle rate is 12%. Data for the two proposals follow.

	Proposal X	Proposal Y
Required investment.	$190,000	$190,000
Annual after-tax cash inflows	42,000	—
After-tax cash inflows at the end of years 3, 6, 9, and 12.	—	126,000
Life of project	12 years	12 years

Using net present value analysis, which proposal do you find to be the more attractive? If Hermson has sufficient funds available, should both proposals be accepted?

LO6 **E25-7B.** **Internal Rate of Return Analysis** Refer to the data in E25-6B. What is the internal rate of return of Proposal X? For Proposal Y?

LO6 **E25-8B.** **Internal Rate of Return Analysis** White Mountain Mining, LLC is considering the purchase of a new piece of machinery. The initial cost of the machine will be $6,250,000 and the machine will have a useful life of five years. The company's hurdle rate is 8%. The following cash flow projections have been made:

Year 1	$1,200,000
Year 2	$1,850,000
Year 3	$2,500,000
Year 4	$1,950,000
Year 5	$1,500,000

Calculate the internal rate of return for the machinery. Should White Mountain purchase the machinery?

LO7 **E25-9B.** **Cash Payback** Refer to the data in E25-6B. What is the cash payback period for proposal X? for proposal Y?

LO7 **E25-10B.** **Average Rate of Return** Thompson Furniture is considering the purchase of equipment for $120,000. The equipment will expand the company's production and increase revenue by $30,000 per year. Annual cash operating expenses will increase by $7,000. The equipment's useful life is 10 years with no salvage value. Thompson uses straight-line depreciation. The income tax rate is 35%. What is the average rate of return on the investment?

PROBLEMS—SET A

LO4 **P25-1A.** **After-Tax Cash Flows** Below is a list of aspects of various capital expenditure proposals that the capital budgeting team of Anchor, Inc., has incorporated into its net present value analyses during the past year. Unless otherwise noted, the items listed are unrelated to each other. All situations assume a 40% income tax rate and an 11% minimum desired rate of return.

1. Pre-tax savings of $4,000 in cash expenses will occur in each of the next three years.
2. A machine is purchased now for $37,000 cash.
3. A long-haul tractor costing $27,000 will be depreciated $9,000, $12,000, $4,050, and $1,950, respectively, on the tax return over four years.
4. Equipment costing $200,000 will be depreciated over five years on the tax return in the following amounts: $25,000; $50,000; $50,000; $50,000; and $25,000.
5. Pre-tax savings of $8,800 in cash expenses will occur in each of the next six years.
6. Pre-tax savings of $7,000 in cash expenses will occur in the first, third, and fifth years from now.
7. The tractor described in aspect 3 will be sold after four years for $5,000 cash.
8. The equipment described in aspect 4 will be sold after four years for $20,000 cash.

Required
Set up an answer form with the two column headings as shown below. Answer each investment aspect separately. Prepare your calculations on a separate paper and key them to each item. The answer to investment aspect 1 is presented as an example.

Investment Aspect 1	**A** **After-Tax Cash Flow** **Effect(s) Inflows (Outflows)**	**B** **Year(s) of** **Cash Flow**
	$2,400	1, 2, 3
Calculations:		
1. Pre-tax cash savings.		$4,000
Less income tax at 40%		1,600
After-tax cash inflow		$2,400

a.   Calculate and record in column A the related after-tax cash flow effect(s). Place parentheses around outflows.
b.   Indicate in column B the timing of each cash flow shown in column A. Use 0 to indicate immediately and 1, 2, 3, 4, and so on for each year involved.

P25-2A. Net Present Value Analysis Champion Company is considering a contract that would require an expansion of its food processing capabilities. The contract covers five years. To provide the required products, Champion would have to purchase additional equipment for $58,000. Champion estimates the contract will provide annual net cash inflows (before taxes) of $21,000. For tax purposes, the equipment will be depreciated as follows: **LO5**

Year 1.	$ 8,000
Year 2.	16,000
Year 3.	16,000
Year 4.	10,000
Year 5.	8,000

Although salvage value is ignored in the tax depreciation calculations, Champion estimates the equipment will be sold for $5,000 after five years.

Required
Assuming a 35% income tax rate and a 10% hurdle rate, compute the net present value of this contract proposal. Using net present value analysis, should Champion accept the contract? (Round amounts to the nearest dollar.)

P25-3A. Net Present Value, Cash Payback, and Average Rate of Return Methods Eastern Incorporated is evaluating a possible $64,000 investment in special tools that would increase cash flows from operations for four years. The tools will have no salvage value. The income tax rate is 40%. Western uses a 12% hurdle rate when using present value analysis. Other information regarding the proposal is as follows: **LO4, 5, 6, 7**

	Year 1	Year 2	Year 3	Year 4
Cash inflow from operations (pre-tax)	$25,000	$45,000	$22,500	$18,000
Depreciation on tax return	21,500	28,100	9,800	4,600
Depreciation in financial statements.	16,000	16,000	16,000	16,000
Net income from investment.	5,400	17,400	3,900	1,200

Required
a.   What are the annual net after-tax cash inflows from this proposal?
b.   Compute the net present value and indicate whether it is positive or negative (round amounts to nearest dollar).
c.   Compute the excess present value index.
d.   Compute the cash payback period.
e.   Compute the average rate of return.
f.   Compute the internal rate of return.

LO5, 6, 7   **P25-4A. Excess Present Value Index and Average Rate of Return**   Highpoint Company is evaluating five different capital expenditure proposals. The company's hurdle rate for net present value analyses is 12%. A 10% salvage value is expected from each of the investments. Information on the five proposals is as follows:

Proposal	Required Investment	Present Value at 12% of After-Tax Cash Flows	Average Annual Net Income from Investment
A....................................	$270,000	$310,030	$37,400
B....................................	200,000	236,780	26,000
C....................................	160,000	173,040	19,200
D....................................	180,000	216,300	27,600
E....................................	128,000	136,990	14,960

Required

a.   Compute the excess present value index for each of the five proposals.

b.   Compute the average rate of return for each of the five proposals.

c.   Assume that Highpoint will commit no more than $500,000 to new capital expenditure proposals. Using the excess present value index, which proposals would be accepted? Using the average rate of return, which proposals would be accepted?

LO4, 5, 6, 7

SERVICE AND MERCHANDISING

P25-5A. Cash Payback, Average Rate of Return, and Net Present Value Methods   Landover Amusement Park is considering the construction of a new facility to house a curved, multistory movie screen. The facility will cost $400,000 and be useful for 10 years, with no salvage value. The facility will be depreciated on a straight-line basis over 10 years on both the books and the tax return. The following annual results are expected if the facility is constructed:

Increase in annual cash revenue		$200,000
Increase in expenses:		
Cash operating expenses.......................................	$80,000	
Depreciation	40,000	120,000
Pretax income...		$ 80,000
Income tax expense (40%)......................................		32,000
Net income		$ 48,000

Landover uses a 12% hurdle rate when analyzing capital expenditure proposals using net present value.

Required

a.   What are the annual net cash flows (net inflows) from this project?

b.   Compute the cash payback period.

c.   Compute the average rate of return.

d.   Compute the net present value and indicate whether it is positive or negative.

e.   Compute the internal rate of return.

f.   Assume that Landover decides to use a 10% hurdle rate when using net present value analysis. Compute the net present value using a 10% hurdle rate and indicate whether it is positive or negative.

LO2, 5   **P25-6A. Weighted Average Cost of Capital and Net Present Value Analysis**   Reed Incorporated is considering a proposal to acquire new equipment for its manufacturing division. The equipment will cost $192,000, be useful for four years, and have a $12,000 salvage value. Reed expects annual savings in cash operating expenses (before taxes) of $68,000. For tax purposes, the annual depreciation deduction will be $64,000, $86,000, $28,000, and $14,000, respectively, for the four years (the salvage value is ignored on the tax return). The income tax rate is 40%.

Reed establishes a hurdle rate for a net present value analysis at the company's weighted average cost of capital plus 1 percentage point. Reed's capital is provided in the following proportions: debt, 50%; common stock, 35%; and retained earnings, 15%. The cost rates for these capital sources are debt, 8%; common stock, 10%; and retained earnings, 12%.

Required

a. Compute Reed's (1) weighted average cost of capital and (2) hurdle rate.

b. Using Reed's hurdle rate, compute the net present value of this capital expenditure proposal. Under net present value analysis, should Reed accept the proposal? (Round amounts to the nearest dollar.)

PROBLEMS—SET B

P25-1B. After-Tax Cash Flows Below is a list of aspects of various capital expenditure proposals that the capital budgeting team of Modern Systems, Inc., has incorporated into its net present value analyses during the past year. Unless otherwise noted, the items listed are unrelated to each other. All situations assume a 30% income tax rate and a 10% minimum desired rate of return.

LO4

1. Pre-tax savings of $5,000 in cash expenses will occur in each of the next three years.
2. A machine is purchased now for $82,000.
3. Special tools costing $45,000 will be depreciated $9,000, $18,000, and $18,000, respectively, on the tax return over a three-year life.
4. A patent purchased for $330,000 will be amortized on a straight-line basis over 15 years on the tax return. No salvage value is expected.
5. Pre-tax savings of $8,000 in cash expenses will occur in each of the next seven years.
6. Pre-tax savings of $5,500 in cash expenses will occur in the first, fourth, and seventh years from now.
7. The special tools described in aspect 3 will be sold after three years for $10,000 cash.
8. A truck with a tax book value of $7,200 after two years will be sold at that time for $4,600.

Required

Set up an answer form with the four column headings as shown below. Answer each investment aspect separately. Prepare your calculations on a separate paper and key them to each item. The answer to investment aspect 1 is presented as an example.

Investment Aspect 1	A After-Tax Cash Flow Effect(s) Inflows (Outflows)	B Year(s) of Cash Flow
	$3,500	1, 2, 3
Calculations:		
1. Pre-tax cash savings.		$5,000
Less income tax at 30%		1,500
After-tax cash inflow		$3,500

a. Calculate and record in column A the related after-tax cash flow effect(s). Place parentheses around outflows.

b. Indicate in column B the timing of each cash flow shown in column A. Use 0 to indicate immediately and 1, 2, 3, 4, and so on for each year involved.

P25-2B. Net Present Value Analysis You have an opportunity to invest in a concession at a world exposition. To use the building and exhibits more fully, the venture is expected to cover a six-year period consisting of a preliminary year, the two years of formal exposition, and a three-year period of reduced operation as a regional exposition.

LO5

The terms of the concession agreement specify the following:

1. At inception, a $60,000 deposit is paid to Global Expo, Inc., the promoting organization. This amount is returned in full at the end of the six years if the operator maintains the concession in order and keeps it open during scheduled hours. The deposit is not tax deductible, nor is its return subject to income taxes.
2. The operator must install certain fixtures that will cost $240,000. The fixtures become the property of Global Expo, Inc., at the end of the six years.

After careful investigation and consultation with local experts, you conclude that the following schedule reflects the estimated pre-tax income of the concession (amounts in thousands of dollars):

	Year 1	Year 2	Year 3	Year 4	Year 5	Year 6
Sales (all cash).....................	$150	$435	$488	$300	$240	$180
Operating expenses:						
Cash...........................	$ 75	$228	$279	$170	$140	$106
Tax depreciation	48	77	46	28	28	13
Total expenses	$123	$305	$325	$198	$168	$119
Pre-tax income.....................	$ 27	$130	$163	$102	$ 72	$ 61

Required

Assuming an income tax rate of 35% and a desired annual return of 12%, what is the net present value of this investment opportunity? What is the maximum amount that could be invested and still earning a 12% annual return? (Round amounts to the nearest dollar.)

LO4, 5, 6, 7   **P25-3B.   Cash Payback, Average Rate of Return, and Net Present Value Methods** At a cash cost of $330,000, Monona, Inc., can acquire equipment that will save $100,000 in annual cash operating expenses. No salvage value is expected at the end of its five-year useful life. Assume the machine will be depreciated over five years on a straight-line basis on both the books and the tax return. The income tax rate is 30% and Monona has a 10% hurdle rate when using a net present value analysis.

Required

a.   What are the annual after-tax cash savings in operating expenses?
b.   What are the annual tax savings from the depreciation tax shield?
c.   Compute the cash payback period.
d.   Compute the average rate of return.
e.   Compute the net present value and indicate whether it is positive or negative (round amounts to nearest dollar).
f.   Compute the excess present value index.
g.   Compute the internal rate of return.

LO5, 6, 7   **P25-4B.   Excess Present Value Index and Average Rate of Return** Swanson Corporation is evaluating five different capital expenditure proposals. The company's hurdle rate for net present value analysis is 12%. A 15% salvage value is expected from each of the investments. Information on the five proposals is as follows:

SERVICE AND
MERCHANDISING

Homework
MBC

Proposal	Required Investment	Net Present Value	Average Annual Net Income from Investment
A...	$ 50,000	$ 8,996	$ 9,100
B...	80,000	5,812	12,000
C...	110,000	27,034	18,300
D...	150,000	7,544	21,500
E...	72,000	15,822	13,960

Required

a.   Compute the excess present value index for each of the five proposals.
b.   Compute the average rate of return for each of the five proposals.
c.   Assume that Swanson will commit no more than $200,000 to new capital expenditure proposals. Using the excess present value index, which proposals would be accepted? Using the average rate of return, which proposals would be accepted?

LO4, 5, 6, 7   **P25-5B.   Cash Payback, Average Rate of Return, and Net Present Value Methods** Lyle Company is considering whether to enter into a franchise agreement that would give the company exclusive distribution rights in a three-state region to a quality line of leisure spas. The franchise agreement will extend eight years and cost $600,000. There is no salvage value. The franchise cost will be amortized on a straight-line basis over eight years on both the books and the tax return. The following annual results are expected if the franchise is acquired:

Increase in annual cash revenue		$230,000
Increase in expenses:		
Cash operating expenses	$95,000	
Amortization	75,000	170,000
Pretax income		$ 60,000
Income tax expense (35%)		21,000
Net income		$ 39,000

Lyle uses a 12% hurdle rate when analyzing capital expenditure proposals using net present value.

Required

a. What are the annual net cash flows (net inflows) from this proposal?
b. Compute the cash payback period.
c. Compute the average rate of return.
d. Compute the net present value and indicate whether it is positive or negative.
e. Assume that Lyle decides to use a 10% hurdle rate when using net present value analysis. Compute the net present value using a 10% hurdle rate and indicate whether it is positive or negative.
f. Compute the internal rate of return.

P25-6B. Weighted Average Cost of Capital and Net Present Value Analysis Manchester Company is con- LO2, 5 sidering a proposal to purchase special equipment at a cost of $740,000. The equipment will be useful for five years and has an expected $60,000 salvage value. Manchester expects annual savings in cash operating expenses (before taxes) of $255,000. For tax purposes, the annual depreciation deduction will be as follows (salvage value is ignored on the tax return):

Year 1	$100,000
Year 2	180,000
Year 3	180,000
Year 4	180,000
Year 5	100,000

The income tax rate is 40%.

Manchester establishes a hurdle rate for a net present value analysis at the company's weighted average cost of capital plus 2 percentage points. Manchester's capital is provided in the following proportions: debt, 70%; common stock, 20%; and retained earnings, 10%. The cost rates for these capital sources are debt, 8%; common stock, 12%; and retained earnings, 10%.

Required

a. Compute Manchester's (1) weighted average cost of capital and (2) hurdle rate.
b. Using Manchester's hurdle rate, compute the net present value of this capital expenditure proposal. Under net present value analysis, should Manchester accept the proposal?

EXTENDING YOUR KNOWLEDGE

EYK25-1. Business Decision Case New Haven Corporation recently identified an investment opportunity involving the purchase of a patent that will permit the company to modify its line of CD recorders. The patent's purchase price is $720,000 and the legal protection it provides will last for five more years; there is no salvage value. However, after preparing the capital expenditure analysis below, New Haven's treasurer has recommended to the company's capital budgeting committee that the investment be rejected. Brad Decker, chairperson of the capital budgeting committee, finds it difficult to accept the treasurer's analysis because he "feels intuitively" that the investment is attractive.

For this reason, he has retained you to review the treasurer's analysis and recommendation. You are provided with the following data and summary of the treasurer's analysis:

1. Required investment: $720,000 cash for the patent to be amortized on a straight-line basis, five-year useful life, with a zero salvage value.
2. Projected cash revenue and operating expenses:

Year	Cash Revenue	Cash Expenses
1	$ 620,000	$240,000
2	560,000	200,000
3	400,000	170,000
4	250,000	80,000
5	200,000	50,000
	$2,030,000	$740,000

3. Source of capital: New Haven plans to raise 10% of the needed capital by issuing bonds, 30% by issuing stock, and the balance from retained earnings. For these sources, the capital cost rates are 8%, 9%, and 10%, respectively. New Haven has a policy of seeking a return equal to the weighted average cost of capital plus 2.5 percentage points as a "buffer margin" for the uncertainties involved.
4. Income taxes: New Haven has an overall income tax rate of 30%.
5. Treasurer's analysis:

Average cost of capital		
(8% + 9% + 10%)/3 = 9%		
Total cash revenue		$2,030,000
Total cash expenses	$740,000	
Total amortization	720,000	
Total operating expenses		1,460,000
Projected net income over five years		$ 570,000
Average annual income		$ 114,000
Present value of future returns		$ 443,420
Required investment		720,000
Negative net present value		$ (276,580)

Recommendation: Reject investment because of insufficient net present value.

Required

a. Review the treasurer's analysis, identifying any questionable aspects and briefly comment on the apparent effect of each such item on the treasurer's analysis.
b. Prepare your own analysis of the investment, including a calculation of the proper cost of capital and hurdle rates, a net present value analysis of the project, and a brief recommendation to Decker regarding the investment (round amounts to nearest dollar).
c. Because of his concern for the uncertainties of the CD recorder business, Decker also has asked you to provide analyses supporting whether or not your recommendation would change
   1. If estimates of projected cash revenue were reduced by 10%.
   2. If the "buffer margin" were tripled from 2.5% to 7.5%.

EYK25-2. **Ethics Case** Sandy Williams is the manager of General Company's cutting department, which employs 70 people. The cutting department desperately needs new equipment to increase productivity and thus avoid the layoff of 25 people. This department is one of four departments being considered for new equipment. The budget committee has announced that only one department's capital request will be approved this year.

Williams works up the cost savings from the new machinery and contacts suppliers to learn the equipment's estimated cost. Williams knows that General Company uses the payback method to evaluate capital projects. The estimated costs for the equipment are extremely high, particularly with all the safety shields recommended by the manufacturer. If one of these recommended safety features, electronic safety sensors not on the current equipment, were left off, the cost would be $200,000 less and the payback period would decrease by three years. If only minimum electronic safety sensors required by the union contract were included, the cost would be $70,000 less and the payback period would decrease by one year.

Required
What are the ethical considerations Sandy Williams faces as she prepares the equipment proposal?

ANSWERS TO SELF-STUDY QUESTIONS:

1. c, (p. 1162)   2. a, (p. 1164)   3. d, (p. 1168)   4. d, (p. 1177)   5. a, (p. 1178)   6. c, (p. 1181)

YOUR TURN! SOLUTIONS

Solution 25.1
Capital budgeting is the planning of major plant and equipment investments. These investments are important because they involve *long-term commitments of significant amounts of capital* and the decisions cannot be easily reversed.

Solution 25.2

Bank loan	45% × 12% =	5.40%
Equity capital	55% × 9% =	4.95%
Weighted average cost of capital		10.35%

Solution 25.3
  a. PV = [$3,000 × 0.71178] + [$5,000 × 0.63552] = $2,135.34 + $3,177.60 = $5,312.94
  b. PV = [$2,000 × 3.03735] = $6,074.70

Solution 25.4
  a. [$90,000 × (1 − 30%)] = $63,000
  b. [$45,000 × (1 − 30%)] = $(31,500)
  c. ($10,000 × 30%) = $3,000
  d. [$5,000 × (1 − 30%)] = $3,500

Solution 25.5

Depreciation tax shield:
    [($350,000 − $15,000)/20 years] × 0.30 = $5,025

After-tax cash inflow:
    [$47,200 × (1 − 0.30)] = $33,040

Total cash inflow:
    ($5,025 + $33,040) = $38,065

Present value of cash flows:
    N = 20; i/YR = 8; PMT = 38,065; PV = $38,065 × 9.81815, so PV = $373,727.88.

NPV:
    ($350,000) + $373,727.88 = $23,727.88

Because the NPV is positive, the company should purchase the building.

Solution 25.6

Year 0	$(1,750,000)
Year 1	$225,000
Year 2	$225,000
Year 3	$225,000
Year 4	$225,000
Year 5	$225,000
Year 6	$225,000
Year 7	$225,000
Year 8	$225,000
Year 9	$225,000
Year 10	$225,000
Year 11	$225,000
Year 12	$225,000
Year 13	$225,000
Year 14	$225,000
Year 15	$225,000
IRR	*9.61%*
Formula in Cell B18 . . .	*=IRR (B1:B16)*

Solution 25.7

Cash Payback Period = $1,750,000/$225,000 = 7.78 years

Appendix A

Columbia Sportswear Company

The complete version of Appendix A and Columbia Sportswear's complete 10-K are available on this book's website.

The law requires publicly traded companies to submit an audited annual report to the Securities and Exchange Commission (SEC) within two months of the close of their fiscal year. This annual report is called Form 10-K. Companies also provide their stockholders with an annual report that contains many of the items included in Form 10-K, along with a letter to the shareholders and public relations and marketing material. Although each annual report is different, all annual reports typically include the following elements:

- Letter to the Shareholders
- Management Discussion and Analysis
- Independent Auditor's Report
- Financial Statements
- Notes to Financial Statements
- Report on Internal Control
- Management's Certification of Financial Statements
- Supplemental Information

In addition, many publicly traded companies also provide a voluntary report on their corporate social responsibility commitments. Because this report is voluntary, its content varies to a greater degree from company to company. Most reports, however, discuss the company's commitment in the areas of both social and environmental impact.

The following pages include excerpts from Columbia Sportswear's 2017 Annual Report. The complete 10-K is available on this book's website. Appendix A is organized as follows:

Occasionally, companies restate financial data for previous years, which may cause specific amounts to change in their financial statements. The data in this appendix reflect the most current financial data available at the time this book was written.

REPORT OF INDEPENDENT AUDITORS

Report of Independent Registered Public Accounting Firm

To the Board of Directors and Shareholders
Columbia Sportswear Company
Portland, Oregon

Opinion on the Financial Statements

We have audited the accompanying consolidated balance sheets of Columbia Sportswear Company and subsidiaries (the "Company") as of December 31, 2017 and 2016 , the related consolidated statements of operations, comprehensive income, equity, and cash flows for each of the three years in the period ended December 31, 2017 , and the related notes and the schedule listed in the Index at Item 15 (collectively referred to as the "financial statements"). In our opinion, the financial statements present fairly, in all material respects, the financial position of the Company as of December 31, 2017 and 2016 , and the results of its operations and its cash flows for each of the three years in the period ended December 31, 2017 , in conformity with accounting principles generally accepted in the United States of America.

We have also audited, in accordance with the standards of the Public Company Accounting Oversight Board (United States) (PCAOB), the Company's internal control over financial reporting as of December 31, 2017 , based on criteria established in *Internal Control - Integrated Framework (2013)* issued by the Committee of Sponsoring Organizations of the Treadway Commission and our report dated February 22, 2018 , expressed an unqualified opinion on the Company's internal control over financial reporting.

Basis for Opinion

These financial statements are the responsibility of the Company's management. Our responsibility is to express an opinion on the Company's financial statements based on our audits. We are a public accounting firm registered with the PCAOB and are required to be independent with respect to the Company in accordance with the U.S. federal securities laws and the applicable rules and regulations of the Securities and Exchange Commission and the PCAOB.

We conducted our audits in accordance with the standards of the PCAOB. Those standards require that we plan and perform the audit to obtain reasonable assurance about whether the financial statements are free of material misstatement, whether due to error or fraud. Our audits included performing procedures to assess the risks of material misstatement of the financial statements, whether due to error or fraud, and performing procedures that respond to those risks. Such procedures included examining, on a test basis, evidence regarding the amounts and disclosures in the financial statements. Our audits also included evaluating the accounting principles used and significant estimates made by management, as well as evaluating the overall presentation of the financial statements. We believe that our audits provide a reasonable basis for our opinion.

/s/   DELOITTE & TOUCHE LLP
Portland, Oregon
February 22, 2018

We have served as the Company's auditor since at least 1994; however, the specific year has not been determined.

FINANCIAL STATEMENTS

COLUMBIA SPORTSWEAR COMPANY

CONSOLIDATED BALANCE SHEETS
(In thousands)

	December 31,	
	2017	**2016**
ASSETS		
Current Assets:		
Cash and cash equivalents (Note 20)	$ 673,166	$ 551,389
Short-term investments (Note 20)	94,983	472
Accounts receivable, net (Note 5)	364,862	333,678
Inventories	457,927	487,997
Prepaid expenses and other current assets	58,559	38,487
Total current assets	1,649,497	1,412,023
Property, plant, and equipment, net (Note 6)	281,394	279,650
Intangible assets, net (Note 7)	129,555	133,438
Goodwill (Note 7)	68,594	68,594
Deferred income taxes (Note 10)	56,804	92,494
Other non-current assets	27,058	27,695
Total assets	$ 2,212,902	$ 2,013,894
LIABILITIES AND EQUITY		
Current Liabilities:		
Accounts payable	$ 252,301	$ 215,048
Accrued liabilities (Note 9)	182,228	142,158
Income taxes payable (Note 10)	19,107	5,645
Total current liabilities	453,636	362,851
Note payable to related party (Note 21)	—	14,053
Other long-term liabilities (Notes 11, 12)	48,735	42,622
Income taxes payable (Note 10)	58,104	12,710
Deferred income taxes (Note 10)	168	147
Total liabilities	560,643	432,383
Commitments and contingencies (Note 13)		
Shareholders' Equity:		
Preferred stock; 10,000 shares authorized; none issued and outstanding	—	—
Common stock (no par value); 125,000 shares authorized; 69,995 and 69,873 issued and outstanding (Note 14)	45,829	53,801
Retained earnings	1,585,009	1,529,636
Accumulated other comprehensive loss (Note 17)	(8,887)	(22,617)
Total Columbia Sportswear Company shareholders' equity	1,621,951	1,560,820
Non-controlling interest (Note 4)	30,308	20,691
Total equity	1,652,259	1,581,511
Total liabilities and equity	$ 2,212,902	$ 2,013,894

See accompanying notes to consolidated financial statements

COLUMBIA SPORTSWEAR COMPANY

CONSOLIDATED STATEMENTS OF OPERATIONS
(In thousands, except per share amounts)

	Year Ended December 31,		
	2017	2016	2015
Net sales	$ 2,466,105	$ 2,377,045	$ 2,326,180
Cost of sales	1,306,143	1,266,697	1,252,680
Gross profit	1,159,962	1,110,348	1,073,500
Selling, general and administrative expenses	910,894	864,084	831,971
Net licensing income	13,901	10,244	8,192
Income from operations	262,969	256,508	249,721
Interest income, net	4,515	2,003	1,531
Interest expense on note payable to related party (Note 21)	(429)	(1,041)	(1,099)
Other non-operating expense	(321)	(572)	(2,834)
Income before income tax	266,734	256,898	247,319
Income tax expense (Note 10)	(154,419)	(58,459)	(67,468)
Net income	112,315	198,439	179,851
Net income attributable to non-controlling interest	7,192	6,541	5,514
Net income attributable to Columbia Sportswear Company	$ 105,123	$ 191,898	$ 174,337
Earnings per share attributable to Columbia Sportswear Company (Note 16):			
Basic	$ 1.51	$ 2.75	$ 2.48
Diluted	1.49	2.72	2.45
Weighted average shares outstanding (Note 16):			
Basic	69,759	69,683	70,162
Diluted	70,453	70,632	71,064

See accompanying notes to consolidated financial statements

COLUMBIA SPORTSWEAR COMPANY

CONSOLIDATED STATEMENTS OF CASH FLOWS
(In thousands)

	Year Ended December 31,		
	2017	2016	2015
Cash flows from operating activities:			
Net income	$ 112,315	$ 198,439	$ 179,851
Adjustments to reconcile net income to net cash provided by operating activities:			
Depreciation and amortization	59,945	60,016	56,521
Loss on disposal or impairment of property, plant, and equipment	1,927	4,805	5,098
Deferred income taxes	44,851	(19,178)	(11,709)
Stock-based compensation	11,286	10,986	11,672
Excess tax benefit from employee stock plans	—	—	(7,873)
Changes in operating assets and liabilities:			
Accounts receivable	(24,197)	36,710	(40,419)
Inventories	46,662	(18,777)	(103,296)
Prepaid expenses and other current assets	(19,241)	(5,452)	4,411
Other assets	931	(5,948)	(2,524)
Accounts payable	30,568	1,483	11,418
Accrued liabilities	11,581	4,847	(2,017)
Income taxes payable	58,702	4,768	(10,994)
Other liabilities	5,798	2,468	4,966
Net cash provided by operating activities	341,128	275,167	95,105
Cash flows from investing activities:			
Purchases of short-term investments	(130,993)	(21,263)	(38,208)
Sales of short-term investments	36,282	21,263	64,980
Capital expenditures	(53,352)	(49,987)	(69,917)
Proceeds from sale of property, plant, and equipment	279	97	144
Net cash used in investing activities	(147,784)	(49,890)	(43,001)
Cash flows from financing activities:			
Proceeds from credit facilities	3,374	62,885	53,429
Repayments on credit facilities	(3,374)	(64,825)	(51,479)
Proceeds from issuance of common stock under employee stock plans	19,946	13,167	17,442
Tax payments related to restricted stock unit issuances	(3,662)	(5,117)	(4,895)
Excess tax benefit from employee stock plans	—	—	7,873
Repurchase of common stock	(35,542)	(11)	(70,068)
Cash dividends paid	(50,909)	(48,122)	(43,547)
Payment of related party note payable	(14,236)	—	—
Net cash used in financing activities	(84,403)	(42,023)	(91,245)
Net effect of exchange rate changes on cash	12,836	(1,635)	(4,647)
Net increase (decrease) in cash and cash equivalents	121,777	181,619	(43,788)
Cash and cash equivalents, beginning of year	551,389	369,770	413,558
Cash and cash equivalents, end of year	$ 673,166	$ 551,389	$ 369,770
Supplemental disclosures of cash flow information:			
Cash paid during the year for income taxes	$ 81,045	$ 70,424	$ 87,350
Cash paid during the year for interest on note payable to related party	685	1,049	1,115
Supplemental disclosures of non-cash investing activities:			
Capital expenditures incurred but not yet paid	3,188	2,710	4,698

See accompanying notes to consolidated financial statements

COLUMBIA SPORTSWEAR COMPANY

CONSOLIDATED STATEMENTS OF EQUITY
(In thousands)

	Columbia Sportswear Company Shareholders' Equity					
	Common Stock			Accumulated Other		
	Shares Outstanding	Amount	Retained Earnings	Comprehensive Income (Loss)	Non-Controlling Interest	Total
BALANCE, JANUARY 1, 2015	69,828	$ 72,700	$ 1,255,070	$ 15,833	$ 11,631	$ 1,355,234
Net income	—	—	174,337	—	5,514	179,851
Other comprehensive loss:						
Unrealized holding losses on available-for-sale securities, net	—	—	—	(6)	—	(6)
Unrealized holding losses on derivative transactions, net	—	—	—	(2,908)	—	(2,908)
Foreign currency translation adjustment, net	—	—	—	(33,755)	(1,132)	(34,887)
Cash dividends ($0.62 per share)	—	—	(43,547)	—	—	(43,547)
Issuance of common stock under employee stock plans, net	835	12,547	—	—	—	12,547
Tax adjustment from stock plans	—	7,925	—	—	—	7,925
Stock-based compensation expense	—	11,672	—	—	—	11,672
Repurchase of common stock	(1,386)	(70,068)	—	—	—	(70,068)
BALANCE, DECEMBER 31, 2015	69,277	34,776	1,385,860	(20,836)	16,013	1,415,813
Net income	—	—	191,898	—	6,541	198,439
Other comprehensive income (loss):						
Unrealized holding losses on available-for-sale securities, net	—	—	—	(2)	—	(2)
Unrealized holding gains on derivative transactions, net	—	—	—	686	157	843
Foreign currency translation adjustment, net	—	—	—	(2,465)	(2,020)	(4,485)
Cash dividends ($0.69 per share)	—	—	(48,122)	—	—	(48,122)
Issuance of common stock under employee stock plans, net	596	8,050	—	—	—	8,050
Stock-based compensation expense	—	10,986	—	—	—	10,986
Repurchase of common stock	—	(11)	—	—	—	(11)
BALANCE, DECEMBER 31, 2016	69,873	53,801	1,529,636	(22,617)	20,691	1,581,511
Net income	—	—	105,123	—	7,192	112,315
Other comprehensive income (loss):						
Unrealized holding losses on derivative transactions, net	—	—	1,159	(17,489)	(516)	(16,846)
Foreign currency translation adjustment, net	—	—	—	31,219	2,941	34,160
Cash dividends ($0.73 per share)	—	—	(50,909)	—	—	(50,909)
Issuance of common stock under employee stock plans, net	787	16,284	—	—	—	16,284
Stock-based compensation expense	—	11,286	—	—	—	11,286
Repurchase of common stock	(665)	(35,542)	—	—	—	(35,542)
BALANCE, DECEMBER 31, 2017	69,995	$ 45,829	$ 1,585,009	$ (8,887)	$ 30,308	$ 1,652,259

See accompanying notes to consolidated financial statements

Appendix B

Financial Statements for Under Armour

The complete annual report for Under Armour is available on this book's website.

Under Armour, Inc. and Subsidiaries

Consolidated Balance Sheets
(In thousands, except share data)

	December 31, 2017	December 31, 2016
Assets		
Current assets		
Cash and cash equivalents	$ 312,483	$ 250,470
Accounts receivable, net	609,670	622,685
Inventories	1,158,548	917,491
Prepaid expenses and other current assets	256,978	174,507
Total current assets	2,337,679	1,965,153
Property and equipment, net	885,774	804,211
Goodwill	555,674	563,591
Intangible assets, net	46,995	64,310
Deferred income taxes	82,801	136,862
Other long term assets	97,444	110,204
Total assets	$4,006,367	$3,644,331
Liabilities and Stockholders' Equity		
Current liabilities		
Revolving credit facility, current	$ 125,000	$ —
Accounts payable	561,108	409,679
Accrued expenses	296,841	208,750
Current maturities of long term debt	27,000	27,000
Other current liabilities	50,426	40,387
Total current liabilities	1,060,375	685,816
Long term debt, net of current maturities	765,046	790,388
Other long term liabilities	162,304	137,227
Total liabilities	1,987,725	1,613,431
Commitments and contingencies (see Note 6)		
Stockholders' equity		
Class A Common Stock, $0.0003 1/3 par value; 400,000,000 shares authorized as of December 31, 2017, and 2016; 185,257,423 shares issued and outstanding as of December 31, 2017, and 183,814,911 shares issued and outstanding as of December 31, 2016.	61	61
Class B Convertible Common Stock, $0.0003 1/3 par value; 34,450,000 shares authorized, issued and outstanding as of December 31, 2017, and December 31, 2016.	11	11
Class C Common Stock, $0.0003 1/3 par value; 400,000,000 shares authorized as of December 31, 2017, and 2016; 222,375,079 shares issued and outstanding as of December 31, 2017, and 220,174,048 shares issued and outstanding as of December 31, 2016.	74	73
Additional paid-in capital	872,266	823,484
Retained earnings	1,184,441	1,259,414
Accumulated other comprehensive loss	(38,211)	(52,143)
Total stockholders' equity	2,018,642	2,030,900
Total liabilities and stockholders' equity	$4,006,367	$3,644,331

See accompanying notes.

Under Armour, Inc. and Subsidiaries

Consolidated Statements of Operations
(In thousands, except per share amounts)

	Year Ended December 31,		
	2017	**2016**	**2015**
Net revenues	$4,976,553	$4,825,335	$3,963,313
Cost of goods sold	2,737,830	2,584,724	2,057,766
Gross profit	2,238,723	2,240,611	1,905,547
Selling, general and administrative expenses	2,086,831	1,823,140	1,497,000
Restructuring and impairment charges	124,049	—	—
Income from operations	27,843	417,471	408,547
Interest expense, net	(34,538)	(26,434)	(14,628)
Other expense, net	(3,614)	(2,755)	(7,234)
Income (loss) before income taxes	(10,309)	388,282	386,685
Income tax expense	37,951	131,303	154,112
Net income (loss)	(48,260)	256,979	232,573
Adjustment payment to Class C capital stockholders	—	59,000	—
Net income (loss) available to all stockholders	(48,260)	197,979	232,573
Basic net income (loss) per share of Class A and B common stock	$ (0.11)	$ 0.45	$ 0.54
Basic net income (loss) per share of Class C common stock	$ (0.11)	$ 0.72	$ 0.54
Diluted net income (loss) per share of Class A and B common stock	$ (0.11)	$ 0.45	$ 0.53
Diluted net income (loss) per share of Class C common stock	$ (0.11)	$ 0.71	$ 0.53
Weighted average common shares outstanding Class A and B common stock			
Basic	219,254	217,707	215,498
Diluted	219,254	221,944	220,868
Weighted average common shares outstanding Class C common stock			
Basic	221,475	218,623	215,498
Diluted	221,475	222,904	220,868

See accompanying notes.

Under Armour, Inc. and Subsidiaries

Consolidated Statements of Stockholders' Equity
(In thousands)

	Class A Common Stock		Class B Convertible Common Stock		Class C Common Stock		Additional Paid-in-Capital	Retained Earnings	Accumulated Other Comprehensive Income (loss)	Total Equity
	Shares	Amount	Shares	Amount	Shares	Amount				
Balance as of December 31, 2014	177,296	$ 59	36,600	$ 12	213,896	71	$508,279	$ 856,687	$(14,808)	$1,350,300
Exercise of stock options	360	—	—	—	360	—	2,852	—	—	2,852
Shares withheld in consideration of employee tax obligations relative to stock-based compensation arrangements	(172)	—	—	—	(172)	—	—	(12,727)	—	(12,727)
Issuance of Class A Common Stock, net of forfeitures	1,996	1	—	—	1,996	1	19,134	—	—	19,136
Class B Convertible Common Stock converted to Class A Common Stock	2,150	1	(2,150)	(1)	—	—	—	—	—	—
Stock-based compensation expense	—	—	—	—	—	—	60,376	—	—	60,376
Net excess tax benefits from stock-based compensation arrangements	—	—	—	—	—	—	45,917	—	—	45,917
Comprehensive income	—	—	—	—	—	—	—	232,573	(30,205)	202,368
Balance as of December 31, 2015	181,630	61	34,450	11	216,080	72	636,558	1,076,533	(45,013)	1,668,222
Exercise of stock options	792	—	—	—	971	—	6,203	—	—	6,203
Shares withheld in consideration of employee tax obligations relative to stock-based compensation arrangements	(199)	—	—	—	(276)	—	—	(15,098)	—	(15,098)
Issuance of Class A Common Stock, net of forfeitures	1,592	—	—	—	—	—	7,884	—	—	7,884
Issuance of Class C Common Stock, net of forfeitures	—	—	—	—	1,852	1	25,834	—	—	25,835
Issuance of Class C dividend	—	—	—	—	1,547	—	56,073	(59,000)	—	(2,927)
Stock-based compensation expense	—	—	—	—	—	—	46,149	—	—	46,149
Net excess tax benefits from stock-based compensation arrangements	—	—	—	—	—	—	44,783	—	—	44,783
Comprehensive income	—	—	—	—	—	—	—	256,979	(7,130)	249,849
Balance as of December 31, 2016	183,815	61	34,450	11	220,174	73	823,484	1,259,414	(52,143)	2,030,900
Exercise of stock options	609	—	—	—	556	—	3,664	—	—	3,664
Shares withheld in consideration of employee tax obligations relative to stock-based compensation arrangements	(65)	—	—	—	(78)	—	—	(2,781)	—	(2,781)
Issuance of Class A Common Stock, net of forfeitures	898	—	—	—	—	—	—	—	—	—
Issuance of Class C Common Stock, net of forfeitures	—	—	—	—	1,723	1	7,852	—	—	7,853
Impact of adoption of accounting standard updates	—	—	—	—	—	—	(2,666)	(23,932)	—	(26,598)
Stock-based compensation expense	—	—	—	—	—	—	39,932	—	—	39,932
Comprehensive income (loss)	—	—	—	—	—	—	—	(48,260)	13,932	(34,328)
Balance as of December 31, 2017	185,257	61	34,450	11	222,375	74	872,266	1,184,441	(38,211)	2,018,642

See accompanying notes.

Under Armour, Inc. and Subsidiaries

Consolidated Statements of Cash Flows
(In thousands)

	Year Ended December 31,		
	2017	2016	2015
Cash flows from operating activities			
Net income (loss)	$ (48,260)	$ 256,979	$ 232,573
Adjustments to reconcile net income (loss) to net cash used in operating activities			
Depreciation and amortization	173,747	144,770	100,940
Unrealized foreign currency exchange rate loss (gains)	(29,247)	12,627	33,359
Impairment charges	71,378	—	—
Amortization of bond premium	254	—	—
Loss on disposal of property and equipment	2,313	1,580	549
Stock-based compensation	39,932	46,149	60,376
Excess tax benefit (loss) from stock-based compensation arrangements	(75)	44,783	45,917
Deferred income taxes	55,910	(43,004)	(4,426)
Changes in reserves and allowances	108,757	70,188	40,391
Changes in operating assets and liabilities (net of acquisitions):			
Accounts receivable	(79,106)	(249,853)	(191,876)
Inventories	(222,391)	(148,055)	(278,524)
Prepaid expenses and other assets	(55,503)	(25,284)	(76,476)
Accounts payable	145,695	202,446	(22,583)
Accrued expenses and other liabilities	109,823	67,754	76,854
Income taxes payable and receivable	(39,164)	(16,712)	(2,533)
Net cash provided by operating activities	234,063	364,368	14,541
Cash flows from investing activities			
Purchases of property and equipment	(281,339)	(316,458)	(298,928)
Purchases of property and equipment from related parties	—	(70,288)	—
Purchase of businesses, net of cash acquired	—	—	(539,460)
Purchases of available-for-sale securities	—	(24,230)	(103,144)
Sales of available-for-sale securities	—	30,712	96,610
Purchases of other assets	(1,648)	(875)	(2,553)
Net cash used in investing activities	(282,987)	(381,139)	(847,475)
Cash flows from financing activities			
Proceeds from long term debt and revolving credit facility	763,000	1,327,601	650,000
Payments on long term debt and revolving credit facility	(665,000)	(1,170,750)	(265,202)
Employee taxes paid for shares withheld for income taxes	(2,781)	(15,098)	(12,728)
Proceeds from exercise of stock options and other stock issuances	11,540	15,485	10,310
Payments of debt financing costs	—	(6,692)	(947)
Cash dividends paid	—	(2,927)	—
Contingent consideration payments for acquisitions	—	(1,505)	
Net cash provided by financing activities	106,759	146,114	381,433
Effect of exchange rate changes on cash and cash equivalents	4,178	(8,725)	(11,822)
Net increase (decrease) in cash and cash equivalents	62,013	120,618	(463,323)
Cash and cash equivalents			
Beginning of period	250,470	129,852	593,175
End of period	$ 312,483	$ 250,470	$ 129,852
Non-cash investing and financing activities			
Change in accrual for property and equipment	$ 10,580	$ 16,973	$ 17,758
Non-cash dividends	—	(56,073)	
Property and equipment acquired under build-to-suit leases	—	—	5,631
Other supplemental information			
Cash paid for income taxes	36,921	135,959	99,708
Cash paid for interest, net of capitalized interest	29,750	21,412	11,176

See accompanying notes.

Appendix C

Financial Statements for LVMH Moet Hennessy-Louis Vuitton

The complete annual report for LVMH Moet Hennessy-Louis Vuitton is available on this book's website.

CONSOLIDATED INCOME STATEMENT

(EUR millions, except for earnings per share)	Notes	2017	2016	2015
Revenue	23	**42,636**	37,600	35,664
Cost of sales		(14,783)	(13,039)	(12,553)
Gross margin		**27,853**	24,561	23,111
Marketing and selling expenses		(16,395)	(14,607)	(13,830)
General and administrative expenses		(3,162)	(2,931)	(2,663)
Income (loss) from joint ventures and associates	7	(3)	3	(13)
Profit from recurring operations	23-24	**8,293**	7,026	6,605
Other operating income and expenses	25	(180)	(122)	(221)
Operating profit		**8,113**	6,904	6,384
Cost of net financial debt		(62)	(83)	(78)
Other financial income and expenses		(117)	(349)	(336)
Net financial income (expense)	26	**(179)**	(432)	(414)
Income taxes	27	(2,318)	(2,109)	(1,969)
Net profit before minority interests		**5,616**	4,363	4,001
Minority interests	17	(487)	(382)	(428)
Net profit, Group share		**5,129**	3,981	3,573
Basic Group share of net earnings per share *(EUR)*	28	**10.21**	7.92	7.11
Number of shares on which the calculation is based		502,412,694	502,911,125	502,395,491
Diluted Group share of net earnings per share *(EUR)*	28	**10.18**	7.89	7.08
Number of shares on which the calculation is based		504,010,291	504,640,459	504,894,946

CONSOLIDATED BALANCE SHEET

ASSETS (EUR millions)	Notes	2017	2016	2015
Brands and other intangible assets	3	13,714	13,335	13,572
Goodwill	4	16,514	10,401	10,122
Property, plant and equipment	6	13,206	12,139	11,157
Investments in joint ventures and associates	7	639	770	729
Non-current available for sale financial assets	8	789	744	574
Other non-current assets	9	868	777	552
Deferred tax		1,738	2,058	1,945
Non-current assets		**47,468**	**40,224**	**38,651**
Inventories and work in progress	10	10,908	10,546	10,096
Trade accounts receivable	11	2,737	2,685	2,521
Income taxes		780	280	384
Other current assets	12	2,919	2,343	2,355
Cash and cash equivalents	14	3,738	3,544	3,594
Current assets		**21,082**	**19,398**	**18,950**
Total assets		**68,550**	**59,622**	**57,601**

LIABILITIES AND EQUITY (EUR millions)	Notes	2017	2016	2015
Share capital	15.1	152	152	152
Share premium account	15.1	2,614	2,601	2,579
Treasury shares and LVMH share-settled derivatives	15.2	(530)	(520)	(240)
Cumulative translation adjustment	15.4	357	1,165	1,137
Revaluation reserves		1,472	1,049	949
Other reserves		19,658	17,965	16,189
Net profit, Group share		5,129	3,981	3,573
Equity, Group share		**28,852**	**26,393**	**24,339**
Minority interests	17	1,408	1,510	1,460
Equity		**30,260**	**27,903**	**25,799**
Long-term borrowings	18	7,046	3,932	4,511
Non-current provisions	19	2,474	2,342	1,950
Deferred tax		3,910	4,137	4,685
Other non-current liabilities	20	9,857	8,498	7,957
Non-current liabilities		**23,287**	**18,909**	**19,103**
Short-term borrowings	18	4,530	3,447	3,769
Trade accounts payable	21.1	4,540	4,184	3,960
Income taxes		763	428	640
Current provisions	19	404	352	421
Other current liabilities	21.2	4,766	4,399	3,909
Current liabilities		**15,003**	**12,810**	**12,699**
Total liabilities and equity		**68,550**	**59,622**	**57,601**

CONSOLIDATED STATEMENT OF CHANGES IN EQUITY

(EUR millions)	Number of shares	Share capital	Share premium account	Treasury shares and LVMH-share settled derivatives	Cumulative translation adjustment	Available for sale financial assets	Hedges of future foreign currency cash flows	Vineyard land	Employee benefit commit-ments	Net profit and other reserves	Group share	Minority interests	Total
								Revaluation reserves				Total equity	
Notes		15.1		15.2	15.4							17	
As of December 31, 2014	507,711,713	152	2,655	(374)	492	207	14	931	(133)	17,819	21,763	1,240	23,003
Gains and losses recognized in equity						645	(103)	(25)	33	25	-	575	130	705
Net profit											3,573	3,573	428	4,001
Comprehensive income		-	-	-	645	(103)	(25)	33	25	3,573	4,148	558	4,706
Stock option plan and similar expenses										35	35	2	37
(Acquisition)/disposal of treasury shares and LVMH share-settled derivatives				23						(13)	10	-	10
Exercise of LVMH share subscription options	552,137		35								35	-	35
Retirement of LVMH shares	(1,124,740)		(111)	111							-	-	-
Capital increase in subsidiaries											-	89	89
Interim and final dividends paid										(1,659)	(1,659)	(229)	(1,888)
Changes in control of consolidated entities										(9)	(9)	1	(8)
Acquisition and disposal of minority interests' shares										5	5	(3)	2
Purchase commitments for minority interests' shares										11	11	(198)	(187)
As of December 31, 2015	507,139,110	152	2,579	(240)	1,137	104	(11)	964	(108)	19,762	24,339	1,460	25,799
Gains and losses recognized in equity						28	23	19	113	(55)	-	128	52	180
Net profit											3,981	3,981	382	4,363
Comprehensive income		-	-	-	28	23	19	113	(55)	3,981	4,109	434	4,543
Stock option plan and similar expenses										39	39	2	41
(Acquisition)/disposal of treasury shares and LVMH share-settled derivatives				(322)						(21)	(343)	-	(343)
Exercise of LVMH share subscription options	907,929		64								64	-	64
Retirement of LVMH shares	(920,951)		(42)	42							-	-	-
Capital increase in subsidiaries											-	41	41
Interim and final dividends paid										(1,811)	(1,811)	(272)	(2,083)
Changes in control of consolidated entities										(5)	(5)	22	17
Acquisition and disposal of minority interests' shares										(56)	(56)	(35)	(91)
Purchase commitments for minority interests' shares										57	57	(142)	(85)
As of December 31, 2016	507,126,088	152	2,601	(520)	1,165	127	8	1,077	(163)	21,946	26,393	1,510	27,903
Gains and losses recognized in equity						(808)	184	171	35	33	-	(385)	(147)	(532)
Net profit											5,129	5,129	487	5,616
Comprehensive income		-	-	-	(808)	184	171	35	33	5,129	4,744	340	5,084
Stock option plan and similar expenses										55	55	7	62
(Acquisition)/disposal of treasury shares and LVMH share-settled derivatives				(50)						(11)	(61)	-	(61)
Exercise of LVMH share subscription options	708,485		53								53	-	53
Retirement of LVMH shares	(791,977)		(40)	40							-	-	-
Capital increase in subsidiaries											-	44	44
Interim and final dividends paid										(2,110)	(2,110)	(260)	(2,370)
Changes in control of consolidated entities										(6)	(6)	114	108
Acquisition and disposal of minority interests' shares										(87)	(87)	(56)	(143)
Purchase commitments for minority interests' shares										(129)	(129)	(291)	(420)
As of December 31, 2017	507,042,596	152	2,614	(530)	357	311	179	1,112	(130)	24,787	28,852	1,408	30,260

CONDENSED CONSOLIDATED FINANCIAL STATEMENTS

CONSOLIDATED CASH FLOW STATEMENT

(EUR millions)	Notes	2017	2016	2015
I. OPERATING ACTIVITIES AND OPERATING INVESTMENTS				
Operating profit		8,113	6,904	6,384
Income/(loss) and dividends from joint ventures and associates	7	25	18	27
Net increase in depreciation, amortization and provisions		2,375	2,143	2,081
Other computed expenses		(43)	(177)	(456)
Other adjustments		(66)	(155)	(91)
Cash from operations before changes in working capital		**10,404**	**8,733**	**7,945**
Cost of net financial debt: interest paid		(70)	(59)	(75)
Tax paid		(2,790)	(1,923)	(1,807)
Net cash from operating activities before changes in working capital		**7,544**	**6,751**	**6,063**
Change in working capital	14.3	(514)	(512)	(429)
Net cash from operating activities		**7,030**	**6,239**	**5,634**
Operating investments	14.4	(2,276)	(2,265)	(1,955)
Net cash from operating activities and operating investments (free cash flow)		**4,754**	**3,974**	**3,679**
II. FINANCIAL INVESTMENTS				
Purchase of non-current available for sale financial assets [a]	8, 13	(125)	(28)	(78)
Proceeds from sale of non-current available for sale financial assets	8	87	91	68
Dividends received		13	6	4
Tax paid related to non-current available for sale financial assets and consolidated investments		-	(461)	(265)
Impact of purchase and sale of consolidated investments	2	(6,306)	310	(240)
Net cash from (used in) financial investments		**(6,331)**	**(82)**	**(511)**
III. TRANSACTIONS RELATING TO EQUITY				
Capital increases of LVMH SE	15.1	53	64	35
Capital increases of subsidiaries subscribed by minority interests	17	44	41	81
Acquisition and disposals of treasury shares and LVMH share-settled derivatives	15.2	(67)	(352)	1
Interim and final dividends paid by LVMH SE	15.3	(2,110)	(1,810)	(1,671)
Tax paid related to interim and final dividends paid		388	(145)	(304)
Interim and final dividends paid to minority interests in consolidated subsidiaries	17	(259)	(267)	(228)
Purchase and proceeds from sale of minority interests	2	(153)	(95)	(4)
Net cash from (used in) transactions relating to equity		**(2,104)**	**(2,564)**	**(2,090)**
Change in cash before financing activities		**(3,681)**	**1,328**	**1,078**
IV. FINANCING ACTIVITIES				
Proceeds from borrowings	14.2	5,753	913	1,008
Repayment of borrowings	14.2	(1,766)	(2,134)	(2,443)
Purchase and proceeds from sale of current available for sale financial assets	8, 13	89	(113) [a]	(3)
Net cash from (used in) financing activities	14.2	**4,076**	**(1,334)**	**(1,438)**
V. EFFECT OF EXCHANGE RATE CHANGES		**(114)**	**(47)**	**(33)**
NET INCREASE (DECREASE) IN CASH AND CASH EQUIVALENTS (I+II+III+IV+V)		**281**	**(53)**	**(393)**
CASH AND CASH EQUIVALENTS AT BEGINNING OF PERIOD	14.1	3,337	3,390	3,783
CASH AND CASH EQUIVALENTS AT END OF PERIOD	14.1	3,618	3,337	3,390
TOTAL TAX PAID		**(2,402)**	**(2,529)**	**(2,376)**

(a) The cash impact of non-current available for sale financial assets used to hedge net financial debt (see Note 18) is presented under "IV. Financing activities", as "Purchase and proceeds from sale of current available for sale financial assets".

Appendix D

Accounting for Investments and Consolidated Financial Statements

Appendix D is available on this book's website.

Appendix E

Accounting and the Time Value of Money

Road Map

LO	Learning Objective	Page	eLecture	Guided Example	Assignments
LO1	Describe the nature of interest and distinguish between simple and compound interest.	E-2	E-2	E-1	EE1A, EE1B
LO2	Calculate future values.	E-3	E-3	E-2, E-3	SS1, EE2A, EE3A, EE6A, EE8A, EE9A, EE11A, EE12A, EE14A, EE2B, EE3B, EE6B, EE8B, EE9B, EE11B, EE12B, EE14B
LO3	Calculate present values.	E-7	E-7	E-4, E-5	SS2, EE4A, EE5A, EE7A, EE10A, EE13A, EE15A, EE4B, EE5B, EE7B, EE10B, EE13B, EE15B

TIME VALUE OF MONEY CONCEPT

Would you rather receive a dollar now or a dollar one year from now? Most people would answer "a dollar now." Intuition tells us that a dollar received now is more valuable than the same amount received sometime in the future. Sound reasons exist for choosing the option of receiving the money sooner rather than later, the most obvious of which concerns risk. Because the future is always uncertain, some event may prevent you from receiving the dollar at a later date. To avoid this risk, we choose the earlier date.

LO1   **Describe** the nature of interest and **distinguish** between simple and compound interest.

A second reason for choosing the earlier date is that the dollar has a time value—that is, the dollar received now could be invested such that one year from now, you could have not only the original dollar but also the interest income on the dollar for the past year. Interest is a payment for the use of money, much like a rent payment for the use of an apartment. Interest is calculated by multiplying an interest rate, usually stated as an annual rate, by a principal amount for a period of time. The principal amount represents the amount to be repaid. The amount of interest can be computed as either a simple interest amount or a compound interest amount.

Time Value of Money: Simple Interest Model

Simple interest involves calculating interest on only the principal amount owed without considering any interest already earned. Simple interest is calculated using the following well-known formula:

$$\textbf{Interest} = \textbf{p} \times \textbf{i} \times \textbf{n}$$

where

    p = principal (total amount)
     i = interest rate for one period
    n = time (number of periods)

For example, if you borrow $3,000 for four years at a simple interest rate of six percent annually, the amount of simple interest would total $720, calculated as $3,000 $\times$ 0.06 $\times$ 4.

Time Value of Money: Compound Interest Model

Compound interest differs from simple interest because it is calculated on both the principal and any previously earned interest that has not been paid. In other words, compound interest involves computing interest on interest, along with the principal amount.

As we can see in **Exhibit E-1**, simple interest only uses the original $3,000 principal to compute the annual interest in each of the four years. In contrast, compound interest uses the entire principal balance, including both the original $3,000 principal and the accumulated interest to date, to compute the next year's interest. This results in increasing interest each year, with the result in **Exhibit E-1** for compound interest yielding a larger ending balance by $67.43.

Because almost all businesses use compound interest, we will assume the use of compound interest in all of the illustrations in this appendix. Simple interest is generally only used in short-term credit arrangements, typically lasting less than a year.

Exhibit E-1	Illustration Comparing Simple Interest to Compound Interest					
	Simple Interest Model			**Compound Interest Model**		
	Interest Calculation	Simple Interest	Principal Balance	Interest Calculation	Compound Interest	Principal Balance
Year 1..	$3,000.00 × 6%	$180.00	$3,180.00	$3,000.00 × 6%	$180.00	$3,180.00
Year 2..	$3,000.00 × 6%	$180.00	$3,360.00	$3,180.00 × 6%	$190.80	$3,370.80
Year 3..	$3,000.00 × 6%	$180.00	$3,540.00	$3,370.80 × 6%	$202.25	$3,573.05
Year 4..	$3,000.00 × 6%	$180.00	$3,720.00	$3,573.05 × 6%	$214.38	$3,787.43
		$720.00			$787.43	

$720.00 ⟶ $67.43 difference ⟵ $787.43

YOUR TURN! E-1

The solution is on page E-15.

MBC GuidedExamples

MBC eLectures

Scott Colin invests $100 in the bank for three years. Calculate the amount of interest that Scott will earn at the end of the three years assuming (1) simple interest at the annual rate of ten percent, and (2) compound interest at the annual rate of ten percent.

FUTURE VALUE OF AN AMOUNT

LO2 **Calculate** future values.

The **future value** of a single sum is the amount that a specified investment will be worth at a future date if invested at a given rate of compound interest. For example, suppose that we decide to invest $6,000 in a savings account that pays six percent annual interest, and that we intend to leave the principal and interest in the account for five years. Assuming that interest is credited to the account at the end of each year, the balance in the account at the end of five years is determined using the following formula:

$$FV = PV \times (1 + i)^n$$

where

$$FV = \text{future value of an amount}$$
$$PV = \text{present value (today's value)}$$
$$i = \text{interest rate for one period}$$
$$n = \text{number of periods}$$

The future value in this case is $8,029, computed as [$6,000 × (1.06)^5] = ($6,000 × 1.33823).

It is often easier to solve time value of money problems with the aid of a time diagram, as illustrated in **Exhibit E-2**. Time diagrams are drawn to show the timing of the various cash inflows and outflows. Note in **Exhibit E-2** that our initial $6,000 cash inflow (the amount deposited in a savings account) allows us to withdraw $8,029 (a cash outflow) at the end of five years.

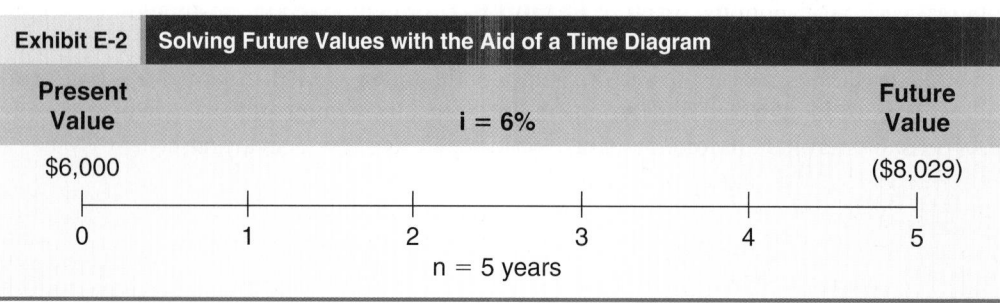

Exhibit E-2	Solving Future Values with the Aid of a Time Diagram

Present Value — i = 6% — Future Value

$6,000 ... ($8,029)

0   1   2   3   4   5

n = 5 years

We can also calculate the future value of a single amount with the use of a table like **Table I**, which presents the future value of a single dollar after a given number of time periods. Simply stated, future value tables provide a multiplier for many combinations of time periods and interest rates that, when applied to the dollar amount of a present value, determines its future value.

Table I	Future Value of $1											
Period	**1.0%**	**2.0%**	**3.0%**	**4.0%**	**5.0%**	**6.0%**	**7.0%**	**8.0%**	**9.0%**	**10.0%**	**11.0%**	**12.0%**
1	1.01000	1.02000	1.03000	1.04000	1.05000	1.06000	1.07000	1.08000	1.09000	1.10000	1.11000	1.12000
2	1.02010	1.04040	1.06090	1.08160	1.10250	1.12360	1.14490	1.16640	1.18810	1.21000	1.23210	1.25440
3	1.03030	1.06121	1.09273	1.12486	1.15763	1.19102	1.22504	1.25971	1.29503	1.33100	1.36763	1.40493
4	1.04060	1.08243	1.12551	1.16986	1.21551	1.26248	1.31080	1.36049	1.41158	1.46410	1.51807	1.57352
5	1.05101	1.10408	1.15927	1.21665	1.27628	1.33823	1.40255	1.46933	1.53862	1.61051	1.68506	1.76234
6	1.06152	1.12616	1.19405	1.26532	1.34010	1.41852	1.50073	1.58687	1.67710	1.77156	1.87041	1.97382
7	1.07214	1.14869	1.22987	1.31593	1.40710	1.50363	1.60578	1.71382	1.82804	1.94872	2.07616	2.21068
8	1.08286	1.17166	1.26677	1.36857	1.47746	1.59385	1.71819	1.85093	1.99256	2.14359	2.30454	2.47596
9	1.09369	1.19509	1.30477	1.42331	1.55133	1.68948	1.83846	1.99900	2.17189	2.35795	2.55804	2.77308
10	1.10462	1.21899	1.34392	1.48024	1.62889	1.79085	1.96715	2.15892	2.36736	2.59374	2.83942	3.10585
11	1.11567	1.24337	1.38423	1.53945	1.71034	1.89830	2.10485	2.33164	2.58043	2.85312	3.15176	3.47855
12	1.12683	1.26824	1.42576	1.60103	1.79586	2.01220	2.25219	2.51817	2.81266	3.13843	3.49845	3.89598
13	1.13809	1.29361	1.46853	1.66507	1.88565	2.13293	2.40985	2.71962	3.06580	3.45227	3.88328	4.36349
14	1.14947	1.31948	1.51259	1.73168	1.97993	2.26090	2.57853	2.93719	3.34173	3.79750	4.31044	4.88711
15	1.16097	1.34587	1.55797	1.80094	2.07893	2.39656	2.75903	3.17217	3.64248	4.17725	4.78459	5.47357
16	1.17258	1.37279	1.60471	1.87298	2.18287	2.54035	2.95216	3.42594	3.97031	4.59497	5.31089	6.13039
17	1.18430	1.40024	1.65285	1.94790	2.29202	2.69277	3.15882	3.70002	4.32763	5.05447	5.89509	6.86604
18	1.19615	1.42825	1.70243	2.02582	2.40662	2.85434	3.37993	3.99602	4.71712	5.55992	6.54355	7.68997
19	1.20811	1.45681	1.75351	2.10685	2.52695	3.02560	3.61653	4.31570	5.14166	6.11591	7.26334	8.61276
20	1.22019	1.48595	1.80611	2.19112	2.65330	3.20714	3.86968	4.66096	5.60441	6.72750	8.06231	9.64629
25	1.28243	1.64061	2.09378	2.66584	3.38635	4.29187	5.42743	6.84848	8.62308	10.83471	13.58546	17.00006
30	1.34785	1.81136	2.42726	3.24340	4.32194	5.74349	7.61226	10.06266	13.26768	17.44940	22.89230	29.95992
35	1.41660	1.99989	2.81386	3.94609	5.51602	7.68609	10.67658	14.78534	20.41397	28.10244	38.57485	52.79962
40	1.48886	2.20804	3.26204	4.80102	7.03999	10.28572	14.97446	21.72452	31.40942	45.25926	65.00087	93.05097
50	1.64463	2.69159	4.38391	7.10668	11.46740	18.42015	29.45703	46.90161	74.35752	117.39085	184.56483	289.00219

Future value tables are used as follows. First, determine the number of interest compounding periods involved (five years compounded annually are five periods, five years compounded semiannually are ten periods, five years compounded quarterly are 20 periods, and so on). The extreme left-hand column indicates the number of periods covered in the table.

Second, determine the interest rate per compounding period. Note that interest rates are usually quoted on an annual or *per year* basis. Therefore, only in the case of annual compounding is the quoted interest rate the interest rate per compounding period. In other cases, the rate per compounding period is the annual rate divided by the number of compounding periods in a year. For example, an interest rate of ten percent per year would be ten percent for one compounding period if compounded annually, five percent for two compounding periods if compounded semiannually, and 2 ½ percent for four compounding periods if compounded quarterly.

Finally, locate the factor that is in the cell at the intersection of the appropriate number of compounding periods and the appropriate interest rate per compounding period. Multiply this factor by the number of dollars involved.

Note the logical progression among the various multipliers in **Table I**. All values are 1.0 or greater because the future value is always greater than the $1 present amount if the interest rate is greater than zero. Also, as the interest rate increases (moving from left to right in the table) or the number of periods increases (moving from top to bottom), the multipliers become larger.

Continuing with our example of calculating the future value of a $6,000 savings account deposit earning six percent annual compound interest for five years, and using the multipliers from Table I, we solve for the future value of the deposit as follows:

Principal × **Factor** = **Future Value**
$6,000 × **1.33823** = **$8,029**

The factor 1.33823 is in the row for five periods and the column for six percent. Note that this factor is the same as the multiplier we determined using the future value formula in our calculation above.

Suppose, instead, that the interest is credited to the savings account semiannually rather than annually. In this situation, there are ten compounding periods, and we use a three percent rate (one-half the annual rate). The future value calculation using the **Table I** multipliers is as follows:

Principal × **Factor** = **Future Value**
$6,000 × **1.34392** = **$8,064**

YOUR TURN! E-2

The solution is on page E-15.

Julie Penn invests $5,000 in the bank for four years. How much will be in her account at the end of the four years if the bank pays compound interest at the annual rate of eight percent?

FUTURE VALUE OF AN ANNUITY

Using future value tables like **Table I**, we can calculate the future value of any single future cash flow or series of future cash flows. One frequent pattern of cash flows, however, is subject to a more convenient calculation. This pattern, known as an **annuity**, can be described as *equal amounts equally spaced over a period*.

For example, assume that $100 is to be deposited at the end of each of the next three years as an annuity into a savings account. When annuity cash flows occur at the end of each period, the annuity is called an **ordinary annuity**. As shown below in **Exhibit E-3**, the future value of this ordinary annuity can be calculated from **Table I** by calculating the future value of each of the three individual deposits and summing them (assuming eight percent annual interest).

Exhibit E-3	Future Value of an Ordinary Annuity					

Future Deposits (ordinary annuity)				FV Multiplier (Table I)		Future Value
Year 1	Year 2	Year 3				
$100			×	1.16640	=	$116.64
	$100		×	1.08000	=	108.00
		$100	×	1.00000	=	100.00
				Total future value		$324.64

Present Value				Future Value
	$100	$100		$100
0	1	2		3

Table II, on the other hand, provides a single multiplier for calculating the future value of a series of future cash flows that reflect an ordinary annuity. Referring to **Table II** in the three periods row and the eight percent interest column, we see that the multiplier is 3.24640, equal to the sum of the three future value factors in **Exhibit E-3**. When applied to the $100 annuity amount, the multiplier gives a future value of $324.64, or $100 × 3.2464. As shown above, the same future value is derived from the several multipliers of **Table I**. For annuities of 5, 10, or 20 years, numerous calculations are avoided by using annuity tables like **Table II**.

Table II	Future Value of an Ordinary Annuity of $1 per Period											
Period	**1%**	**2%**	**3%**	**4%**	**5%**	**6%**	**7%**	**8%**	**9%**	**10%**	**11%**	**12%**
1	1.00000	1.00000	1.00000	1.00000	1.00000	1.00000	1.00000	1.00000	1.00000	1.00000	1.00000	1.00000
2	2.01000	2.02000	2.03000	2.04000	2.05000	2.06000	2.07000	2.08000	2.09000	2.10000	2.11000	2.12000
3	3.03010	3.06040	3.09090	3.12160	3.15250	3.18360	3.21490	3.24640	3.27810	3.31000	3.34210	3.37440
4	4.06040	4.12161	4.18363	4.24646	4.31013	4.37462	4.43994	4.50611	4.57313	4.64100	4.70973	4.77933
5	5.10101	5.20404	5.30914	5.41632	5.52563	5.63709	5.75074	5.86660	5.98471	6.10510	6.22780	6.35285
6	6.15202	6.30812	6.46841	6.63298	6.80191	6.97532	7.15329	7.33593	7.52333	7.71561	7.91286	8.11519
7	7.21354	7.43428	7.66246	7.89829	8.14201	8.39384	8.65402	8.92280	9.20043	9.48717	9.78327	10.08901
8	8.28567	8.58297	8.89234	9.21423	9.54911	9.89747	10.25980	10.63663	11.02847	11.43589	11.85943	12.29969
9	9.36853	9.75463	10.15911	10.58280	11.02656	11.49132	11.97799	12.48756	13.02104	13.57948	14.16397	14.77566
10	10.46221	10.94972	11.46388	12.00611	12.57789	13.18079	13.81645	14.48656	15.19293	15.93742	16.72201	17.54874
11	11.56683	12.16872	12.80780	13.48635	14.20679	14.97164	15.78360	16.64549	17.56029	18.53117	19.56143	20.65458
12	12.68250	13.41209	14.19203	15.02581	15.91713	16.86994	17.88845	18.97713	20.14072	21.38428	22.71319	24.13313
13	13.80933	14.68033	15.61779	16.62684	17.71298	18.88214	20.14064	21.49530	22.95338	24.52271	26.21164	28.02911
14	14.94742	15.97394	17.08632	18.29191	19.59863	21.01507	22.55049	24.21492	26.01919	27.97498	30.09492	32.39260
15	16.09690	17.29342	18.59891	20.02359	21.57856	23.27597	25.12902	27.15211	29.36092	31.77248	34.40536	37.27971
16	17.25786	18.63929	20.15688	21.82453	23.65749	25.67253	27.88805	30.32428	33.00340	35.94973	39.18995	42.75328
17	18.43044	20.01207	21.76159	23.69751	25.84037	28.21288	30.84022	33.75023	36.97370	40.54470	44.50084	48.88367
18	19.61475	21.41231	23.41444	25.64541	28.13238	30.90565	33.99903	37.45024	41.30134	45.59917	50.39594	55.74971
19	20.81090	22.84056	25.11687	27.67123	30.53900	33.75999	37.37896	41.44626	46.01846	51.15909	56.93949	63.43968
20	22.01900	24.29737	26.87037	29.77808	33.06595	36.78559	40.99549	45.76196	51.16012	57.27500	64.20283	72.05244
25	28.24320	32.03030	36.45926	41.64591	47.72710	54.86451	63.24904	73.10594	84.70090	98.34706	114.41331	133.33387
30	34.78489	40.56808	47.57542	56.08494	66.43885	79.05819	94.46079	113.28321	136.30754	164.49402	199.02088	241.33268
35	41.66028	49.99448	60.46208	73.65222	90.32031	111.43478	138.23688	172.31680	215.71075	271.02437	341.58955	431.66350
40	48.88637	60.40198	75.40126	95.02552	120.79977	154.76197	199.63511	259.05652	337.88245	442.59256	581.82607	767.09142
50	64.46318	84.57940	112.79687	152.66708	209.34800	290.33590	406.52893	573.77016	815.08356	1163.90853	1668.77115	2400.01825

If we decide to invest $50 at the end of each six months for three years at an eight percent annual rate of return, we would use the factor for six periods at four percent, as follows:

Periodic Payment	×	**Factor**	=	**Future Value**
$50	×	6.63298	=	$331.65

YOUR TURN! E-3

Kathy Cole invests $100 monthly for 18 months at an annual rate of 12 percent. How much money will Kathy have at the end of the 18 months from her investment.

The solution is on page E-15.

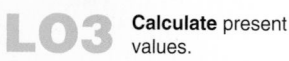

PRESENT VALUE OF AN AMOUNT

LO3 | **Calculate** present values.

We can generalize that (1) the right to receive an amount of money now—its **present value**—is normally worth more than the right to receive the same amount later—its future value; (2) the longer we must wait to receive an amount, the less attractive the receipt is; and (3) the difference between the present value of an amount and its future value is a function of interest (Principal × Interest Rate × Time). Further, the more risk associated with any situation, the higher the appropriate interest rate.

We support these generalizations with an illustration. What amount should we accept now that would be as valuable as receiving $100 one year from now ($100 represents the future value) if the appropriate interest rate is ten percent? We recognize intuitively that with a ten percent interest rate, we should accept less than $100, or approximately $91. We base this estimate on the realization that the $100 received in the future must equal the present value (100 percent) plus ten percent interest on the present value. Thus, in our example, the $100 future receipt must be 1.10 times the present value. Dividing $100 by 1.10, we obtain a present value of $90.91. In other words, under the given conditions, we would do as well to accept $90.91 now as to wait one year and receive $100. To confirm the equality of a $90.91 payment now with a $100 payment one year later, we calculate the future value of $90.91 at ten percent for one year as follows:

$$\$90.91 \times 1.10 \times 1 \text{ year} = \$100 \text{ (rounded)}$$

Thus, we calculate the present value of a future receipt by discounting (deducting an interest factor) the future receipt back to the present at an appropriate interest rate. We present this schematically below:

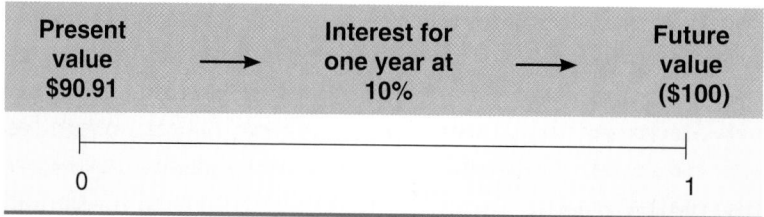

Present value $90.91	→	Interest for one year at 10%	→	Future value ($100)

The formula for calculating the present value of a single amount is determined using the following formula:

$$PV = FV \times [1 \div (1 + i)^n]$$

where

PV = present value of an amount
FV = future value
  i = interest rate for one period
  n = number of periods

As can be seen from this formula, if either the time period or the interest rate is increased, the resulting present value would decrease. If more than one time period is involved, compound interest calculations are appropriate. **Exhibit E-4** illustrates the calculation of the present value of a single amount.

Exhibit E-4	**Present Value of a Single Amount**

How much must be deposited in a savings account today in order to have $1,000 in four years if the savings account pays 12 percent annual interest?

$$PV = \$1,000 \times [1 \div (1.12)^4] = (\$1,000 \times 0.63552) = \$636$$

Table III can be used to calculate the present value amounts in a manner similar to the way we previously calculated future values using **Table I**. As with the future value tables, present value tables provide a multiplier for many combinations of time periods and interest rates that, when applied to the dollar amount of a future cash flow or annuity, determines its present value.

Table III	Present Value of $1											
Period	1%	2%	3%	4%	5%	6%	7%	8%	9%	10%	11%	12%
1	0.99010	0.98039	0.97087	0.96154	0.95238	0.94340	0.93458	0.92593	0.91743	0.90909	0.90090	0.89286
2	0.98030	0.96117	0.94260	0.92456	0.90703	0.89000	0.87344	0.85734	0.84168	0.82645	0.81162	0.79719
3	0.97059	0.94232	0.91514	0.88900	0.86384	0.83962	0.81630	0.79383	0.77218	0.75131	0.73119	0.71178
4	0.96098	0.92385	0.88849	0.85480	0.82270	0.79209	0.76290	0.73503	0.70843	0.68301	0.65873	0.63552
5	0.95147	0.90573	0.86261	0.82193	0.78353	0.74726	0.71299	0.68058	0.64993	0.62092	0.59345	0.56743
6	0.94205	0.88797	0.83748	0.79031	0.74622	0.70496	0.66634	0.63017	0.59627	0.56447	0.53464	0.50663
7	0.93272	0.87056	0.81309	0.75992	0.71068	0.66506	0.62275	0.58349	0.54703	0.51316	0.48166	0.45235
8	0.92348	0.85349	0.78941	0.73069	0.67684	0.62741	0.58201	0.54027	0.50187	0.46651	0.43393	0.40388
9	0.91434	0.83676	0.76642	0.70259	0.64461	0.59190	0.54393	0.50025	0.46043	0.42410	0.39092	0.36061
10	0.90529	0.82035	0.74409	0.67556	0.61391	0.55839	0.50835	0.46319	0.42241	0.38554	0.35218	0.32197
11	0.89632	0.80426	0.72242	0.64958	0.58468	0.52679	0.47509	0.42888	0.38753	0.35049	0.31728	0.28748
12	0.88745	0.78849	0.70138	0.62460	0.55684	0.49697	0.44401	0.39711	0.35553	0.31863	0.28584	0.25668
13	0.87866	0.77303	0.68095	0.60057	0.53032	0.46884	0.41496	0.36770	0.32618	0.28966	0.25751	0.22917
14	0.86996	0.75788	0.66112	0.57748	0.50507	0.44230	0.38782	0.34046	0.29925	0.26333	0.23199	0.20462
15	0.86135	0.74301	0.64186	0.55526	0.48102	0.41727	0.36245	0.31524	0.27454	0.23939	0.20900	0.18270
16	0.85282	0.72845	0.62317	0.53391	0.45811	0.39365	0.33873	0.29189	0.25187	0.21763	0.18829	0.16312
17	0.84438	0.71416	0.60502	0.51337	0.43630	0.37136	0.31657	0.27027	0.23107	0.19784	0.16963	0.14564
18	0.83602	0.70016	0.58739	0.49363	0.41552	0.35034	0.29586	0.25025	0.21199	0.17986	0.15282	0.13004
19	0.82774	0.68643	0.57029	0.47464	0.39573	0.33051	0.27651	0.23171	0.19449	0.16351	0.13768	0.11611
20	0.81954	0.67297	0.55368	0.45639	0.37689	0.31180	0.25842	0.21455	0.17843	0.14864	0.12403	0.10367
25	0.77977	0.60953	0.47761	0.37512	0.29530	0.23300	0.18425	0.14602	0.11597	0.09230	0.07361	0.05882
30	0.74192	0.55207	0.41199	0.30832	0.23138	0.17411	0.13137	0.09938	0.07537	0.05731	0.04368	0.03338
35	0.70591	0.50003	0.35538	0.25342	0.18129	0.13011	0.09366	0.06763	0.04899	0.03558	0.02592	0.01894
40	0.67165	0.45289	0.30656	0.20829	0.14205	0.09722	0.06678	0.04603	0.03184	0.02209	0.01538	0.01075
50	0.60804	0.37153	0.22811	0.14071	0.08720	0.05429	0.03395	0.02132	0.01345	0.00852	0.00542	0.00346

Exhibit E-5 illustrates calculations of present values using the factors in **Table III**.

Exhibit E-5	Present Value of a Single Amount Using Present Value Tables

Calculate the present value of $1,000 four years hence, at 12 percent interest compounded annually:

   Number of periods (one year, annually) = 4

   Interest rate per period (12%/1) = 12%

   Multiplier = 0.63552

   Present value = $1,000 × 0.63552 = $636

   (This result agrees with our earlier illustration.)

Calculate the present value of $116.99 two years hence, at eight percent compounded semiannually:

   Number of periods (two years, semiannually) = 4

   Interest rate per period (8%/2) = 4%

   Multiplier = 0.85480

   Present value = $116.99 × 0.85480 = $100 (rounded)

YOUR TURN! E-4

The solution is on page E-15.

Sabrina Flores wishes to have $2,500 in her bank account in three years. If she can earn seven percent compounded annually, how much will she need to invest today?

PRESENT VALUE OF AN ANNUITY

We can use present value tables like **Table III** to calculate the present value of any single future cash flow or series of future cash flows. For example, assume $100 is to be received at the end of each of the next three years as an annuity. As shown in **Exhibit E-6**, the present value of this ordinary annuity can be calculated from **Table III** as the present value of each of the three individual receipts and summing them (assuming five percent annual interest).

Exhibit E-6	Present Value of an Ordinary Annuity					
Future Receipts (ordinary annuity)				**PV Multiplier (Table III)**		**Present Value**
Year 1	**Year 2**	**Year 3**				
$100			×	0.95238	=	$ 95.24
	$100		×	0.90703	=	90.70
		$100	×	0.86384	=	86.38
				Total present value		$272.32

    Table IV, on the other hand, provides a single multiplier for calculating the present value of a series of future cash flows that represent an ordinary annuity. Referring to **Table IV** in the three periods row and the five percent interest column, we see that the multiplier is 2.72325, equal to the sum of the three present value factors in **Exhibit E-6**. When applied to the $100 annuity amount, the multiplier gives a present value of $272.33 (difference due to rounding).

Table IV	Present Value of an Ordinary Annuity of $1 per Period											
Period	**1%**	**2%**	**3%**	**4%**	**5%**	**6%**	**7%**	**8%**	**9%**	**10%**	**11%**	**12%**
1	0.99010	0.98039	0.97087	0.96154	0.95238	0.94340	0.93458	0.92593	0.91743	0.90909	0.90090	0.89286
2	1.97040	1.94156	1.91347	1.88609	1.85941	1.83339	1.80802	1.78326	1.75911	1.73554	1.71252	1.69005
3	2.94099	2.88388	2.82861	2.77509	2.72325	2.67301	2.62432	2.57710	2.53129	2.48685	2.44371	2.40183
4	3.90197	3.80773	3.71710	3.62990	3.54595	3.46511	3.38721	3.31213	3.23972	3.16987	3.10245	3.03735
5	4.85343	4.71346	4.57971	4.45182	4.32948	4.21236	4.10020	3.99271	3.88965	3.79079	3.69590	3.60478
6	5.79548	5.60143	5.41719	5.24214	5.07569	4.91732	4.76654	4.62288	4.48592	4.35526	4.23054	4.11141
7	6.72819	6.47199	6.23028	6.00205	5.78637	5.58238	5.38929	5.20637	5.03295	4.86842	4.71220	4.56376
8	7.65168	7.32548	7.01969	6.73274	6.46321	6.20979	5.97130	5.74664	5.53482	5.33493	5.14612	4.96764
9	8.56602	8.16224	7.78611	7.43533	7.10782	6.80169	6.51523	6.24689	5.99525	5.75902	5.53705	5.32825
10	9.47130	8.98259	8.53020	8.11090	7.72173	7.36009	7.02358	6.71008	6.41766	6.14457	5.88923	5.65022
11	10.36763	9.78685	9.25262	8.76048	8.30641	7.88687	7.49867	7.13896	6.80519	6.49506	6.20652	5.93770
12	11.25508	10.57534	9.95400	9.38507	8.86325	8.38384	7.94269	7.53608	7.16073	6.81369	6.49236	6.19437
13	12.13374	11.34837	10.63496	9.98565	9.39357	8.85268	8.35765	7.90378	7.48690	7.10336	6.74987	6.42355
14	13.00370	12.10625	11.29607	10.56312	9.89864	9.29498	8.74547	8.24424	7.78615	7.36669	6.98187	6.62817
15	13.86505	12.84926	11.93794	11.11839	10.37966	9.71225	9.10791	8.55948	8.06069	7.60608	7.19087	6.81086
16	14.71787	13.57771	12.56110	11.65230	10.83777	10.10590	9.44665	8.85137	8.31256	7.82371	7.37916	6.97399
17	15.56225	14.29187	13.16612	12.16567	11.27407	10.47726	9.76322	9.12164	8.54363	8.02155	7.54879	7.11963
18	16.39827	14.99203	13.75351	12.65930	11.68959	10.82760	10.05909	9.37189	8.75563	8.20141	7.70162	7.24967
19	17.22601	15.67846	14.32380	13.13394	12.08532	11.15812	10.33560	9.60360	8.95011	8.36492	7.83929	7.36578
20	18.04555	16.35143	14.87747	13.59033	12.46221	11.46992	10.59401	9.81815	9.12855	8.51356	7.96333	7.46944
25	22.02316	19.52346	17.41315	15.62208	14.09394	12.78336	11.65358	10.67478	9.82258	9.07704	8.42174	7.84314
30	25.80771	22.39646	19.60044	17.29203	15.37245	13.76483	12.40904	11.25778	10.27365	9.42691	8.69379	8.05518
35	29.40858	24.99862	21.48722	18.66461	16.37419	14.49825	12.94767	11.65457	10.56682	9.64416	8.85524	8.17550
40	32.83469	27.35548	23.11477	19.79277	17.15909	15.04630	13.33171	11.92461	10.75736	9.77905	8.95105	8.24378
50	39.19612	31.42361	25.72976	21.48218	18.25593	15.76186	13.80075	12.23348	10.96168	9.91481	9.04165	8.30450

Jamal Turner is planning to attend a four-year university. He hopes to save money from his current job so that he will have enough in the bank account when he starts college to allow him to withdraw $10,000 at the end of each of the four years. He expects to earn six percent compounded annually on his investment. How much money will he need in his bank account when he starts college?

YOUR TURN! E-5

The solution is on page E-15.

Guided Examples
MBC

CALCULATIONS USING A CALCULATOR AND A SPREADSHEET

While present value tables can provide a handy method to solve some time value of money problems, they are not suitable for many real-world situations. For example, many real-world interest rates are not even integers like those appearing in **Table I** through **Table IV**, nor are many problems limited to the number of time periods appearing in the tables. While it is still possible to solve these problems with the provided formulas, financial calculators and spreadsheet programs provide a much quicker solution. Financial calculators can be distinguished from other calculators by the presence of dedicated keys for present and future values, along with keys for the number of periods, interest rates, and annuity payments. There are many brands of financial calculators; however, all of them work in much the same way.[1] We illustrate the calculation of bond prices using a calculator and a spreadsheet in Appendix 10A at the end of Chapter 10.

---

[1] It is usually necessary to do some preliminary setup on a financial calculator before performing time value of money calculations. For example, the HP 10BII calculator has a default setting of monthly compounding. This may need to be changed if the problem calls for a different number of compounding periods, such as annual. In addition, the calculator assumes annuity payments occur at the end of each period. This will need to be changed if the problem requires beginning of period payments. See your calculator manual to determine how to make these setting changes.

SUMMARY OF LEARNING OBJECTIVES

LO1 **Describe the nature of interest and distinguish between simple and compound interest. (p. E-2)**
- Interest is payment for the use of money over time.
- Simple interest is computed only on the principal.
- Compound interest is computed on the accumulated principal including any earned interest that has not been paid.

LO2 **Calculate future values. (p. E-3)**
- The future value of a single amount is the amount that a specified investment will be worth at a future date if invested at a given rate of compound interest.
- The formula for calculating the future value of a single amount is $FV = PV \times (1 + i)^n$.
- Future value tables provide a multiplier for many combinations of time periods and interest rates that, when applied to the dollar amount of a present value, determines its future value.
- An annuity represents a special case of a pattern of cash flows where the cash flow amounts are of equal amounts and equally spaced over time.
- A separate table is available that provides a multiplier for the future value of an annuity rather than using separate multipliers from the future value of $1 table.

LO3 **Calculate present values. (p. E-7)**
- The right to receive an amount of money now—its present value—is normally worth more than the right to receive the same amount later—its future value.
- The formula for calculating the present value of a single amount is $PV = FV \times [1 \div (1 + i)^n]$.
- A separate table is available that provides a multiplier for the present value of an annuity rather than using separate multipliers from the present value of $1 table.

KEY TERMS

Annuity (p. E-5)	Interest (p. E-2)	Principal (p. E-2)
Compound interest (p. E-2)	Ordinary annuity (p. E-5)	Simple interest (p. E-2)
Future value (p. E-3)	Present value (p. E-7)	Time value (p. E-2)

Assignments with the logo in the margin are available in BusinessCourse.
See the Preface of the book for details.

SELF-STUDY QUESTIONS

(Answers to Self-Study Questions are at the end of this appendix.)

LO2   1. **Calculate the future value of each of the following items.**
- *a.* $10,000 deposited in a savings account for ten years if the annual interest rate is
  - *1.* Twelve percent compounded annually.
  - *2.* Twelve percent compounded semiannually.
  - *3.* Twelve percent compounded quarterly.
- *b.* $4,000 received at the end of each year for the next ten years if the money earns interest at the rate of four percent compounded annually.
- *c.* $2,000 received semiannually for the next five years if the money earns interest at the rate of eight percent compounded semiannually.
- *d.* $3,000 deposited each year for the next ten years plus a single sum of $17,000 deposited today if the interest rate is ten percent per year compounded annually.

LO3   2. **Calculate the present value of each of the following items.**
- *a.* $75,000 ten years hence if the annual interest rate is
  - *1.* Eight percent compounded annually.
  - *2.* Eight percent compounded semiannually.
  - *3.* Eight percent compounded quarterly.
- *b.* $2,000 received at the end of each year for the next eight years if money is worth ten percent per year compounded annually.

   c. $500 received at the end of each six months for the next fifteen years if the interest rate is eight percent per year compounded semiannually.

   d. $200,000 inheritance ten years hence if money is worth ten percent per year compounded annually.

   e. $3,000 received each half year for the next ten years plus a single sum of $60,000 at the end of ten years if the interest rate is 12 percent per year compounded semiannually.

EXERCISES—SET A

EE-1A. Simple and Compound Interest   **LO1**

   a. For each of the following notes, calculate the simple interest due at the end of the term.

Note	Principal	Rate	Term
1	$20,000	2%	6 years
2	$20,000	4%	4 years
3	$20,000	6%	3 years

   b. Compute the amount of interest due at the end of the term for each of the above notes assuming interest is compounded annually.

EE-2A. Future Value Computation At the beginning of the year you deposit $5,000 in a savings account. How much will accumulate in three years if you earn eight percent compounded annually? **LO2**

EE-3A. Future Value Computation You deposit $5,000 at the end of every year for three years. How much will accumulate in three years if you earn eight percent compounded annually? **LO2**

EE-4A. Present Value Computation You will receive $5,000 in three years. What is the present value if you can earn eight percent interest compounded annually? **LO3**

EE-5A. Present Value Computation You receive $5,000 at the end of every year for three years. What is the present value of these receipts if you earn eight percent compounded annually? **LO3**

EE-6A. Future Value Computation What amount will be accumulated in four years if $10,000 is invested today at six percent interest compounded annually? **LO2**

EE-7A. Present Value Computation You are scheduled to be paid $10,000 in four years. What amount today is equivalent to the $10,000 to be received in four years assuming interest is compounded annually at six percent? **LO3**

EE-8A. Future Value Computation What amount will be accumulated in four years if $10,000 is invested every six months beginning in six months and ending four years from today? Interest will accumulate at an annual rate of ten percent compounded semiannually. **LO2**

EE-9A. Future Value Computation You are scheduled to receive $10,000 every six months for eight periods beginning in six months. What amount in four years is equivalent to the future series of payments assuming interest compounds at the annual rate of eight percent compounded semiannually? **LO2**

EE-10A. Present Value Computation Savanna, Inc., believes it will need $150,000 in five years to expand its operations. Savanna can earn five percent, compounded annually, if it deposits its money right now. How large of a deposit must Savanna make in order to have the necessary $150,000 in five years? **LO3**

EE-11A. Future Value Computation Kate Company deposited $12,000 in the bank today, earning eight percent interest. Kate plans to withdraw the money in five years. How much money will be available to withdraw assuming that interest is compounded (a) annually, (b) semiannually, and (c) quarterly? **LO2**

EE-12A. Future Value Computation Stan Smith deposited $5,000 in a savings account today. The deposit will earn interest at the rate of eight percent. How much will be available for Stan to withdraw in four years, assuming interest is compounded (a) annually, (b) semiannually, and (c) quarterly? **LO2**

EE-13A. Present Value Computation Paul Jefferson made a deposit into his savings account three years ago, and earned interest at an annual rate of eight percent. The deposit accumulated to $30,000. How much was initially deposited assuming that the interest was compounded (a) annually, (b) semiannually, and (c) quarterly? **LO3**

LO2   **EE-14A. Future Value Computation** Kendal Jennings has decided to start saving for his daughter's college education by depositing $3,200 at the end of every year for 18 years. He has determined that he will be able to earn six percent interest compounded annually. He hopes to have at least $90,000 when his daughter starts college in 18 years. Will his savings plan be successful?

LO3   **EE-15A. Present Value Computation** Kershaw Bales won the state lottery and was given four choices for receiving her winnings.

    1. Receive $500,000 right now.
    2. Receive $540,000 in one year.
    3. Receive $50,000 at the end of each year for 20 years.
    4. Receive $45,000 at the end of each year for 30 years.

Assuming Kershaw can earn interest of eight percent compounded annually, which option should Kershaw choose?

EXERCISES—SET B

LO1   **EE-1B.   Simple and Compound Interest**

    a.   For each of the following notes, calculate the simple interest due at the end of the term.

Note	Principal	Rate	Term
1	$6,000	8%	8 years
2	$6,000	12%	5 years
3	$6,000	4%	2 years

    b.   Compute the amount of interest due at the end of the term for each of the above notes assuming interest is compounded annually.

LO2   **EE-2B.   Future Value Computation** At the beginning of the year you deposit $1,500 in a savings account. How much will accumulate in four years if you earn six percent compounded annually?

LO2   **EE-3B.   Future Value Computation** You deposit $1,500 at the end of every year for four years. How much will accumulate in four years if you earn six percent compounded annually?

LO3   **EE-4B.   Present Value Computation** You will receive $1,500 in four years. What is the present value if you can earn six percent interest compounded annually?

LO3   **EE-5B.   Present Value Computation** You receive $1,500 at the end of every year for four years. What is the present value of these receipts if you earn six percent compounded annually?

LO2   **EE-6B.   Future Value Computation** What amount will be accumulated in six years if $5,000 is invested today at four percent interest compounded annually?

LO3   **EE-7B.   Present Value Computation** You are scheduled to be paid $5,000 in ten years. What amount today is equivalent to the $5,000 to be received in ten years assuming interest is compounded annually at six percent?

LO2   **EE-8B.   Future Value Computation** What amount will be accumulated in five years if $4,000 is invested every six months beginning in six months and ending five years from today? Interest will accumulate at an annual rate of four percent compounded semiannually.

LO2   **EE-9B.   Future Value Computation** You are scheduled to receive $5,000 every six months for 12 periods beginning in six months. What amount in six years is equivalent to the future series of payments assuming interest compounds at the annual rate of eight percent compounded semiannually?

LO3   **EE-10B. Present Value Computation** Mimi, Inc., believes it will need $150,000 in ten years to expand its operations. Mimi can earn eight percent, compounded annually, if it deposits its money right now. How large of a deposit must Mimi make in order to have the necessary $150,000 in ten years?

LO2   **EE-11B. Future Value Computation** Zeus Company deposited $10,250 in the bank today, earning eight percent interest. Zeus plans to withdraw the money in five years. How much money will be available to withdraw assuming that interest is compounded (a) annually, (b) semiannually, and (c) quarterly?

EE-12B. Future Value Computation Jason Smithton deposited $2,500 in a savings account today. The deposit will earn interest at the rate of 12 percent. How much will be available for Jason to withdraw in three years, assuming interest is compounded (a) annually, (b) semiannually, and (c) quarterly?

LO2

EE-13B. Present Value Computation Rose Gomez made a deposit into her savings account four years ago, and earned interest at an annual rate of 12 percent. The deposit accumulated to $60,000. How much was initially deposited assuming that the interest was compounded (a) annually, (b) semiannually, and (c) quarterly?

LO3

EE-14B. Future Value Computation Herman Lett has decided to start saving for his daughter's college education by depositing $3,000 at the end of every year for 15 years. He has determined that he will be able to earn six percent interest compounded annually. He hopes to have at least $65,000 when his daughter starts college in 15 years. Will his savings plan be successful?

LO2

EE-15B. Present Value Computation Kelly Fullerton won the state lottery and was given four choices for receiving her winnings.

LO3

1. Receive $800,000 right now.
2. Receive $832,000 in one year.
3. Receive $120,000 at the end of each year for eight years.
4. Receive $46,400 at the end of each year for 30 years.

Assuming Kelly can earn interest of four percent compounded annually, which option should Kelly choose?

ANSWERS TO SELF-STUDY QUESTIONS:

1. *a.* 1. $10,000 × 3.10585 = $ 1,059
     2. $10,000 × 3.20714 = $32,071
     3. $10,000 × 3.26204 = $32,620

   b. $ 4,000 × 12.00611 = $48,024

   c. $ 2,000 × 12.00611 = $24,012

   d. $ 3,000 × 15.93742 = $47,812
        $17,000 × 2.59374 = $44,094
                         $91,906

2. *a.* 1. $ 75,000 × 0.46319 = $34,739
     2. $ 75,000 × 0.45639 = $34,229
     3. $ 75,000 × 0.45289 = $33,967

   b. $ 2,000 × 5.33493 = $10,670

   c. $ 500 × 17.29203 = $ 8,646

   d. $200,000 × 0.38554 = $77,108

   e. $ 3,000 × 11.46992 = $34,410
        $ 60,000 × 0.31180 = $18,708
                         $53,118

YOUR TURN! SOLUTIONS

Solution E-1

(1)

Year	Calculation	Interest
1	$100 × 0.10 =	$10.00
2	$100 × 0.10 =	$10.00
3	$100 × 0.10 =	$10.00
Total		$30.00

(2)

Year	Calculation	Interest
1	$100 × 0.10 =	$10.00
2	$110 × 0.10 =	$11.00
3	$121 × 0.10 =	$12.10
Total		$33.10

Solution E-2
$5,000 × 1.36049 = $6,802.45

Solution E-3
$100 × 19.61475 = $1,961.48

Solution E-4
$2,500 × 0.81630 = $2,040.75

Solution E-5
$10,000 × 3.46511 = $34,651.10

Appendix F

Data Analytics and Blockchain Technology

Road Map

LO	Learning Objective	Page	Assignments
LO1	**Identify and define the four types of data analytics.**	F-2	SS1, EF1, EF2, EF3, EF4, EF5, EF6, EF7, EF8, EF9 EF10
LO2	**Describe the use of data analytics within the accounting profession.**	F-3	SS1, EF1, EF2, EF3, EF4, EF5, EF6, EF7, EF8, EF9 EF10
LO3	**Describe how blockchain technology works.**	F-4	SS2, E11, EF12, EF13, EF14
LO4	**Describe the use of blockchain technology within the accounting profession.**	F-5	SS2, E11, EF12, EF13, EF14

DATA ANALYTICS

Identify and define the four types of data analytics.

Data analytics can broadly be defined as the process of examining sets of data with the goal of discovering useful information from patterns found in the data. Increasingly, this process is aided by computers running programs ranging from basic spreadsheet software, such as **Microsoft Excel** and **Google Sheets**, to specialized software, such as **Tableau**. This technology can reveal trends and insights that would otherwise be lost in the overwhelming amount of data.

Data analytics can be categorized into four mains types, ranging in sophistication from relatively straightforward to very complex. The first category is **descriptive analytics**, which describes what has happened over a given period of time. Simple examples include determining sales trends over a period of time and the relative effectiveness of various social media promotions based on click-through rates. Microsoft Excel and other spreadsheet programs include built-in functions that greatly simplify performing descriptive analytics.

Diagnostic analytics focuses more on why something occurred. This data analytics technique is used to monitor changes in data and often includes a certain amount of hypothesizing: Did the marketing campaign lead to the increase in sales? Did changing the beverage items affect food choices? Did the opening of competing restaurants negatively impact sales growth? Diagnostic analytics is useful because past performance is often a reliable predictor of future outcomes and can greatly aid in planning and forecasting.

Whereas descriptive and diagnostic analytics use data to try to understand what happened and why, **predictive analytics** uses data to try to determine what will happen. The movie, *Moneyball* made the general manager of the **Oakland Athletics**, Billy Beane, famous for using predictive analytics to make personnel decisions in professional baseball. In his evaluation of baseball players, Beane used data to predict player performance so he could assemble the team with the greatest likelihood of winning the World Series. Banks also use predictive analytics to identify and prevent fraudulent transactions by monitoring customer credit card transactions and red flagging those that deviate from a customer behavior profile that was developed from previous transaction and geographic data.

Prescriptive analytics moves beyond what is going to happen to suggesting a course of action for what should happen to optimize outcomes. The forecasts created using predictive analytics can be used to make recommendations for future courses of action. For example, if we own a sports bar and determine there is a high likelihood of our local sports team winning the championship this year, we should expand the bar area and add more big-screen televisions to maximize revenues. **Exhibit F1** summarizes the four types of data analytics.

Exhibit F1		
Type of Data Analytics	**Purpose**	**Example**
Descriptive	To explain what happened	Sales trends for last year
Diagnostic	To understand why it happened	Did the new advertising campaign cause sales to increase last quarter?
Predictive	To predict what will happen	Predicting fraudulent charges based on past behaviors
Prescriptive	To determine what should happen	Expand business to optimize sales based on predicted championship

Data Analytics in the Accounting Profession

Most accountants are likely already performing descriptive analytics in their regular work. This includes, for example, determining sum totals, averages, and period-to-period changes in such measures as net sales and net income. Other examples include average collection periods and day's sales in inventory by product type. Data analytics has other usefulness and should not be limited to only descriptive analysis. Accountants can provide far more value by employing predictive and prescriptive analytics.

LO2 Describe the use of data analytics within the accounting profession.

Accountants can obtain data from a variety of company sources, including enterprise resource planning systems, customer relationship management systems, and point-of-sale systems, to aid them in obtaining insight into future outcomes and providing guidance for future actions. The area of credit granting provides an example. Predictive analytics can help compute credit scores to predict the likelihood of future payments. As a result, prescriptive analytics can aid in suggesting terms for granting credit.

Many other opportunities exist for accountants to utilize data analytics. Tax accountants can apply data analysis to unique tax issues to suggest optimal tax strategies. Accountants serving as investment advisors can use big data to find patterns in consumer behavior that others can use to build analytic models for identifying investment opportunities.

Perhaps no area of accounting can benefit more from an understanding of data analytics than auditing. Auditors employ data analytics to shift from the sample-based audit model to one based on continuous modeling of much larger data sets. This allows auditors to identify the riskiest areas of an audit by focusing on outliers and exceptions.

The major accounting firms have fully embraced the power of data analytics. **PricewaterhouseCoopers** (PWC), **Deloitte**, **Ernst & Young** (EY), and **KPMG** all devote significant staffing resources to provide data analytics services to their clients. These firms claim they can help their clients optimize their data assets to aid in faster and better decisions. For example, PWC provides a flowchart starting with the building of a data foundation and applies advanced analytics to improving business performance, ultimately leading to opportunities for innovation.

While computers and software are instrumental in the entire process, the human element is the most critical factor in the success of any data analytics program. One commonality among surveys of top company managers is the value placed on data analytics for the company's future. Another commonality is the need for professionals trained in data analytics to help the company attain its goals.

Data Analytics in Accounting

Benford's Law, discussed in Chapter 7, provides an example of how data analytics has been used to uncover fraud in a national call center. Forensic accountants utilized their knowledge of Benford's Law to form evidence of a problem by observing patterns in the data. According to Benford's Law, in any list of financial transactions, the number one should occur as the first digit 30.1 percent of the time, with each successive number occurring as the first digit in lesser percentages, with the number nine occurring less than 5 percent of the time. Forensic accountants examined issued refunds and noticed an excessively high occurrence of the number four. The forensic accountants learned that the company had a policy that required supervisor approval of refunds that exceeded $50. The accountants were able to identify a small group of operators who had been issuing fraudulent refunds to family, friends, and themselves. These fraudulent $40 refunds totaled several hundred thousand dollars.

BLOCKCHAIN TECHNOLOGY

LO3
works.

Describe how blockchain technology

Blockchain technology differs from the traditional accounting ledger in a fundamental way that has immense implications for the accounting profession. A traditional ledger system is a closed system controlled at a centralized location with individuals at the centralized location responsible for the maintenance and integrity of the ledger. In contrast, a blockchain is an open, decentralized ledger, where the ledger is distributed across multiple computers called **nodes**. The blockchain ledger is managed autonomously by the distributed nodes such that data is authenticated by mass collaboration rather than by a central authority. Each node on the blockchain maintains a complete copy of all past transactions that have been added to the ledger. Thus, by comparing to the other nodes' copies, the ledger is continuously synchronized. Unlike traditional accounting ledgers, none of the nodes has any special rights that differ from those of the other nodes.

Blockchains get their name because new ledge data are periodically bundled into blocks, which are then added to previous blocks to form a chain. Each block can contain a cryptocurrency exchange, as is the case with **Bitcoin**, but other possibilities include sales transactions, equity trades, loan payments, election votes—pretty much any contract transaction. In addition, the block contains a **time stamp** and a **hash #**, which together form a cryptographic signature associated with the previous blocks. This timestamp and hash make the blockchain essentially tamper-proof because the blocks cannot be changed without the change being apparent to all other nodes. While the chain propagates in only a single chronological order, it can be audited in both directions. **Exhibit F-2** is a visual depiction of the blockchain process.

Exhibit F2

How a Blockchain Works

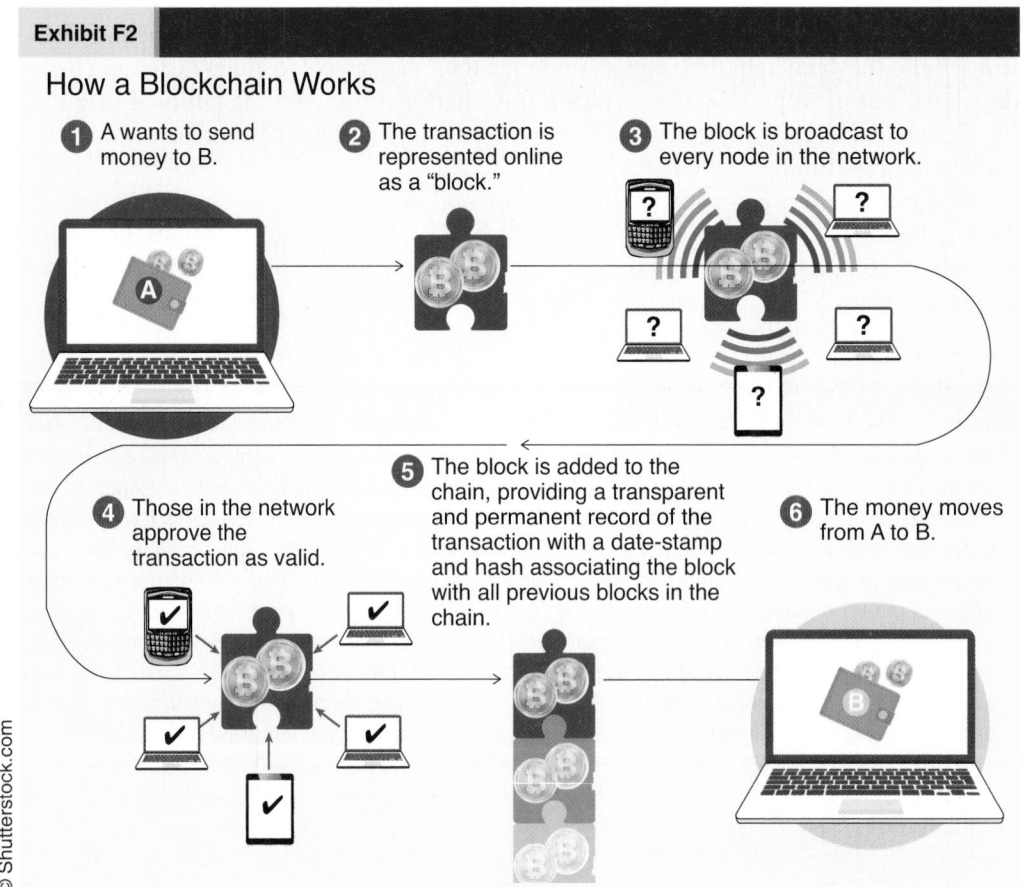

1. A wants to send money to B.
2. The transaction is represented online as a "block."
3. The block is broadcast to every node in the network.
4. Those in the network approve the transaction as valid.
5. The block is added to the chain, providing a transparent and permanent record of the transaction with a date-stamp and hash associating the block with all previous blocks in the chain.
6. The money moves from A to B.

© Shutterstock.com

The accounting profession has seen changes arising from a vast array of technological innovations, from computer spreadsheets to general ledger software to enterprise resource systems. Blockchain technology represents another innovation in the way accounting is and will be performed. The invention of double-entry accounting, the bedrock of financial accounting, allowed managers to trust their own financial recordkeeping. Unfortunately, the same level of trust does not exist with outsiders, which is why companies rely on independent auditors for an opinion on the integrity of an entity's financial statements. These audits are often very time consuming and costly.

LO4 Describe the use of blockchain technology within the accounting profession.

Accountants working in the traditional centralized-ledger environment are likely to spend a large amount of time reconciling accounts and amounts. This involves comparing balances at their company with external documents from outside entities, including banks, brokerages, and business partners, among others. In addition to the time-consuming process of acquiring all the needed sources of information and performing the comparisons, additional time and effort are often needed to reconcile any differences. In a blockchain's distributed ledger system, all node participants can continually confirm all transactions, greatly reducing the effort involved in periodic reconciliations.

Accountants working in the traditional environment are expected to produce internal, ad hoc reports. This often requires considerable effort reconciling internal documents, perhaps from multiple departments or divisions. In a blockchain environment, accountants spend far less time verifying transactional data, freeing up time for more valuable advisory activities.

As a final example of the many ways blockchain technology will change the way accountants work, consider the traditional closing of the books at the end of each period. Instead of needing to acquire the necessary data, verify its accuracy, and make all the necessary adjustments, one could envision a far more automated process with the use of blockchain technology. Financial statements could be updated continuously from data provided by the blockchain, making the period-ending closing process much less time-consuming.

Blockchain technology is widely viewed as the next major step in financial accounting. Instead of keeping separate records documenting each transaction, transactions can be written directly into the decentralized ledger. Thus, each transaction is distributed and cryptographically signed to ensure against later falsification or destruction. This has the potential to allow auditors to automatically verify much of the data in a traditional audit, freeing them to provide value in more important areas, such as the analysis of complex transactions or operational efficiencies.

Some accountants may worry that these evolving technologies will diminish the need for accountants. If history is any indication, the opposite is likely. The accountant's role in the financial process will certainly change, but this change will be evolution, not extinction. Information will still need to be interpreted and categorized before entering the blockchain, and this is where future accountants will provide their value. The Big Four accounting firms realize this and are at the forefront in research on how blockchain technology will be used.

SUMMARY OF LEARNING OBJECTIVES

Identify and define the four types of data analytics. (p. F-2)

LO1

- Data analytics can broadly be defined as the process of examining sets of data with the goal of discovering useful information from patterns found in the data.
- Data analytics can be categorized into four types: descriptive, diagnostic, predictive, and prescriptive.

LO2   **Describe the use of data analytics within the accounting profession. (p. F-3)**
- Many accountants are already performing descriptive data analytics.
- Accountants can add much more value by performing predictive and prescriptive data analytics.
- The large accounting firms have devoted large resources to data analytics.
- Being well trained in data analytics is important for future accountants.

LO3   **Describe how blockchain technology works. (p. F-4)**
- A blockchain represents a decentralized ledger system.
- Each decentralized computer on the blockchain is called a node.
- Unlike a traditional ledger system where authority for maintenance and integrity rests at a centralized location, each node on the blockchain has the same rights as each other node.
- Each block in the blockchain contains information, such as transaction details, along with a time stamp and a hash linking the block to previous blocks in a chronological order.
- Blockchains are essentially tamperproof because alteration to a block by a node would be apparent to every other node on the blockchain.

LO4   **Describe the use of blockchain technology within the accounting profession. (p. F-5)**
- Blockchain technology represents another innovation that will change the way accountants perform their work.
- Blockchain technology will fundamentally change the way audits are performed because all parties to the blockchain will be able to independently verify all transactions.
- Blockchain technology will greatly reduce the time and effort accountants spend on other tasks, such as reconciling source documents, producing ad hoc reports, and performing period-ending book closings.

KEY TERMS

Blockchain technology (p. F-4)	Diagnostic analytics (p. F-2)	Predictive analytics (p. F-2)
Data analytics (p. F-2)	Hash # (p. F-4)	Prescriptive analytics (p. F-2)
Descriptive analytics (p. F-2)	Nodes (p. F-4)	Time stamp (p. F-4)

SELF-STUDY QUESTIONS

(Answers to the Self-Study Questions are available at the end of this chapter.)

LO1, 2   1. **Which of the following are the four categories of data analytics?**
   a. Descriptive, diagnostic, predictive, prescriptive
   b. Expressive, diagnostic, predictive, prescriptive
   c. Descriptive, analytical, predictive, prescriptive
   d. Descriptive, diagnostic, prognostic, prescriptive

LO3, 4   2. **The glue that binds blocks in a blockchain consist of what?**
   a. Time stamps
   b. Sequential numbering
   c. Regulatory approval
   d. Hashes
   e. Both *a.* and *d.*

EXERCISES

A video demonstrating the use of Microsoft Excel's built-in functions for data analysis is available on the textbook's website to assist in solving exercises EF-1 through EF-3.

LO1, 2   **EF-1.   Using Microsoft Excel for descriptive analytics.** Go to the book's website and download the file Employee data.xlsx, **link**. You will need to have the Analysis Toolpak add-in installed in Excel. It can be found under the Tools tab. If it does not appear, select Excel Add-ins under the Tools tab, and then check Analysis Toolpak. From the Excel ribbon, select Data and then Data Analysis. From the pop-up window, choose Descriptive Statistics, then click OK. Select the salary column as the input range, and check the box for labels in first row. Choose "New Worksheet" as the output option, click summary statistics, and click OK. Report the following:

a. Mean (average) salary
b. Median salary
c. Minimum salary
d. Maximum salary
e. Number of salary observations in the database

EF-2. **Using the Microsoft Excel PivotTable function for descriptive analytics.** Go to the book's website and download the file Employee data.xlsx **link**. Place your cursor anywhere in the table of data. From the Excel ribbon, select Insert and then Pivot Table. The entire table should be selected automatically along with the choice to output the PivotTable to a new worksheet. Select OK. From the PivotTable Fields section, select and drag "Gender" and "Minority" to the "Rows" box below. Select and drag the variable "Education" to the "Columns" box. Select and drag the variable "Salary" to the "Values" box. Change the sum of salary to the average of salary by clicking the "i" icon to the right of the "Sum of Salary," choosing "Average," then clicking OK. Report the following: **LO1, 2**

a. Does additional education appear to be associated with a higher average salary?
b. Do males (1) or females (0) appear to earn higher average salaries?
c. Do minorities (1) or nonminorities (0) appear to earn higher average salaries? Does this hold for both genders?
d. What is the average salary of the entire population? What is the average salary of the entire population of males? What is the average salary of the entire population of females? What is the average salary of the entire population of male minorities? What is the average salary of the entire population female minorities?

EF-3. **Using Microsoft Excel for diagnostic analytics.** Go to the book's website and download the file Employee data.xlsx **link**. You will need to have the Analysis Toolpak add-in installed in Excel. It can be found under the Tools tab. If it does not appear, you will need to select Excel Add-ins under the Tools tab and then check Analysis Toolpak. From the Excel ribbon, select Data and then Data Analysis. From the pop-up window, choose "Regression," then click OK. Select values in the "Salary" column as the Input Y Range and values in the columns for "Gender" through "Education" for the Input X Range. Choose "New Worksheet" as the output option, then click OK. Report the following: **LO1, 2**

a. A measure on how well the independent variables gender, minority, and education are able to explain the variation in average salary is the adjusted R Squared. What percentage of the variation in average salaries is described by these variables?
b. The t Stat is a measure of how an individual independent variable explains variation in the dependent variable average salary. An absolute value greater than 2 is generally considered a significant value in explaining variation. What do the t Stats tell us about the ability of the variables gender, minority, and education to explain average salary?

A video demonstrating the use of Tableau Public for data analysis is available on the textbook's website, to assist in solving exercises EF-4 through EF-6. In addition, a series of tutorial videos is available on the Tableau website https://public.tableau.com/en-us/s/resources.

Go to the Tableau website, https://public.tableau.com/en-us/s/, and download the app in order to complete exercises EF-4 through EF-7.

EF-4. **Using Tableau to create summary statistics.** Go to the book's website and download the file Employee data Tableau.xlsx, **link**. Connect Tableau Public to this Excel file. Go to the worksheet and drag the measures "Education," "Jobcat," and "Jobtime" up to Dimensions. Compare the average salaries by gender and minority status by dragging "Gender" to Rows and "Minority" to Columns and then "Salary" to the canvas. Change salary from a sum to an average. **LO1, 2**

a. How do average salaries compare by gender and minority status?

Next, explore how education level affects this relation by dragging "Education" to Columns. It may be easier to make this comparison by switching the order of "Minority" and "Education" on the Columns bar.

b. Does education level affect how average salaries compare by gender and minority status?

Next, change salary from average to maximum.

c. Does education level affect how maximum salaries compare by gender and minority status?

LO1, 2   **EF-5.**   **Using Tableau to calculate a visualization.** Starting with the results from EF-4, change salary back to average. Select the side-by-side bar chart (ninth selection) from the "show me" selections.

Based on this visualization of the data, what can you say about relative salaries for males and females and for caucasians and minorities?

LO1, 2   **EF-6.**   **Using Tableau to forecast future values.** Go to the book's website and download the file Employee data Tableau.xlsx, **link**. Connect Tableau Public to this Excel file. Go to the worksheet and drag the measures "Education," "Jobcat," and "Jobtime" up to Dimensions. Forecast average salaries for males and females based on Jobtime by first dragging "Gender" to Rows and "Jobtime" and "Salary" to Columns. Drag "Salary" to the canvas. Change salary from a sum to an average. From Analytics, select Forecast.

At 100 months of job time, how do the forecasts of average salary for males compare with females?

LO1, 2   **EF-7.**   **Public accounting firms and data analytics.** Go to PWC.com and select "Services" and then "Data and Analytics." Choose a topic and write about how PWC is using data analytics to help its clients.

LO1, 2   **EF-8.**   **Public accounting firms and data analytics.** Go to KPMG.com and select "Insights" and then "Data and Analytics." Choose a topic and write about how KPMG is using data analytics to help its clients.

LO1, 2   **EF-9.**   **Public accounting firms and data analytics.** Go to Deloitte.com and select "Services" and then "Analytics." Choose a topic and write about how Deloitte is using data analytics to help its clients.

LO1, 2   **EF-10.**   **Public accounting firms and data analytics.** Go to EY.com and click on the three horizonal lines in the upper right corner. Next, choose "What we do" and then select "Our services" from the menu on the right side. Finally, click "Analytics and big data" from the popular quick links. Choose a topic and write about how Ernst & Young is using data analytics to help its clients.

LO3, 4   **EF-11.**   **Public accounting firms and blockchain technology.** Go to PWC.com and search for "blockchain." Choose a topic and write about how PWC is using blockchain to help its clients.

LO3, 4   **EF-12.**   **Public accounting firms and blockchain technology.** Go to KPMG.com and search for "blockchain." Choose a topic and write about how KPMG is using blockchain to help its clients.

LO3, 4   **EF-13.**   **Public accounting firms and blockchain technology.** Go to Deloitte.com and search for "blockchain." Select "Blockchain—Perspectives, insights, and analysis." Choose a topic and write about how Deloitte is using blockchain to help its clients.

LO3, 4   **EF-14.**   **Public accounting firms and blockchain technology.** Go to EY.com and search for "blockchain." Choose a topic and write about how Ernst & Young is using blockchain to help its clients.

ANSWERS TO SELF-STUDY QUESTIONS:

1. a. (p. F-2)   2. e. (p. F-4)

Index

Exhibits and notes are included in the index with a corresponding e or n following the page numbers.

Exhibits and notes are included in the index with a corresponding e or n following the page numbers.

Exhibits and notes are included in the index with a corresponding e or n following the page numbers.

Exhibits and notes are included in the index with a corresponding e or n following the page numbers.

Exhibits and notes are included in the index with a corresponding e or n following the page numbers.

Exhibits and notes are included in the index with a corresponding e or n following the page numbers.

Exhibits and notes are included in the index with a corresponding e or n following the page numbers.

Exhibits and notes are included in the index with a corresponding e or n following the page numbers.

Exhibits and notes are included in the index with a corresponding e or n following the page numbers.

Exhibits and notes are included in the index with a corresponding e or n following the page numbers.

Exhibits and notes are included in the index with a corresponding e or n following the page numbers.